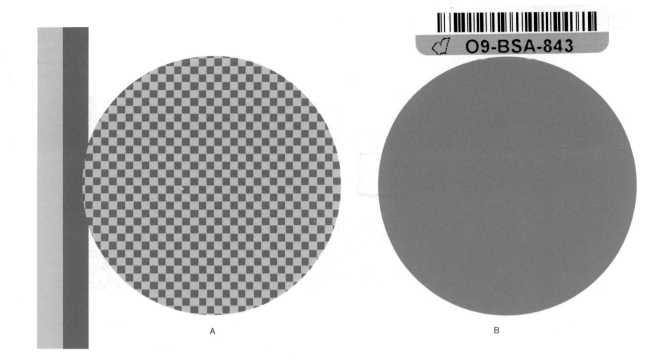

A

B

Color Plate 4

Color Plate 5

Color Plate 6

SENSATION AND PERCEPTION

FIFTH EDITION

SENSATION AND PERCEPTION

FIFTH EDITION

Stanley Coren
Lawrence M. Ward
James T. Enns

Harcourt Brace College Publishers

Fort Worth   Philadelphia   San Diego   New York   Orlando   Austin   San Antonio
Toronto   Montreal   London   Sydney   Tokyo

Publisher	Earl McPeek
Associate Acquisitions Editor	Lisa Hensley
Market Strategist	Kathleen Sharp
Developmental Editor	Janie Pierce-Bratcher
Project Editor	Elaine Richards
Art Director	Don Fujimoto
Production Manager	Andrea A. Johnson

Cover credit: © H. Kuwajima/Photnica

ISBN: 0-15-508050-4
Library of Congress Catalog Card Number: 98-72167

Address for Domestic Orders
Harcourt Brace College Publishers, 6277 Sea Harbor Drive, Orlando, FL 32887-6777
800-782-4479

Address for International Orders
International Customer Service
Harcourt Brace & Company, 6277 Sea Harbor Drive, Orlando, FL 32887-6777
407-345-3800
(fax) 407-345-4060
(e-mail) hbintl@harcourtbrace.com

Address for Editorial Correspondence
Harcourt Brace College Publishers, 301 Commerce Street, Suite 3700, Fort Worth, TX 76102

Web Site Address
http://www.hbcollege.com

Harcourt Brace College Publishers will provide complimentary supplements or supplement packages to those adopters qualified under our adoption policy. Please contact your sales representative to learn how you qualify. If as an adopter or potential user you receive supplements you do not need, please return them to your sales representative or send them to: Attn: Returns Department, Troy Warehouse, 465 South Lincoln Drive, Troy, MO 63379.

Printed in the United States of America

9 0 1 2 3 4 5 6 7   043   9 8 7 6 5 4 3 2

Harcourt Brace College Publishers

Preface

Take away the sensations of softness, moisture, redness, tartness, and you take away the cherry. Since it is not a being distinct from these sensations; a cherry, I say, is nothing but a congeries of sensible impressions or ideas perceived by various senses; which ideas are united into one thing....

George Berkeley, 1713

Virtually everything we know about our world entered our minds in some form through our senses. We all realize that without even some of our senses, our experiences would be incredibly limited. Consider the impossible problem of explaining the difference between the color blue and the color green to a person who has been blind since birth. Or how would you explain to a person who has no taste buds how the taste of chocolate and vanilla differ from each other? Such aspects of the world will never exist for these individuals. For the blind person, salt and pepper differ only in taste. For the person with no ability to taste, salt and pepper differ only in color. For those of us who have senses of sight, hearing, taste, touch, and smell, our world is a continuous flow of changing percepts. Each new sensation carries with it information about our world.

This book provides an introduction to the study of sensation and perception. This fifth edition of *Sensation and Perception* has been revised substantially since the fourth edition and updated with over 700 new literary citations making this, we believe, the most up-to-date textbook available at this level. These changes reflect many of the recent findings that have emerged, or coalesced, into meaningful patterns since the completion of the fourth edition. We have rewritten all of the chapters, with some sections revised "from the ground up." We have retained the general structure and organization of the fourth edition so that the book will still feel familiar to our previous users, although the chapter sequence is a bit different in this edition. We have also retained all those features that instructors felt made the previous editions such a useful teaching tool. For instance, we use concrete examples throughout the text in order to make the subject matter "come alive" for students. Whenever possible, we describe common or natural instances of perceptual phenomena during the discussion of the concepts underlying them. Each chapter is preceded by an outline, which serves as a preview to its contents. These outlines also provide a structure that can guide students as they review the chapters. We have added short chapter summaries for each of the chapters as well.

Although we define all important terms when we introduce them in the text, we also provide, at the end of each chapter, a list of *key terms*. Any item printed in bold letters in the text is also listed both as a key term and in the glossary at the end of the book. Students will find that these key term lists will provide a study aid because they can also be used for self-testing and review purposes, with the glossary used as the "answer key."

One special feature of our text is the inclusion of over 100 *Demonstration Boxes*. Each box describes a simple demonstration designed to allow the students to actually experience many of the perceptual phenomena described in the text. Most require only the stimuli in the box itself or commonplace items that can be found in most homes and dormitory rooms. The majority of these demonstrations require only a few moments of preparation, and we feel that this is time well spent in improving understanding of the concepts under discussion and in maintaining student interest. Some instructors report that having students perform the demonstrations in class has been very useful. In such cases, the demonstrations may also serve as the focal point for a lecture or for classroom discussion. There are also four special Demonstration Boxes which allow individuals to screen their own sensory capacities without the use of special equipment. A test for visual acuity is found in Chapter 4, for color vision in Chapter 5, for uncorrected stereopsis in Chapter 9, and for hearing sensitivity in Chapter 16. These are behaviorally validated screening tests which allow for quick testing of these abilities and may prove quite useful in a variety of research projects; moreover, they provide students with useful information about their own sensory capacities.

This text is designed to survey the broad range of topics generally included under the heading of "sensation and perception." The reader will notice that we champion no single theory of perception. In general, we attempt to be as eclectic as possible, describing various viewpoints in areas of controversy and attempting to present a balanced viewpoint so that instructors of different opinions will be comfortable using the text.

We selected the topics in this book on the basis of our experience in teaching our own courses; therefore, much of the material has already been class tested. We have included three chapters, *Attention*, *Speech and Music*, and *Individual Differences*, that are not always seen in sensation and perception textbooks. These areas have attracted a good deal of experimental work in recent years, and they

are sufficiently relevant to many issues in perception that we believe students should be aware of their existence.

In order to keep the book to a manageable size, we have occasionally been selective in our coverage. It is our first priority to cover the central concepts of each topic in enough detail to make the material clear and coherent. To have included all of the topics ever classified as part of the field of sensation and perception, we would have had to present a "grocery list" of concepts and terms, each treated superficially. Such an alternative was unacceptable to us.

Each of the chapters has been written so that it is relatively self-contained and independent of the other chapters. When this is not completely possible, such as when material from other chapters is used in a discussion, the location of that information is always cited at the relevant place in the text. This has been done to provide instructors with the maximum flexibility as far as chapter sequence presentation is concerned. By altering the sequence in which chapters are presented, an instructor can impress his or her orientation on the material. We also provide a brief Appendix on some basic aspects of neurophysiology, which professors may use when needed.

We have organized the book by sensory systems, with the first half of the book covering the basic physiology and sensory responses and the second half covering those topics involving more complex and cognitive interactions. Chapters 1 and 2 provide an introduction to the problems of sensation and perception along with methodological and theoretical aspects of psychophysical measurement. Chapters 3, 4, and 5 cover the physiology and basic sensory qualities of vision, while Chapters 6 and 7 do the same for audition. Chapter 8 covers the chemical and mechanical senses. Thus, these first eight chapters cover the major topics usually grouped together under the heading of "sensation." Chapters 9 through 15 cover the perception of space, form, speech and music, time, and motion, perceptual constancies, and the perceptual aspects of attention. Chapters 16, 17, and 18 look at how individual factors, such as age, experience, learning, gender, culture, drugs, and personality variables may affect the perceptual response. Thus, the last 10 chapters cover the topics most frequently grouped together as "perception."

Acknowledgments and Dedication

We would first like to acknowledge all of those who have reviewed the previous four editions of our text. Their comments and insights have helped us shape this text into what it is today. We would specifically like to recognize those who contributed directly to this fifth edition: Deborah J. Aks, University of Wisconsin–Whitewater; Robert Patterson, Washington State University; Dan Swift, University of Michigan–Dearborn; Benjamin Wallace, Cleveland State University; and Stephen A. Wurst, SUNY–Oswego.

Finally, the reader might notice that there is no dedication page. This is not to say that we do not wish to dedicate the book to anyone; it merely reflects the fact that there are too many people who have been important in our personal and professional lives to list on any single page (no matter how small the print). Perhaps it is best to simply dedicate this book to all of those researchers who have provided the knowledge that we have attempted to organize and review between these covers, and to all of those researchers who will provide further insights into sensation and perception for future authors to collate, review, digest, wonder at, and learn from.

S.C.
L.M.W.
J.T.E.

Contents

Sensation and Perception

FIFTH EDITION

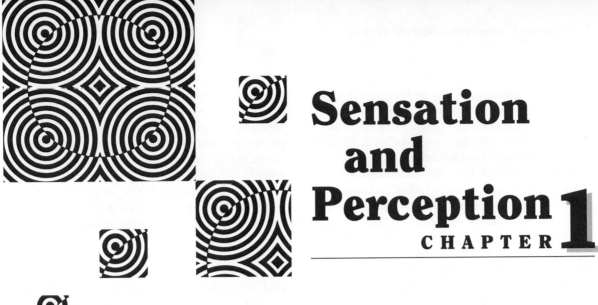

Sensation and Perception

CHAPTER 1

Can you answer the following questions? What color is the sky? Which is warmer—fire or ice? Which tastes sweeter—sugar or vinegar? Which has a stronger smell—burning wood or burning rubber? Which sounds louder—the chirp of a bird or the crack of a rifle? Such questions probably seem quite trivial and the answers obvious. Well, perhaps we should phrase the questions differently. How do you know what color the sky is? How do you know how hot fire is relative to ice? How do you know that sugar is sweet? Again, you might feel that the answers are obvious. You see the color of the sky, you feel the temperatures of a flame and an ice cube, and you taste the sweetness of sugar—in other words, the answers come through your senses.

Let us push our questioning one step further. How do you know anything about your world? You might say that you learn from books, television, radio, films, lectures, or the actual exploration of places. And how do you obtain the information from these sources? Again, the answer is through your senses. In fact, without your senses of vision, hearing, touch, taste, and smell, your brain, the organ that is responsible for your conscious experience, would be an eternal prisoner in the solitary confinement of your skull. You would live in total silence and darkness. All would be a tasteless, colorless, feelingless, floating void. Without your senses, the world would simply not exist for you. The philosopher Thomas Hobbes recognized this fact

1

in 1651 when he wrote: "There is no conception in man's mind which hath not at first, totally or by parts, been begotten upon the organs of sense." The Greek philosopher Protagoras stated the same position around 450 B.C. when he said, "Man is nothing but a bundle of sensations."

You may protest that this is a rather extreme viewpoint. Certainly, much of what we know about the world does not arrive through our eyes, ears, nose, and other sense organs. We have complex scientific instruments, such as telescopes, that tell us about the size and the shape of the universe by analyzing images too faint for the human eye to see. We have sonar to trace out the shape of the sea bottom, which may be hidden from our eyes by hundreds of feet of water. We have spectrographs to tell us about the exact chemical composition of many substances, as compared to the crude chemical sensitivity of our noses and tongues.

Although such pieces of apparatus exist, and measure phenomena not directly available to our senses, this does not alter the fact that it is the *perception of the scientist* that constitutes the subject matter of every science. The eye of the scientist presses against the telescope or examines the photograph of the distant star. The ear of the scientist listens to the sound of sonar tracing out the size and distance of objects, or his eyes read the sonograph. Although the tongue of the scientist does not taste the chemical composition of some unknown substance, her eye, aided by the spectrograph, provides the data for analysis. Really, the only data that reach the mind of the scientist come not from instruments but rather from the scientist's senses. The instrument he or she is looking at can be perfectly accurate, yet if the scientist misreads a digital readout or does not notice a critical shift in the operation of a measurement device, the obtained information is wrong and the resulting picture of the world is in error. The minds of the scientist, the nonscientist, our pet dog sniffing about the world, or a fish swimming about in a bowl, in fact, the minds of all living, thinking organisms are prisoners that must rely on information smuggled in to them by the senses. Your world is what your senses tell you. The limitations of your senses set the boundaries of your conscious existence.

Because our knowledge of the world is dependent on our senses, it is important to know how our senses function. It is also important to know how well the world that is created by our senses corresponds to external reality (i.e., the reality measured by scientific instruments). At this point, you are probably smiling to yourself and thinking, "Here comes another academic discourse that will attempt to make something that is quite obvious appear to be complex." You might be saying to yourself, "I see my desk in front of me because it is there. I feel my chair pressing against my back because it is there. I hear my phone ringing because it contains a bell that makes sounds. What could be more obvious?" Such faith in your senses is a vital part of existence. It causes you to jump out of the way of an apparently oncoming car, thus preserving your life. It provides the basic data that cause you to step back from a deep hole, thus avoiding a fall and serious bodily harm.

Such faith in our senses is built into the very fabric of our lives. As the old saying goes, "Seeing is believing." Long before the birth of Christ, Lucretius stated this article of faith when he asked, "What can give us surer knowledge than our senses? With what else can we distinguish the true form from the false?" Perhaps the most striking example of this faith is found in our courts of law, where people's lives and fortunes rest solely on the testimony of the eyes and ears of witnesses. A lawyer might argue that a witness is corrupt or lying, or even that his memory has failed, but no lawyer would have the audacity to suggest that her client should be set free because the only evidence available was what the witnesses saw or heard. Certainly no sane person would charge the eye or ear with perjury!

The philosophical position that perception is an immediate, almost godlike knowledge of external reality has been championed not only by popular sentiment but also by philosophers of the stature of Immanuel Kant (1724–1804). Unfortunately, it is wrong. Look at the drawings shown in Figure 1-1. Clearly, they all are composed of outlined forms on various backgrounds. Despite what your senses tell you, *A*, *B*, and *C* all are perfect squares. Despite the evidence of your senses, *D* is a perfect circle, the lines in *E* both are straight, and the lines marked *x* and *y* in *F* both are the same length.

The ease with which we use our senses—seeing, apparently through the simple act of opening our eyes, or touching, apparently by merely pressing

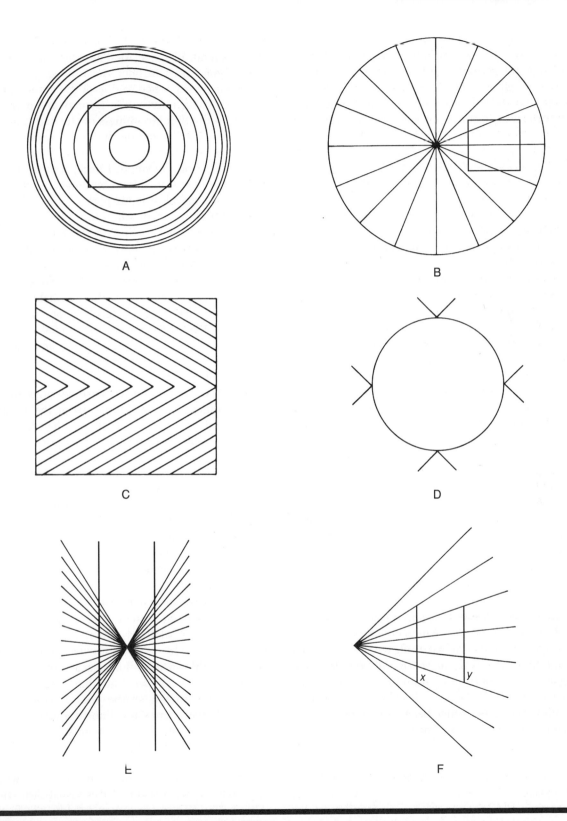

FIGURE 1-1   Some instances where the senses tell lies.

our skin against an object—masks the fact that perception is an extremely sophisticated activity of the brain. Perception calls on stores of memory data. It requires subtle classifications, comparisons, and myriad decisions before any of the data in our senses become our conscious awareness of what is "out there." Contrary to what you may think, the eyes do not see. There are many individuals who have perfectly functioning eyes yet have no sensory impressions. They cannot perceive because they have injuries in those parts of the brain that receive and interpret messages from the eyes. Epicharmus knew this in 450 B.C. when he said, "The mind sees and the mind hears. The rest is blind and deaf."

"So what?" you mutter to yourself. "So sometimes we make errors in our perceptions; the real point is that the senses simply carry a picture of the outside world to the brain. The picture in the brain represents our percept. Of course, if we mess up the brain we will distort or destroy perception." Again, this answer is too simple. If we look outside and see a car, are we to believe that there is a picture of a car somewhere in our brains? If we notice that a traffic light is green, are we to believe that some part of the brain has turned green? And suppose that there were such images in the brain, carried without distortion from the senses; would this help us to see? Certainly, images in the brain would be of value only if there were some other eyes in the head, which would look at these pictures and interpret them. If this were the case, we would be left with the question of how these internal eyes see. Thus, we would eventually be forced to set up an endless chain of pictures and eyes and pictures and eyes because the question of who is perceiving the percept, and how, still remains.

If we are to understand perception we must consider it in its natural context. Sensation and perception are some of the many complex processes that occur in the continuing flow of individual behavior. There is no clear line between perception and many other behavioral activities. No perception gives direct knowledge of the outside world; rather, such knowledge of the outside world is the end product of many processes. The wet-looking black spot on the edge of a desk could be the place where ink was spilled. Of course, this percept could be wrong. The ink may be dry, or the spot might not be there at all. The desk that is

seen and touched might not really exist. We might be dreaming, drugged, or hallucinating. Too extreme, you say? Consider the following example that actually happened to one of the authors. One night he walked across the floor of his darkened home. In the dim gloominess of the night, he saw one of his dogs resting on the floor, clearly asleep. When he bent to touch the dog, he found that it was a footstool. He stepped back, somewhat startled at his stupidity, only to bump against the cold corner of a marble-topped coffee table. When he reached back to steady himself, he found that the corner of the table was, in fact, his dog's cold nose. Each of these perceptions, dog, stool, table, and dog again, seemed, when first received in consciousness, to be accurate representations of reality. Yet, sensory data are not always reliable. Sometimes they can be degraded or not completely available. There seems to be no sudden break between perceiving or sensing an object and guessing the identity of an object. In some respects, we can say that all perception of objects requires some guessing. Sensory stimulation provides the data for our hypotheses about the nature of the external world, and it is these hypotheses that form our perceptions of the world. What's important about what we have been discussing is that no matter how convincing a percept may be, it still may be wrong, as is shown in Demonstration Box 1-1.

Many human behaviors have been affected by the fallible and often erroneous nature of our percepts. For example, the most elegant of the classic Greek buildings, the Parthenon, is bent. The straight clean lines, which bring a sense of simple elegant grandeur, are actually an illusion. Figure 1-2A shows the east wall of the building as it appears. It looks quite square, and the columns look quite vertical. Actually, the Parthenon was built in a totally distorted fashion in order to offset a series of optical illusions. There is a common visual distortion in which we find that placing angles above a line (much as the roof is placed over the architrave) causes the line to appear slightly bowed. One form of this illusion is shown as Figure 1-2B where the ends of the horizontal line appear slightly higher than the center. If the Parthenon were built physically square, it would appear to sag as a result of this visual distortion. This is shown in an exaggerated manner in Figure 1-2C. The sagging does not appear because the

---

DEMONSTRATION BOX 1-1
The Fraser Spiral

Look at the figure here. It clearly looks like a spiral, converging toward the center. How much would you be willing to bet that it is a spiral? On the basis of your perception alone, would you ever believe that it is actually a set of concentric circles? It actually is a set of circles, which you can verify for yourself. Place one finger on any line making up the "spiral." Place a finger from the other hand beside it, and carefully trace the line around with this finger while not moving the first finger. Eventually the moving finger will come back to the stationary one because the lines that appear to spiral all are part of a set of concentric circles (see Fraser, 1908; Stuart & Day, 1988; Taylor & Woodhouse, 1980, for variations of this illusion). This shows that no matter how convincing a perception might be, because it is based on a hypothesis or conclusion used to interpret stimuli reaching us, our conscious interpretation may be wrong!

---

building has been altered to compensate for the distortion. Figure 1-2D illustrates what an undistorted view of the Parthenon would look like. The upward curvature is more than 6 cm on the east and west walls and almost 11 cm on the longer north and south walls.

The vertical features of the Parthenon (such as the columns) were inclined inward in order to correct

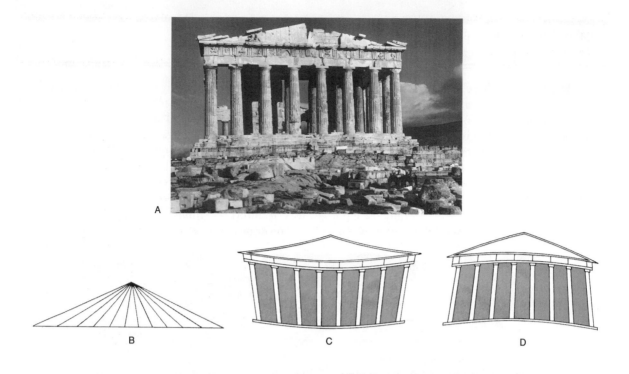

FIGURE 1-2   (A) The Parthenon, looking square and elegant; (B) an illusion that should cause the Parthenon to appear as (C); (D) the way the Parthenon is built to offset the illusion.

for a second optical illusion in which the features of rising objects appear to fall outward at the top. Thus, if we projected all of the columns of the Parthenon upward, they would meet at a point somewhat less than 2 km above the building. Furthermore, the corner columns were made thicker because it was found that when these columns were seen against the sky, they appeared to be thinner than those seen against the darker background formed by the interior wall.

These were conscious corrections made by the Greek architects. To quote one of them, Vitruvius, writing around 30 B.C.: "For the sight follows gracious contours, and unless we flatter its pleasure by proportionate alterations of these parts (so that by adjustment we offset the amount to which it suffers illusions) an uncouth and ungracious aspect will be presented to the spectators." In other words, the Parthenon appears to be square, with elegant straight lines, because it has been consciously distorted to offset perceptual distortions. If it were geometrically square, it would not be perceptually square.

It is amazing to discover the degree to which our conscious experience of the world can differ from the physical (scientific) reality. Although some perceptual distortions are only slight deviations from physical reality, some can be quite complex and surprising, such as that shown in Demonstration Box 1-2.

Such distortions, in the form of disagreements between percept and reality, are quite common. We call them **illusions**, and they occur in predictable circumstances for normal observers. The term *illusion* is drawn from the Latin root *illudere*, meaning "to mock," and in a sense illusions do mock us for our unthinking reliance on the validity of our sensory impressions. Every sensory modality is subject to distortions, illusions, and systematic errors that misrepresent the outside environment to our consciousness. There are illusions of touch, taste, and hearing, as well as of vision. Virtually any aspect of perception you might think of can be subject to these kinds of errors. For instance, such basic and apparently simple qualities as the brightness of an object or its color may be

DEMONSTRATION BOX 1-2
Gears and Circles

The pattern shown in this box should be viewed in motion. Move the book around so that the motion resembles that which you would make if you were swirling coffee around in a cup without using a spoon. Notice that the six sets of concentric circles seem to show radial regions of light and dark that appear to move in the direction you are swirling the book. They look as though they were covered by a liquid surface tending to swirl with the stimulus movement.

A second effect has to do with the center circle that seems to have gearlike teeth. As you swirl the array, the center gear seems to rotate, but in a direction *opposite* to that of the movement of the outer circles. Some observers see it moving in a jerky, steplike manner from one rotary position to another, and other observers see a smooth rotation. Of course, there is no *physical* movement within the circles, and the geared center circle is also unchanging, despite your conscious impression to the contrary.

DEMONSTRATION BOX 1-3
A Subjective Color Grid

The figure in this box consists of a series of thinly spaced diagonal black lines alternating with white spaces. Study this figure for a couple of seconds, and you will begin to see faint, almost pastel streaks of orange-red and other streaks of blue-green. For many observers, these streaks tend to run vertically up and down the figure crossing both white and black lines; for others, they seem to form a random, almost fishnet-like pattern over the grid. These colors are not present in the stimulus; hence they are *subjective*, or *illusory*, colors.

perceptually misrepresented, as shown in Demonstration Box 1-3.

Many perceptual errors are merely amusing, such as those in Demonstration Boxes 1-1 and 1-2, whereas others may be thought provoking, as in Demonstration Box 1-3. Others may lead to some embarrassment or annoyance, such as might have been felt by the artisan who created the picture

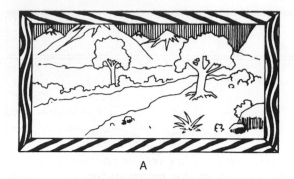

A

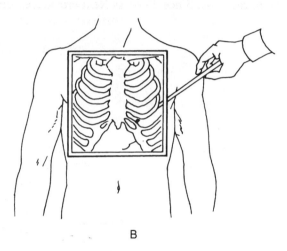

B

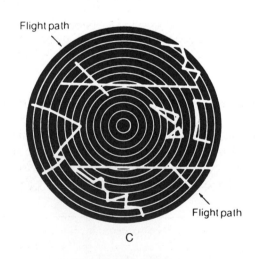

C

FIGURE 1-3   Some perceptual distortions in common situations.

frame shown as Figure 1-3A. Although his workmanship is faultless, he appears to be a sloppy craftsman because the grain of the wood is too prominent. Despite the fact that the picture is perfectly rectangular, it appears to be distorted. Unfortunately, some perceptual errors or illusions are quite serious. In Figure 1-3B, we have shown a surgeon probing for a bullet. She is using a fluoroscope, which presents the outline of the patient's ribs, and her probe is positioned so that it is exactly on line with the bullet lodged below the rib. As you can see, it appears that she will miss and that her probe will pass above the bullet despite the fact that the probe is angled perfectly. Figure 1-3C shows an even more disastrous occurrence of an illusion. It represents a radar screen with various flight regions marked across its face. The two oblique streaks represent jet aircraft approaching the control region, both flying at about 950 kph. The information displayed is similar to that which an air traffic controller might use. From it he might conclude that if these two aircraft continue in the same direction they will pass each other with a safe distance between them. At the moment represented here, however, these aircraft are traveling toward each other on the same line. If they are flying at the same altitude it is very likely that they will collide.

These examples illustrate how important discrepancies between perception and reality can be. Therefore it becomes important for us to know how our perceptions arise, how much we can rely upon them, under what circumstances they are most fallible, and under what conditions our perceptions most accurately present a picture of the world. An exploration of these questions is the purpose of this book.

ASPECTS OF THE PERCEPTUAL PROCESS

The study of perception is diverse. This is partly because perceptual problems have been studied for a long time. The Greek philosophers, the pre-Renaissance thinkers, the Arabic scholars, the Latin scholastics, the early British empiricists, the German physicists, and the German physicians who founded both physiology and psychology considered issues in sensation and perception to be basic questions. When Alexander Bain wrote the first English textbook on psychology in 1855 it was titled *The Senses and the Intellect*, with the most extensive coverage reserved for sensory and perceptual functions. The major portion of both the theorizing and the empirical work produced by Wilhelm Wundt, who is generally credited with the founding of experimental psychology, was oriented toward sensation and perception. In addition to the diversity caused by a long and varied history, perception has been affected by many "schools" of thought. Each has its own major theoretical viewpoint and its own particular set of methodological techniques. Thus we encounter psychophysicists, gestaltists, functionalists, analytic introspectionists, transactionalists, sensory physiologists, sensory-tonic theorists, "new look" psychologists, efferent theorists, artificial intelligence experts, and computational psychologists, to name but a few. There are even theorists (such as some behaviorists) who deny the existence of, or at least deny our ability to study, the conscious event we call *perception*. Despite this chorus of diverse voices, there seems to be a consensus about the important aspects of perceptual study.

Before we look at the major areas of emphasis in the study of the perceptual process, let us first offer a disclaimer. We recognize that it is difficult, perhaps impossible, and most certainly unwise to attempt to draw sharp lines separating one field of inquiry from another. However, there are certain problem areas, or orientations, that characterize certain groups of investigators, and these seem to be definable. The study of sensation, or sensory processes, is concerned with the first contact between the organism and the environment. Thus, someone studying sensation might look at the way in which electromagnetic radiation (light) is registered by the eye. This investigator would look at the physical structure of the sense organ and would attempt to establish how sensory experiences are related to physical stimulation and physiological functioning. These types of studies tend to focus on less complex (although not less complicated) aspects of our conscious experience. For instance, this investigator might study how we perceive brightness, loudness, or color; however, the nature of the object having a given brightness, sound, or color would not make much difference to the investigator.

Someone who is interested in the study of **perception** is interested in our conscious experience of objects and object relationships. For instance, the sensory question might be "How bright does the target appear to be?" whereas the perceptual questions would be "Can you identify that object?" "Where is it?" How far away is it?" and "How large is it?" In a more global sense, those who study perception are interested in how we form a conscious representation of the outside environment and in the accuracy of that representation. For those of you who have difficulty in drawing a hard and fast line between the concepts of perception and sensation, rest easy. Since Thomas Reid introduced the distinction in 1785, some investigators have championed its use, and others have totally ignored the difference, choosing to treat sensation and perception as a unitary problem.

Cognition is a term used to define a very active field of inquiry in contemporary psychology. The word itself is quite old, probably introduced by St. Thomas Aquinas (1225–1274). He divided the study of behavior into two broad divisions: *cognition*, meaning how we know the world, and *affect*, which was meant to encompass feelings and emotions. Today's definition of *cognition* is equally as broad as that of Aquinas. Although many investigators use the term to refer to memory, association, concept formation, language, and problem solving (all of which simply take the act of perception for granted), other investigators include the processes of attention and the conscious representation and interpretation of stimuli as part of the cognitive process. In other words, cognition tends to be somewhere between the areas that were traditionally called *perception* and *learning*, and it incorporates elements of both. The similarity between many of the problems studied by cognitive psychologists and those studied by perceptual psychologists is best seen by the fact that both often publish in the same journals and on similar topics.

Information processing is a relatively general term but is used to emphasize the whole process that finally leads to identification and interpretation of stimuli. This approach focuses on how information about the external world is operated on (processed) to produce our conscious percepts and guide our actions. Information processing is typically assumed to include a *registration* or sensory phase, an *interpretation* or perceptual phase, and a *memoric* or cognitive phase. Thus, rather than being a separate subdiscipline, the information processing approach attempts to integrate sensation, perception, and cognition within a common framework. It relies on a **levels-of-processing** analysis in which each stage of sensory processing, from the first registration of the stimulus on the receptor to the final conscious representation entered into memory, is systematically analyzed.

None of these labels should be taken as representing inflexible, or completely separate, areas of study. At a recent professional meeting one well-known psychologist lamented, "When I first started doing research, people said I studied perception. After a while, they said I studied cognition. Now they say that I am studying human information processing. I don't know what is going on—I've been studying the same set of problems for the last ten years!"

THEORIES OF PERCEPTION

In the same way that there are many aspects of perception, there are also many theoretical approaches to perceptual problems. One important approach may be called **biological reductionism.** It is based on the presumption that for any given aspect of the observer's sensation there is a corresponding physiological event. According to this approach, the main goal of the perceptual researcher is to isolate these underlying physiological mechanisms. The search for specific neural units, pathways, or processes that correspond to specific sensory experiences is common to such theories. One recent example is the work of Margaret Livingstone and David Hubel (1988), who view the visual system as a set of channels, each containing specific neural units that process or extract specific information from incoming information.

Other theoretical approaches are often less bound to a specific class of mechanism. For example, **direct perception** involves a set of theories that begins with the premise that all the information needed to form the conscious percept is available in the stimuli that reach our receptors. Even though the image in our eye is continually changing, there are certain aspects of the stimulation produced by any particular object or environmental situation that are *invariant* predictors of certain

properties, such as the actual size, shape, or distance of the object being viewed. These perceptual **invariants** are fixed properties of the stimulus even though the observer may be moving or changing viewpoints, causing continuous changes in the optical image that reaches the eye. This stimulus information is automatically extracted by the perceptual system because it is relevant to survival. Invariants provide information about **affordances,** which are simply action possibilities afforded or available to the observer, such as picking the object up, going around it, and so forth. The label of *direct perception* was given to such theories by J. J. Gibson (e.g., 1979), who argued that this information is directly available to the perceiver and is not based on any higher level cognitive processing or computation.

A number of perceptual theorists, whose thinking has been influenced by developments in artificial intelligence systems, have adopted an alternative approach. Their theories are usually presented in the form of computer programs or computational systems that might allow machines to directly interpret sensory information in the same manner that a human observer might. Typical of such theorists is David Marr (1982), who began with the general presumption made in direct perception that all of the information needed is in the stimulus input. This approach differs from direct perception in that it describes the piecing together of information based on some simple dimensions in the stimulus, such as boundaries and edges, line endings, particular patterns where stimuli meet, and so forth. This process of interpretation or synthesis is believed to require a number of computations and several stages of analysis that often can be specified as mathematical equations or steps in a computer program. This added requirement of calculating features of objects or aspects of the environment from aspects of the stimuli reaching the observer has resulted in the label of **computational theories** for this approach. Certain aspects of specific computational theories often involve fairly difficult mathematics, including non-Euclidean geometry, Lie transforms, Fourier analysis, and so forth.

A much older (but still active) theoretical approach begins with the recognition that our perceptual representation of the world is much richer and more accurate than might be expected on the basis of the information contained in the stimuli available at any one moment in time. Theories to explain this fact often begin with the suggestion that perception is much like other logical processes. In addition to the information available to our sense organs at the moment, we can use information based on our previous experience, our expectations, and so forth. This means that, for example, a visual percept may involve other sources of information, some nonvisual in nature, some arising from our past history and cognitive processing strategies. The similarity of some of these mechanisms to reasoning leads us to refer to this type of theory as **intelligent perception**. This approach probably originated with Helmholtz in 1867 and survives today in the work of researchers such as Irvin Rock (1983), who have a more cognitive orientation. These theories are also called **constructive theories** of perception because our final conscious impression may involve combining a number of different factors to "construct" the final percept.

It is quite likely that each of these approaches is useful in describing some aspects of the perceptual process (see Coren & Girgus, 1978; Uttal, 1981); however, different orientations tend to lead researchers in different directions, searching for different types of mechanisms. Each approach is likely to be valid for some parts of the problem and irrelevant to others. This is a common occurrence in many areas of endeavor. For instance, a metallurgist might look at a bridge and consider its material components, whereas a civil engineer might look at the load-bearing capacity of the entire structure, and a city planner might look at the same bridge in terms of traffic flow. At first glance there may seem to be very little overlap between the various views because the city planner does not care about the specific shape of the bridge structure, and the engineer cares only about the structural aspects of the beams, not their specific alloy constituents. Yet, each level of analysis is valid for some specific set of questions. This book addresses the problem of how people build a conscious picture of their environment through the use of information reaching their senses. We follow the lead of many contemporary theorists and try to use data from all levels of the perceptual process—and discussions in terms of several different theoretical positions—in order to give an integrated picture of

the process of perception. After all, the label that we apply to our approach is of considerably less importance than the answer itself.

Perceptual factors are important, not only for theories of perception but also for other theories. Many times in science perceptual contributions have been ignored, and the result has been an inadequate, or perhaps quite wrong, explanatory theory. One important example concerns the effect of aging on intelligence and cognitive functioning. This story is told in Application Box 1-1.

THE PLAN OF THE BOOK

The orientation of this book is implicit rather than explicit. Although theories are introduced and discussed in the various chapters, no all-encompassing theoretical orientation has been adopted. We have chosen to be "militantly eclectic" in our orientation. Thus, this text is mostly concerned with perceptual and sensory *processes*. In general, the presentation of the material follows a levels-of-processing approach, in that the first half of the book is concerned with the more basic sensory processes and is organized around specific sensory systems, such as vision or audition, and the second half of the book is concerned with the more clearly perceptual processes that have strong cognitive influences and are often not bound to any single sensory modality. We have tried to make the individual chapters relatively self-contained. We begin by explaining how sensations and perceptions are measured (Chapter 2). We then proceed with the physiological structures and the basic sensory capacities associated with vision (Chapters 3 through 5), hearing (Chapters 6 and 7), and the chemical and mechanical senses (Chapter 8). For those who feel a bit "rusty" about some of the very basic physiological facts, we have also included a "Primer of Neurophysiology" as an appendix. Chapters 9 through 15 deal with those problems that have traditionally been treated as part of classical perception, our perceptual representation of space, time, motion, form, and size. The more cognitive aspects of perception are also introduced in those chapters that deal with music and speech perception and attention. The last three chapters (16 through 18) deal with perceptual diversity, which includes many of the factors that make the perceptual experience of one individual

---

APPLICATION BOX 1-1
Aging and Reduced Intellectual Functioning

How many times have you heard your parents or grandparents say something like "I just don't remember as well as I did. I must be getting old" or "Do you want to add these numbers for me? Now that I am older my mind just doesn't work as well as it used to"? The idea that our cognitive and intellectual functioning diminishes with age is a well-accepted concept in *folk psychology*, which is just a collection of beliefs that the average person has about the way the mind works. In this case, the scientific evidence seems to support these findings. There seems to be lots of evidence that older people do a lot worse on a variety of cognitive tests. Some people have said that this is evidence that the older brain just doesn't work as well—just proof of the saying that "you can't teach an old dog new tricks." However, we now know that these conclusions may be wrong.

When we look at the way in which perceptual ability changes as we grow older, we usually find a decline with age for both our visual acuity (the ability to see fine details) and our auditory sensitivity (the ability to hear faint sounds and to discriminate the differences between tones). These age changes are shown in Figure A, plotted in relative scores (where the average is 50 and each standard deviation away from the mean is 10). Until recently, very few researchers considered the possibility that the apparent decline in mental functioning may be related to the decline in cognitive abilities. There is a reason, however, why you might expect a relationship. People with poor sensory ability don't register all of the details of what is in their environment, and some of what they do register is distorted or incomplete. In the end, this *sensory restriction* will reduce the quality of information that they have to think about. In some instances people with poor perceptual abilities may simply stop processing a lot of what is going on because it is often unreliable or difficult to interpret. Imagine what this might do to a person's thinking ability over the course of many years. To take just one area as an example, people with poor auditory sensitivity would process less verbal information; hence their verbal skills would get "rusty" through disuse. Then, when they were called on to solve verbal problems, they would simply no longer be as good, and we would conclude that their verbal intelligence had dropped. This is what actually happens with age.

Figure B shows a typical experimental result, where people aged 25 to 103 years of age were tested on five different cognitive tests that are commonly used to measure intelligence, such as a test of reasoning or of memory. The test scores were then averaged into a composite "intellectual functioning" score (Baltes & Lindenberger, 1997). Notice that we find the usual decrease in overall mental ability with age.

---

different from that of another. These factors include the changes that occur in the developing individual because of the normal aging process, life history, experience, learning, and personality factors, to name a few.

You will notice that each chapter includes a series of Demonstration Boxes. These are experimental demonstrations that you can perform for yourself using stimuli provided in the book or materials that are easily found around a house or other living quarters. They illustrate many aspects of the perceptual process. Quite often they demonstrate concepts that are very difficult to put into words but that, when experienced, are immediately understandable. You are encouraged to try these demonstrations because they are an integral part of the book. In the same way that perception involves interaction with the world, these demonstrations allow you to interact with your senses in a controlled manner and to gain insight into yourself.

We hope that this book will provide you with some understanding of the limits and the abilities

However, when we statistically remove the effects of the decreasing visual and hearing abilities of older people, the picture changes dramatically. Now we find only a very small decline in mental ability with age, as is shown in the figure.

The first moral of this story is that you *can* "teach an old dog new tricks" but only if the old dog can see and hear well enough to know what is required to perform the tricks. The quality of our thinking depends on the quality of the sensory information that we have to think about. It is not so much that the aging mind is less intelligent but, rather, that the aging sense organs are not allowing the aging mind to perform at the level that it is capable of. The second moral is that failure to consider possible perceptual factors has led people to reach the wrong conclusions about aging for many years.

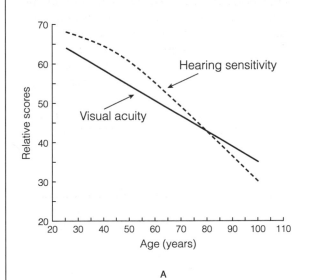

A

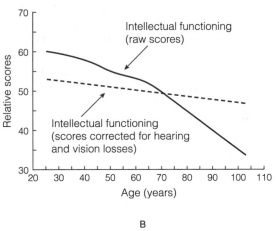

B

APPLICATION BOX FIGURE   (A) Visual acuity and hearing sensitivity decrease with age; (B) the solid curve shows the usually obtained decrease in intellectual functioning obtained, here, as the average of five tests of mental ability; however, when the effects of vision and hearing declines are removed (in the broken line), there is very little evidence of an age-related decline in intellectual functioning (based on Baltes and Lindenberger, 1997).

of your senses. This knowledge should expand your comprehension of many behavioral phenomena that depend upon perception as a first step. Perception seems to be the final judge of the truth or the falsity of everything we encounter as part of our human experience. How often have you heard the phrase "Seeing is believing" or "I didn't believe it until I saw it with my own two eyes"? Yet, you have already seen in this chapter that such faith in the truthfulness of our conscious percepts is often misplaced. In 500 B.C. Parmenides considered how perception can deceive us, summarizing his feelings in these words: "The eyes and ears are bad witnesses when they are at the service of minds that do not understand their language." In this book we will try to teach you their language.

CHAPTER SUMMARY

Perception is important in our study of psychology because all of the information that we have about the external world comes in through our senses. Our conscious representation of the world can be affected by a number of factors, leading to illusions and misperception of the external reality.

Aspects of the perceptual process include **sensation,** which is concerned with the first contact between the sense organs and the external world. Sensation deals with more basic aspects of experience, such as the brightness or color of a light. **Perception** deals with the attempt to identify objects and relationships in the external world. **Cognition** deals with how memory and interpretive processes affect what is perceived, whereas **information processing** attempts to understand the interactions of the various **levels of processing** from the sensory through to the cognitive mechanisms.

Theories of perception vary in nature and approach. **Biological reductionism** is based on the presumption that for any given aspect of the observer's sensation there is a corresponding physiological event. **Direct perception** begins with the presumption that perception involves isolation of **invariants** in the stimuli that surround us and the discovery of action possibilities called **affordances.** **Computational theories** describe mathematical rules by which information about the world can be extracted from the flow of stimuli in the world. **Constructive theories** or **intelligent perception** describe how our cognitive strategies, personal history, problem-solving techniques, and even our memories can alter the world that we perceive in consciousness.

Failure to take perceptual processes into account can lead to misinterpretation of behavioral processes. For instance, the often-cited slowed thinking ability and reduced intelligence of older individuals as measured by some tests disappear when we take into account the reduction in visual acuity and hearing ability that occurs as a simple consequence of aging.

KEY TERMS

illusions
sensation
perception
cognition
information processing
levels of processing
biological reductionism

direct perception
invariants
affordances
computational theories
intelligent perception
constructive theories

Psychophysics

CHAPTER 2

The first issue we have to deal with in the study of sensation and perception is how we can measure a perceptual experience. This is a difficult issue because percepts don't have length, weight, or a physical shape; hence we must rely on what people tell us they are perceiving, and that can sometimes lead to problems. **Psychophysics** is the name given to the study of the relationship between the physical stimuli in the world and the sensations that we experience. The name comes from Gustav Teodor Fechner (1801–1887), a physicist and philosopher who set out to solve the mind-body problem of philosophy, and is based on the Greek roots *psyche*, or "mind," and *physike*, which refers to naturally occurring phenomena. In order to describe the relationship between our physical bodies and our mental experiences, Fechner had to solve three problems. First, he had to find a way to measure the minimum intensity of a stimulus that we can perceive, which is the problem of **detection**. Second, he had to devise a way to measure how different stimuli must be before they no longer appear to be the same, which is the problem of **discrimination**. Finally, Fechner attempted to describe the relationship between the intensity of the stimulus and the intensity of our sensation, and in doing so addressed the problem of **scaling**.

Fechner not only established the philosophical rationale for studying the relations between sensations and physical stimuli but also developed many of the experimental methods still in use today. These methods for collecting and analyzing data are used in every aspect of the study of sensation and perception and in many other areas of psychology, including social, personality, environmental, developmental, clinical, and environmental psychology (Baird & Noma, 1978; Gescheider, 1997; Grossberg & Grant, 1978). As you read this chapter, keep in mind that although psychophysics emphasizes methods, the fundamental concepts it introduces can also be influential in our understanding of every aspect of mind and behavior (e.g., Link, 1993; Norwich, 1993; Ward, 1992).

DETECTION

Our sensory systems are responsive to energy changes in the environment. Energy changes may take the form of electromagnetic (light), mechanical (sound, touch, movement, muscle tension), chemical (tastes, smells), or thermal (heat, cold) stimulation. The problem of detection is the problem of how much of an energy change, starting from zero, is necessary for a sensory system to register its presence (e.g., for an individual to see, hear, or otherwise sense it). Classically, this minimal amount of energy change from zero has been called the **absolute threshold.** In 1860 Fechner defined a threshold stimulus as one that "lifted the sensation . . . over the threshold of consciousness." The idea is that below some critical intensity of the stimulus, a person would not be able to detect it. As soon as this threshold intensity is exceeded, however, we would expect the observer to always detect its presence.

This hypothetical relation can be described using a graph called a **psychometric function.** The *ordinate* (or vertical axis) of the graph is the proportion of stimulus presentations on which an observer says "yes" to the question "Did you see (or hear, feel, etc.) the stimulus?" The *abscissa* (or horizontal axis) of the graph is stimulus intensity. Figure 2-1 shows such a graph using arbitrary units for stimulus intensity. Notice that the proportion of "yes" responses takes a sudden step up from 0 to 1.0 when the stimulus reaches a value of 3.5. The absolute threshold indicated by this ideal psychometric function is thus 3.5.

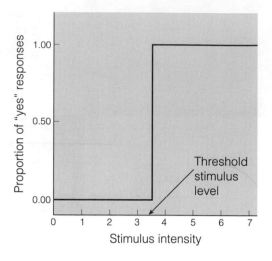

FIGURE 2-1   Absolute threshold.

Method of Constant Stimuli

How do we measure the absolute threshold? We will describe a relatively simple but typical experiment to measure the absolute threshold of hearing. In this experiment a listener sits in a quiet room wearing headphones. The experimenter selects a set of tones to present. The tones differ in their intensity, some clearly easily heard, some not heard at all. She presents these tones, one at a time, to the listener. Each is presented many times in an irregular order. The listener is required to respond "yes" when he detects the stimulus and "no" when he does not. This procedure is called the **method of constant stimuli** because a fixed or constant set of stimuli is chosen in advance. Some typical data obtained with this method are presented graphically in Figure 2-2.

We see in Figure 2-2 that as the stimulus energy increases, the proportion of "yes" responses, indicating that the person heard the stimulus, gradually increases. These S-shaped curves are obtained commonly with the method of constant stimuli in all sensory systems. Notice that our psychophysical experiment did not find the sharp transition from "not sensing" to "sensing" illustrated in Figure 2-1. Instead, the likelihood that a person reports perceiving the stimulus increases gradually as the stimulus intensity increases. So where is the

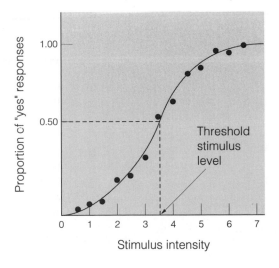

FIGURE 2-2 Typical data from method of constant stimuli in detection.

absolute threshold? Because there is no dramatic transition point to define the absolute threshold, we must make a somewhat arbitrary decision as to what the threshold stimulus intensity is. Most psychophysicists would agree to define the absolute threshold as the stimulus intensity that observers detect 50% of the time. This corresponds to the intensity for which the probability of saying "yes" is the same as the probability of saying "no": Each equals 0.50 because the two must sum to 1.00. Notice that we use the term *probability* in this context. Proportions (as in Figure 2-2) represent actual data, whereas probabilities are theoretical proportions. In Figure 2-2 we show graphically how the threshold can be determined. First, the data points are fitted with a smooth curve. Then, the abscissa value yielding the 50th percentile of the smooth curve is found (this corresponds to drawing a horizontal line from the 0.50 value on the ordinate until it intersects the smooth curve and then dropping a line vertically from this point to the abscissa). The absolute threshold is about 3.5 energy units for this listener. Although this halfway point on the psychometric function (a detection probability of 0.5) is the generally agreed-on value for the threshold, it is an arbitrary value.

Although the method of constant stimuli can produce quite useful estimates of absolute threshold, it does have some drawbacks. First, it is quite time

consuming. Pretesting is often needed to make a sensible advance estimate of the threshold so that the stimulus set can be centered around it, and then many trials must be presented at each intensity level. Although fewer trials are sometimes used, the method is not time efficient because trials presenting intensities far from threshold are not very informative (Simpson, 1988; Watson & Fitzhugh, 1990). Minimizing the time spent determining a threshold is often important, especially in clinical settings, such as a doctor's office where an individual's hearing is being tested for a hearing aid or in situations where there might be short-term fluctuations in sensitivity you want to measure.

Method of Limits

One way to avoid some of the problems of the method of constant stimuli is to focus on stimuli near the absolute threshold rather than to trace out the entire psychometric function. The method of limits, named by Emil Kraepelin in 1891, does just that. In this technique, the experimenter begins by presenting an observer with a stimulus, for example, a pure tone, at an intensity high enough to be easily heard and then decreases its intensity in small steps until the observer reports, "I no longer hear it." This is called a *descending* series. On alternate trials the experimenter starts with a tone that cannot be heard and increases the intensity until the observer reports, "I hear it." This is called an *ascending* series. It is assumed that the response changes when the threshold is crossed, and so each series gives an estimate of the absolute threshold as an intensity somewhere between the last two stimuli presented.

When we estimate thresholds from single series of trials in the method of limits, we find that the "absolute threshold" is not a fixed value as we first thought. For instance, we might find that in one descending series the observer could no longer detect the stimulus when presented with a tone intensity of 50 but in the next descending series a stimulus intensity of only 43 was still detected. Moreover, on average, the descending series yield lower thresholds than the ascending series. It seems that the threshold varies from measurement to measurement, or from moment to moment. Why does this occur? In 1888 Joseph Jastrow

---

DEMONSTRATION BOX 2-1
The Variability of the Threshold

For this demonstration you will need a wrist-watch (or a clock) that ticks. Place the watch on a table, and move across the room so that you can no longer hear the ticking. If the tick is faint, you may accomplish this merely by moving your head away some distance. Now gradually move toward the watch. Note that you are actually performing a method of limits experiment because the sound level steadily increases as you approach the watch. At some distance

from the watch you will begin to hear the source of the sound. This is your momentary threshold. Now hold this position for a few moments, and you will notice that occasionally the sound will fade and that you may have to step forward to reach threshold, whereas at other times it may be noticeably louder, and you may be able to step back and still hear it. These changes are a result of your changing threshold sensitivity.

---

proposed that lapses of attention, slight fatigue, and other psychological changes could cause fluctuations of the threshold. Demonstration Box 2-1 shows how you can experience this threshold variability in a simple experiment.

Because of our presentation so far, you might assume that in a threshold measurement experiment the only stimulus present is the stimulus we are asking our observer to detect. This is not the case. A constantly present and ever-changing background of sensation exists no matter what stimulus we present to the observer. If you place both of your hands over your ears to block out external noises, you will hear a sound one observer poetically called "the sound of waves from a distant sea" and another, somewhat less poetically, "the faint hissing of radio static." Similarly, if you sit in a completely lightproof room in absolute darkness, you do not see complete blackness. Your visual field appears to be filled with a grayish mist, called "cortical gray," and occasionally you can even see tiny "light" flashes here and there. Any stimulus that we ask an observer to detect is superimposed on a background of noise generated within the observer. By *noise* we mean any background sensation other than the one to be detected, which means that we can have visual as well as auditory noise. Because of various factors over which we have no control, such as the rushing of blood in our veins and arteries, this *endogenous*, or internally generated, noise varies in intensity from moment to moment. And as this endogenous noise level changes, so does our measured threshold: The higher the

noise intensity, the higher intensity a (threshold) sound must be to be detected against it.

Because the endogenous noise level cannot be easily controlled, some experimenters have introduced experimentally controlled background noise caused by external stimuli other than the one to be detected (*exogenous* noise). Under these conditions they have a more accurate idea of the noise level with which the stimulus is competing because the exogenous noise is much more intense than, and thus overwhelms, the endogenous noise. Many of the experiments we will discuss have employed such a controlled background noise level.

Adaptive Testing

The method of limits is still somewhat inefficient because it is only the stimuli that bracket the threshold (the last two in each testing series) that give any information; the rest tell us nothing. Adaptive testing keeps the test stimuli "hovering around" the threshold by *adapting* the sequence of stimulus presentations to the observer's responses. Consider, for example, the staircase method (Bekesy, 1947; Cornsweet, 1962). In this procedure we might start with a descending series of stimuli. Each time the observer says, "Yes, I hear it," we *decrease* the stimulus intensity by one step. At some point the stimulus will become too weak to be heard, and the observer will say, "No, I don't hear it." At this point we don't end the series, as we

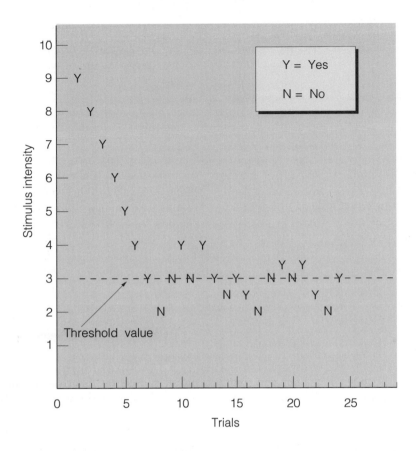

FIGURE 2-3 A portion of a trial-by-trial record (called a *track*) from a run of an adaptive testing technique using a descending staircase procedure where the stimulus intensity was decreased when detected ("yes") and increased when not detected ("no").

did in the method of limits, but rather we reverse its direction, *increasing* the stimulus intensity by one step. We continue for as long as required, decreasing the stimulus whenever the observer says "yes" and increasing it whenever the observer says "no." In this way the value of the test stimulus varies around the threshold value as shown in Figure 2-3. This procedure allows the experimenter to "track" the threshold over time, even if sensitivity is changing, such as after administration of some drugs or after adaptation to different background stimuli. When we wish to, after several *reversals* of direction, we can average the stimulus values at which the reversals occurred to obtain an average threshold value.

The staircase method is the simplest example of the use of adaptive testing to find thresholds. Using the observer's previous responses to determine the stimulus series allows the experimenter to zero in on the threshold quickly and efficiently, with few wasted trials and with a high degree of reliability (Kaernbach, 1991; Meese, 1995). In our example we used the rule "increase intensity by one step if the response to the previous stimulus was 'no' and decrease intensity by one step if the previous response was 'yes.'" This is called a "one up-one down" rule. Other rules can be used, however, to increase the precision of the method, to avoid judgment biases, or to achieve certain statistical proportions in the data (Brown, 1996; Levitt, 1971; Macmillan & Creelman, 1991). Moreover, the intensity step size can also be changed adaptively from trial to trial to achieve even greater efficiency and precision (Kaernbach, 1991). If the series of trials is long enough, there are even some statistical techniques to estimate the entire psychometric function from this trial-by-trial data (Leek, Hanna, & Marshall, 1992).

Here are some examples of approximate absolute threshold values as measured by the methods we have just discussed. The human visual system is so sensitive that a candle flame can be seen from a distance of more than 48 km (30 mi) on a dark, clear night. The human auditory system can detect the ticking of a wristwatch in a quiet room at a distance of 6 m (20 ft)—sensitivity beyond this would allow us to hear the sound of air molecules colliding. Furthermore, the average human can taste 1 teaspoon of sugar dissolved in 7½ liters (2 gallons) of water and smell one drop of perfume diffused through the volume of an average three-room apartment (Galanter, 1962).

Signal Detection Theory

All of the techniques we have described so far are based on simply recording the observer's responses of "Yes, I hear it" or "No, I don't hear it." These could be pretty tenuous data on which to base our theories. Suppose that an observer felt that this was a "test" of some sort in which it would be good for him to appear to be quite sensitive; he might say "yes" on almost every trial. What would prevent this from happening? Even trustworthy and dedicated people, which includes most observers in psychophysics experiments, might be unsure as to whether or not a very weak stimulus was peeking out from the always-present noise. Under these conditions observers must adopt some decision strategy for responding when they are uncertain. For example, observers could limit the number of "no" responses, feeling that too many "no" responses would make them appear to be "hard of hearing."

To control such response strategies, early experimenters inserted catch trials, in which no stimulus was presented, into the series of trials. They reasoned that accurate observers would always respond "no" on catch trials because no stimulus was present; a "yes" response on such a trial would be just a guess. Thus, if observers responded "yes" too often on catch trials they were cautioned against guessing, the calculated threshold was adjusted to account for the guesses, or the data were discarded altogether. Over many experiments, however, it became clear that "yes" responses on catch trials were not always guesses. Sincere, honest observers were reporting that they had really heard something that sounded like the sound they were trying to detect, even when it was not there! Were observers in psychophysical experiments experiencing hallucinations? It seemed absurd to believe that, but there was no way to account for such experiences within classical psychophysical theory. The stage was set for a completely new approach to the problem of detection.

The absolute threshold as measured by the methods discussed so far is a useful statistical fiction. However, threshold measures vary not only with changes in an observer's sensitivity, as we would wish them to, but also with changes in the observer's decision strategies, which is not desirable. Signal detection theory attempts to deal with this problem. This is a mathematical theory that was derived from the same statistical decision theory that is used to analyze scientific experiments (Green & Swets, 1966/1974; Macmillan & Creelman, 1991). Signal detection theory assumes that any stimulus must be detected against the background of endogenous noise in our sensory systems. Thus, on each trial the observer has to decide whether the signal was present in all that noise or whether there was only the usual fluctuating neural noise. For example, a radar operator might be trying to detect on the radar screen the visual signal denoting a radar echo of an approaching airplane against a background of false echoes (of clouds, birds, etc.) and static from the display apparatus. In signal detection theory there is no absolute threshold; there is only a series of observations, each of which must be categorized as either signal present or signal absent. A series of such decisions can be used to deduce how sensitive a person is to a given signal, independent of any motivational or expectation effects that might bias the decisions.

Signal detection theory requires a special type of experiment in order to measure sensitivity and bias. The basic paradigm is shown in Table 2-1. The experiment uses two types of "stimulus" presentations (shown at the left of the table). A *signal absent* trial is like a classical catch trial on which no stimulus is presented and observers see or hear only the noise generated by their sensory system or by the experimenter. On a *signal present* trial the experimenter actually presents the target stimulus (which is, of course, superimposed on the endogenous noise and any exogenous noise). The two possible responses are shown at the top of Table 2-1. *Yes* indicates that the observer has decided that the signal was present on a particular trial (that it was a signal present trial), and *No* indicates that the observer has decided the signal was not present (that it was a signal absent trial). The combination of the two possible types of trials and the two possible responses leads to four possible outcomes on each trial (indicated by the four cells of Table 2-1). A "yes" to a signal present trial is called a **hit**, whereas a "yes" to a signal absent trial is called a **false alarm**. Similarly, a "no" to a signal absent trial is called a **correct negative**, and a "no" to a signal present trial is called a **miss**.

Consider a typical signal detection experiment designed to measure an observer's ability to detect a tone of a given (very low) intensity and frequency in a background of white noise (like the static hiss when a radio is tuned between stations). After a ready signal, the observer is required to respond by pushing one button to indicate, "Yes, it was a signal present trial" and a different button to signify, "No, it was not a signal present trial." Table 2-2 shows a typical response pattern for an experiment with 50% signal present trials and 50% signal absent trials. This **outcome matrix** shows the *proportion* of trials on which the four possible results occurred. Notice that the proportions in each row must sum to 1.00 because we consider the two types of trials separately.

Notice that on 25% of the signal absent trials the observer responded, "Yes, the signal was present." Why should the observer report that a signal was present when it was not? First, the observer is not always sure that whatever was heard

was actually the signal. Thus, many nonsensory aspects of the situation might influence the pattern of responding. For example, if the signal is expected to be present on almost every trial, the observer might respond "yes" to even the faintest or most ambiguous of sensations, whereas if the signal is expected to occur only rarely, the observer would be less tempted by ambiguous, faint sensations and might wait until a very strong sensation was experienced before saying "yes." If the signal was expected to occur about half the time, as in Table 2-2, the observer might respond "yes" whenever the sensation was moderately strong.

If this analysis is correct, then we should be able to change the observer's response pattern by changing only his expectations and leaving everything else the same so as not to change his sensitivity. Typical results from additional experiments with the same observer are presented in Table 2-3. In one case there were 90% signal present trials and in the other only 10%. Notice that when the signal occurred frequently the observer said "yes" often. This resulted in a high proportion of hits, but also in a high proportion of false alarms. The observer said "no" more often when the signal was expected to occur only occasionally, thus reducing the proportion of false alarms but also reducing the proportion of hits.

Another way to change the observer's response pattern is to vary the perceived importance of the two possible responses. This is most effectively done by establishing monetary rewards and penalties for the responses according to a **payoff matrix** such as that in Table 2-4. The payoff matrix shown in Table 2-4 would be expected to produce a symmetric outcome matrix similar to that in Table 2-2 because the relative value of a "yes" response, given by adding algebraically the two entries in the "yes" column $[10¢ + (- 5¢) = 5¢]$, is equal to that of the

Table 2-1   Outcomes of a Signal Detection Experiment

	RESPONSE	
Signal	Yes	No
Present	Hit	Miss
Absent	False alarm	Correct negative

Table 2-2   Outcome Matrix (Proportions) When Stimulus Is Present 50% of the Time

	RESPONSE	
Signal	Yes	No
Present	0.75	0.25
Absent	0.25	0.75

Table 2-3   Outcome Matrices (Proportions) for Two Different Conditions

STIMULUS PRESENT 90% OF THE TIME

	Response	
Signal	Yes	No
Present	0.95	0.05
Absent	0.63	0.37

STIMULUS PRESENT 10% OF THE TIME

	Response	
Signal	Yes	No
Present	0.35	0.65
Absent	0.04	0.96

Table 2-4   A Typical Payoff Matrix for a Psychophysical Experiment

	RESPONSE	
Signal	Yes	No
Present	10¢	−5¢
Absent	−5¢	10¢

"no" response, making both responses equally valuable. If we paid observers according to a payoff matrix with 10¢ for a hit, 1¢ for a correct negative, and nothing for the other responses, we would expect an outcome matrix similar to that in the top of Table 2-3 because the higher relative value of "yes" responses should make the observer want to say "yes" most of the time. The complementary payoff matrix, with only 1¢ for a hit and 10¢ for a correct negative, would yield an outcome matrix something like that at the bottom of Table 2-3. However, even if we did not establish an explicit payoff matrix, we can be sure that observers would use their own implicit payoff matrices, with unknown-to-us relative values of "yes" and "no" responses.

Because changes in an observer's response strategy change the proportions of hits and misses on which we must base estimates of sensitivity, how is it possible to measure sensitivity independent of those changes? To do this, signal detection theory creates a theoretical picture of how the signal and noise must have appeared to the observer over the course of the experiment so as to generate the obtained outcome matrix. This picture is based on several assumptions. First, as we already mentioned, it is assumed that the amount of noise an observer must cope with varies from moment to moment. These fluctuations in noise level are caused by physiological, attentional, and other variables in the sensory and perceptual systems of the observer as well as by random fluctuations in the environment, such as the fluctuating light patterns on a radar screen even in the absence of echoes. Signal detection theory represents these variations across time as a **probability distribution** like that shown in Figure 2-4, called the *signal absent distribution*. In Figure 2-4, the abscissa is the sensory activity level during a trial when no signal was presented, and the ordinate is the relative likelihood of occurrence of any particular sensory activity level over all of the trials in the experiment. On trials when the signal is present, the sensory response produced by the signal adds to whatever activity level was present at that moment, producing the *signal present distribution* also shown in Figure 2-4. In Figure 2-4 the two distributions have been drawn on different copies of the same axes so that each can be seen clearly. In the theory they always overlap. You can see from Figure 2-4 that many different levels of sensory activity could result with some likelihood greater than zero either from signal present trials or from signal absent trials.

In signal detection theory, the observer is considered to be an optimal decision maker (see, e.g., Green & Swets, 1966/1974). Such a decision maker uses a simple rule to make a response on each trial. If the sensation level is above a particular level, called the **criterion** and symbolized with the Greek letter **β (beta)**, the observer says "yes"; if it is below the criterion level the observer says "no." This strategy can be shown to result in the best possible series of decisions in this situation. Signal detection theory assumes that this optimal strategy is used on every trial of an experiment, resulting in the proportions of hits, false alarms, misses, and correct rejections that we would observe in an outcome matrix. In the theory, the area under the appropriate probability distribution to the right or left of the

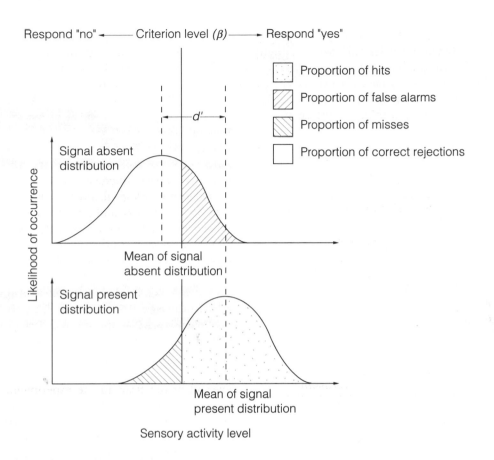

FIGURE 2-4 Illustration of how signal absent and signal present distributions result in hits, misses, false alarms, and correct negatives for a particular criterion setting. Notice that the two curves are actually plotted on the same axes—they are separated for clarity. The curves would overlap if plotted together.

criterion represents the proportions of the various types of responses given over the course of an experiment, as illustrated in Figure 2-4. For example, the area under the signal present distribution to the right of the criterion (where the observer responds, "Yes, I perceived it") represents the proportion of hits observed in an experiment, whereas the area to the right of the criterion in the signal absent distribution represents the proportion of false alarms.

Motivation and expectation will determine where the criterion is placed. For instance, suppose the observer is a radiologist looking for a light spot as evidence of cancer in a set of chest X rays (see, e.g., Swensson, 1980). If the radiologist thinks she has found such a spot, she calls the patient back for additional tests. The penalty for a false alarm (additional tests when no cancer is present) involves only

some added time and money on the part of the patient, whereas the penalty for a miss (not catching an instance of real cancer) might be the patient's death. Thus, the radiologist may set a criterion value that is quite low (high relative value of "yes" responses), not wanting to miss any danger signals. This means she will have many hits and few misses, but also many false alarms. The signal detection theory picture of such a situation, portraying an outcome matrix similar to that at the top of Table 2-3, would look like the one shown in Figure 2-5A. Conversely, if the observer is a witness to a crime who is trying to identify suspects from a set of mugshots, he might be more conservative. Here the penalty for a false alarm could be the arrest, trial, and conviction of an innocent person, whereas the penalty for a miss might be only that the prosecution would have less evidence available to prosecute the guilty parties. The witness might set a high criterion (high relative value of "no" responses) in order to avoid false alarms, but at the penalty of reducing the number of hits. The picture for this situation, with an outcome matrix

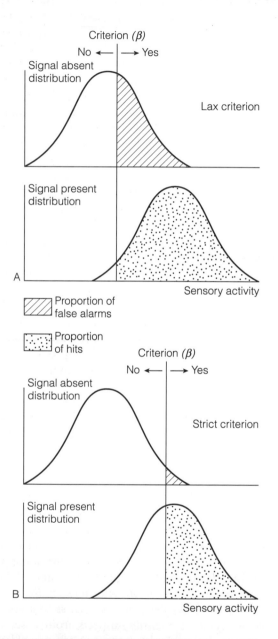

Proportion of false alarms

Proportion of hits

FIGURE 2-5 The effect of motives or expectations on criterion placement and proportion of hits and false alarms.

similar to that shown at the bottom of Table 2-3, would resemble that shown in Figure 2-5B.

Although the location of the criterion alters the response pattern, location of the criterion has no effect at all on the sensitivity of the observer. In signal detection theory, *sensitivity* refers to the average amount of sensory activity a given signal adds to the average amount of sensory activity present in the absence of the signal (noise). This is similar to the everyday use of the word *sensitivity*. Thus, a radio receiver that produces a large electrical response, allowing a weak signal to be heard above the background static, is more sensitive than one that produces only a small electrical response to that signal, which may then be obscured by static and noise.

In signal detection theory sensitivity is measured by the distance between the centers (means) of the signal absent and the signal present distributions. This could be interpreted as the difference in average sensation levels as a function of the presence or absence of a signal. We call this distance measure of sensitivity d', which is pronounced "dee prime" (see Figure 2-4). When the two distributions are far apart, and overlap less, as in Figure 2-6B, d' is larger. When they are close together, and overlap more, d' is smaller, as in Figure 2-6A. Signal detection theory measures an observer's sensitivity to a signal independent of the response strategy by making specific assumptions about how responses are made in the experimental setting. It has become an indispensable part of modern psychophysics, appearing in adaptive measurement techniques (e.g., Kaernbach, 1990) and other commonly used procedures, such as same-different tasks (Dai, Versfeld, & Green, 1996; Irwin & Hautus, 1997). Instructions for calculating d' and β using proportions of hits and false alarms obtained from any typical signal detection experiment (e.g., Tables 2-2 and 2-3) can be found in Computation Box 2-1. Discussions of methods for doing statistical tests on d' and β can be found in Macmillan and Creelman (1991) and Miller (1996).

DISCRIMINATION

The recipe called for dividing the gooey dough mixture into two equal-sized portions, one for the

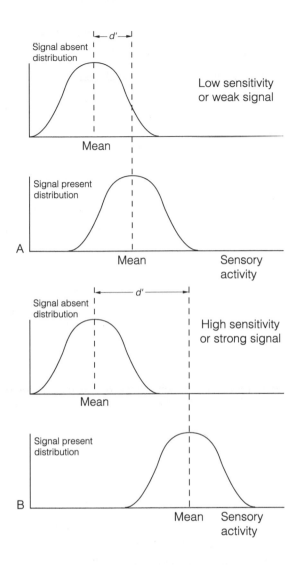

FIGURE 2-6 The effect of sensitivity and signal strength on d'.

could have been 200 g or 1,000 g. He cared only whether the two bowls had the same amount. Discrimination problems ask the question "Is this stimulus different from that one?"

The study of discrimination has focused on the question "By how much must two stimuli differ in order to be discriminated as not the same?" Suppose we are comparing a computer and a typewriter. Are they the same or different? The answer depends on what aspects are being compared. Both have keyboards and can print words, so they are the same in that way. But computers can compute, and typewriters cannot, so they are different, too. To avoid such confusions, the standard discrimination experiment involves variation of stimuli along only one dimension. Thus, in a study of the discrimination of weights, we might hold the size and shape of our stimuli constant and vary only their weight.

In a typical study, observers are presented with pairs of stimuli and asked to make the responses "heavier" or "lighter" or some similar set of judgments appropriate to the stimulus dimension being judged. In this experiment observers are not permitted to say "same" because it has been shown that even when they feel they are just guessing, observers are more often correct than incorrect. Thus, not allowing "same" judgments yields a more accurate measurement of discrimination performance (Brown, 1910). One stimulus intensity, called the standard, is the stimulus that the others are compared with. The standard appears on every trial and is compared to a set of similar stimuli differing only along the dimension being studied. These stimuli make up the set of comparison stimuli. This experiment is a variant of the method of constant stimuli (which, you may remember, is used to determine the absolute threshold) to which the standard has been added. We are also measuring a threshold here, but this is a threshold for the perception of a difference between the standard and the other stimuli. It is called the difference threshold.

Typical results from an experiment in discrimination of lifted weights are displayed in Figure 2-7. In this experiment, the standard (a 100-g weight) was presented with each comparison stimulus (82 g to 118 g in 1-g steps) over 700 times. We need plot only the proportion of the presentations on which each comparison stimulus was judged "heavier"

top and the other for the bottom of the deep-dish apple pie the cook was preparing. He put about half of the mixture into each of two bowls and then compared them. He decided they were not the same, took about a teaspoonful from one and put it into the other. "There," he said, "now they are equal. My pie is going to be delicious!" This somewhat obsessive cook was engaged in an act of discrimination. He was determining whether two amounts of dough were the same or different. He did not care how much dough was in each bowl; it

COMPUTATION BOX 2-1
Calculation of Signal Detection Measures d' and β

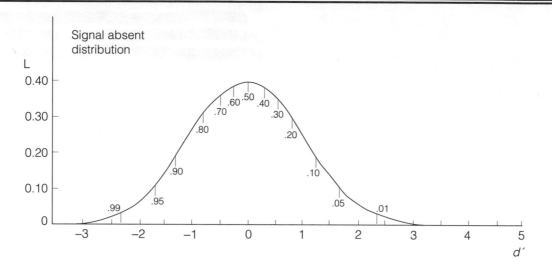

To calculate d' and β using a simple graphic procedure, you will need the sheet of transparent overlay (found inside the front cover) and the diagram of the signal absent distribution above. First, tear the overlay along the perforated line to separate the *criterion* and *signal present distribution* portions as indicated.

Next, from the outcome of a signal detection experiment, you will need the proportions of *hits* and *false alarms*. As an example, we will use the data from Table 2-2.

TO CALCULATE d'

1. Put the sheet containing the criterion on top of the diagram of the signal absent distribution. Make sure that the horizontal line of the criterion sheet is superimposed on the horizontal axis of the distribution.
2. Slide the criterion sheet across the sheet below until the criterion (vertical line) is positioned so that it cuts the signal absent distribution curve at the point that represents the proportion of false alarms. From Table 2-2 this is 0.25, so you must estimate the placement between the marked numbers.

3. Holding the criterion sheet stationary, add the *signal present distribution* sheet to the stack, positioning it so that the horizontal axis is aligned with the other horizontal axes. Adjust it so the criterion meets the signal present distribution curve at the point representing the proportion of *hits* (in this example it is 0.75).
4. The final stack of two overlay sheets on top of the signal absent distribution should look something like the figure on page 27. Notice that you can see through the overlay sheets to the d' scale printed on the signal absent distribution diagram. The d' value can then be read off that scale as the point where the vertical line (which is marked "Read d'" and represents the mean of the signal present distribution) intersects the d' scale (about 1.35 in the figure on page 27—interpolate carefully).

Now try calculating the values of d' for the two sets of data in Table 2-3. You should find that d' is about 1.35, the same as for the data of Table 2-2, in spite of the vast differences in hit and false alarm rates (compare with Figure 2-6).

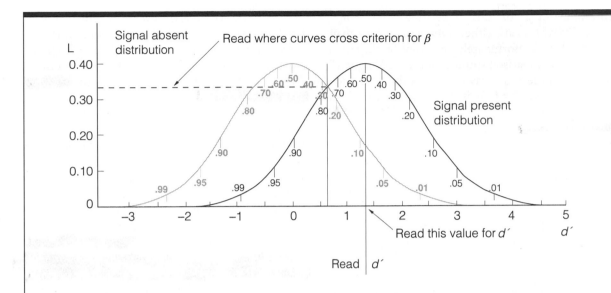

TO CALCULATE β

To measure the criterion, calculating β requires one small computational step in addition to looking at the graphs.

1. Align a straightedge (ruler or piece of paper) parallel to the superimposed horizontal axes of your pile (without sliding the sheets around), and position it vertically so that you are measuring the height of the curve where the criterion and the *signal present curve* meet. Read off the value corresponding to the height from the vertical axis (labeled "L" for "Likelihood") where the straightedge crosses it (around 0.34).

2. Next read the height of the curve where the criterion crosses the *signal absent curve*. (In this example this is the same, with a height of 0.34).

3. To calculate β, divide the height (the L axis value) for the *signal present distribution* by the

height for the *signal absent distribution*. In the figure below, this is 0.34/0.34 = 1.00, or β = 1.00.

Try calculating β for the two sets of data in Table 2-3. You should find that, because of the very different hit and false alarm rates in the two data sets, the β values are also very different. The top data set shows a lax criterion with β less than 1.00 (here around 0.30), whereas the lower data set demonstrates a conservative criterion with β greater than 1.00 (here a bit more than 4.00).

You should save your sheets of transparent overlay with the book so that you can use them for other d' and β calculations. Also note that, although this graphical method is accurate enough for quick estimates of d' and β, psychophysicists use precise numerical tables or complex equations to arrive at these measures with the accuracy needed for research.

---

than the standard because the proportion of "lighter" judgments can be obtained by subtraction (proportion "lighter" = 1 − proportion "heavier"). Notice that the shift from reports of "lighter" to reports of "heavier" is not very abrupt, as it would be if the difference threshold were always a single unique value (as it is in Figure 2-1). Rather, there is a gradual change in the probability of a "heavier"

response as the comparison stimulus changes from much lighter than the standard to much heavier. Again, this S-shaped psychometric function can be fitted with a smooth curve. We have done this (by eye) to the data in Figure 2-7. Just as in the case of measuring the absolute threshold using the method of constant stimuli, because the curve changes gradually, we must decide how we will define the threshold for a stimulus to be called "different." Here *different* means either lighter or heavier than the standard. Unfortunately, the point on the curve where the comparison stimulus was called "lighter" half of the time and "heavier" half of the time (proportion "heavier" = 0.5) is not appropriate. This stimulus intensity, usually called the **point of subjective equality**, represents the stimulus that appeared to be most like the standard, not the difference from the standard that can just be discriminated. A more defensible choice would be the stimulus intensity at which the proportion "heavier" equals 0.75, halfway between perfect discrimination, a proportion "heavier" of 1.00, and no discrimination, the point of subjective equality. At this point the *difference* in the "heavier" direction is noted 50% of the time. Following similar reasoning, the stimulus intensity for which the proportion "heavier" equals 0.25 is the point at which a stimulus difference in the "lighter" direction is noted 50% of the time. By convention, we take the interval from the 0.25 point to the 0.75 point, the **interval of uncertainty**, and divide it by 2 to obtain the **difference threshold**. The difference threshold for the data in Figure 2-7 is about 4 g. This means that when a pair of stimuli in this experiment were separated by 4 g, the subject was able to detect the difference between them about half the time. The

difference threshold is the average of the threshold for "greater than" and the threshold for "less than." It represents the threshold for "different" averaged across the direction of the differences. This value is sometimes referred to as the **just noticeable difference**.

If discrimination is good, the difference threshold will be small, and small differences between stimuli will be noticed. In Figure 2-8 the black line shows the psychometric function of an observer with relatively good discrimination ability who has a difference threshold of 0.50 units. The white line shows that of an observer who is less able to discriminate these stimuli and who has a larger difference threshold of 2.00 units. The worse the discrimination ability, the flatter is the psychometric function and the larger is the difference threshold. The extreme of no discrimination at all would be represented by a horizontal line parallel to the abscissa.

You may have noticed that in the data of Figure 2-7 the point of subjective equality is not equal to the standard. The stimulus that *appears* to be equal to the standard of 100 g is actually 1 g lighter. This is a typical result in many psychophysical experiments involving the presentation of stimuli that are separated in time. The stimulus presented first (generally the standard) is judged to be less intense than the later stimulus. This effect has been named the **negative time error** (because the standard is judged to be *less* intense than it should

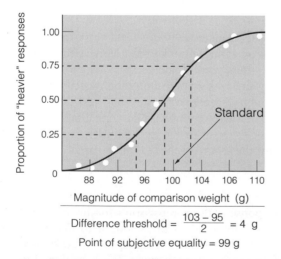

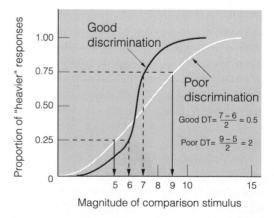

FIGURE 2-7 Typical data from the method of constant stimuli in discrimination with calculations of difference threshold and point of subjective equality.

FIGURE 2-8 Difference thresholds (DTs) for observers of different sensitivity.

be). Fechner (1860/1966) and Wolfgang Kohler (1923) thought this error is caused by the fading of the image or the memory trace of the sensation of the standard with the passage of time. However, work done with auditory stimuli has shown that with proper selection of a time interval the error can be positive rather than negative (Kohler, 1923). Such errors are probably the result of particular cognitive or judgmental factors involved in judging stimuli in the context of others, such as weighting some stimuli more than others (Hellstrom, 1979, 1985). Such comparison processes, as we shall see later, influence even the most apparently simple perceptual tasks.

Weber's Law

Having a way to reliably measure the difference threshold made it possible to ask how it varied with stimulus conditions or the state of the observer. Following the earlier work of Ernst Heinrich Weber (1834), Fechner (1860/1966) conducted experiments in which he measured the difference thresholds for lifted weights using standard weights of different magnitudes. In Figure 2-9 we have plotted for some illustrative data similar to Fechner's, the size of the difference threshold versus the magnitude of the standard. First, notice that the difference threshold is not a constant value. It is larger for larger standards. In fact, the difference threshold increases roughly linearly with the magnitude of the standard. For example, if a room contained 10 lit candles and you could just detect the addition of 1 candle, then if the room contained 100 candles it would take an additional 10 candles for you to notice it. This relation between the size of the difference threshold and the magnitude of the standard is called **Weber's Law.**

Weber's Law is written as

$$\Delta I = kI$$

where ΔI *(delta I)* is the difference threshold, I is the intensity (magnitude) of the standard stimulus, and k is a constant. The constant k, called the **Weber fraction,** is equal to $\Delta I / I$. This constant, which is usually less than 1, indicates the *proportion* by which a standard stimulus must be changed so that the change can be detected 50% of the

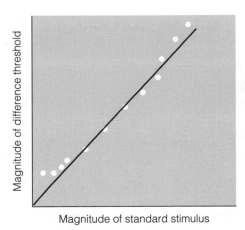

FIGURE 2-9   Effect of intensity of standard on difference threshold.

time. Weber's Law asserts that the Weber fraction is the same for any intensity of standard stimulus. For example, if the Weber fraction for lifted weight is 0.02, a comparison weight must be only 0.04 g heavier than a 2-g standard (2 g × 0.02 = 0.04 g) to be discriminated 50% of the time. However, a comparison weight must be 4 g heavier than a 200-g standard (200 g × 0.02 = 4 g) to be discriminated 50% of the time. A simple demonstration of Weber's Law is given in Demonstration Box 2-2.

Table 2-5 presents typical Weber fractions for a variety of continua. As you can see, some of the ks are relatively large (for example, those for light and sound intensity), and some are smaller (for example, electric shock). Generally speaking, if we have equivalently measured Weber fractions, then larger Weber fractions mean poorer sensitivity to differences along that continuum. For example, the fact that Weber fractions for light intensity are larger in elderly individuals can be interpreted to indicate that such individuals are less sensitive to differences in light intensity than are younger individuals. Also, if we are willing to make some reasonable, although technically tricky, assumptions, it may be possible to compare sensitivities across different sensory systems (Narens & Mausfeld, 1992; Teghtsoonian, 1971; Ward, 1991).

Weber's Law turns out to be a remarkably good description of our ability to make discriminations.

DEMONSTRATION BOX 2-2
Weber's Law

It is easy to demonstrate Weber's law for the perception of heaviness. You will need three quarters, two envelopes, and your shoes. Take one quarter, and put it into one envelope, and put the remaining two quarters in the other. If you now lift each envelope gently and put it down (use the same hand), it is quite easy to distinguish the heavier envelope. Now insert one envelope into one of your shoes and the other envelope into your second shoe, and lift them one at a time. The weight difference should be almost imperceptible. In the first instance the targets differed by the weight of the quarter, and the difference was discriminated easily. In the second instance, although the weight differential was the same (one quarter), the overall stimulus intensity was greater because shoes weigh much more than the envelopes and the quarters alone.

Measurements have been taken in many sense modalities to check the relation. The clearest picture of the results is given by plotting the value of the Weber fraction, $\Delta I/I$, against the standard stimulus intensity. If the Weber fraction is actually constant, we should see a horizontal line, parallel to the horizontal axis. Figure 2-10 shows a composite of data from many sound intensity discrimination experiments. Deviation from the expected constancy occurs at low stimulus values, where internal noise becomes a factor, and at high values, where the sensory systems act in a distorted manner. These deviations look large only because we have plotted the stimuli in logarithmic units. The flat part of the curve actually covers nearly 99% of the total range of intensities used.

Signal Detection Theory in Discrimination

Although signal detection theory was presented (and first developed) to measure detection, it can be extended readily to discrimination. To use the theory in this way, we must redesign the signal detection experiment. In the discrimination version, instead of trying to determine whether the sensation experienced on a given trial came from the signal present or the signal absent distribution, the observer is asked to decide whether it came from the Signal 1 or Signal 2 distribution. Because the signals used are very similar, the sensory activity curves overlap when plotted on the same set of axes, and an observer would be faced with a situation very much

Table 2-5 **Typical Weber Fractions ($\Delta I/I$)**
(based on Teghtsoonian, 1971)

CONTINUUM	WEBER FRACTION
Light intensity	0.079
Sound intensity	0.048
Finger span	0.022
Lifted weight	0.020
Line length	0.029
Taste (salt)	0.083
Electric shock	0.013
Vibration (fingertip)	
60 Hz	0.036
125 Hz	0.046
250 Hz	0.046

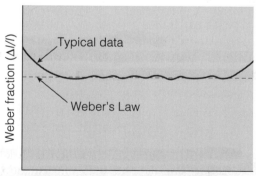

FIGURE 2-10 Typical data for test of Weber's Law. The dotted line is predicted by Weber's Law: $\Delta I/I = K$.

like that faced by the observer in the absolute detection situation. Look back at Figure 2-4 and mentally relabel the two distributions "Signal 1" and "Signal 2." The two stimuli each give rise to a variety of different sensation levels over many trials, with different probabilities. Because the resulting probability distributions cover the same general area of the sensation axis, there is no way to be certain which stimulus elicited a given sensation level on any one trial. The best the observer can do is to place a criterion somewhere on the sensation axis and then to determine whether the sensation level experienced on a particular trial is above or below that criterion. If above, the appropriate response would be that the presented stimulus was a 2; if below, a 1. Just as in the absolute detection situation, where the observer places the criterion will greatly affect the proportions of different responses. In turn, criterion placement will be affected by the observer's expectations as to the relative frequency of presentation of the two stimuli and by the observer's motivational biases.

As in the detection experiment, the measure of sensitivity to the difference between the two stimuli is called d' and is unaffected by changes in the criterion, β. The value of d' is determined by the physical difference between the two stimuli and the sensitivity of the observer's sensory system; both are factors that determine the difference between the average levels of sensation evoked by the stimuli. Thus, d' represents a measure of just how discriminable two very similar stimuli are. As such, it is closely related to the difference threshold and to the Weber fraction (Treisman, 1976).

Reaction Time

We have been discussing situations in which discrimination is very difficult. However, even when stimulus differences are well above the difference threshold, we may feel that some discriminations are easier to make than others. For example, most people feel that red is more easily differentiated from green than it is from orange, even though we would never actually make an error in discriminating these colors. Because methods like signal detection theory experiments depend on observers making errors, they cannot be used to measure detectability or discriminability in situations where

all of the stimulus differences are far enough above threshold to be easily perceived. To measure discriminability in such situations, we must measure **reaction time.** *Reaction time* is defined as the time between the onset of a stimulus and the beginning of an overt response to it. The concept was introduced in 1850 by one of the most influential early workers in perception and physiology, Hermann von Helmholtz, who used it as a crude measure of how quickly nerves conduct information.

There are two varieties of reaction time. **Simple reaction time** involves pressing or releasing a button (or making some other simple response) immediately on detecting a stimulus. **Choice reaction time** involves making one of several different responses depending on the stimulus presented (for example, press the button on the right for a red light and the button on the left for a green light).

Simple reaction times commonly are measured when we are interested in detectability. We have known for a long time that the less intense a stimulus, the slower the reaction time. Figure 2-11 shows typical median reaction times to the onset of a tone plotted against the intensity of the tone collected in a classic experiment by Chocolle (1940). With lower tone intensities, we near the detection threshold, and, although the tone is still always detectable, the reaction times are longer. Similar results have been obtained for visual stimuli (Cattell, 1886; Grice, Nullmeyer, & Schnizlein, 1979).

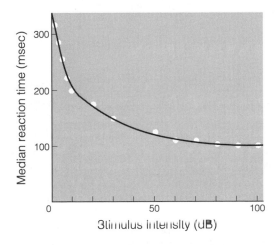

FIGURE 2-11 Effect of stimulus intensity on simple reaction time (based on Chocolle, 1940).

DEMONSTRATION BOX 2-3
Reaction Time and Stimulus Discriminability

A fun-to-do example of the relation between choice reaction time and discriminability involves card sorting (e.g., Shallice & Vickers, 1964). Take a deck of common playing cards and select out of it 10 of the picture cards (kings, queens, and jacks) and 10 numbered cards from the red suits (hearts and diamonds) to make a new deck of 20 cards. Compose another deck of 20 by using the numbered cards (include the aces) of the black suits (clubs and spades). Shuffle each deck separately and place it in front of you, face down. Next you need a clock or a watch with a sweep second hand.

Wait until the second hand reaches the "12", pick up one of the decks, and begin to sort it into two piles. The first deck gets sorted into number and picture cards; the second gets sorted into spades and clubs. Note the time it takes to sort each deck. You may want to repeat the task a couple of times so that you are sorting smoothly. Notice that the sorting time for the spades and clubs (a more difficult task because it involves making small form discrimination on similarly colored cards) is longer than the easier discrimination task of sorting picture and number cards.

Choice reaction time has been used mostly in studies of discrimination and identification. The classic discrimination experiment utilizing reaction time was done by Henmon (1906). In one study, the observer was presented with pairs of lines differing only in length and was told to depress the one of two keys available that corresponded to the side on which the line was longer. Henmon found that the smaller the difference between the line lengths, the longer was the reaction time. He reported similar results for colors and tones. You can experience another example of this effect in Demonstration Box 2-3.

IDENTIFICATION

A doctor who is listening to heart sounds through a stethoscope might be considered to have a discrimination problem to solve, namely, "Are these heart sounds normal or abnormal?" However, if he concludes that the sounds are abnormal, he must still determine what kind of abnormality the sounds represent. This is more complex than the simple discrimination between two alternatives because it involves the recognition of which of a number of possible stimuli are present. It involves remembering and using an *identification function*, which is a rule that links some attribute of each stimulus (such as its intensity) to the label it is to receive. It also involves remembering previous perceptual experiences because, for example, you can identify the smell of mint now only because at some time in the past you experienced that smell and labeled it "mint." To understand identification we must first introduce you to information theory.

The difficulty of any identification task depends, in part, on the number of possible stimulus alternatives an observer is asked to distinguish among. Consider someone who claims he can always identify his favorite brand of beer. Suppose we gave him two unmarked glasses of beer and asked him to sample them and to try to identify his favorite brand. If he did select the correct brand, we would not be very surprised because he would be expected to select his own brand 50% of the time by chance alone, even if his taste buds were nonfunctional and he were just guessing. If our "expert" selected his own brand out of 25 brands presented to him, we would be much more likely to take his claim seriously because the probability that he would by chance alone find his brand out of 25 alternatives is only 1 in 25.

Information Theory

To solve the problem of specifying the difficulty of an identification task, psychologists in the early 1950s turned to ideas developed by engineers to assess the performance of radio and telephone communications systems. Books by Shannon and Weaver (1949) and by Wiener (1961) made it clear that the problems faced by the psychophysicist and by the communications engineer were quite similar. The engineer deals with a message that is transmitted through a communication channel and decoded by someone or something at the receiver end. The degree to which the final decoded message reflects the original message depends, in part, on the ability of the system to transmit information without distortion (this is what is meant by the fidelity of a system) and on the complexity of the input. The psychophysicist has an analogous problem. Stimulus information is transmitted to an observer through a sensory system, and it is then decoded in the central nervous system. The degree to which the observer's identification of the stimulus corresponds to the actual stimulus input will be affected by both the ability of the sensory system to handle the stimulus input without distortion and by the complexity of the input.

The quantitative system for measuring the performance of a communication channel is known as *information theory*. In this theory, the amount of information is defined in a very general way so that the content of the "message" is irrelevant. What, then, do we mean by *information*? We mean what the everyday use of the word implies: reduction of uncertainty. If you tell us that this week will contain a Sunday morning, you have conveyed very little information because we know that every week contains a Sunday morning. If you tell us that this Sunday morning there will be a parade in honor of Jiffy the Kangaroo, you have conveyed a great deal of information because you have specified which one out of a large number of possible alternative events is going to occur.

A useful way to quantify this kind of information is to count how many questions a person must ask to discover which member of a stimulus set has occurred. Suppose there were only two possible alternatives, A or B, and you wanted to determine which of them was the target. You need ask only "Is it A?" to determine unambiguously which alternative had been designated as the target. If you received an answer of "no" you would know immediately that the target was B. If you wanted to determine which of four stimuli, A, B, C, or D, had been chosen as the target, you could do it with two questions. The answer to the question "Is it A or B?" reduces your number of possible alternatives to two because a "no" answer reveals that it is ei-

ther C or D, whereas a "yes" answer indicates that it is A or B. We already know that only one more question is necessary in order to identify the correct item. Each necessary question, structured to eliminate exactly *half* of the alternatives, defines a **bit** (from *bi*nary digi*t*) of information.

The number of bits of information needed to determine exactly one stimulus alternative is the logarithm to the base 2 of the total number of possible stimulus alternatives. The logarithm of a number n to the base 2, which is written $\log_2 n$, is the power to which the number 2 must be raised to equal n. Thus, if we have four alternatives we must raise 2 to the second power (i.e., $2^2 = 2 \times 2 = 4$) and $\log_2 4 = 2$. Similarly, $\log_2 1 = 0$, $\log_2 2 = 1$, $\log_2 8 = 3$, $\log_2 16 = 4$, and $\log_2 32 = 5$ (a detailed table can be found in Garner, 1962). Each time the number of events is doubled, the amount of information rises by one bit. Of course, for intermediate values the number of bits will not be a whole number (for example, seven alternatives gives 2.81 bits).

Channel Capacity

Let us consider an observer as a sort of communication channel. Our observer may be represented as in Figure 2-12. A stimulus is presented, and the observer is asked to try to identify it. By "identify" we mean to give a response that is the correct agreed-on label for the particular stimulus presented. To the extent that the observer's responses match the labels of the stimuli presented, **information transmission** is occurring. That is, if the observer is presented with a stimulus and gives the correct label as a response, information (the correct label) has been transmitted through the channel represented by the observer. If the response matches the stimulus perfectly for all stimuli, then the observer is a perfect information transmitter.

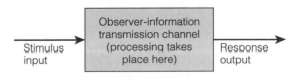

FIGURE 2-12 A human information channel.

Consider an example in which we are randomly calling out letters from a set of eight: *A B C D F G H X*. If an observer correctly identifies (response) the letter that we have called out (stimulus), then she has transmitted three bits of information ($\log_2 8 = 3$). Suppose identification is not perfect; that is, only some of the information available (three bits) is being transmitted. For instance, if the observer hears a faint "eee" sound, with the first part of the letter cut off, she does not know exactly which letter was called out. However, she can eliminate *A*, *F*, *H*, and *X*, which have no "eee" sound. Hence, she has reduced the number of stimulus alternatives by half, and we would say that she will transmit one bit of information in her response, which will be a guess among the other four alternatives. In general, the greater the probability that the observer will correctly identify the stimulus—that is, the more she "picks up" from the presentations, the more information she is capable of transmitting.

Consider a hypothetical experiment in which each of four stimuli was presented 12 times in a random order and an observer was asked to identify which stimulus was presented on each trial. The data from such an experiment can be summarized in a **confusion matrix,** as shown in Table 2-6 for three different observers. Observer A shows perfect transmission of the two bits of information available ($\log_2 4 = 2$) because the correct response was given to the stimulus on every trial. There are never any errors, or *confusions*. Observer B shows poorer information transmission. Note that when Stimulus 2 was presented, it was called "2" most of the time but sometimes it was called "1" and sometimes "3." When the response was "2," however, there is a fair likelihood that the stimulus was Stimulus 2. Observer B is much better than Observer C, who seems to have been responding without reference to the stimulus presented. Observer C transmitted none of the available stimulus information. Formulas for computing the amount of information transmitted in such confusion matrices may be found in Garner and Hake (1951).

How many different stimuli can an observer identify perfectly? Consider first a group of stimuli selected to vary only along a single physical dimension, such as sound intensity or frequency. The number of stimuli from one dimension that a

Table 2-6   Stimulus-Response Matrices for Three Observers

OBSERVER A:
PERFECT INFORMATION TRANSMISSION

Stimulus	Response			
	1	2	3	4
1	12			
2		12		
3			12	
4				12

OBSERVER B:
SOME INFORMATION TRANSMISSION

Stimulus	Response			
	1	2	3	4
1	8	4		
2	2	8	2	
3		2	8	2
4			4	8

OBSERVER C:
NO INFORMATION TRANSMISSION

Stimulus	Response			
	1	2	3	4
1	3	3	3	3
2	3	3	3	3
3	3	3	3	3
4	3	3	3	3

subject can identify perfectly has been found to be surprisingly small. For the identification of tones varying only in frequency, Pollack (1952) found it to be about five different tones, which is equivalent to about 2.3 bits of stimulus information. Garner (1953) found much the same result for sound intensity, around 2.1 bits. Eriksen and Hake (1955) measured several visual continua and found information transmission to be limited to 2.34 bits for light intensity, 2.84 bits for size, and 3.08 bits for wavelength. Overall, the number of stimuli varying only on a single physical dimension that can be identified without error is approximately seven plus or minus two (7 ± 2), depending on the particular stimulus dimension involved (Miller, 1956).

This limit is called the observer's **channel capacity.** Figure 2-13 illustrates how channel capacity is measured; each white dot represents the information transmission calculated from a separate confusion matrix. Notice that even when the amount of information available in the display is greater than 2.5 bits, the observer can transmit no more information than that, the channel capacity in this situation.

Several theories have been proposed to explain this general finding. In the most popular type of theory, the limit reflects cognitive or response processes (e.g., Braida & Durlach, 1988; Gravetter & Lockhead, 1973). A less accepted theory is that the limit is set by the response characteristics of sensory neurons and is thus an absolute limit for a single sensory continuum (Norwich, 1993).

Seven seems to be a very small number of stimuli to be able to identify. We know that musicians, for example, seem able to identify (indeed, sing) hundreds of different songs. Every one of us can certainly identify dozens of faces and thousands of words. How can this be, in light of our inability to transmit more than about three bits of information per stimulus dimension?

Perhaps stimuli in the everyday world are more discriminable than typical laboratory stimuli. However, there is no simple relationship between discriminability and identification performance (Norwich, 1993; Pollack, 1952). Another possible explanation is that our everyday performance is better because of practice or repetition. Except in extreme cases, in which a person might have years of intensive training on a single dimension, the practice effect is also not large enough to explain our everyday performance. For instance, you hear a new word today and later identify that word with ease, even though you have encountered it only once. You can also distinguish the new word from every other word in your vocabulary. We are not at all surprised at such a performance, yet it may involve the transmission of 16 bits of information or more, depending on the total number of words in your vocabulary. If channel capacity is so limited for any single stimulus dimension, how

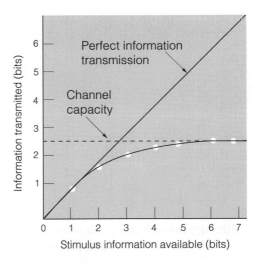

FIGURE 2-13 Channel capacity. The straight diagonal represents perfect information transmission. The curve represents typical performance. The dashed horizontal line is channel capacity.

can this occur? Part of the answer involves the *number of dimensions* along which the stimuli can vary simultaneously.

For example, Pollack (1953) found that if he varied only sound frequency, information transmission averaged about 1.80 bits, whereas if he varied only sound intensity, information transmission was about 1.70 bits. When both dimensions were varied simultaneously, however, information transmission was 3.10 bits. This is more than was obtained for either dimension separately, although not the 3.50 bits expected if the information transmissions on the separate dimensions added perfectly. Nonetheless, the more dimensions along which a set of stimuli varies, the better is the identification performance on that set of stimuli.

Certain ways of combining dimensions also seem to produce better performance by making stimuli "stand out" more clearly from the others of the set or by capitalizing on the small gains obtainable by familiarity (Lockhead, 1970; Monahan & Lockhead, 1977). Thus, by proper selection of stimulus dimensions, Anderson and Fitts (1958) were able to have information transmission levels of 17 bits for a single briefly flashed stimulus. This means that their observers could perfectly identify 1 stimulus out of more than 131,000 alternative stimuli.

The importance of stimulus dimensions and how they are combined has led modern investigators to place less emphasis on the *quantity* of information available and more emphasis on the *quality*, or kind, of information and the characteristics of the information processor (Cutting, 1987; Garner, 1974; Neisser, 1967). The basic ideas of information theory, especially those associated with the effect of the number of stimulus alternatives on performance, have been important in calling attention to critical issues in identification. And although other methods, based on signal detection theory, are used increasingly often to measure identification performance (e.g., Braida & Durlach, 1988), information theory has taken its place as a foundation concept, and modern researchers use its methods and assumptions in many different situations.

The amount of information involved will also affect some of the other measures that we have looked at, such as reaction time. Crossman (1953) argued that reaction time differences are related not only to the discriminability of the stimuli but also to the amount of information they contain. If this is the case, then choice reaction time should be larger the larger the number of response alternatives. This result has been known since Merkel (1885) found that the more numbers his observers had to choose between, the longer the choice reaction time (see Table 2-7).

Hick (1952) attempted to explain these results by postulating that the observer extracts information

Table 2-7   Reaction Time as a Function of Number of Stimulus Alternatives (based on Merkel, 1885)

NUMBER OF ALTERNATIVES	REACTION TIME (ms)
1	187
2	316
3	364
4	434
5	487
6	534
7	570
8	603
9	619
10	632

from the stimulus display at a constant rate (cf. Norwich, 1993), so the more information that must be obtained from the display, the longer the reaction time. In an experiment in which observers pressed telegraph keys in response to lights, he found that a straight line related reaction time to the logarithm of the number of stimulus alternatives. This relation, called **Hick's Law**, states that choice reaction time is a linear function of the amount of information in the stimulus (at least up to three bits; Longstreth, 1987). This means, for example, that we can directly compare reaction times only between conditions in which the number of stimulus alternatives is the same. Demonstration Box 2-4 shows how to produce effects like those of Hick's Law in a card-sorting task.

DEMONSTRATION BOX 2-4
Number of Stimulus Alternatives and Reaction Time

Take a deck of playing cards and separate 16 cards using only the low numbers ace, 2, 3, and 4. Next, make up another deck of 16 cards using 2 each of the 5, 6, 7, 8, 9, 10, jack, and queen. Now shuffle each deck. Measure the time it takes to sort each deck into piles by number (four piles for the first and eight for the second deck) using a watch or clock with a sweep second hand as you did in Demonstration Box 2-3. Notice that the reaction time becomes longer (measured by sorting time) as the number of alternative stimuli that must be recognized and responded to becomes greater. Thus, sorting the four-stimuli deck is more rapid than sorting the eight-stimuli deck.

SCALING

The dog trainer glanced at her new St. Bernard pupil and estimated his shoulder height to be 65 cm (26 in.) and his weight to be 70 kg (150 lb). In so doing she was engaged in the process of estimating scale values of her pupil's height and weight. **Scaling** attempts to answer the question, "How much of X is there?" X can be a stimulus intensity in the real world, a sensation magnitude, or the magnitude of such other complex psychological variables as pleasantness or annoyance.

A **scale** is a mathematical rule by which we assign numbers to objects or events. The scale attempts to represent numerically some property of those objects or events (see Mitchell, 1986). A variety of types of representations may be established, and each has its own characteristics (Luce & Narens, 1987; Narens & Luce, 1986; Stevens, 1946). The most primitive and unrestricted type of scale is a **nominal scale** (from the Latin *nomin* meaning "name"). When numbers are assigned in a nominal scale, they serve only as names, such as the numbers on a football uniform. The nominal scale values signify only the identity of the items and say nothing about value. Thus the team member with the "10" on his jersey is not necessarily larger, faster, or better than the player with the "5" on his jersey.

Whenever it is possible to say that one object or event contains more or less of some property than does some other object or event, we can create an **ordinal scale** of that property. An ordinal scale ranks items on the basis of some quantity. An example might be the "Best-Seller" or "Top 50" lists that order books or records on the basis of how many have been sold. Although this scale is more useful for measurement than is a nominal scale, we are still very restricted in what we can do with the numbers on such a scale because all that is represented is *order* or ranking, not actual quantities.

A third type of scale is the **interval scale**. It not only signifies "more" or "less" but also tells "by how much." It employs not only the sequential properties of numbers but also their spacing, or the *intervals* between them. A good example of an interval scale is the scale of temperature represented by the common household thermometer. Here the temperature difference between 10° C and 20° C (50° F and 68° F) equals that between 40° C and 50° C (104° F and 122° F). Such scales are very useful because most statistical techniques can be meaningfully applied to interval scale values. Interval scales suffer from one major drawback, however. They do not have a *true* zero point; rather, convenience or convention usually dictates where the zero will be. Thus, on the centigrade scale of temperature, zero is the freezing point of pure water, whereas on the Fahrenheit scale zero is the freezing point of a saltwater mixture.

The most scientifically useful scale is the **ratio scale**. Creation of this type of scale is possible only when equality, rank order, equality of intervals and of ratios, and a true zero point can be experimentally determined. Unfortunately, ratio scales are more often found in the physical than in the behavioral sciences. Such things as mass, density, and length can be measured on ratio scales because the zero points are not arbitrary. For example, 0 g represents the complete absence of mass, and we can meaningfully say that 10 g is twice as massive as 5 g. Negative values of mass exist only in the fantasies of dieters.

Not all psychological quantities can be measured in the same way. Some perceptual experiences have an underlying aspect of intensity (for instance, brightness), whereas others do not (such as hue). When we are dealing with an experience in which it makes sense to ask, "How much?" or "How intense?" we have a **prothetic continuum** (Stevens & Galanter, 1957). With prothetic continua, changes in the physical stimulus result in a change in the apparent *quantity* of the psychological experience. For example, louder sounds seem to have "more" of something than softer sounds do; that something is "loudness." This experience can often be connected to the way the sensation is represented in the brain; for example, loudness seems to depend on the total amount of neural activity in auditory areas of the brain, with louder experiences represented by more activity than are softer experiences. Such prothetic continua as loudness can be meaningfully measured on scales of any of the types we have discussed (although some restrictions are necessary—see Gescheider, 1997).

With nonprothetic continua, a change in the physical stimulus results in a change in the apparent *quality* rather than the apparent *quantity* of a stimulus. When we have an experience in which the only question it makes sense to ask is "What kind?" we are dealing with a **metathetic continuum**. Thus, a change in the wavelength of a light may cause its appearance to change from red to green. Psychologically, there is no quantitative difference between these two hues; they simply appear to be different. It makes no sense to ask if red is "more" or "less" than green. Occasionally both types of continua will be present in the same sense impressions. For instance, in touch, the amount of pressure applied is a prothetic continuum, but the location of the touch is a metathetic continuum. Metathetic continua must be dealt with using nominal scales (cf. Schneider & Bissett, 1981).

Indirect Scaling: Fechner's Law

There are two very different approaches to establishing a scale on which numbers will be assigned to the intensity of sensations. The first is **direct scaling**, in which individuals are asked to assign a number directly to the magnitude of a sensation. This seems easy and straightforward. However, many early psychologists distrusted the accuracy of such direct reports. For this reason **indirect scaling** methods, based on discrimination ability, formed the basis for the first psychological scales. Using an indirect procedure is not necessarily to be construed as resorting to an inferior technique. After all, we measure temperature indirectly, using the height of a column of mercury as our indicator. In fact, some have argued that the best way to measure psychological magnitude would be very similar to how temperature is measured (e.g., Ward, 1991).

When Fechner initially attempted to describe the relation between stimulus intensity and sensation, he first had to invent a way to measure the magnitudes of sensations. As his starting point, he assumed that because the minimal difference in stimulus intensity that can be sensed is the difference threshold, our subjective experience of the sensation difference between any two stimuli separated by the physical amount of one difference threshold or *just noticeable difference* (*jnd*) must always be the same regardless of the physical magnitudes of the two stimuli. Thus, if we take two dim lights that are separated by one *jnd* and we take two lights that are much more intense, but again separated by one *jnd*, we should perceive the two pairs

of stimuli as differing by equal sensory steps. This assumption allowed Fechner to create a scale of sensation magnitude by counting *jnd*s of sensation. A stimulus at absolute threshold intensity was assumed to generate 0 units of sensation magnitude; a stimulus intensity 1 difference threshold above absolute threshold was assumed to generate 1 unit of sensation magnitude (1 *jnd* of sensation); a stimulus intensity 1 difference threshold above the 1-unit stimulus to generate 2 units of sensation magnitude (2 *jnd*s of sensation); and so forth. Thus the number of *jnd*s of sensation "measured" the sensation intensity. The *jnd* of sensation was the "unit" of a sensation scale (because all were assumed to represent equal increments of sensation) just as the degree centigrade (or degree Fahrenheit) is the unit of a temperature scale (because all represent equal increments of temperature).

Finally, Fechner assumed that Weber's Law (which states that the difference threshold is a fixed proportion of the stimulus magnitude) is correct. As we have seen, this is reasonable for most of the perceptible stimulus range.

The relation between the sensation intensity and the intensity of the physical stimulus implied by Fechner's assumptions (and a few other technical ones) is shown graphically in Figure 2-14. This curve is described by the equation

$$S = (1/k) \log_e (I/I_o)$$

where S is the magnitude of sensation a stimulus elicits (the number of *jnd*s of sensation above 0 at absolute threshold), I/I_o is the physical magnitude of the stimulus (intensity *[I]* relative to the absolute threshold stimulus magnitude *[I_o]*), *1/k* is the inverse of the Weber fraction ($k = \Delta I/I$), and $\log_e$ is the natural logarithm (logarithm to the base *e*). This equation is called **Fechner's Law** (Baird & Noma, 1978, and Falmagne, 1985, show how it can be derived). The value of *1/k* will be different for different sensory and psychological continua because it is the inverse of the Weber fraction for the continuum scaled. Basically, this law says simply that as we increase the magnitude of a physical stimulus, the magnitude of our sensory experience increases rapidly at first, but then more slowly as the stimulus becomes more intense.

For many years Fechner's Law was used in practical applications, such as building concert halls, to

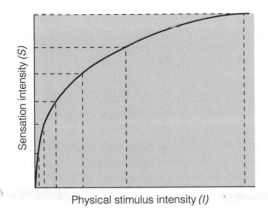

FIGURE 2-14 Fechner's Law. It takes larger and larger differences between stimuli (*I*s) as stimulus intensity increases to give rise to the same size differences between sensations (*S*s).

predict how people would respond to stimuli of various intensities. In addition it was thought to be consistent with physiological data, such as the approximate logarithmic increase in firing rate in sensory neurons with increases in stimulus intensity. Most recently, psychophysicists have often found that scales of sensation intensity based on discrimination measures, such as d', are logarithmically related to stimulus intensity.

Direct Scaling

Since Fechner's time, many psychophysicists have insisted that indirect scaling is neither necessary nor preferable. Because we are interested in the magnitude of the sensation aroused in an observer by a stimulus, why not simply ask the observer to tell us directly how intense the sensation is? If the observer used numbers in a consistent way to report the sensation magnitude, then those numerical responses could be used directly to establish a scale of measurement. For example, the well-known 1-to-10 category scale requires observers to place the sensation created by each physical stimulus into 1 of 10 categories, from weakest to strongest. Stimuli are presented one at a time, and observers' mean (or median, or geometric mean) judgment for a particular stimulus intensity is

treated as the scale value of sensation magnitude for that intensity.

A similar technique was used in an early study by Sanford (1898). He had observers sort envelopes containing weights into five categories, labeled "1" (for the lightest weights) to "5" (for the heaviest). When he plotted the average weight (*x* axis) assigned to each category (*y* axis), he obtained a curve that was concave downward, very similar to the curve predicted by Fechner's Law (Figure 2-14). Sanford took this as additional support for Fechner's Law. Even today, some psychophysicists believe that category scaling is the most useful technique for measuring sensation magnitude (e.g., Anderson, 1992; Krueger, 1991). However, it is acknowledged that category scales are limited in that they are at best interval scales and have no true zero point.

Magnitude Estimation: Stevens's Law

Although in category scaling observers are responding directly to their sensation magnitude, there is still some "indirectness" involved. Most important is that available responses are limited to a few arbitrary category labels. Thus, stimuli that are similar but that give rise to different magnitudes of sensation are often grouped into the same category. S. S. Stevens popularized a procedure called **magnitude estimation** that avoids these problems to some extent. The procedure is so simple and direct that one wonders why it had to be "invented" at all. In this procedure, observers are asked to assign numbers to the magnitudes of the sensations elicited by a set of stimuli that vary on some prothetic dimension. Stimuli are usually judged one at a time, and the only restriction on responses is that only numbers larger than zero can be used.

Consider a typical modern magnitude estimation experiment (e.g., Zwislocki & Goodman, 1980), in which we wish to scale the loudness of a set of pure tones. We would ask observers to assign a number to the sensation (loudness) elicited by each tone in such a way that their impression of the magnitude of that number matched the loudness of the tone. We would tell the observers that they could use any positive number, including decimals or fractions. We would also tell them not to pay attention to any stimuli presented earlier or to the responses they might have given to such stimuli but, rather, to concentrate on matching a number to the loudness of the current stimulus.

This is a very direct way to measure sensation magnitude. As you might also guess, the numbers chosen may vary quite a bit from observer to observer or even from stimulus to stimulus. This method usually requires either an average over many observers or an average over many trials per observer to achieve stable results. Although many researchers prefer magnitude estimation because they believe that the resulting scale has ratio scale properties, there is still some lively debate on this issue (Bolanowski & Gescheider, 1991; Stevens, 1975).

Stevens originally expected the results of magnitude estimation experiments aimed at describing the relation between sensation magnitude and stimulus magnitude to confirm Fechner's Law, even though some earlier direct tests had failed to do this. The earliest was probably in 1872 by one of Fechner's contemporaries, a Belgian investigator named Plateau. Plateau asked artists to mix a gray that was halfway between a particular black and a white. Fechner's Law predicts that this psychological midpoint should correspond to the average of the logarithm of the physical intensity of the black stimulus and that of the white stimulus. Unfortunately, the grays mixed by Plateau's artists seemed to fall halfway between the cube roots (⅓ power) of the intensities of the black and the white stimuli. Plateau suggested that the relation between physical and sensory intensity would be better described by a power function such as $S = I^{1/3}$, rather than Fechner's logarithmic function.

Stevens (1956) confirmed this earlier conjecture when he analyzed the data from an experiment in the magnitude estimation of loudness of pure tones. The equation he found that best described the relation of the median magnitude estimates to the stimulus intensities was

$$L = aI^{0.60}$$

where L (for "loudness") represents the median magnitude estimates, a is a constant, I is the physical intensity of the sound (sound pressure), and 0.60 is a power to which I is raised. In succeeding years, Stevens and a host of others produced magnitude estimation scales for many other sensory continua. All of these scales seemed to be related

to the physical stimulus intensities by the general relation

$$S = aI^m$$

where S is the measure of the sensation intensity and m is a characteristic exponent (power) that differs for different sensory continua. Because this relation states that the magnitude of the sensation is simply the intensity of the physical stimulus raised to some power (m), this relation is often called the **power law** or, after its popularizer, **Stevens's Law.**

In the power law the magnitude of the sensation elicited by a particular stimulus intensity depends on the size of the exponent. In general, the exponent for any one continuum is quite stable. As long as the experimental situation is kept reasonably standard and the same measures of physical stimulus intensity are used (Myers, 1982), the average exponents produced by different groups of observers for the same continuum are quite similar. Some of them are small fractions (0.3 for brightness), some are close to 1 (for line length), and others are substantially greater than 1 (up to 3.5 for electric shock). Some typical exponents for several sensory continua are given in Table 2-8.

In Figure 2-15 we show plots of some power functions relating directly scaled sensory intensity and physical stimulus intensity. Notice that the curves for power functions with different exponents (m) have dramatically different shapes. The curve is concave downward when the exponent is less than 1 (for example, brightness), whereas it is concave upward when the exponent is greater than 1 (for example, electric shock) and a straight line when the exponent equals 1 (for example, apparent length). The immense appeal of the power law is that it allows a vast range of different sensation-magnitude versus stimulus-intensity curves to be captured in the same mathematical function. Moreover, it is relatively easy to estimate what that curve will look like for any set of magnitude estimation judgments. If the power law is a correct description of the relation between magnitude estimations of sensation intensity and stimulus intensity, then logarithms of the magnitude estimates plotted against the logarithms of the stimulus intensities will form a straight line. In Figure 2-16 the curves in Figure 2-15 have been replotted

Table 2-8 **Representative Exponents of the Power Functions Relating Sensation Magnitude to Stimulus Magnitude (based on Stevens, 1961)**

CONTINUUM	EXPONENT	STIMULUS CONDITIONS
Loudness	0.60	Both ears
Brightness	0.33	5° target—dark
Brightness	0.50	Point source—dark
Lightness	1.20	Gray papers
Smell	0.55	Coffee odor
Taste	0.80	Saccharine
Taste	1.30	Sucrose
Taste	1.30	Salt
Temperature	1.00	Cold—on arm
Temperature	1.60	Warmth—on arm
Vibration	0.95	60 Hz—on finger
Duration	1.10	White noise stimulus
Finger span	1.30	Thickness of wood blocks
Pressure on palm	1.10	Static force on skin
Heaviness	1.45	Lifted weights
Force of handgrip	1.70	Precision hand dynamometer
Electric shock	3.50	60 Hz—through fingers

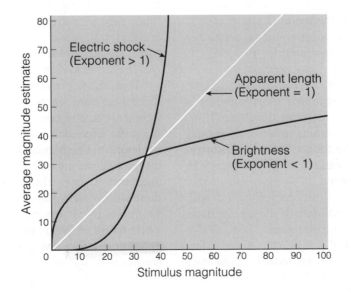

FIGURE 2-15 Power functions for brightness, length, and electric shock. Notice how different exponents give rise to different curves.

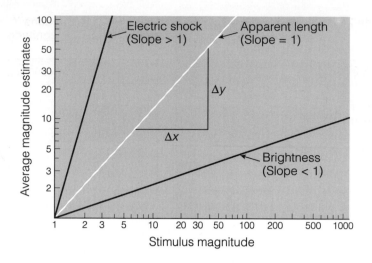

FIGURE 2-16   The same power functions as in Figure 2-15 plotted on logarithmic axes. In such "log-log" plots, all power functions become straight lines, with the slope of the straight line determined by the exponent *(m)* of the power function.

in this way. We can now estimate *m* from the plotted data by measuring the distances marked Δ*y* and Δ*x* in the figures and computing *m* = Δ*y*/Δ*x*. The constant *a* is the point at which the line crosses the ordinate. More sophisticated methods of estimating the parameters in Stevens's Law and those in Fechner's Law are described by Thomas (1983). Demonstration Box 2-5 allows you to perform a magnitude estimation experiment for yourself.

You might wonder why category scaling seems to support Fechner's Law, whereas magnitude estimates are related to stimulus magnitude by a power law. Actually, Stevens and Galanter (1957) found that category judgments only approximately fit a logarithmic relation. Since then several investigators (Gibson & Tomko, 1972; Marks, 1968, 1974; Ward, 1971, 1972, 1974) have shown that category judgments also fit the power law, but with exponents *(m)* that are about half the size of those produced by magnitude estimation. Marks (1974) and Torgerson (1961) suggested that these different results reflect different but equally valid ways of judging the same sensory experience. For example, if my 10-kg dog and my 100-kg brother both gain 1 kilogram in weight, we may ask, "Which one gained more?" If we consider the intervals between weights (as is done in category scaling), the answer is "neither" because both have increased by

1 kilogram. If we consider the ratios between weights (as is implicitly required in magnitude estimation), my dog has increased his body weight by 10% and my brother by only 1%. Thus, my dog exhibited a much greater proportional weight gain. Both types of judgments require estimates of the magnitude of a single event, and both are useful, but the scales (and resultant stimulus-sensation curves) are different (see also Marks, 1979b; Popper, Parker, & Galanter, 1986).

When scaling techniques are used to measure differences between groups, conditions, or changes in sensory acuity over time, it is often found that the sensitivity of the measures can be improved through training. Observers can learn how to give magnitude estimations according to a power function with a particular exponent, thus providing them with a sort of internal "master" scale of sensory intensity (Berglund, 1991; King & Lockhead, 1981; Ward, 1992). This has been called **constrained scaling** because observers were being constrained to use a particular standard scale (West & Ward, 1994). The advantage of this is that when all sensations are judged against the learned scale, the data are less variable, making comparisons across conditions more reliable (West, 1996; West & Ward, 1998). For example, using constrained scaling techniques Marks, Galanter,

DEMONSTRATION BOX 2-5
Magnitude Estimation of Loudness

To produce a graded set of sound intensities for this demonstration, you will need a long ruler, a coin (we have designed the demonstration for a quarter), an empty tin can or water glass, a soft towel, and a friend. Place the can onto the folded towel and have your friend drop the coin from the designated height so that the coin hits the can on its edge only once and then falls onto the towel (silently, we hope). You should sit with your back to the apparatus.

Ask your friend to drop coins onto the can from heights of 1, 10, 70, 100, and 200 cm in some mixed order. For each sound so produced, call out a number whose magnitude you feel matches the loudness of the sound. You may use any numbers you think appropriate as long as they are greater than 0, including decimals and fractions. Your friend should record the height from which the coin was dropped and the number you gave in each instance. Do this for two or three runs through the stimuli (in different

irregular orders), and then average the numbers you called out for each height.

To determine if these judgments follow a power law, plot them on the log-log coordinates provided on the accompanying graph. The vertical axis represents the average magnitude estimates spaced logarithmically, and the horizontal axis represents the sound intensities spaced logarithmically (based on the height of the coin drop). Draw the straight line that best fits (by eye) the data points. Usually the data points fall close to such a line, and any deviations around it are usually fairly random. You can compute the exponent directly (*m* in the power law $S = aIm$) by computing the slope of the straight line on the graph. To do this, pick two points on the line and measure Δx and Δy with a ruler as done in Figure 2-16. Now divide Δy by Δx, and you should get a value somewhere around 0.30. This is half of the 0.60 value for loudness in Table 2-8 because we have measured sound intensity differently here.

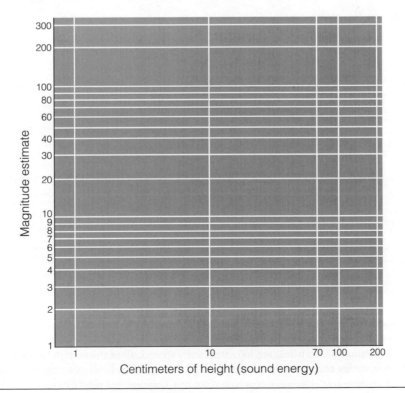

and Baird (1995) were able to demonstrate that the loudness of binaural tones (tones presented to both ears) was roughly twice that of monaural tones (tones presented to only one ear). Obviously, in cases such as this, because we have pretrained observers for a given internal scale, we are not interested in the absolute value of their exponents, as we normally are in scaling experiments. Rather, we are seeking sensitive ways to see how conditions change the scaling exponents. These differences provide us with information about the nature of the underlying sensory experiences.

Cross-Modality Matching   Because the size of the power function exponent varies with how response numbers are used, it might seem that these scales tell us more about how humans use numbers than they do about how sensation varies with stimulus intensity (see Baird, 1975; Baird, Lewis, & Romer, 1970). To counter such criticism, Stevens invented a scaling procedure that does not use numbers at all. In this procedure, an observer ad-

justs the intensity of a stimulus on one sensory continuum until the magnitude of the sensation it elicits seems to be equal to that elicited by a stimulus from a different sensory continuum. Thus, you might be asked to squeeze a handgrip until the pressure feels as strong as a particular light is bright. This procedure is called **cross-modality matching** because the observer is asked to match sensation magnitudes across sensory modalities. Actually, the version of magnitude estimation described earlier is also a form of cross-modality matching in which the number continuum is matched to a stimulus continuum (cf. Oyama, 1968; Stevens, 1975). When we plot the data from cross-modality matching experiments on logarithmic axes (as we did for magnitude estimation experiments), we find that the average matches fall onto a straight line. Despite the fact that the observers no longer make numerical estimates, the data still obey the power law for sensation intensities. Figure 2-17 shows this for a number of modalities matched against handgrip pressure.

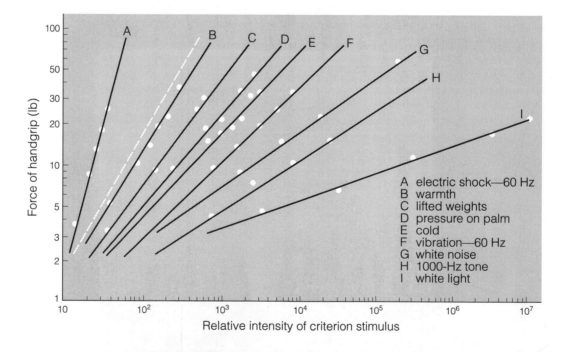

FIGURE 2-17   Cross-modality matching data for nine stimulus continua with force of handgrip as the response continuum. Because the values on both axes are logarithmically spaced, all of the straight lines indicate power function relations between stimulus and response magnitude. The dashed white line has an exponent of 1.0. (From S. S. Stevens, in W. A. Rosenblith (Ed.), *Sensory Communication*. New York: Wiley, 1961. Copyright 1961 by MIT Press)

Cross-modality matching is often more difficult to use than direct magnitude estimation because the subject must adjust stimuli on one of the sensory continua in order to give a response, rather than simply report a number or category label. A recent modification of the cross-modality matching technique makes the task somewhat easier for the observer and seems to give somewhat more reliable results. In *mixed-modality scaling* (Ward 1982a), observers don't actually match sensation magnitudes. Instead, they judge two different sets of sensory stimuli (for instance, lights and sounds), both of which are intermixed in the same experiment. Observers try to use the same scale as the stimuli alternate between the modalities. This technique produces useful cross-modality matching functions with much less effort on the part of the observers, and the power function exponents derived from the matching functions usually agree with those obtained from separate magnitude estimates and cross-modality matching (Nordin, 1994; Stevens & Marks, 1980; Teghtsoonian, 1975; Ward, 1986).

Multidimensional Scaling

Sometimes researchers have difficulty demonstrating the exact relationship between variations in stimuli and our sensory impressions. This is a particular problem for metathetic continua where, as we noted earlier, differences between physical stimuli result in differences in quality, rather than intensity, of the resulting sensations. It is also a problem in situations in which the relevant physical dimensions are complex, are unknown, or do not seem to correspond directly to any psychological dimension. For example, Ekman (1954) obtained observers' ratings of the similarity between many pairs of colors ranging in wavelength from 434 nm to 674 nm. As we explain in Chapter 5, the hue aspect of color varies with wavelength qualitatively rather than quantitatively. Ekman (1954) presented his data in the form of a **similarity matrix** in which pairs of lights that seemed more similar received higher similarity ratings. In the example shown in Table 2-9, each entry represents the similarity rating (on a 1–10 scale) for the pair of stimuli with the wavelengths in the corresponding row and column. Notice that low-wavelength stimuli, which appear blue, have higher similarity ratings with the high-wavelength stimuli, which appear red, than with the medium-wavelength stimuli, which appear yellow. Table 2-9 contains many numbers, and it is not easy to discern a simple relationship from data presented in this way.

An elegant procedure for uncovering the psychological structure contained in such data matrices was developed by Torgerson (1958) and Shepard (1962, 1974, 1980) and was elaborated and extended by several others (e.g., Carroll & Chang, 1970; Kruskal, 1964). The central idea behind this procedure, known as **multidimensional scaling**, is that data representing psychological similarity can be represented as physical distances in a spatial map. The more similar two psychological entities are, the closer together they are placed in the map, whereas the more dissimilar they are, the farther apart. Although these ideas are quite simple and intuitive, a computer program is required

Table 2-9 **A Similarity Matrix for the Observers in Ekman's (1954) Color Perception Experiment**

WAVELENGTHS	445	465	504	537	584	600	651	674
445	—	9	7	6	2	2	7	8
465		—	8	7	2	2	6	7
504			—	9	6	5	2	2
537					7	6	3	2
584					—	8	4	3
600						—	5	4
651							—	9
674								—

to discover the map implied by the data (see Shiffman, Reynolds, & Young, 1981).

An illustration of a spatial map that represents the data collected by Ekman (1954) is shown in Figure 2-18. The computer program provided the positioning of the points representing the various wavelength stimuli. The lines and labels that have been drawn on the map are there simply to help you "see" the structure uncovered by the program. The structure illustrated in Figure 2-18 is the color circle that has been found to be so useful in predicting color mixtures (see Figure 5-4). The axes of the space in which this color circle appears can be interpreted as two *dimensions,* one representing a red-green opponent process and the other a blue-yellow opponent process. As Chapter 5 explains, these opponent processes have been shown to result from characteristic response patterns of neurons in some brain centers of the visual system. Finally, the coordinates of the points representing the stimuli can be interpreted as interval scales of the psychological or physiological dimensions revealed by the map. Thus, multidimensional scaling provides both a way to represent the structure of complex data matrices and a way to obtain meaningful scales of psychological attributes that do not correspond in any simple way to physical dimensions.

Some psychological entities are best thought of in terms of common and distinctive features, rather than in terms of continuous spatial dimensions (Tversky, 1977). For example, the letters of the alphabet have been characterized in terms of distinctive features such as lines of different orientation and curvature (see Chapter 10). **Hierarchical clustering,** a procedure related to multidimensional scaling but differing in the final representation, is sometimes helpful in describing relationships among such sets of stimuli (Johnson, 1967). This procedure also relies heavily on the use of computer programs, but instead of stimuli being represented as points on a map, stimuli are represented as the "leaves" on a "tree," or as "clusters" of stimuli of different degrees of similarity. Together, hierarchical clustering analysis and multidimensional scaling provide a set of very powerful and useful methods of psychophysical scaling when stimuli vary in ways that cannot be described as simple variations in intensity along a single physical continuum.

Context and Bias

Part of the circus strongman's job was to carry various members of the animal cast onto the circus train. One visitor watched in amazement as one after another the strongman lifted the dancing ponies and placed them into their railroad car. "Aren't they heavy?" asked the visitor. "Not if you've just carried three elephants," came the reply.

The essence of this apocryphal tale is that no stimulus is appreciated in isolation. Stimuli are always perceived in the context of the stimuli that precede and surround them. Thus, sportscasters of average height look like midgets when interviewing professional basketball players but look like giants when interviewing professional jockeys. The sportscasters have not, of course, changed size, but their apparent size has changed as a result of the differing frames of reference provided by the heights of those around them. Context effects have long been known to influence judgments of sensory magnitude in many psychophysical tasks, even when the context is in another modality than the one being judged. You can experience this kind of context effect by using Demonstration Box 2-6.

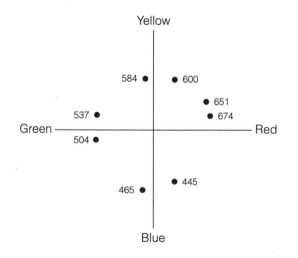

FIGURE 2-18 A *multidimensional scaling* map based on the color similarity data in Table 2-9 (based on Shepard, 1962).

DEMONSTRATION BOX 2-6
The Effect of Visual Context on Judged Weight

You will need two envelopes for this demonstration. One should be rather small (about 7 cm by 13 cm or so), and one should be large (about 20 cm by 28 cm). Put 15 nickels into each envelope. With the same hand, lift the large envelope and next lift the small. Which appears to be heavier? You will probably feel that the small envelope is considerably heavier although the weights are physically equal. This is an example of how a visual context (the envelope size) can alter our perception of heaviness. The same weight in the context of a smaller container seems heavier than when judged in the context of a larger container.

Helson (1964) attempted to explain how context can affect judgments of sensation magnitudes. In Helson's theory, an organism's sensory and perceptual systems are always adapting to the ever-changing physical environment. This process creates an adaptation level, a kind of internal reference level to which the magnitudes of all sensations are compared. Sensations with magnitudes below the adaptation level are perceived to be weak, and sensations above it are perceived to be intense. Sensations at or near the adaptation level are perceived to be medium or neutral. It is significantly more difficult to discriminate stimuli that give rise to sensations that are both on the same side of the adaptation level than to discriminate stimuli, equally close together, whose sensations are on different sides of the adaptation level (Streitfeld & Wilson, 1986). This implies that all perceptions of sensation magnitude are relative. A sensation is not simply weak or intense; rather, it is weak or intense compared to the adaptation level.

For Helson, the adaptation level consists of a combination of the effects of three classes of stimuli. Focal stimuli are at the center of an observer's attention and are usually the ones being judged. Clearly the magnitude of these stimuli will in some way determine the observer's judgments, which is the basic assumption of all scaling procedures. Background stimuli occur close in space and/or time to the focal stimuli, providing the immediate context in which a focal stimulus is judged. Residual stimuli are not current for the observer; they are memories of stimuli the observer has experienced in the past. To be more concrete, consider the sportscaster surrounded by basketball players or jockeys. The physical height of the sportscaster is the focal stimulus. The background stimuli are the heights of the surrounding athletes. The residual stimuli are the heights of all persons previously encountered, including athletes. The adaptation level is a weighted combination (like an average) of all of these stimuli.

Adaptation level theory can explain many perceptual context effects, such as certain visual illusions (Coren & Girgus, 1978). For instance, consider Figure 2-19. The two black circles are physically the same size, although they appear to be

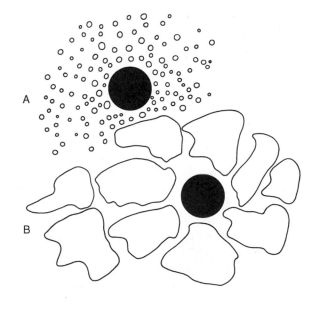

FIGURE 2-19 The circle surrounded by smaller elements appears larger than the circle surrounded by larger elements, although both are the same size (based on Coren & Girgus, 1978).

different. The explanation for this difference in appearance is that when you look at Circle A, your adaptation level for visual size is lower because of the small surrounding elements than when you look at Circle B, which is surrounded by large elements. Circle A is above the adaptation level established for its immediate vicinity and hence appears to be "large," and Circle B is below the adaptation level in its vicinity and hence appears to be "small."

Context can have major effects on judgments of perceptual quantities, such as sensation magnitude (Coren, 1994). Researchers disagree about the specifics of how stimuli interact, which stimuli are involved, and the specific way in which comparisons with a context occur, although all accept the fact that context does affect perception (Coren, 1992; DiCarlo & Cross, 1990; Marks, Szczesiul, & Ohlott, 1986). Context effects have been shown to affect all aspects of psychological scaling, including category judgments, magnitude estimations, and cross-modality matches (e.g., Marks, 1988; Poulton, 1985; Ward, 1987; Ward, Armstrong, & Golestani, 1996).

Context effects suggest that there may be no simple relation between stimulus magnitude and sensation magnitude (Algom & Marks, 1990; Marks, Galanter, & Baird, 1995; Schneider & Parker, 1990). What we perceive is not simply a photographic reproduction of the stimuli in the environment but, rather, is affected by all the myriad stimuli that impinge on us now and have impinged on us in the past because these stimuli provide the context for the perceptual situation in which we presently find ourselves. Perception is active, and processes occurring within the observer can sometimes be just as important in determining a perceptual or sensory experience as are factors in the external environment (Coren, 1994).

The psychophysical measurement techniques introduced in this chapter appear in many disguises throughout the rest of the book. However, psychophysics can involve more than measurement techniques. Many perceptual and cognitive psychologists today continue to work on Fechner's original problems. These psychologists have been called "fundamental psychophysicists" because they study the fundamental psychophysical concepts themselves (such as detection or discrimination) rather than use psychophysical methods to study a sensory system such as vision or audition

(e.g., Link, 1993; Norwich, 1993; Ward, 1992). Despite the cumulative progress of more than 130 years of psychophysical research and the development of many precise ways of measuring perceptual experience, there are still important basic questions that are yet to be answered.

CHAPTER SUMMARY

Psychophysics attempts to describe how our perceptual experiences are related to external stimuli and also provides us with a series of important measurement techniques.

Detection deals with the minimum stimulus intensity needed to actually be perceived. The **absolute threshold** for detection can be measured using a variety of techniques, such as the **method of constant stimuli,** the **method of limits,** and **adaptive testing.** Because the observer's decision strategies have proved to be an important factor, **signal detection theory** was developed. It provides mathematical procedures that allow the separate measurement of sensitivity (d') and the observer's judgmental criterion (β).

Discrimination deals with our ability to tell whether two stimuli are the same or different. **Weber's Law** demonstrates that we can detect smaller differences in weaker stimuli than in more intense stimuli. **Reaction time** measures can often show discrimination differences that are not apparent using measures based on error rates. **Identification** is similar to discrimination except that the observer must recognize one stimulus from a set of more than two stimuli. **Information theory** shows that our identification ability for one stimulus dimension is not very acute, allowing us to recognize a stimulus from only about seven plus or minus two stimulus alternatives. Adding stimulus dimensions increases the observer's **channel capacity.**

Scaling refers to a description of the way in which the experienced sensation intensity is related to the intensity of the physical stimulus. Sensory scales can be created through **indirect scaling** methods, based on measures of **discrimination,** or through **direct scaling** methods, such as sorting stimuli into categories or using **magnitude estimation.** Indirect measures produce a logarithmic relationship between sensation magnitude and stimulus intensity, known as **Fechner's Law,** whereas direct methods produce a power function often called **Stevens's Law.** Special variations in scaling, such as **cross-modality matching, constrained scaling,** and **multidimensional scaling,** have been developed to address specific perceptual questions.

The perception of a stimulus is not an isolated event. **Context,** in the form of other stimuli present, can often alter our judgments of stimulus magnitude. **Adaptation level theory** points out how we often establish an internal reference level that we use to judge stimulus intensities.

KEY TERMS

psychophysics
detection
discrimination
scaling
absolute threshold
psychometric function
method of constant
  stimuli
method of limits
adaptive testing
staircase method
signal detection theory
hit
false alarm
correct negative
miss
outcome matrix
payoff matrix
probability distribution
criterion
beta
d'
standard
comparison stimuli
difference threshold
point of subjective
  equality
interval of uncertainty
just noticeable difference
negative time error
Weber's Law
Weber fraction

reaction time
simple reaction time
choice reaction time
information theory
bit
information transmission
confusion matrix
channel capacity
Hick's Law
scaling
scale
nominal scale
ordinal scale
interval scale
ratio scale
prothetic continuum
metathetic continuum
direct scaling
indirect scaling
Fechner's Law
magnitude estimation
power law or Stevens's
  Law
constrained scaling
cross-modality matching
similarity matrix
multidimensional scaling
hierarchical clustering
adaptation level
focal stimuli
background stimuli
residual stimuli

The Visual System

CHAPTER 3

Although perception occurs within the brain, the brain makes contact with the external environment only through the sense organs. The old saying "The eyes are the windows to the world" makes it clear that the physical properties of this "window" will affect your visual perception in the same manner that the physical properties of a glass window will affect your view. If the window is colored, your perception of the world will be tinted. If the window is curved, so as to magnify the images, your perception of the size of objects viewed through the glass may also be distorted. Thus, it is important for you to understand the physiological makeup of the eye, as well as the way in which information about light is represented in the brain, because these physiological structures are responsible for your perceptions of the world.

LIGHT

Each of the sensory systems is maximally responsive to a different form of physical stimulation. Taste and smell respond to chemical stimuli, touch to mechanical pressure, and hearing to the vibration of air molecules. The physical stimulus for sight is electromagnetic radiation, and the particular form of radiation that produces a visual response is called *light*.

In 1704 Sir Isaac Newton advanced the theory that light acts as if it were a stream of particles traveling in a straight line. Each particle of light is called a **photon,** and so the intensity of light can be measured by the number of photons. Although this conception of light is extremely useful in physics, it is important to the understanding of vision only when we are dealing with stimuli that are very dim. At low levels of light, intensities are often described as the number of photons reaching the visual receptors. As it turns out, the smallest amount of light that is sufficient to activate a receptor cell in the eye is also the smallest possible unit of light, a single photon (Hecht, Schlaer, & Pirenne, 1942).

Light often acts as if it were a stream of particles, but at other times it acts as if it were made up of waves. James Clerk Maxwell (1873) showed that light travels not only in a straight line but also as an oscillating wave. He suggested that if we consider the change in the electromagnetic field surrounding the train of photons, we can treat light as purely a wave phenomenon, with the wavelength defined as the physical distance between the peaks of the photon waves.

Electromagnetic energy can have wavelengths over a broad range, varying from trillionths of a centimeter to many kilometers in length. Very short wavelengths are not visible, nor are very long wavelengths. As can be seen in Figure 3-1, very short wavelengths include gamma rays, X rays, and ultraviolet rays. Longer wavelengths range from those that we call electricity to the broadcasting wavelengths associated with TV and radio (which may be more than 100 m in length). The section of the electromagnetic spectrum that we see as visible light is really quite small, extending from 380 to about 760 nanometers. A **nanometer** is a billionth of a meter and is usually abbreviated *nm*. Perceptually, variations in wavelengths correspond roughly to the hue or color of light. In normal eyes, wavelengths of about 400 nm are seen as violet, 500 nm are seen as blue-green, 600 nm are seen as yellow-orange, and 700 nm are seen as red. However, the perception of color depends on much more than simply wavelength, as you will find out in Chapter 5.

THE STRUCTURE OF THE EYE

Most vertebrate eyes, from those of fish to those of mammals, have a similar basic structure (Berman, 1991; Dawkins, 1996). That is, they contain light-sensitive receptors, protected within a dishlike structure, through which light enters by way of a

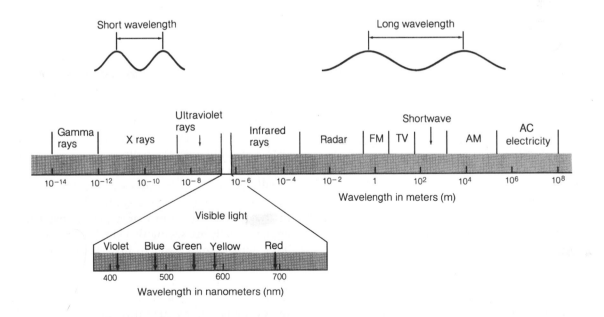

FIGURE 3-1 Electromagnetic radiation spectrum, with the region containing visible light enlarged.

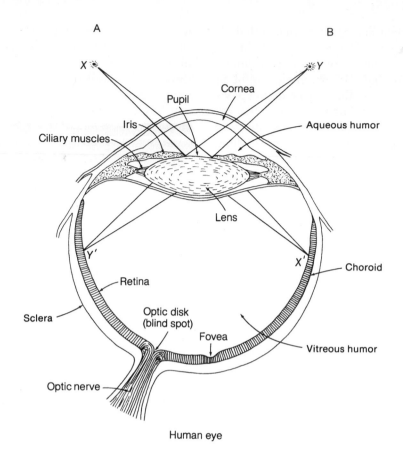

FIGURE 3-2   Structure of the human eye, with a demonstration of the image formation of two targets (*X* and *Y*).

lens. A schematic diagram of the human eye is shown in Figure 3-2. Each eye lies in a protective bony socket within the skull and is a spherical structure about 20–25 mm in diameter. The outer covering, which is seen as the "white" of the eye, is a strong elastic membrane called the **sclera**. Because the eye is not made of rigid materials, it maintains its shape by means of fluid pressure from within.

The front of the eye contains a region where the sclera bulges forward to form a clear, domelike window, about 13 mm in diameter, called the **cornea** (Martin & Holden, 1982). The cornea is the first optically active element in the eye. It serves as a simple fixed lens that begins to gather light and concentrate it. Because the cornea is extended forward, it actually allows reception of light from a region slightly behind the observer, as is shown in Demonstration Box 3-1.

Behind the cornea is a small chamber filled with a watery fluid called the **aqueous humor.** This fluid is similar in nature to the cerebro-spinal fluid that bathes the inner cavities of the brain. This is not surprising because the neural components of the eye actually develop from the same structures that eventually form the brain.

When we look at a human eye, our attention is usually captured by a ring of color. This colored membrane, surrounding a central hole, is called the **iris.** When we say that a person has brown eyes, we really are saying that she has brown irises. The actual color, which may vary from blue through black, is genetically determined in the same way as skin color. The function of the iris seems to be to control the amount of light entering the eye. The light enters through the hole in the iris, which is called the **pupil.** The size of the pupil is controlled by a light reflex. When the light is

DEMONSTRATION BOX 3-1
Vision "Behind" the Eye

It is easy to demonstrate that the visual field actually extends to a region somewhat behind the eye. In order to do this, simply choose a point that is some distance in front of your head and stare at it. Now raise your hand to the side of your head as shown in the figure, with your index finger extended upward. Your hand should be out of view when you stare at the distant point. Now, wiggle your finger slightly, and bring your hand slowly forward until the wiggling finger is just barely visible in your peripheral vision. At this point stop and, with your head as still as possible, move your finger directly in toward your head. You will notice that your hand will touch a point on your temple somewhat behind the location of the eye, indicating that you were actually seeing somewhat "behind yourself."

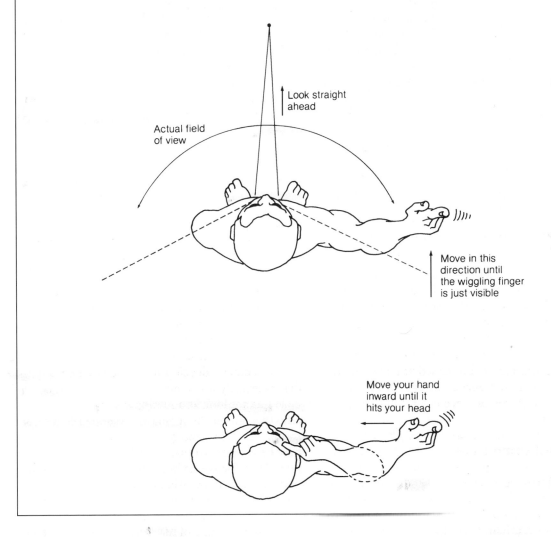

Look straight ahead

Actual field of view

Move in this direction until the wiggling finger is just visible

Move your hand inward until it hits your head

bright the pupil may contract to as little as 2 mm in diameter, whereas in dim light it may dilate to more than 8 mm. This is about a 16-fold change in the area of the aperture. Demonstration Box 3-2 shows how you may observe the effect of light on pupil size.

DEMONSTRATION BOX 3-2
The Pupillary Light Reflex

For this demonstration you need a friend. Dim the light in the room, but leave enough light so that you can still see the size of the pupil of your friend's eye. Notice how large your friend's pupil appears to be under these conditions. Now turn on an overhead light or shine the beam of a flashlight into your friend's eye and note how the pupil constricts. Removal of the light will cause the pupil to dilate again. The light reflex of the pupil was the first reflex ever studied by Whytt (1751), who is credited with the discovery of reflex action. It is still sometimes called *Whytt's reflex*.

The constriction of the pupil serves an important function. Despite the fact that the eye needs light to function, there are some advantages to viewing the world with a small pupil. Although the amount of light entering the eye is reduced, imperfections in the lens produce fewer distortions with a small pupil, and the depth of focus (which is the range of distances over which objects are simultaneously in focus) is vastly increased. We might say that the eye takes advantage of better light by improving its optical response. In dim light, the ability of the eye to discriminate details is less important than the increased sensitivity obtained by increasing the amount of light entering the eye. Thus, the pupil increases in size to let in more light. The pupil size also changes as a function of emotional and attentional variables. Under conditions of high interest the eye tries to gather more light, and the pupil tends to be large, a cue often used by smart traders as an index of a customer's interest in an item. Clever customers often negate the usefulness of this cue in bargaining situations by wearing dark glasses. Similarly, the dimness of candlelight dilates the pupils and makes lovers appear to be more attentive and interested.

The Crystalline Lens

Most vertebrate eyes contain a lens, located directly behind the pupillary aperture. Because the curvature of the lens determines the amount by which the light is bent, its shape is critical in bringing an image into focus at the rear of the eye. The process by which the lens varies its focus is called **accommodation.** The lens changes focus by changing its shape (Dalziel & Egan, 1982). The natural shape of the human lens tends to be spherical, but when the ciliary muscles that control it relax, the pressure of the fluid in the eyeball and the tension of the zonal fibers connecting the lens to the inside wall of the eye cause it to flatten. Under these conditions, distant objects should be in focus. Contraction of the ciliary muscles, from which the lens is suspended, removes some of the tension from the lens, and it takes on a more spherical shape. When it is rounder, near objects are in focus. The effect of lens shape on point of focus is shown in Figure 3-3.

An individual's age is important in determining the focusing ability of the lens. For example, the lens of a newborn infant is in focus only for objects that are approximately 19 cm away, although it is able to accommodate quite well by about 2 months of age (see Chapter 16). After about 16 years of age, the ability of the lens to change focus again decreases with age because the inner layers of the lens die and lose some of their elasticity (Weale, 1986). This results in a form of **refractive error** (light-bending or focusing error) called **presbyopia,** which translates to "old sighted." Functionally, this condition increases the **near point** distance. The near point refers to how close an object may be brought to the eye before it can no longer be held in focus and becomes blurry. Thus, older persons without corrective lenses often may be seen holding reading material abnormally far from their face in order to focus on it adequately.

Another feature of the lens that warrants mention is the fact that it is not perfectly transparent. The lens is tinted somewhat yellow, and the density of this yellow tint increases with age (Coren &

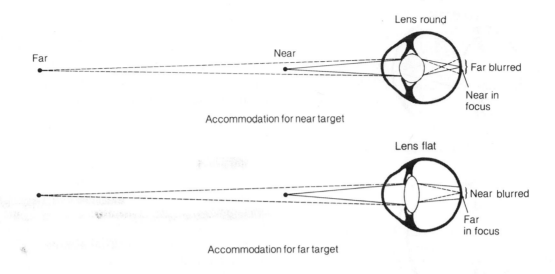

FIGURE 3-3 Accommodation (focusing) of an image by changing the shape of the crystalline lens of the eye.

Girgus, 1972a). The yellow pigment serves to screen out some of the ultraviolet light entering the eye. Animals with clear lenses (such as many birds and insects) can see ultraviolet light, as can people who have had their lenses surgically removed (e.g., Emmerton, 1983; Hardie & Kirschfeld, 1983). The yellow pigment in the lens also screens out some of the blue light and thus alters our perception of color somewhat. For example, you may have heard individuals arguing over whether a particular color is blue or green. If they are different ages, the source of the argument may lie in the fact that because the lens yellows with age, each is viewing the world through a different yellow filter.

As we noted, the major purpose of the lens is to focus the image in the eye. An eye having normal accommodative (focusing) ability is called **emmetropic**. Sometimes there is too much or too little curvature in the cornea or, alternatively, the shape of the eye is too short or too long so that the accommodative capacity of the lens is not sufficient to bring targets into focus. If the eye is too short or if the light rays are not bent sharply enough by the cornea, distant objects are seen quite clearly, but it is difficult to bring near objects into focus. The common term for this is *farsightedness*, and the technical term is **hypermetropia.** If the eye is too long or if the light rays are bent too

sharply by the cornea, near objects are sharply in focus; however, distant objects are blurry. This condition is called *nearsightedness* or **myopia.** The optical situations that result from these difficulties are shown in Figure 3-4.

The Retina

The large chamber of the eye is filled with a jelly-like substance called the **vitreous humor.** This substance is generally clear, although shreds of debris can often be seen floating in it. Try steadily viewing a clear blue sky and note the shadows that move across it as your eyes scan back and forth; these shadows are from floating debris in the vitreous humor.

The image formed by the optical system of the eye is focused on a screen of neural elements at the back of the eye called the **retina.** The term *retina* derives from the Latin word meaning "net" because when an eye is opened up surgically (or its interior viewed with an optical device such as an ophthalmoscope) the most salient feature is the network of blood vessels lining the inner cavity of the eye. Demonstration Box 3-3 shows how you can observe these blood vessels in your own eyes.

The sheet of neural elements that makes up the retina extends over most of the interior of the eye.

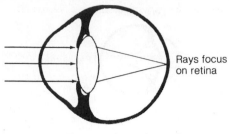

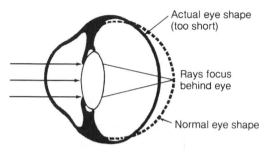

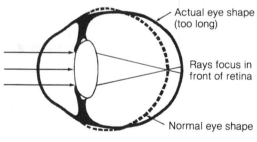

FIGURE 3-4 Three common refractive conditions of the eye.

In diurnal, or daylight-active, animals, the retina is backed by a light-absorbing dark layer called the pigment epithelium. This dark pigment layer serves the same purpose as the black inner coating in a photographic camera, reducing the amount of reflected and scattered light that could blur or fog the image. In nocturnal, or night-active, animals, where the detection of light is more important than image clarity, the light that penetrates the retina is reflected back through the retina by a shiny surface known as the reflecting tapetum. This permits the light to pass through the retina twice (once as it enters and once as it is

reflected out), effectively doubling its intensity. Although this results in a sizeable increase in sensitivity, the increase is obtained at the expense of a considerable degrading of the image through fogging and blur. This is especially true at higher illumination levels. The existence of this reflecting surface explains why cats have eyes that seem to glow in the dark when a flashlight is pointed toward them.

The retina consists of three major layers of neural tissue and is about the thickness of a sheet of paper (see Figure 3-5). It is here that the light is changed or *transduced* into a neural response. The outermost layer of the retina, closest to the scleral wall, contains the photoreceptors. There are two types of photoreceptors, which are distinguishable on the basis of their shapes—long, thin, cylindrical cells, called rods, and shorter, thicker, somewhat more tapered cells, called cones. The outer segments of these cells contain pigments that absorb light and start the visual process. The next level of the retina consists of bipolar cells, which are neurons with two long extended processes. One end makes synapses with the photoreceptors; the other end makes synapses with the large retinal ganglion cells in the third layer of the retina.

In addition to photoreceptors, bipolars, and ganglion cells, there are two types of cells that have lateral connections. Closest to the receptor layer are the horizontal cells. These cells typically have short dendrites (see Appendix for information about neurons) and a long horizontal process that extends some distance across the retina. The other cells that are lateral interconnecters are called amacrine cells. These large cells are found between the ganglion and bipolar cells and interact with spatially adjacent units. More than 30 types of amacrine cells, differing in size and chemical properties, have been isolated (Masland, 1986). Both the horizontal and amacrine cells modify the visual signal and allow adjacent cells in the retina to communicate and interact with one another (Kolb, Nelson, & Mariani, 1981; Naka, 1982; Tomita, 1986).

Light reception occurs within the rod and cone cells. Contrary to what we might expect, the orientation of rods and cones is inverted, with the pigment-bearing end pointing toward the back of the eye rather than toward the lens. Thus, the

---

DEMONSTRATION BOX 3-3
Mapping the Retinal Blood Vessels

For this demonstration you will need a pocket penlight and a white paper or light-colored wall. Hold the penlight near the outside canthus (corner) of your eye. Now, shaking the bulb of the penlight up and down you will see a netlike pattern on the light surface. This pattern is generated by the movements of the shadows of your retinal blood vessels across your retina. By steadily shaking the bulb with one hand and tracing the shadows with the other, you can produce a map of your own retinal blood vessels.

---

retina may be viewed as if it were a transparent carpet lying upside down on the floor of the room, with the pile of the carpet corresponding to the rods and cones. The incoming light must therefore pass through the carpet (the retina) before reaching the photoreceptors. Although this arrangement might appear to be somewhat counterproductive, it actually makes good sense. The photoreceptors need a rich oxygen supply, and to meet this need there are many blood vessels in the epithelial layer at the rear of the eye. If the retina were "right-side up," so many blood vessels would be needed that the light input would be partially blocked. Therefore, the "upside-down" organization is more functional.

The Fovea

Not all parts of the retina are of equal importance in the perceptual process. The most important section of the human retina is located in the region around the **optic axis,** an imaginary line from the center of the retina that passes through the center of the pupil (see Figure 3-7). If we view a human retina through an ophthalmoscope, we note a yellow patch of pigment located in the region of the origin of the optic axis. This area is called the **macula lutea** (or just *macula*), which translates to "yellow spot." Demonstration Box 3-4 describes a procedure in which you can see your own macula. In the center of the macula is a small depression

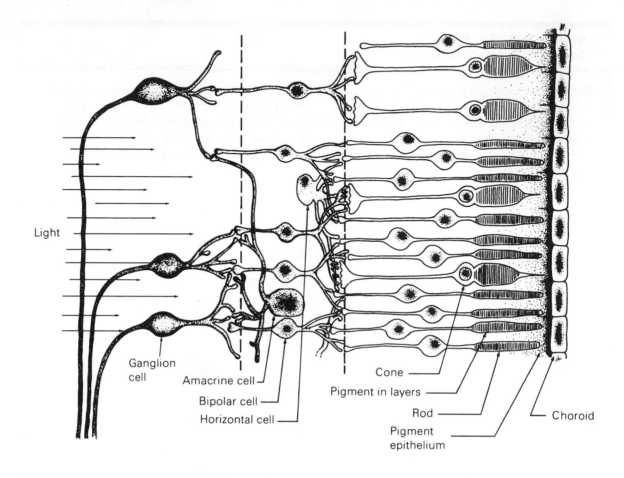

Light

Ganglion
cell

Amacrine cell

Bipolar cell

Horizontal cell

Cone

Pigment in layers

Rod

Pigment
epithelium

Choroid

FIGURE 3-5 Schematic diagram of the human retina.

that looks much like the imprint of a pinpoint about ⅓ mm in diameter. This small circular depression is called the **fovea centralis**, or, translated, the "central pit." The fovea is critical in visual perception. Whenever you "look" directly at a target, it means that the eyes are rotated so that the image of the target falls on the foveal region.

, The fovea is quite unique in its structure and is schematically depicted in Figure 3-6. In the center of the foveal depression, the upper layers of cells are apparently pushed away so that the light passes through a much thinner cellular layer before reaching the photoreceptors. The photoreceptors themselves are very densely packed in this region. This section of the retina contains only cones; there are no rods at all (Osterberg, 1935). Foveal cones have a different shape than the more peripheral cones depicted in Figure 3-5. They are much

longer and thinner (often only 0.001 mm in diameter) and thus somewhat resemble rods.

Outside of the fovea the number of cones rapidly decreases. The number of rods, on the other hand, rapidly increases as one leaves the foveal region, reaching a peak concentration at about 20° of visual angle from the fovea and then decreasing again. This general distribution (which is shown in Figure 3-7) has been verified in computer mappings of the retina (Curcio, Sloan, Packer, Hendrickson, & Kalina, 1987).

Rods and Cones

The presence of two types of retinal photoreceptors suggests the existence of two types of visual functions. In the early 1860s the retinal anatomist

---

DEMONSTRATION BOX 3-4
The Macular Spot

Under appropriate conditions it is possible to see the macular spot in your own eye. In order to do this you will need a dark blue or purple piece of cellophane. Brightly illuminate a piece of white paper with a desk lamp. Now, while looking at the paper with one eye, quickly bring the piece of cellophane between your eye and the paper. Now as you look at the paper you see what appears to be a faint circular shadow in the center of it. The sight of the shadow may last for only a couple of seconds. Sometimes its visibility can be improved by moving the cellophane in front of and away from your eye so that you have a flickering colored field. Some individuals can see the spot when staring at a uniform blue field, such as a clear summer sky. This percept is caused by the fact that the yellow pigment in the macula absorbs the blue light and does not let it pass. This causes a circular shadow, which can be briefly seen. It is often called *Maxwell's spot*, after James Clerk Maxwell, who noticed its presence during some color-matching experiments.

Max Schultze found that nocturnal animals, such as owls, have retinas that contain only rods. Animals that are diurnal, or active only during the day, such as chipmunks or pigeons, have retinas that are all cones. Animals that are active in the twilight, or during both day and night, such as rats, monkeys, and humans, have retinas composed of both rods and cones. On the basis of these observations, Schultze offered what has been called the duplex retina theory of vision. He maintained that there are two separate visual systems. One is for vision under dim light conditions and is dependent on the rods; the other is for vision under daylight or bright conditions and is dependent on the cones. Vision under bright light is called photopic ("light vision"), whereas vision under dim light is called scotopic ("dark vision").

Some early clinical data showed that the eye contains two different visual systems (von Kries, 1895). Individuals whose retinas contain no rods, or only nonfunctioning rods, seem to have normal vision under daylight conditions. However, as soon as the light dims beyond a certain point (into what we might call twilight), they lose all sense of sight and become functionally blind. These individuals suffer from night blindness.

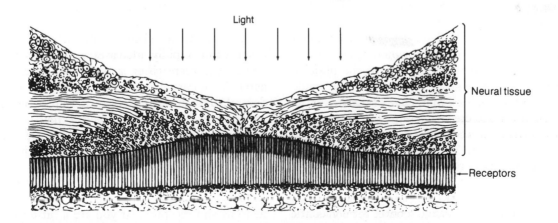

FIGURE 3-6 Sketch of a cross section through the fovea. Light comes from the direction of the top of the page.

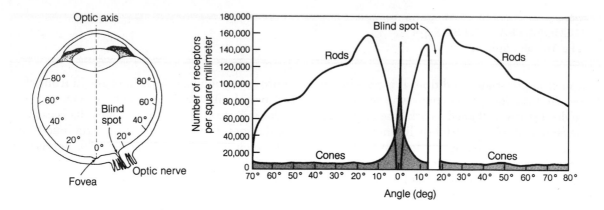

FIGURE 3-7 The distribution of rods and cones in the human retina. The left figure gives the locations on the retina of the "angle" relative to the optic axis on the right figure (based on Lindsay & Norman, 1977).

The implication is that in the absence of rods, scotopic vision is absent. A quite different pattern is found for individuals lacking in functioning cones. These people find normal levels of daylight quite painful, totally lack color vision, and have very poor visual acuity. Under dim levels of illumination, however, they function normally. Such individuals suffer from **day blindness** and provide evidence that a functioning cone system is necessary for normal photopic vision and also for the perception of color. The perception of brightness and of color are discussed in Chapters 4 and 5.

Before a rod or a cone can signal the presence of light, it must first interact with the light in some way. Such interaction involves absorbing, or capturing, one or more photons. Any substance that absorbs light is called a *pigment*. A substance that absorbs a lot of light would appear to be darkly pigmented because most of the photons hitting it would be absorbed and very few would be left to bounce back to the eye of the viewer. As we noted earlier, the outer segments of both the rods and the cones contain visual pigments. If you turn back to Figure 3-5, you will see the pigments arranged in layers in the outer segments of the photoreceptors. For rods, the photosensitive pigment is arranged in a stack of around 2,000 tiny disks, like coins inside a tube; for cones, the pigment is part of a single large, elaborately folded membrane that forms the layers of photosensitive material.

Rods and cones do not contain the same pigment. In 1876 Franz Boll first isolated a brilliant red pigment from a frog retina (which contains predominantly rods). He noted that this pigment bleached, or lost its apparent coloration, when exposed to light. This reaction indicated that the substance was photosensitive. He further noted that the pigment regenerated in the dark. Thus, it fulfilled the elementary requirements of the visual pigment. Kühne took up the study of this pigment in 1877 and, in one extraordinary year, laid the groundwork for our understanding of its action. This pigment has been named **rhodopsin** (which means "visual red").

Rhodopsin is a compound that is made up of two parts: **retinal,** a complex organic molecule derived from vitamin A, and **opsin,** a protein with large complex molecules that have the capacity to act as an enzyme. When a molecule of rhodopsin absorbs a photon of light, it *isomerizes,* or changes shape, and then splits into its two component parts. A complex sequence of events then begins. Several different enzymes are activated, resulting in the breakdown of the molecule that normally keeps the cell membrane open to allow the flow of sodium ions (Schoenlein, Peteanu, Mathies, & Shank, 1991; Stryer, 1987). (In order to understand what happens next, you should know a little about how information is transmitted to and by neurons and receptors. If you are a bit unsure in this area, you should stop and read the "Primer of Neurophysiology" that we've included as an appendix at the back of this book.)

Because of the flow of sodium ions into the rod, the rod cell undergoes **hyperpolarization**, meaning that the normally negative charge of −40 millivolts (mv) across the cell membrane becomes even more negative, perhaps −70 to −80 mv. This indicates that the rod has been stimulated by light (Hubbell & Bownds, 1979; Schnapf & Baylor, 1987). To maintain a sufficient supply of rhodopsin in the rod, this process must be reversed. The rhodopsin regenerates in the dark from the retinal and opsin with the help of vitamin A and a set of enzymes. Because vitamin A is vital to the resynthesis of rhodopsin, the absence of vitamin A in the diet can show up in "epidemics" of night blindness (Wald, 1968). This sometimes happens in isolated communities where fish products or appropriate vegetables are not available. Folk wisdom tells us that eating carrots will improve our vision because carrots are a rich source of vitamin A.

The analysis of cone pigments has proved to be more difficult and elusive than that of rhodopsin. However, we have learned that a purple pigment, **iodopsin** ("visual purple"), is present in the cone cells of some birds. On exposure to light, iodopsin breaks down into retinal and another form of opsin. This is called **photopsin** in cones to distinguish it from the slightly different protein found in rods, which is called **scotopsin**. The retinal, however, appears to be the same as is found in rods.

The biochemical events leading to hyperpolarization in the presence of light are similar for rods and cones (Bridges, 1986; Schnapf & Baylor, 1987). This hyperpolarization stimulates the bipolar cells, which in turn stimulate the ganglion cells. At the same time, complex interactions occur between neighboring bipolar and ganglion cells via the horizontal and amacrine cells that connect to them. The axons of the ganglion cells then carry the resulting neural signals out of the eye toward the brain.

NEURAL RESPONSES TO LIGHT

In order to transmit the visual information from the eye to the brain, the axons of the retinal ganglion cells gather together to exit from the eye by means of a hole through the retina and the scleral wall. The resulting bundle of axons forms the **optic nerve.** Through the center of the optic nerve come the blood vessels that sustain the metabolic needs of the eye. Because the bundle of axons must exit through the retina, there are no photoreceptors in this region. Because of this there can be no visual response to light striking this portion of the retina, and it is appropriately called the **blind spot.** The neural axons that form the optic nerve form a distinctive circular pattern as they exit the eye, and this has led anatomists to refer to this region as the **optic disk.** You may demonstrate the absence of vision in this region of the retina by referring to Demonstration Box 3-5.

The nerve impulses transmitted to the brain via the ganglion cell axons that make up the optic nerves are not "raw" sense data but, rather, are the result of a large amount of neural processing that has already taken place in the retina itself. In order to understand how much processing has occurred, you might consider that there are 120 million rods and 5 million cones in each human eye. Yet, there are only about 1 million axons in each optic nerve. Clearly, each receptor cell does not have its own private pipeline to the brain, but, rather, the responses of a very large number of photoreceptors may be represented in the activity of one optic nerve fiber. This comes about when the combined activity of the 125 million rods and cones, plus the output of several million more intervening bipolar, horizontal, and amacrine cells, converges on the much smaller number of ganglion cells. We will soon see how the information is modified as it is collected.

The Receptive Field of a Visual Neuron

Because the information carried to the brain by a single ganglion cell can represent the combined activity of a large number of rods and cones, a single ganglion cell may respond to a light incident on a sizeable region of the retina. Such a region of the retina, on which the incidence of light alters the firing rate of a cell, is called that cell's **receptive field.** Thus, each ganglion cell processes information coming from a substantial zone of receptor cells in the retina. In order to understand how this visual information is processed, you need to know how specific ganglion cells respond to various forms of light stimuli presented in their

---

DEMONSTRATION BOX 3-5
The Blind Spot

The region of the retina where the optic nerve leaves the eye contains no photoreceptors and thus is blind. You may demonstrate this for yourself by using the figure here. Close your left eye, and with your right eye look at the *X* in the figure. Keeping your eye on the *X*, move the page toward you. At some point the little open square will seem to disappear. At this point its image is falling on your blind spot. Notice that when you have the page at the correct distance, not only does the square seem to disappear, but also the line appears to run continuously through the area where the square should be. This indicates that we automatically "fill in" missing information. We fill it in with material that is similar to nearby visible material. This accounts for why you are not normally aware of the blind spot. You are simply supplying the missing information to fill in this "hole" in the visual field.

---

receptive field. Before attempting to learn this, however, it is important for you to understand the nature of neural responses in general and how they are measured experimentally. If you have not already done so, this might be a good time to read the "Primer of Neurophysiology" appendix.

Most contemporary studies of the response of retinal ganglion cells to light have followed the lead of Hartline (1940) and Kuffler (1953), who inserted an electrode through the eye of an anesthetized cat and recorded from single ganglion cells in the retina. Generally one finds that when a single small spot of light is displayed on the screen, thereby stimulating the retina of the animal observing it, three different types of responses from a ganglion cell may be elicited. The first type of response is the one typically expected when a neuron is excited: a burst of neural impulses immediately following the onset of the stimulus. This response has been dubbed an **on response.** Alternatively, the cell can give a burst of impulses coincident with the termination of a stimulus. Such a response is termed an **off response.** Some responses are hybrids because both the presentation of and the removal of the stimulus cause a burst of neural impulses. These are designated as **on-off responses.** Typical examples of these responses are shown in Figure 3-8.

When investigators use very small lights (about 0.2 mm in diameter in its retinal image), the retinal ganglion cell response tends to vary from on, through on-off, to off, depending on the location of the stimulus. A map of the shape of the overall receptive field of the retinal ganglion cell (the region of retinal stimulation to which the cell responds) shows that the responses are distributed circularly with two distinct zones within each

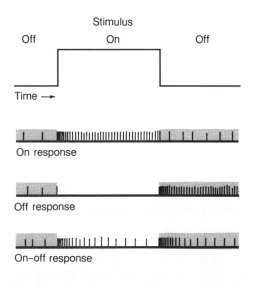

FIGURE 3-8 On, off, and on-off neural responses in the retinal ganglion cells.

receptive field. Typically, the receptive field has a roughly circular center in which the onset of a light stimulus causes the ganglion cell to respond with an on response. The outer portion of the receptive field gives the opposite result. That is, the onset of a light does not produce a response, but its offset does. Between these two regions, roughly at the boundary between the on and off regions, is a narrow region where on-off responses occur. Typical receptive fields are shown in Figure 3-9, where on response regions are marked by "+" and off by "–" (remember, on-off responses occur at the border between these regions).

As Figure 3-9 indicates, some receptive fields have the opposite organization, with the central region giving rise to off responses and the surrounding region showing on responses. There are approximately equal numbers of off-center cells and on-center cells in the retina. The ganglion cells that show the on- and off-center responses are visibly different under the microscope. In addition, the off-center cells make contact with their respective bipolar and amacrine cells at a more peripheral level in the retina (closer to the photoreceptors) than do the on-center cells (Kaneko, Nishimura, Tachibana, & Shimai, 1981; Nelson,

Kolb, Robinson, & Mariani, 1981). Some evidence even suggests that specific amacrine cells, with different neurotransmitters, may shape particular receptive field properties in ganglion cells (Dacey, 1988; Masland, 1986).

Parvo and Magno Ganglion Cells

It has long been known that ganglion cells come in many shapes and sizes (Cajal, 1893). However, only quite recently have researchers come to general agreement on a classification system (Rodieck & Brening, 1983). As shown in Figure 3-10, the most obvious dimension along which ganglion cells vary is that of size. The cells with the smaller bodies have come to be known as **parvo** cells, whereas those with larger bodies are called **magno** cells (*parvo* and *magno* are Latin terms for *small* and *large*, respectively).

We now know that there is a wide range of anatomical and physiological characteristics that are associated with these obvious difference in size (Bishop, 1984; Schiller, 1986; Shapley, 1990). To begin with, Figure 3-10 shows that parvo ganglion cells have branches that extend over a much smaller

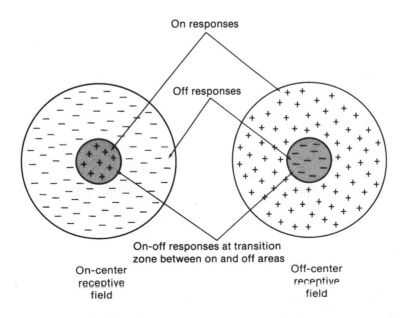

FIGURE 3-9   Circular center-surround retinal receptive fields of two types.

Parvo cell   Magno cell

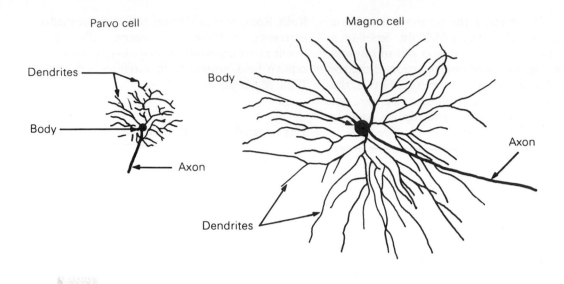

FIGURE 3-10 Examples of parvo and magno cells, taken from a cat retina and laid flat for illustration purposes (based on Boycott & Waessle, 1974).

area than do the branches of magno ganglion cells. This means that magno cells have a much broader range when it comes to communicating with neighboring cells. Proportionally, there are many more parvo cells than magno cells, and they differ in terms of their distribution across the retina. Virtually no magno cells have been found in the foveal region, and the number of magno cells increases as we move outward into the peripheral retina.

Also associated with these differences in anatomy are a number of important functional characteristics. These have been summarized in Table 3-1. For instance, magno cells send neural impulses along their axons at speeds of about 40 m per second. This is very fast when compared with parvo cells, which have conduction speeds of only 20 m per second. Although both parvo and magno cells have receptive fields with the center-surround, on-off arrangement that we have described, the smaller parvo cells also have smaller center-surround receptive fields.

The characteristic neural response patterns of parvo and magno cells also differ. When parvo cells are stimulated they respond in a sustained manner, continuing their neural activity as long as the stimulus remains. Magno cells, on the other hand, have a much more transient response. They tend to give only a brief burst of activity when the

stimulus comes on, or when it goes off, and they tend to cease responding quickly thereafter.

Another parvo-magno difference is illustrated in Figure 3-11. Figure 3-11A shows a schematic drawing of the receptive field of a retinal ganglion cell in which half of the field is evenly illuminated with light and the other half is dark. Suppose that we now switched the illumination to the pattern shown as Figure 3-11B or Figure 3-11C. If we were stimulating a parvo cell, it would continue to respond exactly as it had been responding. In other words, as long as the same amount of illumination is present in the

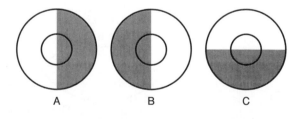

A   B   C

FIGURE 3-11 If the illumination pattern on a center-surround receptive field was half light and half dark, as shown in *A*, and then was shifted to a new orientation (either *B* or *C*), a parvo ganglion cell would not respond to a change, whereas a magno ganglion cell would.

Table 3-1 Selected Anatomical and Physiological Differences Between Parvo and Magno Ganglion Cells, Along With Some Possible Consequences for Behavior

	PARVO GANGLION CELLS	MAGNO GANGLION CELLS
Anatomical Differences	small cell body dense branching short branches majority of cells	large cell body sparse branching long branches minority of cells
Physiological Differences	slow conduction rate sustained response small receptive field low-contrast sensitivity color sensitive	rapid conduction rate transient response large receptive field high-contrast sensitivity color blind
Possible Behavioral Consequences	detailed form analysis spatial analysis color vision	motion detection temporal analysis depth perception

center and surround, the parvo cell does not distinguish between the different locations of illumination. However, any switch in the pattern of illumination will provoke a vigorous response in a magno cell. Because changes in the distribution of illumination across a region of the field are usually caused by movement of an object, this difference means that magno cells are specialized for movement detection, whereas parvo cells are specialized for the analysis of stationary patterns (Kruger, 1981).

THE VISUAL PATHWAYS

The most important concept in the modern understanding of the neural basis of vision is that of *mapping*. The concept of a map is very helpful because of the properties that naturally spring to mind when we think of everyday maps such as roadmaps. A map is an organized representation of information. The lines on the map are not themselves roads and rivers; they refer only to the relationships between these landmarks. In the same way, it is important to remember that the neural signals in a brain map of the visual field are merely one of many possible ways to represent the original pattern of light. Second, a map preserves certain *spatial relations* among landmarks but distorts others. For instance, the relative distance between two towns is accurately preserved in a roadmap, as is the relative direction one must travel to move from one town

to the other. However, the absolute distance can be determined only by converting the scale units of the map into kilometers or miles; the actual direction can be determined only by referencing the roadmap to true north. The same is true of visual maps in the brain. Relative distances and directions between points of light are preserved, although absolute distances and directions may be greatly distorted. Vision researchers often refer to this kind of representation as being a **topographic map.**

Visual Maps

We can begin our story of how the eye and brain map visual information by examining the relationship between points of light in the visual field (the field of view) and specific points on the retina, as shown in Figure 3-12. Imagine the field of view for each eye divided into four quadrants, corresponding to the upper and lower visual field and the nasal and temporal visual field. Then, because of the way in which the cornea and the lens diffract light onto the retina, light from the upper visual field is projected onto the lower retinal surface, light from the *nasal* visual field is projected onto the *temporal* retinal surface, and so on. In short, the visual image of the world is represented as both upside down and left-right reversed on the retinal surface. Long ago, some philosophers were quite concerned about the problems such transformations

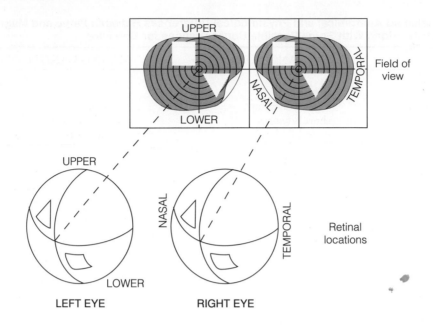

FIGURE 3-12 The relationship between points of light in the visual field and corresponding points on the retina.

of mapping might pose for the brain, but this is no longer considered to be a concern, largely because the image on the retina preserves all the important spatial relations in the field of view. Just like a roadmap, no information is lost simply because the roadmap is turned upside down or viewed in a mirror.

But the mapping of light into neural signals in the retina is only the first of many maps that are constructed by the visual system. As we noted earlier, the axons of the retinal ganglion cells gather together and exit from the eye at the blind spot. This bundle of axons, which forms the optic nerve, is the beginning of a pathway that eventually ends in the brain. However, there are two distinct anatomical routes that lead to the common end point, and each carries somewhat different information, thereby producing different kinds of maps along the way. The oldest visual pathway, in evolutionary terms, is the **tectopulvinar system.** It is a pathway we share with many other animals, including birds. In humans, however, it is no longer the dominant neural pathway of visual information. The dominant pathway for humans and other primates, such as monkeys, is the **geniculostriate system.** Both begin in the same fashion, with the information

traveling out of the eyes along the optic nerves. As can be seen in Figure 3-13, the two optic nerves come together at a point that looks like an X. This point is called the **optic chiasm** (from the Greek letter X, which is called *chi*). In lower animals, the optic nerve from the right eye crosses completely to the left side of the head and vice versa. In many mammalian species, particularly those who use combined input from the two eyes to obtain better depth perception, some of the fibers do not cross (this will be discussed more fully in Chapter 9). In primates, such as humans, approximately one half of the optic nerve fibers cross to the opposite side of the brain. These are the fibers that represent the two inside or nasal retinas. Those from the outside or temporal halves of each retina do not cross but continue on the same side.

This arrangement means that neural signals from temporal retina of each eye are projected to the side of the brain on the same side as that eye, whereas signals from the nasal retina of each eye are projected to the side of the brain that is opposite to that eye. A simpler way to understand this is to remember that all light from the left side of the visual field is mapped onto the right brain and all light from the right side of the visual field of view is mapped onto the left brain.

A. TECTOPULVINAR PATHWAY

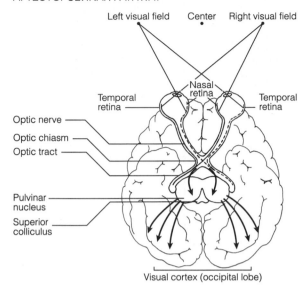

B. GENICULOSTRIATE PATHWAY

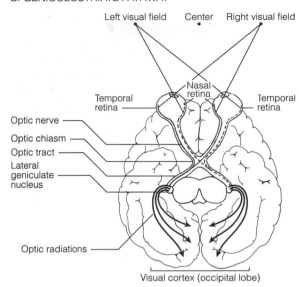

FIGURE 3-13   The two visual pathways from the eye to the visual cortex. (A) The tectopulvinar pathway. (B) The geniculostriate pathway.

The Tectopulvinar System

The brain structures in the tectopulvinar pathway to the visual cortex are indicated in Figure 3-13A. Beyond the optic chiasm the visual pathway going to the cortex is no longer called the *optic nerve* but, rather, the **optic tract.** The tectopulvinar pathway begins when a number of fibers from the optic tract branch off to the brain stem instead of to the midbrain. The visual region of the brain stem is, in an evolutionary sense, a much older and more primitive visual center than is the cortex. In animals it is known as the **tectum,** and for some animals, such as birds, almost all visual processing occurs here. The part of the tectum that receives most of the incoming fibers is the upper pair of what appear to be four bumps on the roof (or dorsal surface) of the brain stem; these are known as the **superior colliculi.** Not all of the retinal ganglion cell types project to the superior colliculi, however. The vast majority of cells appear to be of the magno type in primates (Orban, 1984), meaning that they have rapid responses and are more sensitive to sudden changes in illumination than they are to stationary stimuli.

Cells in the upper and intermediate layers of the superior colliculi have receptive fields that are arranged in an orderly topographic manner—the front (or anterior) portion represents the central visual field, whereas the back (posterior) portion represents the visual periphery. The colliculus on the right receives input from ganglion cells that have been stimulated by stimuli in the left visual field; the colliculus on the left responds to stimuli in the right visual field. As one might expect, given the magnocellular input from the retina, these receptive fields are not very sensitive to details of shape, such as orientation, or to color, but they are quite sensitive to motion and location. In the deeper layers the cells begin to exhibit a very interesting property—in addition to being activated by visual stimuli, they can also be driven by auditory and tactile stimuli. This suggests that the superior colliculi are locations where information from the various senses is combined and integrated.

As with other visual centers in the brain, we must keep in mind that the inputs to the superior colliculi do not come only from the retina. This area receives extensive inputs from the primary visual area of the cortex (Area V1) as well as from a cortical visual area thought to be a center for visual motion processing (Area V5). These returning signals are called **back projections** because they represent a form of feedback based on previous information that has already been sent to the brain. Both of these back projections to the superior colliculi are primarily of the magnocellular type, thus contributing to the view that this brain region is important in the analysis of movement and location (we will return to this topic in Chapter 15).

From the superior colliculi the pathway continues on to the **pulvinar** and the **lateral posterior nuclei,** which are located nearby in the thalamus. From here, the fibers project to the cortex. Interestingly, none is destined directly for the primary visual cortex (Area V1), but, rather, they connect to cells in the secondary visual areas (Area V2 and beyond).

The tectopulvinar pathway in primates is specialized for the control of eye movements and eye fixations. Much of the detailed neural circuitry involved is known because of research over the past 25 years using single-cell recording techniques in awake and behaving monkeys. Some researchers believe it is now the best understood of all sensorimotor systems in primates (e.g., Wurtz, 1996).

Figure 3-14 illustrates some of the important features of cell activity in the upper and intermediate layers of the superior colliculus before, during, and after an eye movement. During a period of steady eye fixation, such as if a monkey were looking at the center of a computer screen, waiting for a new target to appear, a population of **fixation** cells is active in the front portion of the intermediate layers (Munoz & Wurtz, 1993). At the onset of a new target stimulus, but before the monkey can physically move its eyes to the new location, other cells in the same layer begin to become active, with their activity being centered around the location of the new target. This is shown to be at the location indicating 40° in the example in Figure 3-14 because the new target is presented 40° to one side of fixation. These cells, whose activity anticipates the eye movement, are called **buildup** cells because they become active as soon as the new target appears (Munoz & Wurtz, 1995). The eye movement itself may not begin for another 100–200 ms.

The actual eye movement is associated with activity in the upper layers, also centered on the

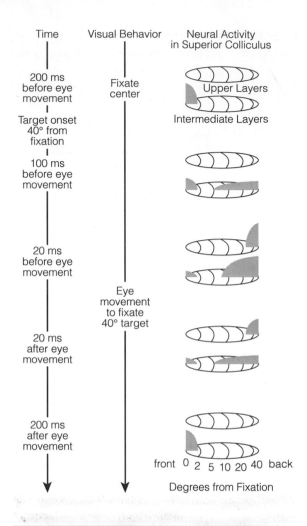

FIGURE 3-14   The pattern of neural firing that occurs in the superior colliculus in response to an eye movement. The height of the gray distributions indicates the number of cells that are active; the location of the gray distributions indicates where on the surface of the superior colliculus the cells are active.

location of the new target. The activity in these **burst** cells begins only about 20 ms before the eye movement and terminates with the end of the movement, which itself takes only 10–20 ms (Munoz & Wurtz, 1995; Sparks, 1978). Burst cells and fixation cells are rarely active at the same time, as though they are involved in mutual inhibition that is based on their own levels of activity. After the eye movement is complete and the new target is being fixated, the fixation group of cells is once again active at the front of intermediate layers of cells in the superior colliculus. Unlike the buildup and burst types of cells, which are active on only one side of the brain stem (the side opposite to the direction of the eye movement), fixation cells are active on both sides.

Thus, even the control of simple eye movements, which are almost always made without conscious thought and occur as frequently as three to four times a second, are governed by an intricate network of neurons. Not only are these neurons highly organized within each of the superior colliculi, but also they receive and send messages to several important regions of the cortex that are visually sensitive. These include regions in the posterior parietal cortex, the frontal cortex, and other regions of the brain stem and midbrain.

The Geniculostriate System

The major termination for the optic tract nerve fibers in the primary visual pathway is a structure in the thalamus called the **lateral geniculate nucleus,** shown in Figure 3-13. The lateral geniculate is arranged in six distinct layers of cells, each of which contains a topographic map of the visual field.

As is the case with the retinal ganglion cells, lateral geniculate cells do not respond to visual stimuli unless the stimulation occurs within their receptive fields. Thus, a particular lateral geniculate neuron provides information about the location of an object in space because it responds only to those objects projected onto the patch of retinal receptors that defines its receptive field. These receptors, in turn, respond only to objects in a particular region of the visual field. Generally, the receptive fields of the lateral geniculate cells are similar to those of the retinal ganglion cells. If we map the response of a lateral geniculate cell by projecting points of light onto a screen in the visual field in front of an animal, we find that the receptive fields of such cells have an on center and an off surround, or the reverse.

Figure 3-15 shows the layering of cells in the lateral geniculate nucleus. Note first that the layers alternate between those receiving input from the eye on the same side and those receiving input from the eye on the opposite side. Another important difference across the six layers is the concen-

tration of small (parvo) cells and large (magno) cells (Lennie, Trevarthen, Van Essen, & Waessle, 1990; Livingstone & Hubel, 1988; Shapley, 1990). Parvo cells are located in the upper four layers of the lateral geniculate nucleus and receive their input primarily from the parvo ganglion cells in the retina, whereas magno cells are located in the lower two layers and receive input from the magno ganglion cells. It should not be surprising, then, that these two cell types show parvo-like and magno-like responses to stimuli. For instance, receptive fields of parvo cells have a color-opponent organization, whereas those of many magno cells are equally sensitive to all wavelengths of light. Magno cells are also more sensitive than parvo cells to the magnitude of the change in luminance at an edge (Lehmkuhle, Kratz, Mangel, & Sherman, 1980; Shapley, 1990). Thus, the division into two parallel streams of processing that began in the retina—a slower-acting one for detailed form and color vision and a faster-acting one for movement perception—continues into the brain. As we will see, this division is maintained by many areas of the brain that process visual information (Bishop, 1984; Schiller, 1986).

Electrophysiological studies of the lateral geniculate have shown that these neurons are spontaneously active. This means that these cells are always emitting some neural impulses, even in the dark. Although this may seem a bit surprising, spontaneity is a characteristic of brain cells. We do not fully understand why this activity maintains itself. It may simply be because the neurons are alive and announce this by occasional random responses. This continuing train of responses does augment the information-coding capacity of the cells because signals may now either be excitatory (cause an increase in the firing rate over the baseline activity level) or inhibitory (cause a decrease in activity relative to the resting response rate).

Another important feature of cells in the lateral geniculate nucleus is that they receive neural signals not only from the retina but also from higher visual centers in the cortex. Some estimates of the percentage of lateral geniculate inputs that are "back projections" of this kind are as high as 80–90% (Schiller, 1986; Zeki, 1993). This is the first instance we have encountered along the visual pathway where the processing of information is being influenced both in a *bottom-up* fashion, involving input coming "up"

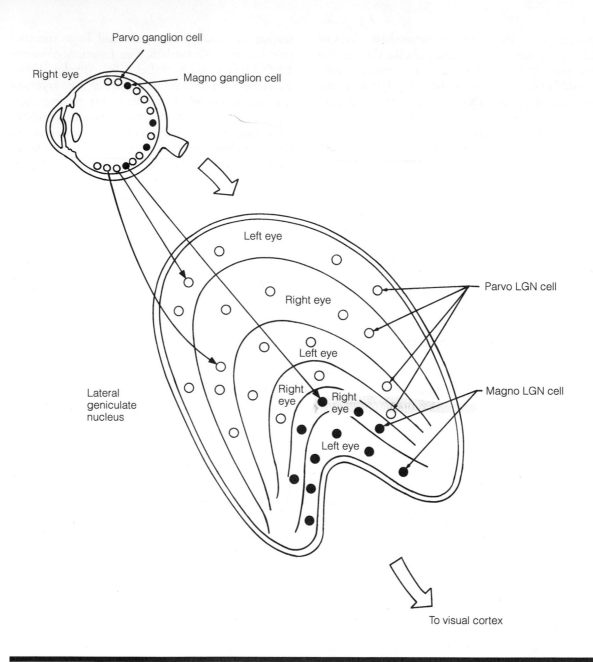

FIGURE 3-15 Layering of cells in the right lateral geniculate nucleus.

from the retina, and in a *top-down* fashion, involving input coming "down" from higher cortical centers. Actually, this kind of interaction is quite common in the processing of visual information.

When the axons of the lateral geniculate neurons leave the geniculate, they form a large fan of fibers called the **optic radiations,** as shown

in Figure 3-13B. These fibers eventually synapse with cells in the cortex in the rear (or posterior) portion of the brain. This general area is known as the **occipital lobe.** Several other labels are now commonly used to refer to different subregions within the occipital lobe. The most popular labeling scheme among vision researchers denotes the different subregions within the occipital lobe as **Visual Area 1 or V1, Visual Area 2 or V2,** and so on. In all there are now more than 36 different regions of the cortex containing neurons that are visually sensitive (e.g., DeYoe & van Essen, 1988; van Essen, 1984). We will restrict our discussion to only the few of these that are reasonably well understood.

THE PRIMARY VISUAL CORTEX

There are over 100 million neurons in the visual cortex. Only the smallest fraction of these has been thoroughly studied in attempts to discover their response characteristics. What we do know is based largely on research in which electrical impulses are recorded (using microelectrodes) from single cells, employing techniques similar to those used in the mapping of the receptive fields for the retinal ganglion and lateral geniculate cells. Current techniques in this area still owe much to the pioneering work done by David Hubel and Torstein Wiesel, who received the Nobel prize in 1981.

With the single-cell technique, a researcher can, in principle, probe any one of the millions of neurons in the cortex to see whether that cell is visually sensitive. However, using this technique alone to determine the visually sensitive regions of the cortex is a little like playing the lottery; you have to be extremely lucky to be presenting the cell's favored stimulus to the relevant portion of the retina at the same time that you are recording that particular cell's responses with a microelectrode. As you can see, this is much less likely to occur at random than is finding that proverbial needle in a haystack.

At present, researchers use a number of additional techniques to assist them in their search for visually sensitive regions in the cortex. One of the most important of these involves examining the anatomical structure of the cortical cells along with their connections to other cells. One of the general principles of brain organization seems to be that a region devoted to a specialized function also has a unique anatomical structure. This means that the cells within the region differ in their appearance from cells in neighboring regions and that the cells within the region have a unique pattern of connection to cells in other regions. These

differences often become visible when we use one of the many modern methods for chemical staining. The effects of these stains can be seen when a slice of cortical tissue is placed under a microscope. What one often finds are patches and stripes of cortical tissue that have been affected differently by the stain, suggesting that these regions have common features and may be candidates for distinct brain areas that process specific kinds of information. Single-cell recordings can then be used to determine whether one of the functions served by that region is a visual one.

Another important criterion used in identifying a cortical region as a visual area is evidence that the region really does represent some sort of a topographic map of the retina. This means that each location that we stimulate on the retinal surface should be directly related to a location where there is activity on the cortical surface. For example, if we have two points, A and B, that we stimulate on the retina, and then we stimulate a Point C that is at a location halfway between A and B, we would expect that in the cortex, the cells responding to C would also lie between the locations of the cells responding to A and B. However, finding such exact maps on the cortex can sometimes be very tricky because the cortical surface is not flat but, rather, is folded, with convoluted wrinkles, rises, and deep indentations.

A final consideration used to determine if we are looking at a distinct visually sensitive cortical area is a functional one. Specifically, the receptive field properties of the cells in a given area should differ from the receptive field properties of other visual areas. As we will see later in this chapter, some visual areas contain topographic maps of the retina that are specialized for representing color, others are specialized for orientation of edges, and still others for the direction of motion.

Despite the wide-ranging differences that exist between the various topographic visual maps, they have a number of interesting features in common. One principle concerns a direct relationship between the amount of cortical tissue devoted to a function and the perceptual importance of that function. In visual topographic maps, it is very common to find large regions devoted to the central retina, with smaller areas of cortical "real estate" devoted to retinal locations farther from the fovea. This allows the average sizes of the receptive

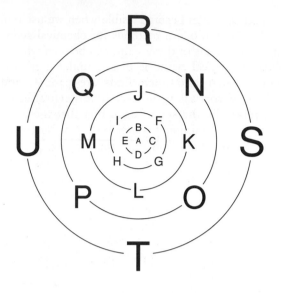

FIGURE 3-16   Letter sizes have been scaled so that when the central *A* is fixated, all other letters are approximately equally easy to read. This illustrates the cortical magnification factor.

fields of neurons to be small in foveal regions, whereas they become increasingly larger as we move away from the center of the retina. Functionally this means that the neurons at the center of the map are able to register much finer details than those in outer reaches of the map. This relationship has been quantified for Area V1, where it has come to be known as the **cortical magnification factor** (Daniel & Whitteridge, 1961; Hubel & Wiesel, 1974). A functional illustration of the cortical magnification factor can be seen in Figure 3-16, where letters have been scaled in size so that regardless of how far they are from the fovea they each approximately equal in their readability.

The most important cortical region for visual processing is Area V1 because it is the first stop in the cortex and almost all of the signals that the other cortical regions get must pass through it. For this reason, Area V1 is often referred to as the *primary* visual cortex. Another popular term for the same region is the **striate** (which means "striped") **cortex** because when it is chemically stained and vertical slices are examined under the microscope, it has a distinct dark stripe through the middle. These stripes occur because the stain-sensitive variety of cells is more concentrated in middle layers

of Area V1 than it is in other neighboring regions of the cortex.

As so often seems to be the case, the topographical mapping of Area V1 was discovered long before the development of modern cellular staining and microelectrical recording techniques. The general mapping can be seen by examining clinical data from cases of accident or war injury, where penetrating missile wounds have injured specific parts of the cortex. When a piece of visually sensitive cortex is so damaged, the patient is blind in the corresponding part of the visual field. Such a damaged area is technically called a *lesion*, and the blind patch in the visual field is called a **scotoma** (meaning "dark spot"). If the blinded region is so large as to encompass an entire quadrant of the visual field, it is called a **quadrantanopia.** If it encompasses an entire half of the visual field, it is referred to as a **hemianopia.** The complete loss of vision as the result of occipital lobe lesions is sometimes called **cortical blindness**, to distinguish it from the blindness caused by damage or malfunction of the eyes and optic tract. The consequences of various kinds of lesions can be seen in Figure 3-17.

The foveal region of the retina is represented at the extreme rear of the cortex, sometimes referred to as the **occipital pole.** As one moves away from the pole, toward the front of the cortex, more peripheral visual field locations are represented among cells that are farther away from the pole. The cortical map of the visual field is inverted and left-right reversed like the image on the retina. Locations in the upper half of the visual field locations are represented below a major convolution at the back of the cortex, known as the **calcarine fissure,** whereas locations in the lower half of the visual field are represented just above the calcarine fissure. The left half of the visual field is represented in the right occipital cortex, whereas the right half of the visual field is represented in the left occipital cortex. Thus, if we divided the V1 cortex into four equal quadrants, damage to the upper-right quadrant would result in blindness for the lower-left quadrant of the visual field.

Following the methodological procedures of Hubel and Wiesel (1962, 1979), many investigators have mapped receptive fields of cortical cells in animals. Not surprisingly, given the nature of receptive fields in retinal ganglion cells and cells of the lateral geniculate nucleus, the familiar circular

OCCIPITAL LOBE
DAMAGE

VISUAL FIELD LOSS

A. HEMIANOPIA

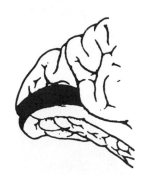

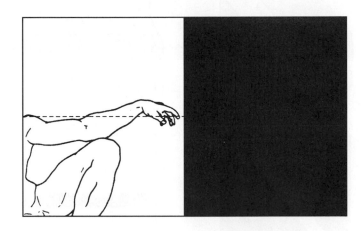

B. SCOTOMA

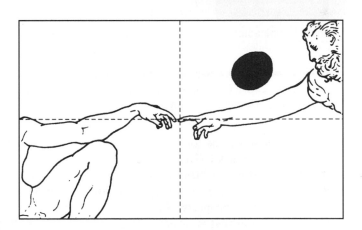

C. QUADRANTANOPIA

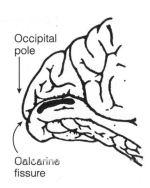

Occipital
pole

Calcarine
fissure

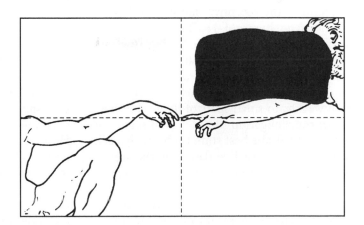

FIGURE 3-17   The consequences of various kinds of lesions to regions of Area V1.

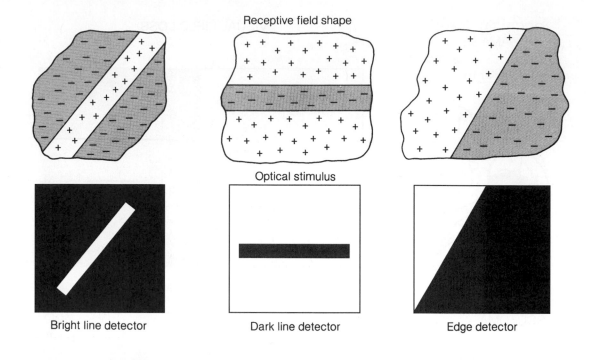

Receptive field shape

Optical stimulus

Bright line detector   Dark line detector   Edge detector

FIGURE 3-18 Receptive fields of "simple" cortical cells: "+" indicates a region in the receptive field that gives an on response, and "–" indicates an off response.

on and off regions also can be found in the receptive fields of cells of Area V1 (DeValois, Yund, & Hepler, 1982; Heggelund, 1981a, 1981b). However, the majority of the measured receptive fields have another interesting property: They have an elongated central region that is oriented at a particular angle.

A diagram of the receptive fields of some such cells is shown in Figure 3-18. This type of cell, which Hubel and Wiesel labeled a simple cell, generally has little spontaneous activity and never seems to respond to diffuse illumination covering the whole screen. Sometimes such cells respond, although weakly, to small spots of light. However, because of the elongation of the central region of the receptive field, the best stimulus for such a cell is a dark or light bar or line flashed in the appropriate location and orientation in the receptive field. Figure 3-18 shows the receptive fields that might be mapped from several different simple cells. Beneath each of them you will see the stimulus that produces the maximal response for each of these receptive fields. Notice that in every case the edge between the light and the dark must be at a

particular location and also at a particular angle of inclination. If the edge is flashed on the receptive field at a different angle, a greatly reduced response, or perhaps no response at all, may be obtained. For this reason such cortical cells are said to have orientation specificity, which is something circular center-surround cells do not have.

Other kinds of neurons in Area V1 seem to be tuned to even more complicated pattern properties of the stimulus. These more elaborate feature-analyzing neurons have been labeled complex cells. They have larger receptive fields than do simple cells, although their size may vary tremendously. Like simple cells, complex cells respond maximally to stimuli when they are in a particular orientation. However, they rarely respond to any flashing patterns. What they prefer is a bar or edge moving somewhere within the receptive field, and its location within the receptive field does not appear to be particularly important. In other words, the complex cells seem to generalize their response over a wider area of the visual field. Figure 3-19 shows the response of a complex cell to two different moving light slits, one in the optimal orientation and the

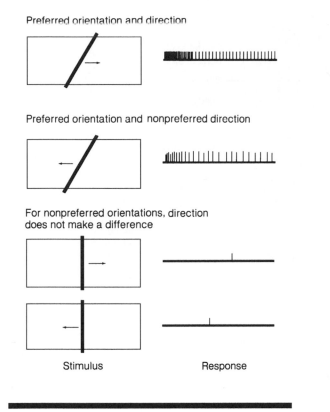

FIGURE 3-19   Some typical complex cortical cell responses.

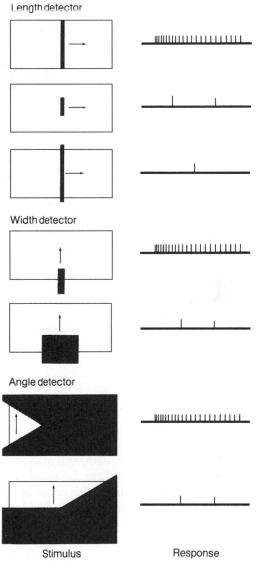

FIGURE 3-20   Some typical hypercomplex or "special complex" cortical cell responses.

other in a nonoptimal orientation. Notice that both direction of movement and orientation are important factors in determining the response.

At an even more sophisticated level of analysis than the complex cells are cells that respond not only to the orientation and direction of movement of the stimulus but also to the length, width, or other features of shapes, such as the presence of corners. For this reason, these cells are sometimes referred to as hypercomplex cells. Figure 3-20 shows an example of some hypercomplex cell responses.

Cells with these various receptive field properties are not randomly intermixed in the visual cortex. Instead, particular cell types are organized vertically into an incredibly detailed spatial structure. The cells in Area V1 are arranged in six layers, numbered 1 to 6, beginning with the outermost (surface) layer. These layers are depicted in Figure 3-21. Over time some of these layers have been studied in greater detail, and as a result several additional sublayers have been identified, as can be

seen, for example, in Layer 4. To assist your understanding of these layers, you should be aware of a general organizing principle of the visual cortex, namely, that cells in the middle layers tend to receive input directly from the preceding visual map. In the case of Area V1, this is the lateral geniculate nucleus. Cells in the outer layers send signals on to other visual regions of the cortex, whereas cells in the innermost layers receive back projections in

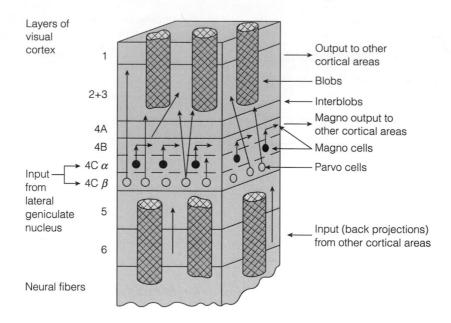

FIGURE 3-21 Location of various visually responsive cells in the layers of the striate cortex (also known as *V1* or the *primary visual cortex*).

the form of inputs from these other visual centers in the brain.

The cell layer in Area V1 receiving inputs directly from the lateral geniculate body is Layer 4C. A majority of the cells here have the simple circular center-surround receptive fields found at lower levels of the visual system. The cell classification system we saw in the retina and in the lateral geniculate nucleus is also preserved in Layer 4C— magno cells are found in the top half (labeled "4C α"), and parvo cells are found in the lower half (labeled "4C β"). This is illustrated in Figure 3-21.

Closer to the cortical surface, specifically in Layers 2, 3, and 4B, we find cells that connect with other visual centers in the cortex. They, too, appear to preserve the parvo-magno distinction, although in a somewhat different form. All of the magno cell inputs from Input Level 4C go directly into Sublayer 4B. This starts a motion-processing channel because these cells are not sensitive to color but are selective for both orientation and movement. Magno outputs go directly from Layer 4B to other cortical areas.

The parvo cell channel is a bit more complex because it divides into two channels. A cell-staining

technique has shown that there are roughly cylindrical patterns of darkly stained cells in Layers 2 and 3, about 0.2 mm in diameter, that can be seen against a background of lighter cells (Wong-Riley, 1979). These dark regions have been called blobs and the light regions interblobs. The parvo cells that go into the blobs carry color and contrast information and may be viewed as the origin of a color channel. The cells in the interblob region respond selectively to the orientation of an edge but do not differentiate between edges of different colors (Livingstone & Hubel, 1988; Shapley, 1990; Zeki, 1993).

Layers 5 and 6 receive back projection inputs from other areas of the visual cortex and contain specialized cells that are reminiscent of the parvo-magno distinction. Receptive fields of cells in Layer 5 are quite large and sensitive to the direction of stimulus movement, whereas those of cells in Layer 6 are rather long, narrow, and orientation sensitive.

The organization of cells across the horizontal surface of the cortex is not random with respect to their receptive field. Instead, cells with a particular orientation sensitivity tend to be grouped

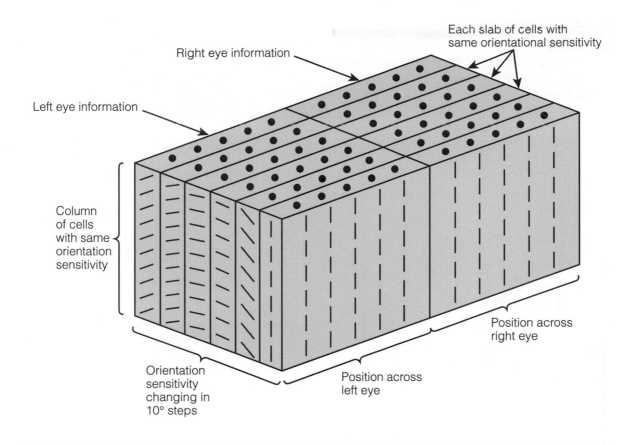

Left eye information

Right eye information

Each slab of cells with
same orientational sensitivity

Column
of cells
with same
orientation
sensitivity

Orientation
sensitivity
changing in
10° steps

Position across
left eye

Position across
right eye

FIGURE 3-22 Diagram of a hypercolumn, which is a small region of visual cortex containing inputs from both eyes and all visual orientations, separated spatially.

into slabs and columns, as diagrammed in Figure 3-22. As we move across the top of the cortex in one direction, the orientation specificity shifts by about 10° per column. Moving in the other direction, we encounter columns of cells that have the same orientation sensitivity but that are more responsive to one particular eye than to the other, hence showing a relative **eye dominance.** The spatial arrangement here seems to be that of alternating stripes, with a slab of cells responding to one eye located next to one responding to the other eye. A region of cortex containing all 360° of orientation specificity, and including a region responsive to both the left eye and the right eye, forms a larger unit that is sometimes called a **hypercolumn.** Such a piece of cortex might be between 0.5 and 1 mm square and 2 mm deep and is diagrammed in Figure 3-22.

MULTIPLE PARALLEL PATHWAYS

In addition to all of the functions we have already described for the primary visual cortex, one of its most important functions is to serve as a source for almost all of the other cortical visual maps. From V1, axonal fibers send neural messages directly and in parallel to several other visual maps. As a group, these other visual areas in the cortex are sometimes referred to as **prestriate cortex,** because they all lie in front of Area V1, or even as **extrastriate cortex,** where the term *extra* means "beyond" the striate cortex. It is important to note that axons arriving at the other visual areas from Area V1 do not carry the same information to each of these other cortical maps of the visual field. V1 segregates three major types of visual information: form, color, and motion and routes these outputs to separate cortical regions for processing.

The visual area that is the nearest neighbor to V1 is (not surprisingly) called *V2*. It is not readily visible from the cortical surface because much of it is hidden in deep convolutions. Its position in the cortex is shown in Figure 3-23. Area V2 receives some input directly from the geniculate fibers as well as being connected point-to-point with Area V1. One of the most distinctive anatomical features of Area V2 is revealed in response to the same chemical stain that makes the blobs visible in V1 (Wong-Riley, 1979). In Area V2 this stain reveals a set of dark stripes running vertically through the cortical tissue, interspersed between lighter stripes. Some of the dark stripes are relatively thick, whereas others are thin. Moreover, in the monkey, thick stripes and thin stripes appear in a repeating pattern separated by the lighter interstripes.

The pattern of connections between Area V1 and the cells in these V2 stripes carries on the idea of separate information channels. The color information from the blobs in V1 is routed directly to the thin stripes in V2; the motion information from Layer 4B in V1 is routed to the thick stripes in V2, and the form and orientation information from the interblob areas in V1 is directed into the interstripe areas of V2. Because Areas V1 and V2 represent visual information in similar ways and because both of these visual areas send axons to almost all of the other prestriate visual areas, some researchers now refer to the two areas together as the *V1-V2 complex* (Zeki, 1993).

Area V3: A Visual Map for Form and Local Movement

Area V3 contains a visual map, separate from Areas V1 and V2, that lies largely buried within a fold of the cortex immediately in front of V1. It is shown in Figure 3-23. Although some of its input comes from V2, some of its input also comes directly from V1, without an intermediate stopover in V2. It is a complete point-to-point correspondence map of the visual field. One of the unique curiosities of V3 (perhaps because of its two sources of input) is that it has two representations of the foveal region of the retina.

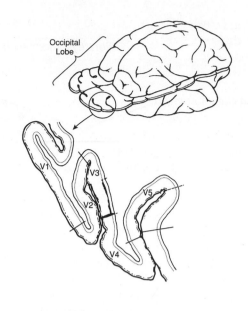

FIGURE 3-23 The locations of Areas V1–V5 in the occipital lobe of the cortex. An imaginary slab has been pulled out from the top drawing and expanded to show more detail.

Cells in V3 receive their input both from the magno-like pathway (Layer 4B, thick stripe) and from the parvo-like pathway (interblob, interstripe). Their receptive fields tend to be specific for edges of particular orientation, many are sensitive to motion, and most are not sensitive to color. Some researchers now see this area as a region specialized for the perception of forms, with additional information about how the forms or figures are moving, rotating, or changing (Zeki, 1993).

Area V4: A Visual Map for Color

An important clue to the specialized function of Area V4, shown in Figure 3-23, was seen over 100 years ago in a report concerning a 61-year-old woman who had suffered a stroke affecting the occipital lobe of her left hemisphere (Verrey, 1888). What we know now, with much greater precision than could be known at the time, was that the woman's principal lesion lay well outside of Area V1, closer to the area known as V4. The most striking feature of the visual deficits that resulted from the stroke was an inability of the woman to see the world in color in the right half of her field of view. Colors in the left half of her visual field appeared normal, but everything in the right half was seen in shades of gray. Since the time of that report, many other patients have had similar problems stemming from cortical lesions (for a review see Zeki, 1990). At times they report a loss of color vision only on one side, and at other times they report a complete loss of color vision. To distinguish this from other forms of color blindness involving abnormal functioning of the retinal cones, this condition is called cerebral achromatopsia.

At first, many neurologists were very reluctant to accept the idea that color blindness could come about solely through a cortical lesion because they believed that the connections between retinal cones and Area V1 were sufficient to produce color vision. However, it is now clear that color vision is absent, or at least very abnormal, unless Area V4 also is functioning properly.

One of the curious features associated with this kind of color blindness is that it is often accompanied by a more general scotoma in the visual periphery. This at first seems paradoxical because color vision is primarily a visual function that is seen in the center of the visual field. However, the related conditions make perfect sense when we consider the locations of Areas V1 and V4 on the cortical surface (see Figure 3-23). It is not at all difficult to see that because of their closeness, an injury that could cause a brain lesion in V4 might also cause some damage to the anterior portion of V1, where the peripheral field of view is mapped.

When we looked at the distribution of cones in Figure 3-7, we found that they were most densely concentrated in the central region of the retina in and around the fovea. Because cones carry the color information, it should not be surprising to find that Area V4 is an incomplete map of the visual field, with inputs mostly from the foveal regions of V1 and V2 and including only the central 40° (Zeki, 1973, 1977). Perhaps the most interesting property of these cells is that they respond to the perceived color of a surface, rather than to the actual wavelength composition of light that enters the eye (Zeki, 1983). As we will see in Chapters 5 and 11, our perception of colors depends not only on the wavelength of the light but also on the

viewing conditions, type of illumination, and other stimuli in the environment. For instance, studies of monkeys with damage to V4 show that their basic ability to discriminate different wavelengths of light is still good; however, their ability to accurately perceive the color of surfaces under changing conditions of illumination is greatly impaired (Heywood, Wilson, & Cowey, 1987; Wild, Butler, Carden, & Kullikowski, 1985).

Area V5: A Visual Map for Global Motion

Area V5 (see Figure 3-23) seems to be specialized for detecting the speed and direction of motion, rather than the identity of the object that is moving. The importance of this visual area to everyday perception is made clear in the case of a 43-year-old female patient who had suffered a fairly small localized lesion in Area V5 because of a vascular disorder (Zihl, von Cramon, & Mai, 1983). Along with some lesser problems in performing arithmetic calculations and finding words for common objects, the most striking observation was the patient's inability to see objects in motion. The patient had difficulty, for example, in pouring a cup of coffee because at any moment in time the fluid appeared to be frozen. As a result, she couldn't stop pouring at the right time. Her inability to see movement in a speaker's mouth also made it difficult to follow a conversation. Crossing the street was especially dangerous because she seemed unable to predict the speeds of approaching cars. This condition has been called cerebral akinetopsia because it is a form of motion (kinesthetic) blindness that is entirely cortical in nature.

Cells in Area V5 receive their input from the thick stripes in V2 and some additional information directly from cells in Area V1. Researchers have found that all cells in V5 are sensitive to motion in one way or another and that over 90% of them are tuned to favor a particular direction. None of the cells seems concerned with the color of the stimulus (Zeki, 1974, 1993). There is an important distinction to be made for the way in which the cells are motion sensitive, relative to those in V3. That is, V5 cells are sensitive to the overall direction of motion of an entire object, whereas the cells in V3 seem to be mostly responsive to motion produced

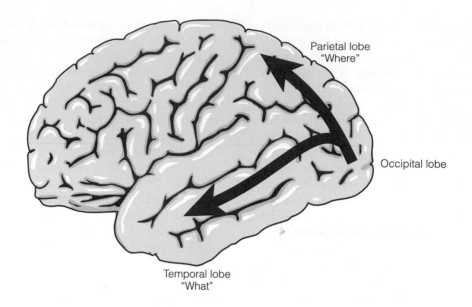

FIGURE 3-24 Two visual pathways that extend beyond the occipital lobe.

along particular edges, such as might occur when an object remains in one place but tilts or rotates (Movshon & Newsome, 1992; Zeki, 1993). To be this sensitive to properties of whole objects, rather than to local attributes of small regions on the retina, cells in Area V5 have very large receptive fields, indicating that they integrate information over a large retinal area (Zeki & Shipp, 1988). The receptive fields of some cells in this region have been found to be nearly one half of the entire visual field, meaning that this area is really concerned with whether or not an object is moving rather than precisely where it is at any moment in time.

The Parietal Lobes: A System for Knowing "Where?"

Up to now we have seen that there are different channels for carrying form, motion, and color information and specialized cortical maps for the representation of this information (Mishkin, Ungerleider, & Macko, 1983; Van Essen & Waessle, 1990; Zeki, 1993). These channels and maps must interact and communicate with one another to produce the many varied aspects of our visual experience. Beyond the occipital lobe, there appear to be at least

two distinctly different regions of the brain involved in visual processing, and these are in the parietal and the temporal lobes of the brain (Mishkin, Ungerleider, & Macko, 1983; Rockland & Pandya, 1981). These areas contain additional maps of the visual field, and some very complex visual processing takes place there. A diagram to help you localize these *tertiary* or "third-order" visual areas is shown in Figure 3-24.

The **parietal** area of the cortex seems to be specialized to answer the question "Where is it?" Monkeys with lesions in the parietal cortex have no difficulty learning to identify objects by sight alone; however, they have a great deal of difficulty learning to respond correctly to information about the location of objects (Mishkin & Lewis, 1982; Mishkin & Ungerleider, 1982; Pohl, 1973). For instance, monkeys trained to respond to the food source that is "closer to the landmark object" are unable to perform this task following parietal lesions, although similar lesions in the temporal cortex leave performance on this task at a high level. Humans with brain damage to the parietal cortex also appear to be impaired on tasks that require relative location judgments but not on tasks that require simple object identification (e.g., Posner, 1988). We will take up this topic in greater detail in Chapter 15.

The Temporal Lobes: A System for Knowing "What?"

The temporal lobes seem to be specialized to answer the question "What is it?"—that is, to identify objects. The visual significance of the lower portion of the temporal lobe, or inferotemporal cortex, was accidentally discovered by Kluver and Bucy in 1937 while observing monkeys who had undergone surgery that removed most of both temporal lobes. They called the syndrome psychic blindness. The animals could reach for, and accurately pick up, small items, and so they were clearly not blind. However, they appeared to have lost the ability to identify these objects by sight. An example of this was shown in a simple laboratory test. A piece of food or a metal object was presented to a monkey approximately every 30 sec. Generally, a normal monkey will eat the food and discard a nail or steel nut after examination by mouth. Within a few trials, a normal monkey will let the metal objects pass by and select only the food. For the animals with inferotemporal lobe loss, however, both the food and the inedible object were picked up on virtually every trial. The animals could easily use vision to grasp each object but yet were unable to learn to discriminate between them. Wilson (1957) found that such monkeys could discriminate between an inverted and an upright *L* by touch, yet with inferotemporal lesions they could not make the same discrimination visually.

This syndrome is similar to a human defect called visual agnosia (Kolb & Whishaw, 1985), which recently received popular attention in the book *The Man Who Mistook His Wife for a Hat* (Sacks, 1987). Patients with visual agnosia can see all parts of the visual field, but the objects that they see mean nothing to them. Patients with lesions of the right temporal lobe also show deficits on a variety of other visual tests. For instance, they have difficulty in placing pictures in a sequence that relates a meaningful story or pattern. They also have difficulty in learning to recognize new faces, in making estimates of the number of dots in an array, in recognizing overlapping figures, and in memory for nonsense forms and pictures. We'll have more to say about such agnosias when we consider some clinical conditions in Chapter 18.

Some investigators have begun to map single neurons in the inferotemporal cortex. Some microelectrode measurements in the monkey brain have produced startling results, suggesting that neurons in this part of the brain have amazing response specificities. Although research on this area of the brain has only recently begun, neurons sensitive to size, shape, color, orientation, and direction of movement have already been discovered (Desimone, Albright, Gross, & Bruce, 1980; Desimone & Gross, 1979; Desimone, Schein, Moran, & Ungerleider, 1985). There are even reports of neurons that are extremely specialized to identify particular targets. For instance, one neuron in a monkey produced its most vigorous response when the stimulus was in the shape of a monkey's paw. Gross, Rocha-Miranda, and Bender (1972) reported that one day they discovered a cell that seemed unresponsive to any light stimulus. When they waved their hand in front of the stimulus screen, however, they elicited a very vigorous response from the previously unresponsive neuron. They then spent the next 12 hours testing various paper cutouts in an attempt to find out what feature triggered this specific unit. When all the stimuli of the set were ranked according to the strength of the response they produced, the experimenters could not find any simple physical dimension that correlated with this rank order. However, the rank order of stimuli, in terms of their ability to drive the cell, did correlate with their apparent similarity (at least for the experimenters) to the shadow of a monkey's paw.

Even more startling degrees of stimulus analysis seem to characterize a region of the temporal lobe called the superior temporal cortex. In monkeys cells in this region have been found to respond selectively to faces (Bruce, Desimone, & Gross, 1981) and to particular movements of faces, such as back and forth or rotation (Perrett & Mistlin, 1987). The more realistic and the more monkeylike the face, the stronger the response. Distorting the stimulus by removing the eyes, scrambling the features, or presenting a cartoon caricature results in a weaker response. Kendrick and Baldwin (1987) have found in sheep similar cells that respond preferentially to sheep faces and, interestingly, to human faces as well. Thus, it seems possible that in your temporal cortex there might be cells that respond best to your grandmother, your car, or many other familiar stimulus shapes.

THE PROBLEM OF VISUAL UNITY

By now you must be impressed by the large number of different maps of the visual field that can be found in the cortex. All of these maps are operating at the same time or, as vision researchers say, *in parallel*, performing specialized tasks that are critical for visual perception, such as identifying and localizing objects and determining their color, shape, and state of motion. We have seen how each of these maps is constructed by careful selection of only some of the information available in the entire field of view. A convenient summary of the pathways leading to these maps, and interactions among them, is shown in Figure 3-25. As the summary shows, the motion map in Area V5 is based largely on the information conveyed by the magno-like pathway that begins in the ganglion cells of the retina and that is further refined in the cells of Layer 4B in Area V1 and the thick-stripe regions of Area V2 before arriving in Area V5. The color map in Area V4, on the other hand, gets its information from parvo cells in the retinal ganglion cells via the blob regions of Area V1 and the thin stripes of Area V2.

This specialization of function of areas within the cortex leads to the obvious question "Why are there so many different maps of the visual field?" Wouldn't one map containing all of the information be enough? To help us think about this, we must first remember that the function of the visual system is not to re-create an image of the outside world in the brain. Remember, there is nobody inside your brain who could look at such an image even if it were there. The function of the visual system is to recognize objects, to locate them in space, and to assist individuals to respond appropriately to objects and events in their environment. Many investigators have suggested that the multiple maps in the visual field were created to increase perceptual speed. Processing several lines of information in parallel is very fast and efficient—much like having a series of diagnostic medical tests (e.g., blood, urine analysis, and X rays) all run at the same time and analyzed in different laboratories, rather than waiting for the first set of test results and then starting the next in some sequential manner (Cowey, 1981; Desimone et al., 1985; Livingstone & Hubel, 1988; Phillips, Zeki, & Barlow, 1984). Others have pointed out that the computations involved in processing such

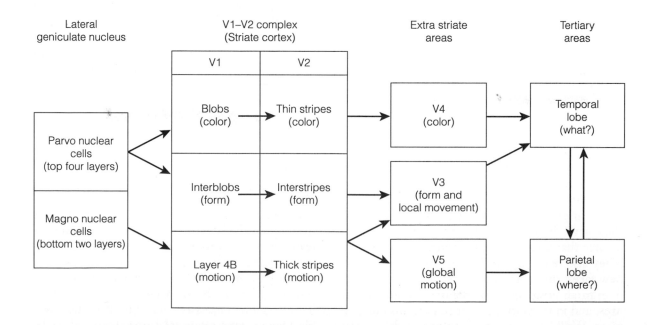

FIGURE 3-25   A highly schematic overview of the geniculostriate visual pathway to the cortex.

attributes as motion and color are themselves so different that it is almost a necessity to keep them isolated from one another (Ballard, Hinton, & Sejnowski, 1983; Zeki, 1993).

Given that there are so many maps, the next scientific (and perhaps philosophical) question is "How can our visual experience be that of a single, coherent visual world, given the fact that the processing of the information is fragmented into many separate maps, in many places in the brain, each with separate information processing aims?" Because theorists are just now beginning to seriously look at this question (e.g., Crick, 1994; Damasio, 1994; Dennett, 1991; Pinker, 1997; Zeki, 1993), our answers for now must be tentative.

One possible answer is that the various areas communicate and coordinate with each other through *back projections*. In this way, for instance, a global motion computed by V5 can be sent back to V1 for further processing and then finally to the parietal centers, which will combine the information so that we can successfully intercept or avoid a moving object (Zeki, 1993). Another possibility is *temporal synchrony*, which means that the results of neural activities taking place at the same time in the various far-flung visual areas become linked together in consciousness because they all are likely to be the result of a single stimulus. Synchronization could be assisted by the fact that there seems to be a rhythmical or oscillatory aspect to the firing of cells in the retina, the lateral geniculate nucleus, and the cortex (e.g., Gray, Konig, Engel, & Singer, 1989; Podvigin, Jokeit, & Poppel, 1992). Direct physiological evidence for synchronous firing in response to a single stimulus has been observed for cells in Area V1 that had similar orientation preferences, even though their receptive fields did not overlap (Gray et al., 1989), and in neurons in separate hemispheres that were stimulated by continuous contours (Engel, Konig, Kreiter, & Singer, 1991). Neurons in V1 and in the lateral geniculate nucleus have been observed firing in synchrony in response to stimuli moving in a predictable direction (Sillito, Jones, Gerstein, & West, 1994).

Alternatively, the very fact that we are dealing with maps may hold the answer. Perhaps there are so many topographic maps of the visual field so that the retinal location can define what goes together. In this way we start with the same retinal location on our various maps, and this common location specifies "an object," while each map simply adds to the set of properties, and these combine in some center, perhaps in the temporal lobes. We will encounter these concepts again when we talk about object and form perception in Chapter 10 (cf. Treisman, 1986b). For now, however, one important consequence of the parallel mapping of visual brain function is that the destruction of any one of these cortical maps may produce only complex and subtle disruptions of visual processing, rather than massive and global deficits, such as a total loss of the ability to read type on paper or to recognize the objects depicted in drawings.

CHAPTER SUMMARY

The eye is designed to respond to **light,** which is electromagnetic radiation with wavelengths between 380 and 760 nm. Light is collected by the **cornea** and passes through the anterior chamber, then through the **pupil,** which is an aperture in the **iris diaphragm,** to the **crystalline lens.** The lens focuses the light by changing shape in a process called **accommodation.** The image passes through the **vitreous humor** in the **posterior chamber** and is projected onto the **retina.** The retina contains two kinds of **photoreceptors: rods,** which are sensitive to dim light, and **cones,** which are used in bright light and convey color information. The central region of the retina, which provides the best visual acuity, is the **fovea,** which contains only cones. Information from the photoreceptors passes through the **bipolar cells** and the **ganglion cells** before passing out of the eye via the optic nerve. Lateral neural interactions across the retina are accomplished via **horizontal cells** and **amacrine cells.** The neural response to light can be either an **on response** or an **off response.** On and off regions are spatially arranged in circular receptive fields. **Parvo** ganglion cells are small cells that respond to the distribution of light on the receptive field and are specialized for detail viewing, whereas larger **magno** ganglion cells respond to movement.

There are two major visual pathways. The **tectopulvinar system** evolved earlier and is mostly made up of magno cell inputs. They pass through the **superior colliculus,** then to the **pulvinar** and

lateral posterior nuclei of the thalamus, and then on to the secondary areas of the visual cortex. This system is involved in processing location and movement for functions such as eye movements. The **geniculostriate system** passes through the **lateral geniculate nucleus** of the thalamus, which maintains separate layers for magno and parvo cells. Information is then sent to the **primary visual cortex,** or **striate cortex** (V1).

Area V1 contains **simple cells** with receptive fields that have **orientation specificity** to detect lines at various inclinations, **complex cells** that detect motion and have **direction specificity,** and **hypercomplex cells** that detect unique visual features. These feature-specific cells are arranged in orderly patterns to form **hypercolumns.** V1 is one of many maps of the visual field. Information from V1 is processed in the cortex in **multiple parallel pathways.** Color information passes through the **V1 blobs** and **V2** thin strips to Area V4. Global motion information passes through **V1** Layer 4B and **V2** thick stripes to V5. Form and local movement information passes through **V1 interblobs** and **V2** interstripes to V3, with some inputs from the motion pathway. All of these inputs are passed on to the **parietal lobes,** which answer the question "Where is it?" and to the **temporal lobes,** which answer the question "What is it?"

KEY TERMS

photon
nanometer
sclera
cornea
aqueous humor
iris
pupil
lens
accommodation
refractive error
presbyopia
near point
emmetropic
hypermetropia
myopia
vitreous humor
retina
pigment epithelium
reflecting tapetum
photoreceptors
rods
cones
bipolar cells
ganglion cells
horizontal cells
amacrine cells
optic axis
macula lutea
fovea centralis
duplex retina theory
photopic
scotopic
night blindness
day blindness
rhodopsin
retinal
opsin
hyperpolarization
iodopsin
photopsin
scotopsin
optic nerve
blind spot
optic disk
receptive field
on response
off response

on-off response
parvo
magno
topographic map
tectopulvinar system
geniculostriate system
optic chiasm
optic tract
tectum
superior colliculi
back projections
pulvinar and lateral posterior nuclei
fixation
buildup
burst
lateral geniculate nucleus
optic radiations
occipital lobe
Visual Area
cortical magnification factor
striate cortex
scotoma
quadrantanopia
hemianopia
cortical blindness
occipital pole
calcarine fissure
simple cells
orientation specificity
complex cells
hypercomplex cells
blobs
interblobs
eye dominance
hypercolumn
prestriate cortex
extrastriate cortex
cerebral achromatopsia
cerebral akinetopsia
parietal
temporal lobes
inferotemporal cortex
psychic blindness
visual agnosia
superior temporal cortex

Brightness and Spatial Frequency

CHAPTER 4

The following scene must have played countless times in horror films and in episodes of *The X-Files:* It is night, and in the darkness two ragged old beachcombers can barely be seen moving along the water's edge. Suddenly, one stops.

"Hey, Charlie, I think there's something out there."

"W-What is it?"

"I can't make it out. It's some sort of glow. It's too dim to make out what it is."

This scene illustrates the most basic property of vision, namely, that it depends on the presence of light. The most primitive visual percepts are simply reactions to the intensity of the incoming energy. These responses are represented in consciousness as a brightness or glow. We often sense the presence of light before sufficient energy exists for us to apprehend shape or form. Thus, the next line of dialogue in the preceding scene usually goes, "It's getting brighter," and then as the energy becomes sufficient for the two characters to apprehend the object itself, "Oh, my God! It's some sort of creature!" As we shall see, the perception of brightness is much more complex and surprising than the script of this particular film.

PHOTOMETRIC UNITS

Electromagnetic energy, or light, can vary along three dimensions: intensity, wavelength, and duration (see

Chapter 3). All dimensions are important in the perception of brightness, although brightness varies most directly with intensity. Of course, to make sense of the perceptual effects, we must first be able to specify the physical intensity of the stimulus. This is not as simple as it might seem.

Light measurement is actually based on the visual effects produced by visible radiation and is called **photometry**. Photometric units are used to describe the light stimulus, and these units are, by convention, expressed in terms of energy. Unfortu-nately, over the years a confusing array of photometric units were developed, most of them designed for some specific purpose by some technical or academic subdiscipline. The result was chaos. Even among the most scholarly, few can tell you how many *nits* there are in an *apostilb* or a *blondel* or how any of these units are related to a *candle* or a *lambert*. In 1960 an International Conference on Weights and Measures established the *System International d'Unites*, which is a uniform system of measurement (known commonly as the SI System).

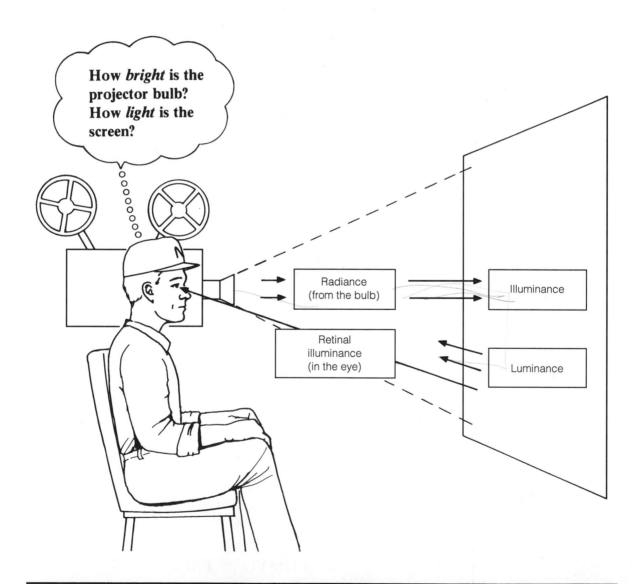

FIGURE 4-1 The relationship between various physical measures of light and psychological judgments of brightness and lightness.

Throughout this book we use these **standard units.** Should your reading bring you into contact with some of the older forms of photometric measurement, we suggest that you look at a more advanced text, such as Wyszecki and Stiles (1967), to make sense of the quantities involved.

There are two ways by which light can reach the eye: (a) directly from a radiating source such as a lightbulb, fluorescent tube, a firefly, or the sun or (b) indirectly by reflection from surfaces that have radiant energy falling on them, such as trees, walls, and paper. Different types of measures are used for these different types of light input. All photometric units, however, are ultimately based on the amount of light emitted from a single candle. The nature of this *standard candle*, its photic energy, and the specific measures derived from it have been fixed (albeit somewhat arbitrarily) by an international body called the *Commission Internationale de l'Eclairage*, usually known as the CIE.

Each different aspect of light is designated by its own name and requires a different measurement unit, and these are summarized in Figure 4-1 for a situation where we have a projector shining light on a screen. Let us begin with the light measures that can be taken with a photometer (a physical light-measuring device). The amount of energy coming from a light source (e.g., the projector bulb) is called its **radiance.** The unit of radiance is the standard candle, which produces an energy of slightly more than 0.001 watt at a wavelength of 555 nm. This quantity of luminous energy is called a **lumen.** The amount of light falling on a surface (e.g., the screen) is another photometric quantity called **illuminance.** The amount of light reflected from a surface is called its **luminance,** and the *percentage* of light falling on a surface that is reflected is called its **reflectance.** Reflectance is thus simply the percentage of luminance compared to illuminance. The amount of light reaching the retina is called the **retinal illuminance.** Table 4-1 summarizes these photometric quantities, along with how they are measured, the units used, and some of their specific properties.

There are two important measures of our subjective impressions of light intensity in which vision

Table 4-1   Photometric Units

PHOTOMETRIC TERM	WHAT IS MEASURED	UNIT	HOW MEASURED	COMMENTS
Radiance or luminous flux	Radiant energy from a light source	Lumen	A candela is the light of a 1-lumen source at a distance of 1 m shone on a square meter	Defined in terms of a standard candle (candela)
Illuminance	Light falling on a surface	Lux	1 lumen/m^2	As the source moves farther away illuminance decreases
Luminance	Light reflected from a surface	Candelas per square meter	Luminance = $\dfrac{\text{Illuminance} \times \text{Reflectance}}{100}$	Independent of distance of eye from surface
Reflectance (albedo)	Proportion of light reflected from surface	Percentage reflectance	Reflectance = $\dfrac{\text{Luminance}}{\text{Illuminance}} \times 100$	Really ratio of reflected to incident light
Retinal illuminance	Amount of light incident on the retina	Trolands	1 candela/m^2 seen through pupil of 1 mm^2 area	Roughly 0.0036 lumens/m^2 through a 1-mm^2 pupil

researchers are interested. These are not physical measures, but instead are measures of our perceptual responses (see Arend & Spehar, 1993a, 1993b). The first of these is **brightness,** the phenomenal impression of the amount of light that is being emitted from a source or reflected from a surface. Thus, a subject might be asked to "make the amount of light coming from this adjustable patch appear to be the same as the amount of light coming from the test patch." *Brightness* is therefore the psychological attribute corresponding roughly to the physical measures of *illuminance* (if the light source is being viewed directly) and *luminance* (if the light source is being judged indirectly by its effect on a reflecting surface). The second measure is **lightness,** the phenomenal impression of the percentage of reflected light relative to the total light falling on a surface. *Lightness* (sometimes referred to as "whiteness") is the psychological correlate of the physical measure of *reflectance*. In this case a subject might be asked to "make this adjustable patch appear as if it were cut from the same piece of paper as the test patch." Thus, it refers to the observer's impression of whether the pigment of a reflecting surface is white, gray, or black (Fiorentini, Baumgartner, Magnussen, Shiller, & Thomas, 1990; Walraven, Enroth-Cugell, Hood, McLeod, & Schnapf, 1990). In this chapter we will focus on *brightness* perception, returning to the discussion of *lightness* perception in Chapter 14.

Why is it necessary to distinguish between the various physical measurements that we can make and the psychological experience of brightness? It is necessary because the perception of brightness cannot be explained simply by the amount of light reaching the eye. As we noted in Chapter 2, when we plot the sensation of brightness against the physical stimulus intensity, we get a nonlinear relationship. The brightness measured by a direct scaling technique (such as magnitude estimation) grows approximately as the cube root of the physical intensity (to be precise, the phenomenal sensation grows at a rate equivalent to the light intensity raised to the 0.33 power). This means that if we had a theater stage illuminated by eight lights and we wished to increase the perceived brightness of the area, doubling the number of lights to 16 would not double the perceived brightness but instead would increase it by only one third. If we wanted to double the phenome-

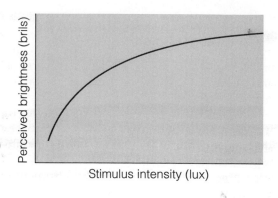

FIGURE 4-2   The nonlinear relationship between stimulus intensity and brightness.

nal brightness, we would have to increase the number of lights to 64!

Figure 4-2 shows the general shape of this relationship graphically. Notice that the curve in Figure 4-2 resembles the logarithmic curve of Fechner's Law (remember Chapter 2 and particularly Figure 2-14). For this reason, various photometric values, such as the brightness scales used in television studios, are frequently presented in logarithmic units, especially when designed for visual purposes. This serves to equalize the sizes of the sensory changes as a function of changes in physical intensity. The unit of brightness in the graph in Figure 4-2 is the **bril,** which was suggested by S. S. Stevens. Each bril represents about ⅒ of a log unit above threshold, in much the same way that a decibel (see Chapter 6) represents ⅒ of a log unit above threshold in audition. Some recent evidence suggests that the magnitude of neural responses in the primary visual cortex is more closely related to our perception of brightness than to the amount of illumination on the retina (Rossi, Rittenhouse, & Paradiso, 1996).

FACTORS IN BRIGHTNESS PERCEPTION

Dark and Light Adaptation

The perception of brightness depends on the current state of sensitivity of your eye, in much the same way that the brightness of the final photographic image depends on the sensitivity of the film. An amount of light that may produce a faint image on insensitive film may produce an overly bright image on very sensitive film. You are probably aware of the effects of your eyes' changing sensitivity when you walk from a darkened room into the bright sunlight, only to find that everything appears to be so bright and "washed out" that a few moments must pass before objects are clearly visible. The opposite occurs when you walk from a bright outside into a darkened movie theater. Now everything appears to be very dark, and objects are difficult to resolve in the gloom. After a while you can discern objects, although the adaptation to the darkness takes somewhat longer than the adaptation to the brighter environment. We call the process of adaptation to a darker environment **dark adaptation** and that to a brighter environment **light adaptation**. Although we cannot slip off our daylight retina and put on the twilight one in the way that we change film in a camera to accommodate changes in lighting conditions, the sensitivity of our eyes does change through these two adaptation processes.

We can monitor directly the changes in sensitivity associated with dark adaptation. First, we adapt an observer to bright light by putting him in a brightly lit room for a few minutes; then we turn off the lights. Now we test to find the observer's *absolute threshold* for the detection of a light that is shone onto the visual periphery. This is done at fixed time intervals after the onset of darkness, using one of the standard psychophysical methods outlined in Chapter 2. Such an experiment usually reveals that the observer at first needs relatively strong stimuli to reach threshold; however, the eye rapidly becomes more sensitive over the first minute or two, at which point it begins to stabilize at a level that is about 100 times more sensitive (2 log units) than when we initially turned off the lights. After about 10 minutes of darkness, the sensitivity begins to rapidly increase again. During this second period, the threshold drops quickly for 5 or 10 minutes, then again stabilizes, reaching a relatively constant level after about a half hour. When we graph the change in threshold for a typical observer, as we have done in Figure 4-3A, we can see a break, or *kink*, in the sensitivity curve. The kink indicates a change in the rate of dark adaptation.

When a sudden transition or break is found in a curve, it often suggests that a second mechanism or process has come into operation. This is confirmed in the present case by the fact that there is a marked change that occurs in your conscious perception near this sharp break in the curve. For

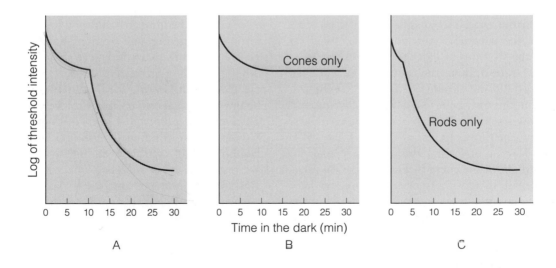

FIGURE 4-3 (A) The normal time course of dark adaptation, (B) dark adaptation in the cones (or central fovea), and (C) dark adaptation in the rods (or periphery).

instance, if we used a greenish light (or nearly any color, for that matter) to measure the threshold, the observer would be able to identify the color throughout the first 10 minutes or so of the test session. At about the point at which the threshold suddenly begins to drop again, the test stimulus would seem to lose its color and become grayish. An old proverb is based on this loss of color vision under dim levels of illumination: "At night, all cats are gray."

In Chapter 3 we talked about the differences between rods and cones. At that time, we reviewed some evidence indicating that rods are found predominantly in animals active during the twilight hours (or in conditions of dim illumination), whereas cones are found predominantly in the retinas of animals that are active during daylight. It was suggested that cones provide **photopic** or daylight vision (including the perception of color), and rods provide **scotopic** or twilight vision. Humans have rods *and* cones; hence, the two segments of the dark adaptation curve represent separate rod and cone contributions. The cones seem rapidly to reach their level of maximal sensitivity. The rods take longer to adapt. When they do, the threshold is lower, but at the expense of a loss in color vision. The point at which the adaptation of the rods catches up to that of the cones is the break in the dark-adaptation curve shown in Figure 4-3A.

We can verify this experimentally. Suppose we return to the experimental situation that we used to track the course of dark adaptation. Now we change the stimulus so that we are focusing a tiny pencil of light only on the central fovea when we take threshold measurements. Because the central fovea contains only cones (Chapter 3), this method will allow us to track dark adaptation in cones. Such an experiment gives us the data shown in Figure 4-3B. Notice that this looks just like the first segment of the curve in Figure 4-3A. No second increase in sensitivity occurs, no matter how long we continue in darkness. To demonstrate the lower or rod portion of the curve we repeat the experiment, except that now we focus our pencil of light about 20° from the center of the fovea, where the retina contains predominantly rods. When we do this, we get the curve shown in Figure 4-3C, in which the first rapid change (attributable to cone action) is almost completely absent.

An even more spectacular way to show the separate rod and cone origin for the two portions of the dark adaptation curve was provided by Hecht and Mandelbaum (1938). They placed a normal observer on a diet deficient in vitamin A for 57 days. Because this vitamin is critical for the synthesis of rhodopsin, the pigment in rods, the diet effectively eliminated the action of these receptors. After 57 days, the observer had a dark adaptation curve similar to that in Figure 4-3B. Not only was the rod portion of the curve almost totally absent, but also the individual was almost completely night blind and unable to see dimly illuminated targets. By the way, the observer completely recovered when he went back to his normal diet. Perhaps similar naturally occurring instances have given carrots (a vegetable high in vitamin A) their reputation for being "good for the eyes." This experiment tells us that the advantage found in carrots is specific to scotopic, or "night," vision.

Overall, these experiments indicate that two separate physiological mechanisms are involved in the perception of brightness: the cone system for brighter illumination and the rod system for dimmer illumination. There is even some evidence suggesting that when bright light is present and the cones are active, they actually inhibit or "turn off" the action of the rods (Drum, 1981).

There is still much to be learned about the nature of the adaptation process. Clearly, any incoming light will bleach the available photopigments in the rods and cones, and time will be needed for them to regenerate. As more pigment becomes available, the sensitivity of the eye should increase. Although such a process does seem to play a role (MacLeod, 1978), dark adaptation involves changes in the sensitivity and responsiveness of neural processes as well (Green & Powers, 1982; Shapley & Enroth-Cugell, 1984). Later in this chapter we shall see that even higher level cognitive responses may influence our perception of brightness. Demonstration Box 4-1 allows you to see the effects of dark adaptation for yourself.

Retinal Locus

As we saw in Figure 3-7, rods and cones are unevenly distributed across the retina. The central fovea contains only cones, which are less sensitive

---

DEMONSTRATION BOX 4-1
Dark Adaptation

To show the dramatic increase in sensitivity associated with dark adaptation, you should first carefully blindfold one eye. Use a couple of cotton balls and some tape to do this. After about 30 minutes darken the room, or step into a reasonably dark closet. Remove the blindfold and compare the sensitivity of your two eyes by alternately opening one eye at a time. The dark-adapted eye should see quite well in the dim illumination, but the other eye will be virtually blind.

---

to weak stimuli, whereas the more sensitive rods are more plentiful in the periphery. Suppose the brightness of a light depended directly on the sensitivity of the stimulated receptors, as well as on the intensity of the light. If that were the case, then moving a constant light stimulus across the dark-adapted retina, stimulating less-sensitive cones near the fovea and more-sensitive rods in the periphery, should change the apparent brightness of the light. This has been verified experimentally (Drum, 1980; Osaka, 1981). Peripheral targets appear brighter. This finding is also embodied in a bit of folk wisdom. At some time in antiquity people noted that looking directly at a dim object, such as a star, could cause it to disappear from view. For this reason, early astronomers would often look at a point off to the side of a star in order to let its image fall upon the more sensitive peripheral retina (containing mostly rods). This technique allows such a dim target to be perceived more clearly. If you try this yourself, look at a point about 20° from the star that you wish to see. This would allow the star's image to fall on the part of the retina where the density of rods is greatest and would give you maximum sensitivity.

Wavelength

The wavelength of the light stimulating the eye will also affect our perception of its brightness. For instance, yellow light (medium wavelengths) almost always appears to be brighter than blue light (short wavelengths). The usual procedure for assessing the relative brightness of lights of different colors is to use a *bipartite target.* This is simply a circular target that has been divided in half. One half contains the *standard color* that is to be matched

in brightness, and the other half contains the *comparison color* that is adjustable. Systematically pairing various colors and then matching their brightness provide a set of measures of the relative amounts of energy needed to produce equal sensations of brightness for various wavelengths of light. For convenience, the wavelength requiring the least energy to equal the brightness of the standard is set at a value of 1.0. All other wavelengths, being less effective in producing the brightness sensation, are assigned values less than 1.0, depending on their relative brightnesses.

After this conversion has been made, a curve can be plotted as in Figure 4-4. Such a curve is called a **luminosity curve.** Notice that we actually have two curves in this figure. The first is labeled *photopic* and represents the results that we would obtain from the matching experiment if the standard were at daylight levels of light intensity. It has a peak sensitivity for wavelengths around 555 nm, and the brightness falls off rapidly for shorter (toward the blue) or longer (toward the red) wavelengths. If we repeat this matching experiment under conditions in which the standard is quite dim, so that only rod vision is operating, the observer will not be aware of the color of the stimuli, and both halves of the field will appear gray regardless of their wavelength. Nonetheless, some wavelengths will still look brighter than others. Thus, we can map out the luminosity curve that is marked *scotopic* in Figure 4-4. Under these conditions the curve is somewhat different, with a peak around 505 nm. This curve is shifted toward the short wavelengths, suggesting that we are more sensitive to blue-green light under dim viewing conditions.

The change in the brightness of light of different wavelengths as the intensity is changed was first described by the Czechoslovakian phenomenologist

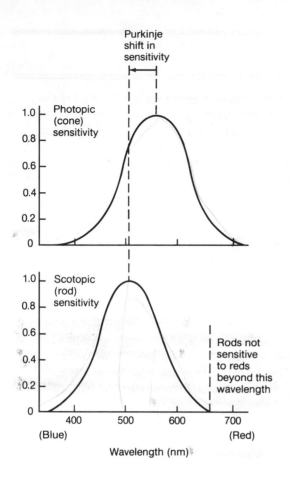

FIGURE 4-4 Differences in relative sensitivity to various wavelengths under photopic and scotopic illumination conditions.

Johannes E. Purkinje, and in his honor this phenomenon is referred to as the **Purkinje shift**. He first noted the change while looking at his garden as twilight was falling. As the light dimmed, the brightnesses of the various colors began to change. Reds that had been bright relative to blues and greens began to look darker, whereas the bluer tones appeared relatively brighter. Because scotopic vision lacks the sensation of color, daylight greens or blues change to moonlight grays, whereas daylight reds change to moonlight blacks. Demonstration Box 4-2 allows you to experience this shift in visual sensitivity for yourself.

There is an interesting application of the Purkinje shift. You may remember from watching war movies that the briefing rooms next to airstrips or the control rooms of ships and submarines are often depicted as illuminated by red light. This red is not used solely for dramatic effect in the film, but is actually used in such real-world settings. Rods are relatively insensitive to the red end of the spectrum; hence red light is virtually equivalent to no light at all for the rods. However, the cones still function at these longer wavelengths if there is sufficient stimulus intensity, so the cones may be used while the rods are beginning to dark adapt. The dashed line in the bottom part of Figure 4-4 shows a wavelength beyond which the rods no longer function while the cones still do. Thus, pilots about to fly night missions, or sailors about to stand the night watch, can be briefed or can check their instruments under red illumination, then function efficiently in the dark without waiting the many minutes necessary to completely dark adapt.

Time and Area

In addition to depending on the intensity, wavelength, and retinal location of the stimulus, our ability to detect a spot of light depends on other stimulus properties. For instance, a photographer knows that when she is taking a picture under dim illumination she may have to lengthen the exposure time in order to collect enough light to adequately register the image on the film. In bright sunlight a short exposure will usually do. Actually, the same amount of physical energy is necessary to expose the film properly in each case; it just takes longer to collect the requisite amount under dim illumination. In physics this relationship is known as the **Bunsen-Roscoe Law**. This law describes the photochemical reaction of any light-sensitive substance, whether it be film or visual pigment. We find that there is a similar tradeoff between stimulus duration and stimulus intensity in vision when we are dealing with the problem of the absolute threshold for brightness perception. We can express this relationship using simple algebra. If we define C as the critical amount of light energy necessary to reach threshold, I as the stimulus intensity, and T as the stimulus duration, the relationship is $T \times I = C$.

This is known as **Bloch's Law**. This means that a weak stimulus must be presented for a long time in order for it to be detected, whereas a more intense

---

DEMONSTRATION BOX 4-2
The Purkinje Shift

For this demonstration you will need a dark room and some way of providing a light whose intensity you can vary without altering its color. A good method is to use a television set as a light source. This may be done by tuning the set to an unused channel and turning the contrast control to a minimum. This reduces the visibility of the random dots that normally appear on the screen. Now, if you darken the room so that the television is the only source of illumination, the brightness control on the set will be a means of controlling the room light. An alternate procedure in the absence of a television is to turn on a light in a room and enter a closet, shutting the door after you. The amount of light entering the closet can be controlled by opening the door by differing amounts. Turning your back to the door allows for a diffusion of the light to any target that you wish to be illuminated. Unfortunately, if the outside room is well lit, opening the door by a few centimeters will provide a good deal of light: Hence, control of illumination may be improved by dimming the light in the outside room.

Now, look at Color Plate 1 inside the front cover of this book. Here we have two colored spots, one blue and one red. When viewed in moderate or bright light (the brightness control on the television is set to high, or the closet door is more widely ajar), the blue spot and the red spot appear to be approximately equal in brightness. Now, make the light very dim (close the door almost completely, or turn down the brightness control on the television). In the bright light, you were viewing the spots with cone vision. Now, if you dim the lights sufficiently, only rod vision will be activated. After 5–10 minutes, as your eye dark adapts, the blue spot will appear to be significantly brighter than the red spot. In fact, the red spot may actually disappear. The effect may be accentuated by staring at the white spot. This shifts the images away from the fovea to an area of the retina containing a greater number of rods.

---

stimulus can be presented for a shorter duration and still be detected. This time-versus-intensity tradeoff works only over stimulus durations less than about $\frac{1}{10}$ of a second. This limiting value may vary a bit, being somewhat longer if the observer is completely dark adapted and somewhat shorter if the observer is very light adapted (Montellese, Sharpe, & Brown, 1979). In general, however, if the duration of a stimulus is greater than about $\frac{1}{10}$ of a second, the probability that you will detect it is no longer affected by its duration, but depends only on its intensity. Like many other things in vision, Bloch's Law holds only under certain circumstances. For instance, it holds better in the periphery (where there are many rods) than in the fovea (Gottlieb, Kietzman, & Bernhaus, 1985) and may also depend on the wavelength of the stimuli used (Schwartz & Loop, 1984).

The size of a stimulus is also important in determining its detectability. In Chapter 3 we noted that there is a good deal of convergence in the visual system, meaning that a number of rods or cones may synapse with the same bipolar cell and several bipolar cells may converge on the same retinal ganglion cell. Consider a hypothetical example. Suppose that four neural responses per second are sufficient to activate a bipolar cell and that a bipolar cell has four receptors making synapses with it. If we provide a tiny spot of light that is strong enough to elicit only 1 unit of neurotransmitter per second from the retinal receptor and the light is wide enough to stimulate only two receptors, clearly the bipolar cell will not respond. If we double the size of the stimulus so that all four receptors are illuminated, however, the bipolar cell will receive a total of 4 units of neurotransmitter per second and will become activated. Thus, as the area of a stimulus increases (even though its intensity does not change), the likelihood increases that we will recruit enough photoreceptors to begin a chain of neural activity that will allow us to detect it. An alternative way of conceptualizing this is in terms of retinal receptive fields, such as those illustrated in Figure 3-9. Increasing the stimulus size might be thought of as simply "filling in" the center of the receptive field with light, thus adding more "on" responses to the overall activity.

For relatively small areas, covering visual angles of 10 min (10′) of arc or less (about 1 mm viewed at arm's length), there is a tradeoff relationship between area and intensity. If A signifies the area stimulated and I and C are stimulus intensity and threshold amount of light energy, respectively, as before, we can describe the relationship as $A \times I = C$. This is known as **Ricco's Law.** Thus, if we increase the intensity of a stimulus, we can decrease its size and still be able to detect it and vice versa for a decrease in stimulus intensity.

For stimulus sizes greater than 10 min of visual angle, increasing the area has a reduced effect. The effect of area on detection for larger stimuli is described by square root $(A) \times I = C$. In other words, for larger stimuli a greater increase in area is needed to achieve the same compensation for a given decrease in stimulus intensity. This second area-intensity relationship is known as **Piper's Law.** Beyond 24° of visual angle no further benefit is gained by increasing the size of the stimulus, and the likelihood of detection depends solely on its intensity. The difference between the two laws seems to arise from differences in the nature or degree of neural convergence in the periphery (Lie, 1980; Ransom-Hogg & Spillman, 1980).

The brightness effects arising from the summation of neural responses converging on a single retinal ganglion cell can be used as a tool to study the underlying neural organization in the retina. For instance, the circular receptive field of a ganglion cell, with an on center and an off surround (see Chapter 3), affects brightness sensitivity (Spillmann, Ransom-Hogg, & Oehler, 1987; Teller, 1980; Westheimer, 1965, 1967). The experimental procedure is in most ways like any other test of visual sensitivity—an *absolute threshold* is measured for a small spot of light at a specific location in the visual field. The way the procedure differs from most is that the threshold is measured when the test spot, instead of being presented in total darkness, is actually superimposed on top of a disk of light that is above threshold, and the subject has to detect the slightly brighter small spot. Figure 4-5 shows the results of an experiment in

which a small spot (2 min in diameter) is used as the test stimulus and is shown on disks of varying diameter. As the size of the background disk increases initially, the intensity of the test spot must be increased to maintain threshold detection. This is because the background disk is exciting more of the same central (on-responding) region of the receptive field than the test spot is exciting. In other words, the test spot is competing with the background disk and making less and less of a contribution to the overall apparent brightness. However, at a disk size of 10 min of arc, something interesting begins to occur. Further increases in the size of the background disk actually make the test spot easier to detect. This suggests that the inhibitory (off-responding) surround of the receptive field has been stimulated by the background disk, thereby allowing the test spot to once again make a larger relative contribution to the excitation of the on-center region. Researchers often use the peak in the threshold function in Figure 4-5 as a measure of the diameter of the on center of a receptive field and use the point where the curve levels off again as a measure of the size of the off or inhibitory region (Spillman, Ransom-Hogg, &

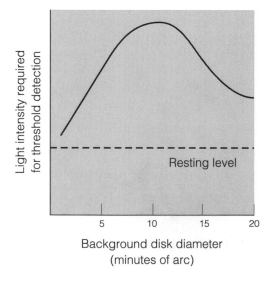

FIGURE 4-5 The intensity required for threshold detection of a spot of light that is 2 min of arc in diameter, plotted as a function of the diameter of a background disk of light that is above threshold (based on Westheimer, 1967).

Oehler, 1987). Some researchers refer to this curve as the **Westheimer function,** after the researcher who first reported it (Westheimer, 1965, 1967).

Maximum Sensitivity

After this discussion, you may be wondering just what the ultimate limit of sensitivity might be if the stimulus were adjusted to the optimal wavelength, size, duration, and retinal position and if the observer were fully dark adapted. The classic experiment to answer this question was conducted by Hecht, Schlaer, and Pirenne (1942). They found that the minimum threshold for the perception of a brightness sensation occurred when only 6 quanta of light (photons) were stimulating the retina. Further computations showed that when detection occured, each of the 6 photons was stimulating a different one of six rods. Theoretically we can't get any more sensitive than this! Even at higher levels of illumination, however, it is possible to show that fluctuations of only a few photons may affect our perception of brightness, thus showing the exquisite sensitivity of the eye as a light detector (Krauskopf & Reeves, 1980; Zuidema, Gresnight, Bouman, & Koenderink, 1978).

VISUAL ACUITY

Visual acuity refers to the ability of the eye to resolve details. There are different types of visual acuity, each dependent on the specific task or specific detail to be resolved. The type of visual acuity most commonly measured is **recognition acuity,** which was introduced by Herman Snellen (1862). He created the familiar *eye chart* found in most ophthalmologists' or optometrists' offices, consisting of rows of letters of progressively smaller size. The observer is asked simply to identify the letters on the chart, and the size of the smallest letters that are identified determines acuity. Acuity is usually measured relative to the performance of a normal observer. Thus, an acuity of 6/6 indicates that an observer is able to identify letters at a distance of 6 meters that a normal observer can also read at that distance (you may be more familiar with the designation *20/20;* 6 m is equivalent to 20 ft). In other words, the measured acuity is normal. An acuity of 6/9 (or 20/30) would mean that an observer is able to read letters at 6 m that are large enough for a normal observer to read at a distance of 9 m. Here, the visual acuity is less than normal.

A more general means of specifying the limits of acuity is to use the minimum **visual angle** of a detail that can be resolved. The visual angle is a measure of the size of the retinal image. Figure 4-6 shows what is meant by *visual angle* and demonstrates a simple computation based on the size and the distance of the object. Generally speaking, a normal observer can reliably resolve details of 1 min of arc (about the size of a quarter seen at a distance of 81 m, which is nearly the length of a football field), although different tasks often produce different limits of acuity (Beck & Schwartz, 1979).

The identification of letters on a Snellen chart is not the best way to measure acuity because letters differ in their degree of identifiability. For instance, *O* and *Q* and *P* and *F* are letter pairs that are easily confused, whereas *L* and *W* and *O* and *I* are quite easy to discriminate. Because these differences

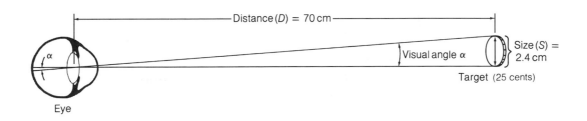

FIGURE 4-6   Computation of the size of the visual angle of the image of a quarter viewed a distance of 70 cm (approximately arm's length), where the observer's line of sight is perpendicular to the lower edge of the coin. Tangent of Visual Angle = Size/Distance; therefore tan $\alpha = S/D = 2.4/70 = 0.034$. Thus, α is approximately 2°.

might affect acuity measurements, E. Landolt (1889) introduced a different recognition task that used circles with a gap in them as targets (see Figure 4-7). The gap can be oriented either up, down, to the right, or to the left, and the observer's task is to indicate the position of the gap. The circles differ in size, and the smallest detectable gap is the measure of acuity.

Several other tasks are used to measure visual acuity. The most primitive measure of acuity is the specification of the smallest target of any type that can be detected. The relationship between brightness perception and the acuity task is most apparent for this task where the target is a light line or spot against a dark background or a dark line or spot against a light background. **Vernier** or **directional acuity** requires an observer to distinguish a broken line from an unbroken line. **Resolution** or **grating acuity** is measured by an observer's ability to detect a gap between two bars or the orientation of a grid of lines. This particular form of acuity task has certain theoretical implications, which we will discuss in the next section. Figure 4-7 shows examples of the previously mentioned acuity targets with arrows pointing to the crucial detail. Notice that each detail is merely a region of the visual field where there is a change in luminance.

It is even possible to estimate people's visual acuity without using any visual targets by simply asking people about their everyday experiences in viewing the world. Because we normally use both eyes and our ability to see a detail will depend on the eye with the better acuity, such an estimate will really be of our "best eye" acuity. Coren and Hakstian (1989) developed a self-report acuity screening inventory that correlates 0.83 with laboratory measures of best-eye visual acuity. You can test yourself with it, using Demonstration Box 4-3.

It is reasonable to expect that the minimum resolvable detail size would be determined by the size of the retinal receptors or the size of the retinal receptive fields. Thus, in order to distinguish whether one or two spots of light are present, it might be expected that it would be necessary to have at least one unstimulated retinal receptor (or receptive field) between two light-stimulated retinal receptors (or receptive fields). Surprisingly, for tasks such as vernier acuity, people can resolve much finer details than might be expected on the basis of these considerations. Under optimal conditions, acuities of 5 sec (a second of arc is $\frac{1}{3600}$ of a degree) or less are possible, despite the fact that the smallest receptive fields are around 25 times larger than this (Klein & Levi, 1985; Westheimer, 1979). In fact, this is about one sixth the diameter of the smallest retinal cones. Resolution of details less than about 10 sec is often referred to as **hyperacuity** because visual performance seems to have gone beyond the resolution imposed by the physical size of the receptors. Some theorists explain this paradox by proposing models of complex neural circuitry and statistical pooling of neural responses (Carlson, 1983; Wilson, 1986). Others believe that the responses of single cells can account for hyperacuity but that these cells are higher up in the chain of processing than ganglion cells. For instance, there is electrophysiological evidence that a vernier stimulus (like the broken line in Figure 4-7) excites a different orientation-tuned simple cell in the primary visual cortex (see Chapter 3) than does a line

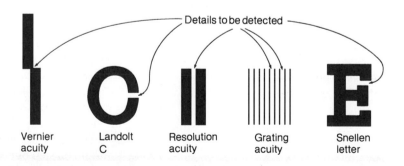

Vernier acuity   Landolt C   Resolution acuity   Grating acuity   Snellen letter

FIGURE 4-7   Some typical acuity targets and the details to be discriminated.

DEMONSTRATION BOX 4-3
Acuity Screening Inventory

To get an estimate of your own best-eye visual acuity, simply take this test, which is the *Acuity Screening Inventory* developed by Coren and Hakstian (1989). The questionnaire deals with a number of common visual situations. For each question you should select the response that best describes you and your behaviors. You can select from among the following response alternatives: Never (or almost never), Seldom, Occasionally, Frequently, Always (or almost always). Simply circle the letter that corresponds to the first letter of your choice.

1. Do you find most book print too small to read easily without glasses or contact lenses? N S O F A

2. Can you recognize people if you see them at a distance when you are not wearing any corrective lenses? N S O F A

3. Do you notice that *far* objects appear fuzzy when you are not wearing glasses or contact lenses? N S O F A

4. Do you notice that *near* objects appear fuzzy when you are not wearing glasses or contact lenses? N S O F A

5. Do you wear glasses or contact lenses? N S O F A

6. Can you read easily in dim light without any corrective lenses? N S O F A

7. Do you think that you may need glasses? N S O F A

8. Would you say that your vision is as good as most people's? N S O F A

Answer the following two questions using Good, Average, Slightly below average, Poor, Very poor (circle the first letter corresponding to your choice).

9. Without glasses or contact lenses, the clearness or sharpness of vision in my *right* eye is G A S P V

10. Without glasses or contact lenses, the clearness or sharpness of vision in my *left* eye is G A S P V

Scoring instructions:
For Questions 1, 3, 4, 5, and 7 responses are scored from 1 for "Never," 2 for "Seldom," 3 for "Occasionally," 4 for "Frequently," and 5 for "Always." For Questions 2, 6, and 8 reverse the scoring so that responses are scored from 1 for "Always" up to 5 for "Never." For Questions 9 and 10 scoring goes from 1 for "Good" to 5 for "Very Poor." Your acuity score is just the sum of these 10 items. Now just check the following table for your predicted Snellen acuity score (this prediction should be plus or minus one line on the eye chart).

ASI SCALE TOTAL	PREDICTED BEST-EYE SNELLEN ACUITY
10 to 18	20/20 (or better)
19 to 25	20/30
26 to 32	20/40
33 to 38	20/60
39 to 50	20/100 (or worse)

---

without the break (Swindale & Cynader, 1986). This would suggest that hyperacuity might exist because high-level cells are specifically tuned to particular "acuity details," like gaps, breaks, or offsets. Because vernier acuity is so sensitive, it has been suggested that the patterns of "range lights" or "leading lights" that are used to assist the navigation of ships would be more effective if the lights appeared as line segments, rather than as points of light on the navigational towers (Coren, Whitehead, Baca, & Patten, 1995).

Because acuity tasks are closely related to brightness discrimination, it is not surprising to find that acuity varies as a function of the many factors shown to be important in the perception of brightness. For instance, the adaptive state of the eye determines the minimum details that can be discriminated under particular viewing conditions (Lie, 1980). Thus, if you step out of the bright sunlight into a dim room, you may find it impossible to read even the large type of the headlines of a newspaper for a few moments. As your eyes adapt to the dim surroundings, however, you can soon easily read even fine print. Even a brief flash of light, bright enough to alter an observer's state of adaptation, markedly reduces an observer's ability to detect and recognize acuity targets (Miller, 1965).

The detection of details in acuity targets also shows an interaction between time and stimulus intensity, very much like that described by Bloch's Law for brightness detection. This means that we can increase the likelihood that a detail will be detected either by increasing the difference between the intensity of the target and that of its background or by increasing the amount of time that the observer views the stimulus. Although Bloch's Law holds only for times less than 100 milliseconds (ms) for brightness detection, the trade-off between time and intensity holds for up to 300 ms in acuity tasks in which observers are trying to detect pattern details (Kahneman, 1966; Kahneman, Norman, & Kubovy, 1967).

Retinal position is also as important for acuity as it is for brightness perception (Jennings & Charman, 1981). The figure in Demonstration Box 4-4 allows you to experience the drastic reductions in visual acuity for targets that are imaged some distance from the fovea. When we measure relative acuity for various locations on the retina, we find that it varies as shown in Figure 4-8. Notice that acuity is best in the central fovea and drops off rapidly as we move into the periphery. This curve looks remarkably like the distribution of cones across the retina diagrammed in Figure 3-7. It also looks much like the distribution of

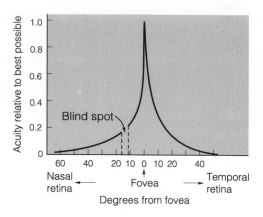

FIGURE 4-8 The distribution of visual acuity across the retina.

parvo ganglion cells in the retina (Peichl & Wassle, 1979). Direct physiological measurement of the responsiveness of parvo and magno cells shows that parvo cells have smaller receptive fields and sustain their responses to stationary stimuli. This has led several researchers to suggest that the limits of visual acuity are set by the prevalence of parvo cells, or cells with characteristics similar to parvo cells, which are best designed for detection and analysis of small details in stationary visual arrays (Andrews & Pollen, 1979; Robson, 1980).

The part of the retina that is highest in visual acuity contains mostly cones, which send their signals to parvo ganglion cells. Because cones operate only at high levels of illumination, we could then

---

DEMONSTRATION BOX 4-4
Visual Acuity as a Function of Retinal Location

Visual acuity is best in the fovea. The range of clear vision extends less than 10° away from the foveal center. Lay this book flat on the table and view the accompanying diagram from a distance of approximately 12 cm. Cover your left eye with your left hand and look directly at the point marked "0°." Without moving your right eye, you will note that the letter over the 0° mark is relatively clear and that the letter at 5° is also legible. However, the letters at 10° and beyond begin to appear fuzzy, and the letters at 40° and 50° are virtually unreadable.

K	B	X	M	P	A	S
+	+	+	+	+	+	+
50°	40°	30°	20°	10°	5°	0°

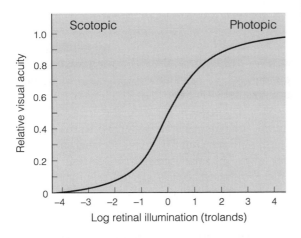

FIGURE 4-9   The effect of illumination on visual acuity.

predict that there would be better acuity at high illumination levels. When we measure the relationship between acuity and illumination directly, we obtain the curve shown in Figure 4-9. Notice that when the illumination is low, in the scotopic (rod) range, acuity is poor, and it improves only slightly as the light intensity is increased. However, as we begin to shift into the photopic (cone) range, acuity improves rapidly. Of course, at too high a light level the acuity is reduced again because of the effects of glare (not shown).

One aspect of the relationship between acuity and illumination has important implications for some common situations. In 1789 Lord Maskelyne, director of the Royal Greenwich Observatory, noticed that he became noticeably nearsighted at night. This tendency to accommodate the eye inappropriately near, even when the object of interest is far away, is called *night myopia* (Leibowitz, Post, Brandt, & Dichgans, 1982). One of the contributing factors is the fact that the pupil is usually quite dilated under dim lighting conditions, contributing to the amount of light scatter in the eye. This degrades the sharpness of the retinal image, interfering with our ability to see details under twilight and nighttime observation conditions. Such an additional reduction of acuity under dim illumination may be an important component in nighttime driving accidents (Leibowitz & Owens, 1977).

SPATIAL FREQUENCY ANALYSIS

Spatial Fourier Analysis

A complete description of the relationship between brightness perception and acuity must take into account a great deal of information. Imagine any test pattern of light. Next realize that when this pattern stimulates the eye there are 125 million or more retinal receptors per eye, each receiving an amount of light ranging from 0 up to many millions of units. Pity the poor perceptual researcher who must now find a method of describing all of this activity (not to mention the poor brain that must interpret it). If we had to catalog every point of light and its intensity before we could understand the major phenomena associated with brightness and acuity, our information about these topics would be limited indeed. Many researchers realized this and began to look for some reasonably small set of relationships among the variables that affect brightness perception that could be used to describe visual arrays, hoping that such a simplified description might yield deeper insight into these phenomena.

In some ways, the most successful attempt to summarize brightness and acuity data to date has involved the use of a mathematical technique based on **Fourier's Theorem**. This theorem states that it is possible to analyze any pattern of stimuli into a series of sine waves. In Chapter 6 we apply this theorem to complex sound waves, in which sound pressure level at some point in space varies over time in an irregular but repeated pattern. For our current problem we are concerned with how light intensity varies across space, namely across the retinal image. According to Fourier's Theorem we can analyze *any* such complex pattern of light intensity across space into a series of simpler sine wave patterns, each of which would be seen as a regularly varying pattern of light and dark if seen alone.

You might recall from your study of trigonometry that a sine wave is simply a regular, smooth, periodically repeating function that can be precisely specified mathematically. Figure 4-10A shows a graph of a sine wave and beside it a distribution of light that varies in the same way, growing more intense where the function rises and less intense where it falls. Such a light distribution is called a

sine wave grating because the intensity of reflected light from the page varies sinusoidally as we move horizontally across the figure, and the whole pattern forms a sort of blurry grating or grid. When applied to light distributions, Fourier's Theorem states that by adding together (scientists call this *synthesizing*) a number of such gratings we can produce *any* specified light distribution. Moreover, although individual sine wave patterns have only gradual changes in intensity, by adding many of them together we can produce even light distributions that contain sharp corners, such as that shown in Figure 4-10. Figure 4-10B is called a **square wave grating** because the light changes are sharp and give a boxlike intensity pattern. Successive addition of the appropriate frequencies of sine waves (or more accurately, the sine wave variations in light intensity that they represent) gradually gives a better and better approximation of the sharp corners of the square wave grating, as can be seen in Figure 4-11. Figure 4-11 shows this graphically for both the square wave grating and a bar.

You might think that adding sine waves can give you only repeating patterns or gratings, such as in Figure 4-10. This is not true. According to the rules of Fourier synthesis *any* pattern, whether repeating or not, can be created by combining appropriate sine waves. Thus, Figure 4-12 shows a single bright bar on a dark background. Below it are the first few sine wave variations in intensity that would be added to produce the bar. Notice that after only the fourth wave pattern has been added, we have already started to create a single bright feature. Addition of other sine waves will ultimately make the bar sharper.

If we take this approach to describing the patterns of light that act as stimuli to our visual systems, we no longer have to catalog the intensity of every point in the pattern. Now we can describe a light pattern precisely with a relatively compact mathematical expression indicating the particular set of sine wave gratings to be added together to reproduce it. Even if the mathematics sometimes become complex, the resulting description is still

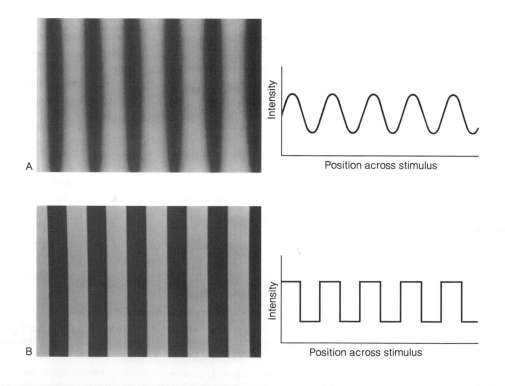

FIGURE 4-10   (A) A sine wave spatial distribution of light and (B) a square wave spatial distribution of light (based on Cornsweet, 1970).

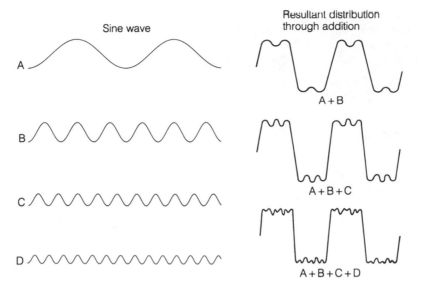

FIGURE 4-11 Gradually adding higher frequency sine waves of lower amplitude to the distribution leads to better approximations of a square wave through the process of Fourier synthesis.

far simpler than a catalog of the light hitting 125 million or more individual retinal receptors. (See Graham, 1989; Levine & Shefner, 1981; or Weisstein, 1980; for a more complete introduction to Fourier analysis of visual patterns.)

Modulation Transfer Function

Fourier analysis (breaking up a pattern into its component sine waves) and *Fourier synthesis* (adding together a set of sine wave variations to create a more complex pattern) provide more than a simple shorthand for the description of light patterns. They serve as powerful tools that may be used to analyze how the visual system responds to stimuli. Consider for a moment how we might test the fidelity of a photographic system (that is, how well the final photo reproduces the actual light variations in the real world). The simplest way of doing this is to use a series of gratings, such as those shown in Figure 4-13. Some of the gratings will have very broad bars and spaces. In such gratings the light intensity rises and falls slowly as we move across the spatial extent of the surface, hence they

are said to have *low spatial frequencies* (the frequency of changes in light intensity across each unit of space is low). Other gratings will have narrow bars and spaces. In these gratings the light intensity changes many times as we move across space; hence they are said to have *high spatial frequencies*. Now we will photograph each grating to see how well it is reproduced. At some point, when the bars and spaces become quite narrow, the system will reach its limit. The photographic lens will no longer be able to resolve the individual bars, and all of the bars and spaces will merge into a gray blur. This is exactly the same type of task that we would use to measure the *resolution acuity* or *grating acuity* of human observers, except that here we are looking at the resolution acuity of an optical system.

When photographic engineers do this type of analysis for an optical system, they measure its resolution in terms of the maximum number of lines per inch that can be resolved. Because very finely packed arrays of lines, corresponding to high spatial frequencies, cannot be resolved and are simply blurred, we say that optical systems *attenuate* the high-frequency components of the pattern. A graphic or mathematical description of the way in

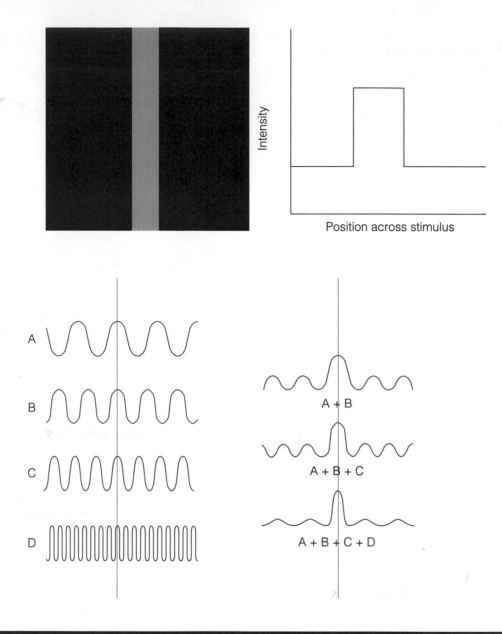

FIGURE 4-12   Gradually adding higher frequency sine waves of the same amplitude to the distribution leads to an approximation of a single bright bar of light (based on Weisstein, 1980).

which certain spatial frequencies are accurately reproduced whereas others are lost because the system cannot resolve them is called the **spatial modulation transfer function.** Any *modulation* is just a change, so *spatial modulation* refers to luminance changes over some spatial distance. Thus, the spatial modulation transfer function measures a system's ability to accurately "transfer" the original

image of the spatial modulation from the target stimulus through the system to final decoding.

Spatial modulation can be described using physical measurements of light on both the light and dark regions of an image. From these measurements, vision scientists construct a value called a **contrast ratio.** There are various specific forms of this ratio, but the most commonly used calculate

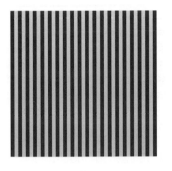  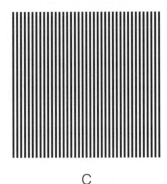

A   B   C

FIGURE 4-13 The effect of spatial frequency on the apparent brightness and contrast of patterns. Notice that the higher frequency pattern (C) has less apparent contrast than the lower frequency pattern (B).

the *difference* between the most and least intense illuminations and divide this number by some average or pooled estimate of the overall amount of light. One example of this, called the *Michaelson contrast ratio*, takes the form

$$\text{Contrast Ratio} = (L_{max} - L_{min}) / (L_{max} + L_{min})$$

where L_{max} refers to the maximum luminance value in the image and L_{min} refers to the minimum luminance value. The *contrast ratio* is very useful as a summary of spatial changes in an image because it is not affected by overall changes in illumination, only by the magnitude of the difference between the most and least intense illuminations. Thus, uniformly increasing the total amount of light falling on an image or grating will have the same effect as multiplying each L term in the equation by a constant value. This would leave the computed contrast ratio unchanged since the multiples on top and bottom of the equation will cancel (see Walraven et al., 1990, for a more complete discussion of contrast ratios).

To assess the visual system's limitations in resolving changes in light intensity over space, a procedure called **contrast matching** is used to measure the modulation transfer function in humans. Consider Gratings A and B in Figure 4-13. Although both are square wave gratings, they differ in terms of their physical *contrast ratio*—Grating A has a smaller contrast ratio than Grating B because the maximum difference in A is between black and

midgray, whereas in B it is between the same black and a higher intensity, white region. Now consider the difference between Gratings B and C. Both are square wave gratings, but B has a lower spatial frequency (wider bars) than C. Despite the fact that the physical contrast is the same (both are the same black ink with the same white interspaces), the perceived contrast (the apparent difference between light and dark regions) is less for the higher frequency, with the black looking a bit lighter and the white a bit darker in C than in B. You can increase this difference by propping the book up and stepping back a foot or two. In a contrast matching task, observers would be asked to match the apparent contrast of such targets (or more usually, sine wave gratings) by adjusting the intensities of the light and the dark regions until the two patterns matched. In this way, we could map the differences in visibility of various spatial frequencies. The reduced contrast in C suggests that the visual system is not doing as good a job in transferring the image from the real world to your consciousness.

An alternative method of measuring sensitivity to various spatial frequencies involves measuring the contrast threshold. This is the amount of contrast difference needed for you to detect that there is a grating present, rather than a uniform gray. Either of these techniques will give us a representation of how sensitivity changes as we change the spatial frequency of the stimuli. In these ways we can map out the modulation transfer function

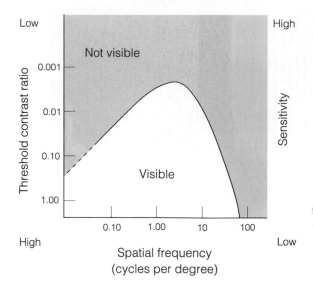

FIGURE 4-14   The modulation transfer function, which shows the relative visibility of targets of various spatial frequencies.

where the stimulus modulations (or intensity changes in the environment) are being transferred to (detected in) the observer's conscious experience of the pattern.

When we measure a typical modulation transfer function for a human observer, it looks like the solid line shown in Figure 4-14. Notice that the threshold contrast ratio is plotted backward (e.g., with higher contrast thresholds lower on the vertical axis). This is done so that when we look at the figure the height of the curve will represent the observer's sensitivity. Clearly, the curve is highest at around 6 cycles per degree (6 cycles of the sine wave over each degree of visual angle), meaning that human observers are most sensitive in this region; we can see stimuli with this spatial frequency even if the contrast ratio is quite low. Sensitivity decreases rapidly for the higher spatial frequencies, meaning that we need more contrast to see these stimuli. This loss at higher frequencies is probably a result of the fact that the eye is an optical system, containing a lens, and any such system has a high-frequency cutoff. Notice also that there is some loss of resolution in the lower spatial frequencies (less than 6 cycles per degree). This loss results from the fact that as the bars and spaces

become wider, the neural sharpening processes (lateral inhibition, which we will talk about later) become less effective. It appears that intensity changes are most effective in producing the phenomenal impression of a brightness difference when these changes occur at intermediate spatial frequencies (as determined by the Fourier analysis). When intensity changes occur too frequently within the visual image, they are difficult to resolve. Similarly, when the physical changes are too infrequent, there is no perception of brightness differences.

The modulation transfer function provides a convenient basis for predicting the apparent brightness of many types of stimulus configurations. Furthermore, as a summary of the spatial frequencies that we can detect at any given contrast level, it serves as a measure of our visual acuity. For instance, if you draw a horizontal line across Figure 4-14 at any contrast level, only the frequencies for which the transfer function curve is above the line will be visible.

Because the modulation transfer function serves as a sort of a summary of our visual acuity and responsiveness to light, we can use it to compare the

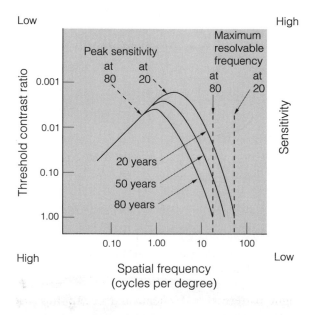

FIGURE 4-15   Changes in the modulation transfer function with age, showing the loss of sensitivity for high spatial frequencies and a general reduction in sensitivity (based on Owsley, Sekuler, & Siemensen, 1983).

visual resolution ability of various groups of individuals. For instance, we know that there are changes in the modulation transfer function as we grow older, with a general reduction in sensitivity to higher spatial frequencies. These changes accurately predict not only reductions in visual acuity with age but also changes in certain aspects of our depth perception (stereopsis) measured by other techniques (Greene & Madden, 1987). Figure 4-15 shows the modulation transfer functions from groups of 20-, 50-, and 80-year-olds (Owsley, Sekuler, & Siemensen, 1983). Notice that the highest frequency visible steadily drops with age (meaning that smaller details or narrower stripes can't be seen). This might be expected if the optical or focusing ability of the lens was diminishing (see Chapter 16). Notice that the peak sensitivity (the highest point on the curve) is lower with age, indicating that visual responsiveness is lower (needs more contrast to reach threshold). Finally, the peak sensitivity, representing the spatial frequency that would appear to have the greatest contrast, is also shifting toward lower frequencies, suggesting that wider stripes or gratings are relatively more effective stimuli when we are older. All of this acuity and brightness response information, and more, can be derived from comparing modulation transfer functions, which explains the popularity of this method of data presentation.

Neural Spatial Frequency Channels

Imagine an extremely self-assured scientist sitting at his home computer, complete with all of the programs necessary to do Fourier analyses of any light patterns that might happen to be of importance or interest, muttering to himself, "If I find Fourier analysis so useful in analyzing patterns of light, maybe the visual system does, too. Perhaps the visual system is set up to conduct some sort of spatial frequency analysis for any given pattern of light. Certainly, if it did, it would benefit from the same sort of concise description of the incoming light pattern that I obtain and could thus also avoid the separate analysis of millions of responses of millions of individual photoreceptors."

Actually, this suggestion is not as strange as it might seem. At a general level, the first stage of spatial frequency analysis can be accomplished by

mechanisms that we know exist and have already discussed. These mechanisms are the circularly organized retinal receptive fields described in Chapter 3. Recall that each of these has an excitatory, or *on*, region that, when stimulated by light, gives an increase in neural response rate, and an inhibitory, or *off*, region that gives a decrease in the neural response rate when stimulated by light (and a burst of responses upon the light's termination). Before we discuss how such an arrangement can do a spatial frequency analysis, we must introduce a bit of terminology. Every cycle of a sine wave grating has both a dark and a light phase, as we saw in Figure 4-10. This means that the dark stripe (or the light stripe) would be one half of the sine wave cycle. Now we can tell you that every circular receptive field is "tuned" to a sine wave frequency whose *half cycle* is equal to the size of its central excitatory or inhibitory region. To visualize this type of structure, consider Figure 4-16.

Suppose that we have an *on-center* receptive field of the size illustrated in the figure. If the spatial frequency is too low, that is to say the stripes are too wide, the fields of illumination will fall on both the center and the surround. Even though the central *on* region (+) of the field is stimulated, there is an equal degree of stimulation of the inhibitory surrounding *off* regions (–) of the receptive field. Because of lateral inhibitory interactions, the two types of responses tend to cancel each other out. Thus, the total response of the ganglion cell with this receptive field is low. Now consider the other extreme, where the spatial frequency is very high, and there are many stripes falling across the field. The *on* and *off* regions of the field would each be stimulated by about equal proportions of light and dark, again producing little or no net response. Finally, consider a spatial frequency in which the half cycle width is approximately the same as the central region of the receptive field. If the bright stripe now covers the central region of the *on* center cell, there will be a vigorous *on* response. There will be little inhibition from the surrounding *off* region, which lies mostly in darkness from the dark half of the cycle. Thus, the net response to this grating would be relatively stronger than to any other grating. Notice that the same sort of analysis of spatial frequency can occur in the *off-center* cell, except that here the optimal response is obtained when the

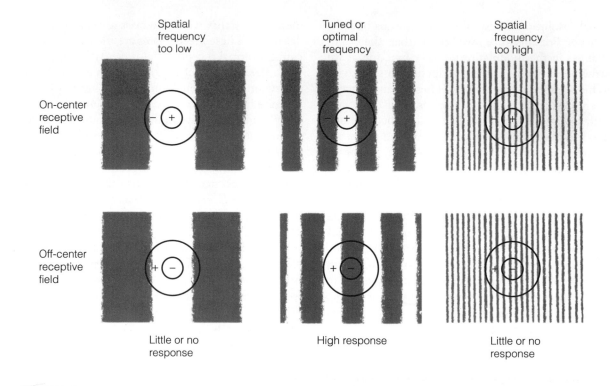

FIGURE 4-16 A demonstration of how a circular receptive field organization of a particular size can perform a crude spatial frequency analysis.

dark half of the cycle is over the central region of the receptive field. Each receptive field is maximally responsive to a specific spatial frequency of light intensity changes.

This crude analysis of spatial frequencies could serve as the first step of a Fourier decomposition of the incoming stimulus pattern if a few additional requirements were met. First, there must be a broad range of receptive field sizes so that "tuning" would be fine enough to approximately determine sufficiently many of the spatial frequencies that make up the pattern. This requirement seems to be easily fulfilled because, as we noted in Chapter 3, parvo and magno cells differ quite a bit in the speed of and nature of their responses. They also differ in their ranges of receptive field size, with parvo cells tuned for higher spatial frequencies than are magno cells. Thus, there may be a number of different channels in the visual system, each tuned to a different range of spatial frequencies. There is some evidence that the magno-like low

spatial frequency channels interact with, and can inhibit, the parvo-like higher spatial frequency channels (Hughes, 1986; Olzak, 1986). Moreover, a model assuming as few as six such channels (or receptive field sizes) can explain some of the remarkable feats of acuity that people are capable of, namely the hyperacuity that we discussed earlier in which resolution ability is better than would be predicted on the basis of the physical size of the retinal receptors (Bradley & Skottun, 1987; Wilson, 1986).

Of course, for such Fourier analysis to be of value perceptually, there must be high-level cells, perhaps in the visual cortex, that preserve the spatial frequency information extracted by the tuned receptive fields of the retinal ganglion cells. There is evidence that such cells exist in the cortex. These cells have not only preferred edge orientations to which they respond maximally but also preferred ranges of spatial frequency (Derrington & Fuchs, 1981; DeValois, Albrecht, & Thorell,

1982; DeValois & DeValois, 1987). Although the existence of such cells does not prove that Fourier analysis occurs in the visual system, it at least suggests that the equipment to perform such an analysis does exist.

Neurons as Spatial Filters Visually sensitive cells in the brain that, working together, are able to perform a crude Fourier analysis of the visual image are often referred to as neural filters. The term *filter* is used here because these cells are thought to respond by firing most rapidly when a specific visual pattern excites them and to fire much less rapidly to any other patterns. In effect they are filtering out all but a select set of stimuli and passing on information about only those that they are "tuned" for, much like a radio tuner passes on to the amplifier only information carried on a specific radio frequency. The cells that we are considering respond by firing more or less, depending on the extent to which the spatial frequencies in the image match the filter characteristics.

It has been suggested that the center-surround cells that we described in Figure 4-15 are themselves the results of the actions of neural filters occurring earlier in the visual system, some of which are still hypothetical and have not yet been physically isolated. They probably result from particular neural networks of connections in the retina. These earlier filters are really quite simple. If we look at their response pattern over a single slice of space, most of them increase their responsiveness toward the center of the field and then tail off again, giving us a familiar bell-shaped distribution, as is shown in the left-most part of Figure 4-17A. These distributions were mathematically described by Carl Fredrich Gauss and hence are called *Gaussian distributions*. Filters with such distributions of response can have either wide or narrow spreads and low or high peaks (compare the left-most distributions in 4-17A and 4-17B). Another important feature is that these filters can be either excitatory (meaning that neural responses increase toward the center of the filter's field) or inhibitory (meaning that neural responses actually decrease the likelihood that other nearby neurons will react). Combining an excitatory and an inhibitory distribution has the same arithmetic effect as subtracting the actual numbers representing the inhibitory distribution of responses from those representing the excitatory. Hence, the spatial filter that results from the combination of these is referred to as the **difference of Gaussian filters,** or, more affectionately, **DOG** filters (Marr, 1982). Note that the net effect of combining two bell-shaped spatial filters, where the wider one is effectively subtracted from the narrower, is to create a filter with all the essential characteristics of an *on-center* receptive field, as shown in 4-17A. An *off-center* receptive field can be modeled by simply subtracting the narrower of the two bell-shaped curves from the wider one, as shown in 4-17B. Both of these arrangements are certainly plausible for ganglion cells because these cells have inputs from other cells with receptive fields in a variety of sizes. This has led many computational vision scientists to build models of the retina with DOG filters (Fiorentini et al., 1990; Marr, 1982; Rodieck, 1965; Wilson & Bergen, 1979; Wilson & Gelb, 1984).

Simple cortical cells have also been modeled as filters represented by other mathematical equations; one of the more popular involves a combination of a bell-shaped curve with another well-known and mathematically describable distribution of responses, namely the sine function. This combination is referred to as a **Gabor filter,** after Dennis Gabor, the Nobel prize–winning physicist who analyzed such filters and used them to develop the theory on which holography is based. The main characteristic that distinguishes the Gabor filter from the DOG filter is that when a sine wave filter is multiplied with a Gaussian filter, it results in a new filter that has orientation in two dimensions, allowing it to detect bars of a specific tilt in the image or edges, depending on how the peaks of the sine wave are aligned with the peak of the bell-shaped filter. This can be seen in 4-17C and 4-17D. As with the DOG filter, Gabor filters are used by many computational vision scientists because they are thought to be plausible models of the way in which the primary visual cortex processes a visual image (Daugman, 1980; Watson, 1983; Webster & DeValois, 1985; Wilson et al., 1990). Notice that DOG filters give us center-surround receptive fields, whereas Gabor filters give us orientation-specific line and edge detectors, such as those described in Chapter 3. Some visual physiologists are beginning to regard the processing of information in the visual system as the application of a complex series of filters to the incoming information (e.g., Van Essen, Anderson, & Felleman, 1992).

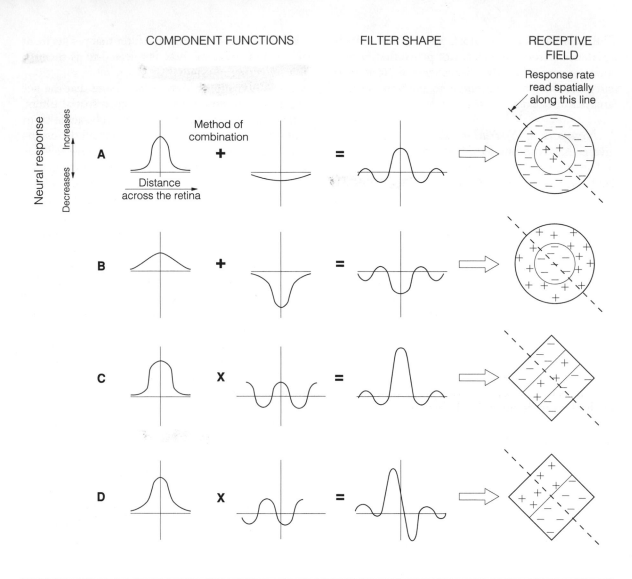

FIGURE 4-17   Subtracting one bell-shaped curve from another of a different width yields a *difference of Gaussian* function that performs spatial filtering like a center-surround ganglion cell (as in A and B). Multiplying a bell-shaped curve with a sine function produces a *Gabor* function that performs like an orientation-specific line detection (C) or edge detection (D) cell in the visual cortex.

Others argue that even if we cannot find specific physiological mechanisms that correspond to Gaussian and sine wave filters, the use of these mathematical concepts to describe differences among various visual feature detectors may help to simplify our understanding of them. At the very least, it allows computational vision scientists to represent feature-specific cells in mathematical terms for later use and manipulation in their theories.

Although spatial frequency analysis and visual filtering seem to provide useful or promising approaches to the problems of brightness and acuity, they do not provide us with the complete answer. Our final perception of a particular brightness, size, or detail resolution involves the operation of all levels of the perceptual system. In later chapters we shall see how spatial frequency analysis is useful in understanding some aspects of form perception

(Chapter 11) and also how cognitive and other high-level factors interact with the basic sensory mechanisms that we have discussed so far to determine our perception of complex stimuli in our environment (Chapters 14 and 15).

SPATIAL CONTEXT EFFECTS

Brightness Contrast

Strange as it may seem, our perception of the brightness of targets often depends more on the luminance of adjacent objects than on the actual luminance of the target itself. Figure 4-18 demonstrates this. Here we have four small squares, each of which is surrounded by a larger square. The central squares all are actually printed in the same gray; thus, the amount of light that reaches your eye from each is the same. Notice, however, that the apparent brightnesses of these small squares are not equal. Their brightnesses vary depending on their background, with the grays printed on dark backgrounds appearing lighter than the grays printed on light backgrounds. This effect is called simultaneous brightness contrast.

Everyday experience tells us that our conscious experience of brightness will increase as the amount of light reaching the eye increases. Unfortunately, our perceptual experiences often defy such "common sense." Despite increases in the amount of light reaching the eye, the brightness of a surface may actually *decrease* depending on the illumination of the background on which it rests because simultaneous brightness contrast is greater

at higher levels of illumination (Arend, 1993). You can see this effect by following the instructions in Demonstration Box 4-5.

The fact that a light surround depresses the apparent brightness of a target suggests that some form of spatial interaction is present. This interaction is in the form of inhibition, where an actively stimulated portion of the retina will suppress other nearby retinal activity. Remember that in the previous section we also encountered the idea of inhibition during our discussion of spatial filters. There we saw that the responses of some spatial filters are supposed to subtract from the responses already going on in another.

Physiological evidence for such inhibitory spatial interaction was first collected using *Limulus* (the horseshoe crab), which has a compound eye that makes dissection of individual visual fibers somewhat easier. Nobel prize winner H. K. Hartline and his frequent collaborator, Floyd Ratliff, were able to demonstrate the inhibitory neural interactions between nearby receptors using a very simple but elegant experiment (Hartline & Ratliff, 1957). They monitored the responses from a cell in *Limulus* that is functionally equivalent to a ganglion cell. When the receptor attached to this cell was stimulated, of course, the onset of the light increased the activity of the cell. However, while this cell was being stimulated, if Hartline and Ratliff illuminated a receptor located a short distance away it caused a decrease in the response level of the cell that they were monitoring. The importance of this finding is that it demonstrates that visual cells may be inhibited by the activity of adjacent visual units. This process is called lateral inhibition because

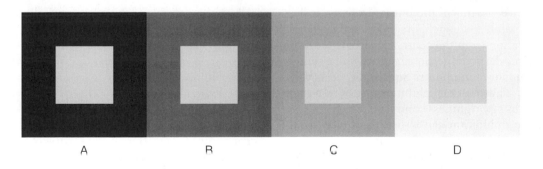

A   B   C   D

FIGURE 4-18 Simultaneous brightness contrast, showing how the background can alter the perception of the central gray regions.

DEMONSTRATION BOX 4-5
The Interaction of Luminance and Background

For this experiment you will need your variable light source again (either the closet or the television). Hold up Figure 4-18 and look at the central squares, with your light source providing a low (but not dim) level of illumination. As you increase the level of illumination from its lowest value, the center target in Square A should grow brighter. Now repeat the procedure while looking at the center target in Square D. Notice that as the luminance level increases, this target square actually gets darker. Because all the center squares are identical in reflectance, the differences in their apparent brightness depend solely on their backgrounds. This may seem strange because we tend to associate black with the absence of light. Because you are already in a room or a place that potentially can be darkened, turn off all the light sources and close your eyes (to eliminate any stray illumination). Notice that what you are seeing is not black but, rather, a misty gray (often called *cortical gray*). Thus, the absence of light is gray, not black. Only in fields that contain some areas of bright illumination can real black be seen.

---

the inhibition acts laterally (sideways) on adjacent cells. The amount of inhibition that any given cell applies to its neighbors depends on how strongly it is responding and on how close the cells are to each other. The more a cell is stimulated and the closer it is to another cell, the more intensely it will inhibit the other.

It is now easy to understand why the surface in Square A is seen to be brighter than the surface in Square D in Figure 4-18. In the part of the retina exposed to the light surround (Square D), many cells are active and, as a consequence of this activity, are actively inhibiting their neighbors. This inhibition from the light surround should reduce the neural response rate of the receptors exposed to the central square, making it appear dimmer. The cells exposed to the target on the dark background do not receive as much inhibition from their less strongly stimulated neighbors. Because the amount of stimulation from the central squares is the same but the cells exposed to Square A are undergoing a lesser amount of inhibition, Square A appears to be brighter. Thus, lateral inhibition provides a basis for explaining brightness contrast effects.

Lateral inhibition can also explain more complex effects observed in other stimulus configurations. Ever since the 1860s, when physicist and natural philosopher Ernst Mach studied patterns with an intensity distribution like that shown in Figure 4-19B, investigators have been intrigued by a particular brightness phenomenon that such a distribution generates (Weale, 1979). In this figure, we have a uniform dark area and a uniform light area, with an intermediate zone that gradually changes from dark to light. However, when we look at the actual stimulus depicted in Figure 4-19A, we do not see a gradual change in brightness flanked by two uniform areas. Instead, two bands or blurry lines are visible at the points marked by the arrows in the figure. One is darker than any other part of the figure, and the other is brighter. They are called **Mach bands,** in honor of their discoverer. Their presence can be explained by lateral inhibition.

We have indicated the location of some retinal cells illuminated by the Mach band–producing pattern in Figure 4-19C. Cell *b* is stimulated by bright incoming light, but it is also strongly inhibited by the activity of the adjacent Cells *a* and *c*. Cell *d* is stimulated to the same extent as Cell *b*. But on one side it is strongly inhibited by *c*, whereas on the other side it is somewhat more weakly inhibited by *e*, which is not receiving as much light. The important thing to derive from this discussion is the fact that Cells *b* and *d* have the same degree of stimulation, but *d* is less strongly inhibited. In this case, we might expect that *d's* corresponding response will be more vigorous than that in cells like *b*. This should cause the region around *d* to appear relatively brighter. Next consider Cell *i*. It is not stimulated very much, but neither are the nearby Cells *h* and *j*.

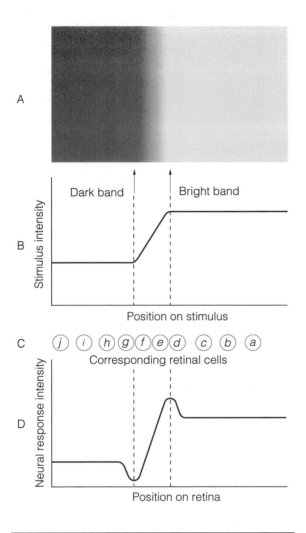

A

B

Dark band

Bright band

Stimulus intensity

Position on stimulus

C   Corresponding retinal cells

D

Neural response intensity

Position on retina

FIGURE 4-19   (A) A Mach band pattern, (B) the actual distribution of stimulus intensity, (C) corresponding retinal cells (see the text), and (D) neural response intensity distribution (*A* and *B* based on Cornsweet, 1970).

This means that *i* is not being strongly inhibited by surrounding units. Cell *g* is receiving the same small amount of stimulation as *i*. However, whereas *g* is weakly inhibited on one side by *h*, it is more strongly inhibited on the other side by *f*, which is responding more vigorously because of the higher intensity of light falling on it. Thus, although *g* and *i* receive the same amount of stimulation, *g* is more strongly inhibited than *i*. This means that its response will be decreased, causing an apparently darker region to appear there. The

relationship between the input and the neural (and perceptual) response is diagrammed in Figure 4-19D. It is quite easy to produce a Mach band pattern for yourself, as shown in Demonstration Box 4-6. It seems likely that a very wide array of brightness perception phenomena can be explained by theories that assume particular patterns of inhibitory and excitatory interactions between sensory neurons (see Arend & Goldstein, 1987; Cornsweet, 1985; Grossberg, 1987).

Lateral inhibition, however, does not provide the whole answer to brightness contrast effects. The physiology of the retina implies that such inhibitory effects should take place over a very limited distance and that targets that are relatively far away from one another should not be affected. Many recent studies have used what are called *Mondrian patterns* to show that this is not the case. Mondrian patterns are named after abstract artist Piet Mondrian, whose works often consisted of a complex arrangement of squares of different hues and lightnesses. If we have a pattern of squares of varying degrees of lightness, it has been observed that introducing a very light one *decreases* the apparent brightness of all of the others, even if they are a long distance away. To explain such "global" effects, some more cognitive and computational mechanisms have been suggested.

Perhaps the most researched global mechanism is based on **brightness anchoring**. This principle suggests that the highest luminance in a pattern tends to appear white and serves as a standard by which all of the other luminances are judged. When that highest luminance increases, the standard against which the others are judged is raised, and all other surfaces in the scene appear to be darker, not because they have changed, but, rather, because they are now darker with respect to the highest. Several recent studies suggest that some sort of cognitive or computational process much like this is taking place (Bruno, Bernardis, & Schirillo, 1997; Cataliotti & Gilchrist, 1995; Gilchrist & Bonato, 1995).

Brightness Assimilation

Given that brightness effects such as simultaneous brightness contrast need more than lateral inhibitory interactions to explain them fully, it should not surprise us to find that high-level

DEMONSTRATION BOX 4-6
Mach Bands

Mach band patterns do not reproduce well in print. This is probably because the range of luminances possible from ink on paper is not very large. It is actually quite easy to produce your own Mach band pattern using a distribution of light. All you need is a card or a book that is opaque and has a straight edge, and a large light source. If you are in a room that has fluorescent or large frosted light fixtures in the ceiling, these produce a fine uniform source of illumination.

When you hold the card near a surface, you cast a shadow. As shown in the accompanying diagram, a full shadow appears under the surface and full light on the other side. In between is a graded shadow, the *penumbra*, which gradually moves from light to dark. Hold the card still and look at the brightness pattern—you will easily see the dark and light Mach bands. You may increase the visibility of the bands by moving the card closer to the surface. This reduces the size of the penumbra and makes the area of gradual change in intensity steeper, as shown in the diagram. Because this puts the bright and dim areas nearer one another, it enhances the effect of the inhibitory process.

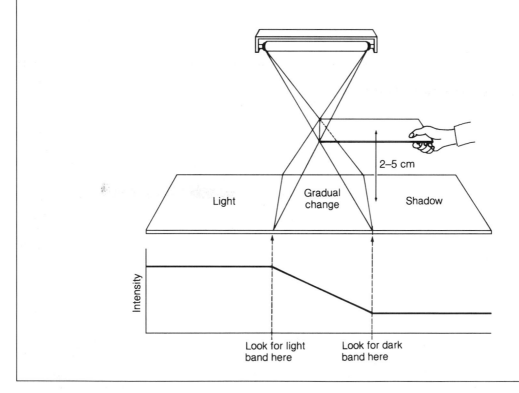

cognitive processing and computational mechanisms may play a role in other brightness phenomena. For example, in many instances predictions made from either lateral inhibitory or excitatory considerations can be wrong. One example of such an effect can be seen in Figure 4-20. The two rings shown in this figure are composed of the same color of gray and lie atop the same sharp background edge of black and white. The only difference between the two rings is that thin black lines have been drawn through the ring in Figure 4-20B to connect the background edge from top to bottom. Despite the fact that lateral inhibition would lead us to expect that the half of the ring on the

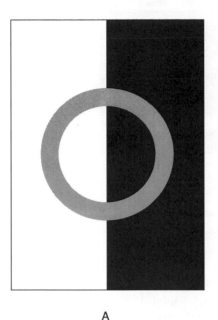
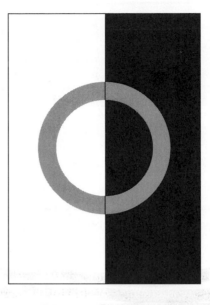

A   B

FIGURE 4-20   Brightness contrast is influenced by the cognitive interpretation given to a form. The gray rings in *A* and *B* are identical, except for the thin black lines in *B*.

white background will be seen as darker than the half on the black background, the gray ring in *A* appears to be uniform in brightness. Compare this with the ring in *B*, which does show the expected simultaneous brightness contrast. It appears that the thin lines are enough to bias the interpretation of the display so that it is seen as two half rings of different brightness laid side by side. The absence of the lines in *A* biases the perception of the ring toward a single-colored object, and thus no contrast effects are seen, and both sides of the ring appear to be an "average" gray (Koffka, 1935).

Another example where cognitive effects may alter or override the effects of lateral inhibition on brightness is seen in Figure 4-21. The gray under the white stripes is identical to that under the black stripes. Notice, however, that the gray under the white stripes appears to be lighter than the gray under the black stripes. This is the opposite of the prediction that we would make based on the action of lateral inhibition. The white stripes should *darken* the gray rather than *lighten* it. The phenomenal impression, then, is the reverse of brightness contrast, and it is called **brightness assimilation** (Shapley & Reid, 1985).

Physiological contributions to brightness assimilation are suggested by the fact that it seems to occur only when the test stripes of white or black fall within the spatial summation zones of ganglion receptive fields as estimated by the Westheimer function that we discussed earlier in this chapter (Westheimer, 1967). If the stimuli are increased in size to the point where the gray and white (or black) stripes taken together fall into the off or inhibitory region of the receptive field, then *brightness contrast* is once again observed (Anstis, 1975). However, higher level processes may play a role in this effect, too. Some of these higher level processes involve computation of some form of average illumination level across the scene. As this average goes up or down, our judgments of the brightness of individual regions are "dragged" in the direction of the average as long as they are not too extreme (Heinemann & Chase, 1995). This is much like the social inference that we might make when we infer that a person is wealthy because that person lives in the same neighborhood where many wealthy people live.

There is some evidence that how we distribute our attention over a pattern influences whether brightness contrast or brightness assimilation

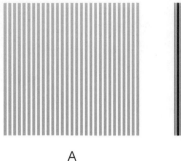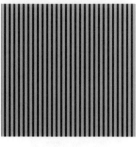

A   B

FIGURE 4-21   Brightness assimilation, where the gray under the white stripes appears lighter than the gray under the black.

occurs. In general, the part of the visual field to which we are attending—or at least the part that is viewed as the figure or object, rather than the background—shows greater brightness contrast (Brussell & Festinger, 1973; Coren, 1969). The background regions that are not directly attended to then show brightness assimilation (Festinger, Coren, & Rivers, 1970). Observers usually describe the pattern shown in Figure 4-21A as a gray field with *white lines on* it and Figure 4-21B as a *set of black lines on* a gray background. Festinger et al. (1970) reasoned that the lines have a "figure-like" quality that captures the attention of observers. Because the gray is then a nonfigural background to which we pay little attention, it shows assimilation. If this is the case, then voluntary shifts in attention that focus concentration on the gray regions should alter the brightness effect from one of assimilation to one of contrast. The gray under the white stripes should now appear to be the darker member of the pair. This is exactly what happens (Festinger et al., 1970). You can demonstrate this for yourself by focusing your concentration on the gray for a few moments. Soon the grays will appear to differ in a contrast direction rather than show brightness assimilation.

Some brightness effects depend on other cognitive factors, namely, the assumptions that the observer makes about the nature of the world or even the way in which regions of the visual field *appear* to be arranged, as well as on simple lateral inhibitory interactions (Agostini & Proffitt, 1993; Flock & Nusinowitz, 1984; Gilchrist, Delman, &

Jacobsen, 1983). We will have more to say about this in Chapter 14 when we discuss the issue of *lightness constancy*.

TEMPORAL CONTEXT EFFECTS

Brightness perception is affected not only by stimuli that lie adjacent to the test stimulus in space but also by events that occur immediately prior in time. The temporal equivalent of simultaneous brightness contrast is called successive brightness contrast. It is most frequently studied by a procedure referred to as selective adaptation. The use of the word *adaptation* here involves the concept of neural satiation, or fatigue, which makes this type of adaptation quite different than the dark or light adaptation discussed earlier in this chapter. In this procedure, an observer is exposed to a stimulus with a specific attribute (e.g., spatial frequency of 6 cycles per degree) for a moderately short time (from 20 sec to several minutes). If there is a specific group of neurons tuned to that particular frequency, they will, of course, immediately start responding when their optimal stimulus appears. If the stimulus remains in view for a long period of time, these neurons will continue to respond, until they are eventually too fatigued to respond vigorously any longer. Because this fatigue might last for a minute or two after exposure to the *adapting stimulus*, we have then effectively eliminated, or temporarily disabled, a particular group of spatial frequency channels, and this should be detectable perceptually.

Many of the findings supporting the idea of spatial frequency channels in the visual system arise from selective adaptation studies. For example, suppose we began by measuring the modulation transfer function of an observer, just as we did to produce the solid line in Figure 4-22. Now we have an observer stare for a while at a grating of about 6 cycles per degree (the adapting stimulus) in order to fatigue the spatial frequency channels associated with this middle range of frequencies. When we next measure the observer's transfer function, we get the results shown as the dotted line in Figure 4-22. Notice that there is a depression in sensitivity around the adapted spatial frequency. This means that it is now harder to detect gratings in this range of spatial frequencies and that larger variations of physical contrast are needed to produce the same perceptual effects. This is exactly what we would expect if the channels tuned to the adapting stimulus frequency have been fatigued and hence no longer responded as effectively. Of course, if we used a different adapting stimulus, the region of reduced sensitivity would be different, depending on its spatial frequency (Graham, 1980; Harris, 1980).

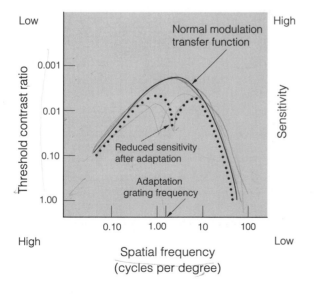

FIGURE 4-22 Selective adaptation of a particular spatial frequency grating reduces the contrast sensitivity for a range of spatial frequencies similar to the adapting frequency.

One particularly interesting perceptual effect can be produced using this technique. Remember that spatial frequency roughly corresponds to the size of elements in a pattern. Thus, low spatial frequencies correspond to large elements or, in our gratings, to wide stripes, whereas high spatial frequencies correspond to smaller elements. Suppose we had somehow disabled all of the low spatial frequency channels. With only the high-frequency channels operating, they would be the major determinant of our responses to any stimuli because the other channels are responding more weakly due to fatigue. Because the action of these higher frequency channels usually signals the presence of higher spatial frequencies, we might expect that the pattern would appear to be dominated by high-frequency (smaller) elements, compared with a situation in which all channels were operating normally. Demonstration Box 4-7 allows you to demonstrate this effect for yourself.

One of the most important findings to emerge from selective adaptation studies of spatial frequency is that the adaptation, or neural satiation, is highly specific to a number of other features in addition to spatial frequency itself. For instance, adaptation to a particular spatial frequency is seen most strongly when the adapting and test gratings are equal in orientation, contrast, and wavelength (Anstis, 1975; Blakemore & Nachmias, 1971; Lovegrove & Over, 1973). You can observe this for yourself by trying out Part 2 in Demonstration Box 4-7. The original adaptation that you experienced for vertical gratings should not transfer to horizontal gratings. This means that selective adaptation often involves several attributes, including not only spatial frequency but also orientation, color, and other factors.

Although these interdependencies among adapted stimulus dimensions might at first appear to make the study of vision very difficult, researchers have also learned how to take advantage of them to learn more about the structure of the visual system. For instance, some have estimated how finely tuned orientation channels are by studying the extent to which spatial frequency adaptation generalizes to gratings that differ systematically in orientation from the adapting stimulus (Wilson, Levi, Maffei, Rovamo, & DeValois, 1990). In Chapter 5 we will see how the dependency between orientation and color response has also been studied using this technique.

DEMONSTRATION BOX 4-7
Selective Adaptation of Spatial Frequency Channels

Part 1

If you look at the figure, you will see that one of the squares on the left has broad bars (low spatial frequency) and that the other has narrow bars (high spatial frequency). The pattern in *B* contains two gratings, both of which have the same spatial frequencies, but they are neither as high nor as low as the ones on the left. Hold the illustration about 80 cm away from you. Now look at the horizontal bar between the upper and lower patterns on the left for about 20 to 30 sec. Move your gaze from one portion of the bar to another, but keep your eyes on the bar. As you look steadily at the bar, the channels tuned to low spatial frequencies from the upper part of your visual field and those tuned to the high spatial frequencies from the lower part of your visual field are fatiguing, or adapting. Now if you transfer your gaze quickly to the dot between the identical grat-

ings, in *B*, you will notice that they no longer seem to be the same. The top part of the grating now appears to be spaced more finely, with thinner stripes than those on the bottom. The low frequency channels have been disabled in the upper region of the visual field. With more high spatial frequency channels active, the percent is shifted toward higher frequencies; hence, the stripes are seen as smaller and more dense. The opposite effect is occurring in the lower region of the field.

Part 2

Now adapt yourself once again to the pair of gratings in *A* for 20 to 30 sec. Then transfer your gaze to the pair of gratings in *C*. These horizontal gratings should not be influenced by the adaptation to *A* because spatial frequency adaptation is sensitive to orientation.

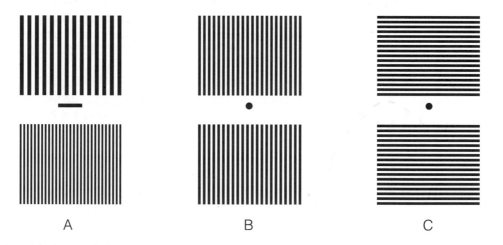

A   B   C

DARKNESS VERSUS BRIGHTNESS PERCEPTION

Although it might seem reasonable to assume that the perception of brightness and the perception of darkness are two ends of a single continuum, there is emerging evidence that brightness perception

and darkness perception are qualitatively different phenomena. This hypothesis was proposed over 30 years ago, based on an observation that we have already mentioned, namely, that increasing the illumination in a display does not cause all objects to appear brighter. Indeed, the brighter objects in the display become even brighter, but the objects that

DEMONSTRATION BOX 4-8
Independence of Brightness Perception and Darkness Perception

For this demonstration you should first cover up the pair of gratings in *B* and then look at the gratings in *A* for about 30 to 60 sec. Do this by moving your eyes back and forth along the dash between the two gratings so that each grating falls on a region of your retina that is equally far from the fovea. Now look at the pair of gratings in *B*. The black lines in the upper grating appear to be finer than those in the lower grating, even though they are physically identical to one another. The interpretation of this illusion is based on separate systems for brightness and

darkness perception. The black bars in the upper grating in *A*, which are wider and hence more dominant, fatigue the *darkness* system more, whereas the wider white bars in the lower figure fatigue the *lightness* system more. When you are presented with equal white and dark stimuli in *B*, the dark response is weaker in the upper pattern, so dark appears less visible (finer bars), whereas the light response is weaker in the lower part of the visual field, making the white bars appear finer (based on Burton, Nagshineh, & Ruddock, 1977).

A   B

appeared to be dark originally now become even darker—not brighter as you might expect (Jameson & Hurvich, 1964; Jung, 1961).

A physiological basis for separate brightness and darkness systems is already apparent at the retina. We saw in Chapter 3 that ganglion cells can be divided into two classes based on their receptive field organi-

zation. On-center, off-surround cells can be thought of as relative brightness detectors, whereas off-center, on-surround cells could serve as relative darkness detectors. What adds weight to this idea is that these two classes of receptive fields can be seen in both parvo and magno cells, they are regularly distributed throughout the retina, and their connections with higher visual centers are independent of one another (Perry & Silveira, 1988; Wassle, Peichl, & Boycott, 1983). It is therefore tantalizing to believe that there are two systems of ganglion cells: one for the perception of brightness and one for the perception of darkness. The existence of two systems would certainly increase the ability of the visual system to respond to a much wider range of luminance levels than would only one system (Fiorentini et al., 1990).

An important discovery by Slaughter and Miller (1981) makes it possible to test directly for the independence of the brightness and darkness systems in the retina. They applied a certain neurotransmitter (called *2-amino-4-phosphonobutyrate*, or *APB*) to the retina of the mud puppy (an aquatic salamander). This caused all of the on-center ganglion cells to become unresponsive to light; however, the off-center cells maintained their normal responses. Since then others have shown that APB blocks the responses of on-center ganglion cells and lateral geniculate nucleus cells in the cat and the monkey (Horton & Sherk, 1984; Sherk & Horton, 1984; Shiller, 1984; Shiller, Sandell, & Maunsell, 1986). Animals treated with APB show normal responses to *decreases* in light but are almost completely unable to detect light *increases*. However, they still show a normal response to oriented edges and to the motion of an edge in a particular direction, provided that the edge is defined by a decrease in light relative to the background.

Several researchers have now also demonstrated the independence of brightness and darkness systems in humans using selective adaptation. When observers were adapted to black gratings of a particular width (Burton, Nagshineh, & Ruddock, 1977) or to a black bar moving at a certain velocity (DeValois, 1977), they showed temporary fatigue in their ability to detect *black* gratings and black moving bars of similar size. However, they showed no evidence of fatigue to *white* gratings or white moving bars of the same size. Demonstration Box 4-8 allows you to observe the independence of the brightness and darkness perception systems for yourself.

CHAPTER SUMMARY

Simply describing a visual stimulus in terms of its intensity in **photometric units** is not adequate to describe our perceptual experience of its **brightness.** This relationship is nonlinear, and our sensation of the brightness intensity will depend on factors such as the state of **dark** or **light adaptation** of the eye. It will also vary depending on which part of the retina is stimulated, with the peripheral retina more sensitive to low-intensity illumination. The wavelength of the light will also affect brightness. The **Purkinje shift** shows that the dark-adapted eye is less sensitive to long-wavelength stimuli and more sensitive to short-wavelength stimuli. At low levels of illumination, increasing the duration of a stimulus can increase the likelihood that it can be detected **(Bloch's Law)**, as can increasing its size **(Ricco's Law** and **Piper's Law)**.

Visual acuity refers to our ability to see stimulus details, usually defined as changes in illumination. Stimuli with a smaller **visual angle** can be resolved in the foveal region of the retina and at high levels of illumination.

Spatial frequency analysis uses **Fourier's Theorem** to analyze patterns into a series of sine waves of different frequencies. These can be represented by grating stimuli with dark and light stripes of different widths. The **spatial modulation transfer function** is a graphic representation of the visual system's ability to resolve **spatial modulations,** depending on their **contrast** and **spatial frequency.** The visual system appears to have different spatial frequency channels that filter the inputs. These may depend on the size of the neural receptive fields.

Spatial context effects refer to the fact that the brightness of a stimulus depends on the intensity of its surround. **Brightness contrast** occurs when addition of more intense stimuli perceptually dims other stimuli, whereas **brightness assimilation** would be the reverse, where more intense stimuli increase apparent brightness. Some of these effects depend on neural interactions, such as **lateral inhibition,** which also causes **Mach bands.** Cognitive and computational effects, such as the distribution of attention, anchoring, or stimulus averaging, may also explain some brightness phenomena. These context effects are affected by temporal factors and adaptation effects as well. There are also some suggestions that there may be separate channels or processing mechanisms for the perception of brightness versus the perception of darkness.

KEY TERMS

photometry
standard units
radiance
lumen
illuminance
luminance
reflectance
retinal illuminance
brightness
lightness
bril
dark adaptation
light adaptation
photopic
scotopic
luminosity curve
Purkinje shift
Bunsen-Roscoe Law
Bloch's Law
Ricco's Law
Piper's Law
Westheimer function
visual acuity
recognition acuity
visual angle
vernier or directional
   acuity

resolution or grating
   acuity
hyperacuity
Fourier's Theorem
sine wave grating
square wave grating
spatial modulation
   transfer function
contrast ratio
contrast matching
neural filters
difference of Gaussian
   (DOG) filters
Gabor filters
simultaneous brightness
   contrast
lateral inhibition
Mach bands
brightness anchoring
brightness assimilation
successive brightness
   contrast
selective adaptation
neural satiation

Color

CHAPTER 5

"My dad was color blind but didn't find out until he was nearly 50. He was always doing strange things. He couldn't be trusted to pick tomatoes from the garden because he was always mixing up the ripe and the green ones. We finally suspected that something was wrong when he commented that he really admired cherry pickers for their ability to recognize shapes. 'After all,' he said, 'the only thing that tells 'em it's a cherry is the fact that it's round and the leaves aren't. I just don't see how they find 'em in those trees!'"

Like the student who told this tale, you may be surprised to find out how important a factor color is in determining our ability to acquire information about the world. For instance, consider Figure 5-1. Although the figure appears to be a random collection of gray shapes, there is a word hidden in it. Each letter is spelled out by a series of similar shapes. If you study the figure for a moment, you will begin to see how difficult it is to pick out the word (if you can do it at all), despite the fact that the shape and brightness information is there. In this task you are much like the color-blind person trying to pick out bunches of cherries, among the leaves, by shape alone. Now flip to Color Plate 2, where we have added the dimension of color to the figure. Notice that in this color plate the word seems to "leap out." Thus, color provides an important stimulus dimension that aids in the localization and identification of targets, which explains why some occupations, such as air traffic controller and electronics technician, require normal color vision (Kuyk, Veres, Lahey, & Clark, 1986).

For some species, color vision is a matter of life and death. For instance, if bees lacked color vision, their task of locating the nectar-bearing flowers hidden among shrubs, grasses, or leaves would be almost impossible. The very survival of bees depends on the ability to spot a glint of color that indicates the presence of blossoms. Some evolutionary psychologists speculate that human ancestors developed the particular kind of color vision system we now have in response to a specific environment (Mollon, 1995). This was one of tropical trees bearing fruit that were too large to be taken by birds and that were yellow or orange in color when ripe. One example is the tree family *Sapotaceae*. These trees offer a color signal of their nutritious fruit only to animals such as monkeys and humans, whose visual systems contain at least three different types of "color-tuned" light receptors.

COLOR STIMULUS

The human eye registers as light wavelengths between 360 nm and 760 nm. Sir Isaac Newton was able to show that stimuli of different wavelengths within this range produce different color sensations. Newton's experiment was quite simple. He took a glass prism and allowed some sunlight to pass through it from a slit in a window shade. When he held a sheet of white paper on the other side of the prism, the light no longer appeared to be white; rather, it took the form of a colored spectrum, looking much like the arrangement of lights in a rainbow (see Figure 5-2A). Newton knew that light bends when passing through a prism and that the amount of bending (technically called *refraction*) depends on wavelength. There is less refraction of the longer wavelengths (600–700 nm) and more of the shorter (400–500 nm). Thus, a prism takes various wavelengths of light, which make up sunlight, and separates them according to wavelength. The fact that we see this spread of light as

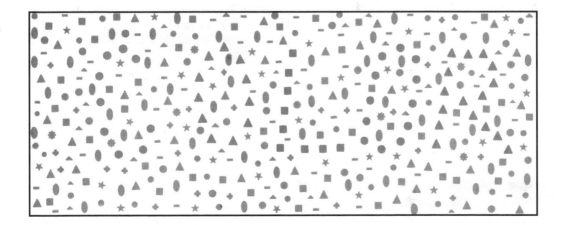

FIGURE 5-1   Can you find the hidden word? If not, turn to Color Plate 2.

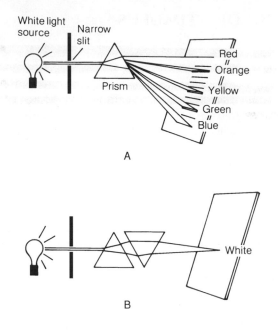

A

B

FIGURE 5-2   Newton's experiments: (A) separation of white light into its various wavelengths gives the color spectrum; (B) recombination of spectral lights gives white light.

varying in hue seems to show that color perception depends on the wavelength of the light. Table 5-1 shows some typical color names associated with some selected wavelengths of light.

Newton also inserted another prism (in the opposite orientation) so that the light was now refracted in the direction opposite to the effect of the original prism. This, of course, recombined all of these wavelengths into a single beam. Now when he placed a piece of paper into this beam it again appeared to be white, with no hint of the original colors that went into the combination. This indicates that the sensation of white results from a mixture of many different wavelengths (see Figure 5-2B).

An important technical distinction should be made here. Figure 5-2 does not describe how white light is broken up into "colored light." Colored light does not exist; rather, what does exist is visible radiation of different wavelengths. If there were no observer there would be no color. Newton pointed this out when he said, "For the rays, to speak properly, are not coloured. In them is nothing else than a certain *Power* and *Disposition* to stir up a sensation of this or that Colour." When we talk about the color stimulus, we should actually speak of radiation of different wavelengths because the sensations of red, green, blue, or any other color reside in the observer. Having made this technical distinction, we must admit that it is extremely convenient to talk about red light or green light, and for the sake of brevity we will not hesitate to do so in some of our later descriptions. Remember, however, that when we refer to a "blue light," we are referring to those wavelengths of light that elicit the sensation of blue, namely, the shorter wavelengths in the visible spectrum.

Objects appear to be the color they are because they reflect to our eyes only selected wavelengths of light. Consider a common object, such as an apple with white light falling on it. It appears to be red. We have already seen that white light, such as sunlight, is a combination of all wavelengths. Because the light stimulus that reaches your eyes produces the sensation of red, all of the wavelengths except the longer (red-appearing) ones must have been absorbed by the surface of the apple. Colored objects or surfaces contain pigments that selectively absorb some wavelengths of light, whereas the rest are reflected and thus reach your eye. It is this selective "subtraction" of some wavelengths from the incoming light that gives an object its color. If a surface does not selectively absorb any of the visible wavelengths reaching it but reflects them all uniformly, it appears white, rather than colored.

Table 5-1   **Wavelengths of Light and Associated Color Sensations**

COLOR NAME	WAVELENGTH (nm)
Violet	450
Blue	470
Cyan	495
Green	510
Yellow-Green	560
Yellow	575
Orange	600
Red	660
Purple	Not a spectral color but a mixture of "red" and "blue"

Color filters work in much the same way, that is, by absorbing some wavelengths of light. For instance, if a white light is projected through a green filter, the resulting beam is green. This means that the filter has absorbed most of the long and short wavelengths, allowing only the medium-range, or green-appearing, wavelengths to reach the eye.

You should be alerted to the fact that simply specifying the wavelength, or wavelengths, in a stimulus does not seem to fully describe the way the color appears to an observer. For instance, a stimulus with a dominant wavelength of 570 nm may appear yellow, whereas another with the same dominant wavelength might appear brown. For this reason, additional factors other than the dominant wavelength are used to classify colors.

Color Appearance Systems

Suppose you were marooned on a desert island that had a beach covered with many colored pebbles. Lacking anything else to do, you set about the task of classifying the colors of all of the pebbles in some meaningful way. The first classification scheme that might come to mind would involve grouping stones together on the basis of their hues. Thus, you would end up with a pile of red stones and another of green stones and so forth. After you have your piles of stones, you would next have to look for some meaningful arrangement for the piles. For instance, you might notice that orange seems to fall, in terms of appearance, somewhere between red and yellow. The yellow-greens, of course, seem to fall between yellow and green. After you reach the blue end of your line of stones, however, you might find yourself running into a bit of a problem. The purple stones seem to fall somewhere between the blues and the reds. This means that a straight line arrangement is not adequate. Instead, you might arrange the pebbles as shown in Figure 5-3.

This crude color arrangement scheme is circular in form. You have probably seen it before in books on art, decorating, or design, where it is usually called the color circle or color wheel. In this arrangement, you have separated the colors according to hue, which is the psychological dimension that most clearly corresponds to variations in wavelength. Very often when we use the word *color*, in

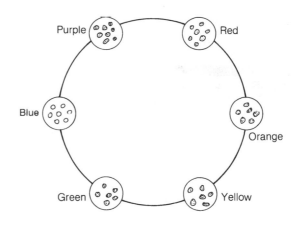

FIGURE 5-3 A primitive color circle for encoding the colors of pebbles.

everyday life and in this chapter, we are actually referring to *hue*. Let us consider the effect of wavelength on sensation by looking at the effects produced by pure or monochromatic stimuli. Monochromatic (from the Greek *mono* meaning "one" and *chroma* meaning "color") stimuli contain only one wavelength. These stimuli are similar to those found in the spectrum generated by Newton's prismatic separation of light and therefore are often called spectral colors. Such monochromatic stimuli do not produce all the hues found in the color wheel. For instance, we find that there is no single wavelength that produces the sensation of purple. This sensation requires a mixture of blue and red wavelengths. Similarly, there is no place in the spectrum where we can find a red that doesn't appear to have a tinge of yellow. In order to achieve such a hue, we must add a bit of blue (short-wavelength) light.

Meanwhile, back on the beach, it has become clear that our color wheel classification scheme based only on the psychological attribute of hue seems incomplete. A close look at the piles of pebbles reveals marked color differences. For instance, among the red pebbles you might find that some are a deep red color and others are pink; another group may be almost pure white with only a hint of red coloration. This observation corresponds to the physical dimension of purity. Clearly the purest color you could get would correspond to a monochromatic or spectral hue, and as you add other wavelengths, or white light, the color would appear to become "washed out." This psychological attribute of color appearance is called **saturation.** It is quite easy to integrate saturation into the color circle by simply placing white in the center. Now imagine that the various degrees of saturation correspond to positions along the spokes or radii emanating from the center of the wheel. The center represents white (or gray), and the perimeter represents the purest or most saturated color possible. Figure 5-4 shows the color wheel now modified to include saturation. Notice that the point corresponding to pink (a moderately desaturated red) is plotted near the center along the line connecting red and white, whereas a crimson is plotted farther away from the center along the same line.

To the average observer, hue and saturation do not completely describe all of the visible nuances of color. It is quite possible to have two colors match in both of these attributes but still appear to be different. For instance, a blue spot of light projected onto a screen would not appear to be the same as another spot identical in all regards except that it has been dimmed by putting a light-reducing filter in front of it. Thus, the sensory quality of **brightness** (which we discussed in Chapter 4) must be worked into our system of describing

colors. Because we have already used the two dimensions capable of being reproduced on a flat piece of paper, it is clear that the addition of a third color dimension (brightness) forces us to use a solid instead of a flat representation.

The shape of the three-dimensional color "space" can be derived from common observation if we recognize that at high brightness levels colors appear to be "washed out," whereas at low brightness levels colors appear to be "weak" or "muddy," meaning that they are of low saturation. Thus, the hue circle must shrink at these extremes because saturation seems to vary over a confined range, and very high degrees of saturation are never observed at very high or low levels of brightness.

If we combine the three psychological attributes of hue, saturation, and brightness, we get something that looks like Figure 5-5. It appears to be a pair of cones placed base to base. This is usually called the **color spindle** or the **color solid.** The central core as we move up or down represents brightness and is composed of all the grays running from white (at the top) to black (at the bottom). We can imagine that at each brightness

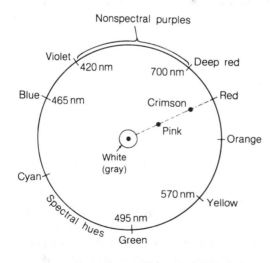

FIGURE 5-4 The color circle modified to allow the encoding of both hue and saturation. Spectral colors are on the outer rim; white is in the center.

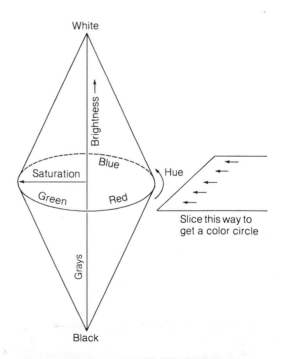

FIGURE 5-5 The color solid.

level, if we sliced through the color solid in the direction shown in the diagram, we would get a color circle in which the hue would be represented along the perimeter. Totally desaturated colors (the grays) are at the central core, as we've already noted; hence saturation is represented by moving from the center outward. This is the basic representation used in many color appearance systems. Probably the most popular in use among psychologists is the one developed by Munsell (1915) and modified by Newhall, Nickerson, and Judd (1943) to agree with the way typical observers arrange color stimuli. To actually classify colors we use a color atlas, in which each page represents a horizontal or a vertical slice through the color solid. Color samples that illustrate colors found in varying locations in the color solid are given in such atlases, allowing the observer to identify and label any given test color.

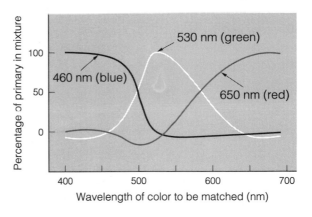

FIGURE 5-6 The proportion of each primary (a 460-nm blue, a 530-nm green, and a 650-nm red) needed to match any spectral color.

Mixing Colors

One of the most important facts about color vision was discovered in the 1850s by a German physicist and physiologist, Hermann von Helmholtz (1821–1894), and by a Scottish physicist, James Clerk Maxwell (1831–1879). These researchers found that human observers were sometimes completely unable to tell the difference between two colored stimuli, even though one stimulus was composed of a monochromatic light and the other was composed of three monochromatic lights in various amounts. They reported that by combining an appropriate set of three different colored monochromatic light sources in appropriate amounts, they could create a color that perfectly matched another monochromatic color. Three monochromatic wavelengths that allow such matches are generally called primaries. Actually, the choice of the wavelengths for the primaries turned out to be rather arbitrary. Primary colors need be only reasonably far apart from one another, with the additional requirement that the mixture of any two of them alone will not match the third one. Any two colors that appear to be the same, even though they are really made up of different wavelengths of light, are called metameric colors.

The results of very careful color-matching experiments are shown in Figure 5-6. The graph in-

dicates the relative amount of each of three primaries needed to create a *metamer* match for any monochromatic color (Wright, 1929). The primary colors used were a red of 650 nm, a green of 530 nm, and a blue of 460 nm. Observers were permitted to adjust the amounts of each of these primaries until the appearance of the color mixture matched the color of a monochromatic test color. You might notice that some of the values in the graph are slightly negative. This indicates that some of that particular primary had to be added not to the mixture, but to the monochromatic test sample in order to reduce its saturation to the point where it could be matched by a mixture of the two remaining primaries.

The fact that any given color can be matched by a mixture of three appropriately selected primary colors suggests an alternate way of specifying the hue of a stimulus, namely, in terms of the proportion (sometimes "negative") of the three primaries needed to reach this match. Geometrically this suggests a triangular space with a primary color at each corner. Color mixtures may then be represented in the same way as they are on the color circle. Thus, yellow—which is a mixture of red and green—is represented by a point on the line between red and green. If we add more red the point moves toward the red primary, and if we add more green it moves toward the green. As in the color

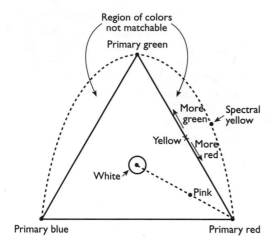

FIGURE 5-7 Specifying colors using a color triangle.

circle, white is represented by a point in the middle and is composed of an equal proportion of the three primaries. Also, as in the color circle, a red of lower saturation (the whitish red or pink) would be represented by a point moved inward toward the center. Such a diagram is shown in Figure 5-7.

Monochromatic colors can usually be produced only under precise laboratory conditions. Most of the light reaching your eye is composed of a mixture of many different wavelengths. Generally, the dominant wavelengths determine the hue that we see as being the "color" of a stimulus. But as the color-matching experiments show, after several wavelengths of light have been combined, the eye can no longer determine the individual wavelengths that went into the mixture. For example, you can have a pure yellow made up of only 570-nm light and another that matches it, composed of a mixture of a 500-nm green and a 650 nm-red. You will not be able to distinguish between these hues, nor will you be able to isolate the red and the green that are in the mixture.

Additive Mixing of Lights The process of combining different wavelengths of light in order to produce new colors is called **additive color mixing.** The consequences of mixing lights from the three primary wavelengths red, green, and blue are shown in Figure 5-8A. Let's begin by imagining that we projected a red disk of light onto a screen, perhaps by placing a red filter in front of a spotlight. If we now projected a deep blue (almost violet) disk onto the screen (using a blue filter and a second spotlight) so that it partially overlapped the red disk, the light reaching our eyes from the overlapping region would contain both red and blue light. Finally, if we repeated the procedure with a third spotlight and a green filter, arranging things so that a green disk of light was partly overlapping both the red disk and the blue disk, we would create a region in the center containing red, blue, and green light. Each time we created a new overlap of color disks, we would be *adding* to the mixture of wavelengths reaching the eye.

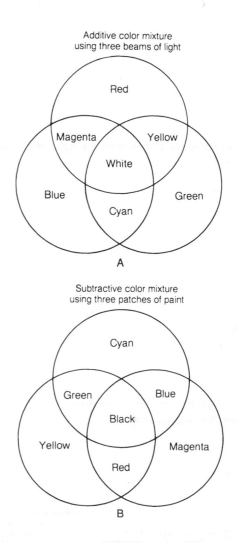

FIGURE 5-8 Color-mixture systems: (A) additive, (B) subtractive.

What many people find surprising about mixing different colored lights to produce new colors is that the colors produced by these mixtures are lighter in appearance than each of the original primary colors. But a moment's reflection will reveal why this must be so. Combining two lights, each of a given intensity, can produce only a light that is more intense than the component lights. So at the place where red and the deep blue overlap, we see a lighter hue that is reddish-purple, often called *magenta*. Where the deep blue and the green overlap, we see a lighter hue that is greenish-blue, usually called *cyan*. Where the red and green overlap, we see a lighter color, *yellow*. Finally, where all three beams overlap, we see only white, which appears as though it contains no color at all. Demonstration Box 5-1 shows another way to produce additive color mixtures that does not require spotlights or filters.

One of the most important insights for a student to grasp concerning additive color mixing is that the perceptual results of color mixing are not predictable from the physics of light and wavelengths. From a purely physical point of view, all light can be characterized as being composed of a collection of wavelengths at different intensities. However, there is nothing in such a physical description to indicate that a monochromatic yellow made up of only 570-nm light will appear identical to light consisting of a mixture of a 500-nm green and a 650 nm-red. This can be predicted only if one understands the physiological basis of color vision in the human eye, which we will turn to in the next section of the chapter.

Subtractive Mixing of Pigments   A form of color mixing that most students are more familiar with, and that is perfectly predictable from the physics of light, is the perceptual consequences of mixing paints or pigments. Mixing paints in order to produce new colors is called **subtractive color mixing** because each addition of pigment to the mix results in more wavelengths being absorbed by the pigments and thus in less light being reflected toward the eye of the observer. As every student learns in grade school, if you mix all the paints in your palette together, you will certainly not produce white. Instead, you will get a dark shade of gray or even black.

As an example, consider an object with a red surface, such as a tomato. Its red appearance means that the surface pigment absorbs most of the short and medium wavelengths, reflecting to your eyes only the long (red) wavelengths. A pigment that looks similar to grass green might absorb most of the long wavelengths and the short

---

DEMONSTRATION BOX 5-1
Color Mixture

There is a simple way to obtain additive color mixtures without using projected beams of light. Consider Color Plate 4A (found inside the front cover of this book), in which you see a checkerboard of tiny red and green squares. In Color Plate 4B you see a yellow disk. Prop up the book so that you can see the color plates when you move across the room. Now, standing at a distance, look back at the figures. What formerly appeared to be red and green now appears to be yellow and should match the yellow disk. At a distance, the optics of the eye can no longer resolve the individual squares. The light from each of them smears, or blurs, across the retina, giving rise to the color mixture effect.

This technique is similar to the technique used in your color television set. If you take a magnifying glass and hold it up to the screen, you will see that each region is made up of a series of tiny dots. When you sit at normal viewing distance, you can no longer resolve the individual dots. They have combined within the eye to give you an additive color mixture. A similar technique was used by the French painter Georges Seurat, who replaced the traditional irregular brush stroke used in painting with meticulously placed dots of color. Thus, instead of mixing paints on his palette, he allowed the mixture to be accomplished optically within the eye of the onlooker viewing the painting from an appropriate distance.

wavelengths, reflecting to your eye mainly middle wavelengths. Thus, when you mix red and green paints together, you end up with a mixture in which only the middle wavelengths are reflected by the green; yet, these are absorbed by the red pigment. Hence, you are essentially subtracting all of the wavelengths, leaving only a muddy gray appearance.

Some consequences of mixing paints are illustrated in Figure 5-8B. Note first of all that in order to produce the full range of colors from only three primary pigments you have to begin with primaries that are not pure in wavelength. Indeed, you will get the best results if you begin with pigments that reflect a rather broad range of wavelengths. This is because mixing pigments can only decrease the range of wavelengths that are being reflected. That is, each addition of pigment to the mix will prevent some additional wavelengths from being reflected to the eye. Therefore, the brightest colors will be found at the periphery of the subtractive color mixing diagram in Figure 5-8B, with the darkest possible color, black, appearing in the center.

In the diagram we can see the consequences of mixing cyan (reflecting the short and middle wavelengths), magenta (reflecting the long and short wavelengths), and yellow (reflecting the middle and long wavelengths). Because the cyan pigment absorbs all the long wavelengths and the magenta absorbs all the middle wavelengths, their mixture absorbs both the long and the middle wavelengths, leaving us only with the short or blue-appearing portion of the spectrum. Similarly, a mixture of magenta and yellow absorbs both the short and middle wavelengths, leaving us with long-wavelength or red-appearing pigment. Finally, when we combine yellow with cyan, we find that the yellow subtracts the short wavelengths and the cyan subtracts the long wavelengths; hence only the middle or green-appearing wavelengths remain.

In the everyday world pigment mixtures are actually much harder to predict than this because the wavelength-absorbing property of pigments is very complex. For example, Figure 5-9 shows the wavelengths reflected by some typical pigments. Notice how irregularly they reflect the light, and imagine the problems in predicting what the resultant mixes might reflect and absorb.

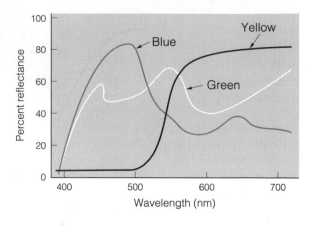

FIGURE 5-9 The relative wavelength composition of a blue, a yellow, and a green pigment.

Color Spaces

The color circle, which we have already discussed, provides a convenient means of predicting the appearance of additive color mixtures. Note that the spacing of colors around its circumference corresponds to the way the various hues appear to an average observer—which is not identical to a regular spacing according to wavelength. To use the color circle to predict a color mixture is actually quite simple. Suppose we mix a spectral red (about 650 nm) with a spectral yellow (about 570 nm). We can depict this as in Figure 5-10, where the resultant mixture is represented by the line connecting these two colors. If we combine the yellow and the red in equal proportions, we will get a color that corresponds to the dot in the center of the line. We can determine what this color will look like by simply drawing a line from the center of the color circle through the dot to the perimeter. When this is done, we find that we get an orange corresponding to about a 600-nm spectral stimulus. Increasing the amount of yellow shifts the point along the line in the direction closer to the yellow hue. Adding more red shifts the point along the line in the other direction. You will notice that we started out with two spectral, or pure, hues (marked on the perimeter); however, the resultant mixed color is no longer on the perimeter but is closer to the

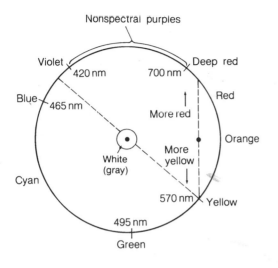

FIGURE 5-10 Using the color circle to predict color mixtures.

center of the color circle. The purest colors possible (the spectral colors) are placed on the perimeter of the color circle; more desaturated colors are found closer to the center of the circle (nearer white or gray). From this we can conclude that any color mixture is less saturated than either of the two component colors that went into it. No mixture of colors can ever be quite as saturated as a monochromatic or spectral color.

Mixing more than two hues (or hues containing more than a single wavelength) is a little more complex. If we mix three colors, the resultant color sensation would be given by the center of a triangle produced by connecting the three colors. If the amount of each hue differs, the center point of the triangle shifts toward the dominant hue.

An interesting effect occurs when we mix two colors that are exactly opposite to each other on the color circle. For instance, mixing a violet with a yellow along the line shown in Figure 5-10 results in a colorless gray. This is because, when the proportions are correct, this mixture lies in the center of the circle. Colors whose mixture produces such an achromatic gray are known as **complementary colors**.

In 1931 a special body of the Commission Internationale de l'Eclairage (CIE) standardized the procedure for specifying the color of a stimulus.

The members of this group decided to use a color space created by the mixing of three primaries as described earlier. Unfortunately, if we select any three *spectral* primary colors, a number of perceptual and mathematical problems result. The major perceptual problem is the fact that there are other spectral colors that cannot be represented within the triangle. For instance, a pure spectral yellow cannot be represented (unless it is one of the primaries, which creates other problems) because any color mixture can never be as saturated as the pure spectral color itself. To solve this perceptual problem, the CIE members selected three *imaginary* primary colors. They arranged the primaries at the corners of the triangle shown in Figure 5-11. These imaginary primary colors are more saturated than any real colors can be. (Remember that this is done so that all perceptually visible colors can be represented *within* the space.) Notice that we have labeled the horizontal and vertical axes of the triangle with the labels x and y.

We can now represent *any* color as a point in the color space. The reason that we can plot a mixture of three colors by using a point that has only two spatial coordinates is because the **CIE chromaticity space** has been arranged so that y represents the proportion of green in the mixture and x represents the proportion of red in the mixture. Clearly the proportions of red and green and blue in any mixture must sum to a proportion of 1.0 (you can think of these as representing percentages where all the items must sum to 100% of the light). If we know the total proportions of green and red in the mixture, we need only subtract these from 1.0 to find the proportion of blue. The actual colors that can be perceived do not fill the full triangle (remember that the primaries we are using are imaginary "supersaturated" colors). Instead, they fill a horseshoe-shaped area with the spectral colors forming the outside boundary. We have labeled this area on the figure so that you can see the regions filled by various colors. Thus, if we had a color specified as $0.2x$ and $0.6y$, we would know that it is composed of 20% red, 60% green, and (subtracting from a total of 100%) 20% blue. Looking at the figure you can find the point described by these x and y coordinates and see that this color would look green.

Notice that brightness is not represented anywhere on this diagram. As in the color space

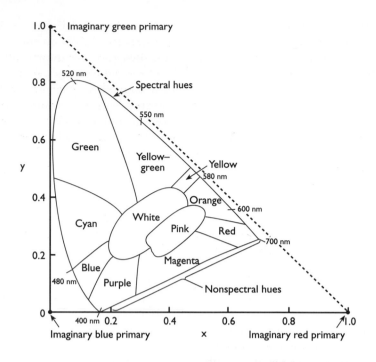

FIGURE 5-11 The CIE chromaticity space, which is a variant of the color triangle system using three imaginary "super" primaries.

we discussed earlier, brightness requires a third dimension. The color space in the figure can be pictured as a single slice through a three-dimensional color space, just as we demonstrated in Figure 5-5. This third dimension is called z. Using the CIE color system we can specify any color stimulus by its **tristimulus values, which are simply the x and y coordinates for the hue of the stimulus and a z coordinate for the brightness of the stimulus.**

Another kind of color space that is becoming increasingly important in everyday life is the color space used in modern color televisions and computer screens. These devices are becoming very common, and more and more people are finding themselves in front of these devices for a large part of their day. For the purposes of producing a color image, a screen of this kind is divided into many distinct columns and rows. At the intersection of each column and row is a tiny square element called a *pixel*, which is short for "picture element." Each pixel on the screen is illuminated by light from three different electron guns, a red or long-wavelength-emitting gun, a green or middle-wavelength-emitting gun, and a blue or short-wavelength-emitting gun. By varying the relative contribution of each of these three guns, a very large number of colors can be shown at each pixel location. For example, if all three guns are turned off, the pixel will appear to be black; if all three guns are turned on to their maximum amount, the pixel will appear to be white; if only one of the guns is turned on to its maximum, the pixel will appear to be a highly saturated red, green, or blue, respectively.

The color space underlying this form of color imaging is called **red-green-blue (or simply RGB) space** and is shown in Figure 5-12. As you can see, it is a three-dimensional space, just as the color solid (Figure 5-5) and the CIE color space (Figure 5-11) are three-dimensional. However, it differs from each of these spaces in interesting ways. At the origin of RGB space, where the red, green, and blue dimensions are set to values of zero, is the color black. As any one of the color dimensions is increased in value, the screen will take on the appearance of that primary color. If two of the primaries are increased together, the appearance will be that predicted by the additive mixing of light (Figure 5-8A). These are the colors represented at the corners of the cube in Figure 5-12 that are two steps away from the origin. Finally, at the corner of the space farthest from the origin is the color white, which is the consequence of fully turning on all three colors. Each point in the RGB space is represented by three values, the first representing the intensity of the red signal, the second the green, and the third the blue. Each goes from 0 (meaning off) to 1 (meaning full power on). Thus, the most saturated red signal would be 1,0,0, whereas the most saturated magenta (red plus blue) would be 1,0,1.

Imagine that there is a line running through RGB space, from the corner representing black to the far corner representing white. This imaginary line represents all the different levels of gray that can exist between black and white. Deviating from this line of grays, toward any corner of the cube, increases the purity or saturation of a color. In other words, the RGB space is really very similar

to the color solid in Figure 5-5, if we are willing to imagine the RGB space standing upright, balanced on the corner representing black, with the corner representing white in the highest position.

The most important practical difference between the color solid and RGB space is that the color solid is intended to represent all of the colors that a human observer can possibly see. The RGB space, on the other hand, describes only those colors that can be produced by a particular digital screen. Each screen has its own limitations, often based on the particular phosphors (light-emitting substances) that are used for each color gun (Hung & Berns, 1995). For instance, you may have noticed that it is very difficult to find a television or computer screen that is able to render a pure white. Most screens in use today are quite blue in appearance even when all three color guns are fully engaged. If you haven't been aware of this before, just think of the color appearance of a television screen that is turned on when other lights are off. It is very blue. The red and green phosphors available to engineers who design these screens are

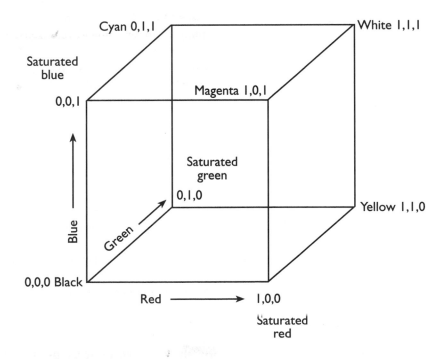

FIGURE 5-12   The RGB color space.

simply not strong enough to balance the intensity of the blue phosphors that are available. During the daytime and in normal room lighting, this effect is less noticeable because of the mechanisms of color constancy and brightness constancy (see Chapter 11).

THE PHYSIOLOGY OF COLOR VISION

To this point, we have dealt with the physical stimulus, some aspects of combining various wavelengths of light, and some methods of specifying the appearance of a color. None of the foregoing descriptions specifies how a particular color sensation arises. In order to understand this, we must deal with both physiological and psychological factors. Let us consider these in light of the two major theoretical positions that have emerged during the past 150 years.

Trichromatic Color Theory

Much research has gone into the search for the physiological basis of color vision. One of the earliest findings was discussed in Chapter 4, where you learned about scotopic (that is, dim) levels of illumination, when only the rods are active and no color vision is found. On the basis of these observations, it was concluded that cones are the retinal receptors that provide the first stage of the color response. Therefore, how the cones provide information about the wavelength of the incoming light becomes the first question to be answered.

Most normal people can discriminate among thousands of colors under a myriad of conditions. If we are careful to hold constant the dimensions of brightness and saturation, the average human observer can reliably discriminate among at least 200 different hues. Suppose that we wished to create an artificial eye with this same ability. The simplest procedure might seem to require a separate cone that responds to each of the discriminable hues. Unfortunately, such a scheme is not practical. For any given colored stimulus, we would have only $\frac{1}{200}$ of the cones active, which means that our visual acuity would be much poorer than research has shown it to be. In addition, such a system would

mean that our acuity measured under white illumination would be many times better than our acuity measured under monochromatic stimulation. Although visual acuity is a bit less when there are only color differences and no brightness differences in a pattern of stimuli, the acuity reduction is not very large (Mullen, 1990).

An alternate scheme would be to have only one type of retinal cone with 200 different code signals by which it could indicate the discriminable hues. This could be done via a sort of neural Morse code. However, nature does not always act like an engineer might act. Anatomical studies of eyes capable of color vision indicate that each cone contains only one pigment. With only one pigment, the only thing that an individual cone "knows" is the amount of its pigment that has been bleached. Although different wavelengths of light may bleach more or less pigment, simply increasing or decreasing the intensity of any colored light stimulus will also cause the same kinds of changes in the amount of pigment bleached. It is therefore impossible for a single cone to be able to discriminate each of 200 hues, let alone provide a distinctive output signal code for each.

The first good solution to how we discriminate colors was suggested almost 200 years ago by Thomas Young (1773–1829). Young concluded that we need only a few different retinal receptors, each with a different wavelength sensitivity, to allow us to perceive the number of colors we do. He speculated that perhaps as few as three different kinds of receptors would do. His theory was revived in the 1850s by Helmholtz. Remember that Helmholtz and Maxwell were able to show that normal observers needed a mixture of only three primaries to match any color stimulus. This fact was taken as evidence for the presence of three different types of cones in the retina, long before it was possible to make a direct observation of the anatomy of a cone. Because the usual color-matching primaries consisted of a red, a green, and a blue, it was presumed that there are three types of receptors, one responsive to long wavelengths, one to medium wavelengths, and one to short wavelengths of light. Because cones operate by the bleaching of pigment, this suggested three hypothetical pigments. The first was called **erythrolabe** (translated from the Greek, this means "red-catching"), the second was called **chlorolabe** (meaning "green-catching"), and the third was called **cyanolabe** (meaning "blue-catching"). This **trichromatic theory** (from the Greek *tri* meaning "three" and *chroma* meaning "color") finds some very convincing support from studies of people with defective color vision.

Color Vision Defects Virtually all individuals differ from what is usually called "normal" or "average" color vision in some way or another (Neitz & Jacobs, 1986). However, some people show drastic deficiencies in their ability to discriminate colored stimuli and, in popular language, are said to suffer from **color blindness.** This term is much too strong because only a very small percentage of individuals are totally incapable of discriminating hues. According to a trichromatic theory of color vision, we can predict five different varieties of color abnormality. The first, and most drastic, would be found in those who have no functioning cones. Because all of their seeing would be done only with the rod system, they would be expected to have no color discrimination ability. In addition, they should have relatively poor visual acuity (20/200 or less) and find photopic, or daylight, levels of illumination to be quite uncomfortable. Their night vision, on the other hand, should be normal. It is estimated that only 1 in 300,000 individuals has no functioning cones at all (Sharpe & Nordby, 1989).

A slightly less drastic malady is one in which only one variety of cone is functioning in addition to the rods. With this problem, vision should be possible under both photopic and scotopic conditions, but there would still be a lack of any color discrimination ability. Any wavelength of light hitting one of the functioning cones (or one of the rods) would produce some bleaching of the pigment. Even though different wavelengths might bleach different amounts, this is not enough to allow color discrimination because the response produced by any one wavelength of light can be matched by merely adjusting the intensity of any other. In other words, the individual with no functioning cones, or the one with only one functioning cone type, responds to light in much the way that a sheet of black and white film does. All colors are recorded simply as gradations in intensity of the response. Such individuals are called **monochromats** (from the Greek *mono* meaning "one" and *chroma* meaning "color").

One might also suppose that some individuals, rather than lacking two sets of cones, as does the monochromat, might have only one malfunctioning cone system. Given two functioning cone systems, they should have some color perception, though it would differ from that of a normal observer. In effect, they should be able to match all other colors with a mixture of only two primaries. Such individuals are usually called **dichromats** (the Greek *di* means "two"). The existence of such individuals has been known since the 1700s. The English chemist John Dalton (1766–1844) was a dichromat, a fact he learned rather late in his life. Supposedly, it first came to his attention when he wore a scarlet robe to receive his Ph.D. degree. Because he was a Quaker, a sect that shuns bright colors, this caused quite a stir, until it became clear that yarn dyed scarlet, gray, or dark blue-green all appeared to be the same to him.

There are three predictable forms of dichromacy, depending on whether it is the red-, green-, or blue-responding cones that are inoperative. The specific confusions are predictable from the color-matching curves of normal observers shown in Figure 5-6. Dalton's type of color defect is usually referred to as **protanopia** (the Greek prefix *prota* means "first," and red light is generally designated as the first primary). A protanope would be insensitive to long wavelengths normally perceived as red light. If a red light were made very much brighter than a green light, a protanope could easily confuse them, whereas a color-normal observer would perceive both that the red light was brighter than the green and also that they differed in hue. Dalton described his subjective experiences when viewing a spectrum such as that produced by Newton's prism. Most individuals perceive six different colors, blending one into another. Dalton reported: "To me it is quite otherwise. I see only two, or at most three distinctions. These I should call yellow and blue, or yellow, blue, and purple. My yellow comprehends the red, orange, yellow, and green of others and my blue and purple coincide with theirs."

The most common form of dichromacy is called **deuteranopia** (the Greek prefix *deutera* means "second," and green light is by convention the second primary). Individuals with deuteranopia have a malfunction in the green cone system. They are still able to respond to green light; however, they cannot distinguish green from certain combinations of red and blue.

Trichromatic theory also predicts that there is a third form of dichromacy that is caused by the absence or malfunction of the blue cone system. Although a name existed for this phenomenon, **tritanopia** (from the Greek *tritan*, for the "third" primary), there was no confirmed report of this difficulty until about 1950, when a magazine article containing a color-vision test plate appeared as part of an intensive search throughout England. This national search resulted in the discovery of 17 tritanopes (Wright, 1952). These individuals, instead of seeing the spectrum as composed of blue and of yellow as do other dichromats, see the long wavelengths as red and the shorter ones as bluish-green. The discovery of this last class of individuals provides strong support for a trichromatic theory of color vision.

Color defects are a fairly common problem. Some instances of it are relatively mild and result in what is called **anomalous trichromatism**. Color matches of individuals with this problem require more red **(protoanomaly)** or more green **(deuteranomaly)** than do color matches of normal observers. If we count all individuals with any form of color deficiency, we find that just over 8% of males show color weaknesses, whereas slightly less than 0.05% of females show similar weaknesses. Color defects are genetically transmitted on the X chromosome,

accounting for their uneven transmission in males and females, and recent studies have conclusively mapped the pattern of this transmission (Botstein, 1986; Nathans, 1987; Nathans, Piantanida, Eddy, Shows, & Hogness, 1986).

Which colors does a dichromat actually see? It is difficult to know how the colors seen by a dichromat compare with those seen by a color-normal observer. However, a glimpse into the visual world of the color defective has been provided by a rare person who was deuteranopic in her left eye but color normal in her right eye. Graham and Hsia (1958) had this observer adjust the color seen by her normal eye so that it appeared to be the same hue as the color seen by her defective eye. The results of her matches are shown in Figure 5-13. As can be seen from this figure, the colors over the entire range of red to green (from about 700 nm to 502 nm) all appeared to have the same yellow hue (about 570 nm), and all of the colors from green to violet appeared to be blue (matching a 470-nm stimulus). The region that appears to be blue-green to the normal observer (around 502 nm) was perceived as being a neutral gray in the defective eye. Researchers have more recently confirmed these results by comparing the color-matching and color-naming performance of dichromats with color-normal observers (Paramei, 1996). Knowledge of the nature of the color confusions among dichromats allowed Coren and Hakstian (1988, 1995) to

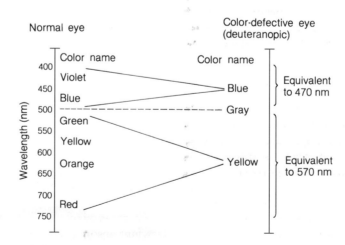

FIGURE 5-13   Color matches of a normal eye to a "color-blind" eye (deuteranopic) in the same observer (based on Graham & Hsia, 1958).

DEMONSTRATION BOX 5-2
Color Vision Screening Inventory

To see if you may have a color-vision deficit simply take this test, which is the *Color Vision Screening Inventory* * developed by Coren and Hakstian (1987, 1988). For each question you should select the response that best describes you and your behaviors. You can select from among the following response alternatives: *Never* (or almost never), *Seldom, Occasionally, Frequently, Always* (or almost always). Simply circle the letter corresponding to the first letter of your choice.

1. Do you have difficulty discriminating between yellow and orange?   N S O F A
2. Do you have difficulty discriminating between yellow and green?   N S O F A
3. Do you have difficulty discriminating between gray and blue-green?   N S O F A
4. Do you have difficulty discriminating between red and brown?   N S O F A
5. Do you have difficulty discriminating between green and brown?   N S O F A

6. Do you have difficulty discriminating between pale green and pale red?   N S O F A
7. Do you have difficulty discriminating between blue and purple?   N S O F A
8. Do the color names that you use disagree with those that other people use?   N S O F A
9. Are the colors of traffic lights difficult to distinguish?   N S O F A
10. Do you tend to confuse colors? N S O F A

Scoring instructions: Responses are scored 1 for *Never*, 2 for *Seldom*, 3 for *Occasionally*, 4 for *Frequently*, and 5 for *Always*. Simply add together your scores for the 10 questions. If your score is 17 or higher, you have an 81% likelihood of failing a standard screening test for color vision. If your score is in this range, you might want to get your color vision tested by your doctor or in a perception laboratory.

*The *Color Vision Screening Inventory* is copyrighted by SC Psychological Enterprises Ltd. and is reprinted here with permission.

---

develop a simple questionnaire that assesses whether individuals are likely to be color blind. You can test yourself with this questionnaire using Demonstration Box 5-2.

Physiological Basis of Trichromatic Theory

Although the data from color mixing and color defects seem to support a trichromatic theory of color vision, direct physiological evidence for the three cone pigments did not appear until the 1960s. The measurement procedure involved is conceptually simple but technically quite difficult (Bowmaker & Dartnall, 1980; Brown & Wald, 1964; Marks, Dobelle, & MacNichol, 1964). It involves a device called a **microspectrophotometer**. With this device a narrow beam of monochromatic light is focused on the pigment-bearing outer segment of a cone. As tiny amounts of light of various wavelengths are passed through the cone, the amount of light absorbed at each wavelength is measured. The

more light of a given wavelength that is absorbed by the cone pigment, the more sensitive is the cone to light of that particular wavelength. Such measurements were taken using cones from the retinae of goldfish, monkeys, and finally from humans.

Although researchers are still refining the detailed description of the cone pigments (e.g., Mac-Nichol, 1986), the general pattern of the results is clear. There are three major groups of cones. A typical set of measurements, taken from a human eye that had to be surgically removed (Bowmaker & Dartnall, 1980), shows maximum absorptions in the ranges of 420 nm, 534 nm, and 564 nm, respectively. Figure 5-14 shows the relative absorption of these three pigments (where 1.0 is the maximum amount absorbed by the pigment). Clearly, on the basis of their sensitivity peaks, we should call the short-wavelength-absorbing pigment "violet," the middle "yellow-green," and the long wavelength "orange" if we wish to be more precise than the "blue," "green," and "red" labels we have been using. Also shown in Figure 5-14 is the relative sensitivity function for the rods in this same eye. These receptors have a maximum absorption of 498 nm when measured with the same technique. Rushton (1962, 1965) introduced a similar technique without using a microspectrophotometer. First, he sent a beam of light into the eye and then took measurements on the amount of light reflected back out of the eye. By taking the difference between the amount of light sent and the amount reflected, he obtained an estimate of the amount of light at each wavelength absorbed by the photopigments in the intact human eye. Next he flooded the eye with light of a particular distribution. Thus, red light might be expected to activate the long-wavelength-catching pigment most strongly; hence it would, with continued exposure, be "bleached out." When he remeasured the amount of light absorbed at each wavelength, the difference between light reflected back by the "bleached" and "unbleached" retinas gave absorption curves similar to those shown in Figure 5-14 for pigments marked "red" and "green" in the fovea.

Rushton reasoned further that protanopes and deuteranopes, according to trichromatic theory, should be missing one or the other of the two longer-wavelength pigments. When he used his procedure with color-defective observers, he found that they were missing the appropriate pigments. The receptors are physically there because the density of cones is the same for normal and color defective individuals (Cicerone & Nerger, 1989). However, the differences in pigment seem to be absent.

Rushton could not find evidence for cones containing blue-matching pigment in the fovea, which suggests that all observers are dichromats, specifically tritanopes, for small targets seen in central vision. This conclusion has been verified using psychophysical techniques as well (Bornstein & Monroe, 1978; Tuck & Long, 1990; Williams, MacLeod, & Hayhoe, 1981). Recent evidence based on destruction of blue cones in the monkey retina by prolonged exposure to short-wavelength light has confirmed the fact that there are no blue cones in a circular region 25 min of arc in diameter in the central fovea (e.g., Sperling, 1986). The relative rarity of blue cones probably also explains why blue contributes less than red or green to many aspects of the visual process (e.g., Kaiser & Boynton, 1985).

Because the cones are differentially distributed across the retina, our color response is different over

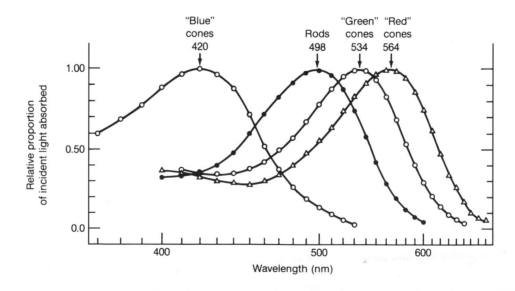

FIGURE 5-14 The relative absorption of various wavelengths of light by the three different cone types and the rods of a human (based on Bowmaker & Dartnall, 1980).

different portions of the eye. The central foveal region is relatively blue blind, and sensitivity to blue light first increases and then decreases with increasing distance from the fovea. Sensitivity to green light diminishes with increasing distance from the fovea and disappears at about 40° from the fovea. A similar pattern holds for sensitivity to red and yellow light, with color responses disappearing in the order green, red, yellow, and blue as distance from the fovea increases. In the far periphery of the retina, we are totally color blind. The exact distance, however, depends on the size of the stimulus. We can discriminate the colors of larger stimuli farther out on the peripheral retina (Johnson, 1986). To see how your own color discrimination varies across the retina, try Demonstration Box 5-3.

Color responses are also sufficiently different between observers, even among those with normal color vision, to suggest that there may be systematic individual differences in cone photopigments (Alpern, 1979). One study involving 200 observers discovered that color-normal males formed two groups based on color-matching tests involving red light (Neitz & Jacobs, 1986). Color-normal females formed a single group, but it was different from either of the two male groups. The genetic basis for this variation is now understood. Using the techniques of molecular genetics, Nathans and his colleagues (Nathans, 1987; Nathans, Piantanida, Eddy, Shows, & Hogness, 1986) have identified the location and molecular structure of at least three genes on the X chromosome that determine the photopigments of the red-light cones. The genes responsible

for the different photopigments are *autosomal recessive*, meaning that they are not usually expressed in females (females have two X chromosomes, and so the gene that might express a distinctive variation on one chromosome is usually blocked by the corresponding typical gene on the other). However, the pattern is quite different for males (males have both an X and a Y chromosome). Because males have only one X chromosome, if that X chromosome carries a gene for the distinctive red photopigment, it will usually be created. This is similar to the explanation for why more males than females have color deficiencies.

Opponent-Process Theory

The German physiologist Ewald Hering (1878–1964) was not completely satisfied with a trichromatic theory of color vision. It seemed to him that human observers act as if there are four, rather than three, primary colors. For instance, when observers are presented with a large number of color samples and asked to pick out those that appear to be *pure* (defined as not showing any trace of being a mixture of colors), they tend to pick out four, rather than three, colors. These unique colors almost always include a red, a green, and a blue, as trichromatic theory predicts (Fuld, Wooten, & Whalen, 1981); however, they also include a yellow (Bornstein, 1973).

Boynton and Gordon (1965) showed that with the color names *red*, *yellow*, *green*, and *blue*

DEMONSTRATION BOX 5-3
Color-Sensitive Zones on the Retina

Color perception is best in the central region of the retina (excluding the small central region of the fovea, which is blue blind). You can observe the changes in color discrimination for different parts of the retina by taking a small orange piece of paper and placing it on a gray surface. Keeping your head fixed, look off to the side of the orange target. If you keep moving your eyes outward (away from the target), you stimulate more peripheral parts of the

retina. Eventually you will reach a point where the orange will look yellowish, meaning that you have now imaged it beyond the red-sensitive zone. If you continue moving your eyes outward, you may even hit a point where the orange no longer looks colored at all but merely appears gray. Your eye will have to move farther to get these changes in color appearance if the orange patch is larger (see Johnson, 1986).

English-speaking observers can categorize the entire range of visible hues (some stimuli seem to require a combination term containing two primaries, such as *yellow-green*). The way in which adult observers distribute their hue names is shown in Figure 5-15, which indicates four overlapping hue name categories corresponding to red, yellow, green, and blue. These results cannot be attributed simply to learning or language use. For example, Bornstein, Kessen, and Weiskopf (1976) showed that 4-month-old infants tend to see the spectrum as if it were divided into four hue categories. They did this by repeatedly presenting a given wavelength of a light until the infants became visually bored and stopped looking at the light (a process called **habituation**). They next monitored how much time an infant spent looking at a second wavelength of light. They found that when the second wavelength was selected from another hue name category (based on the adult data), the infants spent more time looking at it than they did at a wavelength selected from the same hue category. The infants acted as if stimuli in the same hue category were more similar than those from different categories; hence it seems they were categorizing hues into the same four groups that the adults do.

Hering looked at another aspect of the subjective experience of hue. He noted that certain color combinations are never reported by observers, for instance, a yellowish blue or a greenish red. This led Hering to suggest hypothetical neural processes in which the four primaries are arranged in opposing pairs. One **opponent process** would signal the presence of red or green, and a separate process would signal blue or yellow. An example of such a process would be a single neuron whose activity rate increased with the presence of one color (red) and decreased in the presence of its opponent color (green). Because the cell's activity cannot increase and decrease simultaneously, one could never have a reddish green. A different opponent-process cell might respond similarly to blue and yellow. A third unit was suggested to account for brightness perception. This was called a *black-white opponent process*, after the fact that black and white are treated psychologically as if they are "pure colors" (see Quinn, Wooten, & Ludman, 1985). But we need not limit the discussion to speculation based on color appearances alone because physiological evidence bears directly on the issue of opponent-process coding of color information.

Physiological Basis of Opponent-Process Theory When Hering first suggested an opponent-process mechanism for the neural encoding of hue information, there was no physiological evidence to support such a speculation. Perhaps the single most important finding of 20th-century sensory physiology was that neural responses are subject to both excitatory and inhibitory influences caused by interaction between neighboring units. We introduced several such systems in Chapters 3 and 4. In fact, in Chapter 4 you saw that many brightness phenomena can be explained by the presence of a *spatially* opponent mechanism on the retina, where excitation in one region might cause inhibition in another. If we could also find *spectrally* opponent organization, where stimulation by one wavelength of light causes excitation in a neuron and stimulation by a wavelength in another region of the spectrum causes inhibition of that cell's neural response, then we would have a physiological unit that corresponds to the mechanism postulated by Hering.

The first evidence that different wavelengths of light could cause opponent effects in neural response was reported by Svaetichin (1956), who inserted an electrode into the cell layers of the retina of the goldfish. When he recorded the responses to light transmitted by the horizontal cells (units at the first cellular layer beyond the cones, as

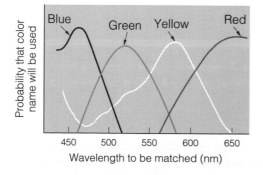

FIGURE 5-15 The relationship between color names and light wavelengths.

described in Chapter 3), he found that responses varied depending on the wavelength of the light reaching the cones. These neural responses were not in the form of the typical action potential found in most neurons but, rather, were graded shifts in the electrical polarization of the cells. Svaetichin found not only that the strength of response varied as the wavelength changed but also, more important, that the electrical sign of the response was different for long and short wavelengths.

Figure 5-16 shows the pattern of responses recorded by Svaetichin and MacNichol (1958). Notice that the spectral sensitivities of the first two units are exactly what we would need for a blue-yellow cell and a red-green cell. For instance, the cell marked *red-green* would respond with a large positive signal if the unit were stimulated with a long-wavelength light (around 675 nm). This positive response could signal red. If the unit were stimulated with a greenish hue (around 500 nm), it would give its peak negative response, thus signaling the presence of green. If we simultaneously stimulated this unit with both a red and a green stimulus, the positive and negative responses would cancel each other and no signal would result. Thus, red and green oppose each other, and the same unit can never simultaneously signal both red and green. Such graded potentials are usually called **S potentials** after their discoverer, Svaetichin. Also notice that there is another form of cellular response shown in the figure; it is marked *luminance*. This type of cell responds to the intensity of the light regardless of the wavelength and thus could be the basis for the black-white response hypothesized by Hering.

When we reach the level of the retinal ganglion cells, there is clearly an opponent-process coding. In addition, there is a spatial distribution to these responses that is similar to the center-surround organization of receptive fields we discussed in Chapter 3 (Boynton, 1979; De Monasterio, 1978). Suppose we shine a tiny red spot on the eye while recording from a retinal ganglion cell. In some cases, as the size of the spot increases, the vigorousness of the neural response increases up to some point. After that, further increases in the size of the red spot have no further influence on the cell's response. Notice that this is very different from the type of response seen when white light is used (as in Chapters 3 and 4),

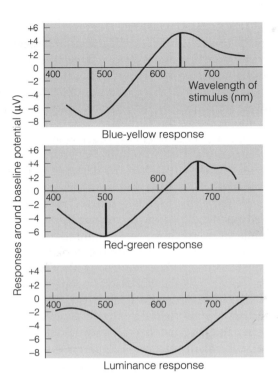

FIGURE 5-16   Graded response of retinal cells to various wavelengths of light (based on Svaetichin & MacNichol, 1958).

where increasing the size of the spot starts to produce a reduction of response rate as it begins to enter the inhibitory region of the receptive field. If we repeat the experiment with a green spot, we find that the cell appears unresponsive when the green spot is in the center of the receptive field. However, as the spot becomes larger or as it is moved into the surround field, the resting level of activity is reduced. Thus, we have a cell that has the property of being excited by red and inhibited by green if the stimulus is the appropriate size and in the appropriate location on the retina. Of course, an equal number of cells with the opposite organization (green excitatory center, red inhibitory surround), plus cells in which the centers are inhibitory and the surrounds are excitatory, are also found. The visual system, after having come on a particular organizational scheme, seems to like to exhaust all possible combinations (see Gouras & Zrenner, 1981; Jacobs, 1986).

Farther along in the visual system at the lateral geniculate nucleus, this particular arrangement can easily produce cells that generate a spectrally opponent signal with appropriate stimulus arrangements. DeValois and DeValois (1980) found that neurons in the lateral geniculate of monkeys are also color coded, similar to the color-coded retinal ganglion cells. These units showed a resting level of activity (in terms of neural responses per unit time) even in the absence of any light stimulation. When the eye was stimulated by large spots of light, the response pattern changed. Some cells responded more vigorously when the eye was stimulated with short wavelengths of light and decreased their response rate below their spontaneous (dark) activity level for long wavelengths of light. Other cells acted in exactly an opposite manner. As with the S potentials, two different classes of cells were reported. Each had different patterns of response as a function of wavelength, similar to what is needed for a red-green cell and a blue-yellow cell. Because the lateral geniculate receives its input directly from the retinal ganglion cells, this is exactly the pattern of results that we would expect. Thus, returning to our example, if we have a red excitatory center in a receptive field, we should get increased response for a large-area red light, whereas the green inhibitory surround would completely ignore its presence. Conversely, a large green spot would cause an inhibitory response and be ignored by the red excitatory center, and so forth.

Typical responses from lateral geniculate cells can be seen in Figure 5-17. There are three cell types. One responds differentially to short and moderately long wavelengths (blue-yellow), one responds differentially to moderately short and long wavelengths (red-green), and one does not show different opponent processing but, rather, responds simply to the amount of luminance reaching the eye. The spectrally tuned cells code both chromatic and spatial information in the responses. This means that whether a given wavelength will produce an increase or a decrease in neural response may also vary as the spatial position of the stimulus spot is varied within the receptive field of the cell.

How can a four-primary, opponent-process (or "push-pull") system exist when we already have provided physiological and psychophysical

evidence indicating that the retina operates with a three-color pigment system? Hurvich and Jameson (1974) suggested a *neural wiring diagram* that indicates the way in which cones, each containing only one of three pigments, could produce opponent responses at the postretinal level. An example of how such a wiring diagram might work is shown in Figure 5-18. It requires only that certain cones excite cells farther along in the system and that other cones inhibit the response rates of those cells. Engineers hit on a similar system when they designed color television transmission. The color in the original scene is first analyzed into its red, green, and blue components by the camera and then transformed into two color-difference (or opponent-process) signals (plus an intensity signal). After reception at their distant location, the signals are reconverted into red, green, and blue signals by the television set. This technique was selected because it requires considerably less information

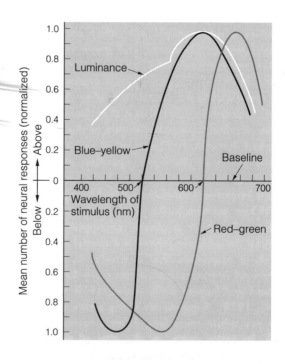

FIGURE 5-17   The neural response rate for cells in the lateral geniculate relative to their resting response rate, for stimulation by lights of different wavelengths (based on DeValois & DeValois, 1975).

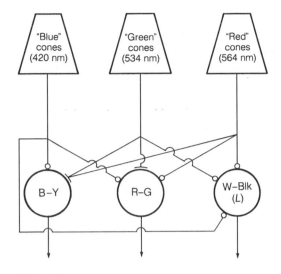

FIGURE 5-18   Schematic diagram indicating how a three-pigment system might be connected to produce opponent-process neural responses. The lines represent the connections. The round and the flat connections differ in that one is excitatory and the other is inhibitory (which is which is arbitrary). Numbers indicate the wavelength of maximum sensitivity.

to be transmitted through each channel, thus providing good fidelity and increased economy. Perhaps similar considerations underlie the organization of our visual systems.

Color Channels and Cortical Coding

There has been a recent explosion of knowledge about how color information is encoded in the nervous system. Let us begin with the lateral geniculate, where the opponent-process color cells are found. As we indicated in Chapter 3, the lateral geniculate is composed of six well-defined layers (three receiving input from each eye). These layers can be subdivided on the basis of the size of cells in each. The upper four tiers are small cells and hence are called the **parvocellular** layers (from the Latin *parvo* meaning "small"), as opposed to the bottom two tiers, which are called the **magnocellular** layers (from the Latin *magno* meaning "large").

The opponent color cells, which actually make up about 90% of the cells in the geniculostriate system, seem to be concentrated in the four parvocellular layers (Schiller & Logothetis, 1990). This has led to the hypothesis that we are dealing with two separate channels of visual information: the parvocellular channel, which carries color information, and the magnocellular channel, which carries brightness information (Livingstone & Hubel, 1988; Shapley, 1990).

As we saw in Chapter 3, the separation of color and brightness channels continues on up through the cortex. New physiological techniques have allowed us to study the organization of color processing in the brain. For example, one staining technique has shown that the distribution of color-sensitive neurons in the primary visual cortex (V1) is not uniform; rather, there are patches of such neurons, which show up when stained as dark, slightly irregular oval regions, each about 0.2 mm in diameter. These regions, given the unsophisticated name of **blobs** by researchers, are shown in Figure 5-19. Many of the color-coded cells from the parvocellular channel have connections in the blobs of V1 (Zrenner, Abramov, Akita, Cowey, Livingstone, & Valberg, 1990), whereas the regions between the blobs (**interblobs**) receive parvocellular and magnocellular inputs that are concerned with brightness, form, motion, and other information that is not color related (Tootell, Silverman, Hamilton, DeValois, & Switkes, 1988).

If we use an electrode to record from the cells in a cortical blob, we find the usual opponent process that involves an increase in response when the eye is stimulated with some colors and a decrease in response when stimulated with others. Once again, there is a spatial factor in this response. For example, stimulating the center of the cell's receptive field with red light would cause the cell to increase its activity, whereas stimulating the surrounding with green light would cause the cell to decrease its activity. Cells in the blob regions have generally circular receptive fields and thus are not very sensitive to differences in edge orientation. They are also not very sensitive to motion signals (Shapley, 1990).

In Layer 4 of V1 in the cortex and in Area V4 of the extrastriate cortex, there are cells that have a *double* opponent organization. Such a cell might increase its activity when the center of its receptive field is stimulated with red light but actually decrease its firing when the surround is stimulated

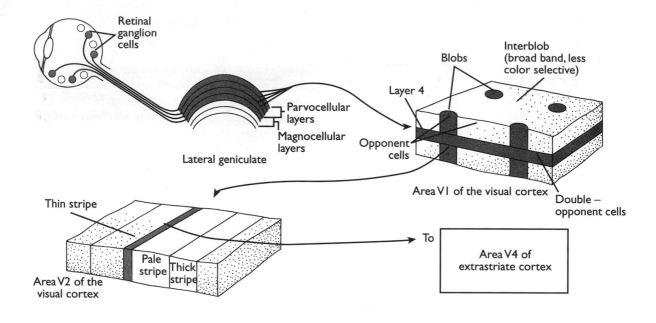

FIGURE 5-19   The major color channel in the visual system is part of the parvocellular system and is shown here, beginning with the eye, passing through the lateral geniculate and then through Cortical Regions V1 and V2.

with red light. The opposite organization is seen for responses to green light in the same cell, with a green spot on the center of the receptive field producing a decrease in response and a green spot on the surround producing an increase in firing (Michael, 1985). A diagram of both a simple opponent-process cell and a double opponent-process cell is given in Figure 5-20.

The most important feature of the double opponent arrangement is that the cell is responsive to the *difference in wavelength* between light in the center and light in the surround of its receptive field. This means that such a cell would signal the same level of activity, for example, regardless of whether the center was stimulated by red and the surround by gray or the center was stimulated by gray and the surround by green, provided that the red-green difference was equivalent in the two cases. Such a cell is ideally suited to being sensitive to the color differences between surfaces, even though the surfaces are both illuminated by light of yet another wavelength. This is exactly what is required for us to be able to see colors as the same under different illumination conditions, such as those introduced by shadowing, colored

filters such as sunglasses, and unusual lighting. We will take up this topic of *color constancy* again in Chapter 11.

The separation of color processing from other visual attributes in the visual cortex continues up through higher levels, with the color-blind magnocellular channel ending up in a different place than does the color-coded parvocellular channel. In area V2, the organization shifts to "stripes" (this term is again based on the way in which regions accept various stains). The color-only neurons concentrate into what appears as dark *thin stripes;* the color-blind magnocellular inputs go into dark *thick stripes;* whereas mixed inputs form wide *pale stripes* (see Figure 5-19).

Beyond the V1–V2 complex, there is growing evidence for a specialized color processing center in Area V4, as we described in Chapter 3. This evidence includes *positron emission tomography* (PET), which measures blood flow from increased metabolic activity in the cerebral cortex, in studies of humans viewing colored images (Lueck, Zeki, Friston, Deiber, Cope, Cunningham, Lammertsma, Kennard, & Frackowiak, 1989) and reports of patients who have sustained injuries to the temporal

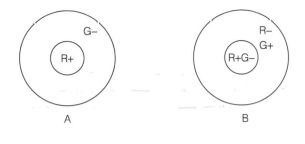

A   B

FIGURE 5-20   Receptive fields of typical color-opponent (A) and double-opponent (B) cells, recorded in the cortex.

region of the brain (near V4) and who have as a result lost the ability to discriminate colors, although they are still sensitive to differences in brightness (e.g., Heywood, Wilson, & Cowey, 1987).

Although our knowledge about the neural coding of colors is increasing, there are still some obvious puzzles left to be solved. One deals with the appearance of **subjective colors.** These are perceived colors, in the absence of the appropriate wavelengths of light, that can be made to appear in certain flickering black-and-white displays (Festinger, Allyn, & White, 1971; Jarvis, 1977; Piggins, Kingham, & Holmes, 1972). The appearance of these colors seems to be more consistent with some sort of neural Morse code carrying color information than with the spatial opponent-process system, which contemporary physiological data seem to support (Young, 1977). Because of this inconsistency, subjective colors remain a puzzle. A procedure for creating subjective colors for yourself is shown in Demonstration Box 5-4. It is interesting to note that people who show color defects for real colors also show the same color defects for subjective colors (White, Lockhead, & Evans, 1977).

COLOR PERCEPTION

Although subjective colors baffle us at the moment, they do demonstrate that the wavelengths of light that are present are not the only factors that determine our perception of hue. A number of other factors, such as stimulus intensity and duration, as well as the characteristics of surrounding stimuli, can alter the perceived color.

Intensity and Duration

Both physiological and psychophysical evidence suggest that color information and brightness information are carried by different visual channels (Bowen, 1981; Boynton, 1988; Favreau & Cavanagh, 1981). Nonetheless, it is also clear that the perception of hue may be affected by the intensity of the stimulus (e.g., Emmerson & Ross, 1986). If intensity levels are low, only rods will be active and no color will be seen. But even beyond the cone threshold the perceived hue of a stimulus will change depending on the stimulus intensity. Specifically, if we increase the intensity of red or yellow-green stimuli, they not only appear brighter but also begin to take on a more yellow hue. Similarly, blue-greens and violets begin to appear bluer when the intensity is increased. This phenomenon is called the **Bezold-Brucke effect,** in honor of its two discoverers. It is quite easy to demonstrate, as is shown in Demonstration Box 5-5. Some researchers believe that the Bezold-Brucke effect comes about because the red-green opponent-process cells are slightly more sensitive than the blue-yellow cells (Coren & Keith, 1970; Nagy, 1980). Thus, we can discriminate between red and green at lower intensity levels. Because the blue-yellow units become active only at higher intensity levels, hues may tend to be dominated by these colors when stimuli are bright (Hurvich, 1981).

Prolonged exposure to colored stimuli also produces a shift in the perception of hue. For instance, if you viewed the world through a deep red filter for a sufficient period of time, you would find that when the filter was removed the world would take on a blue-green tint. This fatiguing of a specific color response is called **chromatic adaptation.** It is believed that these adaptation effects are due either to selective bleaching of one particular photopigment or to fatigue of one aspect of the neural response of an opponent-process system (e.g., Vimal, Pokorny, & Smith, 1987). Imagine looking through a red filter for a long period of time. The red-catching pigment becomes bleached, or the red response in the red-green opponent-process cells becomes fatigued. Now, when you view a white surface, the absence of red pigment (or the weakness of the red response) causes the blue and green systems to account for a greater proportion of the total activity. This gives the white a cyan

DEMONSTRATION BOX 5-4
Subjective Colors

You have already encountered subjective colors in Demonstration Box 1-2, where colors appeared in a stationary stimulus. A more powerful set of subjective colors, produced by flickering black-and-white patterns, began as a toy invented by C. E. Benham in 1894. It was painted on a top and meant to be spun; hence the pattern is often referred to as **Benham's top.** The pattern is shown in the figure. Cut out this pattern (or carefully reproduce it), and mount it on a piece of thin cardboard. Punch a hole in the marked center region, and insert a nail or a round pencil. Now spin the pattern as shown. Colors should appear when the pattern is spun at a moderate speed. If you are spinning it clockwise, the inner bands should be slightly red, the next yellow, then green, and the last blue or violet. The order of the colors should reverse if you spin the pattern counterclockwise. The color effects arise because of the specific patterns of flickering white and black set up by each band. These patterns mimic the flashing on-and-off light patterns used to study subjective colors in a laboratory setting.

If you alter the adaptive state of your eye by staring at a white surface for a minute, you will notice that the perceived colors on each line will be different (Karvellas, Pokorny, Smith, & Tanczos, 1979).

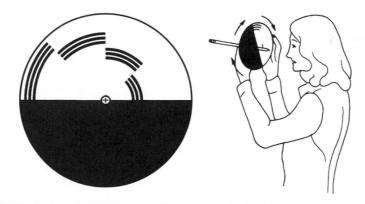

(blue-green) tint. When such fatigue effects due to prolonged stimulation are localized to only one region of the retina, they are called afterimages. Demonstration Box 5-6 provides a stimulus for the production of color afterimages. You will notice when performing this demonstration that the hue of the afterimage tends to be a complementary hue of the stimulus producing the afterimage.

Spatial Interactions

In Chapter 4 you learned that the brightness of a stimulus can be affected by the intensity of adjacent stimuli. The general nature of the interaction is inhibitory, so a bright surround makes a central area appear dim. Inhibitory interactions between adjacent color systems can also occur, and they result in hue shifts. The phenomenon is called simultaneous color contrast. Consider Color Plate 3. Notice that this figure has four brightly colored patches, each of which surrounds a small central square. The square on the red patch appears to be slightly green, and that on the green appears to be slightly red. The square on the blue patch appears to be slightly yellow, and that on the yellow patch appears to be slightly blue. However, each square is exactly the same gray. You might be able to increase the strength of this effect by viewing Color Plate 3 through a sheet of tracing paper or thin tissue.

DEMONSTRATION BOX 5-5
The Bezold-Brucke Effect

For this demonstration you will need three pieces of colored cellophane, glass, or celluloid to serve as color filters. One should be red, the other green, and the last yellow. Take a white sheet of paper that is brightly illuminated with room lighting, and cast a shadow over one half of the paper. Looking through the red filter, you will notice that the hue of the red seen on the bright half of the paper is noticeably yellower than the hue seen on the shadowed portion. When you peer through the green filter, you should experience the same effect. However, looking through a yellow filter should not cause an apparent change in hue. Thus, the brighter you make a red or a green, the more yellow it

will appear. This is a demonstration of the hue shift, associated with increasing stimulus intensity, called the Bezold-Brucke effect.

Another way to see this effect is simply to look at an incandescent lightbulb (60–100 W) through the red or green filter. You will notice that the lightbulb appears to be yellow, despite the presence of the filter. Because the red filter allows only the long (red) wavelengths of light to pass and the green allows only the middle (green) wavelengths through, no yellow is reaching your eye. The yellow appearance of the bulb is caused by the Bezold-Brucke hue shift that occurs when the intensity of the stimulus is high.

Jameson and Hurvich (1964) suggested that color contrast arises from mechanisms similar to those that cause brightness contrast, namely, an active retinal neuron tends to inhibit the responding of adjacent neurons. In the case of the gray square on the red background, for example, we have a situation where the red response systems exposed to the surround are highly activated. In turn, these active neurons will inhibit the red response in the neurons exposed to the central gray patch. Because the red and green responses are usually in balance, inhibition of the red response results in the emergence of the complementary, or opponent, green response in this region. A tinge of green hue is then seen in the gray. The double color opponent-process cells that we discussed earlier might play a role in this process as well. As one might expect, if this is truly an inhibitory interaction such as we observed in brightness effects, it is possible even to produce colored Mach bands (Ware & Cowan, 1987).

Contrast-induced colors act very much like real colors in their ability to produce other perceptual effects. For instance, Anstis, Rogers, and Henry (1978) induced very strong contrast colors on surrounded gray patches (as in Color Plate 3) and found that observers developed negative afterimages to the contrast colors, just as though they had been viewing real colors!

Age and Physical Condition

An individual may have normal color vision when tested at one stage in the life span but may show color discrimination defects when tested at a later stage. Color vision is present in newborn infants; however, it changes over the life span, and these changes can be quite dramatic in old age. (Adams & Courage, 1994; Mercer, Courage, & Adams, 1991). Perhaps this is because the crystalline lens of the eye grows more yellow as we age; hence we look through a gradually darkening yellow filter (Coren, 1987; Coren & Girgus, 1972a). Other effects, such as the loss of cone pigment with age (Kilbride, Hutman, Fishman, & Read, 1986), may also account for changes in color vision. Generally speaking, aging seems to bring about a faster deterioration of blue vision (Schefrin & Werner, 1990; Verriest, 1974). Most individuals are unaware of such changes because the onset is quite slow; however, the effect gradually accumulates. Because the perception of hue is subjective, we seldom have the opportunity to assess whether our hue perception agrees with that of others. Does your red appear to be the same as that of your friends? Clearly, this is only answerable with careful comparisons in a laboratory.

Physical conditions can also result in losses in the ability to discriminate colors. Such acquired

---

DEMONSTRATION BOX 5-6
Color Afterimages

You can easily demonstrate negative or complementary color afterimages using Color Plate 7. Here you see four square patches of color: red, green, blue, and yellow. Notice the black *x* in the middle of this pattern. Stare at the black *x* for about 2 min while keeping the plate under reasonably bright illumination. At the end of this period, transfer your gaze to the black *x* to the right of the figure. You should see a pattern of colored squares that is the exact complement of the pattern originally viewed. Where the red patch was, you will see green; where the green patch was, you will see red; where the blue patch was, you will see yellow; and where the yellow patch was, you will see blue. These are the complementary color afterimages caused by the fatiguing of the various color responses during the time you were staring at the color patches.

---

color vision losses are called **dyschromatopsias.** There are several diseases or physical conditions that lead to such dyschromatopsias. One typical cause for loss of color vision is exposure to certain solvents and neurotoxins (Braun & Daigneault, 1989; Mergler, Bowler, & Cone, 1990). As in the case of aging, the most commonly observed losses are for sensitivity to blue (see Pokorny & Smith, 1986). These blue losses are observed in diabetics (Lakowski, Aspinall, & Kinnear, 1972), individuals with glaucoma (Lakowski & Drance, 1979), individuals with Parkinson's disease (Haug & Kolle, 1995), and alcoholics (Reynolds, 1979). These color vision losses can be aggravated by a number of factors. For instance, diabetic women who take oral contraceptives show significantly greater discrimination losses in the blue range (Lakowski & Morton, 1977). Acquired problems with the red-green system are rarer and usually are associated with cone degeneration or optic nerve diseases (Pinkers & Marre, 1983).

Cognitive Factors in Color Perception

Although color is a basic sensory experience, there are also nonsensory factors that affect the perceived color of an object. In addition, color may interact with other nonperceptual behaviors.

Memory for Color   The remembered color of familiar objects often differs from the objects' actual color. When observers are shown color samples and later asked to match them from an array of colored chips, systematic errors are made. Observers tend to pick chips of greater brightness when asked to remember bright colors and of greater darkness when asked to remember dark colors (Bartleson, 1960; Newhall, Burnham, & Clark, 1957). When asked to remember and match colors of familiar objects with characteristic hues, we remember apples or tomatoes as being more red than the actual objects, bananas are more yellow in memory than in the bunch, and grass is greener than it is on the lawn. Because of this memory effect, many film manufacturers have chosen to modify the spectral reproduction ability of color film so that the reproduced colors are richer than they are in nature. Because television engineers have not made a similar correction, color memory distortions may account for part of our feeling that the picture reproduced on a color television set is an unfaithful reproduction of real color.

Memory color effects tend to creep into certain other matching tasks. For instance, if you are asked to match the color of a Valentine's Day heart or an apple, both of which have been cut out of orange paper, you will match them with a redder hue than you would use to match an oval or a triangle cut out of the same material. A banana-shaped figure, or one labeled *lemon*, is matched with a yellower hue. It seems as if the remembered color blends with the observed stimulus, altering the percept toward the ideal, or prototypical, color of an object (Bruner, Postman, & Rodrigues, 1951; Delk & Fillenbaum, 1965; Harper, 1953; White & Montgomery, 1976). The color you remember is probably "better" than the color that is present;

however, the color you see now may be tinged by your memory's hue.

There is an interesting color phenomenon that some investigators believe is also due to a learning or memory type of process, called the McCollough effect, which is shown in Demonstration Box 5-7.

Culture and Color   As we noted earlier, an English speaker is content to describe hue differences using four basic categories: red, yellow, green, and blue. This is not the case for many other languages, some of which have no separate names for green and blue or red and yellow. There are some languages that distinguish only red as a separate color and have no names for the other hues. It is often argued that there is an interaction between language and perception and that when separate names for separate sensory experiences exist, these labels make discriminations easier. In other words, the Lakuti tribe, whose members have only a single term for blue and green, may see the two colors as being more similar to each other than would English speakers, who have separate words for these stimuli (Whorf, 1956).

Actually, when the ability of individuals to match, discriminate, or reproduce colors (rather than just to name colors) is measured directly, the picture changes. It seems as if the number of color names in a language does *not* affect the ability to make such discriminations (Berlin & Kay, 1969; Bornstein, 1973; Bornstein, 1975). These findings indicate the danger, in the absence of perceptual measurements, of assuming that language usage directly reflects perceptual abilities.

On the other hand, there is some suggestion that the pattern of development of language terms in any culture may represent a record of the actual evolutionary development of the color-perceiving ability of humans (e.g., Robertson, 1967). Thus, most languages develop color word usage in the same order, with *black*, *white*, and *red* appearing first and *pink*, *purple*, *orange*, and *gray* last. Mc-Manus (1997) recently looked into the frequency of use of the 11 English basic color words in over a half-million cases. These were from records found in eight large computerized data banks covering science and literature. He found that frequency of use of color words in English follows this same pattern, with *black*, *white*, and *red* used the most and *pink*, *purple*, *orange*, and *blue* the least. Thus,

although color labels may not determine how we see colors today, they may well contain information about how the categories that we use in color recognition tasks came about.

Color Impressions   Color does more than provide us with additional information about stimuli; it has emotional consequences (Hamid & Newport, 1989). It delights and depresses. It makes humans feel warm or cold, tense or relaxed. For instance, a manufacturer of detergent found that the color of the detergent box made a difference in how the user evaluated the strength of the detergent (Kupchella, 1976). Other data suggest that the color of pills or drug capsules may affect whether patients will take prescribed medications (Coffield & Buckalew, 1988). Apparently medications that are black, gray, tan, or brown are rejected, whereas blues, reds, and yellows are preferred colors.

Color can even produce sensory impressions that are characteristic of other senses. It is almost universal to call the short-wavelength (blue) colors "cool," whereas the longer wavelengths (yellow) tend to be called "warm." Perhaps these labels arise because the cool of the night is first broken by the red of the dawn, with midday characterized by the yellow of sunlight and warmth. As the yellow begins to disappear and the blue of twilight begins to predominate, temperatures again grow cool. Many years and many generations of such an association might stamp this warm-cool relationship into our languages. In an era when the conservation of energy is important, it is interesting to note that people will turn a heat control to a higher setting in a blue room than they will in a yellow room. It is as if they are trying to compensate thermally for the coolness that has been visually induced (Boynton, 1971). Similarly, Alexander and Shansky (1976) have shown that dark saturated colors are perceived as being associated with a greater sensation of "weight" or "heaviness." There is even some suggestion that the color of a substance can affect how it appears to smell to us (Gilbert & Martin, 1996; Zellner & Kautz, 1990). All of these findings emphasize that color is a psychological achievement, not simply a direct effect of the physical variation of wavelengths of light. If you still doubt this statement, it will probably be

---

DEMONSTRATION BOX 5-7
The McCollough Effect

The idea behind this demonstration is that, through repeated exposure to colored lines of a particular orientation, we develop a color aftereffect that is different for lines of different orientation. Some investigators feel that this process comes about because, with continued inspection, the cortical cells that are tuned to a particular combination of stimuli become fatigued. Thus, when we subsequently inspect a set of noncolored stimuli at the same orientation, these cells respond more weakly, which gives us color aftereffects (e.g., Houck & Hoffman, 1986). The particular color seen is usually the complement to the fatigued color. Thus, for instance, if you fatigue the green response, normally white light will appear tinged with red; fatigue of the blue response will produce a yellow aftereffect; and so forth.

Several alternate explanations of the McCollough effect have been offered (e.g., Day & Webster, 1989; Dodwell & Humphrey, 1990). One interesting possibility is based on learning effects similar to Pavlov's classical conditioning

(Allan & Siegel, 1986; Skowbo, 1984; Sloane, Ost, Etheredge, & Henderlite, 1989). In this process the grid of lines serves as the conditioned stimulus (CS) and the color as the unconditioned stimulus (UCS) that produces the unconditioned response (UR—which might be seeing red bars). The pairing over time produces a conditioned color response (CR) that is the opposite of the UR (in this case, seeing green bars) that is evoked when a lined grid is presented by itself. Such a learning mechanism could explain why, under appropriate conditions, the color aftereffect may last for hours, days, or even weeks (Wolfe & O'Connell, 1986).

To see the effect for yourself, first notice that the figure in this box is completely achromatic. Now turn to Color Plate 6 and note the two colored grids, one containing vertical green lines and the other horizontal red lines. To selectively condition your visual system, simply look at the green grid for about 5 sec, and then shift your gaze to the red grid for another 5 sec. Continue this alternation for about 2 or 3 min.

---

instructive to turn back to Demonstration Box 1-3 (p. 7) or Demonstration Box 5-4 in this chapter to see colors develop in your mind where no physical variations in wavelength exist.

CHAPTER SUMMARY

By passing light through a glass prism to create a spectrum, Sir Isaac Newton was able to show that different wavelengths of light correspond to different color sensations. Over the visible range between 360 nm and 760 nm, colors vary, with the shorter wavelengths appearing as blue and the longer wavelengths as red. Color appearance varies in three dimensions and can be described by the **color spindle** or **color solid:** (1) **hue,** the nameable aspect of color (e.g., red or green, etc.), (2) **brightness,** and (3) **saturation,** which corre-

sponds to **purity,** with **monochromatic** stimuli being the most saturated. **Additive color mixtures** result from the addition of light of one wavelength to light of another (e.g., projection of a green light on top of a red light on a screen to produce yellow). Only three color **primaries** (red, green, and blue) in the mixture are needed to match all other colors, with white resulting from the mixture of all three. **Subtractive color mixtures** result from mixing pigments, which subtract or absorb light of various wavelengths (e.g., the mixture of yellow and blue pigments to produce green). The three subtractive-mixture primaries are magenta, yellow, and cyan, with black resulting from the mixture of all three. **Metameric colors** are colors that appear the same but have different wavelength compositions. Mixture colors are always less saturated than monochromatic colors. **Complementary colors** when mixed produce an

Then look back at the figure in this box, and you will find that it appears to be colored: The vertical white bars appear reddish, and the horizontal bars appear greenish. Notice also that turning the book sideways, or tilting your head so the orientation of the lines changes on your retina, will change the colors of the lines.

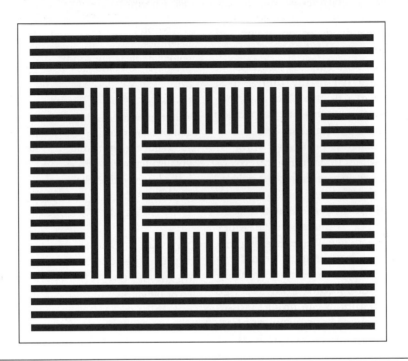

achromatic gray. The **CIE chromaticity space** is a standard system used to describe colors. It gives **tristimulus values,** which are coordinates in the color space representing the proportion of the three primary colors that produce that color appearance, where x and y represent hue and z represents brightness. **Red-green-blue** (or simply **RGB) space** is a means of representing colors on a video screen based on the proportions of the red, green, and blue signals emitted by the electron guns that activate screen pixels.

Trichromatic color theory (originally postulated by Young & Helmholtz) maintains that color is encoded by three different cones, selectively absorbing either short, medium, or long wavelengths of light. This theory was initially inferred from color mixture data and from evidence obtained from **color-blind** individuals. Color blindness is determined genetically by a location on the X chromosome and is 16 times more likely in males. In addition to **monochromats,** who have no color discrimination, there are three forms of color blindness: (1) **protanopia** (loss of long-wavelength vision), (2) **deuteranopia** (loss of middle-wavelength vision), and (3) **tritanopia** (loss of short-wavelength vision). More recently, recording the light absorption of single cones with a **microspectrophotometer** has confirmed that there are three cone types. Color-sensitive cones vary in density across the retina, with the fovea being relatively blue blind and color responsiveness diminishing toward the peripheral retina where cones become rarer.

The **opponent-process theory** of color vision (originally proposed by Hering) suggests that there are neural processes that signal the presence of one color by increasing activity and of an opposing color by decreasing activity. The opponent pairs are red-green and blue-yellow. Cells with this pattern of activity have been found at the retinal ganglion cell level and in the **parvocellular** layers of the lateral geniculate. Brightness is coded in the **magnocellular** layer. In Cortical Area V1, color information is coded by neurons located in the **blobs,** where color responses are keyed to spatial regions in the receptive fields of opponent and double opponent cells. **Interblob** neurons carry only brightness information. In Cortical Area V2, color information is carried in the thin stripes, brightness in the thick stripes, and mixed information in the pale stripes. The final steps in color processing seem to be in Cortical Area V4.

Color perception depends on several stimulus factors other than wavelength. Certain patterns of flickering lights can produce **subjective colors.** The apparent color of a stimulus also varies with intensity, as shown in the **Bezold-Brucke effect.** Prolonged viewing of a stimulus will produce **chromatic adaptation,** hence weakening the sensation and often creating **afterimages.** Colors also interact in an opponent process manner spatially, as is seen in **simultaneous color contrast.** Age and certain physical conditions can produce losses in color perception known as **dyschromatopsias.** Color perception can also be altered by learning and cognitive factors. This can be seen in the systematic distortions in memory colors and perhaps in phenomena such as the McCollough effect. In turn, color percepts can also affect other perceptual modalities, making us feel warm or cool or even affecting our emotional state.

KEY TERMS

color circle (color wheel)
hue
monochromatic
spectral colors
purity
saturation
brightness
color spindle (color solid)
color atlas
primaries
metameric colors
dominant wavelengths
additive color mixing
subtractive color mixing
complementary colors
CIE chromaticity space
tristimulus values
red-green-blue (RGB)
   space
erythrolabe
chlorolabe
cyanolabe
trichromatic theory
color blindness

monochromats
dichromats
protanopia
deuteranopia
tritanopia
anomalous trichromatism
protoanomaly
deuteranomaly
microspectrophotometer
habituation
opponent process
S potentials
parvocellular
magnocellular
blobs
interblobs
subjective colors
Bezold-Brucke effect
chromatic adaptation
afterimages
Benham's top
simultaneous color
   contrast
dyschromatopsias

The Auditory System

CHAPTER 6

It is one of those strange twists of history that while studying the physiology of the ear in order to help the deaf, Alexander Graham Bell developed the telephone. Modern scientists are still studying auditory physiology, and others are realizing Bell's dream by developing implanted prostheses that allow the deaf to hear again. In this chapter we will join these workers in a fascinating journey down the ear canal to explore the physiological structures that play a role in our perception of sounds in the world. In doing this we will get a chance to look at a mechanical marvel, the cochlea, which fills a space of only 2 cubic cm but has over 1 million moving parts (Hudspeth, 1985).

SOUND

Sound is a mechanical pressure wave in a medium, such as air or water. When sound is very intense, such as at a rock concert, you can actually feel with your skin the amplified mechanical pulsations being transmitted through the air, especially those from the bass instruments, which may cause the floor, your seat, and your body to vibrate in resonance with them. Think about what happens when the bass guitarist plucks a guitar string, causing a sound. The string vibrates, moving rapidly back and forth in space. This movement causes the strand of steel to collide with the air molecules

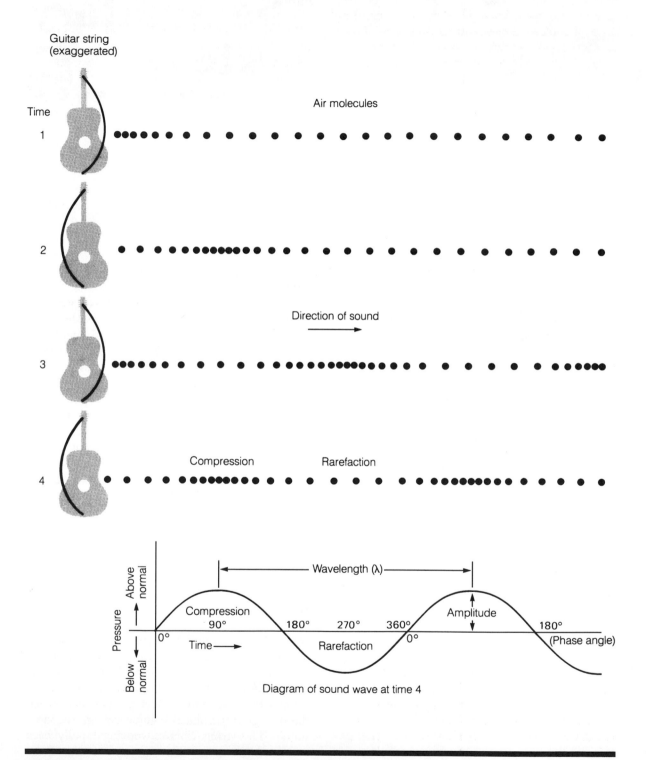

FIGURE 6-1   The nature and description of a simple sound wave in air.

around it. These molecules in turn collide with others, causing air *compression* as the string moves forward and *rarefaction* as it moves back. The result is a **wave** of mechanical energy, as shown in Figure 6-1, which is then picked up by a microphone, amplified electrically, and sent out to your ears.

Sound waves are alternations of rarefaction and compression of the elastic medium (e.g., water, air, or walls) in which they travel and are created by rapid movements of a source in mechanical contact with it. The medium acquires some of the movement energy of the source and transfers it to other locations by means of collisions between the molecules of the medium. Sound waves can be transmitted for great distances, although the individual molecules of the medium vibrate only over very small distances. The interactions of molecules, of course, are not perfectly efficient in transferring the original collision energy, so the sound wave loses energy as it moves away from the source. Consequently, its ability to move or vibrate other objects, such as our eardrums, is less the farther they are from the source. Because sound involves the vibration of parts of the medium through which it travels, it cannot pass through a vacuum. The necessity of a medium for the existence and propagation of sound waves was demonstrated by Robert Boyle in 1660. He suspended his watch by a thread in a jar and observed that its ticking sound gradually faded to inaudibility as he pumped the air out of the jar.

A Simple Sound Wave

The simplest sound wave is what trigonometry calls a *sine* wave. For such a sound wave in air, when we plot air pressure as it varies over time we get the picture shown in the lower part of Figure 6-1. The **wavelength** (represented by the Greek letter λ named *lambda*) is the distance from one peak of the wave to the next, representing a single **cycle.** The **frequency** (f) of the wave is the number of cycles the wave is able to complete in one second. Frequency is expressed in **Hertz** (Hz), named after the German physicist Heinrich R. Hertz. One Hertz is equivalent to one **cycle per second.** The frequency of a simple sound wave is the most important (but not the only) determinant

of the psychological dimension of pitch. Just as in music, *pitch* refers to whether we are experiencing a high or a low note or tone. The range of frequencies that seem to have pitch for people with normal hearing is from about 20 Hz to 20,000 Hz. Sounds below 20 Hz are experienced as vibration, whereas sounds above 20,000 Hz are not heard at all except by young children.

The **pressure amplitude** is the change in pressure in any medium produced by the sound wave as compared to the normal undisturbed pressure. For the simplest sound wave in air, the pressure amplitude is the maximum amount by which the wave causes the air pressure (force per unit area expressed as dynes/cm^2) to differ from normal atmospheric pressure (about 1,000,000 dynes/cm^2 at sea level). The maximum *pressure variation* the human ear can tolerate is about 280 dynes/cm^2 above or below atmospheric pressure, whereas the minimum pressure variation detectable is about 0.0002 dynes/cm^2. For a sound wave with pressure amplitude equal to 0.0002 dynes/cm^2, the air molecules are displaced by about 0.0000000001 cm, which is about 1/10 the diameter of the average air molecule. Obviously the ear is an extremely sensitive organ with a broad response range.

In order to conveniently express this wide range of sound sensitivity, we use a special unit of measurement called the **Bel** (which was named in honor of Alexander Graham Bell). In this measure we represent the sound pressure amplitude as the number of powers of 10 (the logarithm) by which it exceeds some reference level of pressure. Because the Bel is a rather large unit relative to normal hearing levels, we typically use the **decibel** (dB), which is 1/10 of a Bel, as indicated by the prefix *deci*. We call this measure the **sound pressure level.** The formula for sound pressure level (in dB) is

$$\text{number of dB} = 20 \log (P/P_0)$$

where P is the sound pressure amplitude we wish to express in decibels and P_0 is the standard reference level. Table 6-1 gives typical values of sound pressure levels expressed in decibels for some representative sounds. The table shows that as the measured pressure amplitude of a sound increases, loudness also increases. Sound pressure amplitude is the most important (but not the only) determinant of the psychological dimension of loudness.

Table 6-1 **Sound Pressure Levels of Various Sound Sources (P_0 = 0.0002 dyne/cm²)**

SOURCE	SOUND LEVEL (dB)
Manned spacecraft launch (from 45 m)	180
Loudest rock band on record	160
Pain threshold (approximate)	140
Large jet motor (at 22 m)	120
Loudest human shout on record	111
Heavy auto traffic	100
Conversation (at about 1 m)	60
Quiet office	40
Soft whisper	20
Threshold of hearing	0

A final psychologically important parameter of sound waves is **phase angle.** Phase angle refers to the particular part of the compression-rarefaction cycle a wave has reached at a particular instant of time. A single cycle of a sine wave is assigned 360° (as in circular motion). A sinusoidal sound wave begins with 0° at a point of 0 pressure difference, followed by the compression peak at 90°, another 0 pressure difference point at 180°, and the rarefaction "peak" at 270° (see Figure 6-1). This means that any portion of a cycle can be specified by number of degrees from 0 to 360. If two waves are at exactly the same place in their respective cycles (so that their peaks and valleys coincide), they are said to be **in phase.** If their peaks and valleys do not coincide, the two waves are **out of phase.** How much they are out of phase is expressed in terms of **relative phase,** the difference between their respective phase angles. If one wave is at its 90° point (its peak) when another wave is at its 180° point (crossing the 0 pressure-difference line), then the two waves are 90° out of phase.

Because sound waves consist of variations of mechanical pressure over time, different sound waves (patterns of pressure) that occur at the same time can interact with each other within the medium conducting them. If two waves of the same frequency are perfectly in phase (0° out of phase), their pressure changes coincide and they add to each other. When two waves of the same frequency are 180° out of phase, one reaches its minimum

when the other is reaching its maximum and they tend to subtract from each other's effects. If the two waves were of the same pressure amplitude as well, we would not be able to hear the interacting sound waves because the net pressure deviation from atmospheric would be zero. This principle is used in what is called *active noise suppression* to reduce unwanted noises. In a typical system a computer analyzes inputs from a microphone and then generates through a speaker sounds that are 180° out of phase with the unwanted sounds. The broadcast sounds cancel the noise, and it is not heard. Active noise suppression systems are currently being designed for cars, airplanes, and other noisy environments where the characteristics of the noise do not change too rapidly.

Everyday sounds are more complex than the simple sine wave sounds we have been discussing. Only a few sound sources, such as tuning forks or electronic instruments, produce "pure" sine wave sounds. Sounds produced by musical instruments, the human voice, automobiles, waterfalls, and so on have much more complex patterns of compression and rarefaction. These complexities result from the interaction of many different waves of different frequencies and phases. Complex sounds have an additional psychological property called

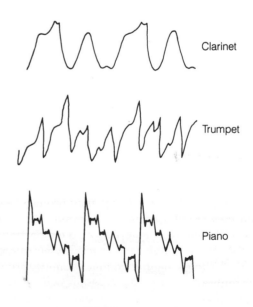

Clarinet

Trumpet

Piano

FIGURE 6-2 Complex sound waves produced by three musical instruments.

DEMONSTRATION BOX 6-1
Perception of Timbre

Perhaps the most primitive musical instrument is the human hand, used (usually in pairs) to clap rhythms. As in any musical instrument, the shape and orientation of the surrounding parts will alter the complex components of the resultant sound, hence the *timbre* that we hear. There seem to be only a few basic ways of clapping, and people have the remarkable ability to distinguish which is occurring from the sound alone (Repp, 1987). Try holding your hands in the configuration shown in Configuration A of the figure so that your hands are aligned and flat. Clap a few times, listening closely to the sound. Now hold your hands in Configuration B, with your hands oblique and slightly cupped. Clap a few times,

again listening closely to the sound. Configuration B generates more low-frequency sounds in the mixture than Configuration A. You should be able to distinguish the different claps quite clearly. You can also hear differences if the palms are crossed while clapping, if you clap with your fingers around your palm, and so forth. It might be fun to have someone else now clap while you are not looking, and see if you can approximate what his or her hand positions are. If you can, you are responding to the timbre of the sounds and performing some form of analysis of the complex sounds actually present into their constituent components, which then allows you to recognize their source.

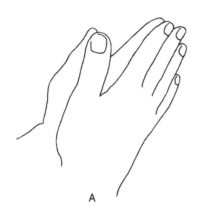

A

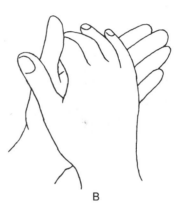

B

---

timbre (see Chapter 7 for a discussion of how this occurs). We can differentiate among the sounds of a trumpet, a clarinet, a piano, and a violin quite easily because the wave forms they produce, even when they are playing the same musical note, are quite different (see Figure 6-2). Demonstration Box 6-1 shows you how to experience our extraordinary ability to identify complex sounds through their timbres.

Complex sounds, such as those in Figure 6-2, can be described usefully by analyzing them into sets of simpler waves, which when added together produce the more complicated wave forms. This method

was invented by the French scientist Jean B. J. Fourier in the course of his studies of heat conduction. Fourier proved a mathematical theorem that states, in essence, that *any* wave form that is continuous and periodic can be represented as the sum of a set of simple sine and cosine waves with appropriate wavelengths, phases, and amplitudes. Figure 6-3 shows an example of the decomposition of a complex wave form into such a set of sine waves, called **Fourier components.** Speech sounds also may be analyzed into their Fourier components, with results that are very useful for the understanding of speech perception (see Chapter 12). In fact, the

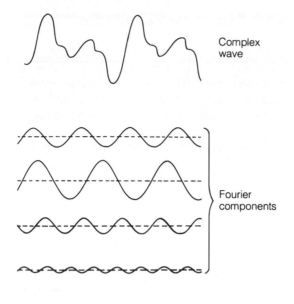

Complex wave

Fourier components

FIGURE 6-3 Fourier components (sine waves) of a complex sound wave.

cochlea of the ear performs a crude mechanical Fourier analysis on complex sounds, with different parts responding optimally to different frequency components of the sound. This fact is known as **Ohm's Acoustical Law** after the physicist George Ohm. You may demonstrate this effect for yourself using Demonstration Box 6-2.

THE STRUCTURE OF THE EAR

Evolution and the Anatomy of the Ear

The human ear is an extremely complex biological system, yet biologists have traced its origins to simple organs in quite primitive animals (Stebbins, 1980; van Bergeijk, 1967). All vertebrate ears seem to have evolved from the sense of touch. Whether primitive or advanced, they seem to be specializations of groups of cells with protruding hairs that, like the hairs on the skin of your arm, are designed to respond to mechanical stimulation. In fact, the skin can be used to demonstrate several phenomena associated with human hearing (Bekesy, 1960).

One of the first developments in the evolution of the mammalian ear was the *lateral line*. The lateral line is a row of nerve endings in the skin of fish and some amphibians that gets its name from the fact that it shows up as a visible line of contrasting color on the skin. These nerve endings are wrapped around sensory hairs that are embedded in jelly-like masses that are exposed to the surrounding water. As the water vibrates from the motions of prey, predators, or other events, the water-like jelly vibrates as well, causing the sensory hairs to bend, thus stimulating the nerve endings and signaling the vibration to the animal's brain. Detection of such vibrations is useful to such animals, especially when vision or other sensory systems cannot function well. For example, the lateral

---

DEMONSTRATION BOX 6-2
Ohm's Acoustical Law

This demonstration is done with a piano or a guitar, but if neither is available use three glasses filled with water to different heights so that they produce a fairly high note, a middle note, and a low note when tapped with a butter knife. Now have some friends strike the high, middle, and low notes simultaneously a few times. Without their telling you, have them drop out one note, sounding only two a few times, then put it back in. Notice that it is quite easy to determine which of the three

notes was added or subtracted, despite the fact that the chord formed by these notes is quite a complex sound pattern. The individual sounds do not lose their identities and can be discriminated from the others in the complex sound. With enough practice a person can learn to separate as many as six or seven different components of a complex chord or "clang." The separation of sound components by the auditory system is known as *Ohm's Acoustical Law*.

line system in one Antarctic fish is tuned very precisely to the vibrations made by the plankton it feeds on, helping the fish find prey during the 6 months of darkness the region experiences (Montgomery & MacDonald, 1987).

In addition to the lateral line system, some types of fish have primitive internal ears that work on much the same principles as do human ears. These internal ears probably evolved from a specialized, deeply sunken part of the lateral line system. This part of the lateral line developed into a primitive **labyrinth,** whose looping passages are filled with fluid. Inside the labyrinth tiny hairs protrude into the fluid and bend when the fluid moves in response to sound stimulation from the water outside. The bending of the hairs is signaled to the fish's brain by way of sensory nerves that synapse with them. In many of its elements, this system is quite similar to that found in humans, even to the composition of the fluid in the labyrinth.

Mammals, birds, and the crocodilian reptiles have a more complex labyrinth that contains a **cochlea.** The cochlea is a specialized extension of the primitive labyrinth that contains a long membrane covered with sensory cells from which (of course) tiny hairs protrude. Its name, which means "shell," is derived from its coiled snail-shell appearance in mammals.

All mammalian ears have the same basic parts, although they differ somewhat in proportions (with the elephant, of course, having one of the largest). They also differ in sensitivity. Bats, whales, and dogs have extraordinarily keen hearing over a very wide range of frequencies. The ears of mammals differ from those of birds, reptiles, and fish in that mammalian ears typically have three small bones to transmit vibrations to the labyrinth, rather than a single bone, as found in these other species. Bekesy (1960), in a series of detailed studies, established that all of these various types of ears function in a similar manner. He was able to link many of the performance differences with differences in the physical properties of the ears (such as the size of the ear canal and the length of the cochlea). Thus, the human ear, with which we will be concerned in this chapter, is a part of a large family of roughly equivalent organs. This makes it possible to extend the results of studies of other mammalian ears to the human auditory system.

Physiology of the Human Ear

We shall now follow a sound wave through the structures of the human ear. The ear can be divided into three major parts: the **outer, middle, and inner ears.** Figure 6-4 is a schematic representation of the human ear. The **pinna** is the fleshy part of the outer ear visible from the outside. Only mammals have pinnae, and they function to channel the sound waves into another part of the outer ear, the **external auditory meatus,** or *ear canal.* Pinnae also aid in the localization of sound, as you will see in the next chapter. Some mammals, such as bats and dogs, have highly mobile pinnae that allow them partially to select the direction from which sounds are received.

The sound waves that enter the ear canal move along it until they encounter the **eardrum** (or **tympanum**). The ear canal acts as a passive amplifier increasing the amplitude of certain sound frequencies through resonance. Notably in humans, sound waves with frequencies between 2,000 Hz and 7,000 Hz (which are vital for understanding speech sounds) benefit from such amplification. The eardrum vibrates in phase with the incoming sound waves, moving faster for high-frequency sounds and more slowly for low-frequency sounds. As we mentioned when discussing sound, these vibratory movements are quite small. The detailed structures of the ear canal, the eardrum, and the air chambers of the middle ear all are important in shaping the way the ear responds to sounds (Rabbitt, 1990; Stinson & Khanna, 1989).

The vibrations of the eardrum are transmitted to the transducer mechanism in the inner ear by three tiny bones *(ossicles)* in the middle ear: the **malleus** ("hammer"), the **incus** ("anvil"), and the **stapes** ("stirrup"). The stapes connects to the inner ear via a small membranous opening called the **oval window.** In some people the ossicles cannot conduct sound vibrations for various reasons, causing *conduction deafness.* Surgery may sometimes restore a vibratory connection between the eardrum and the oval window, partially relieving this condition. In addition to conducting vibrations to the oval window, the middle ear amplifies the strength of the sound-induced vibrations. Amplification is necessary because the eardrum, to which the malleus is attached, is a large, easy-to-move flap of skin, whereas the part of the inner ear that

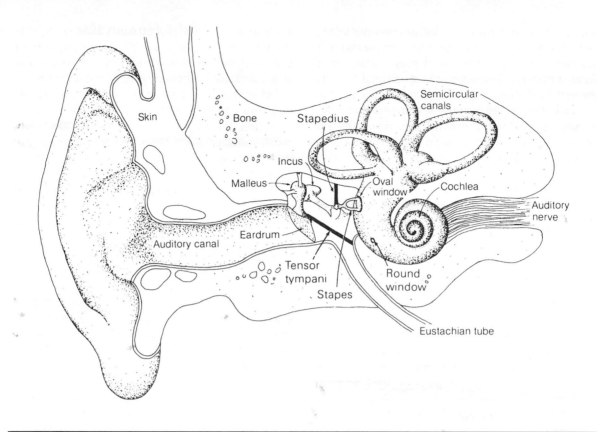

FIGURE 6-4   The human ear (based on Lindsay & Norman, 1977).

must be moved by the stapes, the oval window, is small and difficult to move because it is at the bottom of a long tube filled with fluid. The middle ear increases the pressure applied to the oval window in three ways (Pickles, 1988). First, and most important, the area of the oval window is only about ⅟₁₅ that of the vibrating area of the eardrum. From physics we know that when the same force is applied uniformly to two surfaces of different areas, the smaller surface will receive the greater force per unit area. Hence, the difference in vibrating area between the eardrum and oval window means that the pressure exerted by the vibration on the oval window will be about 15 times greater than that of the sound wave on the eardrum. The other two pressure-increasing mechanisms are more subtle. They depend on the lever action of the malleus and incus and on the way the eardrum buckles as it moves. These two processes increase the force applied by the stapes to the

oval window by decreasing its velocity of movement relative to that of the eardrum. In total, the force applied at the stapes is amplified by a factor of about 30 over that of the sound wave on the eardrum by these properties of the middle ear. This mechanical amplification allows us to hear much fainter sounds than would be possible in its absence.

Somewhat paradoxically, the middle ear can also *decrease* the pressure at the oval window relative to that at the eardrum. This mechanism lessens the damage to the ear caused by high sound pressure levels. Low to moderate sound pressures cause the stapes to push directly on the oval window. For high sound pressures, however, the stapes moves at a different angle, and the force it applies to the oval window is greatly reduced. In addition, high-pressure-level sounds of low frequency cause muscles attached to the malleus (*tensor tympani*) and to the stapes (*stapedius*) to contract reflexively, thus decreasing the movements of the ossicles and decreasing the force applied at the oval window (see Figure 6-4 for the locations of these muscles). These mechanisms reduce the pressure and help to protect the ear from long-lasting excessive stimulation by damaging sounds.

The ossicles of the middle ear are surrounded by air. The pressure of this air in the middle ear is kept approximately equal to that of the surrounding atmosphere by means of the **eustachian tube**, which opens into the back of the throat. Equalization of pressure on either side of the eardrum is important because a pressure differential would cause the membrane to bulge and stiffen, resulting in less responsiveness of the eardrum to the sound striking it (Rabbitt, 1990). If the eustachian tube were not present, the pressure in the middle ear would gradually drop because of absorption of the air by the surrounding tissue. However, the two eustachian tubes open briefly every time we swallow, allowing air to flow into the two middle ear cavities from the mouth and lungs. This equalizes the air pressure on both sides of the eardrum. Sometimes, for example, when we have a head cold, the eustachian tubes become blocked, and the pressure in our middle ears cannot be equalized to that of the outside air. Also, when we are climbing or descending in an airplane, the cabin pressure may become considerably lower or higher than the

pressure within our middle ears unless we equalize the pressure by swallowing or by pressing our nostrils together and blowing gently. However they arise, inequalities between internal and external air pressure can cause temporary hearing loss and even pain. The eustachian tubes can also be a route by which bacteria can travel to the middle ear and cause infections that can also result in temporary hearing loss. This problem, called *otitis media*, often happens when infants or young children get colds because their eustachian tubes are so short. In otitis media, fluid builds up in the middle ear, causing the eardrum to bulge painfully and sometimes to burst before the infection subsides, either naturally or through treatment with antibiotics.

Vibrations of the stapes are transmitted to the inner ear via the oval window, the boundary between the middle and inner ears. The oval window is at the *base* of the **vestibular canal**, one of three tubes that run the length of the cochlea (Figure 6-5). The vestibular canal is connected at the *apex* of the cochlea to another tube, the **tympanic canal**, by an opening called the **helicotrema**. The tympanic canal has its own membranous window, called the **round window**, at its base, dividing it from the middle ear airspace. These canals are filled with *perilymph*, a fluid resembling saltwater. Because perilymph is relatively noncompressible, when a movement of the stapes causes the fluid to

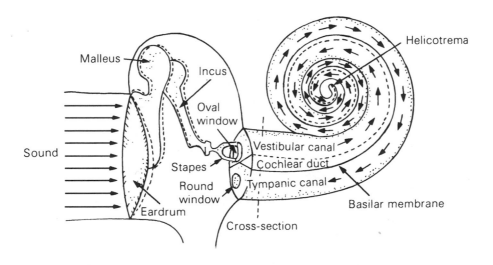

FIGURE 6-5 Movements of the eardrum in response to sound are transmitted by the ossicles to the fluid in the canals of the coiled cochlea.

move, the movement is transmitted by the fluid to the round window, and it bulges into or away from the middle ear airspace. Movement of this fluid causes corresponding movements of membranes inside the cochlea.

The third canal of the cochlea, the **cochlear duct** (or *scala media*), is relatively self-contained. It neither contacts the middle ear nor joins the vestibular or tympanic canals. It is formed by two membranes that run the length of the cochlea: **Reissner's membrane** and the **basilar membrane**. Together they form a crude triangle with the wall of the cochlea (Figure 6-6). The cochlear duct is filled with *endolymph*, a fluid that is more viscous than perilymph and contains many potassium ions. Reissner's membrane is very thin (only two cells thick) and has no function other than to form one wall of the cochlear duct. The basilar membrane supports the structures that transduce the movements of the cochlear fluid into neural signals. In humans the basilar membrane is about 3 cm long. It is narrower (0.08 mm) near the base and wider (0.5 mm) at the apex and is about 100 times stiffer at the base than at the apex. This tapering of the basilar membrane is necessary to maintain the efficient transfer of energy between middle and inner ears at low frequencies (Shera & Zweig, 1991). A third membrane within the cochlear duct is also important. The **tectorial membrane** extends into the cochlear duct from Reissner's membrane, and hairs from some of the cells of the **organ of Corti** are embedded in it (Figure 6-7). The organ of Corti contains the cells that transduce mechanical action in the cochlea into neural signals that are sent to the brain.

The organ of Corti rests on the basilar membrane along its entire length. It contains about 15,000 cells that resemble the cells of the skin in that hairs protrude from them. The hairs are formed from a core made of a protein called *actin* and a covering of another protein called *myosin*. The **tunnel of Corti** separates two sets of hair cells. A single row of about 3,000 **inner hair cells** is found on the inner side (*inner* relative to where the tectorial membrane begins—left side in Figure 6-7), and three to five rows of **outer hair cells** are located on the outer side. Inner hair cells have about 40–60 hairs each. These hairs extend into endolymph that fills the cochlear duct but do not touch the membrane (Lim, 1980). Each outer hair cell may have as many as 100–120 very tiny hairs protruding from it. The tallest of these hairs are firmly embedded in the tectorial membrane; the shorter hairs apparently do not touch the membrane. The hairs on outer hair cells are arranged in V- or W-shaped rows, whereas those on the inner hair cells form straight rows (Photo 6-1).

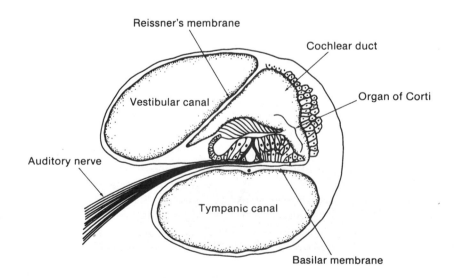

FIGURE 6-6   Cross-section of the cochlea reveals its three canals and the organ of Corti, the auditory receptor.

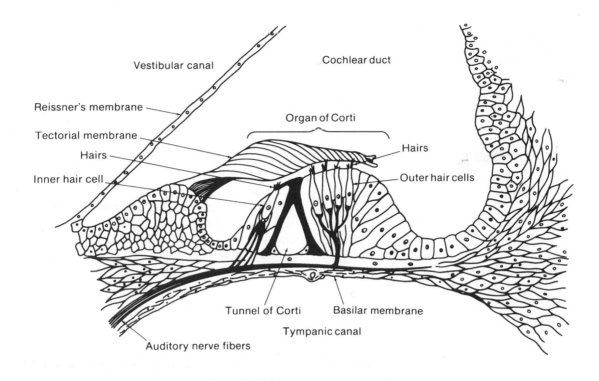

FIGURE 6-7   The detailed structure of the organ of Corti (based on Gulick, 1971).

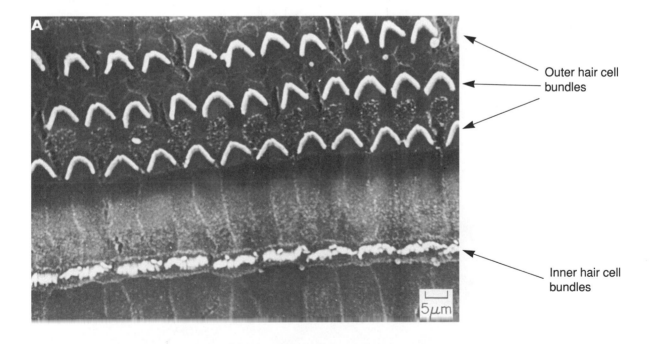

PHOTO 6-1   Scanning electron micrograph of the organ of Corti from the top with the tectorial membrane removed to expose the hair bundles of the outer and inner hair cells (from Pickles, 1988).

For both inner and outer hair cells, the set of hairs of different sizes protruding from a single cell is arranged in order of size and forms a **hair bundle.** Each hair in a bundle is connected to nearby hairs in the same bundle by a broad band of linking filaments. In addition, for all but the tallest hairs, each shorter hair is connected at its tip to the side of its taller neighbor by a thin filament, called a **tip link,** which appears to have a core of actin, similar to the hairs themselves (Photo 6-2; Osborne, Comis, & Pickles, 1988; Pickles, 1988; Pickles et al., 1989). Thus, all of the hairs in a hair bundle tend to move, or bend, as a unit. When they bend toward the longer hairs, the tip links will pull on the cell membrane at the tips of the shorter hairs and on the sides of the taller hairs. This arrangement of hairs and filaments is important for the transduction of sound in the organ of Corti, as we will discuss in the section "Mechanism of Transduction." It has recently been shown that mutations in the genes that regulate the structure of actin and myosin can cause deafness, presumably by causing structural defects in the hairs and their bundles that interfere with their function in transduction (e.g., Lynch et al., 1997). Hair cells can also be damaged by stimulation from high-pressure-level sounds. It was long believed that such damage, causing sensorineural deafness, was irreversible in mammals. However, there is mounting evidence that hair cells can be stimulated to regenerate, even in humans (Forge, Li, Corwin, & Nevill, 1993; Lefebre et al., 1993; Warchol et al., 1993).

About 30,000 nerve fibers, each projecting from a neuron located in the **spiral ganglion,** make connections with the bases of the hair cells of each cochlea. Each one of about 95% of them, called **type 1 fibers,** makes a single connection with a single *inner* hair cell located at about the same place where it enters the cochlea. About 15 type 1 fibers connect to each inner hair cell in the middle of the cochlea, whereas there are only about 3 or 4 fibers connected to each inner hair cell at the base and apex (Spoendlin & Schrott, 1989). The remaining 5% of the fibers are called **type 2 fibers.** Each type 2 fiber connects to about 10 *outer* hair

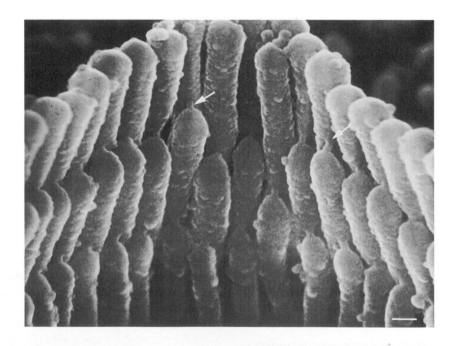

PHOTO 6-2 Scanning electron micrograph of an outer-hair-cell hair bundle, showing the graded sizes of the hairs and the tip links connecting the tips of the shorter hairs to the sides of the taller ones (from Pickles, 1988).

cells. No individual outer hair cell receives more than about four such contacts (Spoendlin, 1978). Figure 6-8 shows how projections of the spiral ganglion neurons innervate the cochlea.

The type 1 fibers have a large diameter and are myelinated, whereas the type 2 fibers are smaller in diameter and are unmyelinated; hence they have slower neural conduction speeds. In addition, the two types of fibers come from spiral ganglion cells that have a noticeably different shape (Kiang, Rho, Northrop, Liberman, & Ryugo, 1982). These differences suggest that these two different sets of fibers may carry different types of auditory information. A likely possibility is that information about sounds is carried by the fibers that innervate the inner hair cells, whereas the fibers that innervate the outer hair cells participate in a feedback loop that controls their mechanical properties and thereby modifies the responsiveness of the inner hair cells to sound (Kim, 1985). The axons of the spiral ganglion cells make up the auditory nerve—the neural pathway to the higher auditory centers in the brain (Figure 6-8).

The hair cells not only send information to the central nervous system via *afferent* innervation from the spiral ganglion but also receive *efferent* signals from nuclei in the **superior olive** (see Figure 6-17;

also see Sahley, Nodar, & Musiek, 1997, for a detailed review). The outer hair cells receive most of their efferent input from cells in the superior olive on the opposite, or *contralateral,* side of the head through what is called the **crossed olivocochlear bundle.** These myelinated nerve fibers are connected to the cell bodies of the outer hair cells. In contrast, the inner hair cells receive most of their efferent input from cells in a different part of the superior olive on the same, or *ipsilateral,* side of the head as the hair cell. Why should we have signals from higher centers coming into the ear? These efferent inputs, especially those to the outer hair cells, are probably used to control the processes that are designed to protect the ear from damage by intense sounds (Puel, Bobbin, & Fallon, 1988) and to sharpen the mechanical tuning curves of the basilar membrane, which we will discuss in the next section. They also may be associated with the focusing of attention on certain aspects of the auditory stimulation (Pickles, 1988, and Chapter 15).

Mechanical Tuning on the Basilar Membrane

The movements of the perilymph produced by vibrations of the stapes cause pressure waves across the cochlear duct. These pressure waves in turn induce mechanical waves to travel down the basilar membrane from the stiffer, narrower base (near the oval window) to the looser, broader apex in only 3 msec (Kitzes, Gibson, Rose, & Hind, 1978). The traveling wave is like a kink that moves down the length of the membrane, much like what happens when a whip is cracked. Figure 6-9 is a schematic drawing of such a wave. You can explore the properties of traveling waves for yourself by fixing a piece of cloth, such as a scarf, at one end with a pile of heavy books and moving the other end up and down (as uniformly as possible) at various frequencies. The speed and distance of travel will vary with the frequency with which you move the free end. The existence of traveling waves on the basilar membrane was demonstrated by Georg von Békésy (e.g., 1960), who received the Nobel prize for his work on the mechanics of the ear.

Variations in elasticity and width of the basilar membrane are responsible for the direction and the speed of the traveling wave. They are also

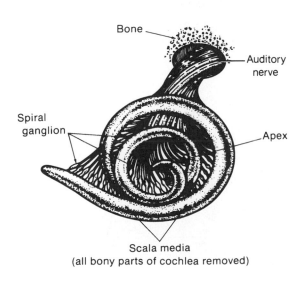

Bone

Auditory nerve

Spiral ganglion

Apex

Scala media
(all bony parts of cochlea removed)

FIGURE 6-8 A view of the cochlea with the bone and other covering removed, leaving only the soft membrane and neural tissue.

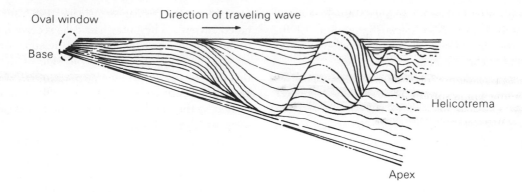

FIGURE 6-9 A traveling wave on the basilar membrane.

mostly responsible for differences in the amplitude of the wave. Bekesy demonstrated that the basilar membrane reacts differently to sound stimuli of different frequencies. Traveling waves caused by low-frequency sounds grow steadily in size as they travel toward the apex and do not reach a maximum until they reach a place near the apex. Those caused by higher frequency sounds, however, don't travel as far down the basilar membrane. The maximum wave amplitude for a high-frequency tone is much nearer to the base of the membrane where the stapes is attached to the cochlea, and the energy of such a wave then quickly dissipates. This is shown in Figure 6-10, which displays traveling wave amplitude at different places along the basilar membrane for pure tones of different frequencies (see also Greenwood, 1990). This mechanical analysis of sound by the basilar membrane is the basis for Ohm's Acoustical Law. Demonstration Box 6-3 shows you how to demonstrate the differences in the ability of low- and high-frequency waves to travel down a membrane.

Modern measurements have demonstrated that the response of the basilar membrane is very sharply tuned to the frequency of the stimulating sound (Sellick, Patuzzi, & Johnstone, 1982), that is, the curves shown in Figure 6-10 are sharply peaked. Variations in the stiffness and thickness of

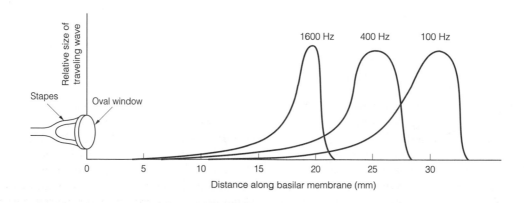

FIGURE 6-10 A graph of the relative sizes of traveling waves along the basilar membrane for three different frequencies of tone. Notice that as the frequency increases, the waves reach their maxima nearer the oval window and stapes (base).

DEMONSTRATION BOX 6-3
The Skin as a Model for the Basilar Membrane

The basilar membrane is set into vibration by incoming sound stimuli. How the membrane vibrates, however, depends on the frequency of the sound input. Low frequencies tend to cause vibrations of significant magnitude along the entire length of the membrane; high frequencies cause vibrations that are significant only near the base. You can easily demonstrate the frequency-specific nature of the vibration by using your finger as a model of the basilar membrane because skin has about the same resiliency and elasticity. Place your finger in your mouth, resting your fingertip firmly against the front of your teeth.

Now make a loud, low sound (try to imitate the low sound of a foghorn), and notice that your entire finger seems to vibrate, perhaps all the way down to the knuckle at its base. Next make a high-pitched sound (try to imitate the whistling of a teakettle or the test tone on a TV station that has ended the day's broadcasting). Notice that the feeling of vibration covers only a tiny region, perhaps your fingertip or down to the first joint. In a similar fashion, low sound frequencies induce waves that extend over the length of the basilar membrane, whereas higher frequency waves are restricted spatially in their effects.

---

the basilar membrane along its length are not sufficient to explain these very sharp mechanical tuning curves (see Pickles, 1988). It is very likely that there is also some kind of active process that modifies the mechanical vibrations before they reach the inner hair cells, thus sharpening the mechanical tuning of the basilar membrane. Figure 6-11 illustrates how this process might work by adding energy to the traveling wave just before it peaks, thereby raising the peak and making the dropoff after the peak even sharper. Current thinking suggests that this active process involves the outer hair cells. The outer hair cells seem to change length in response to changes in voltage across their cell membrane (e.g., Brownell, Bader, Bertrand, & De Ribaupierre, 1985). It has been shown that these length changes provide sufficient force to change the motion of the basilar membrane (Mountain & Hubbard, 1994). One possibility is that the outer hair cells actively push or pull at the tectorial membrane, thus reflecting or absorbing energy from basilar membrane motion (e.g., Geisler, 1991; Kim, 1985; Reuter & Zenner, 1990). Another is that the outer hair cells alter the response of the basilar membrane to the pressure waves in the cochlear canals without involving the tectorial membrane (Neely, 1993; Zwicker, 1986). It is also possible that changes in the stiffness of the outer hair cells may play a role in sharpening

the peak of the traveling wave (Kohlston, 1988). All of these possibilities require efferent inputs from other neural centers to initiate the length or stiffness changes that result in the mechanical action of the outer hair cells on the basilar membrane (Kim, 1985; Pickles, 1988).

An interesting consequence of mechanical activity in the cochlea is that sounds are actually *emitted* by the ear (Kemp, 1978). Some of these otoacoustic emissions occur spontaneously, whereas others are evoked by a sound input. Otoacoustic emissions can be fairly intense (over 20 dB), and they differ depending on how they are stimulated (Lonsbury-Martin et al., 1990). Stimulation of one ear by sound can alter spontaneous otoacoustic emissions from the other ear (e.g., Harrison & Burns, 1993).

At least some of these otoacoustic emissions probably arise from the operation of the active process that amplifies the traveling waves. Evidence for this comes from examination of the effects of some common drugs, such as aspirin and quinine sulfate, which can cause both hearing loss and tinnitus (ringing in the ears). Both of these drugs also reduce the ability of the outer hair cells to move. Administration of aspirin eliminates spontaneous otoacoustic emissions in monkeys (Martin, Lonsbury-Martin, Probst, & Coats, 1988) and humans (Wier, Pasanen, & McFadden, 1988),

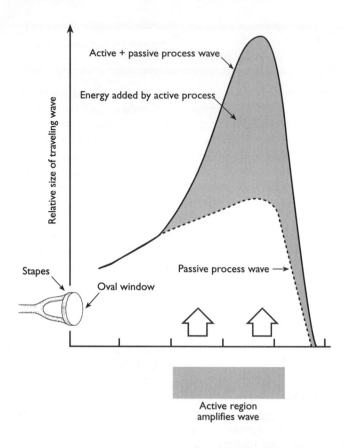

FIGURE 6-11 Illustration of how the active process in the organ of Corti might sharpen mechanical tuning curves by amplifying traveling waves just before their peaks (based on Pickles, 1988).

although it does not alter otoacoustic emissions that are evoked by external sound stimuli. Administration of quinine sulfate eliminates or reduces both spontaneous and evoked otoacoustic emissions in humans (McFadden & Pasanen, 1994). Thus, drugs that reduce the ability of the outer hair cells to move also reduce otoacoustic emissions, suggesting that these internally generated sounds may be due to the activity of these hair cells.

Mechanism of Transduction

The mechanical motions of the ear that we have discussed so far must eventually be changed into electrochemical fluctuations, which are the code of the central nervous system, through a process known as *transduction*. This occurs at the organ of Corti, which rests on the basilar membrane. Traveling waves that move down the basilar membrane also cause it to move sideways with respect to the tectorial membrane. Both inner and outer hair cells are attached at their base to structures connected to the basilar membrane. Because the longest hairs of the outer hair cells are embedded in the tectorial membrane, the shearing force between the two membranes results in a mechanical pressure that causes these hairs to bend. The inner hair cell hairs, which are not attached to the tectorial membrane, are bent when they are swept through the viscous fluid (endolymph) in the cochlear duct by the movement of the basilar membrane (Dallos, 1978; Freeman & Weiss, 1990; Raftenberg, 1990). Although this seems to be a less-efficient way of producing bending, there appear to be no differences in the absolute sensitivities of the inner and outer hair cells (Dallos, Santos-Sacchi, & Flock, 1982).

The bending of hairs is transduced into electrical changes in the hair cells by a mechanism that involves the tip links of the shorter hairs to their longer neighbors (Hudspeth, 1985; Pickles, Comis, & Osborne, 1984). Figure 6-12 illustrates one way in which this mechanism could work. As shown in the figure, the tip of each shorter hair

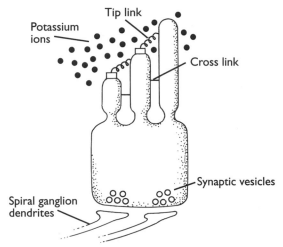

A. Hairs not bent—trapdoors closed

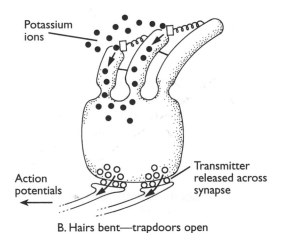

B. Hairs bent—trapdoors open

FIGURE 6-12 Model of transduction in hair cells. (A) No sound, hairs not bent, trapdoor closed, potassium ions excluded, no transmitter released, no action potentials; (B) sound present, hairs bent, trapdoor open, potassium ions enter, transmitter released, action potentials in auditory nerve.

seems to have a pore that functions like a little "trapdoor" (Hudspeth, 1985). When the hair is standing straight, the trapdoor "rattles around" a bit because of impacts with the surrounding molecules but is open only about 20% of the time (shown closed in Figure 6-12A). Potassium ions, which have a positive charge, flow into the hair whenever one or more pores are open. The inward flow of positive charge is just balanced by the outward flow of positive charge caused by other ion "pumps" elsewhere in the cell, maintaining the cell's resting membrane potential at about −60 mV (see Appendix). When the hair is bent in the direction of the tallest hairs, however, the tip link attached to the trapdoor pulls on it and keeps it open more of the time, allowing more positively charged potassium ions to flow into the cell (Figure 6-12B). This causes a depolarization (making the inside of the cell more positive relative to the outside) of up to 20 mV, which in turn releases neurotransmitter substances from the bottom of the hair cell. These neurotransmitters stimulate the dendrites of the spiral ganglion cells, which then generate the action potentials that ascend the auditory nerve to higher brain centers.

ELECTRICAL ACTIVITY OF THE AUDITORY NERVE

We have followed sound energy to the point where it is converted into patterns of electrical activity in the auditory nerve. To study the neural processing of auditory information, we use the same techniques of electrophysiological recording that we used to investigate the visual system. The most common technique involves inserting tiny electrodes into neurons in the auditory pathways and recording their electrical activity in response to various sound stimuli. If you are unfamiliar with these procedures, now would be a good time to glance back at the Appendix.

Recording the spike potentials jumping along the axons of spiral ganglion neurons that make up the auditory nerve reveals several types of responses to sounds played to the ear. Figure 6-13 shows the minimum sound pressure levels of pure tones of various frequencies needed to stimulate some auditory nerve neurons to respond above their resting rate. These are the neural equivalent of absolute thresholds (see Chapter 2). The resulting curves are called **threshold response curves**, and, as can be seen from the figure, each neuron has a best, or characteristic, frequency for which its neural absolute threshold is lowest. Neurons that respond to pure tones in this way are called **tuned neurons** (tuned in the same sense that we tune a radio to accurately receive one particular station's broadcast frequency). The sensitivity of such neurons decreases (the threshold is higher) as we move away from the characteristic frequency in either direction. Another way of expressing the tuning of such auditory neurons is to describe how the rate with which they produce spike potentials to a fixed-level tone varies as the frequency of the tone is varied. A graph of the response rate of a tuned neuron versus frequency is called a **tuning curve**, one example of which is shown in Figure 6-14. The auditory nerve contains neurons tuned to frequencies spanning the entire range of hearing.

The tuned nature of auditory nerve neurons probably arises from the mechanical properties of the basilar membrane (Khanna & Leonard, 1982; Pickles, 1988). Most of the tuned auditory nerve fibers that have been studied are connected to inner hair cells (Kiang et al., 1982; Liberman, 1982). Remember that different locations along

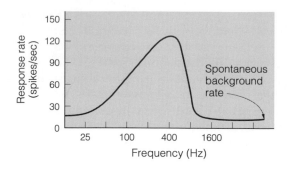

FIGURE 6-14　Tuning curve of a typical auditory nerve fiber (based on Lindsay & Norman, 1977).

the basilar membrane are vibrating vigorously to different frequencies of sound (see Figure 6-10), and it is this vibration that causes the inner hair cells to bend and in turn to initiate the neural response. An inner hair cell responds most strongly when a tone of a certain frequency creates a traveling wave on the basilar membrane that has its maximum amplitude near the location of that hair cell. The frequency of this tone will be the frequency to which the neuron that synapses with that hair cell is tuned. Other frequencies of sound of this same intensity will cause less vigorous movement of the basilar membrane at that location, which in turn results in less vigorous bending of the hair of the hair cell and finally in less vigorous responding of the neuron. The outer hair cells also show frequency tuning. However, their responses probably only indirectly affect the responses of the inner hair cells by altering their own mechanical properties through the feedback loop we discussed earlier (Kim, 1985; Pickles, 1988).

Some evidence for the interaction between inner and outer hair cells comes from a phenomenon called **two-tone suppression** (Rose, Galambos, & Hughs, 1959; Sachs & Kiang, 1968). Suppose that we record from an auditory nerve fiber that is responding vigorously to a tone at its characteristic frequency. Now if a second tone of a different frequency (but moderately close to the tuned frequency) is briefly presented, the response rate in the tuned neuron drops. It is argued that this is the result of mechanical action of outer hair cells stimulated by the second tone that reduces the response of the basilar membrane, and thus of the inner hair

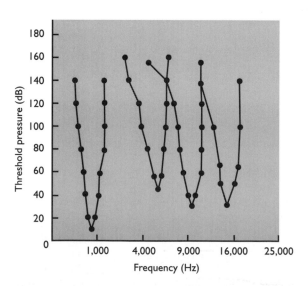

FIGURE 6-13　Threshold response curves for auditory nerve fibers in the cat (based on Whitfield, 1968).

cells, to the first tone. This is supported by the fact that two-tone suppression disappears when outer hair cells have been selectively damaged by a drug (Schmiedt, Zwislocki, & Hamernik, 1980) and by the fact that it can be caused directly by stimulation of the outer hair cells (Geisler, Yates, Patuzzi, & Johnstone, 1990). Moreover, two-tone suppression also occurs with otoacoustic emissions, which are supposed to reflect the active process by which outer hair cells sharpen basilar membrane tuning curves, thus affecting inner hair cell responses (Brass & Kemp, 1993).

The firing rate in auditory nerve neurons changes not only with the frequency of the stimulating sound but also with the time since the sound was presented. **Neural adaptation** is a common effect seen in most sensory neurons. When first stimulated a neuron responds vigorously. However, if the stimulation continues unchanged, the response level drops over time, eventually reaching a much lower response rate. Different neurons display different time courses for adaptation. Some show an initially very rapid stage of adaptation and one or more later slower stages, and others show only the slower later stages. The adaptation curve of a neuron displaying an early very rapid adaptation stage

and a somewhat later slower stage is shown in Figure 6-15. In this typical spiral ganglion neuron from a guinea pig, the firing rate fell to about one third of the initial rate by about 25 ms after stimulus onset and then decreased more gradually over the next several hundred milliseconds (Yates, Robertson, & Johnstone, 1985). Some auditory nerve neurons continue to adapt for several seconds (*long-term adaptation*) or even several minutes (*very long-term adaptation*—Javel, 1996). It is thought that the various phases of adaptation correspond to various stages in the depletion of available neurotransmitters at synapses with the inner hair cells (see Javel, 1996). The long-term adaptation effects are thought to be the cause of *auditory perceptual adaptation*, which is the decrease in the perceived loudness of a pure tone listened to for a long period of time (see Chapter 7).

In the next chapter we will consider a number of theories about how information about intensity and frequency of sound is represented in the auditory system. Some hints about this can be derived from the physiology of the ear that we have already discussed. For example, we know that there are tuned neurons that respond best to a limited range of frequencies. In addition, the frequency of

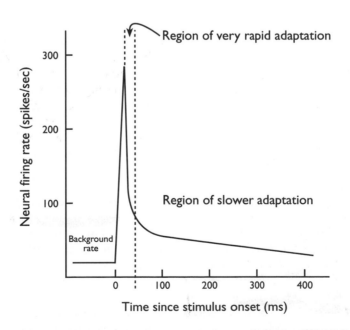

FIGURE 6-15   Neural adaptation in a typical auditory nerve fiber.

low-frequency sounds is encoded directly in the frequency of firing in the auditory nerve (Johnson, 1980; Rose, Brugge, Anderson, & Hind, 1967). Consider a sound with a frequency of 100 Hz. If some neurons fire at each compression peak in the sound wave, the firing rate in the auditory nerve also will be around 100 Hz. Notice that no individual neuron has to fire at 100 Hz for the overall firing to occur at that frequency. It is necessary only that each neuron have the greatest probability of firing at some fixed point in the sound wave cycle, such as at the compression peak. Thus, each neuron would tend to fire in phase with the sound wave, although one may fire only about every second peak, whereas another fires only about every fifth peak. This is called **phase locking.** For many neurons firing out of phase with one another but phase locked to a sound wave there will tend to be at least several spikes occurring at every peak of the wave, and thus the composite response traveling down the auditory nerve will have peaks that occur at a rate equal to the frequency of the stimulating sound. Also, even if each individual neuron is adapting to the sound and firing ever more slowly, the overall firing in the auditory nerve will still occur at the stimulating frequency as long as at least a few neurons fire at each peak. The ability of the whole auditory nerve to fire at the frequency of the stimulating sound wave up to a limit of about 4,000 Hz is a central component of several theories of pitch perception that will be discussed in Chapter 7. What is important here is that the pattern of response of the whole auditory nerve as well as the responses of individual neurons can be used to signal the sound frequency to higher brain centers.

Intensity information is coded differently. Remember that the spiral ganglion neurons are tuned for particular frequencies. Although there may be many cells tuned to the same frequency, different cells can have response thresholds for sounds of that frequency that can differ over a range of 20 dB (Evans, 1975). These tuned neurons fire more rapidly as the intensity of sound increases, but only up to a level about 30 dB to 50 dB above their threshold. At this point the cell is firing as fast as it can, so further pressure increases cannot increase its rate of firing. Such a cell would be said to be **saturated.** With this ceiling on firing rates, the rate that a tuned neuron fires can encode only a limited range of low to moderate sound pressures.

On the other hand, the greater a sound's pressure amplitude, the more individual neurons will fire in response to it. If the sound has a high enough pressure it will even recruit responses from other neurons, which are not exactly tuned to the specific stimulus frequency but, rather, are tuned to nearby frequencies and thus have a much higher threshold for this slightly "mismatched" sound. This allows a much wider range of sound pressures to be encoded by *how many* neurons are firing.

Thus, for any given sound input there is a population of neurons all firing at different response rates. This situation is represented in Figure 6-16A for two levels of pressure. Stimuli of different frequencies tend to cause different populations of neurons to fire above their background rates, as is shown in 6-16B. The entire pattern of auditory nerve activity is different for different stimuli. Frequency seems to be encoded by *which* tuned neurons are firing and for low-frequency sounds by *how fast* the auditory nerve as a whole is firing, whereas pressure seems to be encoded by *how many* tuned neurons are firing (Whitfield, 1978) and for low-pressure sounds by *how fast* specific tuned neurons are firing (Viemeister, 1988).

Our increasing understanding of how the auditory nerve encodes frequency and pressure has allowed people with certain kinds of hearing disabilities to recover some auditory function. As mentioned earlier, if the hair cells do not function normally, either because they were damaged or congenitally malformed, a person has a *sensorineural* hearing loss. This results in raised thresholds, distorted tuning curves, and sometimes in ringing in the ears *(tinnitus)* caused by hair cell or neural activity in the absence of sound. Although it is so far difficult to do anything about too much neural activity, other than to mask it, it is possible to help people who have too little neural response to sounds. Recently, otologists have been able to insert **cochlear implants** into the ear. Under the control of microcomputer chips, these tiny devices stimulate the auditory nerve electrically in response to external sounds (see Schindler & Merzenich, 1985). The implant itself consists of a series of electrodes that have been implanted at different points along the basilar membrane where traveling waves corresponding to different sound frequencies might peak. A microphone worn by the deaf person then analyzes the frequencies of

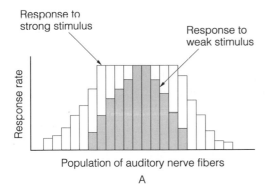

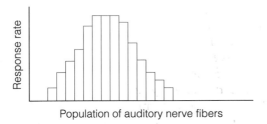

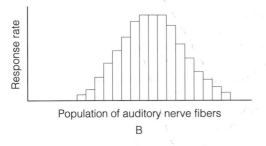

FIGURE 6-16 Hypothetical distributions of response rates for the population of auditory nerve fibers firing in response to (A) weak versus strong stimuli of the same frequency and (B) stimuli of the same strength but of different frequencies.

the incoming sounds and causes the various electrodes to provide appropriate levels of stimulation. If there are enough electrodes implanted along the length of the basilar membrane, the auditory nerve will receive stimulation that mimics the way in which traveling waves stimulate the hair cells for various frequencies. Deaf patients with such devices can discriminate the frequencies of different sounds (Townshend, Cotter, Van Compernolle, & White, 1987) and can even recognize speech sounds quite well, especially when a speech preprocessor is attached to the cochlear implant to isolate certain speech-relevant frequency changes (Blamey, Dowell, Brown, Clark, & Seligman, 1987). People who have been deafened later in life seem to benefit more than those who have been deaf from an early age, although not all speech-encoding strategies available have as yet been tried (Busby, Tong, & Clark, 1993). There is some promise that, in the future, such devices will allow nearly a full range of hearing experience for people with this form of deafness (Miller & Spelman, 1990). There is now hope even for people who lack a functioning auditory nerve because more central implants, farther along the pathway to the brain, are currently being researched (Shannon & Otto, 1990).

THE AUDITORY PATHWAYS

Let us now follow the auditory information as it is processed by various specialized parts of the brain. Figure 6-17 diagrams the principal auditory pathways. The axons of the spiral ganglion neurons make up the auditory nerve, which projects to the **cochlear nucleus,** located in the lower rear part of the brain. As shown in the figure, the auditory nerve axons enter the **ventral** (front) **cochlear nucleus,** where each divides into at least two branches. One branch connects to neurons in the ventral cochlear nucleus, and the other proceeds to the **dorsal** (back) **cochlear nucleus**. The output of the neurons of the ventral cochlear nucleus divides, with about half of the neurons going to the *superior olive* located on the same side of the brain and half to the superior olive on the opposite side of the brain. The axons from the dorsal cochlear nucleus all cross over to the opposite side of the brain and eventually terminate in the **inferior colliculus**. Thus, it appears that much of the auditory information from the right ear is initially sent to the left side of the brain and vice versa. The two superior olives send most of their *afferent* (sensory input) fibers to the inferior colliculi (which are located just below the superior colliculi, discussed in

Chapter 3). As mentioned earlier, special neurons in the superior olives also send *efferent* fibers back to the cochlear nuclei and to the hair cells in the cochlea to modify their response to incoming sounds (Sahley, Nodar, & Musiek, 1997). One group of neurons sends efferent fibers to synapse on the afferent fibers innervating the inner hair cells, mostly on the same side of the brain. Another group sends efferent fibers to synapse directly on the outer hair cells, mostly on the other side of the brain, via the crossed olivocochlear bundle. At the level of the inferior colliculus, considerable fiber crossing takes place from one side of the brain to the other so that each inferior colliculus has information from both ears.

Some neurons in the inferior colliculi send axons to the **medial geniculate** nuclei, and some send axons to the deep layers of the superior colliculi.

The deep layers of the superior colliculi contain neurons that respond to the locations of lights, sounds, and touches (Stein & Meredith, 1993). One function of the superior colliculus appears to be the integration of visual and even tactile information about the location of the source of the sound relative to the listener. This can then be used to control eye, head, and body movements, and it may possibly play a role in how we direct our attention to objects in the world.

From the medial geniculate nuclei, fibers project to a part of the temporal cortex called the **primary auditory projection area,** or A1 (alternatively designated as Brodmann's Area 41). An adjacent area, called A2 (Brodmann's Area 42), also receives axons directly from the medial geniculate, although fewer of them. The general locations of these brain regions are pictured in Figure 6-18.

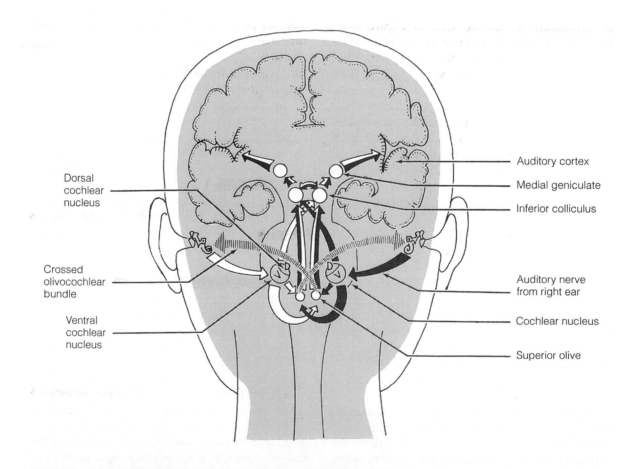

FIGURE 6-17   The major auditory pathways in the brain.

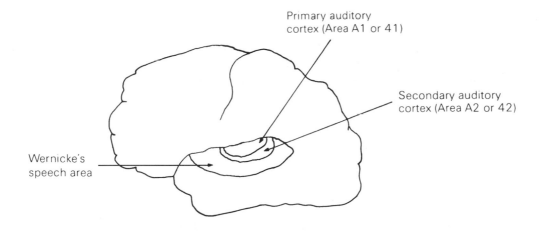

Primary auditory
cortex (Area A1 or 41)

Secondary auditory
cortex (Area A2 or 42)

Wernicke's
speech area

FIGURE 6-18   The principal regions of the cortex responsive to sound (much not visible because they go into the fissures), with Brodmann's numbering of the areas and alternate labeling systems.

Unfortunately, as can be seen in Figure 6-17, much of the auditory cortex is not on the surface but, rather, is tucked into a fold and is not visible in the view of the brain shown in Figure 6-18. Several other areas also process auditory stimuli, including areas adjacent to A1 and A2, some of the somatosensory cortex, and Wernicke's area (Brodmann's Area 22), which processes speech stimuli. Like the primary visual cortex (V1), the primary auditory cortex (A1) is arranged in layers (six of them).

Electrical Activity of the Lower Auditory Centers

Remember that the majority of auditory nerve neurons are tuned for some "preferred" frequency, although some may have "special tuning" and respond only to clicks or other stimuli that are not pure tones. Similar "tuned" neurons are found in the cochlear nucleus, superior olive, inferior colliculus, and medial geniculate. Also, as described earlier for the auditory nerve, there is a region of nearby frequencies that produces an inhibition of response (as in two-tone suppression) in these same cells.

In addition to the frequency tuning of neurons, several more complex or "special tuning" response patterns appear in the more central nuclei of the auditory pathway, and these seem designed to register specific aspects of the sound stimulus. For instance, neurons in the cochlear nucleus of adult cats can be categorized into several types on the basis of their response to a simple tone (Pfeiffer, 1966). **Onset neurons** give a burst of responses immediately after the onset of a tone and then cease responding, no matter how long the tone persists. **Pauser neurons** exhibit a similar burst of firing at the onset of a tone, but this is followed by a pause and then a weaker sustained response until the tone is turned off. **Chopper neurons** give repeated bursts of firing followed by short pauses, with the vigor of successive bursts decreasing. **Primary-like neurons** give an initial vigorous burst of firing when the tone is turned on; then the firing rate decays to a lower level that is sustained for the duration of the tone. These cochlear nucleus neurons have been shown to be capable of encoding some critical aspects of speech sounds (Palmer, Winter, & Darwin, 1986), especially using phase locking to encode regular variations in sound amplitude (Rhode & Greenberg, 1994).

Several other types of neurons can be found in one or more of these auditory nuclei. For example, **offset neurons** reduce their response rate below their spontaneous activity level at the onset of the tone and then give a burst of activity at its offset. An interesting variation of this is a tuned neuron that *increases* its activity at the onset of a tone at a characteristic frequency but *reduces* its activity at the onset of a tone with a slightly "off-characteristic" frequency. At a conceptual level this kind of responding is reminiscent of the on-center/off-surround neurons observed in the visual system (Chapter 3). Rather than having a receptive field that consists of a region in space, these neurons have receptive fields consisting of a band of frequencies. If we traced out the response pattern for such a neuron in the medial geniculate, it would be the roughly W-shaped pattern that you see in Figure 6-19. Notice that as we vary the frequency of the sound input, we get a response rate well above the normal resting level for the preferred or tuned frequency. For frequencies somewhat higher or lower, but close to that tuned frequency, the firing rate is actually inhibited below the normal base rate. As the frequencies become progressively more distant from the preferred frequency, the firing rate gradually returns to background level (Webster & Atkin, 1975).

Because different points along the basilar membrane vibrate most strongly for different frequencies of sounds, we refer to the response of the basilar membrane as **tonotopic** (from the Greek *tono* for "tone" and *topus* for "place"). This spatial

encoding of frequency is preserved in the auditory nerve and appears throughout all of the auditory pathways (Martin, Webster, & Service, 1988; Pickles, 1988; Rose, Galambos, & Hughes, 1960; Rouiller, Rodrigues-Dagaeff, Simm, De Ribaupierre, Villa, & De Ribaupierre, 1989). The tonotopic organization of the basilar membrane can be seen even at the level of the primary auditory cortex (Phillips, 1993). For example, in Area A1 of the cat brain the preferred tuning of strips of neurons goes from high to low frequencies in an orderly progression from the front to the back of the area (Harrison, Nagasawa, Smith, Stanton, & Mount, 1991; Merzenich, Knight, & Roth, 1975).

The finding that sound frequencies are spatially mapped into regions of the cortex has been confirmed in humans using measurements of the magnetic field created in the brain by its electrical response to sounds. The human map is a bit different from that in cats, though. The maximum brain activity observed in both the primary auditory cortex (Romani, Williamson, & Kaufman, 1982) and secondary areas of the auditory cortex (Cansino, Williamson, & Karron, 1994) varies in depth (rather than from front to back, as in the cat) as the frequency varies. Responses generally come

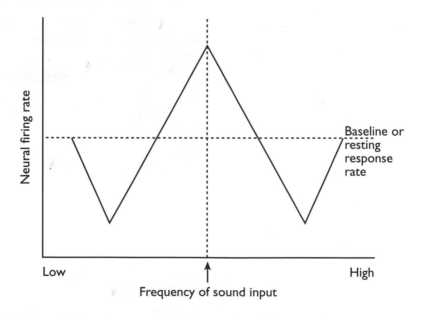

FIGURE 6-19 Schematic representation of a frequency-specific receptive field in the medial geniculate with an excitatory center for the preferred frequency and inhibitory flanks for near frequencies.

from progressively deeper beneath the scalp as tone frequency increases. A similar result has been obtained using *positron emission tomography*, which allows researchers to visualize areas of the brain that are most active during various activities, such as listening to sounds of different frequencies (Lauter, Herscovitch, Formby, & Raichle, 1985—see Appendix). These results are consistent with the idea that the frequency of sound waves is encoded mainly by which neurons are firing throughout the auditory system.

THE AUDITORY CORTEX

Neurons in the auditory cortex exhibit a variety of complex responses to sound stimuli. Among the approximately 60% of the neurons that respond to pure tones, there occur *on* responses, *off* responses, *on-off* responses, and more general *excitatory* and *inhibitory* responses (see Figure 6-20). These responses

closely resemble the response patterns of visual system neurons. The other 40% of auditory cortical neurons seem to respond selectively to more complex sounds, including noise bursts, clangs, or clicks. Ordinary tuned neurons and the specially tuned neurons that respond to more complex sounds seem to be located in separate zones of the human auditory cortex (Alho et al., 1996). Among the tuned neurons in A1, about 30% also seem to have some kind of additional amplitude tuning and respond only to a limited range of sound amplitudes within their preferred frequency ranges (Phillips, 1993). To consider another form of special tuning, there is recent evidence suggesting that there are neurons in the dorsal region of the cat's auditory cortex that are tuned for the duration, rather than the frequency or amplitude, of sounds (He, Hashikawa, Ojima, & Kinouchi, 1997).

An interesting group of specially tuned neurons found in the auditory cortex of the cat are the **frequency sweep detectors** (Whitfield & Evans,

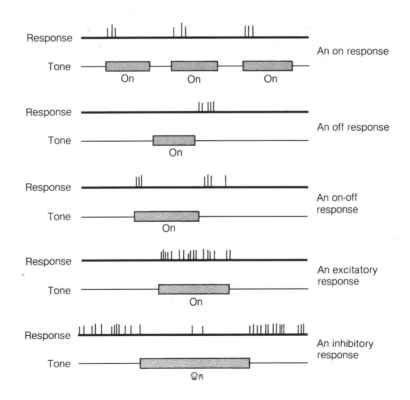

FIGURE 6-20 Different types of response to pure tones recorded from neurons in the auditory cortex of the cat (based on Whitfield, 1967).

1965). These neurons respond only to sounds that change frequency in a specific direction and range. Some frequency sweep detectors respond to increases but not to decreases in frequency within the same frequency range, whereas others respond to decreases in frequency but not to increases. A third type responds only to increases in frequency for low-frequency tones. Such neurons would help the cat discriminate between various types of cat meows, yowls, and screeches. Because these types of stimuli are also often encountered in human speech and music, such detectors, if present in people, could have an important role in our ability to understand spoken language and musical sequences.

Frequency sweep detectors respond selectively to sound patterns in much the same way that visual cortical neurons respond selectively to light patterns. There are even auditory analogs to the face and paw "detectors" observed in the visual parts of the temporal cortex (see Chapter 3). For instance, there are neurons in the cat auditory cortex that respond with a unique pattern of activity to recordings of certain cat vocalizations (Watanabe & Katsuki, 1974). Interestingly, these cortical neurons do not respond with the same pattern of activity to any of the individual components of the cat vocalization—only to the full sound sequence. This indicates that the neurons are integrating the outputs of neurons from lower levels of the auditory pathway that do respond to simpler components of the sound pattern. It seems that the lower level neurons are detecting the various features of the vocalization, and the cortical neuron is responding only to the combination of all of the features (Whitfield, 1980). Similar research has been done in primates. Cells in the auditory cortex of the squirrel monkey seem to be sensitive to the vocalizations of other squirrel monkeys (Swarbrick & Whitfield, 1972). As in the cat, some of these cells are unresponsive to the presentation of simple tones, although they respond vigorously to the presentation of extremely complex vocalizations (Funkenstein, Nelson, Winter, Wolberg, & Newman, 1971).

Sometimes, instead of special tuning of a neuron, there is a special form of coding across the auditory cortex. For instance, the "twitter" call of the common marmoset is faithfully, although abstractly, represented in the synchronized firing of primary auditory cortical neurons dispersed across

Area A1 (Wang, Merzenich, Beitel, & Schreiner, 1995). Particular regions in the brain may be designated for decoding special complex signals. As you will learn later in Chapter 12, in humans there are particular areas, mostly in the left hemisphere of the brain, that are important for analyzing speech sounds. In macaque monkeys, destruction of Areas A1 and A2 on the left side of the brain abolishes their ability to discriminate such complex vocalizations (Heffner & Heffner, 1984). This implies monkeys may have a primitive analog to the speech perception areas of humans. This would be consistent with the fact that temporal response patterns of neurons in the monkey auditory cortex can encode certain important features of human speech, such as voice-onset time, which we will also talk about in Chapter 12 (Steinschneider, Schroeder, Arezzo, & Vaughan, 1995). This may be a fairly specialized ability in higher species, such as primates, because an investigation of the auditory cortex of cats failed to reveal an ability to encode this information (Eggermont, 1995).

The human brain does seem to have specialized mechanisms to analyze speech sounds. Modern imaging studies of the human brain, especially functional magnetic resonance imaging (fMRI—see Appendix), have revealed that in the left hemisphere of the brain the auditory cortex and other areas are extensively involved in the processing of speech sounds (e.g., Binder et al., 1996). Auditory cortex responses to speech sounds are more widespread than those to white noise. (Binder et al., 1994). It has been suggested that these mechanisms may be language specific rather than sound specific because the auditory cortex in the left hemisphere is active even during lipreading in the absence of auditory stimuli (Calvert et al., 1997). On the other hand, some aspects of music perception seem to be processed mostly by the auditory cortex on the right side of human brains (Zatorre, 1985, or see Coren, 1993, for a review).

Although these physiological findings are quite intriguing and suggestive, the ultimate test of any hypotheses about the significance of neural encoding or analysis of auditory patterns rests on data about people's actual auditory perceptions. In Chapter 7 we will consider *what* is heard and try to integrate it with what we have already learned about *how* it is heard.

DEMONSTRATION BOX 7-2
High-Frequency Hearing Limits

You can make a simple test of your own high-frequency hearing using your television set. Turn it on, and then lower the sound completely. Now lean over the back of your set and listen for a soft, high-pitched whine. If you can hear it, this means that you can detect frequencies on the order of 16,000 Hz. Now, try this test on someone who is considerably older than you are and then with someone who is much younger. You should find that the older individual cannot hear this sound, whereas the younger one can. You might also try moving away from the set (if possible) until you can just hear the sound. This is your *threshold distance*. Now have your other observers do the same, and determine their threshold distances. The greater your threshold distance, the more sensitive your ear is to these high-frequency sounds.

Another type of summation in the auditory system is across ears. Sound presentations to one ear are called **monaural** (from the roots *mon* for "one" and *aural* for "ear"), whereas those to two ears are called **binaural** (from the root *bi* for "two"). The threshold for binaural presentation is about one half that for monaural presentation (Chocolle, 1962). An interesting fact is that binaural thresholds are lower than monaural ones even if in the binaural case the sounds are not presented simultaneously to the two ears. For example, if two subthreshold tones are presented to the ears one at a time, within a total duration of less than 200 ms, the combined sound will be detected 50% of the time even if each individual tone is only one half the monaural threshold level (Schenkel, 1967). In this case, temporal summation has combined with summation across the two ears.

Auditory Masking

Most of us have probably experienced the frustration of trying to carry on a conversation in a noisy nightclub or at a loud concert. Even if our conversational partner is shouting, it is difficult to hear what he or she is saying. If the music stops or the crowd quiets, however, we find that our friend's voice is audible immediately. Whether or not a particular sound can be heard depends not only on its own pressure but also on the presence of other sounds. We just discussed how subthreshold sounds can interact to facilitate detection. When sounds that are clearly above threshold interact, the effects are reversed. If we present an observer with a sound that is audible by itself, adding another sound may result in the observer's losing the ability to hear the first one. We usually say that the second sound is **masking** the first (the **target**); hence we will call this added sound a **masker**. When target and masker are presented at the same time, we have **simultaneous masking**.

A masking sound does not make *all* other sounds more difficult to hear. Masking sounds act rather selectively. An elegant experiment demonstrating this was done by Zwicker (1958). He measured the threshold sound pressures for target tones of various frequencies presented both alone

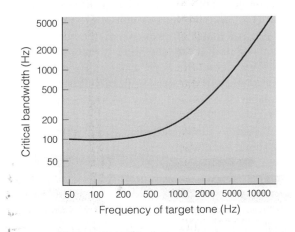

FIGURE 7-2   The relation between critical bandwidth, within which added tones will facilitate detection, and frequency of target tone.

and simultaneously with a narrow band of noise with a middle frequency of 1,200 Hz. He obtained the results shown in Figure 7-3. As you can see from the figure, the higher the level of the masking noise, the higher the level of the target tone had to be for it to be audible. The most striking aspect of Figure 7-3, however, is the asymmetry of the masking effect. The greatest masking (highest target thresholds) is found for tones that have frequencies that are very similar to that of the masker (1,200 Hz). However, there is also substantial masking of tones higher in frequency than the masking sound (the masked threshold curves on the right side of Figure 7-3 are flatter), whereas tones of a lower frequency are relatively unaffected by the masker (the masked threshold curves on the left of Figure 7-3 are steeper). For people with sensorineural hearing loss (caused by damage to hair cells or auditory nerve cells), this "upward spread of masking" effect is even more pronounced (Gagne, 1988). You can experience some aspects of the frequency-specific effect of a masker by performing Demonstration Box 7-3.

Why does simultaneous masking spread upward in frequency? Turn back to Figure 6-10, which shows how the vibration pattern of the basilar membrane varies with the frequency of a pure tone. Notice that tones of low frequencies produce

a very broad vibration pattern, extending over much of the membrane, whereas tones of higher frequencies produce vibration patterns nearer to the oval window that don't extend as far along the membrane. Now look at Figure 7-4, which shows the effects of two tones on vibration of the basilar membrane. In the top row (left column) you see that when the target tone is weak and the target tone is of a lower frequency than the masking noise, the target tone's vibration pattern extends beyond the flank of the vibration pattern produced by the masker, allowing the target to be detected. However, when the target tone is of a higher frequency than the masking noise (top row, right column), the target tone's vibration pattern is completely covered by that of the masker, and the target is not detectable as a separate tone. The sound pressure of the higher frequency test tone in the presence of lower frequency noise must be increased substantially (bottom row, right column) before its vibration pattern at last extends beyond that of the masker and it can be detected as a separate tone.

We have seen how the upward spread of masking is caused by the interaction of the patterns of excitation produced on the basilar membrane by target and masking sounds. These vibration patterns would have their effects on hearing through stimulation of the hair cells located on the basilar membrane. However, the interaction between responses to the target and masker doesn't end at the basilar membrane. Similar to two-tone inhibition (see Chapter 6), neurons responding to the masker could be suppressing the activity of neurons responding to the target tone. Studies of auditory nerve fibers in cats indicate that this additional mechanism is important for target frequencies that are well above the masker frequency (Delgutte, 1990).

Masking sound can decrease audibility of a target sound even when presented before or after the target. If the masker is presented before the target, any increase in the absolute threshold for the target is called **forward masking**. Forward masking increases with the level of the masking sounds and decreases with the **interstimulus interval**, which is the time interval between the mask and the target (see Zwislocki, 1978). For interstimulus intervals longer than 300 ms there is no measurable forward masking. Longer duration masking sounds

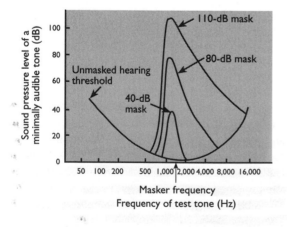

FIGURE 7-3 Thresholds for a pure-tone target in the presence of a narrow band of masking noise centered at 1,200 Hz. The higher the curve, the higher the threshold, hence the more effective the masking (based on Zwicker, 1958).

DEMONSTRATION BOX 7-3
Auditory Masking

To experience several different masking phenomena, you need two major sources of sound—one for a masking sound and one for the target sound that will be masked. Good sources are the noise of a car engine for a masking sound and the car radio for a source of target sounds. If you have a car with a radio, get into it and turn on the radio without starting the engine. Find some music with a good range of frequencies. Classical music is best, but any music will do. Modern music with a lot of steel guitar (country) or electrically amplified guitar (rock) is also good. Take particular note of sounds at the high and the low frequencies. Turn the volume knob on the radio to a level where you can just barely hear these frequencies. Now start the car motor. Press on the accelerator (with the car out of gear!) to make the engine turn over at high revolutions per minute. This creates a source of intense broad-band masking noise. Now listen for the high and the low frequencies that were clearly audible in the music before you started the car

engine. Turn up the volume until the high and low frequencies (which should now be masked) are just barely audible again, and take notice of the difference between the volume settings before and after the noise was introduced. You could map out a masking curve for particular frequencies in a piece of music by varying the revolutions per minute of the motor to vary the level of the noise and by varying the frequency of the sounds whose audibility you are using as a criterion for radio volume adjustment. Note that even with high-level masking noise, you can still hear the middle frequencies, where most of the singing is, whereas the higher and lower frequencies are masked. This is a reflection of the superior sensitivity of the ear to these frequencies. You also experience *speech masking* in your car. When the masking noise is of sufficient level (be careful not to damage your engine), even the middle frequencies (where most speech sounds occur) are masked, and you cannot understand the singer or the radio announcer.

---

produce more forward masking than do shorter duration ones, especially when we are dealing with very short intervals (shorter than 40 ms) to start with (Carlyon, 1988). In general, the lower the frequencies of *both* the target and mask, the more masking takes place (Jesteadt, Bacon, & Lehman, 1982). In addition, the same asymmetry found for simultaneous masking shows up in forward masking: There is little masking of target tones with frequencies lower than the masker but a great deal with target tones of frequencies higher than the masker. However, we cannot explain all of these effects by interaction of excitation patterns on the basilar membrane or by suppression of the neural response to the target by that to the masker because the masker is no longer present when the target is presented at a later time. More central neural processes must be involved. In forward masking, it is likely that the masker is lowering the sensitivity of the hair cells, or their synapses with auditory nerve fibers, to stimulation by the target

tone, thus raising the threshold for the target. It is also possible that more intense maskers cause the basilar membrane to "ring," or continue to vibrate, for up to 10 ms after it is turned off (Carlyon, 1988).

What about **backward masking,** in which the masker occurs after the target? How could the masker affect our perception of the target when it occurs *after* the target sound has already affected the auditory system? Backward masking does occur, but it acts differently from forward masking. For instance, the ability to hear a click sound is reduced if a more intense click follows it by up to 25 ms. And a noise masker may increase the threshold for a tone that is turned on up to 40 ms earlier (Wright, 1964). Unfortunately, at this time the mechanism causing backward masking is not well understood.

Masking also occurs when target and mask are presented to different ears. Such masking is called **central masking** because there is no interaction of vibration patterns on a single basilar membrane,

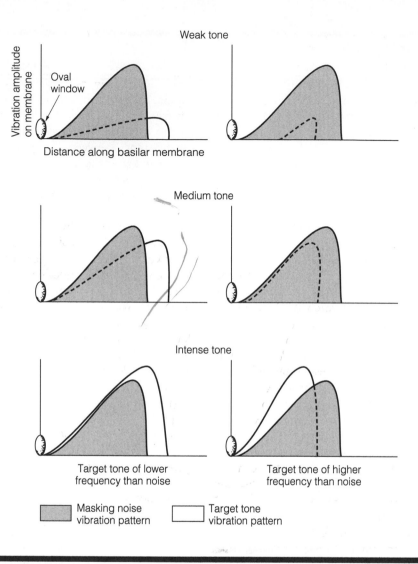

Weak tone

Medium tone

Intense tone

Target tone of lower frequency than noise

Target tone of higher frequency than noise

Masking noise vibration pattern

Target tone vibration pattern

FIGURE 7-4 The interactions of patterns of vibration of the basilar membrane resulting from a target and a noise stimulus (based on Scharf, 1964).

and the masking is therefore assumed to occur in more central brain areas. When masker and target are presented to different ears, the masker must be about 50 dB more intense than when both are presented to the same ear. Under these conditions the effect of the mask is more symmetrical and does not spread so widely with the frequency of the test tone (Zwislocki, Damianopoulos, Buining, & Glantz, 1967). Only when the frequency of the masking sound is quite low (less than 200 Hz) is there appreciable upward spread of masking (Billings & Stokinger, 1977).

It is sometimes impossible to ignore components of complex sounds that are far from the target in frequency, resulting in what is called **informational masking** (Pollack, 1975; Watson, Kelly, & Wroten, 1976). This form of masking occurs when a masking sound is made up of several different frequencies that are chosen at random from trial to trial. When the mask is presented simultaneously with a target, the target is more difficult to detect *even if none of the frequencies is particularly close to the target frequency* (Neff & Green, 1987). However, there is no backward informational masking when the masking sound ends before the target tone begins (Neff, 1991). It has been estimated that about 20% of the simultaneous masking of tones by noise is caused by informational masking (Lufti, 1990). Although the frequencies making up the masker don't have to be very near the frequency of the target tone, the further they are from the target tone's frequency, the less informational masking there is (Leek, Brown, & Dorman, 1991). Moreover, when the masking sound can be segregated from the target in some way, either by appearing to arise at a different location or to have different frequency components or a different time course, informational masking is lessened (Kidd, Mason, Deliwala, Woods, & Colburn, 1994). This suggests that informational masking is probably more cognitive in origin and may be associated with conditions in which it is difficult to focus an individual's attention on the target because of the presence of competing sounds.

Surprisingly, masking can also be *decreased*, and detectability improved, by presenting additional sounds under certain conditions. As we saw earlier, a target tone is masked by a simultaneous noise made up of a narrow band of frequencies centered at the target frequency. However, if the overall amplitude of this noise is slowly varied and if another narrow-band noise that is far from the target frequency and that is fluctuating in phase with the masking noise is added to the situation, masking of the target by the first noise is substantially *reduced* (Buus, 1985; Hall, Haggard, & Fernandes, 1984). One popular explanation of this *release* from masking is called "dip-listening," in which listeners try to listen for the target at the "dips" in the amplitude of the slowly varying masker, when the signal-to-noise ratio is highest and detectability best, and these dips are easier to spot when several noises at different frequencies are "dipping" at once (Buus, 1985; Hirsh & Watson, 1996). Another explanation is that listeners compare the overall pattern of sound level change over time (the "envelope") at the target and outside-noise frequencies; because the envelope at the target frequency contains the target and the other one doesn't, when the two are substantially different the target must be present. The latter explanation is more compatible with the fact that release from masking occurs only for detection of a target, not for discrimination of one target from another of a different level (Hall & Grose, 1995). This is because dip-listening predicts that a better target-to-noise ratio would help in any task, whereas envelope comparison requires that one envelope be different from the rest, and, in a discrimination task, the envelopes of both tones to be discriminated would differ from the remote noise envelope but not very much from each other.

Sound Discrimination

Detecting a masked tone is really a type of discrimination problem, similar to those discussed in Chapter 2. In a masking paradigm, the observer's task usually is to discriminate a target-plus-noise sound from a sound containing only noise. We also obtain useful answers when we ask the discrimination question about simpler sounds: pure tones differing only in sound pressure or in frequency. By how much must these simple sounds differ in order to be heard as different?

We begin by considering our sensitivity to sound pressure differences. Riesz (1928), working at the Bell Telephone Laboratories, did the classic study of sound pressure discrimination. He measured the Weber fraction for sound pressure (the proportion by which the pressure of a sound must be different from that of a standard in order for the difference to be detected 50% of the time—see Chapter 2) for pure tones at a range of standard pressures for each of several different sound frequencies. Figure 7-5 shows Riesz's (1928) results for four different frequencies. As you can see, the Weber fraction for sound pressure differences is smallest (discrimination is best) for stimuli in the middle range of frequencies (1,000 Hz and 4,000 Hz). Our ability to discriminate sound pressure differences is somewhat worse at higher or lower frequencies, although the difference is not always as large as Riesz (1928) found it to be (e.g., Florentine, Buus, & Mason, 1987; Jesteadt, Wier, & Green, 1977), nor is the Weber fraction always found to drop off so smoothly with level (Long & Cullen, 1985). For middle sound levels and frequencies, however, the Weber fraction is rather constant. In general, however, modern studies have found that Riesz's description of discrimination changes with sound pressure and frequency replicates well (Ward & Davidson, 1993), although some investigators find

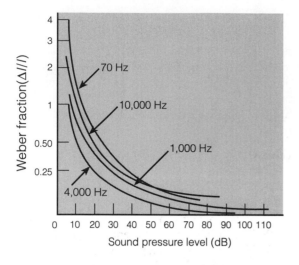

FIGURE 7-5 Sound pressure discrimination measured in terms of the Weber fraction for various sound pressure levels and frequencies of standard stimuli. Note that the Weber fractions are given in intensity (I) units, which are equivalent to pressure squared (based on Riesz, 1928).

some differences in specific values of the Weber fraction that may reflect differences in the testing conditions or the stimulus range chosen (Green, Nachmias, Kearny, & Jeffress, 1979; Hanna, von Gierke, & Green, 1986). To summarize, the auditory system can detect differences of about 10% to 20% in sound pressure (as low as 5% under optimal conditions) across a broad range of frequencies and pressures, covering the range of sounds we most often hear in everyday life.

Just as we observed in our discussion of sound detection, sound pressure-difference thresholds are about 33% smaller for sounds presented simultaneously to both ears (binaural presentation) than for those presented only to a single ear (monaural presentation—Jesteadt & Weir, 1977). This is because the binaural presentation gives the observer two chances to hear the difference (one in each ear), rather than just the single chance available when monaural presentation is used. Similarly, the pressure-difference threshold is smaller the longer a sound lasts, over a range of 2 ms to 2 sec (Florentine, 1986). The longer stimulus durations give more information about the pressure difference and thus more opportunity to detect it.

A special case of pressure discrimination arises in what has been called **profile analysis** (Green, 1987). In this situation, a listener is presented with two complex sounds, each made up of many different frequencies (often more than 20 of them), and is asked to discriminate a slight difference in the level of just *one* of the component sounds. For example, a standard "flat" profile sound might consist of 60-dB pure tones with frequencies of 250 Hz, 500 Hz, 1,000 Hz, 2,000 Hz, and 4,000 Hz. A comparison sound could consist of tones with the same frequencies and levels, except, for instance, the 1,000-Hz tone might have been increased to a level of 65 dB. A listener would be asked to say which of two successive intervals contained the sound with the higher level 1,000-Hz component (this is called a *two-interval forced-choice technique*).

Under these conditions pressure-difference thresholds can be much smaller than for single tones. Thresholds for signal frequencies between 500 Hz and 2,000 Hz can decrease by nearly 10 dB as the number of nonsignal component frequencies is increased from 3 to 21 (Kidd, Mason, Uchanski, Brantley, & Shah, 1991; Robinson & Green, 1988). The auditory system seems to carry out a "profile analysis," in which the level of the tone at the signal frequency is compared with a weighted average of the level of the other components (Berg & Green, 1990). The more component frequencies there are, the more stable, and thus the more useful, such an average would be, and thus the more a "bump" in the profile (difference in a single component) would stand out. Of course, if the profile is very "bumpy" already (e.g., has tones of many different levels), it is more difficult to detect any particular bump (Lufti, 1993; Robinson & Green, 1988). It is not surprising that many listeners must practice for many trials before they can detect these profile differences (see Hirsh & Watson, 1996). After they can, however, the thresholds so obtained are robust and consistent with thresholds obtained with older methods. For example, profile discrimination is best when the level increment is added to components of intermediate frequencies, as in the earlier example (Bernstein & Green, 1987). Also, profile discrimination is better the longer the duration of the complex sounds, up to a limit of 100 ms, after which it is constant (e.g., Dai & Green, 1993).

We also may ask, "By how much must two tones differ in frequency for the difference to be noticed?" Again, the classic study was done at the Bell Telephone Laboratories—this time by Shower and Biddulph (1931). Figure 7-6 shows Shower and Biddulph's measurements of the Weber fraction for frequency for several different sound pressure levels over a broad range of frequencies. Here the Weber fraction is $\Delta f/f$, where f is the frequency of a continuous standard tone and Δf is the modulation (brief change) in frequency of the standard that can just be detected. Notice that the Weber fraction is fairly constant and quite small (around 0.005) for moderate-level tones above 1,000 Hz. This means that if a continuous 1,000-Hz standard were changed by only 5 Hz, to 1,005 Hz, this small modulation would be detected half the time. At lower levels our discrimination of frequency differences is not quite this good. The most comprehensive of the modern studies of frequency discrimination was done by Wier, Jesteadt, and Green (1977). Their results were similar to those of Shower and Biddulph (1931); that is, the Weber fraction for frequency depended on both frequency and level in a way similar to that shown in Figure 7-6.

Another technique to measure frequency discrimination is to present sounds that may or may not change in frequency (*glide*) while they are on and to ask observers to discriminate which of two such sounds changed or in which direction the change occurred. Weber fractions for discriminating increases versus decreases in frequency (up versus down glides) are about the same as for static differences in frequency (0.002 to 0.005), but those for which of two tones glided while the other was static are significantly higher (0.005 to 0.009) (Dooley & Moore, 1988). Under special conditions, when two tones are presented to the same ear and they interact as described in Chapter 6 to produce otoacoustic emissions, the Weber fraction for frequency modulation can be as low as 0.0005 (meaning that a difference of only 1.5 Hz at 3,000 Hz can be detected half the time—McAnally & Calford, 1990). Finally, as was the case for level discrimination, binaural frequency difference thresholds are about 33% smaller than are monaural ones (Jesteadt & Wier, 1977).

Sound Localization

Sounds are usually perceived as emanating from a location in space, from sources to the right or left of, in front of or behind, and above or below our bodies. Some sounds appear to come from close by, others from a distance. Our auditory systems use several aspects of sound to construct a sort of auditory space, with our bodies at the center, within which sounds can be localized and their sources approached ("Hey, Jan, nice to see you!") or avoided ("Grrrroooowwwlll").

Inter Ear Difference Cues When a sound emanates from some distance away from and at a particular angle to a listener, several cues indicate the **azimuth,** or angle from the straight-ahead direction, of the sound source. Figure 7-7 shows a typical situation where a sound is coming from a source at 45° left azimuth. Notice that one ear receives the sound directly from the source while the other ear is in what is called the **sound shadow.** The shadowed ear receives only those sounds from the source that are *bent* around the head or *diffracted* by the edge of the head. This means that the sound pressure at the shadowed ear is lower than that at the ear receiving the sound directly.

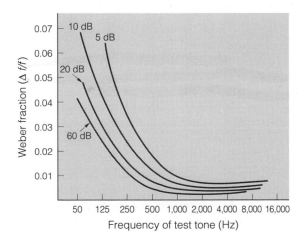

FIGURE 7-6 Frequency discrimination measured in terms of the Weber fraction for various sound pressure levels and frequencies of standard stimuli (based on Shower & Biddulph, 1931).

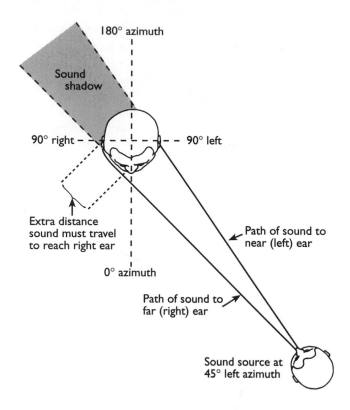

180° azimuth

Sound shadow

90° right

90° left

Extra distance sound must travel to reach right ear

0° azimuth

Path of sound to near (left) ear

Path of sound to far (right) ear

Sound source at 45° left azimuth

FIGURE 7-7 The path of sound to the two ears for a sound source at 45° left azimuth (based on Lindsay & Norman, 1977).

This **sound level difference** between the ears increases as a sound source is moved toward one side (Middlebrooks, Makous, & Green, 1989). Also, although sound waves with frequency lower than 3,000 Hz bend around the head very readily, higher frequency sound waves tend to rush right past the shadowed ear unless deflected into it by some sound-reflecting surface nearby. This exaggerates the level differences caused by the presence of a sound shadow for higher frequency sounds. The increase in sound level difference with increasing azimuth serves as a cue to the direction the sound came from. A large sound level difference between the two ears indicates that the sound source is to one side, at a large azimuth. The greatest level difference occurs when the sound source is at 90° azimuth. The ear receiving the highest level input is closest to the sound source and is perceived to be so.

Unless a sound source is at 0° or 180° azimuth, sound must travel different distances to reach the two ears. Because sound takes time to travel through space, there is a **time difference** in the arrival of the sound at the two ears. For example, for a sound at 90° azimuth in either direction, the ear closer to the sound is stimulated approximately 0.8 ms earlier than is the farther ear. Of course, the time difference is 0 for sounds at 0° or 180° azimuth. Intermediate azimuths result in intermediate values for this time difference (see Figure 7-7). Time difference is a cue to the location of a sound source and results in the experience of an apparent azimuth for it. Under certain circumstances, the time difference between the stimulation of the two ears also results in a **phase difference** in the sound stimulating the two ears. However, although phase difference could be a cue to sound direction, it provides ambiguous information for higher sound frequencies. You may demonstrate the effects of the time difference on azimuth perception for yourself by using Demonstration Box 7-4.

Inter-ear level and time differences occur in a correlated fashion for naturally occurring complex sounds, as illustrated in Figure 7-8. That is, if a complex sound occurs at 45° left azimuth, it will both be louder at the left ear and arrive there earlier. Gaik (1993) showed that sounds for which the two cues are in conflict (for example, louder at the left ear but arriving at the right ear earlier) are perceived differently from those for which the two cues are consistent. In particular, artificial sounds giving conflicting cues are often perceived to be somehow "unnatural" and to emanate from more than one location at once.

Finally, it has also been shown that the pinnae and other parts of the body delay (Batteau, 1967) or amplify (Butler, 1987; Flannery & Butler, 1981) sounds of different frequencies by different amounts. Such differential delays and amplifications provide cues as to the location of complex sound sources, especially their elevation (Asano, Suzuki, & Sone, 1990; Oldfield & Parker, 1984). Because the pinnae and the body generally are not perfectly symmetrical, the effects of their sound shadows differ depending on the direction of the sound source. This shadow effect can actually alter the sound spectra (frequency composition) of complex sounds at each of the two ears (Middlebrooks et al., 1989; Oldfield & Parker, 1986). High frequencies are the most likely to be diminished by such shadowing effects. The resulting differences in sound spectra can serve as learned cues to the directions of the sounds (Butler & Humanski, 1992; Perrett & Noble, 1995). Even brief clicks lasting only 0.025 ms can be localized in this

DEMONSTRATION BOX 7-4
Time Differences and Auditory Direction

For this demonstration you will need a length of rubber hose or flexible plastic tube. Hold one end up to each ear as shown in the figure. Now, have a friend tap the tube using a pencil. At the point where she taps, a sound wave starts moving in both directions down the tube. If she taps so that there is a longer section of tube on one side, the sound must travel farther before reaching one of your ears. This delay is perceived as a shift in direction of the sound. Notice how the sound seems to change direction as different parts of the tube are tapped, causing different patterns of sound delays.

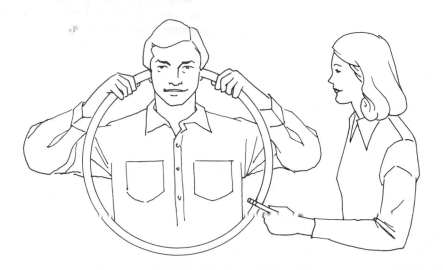

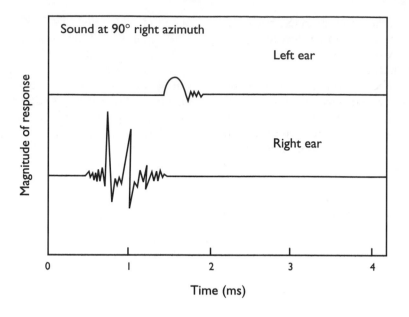

FIGURE 7-8   Responses of the two ears to a brief sound at 90° right azimuth, showing both the sound pressure level and time difference between the responses (based on Gaik, 1993, Fig. 1, p. 99).

manner, although performance decreases with level for such sounds, whereas it is unaffected by sound level for broadband noises (Hartman & Rakerd, 1993). The higher level clicks cannot be accurately localized because they stimulate much of the basilar membrane, and they are not present for long enough that the required subtle comparisons of spectra under these conditions are possible.

In 1907 Lord Raleigh proposed a dual, or two-process, theory of sound localization. He suggested that we localize low-frequency sounds by using time or phase differences, or both, at the two ears and that we localize high-frequency sounds by using the sound level differences at the two ears caused by the sound shadow and differences in their distance from the sound source. This theory was confirmed by later research. For example, Stevens and Newman (1934) recorded localization errors of listeners with eyes closed for azimuths of sound sources of different frequencies. The solid line in Figure 7-9 represents a summary of their data, with errors averaged over all locations at a particular frequency. As you can see, most errors occurred in the region of 1,500–3,000 Hz. There

were fewer errors above and below this frequency range. We can interpret this as indicating the efficient use of at least one cue in the low- and high-frequency ranges. Performance is worst in the midrange, however, where neither cue to localization is particularly useful. This interpretation has been confirmed by work on the **minimum audible angle,** which is the smallest amount of spatial separation of two sequentially presented acoustic events that can just be detected (Mills, 1958). The minimum audible angle varies as a function of frequencies and locations of the sound sources. We are most sensitive to horizontal position changes when a sound source is centered in front of our nose (near 0° azimuth) but most sensitive to vertical position changes when the sound is located directly at the side (90° azimuth; Makous & Middlebrooks, 1990; Perrott & Saberi, 1990). Minimum audible angles for movements of a *single* sound source are somewhat higher than those for two stationary sources presented sequentially, as might be expected because the information from the source is constantly changing (Perrott & Tucker, 1988). These minimum audible angles vary as a function of how fast a sound source is moving, being smallest when movement is in the horizontal or oblique direction at moderate velocities (Saberi & Perrott, 1990). Accelerations and decelerations of moving sound sources can also be detected but only if listeners can hear the sounds for a reasonably long period of time (Perrott, Constantino, & Bell, 1993). On average, we can say that movements of a sound source of only 0.9° can be reliably detected under most conditions (Hartmann & Rakerd, 1989).

Reverberation Cues When we are in an ordinary room, the sound from any source may go bouncing around the room, reflecting from the walls, ceiling, and floor many times. This means that the same sound stimulus can be received at the ear a number of times with various delays. Figure 7-10 illustrates this phenomenon. Why don't we experience an overwhelming auditory confusion as these sounds ricochet around us? Typically, only the *earliest arriving* of the many replicas of a particular complex sound is treated by the auditory system as a separate acoustic event. The echoes that arrive several milliseconds later are treated as part of that original event, not as new events. We do not experience echoes as separate events until the reflecting surface is far enough away that the echoes take a substantial time to reach us (more than 35 ms or so). It is possible, though, to become

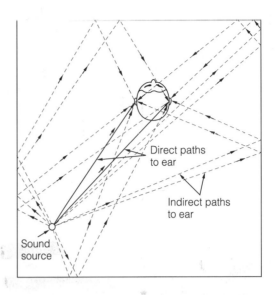

FIGURE 7-10 Some of the echoes produced by sound reflecting from the walls of a room (from Lindsay & Norman, 1977).

aware of changes in echoes that appear to reflect changes in room acoustics through experience and directed attention (cf. Clifton, Freyman, Litovsky, & McCall, 1994). The fact that sounds that arrive at interstimulus intervals of less than 35 ms seem to be fused into one event and that we localize the sound source in space based on information from the earliest arriving sound is called the **precedence effect**. An extensive amount of research has been done on the precedence effect (Rakerd & Hartmann, 1985; Wallach, Newman, & Rosenzweig, 1949; Zurek, 1980), and we now know that it is common in all mammals and occurs even in insects (Wyttenbach & Hoy, 1993).

The experiments of Wallach and colleagues (1949) indicated that the earlier of a pair of fused sounds (separated by 2 ms) was 6–10 times more important than the later of the pair in determining the perceived direction of the sound source. This unequal weighting of the earliest-arriving sound also holds when the two sounds are of different frequencies, providing that the earlier is a low-frequency sound and the later is a high-frequency sound (Shinn-Cunningham, Zurek, Durlach, & Clifton, 1995); high-frequency leading sounds are weighted equally with low-frequency trailing

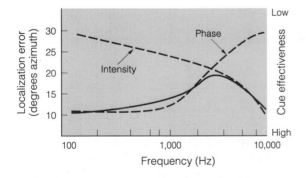

FIGURE 7-9 Relative cue effectiveness in arbitrary units for interaural intensity and phase differences (dashed lines) as a function of frequency. The solid line shows mean localization errors as a function of frequency. (From Gulick, 1971. Copyright 1971 by Oxford University Press, Inc. Reprinted by permission. Data from Stevens & Newman, 1934.)

sounds, and no precedence effect occurs. The precedence effect is an important factor in our ability to listen selectively to one source of sound even though it may be surrounded by a large group of competing sounds (see the discussion of the cocktail party problem in Chapter 15). You can experience the effects of precedence on the localization of sound by using Demonstration Box 7-5.

Under appropriate conditions, echoes can be important to the judgment of the location of sounds. For example, blind individuals apparently use echoes to help them locate and avoid obstacles (Supra, Cotzin, & Dallenbach, 1944; Worchel & Dallenbach, 1947). Animals such as bats and whales have highly developed echolocation systems, similar to sonar, which they can use to locate objects with the same facility with which we use our eyes (Simmons, 1989). These animals may even have special auditory brain pathways analogous to the tectopulvinar visual pathway (serving visual localization—see Chapter 3) to control scanning head movements, which in turn may help to build up a representation of the immediate environment (Kobler, Isbey, & Casseday, 1987), especially complex auditory images of prey (Simmons, 1989).

Echoes also provide cues to the distance of sounds from a listener. As we stated earlier, sound reaches our ears both directly from a source and after being reflected from (or *reverberating* from) various surfaces such as walls (see Figure 7-10). As

a sound source gets farther away from a listener, the amount of sound that directly reaches the ears decreases more rapidly than the amount reaching the ears after reverberation. Thus, the relative amount of "reverberation sound" (which has a distinct quality, like an echo) is a cue to the distance of a sound source from an observer. Bekesy was one of the first to investigate this cue systematically. In 1938 (Bekesy, 1960) he showed that altering the proportion of reverberation sound alters judgments of perceived distances of sounds. More recent work (Butler, Levy, & Neff, 1980; Mershon, Ballenger, Little, McMurtry, & Buchanan, 1989; Mershon & Bowers, 1979) has confirmed and extended this earlier work.

Another cue to distance that seems as compelling as the amount of reverberation is the frequency makeup, or *spectrum*, of a complex sound. Sounds composed mostly of high frequencies seem to come from quite nearby, and the more the sound is dominated by low-frequency components, the farther away its source appears to be. Butler and colleagues (1980) suggested that through experience with a variety of sounds, we learn that more distant sounds typically *are* more dominated by low-frequency components, perhaps because the high-frequency components are more easily blocked by intervening obstructions.

Learning is also involved in the perception that louder sounds are nearer than softer sounds. In fact, everything else being equal, nearer sounds do

---

DEMONSTRATION BOX 7-5
Precedence and the One-Speaker Stereo Illusion

For this demonstration you will need a radio, phonograph, or tape recorder that has stereo speakers located about 2 m apart. Turn on some music, and stand about midway between the two speakers, facing a point between them. You will notice that the sound seems to envelop you. It comes from both sides, and you can clearly identify sounds coming from one speaker or the other. Take a few steps (you need not go very far) toward one side where a speaker is located. After only a step or two you will suddenly find that all the sound seems to be coming from the

speaker nearest you. You no longer get any sensation of sound coming from the more distant speaker (although it still affects sound quality, as you can demonstrate by turning it off). A few steps to the other side will reverse this effect, making it appear as though all of the sound is coming from the other speaker. As you move toward a speaker, you alter the time it takes for the sound to reach your ears. The precedence process then takes the sound arriving first and emphasizes it, giving you the impression that all the sound emanates from that source.

have a higher pressure than do sounds from the same source at a greater distance. Differences in sound distance are thus reliably coded by differences in sound pressure (Ashmead, LeRoy, & Odom, 1990; Mershon & King, 1975). Listeners even make use of this property to direct their motions toward (a friend?) or away from (an enemy?) certain sounds (Ashmead, Davis, & Northington, 1995). Of course, it is always possible that the more distant sound is emitting a stronger signal, making this cue unreliable in deciding the absolute distance of a sound source unless the sound is a familiar one. Through experience we build up memories of what a ringing phone or a car engine sounds like when these sounds are made at different distances from us. In later encounters we can use this knowledge to judge how far away a sound source may be based on the remembered loudness of other similar sound sources.

A final important cue to the distance of a sound source is the presence of a compelling visual object that *could* be the source. The ventriloquist's dummy seems to be talking because its mouth moves and the ventriloquist's does not (if the ventriloquist is any good). Echoes and reverberation play no role in this effect (Mershon, Desaulniers, & Amerson, 1980). In addition, the illusion that a sound is coming from a likely visual object can be so compelling that it can affect the perceived loudness of the sound. If the sound seems to emanate from a visual object that is far away, it sounds louder than if it seems to emanate from one that is close by (Mershon, Desaulniers, Kiefer, & Amerson, 1981). Observers seem to correct for the fact that actual sound pressure diminishes rapidly as the distance from the sound source increases, a phenomenon termed *loudness constancy* (see Chapter 14 for a discussion of constancies).

Virtual Auditory Space   The pinnae, head, neck, shoulders, and other nearby body parts affect different frequencies of sound differently. These effects can be summarized by the head-related transfer function, or HRTF, a mathematical description of exactly how each frequency in a sound from anywhere in surrounding space is amplified or damped by the body parts near the ears. The HRTF describes all of the information available at the two ears regarding the location of a sound source. It is possible to alter sound presented through headphones in the ways it would have been altered in the free field, according to the HRTF, and thus to simulate what a listener would receive in the free field. When this is done the listener has a compelling impression that the sound source is located "out there" in the world rather than is emanating from the headphones (Wightman & Kistler, 1989). Moreover, such "virtual" sound sources can be localized almost as well as real ones, provided that "virtual" head movements are allowed and sufficient exposure obtained (Bronkhorst, 1995; Wightman & Kistler, 1989). The main source of error for virtual localization is in front-back and elevation judgments, both of which also occur with real sources. The HRTFs of different people are, of course, not the same. However, they are sufficiently similar that a "generic" HRTF from a representative listener does create virtual auditory space with headphone-presented sounds for other listeners and permits nearly as good localization performance as do individualized HRTFs (Wenzel, Arruda, Kistler, & Wightman, 1993). This result promises that a new type of human-machine interface technology, a virtual acoustic display, might be constructed using a standard HRTF that would work for most people. Someday, airplane cockpits and air traffic control displays, computers, and advanced communications systems might include virtual acoustic displays that will significantly enhance both the usefulness of the machines and the richness of our experience of them (see ASVA 97, 1997).

Physiological Mechanisms   The auditory system contains neural units that respond to both time differences and sound pressure differences between the two ears and that may, in turn, signal the location of a sound source. For instance, some neurons in the superior olives, inferior colliculi (Semple & Kitzes, 1987), and auditory cortex of various birds and mammals respond best to binaural stimuli that reach the two ears at slightly different times or pressures (see Erulkar, 1972; Phillips, 1993; and Phillips & Brugge, 1985, for reviews). Different neurons have different "best" interaural time differences or different "best" interaural pressure differences. In other words, different neurons are "tuned" to different time differences or sound pressure differences between the two ears. Some of these neurons are also tuned to spectral differences that indicate elevation of the sound source (Aitkin & Martin, 1990). Because these differences are cues to the location of sounds, we could say that these tuned neurons encode sound location much as neurons tuned to sounds of different frequencies encode sound frequency. It is possible that such neurons constitute a kind of map of auditory space, with each neuron having a region of auditory space to which it responds best, a sort of "auditory receptive field" much like the visual receptive fields discussed in Chapter 3.

There are problems with this idea, however. The major one is that the tuning of the neurons is too gross to account for the accuracy with which animals, including humans, can localize sounds. In other words, the "auditory receptive fields" of these neurons are too large to account for the degree of accuracy shown in behavioral data. In some species, such as the barn owl, much smaller, more intricately organized auditory receptive fields have been found using electrophysiological recording techniques (Knudsen & Konishi, 1978a). In the barn owl the receptive fields of these neurons have a center-surround organization (Knudsen & Konishi, 1978b). That is, not only do these neurons fire above their background rate to stimuli in their "best" areas of space, but also they are inhibited in their response by sounds in areas outside their best areas, thus resembling, in many ways, the center-surround organization of neurons at various levels of the visual system (see Chapter 3) and other parts of the auditory system (see Chapter 6). So far there has been no direct evidence that such center-surround neurons exist in the auditory systems of mammals, but it is possible that the time difference and pressure difference detectors are preliminary stages leading to such neurons.

It is possible that interaction of time difference and pressure difference detectors might give rise to higher level neurons that have relatively restricted receptive fields and might allow a fairly accurate mapping of auditory space. One way this could happen is that *change* in time difference and/or pressure difference cues could be coded more precisely than the absolute values of the time difference or pressure difference between the ears. It has been shown psychophysically that the localization mechanism adapts very quickly to sounds that don't change. On the other hand, an adapted localization mechanism responds vigorously again as soon as a stimulus change occurs (Hafter & Buell, 1990). In cats, gerbils, and rats, inferior colliculus neurons respond more accurately to changes in interaural phase than to the interaural phase itself (Spitzer & Semple, 1991).

Another possibility is a map of auditory space that is based on, or calibrated by, the more precise map of visual space. In effect the spatial coordinates used in the visual maps of space could also be assigned to particular auditory neurons. Visual maps of space clearly calibrate auditory maps in the barn owl (Knudsen & Knudsen, 1989), especially in the superior colliculus of the brain (Knudsen & Brainerd, 1991). The deep layers of the superior colliculi of mammals also contain coordinated visual, auditory, and tactile maps of space (Stein & Meredith, 1993), making such a hypothesis even more probable.

A final possibility is that there are no neurons in the auditory cortex that are precisely tuned to sound location. Instead, it is possible that subcortical time difference and pressure difference detectors contribute to location-specific *patterns* of cortical firing, similar to the across-fiber patterns that are thought to encode different smell stimuli (see Chapter 8; Middlebrooks, Clock, Xu, & Green, 1994). In this case, all cortical neurons would be involved in the pattern of firing encoding a sound from any particular location in the auditory field. A specific place would then be coded by a specific pattern of response. For example, something like Neuron A firing vigorously, Neuron B firing moderately, and Neuron C firing minimally might indicate a sound that is near and to the left, whereas Neuron A firing minimally, Neuron B moderately, and Neuron C vigorously might indicate a sound that is more distant and to the right. This approach is supported by the fact that such across-fiber patterns in the auditory cortex of cats seem to give more information about the location of stimulating sounds than do the rates of firing of individual neurons (Middlebrooks et al., 1994).

SUBJECTIVE DIMENSIONS OF SOUNDS

Researchers used to believe that there is a direct and relatively simple correspondence between subjective experiences of sounds and physical properties of sounds. It was taken for granted that every *qualitatively different psychological variable* reflects almost perfectly some corresponding *quantifiable physical variable*. For example, the subjective dimension of **loudness** was thought to be a direct reflection of sound *pressure* and that of **pitch** was thought to reflect sound *frequency*. However, researchers subsequently learned that the subjective qualities of loudness and pitch are complex perceptions that depend on the interaction of several physical characteristics of the stimulus, as well as on the physical and psychological state of the listener.

The deeply rooted older view maintained that at best a listener can be expected to distinguish only two subjective dimensions of sound (loudness and pitch) because there are two predominant physical dimensions of sound (pressure and frequency). In fact, we can differentiate many qualitatively different experiences arising from sound stimuli. These include, in addition to pitch and loudness, the **perceived location** of a sound (where it seems to come from), its **perceived duration** (how extended in time it appears to be), its **timbre** (that complex quality that allows us to distinguish a note played on a clarinet from the same note played on a violin), its **volume** (the sense in which it fills space and seems large or small), and its **density** (a complex feeling of the compactness or hardness of the sound), as well as **consonance** or **dissonance** (how two sounds seem to "go together" or to "clash"). Our auditory experience is rich with these and other sensory qualities—the auditory system is not simply a crude receiver designed to register the frequency and level of sounds.

Recent work has emphasized the interaction of these subjective dimensions of sound rather than their separateness. For example, pitch and loudness are indeed "privileged" dimensions because people can classify sounds faster on the basis of pitch and loudness than on the basis of volume or other subjective qualities (Grau & Nelson, 1988). However, pitch and loudness do interact with one another in such tasks and may even interfere with perception of timbre (Grau & Nelson, 1988; Melara & Marks, 1990). It seems as if the subjective dimensions of sound not only provide additional richness to our conscious experience of sound but also combine with one another to produce complex effects. In the sections that follow

we will discuss a few of these subjective dimensions of sound in more detail.

Loudness

The loudness of a sound is greatly affected by its pressure amplitude. When other properties are held constant, the greater the pressure amplitude of a sound, the greater its apparent loudness. The experience of loudness, however, is *not* identical with sound pressure. Many other factors influence our experience of the loudness of a sound. Thus, decibels are *not* measures of loudness.

To measure loudness we use psychophysical scaling procedures such as those discussed in Chapter 2. S. S. Stevens (1956) used magnitude estimation in a classic study of this type. In his study, observers listened to a set of 1,000-Hz tones that varied in sound pressure, and they assigned a number to each one in such a way that the number was proportional to the tone's loudness relative to a standard pressure that was given the number 100. Thus, a tone that sounded twice as loud as the standard would be called 200, and a tone that sounded half as loud would be called 50. Stevens found that on average loudness is a power function of sound pressure, $L = aP^{0.6}$, where L is the loudness, P is the pressure amplitude of the sound, and a is a constant. The exponent of 0.6 indicates that the power function rises steeply for low sound pressures and then levels off for higher sound pressures (see Chapter 2). The value of the power function exponent for loudness depends on the specific stimuli used and the test conditions employed (Marks, 1974). For example, the exponent varies with stimulus frequency; it is substantially larger than 0.6 for frequencies lower than 400 Hz (Hellman & Zwislocki, 1968; Ward, 1990).

Based on his own and others' work, Stevens suggested a new unit by which to measure loudness based on comparison of loudness to the apparent loudness of a standard sound, a 1,000-Hz stimulus at a level of 40 dB. Any sound whose loudness matches that of the standard is said to have a loudness of 1 **sone**. For most of the range of audible sound pressures there is a linear relationship between the logarithm of loudness in sones and sound pressure in dB. To double the loudness (for instance, from 1 to 2 sones) we have to increase the

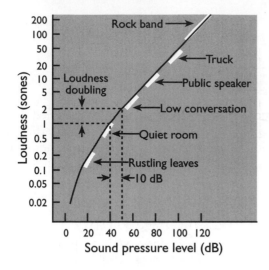

FIGURE 7-11 The relationship between loudness (measured in sones) and sound pressure level (measured in decibels).

level of the sound by about 10 dB. For very weak sounds (below 30 dB), however, doubling the loudness requires much smaller increases in level (e.g., Canévet, Hellman, & Scharf, 1986). This relationship is shown in Figure 7-11, which also shows the loudness in sones of some typical sounds. Table 7-1 summarizes essential aspects of sones and other audiometric units discussed in this chapter.

The loudness of a tone is also affected by its frequency. This relationship can be measured by presenting a listener with a standard tone of a given frequency and level and asking her to adjust the

level of a tone of a different frequency until its loudness matches that of the standard tone. This procedure is repeated for tones of various frequencies. A curve that describes the sound pressure levels at which tones of different frequencies appear to be equally loud as the standard tone is called an **equal loudness contour.**

A series of equal loudness contours is shown in Figure 7-12. Each curve represents a different sound pressure level of the standard tone in decibels. Notice that the contours are not flat. If tones of the different frequencies sounded equally loud when they were the same level, all of the contours would be horizontal straight lines. The fact that the contours rise and fall with frequency, much as the contour for absolute threshold at the bottom of the graph does, means that tones of equal level but of different frequencies appear to differ in loudness. Tones of less than 1,000 Hz or greater than 6,000 Hz must be considerably higher in sound pressure to match the loudnesses of tones between 1,000 Hz and 6,000 Hz. Thus, tones in the middle range of frequencies sound considerably louder than tones of equal level outside this range.

Duration also influences the loudness of a tone. For tones briefer than about 200 ms, we must increase sound pressure level to match the loudness of a longer tone. An equal loudness contour for tones of various durations is shown in Figure 7-13. According to this curve, a 2-ms burst of sound must have a level of about 16 dB in order to sound as loud as a 10-ms, 10-dB burst. This sort of finding suggests that the auditory system sums the energy of sounds arriving over a 200-ms time window (Gulick, 1971).

Table 7-1   Audiometric Units

AUDIOMETRIC TERM	UNIT	WHAT IS MEASURED	HOW MEASURED
Pressure amplitude	Dyne/cm²	Variation of sound pressure from atmospheric	Measure peak compressive force per 1 cm² area
Sound pressure level	Decibel (dB)	Ratio of pressure amplitudes of two sounds	$20 \log (P/P_0)$
Frequency	Hertz (Hz)	Number of cycles of compression/rarefaction	Count cycles per second
Loudness	Sone	Subjective impression of sound intensity	1 sone = loudness of 1,000-Hz tone at 40 dB
Pitch	Mel	Subjective impression of sound frequency	Pitch of 1,000-Hz tone at 40 dB is 1,000 mels

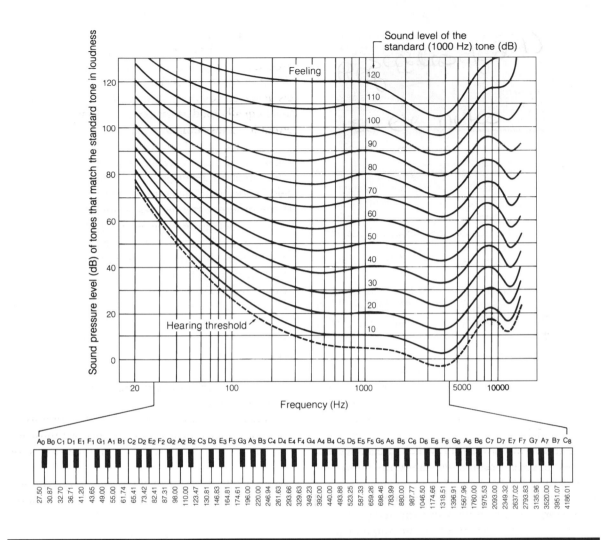

FIGURE 7-12   Equal loudness contours. (From Lindsay & Norman, 1977. Data from Robinson & Dadson, 1956.)

Presentation of the same stimulus to the two ears causes the subjective impressions of loudness from each ear to add together (Algom, Ben-Aharon, & Cohen-Raz, 1989; Levelt, Riemersma, & Bunt, 1972; Marks, 1979b; Schneider & Cohen, 1997). Thus, a binaural presentation will sound about twice as loud as a monaural presentation of the same tone. You can demonstrate this for yourself using a radio, stereo, or television. First, experience the loudness of the sound of the TV when you listen with both ears. Then cover one ear, and notice how the loudness diminishes. The mechanism that sums loudnesses from the two ears appears to be separate from the one that sums loudnesses over time (Algom, Rubin, & Cohen-Raz, 1989).

Other sounds occurring at the same time as, or just before, a sound to be judged also can affect loudness. For example, if a continuous tone is played to one ear and an intermittent one to the other, the loudness of the continuous tone appears to diminish with time (Botte, Canévet, & Scharf, 1982). The reduction in loudness for a continuously presented sound is called **auditory adaptation.** Adaptation is weak for a continuous tone alone, but it can be quite dramatic when the continuous and intermittent tones are presented separately to the two ears. The loudness of the continuous tone in one ear actually diminishes to zero if

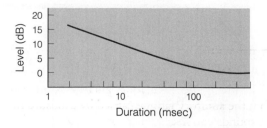

FIGURE 7-13 Equal loudness contour showing the changes in level needed to maintain a constant loudness as the duration of the standard is varied. (From Gulick, 1971. Copyright 1971 by Oxford University Press, Inc. Reprinted by permission.)

the intermittent tone in the other ear is close to it in frequency and is played for 40 sec (Botte, Baruch, & Scharf, 1986). Similar adaptation effects are seen when repeatedly judging the loudness of sounds of two different frequencies if most of the tones at one frequency are higher or lower in sound level than those at the other (Marks, 1993). There is more adaptation of loudness for the higher level tones than for the lower level tones, making the higher level tones sound relatively softer in this context than they would if judged alone. This adaptation is frequency specific and probably takes place in the central auditory system (Marks, 1993, 1994).

A related phenomenon, called **auditory fatigue,** is caused by exposing the ear to a very high level sound. The resultant reduction of loudness of other stimuli presented immediately after the high-level sound stops spreads to other frequencies far from that of the high-level sound (Botte & Mönikheim, 1994). Moreover, the effect of the high-level sound may persist for a long time. Postman and Egan (1949) exposed observers to a 115-dB sound for 20 min. They then measured the sensitivity (sensitivity is usually correlated with loudness) of their listeners over a period of several days. In Figure 7-14 the horizontal line represents listeners' preexposure sensitivity, and the other curves represent the reduction in sensitivity, which can be interpreted as a reduction in loudness, for varying periods of time following the exposure to the 115-dB sound. As you can see, the largest sensitivity reduction immediately followed the exposure to the 115-dB sound; however, it persisted to a measurable extent over a period of 24 hr. You can experience an interesting analog to this experiment (without any risk of damaging your ears) by using Demonstration Box 7-6.

The complexity of a sound also influences its loudness. Most of the sounds we hear in our everyday environment are composed of many different frequencies of sound. We can create a different kind of equal loudness contour by asking listeners to adjust the level of a 1,000-Hz pure tone until its loudness matches that of some complex sound. Consider a complex sound composed of frequencies centered around 1,000 Hz. We

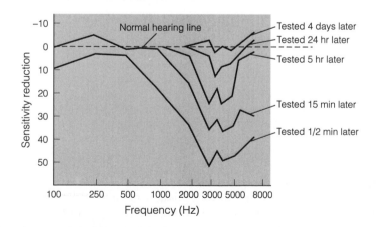

FIGURE 7-14 Prolonged reduction of sensitivity following exposure to a 115-dB sound for 20 min (based on Postman & Egan, 1949).

DEMONSTRATION BOX 7-6
Auditory Fatigue

During an average day you are exposed to many noises and sounds, from individuals who talk with you, stereos, televisions, radios, and numerous other sources. Set a radio or a stereo to an intensity level where the sound seems comfortable for listening in the evening before you go to bed. At the day's end, your auditory system has become fatigued by the ongoing, persistent noise of the day. When you awaken in the morning, however, you may find that the radio,

set to the same sound level, will appear to be too loud. During the night your ears have recovered from the auditory fatigue caused by exposure to the sounds you heard during the previous day. The quiet of the night has given you a chance to recover your sensitivity; hence all sounds now seem louder. This may explain why an alarm clock, whose bell seems low and pleasant when bought one evening in a department store, will seem so jarring and loud the following morning.

---

refer to the range of frequencies included in the sound as its **bandwidth.** As the bandwidth of the sound is increased from narrow to wider, the level of each frequency component is decreased in order to keep the overall level of the sound the same. Figure 7-15 displays an equal loudness contour for such a complex sound. Notice that for bandwidths below about 160 Hz, increasing the bandwidth does not affect the loudness of the sound. This is reasonable because the overall level of the sound is not changing but, rather, only the number of different frequencies included in it. Notice, however, what happens when the bandwidth reaches a critical value of 160 Hz. From this bandwidth onward, loudness begins to increase as we include a greater number of frequencies, although the total level of the sound is unchanged (Cacace & Margolis, 1985; Scharf, 1978).

Pitch

Every time you sing or play a musical scale, you are varying the subjective experience of *pitch*. The *do*, *re*, and *mi* you sing differ in pitch: The *mi* seems "higher" than the *do*. The most important physical determinant of pitch is the frequency of the sound stimulus. The "high" notes on the piano have higher frequencies than the "low" notes. For instance, the dominant frequency of A_4 on the piano (see the extended piano keyboard pictured in Figure 7-12) is 440 Hz, whereas the dominant frequency of A_5 is 880 Hz.

An important demonstration of the strong relationship between frequency and pitch was performed by Robert Hooke in 1681. Hooke placed a card against a wheel that had teeth notched in it and then spun the wheel. The spinning wheel's teeth hit the card, and the resultant vibrations sent out a sound wave—a sort of rough buzzing musical note. When the speed of rotation was increased, the frequency of vibration of the card increased, and so did the pitch of the note. For centuries thereafter, the terms *pitch* and *frequency* were used interchangeably on the assumption that pitch rises and falls in exact step with frequency. However, this assumption is incorrect.

The most commonly used measure of the pitch of a sound is the musical scale. Any note 1 octave

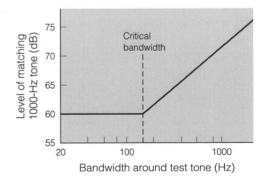

FIGURE 7-15 The effect on loudness of increasing the bandwidth of frequencies in a complex tone (based on Gulick, 1971).

higher than another note of the same name has a frequency exactly two times that of the lower note. For example, A_4 and A_5 on the piano are separated by 1 octave, and the dominant frequency of A_5, 880 Hz, is twice that of A_4 at 440 Hz. This multiplicative definition of *octave* results in all octaves having an equal difference on a logarithmic scale. To see this, consider a set of notes separated by 1 octave: $f_1 / f_2 = 2$ and $f_2 / f_3 = 2$. Then, $\log f_1 - \log f_2 = \log 2$, and $\log f_2 - \log f_3 = \log 2$. Thus, equal frequency ratios imply equal differences of log frequency (log 2 for the octave). The linear relationship between the musical scale and log frequency is shown in Figure 7-16A.

The musical scale has undergone very little change over the years, although some attempts have been made to adjust the spacing between the notes in an attempt to represent more accurately the pitches of different musical notes. For example, the **equal temperament scale** divides each octave into 12 standard intervals (representing equal logarithmic steps) between the musical notes (W. D. Ward, 1970). These intervals are called *semitones*, and each semitone is further divided into 100 *cents*.

Thus, an octave consists of 1,200 cents, and the pitch of any tone can be precisely described in terms of which octave it is in and how many cents it lies above the lowest tone in that octave.

The most useful nonmusical scale for pitch so far is the **mel** scale proposed by Stevens, Volkman, and Newman (1937). Like the sone scale of loudness, the mel scale of pitch was created using psychophysical scaling techniques. For instance, in one experiment the researchers built a sort of electronic piano with 20 keys and 20 corresponding knobs set above the keyboard. Turning a knob varied the pure tone produced by the associated key through a wide range of frequencies. Listeners tuned the piano to produce pitch intervals that appeared to be equally wide. The results were surprising. Subjects did not tune the piano to equal steps on the frequency scale, nor did they tune it to equal steps on a scale of musical intervals.

To specify pitch on the resulting mel scale, as in the case of the sone scale of loudness, we select a standard sound for purposes of definition. The standard sound is the same as that used for sones, namely, a 1,000-Hz, 40-dB pure tone. This tone is

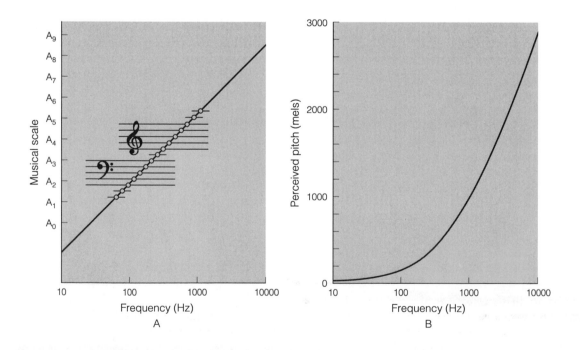

FIGURE 7-16   (A) The relationship between the log frequency and musical scale and (B) the relationship between mels and log frequency (from Lindsay & Norman, 1977).

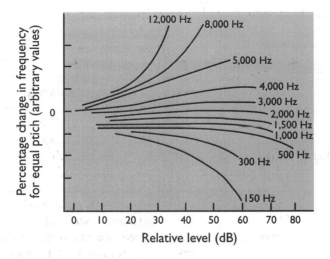

FIGURE 7-17   The relationship between apparent pitch and sound level for one listener (based on Stevens, 1935).

assigned a pitch of 1,000 mels. The standard frequency of 1,000 Hz lies between the notes B_5 and C_6 on the musical scale (see Figure 7-12). However, there are large discrepancies between the mel scale and the musical scale. For instance, the 1-octave difference between C_3 and C_4 corresponds to 167 mels, whereas the 1-octave difference between C_6 and C_7 corresponds to 508 mels. Such measurements confirm the feeling, often expressed by musicians, that the higher musical octaves sound "larger" than the lower ones. It is as if there is more "psychological distance" between the keys at the high end of the piano than between those at the low end. The nonlinear relationship between pitch in mels and log frequency is shown in Figure 7-16B.

Just as factors other than sound pressure level affect the loudness of a sound, factors other than frequency affect its pitch. The major physical factor other than frequency that affects the pitch of a pure tone is its pressure. Using an experimental technique similar to that used in producing equal loudness contours, we can produce **equal pitch contours.** The listener can be asked either to adjust the pressure level of one of two tones that differ in frequency until the two tones match in pitch (Stevens, 1935) or to adjust the frequency of one of two tones that differ in level until the tones match in pitch (Gulick,

1971). Figure 7-17 shows the results from one listener measured by Stevens (1935). The graph shows the percentage change in the frequency necessary to keep the pitch constant as level is changed. The ordinate was chosen so that lines curving upward mean that the pitch is increasing and lines curving downward mean that the pitch is decreasing. As the figure shows, varying the level of a tone alters its pitch. For high frequency tones pitch tends to rise as level increases, whereas for lower frequency tones an increase in level tends to lower pitch.

An interesting illusion, called the *Doppler illusion*, arises from the effects of pressure on pitch (Neuhoff & McBeath, 1996). The *Doppler effect* refers to the change in frequency of a wave when the source of the wave is moving relative to the observer. The Doppler effect is what causes the pitch change of an ambulance siren as the ambulance passes us. However, when a sound source moves at a constant speed past an observer, the observed frequency drops both as the source approaches and as it recedes. Nonetheless, we hear the pitch of this sound rise as the source approaches and then drop dramatically as it passes and recedes. The illusion of increasing pitch (even though frequency is decreasing) as the source approaches apparently arises from the dramatic increase in sound pressure as the source approaches because it can be simulated by changing the pressure of a static source in the same way as that of a moving one would change (Neuhoff & McBeath, 1996).

Another factor that affects the pitch of a pure tone is its duration. A pure tone that lasts for only a few milliseconds is always heard as a click, whatever its frequency. In order to have pitch, tones of frequency greater than 1,000 Hz must last for around 10 ms or longer. For tones of frequency less than 1,000 Hz at least six to nine cycles of the sound wave must reach the ear before it is perceived to have pitch, meaning that most such tones must last for considerably longer than 10 ms before they have pitch (Gulick, 1971). Even for tones that exceed the minimum duration the tonal quality continues to improve as duration is increased up to about 250 ms. Listeners are better able to discriminate between tones of different frequencies when their duration is longer. You may recall that the loudness of a tone also increases as we increase its duration up to around 200–250 ms. Perhaps a quarter of a second represents some sort of fundamental time period for sensory systems such as the ear. Our phenomenal impressions of the world in many modalities seem to be based on averages or sums of energy changes taken over this small window of time (see also Chapter 13).

Theories of Pitch Perception

We now have some inkling of "where" in the cortex pitch is encoded. Studies of patients with parts of their temporal lobes removed (to control epilepsy) suggest that a part of the right temporal lobe called Herschl's gyrus (in Area A1 of the brain; see Figure 6-18) might be where pitch is computed (Zatorre, 1988). "How" pitch is computed, and what information from the ear is used to do this, is a bit more difficult to describe.

Consider a complex sound composed of several different pure tones. The auditory system would conduct a crude Fourier analysis of this complex sound (Ohm's Law), and a listener could discern the presence of the various components. For instance, if two tones are played simultaneously, we hear a musical chord containing two distinct components that differ in pitch—we do not hear a single unitary sound (as you discovered in Demonstration Box 6-2).

We call the lowest, and usually most intense, frequency pure tone in such a complex sound the fundamental. Musical instruments tend to produce complex sounds. In addition to the fundamental there are harmonics, which are frequencies higher than the fundamental. These harmonics all are whole number multiples of the fundamental frequency. For example, we have already noted that a sound wave of 220 Hz corresponds to the musical note A_3. When a musical instrument plays this note, the complex waveform produced also will contain some sound energy at frequencies of 440 Hz, 880 Hz, 1,320 Hz, and so forth. These would be called *high even harmonics* (because they represent even number multiples—2, 4, 6, and so forth—of the fundamental frequency). The timbre of a particular instrument depends on the specific harmonics it produces. Different instruments emphasize different higher harmonics (in music these are often called *overtones*). It is the number of higher harmonics, or overtones, and the relative strength of each that allow us to distinguish a note played by striking a piano key from a note of the same pitch played by plucking a guitar string. The pitch of a complex sound is largely determined by the frequency of the fundamental, whereas the timbre is determined by the harmonics and other, more complex features (McAdams, Winsberg, Donnadieu, De Soete, & Krimphoff, 1995). Nonetheless, the pitch and timbre of complex sounds interact (Beal, 1985). Pitch perception in the context of several complex sounds seems stronger and more resistant to interference from timbre than vice versa (Krumhansl & Iverson, 1992). Nonmusicians seem especially vulnerable to interference between the two dimensions, with timbre differences having a greater effect on judgments of the pitch of isolated sounds than pitch has on timbre (Pitt, 1994). Various combinations of harmonics produce different subjective impressions of the sound. These were described by Helmholtz (1863/1930) back in the mid-1800s and are summarized in Table 7-2.

Because the fundamental frequency is the greatest common denominator of all of the harmonics present in a complex sound, it is easily derived for any complex sound. For example, for a set of harmonics of 600 Hz, 900 Hz, and 1,200 Hz, the fundamental would be 300 Hz. Remember that in natural situations a complex sound usually contains both a fundamental and several higher harmonics.

Table 7-2   Sound Composition and Timbre (based on Helmholtz, 1863/1930)

MAKEUP OF COMPLEX TONE	SUBJECTIVE IMPRESSION
Fundamental alone	Soft
Fundamental plus first harmonic	Mellow
Fundamental plus several harmonics	Broad or full
Fundamental plus high harmonics	Sharp
Fundamental intense, harmonics less intense	Full
Harmonics intense, fundamental less intense	Hollow
Odd harmonics (for example, 1, 3, 5) dominating	Nasal
Frequency ratios of 16:15, 9:8, 15:8, 7:5, or 7:6	Rough or screeching

However, it is possible to artificially create a set of pure tones that is based on a particular fundamental without actually presenting the fundamental itself (for example, 600-Hz, 900-Hz, and 1,200-Hz tones without the 300-Hz fundamental). Such missing fundamental sound complexes can produce an interesting illusion. Suppose you are presented with two complex sounds. One contains the fundamental along with the higher harmonics, and the other contains only the higher harmonics—its fundamental is missing. The illusion is that the pitch of both sounds still appears to be the same, even though the fundamental is not physically present in the waveform of the second sound. Animals, such as cats, birds, and monkeys, are also subject to this illusion (Tomlinson & Schwarz, 1988). Furthermore, magnetic recordings from the primary auditory cortex (A1) of humans show that the same response is produced there when a complex sound with a missing fundamental is presented as when the sound complex contains the fundamental tone (Pantev, Hoke, Lutkenhoner, & Lehnertz, 1989).

Although this auditory illusion may seem of only passing interest, it actually plays an important role in testing the two major theories of pitch. The first of these theories is based on the place principle, and the second is based on the frequency principle. The place principle asserts that different pitches are encoded as different *places* of maximum vibration along the basilar membrane, whereas the frequency principle asserts that pitch is encoded in terms of the overall *frequency* of firing in the auditory nerve.

The place principle was proposed more than 100 years ago, when Helmholtz became intrigued by the fact that the auditory system could separate a complex sound stimulus into its component simple frequencies. He suggested that some parts of the basilar membrane resonate to (that is, vibrate in sympathy with) low-frequency tones, whereas other parts resonate to tones of higher frequency. Thus, if we sounded a complex tone it would be automatically decomposed into its component frequencies on the basilar membrane. Each different tone would cause a different *place* on the membrane to vibrate. This is the *place principle*.

The place principle was supported and modified by Bekesy in a series of precise experiments that ultimately won him the Nobel prize (see Bekesy, 1960). Bekesy discovered that high-frequency tones maximally stimulate the narrow end of the basilar membrane near the oval window, and tones of lower frequencies cause their largest effects farther toward the other (wider) end of the basilar membrane. The action of the basilar membrane is not as simple as Helmholtz's resonance notion, however, because waves of activation were found to travel down the membrane. Moreover, as we discussed in Chapter 6, there are complex interactions between hair cells and the basilar membrane that sharpen the tuning of the basilar membrane (the active process).

The place principle has difficulty explaining the phenomenon of the missing fundamental. Helmholtz attempted to deal with this by suggesting that the transmission process in the middle ear distorts the sound waves before they affect the cochlea and that the distortion creates the fundamental frequency. In this theory, the fundamental is present inside the cochlea even though it is missing in the stimulus that contacts the outer ear. Bekesy (1960) modified this notion somewhat so that the distortion became part of the response of the basilar membrane, which was said to respond "as if" the fundamental were also physically present.

Unfortunately, a dramatic experimental result casts doubt on the distortion hypothesis for the missing fundamental. The experiment involves the presentation of pairs of tones, such as 2,000 Hz and 2,400 Hz, which would produce a missing fundamental of 400 Hz (Patterson, 1969). If a sufficiently high level band of noise, centered around 400 Hz, were now added to the complex sound, we would expect that it would mask the (missing) fundamental because it is vibrating the place on the basilar membrane that the place principle says is vibrating so that the fundamental is heard. Nevertheless, despite the presence of this noise, the pitch of the complex wave is still perceived to be that of the fundamental. This rules out the suggested place theory distortion mechanism for the missing-fundamental phenomenon.

The second major theory is based on the *frequency principle*. The frequency principle also has a long history, having been championed by August Seeback in the 1840s (Green, 1976) and then revived by Wever (1970) and Goldstein (1973). According to the frequency principle, pitch is determined by the overall pattern of spike potentials traveling up the auditory nerve, much as if the neurons were counting the sound wave peaks and reproducing the sound's frequency in the neural response pattern. The greater the frequency, the higher the pitch. We know that neurons in the auditory nerve do tend to fire in phase with the peaks of compression in the stimulating sound wave (phase locking); for tones of up to about 4,000 Hz the overall frequency of firing in the auditory nerve tracks the frequency of the tone (see Chapter 6). A tone of 500 Hz produces about 500 bursts of spike potentials per second in the auditory nerve, and a tone of 1,000 Hz produces twice as many bursts per second.

The frequency principle can explain the missing-fundamental "illusion" and why it is not abolished by masking at the fundamental frequency. According to the frequency principle, the missing fundamental is signaled by the neurons that respond to the higher harmonics (those not higher than 4,000 Hz). The overall pattern of auditory nerve firing would not differ if the fundamental were present because the neuronal response is phase locked to the harmonics. Masking at the fundamental frequency alters only the firing of the neurons that

respond to that frequency; however, someone observing the auditory nerve response frequency would see little difference in the pattern. This may seem topsy-turvy in that we are saying that the fundamental is *not* fundamental, yet consider the example we used earlier in our discussion. Given a sound with harmonics of 600 Hz, 900 Hz, and 1,200 Hz, the fundamental is inferred to be 300 Hz. In much the same way that we *infer* the fundamental from knowledge of the harmonic structure, a higher auditory center ("pitch processor") could infer the fundamental from the pattern of excitation reported by neurons that respond to higher frequencies (Goldstein, 1973; Javel, 1981; Srulovicz & Goldstein, 1983). This idea is confirmed by the following experiment. We again present an individual with a pair of tones, such as 2,000-Hz and 2,400-Hz tones, to produce a missing fundamental of 400 Hz. If we now introduce a high-frequency band of noise, centered at 2,200 Hz and extending for several hundred hertz on either side of it, thus masking the response to the higher harmonics, the missing fundamental is no longer heard (Patterson, 1969).

Additional experiments give a similar picture. If we present one component of a complex tone—say, 600 Hz, to one ear and another, say, 800 Hz, to the other—a missing fundamental corresponding to 200 Hz is perceived (Houtsma & Goldstein, 1972). Here there could be no activity on either basilar membrane corresponding to that created when a 200-Hz pure tone stimulates it because each membrane was stimulated only by a single tone far from 200 Hz. Again, it seems that the central auditory system is inferring the missing fundamental from the pattern of auditory nerve firing in the two ears.

As attractive as it seems, there are several problems with a frequency theory for pitch perception. One problem is that an individual neuron cannot fire at high enough rates to account for the perception of high-frequency sounds. An individual neuron can fire at a maximum of 1,000 Hz. Thus, the ability of the auditory nerve to track frequencies up to about 4,000 Hz has to be explained in terms of a **volley principle** that describes how neural fibers fire in groups or squads (Wever, 1970). While one neuron is "reloading" (actually resting between impulses), its neighbor might be firing. The overall effect in the auditory nerve is a burst of activity for each pressure peak in the sound input, although different neurons are firing at

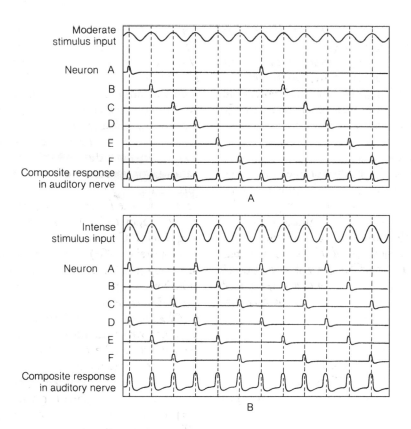

FIGURE 7-18   The volley principle. Note that the composite neural response follows the frequency of the stimulus. However, for the weaker stimulus (A) fewer neurons fire in each volley than fire for the stronger stimulus (B).

different times. An example of how this might work is shown in Figure 7-18. Learning and experience seem to sharpen the ability to interpret the overall pattern of firing delivered by the auditory nerve (Hall & Peters, 1982; Terheardt, 1974).

Another problem with the frequency principle of pitch perception is that it requires the frequency of neural firing to encode both the pressure and the frequency of the sound. One way to resolve this dilemma is to distinguish between the total *density* of neural activity (the actual number of neural responses going down the auditory nerve) and the *number of volleys* (or bursts of firing) per unit of time. An increase in the pressure of a sound, although not changing the volley frequency, would increase the number of neurons firing at each pressure peak, both by stimulating additional neurons that had not previously been firing and by increasing the firing rate in those

neurons that were not yet saturated. If all of the neurons were connected to some higher center (the pitch processor) that computes pitch based on the frequency of volleys and loudness based on the number of responses per volley, the problem would be solved. An example of how this could work is shown in Figure 7-18.

Because both the place principle and the frequency principle seem to be supported by data, it seems likely, as Wever (1970) has suggested, that the ultimate explanation of pitch will include aspects of both theories. Wever proposed that in humans pitch is coded by the frequency principle for frequencies lower than about 4,000 Hz (the theoretical upper limit for volleying). For frequencies from 500 Hz to 20,000 Hz, the place principle can explain pitch perception. Below 500 Hz, however, the vibration pattern on the basilar membrane seems too broad to explain our excellent pitch discrimination by the place theory, so frequency theory is needed to explain performance in this frequency range. Notice that for frequencies between 500 Hz and 4,000 Hz, both principles apply. This could help explain the superior performance of the ear for sounds in this range. For frequencies outside this range we must rely on only one mechanism; therefore, performance is poorer.

The place-frequency compromise is supported by a good deal of research (e.g., Srulovicz & Goldstein, 1983). In one study researchers placed electrodes in the auditory nerve corresponding to different parts of the basilar membrane of a subject's deaf ear (Simmons, Epley, Lummis, Guttman, Frishkopf, Harmon, & Zwicker, 1965). They found that electrical stimulation produced an auditory sensation for this person, as expected. More important, stimulation at different locations produced the perception of different pitches. Similarly, modern cochlear implants (see Chapter 6) produce perceptions of pitch differences by electrically stimulating different places in the cochlea (Townshend et al., 1987). This, of course, supports the place principle. In another direct stimulation study, Simmons and colleagues (1965) varied the frequency of the electrical stimulus from about 20 Hz to 300 Hz. These various rates of stimulation produced the appropriate changes in pitch perception regardless of the specific place where the stimulating electrode was located. This supports the frequency principle. Clearly both mechanisms are needed to explain all of the data.

AUDITORY SCENE ANALYSIS

Everyday sounds are not simple, isolated, and meaningless pure tones or noise bursts. We are surrounded most of the time by a multitude of complex hisses, squeaks, booms, chirps, and roars, as well as a constant stream of words and music that pours out of our social gatherings. All of these sounds are rich sources of diagnostic information about important events happening in our world (Ballas, 1993; Lakatos, McAdams, & Caussé, 1997). How do our auditory systems and the rest of our brains deal with this enormous flow of sound to produce the rich auditory world, filled with sounding objects, events, and locations, that we experience?

The most general way to view our auditory surroundings is as an **auditory scene** (Bregman, 1990). At any moment, the auditory scene may consist of any number of sound-producing events. Each sound source or event varies in spectrum (the amplitude of sound at each frequency), duration, location, time, and so forth. Sounds from these various events all are mixed together in the pattern of acoustic energy received by the ear. The problem we are faced with is to build separate mental representations of the various sound sources from the mixture received. This is called **auditory scene analysis.** To analyze the auditory scene into its components, we must infer backward from the mixture of sounds we receive to the events that generated them. To complicate matters further, in order to build a coherent picture of the world, we must integrate the mental representation of the auditory scene with the representation of the world extracted by our visual analyses of the scene. It is likely that the auditory and the visual maps of the world are "calibrated" against each other as we grow and develop, through multisensory experience with various objects and events. The auditory representation is also affected by processes such as visual capture, which we discussed earlier in this chapter. Figure 7-19 illustrates the problem, where all of the sounds from a trio of musicians mix at the ear but must be sorted out both as to identity and location to create the auditory scene.

The construction of the auditory scene in consciousness appears to involve at least two mechanisms. The first is a fast involuntary process of auditory grouping. The second involves imposition of some structure to guide the grouping and listening process, based on *schemas*, which are higher level hypotheses or expectations based on our knowledge of familiar sounds (Bregman, 1990).

The more primitive auditory grouping mechanism uses several sources of information. First, the continuous flow of sound received by the ear is analyzed into separate time chunks and grouped according to shared frequency ranges. Each time/frequency segment is represented in terms of level, temporal change, frequency change, location, and other variables, which also will include some of the variables that give rise to our perception of sound location (such as time delays between arrival at the two ears and so forth). The mechanism then groups together sounds that have similar patterns over time **(sequential integration)** or that have similar frequency spectra **(simultaneous integration)** into

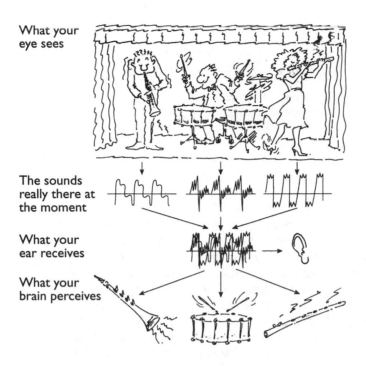

What your
eye sees

The sounds
really there at
the moment

What your
ear receives

What your
brain perceives

FIGURE 7-19 The problem of auditory scene analysis.

separate **auditory streams** (groups of sounds that "belong together" because they appear to emanate from the same source). This mechanism operates according to general rules, probably specified innately, based on patterns of time and frequency similarity. For example, these rules separate the low-pitched, continuous but relatively brief roar of a lion from the high-pitched, intermittent but long-lasting chirp of a bird. Similar rules are followed in the grouping of visual stimuli, as you will see later when we discuss how we perceive visual forms and patterns.

These basic auditory grouping processes have been extensively studied in the laboratory (see Bregman, 1990), and we know a lot about what affects their operation. For example, the faster a series of sounds is presented, the easier it is to separate out the different streams. Similarly, the more different the locations from which two sounds come, the easier it is to hear them as separate streams. Auditory streams in music are facilitated by differences in timbre of the instruments and in the timing of musical notes (Iverson, 1995). After they are separated, perception of the information in each auditory stream is much easier (Barsz, 1991). This low-level grouping

mechanism can create some interesting illusions. For example, when a longer pure tone is repeatedly alternated with a short noise burst, the pure tone is heard as continuing *through* the train of noise bursts, although it is really turned off while each noise burst is on (Warren, 1984). Similarly, frequency glides are perceived to be continuous, even when interrupted by noise bursts (Kluender & Jenison, 1992). Apparently the auditory system is interpreting this auditory scene as if a continuous pure tone, representing one environmental event, were repeatedly being masked by short noise bursts representing another (much like we hear a sustained trumpet note from a radio as continuous, even though parts of it are masked by the clanking of pots or plates in the kitchen as we fix dinner). This illusion of continuity appears to arise from the same processes that produce auditory streaming in different contexts (Bregman, 1990; Tougas & Bregman, 1990). Demonstration Box 7-7 allows you to experience the influence of differences in physical location on the ease of separating a sound mixture into separate streams.

We also depend on the use of learned schemas to help interpret the auditory scene. These schemas contain detailed knowledge about regular patterns of

---

DEMONSTRATION BOX 7-7
Auditory Streaming

One of the most powerful factors in allowing us to create auditory or visual groupings of stimuli involves differences in spatial location. For instance, in the figure accompanying this box you will see an example of a problem involving visual scene analysis. The line of print in the top part of the figure contains a mixture of two messages. They are very difficult to separate. However, when they are separated slightly in location, the two messages are easily understood.

An analogous process operates in interpreting separate but similar sound sources. You can experience this by using two portable tape players or radios with earphones. First tune each so you can hear only static. Now change the tone control so that one of the sounds is a high-pitched static and the other is low pitched, and turn the volume up

on each. Place one earphone from each radio set next to each other (you might use a rubber band to hold them close), and hold the pair of sounding earphones near and slightly in front of one ear. Notice how difficult it is to separate the mixture of sounds into two high- and low-pitched streams. Next, remove the rubber band, and hold one earphone near, but slightly in front of, one ear and the other earphone in the same relative position near your other ear. Notice how much easier it is to separate out the two streams. The intensity differences of the two sounds at the two ears allow them easily to be assigned to different locations, and thus to different streams, and you hear a higher pitched and a lower pitched noise separately, each emanating from a different sound source.

YWOEU   TSAMSETLEL   SLMIOMKEE

Y W O E U   T S A M S E T L E L   S L M I O M K E E

---

sounds that have certain meanings in our lives. For example, a skilled auto mechanic can listen to an ailing engine and separate out the squeaking noise made by a degenerating water pump from the many roars, hisses, clanks, and buzzes made by the other components of the engine. Attention will play a role in this because while listening to the water pump he might not be aware of the flapping sound that indicates that the engine's fan belt is loose. The schema-based process allows a sound that is selected by attention to be processed better, but it doesn't aid processing of the unattended sounds (Bregman, 1990). Schema-based scene analysis processes take longer to operate than the more primitive grouping processes; however, they are also capable of integrating sounds over longer periods of time. Schemas appear to be activated by detecting all or part of a known pattern in the sound input. A schema appears to select out the sounds appearing in "its" pattern for use in constructing "its" event, and this process then contributes to the final interpretation of the auditory scene. Each person's schemas might be different because they depend on each person's unique learning history. However, the schema-based process

and the grouping process work with other perceptual and cognitive processes (such as those of vision) to create our world of perceptual objects from the booming, buzzing confusion confronted by our sensory systems. We will discuss some of the most sophisticated examples of auditory grouping and analysis processes in a later chapter when we look at music and speech perception.

CHAPTER SUMMARY

The auditory detection threshold for humans is so low that if we were any more sensitive we could hear the blood rushing through our capillaries or the sound of air molecules colliding. The **dynamic range** for a particular frequency is the difference between the absolute threshold and the pain threshold and may be up to 150 dB. Different attributes of auditory stimuli interact in perception. **Temporal summation** is one such instance where the energy received over about 200 ms is summed for purposes of detection. In **masking,** a sound interferes with our perception of other sounds near to it (or higher than it) in frequency. The most effective masking is **simultaneous masking,** followed by **forward masking** (where the masker precedes the test stimulus), although **backward masking** is possible under some circumstances.

In terms of sound pressure discrimination, the ear can detect differences in sound levels of 10% to 20% across a broad range of frequencies. In **profile analysis,** two complex sounds made up of many frequencies are compared, with the difference existing in the sound level of only one of these frequencies. Sound frequency discrimination is very acute, with Weber fractions of only 0.005 (e.g., the ability to discriminate 1,000-Hz from 1,005-Hz tones). This discrimination can be made better through the use of glide stimuli.

Sound localization depends on several cues. There is a **sound level difference** between the ear nearest and the ear farthest from the sound, and part of this is due to the **sound shadow** caused by the head. There is also a **time difference** due to the fact that the far ear receives the sound later, and there may also be a **phase difference.** There appear to be neurons in the auditory cortex that are tuned to binaural level and time differences. These are used to make up auditory localization maps, which appear to map visual and auditory locations into a coordinate space. We might expect difficulties in sound localization because of **reverberation** cues from sounds bouncing off of nearby surfaces. However, the **precedence effect** causes us to localize sounds on the basis of the earliest arriving sound in a complex. The pinnae, head, neck, shoulders, and other nearby body parts affect reception of various frequencies of sound differently, and these are described mathematically by the **head-related transfer function (HRTF).**

In our subjective perception of sound there are distinct dimensions or qualities. Some have rough correspondence to physical aspects of the stimulus, such as **loudness,** which mostly depends on sound pressure and is measured in **sones; pitch,** roughly corresponding to frequency and measured either in **mels** or via the musical scale; and **timbre,** which depends on the complex mix of sounds. Other subjective dimensions of sound include **volume, density, consonance,** and **dissonance.** There are interactions among the dimensions, such as when frequency affects apparent loudness, as does the bandwidth of frequencies present. Apparent loudness is also affected by **auditory adaptation** and **auditory fatigue.** Pitch perception is affected by factors such as the duration of the tone and is subject to various illusions, such as the **missing fundamental** and the Doppler illusion. Physiologically, pitch is computed from activity on the basilar membrane using the **volley principle** for low frequencies and the **place principle** for higher frequencies.

Auditory scene analysis refers to how we construct aspects of the world in our consciousness based on auditory inputs. To do this we use schemas and perceptual grouping principles such as **sequential integration** and **simultaneous integration** to define **auditory streams.** This helps us to fill in gaps in the stimulus flow and to separate sounds into meaningful groups.

KEY TERMS

minimum audible pressure
minimum audible field
dynamic range
temporal summation
Hughes's Law
critical band
monaural
binaural
masking
target
masker
simultaneous masking
forward masking
interstimulus interval
backward masking
central masking
informational masking
profile analysis
azimuth
sound shadow
sound level difference
time difference
phase difference
minimum audible angle
precedence effect
echolocation systems
reverberation sound
head-related transfer function (HRTF)

loudness
pitch
perceived location
perceived duration
timbre
volume
density
consonance
dissonance
sone
equal loudness contour
auditory adaptation
auditory fatigue
bandwidth
equal temperament scale
mel
equal pitch contours
fundamental
harmonics
missing fundamental
place principle
frequency principle
volley principle
auditory scene
auditory scene analysis
sequential integration
simultaneous integration
auditory streams

Taste, Smell, Touch, and Pain

CHAPTER 8

People who are both blind and deaf (Helen Keller is one famous example) exist in a perceptual world restricted to smells, tastes, touches, and feelings of warmth and cold and pain. Although such a world may be difficult to imagine for those who can see and hear, these so-called minor senses provide a rich and varied perceptual life. Even linguistic communication is possible, as Helen Keller's teacher demonstrated when she taught her to communicate by finger taps on one another's palms. Moreover, many species of animals rely almost exclusively on taste, smell, touch, and pain for survival-related information about the world. In this chapter we briefly survey these anything-but-minor sensory systems.

TASTE

The sense of taste has a survival function, as well as providing pleasure. A reasonable rule of thumb, at least for natural substances, is that things that taste bad are likely to be harmful, indigestible, or poisonous, whereas things that taste good are likely to be digestible and contain substances the body can usefully metabolize (see Capaldi & Powley, 1990). Taste even helps us avoid ingesting too much of a good thing because the pleasantness and intensity of sweet and salty tastes are more reduced when we are sated (full) than when we are hungry (e.g.,

Scott, 1990). This protective function of taste can lead to paradoxes, such as for foods like hot peppers containing capsaicin, which causes people to experience a "burning" sensation when they chew one. Although nearly everyone initially (and sometimes tearfully) rejects such "hot" foods, most people can learn to appreciate them because a moderate amount of such irritation is not harmful (Zellner, 1991).

The human gustatory sense evolved from direct interactions of the first living things with the giant bowl of chemical soup that formed their environment. Various substances suspended or dissolved in water were important to the survival of those creatures. Some substances provided food, some gave warning, and some caused destruction. The most primitive one-celled organisms clearly could not use anything like visual or auditory sensory systems, which require large numbers of specialized cells. They relied on direct chemical or mechanical interactions with their environment mediated by the cells' outer membrane. As life evolved, multicelled animals could afford a "division of labor" with different cells serving different functions. For a taste/smell system, specialized cells were grouped together to pick up chemical information from the surroundings. For example, fish have pits lined with cells responsive to a variety of chemical and mechanical stimuli. Insects and other invertebrates have such cells located on their antennae.

Although two anatomically separate systems eventually developed, in the sea there was little differentiation between taste and smell. All important chemical stimuli were dissolved or suspended in the same substance: water. When life moved onto land, two chemical receptor systems became differentiated. The taste system became a "close-up" sense, which provided the last check on the acceptability of food. Smell turned out to be useful as a distance sense, although it also retained an important function in dealing with food (Rozin, 1982).

Taste Stimuli and Receptors

The physical stimuli for the taste system are substances that can be dissolved in water. The concentration of a chemical substance present is related to the intensity of the taste we experience. Which property (or collection of properties) of the stimulus gives rise to the various different taste qualities is now becoming known through sophisticated biochemical studies of isolated receptor cells.

Scientists find it useful to distinguish at least four primary taste qualities: *sweet, salty, sour,* and *bitter* (e.g., Bujas, Szabo, Ajdukovic, & Mayer, 1989; Henning, 1916; Schiffman & Erikson, 1971). These taste qualities are associated with some general types of molecules. Sweet taste is generally associated with so-called organic molecules, which are made up mostly of carbon, hydrogen, and oxygen in different combinations. These organic molecules are commonly called sugars, alcohols, and so forth. Other sweet substances, like aspartame and cyclamates, are also organic chemicals, but they are quite different from "natural" sweeteners, such as sugars, in their molecular structure. Bitter taste is related to sweet taste. Many substances that taste sweet in small amounts taste bitter in large amounts (e.g., saccharin). Also, a number of chemicals containing nitrogen (such as strychnine, caffeine, quinine, and nicotine) taste bitter.

Salty taste is elicited by molecules that, when dissolved in water, break into two electrically charged parts called *ions*. For example, each molecule of common table salt is composed of two atoms: one sodium (Na) and one chlorine (Cl). When dissolved in water, the atoms break apart. The sodium atom is now a positively charged ion (written Na^+), and the chlorine atom is a negatively charged ion (written Cl^-). Some salts taste bitter in high concentrations, and in very low concentrations most salts taste sweet.

Sour substances also break up into two parts when in solution, but they are usually acids (such as hydrochloric, sulfuric, acetic, and nitric) rather than salts. In all of these substances, hydrogen is the positively charged ion (H^+). The presence of the hydrogen ion is directly related to the sour taste of such acids, but other properties must also be important because most acids taste sweet or bitter instead of sour.

The receptors that respond to taste stimuli are groups of cells called **taste buds** that are found in three types of little bumps on the tongue called **papillae** (Figure 8-1). *Fungiform papillae* are shaped like little mushrooms (*fungi*) and are found at the tip and the sides of the tongue. *Foliate papillae* make up a series of folds (*folia*) along the sides of the rear portion of the tongue. *Circumvallate papillae* are

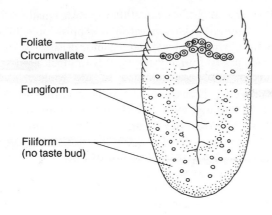

Foliate
Circumvallate
Fungiform
Filiform
(no taste bud)

FIGURE 8-1 A diagram of the human tongue showing the locations of the different types of papillae.

shaped like flattened hills, with a circular trench or valley surrounding them, and are located at the back of the tongue. A fourth type, the *filiform papillae*, contains no taste buds. The arrowhead-shaped filiform papillae help to abrade food into smaller bits that will dissolve more easily. There are also some taste receptors scattered over parts of the mouth other than the tongue, such as on the *soft palate* (which is the back portion of the roof of your mouth). Figure 8-2A shows how the taste buds are

distributed within a circumvallate papilla. Each taste bud consists of several receptor cells (perhaps up to 30) of different types as well as undeveloped basal cells (Figure 8-2B). There are about 10,000 taste buds in your mouth when you are young, although their number decreases with age.

Within each taste bud the individual cells are continually developing. Each taste cell has a life span of only a few days; thus the composition of the taste bud is always changing, with some immature cells (around the outside), some mature cells (near the inside), and some dying cells always present (Beidler & Smallman, 1965). The taste cells in the taste bud seem to be a specialized variation of skin cells. This probably explains their short life span because all skin cells are periodically replaced. Slender projections (called *microvilli*) from the top end (apex) of each cell lie near an opening onto the surface of the tongue called a **taste pore.**

Taste stimuli interact with receptors and ion channels on the microvilli. There are several different transduction mechanisms to turn chemical stimulation into a neural response (see Smith, 1997), and each of the microvilli can have more than one of these. For instance, the transduction of salty-tasting NaCl (table salt) is accomplished by the flow of sodium ions through passive channels in the cell membrane, whereas the transduction of sour-tasting acids is based on the fact that hydrogen

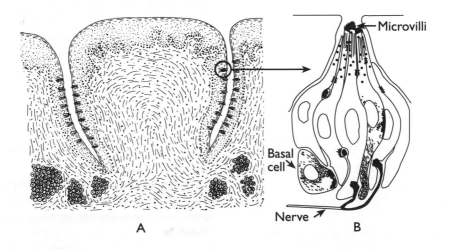

Microvilli

Basal cell

Nerve

A

B

FIGURE 8-2 (A) A typical papilla with taste buds; one is circled (from Wyburn et al., 1964); (B) drawing of a single taste bud (from Smith, 1997).

ions block the usual flow of potassium ions across the same cell membrane. Both sweet- and bitter-tasting molecules are transduced by complicated mechanisms involving specific receptors in the microvilli cell membrane. When appropriate molecules latch onto the receptors, the concentrations of various other molecules inside the cell change in a cascading fashion (McLaughlin, McKinnon, Robichon, Spickofsky, & Margolskee, 1993). Any of these mechanisms can eventually result in the depolarization of the taste receptor cell, which will trigger the release of neurotransmitter molecules that cause spike potentials to travel up the taste nerve (see the Appendix for more about spike potentials).

Neural Pathways and Responses

Three large nerves (the *chorda tympani, vagus,* and *glossopharyngeal*) carry fibers from the taste buds. They run from the tongue to the several nuclei in the **solitary tract,** which is located in the medulla (the place where the spinal cord widens to form the brain stem). In addition, there is information carried from the *common chemical sense.* This system is separate from the taste system and in humans consists mostly of the *trigeminal nerve* of the head and its free nerve endings in the mouth and nasal cavity. The common chemical sense is sensitive to a wide variety of different stimuli, including certain tastes such as those associated with hot peppers and ginger (see Silver, 1987).

From the nuclei in the solitary tract, taste information is carried via a set of pathways called the **medial lemniscus** to the taste center of the thalamus. This taste center is situated at the top of the rear-central portion of the thalamus *(ventral posterior nuclei).* The thalamic taste area projects to three areas in the brain. Two are regions at the base of the primary somatosensory cortex (near from where touch on the face is projected), and the third is the **anterior-insular cortex,** which is a part of the frontal cortex under the front end of the temporal cortex.

Studies of nonhuman animals have shown that taste fibers respond to increasing intensity of the stimulus (which means increasing concentration of the taste chemicals) by raising their overall rate of firing. One of the few human studies capitalized on the fact that taste pathways from the front of the tongue must be cut during a certain kind of ear operation (Diamant, Funakoshi, Strom, & Zotterman, 1963). Before the taste pathway was cut, its electrical activity in response to various concentrations of table salt applied to the tongue was recorded. In all of the patients the amount of neural response was roughly proportional to the logarithm of the concentration of the salt solution. As in most modalities, the neural code for intensity seems to be the overall amount of firing of all of the sensory fibers.

How is taste *quality* or identity encoded? Most receptor cells seem to respond to all of the four basic kinds of taste stimuli although with different sensitivity (Arvidson & Friberg, 1980; Kimura & Beidler, 1961). This implies that several, perhaps all, of the transducer mechanisms described earlier are found in every receptor cell. Most of the taste cells in the thalamus also respond to all tastes (Doetsch, Ganchrow, Nelson, & Erickson, 1969; Scott & Erickson, 1971). The fact that all fibers respond to all tastes is not a problem because each has a different pattern of sensitivities. This means that tastes can still be coded through an **across-fiber pattern** of neural activity (Erikson, 1985; Erickson & Schiffman, 1975; Pfaffman, 1955). Figure 8-3 shows how this might work. Notice that although all of the fibers respond to all taste inputs to some extent, the pattern of firing across the four diagrammed fibers is different for each quality. Thus, for a sugar stimulus (S) we find Fiber A responding vigorously, Fiber B moderately, and Fibers C and D only weakly. For salt (NaCl) Fibers A and D respond weakly, whereas Fiber B responds strongly and Fiber C nearly as vigorously. Erickson (1963) was able to show such distinct across-fiber pattern differences. These patterns become somewhat less distinct in the thalamus (Doetsch et al., 1969; Scott & Erickson, 1971).

Another way to interpret the firing patterns displayed in Figure 8-3 is the **labeled-line theory** (Pfaffman, 1974). The basic idea is that each taste fiber is labeled as if it had one taste quality and that is the one that it is most sensitive to. Thus, when Fiber A in Figure 8-3 responds, because its "best" stimuli are sugars its activity simply signals a sweet taste, whereas Fiber B would signal a salty taste, and so forth. This is consistent with the fact that different sugars are indiscriminable from each other when their taste intensities are equated

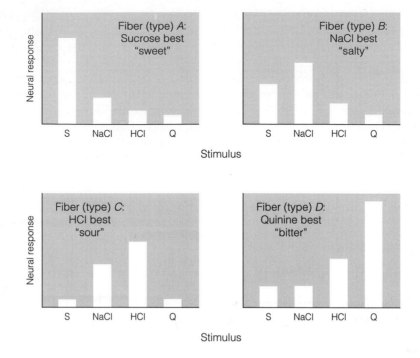

FIGURE 8-3 Using the across-fiber pattern theory, consider each graph to represent the response of a unique taste fiber to the various stimuli. Using the labeled-line theory, consider each graph to represent the average response of a group of more or less equivalent taste fibers.

(Breslin, Beauchamp, & Pugh, 1996). It also means that a simple stimulus, such as table salt (NaCl), could have a complex taste if it activated several types of fibers. This does appear to happen because at different concentrations table salt can trigger both salt and sweet or salt and sour sensations (Bartoshuk, 1978). Moreover, although maltose is indistinguishable from other sugars at low concentrations, it can be discriminated from them at high concentrations, presumably because it activates an additional labeled line (Breslin et al., 1996). Considered in this way, the labeled-line theory is compatible with the across-fiber pattern approach, except that its code for taste quality is a profile across a few fiber types rather than a pattern across many thousands of unique fibers (see also Scott, 1987; Smith, 1985).

Although it is unknown whether labeled lines exist along the entire taste pathway, neurons in the solitary tract nucleus of rats can be categorized into four groups corresponding to the four basic tastes. For instance, an independent channel for saltiness can be demonstrated by blocking the flow of sodium across receptor cell membranes (Scott & Giza, 1990). There is even evidence that the cortical neurons most responsive to the four basic tastes seem to be localized in different parts of the taste cortex (Yamamoto, Yayama, & Kawamura, 1981). There is a suggestion that there may be specific cortical cells that give an "on" response to some taste stimuli and an "off" response to others, similar to the feature-specific cells in the visual cortex discussed in Chapter 3 (Funakoshi, Kasahara, Yamamoto, & Kawamura, 1972).

Taste Thresholds and Adaptation

What are the limits of a human's taste sensitivity? Unfortunately, absolute thresholds vary with the particular taste stimulus and how it is measured. They also vary depending on the viscosity of the substance (Paulus & Haas, 1980), temperature (Paulus & Reisch, 1980), presence of other taste stimuli (J. C. Stevens, 1995), and the part of the tongue or mouth stimulated. This means that several factors have to be controlled when we measure taste sensitivity.

We avoid the problem of thresholds varying with the measure of stimulus intensity by choosing a standard useful measure: the **molar concentration** (Pfaffman, Bartoshuk, & McBurney, 1971). A solution is said to have a concentration of 1 *mole* if the molecular weight of a particular substance (in grams) is dissolved in enough water to make 1 liter of solution. Different solutions with the same molar concentrations have the same number of stimulus molecules in a given volume of liquid.

Figure 8-4 shows how absolute thresholds for various stimuli measured in this way vary across four different parts of the tongue and the soft palate (Collings, 1974). For the bitter substance the lowest absolute threshold on the tongue is at the front, but the soft palate site is even more sensitive to it. The tip and back of the tongue are most sensitive to sweet, whereas the front and sides are most sensitive to salt. The sensitivity of parts of the mouth to "hot" tastes, such as those associated with chili peppers, also differs from place to place. Demonstration Box 8-1 helps you explore these differences.

Individuals often differ dramatically in their absolute sensitivity to certain tastes. In a classic study, Blakeslee and Salmon (1935) measured the absolute thresholds of 47 people for 17 different substances. Most substances, such as table salt or saccharin, had a narrow range of thresholds for different people. For other substances, however, such as vanillin or phenylthiocarbamide (PTC),

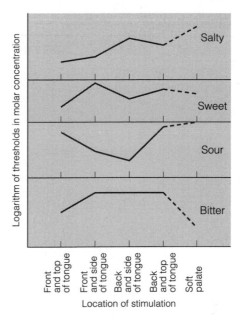

FIGURE 8-4   Average absolute thresholds for four different taste stimuli at four locations on the tongue and at a location on the soft palate (based on Collings, 1974).

large individual differences in sensitivity were found. These latter two substances are interesting because some people are apparently "taste blind" (display *ageusia*) to them. That is, at ordinary concentrations some people cannot taste these substances at all. PTC produces a bitter taste for those who are sensitive to it, but many can't taste it even at high concentrations. If the concentration is high enough,

---

DEMONSTRATION BOX 8-1
Variations in Taste Sensitivity

Although you all have probably experienced spicy "hot" foods on numerous occasions, you may not know that sensitivity to hot spices varies over the mouth. For example, the tip of the tongue is most sensitive to red and black peppers, and the anterior (hard) palate and cheek are least sensitive (Lawless & Stevens, 1988). You could demonstrate this for yourself by placing several drops of Tabasco sauce or other hot sauce (which contain hot red peppers) on the tip of a cotton swab or a bit of paper napkin twirled around a pencil or toothpick. Touch this "taste stimulator" to different parts of your mouth and tongue, and notice how the sensations differ in strength for different locations.

however, even the taste blind can taste PTC. Taste blindness for PTC is similar to color blindness (discussed in Chapter 5) in that both appear to have a genetic component and tend to run in families.

People who are taste blind for PTC also tend to be insensitive to the bitter taste of caffeine in coffee (Hall, Bartoshuk, Cain, & Stevens, 1975). Conversely, people who are sensitive to the taste of PTC also find that the common salt substitute potassium chloride (KCl) tastes bitter and that the taste of a preservative found in many foods, sodium benzoate, is readily noticeable (Bartoshuk, Rifkin, Marks, & Hooper, 1988). Further studies with a chemical relative of PTC, called PROP, revealed that some cheeses taste more bitter and some sweeteners taste sweeter to tasters. In general, those who are most sensitive to PROP (called "supertasters") find many taste stimuli to be more bitter, and "hot" stimuli to be hotter, than those who are less sensitive (Bartoshuk, 1993). This appears to be at least partly because they have more taste buds (and thus receptors) on their tongues. All of these results may eventually be explained by genetic variation in the number and efficiency of the bitter-sweet transduction mechanisms in different individuals.

The taste system adapts very readily to continued stimulation of the same type, and this adaptation temporarily raises the absolute threshold for the particular substance to which it has been adapted. Figure 8-5 shows an example of the effects of previous stimulation with table salt (NaCl) on absolute threshold for the same substance. As you can see from the figure, the absolute threshold varies both with how long the tongue has been exposed to the adapting stimulus and with the strength of the stimulus (Hahn, 1934; Szabo, Bujas, Adjukovic, Mayer, & Vodanovic, 1997). Similar effects can be demonstrated for the effects of adaptation on sensory intensity (Gent, 1979). This sort of adaptation helps explain why at dinner some people resalt their food again and again. As they eat, they adapt to the salty taste and come to need more salt to experience the taste at the same level. You can avoid resalting your food if you eat something that is not salty between bites of salty food (see Halpern & Meiselman, 1980). As Figure 8-5 shows, recovery from adaptation of the threshold sensitivity is virtually complete in about 10 sec, no matter how much salt was tasted previously. Our sensation of the intensity of a taste may take a

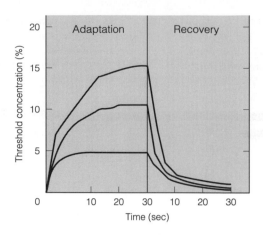

FIGURE 8-5   Adaptation and recovery from adaptation to continued stimulation of the tongue with table salt (NaCl). The three curves represent three different adapting concentrations. The time axis represents the amount of exposure to the adapting concentration, or recovery time, before determination of absolute threshold. Note the resemblance to dark adaptation curves (see Chapter 4; based on Hahn, 1934).

bit longer to recover than our absolute threshold. Given adaptation to a moderately intense stimulus, it may take up to 2 min before the taste seems as strong as it did when you first began to eat (Bujas, Szabo, Adjukovic, & Mayer, 1991). Taken together these results suggest that to experience the full flavor of a meal, one should eat slowly, with many pauses between bites of food.

Adaptation to one substance can also have an effect on the threshold for (and the subsequent taste of) different substances. This is called **cross-adaptation.** For example, adaptation to one salt will raise the threshold to other salts. In some cases, exposure of the tongue to one stimulus may actually *lower* the threshold to another taste stimulus (or make its taste more intense). This special case of cross-adaptation is called **potentiation.** Thus, adaptation to an acid, although reducing the sourness of another acid, may increase the sweetness of a sugar. Adaptation to urea (the bitter substance contained in human urine) will increase the intensity of salty sensations (McBurney, 1969). You can experience dramatic examples of potentiation and cross-adaptation by trying Demonstration Box 8-2.

DEMONSTRATION BOX 8-2
Potentiation and Cross-Adaptation

Have you ever drunk some orange juice right after brushing your teeth in the morning and noticed that it tasted terrible? If so, you were experiencing the effects of sodium laurel sulphate, the detergent in toothpaste, on your taste system's response to citric acid. Citric acid, which is what makes orange juice and lemon juice taste sour, tastes only slightly bitter at very high concentrations. However, stimulation of the taste cells with sodium laurel sulphate causes this bitter taste to increase greatly in intensity, making it noticeable at lower concentrations, such as those found in orange or lemon juice (Bartoshuk, 1988). If you have never experienced this, try the following. Wash your mouth out by swishing with pure water. Then taste

some orange (or lemon) juice. Notice that the bitter taste is very faint if it is there at all. Now brush your teeth, and rinse thoroughly to get rid of the other toothpaste tastes, such as mint, which tastes sweet. Again taste the orange or lemon juice. Notice how the bitter taste has increased in intensity, but the sourness has not changed much at all. Sodium laurel sulphate also decreases the intensity of sweet, salty, and bitter tastes somewhat. You can try to experience these effects by repeating the orange juice experiment just described with sugar water, salt water, and cold coffee. It would be best to do these other experiments on different days so that adaptation effects do not confound your taste sensations.

Taste Intensity

Our ability to discriminate intensity differences in taste, regardless of the stimulus tested, is really quite poor. The Weber fraction (the proportional amount by which the more intense of two stimuli must be larger than the less intense for them to be discriminated, as discussed in Chapter 2) ranges from a relatively poor 0.10 to an awful 1.0, making taste the least sensitive of the senses by this criterion (Pfaffman et al., 1971). Moreover, the Weber fraction for the bitter taste increases as we age, especially for high concentrations of the taste stimulus. For example, for high concentrations of caffeine, the Weber fraction is about 0.4 for young people and around 2.3 for the elderly (Gilmore & Murphy, 1989). This means that to detect a change in the concentration of caffeine the change must be six times larger for the older individual than for the younger one. However, the Weber fraction for sucrose (common table sugar) is about 0.15 regardless of age.

Obviously, the intensity of the taste sensation will be greater if the physical stimulus intensity is greater. For example, magnitude estimations (see Chapter 2) of taste intensity are a power function of stimulus intensity ($S = aI^m$, where S is the

magnitude estimation of how intense the taste is, I is the concentration or intensity of the stimulus, a is a constant, and m is an exponent that describes the rate of change of the perceived intensity of the perceived taste). Under standard conditions the exponent m is usually approximately 1.0 (i.e., for table salt it is about 0.9, for quinine hydrochloride it is about 0.9, for hydrochloric acid it is 1.0, and for sucrose it is 1.0; Meiselman, Bose, & Nykvist, 1972; Norwich, 1984). However, the exponent does vary with state of adaptation (Meiselman et al., 1972; O'Mahoney & Heintz, 1981) and with age, being somewhat smaller for sour and bitter substances for the elderly (see Bartoshuk, 1988).

Several studies have compared neurophysiological recordings from taste nerves with psychophysical data collected at the same time. They have shown that both neural and psychophysical responses vary with stimulus intensity in a similar fashion (Borg, Diamant, Oakley, Strom, & Zotterman, 1967; Diamant & Zotterman, 1969). It seems likely that our sensation of the intensity of a taste is related to the overall amount of neural activity evoked by the stimulus, which in turn depends on the intensity (molar concentration) of the stimulus (see McBride, 1987; Norwich, 1984,

---

DEMONSTRATION BOX 8-3
Putting Out the Fire

You may have had the experience of putting too much pepper or other hot spice in your mouth and finding the burning too much to bear. Or you may have been prevented from eating some tasty dish because it was "too hot." These are circumstances in which you want to reduce the intensity of sensations arising from stimulation of your common chemical sense. Surprisingly, the effectiveness of swishing various liquids in your mouth to put out the fire depends to some extent on how they taste (Stevens & Lawless, 1986). The most effective liquid has a sweet (for example, soda pop) or sour (for example, lemon or other citrus juice) taste and is at a cool tem-

perature. Bitter-tasting substances (for example, quinine or possibly beer) do not seem to help any more than simply waiting for the burning to cease, and salty substances are intermediate in effect. The cool temperature explains some but not all of the cooling effect because different tastants at the same temperature have different effects. If you are daring, you might try swishing some *diluted* Tabasco sauce around in your mouth until it begins to burn and then experimenting with different quenching substances to see whether you can confirm these results. Remember to leave plenty of time between trials for the burning sensation to fade completely.

---

for theoretical discussions of this relationship). However, more than just stimulus concentration is involved in our sensation of the intensity of a single taste because our perception may be affected by the presence of other taste stimuli in mixtures (which is how most tastes are experienced). For example, when half of a 10% fructose solution is replaced by less-sweet-tasting sucrose, the mixture actually tastes *sweeter* (sometimes called *synergism*—McBride, 1993). Similarly, perceived taste intensity from application of a stimulus to one site can be decreased by application of the same taste stimulus elsewhere on the tongue or in the mouth, probably because taste nerves mutually inhibit one another (Bartoshuk, 1988). Mixtures of different taste stimuli display even more complex interactions. For example, adding sucrose to a sour-tasting citric acid solution can decrease its perceived sourness; yet, at the same time it makes the citrus taste more intense—which is a highly profitable state of affairs for soft drink companies making lemon-flavored drinks (McBride, 1993). Similar interactions occur for mixtures of sucrose and NaCl, QHCl (quinine hydrochloride—tastes bitter), and NaCl (e.g., Schifferstein & Frijters, 1993). Demonstration Box 8-3 provides one way in which you can explore a complex interaction between taste intensities.

SMELL

A properly trained police dog can follow the track of a single individual even when it has been entangled with the tracks of many others. The dog is smelling the fatty acids that seep through the shoes of the suspect, even though these are present in incredibly small amounts. For example, each human footprint contains only about 0.00000000004 grams of valeric acid, a typical fatty acid secreted by glands in the sole of the foot. No wonder criminals fear such dogs and often confess voluntarily when tracked and caught through their astounding "nose work."

Because we seldom see a human sniffing the ground to find out who had been there recently or exploring a new room by sniffing the furniture, we tend to think that smell is unimportant. Although much of our perceptual processing of odors seems to be done at a relatively unconscious level, our sense of smell plays a role that is far from minor. For example, for humans as well as other animals, foul odors often signify danger in the sense of putrefied or spoiled substances that are no longer safely edible. Perhaps even more important, although it is very difficult to recall or to name smells, the experience of a particular smell at a particular moment can stimulate a flood of memories of episodes in which that smell was present (Engen, 1987; Herz & Engen, 1996; Schab & Crowder, 1995). These memories of our past are often rich in emotional tones. Thus, the scent of cinnamon might evoke feelings of joy associated with your mother baking apple pies. Such smell-evoked memories may be necessary for normal biological functioning. For example, if a recently mated female mouse smells a strange male's urine before her fertilized egg implants in her uterus, implantation will likely fail. This will also happen if she "forgets" what her mate smells like, either because she was separated from him for 50 days or because a part of the olfactory system responsible for these memories was interfered with (Brennan, Kaba, & Keverne, 1990).

In many common situations, smell works together with taste. If we have experienced nausea after eating a distinctive food, we can acquire a *conditioned taste aversion* to that food, based especially on how it smells, which will make us avoid that food in the future (e.g., Bartoshuk, 1990). When we have a bad head cold, food seems flavorless; yet, our nasal passages are most affected by the cold, not our mouths, where the taste receptors are

located. When our nasal passages are swollen or clogged with extra mucus, smell stimuli cannot reach our olfactory receptors. This affects both our ability to smell and to experience flavor because much of the richness and subtlety of our experiences of the flavors of food and drink come from their odors (Brillat-Savarin, 1825/1971; Hyman et al., 1979; Murphy & Cain, 1980). When we cannot smell, our ability to identify foods by taste alone is significantly inferior, unfortunately for some of the most preferred foods, as Figure 8-6 shows. Demonstration Box 8-4 allows you to experience this for yourself in a controlled way (i.e., you don't have to wait for a head cold).

Smell acts as if it has two separate modes of action that may result in different perceptual experiences and different forms of information extraction (e.g., Bartoshuk & Beauchamp, 1994; Rozin, 1978). The first is associated with our experience of the flavors of food. It is triggered when *odorants* (molecules that can be smelled) are pumped from the mouth into the nasal cavity while we are chewing and swallowing food. The second is a distance sense that occurs when molecules emitted by external objects or organisms are sniffed through the nostrils

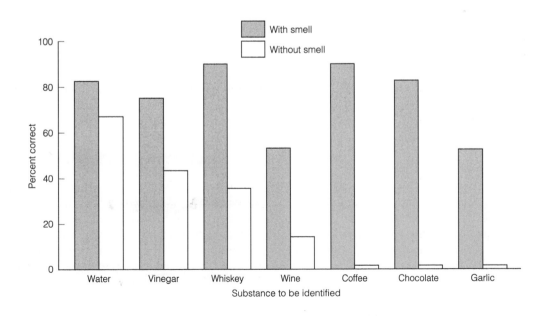

FIGURE 8-6 Identification of some common foods with and without smell (based on Mozel, Smith, Smith, Sullivan, & Swender, 1969).

DEMONSTRATION BOX 8-4
Flavor Without Smell

The simplest way to experience flavor without smell is to pinch your nostrils closed before coming near the substance to be tasted, and then put some of that substance into your mouth and swish it around while paying attention to its flavor. Then release your nostrils, open your mouth slightly, and breathe in gently through both mouth and nose. You should experience a significant change in the flavor when you do this. Try it for the various substances listed in Figure 8-6 and any others you can think of. Your experiences with nose pinched approximate those of elderly people who have experienced large deficits in their sense of smell.

It is rather easy to show that food identification is impaired when the sense of smell is absent. You simply need to get a friend to help you. First prepare several different substances to be identified—the ones listed in Figure 8-6 will do. They should be in a liquid state (mash up the garlic and mix it with water). Then seat your friend at some distance from the solutions, and blindfold him or her. For each substance, first ask him to pinch his nose, and, when he has done that, put some of the solution in his mouth and ask for its name. After he has tried that, tell him to release his nostrils and again attempt to name the substance. Repeat this for each substance, and several friends if you can, and see how closely the results match those of Figure 8-6.

---

into the nasal cavity. It is interesting to note that there are times when the "distant smell" and "food smell" functions give different perceptual experiences. For instance, Limburger cheese has a distant smell that is quite strong and, most people think, offensive, but it has a food smell when in the mouth that contributes in a positive way to the flavor of the cheese, which many people find quite pleasing.

Smell Stimuli and Receptors

Which aspects of a molecule give it the quality of evoking the sensation of smell? First, for humans, it must come from a volatile substance (one that has a gaseous state at ordinary temperatures—in other words, something that can evaporate) because air currents carry the molecules to the smell receptors in the nose. However, the most volatile substances do not necessarily smell the strongest. Pure water, which is very volatile, has no smell at all. In fact, the extent to which a smell stimulus separates itself chemically from water (*hydrophobicity*) is highly correlated with the intensity of its smell (Greenberg, 1981). Conversely, musk (a secretion obtained from some deer and beavers) has low volatility; yet, it is a very powerful odorant and is used in making some of our most expensive perfumes.

In general, any molecule may be described as having a specific size, weight, and shape. In addition, the particular atoms that make up a smell stimulus molecule, the number of electrons available for chemical bonding with receptor molecules on the primary olfactory neurons, and even the flexibility or rigidity of the stimulus molecule can affect how odorants interact with receptor molecules. As yet there is no consensus as to which of these properties is critical; given the large number of molecules that can be smelled, it is likely that several of them are important (for more, Farbman, 1992; Wright, 1982).

The receptive cells of the olfactory system, called **primary olfactory neurons,** are located in a relatively small area in the upper nasal passages (see Figure 8-7) called the **olfactory epithelium,** or "smell skin." Each primary olfactory neuron sends a long extension (called the **olfactory rod**) to the surface of the olfactory epithelium and also sends its axons toward the brain. Thus, the olfactory receptor cells are actually specialized neurons. Remarkably, each primary olfactory neuron functions for only about 4 to 8 weeks before deteriorating; new primary olfactory neurons are continually being produced from the basal cells (see Figure 8-7 and Costanzo & Graziadei, 1987).

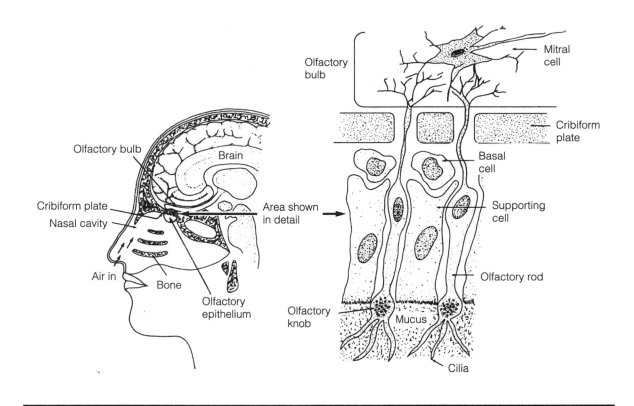

FIGURE 8-7 Anatomy of the olfactory system and a detail of the structure of the olfactory epithelium and olfactory bulb.

A number of **olfactory cilia** protrude from a knob at the end of the olfactory rod. There are around 6 to 8 cilia per olfactory rod in humans but around 100 to 150 in dogs (T. S. Brown, 1975). The olfactory cilia contain the receptor molecules that the smell stimuli attach themselves to (Farbman, 1992). The cilia are hairlike structures embedded in a special type of watery mucus secreted by special glands named Bowman's glands. This mucus contains many substances, some of which protect the receptors and the brain from infections, and many molecules of a special protein called **olfactory binding protein** (or **OBP** for short) that can attach to hydrophobic odorant molecules that would ordinarily be repelled from the watery mucus. It is likely that each odorant molecule bound to an OBP molecule is transported to and detached from each of several receptor molecules on the cilia by the continually moving stream of mucus sweeping across the cilia

(Nickell, 1997; Pelosi & Tirindelli, 1989; Pevsner, Sklar, Hwang, & Snyder, 1989).

The mechanism by which the brief interaction of a stimulus molecule with a receptor molecule causes an electrical response in the primary olfactory neuron is still not completely understood. Most of the evidence supports what has been called the **lock-and-key theory** (Amoore, 1970), in which specific proteins in the cell walls of the cilia form reversible chemical bonds with specific parts of particular odorant molecules (Farbman, 1992; Gesteland, 1986; Getchell & Getchell, 1987; Nickell, 1997). The momentary bonding of stimulus and receptor molecules initiates a cascade of other biochemical processes that results in action potentials in the axon. The chain of events is outlined in Figure 8-8. It starts when an odorant molecule bonds with a receptor activating a specific protein, called G_{olf} (Jones & Reed, 1989). This event, with the help of another

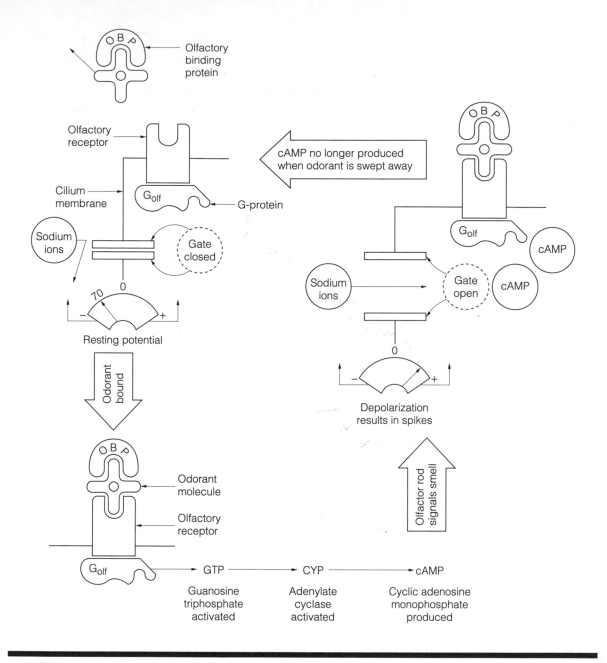

FIGURE 8-8   One of the ways in which olfactory receptors respond to odorant molecules.

molecule (guanosine triphosphate) activates an enzyme called adenylate cyclase, which in turn causes cAMP (cyclic adenosine monophosphate) to be produced (Bakalyar & Reed, 1990; Brand et al., 1989). The cAMP acts as a sort of a key and opens an ion channel in the cell membrane, allowing sodium ions to enter, and this depolarizes the cell and causes spike potentials to travel up the axon (see also Firestein & Werblin, 1989).

Neural Pathways and Responses

The primary olfactory neurons send their axons through tiny holes in a bone at the top of the nasal cavity (the cribiform plate) to form the olfactory nerve. The nerve goes straight to the bottom layer of the many-layered olfactory bulb. This bulb is located in front of and below the main mass of the brain (see Figure 8-7). The passage of the olfactory nerve through the cribiform plate makes it vulnerable to being severed when the head suddenly starts or stops moving in a particular direction. Many people who have had head injuries—for example, in automobile accidents—have lost their sense of smell for this reason.

The axons of the receptors and the dendrites of neurons from the olfactory bulb form complex clusters of connections, called *glomeruli*, in the bulb. These clusters seem to be grouped according to the type of receptor or type of stimulus molecule involved (Kauer, 1980, 1987; Nickell, 1997). One type of olfactory bulb neuron seems to send axons directly along the lateral olfactory tract to the temporal lobe of the cortex, where the primary sensory cortex for smell is located. Another type of neuron sends axons both to the smell cortex and to several lower brain centers, especially the limbic system, which is involved in our experience of emotion and memory (remember how easily smells can evoke memories and feelings). There are about 1,000 times more axons in the olfactory nerve than leave the olfactory bulb, indicating that many receptor cells contribute to the activity of each of the cells in the olfactory bulb and later centers (Allison, 1953). From the primary smell cortex the neural pathways become extremely complex, including projections to the thalamus and several other cortical areas (see Price, 1987).

As is typical for sensory systems, several studies have found that the intensity of the neural response varies directly with the intensity of the stimulus. However, most contemporary investigators have focused on the more difficult problem of how different smell qualities are encoded. They have tried to find evidence of specific types of receptors for different types of stimuli. One major early study was that of Ottoson (1956), who measured the electrical response of the entire olfactory epithelium to various stimuli. He discovered that passing a puff of odor-laden air across the epithelium results in a unique type of electrical response—a slow change in the electrical charge of the receptor cells. This change generates spike potentials in the axons of these cells.

Gesteland, Lettvin, Pitts, and Rojas (1963) recorded both the slow potential change and the spike potentials generated in the axons of single receptors in the olfactory epithelium in response to the same stimuli. These two types of electrical responses are shown one on top of the other in Figure 8-9. As you can see in the figure, this particular receptor responded vigorously to a musky odor, less to nitrobenzene, hardly at all to benzonitrite, and not at all to pyridine. Gesteland and colleagues (1963) thought that these responses indicated the existence of the sought-after receptor types, although they were cautious in making this interpretation. Such caution was well founded because later recordings from single cells in the epithelium, olfactory bulb, and cortical and lower brain centers that receive olfactory information have found that each neuron responds to a broad range of stimuli, much as the taste microvilli do (Cain & Bindra, 1972; Giachetti & MacLeod, 1975; Kauer, 1987; O'Connell & Mozell, 1969).

Across-fiber patterns similar to those found in taste seem to be present in the olfactory system, and it is possible that the "code" for smell qualities will be found in these patterns (Erickson & Schiffman, 1975; Kauer, 1987). At present there is no

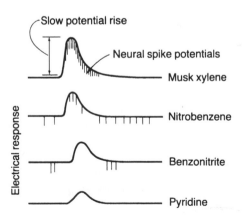

FIGURE 8-9   Slow potential and spike potential responses of olfactory receptor cells to four different smell stimuli (based on Gesteland et al., 1963).

evidence that olfactory fibers fall into groups like the taste fibers seem to, although some investigators have proposed that receptors sensitive to the same stimuli send their axons to the same glomeruli in the olfactory bulb (see Kauer, 1987; Nickell, 1997). There is also some evidence that odorant quality is coded as a pattern of activity across the entire olfactory bulb (Skarda & Freeman, 1987).

Smell Thresholds and Adaptation

De Vries and Stuiver (1961) calculated that it takes at most eight odorant molecules arriving at the olfactory epithelium to activate a single receptor cell in the human. Considering all aspects of the manner in which molecules of odor stimuli are distributed in the nose, they further argued that a single primary olfactory neuron can generate action potentials in response to contact by one stimulus molecule. This is the greatest sensitivity that any single receptor could have. Thus, considering only the primary olfactory neuron, a dog (or any other animal) can't be more sensitive than a human. However, dogs have about 200 times more cilia than humans have. Thus, the likelihood that a very weak stimulus will actually stimulate a primary olfactory neuron and produce a noticeable sensation is greater for the dog (see Marshall & Moulton, 1981).

More traditional measurements of absolute thresholds for various odors give values that vary across psychophysical methods (e.g., Berglund, Hogman, & Johansson, 1988). They depend on the purity of the odorant, the way it is delivered to the olfactory epithelium, and how the stimulus intensity is measured. Moreover, individuals' thresholds for the same substance vary dramatically from moment to moment (Stevens, Cain, & Burke, 1988). Different substances also have different average thresholds.

Smell sensitivity differs reliably across individuals (Rabin & Cain, 1986; Stevens et al., 1988). It is possible to have an "odor blindness," or anosmia, to certain substances (see Engen, 1982). Amoore and colleagues (1969, 1975; Amoore, Pelosi, & Forrester, 1977) have reported 76 different anosmias ranging from the gentle smell of vanilla to the pungent smell of skunk. Some of these anosmias are quite common (for instance, one out of three people cannot smell the camphorous odor of 1,8 cineole), whereas others are quite rare (e.g., only 1 of 1,000 people cannot smell the putrid odor of n-butyl mercaptan; see Pelosi & Pisanelli, 1981). Such specific anosmias are consistent with the idea that in olfaction there are a very large number of receptor types, probably specific receptor proteins in the walls of the cilia, and that each odor stimulates only one or a few types of receptors. It is possible that when a specific receptor protein is missing, perhaps because of a missing or malfunctioning gene, then the person with the missing receptor protein has a specific anosmia.

Prolonged exposure to an odorant causes adaptation that affects thresholds, perceived intensity (Cain & Engen, 1969), and even pleasantness of odors (Cain & Johnson, 1978). One of the great disappointments of wine tasting is that the aroma of even a great wine seems to be experienced strongly only for the first few sniffs. Adaptation rapidly weakens our experience of pleasant smells and flavors unless frequent breaks of about 15 sec are taken. Luckily, continuous sniffing also weakens the less-pleasant odors of sweaty bodies, paint fumes, and air pollution.

Moncrieff (1956) studied the effects of previous exposure to an odorant on the threshold for that same odorant (self-adaptation) and on that of different odorants (cross-adaptation). The largest sensitivity decrease was found for self-adaptation. Cross-adaptation varied with the similarity of the smells of the two stimuli. Odorants with similar smells gave larger cross-adaptation effects than did those that differed in smell. Surprisingly, all of the adapting odors used by Moncrieff had some effect on observers' sensitivity for the others. Sometimes even odorants that are perceptually and chemically different can show cross-adaptation (Pierce & Wysocki, 1996). It seems that the numerous characteristics of odorants that can interact with receptors prevent any simple scheme from reliably predicting cross-adaptation effects. You can experience self- and cross-adaptation for yourself by trying Demonstration Box 8-5.

The unadapted olfactory system seems to be about as sensitive as the visual or auditory system in discriminating changes in intensity, with Weber fractions as low as 0.05, meaning that a change in intensity of only 5% can be detected about half of the time (Cain, 1977). Interestingly, smell intensities can

---

DEMONSTRATION BOX 8-5
Smell Adaptation

You experience self-adaptation of odorants every day. The next time you notice a strong odor, take several deep sniffs, and then take a more usual sniff and pay close attention to the intensity of the odor as compared to what you at first experienced. You should notice a significant decrease in sensation intensity. Alternately, prepare yourself a cup of coffee or aromatic tea, keeping your nostrils pinched while you do. When the steaming cup is in front of you, release your nostrils and take a gentle sniff, noting the intensity of the odor. Then take several deep sniffs followed by another gentle sniff, and compare the odor intensity during the final gentle sniff to that during the first gentle sniff.

It is a bit more difficult to demonstrate cross-adaptation because the effects are weaker and not systematic. You should use your own judgment and explore a range of odorants using the general method described here. When two odorants you wish to test have been obtained, first step into another room, where you cannot smell them, and take several deep sniffs. Then approach the odorants with pinched nose. Release your nostrils near the first (test) odorant, and take a gentle sniff, noting the intensity of the odor. Then take several deep sniffs of the other (adapting) odorant, and return to the test odorant and take another gentle sniff. Compare the odor intensity on this sniff to the first one. If it is less intense, you have experienced cross-adaptation; if it is more intense, you have experienced facilitation, as sometimes happens with biologically significant odors (see Engen, 1982).

---

be discriminated better if the odorants enter the right nostril than if they enter the left nostril (Zatorre & Jones-Gotman, 1990). Because the olfactory pathways stay on the same side of the brain as where they begin, this, along with other evidence, may indicate that the right hemisphere of the brain is more specialized for olfactory processing.

Pheromones

Some smells have been said to have a special biological significance for all animals, including humans. Ellis (1905) pointed out that both men and women often emit strong odors during sexual excitement, and some authors have speculated that human behavior may be strongly influenced by such olfactory stimuli (e.g., Comfort, 1971; Kohl & Francoeur, 1995). Chemicals secreted by animals that transmit information to other animals (usually of the same species) are called **pheromones**. Although it is clear that pheromones strongly influence behavior in many animal species, the possibility that pheromones strongly affect human behavior has been entertained only recently. As you might expect, manufacturers of

colognes and perfumes, ever searching for ways to enhance the sales of their products, have responded to this suggestion by marketing products that contain suspected human pheromones.

Pheromones were discovered and first studied in insects such as ants, bees, and termites, where they are the dominant form of social communication (see Wilson, 1971). There are two major types of pheromones: **releasers,** which "release," or automatically trigger, a specific behavioral response, and **primers,** which trigger glandular and other physiological activities. Insects attract their mates, recruit others for food gathering or fighting, and recognize each other and their own species via releasers. Queen ants, bees, and termites control swarming, new queen production, and the proportion of types of workers using primers. An insect pheromone is usually a *specific chemical* produced by a *specific gland* and detected by a *specific receptor*. Insect behavior is directly under the control of pheromones.

Mammals, of course, are much more complex animals than insects, and the effects of pheromones on their behavior are more subtle. Nonetheless, many pheromone-related effects, both primer- and releaser-like, have been found in several species, including rodents, dogs, and monkeys (see Brown & MacDonald, 1985a, 1985b, for reviews). An example of a releaser-like effect is the effect that the odor of a female dog in heat has on male dogs (Goodwin, Gooding, & Regnier, 1979). In monkeys, female vaginal secretions called *copulins* have a more subtle effect on male sexual behavior in monkeys (Goldfoot, 1981; Goldfoot, Essock-Vitale, Asa, Thornton, & Leshner, 1978; Michael, Keverne, & Bonsall, 1971). In reptiles and mammals, pheromones are secreted by specific glands and detected and processed by the *accessory olfactory system*, which consists of the **vomeronasal organs**—a special set of smell receptors for detecting heavy pheromone molecules—the accessory olfactory bulb, and projections to areas of the brain involved in reproductive behavior (Wysocki & Meredith, 1987).

The behavioral effects of pheromones on humans are likely to be indirect because social and learning factors influence our behavior more than they do that of other mammals. Moreover, humans do not possess a highly developed, clearly functional accessory olfactory system, although recently some evidence for the presence of a vomeronasal organ has been found (Bartoshuk & Beauchamp, 1994; Takami, Getchell, Chen, Monti-Bloch, Berliner, Stensaas, & Getchell, 1993). However, smells may play an important, although probably subordinate, role in some aspects of human social behavior. First, people can reliably detect their own body odor from among a set of similar stimuli contributed by other people (Lord & Kasprzak, 1989; McBurney, Levine, & Cavanaugh, 1977; Russell, 1976; Schleidt, Hold, & Attili, 1981). People also can identify the sex of an odor donor, using both quality ("musky" male versus "sweet" female—Russell, 1976) and intensity (strong and unpleasant male versus weaker and more pleasant female—Doty, 1985), based on hand odor (Wallace, 1977) or breath odor (Doty, Green, Ram, & Yankell, 1982), as well as body odor. Females are better at this (Doty et al., 1982; Wallace, 1977) and at all aspects of odor identification (Doty, Applebaum, Zusho, & Settle, 1985; Lord & Kasprzak, 1989).

Even very young babies can identify the scent of their mothers' breast (MacFarlane, 1975; Russell, 1976) and their mothers' armpit odor (Cernoch & Porter, 1985). Female newborns can even develop a preference for an artificial odorant from mere exposure to it (Balogh & Porter, 1986). However, accurate odor identification in adults requires sufficient experience with the odor and its source (Cain, 1979; Rabin, 1988; Rabin & Cain, 1984; Schab, 1991). Because the relationship between parents and children promotes such experience, we might expect parents to recognize the odors of their own offspring and expect siblings to recognize each others' odors, and they do (Porter, Balogh, Cernoch, & Franchi, 1986; Porter & Moore, 1981).

Because humans are sensitive to biological odors, even without a functioning accessory olfactory system, perhaps they are also sensitive to pheromones. Alpha androstenol is a sex-attractant pheromone for pigs that is also present in human apocrine (a gland in the underarm region) sweat. Does it play a role in human sexual attraction? In spite of several intriguing results, such as small effects of alpha androstenol on ratings of job candidates (Cowley, Johnson, & Brooksbank, 1977), sexual attractiveness (Kirk-Smith, Booth, Carroll, & Davies, 1978), and seat choice in a dentist's waiting room (Kirk-Smith & Booth, 1980), there is no unequivocal evidence that human behavior could be *controlled*, to the extent seen in lower mammals and insects, by such pheromones (Rogel, 1978).

It is possible that there are less dramatic effects of pheromones on human reproductive functioning. For example, male underarm secretions influence the regularity of the female menstrual cycle (Cutler, Preti, Krieger, Huggins, Garcia, & Lawley, 1986), whereas female underarm secretions influence the synchrony of females' cycles (Preti, Cutler, Garcia, Huggins, & Lawley, 1986; see also McClintock, 1971). These are primer-like effects because they involve physiological changes and not specific behaviors. They can be important—for example, menstrual regularity is associated with healthy reproductive functioning and fertility—but they are not direct and powerful immediate influences on human behavior.

TOUCH

Pressure on any part of the skin that covers the surface of our body can evoke the sensation of touch; yet, when we think about sensory experiences we most often ignore this modality in favor of vision or hearing. Nonetheless, the major components of most sexual experiences are touch sensations. The very act of touching another person, in Western society, is considered to be an act of considerable intimacy, whether it is the gentle touch of a friend or lover or the violent punch of an aggressor. The sense of touch, and also those of pain and warmth and cold, arises from receptors located in the skin and their associated neural pathways and structures. Thus, before discussing the senses of touch and pain in more detail, we must describe the structure of the skin and its associated neural machinery.

Skin Stimuli and Receptors

The skin responds to a variety of physical stimuli. When we press an object against the skin, it deforms the surface, and we experience the sensation of touch, or pressure. When an object makes enough contact with any hair on our body to cause it to bend, we also experience touch. The temperature of the object with which we touch the skin also elicits a sensation. Whether it is warmth or cold depends both on the temperature of the stimulus and on the temperature of the skin. Finally, the skin responds to electrical stimulation. For mild electrical stimuli, a type of touch sensation is usually felt, although temperature can also be experienced. When electrical stimulation or pressure becomes intense, or stimulus temperature becomes extreme, the sensation usually becomes painful.

Figure 8-10 is a diagram of the most important structures in **hairy skin,** which covers most of the human body. A different kind of skin, called **glabrous skin,** has no hairs and is found on the palms of the hands, soles of the feet, parts of fingers and toes, and several other places. All skin consists of two basic layers. The outer layer, called the **epidermis,** consists of several layers of tough dead cells on top of a single layer of living cells. The living layer, called the **dermis,** divides constantly to generate the dead protective layers above. Most of the nerve endings in hairy skin are found in the dermis. However, some glabrous skin has a thick outer layer of dead cells that contains many free nerve endings, which makes it effective protection but also extremely sensitive to stimulation. Under the two layers of skin cells is usually a layer of

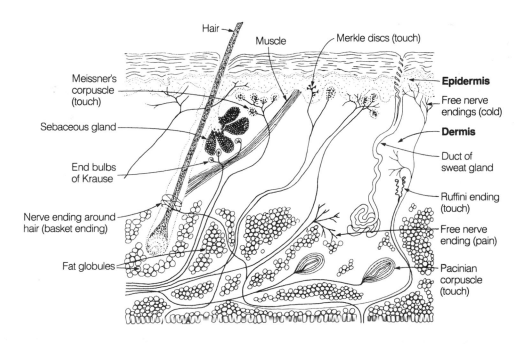

FIGURE 8-10   A piece of hairy skin in cross-section (based on Woolard, Weddell, & Harpman, 1940).

fat cells. In addition to these layers, the skin contains a variety of hairs, muscles, glands, arteries, veins, and capillaries. Some of these are also shown in Figure 8-10.

Figure 8-10 also shows some of the most common nerve endings in the skin. Nerve endings with small bodies or swellings on the dendrites, including the *Pacinian corpuscles*, *Meissner corpuscles*, *Merkel disks*, and *Ruffini endings*, are called "corpuscular" and seem to be associated with various types of fibers that are particularly responsive to touch stimuli. "Noncorpuscular" or **free nerve endings** in subcutaneous fat are associated with pain fibers (Vierck, 1978). Free nerve endings projecting into the epidermis may be associated with cold fibers, which increase their firing rate when skin temperature drops, or with warm fibers, which increase their firing rate when skin temperature rises (Hensel, 1981). They may also be the endings of pain fibers (Perl, 1984).

As an example of how a skin receptor responds to stimulation, consider the very common **Pacinian corpuscle** (Figure 8-10). Loewenstein and his colleagues peeled away the surrounding layers of the cell (much as we would peel an onion) to allow them to touch the axon itself (Loewenstein, 1960). They showed that a mechanical stimulus operates directly on the axon of the nerve by deforming its membrane. This deformation causes numerous tiny holes in the membrane to open, allowing positive ions to flow into the cell and depolarize it. The depolarization generates an action potential in the myelinated axon and carries the message of stimulation to the brain. Temperature probably acts in a similar way, perhaps by controlling chemical reactions that would affect the flow of ions across the cell's membrane. Electrical stimuli probably trigger spike potentials directly. We do not know whether all of the cutaneous nerve endings operate in a similar fashion, but it is reasonable to suppose that they do.

Neural Pathways and Responses

The organization of receptors and neural pathways for the skin senses depends on both the *type of nerve fiber* and *the place of termination* of the pathway in the cortex. The type of nerve fiber is important because different types of nerve fibers carry different kinds of information to the brain. Fibers can be classified in at least three ways: (1) according to the class of stimulus that most easily excites them (mechanical, temperature, or noxious), (2) according to the way they respond to those stimuli (slow or fast adapting), and (3) according to whether they have large, ill-defined receptive fields or small, well-defined ones. By *receptive field* here we mean much the same thing we did for vision (see Chapter 3), except that here it refers to that region of the *skin* that, when stimulated, causes responses in a particular neural fiber. The receptive fields in the skin also possess the same sort of excitatory-center, inhibitory-surround organization found in the visual system (Bekesy, 1967; Gardner, 1983). Demonstration Box 8-6 shows how you can demonstrate this organization for yourself with touch stimuli.

Under the criteria described earlier, humans have been shown to have at least four different types of fibers that respond to mechanical deformation of glabrous skin: fibers with small, well-defined receptive fields that adapt either rapidly or slowly and fibers with large, ill-defined receptive fields that adapt either rapidly or slowly (Greenspan & Bolanowski, 1996; Vallbo, 1981). Such fiber types are reminiscent of the parvo and magno pathways associated with the nerve fibers that leave the retina of the eye (see Chapter 3).

The place on the skin where a particular nerve ending is found determines the location in the brain to which the information is sent, regardless of the type of fiber it represents. All of the sensory information from the skin is sent to the spinal cord through 31 pairs of nerves (one member of each pair for each side of the body). There are also four cranial nerves that collect cutaneous information from the head region. These inputs are gathered into two main pathways to the brain, each of which seems to carry different types of information. Figure 8-11 shows various aspects of these pathways.

The first pathway is called the **dorsal column**. The nerve fibers that comprise it are large, conduct information quickly, and mostly receive inputs from the large, myelinated, fast-conducting Aβ (A-beta) fibers terminating in corpuscular endings in the skin. The pathway goes up the spinal cord on the same side of the body until it reaches

DEMONSTRATION BOX 8-6
Inhibitory Interactions on the Skin

In this demonstration you will see how skin sensations interact. You will need two fairly sharp pointed objects, such as two toothpicks or two bristles from a hairbrush. The demonstration will work better if you ask a friend to control the stimuli. Do not use anything like a knife because you will be pushing the point quite strongly against your skin. First, try pressing one point against the skin of your palm. Notice the spread of sensation around the stimulated point. Now put the two points as close together as you possibly can. Push them together on the same place on your palm. Notice that you feel only one point, although two are present. Now move the two stimulating points slightly apart. You should *still* feel only one point. Repeat this procedure several times, moving the points apart by a little more each time and paying careful attention to whether the sensation feels like two points or one on your skin. If you are pushing hard enough and paying close attention to your sensations, at just about the separation where the two points begin to feel like two distinct points on the skin, you should have a surprising experience. The magnitude of the sensation from the two points should diminish greatly, perhaps vanish altogether for a short time. The sensation should be very faint, even though two toothpicks (or brush bristles) are pushing with some force against the skin. As you then move the points even farther apart, you will perceive two distinct, full-strength sensations, appropriately separate on the skin. This phenomenon is explained by the overlapping of regions of excitation and inhibition in adjacent receptive fields of the skin, as shown in the accompanying figure.

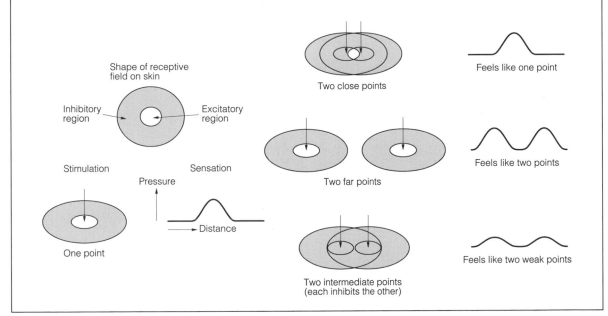

the brain stem, where most of the nerve fibers cross over to the other side. It then continues to the **thalamus** and finally to the **somatosensory cortex,** which is located in the **parietal** region of the brain (the upper-central region, shown in Figure 8-12). Thus, touch information is sent to the somatosensory cortex on the opposite side of the body from where it started. This system has fibers that respond mostly to touch, although temperature fibers have also been found (Hensel, 1981).

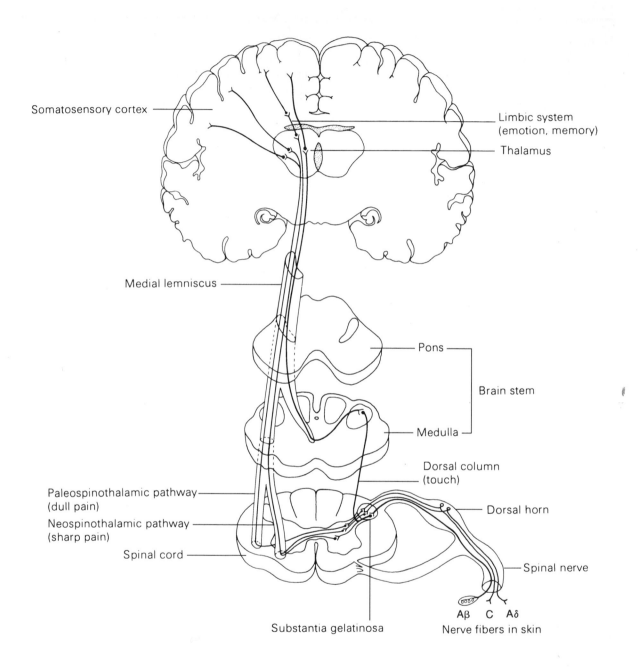

Somatosensory cortex

Limbic system (emotion, memory)

Thalamus

Medial lemniscus

Pons

Brain stem

Medulla

Dorsal column (touch)

Dorsal horn

Paleospinothalamic pathway (dull pain)

Neospinothalamic pathway (sharp pain)

Spinal cord

Spinal nerve

Aβ   C   Aδ

Nerve fibers in skin

Substantia gelatinosa

FIGURE 8-11 Schematic drawing of some of the important neural pathways from the skin to the brain. The sections of the spinal cord and brain stem are horizontal; that of the brain is vertical.

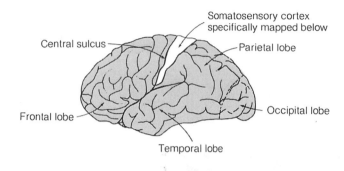

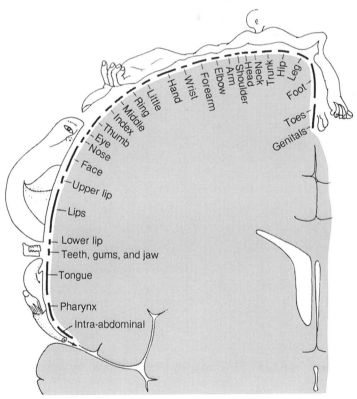

Sensory homunculus

FIGURE 8-12   Penfield and Rasmussen's (1950) topographic map of projections of "touch" nerve fibers on the somatosensory cortex. The length of the line next to the drawing of each body part is proportional to the area of somatosensory cortex subserving that body part. (From *The Cerebral Cortex of Man* by W. Penfield and T. Rasmussen. Copyright 1950 by Macmillan Publishing Co., renewed 1978 by Theodore Rasmussen.)

The second major pathway is called the **spino-thalamic pathway.** This pathway is made up of many short fibers instead of a few long axons. At the brain stem, its two branches, the **pale-ospinothalamic** (*paleo* means "old") and the **neospinothalamic** (*neo* means "new"), join with the dorsal column to form the **medial lemniscus.** The paleospinothalamic pathway is older in an evolutionary sense and seems specialized for sig-naling dull or burning pain—it probably receives most of its input from the small, unmyelinated, slow-conducting C fibers that terminate in the skin. The neospinothalamic pathway seems spe-cialized for signaling sharp or pricking pain and probably receives most of its input from the small, myelinated, but slower conducting Aδ (A-delta) fibers that terminate in the skin. It also receives some input from the large, fast-conducting Aβ fibers. (Aβ, Aδ, and C fibers are described in more detail in the "Pain" section of this chapter.) The two spinothalamic pathways ascend on the oppo-site side of the spinal cord from where their input fibers terminate in the skin and then project to several areas of the brain, the most important being the thalamus and the **limbic system** (re-sponsible for emotion and memory). Fibers from these areas then go to the somatosensory cortex. These pathways seem to carry some information about temperature and touch but signal mostly noxious stimulation.

It is possible to identify two major parts of the somatosensory cortex, which are simply called *S1* and *S2*, and many subsidiary areas (Burton & Sinclair, 1996). S1 has several identifiable layers (Kaas, 1983). Thalamic neurons project mainly to one or more layers in S1, depending on where they come from. S1 neurons then project to S2 (Pons, Garraghty, Friedman, & Mishkin, 1987). Neurons in the many areas of somatosensory cortex connect with each other in very complex ways, following hierarchical rules very similar to those that charac-terize connections in the visual cortex, including back projections between areas (Burton & Sinclair, 1996; see also Chapter 3).

Touch at each location on the body is repre-sented by a corresponding location of activity in the somatosensory cortex (see Burton & Sinclair, 1996, for a review). In effect, the body is mapped onto the cortex. Penfield and Rasmussen (1950) worked out the actual pattern of the relationship

by electrically stimulating the somatosensory cor-tex of patients who were having brain operations. As each place on the cortex was stimulated, the pa-tients reported the sensation felt, such as a tingling of the left leg, an itch of the right hand, and so forth. The resulting map of the body is shown in Figure 8-12. Notice that the spatial location of stimulation on the skin is preserved in the spatial location of activity in the cortex. However, the map may change if sensory input is permanently lost from some region of the skin, even in adult-hood. For example, in monkeys deprived of inner-vation from an arm, the region of S1 that previ-ously encoded touch and pain information from that arm comes after several years to encode infor-mation from adjacent regions of the skin (Pons, Garraghty, Ommaya, Kaas, Taub, & Mishkin, 1991). You can experience one of the consequences of a cortical map that encodes the stimulation of adja-cent regions of the skin into adjacent regions of cortical activity by trying Demonstration Box 8-7.

Touch Thresholds, Adaptation, and Intensity

One of the most striking aspects of our sense of touch is how our sensitivity varies from one region of the body to another. Figure 8-13A shows repre-sentative absolute touch thresholds for several dif-ferent regions of the body. Such thresholds are ob-tained by applying a small rod or hair to the surface of the skin with differing amounts of force per unit area, which changes the tension of the skin. The abrupt change in skin tension, or *strain*, is the stimulus for touch (Frey & Kiesow, 1899), much as an abrupt change in light intensity is the stimulus for vision (see Chapter 4). When the same hair is used for all skin loci, these thresholds can be expressed simply in terms of the amount of force applied to the hair because the area over which the force is applied (the tip of the hair) remains constant. This has been done in Figure 8-13, where the higher the bar, the greater the force needed for absolute threshold and the lower the sensitivity.

Even more dramatic variations of threshold exist within a relatively small area of skin, say, the surface of the arm. To experience this, explore a 2 × 2-cm area on your forearm with a toothpick or hairbrush

DEMONSTRATION BOX 8-7
Aristotle's Illusion

The famous Greek philosopher-scientist Aristotle noticed an interesting illusion of touch that is quite easy to demonstrate. Hold your fingers as shown in Figure A, and touch the point between them with a pencil, as shown. Notice that you feel one item touching you and the sensation of one single touch. Now cross your fingers as shown in Figure B, touching yourself again with a pencil in the place indicated between the fingers. Notice that you feel two distinct touches. The effect may be stronger if you close your eyes during the touches. The simplest and most plausible explanation of the illusion is that when the pencil is stimulating the inside of the two fingers (Figure A), the touch information is being sent to overlapping or adjacent areas of the touch cortex, resulting in the sensation of one touch. When

the pencil is stimulating the outsides of the two fingers because of your finger contortions, the information is being sent to two separate areas of the touch cortex, allowing you to experience two distinct touches. Such a cortical mapping is quite reasonable because commonly a single object between two fingers would be expected to stimulate adjacent skin surfaces and hence should be encoded as a single touch source. It is normally not possible, however, for a single object to stimulate the outsides of two different fingers, and so two different touches should be experienced in these circumstances. The cortical mapping reflects these common situations. It seems that whether the fingers are actually crossed or not, all processing makes the assumption that they are uncrossed (Benedetti, 1985).

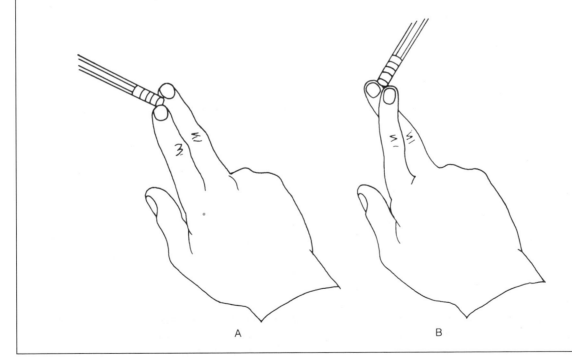

A   B

bristle, pressing with the same very light pressure every time you touch the skin. You will find that you can feel the touch of the bristle distinctly on some spots, whereas on others you will feel only a very faint touch or none at all.

A vibrating touch stimulus is easier to detect than is the single touch of a bristle. The absolute threshold for a vibrating stimulus depends on the vibration frequency, much as the threshold of hearing depends on the frequency of a sound wave.

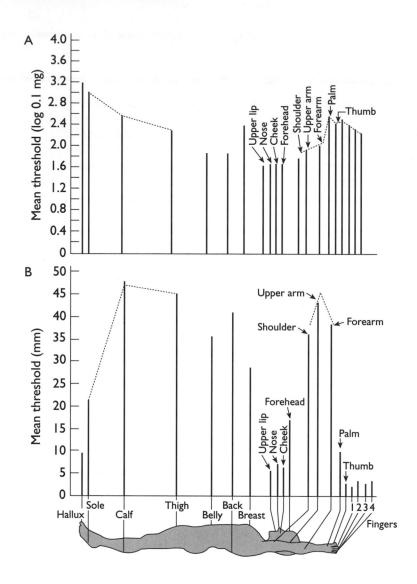

FIGURE 8-13 (A) Representative absolute thresholds for different regions of the skin. (B) Representative two-point thresholds for different regions of the skin (based on S. Weinstein in D. R. Kenshalo (Ed.), *The Skin Senses*, 1968, Charles C. Thomas, Publisher, Springfield, Illinois).

Also, similar to the ear, the skin is sensitive only to a limited range of vibration frequencies, from about 40 Hz to about 2,500 Hz. The absolute threshold for a vibrating stimulus can be affected by skin temperature, being somewhat lower when the skin is warm. This effect is restricted to vibration frequencies over 100 Hz for glabrous skin, but it occurs at all frequencies for hairy skin (Verrillo & Bolanowski, 1986). Cooling increases the touch threshold on the tongue, at least for intermediate vibration frequencies (Green, 1987).

There seems to be a minimum absolute threshold measurable for touch, similar to vision and smell. Vallbo (1983) placed a subcutaneous electrode in a rapidly adapting nerve fiber in the hand of an awake human volunteer. He found that a single spike potential in the fiber, stimulated by a 10-μm movement of a tiny probe placed on the skin, produced a detectable sensation. Obviously, at the neural level, we can't get any more sensitive than the ability to experience a single spike potential as a conscious touch sensation.

One aspect of all tactile experience is that each touch sensation is localized at a particular place on the skin. Our ability to localize a touch sensation accurately is directly related to the amount of neural representation the touched place has in the touch cortex. In general, the greater the representation of a particular area, the smaller are the errors of localization for that area (the relative cortical representation of areas of the body was shown in Figure 8-12). One way of expressing localization accuracy is the **two-point threshold.** This threshold arises from the discovery by Weber in the 1830s that two-touch stimuli (such as the points of a drawing compass) will be felt as a single touch if they stimulate points that are very close together on the skin. The two-point threshold is a measure of how far apart two separate touch stimuli must be on the skin before they are felt as two separately localizable touches. A comprehensive determination of two-point threshold was provided by Weinstein (1968), and a summary of some of his results is shown in Figure 8-13B, where higher bars mean that the points must be farther apart to be discriminated. Notice the remarkable two-point sensitivity of the lower face, the hands, and the feet. Presumably this reflects the use of these areas in manipulation of objects. The high sensitivity of the feet may be a leftover from our primate ancestors, who could manipulate objects with their feet!

Touch sensations adapt, as do all other sensations. This can be shown by simply applying a stimulus to the skin and observing the gradual disappearance of the sensation. For example, when you first get dressed in the morning you may be (uncomfortably) aware of your belt or waistband, but after a while the sensation from it fades from consciousness. Zigler (1932) measured touch adaptation for several different areas of the body. He found that the heavier the stimulus, the longer it took for the sensation to disappear, but that the larger the area covered by the stimulus, the less time it took for the sensation to disappear. You can demonstrate this result by trying Demonstration Box 8-8.

Adaptation can also be measured by asking an observer to adjust the intensity of a briefly presented stimulus until the sensation associated with it matches that associated with another stimulus to which adaptation has been taking place over some time period. The difference between the intensities of the two stimuli is a measure of the amount of adaptation that has taken place, assuming that the two stimuli would be equal in sensation magnitude if they were equal in intensity. Using this technique, Frey and Goldman (1915) determined that adaptation to touch stimuli is similar to that for other modalities. Adaptation is very rapid for the first second or so and then gradually slows down. After 3 sec, the sensation level has decreased to about one quarter of the beginning value.

Bekesy (1959) used this same technique to measure the time course of adaptation for vibratory stimuli, which generally takes longer than adaptation for static stimuli. Again, different parts of the body respond differently. On the lip adaptation is complete after about 20 sec. On the forearm, however, loss of sensation is more gradual, and adaptation is not complete even after 60 sec. These

---

DEMONSTRATION BOX 8-8
Touch Adaptation

For this demonstration, you will need a watch with a sweep second hand, two pieces of cardboard (cut into small circles with diameters of about 1 cm and about 4 cm), and a friend. Lay one piece of cardboard on the skin of your friend's back, and record the amount of time before the sensation of touch disappears. Repeat this with the other piece of cardboard. Try the experiment again, only this time press gently on each cardboard. Notice that the lighter touches and the larger surface-area stimulations disappear faster from consciousness. Thus, they show faster adaptation.

longer adaptation times are consistent with the more effective vibratory stimulus.

Vibrating stimuli are also used to study the intensity of touch sensations. Magnitude estimates of the intensity of a 60-Hz vibratory stimulus on the fingertip follow a power function of stimulus intensity with an exponent of about 0.95—nearly a linear relationship (Collins & Cholewiak, 1994; Stevens, 1959). Magnitude estimates of single mechanical pulses applied to the skin of the hand are also a power function of stimulus intensity, but with a somewhat lower exponent for glabrous skin (about 0.70) than for hairy skin (about 1.05) (Hamalainen & Jarvilehto, 1981).

We mentioned earlier that the action of a vibrating stimulus on the skin is quite similar to that of sound on the ear in that sensitivity is greatest for certain stimulus frequencies (e.g., Gescheider & Verrillo, 1982; Marks, 1979a). Correspondingly, for a given physical pressure, some vibration frequencies give a more intense touch sensation than others. Figure 8-14 shows a set of equal sensation curves, for a vibrating stimulus on the skin, that is very similar to the equal loudness contours presented in Figure 7-12. Every point on a given line represents the same perceived touch intensity. For

touch, maximum sensitivity seems to be in the region of 200–400 Hz. Notice that stimulus intensity in Figure 8-14 is measured in decibels (compared to a displacement of the vibrator surface by one millionth of a meter, which represents 0 dB). This is similar to the decibel scale used in hearing (see Chapter 6).

There are other similarities between responses of the skin to vibrating stimuli and hearing, both because of the similarity of the stimuli involved (both are mechanical vibrations) and because of the evolutionary origins of the cochlea of the auditory system and hairy skin (see Chapter 6). For example, discrimination of the intensities of vibrating stimuli follows Weber's Law as closely as that of sound intensities does (Gescheider, Bolanowski, Verrillo, Arpajian, & Ryan, 1990). Channel capacity is similar for vibratory and sound intensity at about 2 bits maximum (Rabinowitz, Houtsma, Durlach, & Delhorne, 1987). Forward, backward, and simultaneous masking of vibrating stimuli occurs in the presence of another vibrating stimulus, and the amount of masking decreases as the time interval between target and mask increases (Gescheider, Bolanowski, & Verrillo, 1989).

The skin is different from the ear in that, in glabrous skin at least, there seem to be four distinct receptor and afferent nerve systems, often called channels, for touch rather than the single system represented by the cochlea of the ear. Each of the four systems has distinct psychophysical properties, some of which are summarized in Table 8-1. The Pacinian system (composed of Pacinian corpuscles and their nerves) seems to be most sensitive to high-frequency vibrations, in the region around 250 Hz (Verrillo, 1968), whereas each of the three non-Pacinian systems (NP1, NP2, and NP3) has a different, generally lower, operating range of frequencies (e.g., Bolanowski, Gescheider, Verrillo, & Checkosky, 1988; Greenspan & Bolanowski, 1996). The psychophysical properties of each channel depend on both the mechanical properties of the skin and on those of the specific receptor stimulated (e.g., Van Doren, 1989). Although stimulation of only one channel is required for a sensation to be perceived, our touch sensations usually result from a blend of activity in all four channels, as each responds to a different aspect of a particular touch stimulus (Greenspan & Bolanowski, 1996).

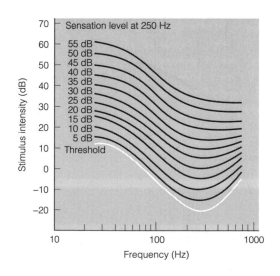

FIGURE 8-14 Equal sensation contours for a vibrating stimulus. These contours are quite similar to equal loudness contours over the same range of frequencies (see Figure 7-12) (from Verrillo, Fraioli, & Smith, 1969).

Table 8-1   The Four-Channel Model of Touch Sensation for Glabrous Skin[a]

CHARACTERISTIC OF CHANNEL	CHANNELS			
	Pacinian	NP1	NP2	NP3
Adaptational property	Rapid	Rapid	Slow	Slow
Receptive field size	Large	Small	Large	Small
Receptor ending	Pacinian	Meissner	Ruffini	Merkel
Sensation	Vibration	Flutter	Buzz-like	Pressure
Frequency range	40–500 Hz	2–40 Hz	100–500 Hz	0.4–2.0 Hz
Temporal summation	Yes	No	No	Indeterminate
Spatial summation	Yes	No	?	No

[a]Based on Greenspan & Bolanowski, 1996.

In addition to passively perceiving vibrating stimuli, we can perceive changes in pressure from textured surfaces as they move relative to our skin surface. The perception of "roughness" varies over the body, with greatest sensitivity on the lips, fingers, and forearms and least sensitivity on the heels, back, and thighs (J. C. Stevens, 1990). These relative sensitivities are similar to those for absolute sensitivity to the pressure of a single point (see Figure 8-13A). Roughness is perceived similarly whether the surface or the body part moves (Heller, 1989). Moreover, although vision and touch perform similarly in discriminating relatively rough textures, touch is superior to vision for discriminating smoother textures (Heller, 1989).

Tactile and Haptic Pattern Perception

The sense of touch can discriminate and recognize complex objects (Klatzky, Lederman, & Metzger, 1985), although it tends to respond best to different aspects of objects than the visual system does (Klatzky, Lederman, & Reed, 1987). Louis Braille exploited this ability when he created his tactile pattern alphabet, which enables blind people to read any suitably translated text. In this alphabet, patterns of raised dots on paper play the role of the patterns of ink on paper that constitute written language for sighted people. The remarkable speed with which an experienced blind person can read a Braille-rendered text reflects not only long hours of practice (as does any form of reading) but also the remarkable sensitivity of the touch system.

Of course, the final interpretation of these patterns of touch stimuli involves a number of complicated cognitive processes (Krueger, 1982).

A way of conveying information by way of touch that more directly substitutes tactile patterns for visual patterns is the vision substitution system (White, Saunders, Scadden, Bach-y-Rita, & Collins, 1970). Here, a television camera scans a visual pattern, and the output of the camera is converted into a pattern of vibrating points on the skin of the back of a blind (or blindfolded) observer. The observer can move the camera to view different parts of the visual scene. When visual stimuli are converted to tactile patterns in this way, observers can recognize up to 25 different stimulus patterns. Even the relative distances of various objects in a scene can be perceived from the tactile pattern, and illusions are experienced as well. These findings raise questions similar to those raised by visual and auditory pattern perception. For example, we might ask if there are feature detectors for touch. These and other findings (e.g., Horner, 1991) also remind us of the importance of high-level cognitive processes in even the simplest types of perceptual experiences.

Reading in Braille requires that the reading material be translated into Braille. This is especially difficult to do with newspapers and magazines, which are published in large numbers. The Optacon (Bliss, Katcher, Rogers, & Shepard, 1970) offers a solution to this problem. It works like the vision substitution system except that the size of the visual field scanned is only about that of a single printed letter, and the pattern of vibrations corresponding to each letter is formed on the fingertip rather than on the back. After 50 hr of training, blind users of the Optacon can read untreated material at 20 words per minute. Experienced users attain rates as high as 60 words per minute. Interestingly, sighted users can also achieve excellent performance, although they exhibit large individual differences (Cholewiak & Collins, 1997).

The tactile perceptual system can also aid the hearing impaired. Several devices have been developed in which an array of electrodes or vibrators is used to transmit speech information to the skin of hearing-impaired people. In these devices, the prominent frequency components in speech are translated into vibration at different places on the skin, and people can learn to recognize the vibratory patterns as words. Devices such as the "Tickle Talker" (Cowan, Alcantara, Blamey, & Clark, 1988), the Queens vocoder (Brooks & Frost, 1983), and the Tacticon (Weisenberger, Broadstone, & Saunders, 1989) all have been shown to be useful, especially in conjunction with lipreading.

The Optacon and similar devices also have been used for research into the mechanisms of tactile pattern perception (e.g., J. C. Craig, 1981, 1983b; Loomis, 1981; Schneider, Hughes, Epstein, & Bach-y-Rita, 1986). Just as in other sensory systems, presentation of one pattern on the skin can *mask* another, making it more difficult to recognize (J. C. Craig, 1978), although some of the difficulty may arise from competing responses to internal representations of the two tactile patterns (J. C. Craig, 1995; Horner, 1997). For example, if a letter pattern is presented on the Optacon and then followed immediately by a rectangular pattern, observers have a harder time identifying the letter than if no masking pattern was presented. This is called **backward masking** because the masking pattern seems to act backward in time to interfere with the perception of the earlier target. **Forward masking** also occurs with tactile patterns; here, the masking pattern is presented first, followed by the target. As in audition and vision (see Chapters 7 and 10), masking studies often reveal basic mechanisms of tactile perception. For example, there is usually more backward masking when the time interval between target and mask is short and more forward masking when the time interval is long (J. C. Craig, 1983a). This is consis-

tent with the idea that perceptual representations of tactile features persist for about 1,200 ms (Craig & Evans, 1987; Evans & Craig, 1986) and reveals something about how those representations are integrated over time (Evans, 1987). Masking effects are similar for all body locations, although pattern discrimination and recognition in the absence of masking varies with location on the body (Cholewiak & Craig, 1984). The ability to localize tactile stimuli is similarly subject to backward, forward, and simultaneous masking and depends on the time interval between mask and target (J. C. Craig, 1989). However, masking of identification is usually most effective when the mask and target occur at the same location (but see Horner, 1997), whereas masking of localizability is most effective when mask and target occur at different locations (J. C. Craig, 1989).

We have been talking about receptors that respond to mechanically encoded information from the world around us when contact is made with our skin. There is also a vast amount of touchlike information available from within our own bodies. Thus, we can determine by feel alone whether our bodies are moving or stationary (see also Chapter 14: "Motion"), and we can also determine the position and movement of our body parts. The neural processing of this information and the sensations we feel, called collectively **kinesthesis**, bear striking resemblances to touch.

In the highest organisms, several specialized receptor systems inform the brain about the position of the limbs or the orientation of the body. Our bodies are literally enmeshed in a web of sensory receptors that accurately monitor the positions of various body parts so that appropriate action can be initiated and controlled. In many cases the signals of these sensory systems are not consciously perceived but, rather, are used in controlling reflex actions that maintain an upright posture. When these signals are perceived, they give rise to the sensations of force or weight, which are often used to help guide our voluntary movements, as in sports or other skilled motor performance, and also our identification of objects that can be touched but not seen.

When we move our limbs about actively through the world, we perceive objects through a combination of tactile and kinesthetic sensations caused by our mechanical interaction with them.

Such experiences play an important role in perceptual development as vision and touch calibrate each other (see Chapter 16), and they can also be important under conditions in which visual and auditory information about the world is missing or impoverished, such as when stumbling about in a dark bedroom. Our experience of the world based on a combination of tactile and kinesthetic sensation is called **haptic perception** (Gibson, 1966).

People are very good at identifying ordinary objects presented haptically (Klatzky, Lederman, & Metzger, 1985). One important type of haptic information about objects is their size (extension in space). Our ability to discriminate lengths using only haptic perception is quite good. For example, the difference threshold for length for objects between 10 mm and 20 mm is about 1 mm, indicating a Weber fraction of 0.05 to 0.10 (Durlach et al., 1989). Haptic length discrimination does not follow Weber's Law very well, however, because the Weber fraction tends to decrease for larger objects. Nonetheless, channel capacity is about 2 bits for haptic length, similar to visually perceived length (Durlach et al., 1989).

Several other haptic attributes of objects can be reliably discriminated and are often used in haptic object identification. One is surface texture (Lederman, Browse, & Klatzky, 1988), which is often integrated with the perception of hardness (Klatzky, Lederman, & Reed, 1989), and also there is perception of any curvature of the object surface (Pont, Kappers, & Koenderink, 1997). Moreover, even a brief "haptic glance" at an object can sometimes suffice to identify it through detection of one or more of these characteristic properties, although free haptic exploration (which means freely feeling around the object) is necessary to achieve the highest levels of accuracy (Klatzky & Lederman, 1995).

Sometimes the cues to haptic shape perception are quite subtle. Figure 8-15 illustrates an intriguing experimental setup that shows that the shape of solid objects can often be identified when they are merely wielded by a handle and their edges and contours are not seen or touched. This appears to occur because observers can sense haptically the moments of inertia and resistance to rotation around various axes of the objects. It also indicates that the distribution of mass of an object can play a

role in the perception of its shape (Burton, Turvey, & Solomon, 1990), orientation (Turvey et al., 1992), and where it is grasped (Pagano, Kinsella-Shaw, Cassidy, & Turvey, 1994). Furthermore, such wielding of a rod can yield information about objects struck with it, such as size (Barac-Cikoja & Turvey, 1993) and distance (Barac-Cikoja & Turvey, 1995). This is the same process by which the information received by tapping a cane aids blind people by providing cues as to both sizes and distances of objects in the world. This same process seems to assist normally sighted individuals in maintaining body orientation and posture in the dark or when their eyes are closed (Jeka, Easton, Bentzen, & Lackner, 1996).

Haptic perception is closely related to vision in some ways, in that we can often recognize an object that we explored only by touch when we later see it, or vice versa, suggesting that there is at least partial equivalence between visual and haptic representations of objects (Gibson, 1966). Another example of the close visual-haptic relationship is that some visual patterns that cause illusions, such as one line being perceived as longer than another, although they are the same length, also occur when three-dimensional models of the patterns are explored by touch alone (e.g., Day, 1990; Heller, Calcaterra, Burson, & Green, 1997; Walker & Shank, 1988; Wenderoth, Criss, & van der Zwan, 1990). Finally, haptic exploration is often used to assist visual recognition when making difficult discriminations (Klatzky, Lederman, & Matula, 1993). In fact, when vision and touch disagree on a difficult-to-judge object property, such as size, touch can dominate vision if responses are rendered haptically as well (Hershberger & Misceo, 1996).

Understanding haptic perception can also be practically useful. For example, the Tadoma method of assisting speech perception by people who are both blind and hearing impaired, as Helen Keller was, is based on haptic perception. In Tadoma, an observer touches the speech articulators (the parts of the face and neck that produce speech sounds, e.g., lips, jaw, etc.). From the motions of the articulators perceived by the "listener," the words said by the speaker can be deduced with a good deal of accuracy (Norton, Schultz, Reed, Braida, Durlach, Rabinowitz, & Chomsky, 1977). You can try Tadoma for yourself in Demonstration Box 8-9.

FIGURE 8-15 Experimental setup for recognition of objects based on haptic information, especially the distribution of mass in the object (based on Burton, Turvey, & Solomon, 1990).

PAIN

Pain is a complex experience. It is usually associated with damage to the body of an animal, and, in humans, its experience is accompanied by myriad emotions and thoughts. Many sensory psychologists consider pain to be a sensation; other psychologists argue that pain is not a sensation at all but, rather, an emotion or a bodily state akin to hunger or thirst (e.g., Wall, 1979). Perhaps the best view is a compromise. There are certainly identifiable sensory characteristics of the experience of pain. Pain has absolute and differential thresholds, it adapts, and it has definable and separate physiological pathways and projection areas in the brain. Furthermore, its intensity dimension is separable from the intensity dimension of non-painful stimuli in the same modality (Janal, Clark, & Carroll, 1991). In these ways pain acts like a sensory system, and we will treat it here as a unique sensory modality.

Pain Stimuli and Receptors

There are at least two aspects of the evolutionary significance of pain. First, it is essential that an animal be able to avoid or terminate environmental situations that could harm it. Light, sound, touch, and temperature, when they occur at very

When perceiving speech using Tadoma, the perceiver places his or her hand on the face and neck of the speaker, with the thumb across the middle of the lips and the fingers fanned out across the face and neck as in the figure in this box. To try this for yourself, get a friend to whisper the words listed below while you monitor the person's articulators as shown in the figure. Pay attention to the in-and-out movements of the lips, the up-and-down movements of the jaw, and the flow of air from the mouth (the cure of larynx vibration is abolished by the need to whisper if you have normal hearing). You should have your eyes closed and put earplugs or cotton in your ears so visual information and auditory information are absent. Your friend should read the words very slowly, in an irregular order, and (because you are new at this method of perceiving speech) with exaggerated movements. There should be a pause after each word for you to guess what the word was. For an even more difficult test, your friend should choose words you have not seen and use normal movements of the articulators, although he or she should still speak slowly. Some words that are relatively easy to discriminate are *you, me, yes, why, but, candy, tree,* and *push.* Reverse roles so your friend can try it, too.

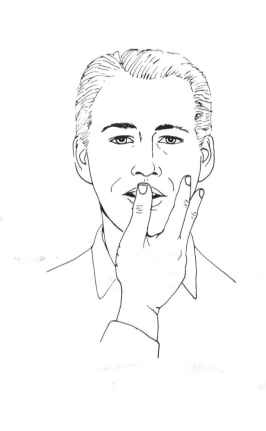

high intensities or for prolonged durations, can destroy the receptors that are specialized to receive them. If such potentially harmful intensities are not recognized quickly, the organism may perish. Second, pain signals individuals so that they may cope appropriately with an injury if it does happen. Sometimes individuals may receive serious injuries, and yet they may not feel pain until sometime later (Melzack, Wall, & Ty, 1982). Under certain circumstances this is adaptive because pain seems to have the function of inducing individuals to be still in order that healing may occur or to seek treatment for the injury. However, sometimes when an injury first occurs, actions such as escaping or fighting for one's life may be required, and pain would only interfere with these. Thus, delaying the perception of pain until such a time when it is safe to engage in behaviors that promote healing may save an individual's life (see Wall, 1979). During the recovery phase, the stimulus for pain is the injury itself, and the function of the pain is not to warn but to promote recovery by reducing activity that may make the injury worse. Without the pain sense to warn and immobilize, we would have a hard time living long enough to reproduce, which is often the unfortunate fate of those humans who are born without a well-functioning pain sense (see Sternbach, 1963). For example, Melzack and Wall (revised edition, 1988) reported such a case, where a woman died at the young age of 29 of massive infections caused by damage to her skin and bones from abrasions and unhealed injuries, especially to her joints, that she simply had not detected because she lacked adequate pain sensitivity.

The best candidates for pain receptors are the free nerve endings with which the skin and the rest of the body are particularly well supplied. As we mentioned earlier in this chapter, free nerve endings in the subcutaneous fat under the dermis of the skin have been found to be connected to nerve fibers associated with pain (see Vierck, 1978). The position of these endings in the subcutaneous fat makes them respond only to high-intensity stimuli, whether mechanical or temperature. Other pain fibers terminate in the epidermis; these endings are wrapped in a Schwann cell sheath (see Appendix), which allows them to retain a high stimulation threshold even in this more exposed location (Perl, 1984).

Another view puts less emphasis on the receptors than on their associated nerve fibers. There are at least three major classes of such nerve fibers. Large myelinated fibers (Aβ) respond especially well to light touch stimuli. These fibers conduct nerve impulses at high speed (as fast as any in the nervous system, at least 40 m/sec) and connect with both the dorsal column and spinothalamic pathways. Smaller myelinated fibers (Aδ) and small unmyelinated fibers (C) are much slower conducting (about 5–20 m/sec for Aδ and less than 2.5 m/sec for C), have higher thresholds, and respond only to noxious stimuli, such as pinches, pin pricks, or extreme temperatures (Lynn & Perl, 1996; Willis, 1985). The Aδ fibers are especially sensitive to noxious mechanical stimuli, whereas the C fibers respond to all kinds of noxious stimuli (they are often called *polymodal nociceptors*). C fibers typically terminate in free nerve endings in the subcutaneous fat of the skin or deep in muscles and joints, whereas the Aδ fiber ends are wrapped in Schwann cells and terminate in the epidermis, and the Aβ fibers terminate in more elaborate corpuscular endings. Aδ and C fibers connect mainly with the spinothalamic pathway and are now generally acknowledged to be "the" pain fibers (see Figure 8-11). Apparently the fast Aβ fibers and dorsal column pathway are specialized for highly discriminative processing of tactile information, whereas the slower Aδ and C fibers and spinothalamic

pathway carry information such as pain, temperature, and only rudimentary touch. This relationship was first suggested in 1920 by Henry Head.

The particular organization of the pain pathways leads to some interesting phenomena. For example, **double pain** is the experience of two distinct peaks of pain, differing in quality and separated in time, arising from a single pain stimulus. It is now generally accepted that the first, sharp or pricking pain, arises from the response of the somewhat faster conducting Aδ fibers to the noxious stimulus, whereas the second, dull or burning pain, arises from the slower conducting C fibers (Cooper, Vierck, & Yeomans, 1986; Torebjork & Hallin, 1973; Willis, 1985). You can experience this for yourself by trying Demonstration Box 8-10.

Neural Responses to Pain Stimuli

The electrophysiology of pain has been studied by applying noxious stimuli, such as electric shock, pinching, or pricking, to animals and recording the responses of neurons at various levels of the nervous system. In this way it has been discovered that certain neurons fire only when their receptive fields are stimulated by stimuli that we perceive as being painful. For example, Poggio and Mountcastle (1960) found such neurons in the cat's thalamus, and Casey and Morrow (1983) and Bushnell and Duncan (1989) found them in the thalamus of awake monkeys. Such neurons also have been found in Area S1 of the somatosensory cortex of rats (Lamour, Willer, & Guilbaud, 1983) and monkeys (Kenshalo & Isensee, 1983) and may also occur in Area S2 (see Willis, 1985). Studies using PET scans (a noninvasive technique described in the Appendix) have identified three different areas in the human cerebral cortex that respond when painful heat or vibration is applied to the skin: the anterior cingulate gyrus, S1, and S2 (Coghill et al., 1994; Talbot et al., 1991). It is clear that both the thalamus and the cortex play roles in pain perception. Probably several brain areas contribute to the pain experience (see Casey, 1978; Willis, 1985).

Perhaps the most interesting electrophysiological fact about pain is that the nerve fibers involved in pain and those involved in tactile and kinesthetic sensations interact, sometimes in opposition

DEMONSTRATION BOX 8-10
The Production of Double Pain

This demonstration uses the method of Sinclair and Stokes (1964) to generate two pains for the price of one. Double pain is experienced only under certain conditions. When these conditions are met, people report a first sharp, stinging sensation, followed about 1 sec later by a more-intense burning pain that may spread to a wider area and fades more gradually. Although most people, under the appropriate conditions, experience this sequence without being told what to expect, we are telling you now so that you will have a good chance to experience it. For this demonstration you will need to find a source of hot water, something to measure its temperature, and two medium-sized bowls to hold it in. You need to produce two water baths: one at 35° C (95° F) and one at 57° C (135° F). If you have access to a thermometer (a meat thermometer is fine for this demonstration), this would obviously be the best way to measure the temperatures of the baths. If you do not have a thermometer, simply mix 3½ cups of very hot tap water with 3½ cups of cold tap water for the 35-° C bath. To keep it at about this temperature, add a little hot water every minute or so. To create the 57-° C bath,

combine 6⅔ cups of hot tap water with ⅓ cup of cold tap water.

Immerse your entire hand in the 35-° C bath for about 10 min. When this time has elapsed, mix the 57-° C bath, and carefully insert your finger into it until the water comes up past the second joint of the finger. Count "one-thousand-one" to yourself, and then withdraw your finger. Pay careful attention to the sensations you experience. Notice that first you feel a sharp stinging and then about a second later a burning feeling. You may try the experiment again and again without fear of any damage if you immerse your hand in the 35-° C bath between trials, and always limit your immersion in the 57-° C bath to 1 sec. If you wish, you can try varying the temperatures of the two baths to find the limits of the conditions under which the phenomenon will occur. Also, in calculating the formulas for the two baths, we assumed that the cold tap water in your area has a temperature of about 10° C (50° F), and the hot tap water a temperature of about 60° C (140° F). If your water temperatures vary significantly from these, you will have to adjust the proportions of each to make up the baths.

to each other. Melzack and Wall (1965, 1988) devised an ingenious conceptual model of pain, called the **gate-control theory,** based on the interaction of two of these fiber types. This theory provides the foundation for most modern accounts of pain phenomena and has received both anatomical and experimental support (Humphries, Johnson, & Long, 1996). It is diagrammed in Figure 8-16.

First, notice in Figure 8-16 that both low-threshold, fast (Aβ) sensory fibers and high-threshold, slow (Aδ and C) sensory fibers have connections with the **substantia gelatinosa** (a group of neurons in the spinal cord; see also Figure 8-11) and with the **transmission cells (T cells).** These T cells are some of the slow-conducting fibers that make up the spinothalamic pathway and send pain information up the spinal cord to the

brain, whereas the substantia gelatinosa serves as the gate that may or may not allow the T cells to send their pain signals. Basically, the fast Aβ fibers close this gate, whereas the slow fibers open it. Notice in Figure 8-16 that the connections of both the fast and the slow fibers to the T cells are marked with a plus sign, meaning that they increase neural activity in those cells. The actions of these fibers on the substantia gelatinosa cells are different, however. The fast fibers excite the neurons in the substantia gelatinosa (+), whereas the slow Aδ and C fibers inhibit their action (−). When the T cells are sufficiently active, we experience pain. A light touch would mostly stimulate the fast fibers, which have lower thresholds. This would excite the substantia gelatinosa neurons, causing them to inhibit the T cells, thus canceling the

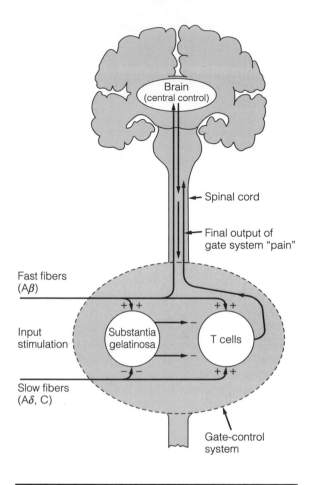

FIGURE 8-16 An illustration of the gate-control theory of pain.

excitation of the T cells by the fast fibers and keeping them below the activity level that is sensed as pain. A noxious stimulus, however, would stimulate the higher threshold slow fibers as well as the fast fibers. Because the slow fibers inhibit the substantia gelatinosa cells, canceling their excitation by the fast fibers, the substantia gelatinosa neurons no longer inhibit the T cells, which can fire more vigorously in response to input from both fast and slow fibers, and pain is experienced.

Generally speaking, chemical analgesics act to inhibit the slow fibers but do not affect the fast fibers. This allows the substantia gelatinosa to inhibit the T cells and keep the pain gate closed. Another way to close the pain gate (at least somewhat) is to rub or vibrate the skin around an area where you have hurt yourself, thus stimulating the

fast fibers in the surrounding skin, which will stimulate the substantia gelatinosa and close the gate. However, higher level processes can also participate because fast fibers transmit information directly through the dorsal column to the brain, which can in turn send information back down the spinal cord to modify the gate-control system, which may explain how some people can mentally reduce their feelings of pain. Melzack and Casey (1968) suggested that this central pathway to the gate may respond to cognitive and emotional events signaled by the brain, which may be capable of changing the nature of a potentially painful experience. There is experimental evidence that the descending pathways can inhibit responses of spinal cord neurons to noxious stimuli (e.g., Dickhaus, Pauser, & Zimmerman, 1985; Light, 1992; Willis, 1983).

Pain Thresholds, Intensity, and Adaptation

To treat pain as a sensation it is useful to define a pain threshold. This is taken to be the intensity of a stimulus that will just barely produce a sensation of pain. As in touch, there are specific tiny points on the skin that respond selectively to pain. These "pain points" give the sensation of pain for stimuli that do not produce painful sensations when applied to other places on the skin. Pain points correspond to the receptive fields of the pain fibers (Lynn & Perl, 1996; Willis, 1985). The distribution of such pain points over the body seems quite variable, as can be seen from Table 8-2. Pain thresholds vary in the oral-facial regions as well, with the tongue and inside of the lip being less sensitive than other parts to heat-induced pain (Green, 1985).

A major advance in measuring pain thresholds was made by Hardy, Wolff, and Goodell (1943). They used a device that focused an intense beam of light on the ink-blackened forehead of a subject in order to produce a precisely measurable and controllable pain stimulus. They called this device a **dolorimeter,** from the Latin *dolor* meaning "pain" and *meter* meaning "to measure." The exact thresholds measured in this way are of little importance because the units of any pain threshold stimulus vary with the pain-producing device or stimulus

Table 8-2 Distribution of Pain Sensitivity[a]

SKIN REGION	PAIN POINTS/CM^2
Back of knee	232
Neck region	228
Bend of elbow	224
Shoulder blade	212
Inside of forearm	203
Back of hand	188
Forehead	184
Buttocks	180
Eyelid	172
Scalp	144
Ball of thumb	60
Sole of foot	48
Tip of nose	44

[a]Based on Geldard, 1972.

modality. More important, Hardy and colleagues (1943) were able to show that pain thresholds act like the thresholds for other sensations. Pain thresholds are relatively stable as long as the conditions are stable, but they vary systematically with changes in the neurological, pharmacological (drugs), or psychological state of the individual. These results have been replicated many times, and more recently even social situations have been shown to affect pain thresholds (Craig, 1978).

Whether two pains are the same or different in intensity can be discriminated, indicating that there is also a meaningful difference threshold for pain. The first good measurement of the difference threshold was done by Hardy, Wolff, and Goodell (1947) using a modification of the dolorimeter. To accomplish this the authors subjected themselves to both a large amount of pain and considerable tissue damage. They even moved the site of the painful stimulation from the forehead to the forearm because the latter was more easily cared for when blistered by the pain stimuli. These rather extreme measures resulted in some very important results. Hardy and colleagues (1947) found that the difference threshold is reproducible under constant conditions. Moreover, they also found that the Weber fraction remains remarkably constant (as Weber's Law would assert) at about 0.04 (a mere 4% stimulus change) over quite a large range of pain intensities. This indicates that we are quite sensitive to variations in pain intensity. Weber fractions increase dramatically at only the highest stimulus intensities. At the extremes, however, the data were not very reliable because the skin damage being sustained made it difficult for the author/observers to concentrate on the pain intensities. More recently, signal detection theory has been successfully applied to the study of pain discrimination, although great care must be taken in doing this (Irwin et al., 1994; Irwin & Whitehead, 1991).

Hardy and colleagues (1947) also created the first scale of pain intensity. Because they had established the validity of Weber's Law for pain, they merely added up *jnd*s, as Fechner had done (see Chapter 2), to create a scale of pain intensity based on the discriminability of painful stimuli. They called this scale the **dol scale**. Later scales of pain intensity were created by more direct methods (see Gracely & Naliboff, 1996, for a review of pain measurement). For example, magnitude estimations of the intensity of pain produced by electric shocks follow a power function with an exponent between 2 and 3.5, making this the sensory modality with the largest power function exponent (see Chapter 2 on exponents and Algom & Lubel, 1994; Rollman & Harris, 1987; Stevens, 1961—for measures of various painful stimuli). The exponent varies as a function of the nature of the pain stimulus and even with the social context in which the pain is measured (Craig, Best, & Ward, 1975; Sternbach & Tursky, 1964).

An interesting aspect of pain perception is that pain experience from different sources can add together to produce a higher intensity of experienced pain than either one alone. This is true both within modalities and across modalities. Thus, stimulating two teeth at the same time lowers the pain threshold compared to stimulating a single tooth and turns mild discomfort into pain (Brown, Beeler, Kloka, & Fields, 1985). Also, pain from shock and loud noise experienced together is roughly the linear sum of the pains experienced separately (Algom, Raphaeli, & Cohen-Raz, 1986).

Does pain adapt? As early as 1939, Dallenbach demonstrated that pain caused by needles, heat, and cold does adapt. Heat-induced pain was studied by having observers judge the degree of experienced pain as they sat with their hands in hot water over a period of time (Hardy, Stolwijk, & Hoffman, 1968). As can be seen from Figure 8-17, adaptation

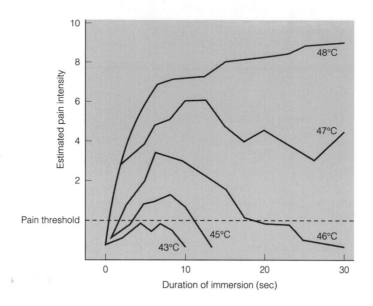

FIGURE 8-17   Average estimations of pain intensity from hot water immersions of different temperatures at different durations.

was complete for the lower temperature pain stimuli, which were only mildly painful, and less complete for the more painful stimuli. Adaptation may not take place at all for extremely painful stimuli, although it has been shown that even dental pain adapts (Ernst, Lee, Dworkin, & Zaretsky, 1986). Demonstration Box 8-11 allows you to experience pain adaptation, but be careful—that water is hot!

Analgesia and Endogenous Opiates

Because pain is unpleasant we seek to minimize it. Yet, pain often persists or may occur for the first time well after a damaging stimulus is gone. As we already mentioned, pain sensations are designed to induce individuals to remain relatively immobile, which aids healing under primitive conditions. However, modern humans are not content to accept this immobilizing pain, nor do they desire to experience the pain from surgery or illness. Thus, we have assembled an impressive array of analgesics (which reduce pain but not the detection of touch, cold, and warmth) and anesthetics (which eliminate all sensation) to rid ourselves of pain. The major focus of much pain research is to discover new ways to get rid of pain. The most potent

and reliable method of pain relief is to ingest (for example, aspirin) or inject (for example, novocaine) chemicals into our bodies. We also apply sprays or salves to cut or burned skin to achieve a local anesthesia. For more severe pain we resort to narcotic drugs (such as morphine, an opium derivative) or opt for unconsciousness (as with ether or chloroform).

It was while studying how opium-based drugs like morphine produce analgesia that researchers discovered **endogenous opiates** (opiates generated from within) that, like the manufactured drugs, interact with specific receptors in the brain to produce analgesic effects (Kosterlitz & McKnight, 1981; Snyder, 1977). At least two major classes of internally generated chemicals, the **enkephalins** and the **endorphins,** have significant analgesic effects and seem to react with the same sites that opiates do (Millan, 1986; Yaksh, 1984). When administered via injection, the endorphins have more potent and longer lasting effects. The opium-like action of these endogenous substances is further demonstrated by the fact that their analgesic effect can be blocked by the administration of *naloxone*, a chemical that blocks the action of opiates such as morphine and heroin and is often administered to those who have taken overdoses. Administration of

---

DEMONSTRATION BOX 8-11
Pain Adaptation

All you need for this demonstration is a fairly hot water bath, hot enough to cause mild pain but not hot enough to burn your skin. A pan or bowl of water at about 46° C would be ideal. You can make such a bath by mixing hot and cold tap water. Assuming your average cold tap water is about 10° C and the average hot is about 60° C, it would take about 1 cup of cold water and 3 cups of hot water. Alternatively you could measure with a meat thermometer, or simply add cold water to the hot until you get a mildly painful sensation when you immerse your finger in the bath.

When you have your bath of water, immediately immerse a finger in it and pay attention to the intensity of the painful sensation. It should begin to diminish after about 5–10 sec and may vanish entirely after about 20 sec. Now place a finger from your other hand into the bath. The sensation of pain you experience on that finger is evidence that adaptation to the pain has taken place, rather than a disappearance of pain because the water cooled down.

---

naloxone by itself makes people who are under stress more sensitive to pain, presumably because it blocks the effectiveness of endogenous opiates released naturally under these circumstances (Schull, Kaplan, & O'Brien, 1981).

Our conscious experience of pain intensity is affected not only by the magnitude of the pain stimulus but also by concentrations of these "chemical regulators," which are generated internally and act directly on specific areas of the central nervous system. Study of endogenous opiate systems may also provide clues to the mechanisms involved in nonchemical methods for the reduction of pain. For example, Willer, Dehen, and Cambier (1981) found that the psychological stress caused by the anticipation of a painful shock resulted in analgesic effects. Presumably the stress triggered the endogenous opiate system to protect the individual from the expected pain (see also Lewis, Terman, Shavit, Nelson, & Liebeskind, 1984). Similarly, women during the last 2 weeks of pregnancy experience significant increases in pain thresholds, which reduces their discomfort (Cogan & Spinnato, 1986). This is not confined to humans. Pregnant rats also experience the same threshold increases, and this effect is reduced by injection of opiate antagonist chemicals (Gintzler, 1980).

The endogenous opiate system may also be involved in some of the more "mysterious" reports of reduced pain sensitivity. Take the case of placebo effects, such as the pain reduction people experience when they take a pill that they think is an analgesic but is really an inert substance. These effects are sometimes reversible by naloxone, suggesting that an endogenous opiate system is involved. Perhaps even more mysterious is the traditional Chinese technique for alleviating pain called *acupuncture* (from the Latin *acus* meaning "needle" and *pungere* meaning "to sting"). In this technique, long, thin needles are inserted at various sites on the body. These needles may be twirled, heated, or have electrical current passed through them. Although Western doctors have been cautious about accepting acupuncture as a valid means of reducing pain, most studies support its effectiveness (see P. E. Brown, 1972; Chapman, 1978; Cheng, 1973; Clark & Yang, 1974). Many studies have now established that pain reduction achieved through acupuncture is mediated by release of endogenous opiates (Akil & Watson, 1980; He, 1987; He, Lu, Zhuang, Zhang, & Pan, 1985; Kosterlitz & McKnight, 1981).

The brain-chemical interaction we have been discussing provides only an incomplete picture of the factors influencing our perception of pain. For instance, many forms of pain reduction, such as that achieved via hypnosis, do *not* appear to be mediated by endogenous opiates (Akil & Watson, 1980; Kosterlitz & McKnight, 1981). It seems that humans have at least two pain control systems, and only one of them involves endogenous opiates (Akil & Watson, 1980; Mayer & Watkins, 1984; Watkins & Mayer, 1982).

Some of the most interesting analgesic procedures involve cognitive processes. These include such techniques as suggestion, attitude, concentration of attention, and social modeling (Craig, 1978; Weisenberg, 1984; Wolff & Goodell, 1943). The efficacy and interpretation of these techniques vary, but there is no doubt that they result in dramatic changes in pain thresholds. For instance, social modeling, where observers see another person's reactions to painful stimuli before judging the painfulness of the same stimuli for themselves, has been reported to affect both d' and physiological reactivity to painful electric shocks (Craig & Coren, 1975; Craig & Prkachin, 1978). Similarly, when people are attending to a stimulus modality that is different from the one in which a painful stimulus is presented, they experience significantly less pain and can less accurately and quickly discriminate levels of the painful stimulus (Miron, Duncan, & Bushnell, 1989).

The perception of pain involves several different mechanisms. These mechanisms may be integrated within the gate-control theory of pain that we discussed earlier. According to this theory, pain is experienced when the T cells are firing at a high enough rate. The theory describes a spinal gate controlled not only by fast- and slow-conducting sensory fibers but also, as we noted earlier, by inputs from higher levels of the nervous system. Thus, cognitive factors, motivational states, attentional factors, or other stimulation, such as high-intensity hissing noises, electricity, or music, could all be responsible for controlling the gate via the pathway *descending* from the brain to the spinal cord gate (Light, 1992; Willis, 1983, 1985). These descending pathways seem to be strongly implicated in analgesia caused by release of endogenous opiates. Perhaps activation of the descending pathways causes release of endogenous opiates into the spinal cord, thus decreasing firing of the T cells (Watkins & Mayer, 1982). However, the mechanism involving the substantia gelatinosa does *not* seem to use endogenous opiates to produce its effects.

CHAPTER SUMMARY

Taste and smell began as a single chemical sense. Taste responds to chemicals that are water soluble. The four primary tastes are *sweet, salty, sour,* and *bitter.* **Taste buds** are the taste-receptive cells that are found in three types of **papillae** called *fungiform, foliate,* and *circumvallate papillae.* In each **taste pore** are microvilli, which respond to taste-related molecules. Taste information is carried through the **solitary tract,** via pathways called the **medial lemniscus,** to the taste centers in the **thalamus,** then to the **anterior-insular cortex** in the frontal cortex. The **labeled-line theory** of taste quality perception claims that each taste fiber is tuned to a single basic taste quality. The **across-fiber pattern** theory presumes that each taste fiber can respond to all taste stimuli with different intensities; hence the taste is determined by the overall pattern. Taste thresholds vary with the **molar concentration** of the substance and the place on the tongue that is stimulated. Individuals can also exhibit *aguesias* (taste blindness) for specific substances. In addition to rapid **self-adaptation** with continued exposure to a substance, there are **cross-adaptation,** which reduces apparent intensity for other tastes, and **potentiation,** which increases the apparent intensity of other tastes.

Smell has two modes of action, related to our experience with food flavors. The first is triggered when *odorants* are pumped from the mouth into the nasal cavity while chewing, and the second is a distance sense from sniffing molecules emitted by volatile external sources. The **primary olfactory neurons** are in the **olfactory epithelium,** and each contains an **olfactory rod** with **olfactory cilia,** which contain the taste receptors. These cilia extend into mucus that contains **olfactory binding protein,** which captures the odorant molecules. According to **lock-and-key theory,** variously shaped molecules fit into holes in the walls of olfactory receptor cells, causing an electrochemical event that triggers neural activity. Smell travels through the **olfactory nerve** to the **olfactory bulb,** then along the **lateral olfactory tract** to the primary olfactory cortex in the temporal lobe. Other neurons carry smell information to the limbic system. For smell identification an across-fiber pattern theory works better than a labeled-line theory. Rapid **self-adaptation** diminishes the apparent intensity of smell stimuli; however, **cross-adaptation** depends on the similarity of the test smell to the adapting smell. Most animals (including humans) can smell and react to **pheromones** (chemicals secreted by animals that transmit information to other animals), and there appear to be special smell receptors for these, as in the **vomeronasal organs** of mammals. Humans can identify relatives and the sex and often the relative age of individuals by smell alone but are probably not directly under the control of pheromones.

Most touch sensations come through the **hairy skin** and **glabrous** (hairless) **skin.** There is a variety of touch receptors, including **Pacinian corpuscles** (specialized for deep pressure sensation), *Meissner corpuscles, Merkel disks,* and *Ruffini endings* and highly sensitive **free nerve endings.** There are center-surround receptive fields for touch similar to those found in vision. There are two main touch pathways to the brain: (1) the **dorsal column** carrying information via Aβ fibers from corpuscular endings in the skin to the **thalamus** and then **somatosensory cortex** (S1 and S2) located in the **parietal** region of the brain on the opposite side of the body from the touch and (2) the **spinothalamic pathway** whose two branches (**paleospinothalamic** and **neospinothalamic**) join with the dorsal column to form the **medial lemniscus.** These project to the **limbic system** and then to the somatosensory cortex. Touches occurring at all parts of the body are systematically mapped onto the somatosensory cortex. The absolute touch threshold, the **two-point threshold,** and the rate of touch adaptation vary dramatically depending on the part of the body that is stimulated. Much information can be carried through touch, and several **vision substitution systems** have been developed to convey images and words to vision-impaired individuals via tactile stimulation. In sequences of tactile stimuli accurate identification may be impaired by **forward** and **backward masking** because sensations caused by tactile stimulation may persist for over a second. **Haptic perception** refers to identifying objects and physical relationships using touch and **kinesthesis** (the sensations of limb position, force, and movement). Haptic perception follows much the same rules as visual pattern perception, and there are even haptic illusions similar to visual illusions.

Pain is a special form of touch perception associated with body tissue damage. It uses several different pathways and brain centers. The slower C fibers (which terminate in free nerve endings) and somewhat faster Aδ fibers (with endings wrapped in Schwann cells) are the main pain fibers. The difference in fiber transmission speed accounts for the perception of **double pain.** Pain reception areas in the cortex are found in S1, S2, and the cingulate gyrus. According to the **gate-control theory** of pain, fast fibers close the pain gate in the **substantia gelatinosa** (located in the spinal cord), whereas the slow fibers open the gate, allowing the **transmission cells (T cells)** to carry the pain signal to the brain. With apparatus such as the **dolorimeter,** it has been shown that pain thresholds vary depending on the location on the body that is stimulated. Adaptation to pain is slow and may not occur at all for intense stimuli. Among the many substances that will produce analgesia are the internally generated **endogenous opiates,** which include two major classes of chemicals: the **enkephalins** and the **endorphins.** These act on the same brain sites that externally administered opiates such as morphine do. Acupuncture seems to work by releasing some of these endogenous opiates. It is possible that cognitive factors may also trigger release of these chemicals or may directly open or close the pain gate. Such cognitively induced effects can account for how some individuals consciously control their pain responses and perhaps why hypnosis can be used as a pain-reducing technique.

KEY TERMS

taste buds
papillae
taste pore
solitary tract
medial lemniscus
thalamus
anterior-insular cortex
across-fiber pattern
labeled-line theory
molar concentration
ageusia
cross-adaptation
potentiation
primary olfactory
  neurons
olfactory epithelium
olfactory rod
olfactory cilia
olfactory binding protein
  (OBP)
lock-and-key theory
olfactory nerve
olfactory bulb
lateral olfactory tract
anosmia
self-adaptation
cross-adaptation
pheromones
releasers
primers
vomeronasal organs
hairy skin
glabrous skin

epidermis
dermis
free nerve endings
Pacinian corpuscle
dorsal column
thalamus
somatosensory cortex
parietal
spinothalamic pathway
paleospinothalamic
neospinothalamic
medial lemniscus
limbic system
two-point threshold
vision substitution
  system
Optacon
backward masking
forward masking
kinesthesis
haptic perception
Tadoma
double pain
gate-control theory
substantia gelatinosa
transmission cells
  (T cells)
dolorimeter
dol scale
endogenous opiates
enkephalins
endorphins

Space

CHAPTER 9

I n 1621 Robert Burton noted that "All places are distant from heaven alike." Perhaps for a clergyman-philosopher such a description of spatial relations was sufficient. Yet, for you, a simple mortal trying to pick up a cup of coffee from the tabletop, much more precision is needed. You must be able to judge how far the cup is from your hand with a good deal of accuracy, lest you end up with a messy puddle of hot fluid. Your very life may depend on your precision in judging depth and distance, as when you sense that you are standing near the edge of a cliff or are driving your car along a mountain road. You cannot get cut by a knife edge pictured in a flat photograph, but the real blade extending toward you in space can produce painful contact. Thus, accomplishing our daily tasks safely depends on the accuracy of our spatial perception.

TYPES OF DEPTH PERCEPTION

Our perception of depth has at least two different aspects. The first involves the perception of the actual distance of an object, such as how far away a pencil is on a desk. This is an estimate of **absolute distance**, which involves a process called **egocentric localization**. Most of us are familiar with the word *egocentric* in its everyday use—you are egocentric if you are concerned only about your own activities and their effect on yourself. In the context

251

of space perception, *egocentric* means that we have a good sense of where our bodies are positioned relative to other objects in the external environment. The second aspect of space perception involves the perception of relative distance, such as whether the pencil is lying nearer to the book or to the coffee cup, which are also on the desk. The judgment of relative distance requires the observer to make **object-relative localizations,** which are estimates of the *distances between objects* in the environment. The judgment of relative distance is also involved in the perception of whether an object is flat (as in a two-dimensional picture) or solid (three-dimensional), in that this requires estimation of the spatial relationships between parts of an object.

The accomplishment involved in seeing objects in depth is quite amazing considering that the basic information available to the nervous system is just a flat image on our retinas. The question of how we convert this two-dimensional image into our three-dimensional conscious impression of the world has stimulated a number of different theoretical approaches. Before discussing the research on this problem we will briefly summarize these approaches. (Recall that we introduced three different theoretical approaches in Chapter 1.)

One approach is called **direct perception** (Michaels & Carello, 1981) and is characterized by the work of J. J. Gibson (e.g., 1979). There are three assumptions that are central to direct perception. The first is that all the information we need to see three-dimensionally is present in the retinal image or in relationships among parts of the retinal image. The second is that the visual scene is analyzed by the brain in terms of whole objects and surfaces, rather than in terms of elementary stimulus attributes such as edges, colors, and specific locations that together make up objects. Finally, direct perception assumes that the impression of depth or distance arises immediately in the observer on viewing the stimulus and needs no further computation or any additional information based on inferences or experience.

An alternative approach is used by scientists who view visual processing as being similar to information processing done by a computer. These scientists have been influenced by developments in *artificial intelligence,* which is a part of computer science that attempts to design machines that behave "intelligently," such as machines that can interpret visual information. There are actually two different types of these scientists. The first is interested in designing robots that can perform tasks for humans based on visual input. The second is interested in designing computer programs that will duplicate the processing steps actually used by a human observer when viewing visual stimuli such as pictures. For this second group the computer program actually serves the same function as a theory, in that it can be used to predict what a person might see in particular circumstances. Because of this, the computer programs, or the description of the processes used to create the programs, are often referred to as **computational theories** of vision. One of the best known of these computational theorists was David Marr (1982). He began with one of the assumptions made in direct perception, namely, that all the information we need to derive three-dimensionality is present in the visual inputs. However, he departed from the direct perception view, in the manner of all computational theorists, when he suggested that the accurate interpretation of three-dimensionality requires a number of complex computations and several stages of analysis. We'll encounter this theory again in Chapter 10 when we discuss the perception of form.

There is yet another important version of perceptual theory that is based on the assumption that our perceptual representation of the world is much richer and more accurate than might be expected on the basis of the information contained in the visual image alone. This approach, which might be called **intelligent perception,** originated with Helmholtz in 1867 and is today best exemplified by Gregory (1978) and Rock (1983, 1997). It suggests that perception is like other mental processes in that, in addition to the information available at the moment, we can use information based on our previous experience, our expectations, and so forth. In other words, our visual perception of space may involve "going beyond" the information given in the visual image. Some of this information may be nonvisual in nature, such as material derived from our past history, and the selection of this information may be affected by our cognitive processing strategies. Because this approach emphasizes the combining of several sources of information to essentially "build" or "assemble" our conscious experience of what is "out there," such theories have also been called **constructive theories** of perception.

Although it is quite likely that each of these approaches is valid for some aspects of the perceptual process (cf. Coren & Girgus, 1978; Uttal, 1981), theorists who favor particular approaches tend to try to isolate different factors when they consider the perception of depth or distance. For instance, a theorist interested in direct perception might concentrate on looking at aspects of the stimulus and relationships between stimuli in the retinal image, whereas a theorist who believes in constructive perception may focus on the cognitive interpretive processes called into play when we attempt to comprehend the three-dimensional nature of the world. All of these approaches, however, usually begin by attempting to isolate the **cues** for depth. These are signals in the stimulus that we are often not consciously aware of but that function to shape our perceptual responses.

PICTORIAL DEPTH CUES

When you look at a realistic painting or a photograph, you find it quite easy to perceive the spatial relationship among the various items portrayed. Your impression of the relative distances in such scenes is based on a set of cues, appropriately called **pictorial depth cues.** These cues are also called **monocular cues** because they not only appear in pictures but also are available when only one eye is used to view a scene. Remember that the image on the retina is essentially a two-dimensional image (we will have more to say about this in Chapter 10). To understand these depth cues we must first recognize that visual experience usually depends on the transfer of light reflected from an object in the external world to the eye of the observer. A number of depth cues depend on characteristic ways in which light travels to the eye and on ways in which it is affected by the medium (usually air) through which it passes. Other depth cues depend on how light interacts with objects and also on the geometry of images.

Interposition or Occlusion

The vast majority of objects in the world are not transparent. Because light reflected from distant objects cannot pass through opaque objects that stand between them and the observer, a nearer object tends to block the view of a more distant one. This depth cue is called **interposition or occlusion.** It is easy to see that the cat in Figure 9-1 is nearer than the man's leg because the view of the leg is partially covered by the image of the cat. Notice that interposition is a cue for relative depth only. It indicates that the cat is nearer than the man's leg but not how far away the cat or the man are.

One of the most interesting findings with regard to interposition is that the absence of stimulation from the part of the man's leg that is behind the cat is only rarely brought into our consciousness. Instead, the visual system usually "fills in" the occluded portion of an object very rapidly and automatically, and we act as if the whole object were present and visible (Gerbino & Salmaso, 1987; Nakayama et al., 1989; Sekuler & Palmer, 1992; Weisstein, Mantalvo, & Ozog, 1972). For example, several studies have shown that subjects are

FIGURE 9-1   Interposition as a depth cue is illustrated by the fact that the cat is seen as closer than the man's leg because it partially blocks the view of the leg.

able to make a speeded "same-different" response to pairs of shapes just as rapidly when one member of the pair is partly occluded as when both members of the pair are completely visible (Gerbino & Salmaso, 1987; Sekuler & Palmer, 1992; Shore & Enns, 1997). Careful investigation of the amount of time needed for the "filling in" to be complete suggests that it occurs within the first 100–200 ms of processing (Sekuler & Palmer, 1992). Increasing the number and quality of other depth cues in the scene can reduce this time to less than 100 ms (Bruno & Bertamini, 1997).

Shading and Shadows

The fact that light cannot pass through most objects gives rise to the interposition cue. The fact that light usually travels in straight lines gives us another cue for relative depth. This means that surfaces

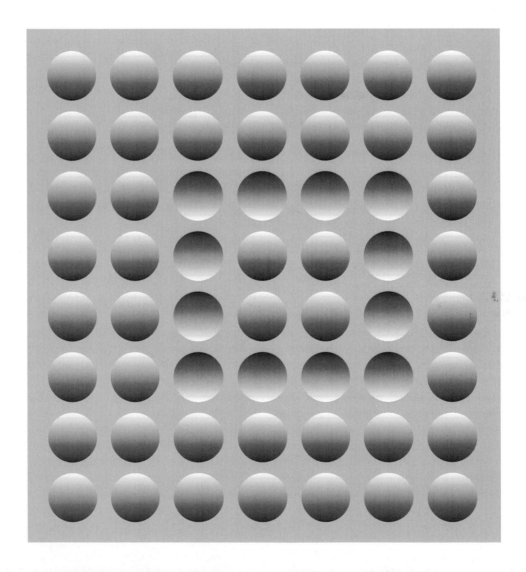

FIGURE 9-2   Shading makes it clear that we are looking at a central square made up of "dimples" or "dents" with a background of "pimples" or "bumps." Turning the figure upside down reverses the shadow pattern and also reverses the perceived depth relationships so that we see a square made up of pimples and a background of dimples.

facing the light source will be relatively bright, whereas surfaces away from the light source will be in shadow. Particular patterns of shadow can provide information about the relative shape of solid objects. Thus, if light comes from above the lower part of an ingoing dent or "dimple," it will catch more of the light, whereas the upper part will be in relative shadow. For an outgoing protrusion or "pimple" the top part will be bright and the lower part in shadow. This is illustrated in the picture of "pimples and dimples" shown in Figure 9-2. As it stands you see a square made up of "dents" or "dimples" surrounded by a field of "bumps" or "pimples." If you turn this book upside down, the light and shadow patterns in the figure reverse, and now the square is made up of protruding bumps, whereas the background is a field of ingoing dents (cf. Berbaum, Bever, & Chung, 1984; Ramachandran, 1988). Clearly, for this shading cue to work consistently in this example, we must be assuming that the light is coming from above (which it usually does in most everyday situations). If the light were coming from another direction, the shading pattern would be different. Observers do seem to use their knowledge or presumptions about the location of the light source to help them accurately perceive the three-dimensional nature of objects using the shading cue (Berbaum, Bever, & Chung, 1983; Enns & Rensink, 1990; Ramachandran, 1988).

The shading pattern on an object or surface is actually only one of the cues associated with shadows. The shading that defines the shape of an object can be called an **attached shadow** because the pattern of light that serves as a cue to its three-dimensional shape is actually distributed over the object itself (see Figure 9-3). However, another factor that can affect the shading pattern is the presence of a second object or surface lying in the path of the light source. Such an object will give rise to a **cast shadow,** such as can be seen in Figure 9-3.

Attached and cast shadows share a number of attributes in the way they signal information about the visual world. For example, the direction from which light in a scene is being cast is given in a similar way by attached and cast shadows: Both shadows fall away from the source of light. The relation between the brightness of a shadow and the surrounding surface is also similar for both kinds of shadows: Shadows are invariably darker than the surfaces on which they are projected. Research

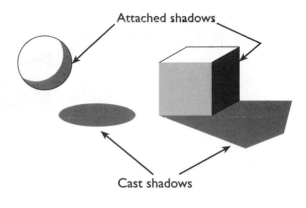

FIGURE 9-3 Two types of shadows that give us different information about depth. *Attached shadows* help to indicate the intrinsic shape of an object, and *cast shadows* indicate the relative distance of an object from another object or surface.

shows that the human visual system has a broad tolerance for the interpretation of shapes as shadows, provided that they follow these rough guidelines (Cavanagh & Leclerc, 1989).

However, research on the perception of shadows also indicates that the visual system uses different information from cast shadows than from attached shadows in analyzing the visual world. Let's begin with the shape of an object. Whereas attached shadows (shading) provide considerable information about surface shape via pattern of light and dark regions, cast shadows signal shape only through a distorted silhouette of the objects casting the shadows (Marr, 1982). When it comes to the determination of relative depth and distance, the two types of shadow again differ in their information content. Whereas the attached shadow can provide only information about object shape, observers are able to use the distance between objects and cast shadows to determine the relative depth of objects (Berbaum, Bever, & Chung, 1984; Cavanagh & Leclerc, 1989). Specifically, the more separated the object is from its cast shadow, the greater will be the perceived distance between the object and the shadowed surface. A very compelling illusion of motion that is based on this principle is illustrated in Figure 9-4. A stationary target shape seen against a checkerboard pattern can be made to appear to move toward and away from the viewer simply by moving a cast

Time 1

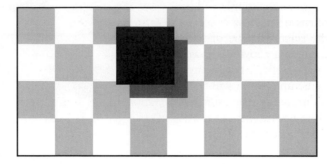

Time 2

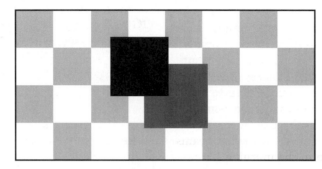

Time 3

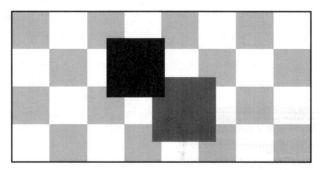

FIGURE 9-4 The stationary black square can be made to appear to move toward and away from the viewer simply by moving the gray cast shadow toward and away from the black square (drawn based on description by Kersten & Knill, 1996).

shadow toward and away from the target shape (Kersten & Knill, 1996).

Aerial Perspective

The partial and complete blockage of light by objects gave us our first two pictorial cues for relative depth. Another cue for depth emerges from the fact that the air is filled with light-absorbing and light-scattering particles even on the clearest of days. As light passes through the air, some of it is absorbed, and other light is scattered by the minute particles of dust and moisture. Large particles (such as dust) scatter the light uniformly, causing a uniform distribution of light or a blurring of the image. For particles that are small in comparison to the various wavelengths of light (such as minute bits of water vapor), the degree of scatter depends on the specific wavelength. In general, shorter wavelengths (blue) are scattered more than longer wavelengths (Uttal, 1981). The combined effect of these phenomena produces the cue called **aerial perspective,** in which the image of a very distant object, such as a distant mountain, will be slightly bluer in hue and hazier or less distinct in appearance than the images of nearer objects that are physically the same in color.

Such changes in appearance can provide information about the absolute distance of relatively faraway objects. In some geographic regions (such as the prairies of the United States and Canada), this can lead to considerable errors in distance judgments because the clear, dry air reduces aerial perspective. Thus, a plateau that appears to be only 1 or 2 miles away on a clear day, when looking across a dry sector of Wyoming, may actually be 20 or 30 miles from the observer. Conversely, this explains why objects seen in the morning fog or a mist appear to be farther away than when seen in bright midday sun (Ross, 1975).

There is an interesting variant of the aerial perspective cue that is usually referred to as **relative brightness.** The light from more distant objects must travel through the atmosphere for a greater distance and may be subject to increased absorption or scattering of the light by the particles in the air. Thus, the more distant object may appear to be less bright, even though the distances may not be as great as those described in the context of the usual aerial perspective cue (Uttal, 1981). Certainly, in the absence of any other cues, you will tend to see the brighter of two identical objects as closer (Ittelson, 1960).

Retinal and Familiar Size

As an object moves farther away, its **retinal image size** begins to diminish. One country song captured this effect in a lyric, "If you see me getting smaller I'm leaving." The geometry of this situation is shown in Figure 9-5, where the more distant person is casting a smaller retinal image. We tend to use these relative differences in retinal image size as a cue for relative distance, as in Figure 9-6, where we see a row of puppies that seems to recede in the distance from us because of their decreasing image size. Thus, the comparison of the sizes of objects in the visual field, relative to each other, is an important part of the process of perceiving relative distance.

Retinal image size is a cue used by both direct perception and computational theories of perception. There is, however, another size cue that is important in constructive theories. This has nothing to do with image size but, rather, with your previous experience with the usual or **familiar size** of the object. For example, playing cards all tend to be around the same size. Ittelson (1951) presented to observers three playing cards, under **reduction conditions.** This was usually a darkened room with all other depth cues removed. One of the playing cards was normal in size, a second was twice normal size, and a third was one half of normal size. He found that observers tended to

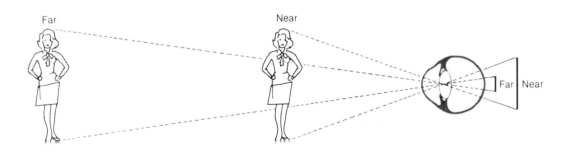

FIGURE 9-5   Objects of the same physical size produce smaller retinal angle sizes with increasing distance from the observer. Thus, relatively speaking, smaller images are perceived to be more distant.

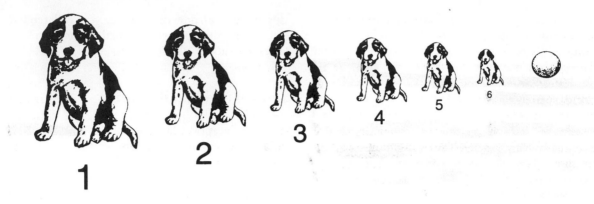

FIGURE 9-6   Relative size differences are interpreted as cues for relative distance. Thus, we see a row of puppies that seems to recede in the distance because of their decreasing image size.

judge the double-sized playing cards as being much closer to them and the half-sized cards as being much more distant than the normal-sized card. This is the same process that causes you to see the dogs in Figure 9-6 as receding into the distance. You assume that all of these images are about the same "dog size" and use this familiar size information in conjunction with the changing retinal size to gain the impression of changes in relative distance.

As long as the objects are commonplace and the distances not too extreme, familiar size can give you absolute depth information, not merely relative depth information (Epstein & Baratz, 1964; Fitzpatrick, Pasnak, & Tyer, 1982). Thus, if we see a very tiny elephant, we can use our knowledge that elephants are relatively large creatures to

deduce that the elephant has not shrunk in size but, rather, is far away from us. You may demonstrate the effect of familiar size for yourself by following the instructions in Demonstration Box 9-1.

Linear Perspective

There is a well-known pictorial depth cue that may be seen as an extension of the retinal-image-size cue to distance. This cue is **linear perspective.** For example, look at Figure 9-7, which is adapted from a book by Jan Vredman de Vries on how to depict perspective in drawings (de Vries, 1604/1968). In this schematic scene we notice that physically parallel lines, such as those defining the paving blocks making up the floor,

---

DEMONSTRATION BOX 9-1
Familiar Size and Distance

Look at Figure 9-6. Notice that the row of puppies seems to recede into the distance. Off to the right is a ball. If we told you that it is a tennis ball or a baseball, you would have no difficulty in deciding which dog is at the same distance away from you as the ball. After you decide this, return to this box.

Now, suppose we told you that the ball is

really a volleyball or a basketball. Which dog is the same distance as the basketball? Notice that the ball apparently "moved backward" in depth when you assumed it was a larger object. This shows how knowledge of the size of an object can affect our judgment of the distance of the object, giving us the *familiar size* cue to distance.

seem to converge as objects become more distant. So do the hypothetical lines that connect all the tops and all the bottoms of the pillars, all of which are supposed to be physically the same size. This illustrates the fact that parallel lines in the real world, such as railroad tracks, appear to converge, and objects appear to get smaller and smaller in a systematic fashion as their distance increases. Eventually they reach a **vanishing point,** where all the perspective lines converge, and objects diminish to invisibility. This point is usually on the horizon, as shown in the figure. This is a simple geometric effect that occurs in the real world and when we project a three-dimensional scene onto a two-dimensional surface. It provides a powerful relative depth cue (e.g., Braunstein & Liter, 1993). Hence, it is easy to determine that Pillar B is farther away than Pillar A by utilizing the perspective cue.

Texture Gradients

James J. Gibson (1966, 1979) suggested an interesting way of combining both linear perspective and relative size information into one cue, which he referred to as **texture gradient.** A visual texture is loosely defined as any collection of objects in the visual image (Caelli, 1982), and the gradient (continuous change) is the change in the relative size and compactness of these object elements. The more distant parts of the texture have smaller elements that are more densely packed together (Gibson, 1966). The depth impression associated with texture gradients is sometimes called *detail perspective.* Figure 9-8A shows a texture of lines. Because the texture is uniform, it shows little depth and looks much like a flat wall or garage door. If we introduce a gradient, however, as is done in Figure 9-8B, with the lines becoming more

Horizon

A

B

FIGURE 9-7 An example of linear perspective, in which physically parallel lines seem to converge as they grow more distant. Notice that the lines have been extrapolated to show a vanishing point on the horizon.

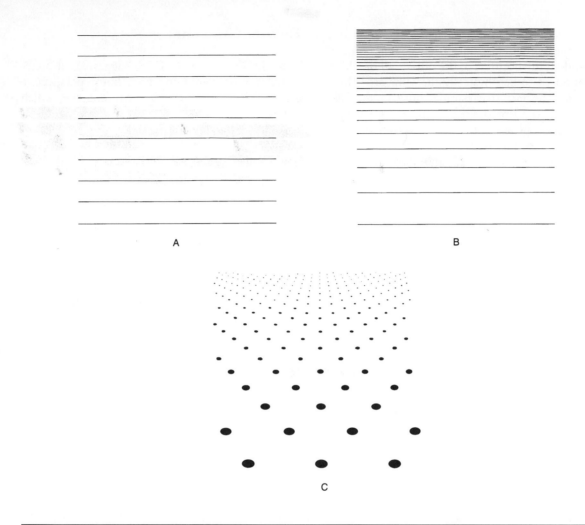

FIGURE 9-8 Examples of texture gradients are shown in B and C, which appear as surfaces receding in depth. In *A* there are no decreases in element size or spacing, and thus the perception is of a flat surface.

compact as we move toward the top, we now get an impression of depth. An even stronger impression of depth appears if we allow the gradient to appear in the horizontal placing of elements as well as the vertical, as can be seen in the texture of dots in Figure 9-8C. One important type of information contained in texture gradients emerges from the fact that sudden changes in texture usually signal a change in the direction or distance of a surface. Thus, Figure 9-9A shows how the gradient changes when we shift from floor to wall, and Figure 9-9B shows how the gradient changes at a cliff or stepdown. The perception of depth obtained from texture gradients can be quite striking. Texture helps us to define the shapes of solid objects (Todd & Akerstrom, 1987; see also Chapter 10) as well as delicate variations in distance, as shown in the undulating surface depicted by texture cues alone in Figure 9-10.

Height in the Plane

Another cue to distance depends on the relationships between objects as their images are projected onto our retinas. This cue is **height in the plane,**

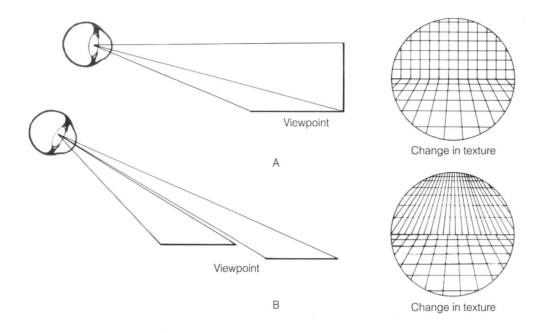

FIGURE 9-9   How texture changes at a corner (A) and an edge next to a sharp drop in depth (B).

FIGURE 9-10   This rippling or undulating surface is defined completely on the basis of variations in texture density.

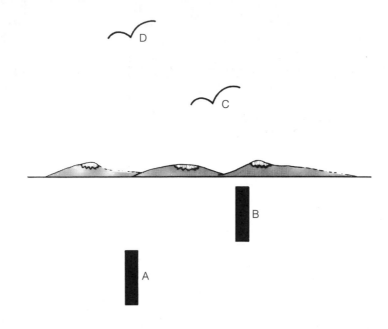

FIGURE 9-11   Height in the plane and proximity to the horizon will determine which elements in the diagram are perceived as more distant. In this case, *B* and *C* are seen as being farther away because they are closer to the horizon.

or *relative height*, and refers to where an object is relative to the horizon line. In Figure 9-11, Post B seems farther away than Post A because the base of Post B is closer to the horizon line. Hence, it is said to be "higher in the plane," or "higher in the picture plane," if we consider this as a two-dimensional projection. The reverse holds for targets above the horizon. Bird C seems farther away than Bird D because Bird C is "lower in the picture plane." In other words, proximity to the horizon line signals the greater distance.

PHYSIOLOGICAL CUES FOR DEPTH

Until now we have considered only cues for depth that can be found in the retinal image itself. There are other cues for distance that come about because of the way the visual system responds to or interacts with the visual stimulus. These may be called **structural** or **physiological cues** because they arise from muscular responses and adjustments of the eye.

Accommodation

When we discussed the physiology of the eye in Chapter 3, we described how the crystalline lens responds to targets at different distances from us. We noted that the shape of the lens must change (actually its amount of curvature changes) in order to keep the retinal image in clear focus (Dalziel & Egan, 1982). This process is called **accommodation**. There is only one particular curvature that will clearly focus the retinal image of an object viewed at a particular distance from the eye. Relaxed accommodation, where the lens is relatively flattened, is necessary if distant objects are to be clearly focused on the retina, whereas a strongly curved lens is needed to image closer objects on the retinal surface. As we change the tension on the ciliary muscles, which control the lens shape, feedback from these muscular changes can provide us with some additional nonvisual information about the distance of the object we are looking at.

In addition to feedback from the act of accommodation, the presence or absence of blur due to an object being out of focus can serve as a cue for relative distance. It has been shown that in the absence of all other depth information, observers can judge that two spots of light presented in complete darkness are at different distances. This is probably because accommodation cannot be correct for two stimuli at different distances at the same time; hence, one of the lights will be slightly blurred and out of focus, suggesting that the targets are not equidistant (Kaufman, 1974).

There is some controversy over the utility of accommodation as a cue to depth in everyday situations. Accommodation is rather slow in its effects and is also limited in the range of observer-to-object distances over which it is useful (Graham, 1965). For example, for objects at a distance of around 3 m, the lens has fully relaxed accommodation and doesn't flatten out any farther, regardless of how far away an object is. There is a similar limit for close objects. If a target is within 20 cm of your face, your lens has reached its point of maximum curvature. Within the range of 20 cm to 300 cm, however, accommodation may provide a useful, if not very precise or rapid, auxiliary cue for distance (Hochberg, 1971; Iida, 1983).

Convergence and Divergence

Another potential distance cue comes from the fact that we have two eyes. Two-eyed perception is referred to as **binocular,** from *bi* meaning "two" and *ocula* meaning "eye." Because (as we learned in Chapter 3) the best visual acuity is obtained when the image of an object is focused on the two foveas, eye movements are executed to bring the image to this region of each eye. If the eyes move in different directions, this is called **vergence movement.** If an object is close to you, you must rotate your eyes inward (toward the nose) in order to focus its image on the fovea. Such a movement is called **convergence** (the root *con* means "toward"). When a target is farther away, the eyes must move away from each other in an outward rotation (toward the temples); hence, this movement is called **divergence** (from the root *di* meaning "apart"). Different degrees of convergence and divergence are shown in Figure 9-12.

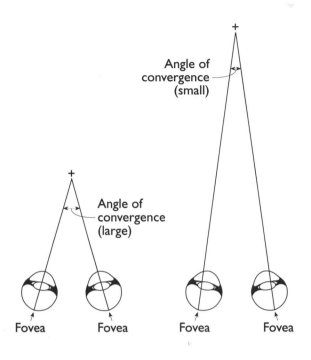

FIGURE 9-12 Convergence angle changes as a function of fixation distance. This may provide some information about target distance.

Each target distance, up to about 6 m, is associated with a unique angle between the eyes called the *convergence angle*, as indicated in Figure 9-12. To achieve each eye position, a unique pattern of muscular contractions must occur. Feedback from such vergence movements could be useful in determining the distances of objects, although there has been some controversy about how useful and reliable such information is as a depth cue (Gogel, Gregg, & Wainwright, 1961; Hochberg, 1971; Rivest & Ono, 1989). However, some evidence suggests that convergence and accommodation together may provide quite accurate absolute depth information, especially when the only visible stimulus is a single point of light whose distance observers are asked to judge (Morrison & Whiteside, 1984). There is also some evidence that the eyes converge and accommodate as if they were looking at objects at various distances in response to the pictorial depth cues found in paintings and line drawings (Enright, 1987a, 1987b).

MOTION AND MOTION PARALLAX

Except for the physiological cues, all of the cues to depth we have discussed so far can be defined with respect to a single static or unchanging image, such as a photograph or a painting. However, most of our perception of depth occurs in an environment in which the observer is in motion (because of body, head, or eye movements) and very often in which objects are in motion as well. This gives the visual system the opportunity to compare multiple images over time, each slightly different depending on the speed of movement. Therefore, it should not be surprising that when we add motion to the incoming visual pattern, we acquire some additional opportunities for depth cues to appear.

One of these movement cues concerns the pattern of motion of an object as you travel past it. Suppose you are traveling in a car or bus and looking at the scene in Figure 9-13. Suppose also that your direction of movement is from right to left and that you are gazing at the spot marked "fixation point." Under these conditions, all of the objects closer to you than the fixation point will appear to move in a direction opposite to your movement, whereas objects that are farther away will appear to move in the same direction you are moving. Not only the direction but also the speed of movement vary with the objects' proximity to you and to your point of fixation—the nearer the object is to the retina, the faster will be its motion across the retina relative to other objects. This cue to distance is called **motion parallax.** Motion parallax can also be generated by swinging your head back and forth while your body is stationary, giving you very good information about the depth of objects if they are not too distant from you (Ono, Rivest, & Ono, 1986; Ono & Rogers, 1988; Rogers & Graham, 1979).

FIGURE 9-13 Motion parallax. When an observer moves, objects at varying distances from the observer will move in different directions at differing speeds. These differences can serve as cues for the relative distances of the objects.

DEMONSTRATION BOX 9-2
The Kinetic Depth Effect

To see how subtle motion parallax effects can create the impression of a three-dimensional form in a two-dimensional pattern, you will need a candle and a piece of stiff wire (a coat hanger or a long pipe cleaner will do). Bend the wire into a random three-dimensional shape. Now light the candle and darken the room. Place the bent wire so it casts a shadow on a blank wall, as shown in the figure. Notice that when the shape is absolutely motionless, the shadow is seen as a flat pattern of lines. Now if you rotate the shape with your hand, the shadow suddenly changes perceptually, becoming a three-dimensional object that cannot be seen as flat, despite the fact that you are viewing a two-dimensional shadow.

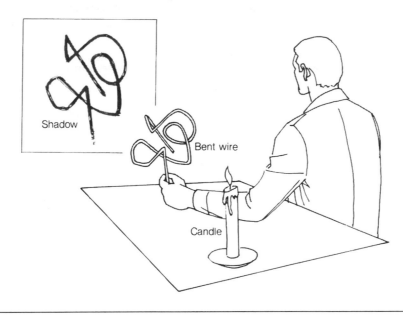

A special form of motion parallax occurs when an object moves or rotates. The relative pattern of movement of parts of the object can give us information about its three-dimensional shape (e.g., Carpenter & Dugan, 1983; Doner, Lappin, & Perfetto, 1984). The fact that motion cues can give us information about the relative depth of parts of an object has been called the **kinetic depth effect** (Gibson, 1966; Kaufman, 1974; Rock, 1975). Demonstration Box 9-2 allows you to see this phenomenon for yourself. In Chapter 14 ("Motion") you will also learn how motion parallax can give you information about the direction of your movements through space.

BINOCULAR DEPTH PERCEPTION

Just as motion provides the visual system with multiple images to compare, thereby giving it additional cues to depth, the fact that we have two eyes confers a great advantage in trying to estimate relative depth. For example, in many common tasks involving judgments of relative depth, such as threading a needle, inserting items into slots, or even placing cards behind alphabetic dividers in a box, many people perform up to 30% faster and more accurately when using both eyes than they do with one eye alone (Sheedy, Bailey, Buri, &

Bass, 1986). For this reason, many occupations or tasks that require good distance-judging proficiency will often screen for **stereopsis,** which is the ability to extract depth information from the binocular views. Poor stereopsis can prevent a person from becoming an airplane pilot or even from driving a car.

Cues for Stereopsis

The specific cue for binocular depth perception (stereopsis) depends on the fact that, in humans and many other animals, the two eyes are horizontally separated but overlap in their view of the world. In humans, the distance between the two pupils can be up to 6.5 cm. Because of this separation, each eye has a different direction of view on the objects seen by both eyes and hence a different image of the world. We call the differences between the two eyes' images **binocular disparity.** You can see how different the images may be by following the instructions in Demonstration Box 9-3.

The process by which we merge these disparate images into a single unified percept is called **fusion.** As a process, however, fusion is fairly limited in its range of operation, and many parts of the total visual image do not fuse. This failure of the

---

DEMONSTRATION BOX 9-3
Binocular Disparity

You can see the difference between the views of your eyes by holding a pencil up near your nose, as shown. The tip of the pencil should be toward you and angled slightly downward. Now alternately close each eye. The pencil seems to swing back and forth. With your right eye open, it appears angled toward the left; with the left eye open, it appears angled toward the right. With both eyes open, the fused view is of a pencil straight ahead of your nose.

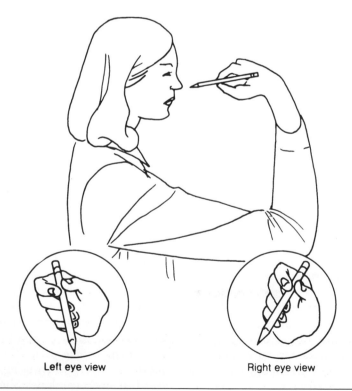

Left eye view   Right eye view

two eyes' views to merge completely gives rise to double vision or **diplopia.** Under normal viewing conditions you are usually not consciously aware of this diplopia; however, you can readily learn to see the double images in the unfused portion of the visual field. Demonstration Box 9-4 shows how this is done.

In Demonstration Box 9-4 you should have noticed that the pattern of double images is different depending on whether the unfused image is in front of or in back of the target you fixated. In the demonstration we defined these patterns as **crossed** versus **uncrossed disparity.** Objects more distant than the point of fixation are seen in uncrossed disparity, whereas closer objects are seen with crossed disparity. Hence, we can use the type of double image as a cue to relative distance. Only objects at about the same distance as the target we are fixating will be fused and seen singly. When we map out all of the points where targets are at about the same convergence or fixation distance in visual space, we trace out an imaginary curved plane called the **horopter.** A narrow region on either side of this hypothetical plane includes all points in visual space that are fused into single images. It is called **Panum's area.** Figure 9-14 contains a diagram of the horopter and Panum's

area. The size and shape of Panum's area actually change a bit with varying fixation distances. However, for every fixation distance there is a zone in the visual field where the disparate images are seen as fused into a single object.

The process of fusion has also been studied in terms of **corresponding retinal points.** These are areas on the retina that represent a common direction or location according to the map of the visual field represented in the visual areas of the brain. The foveas of the two eyes are corresponding retinal points, and, according to this conceptualization, the horopter represents the zone in visual space that stimulates corresponding retinal points for one fixation distance.

There are large individual differences in terms of stereoscopic depth perception. *Percent stereopsis* is a measure of an individual's sensitivity, and it is similar to Snellen acuity or decibels of hearing loss in that it is based on a comparison to a fixed value for "normal" or average stereopsis. In this case *100% stereopsis* refers to an ability to accurately interpret a depth difference based on a binocular disparity difference of 20 sec of visual arc. In most states in the United States an individual must have a minimum of 65% stereopsis (the ability to resolve 59 sec of visual arc) to get an unrestricted automobile driver's

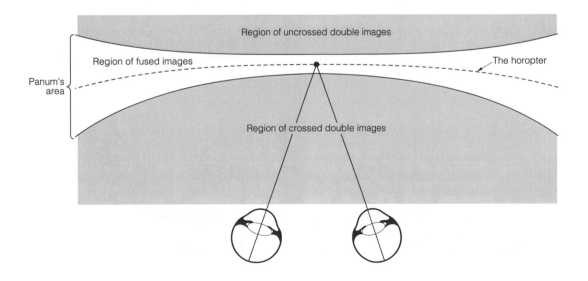

FIGURE 9-14   The horopter and Panum's area for one fixation distance. The regions of fusion and disparate images are shown. Crossed disparity is present at distances closer to the observer than the fixation distance; uncrossed disparity is present beyond the fixation distance. The presence of disparate images may provide a cue to distance.

DEMONSTRATION BOX 9-4
Double Images and Disparity

Find a piece of transparent colored material, such as cellophane (any hue will work). Place it before your right eye. If you wear glasses, you can affix it to the frame over the lens in front of your right eye; if not, use a piece of tape to hold it to your forehead. Now align two index fingers directly in front of your nose with the closer finger about 10–20 cm from your nose and the farther finger about 8 cm behind the closer one.

Now that you have arranged the appropriate situation, fixate your nearer finger. However, simultaneously try to pay attention to what the far finger looks like. This is a pretty difficult feat to accomplish at first, but with practice you should be able to fixate one target while simultaneously paying attention to what is going on beyond the fixated area. When you fixate the near target, you will notice that two images of the far target will be seen. The fact that one eye is viewing the image through a colored filter should help make the presence of double images beyond the fixation point more apparent. If you switch your fixation to the farther object, the closer of the two targets will appear as a double image. Targets that lie away from the area surrounding the point of fixation are not fused into a single image. They produce *disparate* retinal images. Disparate (unfused) images are always present in the visual field; however, we are usually not aware of them unless forced to attend to them, as in this demonstration.

After you have become comfortable with this procedure, fixate the near target and then close your right eye. You should notice that the image of the far target (the uncolored image) appears to lie to the left of the nearer, fixated object. Now close the left eye and open the right, and you will notice the opposite. The image of the far target (the colored image) now appears to lie to the right of the nearer, fixated target. The fact that the right eye is seeing the right disparate image and the left eye is seeing the left disparate image means that when both eyes are open, the far target is seen in *uncrossed disparity*. The opposite will happen if you change your fixation to the far target. Now the closer object appears as *diplopic* (double). If you once again alternately close each eye, you will notice that the right eye is now seeing the image that lies to the left of the fixated target (the colored image), while the left eye is viewing the image that lies to the right. In the case of double images that lie closer to us than the point of fixation, we have a situation of *crossed disparity*. As the text explains, these differences in disparity may be a cue to distance.

---

license. Persons with less than this degree of stereopsis may still be able to ascertain depth differences based on binocular disparity alone if the differences are large enough. People with only 25% stereopsis would require a binocular disparity of 286 sec of arc or almost 5° to detect any depth differences. Such disparity levels will seldom be encountered under most normal circumstances; hence, such people will have no functionally usable stereopsis to assist in the accurate manipulation of objects within arm's length, and they will not benefit from binocular disparity when trying to catch a ball or when engaging in most activities where precise relative depth judgments are important. It is possible for you to estimate your stereopsis ability without the use of laboratory instruments, using the inventory developed by Coren and Hakstian (1996). This Stereopsis Screening Inventory appears in Demonstration Box 9-5. It is important to know your own capabilities in this area because a fairly large number of people (between 5% and 10% of the population) do not have usable stereopsis.

The Process of Stereopsis

In the 1830s two physicists, Charles Wheatstone and Sir David Brewster, independently invented a technique to re-create the impression of depth from flat pictures using only the binocular disparity cue

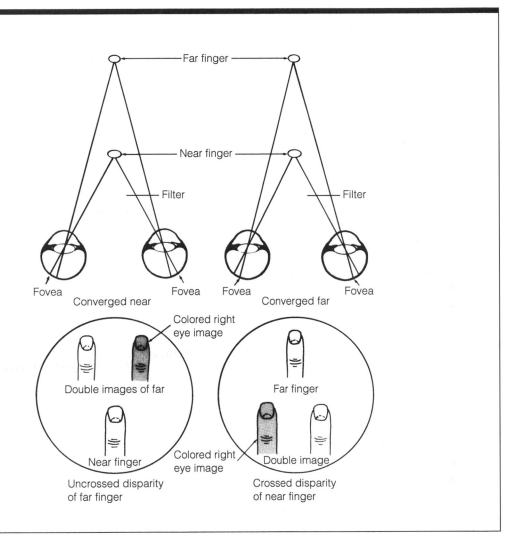

Far finger

Near finger

Filter

Filter

Fovea

Fovea

Fovea

Fovea

Converged near

Converged far

Colored right eye image

Double images of far

Far finger

Near finger

Colored right eye image

Double image

Uncrossed disparity of far finger

Crossed disparity of near finger

(see Wade, 1984). Their technique involves re-creating the disparate views each eye would see and representing them to the eyes in the form of drawings or photographs. Thus, in Figure 9-15A, we have two rods at different distances from the observer. If we drew the image each eye sees, we would get something like Figure 9-15B. Notice that the images are disparate because the rods are more widely separated in the right eye's image than in the left eye's image. Now the resulting images are viewed in an optical instrument known as a stereo-scope, which places different stimuli into the two eyes simultaneously, as shown in Figure 9-15C. When this is done, the disparate images fuse, and the objects are seen as if they were an actual three-dimensional scene. For a period of time every Victorian living room had a stereoscope and a set of travel pictures of famous places that had been taken using a camera with two lenses and shutters. This produced the "visual magic" of depth from flat images.

Understanding how stereopsis is achieved is more difficult than setting up the conditions that allow us to see binocular depth. There have been several computational approaches to this problem, most of which involve selecting a particular location in space, then comparing and computing the relative positions of parts of the images. From such computations it was hoped that the relative depth of the objects being viewed could be derived (e.g., Marr & Poggio, 1979; Mayhew & Frisby, 1980).

DEMONSTRATION BOX 9-5
Stereopsis Screening Inventory

To get an estimate of your own stereopsis, simply take this test. It is the Stereopsis Screening Inventory developed by Coren and Hakstian (1996). Scores on this test correlate $r = 0.80$ with laboratory measures of stereoscopic depth sensitivity. The questionnaire deals with a number of common visual situations. For each question you should select the response that best describes you and your behaviors. You can select from among the following response alternatives: Never (or almost never), Seldom, Occasionally, Frequently, Always (or almost always). Simply circle the letter that corresponds to the first letter of your choice.

1. Do you find most book print too small to be read easily without glasses or contact lenses? N S O F A
2. When you were a child did your parents or teachers tell you that you were holding the book too close to your eyes? N S O F A
3. Are you troubled by temporary losses of vision in one or both eyes? N S O F A
4. Do your eyes feel "tired," especially at the end of the workday? N S O F A
5. Do you wear glasses or contact lenses? N S O F A
6. Do you think that you may need glasses? N S O F A
7. Would you say that your vision is as good as most people's? N S O F A

Answer these last two questions using Good, Average, Slightly Below Average, Poor, or Very Poor (circle the first letter corresponding to your choice).

8. Without glasses or contact lenses, the clearness or sharpness of vision in my *right* eye is: G A S P V

9. Without glasses or contact lenses, the clearness or sharpness of vision in my *left* eye is: G A S P V

Scoring Instructions

Responses to Questions 1 to 6 are scored as 1 for "Never," 2 for "Seldom," 3 for "Occasionally," 4 for "Frequently," and 5 for "Always." Question 7 is reverse scored ("Never" = 5 to "Always" = 1). For Questions 8 and 9 scoring goes from 1 for "Good" to 5 for "Very Poor." You next need to compute a 10th score, which is simply the absolute (unsigned) difference between Questions 8 and 9 (e.g., if the response to Question 8 was "Good" and to Question 9 was "Slightly Below Average," the 10th entry in the total would be the absolute difference of 1 minus 3, which is 2). Now add these 10 scores (your nine answers plus the computed 10th value) to get your total score.

If your total score is 17 or less, you have better than 65% stereopsis, and for most everyday situations your binocular depth perception is quite normal. If your total score is 18 to 30 you have an 84% chance of having a moderate to strong stereopsis deficit (65% to 25% stereopsis). Although you may be able to use binocular depth information if the disparities are quite large, you have enough of a depth loss that you have a high probability of failing the depth perception test used for most automobile driver's licenses. With scores of 31 or higher there is an 81% chance that you are among the 5% to 10% of the population who have no functional stereopsis (stereopsis less than 25%).

Although interesting, these approaches have not yet provided a "breakthrough" conceptualization, although, as will be seen later, they do provide some descriptively useful suggestions.

The most provocative findings about stereopsis have actually come from direct physiological measurement. The first important results date from the late 1960s, when investigators began to find disparity-tuned detectors in the visual cortex of the cat (Bishop & Pettigrew, 1986). These detectors are neurons that are finely tuned to small differences in the relative horizontal placement of

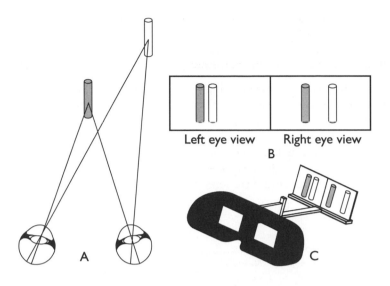

Left eye view   Right eye view

B

A

C

FIGURE 9-15   Disparate retinal images. (A) The two retinal images of a scene are different because the two eyes view the world from slightly different directions. (B) A stereogram is a flat representation that mimics the differences between the two retinal images. (C) A stereogram is viewed in a stereoscope that allows for the separate but simultaneous stimulation of the two eyes. The phenomenon is called *stereopsis*.

images in the two eyes (Bishop, 1981). For example, suppose there is no disparity in the images of the two eyes and a particular neuron responds maximally to this condition. This particular neuron would represent a spatial position that lies on the horopter, or the zone of fused images in external space. In a like manner, other neurons may be tuned to particular disparities that represent locations in space that lie in front of or behind the horopter. This means that rather large populations of cortical neurons would be needed to represent all of the possible disparity values in the visual scene.

It is now clear that the mere existence of disparity-tuned detectors is not enough to explain stereoscopic depth perception. The problem is illustrated in Demonstration Box 9-6, which contains a random-dot stereoscopic display. These displays were introduced by Julesz (1964, 1971), who used them to demonstrate the notion of **global stereopsis,** or the perception of depth in the absence of monocular shape or form. If you follow the instructions in Demonstration Box 9-6 (and if you have normal or at least moderate stereopsis), you will see a dotted square floating in front of the background of random dots. This perception

comes about because of disparity cues built into the dot patterns. Figure 9-16 shows how this disparity, which consists of a horizontal shift in a group of these random dots, is created.

You might suppose that because there is disparity built into the random-dot stimulus, neurons tuned for such information should be capable of detecting depth from these arrays. However, it is not quite that simple, mainly because the stimulus is composed of identical dot elements rather than discrete and identifiable contours. If stereopsis is based on the action of disparity-tuned detectors, each of which responds to one disparity value in the array, any dot potentially could be combined with any other dot. Each of the many possible combinations would produce a different depth perception. The task for the visual system is to find the dots in one eye that correspond to the same dots in the other eye—this is called solving the **correspondence problem** by computational researchers. To solve this problem there must be a method of eliminating or avoiding false combinations and selecting only correct disparity pairs.

Computational theorists have proposed very sophisticated computer programs to do exactly this. Many of these are based on the idea that disparity

DEMONSTRATION BOX 9-6
Random-Dot Stereograms and Global Stereopsis

You may demonstrate how depth cues can bring about the perception of binocular form by using the accompanying figure. You will need a pocket mirror, which should be placed on the dotted center line of Figure B while you hold your head as shown in Figure A. Adjust the images until the two views seem to overlap and the frames around the outside seem to be at the same distance. Viewing it in this way, you will see a square form emerge, floating above the background, created completely by the depth cue of binocular disparity. Notice that this square cannot be seen in either monocular view alone.

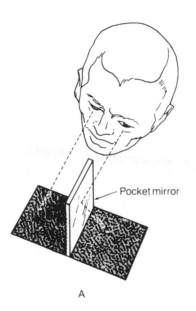

A

B

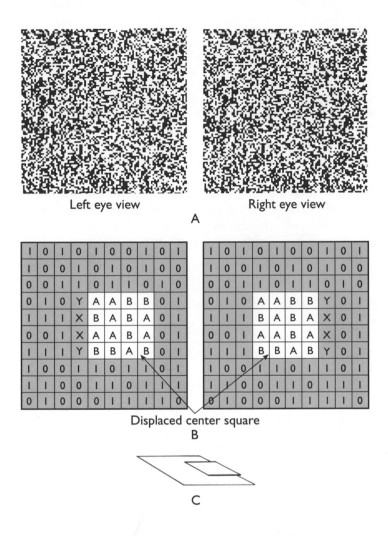

FIGURE 9-16 Figure A is a random-dot stereogram. Figure B shows how Figure A is constructed, and Figure C illustrates that a central square is seen floating above the background when the two views are combined in a stereoscope. (From B. Julesz, *Foundations of Cyclopean Perception*. Copyright 1971 by the University of Chicago Press.)

detectors tuned to the same disparity mutually facilitate one another, whereas those of different disparities inhibit one another (Burt & Julesz, 1980; Marr, 1982; Mayhew & Frisby, 1980). Mathematically it can be shown that with a population of detectors working together in this fashion, only one depth solution would be common to this facilitory-inhibitory process, and only one global stereoscopic view would be seen (Julesz & Schumer, 1981). Together, these programs have come to be called **cooperative algorithms** for achieving stereopsis in the absence of familiar shapes and forms.

In this instance, computational theorists do seem to have reached a solution similar to that suggested by physiological investigators. Both attempt to explain the random-dot stereo problem by assuming that neurons tuned to the same disparity cooperate, whereas those tuned to different disparities inhibit each other. For many years this idea was only a theoretical possibility, based on Hubel and Weisel's (1962) observation that the receptive fields of most cells in the striate cortex (V1) could be stimulated through either eye (Mustillo, 1985). Since the 1970s, however, this idea has received increasing support from electrophysiological recordings made on alert, behaving monkeys. Gian Poggio and his colleagues (Poggio & Fischer, 1977; Poggio & Poggio, 1984; Poggio & Talbot, 1981) have been able to identify two classes of disparity-sensitive neurons in the striate cortex. One type of neuron is sensitive to disparities tuned over a narrow range about the fixation point; the other type is sensitive to crossed (signaling "near") and uncrossed (signaling "far") disparities. Within each of these classes, cells can be further subdivided into those with excitatory responses and those with inhibitory responses. For instance, a cell with an excitatory response to crossed disparity will give an inhibitory response to uncrossed disparities and vice versa. Thus, all of the components for a cooperative algorithm for stereo depth appear to be present already in the first cortical region of visual processing (Aslin & Dumais, 1980; DeValois & DeValois, 1980).

Since the introduction of the random-dot stereo display, most of the research on stereo depth has focused on this form of stimulus (Regan, Frisby, Poggio, Schor, & Tyler, 1990). One of its main advantages over more traditional stimuli is that it completely bypasses the need for monocular form perception. The process of stereo fusion can be understood without first having to explain shape and form identification processes (Julesz, 1986). Another very important by-product of this stimulus is that it ensures that all perceived forms are being assembled in the visual cortex after information from the two eyes has been combined. (Recall from Chapter 3 that information from the two eyes is still in separate layers at the lateral geniculate nucleus but is combined in the primary visual cortex, V1.) This same random-dot type of stimulus allows researchers to see whether perceptual phenomena other than depth perception are occurring prior to, or only after, visual information has reached the cortex. Among the phenomena that have been studied in this way using random-dot displays are visual illusions (Papert, 1961), visual aftereffects (Julesz, 1986; Regan & Beverly, 1973; Tyler, 1975), and apparent motion (Julesz & Payne, 1968).

INTERACTION OF DEPTH CUES

Although each of the cues for depth that we have discussed is sufficient, by itself, to give the conscious impression of a three-dimensional arrangement in space, the accuracy of our perception of distance often depends on the interaction of several cues. Under normal conditions, if a cue such as interposition suggests that your friend Fred is standing closer to you than your friend Maria is, other cues, such as relative size, height in the plane, and binocular disparity, will tend to confirm this relationship. Chaotic and conflicting cues, such as those shown in William Hogarth's 1754 engraving *False Perspective* (Figure 9-17), virtually never occur in "real world" settings.

How do cues for depth combine? Jameson and Hurvich (1959) suggested that an observer's sensitivity to a difference in distance when several cues are available is approximately the arithmetic sum of the sensitivities obtained with each cue alone. This has now been demonstrated experimentally by several investigators. For example, one study showed that information from binocular disparity and linear perspective added together in the final judgment of perceived depth (van der Meer, 1979). Another found consistently additive relations among depth specified by relative size, height in the plane, occlusion, and motion parallax (Bruno & Cutting, 1988). Still another study found additive relations between motion parallax and binocular disparity (Rogers & Collett, 1989). Although the exact form of the addition rule has yet to be determined (Massaro, 1988), it is certainly the case that the more cues available and the more consistent they are, the stronger is the perception of depth (Berbaum, Tharp, & Mroczek, 1983).

One important consequence of the interaction of depth cues is their ability to provide unique information about dynamic events. For example, consider what happens to the image on your retina as you watch an automobile on a highway pass by a house that lies between you and the highway. One cue to the relative depths of these objects is, of course, occlusion—the more distant automobile will be only partially visible for some period of time and perhaps entirely occluded for a brief period. Another cue is given by motion—the car will be moving at a faster speed on your retina than the house as you move your head. However, the combination of these two cues produces an important emergent property with regard to the visible contours of the automobile and the house. Portions of the surface of the auto will disappear as it moves behind the house (*deletion*), and then portions of

FIGURE 9-17   Ambiguity of depth cues gives a confusing, difficult interpretation to a scene, as shown in Hogarth's 1754 engraving *False Perspective*. The more you study this figure, the more contradictory depth cues you find.

the surface will again become visible when it emerges *(accretion)*. **Surface deletion** and **surface accretion** can be powerful cues to depth, even when defined only with random-dot displays. The stimuli that are deleted or accreted over time are perceived to lie in a plane behind the dots that may move but remain visible (Craton & Yonas, 1990; Kaplan, 1969).

Another depth cue that emerges from a combination of simpler cues is that of **stereomotion,** or a difference in the relative rates of motion in the two eyes (Regan et al., 1990; Regan & Beverly, 1973, 1979). If an object such as a baseball is hurtling toward you on a direct collision course with your head, the edge of the ball that projects onto your left eye will be moving across the retina at exactly the same rate, albeit in the opposite direction, as the edge of the ball that projects to your right eye. On the other hand, if the ball is coming toward you at an angle, such as might happen if it were to narrowly miss your head, then the rate of motion in one eye will be faster than in the other. Thus, this cue involves a comparison between motion in the two eyes. Interestingly, investigators have found neurons in the striate cortex of cats and monkeys that are sensitive to leftward motion in one eye at the same time that they are sensitive to rightward motion in the other eye (Cynader & Regan, 1978; Poggio & Talbot, 1981). In fact, some neurons are tuned sharply enough to be able to detect objects on a "near miss" collision course, whereas others are tuned to detect "a hit in the head" (Regan et al., 1990).

PERCEPTION OF DIRECTION

Three-dimensional depth is only one aspect of our perception of space. The perception of the location of an object will also include its direction relative to our bodies. There are actually two types of directional judgments that we integrate in a complex fashion to give us our sense of up, down, right, and left (Howard, 1982). The first one is called **bodycentric** direction. It uses as a reference location the midline of the body, an imaginary vertical line parallel to the spine passing through the navel. The second is called **headcentric** direction, where the midline of the head is used as another reference location for right and left. The midline of the head is an imaginary vertical line centered

on the nose. Of course, bodycentric and headcentric directions are potentially different because it is possible to rotate the head independently of the body. The distinction between these two aspects of direction is shown in Figure 9-18. This distinction is particularly relevant for pilots involved in air and space flight, where the body is strapped into a vehicle that is not necessarily moving in a bodycentric direction. Studies in which the body orientation has been fixed in a misaligned position relative to its motion through space have shown that the perception of heading is quite accurate, provided that the head and eyes are free to move. If the head is also fixed in a misaligned position, then there is a systematic distortion in the perceived heading in the direction of the misalignment (Telford & Howard, 1996).

Most of the research on direction has concentrated on one aspect of headcentric perception we can refer to as the *visual straight ahead*. We tend to usually define our notion of "straight ahead" as a direction in front of us, oriented around the midline of the head, regardless of eye position (Cutting & Vishton, 1997). The visual **egocenter** is the position in the head that serves as our reference point for the determination of headcentric straight ahead. In some respects, this is a very complex judgment because we seem to ignore the directions that the eyes are pointing and to compute a straight ahead that seems to be located in front of the middle of the head. Researchers often refer to this compromise direction as the location pointed to by a hypothetical **Cyclopean eye,** a name derived from the mythical Greek giant Cyclops, who had a single eye in the middle of his forehead. Demonstration Box 9-7 shows how you can experience for yourself the referring of the visual direction of the two eyes to this common egocenter.

Eye Movements and Direction

Several variables affect our sense of the direction of objects. Stimulus factors are, of course, important; the more stimuli available, the more stable our directional judgments, which accounts for the fact that our ability to judge direction is much less stable in the dark. Also, visual configurations influence the judgment of direction. For example, if you are looking at a square or rectangle that is not

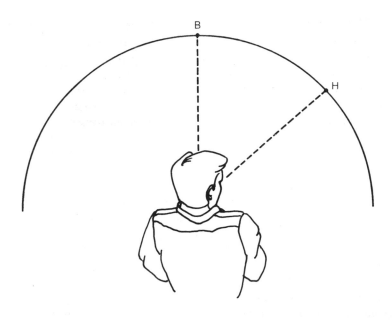

FIGURE 9-18   The distinction between bodycentric and headcentric directions. Point B is straight ahead of the body midline, whereas Point H is straight ahead of the midline of the head. Notice, however, that these two straight-ahead directions can be two different points in visual space.

exactly centered in your visual field, there will be a tendency for you to judge the straight-ahead direction in terms of the center of this displaced square or rectangle. It is as if the perceptual system confuses what is straight ahead of the observer with what is centered with respect to the other contents in the visual field (Roelofs, 1935; Royden & Hildreth, 1996). However, nonvisual factors also play a role in directional localization.

In the previous section we saw how eye movements, in the form of convergence and divergence, convey information about the distances of objects. It would also seem reasonable that feedback from eye movements could help in determining the visual direction of an object. At least two sources of eye movement information could be used to compute the direction of an object in space. The first arises from the movement commands sent to the eye muscles (the **efference copy**); the second (the **afference copy**) arises from feedback from the eye movement itself. One study examined the influence of the efference copy by having subjects judge the straight ahead while pressing a finger lightly against the side of their eyeball—hence moving the eye without efference from the eye muscles

(Bridgeman & Graziano, 1989). Observers showed very little influence of this manipulation when judging straight ahead in a normal visual environment, but their judgments were considerably biased in the direction of the finger press when they were made while viewing a blank field with no landmarks. Although there is controversy about whether efference or afference information is more important (e.g., Matin, 1982; Shebilske, 1976; Stark & Bridgeman, 1983), it seems clear that eye movement information does play a role in localizing targets in space (Banks & Ehrlich, 1996).

There are many examples demonstrating how eye movements affect our localization of targets. The information about target localization seems to be associated with where the eyes are pointing at any given moment. Imagine that the fovea of the eye serves as a reference point. In the absence of other information, we localize a target as being in the direction that the fovea is pointing when we try to look at it. This means that if we accurately image the target on the fovea, we will accurately perceive the direction of the target. If, on the contrary, we inaccurately point our eyes, such as when the eyes lag behind a moving target that we are

---

DEMONSTRATION BOX 9-7
The Common Visual Direction of the Two Eyes

You can experience how the visual directions of the two eyes are referred to one common direction in the center of the head. First, take a sheet of stiff cardboard (20 cm × 27 cm will do), and place it in front of the eyes, as shown in the figure. Put a dot in the middle of the far end of the cardboard, and stare at it while a friend marks the exact center position of each of your pupils on the end of the cardboard closest to your face. Next, draw lines from these marked points until they form an angle, or V (as pictured). Finally, reposition the cardboard in front of your face at a point slightly below your eyes. Now, stare at the far point where the two drawn lines intersect, and you should see, in addition to the two lines you have drawn, a somewhat more shadowy line running between them. This "new" line is the fusion of the views of the two eyes and should appear to point directly at a spot close to the midline of the head. This demonstrates that although the direction of each eye's view is different (as shown by the spatial separation between the two drawn lines

converging on the far point on which you are fixating), the visual direction of the combined binocular view is referred to a common point between the eyes. This point is called the *egocenter*, or the *Cyclopean eye*.

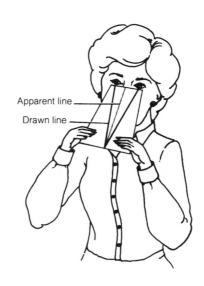

Apparent line
Drawn line

---

trying to track (see Chapter 14 on motion), we should inaccurately localize the target. There is a good deal of evidence that this is exactly what happens (e.g., Coren, Bradley, Hoenig, & Girgus, 1975; Festinger & Easton, 1974; Honda, 1984; Mack & Herman, 1972).

The role of eye movements in target localization can be quite subtle. For example, there is a suggestion that the eye movement does not actually have to be made but that the eye movement we compute in order to move the eye at some later time may bias our perception of direction (e.g., Coren, 1986; Hershberger, 1987). Furthermore, eye movement information both influences and is influenced by other aspects of localization behavior. Thus, Mather and Fisk (1985) were able to show that the information we obtain from looking at a target can aid in accurately pointing to the target. Conversely, information obtained from pointing can assist the eyes in accurately looking at other targets.

Eye Dominance and Perceived Direction

We have considered eye movements of either eye to be interchangeable, but some evidence suggests that the two eyes are not used equivalently in the computation of visual direction. Before we consider this evidence, it is important to understand that there are some tasks we habitually do with one eye. In sighting tasks where only one eye can be used at a time (such as in looking through a telescope) 65% of all observers consistently use their right eye, whereas the remainder consistently use their left (Coren, Porac, & Duncan, 1981). The preferred eye for such tasks is usually called the **sighting-dominant eye** (Porac & Coren, 1981; Ruggieri, Cei, Ceridono, & Bergerone, 1980). Demonstration Box 9-8 shows how you can determine which eye is your sighting-dominant eye.

DEMONSTRATION BOX 9-8
Sighting Dominance and the Straight-Ahead Direction

The visual straight ahead may depend on a single eye (Porac & Coren, 1976, 1981; Walls, 1951). Try the following demonstration to see how this works. Stand in front of a wall at a distance of about 3 m. Pick a point on the wall that is directly in front of you (a small crack or bump will do). Now, with both eyes open, *quickly* stretch out your arm and align your fingertip with the point on the distant wall. When the alignment has been completed, alternately close each eye. You will find that the point on the distant wall will shift out of alignment for one of the eyes. However, the other eye will seem to be aligned with the point on the wall whether one or both eyes are opened. The eye that maintains the alignment is called the *sighting-dominant eye*. You will notice that regardless of which hand you use to perform the alignment, you will tend to line up a near (your fingertip) and a distant (the point on the wall) target in terms of the same eye. The presence of a sighting-dominant eye, and our tendency to make a straight-ahead alignment in terms of this eye, indicates that the locus of the egocentric straight-ahead direction may be shifted toward the side of the sighting-dominant eye.

For the purposes of our discussion of the perception of direction, sighting dominance is important because the visual direction associated with straight ahead is more strongly influenced by the dominant eye (Porac & Coren, 1976, 1981). This certainly does not mean that only one eye is used to determine visual direction (Ono & Weber, 1981). Rather, it means that the location of the egocenter, or Cyclopean eye, is biased toward the side of the sighting-dominant eye (Barbeito, 1981). For instance, Porac and Coren (1986) tested observers in a totally darkened room and had them set a point of light so that it appeared to be visually straight ahead. Whether observers used only one or both eyes, they tended to set the point so that it was closer to the side of the dominant eye, rather than midway between the two eyes.

Another interesting consequence of eye dominance and sighting concerns head posture. Many people display a noticeable head tilt in their everyday posture—a head tilt that becomes more pronounced when they are asked to judge the alignment of objects in depth. Research has shown that individuals with right-eye dominance tilt their heads to the left, whereas those with left-eye dominance tilt their heads to the right. Both types of individuals appear to tilt their heads in order to help maintain a line of sight that is consistent with a body-centered coordinate system (Previc, 1994).

DEVELOPMENT OF SPACE PERCEPTION

One of the most common ways to assess whether there is a constructive aspect to space perception is to observe the behavior of young organisms when they are placed in situations that call on their abilities to perceive distance or direction. Because infants and young animals have limited experience with the world, their abilities to deal with such situations should shed some light on the role of inborn versus learned components in the perception of visual space.

Species Differences

The evidence is quite clear that in certain simpler animals, the perception of direction and distance is inborn. For example, in salamanders it is possible to rotate the eye 180°, thus inverting the retina. When this is done, animals consistently swim and snap in the opposite direction when presented with a food lure (Sperry, 1943). Because the same results occur when similar operations are performed during the animals' embryonic stage, it is clear that visual direction is related innately to the location of retinal stimulation in this species (Stone, 1960). Similarly, immediately after birth chicks peck at small objects with reasonable accuracy. When experimenters optically displaced the images of the targets to one side (using special lenses attached to hoods), the chicks proceeded to peck systematically to one side. This pattern of inaccuracy showed little improvement over time, suggesting that this response to the apparent direction of stimuli was not changeable by experience (Hess, 1950). In higher animals, such as mammals, experience may play a larger role.

Other research shows that several species of young animals, in addition to human infants (Kellman & Spelke, 1983), show evidence of visual "filling in" of the occluded portion of an object. These animals, which include mice (Kanizsa, Renzi, Conte, Compostela, & Guerani, 1993) and newborn chicks (Regolin & Vallortigara, 1995), behave toward partly occluded objects in the same way that they behave toward the objects that are completely visible. Whether or not these animals use the interposition cues of occlusion to interpret the relative depth of the objects is still not known. It is somewhat surprising to find that there are some animals, such as pigeons, that, although tested using the same procedures, do not show this capability (Sekuler & Lee, 1996).

To more exactly determine which factors may be influenced by experience in a species, investigators frequently use controlled-rearing procedures, such as rearing an animal in total darkness from birth until testing. Such dark rearing eliminates all externally generated visual experience. If experience with various visual depth cues is necessary for the development of normal depth perception, these dark-reared animals should have measurable deficits when required to respond to distance cues. If depth perception simply matures as the animal ages, then restricting the animal's visual experience should not affect its behavior, and the only important variable should be its chronological age.

A simple and popular procedure for measuring depth perception in young animals uses an apparatus called the **visual cliff** (Walk & Gibson, 1961). A diagram of a typical visual cliff arrangement is shown in Figure 9-19. Basically it consists of two sections, divided by a "start platform." Each section provides a different depth impression. The "shallow" side is a piece of glass that lies directly over a patterned surface. The "deep" side has the same type of patterned surface but looks like a sharp drop because the surface is placed at some distance below the glass. For testing, a young animal is

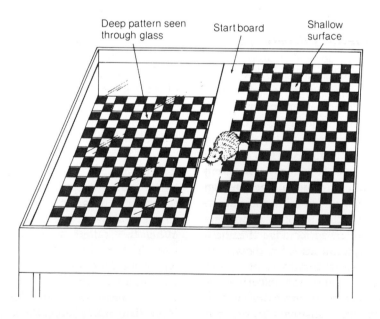

Deep pattern seen through glass   Start board   Shallow surface

FIGURE 9-19 The visual cliff.

placed on the central starting platform that separates the apparently shallow and deep surfaces. It is assumed that from this position the subject can see that the shallow side is safe, whereas the deep side, with its simulated clifflike drop-off, would be perceived as being dangerous. Investigators make the presumption that if the animal consistently chooses the shallow over the deep side, then it can perceive the difference in apparent depth and is attempting to avoid a fall.

Several different types of animals have been tested on the visual cliff, including rats, chickens, turtles, goats, sheep, pigs, cats, dogs, monkeys, and humans (Green & Davies, 1993; Walk & Gibson, 1961). In all cases, even when testing very young animals, there was a preference for the shallow over the deep side of the cliff. There were some interesting species differences, however, which seemed to be related to the habitat features of the natural environment for the various species (Sloane, Shea, Proctor, & Dewsbury, 1978). For instance, aquatic animals, such as certain turtles, did not show the marked preference for the shallow side that the other, more landbound species displayed. Perhaps the survival value of cliff avoidance may not be as pronounced in animals that spend much of their lives swimming because changes in depth of water are not as perilous as sudden sharp drops on land.

Experience and Depth Perception

Although the cross-species differences observed in depth perception are of interest, the visual cliff apparatus has been used primarily to generate data concerning the development of depth perception. A combination of controlled rearing followed by observations of behavior on the visual cliff has been the experimental technique most commonly used in animal studies. In general, the findings have suggested that experience and innate factors interact to produce an animal's ability to perceive depth. For example, when cats or rats are initially reared in the dark, they show little depth discrimination on the visual cliff when first tested. However, as they receive more and more experience in a lighted world, their depth discrimination rapidly improves until they are indistinguishable from normally reared animals (Tees & Midgley, 1978; Walk & Gibson, 1961).

When the visual experience takes place also seems important. There seem to be **sensitive periods** in an animal's development, referring to the fact that there are particular ages and particular durations of time when depriving an animal of a particular type of visual experience may produce the largest perceptual deficits (Aslin, 1981b; Mitchell, 1981; Timney, 1985). For instance, a study by Tees (1974) shows how deprivation of visual experience during a sensitive period can affect later depth perception. Dark-reared rats were compared to light-reared rats on their preference for the deep versus the shallow side of the visual cliff. The amount of time that the animals were dark-reared was varied, and, in addition, the strength of the depth information was varied by varying the distance to the bottom of the deep side of the visual cliff. In this study, the age of the animal, the amount of distance information, and the amount of visual experience all interacted. It was only among the animals that had been dark reared for a comparatively long time (60 to 90 days) that the effects of rearing conditions revealed themselves. For these animals, although depth could be discriminated when the drop-off was large, there was an insensitivity to weaker distance cues. These data indicate that there may be inborn components in the ability of rats to discriminate depth on the visual cliff. These are probably sharpened through experience with depth cues in the environment, a finding supported by other research as well (e.g., Kaye, Mitchell, & Cynader, 1982).

The developmental time course and the effects of experience seem to be different for the various depth cues. Binocular depth perception develops quite early because evidence for the use of binocular disparity for a depth cue may be found in 3- or 4-month-old infants (Birch, Shimojo, & Held, 1985; Braddick, Atkinson, Julesz, Kropfl, Bodis-Wollner, & Raab, 1980; Hutz & Bechtoldt, 1980; Petrig, Julesz, Kropfl, Baumgartner, & Anliker, 1981). Infants at this age are too young to crawl and cannot be tested on the visual cliff, so other techniques must be used. For example, Fox, Aslin, Shea, and Dumais (1980) presented random-dot stereograms, similar to those in Figure 9-16, to infants between 2 and 5 months of age. When viewing with special glasses, these infants saw a square floating in front of a background only if they could combine the disparate information from the two eyes' views. (You saw in Demonstration Box 9-6 that such patterns are meaningless unless you can make use of the disparity cues hidden in each monocular view.) This square was then made to move. When infants could see the square in depth, they tended to follow it with their eyes.

An alternative technique for measuring depth perception in somewhat older infants capitalizes on the fact that infants older than 4 months tend to reach for objects that appear to be near them (Granrud, Yonas, & Pettersen, 1984). Results using this technique verified the finding that binocular depth perception is present by 4 months of age (Granrud, 1986), suggesting either an innate or a rapidly learned process. This confirms earlier animal work, which suggested that the use of monocular cues for depth is much more dependent on specific experience than is binocular depth perception (Eichengreen, Coren, & Nachmias, 1966).

The ability to use kinetic depth information seems to develop at about the same time that the ability to use binocular depth information appears, at roughly 3 to 5 months of age (Kellman, 1984; Owsley, 1983; Yonas & Granrud, 1985b). One biologically important aspect of depth perception, namely sensitivity to information about object motion toward the body (which may indicate an impending collision), seems to be present at an even earlier age. It has been measured at ages as young as 2 to 3 weeks (Ball & Vurpillot, 1976; Yonas, 1981). Even at this young age, infants will blink their eyes when presented with an object that seems to be moving closer and seems to be growing close enough to hit them in the head.

Studies of sensitivity to pictorial depth cues have shown a slower developmental process, by about 3 to 4 months. For example, several studies have shown that 6- to 7-month-old infants respond to linear perspective information (Arterberry & Yonas, 1989; Kaufman, Maland, & Yonas, 1981; Yonas, Cleaves, & Pettersen, 1978), familiar size (Granrud, Haake, & Yonas, 1985), texture gradients (Arterberry & Yonas, 1989; Yonas & Granrud, 1986), and concavity-convexity specified by shading (Granrud & Yonas, 1985). Use of more complex cues, such as the perception of relative depth in a picture based on the direction of shadows cast in the pictorial representation, may not appear until the age of 3 years (Yonas, Goldsmith, & Hallstrom, 1978).

Developmental studies indicate that the perception of depth and distance cannot be fully understood unless we allow some components to be explained by inborn factors, whereas others may require active experience to emerge. These studies suggest that adhering strictly either to a direct perception viewpoint or to a constructive perception viewpoint might be too limiting. Innate components of perception must mature, and certain types of experience can help or hinder the achievement of a high level of perceptual functioning. Some aspects of depth perception seem to be given directly, and others require memory and experience to allow them to properly function.

CHAPTER SUMMARY

The two aspects of depth perception are **egocentric localization** (involving judgments of **absolute distance**) and **object-relative localization** (involving judgments of **relative distance**). The three main theoretical approaches to explaining depth perception are **direct perception, computational theories,** and **intelligent perception** (often referred to as **constructive theories** of perception). All begin with an analysis of depth **cues.** There are a number of **pictorial** or **monocular depth cues.** The characteristics of light transmission produce the **interposition** or **occlusion** cues where near objects obscure more distant ones. Shading (or **attached shadow**) is an important cue for the three-dimensional shape of objects. **Cast shadows** are a cue for the relative distance between objects and other surfaces. **Aerial perspective** and **relative brightness** arise because light is absorbed or scattered as it travels through the air. Geometrical properties of the image also provide depth cues. **Retinal image size** can suggest relative distance and, when combined with **familiar size,** can indicate absolute distance. **Linear perspective** (where objects diminish in size to a **vanishing point**) and **texture gradients** are cues that depend on retinal size variations. **Height in the plane** gives distance information based on the relative position of the object image rather than on its size. **Structural** or **physiological cues** for depth include **accommodation** (changes in lens thickness) and the relative **convergence** or **divergence** of the eyes. Objects in motion provide additional cues through the relative movements of parts of the retinal image. **Motion parallax** can be used to estimate distances, and the **kinetic depth effect** can define the three-dimensional aspects of moving objects. Binocular depth perception or **stereopsis** depends on **binocular disparity** due to the fact that the eyes are spaced apart and have different lines of sight. Normally, disparate objects stimulating **corresponding retinal points,** which are on the **horopter** or in **Panum's area,** will be fused. Images with graphically represented disparities can be fused into a three-dimensional percept in a **stereoscope.** Failure of **fusion** will result in **diplopia,** and the pattern of double vision (**crossed** versus **uncrossed disparity**) can give relative distance information. Between 5% and 10% of people lack functional stereopsis. Stereoscopic depth can arise due to **global stereopsis** in the absence of clear monocular forms (as in random-dot stereograms) if the visual system can solve the **correspondence problem.** Computational theorists have designed various **cooperative algorithms** to do this. When depth cues combine or interact there is the possibility of emergent depth cues, such as **surface deletion, surface accretion,** and **stereomotion.**

The perception of direction can either be **bodycentric** or **headcentric.** Headcentric judgments are based on the **egocenter** and involve positioning a hypothetical **Cyclopean eye.** Eye movements can also affect judgment of direction through, and interaction between, the **efference copy** of the movement command and the **afference copy** based on feedback from the movement. Judgments of straight ahead are also influenced by the direction of the **sighting-dominant eye.**

There are developmental and species differences in depth perception. Some of these have been measured using the **visual cliff.** There appear to be **sensitive periods,** when experience can have a major influence on the development of depth perception. The development of the ability to interpret particular depth cues follows different time courses, with some cue processing, such as binocular disparity, developing early, whereas some of the pictorial depth cues take considerably longer to develop.

KEY TERMS

absolute distance
egocentric localization
relative distance
object-relative localization
direct perception
computational theories
intelligent perception
constructive theories
cues
pictorial depth cues
monocular cues
interposition (occlusion)
attached shadow
cast shadow
aerial perspective
relative brightness
retinal image size
familiar size
reduction conditions
linear perspective
vanishing point
texture gradient
height in the plane
structural (physiological) cues
accommodation
binocular
vergence movements
convergence

divergence
motion parallax
kinetic depth effect
stereopsis
binocular disparity
fusion
diplopia
crossed disparity
uncrossed disparity
horopter
Panum's area
corresponding retinal points
stereoscope
global stereopsis
correspondence problem
cooperative algorithms
surface deletion
surface accretion
stereomotion
bodycentric
headcentric
egocenter
Cyclopean eye
efference copy
afference copy
sighting-dominant eye
visual cliff
sensitive periods

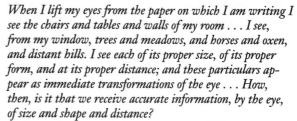

Form
CHAPTER 10

When I lift my eyes from the paper on which I am writing I see the chairs and tables and walls of my room . . . I see, from my window, trees and meadows, and horses and oxen, and distant hills. I see each of its proper size, of its proper form, and at its proper distance; and these particulars appear as immediate transformations of the eye . . . How, then, is it that we receive accurate information, by the eye, of size and shape and distance?

(Mill, 1829, p. 97)

Look around you, as John Stuart Mill did. You will be struck, as he was, with how filled the perceptual world is with *objects*. When you enter your room you see a desk, a chair, some books, and so forth, not the patches of light, brown, gray, red, and green that make up the actual stimulus on your retina. You not only *see* these patches as objects but also identify them as members of particular classes of objects and can recall whether you have seen them before. In this chapter, we tell you something of what we know about the perception of form (Mill's other questions, about distance and size, are dealt with in Chapters 9 and 11, respectively). First we will describe the information about the world that is present in the distribution of light on our retinas, and then we will describe how the visual system transforms that stimulation into perceptual objects. Finally, we will discuss how we recognize and identify these perceptual objects. In several places in this chapter, we will demonstrate the differences between the traditional psychological approach to the perception of form and the newer approaches, some of which involve "computational" mechanisms.

THE PROBLEM OF VISUAL FORM PERCEPTION

The eye receives information in the form of light that is reflected from objects and surfaces in the environment. The total of all the light from the environment that stimulates your eyes at any given moment is called the **visual field.** Figure 10-1 portrays the visual field as seen by the left eye of the physicist/psychologist Ernst Mach as he lay on the couch in his study in Prague, Czechoslovakia, sometime around 1885. Reflected light from the visual field forms a **retinal image,** consisting of a two-dimensional distribution of light of various intensities and wavelengths on his retina. The intensity and wavelength of each point of light in this image are determined by the combination of four general aspects of the environment and its relationship to the viewer, as is shown in Figure 10-2.

The first of these aspects is the **light source** and refers to the direction and intensity of the light-producing regions in the environment. For example, in a natural outdoor scene, there is only one important primary source—the sun. Most light reflected from the various objects in the environment originates from this source, although reflections of light from one surface to another may provide *secondary sources* of illumination. The light

FIGURE 10-1 The visual field as seen by the left eye of Ernst Mach (based on Mach, 1959/1886).

reflected to earth on a moonlit night is an example of such secondary light. In an indoor scene, there may, of course, be more than one primary light source (e.g., several lightbulbs) and many secondary sources (e.g., reflecting walls).

A second factor that determines the nature of the retinal image is the **reflectance** properties of the various surfaces that come in contact with the light. As discussed in Chapter 5, some surfaces absorb light from one region of the wavelength spectrum more than from other regions, leading to the perception of differently colored surfaces. Thus, if one surface absorbs the short and middle wavelengths and reflects only the longer wavelengths, the portion of the retinal image that corresponds to the image of this surface will contain only red-appearing light. In addition to these wavelength reflectance characteristics, surfaces differ in the total amount of light they absorb. Some surfaces are highly reflecting and thus look glossy or mirror-like; others absorb much of the incident light and thus are matte or dull.

A third aspect is the **surface orientation** (relative to the light source and the viewer) of the various reflecting surfaces in the scene. Surface orientation is determined with reference to an imaginary line perpendicular to the surface, which is called the *surface normal.* For instance, a surface oriented for optimal light reflection would be one in which the angle between the direction of the light source and the surface was exactly the same as the angle between the direction of the viewer and the surface normal. As these two angles become more unequal, less and less light will be reflected from the objects onto the image. For example, the surface of the pyramid that is facing the eye in Figure 10-2 is reflecting more light to it than are the block surfaces that are facing the same way. This is because the angle between this surface and the light source is approximately equal to the angle between the surface and the eye.

The fourth aspect is the **viewing position,** specifically the relationship between the viewer's eye and the scene. If Ernst Mach would have gotten off his couch and walked to the bookshelf on the side of the room, the retinal image projected from the room would have changed dramatically from that shown in Figure 10-1. This would occur despite the fact that the light sources, surface reflectance characteristics, and surface orientations

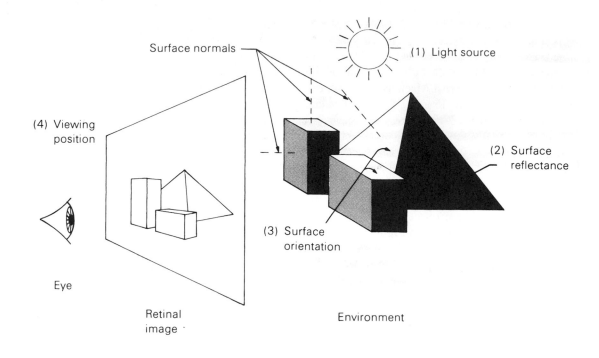

FIGURE 10-2 Four properties of the visual environment that together determine the intensity and wavelength of each point in the retinal image: (1) light source, (2) reflectances, (3) surface orientations, and (4) viewing position. The surface normals are also noted for some surfaces.

had not changed at all relative to one another. Similarly, your own viewing position on the scene depicted in Figure 10-2 is quite different from that for the eye shown in the figure.

These four aspects of the viewing situation, then, determine the distribution of light in the retinal image of the viewer. This simple fact has fooled many people, including even some perception researchers, into thinking that the problem of form perception is fairly straightforward. Their false reasoning goes something like this: "If the two-dimensional retinal image is completely determined by four aspects of the three-dimensional world and our relationship to it (namely: light source, reflectances, surface orientation, and viewing position), then it should be possible to examine the image and decompose it in a way that will give us a precise description of that world and the objects in it." What this reasoning fails to take into account is that any given retinal image could have been produced by a potentially infinite number of scenes.

The ambiguity of the form information in the retinal image is shown in Figure 10-3. Suppose that a viewer is looking at a wire hoop, and the image that it casts in his eye is circular. On the basis of this information alone he really can't say what the shape of the hoop is because the same image would be cast by a circular hoop viewed straight on; a tall, thin hoop tilted back; or a short, fat hoop tilted to the side. The orientation of the hoop relative to the viewing position combines with the shape of the object to determine the shape of the retinal image. Unless the viewer knows something about the orientation of the hoop relative to himself, the retinal image does not contain enough information to differentiate between a glimpse of a circular or an oval hoop. This illustrates how the perception of an object's shape and the assumed viewing position are intertwined aspects of the observer's perceptual experience.

This process of getting from the flat patches of light that make up the retinal image to the world of objects about us is the major problem in the

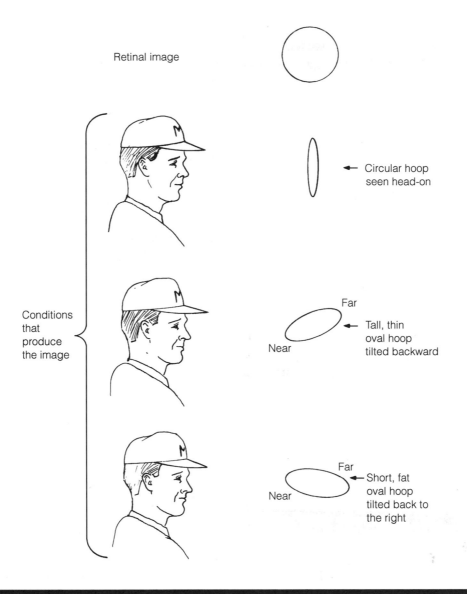

Retinal image

Conditions that produce the image

Circular hoop seen head-on

Far

Near

Tall, thin oval hoop tilted backward

Far

Near

Short, fat oval hoop tilted back to the right

FIGURE 10-3   The inherent ambiguity of the shape of objects in the retinal image.

perception of visual form. What makes it so fascinating to study is that this problem is being solved by our visual systems every moment that our eyes are open, without even a hint of effort on our part. It is only when attempts have been made to understand the visual system with mathematical equations (Grossberg, 1987; Tsotsos, 1988) or to build a functioning visual system by machine (Horn, 1977, 1986; Marr, 1982; Nevatia, 1982) that the enormous complexity of this problem becomes apparent. Because of its complexity, perception

researchers now tend to work on the problem by dividing it into several smaller subproblems, which we will now examine in turn.

CONTOUR PERCEPTION

At the most basic level, the visual system seems to divide the visual field into regions of uniform brightness (Palmer & Rock, 1994), which are commonly referred to as **shapes.** Shapes are separated from the background, or from other shapes, by contours. A contour is a region in the retinal image where the light intensity (or wavelength composition) changes abruptly. Examples of contours in the everyday world can be found at the edge of a blackboard, the outline of the moon against the night sky, and the silhouette of a person. Note that a black line on a sheet of white paper, strictly speaking, consists of two contours: one where the white paper changes to black lead and another where the black lead changes back to white paper. The artistic convention of using a line on a flat surface to represent an edge in the real world seems to be based on a very primitive perceptual tendency to interpret lines as contours (Hochberg & Brooks, 1962).

Generally speaking, shapes are regions in the retinal image that are surrounded by contours. In addition to the spatial dimensions of these regions, shapes may have other attributes, such as color, texture, three-dimensional depth, or even motion. We will refer to these attributes as features of the shape. Under many circumstances the visual system seems to be inherently biased to interpret the shapes in the retinal image as objects in the real world. However, because this is an interpretation, at times we will find that this interpretation can be systematically wrong, to the extent that the misinterpretation leads to visual illusions, as you will see in Chapter 11.

Contours are the basic building blocks of visual perception; in their absence we actually lose our ability to see. We can demonstrate this by looking into a Ganzfeld (German for "whole field"). A Ganzfeld is a visual field that contains no abrupt luminance changes and thus no contours. When observers look into a Ganzfeld, they usually report seeing "a shapeless fog that goes on forever." Any hint of color soon fades to gray, even if the entire field is illuminated with, say, green or blue or red light (Cohen, 1958). Many observers even experience perceptual *blank out*, a feeling that they *can't see*, after prolonged viewing. This feeling quickly disappears the instant any kind of luminance change is introduced into the visual field (Avant, 1965; Cohen, 1958).

Blank out can occur in natural environments as well. For instance, *snow blindness* is a kind of natural blank out, caused by the lack of contour in the retinal image when the visual field contains a lot of

snow and ice. The snow and ice scatter much of the light in all directions and together are often very uniform in texture, which creates a kind of natural Ganzfeld. You can experience some of these sensations for yourself by trying Demonstration Box 10-1.

The perception of a contour does not occur in isolation. We saw in Chapter 4 that the visibility of something as simple as a small disk of light in an otherwise empty field is influenced by both its size (Ricco's Law) and the size of its immediate background (the Westheimer effect). The same principles apply to the detection of a simple contour. Its visibility will be influenced by the other contours that are simultaneously present in the visual field.

One of the most peripheral influences on the perception of a contour seems to arise from the interactions that occur among neurons in the retina. In Chapter 3 you learned that retinal ganglion neurons have receptive fields that have a center-surround organization, meaning that if the center of the field is excited by light, then the surround of the field will be inhibited by light. An equal number of ganglion cells have the reverse arrangement, with an inhibitory response to light at the center and an excitatory response to light in the surround.

One of the effects of these receptive fields can be observed directly by viewing the pattern known as the Hermann grid, shown in Figure 10-4A. When it is viewed from the appropriate distance you will see gray smudges at the intersections of the white spaces separating the black squares. One of the disconcerting aspects of this experience is that the very intersection you are gazing at directly does not appear to be filled with a gray smudge; only those intersections that are not currently being fixated give the illusion of the gray smudge.

The diagram in Figure 10-4B illustrates what is going on at the ganglion cell level. A receptive field that is center-excitatory and aligned with an intersection will have a larger net amount of inhibition in its surround than will a same-size receptive field centered in the space between two squares. This means that, relatively speaking, the intersections will be registered by ganglion cells as containing less light than the vertical and horizontal regions between squares. But why doesn't this illusion occur at the intersection that is being fixated directly? This is because the receptive fields are smallest for neurons in the foveal region of the

DEMONSTRATION BOX 10-1
The Ganzfeld

Although Ganzfeld situations have been produced with elaborate laboratory equipment, there are several simple ways to produce a Ganzfeld that will allow you to experience this contourless field for yourself. You can take a table tennis ball and cut it in half, placing one half over each eye, or you can use two white plastic spoons (like those probably available in any campus cafeteria) to produce a Ganzfeld by placing the bowl of a spoon over each eye as shown in the accompanying figure. Direct your gaze toward a light source (a fluorescent lamp, say) prior to placing the objects before your eyes so that your field of view will be flooded with diffuse, contourless light. Stay in this position for a few minutes and monitor any changes or alterations in your conscious perceptual experience. If the light originally had a tint, you will soon notice that the color will fade into a gray. After a while you will suddenly feel that you cannot see. This feeling of blindness is called *blank out*. It seems that in the absence of contours in the field, vision ceases. If a friend now casts a shadow over part of the field (say, with a pencil across the spoons), vision will immediately return with the introduction of this contour.

Spoon

retina, and they increase in size as distance from the fovea is increased. Therefore, the size of the receptive field that is ideal for producing the illusion in the visual periphery will, by definition, be larger than the receptive fields that are active when the pattern is examined at the center of gaze. Viewing the pattern up very close will increase the retinal size of the spaces in the pattern stimulating the periphery and, as you would predict, will also reduce the strength of the illusion as the contour distances no longer "match" the receptive field sizes.

Another way that contour interactions have been studied is by looking at how detection thresholds for a contour change as a function of

A

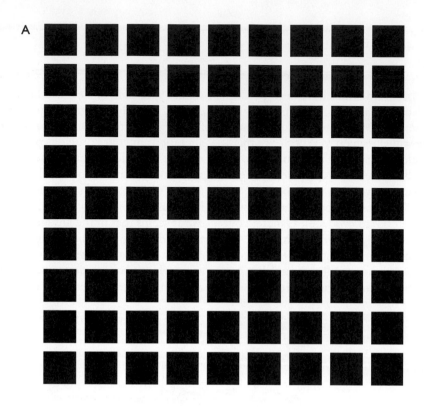

B

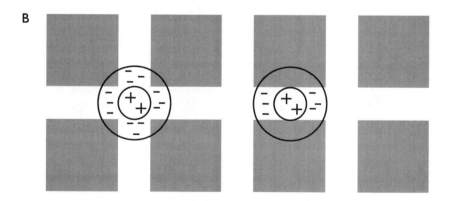

FIGURE 10-4 (A) The Hermann grid. (B) A sketch of the response of two ganglion cell receptive fields, one centered on an intersection of the grid, the other centered on a space between two square elements.

the presence of other contours in the vicinity (Fiorentini et al., 1990). It might be puzzling to learn that a neighboring contour has an influence on the detection of a target contour even when the neighboring contour is itself below the threshold of visibility. Figure 10-5 illustrates the typical

results from an experiment involving the detection of a vertical bar in the presence of a second bar that is just below detection threshold itself. When the second bar is less than 5 min of arc away from the target, it actually facilitates the detection. That is, the target bar can be seen at a much lower contrast than when it is shown in isolation. At intermediate distances, such as 5–10 min of arc, the second bar has an inhibitory effect on the target detection. Finally, when the second bar is farther than 15 min of arc from the target, it has no influence on target detection. As you will probably recognize, the threshold curve shown in Figure 10-5 represents a one-dimensional slice through a typical center-surround receptive field where the center is excitatory. Studies such as this indicate that receptive fields for thin lines are only 4–5 min of arc at the fovea and grow rapidly in size up to about 2° of arc in the visual periphery (Fiorentini et al., 1990).

Interactions such as these do not occur only for the perception of simple contours and are not brought about only by the way that ganglion cells communicate with one another. Indeed it appears that the concepts of **spatial summation** for closely neighboring stimuli and **lateral inhibition** among slightly more distant stimuli are general design principles of the brain. For example,

the perception of many forms, including letters, shapes, and pictures, is influenced negatively by the presence of other forms in the near vicinity. Researchers who study these influences on visual acuity often refer to this effect as **crowding** (Bouma, 1970; Loomis, 1978; Toet & Levi, 1992). Those who study the role that attention plays in visual perception often refer to similar effects as **simultaneous masking** or **flanker effects** (Eriksen & St. James, 1986; He, Cavanagh, & Intriligator, 1996; LaBerge & Brown, 1989). In all cases it appears that neural units that are specialized for the analysis of specific visual attributes actively compete with other units in their region by sending inhibitory signals to neighboring units that are proportional to their current level of activation (Wilkinson, Wilson, & Ellemberg, 1997).

In the natural world the perception of contours can be very complex. If you look around you right now you will notice that some contours defining objects are partly occluded from view by objects that lie nearer to you than the contours. Other contours are not associated with very much contrast because the color and luminance on either side of the edge are very similar. Still other contours do not define the edge of an object at all but are instead the result of shadows cast by other objects standing between a light source and the surface on which the shadows have been cast. Therefore, in order to analyze an image appropriately your visual system must be able to group contours that truly belong together; it must be able to boost the signal of parts of contours that are very faint in the image; and it must be able to assign some contours to the status of "surface edge" and other contours to the status of "shadow edge."

Vision scientists who study the computational aspects of contour detection have discovered a number of ingenious mathematical tools to help them detect contours in an image (Horn, 1986; Marr, 1982). Most of these tools involve examining the gradient of image intensity in a local region of the image in order to find the precise location in which the intensity is changing most rapidly. All of these locations are then represented in a **contour map**, which is a representation of the original image in which only the edges have been preserved and coded as points. Figure 10-6B shows a typical contour map for the photograph shown in Figure 10-6A, generated by using a simple contour-finding algorithm. Note that

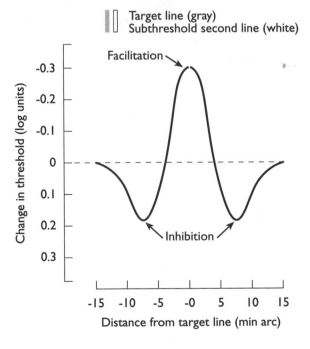

FIGURE 10-5 The change in the threshold of detection for a small target bar (gray) as a function of the distance between the target bar and a second subthreshold bar of similar size (white).

A

B

FIGURE 10-6 (A) A black and white photograph of a scene. (B) The same photograph in which all edges have been replaced by contours.

because of imperfect lighting in the original photograph and because of noise in the edge-finding process, some portions of the real contours have been omitted and other markings that do not represent real contours have been added. The next task for both an artificial vision machine and for a human visual system is to determine which edges belong together, which should be discarded, and which edges need to be added because they are missing from the map.

One way in which contour grouping has been studied in human vision is to ask observers to indicate the shapes hidden in pictures such as those shown in Figure 10-7 (Beck & Rosenfeld, 1989; Field & Hayes, 1993). These are textures generated by randomly sprinkling small elements such as short bars all over an image. However, among the randomly oriented elements is a continuous curved line of elements. Which S shapes are easiest to see? You will probably not be surprised to see that bars that are farther apart, as in Figure 10-7A, are more difficult to group into a continuous line than are bars that are closer together, as in Figure 10-7B. However, note that the relative orientation of the bars is also very important. Figure 10-7C contains the same number of bars as does Figure 10-7B, but instead of being aligned on their long axis each of the bars has been oriented at 90° to its original orientation. As you can see, it is extremely difficult to group the bars on this basis. Only when the density of the bars is increased twofold, as in Figure 10-7D, is the S shape once again easily visible. Findings such as these indicate that there is a cooperative grouping process in human vision that seeks to extend edges as well as a competitive grouping process that seeks to inhibit the grouping of edges that do not have the same orientation.

Finally, it is important to keep in mind that for contour perception to occur, there must be not only spatial variation in the intensity of light but also variation in the pattern of illumination on the retina over time. In Chapter 13 you will see that a variety of temporal factors are important in the perception of contours.

FEATURE EXTRACTION

The shapes that emerge into our consciousness from the retinal image can be said to possess features that differentiate them from other shapes. For example, if you have ever picked raspberries or blackberries, you will recall that the image of a ripe berry consists of a curved and roughly oval shape. Sometimes these shapes overlap the leaves of the plant, and sometimes they are themselves overlapped by leaves or other berries. A ripe berry will tend to be larger than the others, will have a texture of bumps that is coarser than the others, and will reflect a darker "reddish" or "purplish" color. The so-called **relevant features** of the ripe berry are those that help you differentiate it from the others (Garner, 1974). In this case these features are size, texture, and color.

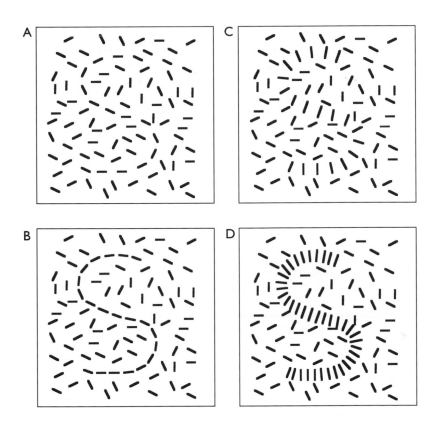

FIGURE 10-7 There is an S-shape configuration in each of these randomly textured patterns. (A) Large spacing between the bars in the S shape. (B) Small spacing between the bars in the S shape. (C) Small spacing between the bars, but the bars are all rotated by 90°. (D) Bars are rotated by 90°, but their spacing has been reduced by one half.

Perception researchers use several different experimental methods to help them determine what the basic features are for the human visual system. One of these is the **visual search** task, in which the subject looks for the presence of a single target item and the experimenter varies the total number of search items in the display from trial to trial. An example of two of these displays is shown in Figures 10-8A and 10-8B. If the time it takes for the subject to find the target stays approximately the same as the number of items is increased, the target is said to "pop out," and the feature that differentiates the target item from the distracting items is thought to be a basic visual feature.

In a related task, subjects are asked to identify the presence or the location of an "odd" region in a briefly flashed display consisting of tiny figural elements. Two examples of displays from such a **texture segregation** task are shown in Figures

10-8C and 10-8D. If subjects are able to find the "odd" region in a display shown for less than 100 ms, the region is again said to pop out, and the feature that differentiates the elements in the "odd" region from background elements is believed to be a basic visual feature.

These two tasks, and others, tend to agree in their identification of a number of basic visual features of shape, including color, brightness, orientation, length, and curvature (Beck, 1982; Cavanagh, 1988; Julesz, 1984; Neisser, 1967; Ramachandran & Anstis, 1986; Treisman, 1986b; Treisman et al., 1990). In addition, these simple features can sometimes be combined in a hierarchical fashion to create **emergent features.** These are *Gestalts* or larger configurations that cannot be explained by simply examining the component parts, as shown in Figure 10-9. These emergent features sometimes behave just like simpler features in visual

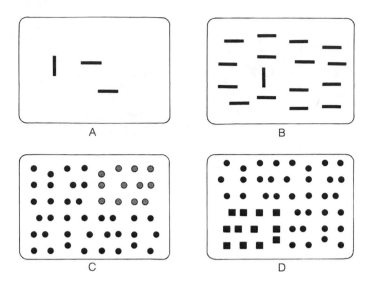

FIGURE 10-8 (A and B) Displays from a typical visual search experiment in which the target is a vertical bar. This target is easy to find, regardless of the number of horizontal bars present. (C and D) Displays from a typical texture segregation experiment in which the elements in the "odd" region differ in brightness or in shape from the elements in the "background" region.

search and other feature detection tasks (Enns, 1990b; Enns & Prinzmetal, 1984; Pomerantz, 1986). Some of the important emergent features identified to date include spatial relations among contours, such as line crossings, line endings, and line closure (Elder & Zucker, 1993, 1994; Julesz, 1984; Treisman & Souther, 1985). Still other emergent features can be traced to the three-dimensional orientation of surfaces (Aks & Enns, 1996; Enns & Rensink, 1991), the direction of scene lighting (Enns & Rensink, 1990; Ramachandran, 1988), and surfaces defined by common motion (Driver & McLeod, 1992), stereo-depth perception (Nakayama & Silverman, 1986), and pictorial depth cues (Enns, 1992). In these latter cases the "features" can no longer be defined with respect to the contours and shapes in the image but instead must be defined with respect to the three-dimensional visual world that has been interpreted from the image.

An alternative way to characterize visual features is to trace them to a physiological base, as, for example, the edge "detectors" of the visual cortex discussed in Chapter 3. A related approach, dealt with in Chapter 4, involves specifying the spatial frequency components that make up a shape as its "features." As was pointed out in Chapter 4, the two-dimensional distribution of light on the retina can be completely described in terms of simple sine wave gratings. Through the process of Fourier analysis, we can determine which sine wave gratings, at which spatial frequencies, need to be combined to create any pattern. One suggestion has been that these sine wave frequencies (called *Fourier components* after they are determined by the appropriate mathematical calculations) are the features used to identify perceptual objects (e.g., Campbell & Robson, 1968; Pollen, Lee, & Taylor, 1971). It has now been shown that this approach cannot work if the Fourier analysis is applied over the entire visual field (e.g., Caelli, 1984; Cavanagh, 1984; DeValois & DeValois, 1987), but it still appears to be useful if the analysis is done over smaller regions, around the size of cortical receptive fields (Fogel & Sagi, 1989; Gurnsey & Browse, 1989; Sutter, Beck, & Graham, 1989).

Unfortunately, the spatial frequency approach is really different from other forms of feature analysis in more ways than simply being describable in terms of mathematical equations. First, the spatial frequency components are not apparent to

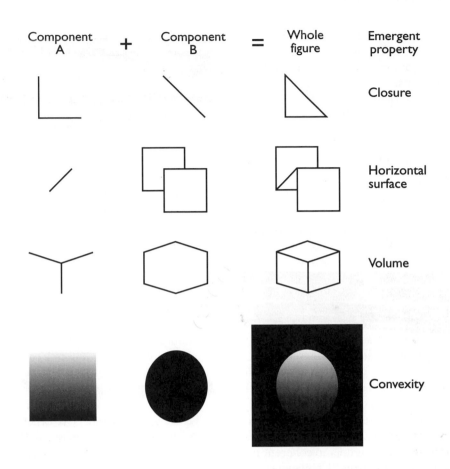

FIGURE 10-9   When component figures are added together, emergent features are sometimes created that cannot be explained by examining the component parts (based on Enns, 1990b; Pomerantz, 1986; Ramachandran, 1986).

consciousness and thus are not useful in describing what we see. Second, they are not always related to texture segregation because regions of the visual array that are clearly different in their Fourier components sometimes do not appear to be perceptibly different (Caelli, 1988; Julesz, 1981; Julesz & Bergen, 1983). However, this approach does have the advantage that the set of possible Fourier components is not as arbitrary as the feature list seems to be and does not change with the set of shapes. Some researchers therefore feel that it may ultimately still prove to be useful for the description of our perception of forms. We will gain a greater appreciation of the complexity of both the feature and the spatial frequency approaches to form perception when we examine the principles of perceptual organization in the next section.

PERCEPTUAL ORGANIZATION

The quotation from Mill beginning this chapter emphasizes that the visual world is filled with *objects*. That is, under normal viewing conditions, our visual systems operate to produce **perceptual objects** from the array of blobs and contours contained in the distribution of light on the retina. There are no perceptual objects on the retina; they exist only in our minds and only as the result of many levels of processing and interpretation applied to the retinal image. The miraculous thing is that the perceptual objects so closely resemble what physics tells us is the nature of the "real" objects "out there" in the world. An apple to our consciousness is very like an apple "out there." How does this come about? Our best guess at this time is that the perceptual object is *constructed* from a group of features (or attributes) detected at a particular spatial location. In what follows we will discuss how this happens.

Figure and Ground

The general question of how all perception comes to be organized into patterns, shapes, and forms was central to a group of psychologists (Max Wertheimer, Kurt Koffka, and Wolfgang Kohler were the most influential) who formed the **Gestalt** school of psychology. *Gestalt* is a German word that can be translated as "form," "whole," or even "whole form." The Gestaltists were interested in processes that cause certain visual elements to seem to be part of the same figure or grouping and certain others to seem to belong to other figures or groups. They formulated several laws of perceptual organization that govern the emergence of a visual figure (Wertheimer, 1923). Their basic observation was that elements or features within a visual pattern do not seem to operate independently. At the phenomenal level, there appear to be attractive "forces" among the various elements that cause them to form a meaningful and coherent figure, much as gravity organizes the planets, sun, and moons of our solar system. The Gestaltists described how certain regular properties of elements within a pattern bring about the emergence of stable figures.

Perhaps the most primitive example of perceptual organization is when we see a two-dimensional **figure** (say, a black spot) on a two-dimensional **ground** (e.g., the expanse of white paper on which the spot is drawn). A figure is simply a group of contours that has some kind of object-like properties in our consciousness. A shape can be a figure, but shapes can also form part of the background (or *ground*) from which the figure emerges. Thus, a ball resting on a field of grass is a figure (here, a round shape) resting on a ground consisting of many elongated shapes (the blades of grass). How can we tell the difference between a figure and its ground? For example, how can you tell the book you are reading from the table on which it rests or the printed words from the page? On your retina the blobs of contours that make up figures and grounds are all run together, intersecting and overlapping, but somehow the visual system separates the book from the table and the words from the page.

To begin with, this separation is a psychological achievement and not a simple description of the physical stimulus. This can be seen in Figure 10-10B. This is the famous Rubin (1915, 1921) face-vase ambiguous figure. When you look at this figure you might see a pair of silhouette faces gazing at each other, or you might see an ornate vase. The vase appears white against a black ground, whereas the faces appear black against a white ground. Notice that as you look at Figure 10-10B for a few moments the two pattern organizations alternate in consciousness, demonstrating that the organization into figure and ground is in your mind, not in the stimulus. Notice also that the faces and the vase never appear together. You "know" that both are possible, but you can't "see" both at the same time. It is impossible for a given part of a visual pattern to be simultaneously interpreted as both figure and ground. Generally speaking, the smaller an area or a shape is, the more likely it is to be seen as a figure (see Weisstein & Wong, 1986). This is demonstrated in Figure 10-10, where it is easier to see the vase when the white area is smaller (10-10A) and easier to see the faces when the black area is smaller (10-10C).

After a particular interpretation has been arrived at—for example, the vase—figure and ground take on distinct properties. When the white area is seen as the vase, it appears to be in front of the black area seen as the ground, and the contours in the pattern seem to belong to the vase. However, when the interpretation changes, the contours are now seen to belong to the faces, and the faces seem closer than, and in front of, the white background. Furthermore, figures appear to be more "thing-like" and appear to have a shape, whereas the ground appears formless. Figures are seen as "richer" and more meaningful and are remembered more easily. Figures also contrast more than the ground, appearing brighter or darker than equivalent patches of light that form part of the background (Coren, 1969). Finally, the stimuli seen as figures are processed or registered in greater detail than stimuli seen as ground (Weisstein & Wong, 1986).

Of course, in natural visual scenes, the distinction between figure and ground is rarely as arbitrary as in Rubin's face-vase figure. There are,

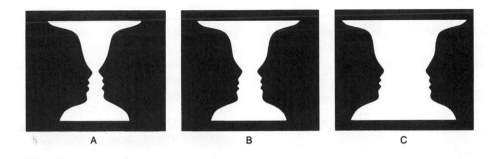

FIGURE 10-10   (B) A reversible figure-ground stimulus in which a pair of black faces or a white vase (or perhaps a bird bath or goblet) is seen alternately. When the white area is smaller (A) the vase is easier to see; when the black area is smaller (C) the faces are more easily seen.

however, some natural conditions where there is ambiguity as to what constitutes a figure. For instance, we are often confronted with scenes in which our view of one figure is partially blocked by the shape of another object. (*Interposition*, or the partial occlusion of one object by another, was discussed in Chapter 9). Look at Figure 10-11*A*. Despite the large amount of black interposed in front of the gray figures, our visual system is effortlessly able to group together the correct portions of the image. In this figure, several copies of a familiar letter of the alphabet *(B)* can be seen lying in various orientations underneath some spilled ink. How are these various letter fragments grouped so effortlessly? Familiarity with the occluded objects is clearly *not* a sufficient condition for this to occur, as is shown in Figure 10-11B. This figure contains the same letter fragments, but the occluding spots of black ink have been removed—subjects find these letters almost impossible to decipher even when they know which letters to look for (Bregman, 1981; Kanisza, 1979). Thus, the grouping that is occurring in Figure 10-11A must be following some rules that work regardless of the meaning of the objects.

One suggestion is that shape contours are "labeled" very early in the grouping process as either **intrinsic contours** (meaning they belong to the figure) or **extrinsic contours** (meaning they are simply a consequence of one object occluding another; Nakayama, Shimojo, & Silverman, 1989). The *intrinsic* contours of the ink spilled in Figure 10-11A can be traced to form continuous shapes. *Extrinsic* contours (where the ink crosses the un-

derlying letters) serve as a signal that allows the *intrinsic* contours of the letter *B* to be "filled in" underneath the occluding black ink. In Figure 10-11B the shape fragments that have been drawn are a combination of *intrinsic* contours of the letter *B* and *extrinsic* contours caused by the ink spill. In this case the visual system has no way of knowing which is which because the interposing figure is not visible; hence the "filling in process" is not invoked. Now examine Figure 10-11C. Here only the *intrinsic* contours of the letter *B* have been retained, and so the letters are once again quite readable (Brown & Koch, 1991). It appears that correct contour labeling can be achieved in a number of ways, including the assignment of contours to different depth planes—such as the ink being seen in front of the *B*s (Nakayama et al., 1989). Sometimes the characteristics of the contours determine the labels. For instance, at approximately T-shaped intersections between contours the stem of the T intersection is labeled *intrinsic* and is seen as part of the more distant figure, whereas the crossbar is labeled *extrinsic* and is part of the nearer, interposing figure (Enns & Rensink, 1991; Kellman & Shipley, 1990).

Contours that are not physically present on the retina but that still affect our perception of figure and ground are called **subjective contours** or **illusory contours** (Petry & Meyer, 1987; Purghé & Coren, 1992). Figure 10-12 illustrates how a figure can emerge from a two-dimensional array without the contribution of any *intrinsic* contours. The only contours that are used to define the rectangle in Figure 10-12A and the triangle in 10-12B

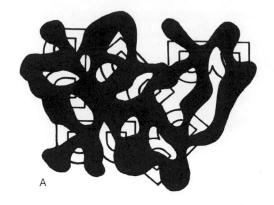

A

B

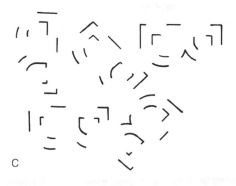

C

FIGURE 10-11 (A) Several copies of the letter *B* are lying beneath some spilled ink, but they are easy to read. (B) The same letter fragments, without the ink as an occluding object, are very difficult to read. (C) When only the *intrinsic* contours of the letters are shown, the letters are easy to read, despite the absence of any ink to act as an occluding object (based on Brown & Koch, 1991).

are *extrinsic* contours that occur when these figures occlude the shapes underneath them. The implicit depth cues derived from these contours cause us to conclude that such a figure must be present, and we then reorganize the perception of the array to perceive a figure (the white rectangle) that actually is not present (Coren, 1972).

Although many factors can contribute to the formation of subjective contours (e.g., Coren, 1991; Halpern, 1981; Ware, 1981), the presence of depth cues seems to provide a powerful impetus to organize parts of the field into simple figures. This is consistent with observers' reports that the figures created by subjective contours appear to lie in front of their backgrounds, even when all other depth cues are carefully removed (Coren & Porac, 1983b). Interestingly, subjective contours act very much like real contours, in that they can mask real contours (Lehmkuhle & Fox, 1980; Weisstein, Matthews, & Berbaum, 1974), improve judgments of the position of a dot (Pomerantz, Goldberg, Golder, & Tetewsky, 1981), be used to create illusion figures that distort size and direction (Coren & Harland, 1994), and cause motion aftereffects (Smith & Over, 1979). If subjective contours are moved across the retina, they can even make real stationary contours such as dots or stripes appear to move with them. This illusion has playfully been called "motion capture" by Ramachandran (1986).

Figural Grouping

Most forms or objects that we see are composed of a number of elements. We have already found that the organization of elements into perceptual objects involves an active constructive process. We can see the action of this "urge to organize" in Figure 10-13, where the many possible organizations of the elements seem to alternate in a rapid, unstable manner.

The Gestalt researchers studied the way in which elements in visual patterns tend to become organized into formlike or object-like perceptions. They listed the various principles that they discovered in the form of what are now called the *Gestalt Laws of Perceptual Organization.* These "laws" help to explain the way in which we organize sounds as well as visual forms, as you will see in Chapter 12 when we discuss the perception of speech and

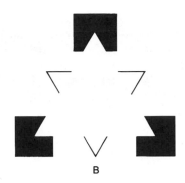

A   B

FIGURE 10-12   The white rectangle across the word *STOP* in *A* and the white triangle in *B* are bounded by subjective contours. They actually do not exist in the stimulus. (From Coren, 1972. Copyright 1972 by the American Psychological Association. Reprinted by permission.)

music. To illustrate these principles of organization we can start with the dots shown in Figure 10-14A, which are equally spaced in the horizontal and vertical directions. These dots can be seen as being organized in rows or columns or even as lying along diagonal paths. Much like the vase and faces we discussed earlier in Figure 10-10 or the unstable pattern in 10-13, if these dots are viewed for an extended period of time, the organization will be seen to change spontaneously. Some patterns, such as rows and columns, seem to be preferred, with diagonal organizations reported less frequently (Kubovy & Wagemans, 1995). However, if the vertical distance between dots is reduced relative to the horizontal distance, as in Figure 10-14B, the column organization will begin to dominate. This is an example of the **Law of Proximity**, which states that elements close to one another tend to be perceived as a unit or figure. That is also the principle that is working to make the *S* in Figure 10-7B more easily seen than in 10-7A.

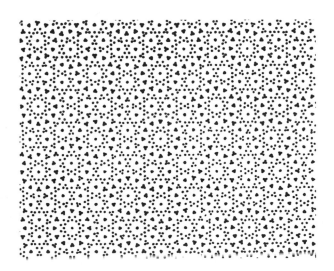

FIGURE 10-13   A stimulus revealing the "urge to organize." There are many possible organizations of the various small elements, and the visual pattern you see is continually changing as you shift from one organization to another.

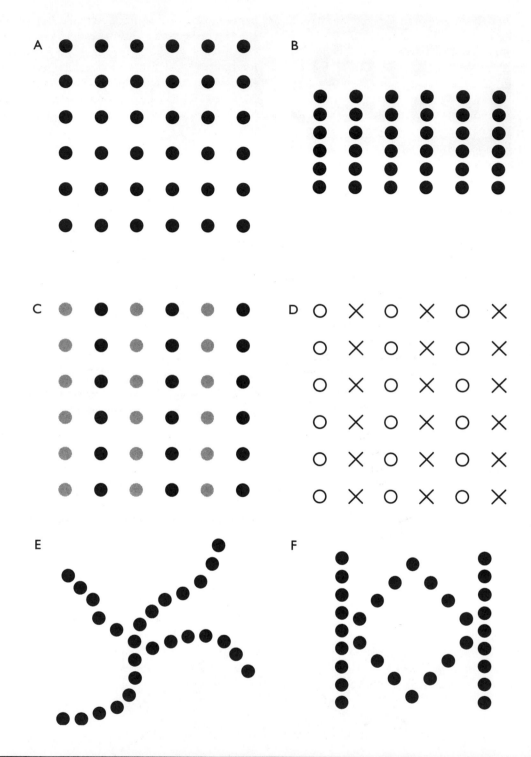

FIGURE 10-14 Examples of the Gestalt principles of figural organization: (A) ambiguous pattern that can be organized as rows, columns, or diagonals, (B) grouping by proximity, (C) grouping by similarity of color, (D) grouping by similarity of shape, (E) good continuation, (F) closure.

If we change the brightness, color, or shape of some of the elements, we can see in operation the **Law of Similarity,** which maintains that similar objects tend to be grouped together. For example, in Figure 10-14C the elements in every other column have been colored gray rather than black. The result is an organization of the square matrix into stripes based on alternating values of element brightness. Figure 10-14D illustrates the same principle, but this time grouping by similarity is based on similarities in shape rather than brightness.

Observers who are asked to describe Figure 10-14E usually say they see two intersecting wavy lines of dots. This is an example of the **Law of Good Continuation,** which states that elements that appear to follow in the same direction (as in a straight line or simple curve) tend to be grouped together. When elements are in motion, elements that move together are said to have **common fate,** which is a sort of variant of good continuation that states that elements that move together tend to be grouped together. This is sometimes referred to as the **Law of Common Motion.** You will see an example of how this can result in perceptual organization into moving objects later in Demonstration Box 14-1.

Figure 10-14F is an example of the **Law of Closure,** which states that when a space is enclosed by a contour it tends to be perceived as a figure. In this case, most people see a diamond positioned between two vertical lines. Actually Figure 10-14F can also be seen as a letter *W* stacked on a letter *M* or a normal *K* and a mirror-image *K* facing each other, were it not for the compelling nature of closure, which in this case produces a tendency to organize the central elements into a diamond shape.

All of the Gestalt laws operate to create the most stable, consistent, and simple forms possible within a given visual array. The Gestalt psychologists called this process the **Law of Pragnanz,** which states that the organization of the visual array into perceptual objects will always be as "good" as the prevailing conditions allow. Here the meaning of *good* encompasses concepts such as *regularity, simplicity,* and *symmetry.* The Law of Pragnanz is also a way of saying that the perceptual systems work to produce a perceptual world that conveys the "essence" of the real world, that is, to assure that the information about the real world is correctly interpreted. In fact, the German word *Pragnanz* means approximately "conveying the essence of something." Because prevailing conditions are sometimes not ideal, as in line drawings or on a foggy night, the essence can be "better" than the reality. Seeing complex patterns of contours as perceptual objects makes further processing of the vast array of information in the retinal image simpler and faster (Oyama, 1986; Yantis, 1992). Demonstration Box 10-2 allows you to explore the concept of Pragnanz further.

DEMONSTRATION BOX 10-2
Pragnanz

Look at the accompanying figures for a moment and (without looking back again) draw them on a separate piece of paper. When you have finished, return to this box.

Now carefully compare the figures you drew to the actual figures. Did you pick up the fact that the "circle" is actually a tilted ellipse? That the "square" contains no right angles? That the "triangle" has two rounded corners and an open one? That the "X" is actually made up of curved lines? Look back at your reproductions. If you drew (or remembered) just a good circle, square, triangle, and X, your percepts have been "cleaned up" by the action of Pragnanz.

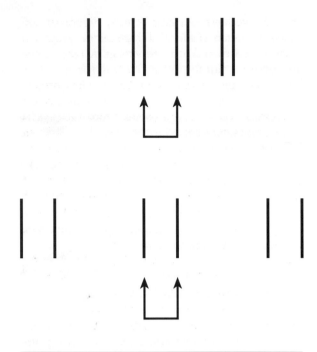

FIGURE 10-15 The perceptual distortion of the distance between elements (the distances marked by arrows are the same) by the principle of proximity.

The Gestalt principles are so powerful that they are responsible for some visual illusions. For example, distances between parts of a pattern that are organized into the same group, or figure, are underestimated relative to the same distances when the same parts belong to different groups (Coren & Girgus, 1980; Enns & Girgus, 1985). Figure 10-15 illustrates these effects. The figure shows two different groupings formed by operation of the Law of Proximity. The distance between the two lines pointed to by the arrows in each part is identical, yet that distance seems larger in the upper part, where the lines are parts of two different groups. Such distortions support and enhance the operation of the Gestalt laws to form perceptual objects from discrete parts of the visual array.

The Gestalt principles also interact in important ways with other aspects of form and space perception. For instance, by studying the perception of arrays of dots such as are shown in Figure 10-16, some researchers have found that both retinal proximity and perceived proximity are

important determinants of the way in which the dots are perceptually grouped (Rock & Brosgole, 1964). If observers see the dots in Figure 10-16 as being attached to a flat surface such as the page, then grouping is influenced primarily by the proximity between dots as measured in the retinal image. On the other hand, if observers perceive the dots as being attached to a surface that is receding away from the observers on the right-hand side, then the apparent proximity between the dots on the perceived surface determines whether row or column organization is seen. Related experiments examining the Law of Proximity and the perceptual completion of partially occluding objects (Palmer, Neff, & Beck, 1996) and the Law of Similarity and perceived lightness (Rock, Nijhawan, Palmer, & Tudor, 1992) have shown that figural grouping often depends on the apparent or perceived proximity, similarity, and continuation. This suggests that the principles of grouping do not operate in isolation from other perceptual mechanisms, such as depth perception (Chapter 9) or shape and color constancy (Chapter 11), but instead both influence and are influenced by these mechanisms.

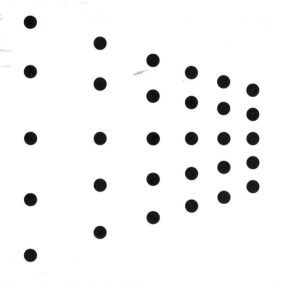

FIGURE 10-16 Grouping into rows or columns depends on the perception of surface depth. If the surface is seen as receding in depth, then the apparent proximity rather than the retinal proximity between dots determines grouping.

Texture Segregation

Shapes and figures can be formed by changes in the stimulus pattern other than intensity or wavelength. For instance, object boundaries may be defined by regions of the retinal image that differ only in **visual texture**. Visual textures are collections of tiny contour elements or shapes that do not differ in average brightness or color. For example, in Figure 10-17 you will see three regions defined by different textures—one a texture of Ls, the second a texture of Ts, and the third a texture of tilted Ts. Notice that there is apparently a boundary, or contour, on either side of the central region populated by upright Ts. These contours are a form of subjective contour because they are not actually present in the stimulation and are generally referred to as **textural contours.**

The ease with which you can make out shapes defined only by textural contours depends on the nature of the textural elements. It has often been suggested that the segregation of parts of the field on the basis of textural elements is really an example of grouping by similarity, which we discussed earlier. From this perspective, the element properties that permit effortless texture segregation can be taken to be those properties that are analyzed automatically by the visual system. Good examples of both weak and strong texture properties are shown in Figure 10-17. Although people judge a T shape in isolation to be less similar to (and therefore more distinctive from) an L shape than to a tilted T shape, these judgments do not predict what happens when entire regions of a texture are made up of these shapes (Beck, 1966, 1982). The texture boundary between the Ls and the upright Ts is much less apparent in Figure 10-17 than the texture boundary between the upright Ts and the tilted Ts. Apparently, the orientation of element contours is a much more important aspect of their contribution to texture regions and edges than is the specific spatial relations between two contours.

Texture segregation is usually easy and automatic when there are differences in the number, density, or type of a few classes of local features that are generically called **textons** (Julesz, 1981; Julesz & Bergen, 1983). Textons include elongated *blobs* of a particular color, length, width, or orientation; line ends (called *terminators*); and blob crossings (*intersections*). For example, if you look carefully you can see a square shape that appears in the upper right central region of Figure 10-18A. It is defined by a boundary between elements that have no terminators and elements that have three terminators. Notice that all of the elements are made up of exactly the same parts or blobs: a slanted line

FIGURE 10-17 Examples of weak and strong texture boundaries.

in two different orientations and a "corner" blob in four different orientations. The local texture elements differ only in how these parts are put together. The pattern becomes easier to see after you have looked at the figure several times.

The square shape in the central region of Figure 10-18B is much more difficult to see. You will probably be able to find its boundaries only if you find two different elements somewhere and then systematically follow neighboring pairs of elements in order to find where the boundary is. The central region in this texture is composed of elements that resemble the number 10 in one of four orientations. The outer region is composed of elements that resemble the letter *S*, either regular or mirror imaged and upright or lying down. Because the *S* element and the 10 element are both composed of the identical blob parts and there are no other textons (e.g., number of terminators or intersections) to distinguish them, this texture-defined square is very difficult to detect even after many viewings of the pattern.

Although Julesz's theory seems to be a useful description of texture segregation, careful experiments have shown that it must be modified somewhat. To begin with, all textons are not equally powerful in their ability to define textural contours. For example, color differences are clearly dominant over shape differences in forming textures, and this differential salience strongly affects texture segregation (Callaghan, 1989; Callaghan, Lasaga, & Garner, 1986; Gurnsey & Browse, 1987). Certain higher level factors, such as closed versus open figures, can often act as a texton when the closed figures are very different from the background figures (Enns, 1986). The best suggestion seems to be that texture segregation is determined by the degree to which textons unique to a particular region of the visual field are salient in the context of textons in other, surrounding regions (Beck, 1982; Enns, 1986; Olson & Attneave, 1970).

Spatial Frequency Analysis

Several investigators have been quite successful in developing computational models of texture segregation that are based on contour-detecting receptive fields such as are found in the striate visual cortex (e.g., see Beck, Sutter, & Ivry, 1987; Gurnsey

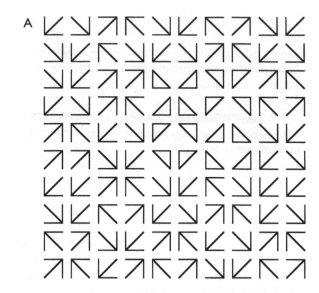

FIGURE 10-18 Texture boundaries defined by (A) a difference in the number of element terminators and closure and (B) a difference only in the presence of closure.

& Browse, 1989; Sutter, Beck, & Graham, 1989; Wilkinson, Wilson, & Ellemberg, 1997). These receptive fields are usually described mathematically as *Gabor* filters, which are templates oriented to detect patterns of particular spatial frequency and orientation (see Chapter 4).

The main idea behind the spatial frequency models is that all regions of an image are analyzed simultaneously with *Gabor* or similar filters and that texture boundaries are detected when the filters that best fit one region of an image are substantially different from the filters that best fit another region. The differences between best-fitting filters can be based either on spatial frequency (e.g., if the grain or coarseness of the texture changes from region to region), on orientation (e.g., if the predominant element orientation changes between regions), or on both spatial frequency and orientation.

One of the important discoveries made in comparing the performance of computational models with that of human observers attempting to detect texture boundaries is that human texture segregation is sensitive to the polarity of the luminance relations between elements and the background (Beck, Sutter, & Ivry, 1987; Sutter, Beck, & Graham, 1989). *Positive polarity* refers to an element's being brighter than the background; *negative polarity* refers to an element's being darker than the background. As shown in Figure 10-19A, if a texture pattern is composed of alternating bands of dark and light elements, then a change in the orientation of the bands from vertical to diagonal is readily detected, and we see two regions defined by their patterns. The orientation of receptive fields suitable for detecting the bands in the vertical region of the texture would be different from the orientation of receptive fields suitable for detecting the bands in the diagonal region.

However, a comparison of Figure 10-19A with Figure 10-19B shows that this is true only if the dark and light elements also differ in contrast polarity. In Figure 10-19A the background level of gray lies *between* the level used to draw the dark and the light elements so that the dark elements are darker than the background (negative polarity), while the light elements are lighter than the background (positive polarity). In Figure 10-19B the same values of gray been used for the dark and light elements, but the background level has been changed so that both the dark and light texture elements have the same polarity in that both are darker than the background. Now the segregation of the two regions of the pattern based on textural differences is much more ambiguous. This sensitivity to the polarity of the contrast between

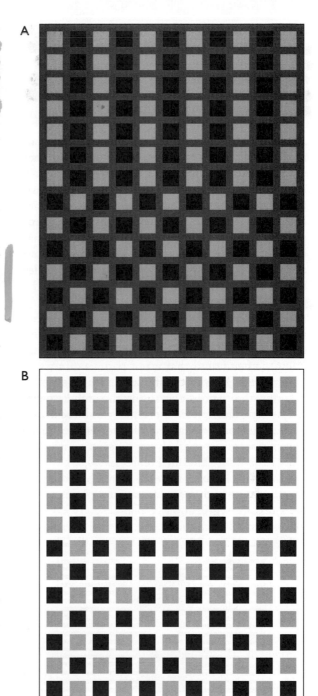

FIGURE 10-19 (A) Dark and light texture elements shown against a background of intermediate gray. (B) The same texture elements shown against a background that is lighter than both elements.

elements and backgrounds indicates that automatic texture segregation is based on some very crude comparisons (e.g., whether the contrast polarity is the same or different) and does not take full advantage of the quantitative information available in the computational models.

In the study of figure and ground, Julesz (1978) argued that texture segregation by these kinds of mechanisms is an "early warning" system that draws attention to regions requiring finer analysis. The texture boundary detection is accomplished by background processes, whereas the finer, more detailed analysis of important shapes is accomplished by figural processes. This argument has been interpreted as meaning that regions that are defined by *higher spatial frequencies* (e.g., smaller details or sharper contours) are more likely to be seen as being figures.

A demonstration of the relationship between spatial frequency analyses and the perception of figures comes from Klymenko and Weisstein (1986). They found that when regions of a visual field were defined by different spatial frequency gratings, the regions containing the higher spatial frequency grating were more likely to be seen as a figure. Regions containing the lower frequency gratings were more likely to be seen as ground. This is demonstrated in Figure 10-20, where the faces are much easier to see as figure because they are filled with high spatial frequency gratings.

FIGURE 10-20   A reversible figure-ground stimulus in which the faces are easier to see than the vase because they are filled with relatively high spatial frequency gratings (based on Klymenko & Weisstein, 1986).

There is an important implication of these results linking spatial frequency to figure perception. Higher frequency analyses are more likely to be accomplished by the parvocellular system (see Chapter 3), which also has the higher visual acuity for finer details. Thus figure perception may be more intimately associated with the parvocellular than with the low-spatial-resolution magnocellular system.

Information, Symmetry, and Good Figures

When we spoke about the Law of Pragnanz we introduced the notion of "figural goodness." Although we referred to "good" figures as being regular and symmetrical, this definition is too imprecise and limited for many situations and stimuli. For example, can we determine whether the letter *F* differs from the letter *R* in terms of figural goodness given that neither demonstrates regularity or symmetry? Several solutions to this problem have been suggested, but there still seems to be no consensus. One reasonable scheme involves defining figural goodness in terms of the amount and complexity of the information that is needed to describe a particular stimulus or perceptual organization (Hochberg & Brooks, 1960; Leeuwenburg, 1971, 1988). Hochberg and Brooks (1960) used a formula to compute figural complexity based on the total number of angles, the number of different-sized angles, and the total number of separate line segments in the image of the figure. This computation was supposed to represent the amount of information needed to identify the figure when perceived in a particular way.

To help illustrate this approach Figure 10-21 shows figures varying in image complexity from *A* (most complex) to *D* (least complex). Figures with the lowest complexity are apt to be seen as two-dimensional; thus Figure 10-21D is usually seen to be a flat puzzle made up of interlocking triangles. When figures are seen as three-dimensional it usually involves greater image complexity. Thus, although it is possible in principle to see Figure 10-21D as a three-dimensional cube (sort of a variation of Figure 10-21A, but tilted a bit), to do so would involve considering 24 angles (4 on each cube face) instead of the 18 angles (3 from each triangle) that are needed to describe the figure as flat. Generally it is the organization with the lowest figural complexity that is most likely to be actually seen, as if the visual system was biased toward doing the least amount of processing possible when viewing any stimulus.

Closely related to the Hochberg and Brooks computations is an alternative method of looking at the amount of information in a figure and its consequences for perception. This method was suggested by Attneave (1955), who tried to quantify the figural goodness of patterns using *information theory* (which we discussed in Chapter 2). To see how information theory applies to patterns, consider Figure 10-22, where we have broken up small parts of larger images into separate smaller *cells* (you can think of these as pixels). We will call the whole stimulus array a *matrix*. Notice that we can construct a variety of patterns by simply filling in cells. Suppose we asked you to guess the figure present, without actually seeing it, by simply guessing whether each cell was black or white. Because each guess deals with two alternatives, the answer to each contains one *bit* of information, as we pointed out in Chapter 2. If we filled in the

pattern randomly, in order to guess the complete pattern you would need 64 guesses (one for each cell) or 64 bits of information (one for each guess needed). If we told you that the left side was the mirror image of the right side, called a *vertically symmetrical* pattern because the mirror images are symmetrical around a vertical line, you would need to guess only 32 cells either on the right or on the left in order to guess the pattern, thus reducing the amount of information to 32 bits. Therefore, a vertically symmetrical figure, such as Figure 10-22B, contains less information than an asymmetrical figure, such as Figure 10-22A. Figure 10-22C, which is symmetrical around vertical, horizontal, and diagonal axes, contains even less information than the other two patterns (16 bits) because only one corner (16 cells) must be known before the entire pattern can be derived.

Because good figures are generally symmetrical and regular, we can now see that they also contain less information. This means that they should thus be easier to remember and easier to recognize. Studies show groupings of simple linear features—those that form closed "good" figures or symmetrical low-information patterns—are much easier to recognize than those composed of the same features in a different arrangement (Attneave, 1955; Pomerantz, Sager, & Stoever, 1977). These data seem to indicate some kind of advantage (faster or earlier) for the perception of good figures. Yodogawa (1982) has given a mathematically rigorous measure of pattern symmetry, based on information theory, that nicely predicts perceptions of pattern symmetry and pattern complexity in such situations.

Actually there appears to be a general bias in perception toward symmetry or figural goodness. Freyd and Tversky (1984) found that symmetrical forms were often matched to even more symmetrical forms. They argued that detection of overall symmetry in a form leads to the observer's assumption that it is symmetric in its details as well, which might explain the results you got when you tried Demonstration Box 10-2.

A final suggestion about goodness that has been influential was made by Garner (1962, 1974), whose definition of the amount of information in a pattern is somewhat different. It depends on the number of possible alternatives that a figure could be drawn from, much like the definition of the difficulty of recognition that we used in Chapter 2

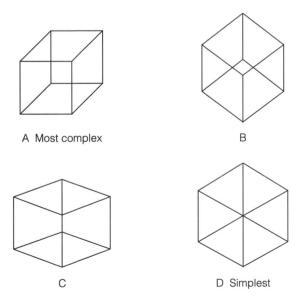

A Most complex   B

C   D Simplest

FIGURE 10-21 Various projections of a cube. The figures are more likely to be seen as two-dimensional as the viewer moves from the most complex (A) to the least complex (D).

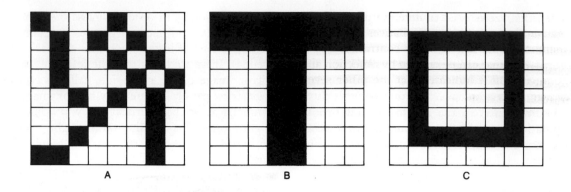

FIGURE 10-22 Examples of symmetry in patterns: (A) no symmetry, (B) symmetry around a vertical axis, (C) symmetry around both horizontal and vertical axes.

when we introduced the concept of information. Garner argued that the smaller the set of possible alternatives that can be created from a figure by rotation and reflection, the less the information and the better the figure. Figure 10-23 shows the set of alternative patterns for three different dot patterns. Clearly, Figure 10-23A is the "best" and Figure 10-23C the "worst" under this definition.

Set of all possible unique rotations and reflections

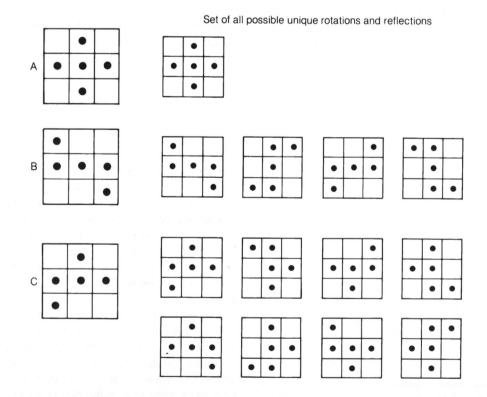

FIGURE 10-23 Relationships between figural goodness and the set of possible alternative stimuli that can be created by rotations and reflections: (A) is the "best" figure, and (C) is the "worst" (based on Handel & Garner, 1965).

Because Figure 10-23A is unique, it is the least informative about its set of alternatives (which has no members); Figure 10-23C, in contrast, is one of eight patterns that can be created by reflection and rotation. Seeing it indicates that the other seven alternatives did not appear and thus conveys three bits of information (because, as you learned in Chapter 2, the amount of information is equal to $\log_2$ of the number of stimulus alternatives). Garner and his colleagues (Garner & Clement, 1963; Handel & Garner, 1965) found that the smaller the set of possible alternatives, the more likely an observer was to rate a pattern as "good" (the observer didn't see the set of alternatives). This approach, and the others described earlier, supports the conclusion that good figures are simple and contain less information. In this sense it doesn't matter which approach we prefer: The Law of Pragnanz is the same in all of them.

OBJECT RECOGNITION AND IDENTIFICATION

Look at Figure 10-24 and study it for a minute or so. You have never seen it before because it was especially constructed to make a point. It is clearly an object, but what is it? Now look at it again. You will recognize it because you have seen it before (just a few seconds or so ago), although you still are not able to identify it (it is not a "real" object). You experience familiarity, but the object makes no sense. Now study it a little longer. Eventually you may begin to be able to classify it into some object class or other; perhaps it resembles a distorted version of a streetside hot dog vendor's cart or perhaps a child's toy. The longer you look at it, the more associations it generates, although it still doesn't have a name. If we told you that it is a "horned wheeler," the name might suggest that it is an apparatus for conveying or transporting things, although how or why still might be a puzzle.

Every day, practically every moment, we recognize and identify perceptual objects like the one in Figure 10-24, although they are seldom as novel. Actually, the ability to see a stimulus as an object is often not sufficient. Our very survival may depend on our recognizing an object as something we have seen before and on our labeling (really, categorizing) that object so that we can retrieve information

FIGURE 10-24 An object you have never seen before (based on Biederman, 1987).

about its likely behavior or the behavior we should perform in its presence. How do we go about identifying objects?

Recognition Versus Identification

The first thing we must do is make our terminology clear. In what follows, when we refer to object **recognition** we mean the experience of "perceiving something as previously known" (Mandler, 1980). Object **identification** means naming an object, correctly classifying it in some categorization scheme, knowing in what context it is usually encountered, knowing its relation to other concepts, and so on—in short, remembering something more about it than merely having seen it before. According to Mandler (1980), the experience of familiarity comes about because the more exposure we have to a perceptual object, the more we have organized the various processes that create and maintain that object out of a particular combination of critical features. The process of perception leaves memory traces, which are then experienced as familiar the next time a similar stimulus is encountered. The more times an object is encountered, the more detailed the corresponding memory trace for it can become, and the more familiar it will seem when it is next encountered.

Identification, however, clearly requires some sort of memory and retrieval process. The representation of the perceptual object created for the moment must be compared to other representations in memory, along with the connections these other representations have to other information stored in memory. Most investigators agree on this much. What they don't agree on is the composition of this representation that is compared to the memory, whether it is features of some sort or spatial frequency components or another system. Let's consider some of their suggestions.

Data- Versus Conceptually Driven Processing

All modern theories of visual object recognition and identification assume at least two major types of psychological processes. One type is referred to as **data-driven processing,** which begins with the arrival of sensory information at the receptors. This type of processing is characterized by a fixed set of rules or procedures that is applied to all incoming data. In a sense, the data themselves *drive* the processing because the rules usually concern the registration of particular patterns in the data. In terms of visual object recognition, data-driven processing would include the registration of distinctive features in the image, such as luminance differences, contours, and other attributes that distinguish one pattern from another. To some extent, figural grouping processes can also be data driven, as we saw in the case of subjective contours and the Gestalt laws. For example, our perception of Figure 10-24 was largely determined by data-driven processes in that we were able to determine its shape and the relations between its various parts without having a previously stored representation with which to compare it.

The second type of processing is called **conceptually driven processing,** and its importance is illustrated in Demonstration Box 10-3. In this type of processing, higher level *conceptual* processes—such as memories of past experiences, general organizational strategies, and expectations based on knowledge of the world and previous events or the surrounding context—guide an active search for certain patterns in the stimulus input.

An example of the role of conceptually driven processing can be seen in the initial perception of a dark thing flashing through the air on a playground. If we were in a playground in which people were playing ball, we might initially treat the stimulus as a ball someone had thrown and quickly check to make sure it wasn't heading in our direction. If instead we were in a quiet garden park, our first tendency might be to treat the stimulus as a bird flying by. This different initial perception would certainly lead to a different outcome for our behavior because we might not check the flight path of the stimulus with the same diligence in the garden park. As this example shows, both data- and conceptually driven processing must occur for perception to be complete. If only data-driven processing occurred, we would not be able to take advantage of our tremendous amount of experience with the visual world to enhance our perceptual functioning and to make it more efficient. This is especially important in poor visual environments and in situations where time to act is of the essence. If only conceptually driven processing occurred, we would see only what we expected to see and would make too many mistakes to survive.

Global Versus Local Processing

Because there is considerable evidence for physiological feature detectors, most approaches to data-driven processing emphasize the role of **local features** in object recognition and identification. Local features may be viewed as the small-scale or detailed aspects of a figure, in contrast to the overall or **global aspect** that gives the whole form its apparent shape. In Figure 10-25B we see the global shape of a letter *H* made up of small *S*s. Each small *S* is made up in turn of local features (e.g., the curved line segments), and each of these features could be subdivided into even smaller local features (such as microdots of ink) if we had a large enough magnifying glass. Thus, the terms *local* and *global* are relative; we must specify what level of detail we are referring to when we use them. You can see for yourself the importance of local features in object identification by trying Demonstration Box 10-4.

An interesting issue arises with respect to global and local levels of detail in visual forms. Navon

DEMONSTRATION BOX 10-3
Conceptually Driven Processing

The figure in this box is a drawing of an animal you have seen many times before. Do you know what it is? If not, turn the page and look at the hint given in the figure there.

In the figure on the next page, the cow's head is outlined. Now look back at the figure here. Having once "seen" the cow, you may wonder how you missed recognizing it in your first glance at this picture.

The difference between your experience during the first look at the figure and your experience during the second look (after you knew what it was a picture of) illustrates the distinction between data-driven and conceptually driven visual processing. In the first viewing, the data-driven processes extracted shapes of various sizes and with various features. You then tried to match this collection of features with objects in your long-term memory. Perhaps you thought it was an aerial photograph of the Great Lakes or some other familiar scene. In the second viewing, your memory representations of a cow influenced the way you grouped the shapes in the picture. From now on, your memory will contain a record of this picture, and you will probably be unable to look at the figure below (even weeks from now) without seeing the cow immediately.

(1977) argued that the detection of global (large-scale) aspects of a form with several levels of detail would always be faster than the detection of the more local details. This position resembles the Gestalt position in that whole forms that are grouped by Gestalt processes seem more immediately available to our consciousness than do the more local constituents that have been so grouped. Navon (1977) did several experiments to test this idea, and one in particular was provocative. In this experiment, observers were asked to name forms like those in Figures 10-25A and 10-25B at either the global level (e.g., *H*) or the local level (e.g., *H* for Figure 10-25A, *S* for Figure 10-25B) as fast as they could. In addition, sometimes the name of the form was the same as that of it constituents (Figure 10-25A), and sometimes the names at the two levels were different (Figure 10-25B). The first result was that regardless of what the stimuli were like, observers were always faster in naming the global level than the local level. Moreover, when they named the global-level form, it didn't matter whether the local

Solution to Demonstration Box 10-3

```
H       H       S       S
H       H       S       S
H       H       S       S
H       H       S       S
H H H H H H   S S S S S
H       H       S       S
H       H       S       S
H       H       S       S
H       H       S       S

    A               B


H       H       S       S

H       H       S       S

H   H   H   S   S   S

H       H       S       S

H       H       S       S

    C               D
```

FIGURE 10-25 Examples of stimuli that have two distinct levels of detail.

constituents had the same name as the global form or not; observers were equally fast. However, when naming the local constituents, observers were greatly slowed down if the global form had a differ-ent name. Based on these data, Navon argued for **global precedence,** the idea that detection of the more global aspects of a visual form is faster than detection of the more local aspects.

Although Navon (1977) did demonstrate one set of conditions under which global precedence occurred, other studies suggest that local and global features are detected simultaneously (in parallel) and at approximately equal speed (Boer & Keuss, 1982; Hughes, Layton, Baird, & Lester, 1984; Paquet & Merikle, 1984; Ward, 1983). More specif-ically, it seems that global precedence for visual forms holds only for a specific set of conditions. When the global form is made a bit harder to see—for example, by spacing out the local features, as in Figures 10-25C and 10-25D—the results are re-versed (Martin, 1979). Now the smaller letters are named more quickly, and the naming of the larger letter is slowed down when the smaller constituents have different names, as in Figure 10-25D. More-over, when low spatial frequencies are eliminated altogether the global advantage disappears (Lamb & Yund, 1996).

The *absolute* size of the figure also may be im-portant in determining whether global or local features are processed more easily. When the stim-ulus is much larger (for instance, when you hold Figure 10-25A or B close to your eyes), you will notice that now the smaller letters are much more

DEMONSTRATION BOX 10-4
The Role of Local Features in Pattern Recognition

Harmon (1973) and Harmon and Julesz (1973) have presented an interesting set of demonstrations that illustrate how local features can interfere with a more global percept. One of their demonstrations is presented in the figure shown in this box—a computer-processed block representation of a photograph. The brightness information from this scan has been locally averaged, so the brightness value in each of the squares is an average of a number of brightness samples taken in that area of the picture. This technique can be used to see if such local brightness information can elicit

the percept of the original photograph. To try this, look at the figure at normal reading distance. Do you recognize the person? Try again, viewing from 2 m this time. (It will also help if you squint your eyes.) If you follow these instructions, you should be able to identify this block portrait as a very famous historical person. If not, the name of the individual is printed upside down in the bottom right-hand corner of this page. (From Harmon & Julesz, 1973. Copyright 1973 by the American Association for the Advancement of Science. Used by permission.)

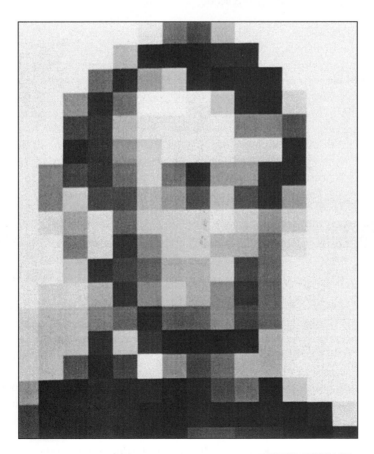

Abraham Lincoln

salient and easier to see and the larger letter is more difficult to see. In the laboratory, observers can tell which of two smaller letters is present in such a display more quickly than they can tell which of two larger letters is present when the display is larger than about 7° of visual angle. When the display is smaller than this (try holding the book at arm's length to view *A* or *B*), the larger letters are more quickly discriminated (Kinchla & Wolfe, 1979). Why is absolute size so important in determining processing priorities? Perhaps because of the fact that various feature-sensitive cells in the cortex are "tuned" for specific-sized stimuli (see Chapter 3). Thus, the visual system may be biased toward a faster reaction to groupings of local features of a particular size (Hughes et al., 1984), although what size that is may be partly determined by the range of absolute sizes in the scene (Lamb & Robertson, 1990).

All of the preceding factors are affected by how observers distribute attention to the figure. Observers are able to voluntarily direct their attention either to global or local aspects of the figure and thus give that level processing dominance (Hoffman, 1980; Kinchla, Solis-Macias, & Hoffman, 1983; Robertson, Egly, Lamb, & Kerth, 1993). If they are forced to switch attention from one level to the other, however, this tends to slow and interfere with their ability to process either level of features (Ward, 1982b, 1985). So the perception of global versus local pattern structure involves a complex interplay of data- and conceptually driven processes and possibly several independent brain mechanisms (Heinze & Münte, 1993; Lamb, Robertson, & Knight, 1990).

Context and Identification

There are many other examples of the importance of conceptually driven processing in the formation, recognition, and identification of perceptual objects. Look at Figure 10-26. Most people would see there two lines of characters, the top line being *A*, *B*, *C*, *D*, *E*, *F* and the bottom line being 10, 11, 12, 13, 14. Now look closely at the forms you saw as *B* and 13. They are identical; the same form was interpreted as a letter *B* in the context of other letters and as a number 13 in the context of other numbers. Notice that the data (the actual stimulus input) are

A, B, C, D, E, F
10, 11, 12, 13, 14

FIGURE 10-26 The effect of context on pattern recognition. The *B* and the *13* are identical figures.

identical for both the perceptual organizations representing the *B* and the *13*. Your identification of those perceptual objects, however, has been affected by conceptually driven processing based on knowledge and assumptions, mostly obtained here from the other stimuli that form the context.

Another example of the effect of context on identification comes from a study by Palmer (1975a). Palmer asked observers to identify objects presented after they had seen either an appropriate context or an inappropriate context for those objects. For example, in Figure 10-27 the loaf of bread (A) would be appropriate in the context of the kitchen counter displayed there, but the mailbox (B) would be inappropriate. Objects presented after an appropriate scene were more readily identified than were the same objects presented after an inappropriate scene. It seems that what you see immediately before the presentation of a stimulus evokes a series of expectations about objects likely to be present. When the next object seen matches these expectations, identification is easier, whereas incongruous or unexpected items become harder to identify.

Palmer (1975b) demonstrated a related idea in relation to face perception. Look at Figure 10-28. Notice that when seen as part of a face, any bump or line will suffice to depict a feature. When we take these features out of context, they do not really portray the objects very well. We actually require more of a detailed presentation (such as those in Figure 10-28C) to identify facial features unambiguously when presented in isolation. Thus, in this situation the conceptually driven contextual expectations compensate for lack of detail in the data-driven feature extraction. It should be clear by now that the final interpretation of a visual scene depends on both data-driven and conceptually driven processing.

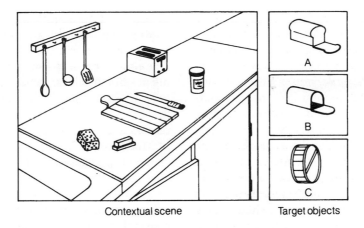

Contextual scene   Target objects

FIGURE 10-27   Context and target stimuli used by Palmer (1975a).

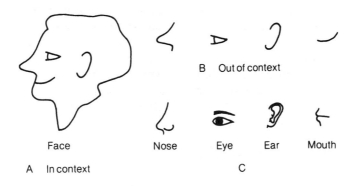

Face   Nose   Eye   Ear   Mouth

A   In context   C

B   Out of context

FIGURE 10-28   Facial components are easily recognized in context (A), but out of context they are much less identifiable (B) unless they are made more detailed (C; Palmer, 1975b). (From Norman, Rumelhart, & the LNR Research Group, 1975. Copyright 1975 by W. H. Freeman and Co. Used by permission.)

THEORIES OF OBJECT IDENTIFICATION

Many different types of theories have been offered to explain how perceptual objects are identified. We have already encountered parts of a few of them in our discussion. One recurring theme in these theories is the presumption that during the first stage of perception information in the retinal image is processed to detect contours and simple features, which are then grouped into figures and regions at a second stage, and finally compared to memories of perceptual objects at a third stage to determine the identity of the stimulus. Expectations and context play their most important role at the stage of comparing the input to memories; the match required for identification doesn't need to be as good if a particular object is expected either because of the context or because it is being searched for. The major disagreements between theories arise in specifying just what aspects of the perceptual object are used in the comparison process.

Pandemonium

One very successful theory of this type emphasizes the data-driven feature extraction processes. It was originally called **Pandemonium** because each stage in the analysis of an input pattern was originally conceived of as a group of *demons* shouting out the results of their analyses (Selfridge, 1959). Figure 10-29 shows how the theory works. In the first stage, an *image demon* passes on the contents of the retinal image to each of a set of *feature demons*. These feature demons shout when they detect "their" feature in the input pattern. These shouts are listened to by the *cognitive demons*, each of which is listening for a particular combination of shouts from feature demons. As the information is analyzed by the feature demons, the cognitive demons start "shouting" when they find a feature appropriate to their own pattern, and the more features they find, the louder they shout. A *decision demon* listens to the "pandemonium" caused by the shouting of the various cognitive demons. It chooses the cognitive demon (or pattern) that is making the most noise as the one that is most likely to be the pattern presented to the sensory system.

Pandemonium is one of many similar models that depend on data-driven analysis of simple features much like those to which cortical cells are tuned (see Chapter 3). In general, such models can account for many aspects of object identification, such as the mistakes people make when trying to identify alphabetic characters (see Ashby & Perrin, 1988; Keren & Baggen, 1981; Townsend & Ashby, 1982). Variations of the basic theory can be constructed to account for between-letter confusions that depend on minute details of the letters, such as size, type font, and the like (Friedman, 1980; Sanocki, 1987).

Model-Based Identification

A second type of theory deliberately avoids the use of any specific features, such as specific shapes or line arrangements. These theories rely instead on detailed conceptual knowledge of the objects that are expected in a scene and so are called **model based** (e.g., Brooks, 1981; Lowe, 1987). Earlier and simpler versions of these theories were often called *template theories*. Object identification occurs

by comparing the projection of the real object on the retinal image with a projection of a model that has been stored in memory (i.e., the template). The projection of the model is adjusted for viewing position until it matches the object in the scene exactly. From this information, the position and distance of the viewer from the object can be determined.

Model-based identification is therefore an example of a completely conceptually driven theory. The only objects that can be "seen" are those for which models have been stored in memory. This theory has been successfully used to design machines that can pick up single objects from a jumbled bin of objects (e.g., razor blades) using only input from a video camera as a guide to action. This success in "artificially intelligent" machines has caused vision researchers to consider it carefully. However, its complete inability to process novel objects means that, at best, it can be only part of the story for human object identification.

Identification by Components

Although Pandemonium is a successful theory, we have seen that one of its shortcomings is that the set of features used to characterize perceptual objects is really quite arbitrary. This gives the theory very little generality. For example, a theory designed to account for letter identification will have a great deal of difficulty explaining how landscape scenes are identified. Model-based theories overcome this problem by "building in" views of all possible objects that might be encountered. Of course, this causes a new problem—novel objects are not identified.

These two problems have been addressed by a recent approach based on the theory that objects can be represented by what some feel is a less arbitrary, primitive set of parts or modules (Guzman, 1971; Leeuwenburg, 1988; Marr, 1982; Pentland, 1986). According to this theory, some simple properties of visual geometry generally remain constant even though the image and the observer are moving and changing in various ways. From these properties, researchers derived a set of simple components of which perceptual objects are said to be composed (Biederman, 1987). All of the components, called **geons,** are variations of a generalized

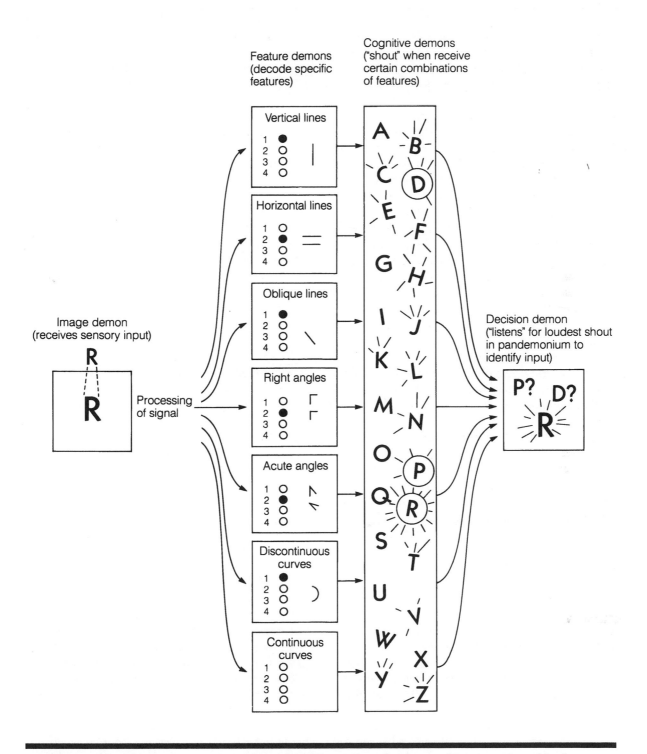

FIGURE 10-29   The Pandemonium model in action. The number of each type of feature registered by the feature demons is indicated by which circle is blackened in each box and by the number of times the feature is printed in the box.

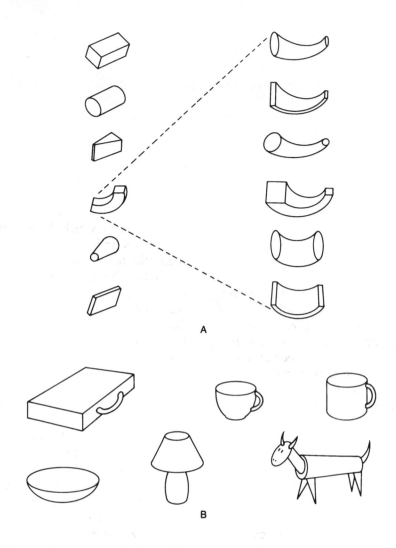

FIGURE 10-30 (A) On the left is a partial set of geons, from any one of which many variants can be created (as on the right for one of them) by varying the basic parameters. (B) Some of the objects that can be created from geons (based on Biederman, 1987).

cylinder. Figure 10-30A displays some of these geons and something of the variety of shapes that can be derived from one of them. Figure 10-30B shows how various combinations of the simple geons give rise to various perceptual objects (see also Figure 10-24). Biederman (1987) calculated that a very small set of such geons (no more than 36) could generate over 150 million 3-geon objects, ample to describe even the richness of human object perception.

Not only does this theory provide a set of primitive features (the geons) with which to describe an object, but also it accounts for some of the major phenomena of object identification. The importance of geons can be seen in that if you degrade a pattern but still permit an arrangement of as few as two or three geons to be seen, it doesn't hinder object identification (Biederman, 1987). The idea is that the description of an object in terms of its geon components is compared to other remembered geon-based descriptions. Moreover, even if you've never seen the form before, as in Figure 10-24, it can still be analyzed into its geon components and even tentatively placed into a category.

Finally, this approach also emphasizes that the Law of Pragnanz applies to the geons that make up an object and not to the whole object. We tend to see the best *geons*, which will then give rise to the best object.

Computational Theories

Most of the modern theories of object perception and identification have been influenced by the attempts of computer scientists and engineers to develop machines that can "see" and identify patterns. Pandemonium models have been used to design machines that can read the account numbers on our bank checks; model-based theories have been used to assist in the sorting and handling tasks that are needed on a manufacturing assembly line; and identification-by-components theories have been used to design robots that can roam around an office picking up empty soda cans. It did not take perception researchers long to recognize that this line of endeavor might lead to some useful insights about alternative ways in which biological organisms see forms because, at the very least, in order to program a machine to perform this function we must be very specific about the way information is selected and processed.

Probably the most influential version of this approach has been that of Marr (1982), who first analyzed the problem of creating such a "seeing machine" into three levels. These three levels should not be confused with the levels of feature extraction, grouping, and object identification that are required for object perception and that we have already discussed. Instead, these are three levels at which the problem of form perception can be studied. They are arranged hierarchically from most abstract to most concrete. However, it is important to realize that none of these levels can be reduced to another; each is essential for a complete understanding.

The first level consists of specifying the *computational theory* behind the visual task to be solved. This usually consists of an attempt to state exactly the nature of the visual problem, the information that may be available in the retinal image, and the information required to achieve the correct solution. We followed this approach at the beginning of this chapter when we discussed "the problem of visual form perception."

The second level, called *representation and algorithm*, has to do with the various ways the required information could be represented and the necessary calculations made. Often at this level several different algorithms are specified, each of which performs the same computational steps. For example, we discussed various ways to quantify the idea of good form or "Pragnanz" in the earlier section on perceptual organization.

Finally, the third level, *hardware implementation*, describes the actual construction and use of a given algorithm in some device. The device can be either a computer, for which the term *hardware* is appropriate, or a brain, in which case some researchers prefer the term *wetware* (Zucker, 1987). Although specifying the neural circuitry underlying form perception is at this point a goal that is still out of reach, we saw in the section on contour perception that some aspects can be modeled fairly accurately by lateral inhibitory connections among retinal ganglion neurons.

This *computational approach* is quite different from the behavioral approach of traditional psychology. For example, perception psychologists typically deal only with the second level (representation and algorithm) and even then usually do not use mathematical language to specify their theories (e.g., see Treisman, 1986b).

In Marr's own approach, the object identification process is broken down into several computable problems, as shown in Figure 10-31. Beginning with the retinal image (Figure 10-31A), a set of routines computes from the retinal image what Marr called a *primal sketch*. This is an abstract representation (described mathematically) of where various contours are located, along with a rough grouping of contours into shapes (blobs) that may belong together (Figure 10-31B). From the primal sketch is computed the *2½-D sketch*, which contains an abstract description of the orientation and approximate depth relationships of potential surfaces in relation to the viewer (Figure 10-31C). Finally, a *3-D model* is computed from the 2½-D sketch. This model, corresponding to what we have called the perceptual object, represents shapes and their spatial organization in terms of their relationship to each other and in terms of volumetric primitives similar to geons (Figure 10-31D). This set of descriptions constitutes the computational theory of object representation,

A

Primal Sketch
B

2 ¹/₂–D Sketch
C

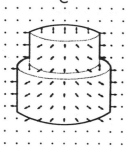

3–D Model
D

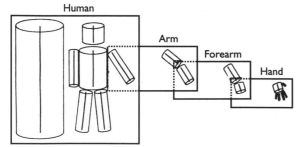

FIGURE 10-31 Object identification according to Marr's (1982) computational model. (A) The original image. (B) The primal sketch. (C) 2½-D sketch. (D) 3-D model.

although we don't provide you here with the mathematical procedures for accomplishing these computations.

Many investigators are still working both to refine the computational theory and to construct representations and algorithms that will do the computations (e.g., Horn, 1986; Pentland, 1986; Ullman, 1996). Ultimately, however, the usefulness to psychology of such approaches will depend on whether they provide us with any insights as to how the brain actually processes the visual information in a biological system, such as in humans. It is truly humbling to realize that understanding the simple act of recognizing that you are looking at a pencil, and that the pencil is not part of the desk on which it rests but, rather, is a separate object in its own right, remains a problem about which there are many theories but still no firm answer.

CHAPTER SUMMARY

The **retinal image** of any particular **visual field** is determined by the nature of available **light sources, surface orientations** and **reflectances,** and the observer's **viewing position.** First the visual system divides the visual field into **shapes,** each of which is bounded by **contours** and defined by a set of **features.** In the absence of visible contours, as in a **Ganzfeld,** conscious perception ceases. Certain retinal mechanisms interact to facilitate or interfere with the perception of contours via **spatial summation, lateral inhibition,** and **crowding** or **simultaneous masking.** These may also produce certain illusions, such as in the **Hermann grid.** In certain computational perception theories, the first step in form perception involves the edge detection and the creation of a **contour map.** Other theories suggest that the first step is the isolation of *Fourier components* based on a spatial frequency analysis. Next the visual field is organized according to **relevant features, emergent features,** and relationships into **Gestalts.** Basic features are studied using experiments involving **visual search** and **texture segregation.** The initial step in analyzing the visual scene involves isolating **perceptual objects** and segregating the field into **figures** and **ground.** This is a psychological process that can be affected by the relative size and brightness of regions of the field, the presence of **intrinsic** and **extrinsic contours,** and the presence of certain implicit cues that may even lead to the illusory perception of **subjective contours.** Next the Gestalt **Laws of Proximity, Similarity, Good Continuation,** and **Common Motion** come into play to organize the visual field. The **Law of Pragnanz** suggests that the final perceptual organization will be as "good" (defined as regular, simple, and symmetrical) as the conditions allow. According to information theory, good figures contain less information, which would explain why regular and symmetrical figures and patterns are much easier to **recognize, identify,** and process. The perception of **textural contours** suggests that certain complex local features, known as **textons,** can affect figural organization, and certain forms of spatial frequency analyses, or the use of Gabor filters, may also be involved.

Object **identification** can be **data driven** (which is processing based directly on the incoming stimulus properties and involves fixed, low-level, rule-based analyses) or **conceptually driven** (which is guided by higher level processes such as memories and expectations). Context effects are examples of conceptually driven processing. Analyses can also be either **global** (oriented toward the overall arrangement of elements) or **local** (oriented toward isolation of specific feature elements). Theories of object identification vary in their emphasis of these aspects. Thus, **Pandemonium** is data driven, involving a series of data-driven feature isolation and recombination steps. **Model-based** theories are more conceptually driven, as in the *identification-by-components* theory, which uses complex **geons** as the primary features. Computational theories attempt to specify processing algorithms that could be used in a "seeing machine" or computer program. For example, Marr's theory involves computation of a *primal sketch* (basic contour map), *2½-D sketch* (abstract representation of depth and orientations), and finally the *3-D model* (involving basic shapes and their organizations).

KEY TERMS

visual field
retinal image
light source
reflectance
surface orientation
viewing position
shapes
contours
features
Ganzfeld
Hermann grid
spatial summation
lateral inhibition
crowding
simultaneous masking
flanker effects
contour map
relevant features
visual search
texture segregation
emergent features
perceptual objects
Gestalt
figure
ground
intrinsic contours

extrinsic contours
subjective contours
illusory contours
Law of Proximity
Law of Similarity
Law of Good
  Continuation
common fate
Law of Common
  Motion
Law of Closure
Law of Pragnanz
visual texture
textural contours
textons
recognition
identification
data-driven processing
conceptually driven
  processing
local features
global aspect
global precedence
Pandemonium
model based
geons

The Constancies

When we look around the world, our perception is of objects and surfaces. Each of these has a relatively enduring set of properties, such as size, shape, and color. Now consider a very simple problem. Suppose that you are presented with two rectangles made of cardboard and asked to say which one is larger. If the difference in their physical size is not too small, you would probably have little trouble giving the correct answer. Now consider a second problem. How did you reach your conclusion? Many people would probably give an answer like this: "The larger rectangle produces a larger image in my eye." However, this answer would be quite wrong, as can be seen from Figure 11-1. There we have three different rectangles; the image of each is the same size on your retina, yet each is a representation of a different-sized cardboard rectangle "out there" in the "real world." The smallest of these pictured objects would be only a few centimeters on each side "out there," whereas the largest would be over a meter in width and length.

To paraphrase Albert Einstein, "We like to keep things simple, but not too simple." Up to now we have been treating perception in a fairly simple fashion, in that we have adopted the general position that for every distinct kind of perceptual experience—color, brightness, distance, size, and the like—there is some unique stimulus or type of stimulus information that affects our sense organs.

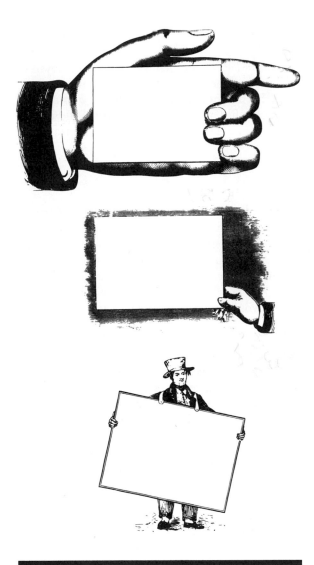

FIGURE 11-1 Three rectangles whose retinal images all are the same size, although each appears to be different in size than the others.

Although we may not fully understand what that stimulus is, we believe that we could potentially discover it. We also have been assuming that our perception is related directly to the stimulus information that reaches us, with, perhaps, room for some minor adjustments caused by interactions with or limitations imposed by the nature of our sensory receptors or the neural processes used to encode the information they receive. However, this assumption that a given perceptual dimension (such as the apparent size of the object we are looking at) is related uniquely to a corresponding identifiable stimulus dimension (such as the size of a retinal image) is too simple.

THE TASK OF PERCEPTION

Before we go any further in our discussion, we must make some distinctions. To begin with, stimuli can be divided into two general classes: A **distal stimulus** is an actual object or event "out there" in the world; a **proximal stimulus** is the information that our sensory receptors receive about that object or event. For example, a tree falling in the forest would be a distal stimulus, whereas the sound of its fall at our ears and the changing light reflected from it to our eyes would be proximal stimuli. The task of perception is to characterize accurately the distal stimulus because that corresponds to an actual object or event in the real world (Brunswick, 1956; Coren, 1984). The problems associated with doing this come from the fact that the proximal stimulus is, by itself, not always an ideal source of information about the distal stimulus, as we saw when we judged the size of the real-world objects depicted in Figure 11-1. Other factors, such as the **context** in which the distal stimulus occurs, must be taken into account. In this sense, our perception of objects may be viewed as being a form of **multidimensional interaction** (Uttal, 1981).

There is some controversy about the nature of the multidimensional interactions that allow us to perceive the properties of objects. One theory, known as **direct perception,** is identified with the work of J. J. Gibson (1979). This theory has an implicit evolutionary background in that it contends that the importance of any object rests in how an animal may respond to it. These response opportunities are called **affordances** (because the object *affords* certain types of action). These affordances depend on the actual size and shape of the object in the real world. According to direct perception theory, there is enough information in the proximal stimulus to derive these affordances. The trick is to isolate stimulus **invariants,** which are features of the stimulus that are always good predictors of the nature of the object. These stimulus invariants may actually be higher level features of the stimulus, such as the comparison of the size of the image of the object to the sizes of images of other objects that form its visual context (Bruce & Green, 1985; Gibson, 1979; Michaels & Carello, 1981). Presumably, if we are considering any aspect of our perception of an object, such as its size, all we need to do is look carefully enough, and we should be able to isolate a set of *purely optical* stimulus factors that determines our perception of the size of that object. The whole process is automatic and should not involve any complex computation or any inferential or cognitive processing.

An alternative viewpoint can be traced back to the works of Helmholtz (1909/1962). It has attracted many supporters (e.g., Epstein, 1973; Rock, 1983; Uttal, 1981) and presents a **constructive theory** of perception, sometimes referred to as **intelligent perception** because thinking processes, as well as perceptual processes, are involved. In constructive theories, perception arises as a form of **unconscious inference,** which is to say that information from the stimulus may be unconsciously combined with other information in an inferential or problem-solving manner to "derive" the perceived object. The nonstimulus information used in this process may come from other sensory inputs, such as feedback from eye movements; from prior experience that has given us a concept as to the usual size or shape of an object; or even from *expectations* and *guesses* as to the nature of the distal stimulus. In other words, our visual perception of an object's properties may depend on some completely nonvisual sources of information, plus some complex cognitive processes that treat the current perceptual situation as if it were a puzzle to be solved.

Somewhere in between the direct and the constructive theories of perception are the **computational theories,** which are often presented as mathematical or computer program models of perceptual processes. These agree with direct perception in that they try to explain as much of perception as possible by analyzing only the optical stimulus. They also agree with constructive theories in their assertion that the perception of objects does require some form of computation. What is unique about computational theories is their multilayered analysis of the perceptual task to be solved and their careful attention to the details of the computations that are needed (Marr, 1982). A typical computational theory would begin by answering the question "What function does a particular perceptual process play in the life of the organism?" It would then undertake an analysis of the information available in the stimulus to perform this function. Finally, the theory would list all the steps that are needed to go from the optical stimulus to the necessary perceptual experience.

PERCEPTUAL CONSTANCIES

If the only information that we had about nature was the proximal stimulus, such as the retinal image of an object, our world would be as chaotic as the *Wonderland* that Alice found at the bottom of the rabbit hole. Because the retinal image of an object is larger the closer an object is, an approaching friend would appear to grow larger as she grew nearer. A piece of white paper would appear black when viewed in the moonlight because the amount of light in the retinal image is no greater under these conditions than in the image of a piece of coal viewed in normal room light. This same piece of paper would appear to change shape continually—the retinal image changing from rectangular to trapezoidal as the paper's angle of tilt was varied—and its color would appear to be blue under fluorescent lighting and yellow under incandescent lighting. Fortunately, our perception of objects is much more *constant* than would be expected if the only information available were the proximal stimulus. Your friend remains the same size but changes her distance from you. The piece of paper remains a white rectangle, although you might sense the fact that the color or intensity of the light falling on it, or its angle of tilt relative to you, has changed. This illustrates a very basic aspect of perception, which is that *the properties of objects tend to remain constant in consciousness although our perception of the viewing conditions may change.* The fact that our perception of the world does not vary as much as fluctuations in the proximal stimulus would lead us to expect is what we mean by the *perceptual constancies.*

Although there are many varieties of perceptual constancies, they fall into three general classes. The first pertains to object properties, such as an object's size and shape; the second to certain qualities, such as the whiteness or color of surfaces; and the third to the locations of objects in space relative to the observer.

Table 11-1   The Relationships Between the Registered and Apprehended Variables in Some of the More Common Perceptual Constancies

| | REGISTERED STIMULUS (may be unconscious) | | APPREHENDED STIMULUS (conscious) | |
Constancy	Focal Stimulus	Context	Constant	Changes
Size constancy	retinal image size	distance cues	object size	object distance
Shape constancy	retinal image shape	orientation cues	object shape	object orientation
Lightness constancy	intensity of light on the retina	illumination cues	surface whiteness	apparent illumination
Color constancy	color of retinal image	illumination cues	surface colors	apparent illumination color
Position constancy	retinal location of image	sensed head or eye position	object position in space	head or eye position
Loudness constancy	intensity of sound at the ear	distance cues	loudness of sound	distance from sound
Odor constancy	amount of odorant in the nose	proprioception from sniff	intensity of smell	strength of sniff

Each constancy has two major perceptual phases. The first phase involves **registration,** the process by which the changes in the proximal stimuli are encoded for processing. There is no need for the individual to be consciously aware of this registration process. The second phase involves **apprehension,** the actual subjective experience. This is the conscious component that is available for you to describe. Normally, registration is oriented toward a **focal stimulus,** which is simply the object that you are paying attention to. In addition, you also register stimuli that are nearby or occurring at the same time; these are the **context stimuli.** During apprehension you become aware of two classes of properties: the **object properties** of the focal stimulus, which tend to remain constant, and the **situation properties,** which indicate more changeable aspects of the environment, such as your position relative to the focal object or the amount or color of the available light and which are derived from cues found in the context. The way these categories interact is shown in Table 11-1, which describes these variables for a number of constancies (cf. Coren, 1990). If all this appears a bit complicated in theory, in practice it is really quite straightforward. Let us look at some of the more common constancies to see how they work.

SIZE CONSTANCY

Before you can understand size constancy, you must understand what happens to the retinal images of objects as our distance from them varies. As the distance between the eye and the object grows larger, the size of the retinal image grows smaller. This relationship is shown in Figure 11-2. As you probably recall from Chapter 4, retinal image size is usually expressed and measured in terms of visual angle. The visual angle for S_1 (Stimulus 1) is α_1 and for S_2 is α_2. Like other angles, these are expressed in degrees, minutes, and seconds of arc. As an example, the image size of a quarter (a 25-cent piece) held at arm's length is about 2°, whereas at a distance of about 80 m the quarter would have a visual angle of 1 min of arc. At a distance of 5 km (around 3 miles) it would have the tiny retinal image size of only 1 sec of arc. Thus, as its distance from an observer increases, its retinal image size decreases.

Consider what happens as we watch someone walk down the street. Suppose we perceived size only in terms of retinal image size. If such were the case, a man who is 180 cm (about 6 ft) tall would look like a small child when he was at a reasonable distance but would appear to "grow" as he approached us. Of course, this does not happen.

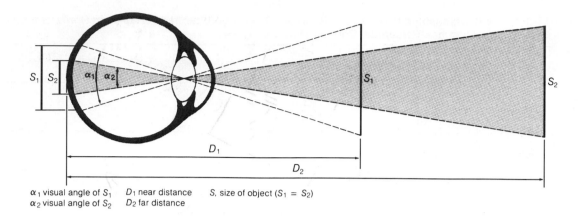

α_1 visual angle of S_1 D_1 near distance S, size of object ($S_1 = S_2$)
α_2 visual angle of S_2 D_2 far distance

FIGURE 11-2   The visual angle. Although the physical size *(S)* of the object does not change, changes in distance *(D)* will result in changes in the size of the visual angle *(α)*. Here α_1 (the image of Object S_1 close to the eye) is larger than α_2 (the image of Object S_2 farther from the eye).

Instead, we perceive him to be "man size" regardless of his distance from us. This stability of perceived size despite changes in objective distance and retinal image size is called **size constancy.** In essence, it involves assigning a constant size to an object in consciousness, no matter what its distance or retinal size may be.

Size Constancy and Distance Cues

Size constancy, as we have seen, is a process by which we "take into account" the apparent distance of an object in order to "adjust" the perceived size to more accurately represent the actual physical size of the object. For example, in Figure 11-3A, we see three men standing in a courtyard. All three appear to be about the same size, even though the retinal image size of the apparently most distant individual is only about one third that of the apparently nearest one. In other words, we estimate distance and size together and adjust our perception of size in accordance with our distance judgment, perceptually "enlarging" more distant objects. You can see how this **constancy scaling** works by looking at Figure 11-3B, where all the images of the men are exactly the same size. Here the constancy scaling correction becomes more obvious when it makes the apparently farthest man appear much larger than we would usually expect

a man to be. This demonstrates that changes in apparent distance alter our perception of apparent size. A more direct example of this process is shown in Demonstration Box 11-1.

How does the perceptual system take distance into account? The simplest answer is that we utilize cues to the distance of the target that are available as part of the visual context. This would suggest that when we increase the number of distance cues, constancy should be better, whereas reducing the number of cues should reduce the tendency toward constancy. Many experiments have demonstrated how the availability of cues in the visual array contributes to the maintenance of size constancy, beginning with the early work by Holway and Boring (1941). Simply stated, the more cues, the better the size constancy (e.g., Chevrier & Delorme, 1983). For example, Harvey and Leibowitz (1967) asked observers to choose a size match for a standard target that was placed at various distances. There were two viewing conditions. One corresponded to natural situations with many distance cues, and the second involved the removal of the surrounding context by having the observers view the standard target through a small opening that blocked the view of everything but the target to be observed. Under natural viewing conditions, size matches conformed very well to the predictions based on the efficient operation of the size constancy mechanism. This was the case

FIGURE 11-3   (A) Three men whose retinal image grows smaller as they appear to be more distant; however, because of size constancy they appear to be the same size. (B) Here, when the images remain the same size, the apparently more distant man appears to be larger.

for all the observer-target distances used in this experiment. However, when the context was removed, size matches conformed to constancy predictions only at viewing distances up to about 120 cm (about 4 ft). After that, size matches began to deviate from the predictions based on size constancy. This experiment shows that depth cues are needed to maintain size constancy and our accurate perception of the size of objects around us.

Why was there still constancy at the closer distances even though the depth cues were removed? Probably because viewing through a small hole removes only the *visible* distance cues. As we discussed in Chapters 3 and 10, when we fixate objects at different distances, the lenses of the eyes change shape to accommodate for changes in fixation distance. Simultaneously, the eyes either converge for near objects or diverge for distant objects to produce stable binocular foveal fixation. When targets are relatively close to you, information about their distance can be gotten from feedback from the accommodation and convergence actions of the eyes. This suggests that these physiological

cues to distance have been incorporated into the multidimensional mix of information resulting in the size constancy.

One important thing to notice in this example is that the source of the distance cues is not really important. The cues do not have to come from the visual array per se but, rather, can come from other sources. We can show this by demonstrating that in the absence of any other information about the distance of the target (such as the pictorial cues to distance cataloged in Chapter 10), changes in accommodation and convergence result in changes in perceived size (Roscoe, 1989). A demonstration of this is found in Leibowitz and Moore (1966). Their observers viewed a white triangle in an otherwise completely dark field. They matched the size of this stimulus by making size adjustments in a similar triangle. Accommodation and convergence were varied by inserting prisms and lenses before the eyes. This forced the observers to adjust their convergence and accommodation to closer or farther distances when viewing the target, although the retinal size remained constant. If these depth cues help to stabilize the perception of size, this

DEMONSTRATION BOX 11-1
Size Constancy and Apparent Distance

An easy way to demonstrate how apparent distance affects apparent size requires that you carefully fixate the point marked *X* in the accompanying white square while holding the book under a strong light. After a minute or so, you will form an afterimage (see Chapter 5) of the square. If you now transfer your gaze to a blank piece of paper on your desk, you will see a ghostly dark square floating there. This is the afterimage, which will appear to be several centimeters long on each side. Now shift your gaze so that you are looking at a more distant, light-colored wall.

Again you will see the dark square projected against the wall, but now it will appear to be much larger in size. Because of the nature of an afterimage, its visual angle does not change. But as you project it against surfaces at varying distances from you, its apparent size changes. It appears to be larger when it is projected on a distant surface. This is an example of how size perception and distance perception interact by means of the size constancy mechanism. The quantitative expression of the relationship is often called *Emmert's Law*.

experimental manipulation should have resulted in changes in perceived size.

The prediction of these investigators was confirmed. The size of the target judged to be equal to that of the standard triangle increased as accommodation and convergence changes were manipulated to indicate increasing target distance (much as the size of the man increased with increasing apparent distance in Figure 11-3B). Hence, it seems that the state of the oculomotor (eye muscle) system, which varies with the distance of the distal stimulus, conveys information that helps to stabilize size perception. Because the perception of size seems to be linked to the perception of distance in some way, this is one way in which structures within the visual system "take distance into account" in computing the size constancy correction. We have seen that visual depth cues trigger size constancy, as do accommodation and convergence. Adding binocular disparity, the depth cue involved in stereopsis (see Chapter 10), can also strengthen size constancy, as shown in Demonstration Box 11-2.

Actually, any source of distance information can be used to obtain accurate size constancy. Removing all or most of the depth information, however, causes size constancy to break down, and, generally speaking, there is an apparent *minification*, by which distant objects now appear to be too small (Mehan, 1993).

DEMONSTRATION BOX 11-2
Additional Depth Cues Strengthen Size Constancy

Hold out both of your hands with their backs toward you. One hand should be relatively near you (about 20 cm or 8 in. should do), and the other should be out at arm's length. At first glance, both hands should appear to be about the same size. Now, remove the binocular disparity depth cue by closing one eye. Keeping your hands at these different distances and your head very steady (to prevent motion parallax as a further depth cue), move your distant hand to the side until its image appears to be just next to the near one. Now when you compare the size of the two hands it should be clear to you that the more distant one appears smaller than the near one, showing a clear weakening of size constancy. You can restore the size constancy by adding additional depth cues—open both eyes and swing your head from side to side, and your hands will again appear to be the same size.

Direct and Constructive Aspects of Size Constancy

Earlier in this chapter we contrasted the *direct* and the *constructive* theories of perception. Direct theories of perception are based on the presumption that all of the information we need for such things as constancy can be found in the proximal stimulus. Geometric regularities, such as the convergence of parallel lines with increasing distance (linear perspective) or the increasing textural density of more distant fields of elements, serve as reliable cues for distance. Such cues may be sufficient to maintain size constancy (Bruce & Green, 1985; Gibson, 1979; Michaels & Carello, 1981).

For example, we can imagine two objects of the same size sitting on a surface at different distances from the observer. As you know from Chapter 10, the fact that textured surfaces show denser gradations of coarseness as they recede into the distance is a very powerful distance cue. If two objects at different distances appear to cover the same number of texture elements (in other words, their relationship to the textured surface remains constant), they will remain perceptually the same size. This principle was first described in detail in 1604 by artist Jan de Vries and was reintroduced by Gibson (1979) within a more modern framework. In Figure 11-4 we have modified one of the drawings used by de Vries. You will notice that here we have two rectangular structures (*A* and *B*) that appear to be about the same size but that appear to vary in distance. Despite the fact that their retinal image size differs, notice that, regardless of its distance, each rectangular object is 3 texture elements long and 3 wide (here the texture elements are the square "tiles"). Notice that this relationship holds even when the viewing angle is different, as for Object *D*. Different sizes are associated with different ratios between the textures and the objects themselves. Thus, *A*, *B*, and *D* appear to be the same height (about 1 texture element), whereas *C* (whose height in the picture is actually smaller than that of *A*) appears to be a taller object because it is about 4 texture elements high. Thus, according to direct perception, the observer could extract the physical size of the objects by comparing the relative size of the objects to the size of the surrounding texture elements. It is this extracted information that results in size constancy. The size estimates based on texture density do not require elaborate computations but occur very quickly, allowing observers to rapidly search for and compare the size of objects at different distances (Aks & Enns, 1996).

Constructive theories of perception allow for sources of information other than the proximal stimulus to shape the final percept. We have already seen how feedback from the accommodative and convergence movements of the eye might serve such a function. However, more important than this type of information for constructive theories is information generated by cognitive judgments and operations or from learned factors

FIGURE 11-4 Rectangles *A*, *B*, and *D* all appear to be the same size because each covers the same number of texture elements (based on de Vries, 1604/1968).

and expectations (e.g., Epstein, 1973; Rock, 1983; Uttal, 1981). In this type of theorizing it is probably inappropriate to speak of "cues." Rather, any factor that results in a change in one aspect of perception (here the distance of the target) can bring about a change in another aspect of perception (here the size of the object), regardless of the source of that information (see Hochberg, 1974). Let us see how some nonvisual sources of information can affect our perception of size.

Our experience with the world has already provided us with much information that assists us in maintaining size constancy. For example, we learn that particular objects have typical physical sizes. This *familiar size* information can be used in the absence of any other information to judge the size of the object after it has been identified or to judge the distance of the object based on its retinal and familiar size, similar to the situation in Demonstration Box 10-1 (cf. Predebon, 1993). Simply put, we have an expectation that familiar objects,

such as playing cards or coins, have customary sizes. If we were presented with a very tiny image of a playing card, we would maintain our size constancy by seeing this as a normal-sized playing card viewed from a long distance rather than as a playing card that is much smaller than usual (cf. Gogel & DaSilva, 1987b; Higashiyama, 1985; Ono, 1969).

Our experience and expectations also explain an interesting breakdown of size constancy that occurs at very large target-observer distances. We need only to climb to the top of a tall building and note that people below appear to be tiny dolls and that cars appear to be little toys. It seems likely that the unusual viewing conditions and exceptional distances are so unfamiliar that they simply do not trigger the size constancy mechanism in this instance (Day, Stuart, & Dickinson, 1980). This is supported by the fact that the range of distances over which size constancy works is greater for adults than for children (e.g., Zeigler &

Leibowitz, 1957), presumably because adults have had more experience with a greater variety of environmental viewing conditions. Introducing anything that makes the viewing situation the least bit unusual will make processing the distance information less reliable and will, therefore, reduce size constancy. For instance, people are quite good at judging the length of lines drawn on a flat surface; however, size constancy breaks down quite a bit if the lines are presented in three dimensions and appear in random orientations relative to the observer because we have to take into account not only the distance from the observer but also the fact that various parts of the lines are at different distances from the observer (Norman, Todd, Perotti, & Tittle, 1996).

Several other considerations support some constructive theory factors in size constancy. Some evidence suggests that we do not actually have to *perceive* the distance. Simply *knowing* the distance, such as being told how far an object is from us, seems to be enough to elicit the size constancy adjustment (Pasnak, Tyer, & Allen, 1985). Furthermore, if our attention is directed elsewhere, so the full measure of cognitive processing is not available, size constancy processing begins to break down (Epstein & Broota, 1986). Demonstration Box 11-3 allows you to see how attention interacts with size constancy.

Neither direct nor constructive theories of perception seem adequate to explain all aspects of size constancy (or any constancy, for that matter). It is

---

DEMONSTRATION BOX 11-3
Attention and Size Constancy

Begin with your right hand in front of you at arm's length. Now look directly at your hand and move it toward your face and away again several times. Although the retinal image size is changing, your hand appears to be the same size because of the operation of size constancy.

Next hold the index finger of your other hand up in front of your face (at about 20 cm) as shown in the figure. Look steadily at the finger. Now, while maintaining fixation on your fingertip, bring your right hand toward and away from your face. Try not to move your eyes from your finger, but try also to pay some attention to the image of your hand as you move it closer and farther from your face. Under these conditions, where your attention is divided and pulled away from simply viewing the target, your size constancy should break down. Now the hand seems smaller when farther and larger when nearer to you, demonstrating that when attention is somewhat diverted, we are more apt to experience the proximal (retinal) stimulus changes rather than apply the constancy correction.

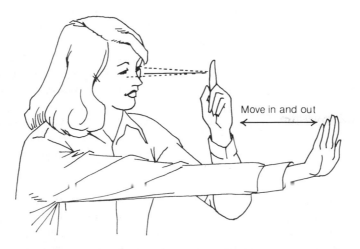

Move in and out

more likely that both processes combine to produce the final perception of size and distance (e.g., Gogel & DaSilva, 1987a).

Size Constancy and Illusion

Size constancy provides stability in our perception of the world by giving our conception of particular objects a consistent set of properties despite variations in the retinal image size. This is usually useful, but under special circumstances it can lead to errors or illusions. To see how this comes about, consider a variation of Figure 11-3: In Figure 11-5A we see two logs lying in the middle of a road. Although they have been drawn to be two different sizes on the paper, the distance cues in the context (perspective, texture, and others) indicate that the upper log is more distant. Because of size constancy we see it as being the same size as the closer log. In Figure 11-5B we have two logs that appear to be different in size, with the more distant one seemingly longer than the closer one, although they have been drawn to be exactly the same physical size on the page. Once again, this represents the operation of size constancy. To the extent that the picture mimics conditions in the real world, the upper log appears to be more distant. In the real world, it could cause the same-sized retinal image as the lower log only under conditions in which it was physically longer. Because in the picture the logs have been drawn the same size, the constancy scaling mechanism has correctly adjusted our perception.

The perceptual problem arises with Figure 11-5C, where we see two converging lines and two horizontal lines. Notice that the upper line appears to be slightly longer. Because, like the logs in Figure 11-5B, the two lines are physically equal in length, this perceptual difference is called a visual-geometric illusion, and this particular version is usually called the **Ponzo illusion**. Actually, this is an illusion only in the sense that no context for depth or distance has been drawn into the figure. It is caused by the fact that there are *registered* cues for distance here (the converging perspective lines) that are sufficiently strong to evoke the size constancy mechanism but that are not sufficiently strong to evoke the conscious *apprehension* of distance (Coren & Girgus, 1977; Gillam, 1980;

Gregory, 1966). Thus, at one level we are treating the stimuli as if they were three-dimensional, whereas we are still representing the stimuli in consciousness as a flat two-dimensional array. If this seems difficult to imagine, let us point out that in some instances there is a very fine distinction between a picture (representing a three-dimensional arrangement where constancy scaling is appropriate) and a simple array of lines that produces a visual illusion. It is possible to imagine someone with poor drawing ability producing a figure like Figure 11-5C when asked to draw Figure 11-5B, where the converging lines were really meant to be depth cues!

Cues that are registered in sufficient strength to inappropriately elicit size constancy are often quite subtle. Consider Figure 11-6, where the vertical line marked *A* appears to be shorter than the vertical line marked *B*, although they are equal in length. This distortion, which is called the **Mueller-Lyer illusion**, probably involves several different mechanisms (Coren, Porac, Aks, & Morikawa, 1988; McClellan & Bernstein, 1984), with one of the most important being size constancy (Coren & Girgus, 1978; Eijkman, Jongsma, & Vincent, 1981; Gregory, 1966; Madden & Burt, 1981; Nijhawan, 1991). For example, the wings turned toward the vertical line might mimic the perspective cues of the outside of a building (shown in *C*), whereas the wings turned away from the vertical line might mimic an interior corner of a room (shown in *D*). Because the closest point in the array is the plane of the paper, it is easy to see that if the wings imply increases or decreases in distance away from that plane, the vertical shaft in *B* is more distant than that pictured in *A*. Hence, the operation of size constancy would enlarge the apparent length of *B* relative to *A*. Notice again that this is an illusion of size only in the sense that no depth or distance was intended; therefore, the application of size constancy is inappropriate in this situation.

If we deliberately add or emphasize the depth cues to the basic Mueller-Lyer figure elements, we can get a particularly powerful illusion effect. This is shown in Figure 11-7, where the depth effects shown in Figure 11-6 are accentuated. Here the two heavy vertical lines are the same physical length but appear to be very different in length because of the action of size constancy. Conversely, if the depth cues at each end of the line are made to

FIGURE 11-5 (A) The two logs lying on the road appear to be at different distances. Therefore, their apparent size is the same despite the fact that the apparently more distant log is physically smaller (on the page) than the other one. (B) The logs are identical in size; however, the one that appears to be more distant looks larger. The application of size constancy can lead to illusions of size, as seen in (C), which is the Ponzo illusion and is similar to (B) except that the context indicating distance and depth has been greatly reduced (based on Coren & Girgus, 1978).

contradict one another, the size of the illusion is greatly reduced (Nijhawan, 1991).

Several other illusion distortions also seem to result, at least in part, from observers' responding to implied depth cues in a configuration (Coren & Girgus, 1978; Ward, Porac, Coren, & Girgus, 1977). Perhaps the most spectacular of these is the **moon illusion**, where the moon on the horizon appears to be larger than the moon when it is high in the sky, despite the fact that it is optically always

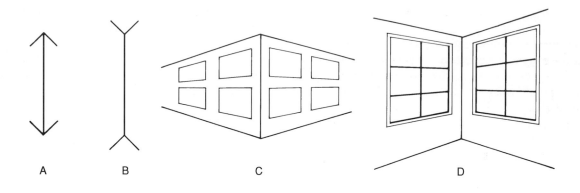

FIGURE 11-6 (A) The underestimated segment of the Mueller-Lyer illusion. (B) The overestimated segment. (C and D) The corresponding perspective configurations.

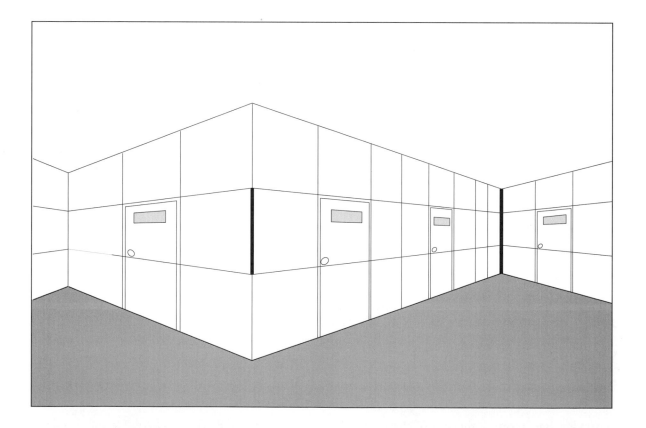

FIGURE 11-7 A version of the Mueller-Lyer illusion in which the depth relationships are accentuated. The two heavy vertical lines are identical in length.

the same-sized disk (Hershenson, 1989). One explanation of this phenomenon is based on size constancy (Kaufman & Rock, 1989). The notion is that the moon is seen as if it were on the "surface" of the sky. If the sky were registered as a uniform hemisphere, there would be no illusion. However, the sky actually is registered as a flattened bowl, with the horizon farther away than the zenith, as shown in Figure 11-8. This is because when you look toward the horizon, you have many depth cues for distance (texture gradients, familiar objects, etc.), whereas when you look up, there is only sky. This means that the moon is registered to be farther when on the horizon than when at zenith, and, hence, by the action of size constancy, its apparent size is apprehended as being larger. This is verified by the fact that the moon illusion occurs in pictures, and its strength seems to be directly related to the number and strength of depth cues in the pictures (Coren & Aks, 1990).

If the moon illusion is caused by the presence of depth cues, then weakening the strength of any depth cues present should affect the magnitude of the moon illusion. If you are athletic enough you can confirm this. Pick a time when the moon is on the horizon and looks quite large. Now, turn your back on the moon and bend over and view it through your legs. With your head and the scene upside down, the depth cues present don't look quite normal, and you will find that the moon illusion is reduced and that the moon looks smaller. Coren (1992) used a more decorous technique (at least for those of us who are overweight and/or out of shape) to accomplish the same thing. He simply turned a scene containing the moon upside down and found that the moon illusion in pictures was

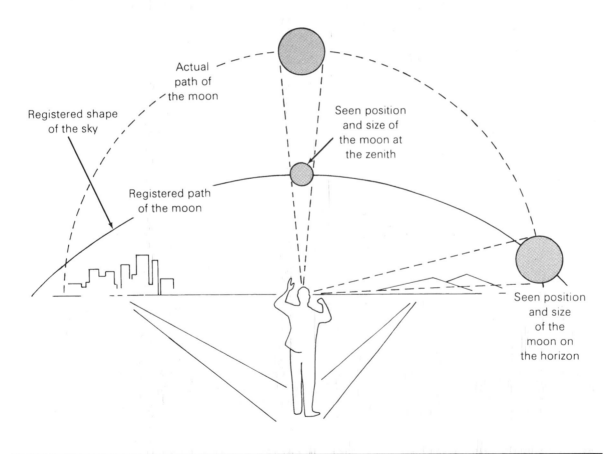

FIGURE 11-8 The fact that the moon is registered to be more distant when it is at the horizon than when it is overhead helps to explain the moon illusion.

also decreased. Again this happens because the depth cues are weakened by viewing them in an unusual orientation.

Although size constancy does not account for all the effects in the moon illusion (see Coren, 1989; Hershenson, 1989; McCready, 1986; Plug & Ross, 1994; Reed, 1989), it does appear to play a role in producing this and several other illusions of size.

SHAPE CONSTANCY

We have spent a good deal of time describing size constancy, mainly because the other constancies have much in common with it. Each involves the registration of either environmental cues or cues about our relationship to an object in the environment and the apprehension of the object properties as being constant while the environment

changes or our own relative condition changes. Thus, Epstein and Park (1964) have defined shape constancy as the relative constancy of the perceived shape of an object despite variations in its orientation. To see why such a form of constancy correction is necessary, consider what happens when you view a rectangular card from different angles, as in Figure 11-9. As we increase the tilt of the card, the retinal image becomes more like a trapezoid with the formerly vertical sides tapering outward. Yet, the object still "looks" rectangular. The same happens when we swing a door outward. The large changes in the shape of the retinal image must be compensated for in some way if the door is still to appear to be rectangular. This requires information from some other sources because the shape of the retinal image alone does not appear to be enough (cf. Rock & Linnett, 1993). In achieving shape constancy, the perceptual system appears to compensate for

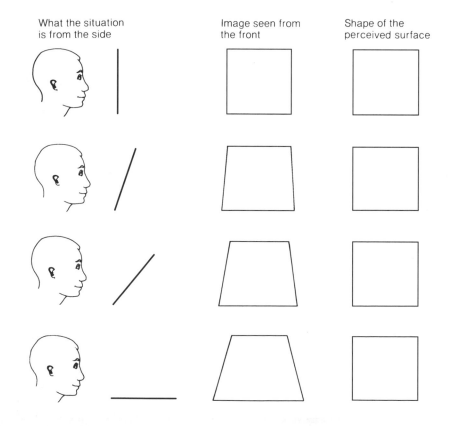

FIGURE 11-9 Shape constancy. Changes in the tilt or slant of objects will cause changes in the shape of the retinal image; however, perceived shape remains constant (based on Lindsay & Norman, 1977).

DEMONSTRATION BOX 11-4
Shape Constancy

Look at the box in the accompanying figure. Most people believe that a dime will fit inside the top of this box. Try placing a dime (flat on one face) into the box. Does it fit?

The reason that the top surface of this box appeared to be large enough to accommodate the dime is that you made a shape (and size) constancy correction. The shape constancy correction changed the appearance of the top of the box into a square; the size constancy correction made the sides of the box appear equal.

Look back at the box and notice that its real physical shape is a parallelogram, not a square.

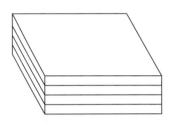

---

changes in slant in a way analogous to the compensation for distance changes in size constancy. Follow the instructions in Demonstration Box 11-4 to see the operation of shape constancy for yourself.

There is an intimate relationship between size constancy and shape constancy—both are related to distance perception. However, for shape constancy the distance information pertains to the *relative distance* of different parts of the object from the observer—in other words, to its orientation in space or its slant. The relationship between size constancy and shape constancy is shown graphically in Demonstration Box 11-5.

In unrestricted viewing, with many contextual cues available, observers tend to perceive the shape and slant of objects with remarkable accuracy (Lappin & Preble, 1975). Just as we saw in the case of size constancy, if we reduce the number of depth cues that are available or prevent observers from using contextual information that would indicate the degree of slant, the operation of shape constancy becomes less effective and the percept comes to reflect the retinal situation rather than the actual object (Leibowitz, Wilcox, & Post, 1978; Niall, 1990).

Observers use several strategies to assist in the judgment of orientation and to supplement contextual information. For example, in Figure 11-10A we have a shape (the letter *E*) that has a common or a *normative* orientation based on our experiences with it. We can use such normative

information to infer whether the shape is upright, rotated, or tilted (e.g., Braine, Plastow, & Greene, 1987; Rock, 1973). In the absence of such prior experience, we make certain presumptions about shapes. For example, we presume that the longest dimension (sometimes called the *principal axis*) represents the upright dimension (Sekuler, 1996). Thus, we are apt to consider the rectangle shown in Figure 11-10C as more tilted than that shown in Figure 11-10B (cf. Humphreys, 1984).

The apparent tilt of objects is also affected by certain other ways in which we use, or infer, aspects of apparent depth. Consider the pair of boxes shown in Figure 11-11A. Notice that the boxes are apparently drawn in three dimensions but with cues suggesting that the orientation in space is different for each of the two objects. Shift your attention to the long lines describing the edges of the sides of each box that are nearest to one another; these are the inside edges that we have indicated with arrows in Part B of the figure. Now consider the relative orientation of these lines, and you will notice that these two lines do not *appear* to be parallel to one another, despite the fact that they have been drawn with physically parallel lines. Instead, the extensions of these edges appear to diverge as they move toward the top of the drawings. To help convince yourself that this is in fact an illusion, simply turn the page upside down. If the lines were physically diverging in the normal orientation, then they now ought to appear to converge as they move up; however, these particular edges of the

---

DEMONSTRATION BOX 11-5
Size and Shape Constancy Interactions

To see how size constancy and shape constancy interact, first consider the two gray box tops in the figure below. Are they the same shape? Next look at the sides marked *A*, *B*, and *C*. Which side is the longest, and which is the shortest?

Actually (as a ruler will confirm), all three marked sides are the same length. If you trace the gray top of one box and superimpose it on the gray top of the other (you will have to rotate it 90°, of course), you will also find that the shapes of the two gray areas are exactly the same.

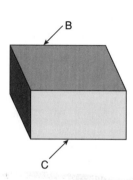

---

two boxes still appear to diverge toward the top of the page. Enns and Coren (1995) called this distortion of apparent orientation the *box alignment illusion.* These researchers were able to show that this illusion depends on our presumptions of the number and location of one aspect of depth information associated with linear perspective, namely the location of the *vanishing point*, which is the place where all of the perspective lines converge (see pages 258–259 in Chapter 9). Even though no vanishing point is drawn into these figures, we still process the perspective information present to infer its location, and this affects our perception of the shape and tilt of the objects. As you might suspect from this line of argument, superimposing such stimuli on pictures that have the vanishing points clearly represented will alter the strength of the box alignment illusion, much like manipulation of depth cues will affect most aspects of shape constancy.

The way in which we approach the task of looking at objects may also affect the degree of constancy that we obtain. For example, some researchers have systematically varied the way that observers are supposed to judge the stimuli by asking them either to report the sizes and shapes of the objects they were viewing (the **objective instruction**) or to report the sizes and shapes of their retinal images (the **projective instruction**). The objective instruction is closest to normal viewing, where the perceptual task is to derive what is "out there." The projective instruction is similar to what an artist must do in trying to translate the scene being viewed onto a canvas consisting of sizes and shapes of colored regions that will represent objects in space when viewed by an observer. It has been shown many times (e.g., Carlson, 1977; Gilinsky, 1989; Kaess, 1980) that when observers are asked to adopt the projective viewing set they show less size and shape constancy, although it appears that they cannot completely turn off the constancy correction (Lappin & Preble, 1975; Lichte & Borresen, 1967).

Other viewing factors affect the degree of constancy obtained. For instance, Epstein, Hatfield, and Muise (1977) showed that, much like any cognitive task, the more processing time that is available, the more shape constancy is found. Epstein and Lovitts (1985) showed that, much like size

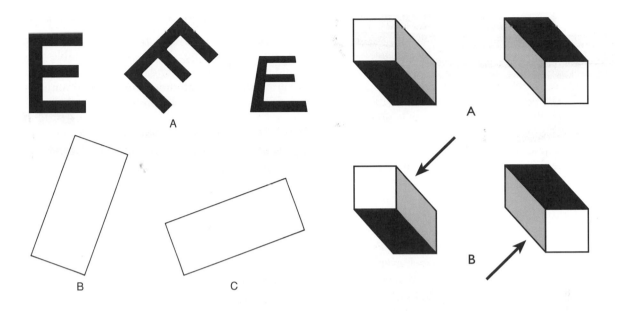

FIGURE 11-10   (A) We can tell how some shapes are tilted in space because of our familiarity with them. For less common shapes we assume that the longest axis indicates "upright"; hence, we will see (C) as more tilted than (B), although they both are tilted the same amount from the horizontal.

FIGURE 11-11   The box alignment illusion: Look at the long inside edges of the boxes in (A)—the edges to look at are highlighted with arrows in (B). Notice that these do not appear to be parallel (even though they are physically parallel) but, rather, seem to diverge toward the top of the figure. Now turn the page upside down and notice that these lines still appear to diverge toward the new top of the figure.

constancy, the more attention you pay to the task, the better the shape constancy correction.

LIGHTNESS OR WHITENESS CONSTANCY

How light or white an object appears to be is also affected by a constancy mechanism. The amount of light at different points in our retinal image coming from an object (the **retinal illuminance**) is determined by two things. The first is the amount of light from any source, such as the sun or a lightbulb, that falls on the object. This is called **external illuminance**. The second is the **reflectance** (sometimes called the *albedo*), which is the proportion of light falling on the object that is reflected to the eye of the observer. The reflectance is the object property that most closely corresponds to how light or white a surface appears. For example, a white surface will reflect

most (perhaps 80%–90%) of the light that falls on it. In contrast, a black surface will absorb a great deal of light, and the proportion reflected will be quite small (often less than 4%–5%). Roughly speaking, the amount of light reaching the eye can be obtained from the simple formula

light at eye = reflectance × external illuminance

Thus, if a surface that reflects 90% (or 0.9) of the incident light receives that light from a source with a physical intensity of 100 units, we would calculate a "light at eye" value of 90 units. Although not all of the light reaching the eye from a surface actually reaches the retina itself because some is absorbed or reflected by the cornea, lens, and the like, the proportion of the "light at eye" that does reach the retina is a constant.

Brightness refers to the apparent intensity of the light source that is illuminating a region of the visual field (e.g., a brightly lit versus a dimly lit part of a room). **Lightness,** on the other hand, refers to the apparent reflectance of a surface, with black objects reflecting little light, white objects a lot, and gray objects intermediate amounts (Jacobsen & Gilchrist, 1988). Because *lightness* actually determines the color of the object on a scale from white through black, this property is sometimes referred to as **whiteness.** Your impression of how white an object is, however, is relatively independent of the amount of light reaching your eye. A piece of white paper will differ in *brightness* depending on whether it is viewed in dim light or bright light. On the other hand, it will always appear to be the same shade of white, thus maintaining a constant *whiteness.* A piece of coal viewed in bright sunlight will still appear black even though it may be reflecting a greater amount of light to the eye than would a piece of white paper viewed in ordinary room light (i.e., 5% reflected to your eye from the 1,000 units of sunlight falling on the coal equals 50 units of light reaching the eye from the coal, which is greater than the 90% of 50 units of room light falling on the paper, which equals only 45 units of light reaching the eye from the paper). These are examples of **lightness** or **whiteness constancy.**

Two types of explanation have been given for lightness constancy. The first fits well with direct perception and computational theories because it maintains that constancy is computed or derived from stimulus relationships. Remember that the direct perception explanation of size constancy involves looking at the ratio or relationship between the size of a visual object and the texture elements around it. In lightness constancy, a similar ratio is considered, but rather than being based on size, it is the ratio or comparison between regions of illuminance on the retina.

This **ratio principle** works as follows. Consider Figure 11-12. Suppose that you are looking at a white table top with a reflectance of 80% on which is resting a gray piece of paper with a reflectance of 40%. They are illuminated by a light source of 100 units of intensity. The amount of light reaching your eye would then be 80 units from the table and 40 units from the paper. Suppose that an identical piece of paper is seen in shadow so that the intensity of the light in the shadow is only half of the original 100 units (50 units). Now the amount of light reaching your eye from the table and the

paper is 40 and 20 units, respectively. On the basis of the amount of light reaching your eye, we might now predict that the shadowed white table top would appear to be gray and similar in lightness to the gray paper viewed under the intense illumination. This, however, is not the case—the white still appears white and the gray appears gray. It is not the total retinal illumination that matters but, rather, the ratio of the intensities of the two patches of light on the retina (Wallach, 1972). In this situation, the light from the white surface is twice as intense as that from the gray surface, regardless of the intensity of the external illumination; hence, the ratio remains 2 to 1 here. Lightness constancy based on predictions from the ratio principle holds over a million-to-one range of illumination (Jacobsen & Gilchrist, 1988).

There have also been a number of elaborations of the ratio principle. One of the better known is a computational model called the **retinex theory** (Land, 1986; Land & McCann, 1971). The retinex theory provides a specific set of conditions under which the ratio principle operates and under which it does not. According to the retinex theory illuminance ratios are computed only from sharp edges where there are substantial illuminance differences. Small or gradual changes in illuminance tend to be ignored in the computations. Items separated by a wide distance in visual field can be compared by computing the illuminance ratios at all of the boundaries between them. This theory has been very successful in allowing the ratio principle to be extended to brightness constancy situations where there are gradual and complex changes in the illumination falling on a number of regions with different reflectance levels.

To explain how the ratio principle might work at a physiological level, some investigators have suggested that lateral inhibition in the retina (which we discussed in Chapter 4 as an explanation for brightness contrast) might play a role in maintaining lightness constancy (cf. Cornsweet, 1985; Gilchrist, 1988; Richards, 1977; Shapley, 1986). In this explanation, we assume that the amount of inhibition is greater the greater the intensity of retinal illumination. The idea is that greater stimulus intensity not only yields a larger neural response in the excited areas but also results in more inhibition generated by adjacent areas. Because the larger amount of inhibition would subtract from the greater excitation,

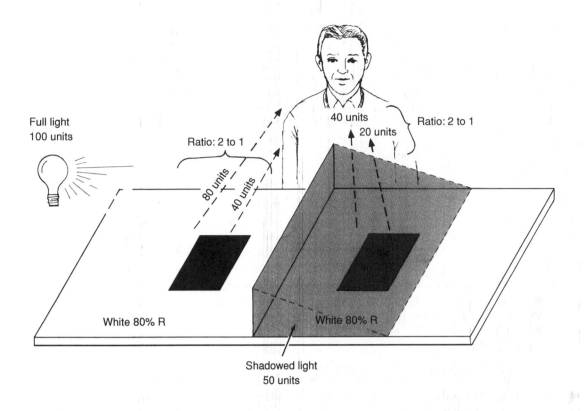

FIGURE 11-12   The ratio principle in lightness constancy. Notice that the ratio of the amount of light reaching the eye of the observer from the background and the target remains constant regardless of the amount of light falling on the two surfaces.

it could offset the larger response of the eye to more intense illumination. This would leave the overall neural response of the eye relatively the same regardless of the average intensity of the light input. If the inhibition and excitation are balanced in this way, it can be shown computationally that changes in the overall illumination will leave the difference in the neural responses to dark and light areas relatively unchanged. One way to fool the system, however, would be to alter the intensity of the background alone because this affects the nature of the neural response even though the illumination of the target area has remained the same. This means that a change in the object's relationship to its background could affect how well lightness constancy works, and this has been shown to be the case (Schirillo & Arend, 1995). Thus, according to this theoretical notion, lightness constancy is the result of neural interactions taking place at the retinal level.

One prediction made by the ratio theory is that lightness constancy should depend on having several different levels of reflectance under the same illumination in close proximity in the visual field. This prediction is confirmed in the results of a classic experiment by Gelb (1929). He used a concealed light source to illuminate an object that was placed in a dimly lit field, as shown in Figure 11-13. The illuminated object was a black disk. However, observers reported seeing a white disk in dim light rather than a very brightly lit black disk. Of course, this represents a complete failure of constancy. If constancy were operating, the observers would see the black disk as black even though it was very brightly lit. Gelb then tried a second manipulation. He placed a piece of white paper in front of the brightly lit black disk. As soon as this was done, observers reported that the disk looked black. In other words, with the addition of the reference white paper, constancy returned.

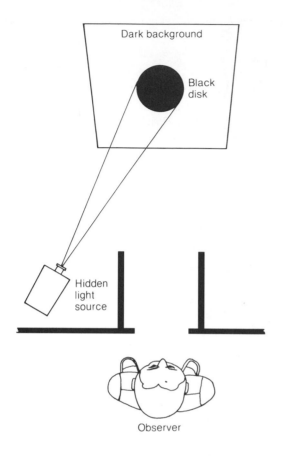

FIGURE 11-13 Experimental situation used by Gelb (1929) to test for lightness constancy when a light source was hidden from view.

However, as soon as the piece of white paper was removed, the black disk returned to its former white appearance. Although these results appear to strongly support the direct perception notion of constant intensity ratios as the basis for lightness constancy, Gilchrist & Jacobsen (1984) have shown that still other factors must play a role because we do maintain lightness constancy even in a world of one reflectance level, such as an all-white room!

A second explanation based on a constructive theory of perception would add a number of factors to the constant ratio explanation of lightness constancy. Such a theory would argue that the observer responds to cues indicating the nature of the illumination falling on the object and adjusts the lightness of the object in consciousness accordingly. Thus, in the Gelb experiment

it could be argued that the introduction of the white piece of paper provides a cue indicating that there is an intense, hidden light source. This information evokes the formerly inoperative constancy correction.

Several such cues seem to be important in triggering lightness constancy. For instance, the presence of visible shadows produces a lightness correction (Gilchrist & Jacobsen, 1984; MacLeod, 1947). Also, cues as to the location of the object relative to the light source seem to provide information to allow us to correct our perception of the whiteness or lightness of the object, despite the retinal illumination intensity (e.g., Beck, 1965; Flock & Freedberg, 1970; Hochberg & Beck, 1954). The shape of the object and the distribution of illumination over it will affect lightness constancy (Pessoa, Mingolla, & Arend, 1996), and even information about the relative spatial relationships among objects seems to contribute to this effect (Gilchrist, 1980; Mershon & Gogel, 1970). Demonstration Box 11-6 shows how our presumptions about the illumination falling on a surface can affect its lightness.

COLOR OR HUE CONSTANCY

We have seen how the perceived size, shape, and lightness of objects remain relatively constant in our consciousness regardless of changes in the retinal image. Similar to the size and intensity changes of the retinal image that are associated with different viewing conditions, the color of the retinal image may also change as a function of the spectral composition of the light falling on it. Nonetheless, within limits, we will still see a red apple as being red whether it is viewed under white light, fluorescent light that has a dominant blue hue, or incandescent light that is basically yellow. Color constancy refers to our ability to abstract a relatively constant color of an object despite variations in the color of the illumination falling on it.

Just as in lightness constancy, our perception of color is not based completely on an object's image on the retina but, rather, also depends on its relationship to surrounding stimuli (e.g., Brou, Sciancia, Linden, & Lettvin, 1986; Jenness & Shevell, 1995; Land, 1986). Color constancy is significantly better when there are many objects around to

DEMONSTRATION BOX 11-6
Lightness Constancy

To a certain extent, lightness constancy depends on assumptions that the observer makes about the nature of the world. Consider the gray tube shown here. Notice that the gray of the interior of the tube appears to be lighter than the gray of the exterior. In fact, they are the same gray. Coren and Komoda (1973) suggested that this apparent lightness difference involves a cognitive adjustment based on presumptions that we make about the environment. If the tube were real, its interior would be likely to receive less light than its exterior. In the tube pictured here, however, the same amount of light reaches the eye from both the apparent interior and the apparent exterior surfaces. This could happen only if the interior surface reflects a greater proportion of the light than reaches it; in other words, the internal surface must have a greater reflectance. This demonstration shows one way lightness constancy operates. The visual system makes presumptions about the amount of light reaching surfaces and adjusts the perceptual experience so that the apparent lightness corresponds to the assumed relative reflectances, rather than to the actual distribution of light reaching the eye.

Also notice one other interesting aspect of the tube shown here, namely that either the right- or the left-hand portion can be viewed as the interior or the exterior surface. A figure that can assume several different orientations depending on one's point of view is called a *reversible figure.* Notice how the apparent lightness difference between the two sides changes, depending on whether you see the right or the left side as the interior surface. The apparent inner surface, regardless of whether it is the right or the left, appears to be the lighter one.

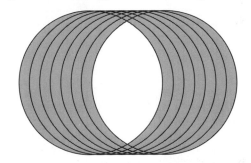

serve as comparison stimuli. You can prove this for yourself by using Demonstration Box 11-7.

There is a certain similarity in the theories used to explain lightness constancy and color constancy. For instance, the direct perception and computational approaches are represented by several very elaborate and often mathematically complex models based on comparison of color and lightness changes occurring at boundaries. These bear much in common with the kind of reasoning that led to the ratio principle and the retinex theory for lightness constancy (Brainard, Wandell, & Chichilnisky, 1993; Dannemiller, 1989; Land, 1986; Worthey & Brill, 1986). There are also constructive theories of color constancy that draw on other sources of information. For instance, cues about the nature of illumination falling on a surface would allow us to correct for color shifts. Our prior knowledge about the identity of the object being viewed can also be used to maintain constancy. Thus, a banana may appear yellow in red light, in part simply because we know that it is a banana (Jameson & Hurvich, 1989; Jin & Shevell, 1996).

In the case of color constancy, however, there are some additional physiological mechanisms that also play a role. These would help to explain why an animal as primitive as the goldfish can demonstrate color constancy (Dorr & Neumeyer, 1996). They are also consistent with the finding that damage to visual Area V4 of the cortex of monkeys does not affect color discrimination over the long run but does produce noticeably poor performance on tasks that require color constancy (Kulikowski, Walsh, McKeefry, Butler, & Carden 1994).

The major physiological mechanisms involved in color constancy are those associated with adaptation processes (Webster & Mollon, 1995). Obviously,

---

DEMONSTRATION BOX 11-7
Context and Color Constancy

The greater the number of other colors in a scene, the better your color constancy tends to be. To demonstrate this you will need Color Plate 5, a piece of dark paper (preferably black) with a small hole (around a quarter of an inch or 7 mm) punched or cut into it, a desk lamp, and a colored filter or piece of colored cellophane (for this you can use the light red acetate insert that is used with Computation Box 2-1). Turn off all of the room lights except for the desk lamp. Now place the paper over the color plate so that only the yellow of the banana is visible. The hole is obviously filled with a yellow color. Now hold the red filter in front of the desk light so that only red illumination falls on this array. Now the color of the banana seen through the hole appears to be reddish or orange in color, indicating that color constancy is not working. Now remove the dark piece of paper so that the whole scene is exposed but still illuminated with red light. In a few seconds you will begin to make out all of the colors of the fruit, and the banana will now look yellow again, despite the fact that this same color looked reddish when it was the only color visible. Thus, color constancy has been restored in the presence of a varied number of different-colored objects in the scene.

---

any changes in the color of the illumination will change the wavelength composition of the retinal image. If, for instance, we shine reddish light on an object, the surface should appear redder because of the increased activity of the red-responsive cones. However, this increased activity leads to faster *chromatic adaptation* (see Chapter 5, page 143), which is the process by which a cone's response to a particular colored stimulus is weakened with continuous exposure. The greater red response leads to more vigorous activity, which in turn leads to faster adaptation in the red cones, which then makes the object seem less red than it otherwise would, thus canceling out the effect of the colored illumination (Werner & Walraven, 1982). In effect, the added red of the illuminant is effectively subtracted by the adaptation process. Obviously, the more that you are exposed to a colored illuminant, both in terms of the time and the area filled by the light, the more adaptation there will be and the more color constancy there will be (e.g., Uchikawa, Uchikawa, & Boynton, 1989). It may take up to 15 min of exposure to the colored illuminant before full color constancy is achieved and objects appear to be the same hues that they would be if they were seen in white light (Kuriki & Uchikawa, 1996).

OTHER CONSTANCIES

There are many other constancies, some well known, some less known. For example, there is an auditory version of size constancy called **loudness constancy.** In this situation, the loudness of a sound source remains constant, even when the sound level at the ear diminishes because of movement away from the source.

There are also several other visual constancies. We encounter one class of these in Chapter 14. There we see that despite the fact that the retinal image moves we do not experience the world as moving but, rather, register this change as arising from eye movements. This phenomenon is known as **position constancy**, which is controlled by feedback of some sort from our eye and head movements combined with the actual movements of the visual image across the retina. Similar, but not the same, is **direction constancy,** in which despite our head and eye movements the egocentric direction of objects (where they lie relative to our bodies) remains constant.

Position constancy and direction constancy can be distinguished from each other in the following way. Eye movements do not change egocentric direction, but head and body movements can. For example, look at an object that is straight ahead of your body. Now shift your head to one side. Because we tend to use the head as the reference for egocentric direction (see Chapter 14), the object no longer seems to be directly straight ahead. Although the object is now perceived to lie in a different direction, its position in space is the same as it was before the head movement. Position constancy and direction constancy are related but still separable phenomena (Shebilske, 1977).

There is even a kind of **odor constancy.** When you are sniffing an object, a deep sniff will tend to pull more of the odorous molecules into your nose. We know that if we artificially give a large puff of some vapors to you, it will smell more intense than a smaller puff (e.g., Rehn, 1978). Yet, when you actually sniff something, its "smelliness" remains constant despite the strength of your sniff, hence demonstrating odor constancy (Teghtsoonian, Teghtsoonian, Berglund, & Berglund, 1978).

As we go through this list of constancies, a pattern ought to be emerging. The purpose of perception is to derive information about the nature of the external environment and the objects that inhabit it. The viewing conditions, our relationship to objects, and our own exploratory behaviors will very frequently change the pattern of the proximal stimuli at our receptor surface. The constancies, then, are complex "corrections" that take into account the ongoing conditions and allow us to extract a stable set of object properties from the continuous flow of sensory inputs at our receptors. Were it not for such constancy corrections, objects would have no permanent properties in consciousness at all. They would continually change size, shape, lightness, color, and direction with every move we make. Consciousness and sanity would be difficult to sustain in a world of such sudden changes.

CHAPTER SUMMARY

The task of perception is to reconstruct the **distal stimulus,** which is an actual object or event in the external world, from a **proximal stimulus,** which is the information that our sensory receptors receive about that object. According to **direct perception** theories, this construction comes about through **invariants** in the stimulus and action **affordances.**

Intelligent perception and **constructive theories** suggest that **unconscious inference** plays a role in deriving the distal stimulus, whereas **computational theories** fall some place between the **constructive theory** and direct theory.

Perceptual constancies refer to the fact that the properties of objects tend to remain constant in consciousness although the viewing conditions and the stimulus registered on our sensory receptors may change. Thus, **size constancy** refers to the fact that our perception of the size of an object is unchanged even though the retinal image grows smaller as the object becomes more distant. Size constancy is maintained by the presence of depth cues and may be supported by other factors, such as the ratio of the size of the target to items that form its background. The differential availability of depth cues to trigger size **constancy scaling** may produce some visual distortions, such as the **moon illusion.** Other visual illusions, such as the **Ponzo illusion,** may come about because we mistakenly treat a two-dimensional drawing as if it were a three-dimensional scene and allow size constancy scaling to be triggered by implicit registered depth cues.

Shape constancy refers to the fact that the shape of an object remains invariant despite changes in our angle of viewing. It depends on our ability to ascertain tilt or relative depth. **Lightness** or **whiteness constancy** refers to the fact that an object with a high **reflectance** under low illumination will still appear lighter than an object with lower reflectance under high illumination, even though less light may be reaching the eye from the first object. The *Gelb effect* demonstrates that lightness constancy depends somewhat on our ability to determine the amount of light falling on the region that we are viewing. Both the **ratio principle** and the **retinex theory** explain how the pattern of light and dark regions in the visual field can trigger lightness constancy mechanisms.

Color (or *hue*) **constancy** refers to the fact that the color of an object remains unchanged even when that object is viewed under a chromatically tinged illuminant. Some computational theories similar to the retinex theory and some constructive theories based on familiarity with the objects viewed and the illuminants have been used to explain color constancy; however, *chromatic adaptation* seems to also play an important role in the process.

Other constancies include **loudness constancy, position constancy, direction constancy,** and **odor constancy.** Each is characterized by the fact that the source of stimulation appears to remain constant in our perceptual apprehension, although the registered stimulation on our sensory receptors is varying with our current relationship to the stimulus source.

KEY TERMS

distal stimulus
proximal stimulus
context
multidimensional
   interaction
direct perception
affordances
invariants
constructive theory
intelligent perception
unconscious inference
computational theories
registration
apprehension
focal stimulus
context stimuli
object properties
situation properties
size constancy
constancy scaling
Ponzo illusion

Mueller-Lyer illusion
moon illusion
shape constancy
objective instruction
projective instruction
retinal illuminance
external illuminance
reflectance
brightness
lightness
whiteness
lightness or whiteness
   constancy
ratio principle
retinex theory
color constancy
loudness constancy
position constancy
direction constancy
odor constancy

Speech and Music
CHAPTER 12

MUSIC

We would probably all agree that the random pounding of a typical 3-year-old on the keys of a piano, although perhaps music to a parent's ears, does not qualify as music for the rest of us. However, if we hear a concert pianist playing a piece by Chopin, even if our tastes do not include classical music, nearly all of us would at least agree that we are listening to music. Both "performers" are using the same 88 piano keys, both are producing a series of sounds that vary in loudness, pitch, timbre, and duration, and yet one produces noise and the other music. The difference lies in the fact that our perception of music is created by the context, or relationship of each sound to those preceding and following it. A child's random pounding of the keys on the piano or your experience when presented with single sounds in a pitch judgment experiment lack those relationships that structure musical sounds. After we perceive a sequence of sounds as music, however, an entirely new set of phenomena emerges, and even the perception of individual sounds will be different (Krumhansl, 1990).

Musical Pitch Versus Acoustical Pitch

One of the most striking examples of the perceptual phenomena that differentiate musical perception from other forms of auditory perception is the difference between musical pitch and acoustic pitch. In Chapter 7 we introduced the *mel scale* for acoustic pitch. This scale was derived from experiments in which listeners were asked to adjust the frequencies of a set of pure tones so that the intervals between them were equal pitch steps. However, as described in Chapter 7, frequency intervals that give rise to equal numbers of mels do not correspond to equal intervals on our common (equal tempered) musical scale. For both the mel scale and the musical scale, sounds vary along the dimension of **height,** which is simply whether a sound appears to be of higher or lower pitch. In music, however, there are additional relationships among the notes that influence the musical pitch described by the musical pitch scale.

One important relationship for musical pitch involves the concept of the *octave*. In the common scale—*do, re, mi, fa, so, la, ti, do*—the second *do* is one octave higher than the first *do*. For any two sounds separated by an octave, the fundamental frequency (see Chapter 7) of the higher is exactly twice the frequency of the lower. Thus, middle C on a piano has a fundamental frequency of 261.6 Hz, and the C one octave higher has a fundamental frequency of 523.2 Hz. Musical notes that have the same relative position in an octave (such as two *do*s, or C notes, separated by one or more octaves) seem more similar to each other than do notes that have different relative positions in the octave (such as C and G, or *do* and *so*). The surprising aspect of this is that it means that notes that are close in frequency (such as C and D) then sound more dissimilar than notes that are farther away in frequency (such as C and C an octave higher).

The tendency for musical notes with similar positions within an octave to sound similar means that the one-dimensional mel scale (with low notes at the bottom and high notes at the top) will not suffice to describe our perception of musical pitch. This is reminiscent of the situation for color perception that we discussed in Chapter 5. Remember that to describe our perception of color we had to resort to a three-dimensional arrangement. For instance, we arranged hues (the nameable aspects of colors) in a circle that went from violet to blue, green, yellow, orange, and red and then back to violet again (with nonspectral purple falling between red and violet). Because hue of a light is independent of its brightness (meaning that we can have

bright and dim lights that are both red in hue), we represented brightness by moving up or down in space. Analogously, in music we can vary the height of a note without changing its identity. If we identify notes on the piano by numbering the octaves, the lowest note on the piano is A_1 and the highest note is A_7. These notes sound similar, even though the A_7 also sounds clearly "higher."

This additional aspect of musical pitch is called **chroma** to emphasize its similarity to hue. Thus, all *do*s have the same chroma, as do all *re*s, and so forth. More precisely, all musical notes with the same name (e.g., C or G) share the same chroma. Like hue, pitch chroma is represented by a circle. To represent both height (one-dimensional) and chroma (two-dimensional) together graphically we must use a three-dimensional scheme, much as we did for color. Such a scheme was first proposed in 1846 by Drobisch, who recommended using a helical representation, an idea that has persisted until the present (Krumhansl, 1990; Shepard, 1982). Figure 12-1 shows the musical pitch helix. The circular component of the helix represents pitch chroma, whereas the vertical component represents pitch height. One complete turn of the helix (a 360° rotation in the horizontal plane) describes a single octave. All notes with the same name fall on a vertical line connecting the helix to the same point on the chroma circle at the bottom, and all sound similar.

The typical laboratory experiment in pitch perception presents isolated pure tones that vary only in height and whose similarity is not affected by changes in chroma. However, the power of chroma is apparent in a dramatic illusion of ever-increasing pitch height produced by playing a series of specially composed sounds that move only around and around the chroma circle (Shepard, 1964; but see also Burns, 1981; Pollack, 1978). You can try this for yourself in Demonstration Box 12-1. An interesting variant of this illusion was reported by Deutsch (1986, 1987; Deutsch & Kuyper, 1987). She found a circular pattern of sounds that is heard as ascending when played in one musical key but descending when played in another, which is contrary to the experience in music that a melody sounds the same when transposed to another key.

Although the musical helix describes the major components of musical pitch, it doesn't tell the

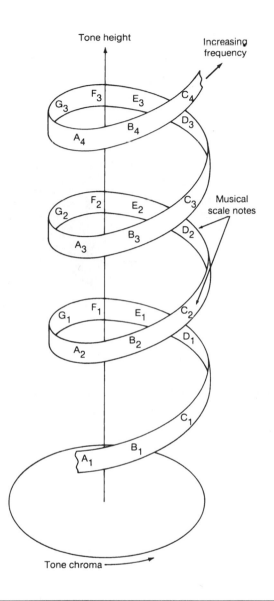

FIGURE 12-1 A regular helix represents the two aspects of musical pitch: height and chroma.

relations between musical notes and between musical keys (e.g., the key of C or F# or any particular group of notes that comprises the musical scale used for a particular melody) require a much more complicated representation, and researchers are still working on this problem (see Bregman, 1990; Krumhansl, 1990; Krumhansl & Kessler, 1982; Shepard, 1982). Such relations play an important role in music theory and seem to indicate aspects of our perceptual processing of musical stimuli.

Musical Notes and Chords

How well can people identify musical notes? In music contexts, we frequently hear of individuals who have *perfect (or absolute) pitch*. Such people, usually musicians, are able to identify a musical note that is played on an instrument even when the note is presented in complete isolation from other notes (although they do occasionally misidentify the octave where it is located because of the perceptual similarity we have already discussed). However, when these people are presented with pure sine-wave tones, they can identify the notes correctly only about half the time (Lockhead & Byrd, 1981). This is still a lot better than those without perfect pitch, who tend to be correct on only about 8% of the trials, but it is nowhere near "perfect."

Remember from Chapter 7 that the pitch of a complex sound is predominantly determined by the fundamental frequency (the lowest and usually most intense frequency component). A pure tone contains only one frequency, which is by definition the fundamental. When a note is played on a musical instrument, however, different harmonic frequencies (multiples of the fundamental) are also sounded, giving *timbre*, or complexity, to the sound. Because people with perfect pitch for musical notes do relatively poorly when identifying pure tones, they must be using more than the fundamental frequency of the musical notes to identify them. Probably they are using the higher harmonics (the same ones that allow us to determine whether a note was struck on a piano or a guitar) to aid in identification. From self-reports we know that people with perfect musical pitch judge chroma by comparing the test note with an internal (remembered) standard for each note, whereas

whole story. Even more esoteric relations between musical notes can also be important, especially for musicians and others who actively listen to music (Krumhansl & Kessler, 1982; Shepard, 1982). For example, when the frequency of one musical note is exactly 1.5 times the frequency of another, a 3-to-2 ratio, or a "perfect fifth" to a musician, the two notes seem to go together better than for any other frequency steps except the octave, which we have already indicated is special. This and other

---

DEMONSTRATION BOX 12-1
The Tonal Staircase

Shepard (1964) invented a series of complex tones generated by a computer that when listened to in sequence seemed continually to increase in pitch. That is, each step between tones was perceived as being a step upward in pitch. Shepard, however, used a trick in generating this series of sounds, and in fact the series ended where it had begun, completing a journey around the chroma circle (see Figure 12-1). The continuing rise in pitch was an illusion. It is rather difficult to produce Shepard's series of sounds without complex equipment, but it may be possible for you to hear the illusion anyway. First, fill a glass partially full of water; a crystal glass would be best, perhaps a wine glass, but any glass with a "ring" should do. Now tap the glass gently with a knife or other implement to make it ring. Continue tapping gently to produce a series of complex sounds. Each sound will be slightly different from the others in its frequency components because of variation in the way the knife strikes the glass. The series of sounds produced this way can often be heard to ascend or descend in pitch continuously, much

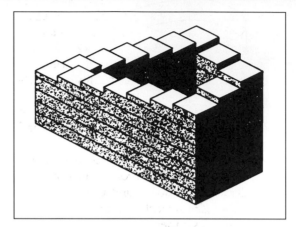

in the way Shepard's sounds did, even though the sounds are highly similar and the fundamental frequency probably does not change. In Shepard's demonstration, this illusion is quite similar to the visual staircase illusion shown here. The stairs seem to climb endlessly but never get anywhere. This is proably the most striking demonstration of the reality of the quality of pitch chroma in musical sounds.

---

people without perfect pitch seem simply to guess at chroma. Actually, the use of an internal standard can sometimes cause the performance of those with perfect pitch to be poorer than that of those without it. For example, those with perfect pitch did well identifying pitch intervals relative to a piano-like C note, a common internal standard, but poorly when the reference note was F#, out-of-tune C, or out-of-tune E. For people without perfect pitch the choice of the standard made no difference (Miyazaki, 1995). It seems that those with perfect pitch rely on it even in relative-pitch tasks, to their detriment when identifying pitch intervals relative to an unfamiliar standard. Perfect pitch does seem to arise from a specialization of the brain: The left-hemisphere auditory association cortex of musicians with perfect pitch is relatively larger than that of musicians without perfect pitch and that of nonmusicians (Schlaug & Jancke,

1995). It can be difficult to see the effects of this difference, however. For example, in a pitch memory task the evoked brain responses to musical stimuli for musicians with perfect pitch were quite different from those of nonmusicians but only marginally different from those of musicians who relied on relative pitch (Hantz & Kreilick, 1995). Musical training seems to give rise to effective pitch judgment strategies and similar brain activity regardless of the presence of absolute pitch-related specializations.

The spacing between musical notes is called a **musical interval.** In music of the Western world, scales have been arranged with logarithmic musical intervals. This is because frequency intervals that are equal on a logarithmic scale are perceived as being approximately equal intervals of musical pitch. For example, if you heard an interval generated by a pair of notes with frequencies of 200 Hz and 400 Hz and another generated by a pair with frequencies of 2,000 Hz and 4,000 Hz, they would seem to be about equally large (because log 400 – log 200 = log 4,000 – log 2,000 = 0.3). One implication of this is that any two intervals separated by the same number of intervening notes will appear to be equal. You don't have to have memorized a table of logarithms to determine if you will have equal-sounding musical intervals because subtracting logarithms is equivalent to dividing raw numbers. Thus, 400/200 = 2, as is 4,000/2,000, so equal log intervals really mean equal ratios and equal-sounding musical differences.

When three or more musical notes are played at the same time, a **chord** is created. Chords give much of the characteristic sound to what we call music (see, e.g., Krumhansl, Bharucha, & Kessler, 1982). Formal music theory provides a somewhat complicated system for naming chords, which we won't go into here. Suffice it to say that chords are also defined in terms of the ratios of the fundamental frequencies of the notes that constitute them. Chords whose respective components stand in the same frequency relationship to each other are given the same name, no matter what octave they are from. For example, an E major chord is composed of the notes E, G#, and B no matter whether the notes are three octaves up from the lowest on the piano (E_4, $G\#_4$, and B_4) or six octaves up (E_7, $G\#_7$, and B_7). This aspect of musical pitch also is consistent with the helix shown in Figure 12-1, if spacings between the notes are equal on a logarithmic scale, because the intervals between the notes remain the same regardless of height or absolute frequency.

Musical Forms

So far we have described a few of the most important local, or individual, aspects of musical sequences or combinations of notes. That is, we have described music at the level of the frequencies of the notes that make it up. Any sequence of notes also has global properties, however, that give an overall pattern to the sound sequence and are very important to its musical character. One important set of global properties, that defining the *melody* of a piece, refers to the sequence of pitch changes that occur, including the proportion and sizes of the various ascending and descending intervals. These are global properties because they are perceived in relationship to one another rather than as individual features (Cuddy, Cohen, & Mewhort, 1981; Deutsch, 1978). Together, these global cues to melody can be called the **contour** of a piece of music. The concept of musical contour closely resembles the concept of visual contour. It is the general shape of the musical sequence of sounds, defined in terms of rises and drops in frequency instead of in terms of changes in direction of an edge in the visual field. Figure 12-2 shows some examples of musical passages that have the same contour even though they are in different positions on the musical scale. Even trained musicians often fail to detect a distortion in the particular notes that make up a piece of music, provided that the contour remains intact (Krumhansl, 1990). The same subjects, on the other hand, are extremely sensitive to changes in contour. In fact, melodies can be recognized even on the basis of such global properties alone, although performance is better when the local cues are also available (Dowling, Kwak, & Andrews, 1995).

A typical piece of music consists of a rather long sequence of different notes and chords, similar to a long string of sounds uttered by a person making a speech. Just as we perceive a complicated hierarchy of words, phrases, and sentences as we listen to someone speaking, we also organize music in a hierarchical fashion (Bharucha, 1996; Palmer & Krumhansl, 1990; Serafine & Glassman, 1989). Combinations of notes form *motifs* (sometimes written as *motive* but still pronounced "*mo-teef*"), combinations of motifs form *phrases*, and so on (Deutsch, 1978).

How are these combinations formed perceptually? We have found that notes are grouped into motifs, then motifs are grouped into phrases, both according to principles that closely resemble those of visual form perception. There are unlearned and primitive processes that operate automatically to group musical notes into different "streams," and there are learned schema-based rules for organizing musical notes into motifs and phrases. The latter are based on musical conventions acquired either through formal training or just through mere exposure to recorded and live music performances (Bregman, 1990; Deliege & Melen, 1996). These learned conventions can be

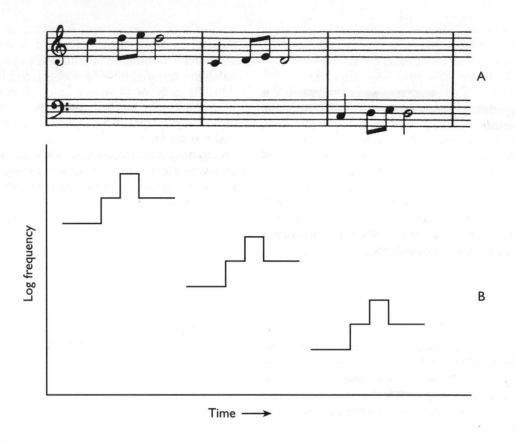

FIGURE 12-2 When a melodic sequence is transposed to different positions on the musical scale (A) it still retains the same contour (B).

so powerful that they can affect preferences for the way musical instruments are tuned (Loosen, 1994, 1995), detection of changes in melodic structure (Trainor & Trehub, 1992, 1994), and perception of musical tension (Bigand, Parncutt, & Lerdahl, 1996). Thus, we can consider the perception of music and melody as a form of auditory form perception that follows the general rules of perceptual organization.

The most general of the principles by which musical notes are grouped are the Gestalt laws that we encountered in Chapter 10 as applied to visual form. At least three of these laws operate on musical notes and chords as well (Deutsch, 1978). The first principle of musical grouping is an application of the Law of *Proximity* (see Figure 10-14B for an example from vision). By this principle, notes that are close together in musical pitch are grouped into the same musical form, whereas notes that are far

apart in musical pitch are grouped into different musical forms. Bregman (1990) created a striking example of the operation of this principle. He first played two familiar melodies to subjects, one to each ear, using a similar range of musical notes and thus a similar pitch range for each. The notes for each melody were alternated in sequence to the two ears (e.g., Note 1 of Melody 1 to the right ear followed by Note 2 of Melody 1 to the left ear, then back to the right ear for Note 3, etc., while Note 1 of Melody 2 was played to the left ear first, followed by Note 2 of Melody 2 to the right ear, and so forth). As you might expect, subjects heard only a mishmash of sound and were unable to identify the two tunes. As the two melodies were separated gradually in pitch range—one becoming progressively higher, the other progressively lower—subjects were able to identify the two familiar melodies even though they were "split" across the two ears.

Another good illustration of grouping by pitch proximity is Deutsch's (1975) *scale illusion*. This occurs when two different sequences of notes are presented, one to each ear, as illustrated in the left panel of Figure 12-3A. The vast majority of listeners hear the sound sequences represented in the right panel of Figure 12-3A, in which all of the higher pitched notes are grouped into an "arc" that falls and then rises, whereas all of the lower pitched notes form an arc that first rises and then falls in pitch. Notice that in this perceptual organization, half of the notes are heard by the opposite ear in which they actually occur. This is a very powerful effect of a musical grouping principle, which must be heard to be believed (see Deutsch, 1995).

This auditory grouping based on pitch proximity is implicitly taken into account by musicians. Whenever the same instrument plays both a melody and an accompaniment, they are played in different frequency ranges so that the melody will be the *figure* (the part that stands out perceptually), and the accompaniment will be the *ground* (or background against which the melody is imaged). An example is in folk-guitar playing, where the performer often keeps a steady accompaniment going on the bass strings of the guitar while playing a melody on the treble strings. Composers have also used this principle to create illusions in music, for example, the segments from works of Tchaikovsky and Rachmaninov in Figures 12-3B

FIGURE 12-3 Three examples of the Deutsch illusion. In all cases, the left part of the figure shows what is played, and the right shows what is usually heard. (A) The original, from Deutsch, 1975. (B) From Tchaikovsky, Sixth Symphony, last movement. (C) From Rachmaninov, Suite for Two Pianos, Opus 17, second movement.

and 12-3C. In Figure 12-3B, two violin sections play the phrases of music transcribed on the left, but the audience hears the notes as if the phrases illustrated on the right were being played. A similar phenomenon occurs for the music in Figure 12-3C in which the parts are played by two pianos.

A second principle of musical grouping is an application of the Gestalt Law of *Similarity* (see Figure 10-14C or D for a visual example). Different types of musical instruments play the same notes with different timbres, which gives them their characteristic sounds and allows us to identify which instrument is playing any given note (see Chapter 7). When several instruments are playing simultaneously, the listener tends to group those of similar timbre into the same stream. In symphonic music, this principle is used to separate phrases that have a similar fundamental frequency range but a different musical message. Also, timbre provides an additional principle of grouping to that of pitch range when different instruments play different parts of a piece (as in the lead and rhythm guitar parts of a piece of modern rock music).

The third musical grouping principle is an application of the Gestalt Law of *Good Continuation* (see Figure 10-14E for a visual example). Sequences of pitch changes in the same direction (for example, successive notes of ever-increasing pitch) tend to be perceived as part of the same sequence, whereas changes in direction of change (for example, three notes of ever-increasing pitch followed by three notes of ever-decreasing pitch) tend to act as boundaries between segments (Deutsch & Feroe, 1981). Interestingly, a good-continuation-based pattern was never reported by subjects in Deutsch's (1975) experiment on the scale illusion, although it is a reasonable one to expect from that stimulus. Good continuation would create a pair of interlocking scales of the notes displayed in Figure 12-3A, one rising and one falling, as shown in Figure 12-4B. This pattern is perceived by nearly every listener when the scales are actually presented to separate ears, so proximity doesn't dominate when laterality and good continuation are arrayed against it (Radvansky, Hartmann, & Rakerd, 1992). However, the good-continuation pattern is heard by about 40% of listeners when single notes are added or subtracted from the original Deutsch sequences, as has been done in Figure 12-4A (Radvansky et al., 1992). Apparently such sequences are

ambiguous musical figures that have competing organizations (Smith, Hausfeld, Power, & Gorta, 1982), analogous to Figure 10-3 for vision. In some cases one organization dominates, but small alterations in the musical figure can dramatically affect which organization is heard.

If you would like to hear these effects, you might try to obtain Dowling and Harwood's (1986) book, which includes taped demonstrations of the scale illusion and other musical phenomena. More recently Deutsch (1995) has issued a CD that also contains examples of the scale illusion and many similar musical illusions and paradoxes.

So far we have concentrated on variations in the frequency of musical notes or combinations of notes, neglecting the other major dimension of musical sounds: their duration. You probably learned in grade school that written sequences of musical notes indicate not only the height (frequency) of each note but also the duration of each note. A whole note is held for one duration unit, a half note is held for one half the duration of a whole note, a quarter note for one quarter the whole-note duration, and so forth. Both the duration and height of notes are vital in determining our perception of melody. You can clearly see this in Figure 12-5, which presents three musical excerpts. All have the same contour. They differ only

FIGURE 12-4 (A) A stimulus configuration that gives rise to a percept resembling that in (B). (B) A possible but unheard percept of the original Deutsch illusion shown in Figure 12-3A.

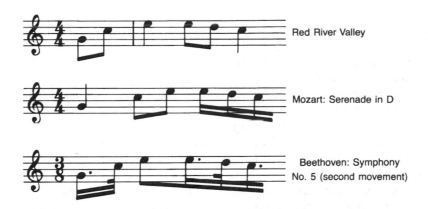

FIGURE 12-5   Three musical phrases in which the melodic sequence of tone height is the same, and the tones differ only in duration.

in the duration for which the notes are held, but this causes a tremendous difference in the melody we perceive. The first excerpt is the beginning of the familiar American folk song "Red River Valley," the second is the opening of Mozart's Serenade in D, and the third is the beginning of the second movement of Beethoven's Symphony No. 5. If you play a musical instrument or sing you may want to try performing these phrases for yourself, just to hear how different they sound. Or you could obtain the three passages on recorded media and compare them on your stereo.

A sequence of sounds of various durations possesses **rhythm** and **tempo**. Tempo is the perceived speed associated with the presentation of the sounds, and rhythm is the perceived organization in time. When listeners are presented with a sequence of sounds, they spontaneously organize it into subsequences consisting of an accented sound followed by at least one, and sometimes several, unaccented sounds (Bolton, 1894). This is why the ticking of a clock seems to go "*tick*, tock, *tick*, tock," despite the fact that every ticking sound emitted by the clock is identical. This spontaneous organization happens when the sounds are presented at rates between 10 per second and 1 every 2 seconds and seems to occur most strongly at rates of 2 to 3 sounds per second. Under some circumstances the percept may vary in the degree of accenting of sounds, so a fairly complex rhythmic structure is perceived despite a physical stimulus that is

absolutely regular. In the perception of music, these induced rhythms are superimposed on the deliberately manipulated rhythmic structure of the music according to principles of grouping similar to the Gestalt-like principles mentioned earlier. The overall rhythmic organization of the music interacts with the organization induced by the variations in pitch of the musical notes, making it easier to perceive the melodic structure of the music (Bigand, 1997; Deutsch, 1978; Handel & Oshinsky, 1981; Palmer & Krumhansl, 1987). This overall temporal structure can be so compelling that people can, from hearing a recording of a popular song many times, sing it from memory—long after their last hearing of it—at just about the tempo at which it was performed on the recording (Levitin & Cook, 1996). Demonstration Box 12-2 shows how sounds may be rhythmically grouped together by variations in timing and also by differences in the timbre of the notes.

To follow the analogy of vision once again, not all perceptual grouping is based on automatic, and perhaps unlearned, organizational principles. There is good evidence that music listeners rely on their experience to "fill in" aspects of the melody and to impose structure on the musical stream. One study showed that musical "filling in" was influenced by several levels of structure, including expectations based on musical key structure, predictions based on Western music styles, and familiarity with specific melodies (DeWitt & Samuel, 1990).

DEMONSTRATION BOX 12-2
Rhythmic Grouping

In this demonstration you will produce a series of tapping sounds as stimuli. In order to indicate how your taps should be distributed in time, let us establish a sort of rhythmic notation. Whenever we present a *V* it indicates a tap, whereas a hyphen indicates a brief pause. First, tap this simple sequence: *VV-V.* Listen carefully, and notice that the first two taps seem to "go together" or form a unit, but the last seems to stand alone. Now, repeat this sequence of taps several times and try to mentally change this organization so you have two groups, with the first tap *(V)* forming one and the last two taps *(V-V)* forming the other. Notice that no effort of will allows you to do this. The two taps that are close together in time seem to go together and the other does not. This is analogous to the Gestalt principle of grouping by proximity that we discuss in Chapter 10.

Next, try the sequence VVV-V-V-VVV-V-V-VVV, and so on. Notice that this is a repetition of three quick taps, followed by two slow taps. Notice that now the three taps from one group, and the two slow taps form another,

perceptually. It is virtually impossible to hear this any other way. This is analogous to the Gestalt principle of similarity (the visual analogue is shown in Figure 11-11).

While you are tapping, you can see that perceptual groups or clusters can be formed by frequency or timbre differences despite the absence of rhythmic differences. Begin by steadily tapping a surface with your pencil. Make sure the tapping rhythm is steady and unchanging. Now take a piece of paper and slip it between the surface and your pencil and notice that the sound quality changes. Without changing your rhythm, slip the paper in and out so that you are tapping *table, table, paper, paper, table, table,* and so on. Notice that the sounds seem to take on a grouping, with the table taps together and the paper taps together, and it seems, despite the fact that you are tapping quite steadily and monotonously, that the sounds have a rhythm that goes *table, table,* pause, *paper, paper,* pause, *table, table,* and so forth. Here, grouping by perceived similarity has imposed an apparent rhythm on the sound sequence.

In another study, when both musically trained and untrained listeners were asked to rate the subjective goodness of various notes within a larger melodic sequence, their responses followed quite closely predictions made from the types of music to which they had been most exposed, even when this violated a Gestalt law such as that of good continuation (Krumhansl, 1985). Studies of brain responses to musical stimuli indicate that such differences seem to arise from the high-level interpretive response to the music rather than the lower level perceptual aspects (Besson & Faita, 1995). On the other hand, these learned differences are supported by differences in brain structure between musicians and nonmusicians, including a larger anterior corpus callosum in the former (Schlaug & Jäncke, 1995). Moreover, musicians tend to use specialized structures in the left hemisphere of the brain (also the language hemisphere

for most people) when musical listening is difficult, whereas nonmusicians tend to rely on the right hemisphere in such situations (Messerli, Pegna, & Sordet, 1995).

The "learned" aspect of musical organization can also be seen in developmental studies. For example, one group of researchers studied the ability of 6-month-old infants and adults to detect "mistakes" in new melodies that were based on their native musical scales (Lynch & Eilers, 1990). North American infants were equally able to detect "mistakes" in a traditional Western major scale and a Javanese *pelog* scale that was not part of their birth culture. Adults, on the other hand, were much better able to detect "mistakes" in their native Western scale. In another experiment, infants' ability to detect changes to melodies was unaffected by whether such changes are predictable from Western musical conventions or not, whereas adults raised in North America did much better with changes that wouldn't occur in Western music (Trainor & Trehub, 1992). This suggests that infants are born with an equal ability to perceive music from all cultures but that the music perception system becomes (pardon the pun) "tuned" by experience. We will see a similar story for language learning later in this chapter.

Music is an important part of every culture, and even the music perception subfield has many more aspects than those few we have space to cover here. Several important books (Bregman, 1990; Deutsch, 1982; Dowling & Harwood, 1986; Krumhansl, 1990; Sloboda, 1985), a special issue of the journal *Perception & Psychophysics* (Dowling & Carterette, 1987), and several journals devoted to the psychology of music (e.g., *Music Perception* and *Psychomusicology*) cover these other aspects in some detail. In the future, comparisons between the music of different cultures may yield some insight into which aspects of music depend on learning the musical vocabulary of a particular culture and which depend on mechanisms that characterize all human beings (Deutsch, 1982; Perlman & Krumhansl, 1996; Serafini, 1995). Similarly, comparisons between species that produce music (e.g., among varieties of songbirds, between songbirds and humans) may shed light on the neural mechanisms that are critical to various aspects of music perception (e.g., Brenowitz, 1991; Hulse & Page, 1988).

SPEECH

"I can't understand it," Janine muttered to herself as she strolled through the famous Prado museum in Madrid. "I've been studying Spanish for two years. I can read it fluently. These descriptions of the paintings are no problem at all. Yet, whenever I try to talk to someone at a party, I can't understand a word anyone is saying. It all sounds like noise." She sighed as she gazed at yet another masterpiece by Goya. "I guess I just don't have an *ear* for Spanish."

Janine's problem is not unique among those learning a second language. We seldom think about how remarkable an accomplishment speech perception is until we are in a situation like the one that frustrates her, where we must listen to what

seems a stream of nearly continuous speech without understanding it. In our native language we can understand speech at rates of up to about 50 discrete sound units per second, although speech usually proceeds at only about 12 units per second (Foulke & Sticht, 1969). This is quite amazing because in one study listeners could determine the order of some nonspeech sounds, such as tones, buzzes, and hisses, only when they occurred at the much slower rate of about two thirds unit per second, or about one unit every 1.5 seconds (Warren, Obusek, Farmer, & Warren, 1969). Advertisers often take advantage of our ability to process rapidly occurring speech sounds by having announcers in TV or radio commercials speak much faster than usual. Because speaking rate has a large effect on the temporal cues that are so important in speech perception, there must be a "normalization" process that adjusts for distortions introduced by variations in speaking rate (e.g., Pind, 1995). This process seems to be tightly coupled with the speech perception process, so variations in speaker rate cannot be ignored, even when irrelevant (Green, Tomiak, & Kuhl, 1997).

Analysis of the nature of speech sound signals does not seem to be sufficient for understanding how people perceive speech sounds of their native language so accurately, because we can understand speech even when the signal is grossly distorted or transformed, for example, when people speak with an accent, with a mouthful of food, or while holding their nose (Remez, Rubin, Pisoni, & Carrell, 1981). Devices like telephones and radios also produce distortions of the sound signal that don't greatly affect the intelligibility of speech (except for a foreign language that you don't know very well!). Normal conversation is possible over the telephone even though telephones transmit only a limited range of frequencies, possibly because the speech perception system can opportunistically use whatever information is available, including context, to develop a meaningful interpretation of the signal (Warren, Reiner, Bashford, & Brubaker, 1995). Other transmission systems can severely *clip* the speech signal (turn it into a series of *on* or *off* pulses) yet still only marginally affect its intelligibility (although it *will* sound different). We can also easily understand conversations despite a background of noise, even when the noise level is only 6 dB less than the speech intensity. In fact, even if the speech and noise are the same intensity, we can identify about 50% of single words, and we can understand speech on a familiar topic even if the speech level is lower than that of the noise.

As a first approach, we might argue that speech perception is merely a particular form of auditory form perception and should follow principles similar to those of music perception. To a certain extent this is true. However, because the function of speech is to convey information and because it plays such an important role in human behavior, it is often necessary to conceptualize speech perception quite differently from that of simple sound stimuli or music. Also, we should warn you in advance that we will present no final answers here. Speech is one of the most controversial areas of perception research, and we are moving only slowly toward the best way to think about the difficult problems that exist.

The Speech Stimulus

When we discussed visual form perception in Chapter 10, we suggested that the visual system constructs perceptual objects that represent objects in the environment. Speech perception is similar, only in this case the perceptual objects are linguistic entities (in the form of meaningful phrases and sentences) based on utterances generated by another person. As Liberman and Mattingly (1985) put it, "the objects of speech perception are the intended phonetic gestures of the speaker" (p. 2). Thus, the goal of the speech perception process is to develop in the listener's consciousness a meaningful representation of what a speaker *intended to say*.

Given the intimate association between speech and language, it was probably inevitable that linguists were the first to describe the speech stimulus. Their description depends on the analysis of speech sounds in terms of how they are produced (*phonetics*) and how specific sounds distinguish words in a language (*phonemics*). Such descriptions are universal, in the sense that speech production and the methods of distinguishing linguistic units follow the same rules in every human language, although the specific sounds and the rules for combining them may be quite different (see Clark & Clark, 1977; Ladefoged, 1975). Although our

discussion will be limited to American English, a similar analysis can be done for any language.

Consonants and Vowels In American English speech, the vocal apparatus produces two basic types of speech sounds: **vowels** and **consonants**. They are produced by alternating sequences of opening and closing the vocal tract (the air passages in our throats, mouths, and nasal areas) while air from the lungs flows through it. Typically, closing movements produce consonants, and opening movements produce vowels.

Consonants are classified according to three major attributes: *voicing, manner,* and *place,* according to how they are produced. The voicing attribute consists of two categories: For *voiced* consonants a constriction of the flow of air out of the mouth is followed in less than about 30 msec by vibration of the vocal cords, whereas for *unvoiced* consonants the vocal cords don't begin vibrating until more than about 40 msec after the constriction. The *b* in "bat" is voiced, whereas the *p* in "pat" is unvoiced. With Demonstration Box 12-3 you can experience an exaggerated version of voiced and unvoiced consonants.

There are three manners in which the air-flow constriction can be produced. *Stops* are formed by completely stopping the flow of air from the lungs and then suddenly releasing the flow. The *p* in "pea," the *t* in "tea," and the *k* in "keep" are examples of stop consonants. *Fricatives* are formed by stopping the flow through the nasal passages but leaving a small opening in the mouth and forcing air through it, producing a "hissing" sound. Examples are the *s* in "best," the *z* in "buzz," and, as is only fair, the *f* in "fricative" (and "fair"!). *Nasals* are produced through the nose, as you might have expected. For these sounds the mouth is closed, and the air from the lungs flows through the nasal passages. Examples are the *m* in "mean" and, of course, the *n* in "nasal."

There are two places in the vocal tract where most of the constrictions occur. In one, the lips or the lips against the teeth control the flow of air from the lungs; consonants produced by such constrictions are called *labial* (*labium* is Latin for "lip"). Examples of labial consonants are the *b* in "bat" (voiced, stop), the *v* in "vat" (voiced, fricative), and the *m* in "mat" (voiced, nasal). The other place of constriction is inside the mouth. Here the

---

DEMONSTRATION BOX 12-3
Voiced and Voiceless Fricatives

Consonants in the English language are produced by a combination of vocal-cord vibration and variations in the passage of air through the oral cavity. *Fricatives* are a class of consonants formed when the mouth moves to a position that nearly blocks the flow of air, so air is forced through the tiny hole. However, fricatives also differ in whether they are voiced (accompanied by vocal-cord vibration) or voiceless (have no vocal-cord vibration). To illustrate this interaction between the flow of air and the quality of voicing, try the following demonstration suggested by Brown and Deffenbacher (1979). Make the sound of a z,

such as in the word "zip." Now try producing a tune (for example, "Oh, Susannah") while you sound the z. You should be able to do this easily; in fact, it will sound something like a kazoo. However, now try the same thing while making the sound of an f, such as in the word "fat." F is a voiceless fricative; therefore, the lack of vocal-cord vibration should make it impossible for you to produce a melody (remember, just produce the sound of f; do not hum simultaneously). The quality of voicing, or vocal-cord vibration, allows one type of fricative to be "melodic," whereas the other is lacking in that quality.

---

tongue is positioned at various places, most often either at the ridge behind the teeth *(alveolar)*, against the hard palate *(palatal)*, or against the velum (the soft palate at the top of the throat, *velar*). Examples are the t in "tin" (unvoiced, stop, alveolar), the n in "gnat" (voiced, nasal, palatal), and the c in "cot" (unvoiced, stop, velar). Try producing these sounds and paying attention to where your articulators (the parts of the vocal tract used to shape speech sounds, such as teeth, tongue, lips, and palates) are while you are doing it.

Vowels are produced very differently from consonants, by vibrating the vocal cords as air moves out of the lungs through the open mouth. Again, which vowel is produced depends on the relative positions of various parts of the vocal tract. First, the position of the tongue in the mouth is important, whether front, center, or back, and so is its relative height. Changes in tongue position and height change the shape of the resonating chamber in your mouth, resulting in the various vowel sounds. For example, the *ee* in "beet" is produced with the tongue at the front and quite high up in the mouth, the *a* in "sofa" is produced with the tongue central and at middle height in the mouth, and the *o* in "pot" is produced with the tongue at the back and low in the mouth. Try saying these sounds and paying attention to where your tongue is. Second, the degree of rounding of the lips is

important in vowel production. The *o* in "who" is called a *rounded* vowel because the lips must be rounded in order to produce it, whereas the *e* in "he" is *unrounded* because the lips are flat when it is produced.

Phonemes Linguists have also created a system of speech sounds that is sufficient to describe any utterance in any language. In this system the basic unit of speech sound is the **phone**. A phone that is used in a language to distinguish one word from another is called a **phoneme**. Every language has its own group of necessary phonemes; some have only a few (Hawaiian has 11), whereas others require as many as 60 (some African dialects) in order to distinguish all of the words. American English has 40 basic phonemes (excluding those specific to regional dialects, such as drawls and twangs). Table 12-1 lists the major phonemes of American English and the symbols used by the International Phonetic Association (IPA) to refer to them. Phonemes are usually set off from text by a pair of slashes (e.g., /p/ or /P/), but to make things more natural we will simply italicize phonemes and give an example word in quotes (e.g., the *p* in "pod"). Try saying the various example words in Table 12-1, paying attention to how the sounds of the phonemes correspond to the way the sounds are produced (their phonetic features).

Table 12-1 **The Major Phonemes of North American English**

CONSONANTS				VOWELS			
p	pea	θ	thigh	i	beet	o	go
b	beet	ð	thy	ɪ	bit	ɔ	ought
m	man	s	see	e	ate	a	dot
t	toy	ʒ	measure	ɛ	bet	ə	sofa
d	dog	tʃ	chip	æ	bat	ɜ	urn
n	neat	dʒ	jet	u	boot	ai	bite
k	kill	l	lap	U	put	aU	out
g	good	r	rope	ʌ	but	ɔi	toy
f	foot	y	year	ɒ	odd	ou	own
ç	huge	w	wet				
h	hot	ŋ	sing				
v	vote	z	zip				
ʍ	when	ʃ	show				

Note: The phonetic symbol is to the left of each column, and its sound corresponds to the part of the word represented in bold type. Some vowel and consonant combinations are also shown.

Every phoneme has a unique description in terms of its articulatory features (e.g., the *b* in "bat" is voiced, bilabial, stop), so there is a one-to-one correspondence between the articulatory and phonemic descriptions of words. Unfortunately, it is often impossible to isolate the acoustic properties of the speech signal that correspond to a particular phone in a particular uttered phrase. This is because in normal speech, movements of our articulators are often producing sounds relevant to three phones simultaneously (the end of one, the middle of another, and the beginning of a third—this is called coarticulation). It is therefore very difficult (some say impossible) to find a clear correspondence between acoustic features and perceived phonemes except in fairly specific, often simplified, instances.

Acoustic Properties of Speech Because phones refer to speech *sounds*, it is useful to have a means of displaying the speech sound signal so that we can describe any relationships between articulatory and acoustic features and the perceived speech units. To do this we use the fact that any complex sound wave can be represented as a set of simple sine waves of different amplitudes and frequencies (see Chapter 6). For speech we must also represent the variations of the speech waveform over time. The result is displayed as a **speech spectrogram**, an example of which is shown in Figure 12-6. In speech spectrograms, the horizontal axis shows time from the onset of the speech sound, and the vertical axis shows the frequencies of the sine wave components. The moment-to-moment variations in amplitudes of the different components are represented by the varying darknesses of the smudges on the spectrogram: The darker the smudge, the greater the amplitude of the component. Figure 12-6 displays large-amplitude components at frequencies from about 300 Hz to 700 Hz in all of the syllables. These components last about 200 ms for the "bab" syllable and about 300 ms for the "gag" syllable.

The bands of dark smudges that are obvious in Figure 12-6 represent **formants**. Formants are bands of especially high amplitude components that arise because the sound waves created by the passage of air from the lungs across the vocal cords and out through the mouth and/or nose are affected by the positions of the various parts of the vocal tract. For each mouth posture and air-flow pattern certain ranges of frequencies are enhanced and others are diminished. The enhanced frequencies are represented by the bands of smudges, whereas the diminished frequencies are represented by the lighter areas on the spectrogram. At least four formants can be distinguished for each of the syllables in Figure 12-6. The one at the lowest frequency (around 500 Hz in the figure) is called the *first formant* and is produced by the shape of the pharynx (wall of the throat). Any change in the shape of the pharynx produces a change in the frequency at which the first formant happens. The *second formant*, at about 1,400 Hz to 1,500 Hz in the different parts of Figure 12-6, is produced by the shape of the oral cavity. Higher formants are produced by complex resonances of the vocal tract, including the nasal passages.

In general, vowels and consonants can be distinguished in speech spectrograms. The relative positions of the various formants roughly correspond to the different vowel sounds. A special apparatus, called a *vocoder*, provides a sort of reverse spectrograph, re-creating the sounds for any pattern that it has been fed and even creating artificial speechlike sounds. Using artificial speech stimuli, it has been shown that only the first two formants are needed to create sounds that listeners readily identify as vowels; hence in our subsequent discussion we will

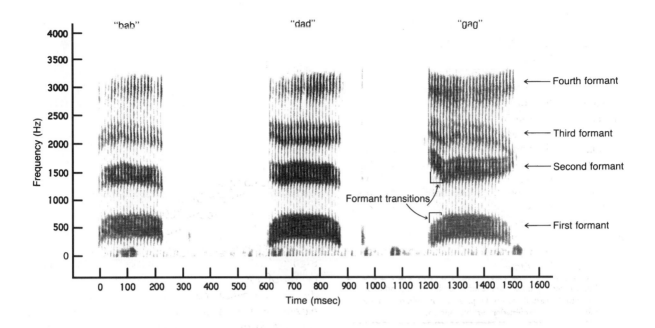

FIGURE 12-6 Speech spectrograms of the words "bab," "dad," and "gag," spoken with a British accent (based on Ladefoged, 1975).

refer to only the first two formants. Figure 12-7 shows the first two formants for a set of vowel sounds spoken by an adult male. Because people have different-sized mouths, noses, and throat passages, they have different ranges of possible shape changes. This means that the first and second formants will appear at a range of different frequencies across different speakers. Figure 12-7 also

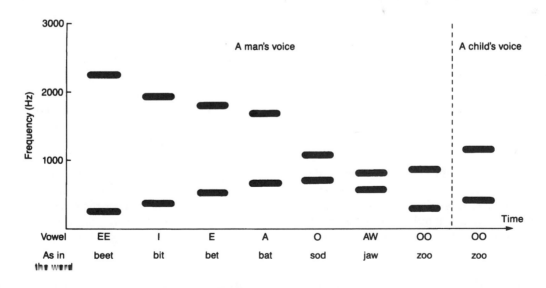

FIGURE 12-7 The first two formants for a series of vowel sounds made by an adult male voice. For comparison, the last vowel sound is shown also as it would be made by a child's voice.

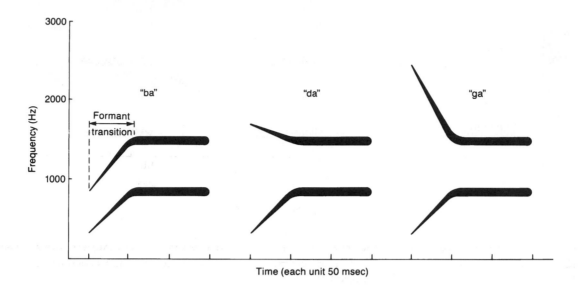

FIGURE 12-8 Changes in the formant transition cause a systematic change in the consonant sound heard for the same vowel. The vowel sound is the *o* in "sod."

shows, for comparison, one vowel spoken by a child. Notice that for the same vowel sound corresponding formants are located at higher frequencies for the child than for the adult.

Consonants are generally indicated by **formant transitions,** which are changes of formants over an interval of less than 100 m. Typical formant transitions are identified in Figure 12-6 and drawn schematically in Figure 12-8. Notice in Figure 12-8 that as the second formant transition changes, the consonant changes from *b* to *d* to *g*, although the vowel sound (represented by the two formants after the transitions) remains the *o* in "sod."

The rate of change in the formant transition is quite important in the perception of the phoneme. Figure 12-9 shows that a short transition before the *e* in "let" is heard as the consonant *b* and a slightly longer one as the consonant *w*. However, when the transition is even longer it doesn't sound like a consonant at all but, rather, like the *ue* in "duet," which is a *diphthong*, or change between two vowels.

Simple speech sounds of the sort described here do produce predictable perceptual responses, yet in natural speech the signal is not so regular. The theoretically expected components are often missing or distorted. Some individuals (such as Victor Zue) seem to be able to "read" speech spectrograms

with an accuracy of about 90% (Cole, Rudnicky, Zue, & Reddy, 1980), but this is a rare quality. Because of coarticulation there is seldom a precise correspondence between the acoustic properties of the stimulus and the perception of the speech signal. Although it is possible to obtain a precise acoustic description of any utterance in terms of a speech spectrogram, it is not always possible to say exactly which aspects of that spectrogram are meaningfully related to speech perception. In some respects this is quite reasonable, suggesting that we should be looking for higher level regularities or patterns of relationships rather than acoustic properties of individual speech units to explain our perceptions. In music we can recognize a melody played on a piano in one key as being the same melody when it is played on the clarinet in another key even though no two sounds corresponding to parts of the melody are ever the same. The melody is carried in the relationships among the individual sounds rather than in the absolute properties of the individual sounds. A global analysis based on relationships instead of individual acoustic components seems to be required in speech perception as well, considering that we are able to comprehend the same message from such a wide variety of speakers.

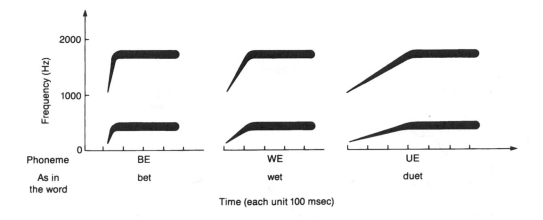

FIGURE 12-9   The duration of the formant transition affects what is heard. When it is short a consonant is heard; when it is long a shift between two vowels is heard.

Issues in Speech Perception

So far we have discussed speech perception as a form of auditory form perception in which the listener's task is to isolate phonemic units and integrate them into speech objects, much like the visual object task we discussed in Chapter 10. To this end, we have been looking at attributes of the speech signal. However, because speech perception is a topic in so many different disciplines— linguistics, electrical engineering, and computer science as well as psychology and speech and hearing science—there is a tremendous diversity of approaches to the field. One way to deal with these diverse views is to focus on the major problems, or issues, common to most approaches. We have chosen a few important issues for discussion here (see Miller & Eimas, 1995).

Ambiguity and Invariance   Although we described earlier some features of the speech signal that generally correspond to the perception of vowels and consonants, this is an oversimplification that holds only under certain controlled circumstances. When speaking naturally we do not simply add together the articulatory movements associated with each vowel and consonant component to produce the final complex utterance; rather, we coarticulate. Conversely, when listening to normal speech, we may perceive a consonant in

the absence of the usual formant transition or hear a vowel that is not the one indicated by the formants in the signal. As we said earlier, because of coarticulation specific features in the acoustic signal do not always predict specific perceptual experiences associated with the speech stimulus.

Our perception of the speech signal differs from its acoustic properties in several ways. For instance, we hear speech in segments that we interpret as phonemes, words, or phrases separated by pauses. In actual fact, the natural speech usually occurs in a continuous stream, without any obvious breaks or other "markers" corresponding to these perceived subdivisions (e.g., Chomsky & Miller, 1963). The speech signal also lacks **linearity,** the idea that for each phoneme in an utterance we should be able to find a corresponding segment of the physical speech signal. Linearity also requires that the order of acoustic segments must correspond to the order of phonemes. Neither criterion is met in the natural speech signal. One example of linearity failure is the children's ditty "mares eat oats and does eat oats and little lambs eat ivy." If you hear someone read it for the first time it will probably sound like "marsee doats and dosee doats . . ." After you know what it means, you will begin to hear "breaks" in the acoustical stream where none physically exists.

Another problem is with **acoustic-phonetic invariance,** the notion that there must be some

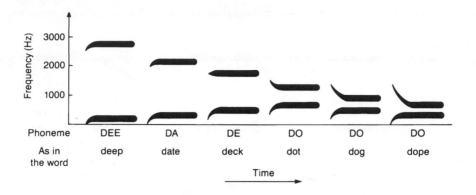

FIGURE 12-10 Despite the fact that the formant transition in the second formant changes from a rise to a drop, depending on the vowel, the same consonant phoneme *d* is heard, violating acoustic-phonetic invariance.

constant set of acoustic features associated with each perceived phoneme. For example, the formant transition representing a particular consonant must be present every time this consonant is perceived. If this acoustic feature is present it means that the associated phoneme was intended, whereas if this acoustic feature is absent it means that the phoneme was not intended. Unfortunately, such invariance does not characterize natural speech. The state of affairs is much more complex.

Figure 12-10 illustrates how very different acoustic signals can be perceived as the same phoneme. In this case the phoneme is the *d* in "date" for all the consonant-vowel combinations illustrated. In the examples in Figure 12-8, it was the second formant transition that determined which consonant was heard. This rule is violated for the examples in Figure 12-10. When we hear *d* in combination with the vowel *ee*, to form the *dee* in "deep," the second formant transition is a rise; when we hear *d* in combination with *o*, to form the *do* in "dope," the second formant transition is a drop; and when we hear the *d* in combination with *e*, forming the *de* in "deck," there is no second formant transition at all! This situation violates linearity because the information about *d* does not correspond to a specific segment of the acoustic signal (for example, the second formant transition). It also violates invariance because the acoustic cue for *d* depends on the context (here the vowel it is paired with) rather than a specific set of

invariant acoustic features. This lack of correspondence between phonemes and acoustic features makes it quite difficult to determine exactly what will be perceived given only the acoustic input. You can see this for yourself in Demonstration Box 12-4.

Is Speech Special? In some respects, speech is quite special and different from other perceptual stimuli. Speech is produced by humans to communicate linguistic information, something only humans do naturally. Speech *sounds* special to the listener; there is a distinct difference between our perception of speech and of other sounds. However, speech researchers usually mean something else by this question. They refer to the proposal by a group of researchers that the perception of speech is accomplished by a specialized set of neural mechanisms in humans (e.g., Liberman, 1982; Liberman & Mattingly, 1989). This is a major point of controversy within the speech research community, and researchers often classify each other by where they stand on this issue. Several lines of research have been used to argue for or against the special quality of speech processing. We discuss a few of them in what follows. The arguments usually take the form of the "speech is special" forces obtaining a dramatic finding that appears to demonstrate a special "speech mode" of processing, followed by the "speech is just a form of auditory form perception" forces showing that the same finding can be obtained using nonspeech

DEMONSTRATION BOX 12-4
Segmenting the Speech Signal

To see how difficult it is to segment the nearly continuous speech signal into words purely on the basis of acoustic criteria, look at the two speech spectrograms in this box, both of which are adapted from Pisoni and Luce (1986). Before reading the next paragraph, look at each segment and try to figure out how many words or syllables are in Phrase A.

Phrase A has five words and six syllables. It was made from a recording of the sentence "I owe you a yoyo." How successful were you? Even knowing the phrase in advance doesn't seem to help very much, does it?

Now look at Phrase B. It represents the spectrogram of the phrase "Peter buttered the burnt toast." There are five occurrences of the phoneme *t* as in "toy" in this phrase. If there is invariance and linearity in the speech signal, you should be able to find five repetitions of the same signal representing this phoneme *t*. Can you find them? It may be of some comfort to know that speech researchers have the same difficulties, and they have not solved them yet. A book devoted to this problem illustrates the variety of approaches that is being tried and provides an excellent summary of the current state of knowledge on this subject (Perkell & Klatt, 1986).

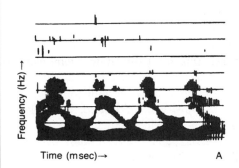

stimuli and proposing a purely acoustic explanation for the phenomenon with both speech and nonspeech stimuli. The results have thus been much like a tennis match, with players lobbing research findings and interpretations back and forth. There is evidence to suggest that speech perception differs from other aspects of hearing in some of its physiological mechanisms. First, there are two special areas in the brain identified with speech processing: Wernicke's area, in the superior part of the left temporal lobe of the cortex, for speech perception; and Broca's area, in the rear part of the left frontal lobe of the cortex, for speech production. In most humans the left hemisphere of the brain seems to be specialized for speech and language (see Coren, 1992). Damage to the left side of the brain is more likely to produce disruption in speech comprehension or production, presumably because the areas damaged are specialized to perform those functions (e.g., Kolb & Whishaw, 1985). The exclusive role of particular parts of the left hemisphere in speech processing (and not in processing of other auditory stimuli) has been identified by the most recently developed brain imaging techniques, including positron emission tomography (PET—Fiez & Raichle, 1995; Söderfeldt et al., 1997; Zatorre, Meyer, Gjedde, & Evans, 1996) and functional magnetic resonance imaging (fMRI—Binder et al., 1994, 1996). (See the Appendix for a description of PET and fMRI.) In fact, the auditory cortex of the left hemisphere contains language-specific memory traces of recently encountered phonemes that are absent for equally complex nonspeech acoustic stimuli (Näätänen et al., 1997). It is reasonable to expect behavioral manifestations of this specialized neural processing of speech. In the next sections we discuss three lines of behavioral evidence that are often cited in support of the view that "speech is special."

CATEGORICAL PERCEPTION

One of the first perceptual phenomena to suggest a special speech mode of auditory processing was that of categorical perception (Liberman, Harris, Hoffman, & Griffith, 1957). A prominent example of categorical perception involves the articulatory attribute of voicing of stop consonants. Remember that for *voiced* consonants such as the *b* in "bad" voicing usually occurs less than 30 ms after a stop, whereas for *unvoiced* consonants such as the *p* in "pad" voicing is delayed until more than 40 ms after the stop. The time at which the onset of voicing occurs can be viewed as a stimulus continuum, ranging from about 0 ms to 70 ms or so after the stop. From basic auditory psychophysics of such a continuum, we would expect that as we varied the voice onset time for a presented stop plus vowel stimulus from 0 ms to 70 ms, we should get a gradual change of the perception of voicing, leading to a gradual change of the identified consonant from, say, *b* to *p*, with perhaps some region around 30 ms to 40 ms in which the identity of the phoneme was ambiguous or a combination of the two. Surprisingly, this does not typically occur. Rather, for all voice onset times less than about 35 ms listeners hear a voiced consonant—say, *b*—and for all voice onset times greater than that they hear an unvoiced consonant, say, *p*. In other words, the entire stimulus continuum of voice onset time gives rise to only two categories of percept, a result we would expect if there were only two separate categories of voice onset time but an unexpected one for a stimulus that can be varied continuously.

Figure 12-11A shows some typical results for a study using artificial speech sounds. The value of voice onset time that divides the *b* (voiced) region from the *p* (unvoiced) region, around 35 ms for the data in Figure 12-11A, is called the phonemic boundary. Moreover, if listeners are presented with pairs of sounds with voice onset times on the same side of the phonemic boundary (say, 10 ms versus 20 ms before voice onset), they have a very hard time discriminating them at all, whereas if the stimuli come from opposite sides of the boundary (say, 30 ms and 40 ms), discrimination is very

good. Consonants show this categorical perception, but vowels do not.

When these findings were first presented, it was thought that nonspeech stimuli did not segregate into perceptual categories but, rather, produce much more gradual perceptual transitions as the stimuli vary along some continuum. Many researchers concluded that some special kind of mechanism must exist to process and categorize acoustic cues defining the various consonants. The data are not so clear now, however (see Pisoni & Luce, 1986, for a review). Several studies have shown that similar dramatic categorization effects can occur for nonspeech stimuli. For example, Cutting (1976) found a fairly sharp categorical boundary for "plucked" versus "bowed" sounds (like those of violins), which differed only in their onset times. Other studies have found similar results for nonspeech "chirps" and "bleats" (Pastore & Li, 1990) and for simple temporal rhythms (Schulze, 1989).

Another group of researchers critical of the "speech is special" view has shown that phoneme boundaries are perceived in a categorical way in nonhuman species such as macaque monkeys (May & Moody, 1989; Morse & Molfese, 1987), Japanese quail (Kluender, Diehl, & Killeen, 1987; Kuhl & Padden, 1983), and border collies (Adams & Molfese, 1987), none of which should be expected to have a special mechanism for human speech processing. The monkey auditory cortex (A1) responds to voicing onset only for a stimulus on the unvoiced side of the phonemic boundary, thus reflecting the perceptual boundary (Steinschneider, Schroeder, Arezzo, & Vaughan, 1995). Even crickets display categorical perception of pure tones that attract (frequency lower than 16,000 Hz) and repel (frequency higher than 16,000 Hz) them (Wyttenbach, May, & Hoy, 1996). These and other data, although still quite controversial, indicate that at the very least, both speech processing and nonspeech processing are based on a rich, abstract auditory code generated from the input sound (Sawusch & Gagnon, 1995).

Categorical perception effects can be obtained for any perceptual continuum by using the *adaptation level* as the category boundary. Recall from Chapter 2 that for any stimulus continuum, the adaptation level represents a sort of neutral point that serves as a reference for subjective judgments.

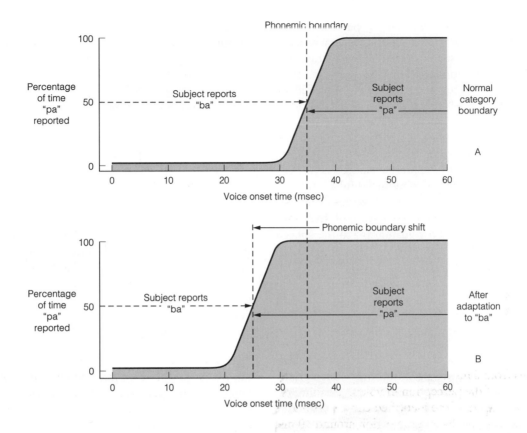

FIGURE 12-11   Typical results of an experiment on categorical perception of phonemes. (A) Before adaptation the phonemic boundary is at about 35 ms voice onset time. (B) After the subject listens to "ba" for 2 min, the phonemic boundary is shifted to about 25 ms voice onset time.

Stimuli above the adaptation level are perceived to be qualitatively different from those below the adaptation level, for example, hot versus cold or loud versus soft. For several stimulus continua, discrimination is considerably worse when stimuli are selected either all from below or all from above the adaptation level (Streitfeld & Wilson, 1986). This pattern of data is much like that observed in categorical speech perception.

Just as the adaptation level varies as a function of previous experience with particular stimuli, the phonemic boundary also varies with experience with speech stimuli. You may have experienced this informally if you have spent time listening to someone speak English with a strong foreign accent. At first, you may have had a difficult time understanding what was being said. However, after some time you may have been startled to realize that you no longer were "hearing" an accent. Al-

though you may have suspected that the speaker's accent had vanished over time, you could hear that this was not so if you were separated for several weeks. What changed was your adaptation level for certain phonemic boundaries.

This phenomenon has been studied systematically by presenting listeners repeatedly with a good example of a phoneme at one end of a continuum such as voice onset time, say, the syllable "ba" with a voice onset time of 10 ms. After 2 min or so of listening to "ba," listeners were then presented with the other voice onset time stimuli as before, such as those used to generate the curve in Figure 12-11A. Adaptation to the repeated "ba" sound shifted the phonemic boundary in the direction of the adapting stimulus so that now a stronger (shorter voice onset time) stimulus is necessary to perceive "ba," as shown in Figure 12-10B. Thus, some stimuli that previously were heard as "ba" are now classified as "pa." Similar results have been obtained with other characteristics of speech stimuli, such as place of articulation and vowel pronunciation (see Diehl, 1981).

Originally, these findings were interpreted by proponents of the "speech is special" view to indicate that there were speech feature detectors that were being fatigued or adapted (Abbs & Sussman, 1971; Eimas & Corbit, 1973; Lisker & Abramson, 1970). However, proponents of "speech is just auditory form perception" obtained similar shifts in categorical boundaries with nonspeech stimuli, depending on the acoustic similarity of the nonspeech stimulus used for adaptation to the speech stimulus used for testing (Samuel, 1986; Sawusch, 1986). These latter results were taken to imply that no special speech feature detectors, or special speech processing, need to be postulated to explain the data. It is not yet possible to conclude that either group of researchers has prevailed.

DUPLEX PERCEPTION

Yet another phenomenon that has been interpreted as evidence for a special speech processing mode is **duplex perception,** in which the same sound can be perceived as having both speech and nonspeech qualities (Rand, 1974). The most common way to create duplex perception is to present a group of synthetically generated formants lacking a critical formant transition, called the *base*, to one ear and the missing critical formant transition, called the *excerpt*, to the other ear. Typically, the base alone is heard as a particular syllable with an ambiguous initial consonant, say, "da" or "ga," whereas the excerpt alone is heard as a nonspeech "chirp." When the base and the excerpt are presented together, listeners simultaneously hear a speech sound in the ear receiving the base, either "da" or "ga," depending on which excerpt was presented, and also a nonspeech "chirp" in the ear receiving the excerpt. When listeners respond to the speech sound, they show many of the phenomena associated with speech processing, such as categorical perception. When they respond to the nonspeech chirp, they do not show these phenomena. Auditory masking studies show that the speech percept and the chirp are influenced differently by the interval between target and masker, arguing further for the separation between speech and acoustic feature perception (Bentin & Mann,

1990). Results such as these are used to argue that responding to speech stimuli involves a different mode of perceptual processing than does responding to nonspeech stimuli (Liberman, 1982; Liberman & Mattingly, 1989).

It is also possible to produce duplex perception by presenting the same specifically constructed stimulus to both ears (Whalen & Liberman, 1987). In this case, the speech percept alone is heard at low intensities, whereas at higher intensities both speech sounds and nonspeech chirps are heard. Interestingly, the "duplexity threshold," at which both sounds are heard, is about 20 dB higher than the threshold for discriminating speech sounds in the same stimuli. At the least this indicates that speech processing dominates nonspeech processing and is consistent with the idea of a separate speech processing mode. However, duplex perception has also been shown to occur for some nonspeech stimuli, such as musical chords (Collins, 1985; Hall & Pastore, 1992; Pastore, Schmeckler, Rosenblum, & Szczesiul, 1983) and the sound of a door slamming (Fowler & Rosenblum, 1990), providing evidence that is inconsistent with the interpretation of these phenomena as due to a special speech processing mode. Data on how duplex perception changes with intensity of the excerpt and on acoustic differences between the excerpt and base have been used to support the notion that duplex perception is a property of the auditory system and does not require a special speech processing mode (Bailey & Herrmann, 1993; Nygaard, 1993). Other experiments show that if an auditory pattern is compelling, it can "capture" the relevant phonetic cues, reducing the phonetic integration normally seen in duplex perception. The idea is that information can be shared between independent phonetic and acoustic processing systems but that what one systems captures the other can't access (Whalen & Liberman, 1996; Xu, Liberman, & Whalen, 1997).

CROSS-MODAL INTEGRATION

A final phenomenon that has implications for the "Is speech special?" controversy is the **McGurk effect** (McGurk & MacDonald, 1976). This involves a form of cross-modal integration in which visual information about articulator movements affects what a listener hears when listening to speech. In this effect, the listener is exposed to a series of speech sounds—for example, "da"—and at the same time to a movie or video of a face articulating speech sounds in synchrony with the speech sounds. When the visually presented articulator movements are congruent with the speech sounds, speech perception is normal. However, when the visual and auditory inputs are incongruent—for example, the sound is "ba," but the face is making the articulatory movements associated with "ga"—the percept is often a compromise phonetic percept, in this case "da." This suggests that visual information and auditory information about speech are being integrated before the phoneme is categorized (see Massaro, 1987). The McGurk effect seems to be stronger for syllables and weaker for complete words (Easton & Basala, 1982). This implies that visual speech information is not powerful enough to overcome a combination of auditory and semantic information. Only when the visual information and auditory information are about equal does the conflict produce the "in-between" percept.

Of course, in normal speech the visual information and auditory information are usually consistent; hence the sight may be a useful means of augmenting the intelligibility of the sound. It is reasonable to suppose that speech perception would involve such a mechanism because most linguistic communication takes place, and is learned by the child, in a face-to-face mode where both types of cues are available. However, we don't *need* visual cues to understand speech. For example, we understand speech on the radio, even at higher than normal presentation rates, as in commercials. Also, other theories can account for such auditory-visual cue integration (e.g., Massaro, 1987). You can experience a similar effect caused by the cross-modal integration of speech cues by trying Demonstration Box 12-5.

The McGurk effect has been interpreted as evidence that visual and auditory phonetic cues converge at some special brain site of speech processing. This site may be the primary auditory cortex or the auditory association cortex because silent lip-reading activates these areas in the same way that auditory speech perception does (Calvert et al., 1997). Some behavioral data seem to be inconsistent with this interpretation, however. For instance, Roberts & Summerfield (1981) set up conditions to measure the adaptation-induced shift in the

---

DEMONSTRATION BOX 12-5
Cross-Modal Integration of Cues

For this demonstration you need access to a television set and a radio. Bring the radio into the same room as the television set and turn them both on. Tune the radio to a point between channels so a hissing or roaring sound comes from the speaker. Tune the television set to a newscast or other show where a person is talking steadily, looking directly into the camera. Set the volume of the television set to a medium setting so that you can comfortably understand what is being said but low enough so that when the radio noise is turned to a high level you can't hear the television. Now, close your eyes and turn up the radio noise until you can't understand what the speaker on the television is saying, then lower the radio noise until you can just barely understand the speaker, and finally raise it a bit so you can't again. Now, open your eyes. In the presence of the visual cues as to what is being said, you will find that you now can understand the television speaker when you see his or her face. The effect will be similar to turning down the noise slightly, except that all you did was add the visual cues. When you close your eyes again, you should find it again impossible to understand the television speaker's speech. The additional information you are obtaining visually by watching the speaker talk is clearly having an effect on the intelligibility of the speech. These visual cues are particularly important anywhere the intelligibility of speech is reduced by the presence of noise, such as at a noisy party or on a noisy downtown street, or if your hearing is not very acute. Thus, many hearing-impaired people find it easier to understand speech when they are looking at a speaker's face.

phonemic boundary (Figure 12-11) for the Mc-Gurk stimuli: The sound was "ba," the visual image mouthed "ga," and the subject heard "da." The question was, Would the listeners adapt to the presented sound, "ba," or to the perceived sound, "da"? The answer was that the phonemic boundary shifted to a place predicted by adaptation to the presented sound, "ba," rather than the perceived sound, "da." The implication that the auditory-visual integration does not affect the low-level auditory processing of speech sounds seems inconsistent with a location of the integration site in the primary auditory cortex.

Let us now reiterate our original question: "Is speech special?" As you can see from the give-and-take nature of the data we have presented, a special speech perception is a possibility, but a simple extension of auditory form perception processes cannot be rejected. It is likely that there is a rich interaction between "ordinary" auditory processing, which, as we have seen in Chapter 7, is really not so ordinary, and the "special" processing of speech sounds.

Development Infants are born with a remarkable ability to respond to human speech (Jusczyk, 1986; Kuhl, 1987). Recordings of the electrical activity of the brain have revealed that even premature infants of 30–35 weeks gestational age can discriminate among vowel sounds (Cheour-Luhtanen et al., 1996). At birth, infants move their limbs in synchrony with connected adult speech but not with other sounds, such as tapping sounds or disconnected vowel sounds (Condon & Sander, 1974). In addition, infants show much the same patterns of responses to spoken phonemes that adults do. For example, infants as young as 1 month of age discriminate speech stimuli better across phonemic boundaries than within phonemic categories, showing categorical perception in the way that adults do (Eimas, Siqueland, Jusczyk, & Vigorito, 1971). Because, at 1 month of age, infants have had only minimal exposure to speech sounds and their utterances consist only of cries, screams, and babbles, they clearly have not yet learned language. Their ability to make speech discriminations similar to those of adults has thus been taken as evidence of an innate mechanism for speech processing.

Other developmental evidence for an innate speech system comes from studies of children's babbling (Lenneberg, 1967; Locke, 1983). By 7–10 months of age infants normally engage in vocalizations that are characterized as repetitive (e.g., saying "dadada") and syllabic in structure (i.e., consonant-vowel clusters), without apparent reference or meaning, and that progress through a well-defined series of stages. Some critics have dismissed babbling as nothing more than evidence that motoric aspects of the vocal speech apparatus are developing. However, severely hearing-impaired infants raised by parents whose only linguistic communication was American Sign Language (ASL) produce "manual babbling" that, although made with hands and fingers, is indistinguishable in its time course, structure, and function from the vocal babbling of hearing infants (Petitto & Marentette, 1991). Thus, babbling seems to be related to the development of an *amodal* language system. Interestingly, hand and finger movements of the hearing infants bear no resemblance to those of the young ASL "signers" in the study of manual babbling.

Another very impressive demonstration of infants' speech perception ability is that infants can integrate auditory information and visual information about speech. In one study, 4-month-old infants were presented with two video displays of the same person's face speaking two different vowel sounds, as illustrated in Figure 12-12. At the same time, each infant was presented (from a loudspeaker midway between the faces) with the sound of the person's voice producing one or the other of the vowel sounds. The voice and the two faces were all in synchrony with each other, but the voice corresponded to only one of the face's articulatory movements. The infant spent about 73% of the time looking at the face that was articulating the vowel sound it was hearing. Thus, very young infants also demonstrate cross-modal integration of speech cues, just as adults do (e.g., the McGurk effect), even though they have had only limited experience with such cues and do not yet speak. Moreover, this ability is apparently a function of the left hemisphere of the brain in infants, just as speech production is a function of that hemisphere in adults (MacKain, Studdert-Kennedy, Spieker, & Stern, 1983).

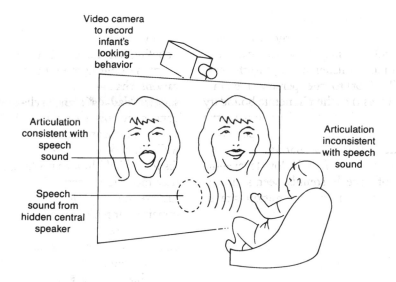

FIGURE 12-12 Illustration of an experiment showing that infants can integrate phonemic information across auditory and visual modalities (based on Kuhl & Meltzoff, 1982).

Although there is a good deal of evidence suggesting that from birth infants can discriminate the entire set of possible phonemes that the human vocal apparatus is capable of making, adults cannot. Thus, a native Japanese speaker may say "ararm crock" when he actually means "alarm clock," not because of sloppy speech but because the Japanese language does not have the two separate phonemes *r* as in "run" and *l* as in "look." Instead, Japanese has a sound that is intermediate to these two consonants in English, one that will often sound like an *r* to the English speaker when *l* is intended and vice versa.

As infants develop, they maintain the ability to make subtle discriminations between the phonemes present in their own language environment, but by 1 year of age they lose much of the capacity to discriminate contrasting phonemes that they are not regularly hearing (Werker, 1989, 1992). This loss occurs earlier for vowels than for consonants (Polka & Werker, 1994). One study demonstrated this with two different *t* sounds, taken from the Hindi language, that are not discriminated in English. For example, nearly all 6- to 8-month-old infants, regardless of their language background, are able to discriminate as accurately as adult Hindi speakers two different Hindi *t* sounds that are not discriminated in English. However, by 1 year of age, only infants from Hindi-speaking families retain this ability (Werker & Tees, 1984). Conversely, both infants and adults, but not monkeys, accept a broad range of variations from the ideal acoustic pattern of a phoneme in their language as representative of that phoneme—the *perceptual magnet effect* (Kuhl, 1991). In one study even 6-month-old American babies were better able to detect slight deviations, such as those produced by different speakers, from the ideal Swedish *y* sound (which is not found in English) than were their 6-month-old Swedish counterparts. The Swedish babies, not to be outdone by this performance, were better able than the American babies to detect slight departures from the English *ee* sound, which is not found in Swedish (Kuhl, Williams, Lacerda, Stevens, & Lindbloom, 1992). The effect appears to result from passive exposure to language and can be accounted for by the way the brain forms neural maps that are biased by exposure (Guenther & Gjaja, 1996—see Chapter 16). Both of these types of studies demonstrate that an infant's linguistic surroundings tune the mechanisms that will later be used to discriminate speech. The result is that adults lose the ability to discriminate phonemes found only in other tongues while developing a greater tolerance for irrelevant deviations from the prototypical sounds of their own language. In addition to increasing the knowledge of the prototypes of the phonemes of a language, experience with correctly producing those phonemes increases the ability to integrate visual information and auditory information about them in perception, as in the McGurk effect (Desjardins, Rogers, & Werker, 1997). Thus, we might say that infants are born with a "language-general" discrimination ability, whereas adults develop a "language-specific" discrimination ability through experience listening to and producing utterances in a particular language (cf. Best, 1992).

One way to conceptualize this language-specific discrimination ability is in terms of the differences between languages in phonemic boundaries. Phones that sound different in one language, because they are opposite sides of a phonemic boundary, might be heard as the same in another, because they are on the same side of a differently placed boundary, similar to the short-term adaptation phenomenon illustrated in Figure 12-11. Experience with a language seems to permanently alter the placement of these boundaries and hence the phonemic categorization of phones. For instance, if you make a continuous z sound as in "zzzzz" and then bring the tip of your tongue close to your teeth, the sound will change into an extended *th* as in "that." The distinction between z and *th* is determined by the tongue position. The boundary between these two phonemes is different for different languages. Thus, adult native French speakers will make sounds that their ears tell them have crossed the boundary from z to *th* but that to native English speakers still appear to be on the z side. That is why a French speaker may be perceived by an English speaker as saying that she is going out to "walk ze dog."

Context We mentioned that a major problem in speech perception is the ambiguity of the speech signal due to the lack of an invariant set of acoustic features that correspond to the perceived speech units. Demonstration Box 12-4 is a fairly dramatic example of this problem. One factor that always helps to interpret patterns, whatever the modality, is the context in which the patterns appear. We saw this for visual patterns in Figure 10-26, where the same pattern elements were seen either as a letter

or a number, depending on the context formed by the surrounding stimuli. In terms of the ultimate function of speech, which is to convey meaning, context is vital because the same sound unit may signify different meanings. This occurs in the case of **homophones,** which are words that sound alike when spoken but convey different meanings—such as *be* and *bee*, *rain* and *reign*, and *no* and *know*. Although acoustic cues might sometimes differentiate these words, most often the surrounding context helps us tell which word was meant by the speaker.

Interestingly, there are other words that sound quite different to us, such as *married* and *buried*, that are produced by speakers using nearly identical movements of the mouth and lips. These are called **homophenes** and are difficult for lipreaders to discriminate out of context. If we are watching a speaker's face for some visual information in a difficult listening context and if the word uttered is a homophene, we will get more help from the semantic context than from the visual indications of the articulatory movements. Demonstration Box 12-6 presents an example of how context affects our ability to extract the meaning of speech stimuli.

The context effect in Demonstration Box 12-6 is based on identifying the general topic with which an utterance is concerned. There are a great many other context effects in speech perception, many of them arising from the meaning attached to the speech sounds (see also Liberman & Mattingly, 1985; Sawusch, 1986). One interesting demonstration of this type of effect was provided by Day (1968, 1970). She presented sound sequences simultaneously to both ears of listeners. For example, if the left ear received *b-a-n-k-e-t* the right ear received *l-a-n-k-e-t*. Many of the listeners fused the two sequences into the word *blanket*, even when *lanket* preceded *banket* by several milliseconds; other listeners heard only the separate sound sequences. But no one heard *lbanket*, which is a sequence of phonemes that does not occur in English. The expectations as to which sounds *can* occur in speech clearly provided a context that influenced what was perceived.

The importance of context is demonstrated by the fact that if trained listeners are asked to provide a phonetic transcription of spoken passages in an unknown language, they do quite poorly, despite their training, simply because of the absence

DEMONSTRATION BOX 12-6
Context and Speech Perception

In the absence of an appropriate context, even common words are often difficult to identify. To see how context interacts with speech perception, read the following phrase in a smooth, rapid conversational style to a friend: "In mud eels are, in clay none are." Ask your friend to write down the phrase exactly as he or she heard it. Now you should provide a context by telling your listener that you are going to read a sentence from a book that describes where various types of amphibians can be found. Then read the above sentence again at the same speed you did before. After your listener writes down what was heard this time, you can compare the sentences (or nonsentences) that were heard with and without the context. Without the context you might find responses such as "In middies, sar, in clay nanar" or "In may deals are, en clainanar" (Reddy, 1976). Here the words in the sentence are difficult to identify when presented rapidly, and a strange and largely meaningless set of segments is generated. When the proper context is supplied, however, the same speech sounds are correctly segmented into words and are interpreted as meaningful elements.

of an adequate semantic and syntactic context (Shockey & Reddy, 1974). Even if we know a language, our ability to identify isolated words extracted from a stream of recorded speech is quite poor. Generally in such tests listeners are capable of identifying less than half of the items (Pollack & Pickett, 1964). If the same words are presented surrounded by longer strings of the words in the original recorded utterance, identification is much better. Thus, the more acoustic, syntactic, or semantic context provided, the better the listeners are at identifying the words.

The context of a sentence can actually induce a listener to supply missing parts of the stimulus to fill in a gap in continuous speech so that it is heard as if it were uninterrupted. Warren (1970) presented listeners with a taped sentence: "The state governors met with their respective legislatures convening in the capital city." The acoustic information corresponding to the first *s* in "legislatures" was deleted and replaced by the sound of a cough. Nineteen of 20 listeners reported nothing unusual about the sentence. They restored the missing phoneme; hence the effect was named the **phonemic restoration effect**. Again, the context of the sentence determined the speech sequence actually perceived. This is a powerful effect. For example, restored phonemes can cause adaptation-like shifts of phonemic boundaries (Samuel, 1997).

Apparently both meaning and acoustic cues play a role in such restoration of missing or obliterated components (Bashford & Warren, 1987; Bashford, Warren, & Brown, 1996; Samuel, 1981, 1996). For example, one study found that the degree of phonemic restoration was related to whether or not visual articulatory cues were available as well as to the place and manner of articulation (Trout & Poser, 1990). Another study found that restoration was more likely for words that had a larger number of possible ways they could be completed in the phrase (e.g., "*l*egion" or "*r*egion") than for those that were unique (e.g., "*le*sion"; Samuel, 1987). Thus, if we delete portions of common words or phrases or present only the distinctive parts of words, the listener is more likely to "hear" the speech as being continuous if the context makes the missing part more predictable (Bronkhorst, Bosman, & Smoorenburg, 1993). In effect, we can then hear the speech units that the immediate context suggests should be in the phrase, even if they are not physically present.

Theories of Speech Perception

Many theories have been proposed to explain the phenomena we have discussed here. It is probably safe to say that no one theory has yet achieved a consensus that it is the most useful, although two

that we will discuss later, *trace theory* and *cohort theory*, seem to be leading the race (Miller & Eimas, 1995). In fact, many researchers feel that theory is an area of significant weakness in speech perception research (e.g., Pisoni & Luce, 1986). The many candidate theories of speech perception can be categorized on the basis of their level of analysis, whether they are oriented toward the identification of phonemes or of words, and on the basis of whether they utilize **active** or **passive processing** (Nusbaum & Schwab, 1986). Passive processing, like the data-driven processing we discussed for visual form in Chapter 10, involves a filtering or feature detection sequence of events that is relatively fixed in nature and works at a sensory level. After the message is sensed and filtered, it is then mapped fairly directly onto the acoustic or articulatory features of the language. Active processing involves a much more extensive interaction between low-level sensing of acoustic features and higher level processes involving analysis of context and knowledge of speech production and articulation. This is reminiscent of the conceptually driven processing in visual form perception that we described in Chapter 10 in that the sequence of processing steps may not be fixed but may vary depending on the results of earlier computations. Both active and passive models may rely on general acoustic processing rules or may invoke "special" speech analysis processes.

Many passive theories incorporate the notions of *feature detectors* or *template matching*. Feature detectors for speech are usually conceptualized as neurons specialized for the detection of specific aspects of the speech signal, much the way specific neurons in the visual cortex selectively respond to aspects of the visual stimulus such as line orientation (see Chapter 3). An auditory template may be viewed as a stored abstract representation of certain aspects of speech that develops as a function of experience and serves the same function as a feature detector. Speech feature detectors or auditory templates in speech identification are employed in "Pandemonium-like" models (see Chapter 10), in which a speech stimulus is identified as the phoneme or word whose "cognitive demon" is most activated by its associated "feature demons."

Some theories that are predominantly passive in nature stress that ordinary auditory processes are sufficient to explain speech perception at the level of phonemes (e.g., Fant, 1967; Massaro, 1987; Samuel & Kat, 1996). These *auditory theories* usually postulate several stages of processing of speech sounds. The first stage consists of "ordinary" auditory processing, including analysis of a complex sound into its simple sine wave components, auditory feature analysis, and auditory pattern processing. For some theorists feature analysis occurs first, then pattern analysis, whereas for others they occur at the same time (in parallel). The next stage then applies more specialized (but not necessarily "special") rules to the output(s) of the first stage(s), integrating them to produce perception of phonemes. A good example of this approach that uses words, rather than phonemes, as the unit is Klatt's (1980) Lexical Access From Spectra (LAFS) model. In this model the listener does a spectral analysis of the input signal, matching the results of this analysis to a set of templates of features stored in memory. Words are then identified from the set of features detected in the input. In this model there is no need to describe segments or phonemes or other linguistic entities; the speech input is directly matched to words in memory by a fixed process.

A passive model that uses "special" speech units is also possible (e.g., Eimas & Corbit, 1973). In such a model the first stages consist of detection of speech features by "special" feature detectors, followed by integration of these features into percepts by (possibly) "special" rules. Figure 12-13A gives a schematic representation of a general passive speech perception theory that contains elements similar to many models that have been proposed.

Active models of speech perception are somewhat more variable because they often involve analysis of the context in which the speech is occurring, the expectations of the listener, the distribution of attentional resources, and memory. Because different researchers place different degrees of emphasis on these various components, active theories often differ dramatically from one another.

One prominent active model of word identification is called **cohort theory** (Marslen-Wilson, 1980, 1989). In this model passive stages of analysis initially extract information about the phoneme(s) of a word. On the basis of this information all the words in memory that have similar phonemes (e.g., all words beginning with *st*, such as "stop," "stall," "stride") are activated in proportion to how

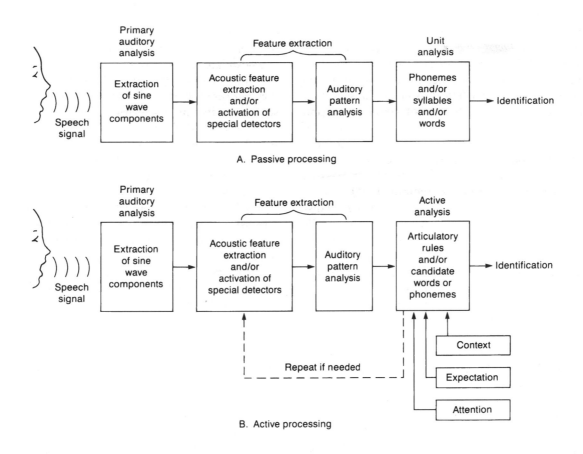

FIGURE 12-13 Diagrammatic representation of the difference between a typical passive model of speech processing (A) and a generalized active model of speech processing (B).

similar they are to the extracted phoneme(s). These words constitute the "cohort" or group of possibilities to be considered. After the cohort is activated, other acoustic or phonetic information and the goodness of fit between cohort members and the ever-developing meaning of the discourse operate to eliminate all the candidates except the most appropriate one.

Another prominent active theory, which has been implemented as a computer model, is McClelland and Elman's (1986) trace theory. This theory begins with passive feature detection at three interacting levels. (1) acoustic feature detectors whose output is the input to (2) phoneme detectors whose output is the input to (3) word detectors. The unique aspect of this model is that the various detectors and other processors, referred to in the

computer model as *nodes*, are highly interconnected. Activating one node tends to activate all the nodes to which it is connected, both at the same level and at other higher or lower levels. This is actually quite a complex model in which various levels may interact with one another in a looping fashion, with high levels "tuning" or altering the weighting given to specific features at lower levels.

All active theories have in common high-level decisional processes superimposed on the initial feature-extraction results. Thus, the speech we "hear" may be determined by factors other than the actual acoustic signal. A diagram of a generalized active speech-processing theory is shown in Figure 12-13B.

One of the first, and most influential, general theories of speech perception is difficult to classify as active or passive because it has elements of both. This is the *motor theory* proposed by Liberman, Cooper, Shankweiler, and Studdert-Kennedy (1967) and more recently revised by Liberman and Mattingly (1985, 1989). It deals with the identification of phonemes considered as the intended phonetic *gestures* of a speaker, that is, what the speaker intends to say. In this theory, speech is clearly "special," in the sense that perception of speech sounds is accomplished by a specialized processing mode that is both innate and part of the more general specialization for language that humans possess. In particular, the theory assumes that the same evolutionary adaptations of the mammalian motor system that made speech possible for humans also gave rise to a system for perceiving the resulting speech sounds based on the way they were produced. In this theory, intended speech gestures are inferred from an acoustic/visual speech signal based on an abstract representation of the articulatory movements the listener would use to produce that speech signal.

An example of how this system might work can be seen by looking back at Figure 12-10 and noting that the *d* in *dee* as in "deep" is perceived as the same *d* as that in *do* as in "dope," although they are quite different acoustically. According to motor theory, both are heard as *d* because the listener would use equivalent articulatory movements to produce the *d* phoneme for both utterances. The fact that the actual sounds of the two *d*s are not the same is irrelevant, just as pitch of voice, speed of speech, and other sound-distorting factors are irrelevant.

The motor theory of speech perception remains controversial. As discussed earlier in the "Is Speech Special?" section, the evidence for a special speech processing module continues to be debated, and new findings seem to stir things up rather than settle the issue. For example, perceived pitch of vowels is much more sensitive to temporal displacements of acoustic components than are nonspeech complex sounds (Hukin & Darwin, 1995); vowel quality (analogous to timbre) of static vowel sounds can be identified at much shorter durations than can the pitch (octave or note) of the sounds (Robinson & Patterson, 1996); and humans perceive the similarities among vowels differently than do monkeys (Sinnott, Brown, Malik, & Kressley, 1997). All of

these findings point to some kind of special processing of speech sounds by humans. Nonetheless, other data continue to indicate that at least some of these special properties of speech sounds are *not* specific to humans (Kluender & Lotto, 1994), and debates continue to rage about whether we hear sounds or "tongues" (Fowler, 1996; Lindblom, 1996; Ohala, 1996; O'Shaughnessy, 1996; Remez, 1996; Stevens, 1996).

No one theory or level of analysis has come to dominate speech perception. In fact, there appears to be a gradual blurring of some of the distinctions. For instance, we have seen that active models begin with a passive-processing, feature-extraction component, whereas some of the passive-processing models may allow active processing when the signal is degraded or conditions are difficult (Fant, 1967; Massaro, 1987). The motor theory also has strong resemblances to both active and passive theories. In addition, some investigators have proposed that both general auditory processes and special speech processes are necessary to account for all the data (e.g., Pisoni, 1973; Werker & Logan, 1985). Certainly there can be no argument as to whether an auditory mode of processing exists. The problem speech theorists still must contend with is just how "special" speech perception is and how much of what is heard is in the signal and how much is constructed in the mind of the listener.

CHAPTER SUMMARY

Whereas acoustical pitch is measured by the mel scale, musical pitch is measured by our common equal-tempered musical scale. Musical tones vary in **height** (high or low pitch) and in **chroma** (where they are in each octave), with items having the same chroma sounding similar although they may differ in height. This gives rise to a helical description of musical pitch. In the Western world, **musical intervals** defining scales are arranged with logarithmic spacings because equal frequency ratios sound like equal musical intervals. The sequence of notes that makes up a melody is recognizable by its **contour** (the sequence of rises and drops in relative frequencies), although musical phrases where contours are similar but where individual notes are held for different durations will no longer appear to be the same melody. Sequences of notes are grouped into motifs, and sets of motifs are grouped into phrases according to Gestalt principles similar to those in visual form perception using proximity, figure-ground, similarity, and good continuation. The scale illusion is an example of grouping by pitch proximity. Some aspects of organization are learned by cultural exposure to particular patterns of music. **Tempo** is the speed of the melody, whereas **rhythm** is its organization in time. Rhythm is affected by internal organization principles, similar to those that produce the perceptual grouping of "tick, tock" on a clock sound, even though each click is identical.

Because the function of speech is to convey information, it is often necessary to conceptualize speech perception quite differently from that of simple sound stimuli or music. **Phonemes** are the basic sounds used to make up each language. The features that make up **consonants** are voicing manner (stops, nasals, and fricatives) and the place of the **articulators** (labial, palatal, alveolar, or velar) where constrictions occur. **Vowels** are produced by vibration of the vocal cords and modified by the location of the tongue in the mouth and by the shape of the lips. The speech stimulus can be displayed as a **speech spectrogram,** which often shows several **formants,** which are frequency ranges of higher intensity. The location of formants best describes vowel sounds, whereas **formant transitions** describe consonants. The speech signal, however, is often ambiguous. It is lacking in **linearity** because each phoneme does not correspond to a definable segment of the acoustical speech signal, and it lacks **acoustic-phonetic invariance,** which requires that there must be some *constant set* of acoustic features associated with each perceived phoneme. This has led to the suggestion that speech is special and is not guided by the normal rules of acoustical perception. Consistent with this suggestion is the fact that there are specific speech centers in the brain removed from the primary auditory areas. It has also been suggested that **categorical perception,** where continuous variations in voice onset times are not heard as continuous changes but, rather, as distinct categories of phonemes on either side of the **phonemic boundary,** is evidence for speech being special; however, recent evidence suggests that nonspeech stimuli are also categorically perceived. The phonemic boundaries are not biologically fixed but, rather, can be affected by adaptation, level effects, and these also differ among various languages. An infant can perceive all possible phonemes; however, adults lose their ability to hear phonemes outside of the languages that they heard and learned when young.

The controversy over whether speech is special continues. **Duplex perception,** in which the same sound can be perceived as having both speech and nonspeech qualities, has been offered as evidence that speech is special. Similarly, cross-modal integration of speech information—as shown by the **McGurk effect,** where the perception of an "intermediate" phoneme can be produced when auditory and visual cues from watching a speaker's lips conflict—has been suggested as evidence that acoustical information and visual information converge at a higher speech center in the brain.

The ambiguity of speech, such as the problem of distinguishing between the **homophones** "no" and "know," is reduced when an observer takes context into account. Context can also allow an observer to fill in phonemes that are missing or obscured, as in the **phonemic restoration effect.**

Theories of speech perception include **passive processing,** which involves a sequence of filtering operations of a relatively fixed nature that works at a sensory level using feature detectors and template matching, as in the Pandemonium or LAFS models. **Active processing** involves a much more extensive interaction between low-level sensing of acoustic features and higher level processes involving analysis of context and knowledge of speech production and articulation. For example, in **cohort theory** low-level passive acoustical analysis activates a cohort, or group, of words with similar phonemes that context and other active comparisons whittle down to the most likely meaning. **Trace theory** is a computer model based on the activation of particular nodes that trigger activity at both high and lower analysis centers. In motor theory the observer circumvents the ambiguity of the speech signal by using the acoustical and visual information to infer the sequence of movements that he or she would use to make the same sound. At this time, no one speech theory seems to dominate, and the issue of whether speech is special and different from acoustical perception remains unresolved.

KEY TERMS

height
chroma
musical interval
chord
contour
rhythm
tempo
vowels
consonants
articulators
phone
phoneme
coarticulation
speech spectrogram
formants
formant transitions

linearity
acoustic-phonetic
 invariance
categorical perception
phonemic boundary
duplex perception
McGurk effect
homophones
homophenes
phonemic restoration
 effect
trace theory
cohort theory
active processing
passive processing

Time

CHAPTER 13

Nobel prize–winning physicist Albert Einstein often thought about the meaning of time and ultimately concluded that "the distinction between past, present and future is only an illusion, however persistent" (Einstein & Besso, 1972). From the psychological point of view, a better conclusion might be that time and space are modes by which we perceive and think about our world, rather than the physical conditions under which we live. As we will see in this chapter, the time dimension is every bit as important as the space dimension in our perception of the world and events occurring in it.

THE IMPORTANCE OF TIME TO PERCEPTION

If you were to read only the chapter on space (Chapter 9), you might be forgiven for thinking that the spatial arrangement of stimuli is the most important aspect of visual perception. The perceptions of three-dimensional depth, of visual direction, and of the sizes and locations of objects all are based on our brain's ability to process information about the spatial layout of the environment. You might think that all of the information needed to extract this information comes directly from the retinal images or the relationship between the retinal images of our two eyes; however, much of this processing is strongly dependent

379

on the perception of time and the temporal relationship between stimuli.

Events Are the Units of Perception

Do still photographs or videotape provide a more realistic record of the important moments in your life? Most people will say quite confidently that videotape places an observer "inside the action" to a greater extent than does a series of still photographs. What is it that is recorded on videotape that is lost when recorded in a series of still photographs? Is it that videotape merely contains more information, by virtue of the sheer volume of still photographs contained within a video sequence? Research shows that it is more than that. Indeed, it is something deeply related to the way in which information is processed by the brain.

Our brain is designed to respond to change, and the basic unit of our perceptual experience is the event. Events consist of a set of relations among objects and actions. Although object perception is a necessary ingredient for the perception of an event, as is the perception of an action, of greatest importance to the perceiver are the answers to the questions "Who is doing what to whom?" and "What is happening to me or around me?" The answers to these questions permit observers to properly plan future actions of their own.

In many ways, events are similar to sentences or phrases in natural language. Although language consists of single units such as nouns and verbs, its meaning is not in these units themselves but, rather, in the sequence or timing of these units. For instance, there is a great difference between a "man-eating shark" and a "shark-eating man." Although both of these phrases contain the same elements, it is the sequence or timing of the arrival of these stimuli at the eye or ear that determines the actual meaning that we perceive. In the same way, our use of the term *event* refers to a series of stimuli that unfolds over time. Our ability to understand actions or the relations that exist between objects depends on this unfolding. Therefore, our perception becomes quite limited when most of the time dimension is lost, as it is when we are viewing still photographs.

Actually, moment-to-moment changes in stimulation are necessary for us to be able even to perceive a still picture or a drawing. Even if you try to stare at a picture and not move your eyes at all, your retinal image is continually in motion. This comes about because of eye movements over which we have little control. Some of these are small, involuntary, drifting movements. In addition, the eye is jiggling or shivering in its socket because of tiny jerky movements called **microsaccades.** These microsaccades occur many times a second and cause the retinal image to shimmy from place to place on the retina no matter how hard we try to hold our eyes completely still. The end result of all this eye movement is that contours in the retinal image are continually moving over a number of different retinal receptors. This means that the output from any given receptor in the eye will actually vary over time with a series of on and off signals as the image bounces around on the retinal surface.

To see how important this change in the image over time is, we can eliminate it using a **stabilized retinal image** technique. This technique requires an observer to wear a special contact lens that moves with the eye and has a mirror or a tiny projector mounted on it (e.g., Pritchard, Heron, & Hebb, 1960; Riggs, Ratliff, Cornsweet, & Cornsweet, 1953; Yarbus, 1967). The projected image now stays on the same retinal receptors no matter how the eye moves. What do we see when the temporal variations in the retinal image are removed? The answer is nothing. When people view a stabilized image, they find that over a period of only a few seconds the picture fades from consciousness. The contours disappear in chunks, and the color also fades away. If we now flicker the image on and off, the pattern will reappear in consciousness, and, if the flicker rate is high enough, it will stay in view (Cornsweet, 1956). Flickering the image has simply reintroduced some of the temporal changes in the retinal image that we removed through the stabilizing technique. The disappearance of the perception of pattern when the retinal image is stabilized, and its reappearance when the retinal image is flickered, supports the idea that constant change over time is the critical property for stimulating the individual receptors. Without constant change, receptors soon cease to respond differently from neighboring receptors, and thus we lose the ability to detect the presence of a contour (cf. Norwich, 1983). Therefore, for pattern vision to occur, there must be not only spatial variation in the intensity of light, as in contour and light variations distributed over space, but also variation in the pattern of illumination over time.

We have already provided you with a demonstration of the disappearance and the reappearance of a stabilized image with flickering stimulation in Demonstration Box 3-4 in Chapter 3, which you might want to look at again. In that demonstration you mapped the pattern of blood vessels that lies above your retina. Ordinarily you don't see these blood vessels because they create a stabilized image on your retina as light passes through them. They are always in the same place, so they create no temporal changes in stimulation of the receptors. By moving a flashlight placed at the corner of the eye, however, you cause their shadows to move across the retina. With these momentary temporal variations, you have effectively destabilized these images, which is why they become visible. You will note that as soon as you stop moving the flashlight (thus stopping the temporal change), the blood vessels disappear because their image is now stabilized again.

Another demonstration that you can try for yourself takes advantage of the fact that in our visual periphery we are sensitive only to movement. Have someone wave an object or her finger around at the side of your visual field. You will find that the movement is seen but that you cannot identify the shape of the object. Even more important, when the movement stops, the object will become invisible. You may be surprised to learn that only the most complex mammals, including humans, have visual systems that can signal the brain in the absence of movement in the retinal image. More primitive animals cannot see stationary objects at all. That means that the jiggling effects caused by the microsaccades are not a flaw in our visual system but, rather, a mechanism that evolved to provide continuous temporal variation and movement in the retinal image, which, in turn, allows us to see aspects of the stationary environment that are often invisible to lower animals.

Percepts Emerge Over Time

One fact about perception that would be of great interest to mystical philosophers is that our perception of an event does not occur in "real time" but, rather, that we live in the past. Despite what you may believe, our perception of such ongoing ordinary events as an approaching car or of a thrown baseball is not instantaneous. We see the world in what a video technician would refer to as "taped delay," with our consciousness always lagging behind the reality. The puzzle is, If we perceive only events that are already past, then how is it even possible for us to accurately interact with objects in the world? Why don't more of us walk blithely in front of moving cars or fail to duck in time to avoid being hit by projectiles? Before we try to answer these important questions, let us provide you with some important background information about the known temporal relationships between physical events and their perception.

We will begin with the timing between an extremely simple visual stimulus and its associated percept. This relationship is illustrated in Figure 13-1. The stimulus is a 1 ms flash of light (a millisecond equals $\frac{1}{1000}$ of a second) over a small region of the retina, say $\frac{1}{10}$ of a degree. The neural activity associated with this flash of light begins with a small delay following the onset of the light, but, once started, the neural activity will continue for a duration that is much longer than the duration of the original brief flash. Our conscious experience of the flash depends on the duration of the neural activity, not the physical duration of the flash. This means that the perceived duration of the light will be a sort of illusion in that it will appear longer than it actually is. Technically we refer to this overestimation of the length of a stimulus as **visible persistence**. The length of this visible persistence depends on the adaptive state of the eye. Thus, our conscious experience of a 1 ms flash will last approximately 100 ms under light-adapted conditions (predominantly cone vision) and as long as 400 ms under dark-adapted conditions (rod vision; Coltheart, 1980; Di Lollo, 1980, 1984; Di Lollo & Bishof, 1995).

Some of you are probably relieved by Figure 13-1 because it indicates that the delay between the eye receiving a stimulus and the onset of the associated neural response (our "taped delay") is really quite small and might not have much impact in our everyday life. However, we must remind ourselves that the relationship shown in Figure 13-1 refers only to the first layers of neurons that

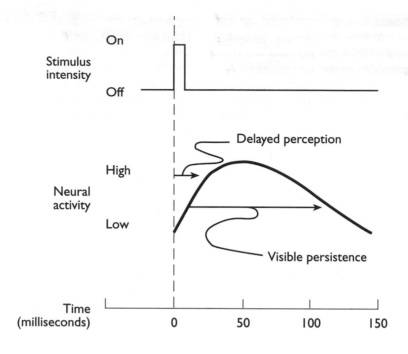

FIGURE 13-1   The temporal relationship between a flash of light and associated activity in visually sensitive neurons.

respond in the visual system. It takes between 10 ms and 50 ms for visual signals to reach the lateral geniculate nucleus of the brain, and it takes another 20 ms to 50 ms for information to reach the primary visual cortex. From the visual cortex it takes yet another 50 ms to 100 ms for information to reach centers in the frontal parts of the brain that are responsible for action and planning and perhaps even consciousness (DeValois & DeValois, 1991). Therefore, the time that elapses between a visual stimulus impinging on our retina and our acting in response to it can be quite long, potentially posing significant problems in being able to respond effectively to threats and opportunities in our visual environments. To put this in perspective, consider that under optimal conditions, it takes an automobile driver over 200 ms to perceive a stimulus that requires the decision to apply the brakes. A sizeable portion of this time is spent simply in passing neural information through the nervous system. After the stimulus is perceived and interpreted, the initiation of muscle responses is, by comparison, quite fast, taking only 10–15 ms (Woodworth, 1938). Thus, if you are traveling at a

speed of 65 mph (around 100 kph), by the time you have become conscious of a stimulus that will require you to stop, your car has already traveled an additional 20 ft (6 m), and you still haven't made even the slightest movement toward the brake pedal.

Some recent experiments have helped to shed light on the ways in which the brain compensates for the handicap of registering visual information in "taped delay." In short, the brain appears to have built-in mechanisms to anticipate where stimuli will be a short time in the future. In one study (Nihjawan, 1994), observers viewed a thin bar smoothly rotating about its center on a viewing screen. At unpredictable intervals an extension of the bar was briefly flashed on and off. If perception was instantaneous with the stimulus, or even if there was a constant delay between the presentation of a stimulus and its associated percept, then observers should have seen the brief flash as an outward extension of the rotating bar. However, what they saw in response to the brief flash was a second bar appearing briefly in a location trailing well behind the location of where a true extension would be. It was as though perception of the smoothly rotating bar was made possible by mechanisms of anticipation, and the perception of the briefly flashed extension to the bar was seen as a different stimulus because its unpredictable appearance did not fit into the anticipated pattern.

In a related physiological study (Sillito, Jones, Gerstein, & West, 1994), researchers were able to record activity from cells in the lateral geniculate nucleus of a cat, both when these cells were influenced only by incoming visual information concerning motion and when these cells were also connected to neurons descending from the primary visual cortex. The descending neurons were shown to *prime* the cells in the lateral geniculate nucleus so that these cells needed less activity than usual to respond in favor of the direction of motion signaled by the cortex. The authors suggested that the function of the cortical feedback was to test for the presence of certain patterns in the input and to lock onto them very quickly when they were found. This research therefore reveals a neural circuit that can help the observer overcome the inherent "taped delay" aspect of perception. However, in order for it to work, high visual centers must be given enough information to develop an anticipatory hypothesis that can be used to "tune" the lower visual centers for some expected types of stimuli. Such anticipation could be based on recently acquired information, as in the case of viewing a smoothly rotating bar (Nihjawan, 1994), or it could be based on longer term memories of what to expect in a given circumstance (Stelmach & Herdman, 1991).

As soon as we introduce the possibility of more than one stimulus occurring in succession, even more complex relationships emerge between the timing of physical events and their perception. Remember that we started our discussion with a simple 1 ms flash of light; now let's consider that flash, followed shortly thereafter by another 1 ms flash of light. Two very different percepts will occur, depending on whether or not the second flash occupies the same spatial location as the first flash.

If we have two flashes being shown in succession in separate spatial locations, as shown in Figure 13-2, the perceptual result is **temporal integration,** meaning that the two flashes appear to form a single unified stimulus. Temporal integration has been studied very effectively by using a

pattern of dots, as is also shown in Figure 13-2 (Di Lollo, 1980, 1984). We start out with a square pattern matrix that can contain 25 dots arranged in five rows and five columns. In the first 1 ms flash, we present 12 of these dots in randomly selected positions, whereas in the second 1 ms flash, 12 different dots are shown. This means that 1 dot is missing. The observers' task is to locate the position of the missing dot. The only way that observers can do this is by integrating information about dot locations across the two flashes. The large number of dots (12 in each frame) and the randomness of the missing location make it impossible to perform this task by any conventional use of short-term memory, which usually holds only seven or so elements. If the two flashes are shown with an interval of 0 ms to 50 ms separating the two events, then accuracy in identifying the missing dot is quite high because the visible persistence bridges the time gap and integrates the two views. In fact, subjects are often unaware that there were two flashes and appear to see all 24 dots as if they had been flashed on at the same time. However, by the time 100 ms has elapsed in light-adapted viewing conditions, accuracy in the task is approaching chance levels (1 in 25, or 4%), and subjects report seeing two successive groups of dots that they simply can't integrate in any way.

If we have two brief flashes being shown in succession but in the same spatial location, as illustrated in Figure 13-3, the perceptual result is quite different. Here we may find that the second of the two flashes will be perceived more accurately than the first (Breitmeyer, 1984; Michaels & Turvey, 1979). This is often referred to as **backward masking** because it is believed that somehow the stimulus that occurred later in time actually interferes with the processing of the earlier stimulus, much as if it were working backward in time. This phenomenon was studied in an elegant experiment by Bachman and Allik (1976). These researchers presented two simple shapes in rapid succession in the same spatial location. Each shape was flashed for 10 ms, chosen randomly from the set shown in Figure 13-3, and observers were asked to identify both shapes. When the two shapes were shown simultaneously, accuracy was equally poor for both the first and second shapes, showing the difficulty of identifying each shape in the composite display of two shapes. However, as the interval between

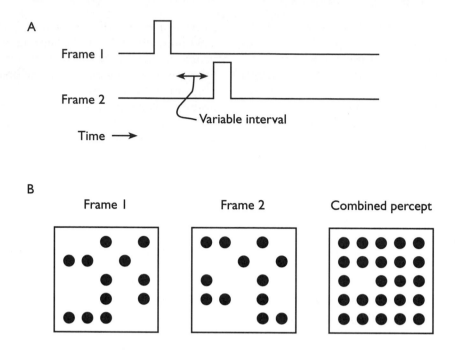

FIGURE 13-2 A method for studying temporal integration involving two display frames, each presented for 1 ms and at varying intervals from one another. Twelve dots are displayed in each frame such that when the frames are superimposed, one dot in the five-by-five matrix is missing. Observers are asked to report the location of the missing dot. Accuracy in this task declines steadily over intervals from 0 ms to 100 ms (based on Di Lollo, 1980, 1984).

the two flashes increased, the patterns of accuracy for the first and second shapes began to deviate substantially from one another. Whereas accuracy for the second shape improved steadily with an increased delay between flashes, accuracy for the first shape plunged even lower before beginning to improve with increased delay. The **J-shaped masking** pattern of accuracy shown for the first shape is evidence that there is a perceptual competition when two objects are flashed in quick succession. The fact that this pattern is seen only for the first object indicates that it is the temporally later stimulus that wins the competition.

Spatial Analyses Require Time

The last point that we want to make in order to convince you that time is as important as space in perception involves the analysis of spatial layout itself. Examine the picture shown at the left in Figure 13-4, which is a reproduction of a famous print

by Dutch artist M. C. Escher. What is involved in understanding the spatial layout depicted in this print? At some time after we begin viewing this picture, we realize that there are some glaring inconsistencies in the three-dimensional structure of the building. Some of the apparently straight posts connecting the lower and upper floors begin on a portion of the building nearest to us and end on a portion of the building that is farthest away. What does it take for us to detect these inconsistencies? Why don't we detect them immediately on being shown the picture?

It turns out that the inconsistencies can be detected only by comparing the depicted spatial structure over regions of the picture that are somewhat removed from each other. What the artist has cleverly done is to draw a building with depth relationships that are locally consistent everywhere. This means that each of the connections shown between two or more contours does not violate any principles of perspective drawing. This is shown for each of the two regions highlighted in

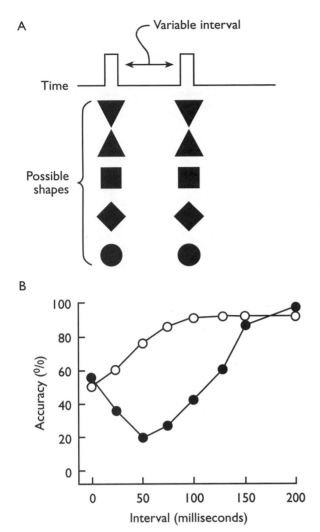

A

Variable interval

Time

Possible shapes

B

FIGURE 13-3   A method for studying visual masking involving the presentation of two shapes in rapid succession in the same spatial location. Observers are asked to report the identity of both shapes. When the shapes are shown simultaneously, accuracy is equally poor for both shapes. However, with an increasing interval between shapes, accuracy for the first shape (shown as black dots) is impaired more than for the second shape (based on Bachman & Allik, 1976).

Figure 13-4B. However, Escher has fooled the eye through violations of global consistency, changing the depth assignment of a given edge somewhere between these two locally consistent regions.

Why can't we detect these global inconsistencies immediately? The main reason is that the fovea of the eye has only a very limited spatial range over which it has acuity for fine spatial detail. The depicted structure in two regions can therefore be compared only after an eye movement has been made; the two regions of detailed structure cannot be seen simultaneously. The same process of integrating successive bits of information over time goes on in the perception of more common stimuli. Thus, you may feel that you see a face all at one time, yet direct measures show that we look at the eyes, the mouth, the nose, and the frame made by the hair over a period of a second and more, and then we integrate the information over the viewing time to make one coherent percept.

You might think that some of the need for temporal integration could be eliminated by viewing stimuli at a distance, or after a proportional size reduction. Such an altered stimulus would allow more of the pattern to stimulate the fovea of the eye, and fewer time-consuming eye movements would be needed. Unfortunately, this is not the case because information-processing time is affected not only by the size of the area being scanned but also by the amount of information in that area. Thus, reducing the size of the stimulus increases the amount of detail that is packed into increasingly smaller portions of the retina. Apparently, the spotlight of attention, or the *mind's eye*, is limited in the amount of detail it can register at once, and so the detection of inconsistency still takes a comparable amount of time, despite no physical eye movements being necessary to acquire all the information (Enns & King, 1990). This demonstration therefore illustrates the need for even apparently simple spatial analyses to require processing over time. Only by comparing information acquired at different points in time can the correct spatial analysis of a scene be completed.

TEMPORAL PROPERTIES OF THE VISUAL SYSTEM

Temporal Resolution

How sensitive are the eye and brain to changes in illumination over time? As with most of the other questions of this sort that we have asked, the

A

B

FIGURE 13-4   (A) *Belvedere* by Dutch artist M. C. Escher. (B) The same picture, highlighting two regions that are locally consistent in their depiction of depth and surface relations but that are globally inconsistent with one another.

answer is not simple because different parts of the visual system have different sensitivities. Physiological studies have shown that the activity of retinal receptors in the eye can resolve a flickering light at rates of up to several hundred cycles per second, although the sensitivity of neurons in the primary visual cortex to change over time is much less. When observers are asked to discriminate a light that is rapidly flickering on and off from one that is steadily on, the measured **critical fusion frequency, or CFF,** is somewhere between 10 cps and 60 cps. This is a very broad range because a stimulus flicking at 10 cps corresponds to a light turned on and off repeatedly for 50 ms durations, whereas at 60 cps on and off periods are only 8.3 ms in length.

Our temporal resolution as measured by the CFF varies over this wide range because it is sensitive to a number of variables, including the current level of light adaptation or dark adaptation, the intensity of the light, the distance of the light from the fovea, and the wavelength composition of the light. Table 13-1 provides a summary of these effects. Note that the CFF showing the greatest temporal resolution (highest frequency) would be obtained with the combination of a light-adapted eye and a light of high intensity but of any hue viewed in the visual periphery. A CFF showing the least resolution (lowest flicker rate) would be obtained with a dark-adapted eye and a light of low intensity and long wavelength (i.e., red) presented on the fovea.

Table 13-1   Factors That Influence Critical Fusion Frequency, the Ability to Discriminate a Flickering From a Steady Light

	CRITICAL FUSION FREQUENCY (CYCLES PER SECOND)					
Variables	10	20	30	40	50	60
adaptation	dark adapted ⟵————————————⟶ light adapted					
luminance	very dim ⟵————————————⟶ very bright					
retinal location				fovea ⟵——————⟶ periphery		
stimulus size				under 0.5° ⟵——————————⟶ over 10.0°		
wavelength						
dim light	red – green – blue					
bright light					⟵———— all hues ————⟶	

A second division of the visual system that has important consequences for our question of sensitivity to temporal changes in illumination is that division between the parvo and magno pathways of the visual system. As we saw in Chapter 3, this important distinction emerged in studies of retinal ganglion cells, where it was observed that some neurons respond primarily to the onset or offset of light in their receptive fields, whereas others respond in a more sustained fashion to the steady stream of light. Psychophysicists subsequently began referring to the *sustained* versus *transient* channels of the visual system.

Recent research has made it clear that the magno pathway (transient channel) is largely responsible for the time-keeping operations of vision. This was demonstrated very convincingly in a recent study (Leonard & Singer, 1997). Observers were asked to determine whether there were one or two flashes of light presented on any trial. The stimuli were either a single 50 ms flash of light or two 50 ms flashes separated by a 50 ms interval. If these were the only stimuli visible, then this task was extremely easy. Observers typically discriminated these two events with an accuracy of over 95%. However, introducing an irrelevant flash of light—anywhere else in the visual field and within approximately 250 ms of the test flash—greatly impaired the observers' accuracy in discriminating the single flash from the double flash.

Leonard and Singer (1997) subsequently examined the important characteristics of this distracting flash in relation to the test flashes. Low-contrast flashes were used to selectively activate the magno pathway; equiluminant chromatic flashes were used to selectively activate the parvo pathway; and high-contrast flashes were used to activate both pathways simultaneously. The researchers found that a low-contrast distracting flash could disrupt accuracy for all kinds of test flashes. On the other hand, accuracy for low-contrast test flashes was not disrupted by high-contrast and colored distracting flashes. This indicates that information about the precise timing of flashes is conveyed by the specialized magno pathway. It can therefore be disrupted by other magno signals that are irrelevant to the task, and it can influence the perceived temporal structure of information conveyed primarily by the parvo system.

Visible Persistence

Is the phenomenon of visible persistence that we discussed earlier of general benefit to the visual system, or is it a nuisance? Does visible persistence give us the ability to perform some tasks that would be impossible without it, or does it simply reflect the inherent sluggishness of a visual system that is built from relatively slow-acting neurons? Actually, visible persistence can be a boon or a bane, depending on the task we are asked to perform.

One realm where our technological society has come to rely completely on visible persistence is that of video display devices. A modern television or computer screen consists of many rows and columns of picture elements, affectionately called **pixels** by engineers. Each pixel can be triggered to project a light of a certain intensity and wavelength composition by turning on an electron gun pointed at that location. However, the electron gun activates any given pixel at some specified place on the screen for only an extremely brief time. In fact, each pixel is turned on and off in succession, starting from the upper left-hand pixel and moving to the lower right-hand pixel. Each pixel is illuminated once every 15–16 ms so that all the pixels are lit, or, technically, *refreshed*, 60–75 times a second. The chemical phosphor used at each pixel location on the screen does permit light to persist for some time longer than when the electron gun is actually on, but for the vast majority of the cycle, each pixel is turned off.

If our visual systems did not have visible persistence and were sensitive to the actual times of related changes going on across the television screen, we would see a single dot of light changing color while it traveled rapidly from left to right and from the top to the bottom of the screen. This would be repeated more than 60 times a second. If we add just a little visible persistence, then the screen would appear as a snowy flickering pattern with alternating regions of light and dark, and we would not see very realistic images. However, because our visual system has much lower temporal resolution than the television, we see a stable picture in which all the pixels appear to be illuminated simultaneously. The visual systems of dogs have a higher temporal resolution than do those of humans, so that dogs do see an unstable flickering image. That is one reason why a dog's attention is not usually captured by the TV, even if it is showing a picture of Lassie romping across the screen.

Despite the marvelous invention that is modern television, we suspect that humans did not evolve a visible persistence function primarily to facilitate our television viewing pleasure. Are there places in the natural world where visible persistence would be of benefit? The answer is "yes," and the reason is best understood when we compare some of the functions of the human visual system to that of a camera. In the design of any optical device, whether biological or artificial, some decision must be made with regard to the trade-off that exists between the duration of light exposure and the intensity of exposure. If there is plenty of illumination, then the stimulus has to be exposed for only a brief time to register the pattern of light.

This corresponds to a fast shutter speed on a camera and little persistence of neural activity in the low visual levels of humans. If illumination levels are low, however, then a longer time window of persistence—and a slower shutter speed—is needed to register the same pattern of light. We have already seen another example of this effect in **Bloch's Law** (Chapter 4). This relationship describes how the intensity of the light stimulus and the time that it is exposed determine its visibility. Generally speaking, the dimmer the stimulus, the longer that it must be exposed in order for us to detect its presence.

In the course of human evolution, numerous compromises have been made to achieve a degree of visible persistence that is sufficient to activate neurons at high levels but that is not so great that the temporal resolution necessary for our survival is lost. Furthermore, we have seen that nature has determined that the duration of persistence is changed dynamically, such that when we are dark adapted or when we are looking at dim stimuli, visible persistence is longer, giving us a greater opportunity to detect the presence of the pattern.

There are cases, however, where the degree of visible persistence that exists in human vision is clearly detrimental to optimal visual functioning. But, here again, we see that some attempt has been made by the highest brain processes to compensate for the task-specific deficiencies of lower visual processes. A good example is **motion smear**, which refers to the trail of visible persistence that is left by an object in motion. You have probably seen this in the dark, when quickly moving a light, such as a small flashlight, a lit cigarette, or a burning ember from a campfire, causes a streak to be visible. The persistence of the streak is long enough to allow you to make visible circles and other forms. Motion smear, however, does not require either dark conditions or very bright stimuli to be present. Demonstration Box 13-1 shows how to experience this phenomenon.

In general, motion smear contributes to difficulty in seeing the precise shape of an object in motion, although it may assist in determining the trajectory of a moving object. Research has shown that there is substantial **suppression of motion smear** when an object in motion follows a predictable path (Breitmeyer, 1989). In one study (Hogben & Di Lollo, 1985), observers were asked

---

DEMONSTRATION BOX 13-1
Motion Smear

Motion smear is the result of visible persistence when an object moves quickly across your visual field. You can easily experience this smear in daylight by holding one finger in front of your face and wagging it back and forth quickly, as shown in the figure. You will see an image with two fingers, one at each end of the swing, plus an additional blurred shape corresponding to your moving finger in the midportion of the movement path. The multiple fingers and the blur are evidence of visible persistence. This same persistence can decrease your ability to resolve more complex moving targets. To see this, now hold up two, three, or four spread fingers. Wag your hand back and forth as you did before. Again you see something at the end of each swing and a blur between, but the images of the various fingers all are superimposed on the still-persistent images of the others, making it virtually impossible to clearly make out how many separate fingers are moving back and forth in front of your face.

In the dark, motion smear is even greater, permitting you to spell out letters of your name in the air with a burning ember from a campfire or a lit cigarette.

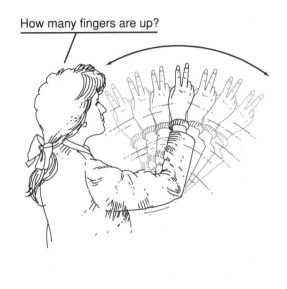

How many fingers are up?

---

to indicate the number of dots that could be seen simultaneously on an imaginary circle. In reality, a single dot was being plotted on the screen at any point in time, but its location changed from moment to moment. Visible persistence was the basis for observers' seeing simultaneous dots. When the dot was plotted randomly on the circle, observers could see six to seven dots because of visible persistence. However, when the dot followed a predictable circular path on the screen, observers could see only two to three dots, meaning that the visible persistence was reduced. The same thing happens for continuously moving targets. If you know where the target is going, some of the smear is suppressed. Studies of patients with selectively compromised magno visual pathways do not show as strong a pattern of suppression, suggesting that the suppression of motion smear is accomplished by the magno pathway inhibiting the parvo stream (Tassinari, Campara, Laercia, Chilosi, Martignoni, & Marzi, 1994).

Visual Masking

The likelihood that you can see a target is greatly reduced if the stimulus is presented when there is another target nearby in both location and time. This is referred to as **visual masking**. In principle, masking could be **forward,** meaning that when two stimuli are presented, the first stimulus interferes with the perception of the second; masking could be **simultaneous,** meaning that perception is impaired by the presence of an extraneous stimulus presented at the same time; and masking could be **backward,** meaning that the presence of the second stimulus interferes with the perception of the first. Forward masking is actually the weakest of the three types. It occurs only if the first stimulus is very close in time (100 ms or less) and gets stronger as the interval between stimuli approaches zero. Thus, although in a strict sense this can be called *forward masking*, it is likely that this is really simultaneous masking; however, the

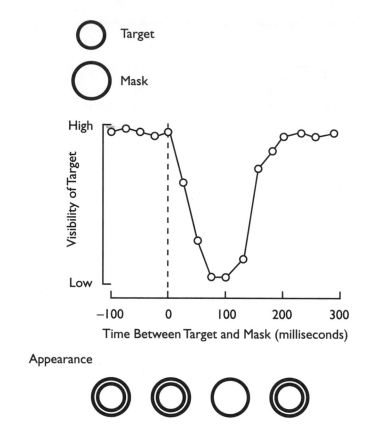

FIGURE 13-5 A typical masking function where the visibility of the target is most strongly interfered with when the masking stimulus follows the target stimulus by around 100 ms.

visual system is responding too slowly to recognize that the two stimuli did not appear at the same time. In the case of simultaneous or forward masking, the masking stimulus is making target identification difficult through the addition of visual noise to the target signal—a kind of camouflage.

Backward masking is quite different in that more than one mechanism appears to be responsible for the interference between target and mask. One of the ways that these mechanisms have been distinguished is by comparing **monoptic masking**, in which the target and mask are presented to only one eye, with **dichoptic masking**, in which the target is presented to one eye and the masking stimulus to the other (Breitmeyer, 1984; Michaels & Turvey, 1979). If masking occurs under dichoptic conditions, then we can be confident that low-level or early mechanisms involving interactions in the retinal or optic nerve cannot be responsible for the

interference because the information from the two eyes combines to form a single view only higher up in the visual system. Some studies of dichoptic masking have found that the curve describing the visibility of the target as a function of the interval between target and mask is J- or even U-shaped, as can be seen in Figure 13-5. Notice that this kind of curve indicates that the target is still relatively visible when the mask is presented simultaneously but that masking increases (visibility decreases) as the interval between the target and the mask approaches 50 ms to 100 ms. If we make the time between the stimuli even greater, approaching 200 ms or more, then the masking effect decreases, and the target becomes visible again.

Varying the number of potential target stimuli gives us additional information about the mechanisms responsible for backward masking (Breitmeyer, 1984; Sheerer, 1973; Spencer & Shuntich,

1970). When only one potential target is presented in a display, followed by a mask, accuracy impairments occur only when the mask arrives within 100 ms or so. However, when there are 12 potential items, backward masking extends to almost half a second (500 ms). Multiple targets act differently in other ways as well. For instance, the degree of masking with a single item is also strongly influenced by the intensity of the mask, with brighter masks producing more masking. When there are a number of targets, however, varying brightness of the mask seems to have little effect.

Findings such as these have led some to theorize that there are two important mechanisms of backward masking: masking by **integration** and masking by **interruption** (Bachman & Allik, 1976; Breitmeyer, 1984; Enns & Di Lollo, 1997). Masking by integration essentially applies to forward and simultaneous masking, as well as to backward masking that occurs within a 100 ms window. The problem for the visual system is that the target and mask patterns are essentially fused or integrated into a single pattern, making the resolution of the two separate stimuli difficult.

Backward masking by interruption involves a very different kind of perceptual problem. It is based on the presumption that we need a certain amount of time to process a target well enough that we can recognize it. Masking then comes about when processing of a first pattern (the target) is interrupted by a second pattern (the mask) that appears in the same spatial location and presumably is demanding use of the same visual analyzing units. This conflict does not involve the early visual stages of processing where contours are defined but instead involves a competition for the higher level mechanisms involved in object recognition (Enns & Di Lollo, 1997).

PERCEPTUAL ORGANIZATION OVER TIME

Time becomes a problem when we try to figure out which parts of the flow of visual information belong together because they are part of a stream of stimuli that simply takes a while to appear, as compared to those stimuli that should be seen as separate because they are really from different events but just happen to be occurring very close

in time. These are fundamental problems confronted by every perceptual system. Some researchers have referred to these problems as the *temporal stability versus plasticity dilemma* (Grossberg, 1995) because they seem to highlight a tension between two necessary but opposing forces. One is the force toward perceptual stability, necessary in a world where the information at our receptors from even a rigid and stationary object is constantly undergoing change over time, because we move and change our angle of view or other stimuli enter the visual field, perhaps partly blocking our view. The second force is toward perceptual plasticity, which is the process by which we attempt to segregate the parts of the sensory array because more than one object or event has appeared coincidentally in time.

Perceptual Stability

The force toward perceptual stability has been studied using several important auditory illusions. One of the simplest is called the **auditory continuity illusion** (Grossberg, 1995; Warren, 1984). Suppose that you hear a steady tone that shuts off for a moment and then turns on again. Obviously you will hear a silent gap in the tone. Suppose, however, that instead of silence, we fill that gap with a broadband noise (sort of a burst of static), which turns on just as the tone shuts off and turns off when the tone starts again, as shown in Figure 13-6. Under certain conditions you will hear the tone as though it had been continuously on, even during the noise. The perception that the tone continues through the noise (even though it is not physically present) is the auditory continuity illusion. The illusion disappears if the tone does not turn on again after the noise burst turns off, so now you don't have the illusion that the tone continued during the noise. In the illusion situation it should be obvious that your brain does not know whether the tone will start again until after the noise has been shut off. Therefore, what you experience is a construction of your brain that has been assembled after all the parts of the pattern of signals have been presented. This construction helps to provide continuity for the perception of a single event across breaks or interruptions in the signal that occur because of extraneous stimuli in the

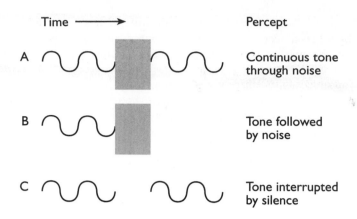

FIGURE 13-6   The auditory continuity illusion. (A) If a stimulus consists of a tone (wavy line), followed by a brief period of noise (rectangle), and then the tone again, you will hear the tone continuing through the noise. (B) If the tone does not turn on again, you will not hear the tone during the noise. (C) If the period of interruption is not filled by noise, the tone will be heard with an interruption (based on Grossberg, 1995).

environment. You might think of this the next time you hear the continuous note of a saxophone on the radio in your kitchen, despite its being interrupted by clanks from the pots or dishes you are working with.

In the previous chapter we saw a related illusion that involved speech in which listeners supplied missing parts of speech when the stream of speech was interrupted by other sounds. We referred to this as the **phonemic restoration effect** (Warren, 1970). There it was the meaningful content of the sentence that determined the speech sequence that was actually perceived. In effect, we hear the speech units that the immediate context suggests should be in the phrase, even if they are not physically present.

The visual system can be shown to behave in similar ways. When we see a target (say, a black disk) that apparently moves behind another target (say, a white square) so that what is really stimulating our retina is a disk with a notch or a bite taken out of it, we still "see" the disk as a complete circle, just partially obscured from view (Shore & Enns, 1997). What is happening here is that the perceptual system is simply "filling in" to effectively "heal" stimuli and make them perceptually whole in order to correct for briefly occurring distortions or gaps. This, by the way, is one reason why we don't see gaps in the stimuli caused by the blind spot. The filling-in process completes the stimuli

as our eyes move over the field. Only by effectively limiting the changes over time and focusing our attention on the unchanging stimulus do we become aware of the blind spot, as we showed you in Demonstration Box 3-5. Perhaps even more striking than the filling-in phenomena is the way in which the visual system provides the illusion of continuity and completeness in object perception, even though, at any given moment, only a small portion of an object may be actually visible. You can demonstrate this for yourself using Demonstration Box 13-2.

Perceptual Plasticity

The force toward perceptual plasticity can be seen in our everyday ability to segment the continuous stream of acoustic information associated with spoken speech into individual words. To remind yourself of the complexity of this problem, think back to the last time you heard a conversation between two people in a language that you did not understand. How well would you do if you were asked to indicate the beginnings and endings of words in that stream of speech? This turns out to be a very difficult task because the pauses in the stream of sounds rarely coincide with the boundaries between words. The raw acoustical information gives us very little reliable information on its

---

DEMONSTRATION BOX 13-2
Figural Integration

It is rare that we see an object in its entirety. Either we or the object are moving about, resulting in glimpses that are partially occluded by other objects (for example, a dog running through some trees). Yet we have no difficulty identifying the object. Parks (1965) studied this phenomenon by moving a shape behind a narrow window, or slit. His surprising result was that a wide variety of shapes could be easily recognized, even though a shape was never seen except as a series of fragments. Because of one of the shapes Parks used, the phenomenon of easy identification of shapes presented by moving them behind a slit has come to be called *Parks's camel.*

In order to experience Parks's camel for yourself, have a friend pass various objects

(including himself or herself) behind a narrow slit created by a door that is slightly ajar (Shimojo & Richards, 1986). Try varying the size of the slit and the speed with which the object passes across it. You will find that over a surprisingly wide range of size and speed conditions the object will be identifiable. Also, pay attention to the strength of the feeling you will have that the *entire* object is present, even though at any moment you are only receiving a fragmentary view of it. When the conditions are optimal, that impression is very strong. This demonstrates the importance of the integration over time required to create the perceptual object out of a chaotic and constantly changing retinal image.

---

own. However, if we are familiar with a language, the problem seems very easy. The difference is that we are familiar with the words that can possibly be spoken, and so we use that knowledge to segment sounds that have no real physical breaks.

Even within the experience of hearing a familiar language, the role of context can be shown to be critically important in the segmentation process. Imagine hearing the sounds associated with "I'd like anicetea" in one of two contexts: first, at an outdoor cafe near the beach on a summer day and then in one of those embroidered French pastry shops in midwinter. The person serving you would undoubtedly hear two very different messages, despite the acoustical streams being identical in the two settings.

The role of context in perceiving visual motion is equally important. Consider two displays created by Ramachandran and Anstis (1986), which consist of alternating the views shown as Frames 1 and 2 in Figure 13-7A. What the person reports seeing here is a single small dot that is flashing on and off beside a stationary larger square. In Figure 13-7B, we have simply added three dots. Alternating Frames 1 and 2 makes those three dots appear to move first right and then left in a repetitive

manner. However, now observers see something completely different happening to the original dot beside the square. It seems to be moving behind the square and then reemerging in a repetitive manner. In the context of other dots that appear to move, the brain acts as if it is now most plausible that the original small dot is doing the same thing, and so a motion signal is attributed to that dot, even though there is no local evidence that the dot is moving. We will learn more about apparent motion in the next chapter.

THE PERCEPTION OF THE PASSAGE OF TIME

Our sense of the passage of time is a perceptual experience. Up to now we have considered the relationship between physical stimuli and our perceptual experiences. However, in the case of perceiving the passage of time the situation is less clear. There certainly is no readily visible "time organ" for such stimuli to impinge on. Our notion of time may be associated with some form of internal clock that we consult like a wristwatch to determine the span of an event, but it also seems tied

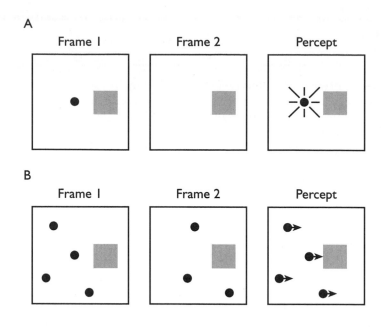

FIGURE 13-7 Visual displays consisting of two frames that are flashed repeatedly. (A) A single small dot is seen flickering on and off beside a stationary larger square. (B) The same small dot is now seen moving behind the square and back again. The only thing in this display that is different than the previous one is that there are other dots that appear to be moving back and forth as a group (based on Ramachandran & Anstis, 1986).

to our experience of successive change (Fraisse, 1963). It is through the concept of change that time and motion become intertwined. Changes that occur in a sequence are often associated with a perception of time passing, whereas, as you will learn later in this book, changes in location over time may, under the proper conditions, be perceived as movement.

The concept of time is fundamental to human beings. For example, every language thus far analyzed has separate tenses for past, present, and future, plus innumerable modifiers to specify *when* more precisely—*yesterday, today, recently, in an hour, while, during, after,* and hundreds more (Bentham, 1985). Despite this position as a fundamental experience, the study of time is complex because "time is not a thing that, like an apple, may be perceived" (Woodrow, 1951). In fact, time involves two qualities of our perception that seem to be added to our consciousness and that do not seem to correspond to simple physical dimensions. These qualities are an awareness of a present moment and the impression that time passes. Let us

call these the concepts of **now** and **flow,** respectively (Michon, 1985).

The concept of *now* is always with us and has been described by William James (1890) as the "saddle-back of time with a certain length of its own, on which we sit perched, and from which we look in two directions into time." Sometimes called the *subjective present,* it is the few seconds of our current experience of ongoing consciousness; all else is either past or future. Although *flow* is an equally fundamental perceptual attribute of time, it actually includes a number of different measurable aspects of experience (cf. Brown, 1990; Poppel, 1978). Each of these additional facets of time perception may be quite different from the others and may involve unique physiological or information-processing mechanisms.

One of the most common judgments that we make about time flow is *duration estimation.* This is simply our perception of how much time has elapsed between two events, such as the time that lapses between when you turn on the stove and when a pot of water boils. We usually use units such as seconds or minutes to describe duration. Next, we have the perception of *order* or *sequence*, which involves the determination of which event came first, second, and so forth. Without this you could never correctly remember telephone numbers that someone has just read to you. The minimal case of the perception of sequence involves determining the time interval that must separate two events before they are perceived as occurring one after the other, rather than at the same moment. This judgment involves the discrimination between the experiences of *simultaneity* and *successiveness*. The last aspect of flow is somewhat less perceptual but still requires time estimation. Anticipating or planning an ordered sequence of events before they occur is especially important in playing musical instruments or in performing actions such as speech production in which we automatically plan and execute an ordered sequence of sounds to produce meaningful utterances.

Two general processes have been suggested by which we perceive times. We may call these "clock" theories because each gives a mechanism that explains how we monitor the passage of time. The first involves a **biological clock** and assumes that there is some physiological mechanism that we can use as a timer for our perception of time. Thus, just as the eye is an organ that monitors light, our biological clock monitors time. The second involves the notion of a **cognitive clock,** in which time is derived via some cognitive process that is based on factors such as how much sensory information is processed, how many events occur within a given interval, or how much attention is paid to ongoing cognitive events. In this latter viewpoint time is constructed rather than simply monitored. Both types of clocks may exist, and each may be used for different types of time perception.

Biological Clocks

Many physical phenomena have their own rhythms or timing. There are day-night cycles, cycles of the moon, cycles of the seasons, and many others. Living organisms often display similar rhythmic activities. Many flowers open and close at particular times of the day. Animals have physiological and behavioral processes that cycle regularly. One proposal about the way time is perceived is based on the idea that the *flow* of subjective time is related to some body mechanism that acts in a periodic manner, with each period serving as one "tick" of the biological clock. Anything that alters the speed of our physiological processes would then be expected to alter our perception of the speed at which time passes.

Circadian Rhythms   Two of the most obvious examples of apparently timed behaviors are the sleep-wakefulness cycle that runs through a regular daily rhythm and the hunting and feeding patterns of animals that repeat every 24 hours (Groos & Daan, 1985; Rijnsdorp, Daan, & Dijkstra, 1981). There are also more subtle physiological processes that have their own periodic changes. For example, the pulse, blood pressure, and temperature of the body show day-night variations in humans as well as in many other animals. There is more than $1°$ C difference in body temperature between the coolest point, which occurs during the night, and the warmest point, which occurs during the afternoon (Coren, 1997). These all are examples of a **circadian rhythm,** which comes from the Latin *circa,* meaning "approximately," and *dies,* meaning "day." Thus, a circadian rhythm is one that varies with a cycle of roughly 24 hours.

So much rhythmic activity in behavior suggests control by some internal *biological clock*. Alternatively, it may be that these repetitive 24-hour changes are simply a function of the regular changes in light and temperature that occur in the day-night cycle. Thus, an animal might become active in the presence of daylight, when it can see more clearly and when the temperature is a bit higher, and it is this activity that then alters the physiological function. The "built-in" approximately 24-hour cycle, however, can be demonstrated experimentally in the absence of light or temperature changes. For example, suppose that we find ourselves in a constant-light environment, where there are no changing cues that show the passage of time. Under these conditions our biological clock will "run free," gaining or losing time like a not-too-accurate physical clock. Although different people will have different cycle lengths, most of us will begin to live a "day" that is approximately 25 hours long (e.g., Aschoff, 1981; Wever, 1979).

If the internal biological clock is set for about 25 hours, why do our internal and behavioral rhythms continue on a 24-hour cycle? Why doesn't our daily activity cycle drift out of phase with local time? This is because there is a mechanism that synchronizes the internal timer with local time. From the behavioral point of view, the most salient aspect of local time is the alternation of light and dark. To be an accurate reference against local time, a biological clock must be synchronized with the local day-night cycle, and it must have a stable period that is relatively free of unpredictable environmental fluctuation. This process of synchronization is called **entrainment.** If there were no such process, when you travel across the continent, where the sun might rise 3 hours earlier relative to the current setting of your biological clock, you would be left 3 hours "out of step" with your new environment. Such trips, of course, cause some disruption of your time sense in the form of *jet lag*, which accounts for the sight of newly arrived Europeans wandering through the lobbies of New York hotels at 4 A.M. or 5 A.M., looking for an open restaurant for breakfast. Because of their great speed of travel, their circadian rhythms are still set to Paris, Moscow, or some other European time.

Body time does eventually adapt to the new time zone at a rate of ½ to 1 hour per day. This adaptation comes about through entrainment of the biological clock to the local environmental sunlight-to-darkness cycle (Coren, 1997).

To use the scientific term, light is the primary *zeitgeber* (German for "time giver"). Much evidence, based on several species of animals including humans, shows that the internal clock is synchronized to light (e.g., Johnson & Hastings, 1986). A flash of light will reset the biological clocks of animals reared in constant darkness, either advancing it or retarding it, depending on when the flash occurs (Aschoff, 1979). If there is no regular light cycle, however, other environmental stimuli, such as daily fluctuations in temperature, may serve as *zeitgebers* to set the internal timer.

Is there a single structure that might serve as the biological clock? Researchers have isolated several regions in the hypothalamus that seem to be important to maintaining the circadian rhythm (Gerkema & Groos, 1990; Rusak & Zucker, 1979). The most important of these is called the **suprachiasmatic nucleus** (which we will abbreviate as the **SCN**), and

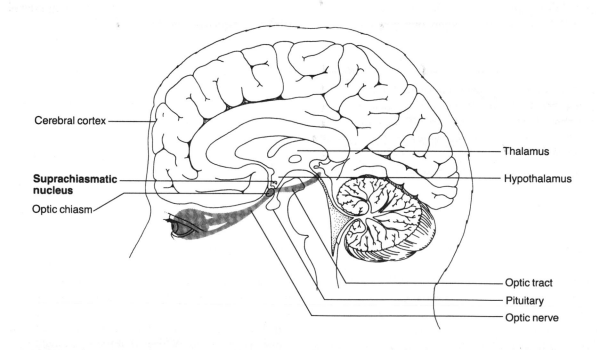

FIGURE 13-8 The location of the suprachiasmatic nucleus of the hypothalamus, which is thought to be the basis of the biological clock that maintains circadian rhythms.

it is located very near the optic chiasm, as can be seen in Figure 13-8. The SCN is really a very tiny organ, containing only a few thousand cells; however, it has a large effect on our behavior. The timing function of this organ is easily demonstrated. For example, rats are nocturnal animals, sleeping during the day and foraging at night. Destroying the SCN abolishes this pattern. The animals still sleep the same amount of time, but the circadian pattern is gone, and they sleep in random periods throughout the day and night (Stephan & Nunez, 1977). Tumors in this region have the same effect in humans (Fulton & Bailey, 1929). Furthermore, electrical stimulation of the SCN in animals will reset the biological clock, in much the same way that flashes of light do for dark-reared animals (Rusak & Groos, 1982). Because light is the primary *zeitgeber* for the circadian clock, we would expect that the SCN would receive inputs from the visual system, and it does (e.g., Groos & Meijer, 1985). It also may be affected by a hormone secreted by the pineal gland (which is also light sensitive). This hormone, called *melatonin*, is normally secreted at night (or after a period of light exposure) and appears to reset the circadian clock in the SCN (Cassone, 1990; Wever, 1990).

If light is needed to keep our internal clocks synchronized to local time, this raises an interesting question. What happens to blind people who can't see light? Can they reset their biological clock? About 76% of blind people report that they have difficulty falling asleep at their usual bedtime and that these difficulties are cyclical in nature, which is exactly what you would expect if blind people had a free-running internal clock that was an hour or so longer than 24 hours. Coren (1997) reviewed several studies that have looked at blind people over a long term and confirmed the fact that their internal circadian timer is not resetting normally. For example, one study of a completely blind man monitored an 80-day period. His periods of sleep gradually drifted, so for a week he was sleeping during the night, but 2 weeks later his maximum periods of sleepiness were during the day. This pattern of behavior was consistent with an individual whose internal clock is set at a day length of 24.9 hours. Thus, the absence of a normal light sense in the blind seems to hamper more than their ability to process visual information. It also condemns them to a situation where

their body time drifts, leaving their normal sleeping and waking cycles out of step with those who have normal sight.

Short-Term Timers   Although our circadian rhythms are maintained by an internal biological clock, we often make estimates of times that are considerably shorter than 24 hours. We can accurately determine which of two time intervals is longer when each is less than a second in duration. A "slow" circadian clock would be quite useless for this task, which suggests that there are probably several biological clocks in animals. For example, destroying the SCN does not affect the cyclic change in body temperature (Fuller, Lydic, Sulzman, Albers, Tepper, & Moore-Ede, 1981), nor does it seem to affect some short-cycling biological rhythms. In much the same way that we might use a stopwatch to measure short intervals, our wristwatch to measure longer ones, and a calendar to measure even longer periods of time, there seem to be different biological clocks for different aspects of behavior. Heartbeats, electrical activity in the brain, breathing, hormonal and metabolic activities, and even walking steps have at one time or another been suggested as candidates for an internal biological timing mechanism (Aschoff, 1981; Ornstein, 1969; Poppel, 1978; Treisman, 1963). Some of these might be useful as biological clocks to measure intervals shorter than the 24-hour circadian period. Therefore, we might view the perception of time as occurring in a "clock shop" rather than in a single biological timer.

Rather than look at long time intervals, some researchers have gone to the other extreme and asked: What is the shortest time interval that we can sense? Experimentally, they asked the question What is the minimum time separation needed for two events to be perceived as occurring at different times (successively) rather than at the same time (simultaneously)? In effect, they were searching for the basic time unit in perception. This idea was discussed in some detail by Stroud (1955), who suggested that psychological time is not a continuous dimension but, rather, consists of discrete bits. These **perceptual moments** are the psychological units of time. Based on several research findings, Stroud estimated that each moment is about 100 ms in duration, which would be the shortest perceived duration that a stimulus can have. In addition, stimuli presented within the same moment either would be perceived as occurring simultaneously or, depending on the nature of the stimulus, would not be distinguishable from each other. Stimuli presented in different moments would be perceived as being successive.

Efron (1967, 1973) demonstrated this aspect of the perceptual moment by looking at *micropatterns*, which are variations in a stimulus that occur so quickly that there is no corresponding change in the perception. For instance, a 20 ms stimulus composed of 10 ms of red light followed by 10 ms of green light is not perceptibly different from one in which the green comes before the red—both appear yellow (if visible persistence is eliminated; Yund, Morgan, & Efron, 1983).

White (1963) attempted to measure the perceptual moment by having observers estimate the number of clicks they heard. He presented the clicks at different rates up to 25 per second. Observers were fairly accurate at rates of up to 5 per second; at the highest click rates, however, observers still estimated a presentation rate of about 6 to 7 clicks per second. This corresponds to a perceived rate of one stimulus per 150 ms. Thus, information could not be processed in "chunks" smaller than 150 ms, which would be the resolution limit of the internal timer.

In another study, Efron (1967) presented two pulses of light and asked observers to say which one was longer. One of the flashes was always 1 ms in duration; the other was of a variable duration. Both flashes were always seen as being of the same length until the exposure time of the variable flash exceeded a value of 60 ms or 70 ms. At this duration, the variable flash was seen as being longer than the 1 ms flash. Efron concluded that the minimum duration of a stimulus in consciousness (which should be one perceptual moment) is 60 ms to 70 ms.

It seems likely that the perceptual moment is different for different tasks and, perhaps, for different sensory modalities (e.g., Kolers & Brewster, 1985). For example, reaction time studies (where observers are asked to react as quickly as possible to a stimulus input) have indicated that short-term memory can be scanned at about the rate of 25–30 ms per item (e.g., Sternberg, 1975). The detection of different vowel sounds in speech may

require only 20 ms (Hermes, 1990). The timing of well-trained motor tasks, such as typing or piano playing, also seems to support a 30 ms internal timing organization (Augenstine, 1962; Shaffer, 1985). In an experiment in word recognition, Eriksen and Collins (1968) used a set of patterns that, if seen by themselves, seemed random and unrelated to any word. If, however, two patterns were superimposed, either physically or psychologically, they formed a particular word. The researchers found that when observers were shown patterns sequentially, recognition for the word was highest when the interval between the patterns was about 25 ms. This implies that the perception of simultaneity is maintained over only a 25 ms interval rather than one that approaches 100 ms. There is also some suggestion that the perceptual moment becomes unstable when judgments involve more than one sensory modality, such as judging the order of presentation of a sound and a light (Ulrich, 1987).

An interesting "reverse" demonstration of the perceptual moment comes from Intraub (1985), who presented a series of pictures to subjects at a rate of one every 111 ms. One of these pictures always had a frame around it, and observers were asked to indicate which picture had the frame. On 54% of the trials, observers reported that the frame was around the picture that appeared before or after the correct one, probably because the two pictures fell within the same perceptual moment. All of these data suggest that, depending on the specific task, the minimum perceptual duration (or the time between ticks of the fastest biological clock) is probably between 25 ms and 150 ms.

Biological Pacemaker To the extent that there is a biological timer that serves as a sort of pacemaker, ticking away internal time, it would be reasonable to expect that it would speed up or slow down along with other physiological processes in the body. Hoagland (1933) verified this when his wife became ill with a high fever. He asked her to estimate the duration of 1 min by counting to 60 at a rate of one number per second. When her body temperature was approximately 39° C (103° F) her perceived minute was only 37.5 sec by objective clock time. This suggests that at higher body temperatures the speed of physiological activities increases, and this causes the pacemaker to tick more rapidly than usual. Thus, when

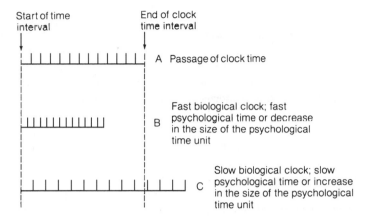

FIGURE 13-9 Each tick mark on these lines represents a unit of time. Those in A are clock time; those in B and C are ticks of the biological clock. Notice that in B the internal clock is faster, so the same amount of clock time seems psychologically longer and time "drags by." For C, the internal clock is slower, and so the same amount of clock time seems much shorter psychologically.

asked to reproduce a given physical time interval, a person with a high body temperature produces an interval that is too short. Similar results have been obtained in rats using natural daily variations in body temperature (Shurtleff, Raslear, & Simmons, 1990). An alternative way of looking at this is to note how our perception of physical (clock) time will seem to change when psychological time is running quickly. A given physical duration will appear to be too long if the psychological clock is ticking faster than the physical clock, therefore

giving more ticks per unit time than normally occur (see Figure 13-9).

If an increase in body temperature increases apparent duration, then lowering body temperature may have the opposite effect. This was found by Baddeley (1966), who tested scuba divers diving in cold water off the coast of Wales. Like Hoagland, he asked his subjects to count to 60 at a rate of one number per second. After the dive, when their body temperature was approximately 1° C lower than it had been before entering the water, his

---

DEMONSTRATION BOX 13-3
Body Temperature and Time Perception

This demonstration is based on an experiment performed by Pfaff (1968). We know that our body temperature can fluctuate as much as 1° C during the course of a day. It is at its lowest point early in the day and tends to rise throughout the afternoon. Given this, try the following observations. On rising in the morning, try counting to 60 at the rate of what you perceive to be one number per second. You will probably need a friend to keep track of clock time for you so that you can relate your perceived minute to a

clock minute. Then take your temperature. (Do not take your temperature before you count; otherwise it may bias your counting rate.) Do this several times throughout the day, and keep a record of your results. If the theory is supported, you should find that your counting time will shorten (relative to a clock minute) as your body temperature increases. Thus, as the body clock speeds up, the passage of time tends to be overestimated, and "clock" time seems to pass more slowly.

subjects required approximately 70 seconds to count to 60. This indicates that their pacemakers were ticking at a slower rate than the external clock. Counting time using the slower ticking rate of their internal timers led them to underestimate the passage of time. In other words, when our internal clock is too slow, physical time seems to whiz by (see Figure 13-9). You may demonstrate the effects of temperature on your own time sense by trying Demonstration Box 13-3.

If we have an internal biological clock, then anything that affects the rate of physiological function might also affect our estimates of time. For instance, fatigue usually slows physiological functioning. Thus, the longer we are awake (or the greater the pressure for sleep), the slower our biological clock and the more likely that when asked to estimate the passage of an hour our estimate will be longer than a physical clock hour (Aschoff, 1984; Daan, Beersma, & Borbely, 1984). Similarly, general anesthetics lead to overestimates of physical time (Adam, Rosner, Hosick, & Clark, 1971; Steinberg, 1955). Conversely, many investigations have found that drugs such as amphetamines and caffeine (both of which are stimulants) lead to underestimates of physical time (Frankenhauser, 1959; Goldstone, Boardman, & Lhamon, 1958). Drugs such as marijuana, mescaline, psilocybin, and LSD also seem to produce a lengthening of perceived time relative to a nondrug state that would lead to underestimates of physical time (Fisher, 1967; Weil, Zinberg, & Nelson, 1968). It has been argued that all these changes in time perception are caused by acceleration or deceleration of the pacemaker that serves as our internal timer.

Cognitive Clocks

When you say that 2 minutes of sitting on a hot stove feels like 2 hours but that 2 hours of sitting with your loved one seems like 2 minutes, you actually are expressing the central aspect of most cognitive clock theories of time perception. These theories are based on the presumption that the perception of the passage of time is based not on physical or biological time but, rather, on the mental processes that occur during an interval. In effect, time is not directly perceived but,

rather, is "constructed" or "inferred" (Fraisse, 1963; Woodrow, 1951). This suggests that the tasks a person engages in will influence that person's perception of the passage of time. Given the variety of potential cognitive activities, it is perhaps not surprising that a number of different variables affect the cognitive clock. Among the variables that have been shown to affect the subjective perception of duration are (1) the number of events occurring during the interval (e.g., Adams, 1977; Block, 1974; Poynter & Holma, 1985), (2) the complexity of stimulus events (e.g., Block, 1978; Ornstein, 1969), (3) the type of cognitive or information processing required (e.g., Hicks, Miller, & Kinsbourne, 1976; Thomas & Weaver, 1975), and (4) the amount of attention given to the passage of time (e.g., Brown, 1985; McClain, 1983). All of these affect the perception of the *flow* or passage of time, and all are consistent with the idea that the rate at which the cognitive clock ticks is affected by how internal events are processed.

Change One notion is that the ticking rate of the cognitive clock is dependent on **event processing** or **change monitoring**. The greater the number of events, or the more changes that occur, during an interval, the faster your cognitive clock ticks, and thus the longer is your estimate of the amount of time that has passed. Several studies seem to support this idea. A duration filled with stimulus events is perceived as longer than an identical time period empty of any external events, a phenomenon known as the **filled duration illusion**. For example, if we fill a time interval with brief tones, this interval will be perceived as being longer than an identical time interval during which no tones (or fewer tones) were presented. This is also true for such events as light flashes, words, or drawings (e.g., Avant, Lyman, & Antes, 1975; Hicks, Miller, Gaes, & Bierman, 1977; Ornstein, 1969; Poynter & Holma, 1985). Conversely, observers engaging in **restricted environmental stimulation technique** studies (where for 24 hours or more they recline in a soundproof, darkened chamber with essentially all typical environmental stimulation removed) tend to underestimate drastically the amount of time they have spent in the chamber (Suedfeld, 1980). This underestimation occurs, presumably, because so few stimulus events have transpired during the interval.

Processing Effort How difficult stimuli are to process and the amount of memory storage that they require have also been shown to affect our perception of the duration of a time interval. For example, we tend to judge the brief presentation of a word to be longer in duration than a blank interval of the same length (Thomas & Weaver, 1975). Furthermore, the presentation interval of familiar words is judged to be shorter than the presentation interval of meaningless verbal stimuli (Avant & Lyman, 1975; Avant, Lyman, & Antes, 1975), and presentations of nonfamiliar words appear to take longer than those of familiar words (Warm & Mc-Cray, 1969). In both instances, an increase in the amount of information processing required during the interval (a word versus a blank and a meaningless group of letters versus a word) leads to an increase in the estimated duration of the interval. This is consistent with a **processing effort model** of time perception. Similarly, the more items you store in memory during an interval of time, the longer you judge the time to be (Block, 1974; Mulligan & Schiffman, 1979), a notion sometimes called the **storage size model** of time perception. Both are based on the presumption that the ticking rate of the cognitive clock is dependent on the amount of cognitive activity actually engaged in.

Temporal Versus Nontemporal Attention Both the *event processing* and the *processing effort* mechanisms seem to affect an observer's cognitive clock time, but the results are complicated by the way the observer is attending to the task. A simple example of this is given by the old homily "A watched pot never boils," which suggests that the more attention you pay to the passage of time, the longer the time interval appears to be (e.g., Block, George, & Reed, 1980; Cahoon & Edmonds, 1980). This may be called the **temporal processing model** of time perception.

One of the best examples of the temporal processing model is the fact that when we are told in advance that we will have to judge the time that a task takes, we tend to judge the duration as being longer than we do when we are unexpectedly asked to judge the duration after the task is completed (e.g., Brown, 1985; McClain, 1983). Simply telling observers that they will later have to estimate the time that has passed causes them to pay attention to, and perhaps to order, internal events and external physical events in a way that increases the perceived duration of the task.

Conversely, anything that draws our attention away from actually monitoring the passage of time should shorten our sense of "time passing." For instance, making the task that we are working on more difficult makes it harder to attend to time directly. For this reason, we find that estimates of the duration of difficult tasks are usually shorter than estimates of the duration of easy tasks (e.g., Arlin, 1986; Brown, 1985; McClain, 1983). Sometimes, directing attention toward or away from the passage of time may even reverse the *filled duration illusion,* which we discussed earlier, because it is more difficult to process many events in an interval while at the same time attending to the flow of time itself (e.g., Miller, Hicks, & Willette, 1978; Zakay, Nitzan, & Glicksohn, 1983). Demonstration Box 13-4 shows how attention to time and task difficulty interact to affect our perception of the passage of time.

It should be clear from the preceding discussion that in the same way that there are a number of biological clocks that can interact in complex ways to give us a sense of the *flow* of time, there are a number of cognitive clocks, or at least a number of ways to set the speed of a single cognitive clock. One interesting aspect of the effects of cognitive processes on the estimation of time is the effect of age. We all remember how when we were children, the time between birthdays seemed endless. There is now a good deal of evidence that as people age, the passage of larger units of time (such as days, months, or even years) seems to be much faster (Joubert, 1990; Lemlich, 1975). One possible explanation for this is that the total amount of time that you have experienced serves as a reference level and that the perceived duration of any time interval is compared to this baseline (Joubert, 1983; Walker 1977). Thus, when you are 5 years old, the passage of a year represents the passage of an interval equivalent to 20% of your life span, so it seems to drag by. When you are 50, however, a year represents only 2% of your elapsed time experience, and so it seems to zip past more quickly.

DEMONSTRATION BOX 13-4
Time Perception and Attentional Factors

For this demonstration you will need a stopwatch or a watch with a sweep second hand. Do each step *before* you read the instructions for the next one.

1. Sitting quietly, note the time and then, with your eyes closed and with no counting, estimate the passage of 30 seconds. Then open your eyes and note the actual amount of time that has passed.
2. Next, note the time, look away from the watch, and start to count backward from 571

by threes (e.g., 571, 568, 565, etc.). Be sure to count out loud. When you feel that 30 seconds have passed, stop counting and note the amount of time that has elapsed.

3. Compare the two time estimates. The first one should be shorter than the second one because your cognitive clock was moving slower when you were attending only to the passage of time and faster when you were dividing your attention between the counting task and the monitoring of time (see Figure 13-2).

CHAPTER SUMMARY

Time is critical to perception. **Events,** defined as sets of relations among objects and actions that take place over time, are the units of perception. Removing the changes that take place over time, as in **stabilized retinal images,** will often result in the complete lack of perception. The **temporal integration** of the perceptual system determines the number of events that we can perceive. Some events continue long after the stimulus has disappeared, as in the case of **visible persistence,** whereas events that occur after a stimulus has been turned off can still affect our ability to perceive it, as in the case of **visual masking.**

Perception is organized over time. Some processes operate to maintain *perceptual stability,* so that perception appears to be continuous even when the stimulus is interrupted, as in the case of the **auditory continuity illusion.** The converse of this is **perceptual plasticity,** in which the percept is divided into temporal segments that make cognitive sense, even though the stimulus is relatively continuous.

Some of our time perception is controlled by a **biological clock,** which is most important in providing the long-term timing, as in **circadian rhythms.** Light plays an important role as a *zeitgeber,* or time giver, that helps to calibrate this clock. Short-term biological timers can be affected by factors such as body temperature and drugs. Other aspects of time perception are controlled by

cognitive clocks, which are affected by factors such as the amount of perceptual change, processing effort, and the distribution of attention.

KEY TERMS

event
microsaccades
stabilized retinal image
visible persistence
temporal integration
backward masking
J-shaped masking
critical fusion frequency (CFF)
pixels
Bloch's Law
motion smear
suppression of motion smear
visual masking
forward masking
simultaneous masking
backward masking
monoptic masking
dichoptic masking
integration
interruption
auditory continuity illusion
phonemic restoration effect
now
flow
biological clock
cognitive clock
circadian rhythm
entrainment
zeitgeber
suprachiasmatic nucleus (SCN)
perceptual moments
pacemaker
event processing
change monitoring
filled duration illusion
restricted environmental stimulation technique
processing effort model
storage size model
temporal processing model

Motion
CHAPTER 14

Perception is not static but, rather, changes continually over time. Many of these changes are like successive "snapshots," such as glancing from one page to another or shifting your gaze from one building to another as you stand in the street, but many other changes are more continuous in nature, such as watching a car moving in the street beside you or a bird flying through the air. These latter perceptual experiences have the added quality of perceived motion.

Your initial feeling might be that the perception of motion is really quite trivial. You might suspect that all you need for motion to be perceived is the image of a visual stimulus moving across your retina. On the contrary, motion perception involves some fairly complex interactions among a number of different systems, and motion across the retinal surface may be only a minor factor (Sekuler, Ball, Tynan, & Machmer, 1982).

For instance, we can perceive movement when the image of the stimulus is not moving across our retina at all, such as when we follow a moving car with our eyes. If we are tracking it well, the image of the car will be relatively fixed on the same retinal location, yet we still see it as moving. There are other times when the retinal image is in motion, but we do not see movement. This occurs when our eyes move from one location to another examining stationary objects. Despite the fact that the images slide across our retinal receptors, we perceive the world as remaining stationary. Finally, there are times when both our eyes and a visual stimulus are stationary, but we still see movement! This can occur when we view a solitary candle glowing in the dark or when we view a stationary object against a moving background. In both of these cases an object that is actually stationary appears to move around against an apparently stationary background (Duncker, 1929). As you can see then, movement of the retinal image does not fully account for the perception of motion. Although it will be important for us to understand the visual stimulus conditions that elicit the perception of motion, you will soon see that there are important nonvisual factors to consider as well.

WHAT IS THE PURPOSE OF MOTION PERCEPTION?

Motion perception serves several important functions. The most obvious, of course, is that of providing the visual system with information concerning the relative velocity (speed and direction) of objects in the visual environment. Animals with relatively poor visual acuity may still be finely tuned to detect motion because any movement in the environment could signal the presence of predators or prey. The detection of motion is a function with which even the lowliest of seeing creatures is equipped. Houseflies, for instance, are exquisitely prepared to adjust the landing configuration of their limbs and body in correspondence with the slant of an approaching surface (Reichardt & Poggio, 1979). However, there are other, less obvious functions of motion perception that are equally important to the larger goals of visual perception. Considering each of these functions briefly will help to provide some insight into the way we have organized the material in this chapter.

One very important function of motion perception is to enable the eye movement system to track an object that is in motion. As we have seen, our retinas are designed with only a very small region around the fovea that is capable of registering fine spatial detail. If it is our goal to visually identify the fine grain of objects that are in motion, then it becomes essential that the image on our retina be fixed. This can be accomplished only by making eye movements that coincide with the movement of the objects.

Another function of motion perception that is less obvious is that of segmenting figure from ground. The general principle here is the Gestalt Law of **Common Fate** (Wertheimer, 1923): Portions of an image that move together tend to be part of the same object or surface. The perceptual power of this law can be observed by following the instructions in Demonstration Box 14-1. Because of common fate, the perception of motion helps us identify objects, quite aside from any precise estimates of speed or direction. Those portions of the image that move together (or don't move when the background is moving) will tend to stand out perceptually and are thus excellent candidates for closer attention by the visual system.

A related but even more sophisticated function of motion perception is the perception of object shape and three-dimensional surface structure from the pattern of motion in the image. Consider those portions of a three-dimensional object that are visible from a single snapshot. Now compare the information gained from watching the same object move through space, or by moving around the object when it is stationary. In both cases, the visual system is given multiple views or vantage points of the same object. Just as the two views given by each of the two eyes can help to resolve the three-dimensional structure of an image, so, too, can the multiple images acquired through motion be used to determine three-dimensional structure.

Finally, the motion characteristics of an object are themselves powerful cues to the identity of the object. Indeed, under certain circumstances, some objects can be identified only by their unique pattern of motion. Take, for example, the problem of identifying a bird in flight. From a sufficient distance, the shape, size, and color cues of the bird have been rendered essentially useless—only a moving dark blob can be discerned. However, the motion cues still tell a powerful story. The larger the bird, the slower will be the beat of its wings. By this technique alone, a large raptor such as an eagle can be distinguished from a finch or a starling. Expert bird-watchers are in fact able to use motion cues alone to discriminate birds of the same size and color, such as bald eagles versus turkey vultures and golden eagles versus hawks.

DEMONSTRATION BOX 14-1
Common Fate

For this demonstration you will need two sheets of transparent plastic, a pen that will write on the sheets, and a white piece of paper. The sheets and pens used for making displays visible by overhead projectors will serve the purpose very well. On one of the sheets draw 30–40 same-size dots at random so that they look like they have been sprinkled on the sheet. On the other, use dots to draw a simple shape, such as a triangle or a letter of the alphabet, using only 4 to 6 dots. Be careful to make these dots the same size and shape as the random dots on the first sheet. Now place the two sheets of transparency on top of one another, preferably on a white sheet of paper. You should no longer be able to see the shape outlined by the few dots on the second sheet. Now keep one of the sheets stationary and move the other. Suddenly the shape will spring to life either as a moving figure over a stationary field of dots or as a stationary figure in a moving field of dots. This illustrates the Gestalt *Law of Common Fate*. Note how quickly your ability to identify the dots belonging to the shape disappears after the motion stops. This is also a very simple example of a *structure from motion* display, which we will discuss later in the chapter.

PHYSIOLOGICAL BASIS FOR MOTION PERCEPTION

It seems reasonable to begin our analysis of the perception of motion by first seeing if there are specific neural units for the detection of motion, much as there are for the detection of colors. In the early history of research in visual perception, before direct physiological evidence was available, a hotly debated question was whether the sensation of motion is primary, like that of color sensation, or secondary, meaning that it is derived from the basic sensations of space and time. To the frustration of researchers, the science of physics could not supply an answer because the relation between motion velocity (V), space (S), and time (T) could be written as $V = S/T$, suggesting that velocity is computed from time and space, or equally well as $S = V \times T$ or even $T = S/V$, suggesting that it is a primary dimension used in our computations of space or time.

However, there were strong hints even then, based only on an analysis of subjective experience, that motion perception is a primary sensation. For instance, researchers appealed to the well known **waterfall illusion.** If you stare at a continuously moving image, such as a waterfall, for a minute or two and then shift your gaze to a stationary image, such as the bank beside the waterfall, you will see an image moving in the opposite direction for a short period of time. This suggests that there are low-level neurons that have become fatigued, in the same way that staring at a large color patch seems to fatigue color-sensitive neurons, thereby influencing subsequent color perception in the direction of the complementary color. In this case, the fatigue seems to bias the system in favor of seeing motion in a direction opposite to that of the original stimulus.

The psychophysical technique used to study the waterfall illusion in the laboratory is called **selective adaptation** (Sekuler, 1975). It involves exposing the eye to a moving pattern, such as a field of stripes. Prolonged viewing of such a stimulus temporarily reduces an observer's ability to detect motion in the same direction as the stripes (e.g., Hunzelmann & Spillman, 1984). However, this drop in sensitivity does not carry over to faster or slower movements, nor does it generalize to movements in the opposite direction (Dawson & Di Lollo, 1990; Sekuler, 1975; Sekuler & Ganz, 1963; Wright & Johnston, 1985). Thus, the selective adaptation procedure gives results consistent with the idea that our brains contain movement-sensitive neurons that are tuned to a particular direction and speed. To experience an interesting illusion that researchers believe is caused by the fatigue of motion-sensitive neurons, try the demonstration in Demonstration Box 14-2.

DEMONSTRATION BOX 14-2
Motion Aftereffect

The form of **motion aftereffect** demonstrated in this box is often called the *spiral aftereffect* because the stimulus used to induce it is a rotating spiral. Photocopy or trace the accompanying stimulus and place it on the turntable of a record player as if it were a record. Let the stimulus rotate for about a minute, while you stare at the center. Stop the turntable and hold it so that it is completely stationary. While the turntable was moving, the spiral appeared to expand. Now it should appear to be (paradoxically) shrinking. This shrinking (without any apparent change in size) is an illusory movement because the stimulus is no longer in motion. It is probably caused by fatiguing, or selective adaptation, of physiological motion detectors, produced by prolonged stimulation in one direction of movement. The 60 seconds of viewing will give you an aftereffect (the paradoxical contraction) that will last about 10 to 15 seconds (compare Hershenson & Bader, 1990). You can demonstrate that the cells are tuned for different stimulus velocities by changing the speed of your turntable and repeating the demonstration. You will notice that this will change the rate of shrinking in the aftereffect.

Another hint of the primary status of motion can be seen in the separate nature of the perceptual experiences associated with an object's motion and with its shape. In many instances, motion can be perceived quite independently of the form giving rise to the perception of motion. An example of this can be seen in **apparent motion** displays, which involve two stationary displays being rapidly interchanged. If one display consists, say, of a white square on the right side of the field and the other consists of a white square on the left side, alternating these views at the correct speed will give the impression of a white square moving left and right in an oscillating manner. This motion seems to depend very little on whether the two objects are identical, similar, or extremely different in color and shape, provided that there is only one object in each frame. Thus, if one display is a white square and the other is a red circle, you will still get the feeling of motion, now accompanied by some sort of magical distortion in color and shape. Thus, the motion signal seems to be generated quite independently of the signal corresponding to shape perception.

During the 1960s and 1970s the hypothesis that motion is a primary sensation was confirmed in physiological studies. These studies revealed that the visual systems of many animals contain individual neurons that are sensitive to movement. Neurons sensitive to a visual target moving in a particular direction were first described in frogs (Maturana, Lettvin, McCulloch, & Pitts, 1960) but soon after in the housefly (for a review see Hausen, 1982), pigeon (Maturana & Frenk, 1963), rabbit (Barlow, Hill, & Levick, 1964), ground squirrel (Michael, 1966), cat (Stone & Fabian, 1966), and monkey (Hubel & Wiesel, 1968).

Motion perception occurs at a peripheral level of processing in simpler organisms. In most lower animals, such as the rabbit, the first neurons that are able to discriminate the direction of motion are found in the retina, specifically, the ganglion layer of neurons. In higher animals, such as the cat, however, less than 1% of the retinal ganglion neurons are direction selective, meaning that motion is processed at higher levels. By the time we get to the monkey, no motion sensitive ganglion neurons can be found (Rodieck, 1979). It is widely believed that the first neurons to show selectivity for motion in primates, including humans, are located in the superior colliculus and in the primary visual cortex.

Neurons that are sensitive to the direction and to the speed of movement are believed by most researchers to arise from a specific arrangement of inputs, such as is shown in Figure 14-1 (Marr & Ullman, 1981; Reichardt, 1961; van Santen & Sperling, 1985). The generic name given to this arrangement of neurons is the **Reichardt detector,** named after the researcher who first proposed it. This model requires at least three different neuronal units to make it work. The two cells at the top of the diagram (A and B) behave like the simple cortical cells we discussed in Chapter 3; their receptive fields are each tuned to edges of a particular orientation. The neural signals from these two cells are compared with one another by the third

cell (C) shown in the lower part of the diagram, but only after the signal from Cell A has been delayed by some small amount of time. The purpose of the delay is to compensate for the movement of the stimulus, which will cause successive neural receptive fields to be stimulated. If the two signals (A and B) arrive at about the same time, then the comparator cell (C) will fire vigorously, signaling a moving stimulus. Each system is tuned for a particular direction and speed of movement. The system drawn in Figure 14-1 will signal the presence of a rightward motion because movement from B to A (leftward) will produce signals that do not arrive at the same time. It is also tuned for a particular speed, and this tuning depends on the length of time that the signal from Cell A is delayed. Shorter delays are needed to synchronize the signals corresponding to a faster moving stimulus.

In Chapter 3 we considered evidence from anatomical, physiological, and clinical neuropsychology that suggested that there are different pathways in the visual system for different kinds of information (e.g., Livingstone & Hubel, 1988; Maunsell & Newsome, 1987; Ungerleider & Mishkin, 1982). If we consider first the two most general visual pathways in primates, we find that it is the *tectopulvinar pathway*, which is much older in evolutionary terms, that is more involved in motion perception than is the newer *geniculostriate pathway*. There are some suggestions that the tectopulvinar pathway may be entirely specialized for the perception of movement, along with the control of responses that involve moving stimuli, such as some kinds of eye movements (Flandrin & Jeannerod, 1981; Guitton, Crommelink, & Roucoux, 1980; van Essen, 1979).

Within the geniculostriate system, however, there is an important subdivision that does seem sensitive to motion perception. Specifically, the *magnocellular system* is more responsive to moving stimuli, whereas the *parvocellular system* seems to be more involved in form perception (DeYoe & van Essen, 1988; Zeki, 1993). However, although many researchers speak as if these pathways are quite separate and distinct (which would suggest that the perception of form and motion involve completely independent physiological mechanisms), there is considerable interaction in the functions of these two pathways.

One of the key neuronal features of both the tectopulvinar pathway and the magnocellular

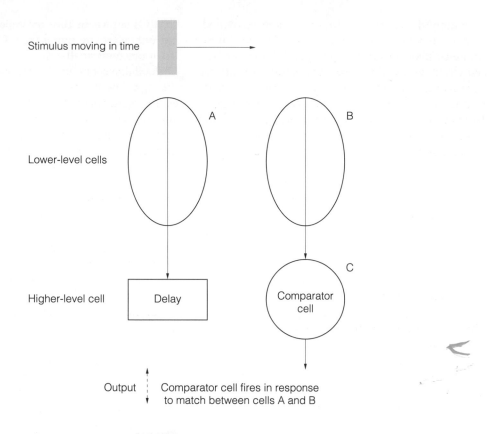

Stimulus moving in time

Lower-level cells

A

B

Higher-level cell   Delay

Comparator cell   C

Output ┊ Comparator cell fires in response
to match between cells A and B

FIGURE 14-1   A computational model of motion detection that is consistent with physiological evidence (based on Reichardt, 1961).

system is that each contains many more cells that have transient rather than sustained responses (see Chapter 3). Transient response cells seem better suited to the perception of rapid rates of movement because they respond to any change in stimulation. Sustained response cells are more oriented toward the detection of details; hence they are better suited for the perception of form or very slow movement. These two types of cells are not distributed equally across the retina. Cells with transient response patterns are more abundant in the peripheral retina. This fact helps to explain why detection of movement depends both on the speed of a moving target and on where in the visual field it is (Campbell & Maffei, 1981). Our ability to detect slow target movements (up to about 1.5° per second) *decreases* with distance from the fovea (Choudhurt & Crossey, 1981; Lichtenstein, 1963; McColgin, 1960). For higher target velocities, however, our ability to detect target movement *increases* with distance from the fovea. For moderate to fast velocities, the peripheral retina seems better able to detect movement (because of the increased proportion of transient response cells) even though the decrease in acuity may be so great that the observer may not be able to recognize the shape of what is moving (Bhatia, 1975; Brown, 1972). This is why we sometimes see a TV screen flickering when we catch a glimpse of it far in the periphery of the visual field. Out there, the transient cells are sensitive enough to detect the movements of the raster that paints each line on the TV screen.

The importance of the magnocellular system in motion perception can be shown quite effectively using a technique involving **isoluminant stimuli.** These are patterns of lines or forms that are distinguished from their backgrounds only on the basis of color. All brightness differences have been eliminated (hence the terms *iso*, meaning "the same," and *luminant*, referring to light). These patterns are used because the magnocellular system responds much better to brightness differences than it does to color differences, whereas the parvocellular system can detect patterns that contain only color differences. Thus, when we look at moving isoluminant stimuli we may be able to see the pattern itself quite well, but the speed and even the direction of movement are often difficult to determine because the magnocellular system is not stimulated by such stimuli. (Cavanagh, Tyler, & Favreau, 1984; Lindsey & Teller, 1990; Ramachandran & Gregory, 1978; Troscianko & Fahle, 1988). This deficiency in motion perception for isoluminent stimuli indicates that the color-blind but luminance-sensitive magnocellular system is more involved in motion perception than is the color-sensitive parvocellular system.

In monkeys and humans there are two main regions of the cerebral cortex that contain many neurons with the characteristics of Reichardt detectors: the primary visual cortex and the temporal lobe (Allman, Miezin, & McGuinness, 1985; Maunsell & Van Essen, 1983; Newsome & Pare, 1988). The specific portions of the temporal lobe that contain these cells are called the *medial temporal* and *medial superior temporal* areas, and they are shown in Figure 14-2.

Many neurons in the primary visual cortex are tuned to the direction of stimulus movement, discharging strongly when a properly oriented stimulus drifts in one direction across the visual field and discharging less strongly (or not at all) when the same stimulus moves through the field in the opposite direction (see Hubel & Wiesel, 1979). The degree of specificity of response to moving stimuli can be quite strong. For instance, there are cells that respond not only to particular directions of movement but also to particular speeds of the moving targets (Maunsell & Van Essen, 1983; Orban, Kennedy, & Maes, 1981a, b).

The importance of the temporal lobe in motion perception has been made vividly apparent in clinical cases where patients with temporal lobe damage can still see stationary shapes and colors but can no longer perceive motion. Consider one case of bilateral brain damage, including the temporal lobe, where a woman reported that she could easily recognize cars when she saw them but could no longer judge their speed. The simple act of pouring a cup of coffee became virtually impossible because she could not see the

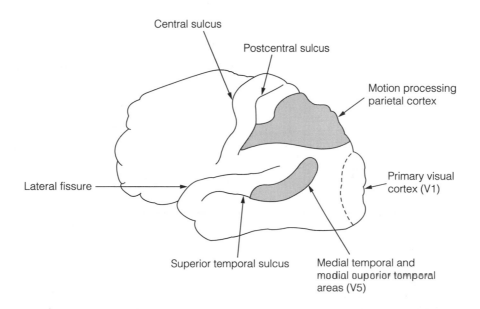

FIGURE 14-2 The regions of the cortex that are most involved in motion perception.

dynamic flow of the fluid nor the steady rise of the liquid level (Hess, Baker, & Zihl, 1989; Zihl, von Cramon, & Mai, 1983).

Laboratory studies combining behavior and physiology in monkeys have helped to illustrate the different roles played by the primary visual cortex and the temporal lobe in the perception of motion (Movshon & Newsome, 1992; Newsome, Britten, & Movshon, 1989). In monkeys the motion-sensitive region of the temporal lobe corresponds to the human region known as Area V5. Recording from single cells in this region in monkeys has shown that almost all the neurons are strongly direction selective. This means that they increase their firing rate above the resting rate in response to stimuli moving in their preferred direction and reduce their firing rate (below the resting rate) in response to stimuli moving in other directions. An important way in which these neurons differ from motion-sensitive cells in the primary visual cortex (called *V1* in monkeys) is that they have large receptive fields. In contrast to the receptive field of a neuron in V1, which may be only a few minutes of arc in size, the receptive fields of neurons in V5 may extend up to one quarter of the entire visual field. This has been interpreted as meaning that these neurons in V5 are integrating the activity of many motion-sensitive neurons in V1.

The unique roles played by neurons in Areas V1 and V5 can be seen by using specifically designed motion stimuli. One of these looks very much like the "snow" on an untuned TV channel. It is actually a rapid series of frames containing dots in randomly chosen locations. This is illustrated in Figure 14-3. The correlation between the movements of dots in successive frames is called **motion coherence**. If the dots in each frame are placed randomly, without any regard to previous or successive frames, then the motion coherence is said to be 0%. However, if 50% of the dots in successive frames move in the same direction, with a consistent trajectory, then the motion coherence of the display is 50%. Finally, if all of the dots are matched so that the entire screen of dots is translated in the same direction and by the same amount from frame to frame, then the motion coherence is 100%.

Human observers are highly sensitive to small correlations in these displays, sometimes being able to detect motion coherence that involves as few as 3% of the dots. The most optimal conditions seem to occur when the correlated dots are moving together at about 2.0° per second, which involves a dot displacement of 0.1° every 50 ms. Sensitivity also increases with the size of the visual field that is taken up by the display. Unlike many other psychophysical tasks, which do not improve when the display grows larger than about 1°, sensitivity to motion coherence continues to improve until the displays are about 20° in diameter.

Studies of monkeys have shown that only the neurons in Area V5 are sensitive to the global

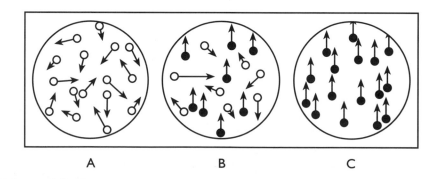

FIGURE 14-3 Schematic illustrations of three random dot kinematograms with different degrees of motion coherence. (A) Motion is said to have 0% coherence because there is no relationship between the locations of dots in successive frames. (B) Motion is partially coherent because half (50%) of the dots have the same trajectory in successive frames. (C) Motion is completely coherent (100%) because all of the dots move in the same direction and at the same speed.

direction of motion in displays such as these (Movshon & Newsome, 1992). Neurons in Area V1, because of their small receptive field size, are sensitive only to the direction of motion for a single dot in a small region of the display. As a result, these neurons are unable to distinguish a dot that is moving coherently with other dots from a dot that is moving completely independently. In sharp contrast to this, a neuron in Area V5 will fire selectively to a random dot display when the motion coherence in the same direction is as low as 5%. One of the most exciting aspects of this research is that the thresholds determined for individual neurons match almost exactly with those determined from the behavior of a monkey who has been trained to indicate the perceived direction of motion in a random dot display. That is, the degree of coherence required to activate an individual neuron is the same degree of coherence required for the accurate discrimination of motion as indicated by the monkey's responses. To further confirm this relationship, studies of small lesions in Area V5 in one hemisphere of the brain have been shown to decrease the behavioral sensitivity of the monkey to coherent motion displays in the opposite visual field. For the visual field corresponding to the unlesioned hemisphere, however, the threshold for motion coherence is unimpaired (Movshon & Newsome, 1992).

STIMULUS FACTORS IN MOTION PERCEPTION

Generally speaking, there are two principal mechanisms by which we perceive motion. The first involves detecting shifts in the relative position of parts of the visual image; the second involves using our eyes to follow a moving target. Many researchers believe these involve different perceptual systems, and so we will refer to the system that responds to image changes the **image-retina system** and to the one that interprets motion from our eye and head movements as the **eye-head system** (Gregory, 1978). Because the image-retina system involves only optical image changes, let us consider it first.

Perhaps the first question to ask is how much movement in the image is needed before we can perceive motion. To answer this question, we usually measure a movement threshold just as we measure thresholds for the minimum amount of light or sound needed for sensation (see Chapter 2). Our sensitivity to the movement of an external target depends on several variables. In experimental settings, absolute movement thresholds have usually been studied using a small point of light that moves against some sort of stationary background, as in one of the earliest studies by Hermann Aubert (1886). He found that observers could detect the movement of a luminous dot in the dark, 50 cm from the eye, when it was moving at about 2.5 mm per second (which is about one fifth of a degree of visual angle per second).

Target movement alone, however, is not enough to allow us to describe the motion thresholds. Motion perception often involves the recognition that relationships are changing between visual stimuli, which means that we are also dealing with relative movement thresholds. Some interaction among visual targets, such as *edge transitions* (where parts of a moving surface systematically block or expose our view of other elements) can assist the perception of motion (Kaiser & Calderone, 1991; Walker, 1975). Perhaps the best situation for detecting target movement is when there is some motionless reference point, such as a stationary feature nearby or on the background, that forms the **visual context**. An example might be a stationary square frame surrounding the target. Under these circumstances we find that observers are much more sensitive (e.g., Palmer, 1986). The minimum movement that can be detected in the presence of a stationary visual context is about .25 mm per second or 0.03° of visual angle per second (as compared to 0.2° per second for a single target with no stationary context). This is an incredible degree of movement sensitivity. If a snail were to crawl across a desk 1.5 m wide at this rate, it would take it 1 hr 40 min to go from end to end.

Our ability to judge the difference between two velocities is similarly facilitated by the presence of other stimuli that are stationary (Bonnet, 1984). Some researchers contend that the image-retina system really involves two different sources of motion information. The first is **subject-relative change**, where the only information is the movement of the target relative to the observer's position in space. The second is **object-relative change**, which is the movement of one target relative to others and creates a sort of "configurational change" in the visible pattern and therefore may involve processes similar to form perception (e.g., Mack, Heuer, Fendrich, Vilardi, & Chambers, 1985; Wallach, Becklen, & Nitzberg, 1985). In terms of the detection and discrimination of motion, we appear to be much more sensitive to object-relative change. Furthermore, our ability to detect object-relative motion is present quite early in development, perhaps as early as 8 weeks of age in human infants (Dannemiller & Freeland, 1991).

As soon as we consider the possibility of seeing the motion of more than a single dot or edge in an image, several new problems arise. One of these is called the **motion correspondence problem.** Consider the stimulus situation shown in Figure 14-4. At the start (Time 1) three spots of light appear at one side of a screen. A fraction of a second later they are replaced by three identical spots of light on the other side of the screen (Time 2). What the observer sees is motion, as though each of the three spots had moved across the screen toward the right. However, this is not the only logically possible motion. Because all of the spots are identical, there is a large number of different patterns of movement that might have been seen, and two examples (which observers never actually see) are shown in Figure 14-4.

Some paths of motion are seen and others are not because the perception of motion follows certain rules (Dawson, 1991). These rules include a preference for *proximity in space*—the shortest possible movement between two images will tend to be seen (Burt & Sperling, 1981)—and also a preference for *proximity in time*—the motion that requires the slowest speed will tend to be seen (Dawson & Pylyshyn, 1988). Thus, the motion correspondence problem is most often solved perceptually by following the shortest distance between two neighboring stimuli in the shortest period of time.

A second problem that occurs with multiple stimuli in motion has to do with the inherent ambiguity of the signal registered by each individual Reichardt motion sensor. Recall that each such sensor can be specifically tuned for motion in a given direction and of a specific velocity. The problem arises when one considers the large number of different stimuli that can activate any single detector. Consider the Reichardt detector shown

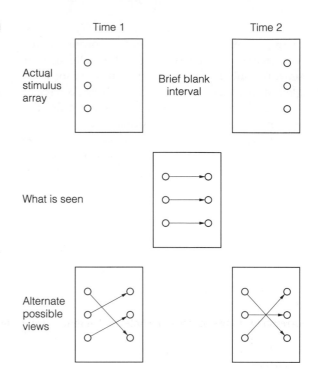

FIGURE 14-4 The correspondence problem. A stimulus involving three spots of light flashed on one side of a screen and then on the other a moment later is seen as the simple apparent movement of the three spots of light as shown in the central frame. Logically, however, there are many other forms of motion that could be seen, including those shown in the bottom frames.

in Figure 14-1. It would be activated by a vertically oriented edge moving horizontally (from left to right) across the retina at a given speed. However, it would also be activated by an obliquely oriented edge that passed over it more quickly. In fact, there are a very large number of combinations involving orientation and speed of a moving contour that would activate the same unit. In principle, then, the output of a single Reichardt detector does not specify the motion of an edge with very much precision. It can indicate only that motion has been detected in a very general direction (e.g., rightward) and of a very general speed (e.g., moderate). This is called the **aperture problem,** based on the fact that if we were viewing a figure moving behind a stationary aperture, we might get erroneous

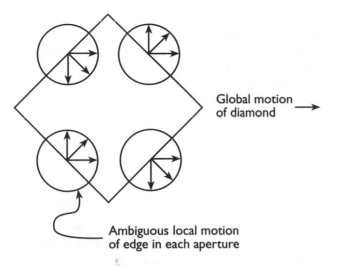

Global motion
of diamond →

Ambiguous local motion
of edge in each aperture

FIGURE 14-5   The aperture problem. An object in motion, such as the diamond shape, has both a motion that corresponds to the object as a whole (global motion) and a number of motion signals that differ from one another (local motions). Because individual motion sensors consider only a small region of any given image, information from the local signals must be integrated by the visual system in order to determine the global direction of an object in motion.

movement information. The nature of this problem is illustrated in Figure 14-5, where the different local motion signals correspond to different regions of a simple shape such as a diamond. Depending where each aperture is, the movement of a local edge of the diamond shape is consistent with different motion signals. In order to see the motion of the shape as a whole, information from these various apertures must be integrated. Studies of the responses of single neurons in the monkey to stimuli such as these indicate that whereas the cells in Cortical Area V1 are sensitive to the local or aperture motion signal (e.g., orthogonal to the local edge orientation), cells in Cortical Area V5 are sensitive to the direction of motion of the shape as a whole (Adelson & Movshon, 1982; Movshon, Adelson, Gizzi, & Newsome, 1985).

Another problem associated with the perception of motion in complex arrays involves determining which objects are moving and which are stationary. A well-known example of a misattribution of motion was first described by Duncker (1929), who studied the perception of a bright dot displayed in an otherwise featureless dark room. When the dot was moved very slowly, observers were not certain whether or not it was moving.

However, when a stationary dot was placed near the moving dot (in effect becoming the visual context), it became quite clear that one of the dots was in motion (due to the object-relative changes). Curiously, observers could not identify which of the two dots was moving. Duncker next changed the context stimulus by making it a rectangular luminous frame that was stationary and surrounded the dot. Under these circumstances there was no ambiguity, and observers were able to tell that the dot rather than the frame was in motion.

Duncker next varied the conditions so that the dot was stationary and the surrounding rectangular frame was moving. Under these circumstances an illusion appeared, in that observers reported that the stationary dot rather than the frame was moving. Duncker called this **induced motion** because the perceived movement of the dot was induced or brought about by the real movement of the surrounding context. This is similar to the perception that the moon is moving behind the clouds, when actually the clouds are moving quickly while the moon's motion is negligible in comparison. The clouds provide a surrounding context that is in motion, and, consistent with the principle that Duncker discovered in the laboratory, they induce an apparent motion of the not-detectably-moving moon.

Induced movement effects are most dramatic when the context is moving slowly rather than quickly (Wallach & Becklen, 1983). Square frame shapes are more effective than circular frames, and large surrounds are more effective than small ones (Michael & Sherrick, 1986), although it appears that it is the part of the visual context that is closest to the target that is most responsible for the illusion (Schulman, 1979). Furthermore, in order to induce motion, the target and the background must be at the same distance from the observer. If the frame that supplies the context is too far in front of or behind the target, no motion will be induced (Gogel & Koslow, 1972). You can produce induced motion yourself by following the instructions in Demonstration Box 14-3.

EYE MOVEMENTS AND MOTION PERCEPTION

Up to now we have focused our discussion on the visual stimulus factors that contribute to our perception of motion, such as movement of the image across the retina. To that extent we have been concerned with the image-retina movement system (see Figure 14-6A). We now turn our attention to the *eye-head motion system*. This system enables us to detect the movement of external objects even when the image remains in a fixed position on the retina. This most commonly occurs when we move our eyes to follow the path of a physically moving object, as when we track an automobile moving down the highway. This kind of eye movement is called **smooth pursuit movement** and is illustrated in Figure 14-6B. It is designed to keep the image of the target on the fovea (the most acute part of the retina). Of course, these eye movements themselves depend on the accurate detection of motion by some part of the visual system that can direct the eye's movements correctly. This system operates largely automatically, meaning that we are not conscious of the motor commands given to the eye to maintain fixation on an object. The neural basis for smooth pursuit eye tracking seems to include both the older tectopulvinar visual system we discussed earlier and the *vestibular system* (see Parker, 1980), which we will discuss later in this chapter. This type of smooth pursuit eye movement is found only in animals that have foveas, and the eye movements give us information about the target's motion (Post & Leibowitz, 1985; Raymond, Shapiro, & Rose, 1984).

Actually, there are two types of smooth pursuit eye movements. The one that we have been talking about might be called **voluntary pursuit movement.** The second type is **reflex pursuit movement,** which keeps images of objects relatively fixed in one place on your retina despite the fact that your head may be moving. An example of this is shown in Figure 14-7, where the individual is steadily looking at the lens of the camera. Notice that the eyes seem to remain stationary while the head seems to rotate around them. Actually the eyes are tracking in the direction opposite to the head movement in order to keep the target on the fovea.

DEMONSTRATION BOX 14-3
Induced Movement

To induce movement in a stationary target, all you need is a sheet of clear cellophane or glass and a sheet of white paper. In the middle of the white paper draw a small dot. On the clear cellophane draw a large rectangle, about 10 cm by 16 cm (4 in by 6 in), using a felt-tip marker or a grease pencil. Now lay the clear sheet over the paper so that the dot is enclosed by the rectangle and is near one of its sides.

Look steadily at the dot and *slowly* move the cellophane across the paper. You will notice that the dot appears to move in the direction opposite the motion of the rectangle. The effect is strongest when the dot is near the sides of the rectangle, where object-relative change plays a role. Increasing the speed of movement should reduce the amount of induced motion you perceive. Why?

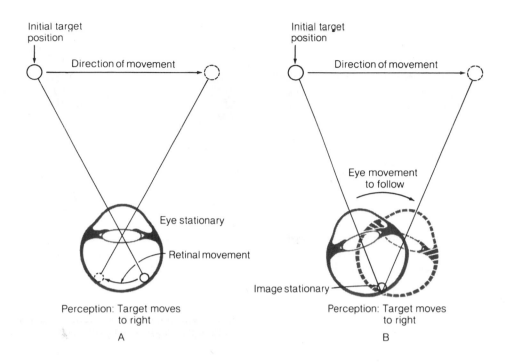

FIGURE 14-6 (A) The image-retina movement system. The image of the moving object stimulates the retina when the eyes are held stationary. This gives information about object motion, possibly as a result of the involvement of movement-detecting cells. (B) One of the functions of the eye-head movement system. When the eye pursues a moving target, the image remains stationary on the fovea of the eye, but we still perceive the movement of the object.

One of the real puzzles of motion perception is how we are able to perceive the motion of a target that remains motionless on our retina, as happens during smooth pursuit eye movements. One important source of information is the *object-relative change* that can be detected between the stationary target image on the fovea and the retinal motion of the background caused by the eye tracking the target (Pola & Wyatt, 1989). However, suppose that the image of the target remains on the fovea but that there is no patterned background to provide object-relative information to suggest movement. The only way the observer can now know the path or the speed of an object is by monitoring the speed and direction of the tracking eye movements (e.g., Epstein & Hanson, 1977; Rock & Halper, 1969). Because we have previously (see Chapter 10) discussed how eye movements can provide us with information as to the size and location of objects (e.g., Coren, 1986), it should not surprise us to learn that spatial and movement information is also provided nonvisually by the eye movement signals themselves.

If our perception of the motion of an object depends on information from the eye movements used to track the object, then this implies that anything that alters the direction or speed of motion of the eye should also alter our perception of the movement of the object. Such alterations or misperceptions occur quite regularly. For instance, the eye does not pursue moving targets with perfect accuracy but, rather, tends to lag some distance behind the target. The degree to which the eye lags behind is dependent on the speed of the target (Fender, 1971; Puckett & Steinman, 1969), and under some circumstances the eye never really catches up to the stimulus (Young, 1971). This may cause distortions in the size or the shape of the path the eye follows (e.g., Festinger & Easton, 1974). For example, Coren, Bradley, Hoenig, and Girgus (1975) have shown that the size of the circular path traced out by a rotating spot of light seems to shrink as the speed of the target increases. At slow speeds, where the eye can track accurately, or at speeds

FIGURE 14-7 Reflex pursuit eye movements are used to keep the image of an object fixed on your retina even though you move your head. Here the individual is looking at the camera while rotating her head. Notice how these vestibularly controlled movements keep the eyes fixed while the head seems to rotate around them.

much too fast for even an attempt at tracking, the judgments are reasonably accurate.

Another example of how eye movements can affect our visual perception of motion is the **Aubert-Fleischl effect**. If we estimate the speed of a target when we are tracking it as it moves in front of a stationary background, it appears to move more slowly than it would if we were holding our eyes still by fixating on a point on the stationary background. This phenomenon is another example of predictable perceptual distortions arising because of lags in our smooth tracking. Because our pursuit eye movements tend to lag behind targets, an observer will not only underestimate the velocity of a target that is tracked with the eye but also will tend to underestimate the distance the target has moved (Mack & Herman, 1972). Demonstration Box 14-4 allows you to see this effect for yourself.

There are some circumstances when our own eye or head movements produce movements of the visual image across our retina that are very similar to those that might occur if the scene were actually in motion. One important function of the eye-head movement system is to compensate for such movements so that we continue to see the world as being stationary even though we are moving. This process of compensating for eye movements is called **position constancy**, and the fact that objects seem to maintain a fixed position relative to us, despite rotations of both our head and eyes, is

called **direction constancy**, which we briefly mentioned in Chapter 11. We are quite accurate in our ability to distinguish image movements caused by target movements from those caused by our own movements (see Wallach, 1987). Although we do not know exactly how this movement compensation system works, it must include a system that monitors the changing position of the eye relative to the position of the head, either when we are tracking a moving target or when we are making eye movements to scan a stationary scene (Howard, 1982). Two classes of theory have been proposed to explain how the eye-head movement system accomplishes this.

Sir Charles Sherrington (1906) suggested that motion is detected via feedback information from the six extraocular muscles that control the eye movements. This feedback information, called *proprioceptive* or *position information* (see Chapter 17), enables the observer to monitor eye position. The proprioceptive information tells the brain that the eyes have moved, and in turn this information allows the brain to interpret movement across the retina as being observer generated rather than object generated. In support of this theory, there is evidence that there are cells in the superior colliculus and visual cortex of the cat that monitor eye position (Berkley, 1982; Kurtz & Butter, 1980). These cells fire at different rates depending on the extent and direction of eye movement (Donaldson & Long, 1980; Kasamatsu, 1976; Noda, Freeman, &

DEMONSTRATION BOX 14-4
Apparent Movement

To see apparent movement similar to that described by Wertheimer, simply hold your index finger vertically a short distance in front of your nose. Look at any distant target (such as a mark on the far wall of the room). Relax your eyes and alternately wink each eye. You should see your finger in a different place with each eye.

Now, begin to rhythmically open and close each eye in turn (remembering to keep your eyes relaxed). At slow rates you should see your finger "jump" from side to side; however, at some moderate rate of winking you should see the finger appear to actually "move" from one position to the other.

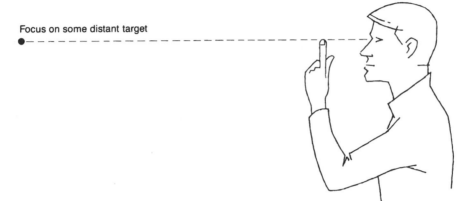

Focus on some distant target

Creutzfeldt, 1972). Sherrington's theory is often called an **inflow theory** because it is the information "flowing in" from the eye muscles to the brain that is the crucial message for the interpretation of movement.

A different theory about how the eye-head movement system compensates for self-generated movements of the visual image was offered by Hermann von Helmholtz (1909/1962). He suggested that when the brain initiates an eye movement, efferent (motor) signals are sent out commanding the eyes to move. Copies of these signals, sent to central regions of the visual system, can be used to indicate that movement information coming from the retina is due to the eyes moving, rather than to movement of stimuli in the world. Because the interpretation of the origin of movement is based on information from the message sent out from the brain to initiate an eye movement, this is called an **outflow theory**. As in the case of inflow information, there seem to be some cells in the cerebellum and the cortex of monkeys

that contain information about eye position. Because these cells respond before the actual movement takes place, they could represent the source of outflow information registering the *intention to move*, rather than the movements themselves (Miles & Fuller, 1975; Wurtz & Goldberg, 1971).

To see how outflow information might compensate for eye movements, try this little experiment suggested by Helmholtz. Place your hand over one eye and try tapping or pushing (through the eyelid) the side of your other (uncovered) eye very gently with your fingertip. This rotates the eye in a movement similar to one that could be initiated by the brain. However, in this case the brain has not sent a signal to the extraocular muscles to move the eye. When the eye is rotated in this passive fashion, the visual field will be seen to jog in the direction opposite to the movement of the eye and to the same extent that the eye actually moved (e.g., Miller, Moore, & Wooten, 1984). Thus, the stability of the visual field holds only for eye movements initiated by signals from the brain. Passive

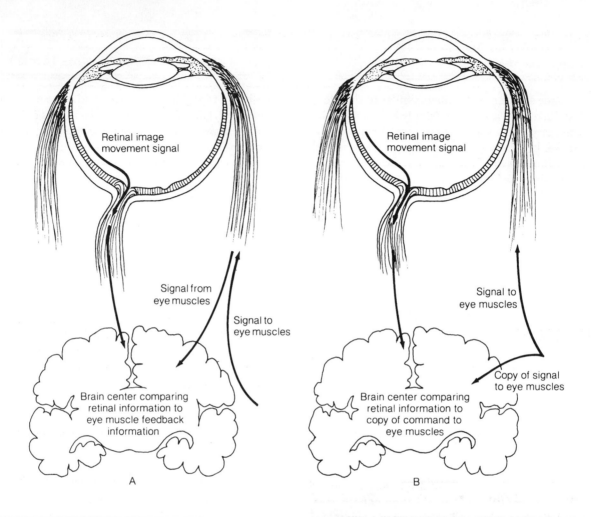

FIGURE 14-8 A major function of the eye-head moment system is to maintain the stability of the visual world during eye movements, thus achieving position or direction constancy. The inflow theory (A) states that this is accomplished by comparing movement signals from the retina with proprioceptive feedback from the eye muscles that indicates that the eye has moved. The outflow theory (B) maintains that commands from the brain to initiate voluntary eye movements cancel the movement information coming from the retina as the eyes move.

eye movements result in an apparent movement of the visual field. It seems as though the action of the eye-head system requires that the signals to and/or from the eye muscles be compared to signals arriving from the retina indicating changes in retinal image position (Matin, 1982).

Figure 14-8 illustrates the difference between the inflow and outflow theories. It now seems very likely that both inflow and outflow are needed to provide a full explanation of the eye-head movement system. There are probably times when the information about eye position from the motor system is more reliable than information from the cortical commands sent to the motor system. Table 14-1 gives a summary of the relationship between the image-retina and eye-head movement systems. Demonstration Boxes 14-5 and 14-6 give other interesting examples that illustrate the relationships between eye movements, visual stability, and the perception of motion.

Table 14-1   The Effect of Retinal Image Change and Eye Movements on the Perception of Motion

TARGET MOTION	MOTOR TO EYE (HEAD)	SIGNAL RETINAL MOTION	PERCEPTION OF TARGET
	Image-Retina System		
No	None	None	Stationary Target
Yes	None	Yes	Target motion
	Eye-Head System		
No	Saccade	Yes	Stationary target
Yes	Pursuit	No	Target motion
No	Passive push with finger	Yes	Target motion in opposite direction

REAL VERSUS APPARENT MOTION

Some of the early psychological researchers noticed that the perception of motion does not require a stimulus that is actually moving in the world. All that is required for a vivid impression of motion is that a stimulus be appropriately displaced in space and time. This observation has since been used to great advantage by advertisers and lighted

---

DEMONSTRATION BOX 14-5
The Aubert-Fleischl Effect

To experience the underestimation of both speed and distance moved when you track a target, begin by practicing a movement that will serve as your tracking target. With your eyes closed, swing your hand back and forth in front of you at a moderate speed and in a rhythmic fashion as shown in the figure. When you are moving with a nice regular tempo, open your eyes, look straight ahead, and judge the speed and the distance your hand is moving. Now look directly at your finger and track it. Notice that your hand seems to be moving more slowly, and the size of the back-and-forth movement (the path length) appears to be shorter. The apparent path length seems shorter probably because when you are tracking the target, information about the extent of the motion comes from the eye-head system, and your tracking movements lag behind the physical target, resulting in a slower overall velocity and a shorter eye-movement path length.

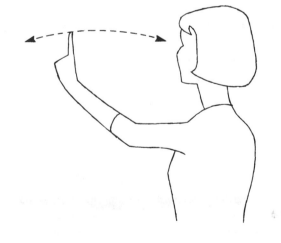

DEMONSTRATION BOX 14-6
Afterimages and Apparent Movement

You can readily experience one of the ways the eye-head movement system differentiates external from observer movement. The first thing needed is to generate a *stabilized retinal image*. Ordinarily, the retinal image is in constant motion and stimulates varying groups of receptors at a rapid rate. However, by quickly satiating or fatiguing a single group of retinal receptors, we can generate an image that maintains its position regardless of eye movements. Many of you are probably familiar with the technique used to give rise to such an image if you have ever had your picture taken with a flashbulb attached to the camera. If you looked at the light while it flashed, you may have noticed a purple dot that tended to linger in your field of view for some time after the picture was taken. This purple dot is called an *afterimage*. It is one example of a stabilized retinal image. The afterimage does not shift position on the retina. It stays in a constant position regardless of how we move our eyes. We can use the afterimage to demonstrate the operation of the eye-head movement system.

Perhaps the easiest way to generate an afterimage is to look at a rather bright but small source of light for a brief period of time. Make a 1-cm hole in an index card and hold it up in front of a lightbulb. Look at the hole for a few moments, and this should provide a clearly visible afterimage when you look away from the light. Now notice that each time you move your eyes the afterimage seems to jump in the same direction. This apparent movement is due to the action of the eye-head system.

Commands have been issued to the eye to move, yet the image remains on the same place on the retina. This could occur only if the image had moved as much as the eye (see Table 14-1). You may also notice that the image sometimes seems to drift smoothly from place to place. Again, the image never moves; the movement is signaled from the movements of your eyes. This is one example of how the action of the eye-head movement system can lead to illusions of motion.

sign manufacturers in every major city of the world. The signs that appear to have moving messages in them, such as bouncing arrows or borders in motion, actually consist of a series of stationary lightbulbs that flash on and off in succession.

One of the early psychological researchers who studied this phenomenon was Max Wertheimer (1912). Beginning with two lines separated in space, which could be flashed on and off sequentially, he varied the time interval between the offset of the first line and the onset of the second (we call this variable period the **interstimulus interval**). When the interstimulus interval was very brief, observers saw two lines appear simultaneously because of the phenomenon of visible persistence that we discussed in Chapter 13. If the interval was made to be quite long, the observers saw a line appear and disappear, followed by a second line appearing in a different location. However, for some intermediate interstimulus intervals

Wertheimer's observers reported that they saw a line appear and then *move* from the first position in space to the second. Although it was initially called *phi movement*, we now refer to this experience of movement between successively presented stationary stimuli as **apparent movement**, to distinguish it from **real movement**, where the stimulus actually moves in space. You can demonstrate this type of apparent movement for yourself by following the instructions in Demonstration Box 14-7.

The fact that the eye and brain can be fooled into seeing motion from a rapidly presented sequence of still stimulus frames might seem to be an interesting but not very useful curiosity. Yet, every time you go to the cinema, you are paying to see 2 hours of an apparent motion illusion. Each frame in the film you watch is actually stationary, being exchanged for a new frame about 24 times a second. Television and computer screens work in much the same way, with static frames changing

---

DEMONSTRATION BOX 14-7
The Autokinetic Effect

There is an interesting phenomenon in which movement is seen in the absence of any physical motion of the target. The word used to describe the occurrence is *autokinesis*, which means "self-moving." For this experiment, you will need a *very* dark room. No stray light of any sort should be visible. In addition, you will need a small, dim point of light (a lighted cigarette works fine). Place the point of light about 2 m away from you and look at it steadily. After a few minutes it should appear to move, perhaps slowly drifting in one direction or another. Of course the light is still stationary; hence the movement is an illusion, which is called the **autokinetic effect.**

The autokinetic effect demonstrates the outflow principle that operates in the eye-head movement system. The visual system monitors only commands to initiate voluntary eye movements. However, these are not the only types of eye movements possible. Our eyes also exhibit involuntary movements. As you may have guessed, these are not monitored by the visual system. One type of involuntary eye movement is *eye drift*, and this is the mechanism implicated in the autokinetic effect (Matin & MacKinnon, 1964). When we steadily fixate or stare at a target, it is difficult for the eyes to maintain steady and accurate fixation on that one point of space (Ditchburn, 1973). The eyes will tend to drift off of the fixation point; however, the visual system does not monitor this movement until it exceeds a critical point. In the autokinetic situation, retinal image movement has been signaled in the absence of commands to initiate voluntary eye movements. This is the situation under which the movement of the retinal image is attributed to an externally moving object (see Table 14-1). There is no information that the eyes have moved, so illusory movement of the dim spot of light is seen.

---

about 30 times a second in television and 60 times a second on your personal computer.

If the perception of motion derived from apparent motion stimuli differs little, if at all, from the perception of motion derived from objects that are really moving in the three-dimensional world, you might be tempted to ask why it is important that researchers even make the distinction between real and apparent movement. The answer, as is so often the case, depends on the perspective we take. From the perspective of the neural motion signals produced in the brain, the two types of stimuli are indistinguishable. Both will stimulate Reichardt-type motion sensors in exactly the same way, provided that the spatial and temporal displacements are comparable (Burr, Ross, & Morrone, 1986). However, from the perspective of the person designing a moving visual display, there is a great deal of difference. In a display with objects that actually move over time, the observer's perception of motion will be limited only by the temporal and spatial limits of the visual system. In a display consisting of apparent motion, the perception of motion will also depend on the rules used by the visual system to fill in the physically absent motion information.

Our impression of apparent motion is dependent on both the distance between the stimuli at successive points in time and the time that elapses between the successive presentations. Generally speaking, when the stimuli are separated by increasingly large distances, longer time intervals between the stimuli are needed for apparent motion to be perceived (Farrell, 1983). However, careful analysis of the temporal aspects of apparent motion displays reveals that there are really three different variables involved. These are illustrated in Figure 14-9. In addition to the *interstimulus interval*, which we have already discussed, there is the duration of the stimulus in each frame **(frame duration)**, as well as the time that elapses between the onset of one frame and the onset of the next frame. This variable is often referred to as **stimulus onset asynchrony** or even simply *SOA*. Systematic comparisons of the

effects of each of these variables, alone and in combination, have revealed that the primary determinant of the perception of motion is the stimulus onset asynchrony. Manipulations of frame duration and interstimulus interval do not have much of an influence on the perception of motion unless they are also associated with a change in SOA. Because of these findings, some researchers have taken to referring to this finding as the **SOA Law** (or **Onset-Onset Law**) of apparent motion perception (Breitmeyer, 1984; Kahneman, 1967).

In trying to characterize some of the other rules of apparent motion perception, researchers have come to the conclusion that there is an important and fundamental difference between two kinds of apparent motion displays. One kind of display corresponds to the motion sequences shown on television and in movies, where each successive frame lasts only a few milliseconds and the spatial displacements of an object from frame to frame are only a few minutes of arc. These are called **short-range motion** displays. The other kind of display is like those studied by the early Gestalt psychologists (e.g., Wertheimer, 1912) and seen in some neon advertising signs, which involve apparent motion of only one or two objects over much larger spatial displacements with longer temporal intervals. These are called **long-range motion** displays.

Short-Range Motion Perception

The short-range motion displays that are usually studied in the laboratory consist of randomly located dots in each frame of the sequence. We have already discussed one version of these, the random dot displays resembling an untuned TV channel that are used to study motion coherence. A more general name that is often used to refer to random dot displays used to create motion sequences is the **random dot kinematogram,** often abbreviated as **RDK.**

If we begin with a single frame of randomly located dots and create an RDK by displacing all of the dots, either horizontally or vertically, by the same amount in successive frames, we can ask questions such as "What is the minimum spatial displacement over which the direction of motion can be discriminated?" "What is the maximum displacement before the perception of motion breaks down?" "What are the minimum and maximum temporal intervals that will still result in the perception of motion?" Many studies addressing questions such as these have shown that reliable motion perception occurs only when the spatial displacements are small (around 5 min to 15 min of arc) and the temporal intervals are short (around 20 ms to 80 ms). With apparent motion generated in this way, as long as the dots in successive frames are of the same luminance, we can produce even

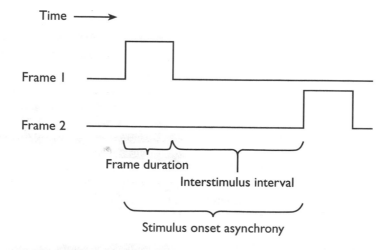

FIGURE 14-9. The three temporal variables of apparent motion displays: frame duration, interstimulus interval, and stimulus onset asynchrony. Of these three, stimulus onset asynchrony is the best predictor of the quality of motion that will be perceived.

motion aftereffects, similar to those described in Demonstration Box 14-2 (Anstis, 1978; Baker & Braddick, 1985; Braddick, 1974; 1980; Nakayama, 1985; Petersik, 1989; Vautin & Berkley, 1977).

Long-Range Motion Perception

Most of the long-range motion displays that have been studied consist of only a small number of stimuli. In these displays, motion is seen over distances much greater than the optimal 15 min of visual angle for short-range motion. Distances may actually include separations of many degrees across the visual field. The time between successive frames that produces the perception of motion can also be much longer—often more than 200 ms. The perceptual processes for long-range motion are less stimulus driven and seem to be based on more complex inferential procedures. For instance, it often seems as though the brain is unwilling to conclude that the disappearance of one stimulus should be followed shortly thereafter by the sudden and independent appearance of an identical stimulus nearby. Therefore, an inference is made that the original stimulus must have moved to this new location. Described this way, the process seems to involve a form of "logic" or simplifying principle that derives apparent motion as a reasonable interpretation of the stimulus changes observed (Hatfield & Epstein, 1985; Ramachandran & Anstis, 1986; Rock, 1983).

However, long-range apparent motion perception also demonstrates a good deal of "tolerance" in its interpretation of the way the motion correspondence problem should be solved. For example, suppose we present a display of alternately flashing and spatially separated stimuli at a rate we know produces the sensation of motion. Now suppose that the target on the right is red and the one on the left is green. Will we still see motion? The answer is that we will see a target both moving *and* changing color as it moves. We can get apparent motion not only between targets of different colors but also between targets with different shapes, sizes, brightnesses, and orientations, and in most of these situations the target seems to be transformed while it is moving (Anstis & Mather, 1985; Bundesen, Larsen, & Farrell, 1983; Kolers & Green, 1984; Kolers & von Grunau, 1976).

The stimulus inputs to the long-range motion process can also be considerably more abstract than stimuli for the short-range process (Cavanagh & Mather, 1989). Figure 14-10 illustrates this point in two ways. When Figure 14-10A is alternated with Figure 14-10B every 200 ms or so, observers see a dot-covered square jumping back and forth with its corners resting on the quartets of large black disks (Ramachandran & Anstis, 1986). To appreciate how much interpretation is involved in this perception note that the "jumping square" is defined by subjective contours alone (Chapter 10). The dots covering the subjective square do not move, nor are they displaced physically at all (this means that the retinal images of the dots are fixed in the same place regardless of whether the square is seen at the right or left). Yet, in our perception there is apparent movement of the dots. It appears not only as though the square jumps back and forth but also as though it takes the dots covering it with them. Thus, all of the dots are also seen jumping right and left, despite the fact that nothing is actually moving across the retina.

Long-range apparent motion perception adapts flexibly to other conditions in the visual field. If

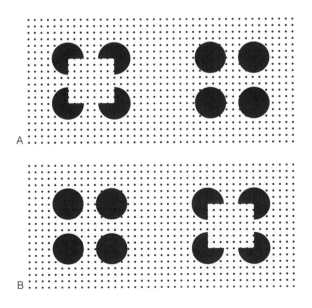

FIGURE 14-10   Two stimulus displays (*A* and *B*) that are alternated to produce the apparent motion of subjective squares (based on Ramachandran & Anstis, 1986).

you place an object in the pathway of the apparent movement, the perceived path of motion will seem to deflect around the object (Berbaum & Lenel, 1983). If a particular pathway is suggested by, for instance, briefly flashing a curved path between the two flickering stimuli, the apparent motion will seem to follow that pathway (Shepard & Zare, 1983). If the stimulus looks like a solid object, the path that the apparent motion follows can be quite complex and can involve even motions that appear to be three-dimensional (rather than simply side to side; e.g., Hecht & Proffitt, 1991). It is as if the observer tries to "figure out" how the object could have gotten from the position and orientation that it had at Time 1 to the position and orientation that it has at Time 2 while still remaining a solid and real object. All of these factors suggest that high-level cognitive processing mechanisms play a role in the perception of apparent motion in long-range displays (Rock, 1983).

Some researchers have considered the empirical differences between the perception of motion in short-range and long-range displays and have theorized that perception in each is determined by two fundamentally different systems—one governed by primitive and preattentive short-range processes and the other by cognitively influenced and attention-limited long-range processes (Braddick, 1980; Petersik, 1989). Others have reasoned that the distinction is really one of different types of motion sensors. The short-range displays are said to activate Reichard sensors, with values of small time and space parameters, that take only luminance changes as input, whereas the long-range displays are said to activate sensors that have much larger spatiotemporal windows and that are stimulated by luminance, color, texture, and even motion (Burr, Ross, & Morrone, 1986; Cavanagh & Mather, 1989).

INTEGRATION OF LOW-LEVEL MOTION SIGNALS INTO HIGH-LEVEL PERCEPTS

Figure-Ground Relations

Motion perception helps us divide the world into coherent figures, objects, and surfaces. One example

of this was described in Demonstration Box 14-1, where we saw how the Gestalt Law of Common Fate allows us to see an otherwise invisible figure. Another example can be seen in the random dot kinematogram illustrated in Figure 14-11. This type of display has been used quite effectively to study the rules of perceptual grouping when relative motion differences are the only cues to shape and surface boundaries. The construction of these displays is very similar to the random dot stereograms illustrated in Figure 9-16 (Chapter 9) except that the two frames are now shown successively in time rather than stereoscopically. In both displays there is a region of dots in one frame that has been displaced horizontally relative to the same region of dots in the other frame. When the two frames are shown in alternating fashion, the displaced region appears to oscillate horizontally over time. Not only does this figural region segregate perceptually from the background as a distinct shape, but also it appears to be closer to the observer than is the background.

The appearance of the oscillating figure as nearer than the background is consistent with what is happening to the individual dots at the edge of the figure. Over time, dots in the background are being successively deleted and redrawn as the oscillating edge moves back and forth over the background (Shipley & Kellman, 1994; Yonas & Craton, 1987, 1990). These are therefore the local cues in the random dot kinematogram to the depth cue identified as *motion parallax* in Chapter 9.

Three-Dimensional Shape and Depth From Motion

Some subtle modifications to a random dot kinematogram can make it useful for studying the role of motion in the perception of three-dimensional shapes and surfaces. Consider the display illustrated in Figure 14-12. It starts once again as a random collection of dots in the first frame, but in successive frames each dot is displaced along the trajectory that would correspond to the location of a randomly chosen dot on the surface of a transparent cylinder. Observers viewing this display see a vivid image of a transparent cylinder rotating in depth. The dots corresponding to the surface that are depicted farther away from the observer are

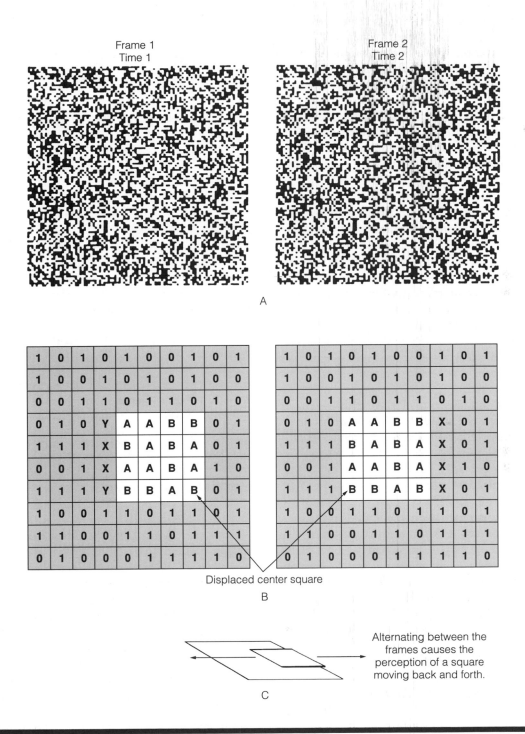

FIGURE 14-11   Figure A is a random dot kinematogram. Figure B shows how *A* is constructed, and *C* shows that alternating between the frames causes a square to be seen moving back and forth in front of the background (based on Julez, 1971).

seen as moving in a different direction and at a different depth plane from the dots corresponding to the apparently nearer surface.

Demonstrations such as the one illustrated in Figure 14-12 show that relative motion information alone is sufficient to enable the processes responsible for shape perception to operate. The process is sometimes called **structure from motion** by researchers who are interested in the computational aspects of three-dimensional vision. Detailed analyses of the geometry of the displays that produce these percepts have revealed that the three-dimensional structure of a rigid object can be determined mathematically from a minimum of four dots viewed over a minimum of three different frames in the sequence (Ullman, 1979).

It is also worth reminding the reader that the structure from motion problem is closely related to the *kinetic depth effect* described in Chapter 9 ("Space"), Demonstration Box 9-2. There we saw that the three-dimensional shape of an object can be determined quite easily from only its silhouette, provided that the object is undergoing rotation about one of its axes. With the random dot kinematogram shown in Figure 14-12 we see that the three-dimensional shape of an object can be recovered successfully by the visual system even when the silhouette of the object is no longer explicitly present.

Biological Motion

As we have seen, patterns of movement among randomly located dots can serve as powerful cues to the shape and identity of objects. One of the more finely tuned skills that humans possess in this regard is the ability to identify other humans and what they are doing solely from the patterns of motion made by their trunk and limbs. Studies examining this ability refer to it as **biological motion** perception (e.g., Johansson, 1976a).

In a series of studies, Gunnar Johansson and his coworkers began by asking, "Will an observer be able to identify the motions associated with the act of walking even in the absence of any other information, such as sight of the person?" To answer this question Johansson and his coworkers developed a clever technique. They attached small flashlight bulbs to the major joints of an individual (shoulders, elbows, wrists, hips, knees, and ankles),

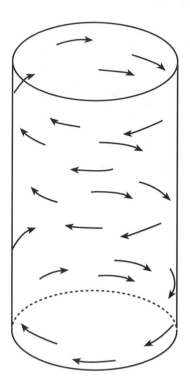

FIGURE 14-12   A random dot kinematogram that appears to the viewer as a cylinder rotating about its vertical axis in three dimensions. Because observers "see" the dots as transparent moving surfaces, even though there is no shading or edge information in the image, these displays are used to study the perception of three-dimensional *structure from motion.*

as shown in Figure 14-13A. They then made a motion picture film of the person as he moved around in a darkened room. When observers later watched the film, they saw only a pattern of lights moving about in total darkness. Nonetheless, they were able to identify the pattern as a person walking or running, even when they got to see the motion only for as short an exposure as 200 ms (Johansson, von Hofsten, & Jansson, 1980). Observers were also easily able to detect abnormalities, such as the simulation of a small limp.

In another experiment, two people with similar arrays of lights were filmed while performing a spirited folk dance. Figure 14-13B shows a series of positions from the folk dance in which the black dots mark the positions of the lights. Once again, even with only a moving pattern of lights,

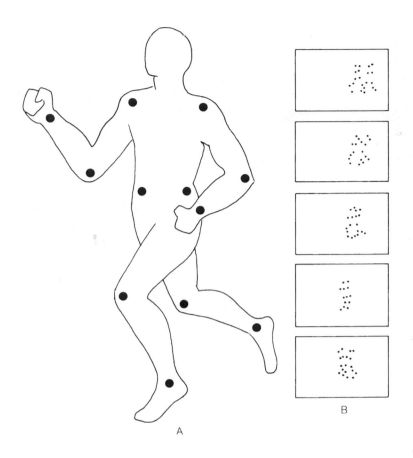

FIGURE 14-13   An example of the type of displays used by investigators to study patterns of humans in motion. *A* indicates the positions of lights affixed to individuals, and *B* shows a sequence of movement positions made by a dancing couple.

observers had no difficulty identifying the motion as a dancing couple (Johansson, 1976b). Infants as young as 4 months of age seem to notice that biological motion is different from other forms of motion and prefer to watch patterns of the sort we have been discussing, rather than random patterns of lights moving (Fox & McDaniel, 1982).

Our precision in recognizing individuals based only on their biological motion patterns is really quite striking. For example, in one study researchers photographed a group of people who were acquainted with one another. These people were photographed with only lighted portions of several joints visible. Several months later these same people were invited to watch the films and to attempt to identify themselves and their acquaintances in the film. People were able to identify

themselves and others correctly on many trials, although their performance was not perfect. The researchers also asked their observers how they went about making their identifications of various individuals in the film. The observers tended to mention a variety of motion components, such as the speed, bounciness, and rhythm of the walker, the amount of arm swing, or the length of steps as features that allowed them to make their identification. In other studies, these same researchers found that observers could tell, even under these conditions, whether a person was a male or a female, despite seeing only a moving pattern of dots. In fact, it was not necessary for all of the body joints to be represented in the light display for people to make correct identifications. Even when only the ankles were represented, observers could detect the sex of the walker. They could also make these gender identifications within about 5 seconds of viewing (Barclay, Cutting, & Kozlowski, 1978; Cutting & Kozlowski, 1977; Cutting & Proffitt, 1981; Kozlowski & Cutting, 1977). Thus, different motion patterns characterize each sex and each individual.

Much work is being done to determine the nature of the information used to identify individuals, and from this some fairly sophisticated computer programs have been developed to create simulated biological motion patterns (cf. Cutting, 1978; Runeson & Frykholm, 1983; Todd, 1983). For instance, Cutting, Proffitt, and Kozlowski (1978) proposed that the torso of the body acts like a flat spring with the limbs in symmetrical motion around it. This, along with certain individual differences in bodily dimensions (such as the relative widths of the shoulders and hips), provides a center of movement that is not necessarily associated with any body part; however, it organizes the coherent motion of the body parts in an individual fashion, making identification possible. Perhaps it is patterns of biological motion such as this that enable us to identify people in light too dim to allow us to see their faces. It also probably explains how you can identify people walking down the street, even though they may be too far away for you to make out their features or may have their backs to you.

Motion of the Self

Back in the 19th century there was a fairground ride called the Haunted Swing. In this ride, people entered a boat-shaped enclosure, and artificial scenery was slowly swung backward and forward outside the windows. This resulted in an incredibly strong illusion that the chamber was rocking, and people felt all of the bodily sensations of real motion, including a feeling of loss of their postural stability that made them sway, and even vertigo (Howard, 1982; Wood, 1985). There is an everyday example of this effect. Probably most of you have had the experience of sitting in a bus or a train parked next to another vehicle. All at once the adjacent vehicle starts to move. However, instead of correctly attributing the movement to the vehicle beside you, you have a powerful sensation

of yourself in motion. This is a case of induced movement, such as we discussed earlier; however, it is an *induced movement of the self*. It is important because it reflects the interchangeability of visual and vestibular factors in the perception of body motion.

If we were not aware of dynamic changes in the visual image as we move, we probably would bump into things much more often as we walk around or not notice that our body has swayed or leaned until we actually incline too far and topple over. Our perception of **self-motion** depends on an analysis of the continually changing aspects of the retinal image as we move. Consider our most typical motion, which is forward in depth. Although a number of sources of information are important in this situation (see Larish & Flach, 1990), some particular features of the visual array seem to be particularly important. As we move forward, the visual array in front of us is a radially expanding pattern in the center of our visual field and a laterally translating pattern in the periphery.

For example, consider the pattern shown in Figure 14-14A. Here the arrows represent the flow of the visual array as if you were moving toward the door marked *A*. Images of objects around Door A—that is, those stimuli to its sides or above or below it—expand radially outward and into the periphery as you move forward. This flow of stimuli has been called **streaming perspective** (Gibson, 1979). If your path were angled so you were going toward the door marked *B*, the optical transformation pattern would be similar to that in Figure 14-14B. In both cases, the center of this outward flow, which is called the **focus of expansion**, indicates the direction of your movement. Although the specific patterns shown by the streaming perspective of targets in the field will vary as you move your eyes (Andersen, 1986; Cutting, 1986; Regan & Beverly, 1982), it is still easy to direct your movements by keeping the door you wish to reach in the center of the outward flow of stimuli (cf. Warren & Hannon, 1988).

If we present you with a steadily moving pattern that is the equivalent of a natural streaming-perspective pattern, you will feel as though you are moving. If the pattern is radially expanding, as in Figure 14-14, you will feel as though your body is moving forward. If the pattern is moved steadily to the side you will feel that you are moving (or

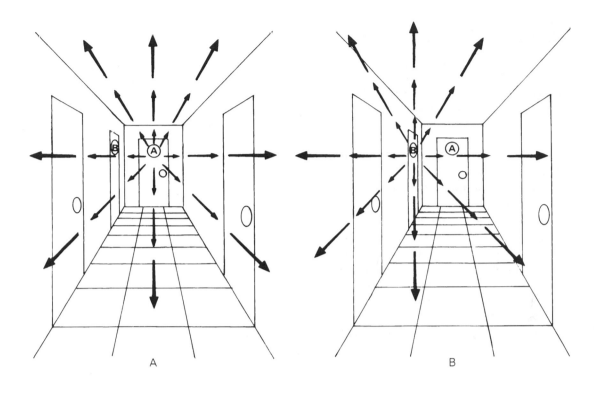

FIGURE 14-14   Streaming perspective. Figure A shows the pattern of flow or expansion of stimuli as it would appear if you were moving toward Door A. The length of the arrows indicates the rate of change or speed of expansion, with longer arrows meaning faster change. *B* shows how the pattern of stimulus flow would change if you were now moving toward Door B, rather than straight down the hallway.

starting to lean or tilt) sideways, or even rotating if the pattern surrounds you. Such induced motion of the self is usually called **vection** (Dichgans & Brandt, 1978). Generally speaking, there is a consensus that the central visual field is more specialized for object motion, whereas stimulation of the peripheral visual field is necessary to induce the feeling of self-motion. Thus, patterns that extend into the periphery tend to produce strong feelings of vection (e.g., Delorme & Martin, 1986; Held, Dichgans, & Bauer, 1975). If the speed of flow is not too fast and the pattern is correct, visually induced self-motion can be experienced even for small central patterns (Andersen & Braunstein, 1985; Stoffregen, 1985). Demonstration Box 14-8 shows how you may experience a form of induced self-motion.

The relatively greater contribution of the peripheral retina to vection may explain why the feelings of self-motion can be so strong when you view motion pictures with an oversized or wraparound screen. In fact, a modern version of the Haunted Swing illusion can be found in some fairs and amusement parks, where viewers are surrounded by the projected pictures associated with riding down a roller coaster, flying in a helicopter, or hurtling down a raceway at high speed. Most viewers feel all of the bodily effects normally associated with the equivalent self-motion, and the effects are sufficiently indistinguishable from actual movement that it suggests that the visual and *vestibular* (see next section) inputs must have some common neural pathways and centers. This would be a sensible arrangement because the vestibular system responds only to accelerations or decelerations of body motions. After any prolonged period of constant velocity, the vestibular system would cease to respond, and the only remaining indication of movement would be the motion in the visual array.

DEMONSTRATION BOX 14-8
Induced Self-Motion

For this demonstration you should have two small light sources (lighted candles will work fine) and a darkened room. Hold the candles out at arm's length and about at eye level, as shown in the figure. Look straight forward (remove your glasses or squint your eyes a bit so that you don't see the surrounding room too clearly). Now slowly move the candles back toward the sides of your head (not too close!). As you do so, you should experience an induced motion of your body so you now feel that you are leaning forward slightly. If you move the candles slowly forward, you should get the impression that you have straightened up or are now leaning backward somewhat. Next, try the same arm movements with your eyes closed to see that this effect does not occur in the absence of the visual stimulation. This means that the feeling of body tilt produced in this situation is a form of vec-

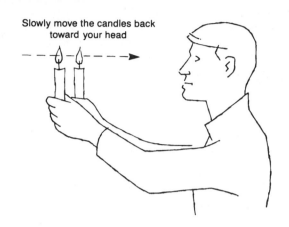

Slowly move the candles back toward your head

tion caused by the streaming perspective simulated by the movements of the lights, which suggested that at least the upper portion of your body was moving forward.

To the extent that vestibular information and visual information can each produce similar feelings of self-motion, it should not be surprising to find that there are cells in the vestibular nuclei whose rates of firing are influenced by signals suggesting bodily motion, whether such signals come from the vestibular organs themselves or from visual motion (e.g., Henn, Young, & Finley, 1974; Waespe & Henn, 1977). There seems to be a complex interaction between the visual and the nonvisual inputs to give us this feeling of self-motion (DiZio & Lackner, 1986; Henn, Cohen, & Young, 1980). However, the situation is really very complicated. In some of the situations that we have described, where the illusion of self-motion is produced, the mismatch between visual and vestibular signals can produce unpleasant feelings. In some individuals there are even symptoms of *motion sickness* (complete with nausea and vomiting) caused by the lack of agreement between visual and vestibular signals (Reason & Brand, 1975; Stern, Koch, Leibowitz, Lindblad, Shupert, & Stewart, 1985). With continued exposure, individuals become used to

this situation, and the symptoms then disappear (Hu, Grant, Stern, & Koch, 1991).

A SENSE OF BALANCE

Another sensory system primarily concerned with motion and motion-related matters tends to interact with visual input to separate bodily motion from stimulus motion. The **vestibular system** functions to inform us about the motion of our body through space, to assist in the maintenance of an upright posture, and to control eye position as we move our heads while viewing various stimuli. For the most part, these operations take place outside of consciousness. Before we consider the high-level interactions that involve this system, let us first consider its basic structure and physiology.

Some of the most primitive organisms have organs that are sensitive to changes in motion of the body. In primitive invertebrates such as the crayfish these are called **statocysts**. Each consists simply of a fluid-filled cavity that is lined with hair cells. In the cavity is a tiny stone, called a **statolith** or "still stone," that rests on the hairs. When the animal accelerates, the stone tends to lag behind because of its inertia, thus bending the hairs on which it rests. This action generates an electrical response to the movement. If the animal is tilted, the stone rolls along over a number of different hairs, bending them and generating a different response, indicating tilt. The function of such organs is to signal the animal's orientation with respect to gravity. More advanced invertebrates, such as the squid or octopus, have multichambered statocysts that approach vertebrate vestibular organs in complexity and that have the ability to detect acceleration in several planes (Stephens & Young, 1982).

Primitive vertebrates have organs that have a similar function; they are called **otocysts,** and the bones they contain are called **otoliths.** Notice that these terms each contain the root *oto* meaning "ear." These organs are usually closely associated with the ears because both the auditory receptors and the vestibular organs probably evolved from pits on the surface of hairy skin. In mammals, these organs are protected by the skull from possibly damaging outside forces. In humans, the **bony** **labyrinth** in the head contains the cochlea (which is the auditory organ) and the **semicircular canals,** the **utricle,** and the **saccule,** which comprise the vestibular organs (see Figure 14-15).

Vestibular Stimuli and Receptors

The effective physical stimulus for any vestibular organ is change of rate of motion, or **acceleration,** which occurs whenever we move through space, whether we jump up and down, take off in a jet plane, or simply stand up and walk. The semicircular canals and their associated receptor organs seem particularly well suited for monitoring rotary acceleration (as when turning around or falling down). The other two organs, the utricle and the saccule, seem mainly to respond to linear acceleration (as when taking off in a plane).

The movement-receptive portion of the semicircular canals is called the **crista,** which is found in a swelling (called an **ampulla**) at the base of each semicircular canal (see Figure 14-16). The crista consists of an array of sensory cells from

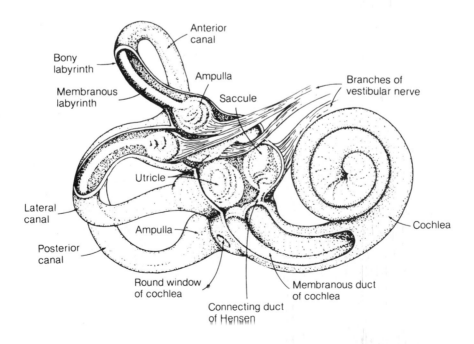

FIGURE 14-15   A diagram of the right inner ear showing the cochlea (which houses the auditory receptor), the semicircular canals, the utricle, and the saccule (from Geldard, 1972).

which tiny hairs protrude, as shown in Figure 14-16A. These hairs are embedded in a jelly-like material called the **cupola**. When your head accelerates, the inertia of the fluid in the canals causes the cupola to move in the opposite direction. This in turn causes the hairs to bend, generating neural responses (just as the hair cells do in the ear; see Chapter 6). As your head continues to move at a particular rate of speed, the cupola gradually comes back to its resting position, no longer bending the hairs and no longer causing a response in the sensory cells. This is why the effective stimulus is acceleration rather than steady movement.

The receptor organ found in the utricle and the saccule is called the **macula**, shown in Figure 14-16B. It functions much like the statocyst we discussed before. As in the crista, tiny hairs protrude from the sensory cells in the macula. These hairs are embedded in a jelly-like substance covered by a membrane containing otoliths, which lag behind when the head is accelerated, bending the hair cells and generating an electrical response. When the jelly and hairs catch up to the rest of the head, which would happen when the acceleration ceases and motion becomes steady, the hairs are no longer bent. This means no response is generated, even though the head can be traveling at thousands of kilometers per hour relative to the earth.

Neural Responses in the Vestibular Sense

The hair cells from both the crista and the macula send their information to the brain stem via the eighth cranial nerve. From there most of the nerve fibers go to the **vestibular nuclei** (still in the brain stem). After this the sensory pathways become complicated and somewhat obscure. There are projections to the cerebellum and to the cortex, but they are different in different animals (see Correia & Guedry, 1978). It is important to note that most of the fibers leaving the vestibular nuclei are motor or **efferent fibers.** One major group of these fibers forms a pathway to the muscles that move the eyes. Szentagothai (1950) discovered that each pair of eye muscles receives fibers from a different semicircular canal. The arrangement indicates that muscles that move the eye in a particular plane are controlled by nerve fibers that originate in one of the semicircular canals that responds to acceleration in that plane. Acceleration in a particular direction causes compensatory eye movements in the opposite direction. This allows the eyes to remain fixed on an object even though the head is turning in various directions. The relationship between eye movements and vestibular stimulation is shown in Demonstration Box 14-9.

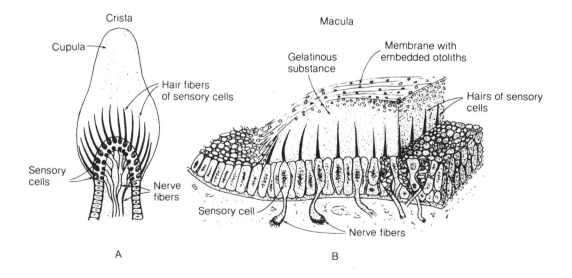

FIGURE 14-16   (A) Diagram of the crista, the receptor found in the ampulla of each semicircular canal. (B) Diagram of the macula, the receptor found in the utricle and the saccule (from Geldard, 1972).

DEMONSTRATION BOX 14-9
Vestibular Stimulation and Eye Movements

For this demonstration you will need a friend and a little space. Have your friend hold her arms out and spin around (like a whirling ice skater) until she becomes dizzy. This continuous rotation sets up currents in the semicircular canals that trigger the compensatory eye-movement system. Now stop your friend from turning and look into her eyes. You will notice that the eyes drift steadily in one direction and then snap back and start to drift again. This type of repetitive eye movement is called **nystagmus.** It is a reflex movement evoked automatically by the vestibular stimulation caused by fluid currents in the semicircular canals.

Lowenstein and Sand (1940) performed a classic study that illustrates the electrophysiology of the vestibular system. They recorded the electrical activity of single nerve fibers from the crista of a ray (a kind of fish) while the entire labyrinth was rotated on a turntable. They found that as long as the head was accelerating, the fibers responded. The fibers increased their firing rate above the resting rate for acceleration in one direction and decreased it below the resting rate when the acceleration was in the opposite direction. Thus, as in other sensory systems, both excitatory and inhibitory responses to physical stimuli occur. Lowenstein and Sand also showed that the magnitude of the response (impulses per second in single fibers) varies directly with the magnitude of the stimulating acceleration. So stimulus intensity seems to be encoded in a manner similar to that in other sensory systems. There are at least two other types of nerve fibers: One always responds to acceleration (regardless of direction) with an increase in firing rate, and the other responds only with a decrease in firing rate. The fibers connected to the hair cells of the macula respond to their stimuli somewhat more simply. Two types of responses have been described. The first is an increase in the rate of neural firing when the head is tilted; the second is an increase in the rate when the head is returned to its original position (Wyburn et al., 1964). Although there have been some studies of cortical responses to acceleration of the head, little is known in detail about these responses. One fact that has emerged is that inputs from vestibular, kinesthetic, and visual systems converge in the cortex, so our sensations of "turning" and the like depend in a complex way on all

of these inputs (Mergner, Anastasopoulos, Becker, & Deecke, 1981; Parker, 1980). One striking example of this complex interaction is the phenomenon of motion sickness, which is often caused by a mismatch between visual and vestibular or kinesthetic inputs. A great deal of effort is being put into studying this aspect of human reaction, especially because of its importance in space travel, which involves zero-gravity conditions.

The perception of motion is therefore a good example of **sensory convergence,** a process by which several inputs may combine to produce a single coherent perception. Of course, we are often not conscious of all of the components that have gone into the computation. In the case of motion perception, we have seen that the apparently *visual* experience of motion may contain proprioceptive inputs from eye movements and the vestibular sense, or copies of efferent commands issued to the eye muscles, even though our conscious impression remains strictly visual. As seems to be so often the case in perception, the percept we experience in our consciousness is an amalgam of many sources even though to us it may seem to be a simple experience.

CHAPTER SUMMARY

Motion perception serves not only to guide our actions with respect to moving objects in the environment but also to compensate for stimulus movement caused by our own body movements. It also helps to segregate the environment into objects, figures, and surfaces via mechanisms such as **Common Fate.** The existence of specific neural units that detect motion has been demonstrated through **selective adaptation,** which produces **motion aftereffects.** An important theoretical neural circuit for the detection of motion is the **Reichardt detector.** The tectopulvinar pathway seems to be specialized to process motion signals. Within the geniculostriate pathway it is the magnocellular system, rather than the parvocellular system, that is most important for motion perception. This has been verified behaviorally using displays involving **isoluminant stimuli.** In the cortex, it is the temporal lobe Area V5 that processes global motion perception and is sensitive to **motion coherence.**

The **image-retina system** is most responsive to optical motion signals. **Object-relative changes** that occur with a **visual context** produce very low thresholds for motion detection. The visual context can also produce illusory **induced motion** under some circumstances. The seen motion paths, however, depend on apparent **motion correspondence** as well as the physical changes in the optical array.

The **eye-head system** uses **smooth pursuit eye movement** information to infer motion in the environment. This information can involve either **inflow** information from eye muscle proprioception or **outflow** information from efferent commands issued to the muscles. Distortions in either source of information can result in errors and illusions involving perceived movements, such as in the **Aubert-Fleischl effect.**

It is often difficult to discriminate between the mechanisms involved in **real** versus **apparent movement.** Within apparent motion, however, **short-range motion** perception seems to be almost completely driven by sensory factors, such as **stimulus onset asynchrony,** whereas **long-range motion** perception seems to involve more inferential processes. Integration of low- and high-level motion mechanisms can be seen in our perception of three-dimensional **structure from motion,** the use of motion to segregate the visual field into figures and surfaces, and in perception of **biological motion,** by which people can be identified from their movement patterns alone.

The perception of **self-motion** involves both optical and physiological processes. On the optical side there are the systematic changes in the array that we call **streaming perspective,** which can also result in apparent self-motion or **vection.** Physiological contributions to perception of self-motion are primarily the product of the **vestibular system,** which also provides us with our sense of balance.

KEY TERMS

Common Fate
waterfall illusion
selective adaptation
motion aftereffect
apparent motion
Reichardt detector
isoluminant stimuli
motion coherence
image-retina system
eye-head system
visual context
subject-relative change
object-relative change
motion correspondence
 problem
aperture problem
induced motion
smooth pursuit
 movement
voluntary pursuit
 movement
reflex pursuit movement
Aubert-Fleischl effect
position constancy
direction constancy
inflow theory
outflow theory
interstimulus interval
apparent movement
real movement
autokinetic effect
frame duration

stimulus onset
 asynchrony
SOA Law (Onset-Onset
 Law)
short-range motion
long-range motion
random dot
 kinematogram (RDK)
structure from motion
biological motion
self-motion
streaming perspective
focus of expansion
vection
vestibular system
statocysts
statolith
otocysts
otoliths
bony labyrinth
semicircular canals
utricle
saccule
acceleration
crista
ampulla
cupola
macula
vestibular nuclei
efferent fibers
sensory convergence

Attention

CHAPTER 15

My experience is what I agree to attend to. Only those items which I notice, shape my mind—without selective interest, experience is an utter chaos.

(William James, 1890, p. 402)

Our sensory receptors are continually receptive to their respective stimulus energies. This provides an enormous amount of information about events in our environment, and yet our ability fully to process all of this information is limited. Most of the time only one of the many streams of sensory input seems to fill our minds, and the others fade to the periphery of consciousness (James, 1890). The various ways by which we select among all that is there to be looked at, listened to, felt, smelled, or tasted are often grouped together under the general label of *attention*.

VARIETIES OF ATTENTION

Imagine the following scenario: You are reading this book, and various extraneous events distract you. You get a cramp in your foot and stretch it; a fire engine screams by outside, and you listen until the siren stops somewhere down the block; a flicker of movement in the periphery of your visual field causes you to look toward the door to the room as your roommate enters bringing you a midnight snack (you wish!). In this fantasy of college life, each of several important events demands an **orienting** response. That is, your attention is drawn, or pulled, to a source of sudden change in your sensory world. Some events you might give only brief attention to, as when you initiate the

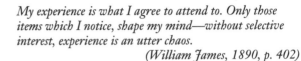

foot stretch. Other events you might listen to (the fire siren) or look at (your roommate) for longer periods of time. Although you attend to some stimuli, you also exclude many others. Hence, while listening to the siren you are probably unaware of the goldfish swimming in its bowl or the refrigerator humming in the next room. Technically we would say that you are **filtering** out the extraneous events, attending to only one of the several available distinct and separable sources of information about the world, which we will refer to as **information channels.**

Continuing the fantasy, perhaps your attention wanders for a moment from the page, and you think of the exam scheduled for tomorrow in calculus. You wonder where your notes are and look up, scanning your room for the green binder you will be poring over in a few minutes. You are **searching** for a relevant stimulus in the environment, scanning your sensory world for particular features or combinations of features. Finally, just as you are about to start studying your math notes, you pause, realizing that it is at about this time every night that the wolves in the zoo next door begin to howl at the moon. You listen for a few moments. Yes, there they are, right on time. You were expecting something to happen and in **preparing** for that event momentarily attended to "empty space" until it did (LaBerge, 1995).

Throughout this fantasy of college life, different forms of attention were called on, and each played a major role in determining conscious perceptual experience.

In what follows, we describe in more detail some of what is known about how attention operates in these four tasks: orienting, filtering, searching, and preparing. Our discussion will be restricted to the visual and auditory modalities because most work has been done on these, but our conclusions apply to the other modalities as well. By way of definition, we also point out that each of the tasks we described can involve paying attention to a single target or event (**focused attention**) or dividing it among several of them (**divided attention**). Figure 15-1 summarizes the framework for describing attention we will use in this chapter.

In recent years several particular issues or problems of attention within this very general framework have generated much research. For example, Egeth and Yantis (1997) singled out three issues for discussion and review: the interaction of the deliberate deployment of attention with its "capture" by aspects of the stimulus display, whether attention is directed to a region of space or to perceptual objects, and the time course of attentional deployment and of its effects on perceptual processing. These issues will arise often as we discuss the major tasks of attention outlined in Figure 15-1.

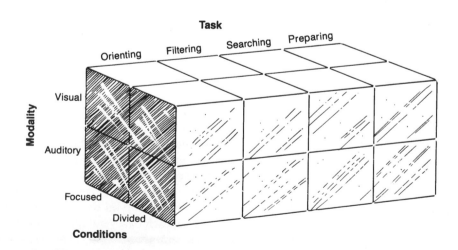

FIGURE 15-1 A representation of various perceptual attention situations dealt with in this chapter.

ORIENTING

The simplest way to select among several stimulus inputs is to *orient* our sensory receptors toward one set of stimuli and away from another. We might say that we do not passively see or hear but, rather, that we actively *look* or *listen* in order to see and hear. In other words, we must pay attention in order to explicitly perceive events in our world (Mack, Tang, Tuma, Kahn, & Rock, 1992).

Orienting Reflex

We have all seen a dog or a cat prick up its ears and turn its head toward a sudden sound. The animal is performing the most primitive form of **orienting response,** which involves adjusting the sense organs so they can optimally pick up information about the event. Responses such as flicking the eye in the direction of a sound or peripheral movement occur automatically and are collectively referred to as the **orienting reflex.** This is such a reliable reflex that eye and head turns toward sounds have been used to test the hearing of newborn infants (Butterworth, 1981; Muir & Field, 1979). The most effective orienting stimuli are loud sounds, suddenly appearing bright lights, changes in contours, or movements in the peripheral visual field that are not regular, predictable occurrences. Interestingly, the sudden offset of a light or sound that has been on for a while can also elicit the orienting reflex. When any of these stimuli occur, the animal, or human, turns its eyes so as to fixate the visual object or sound source and often orients the head and body to face the event as well.

Several other behaviors follow onset of a sudden event, such as postural adjustments, skin conductance changes, pupil dilation, decrease in heart rate, a pause in breathing, and constriction of the peripheral blood vessels (see Rohrbaugh, 1984, for more details). It is as though we had an internal "model" of the immediate world of stimuli around us. When we notice a departure of stimulus input from that model, we reflexively orient to that stimulus in order to update that model as quickly as possible (Donchin, 1981; Sokolov, 1975). If the same stimulus occurs repeatedly it becomes an expected part of our model of the world, and our orienting reflex toward it becomes weaker, even if the stimulus is quite strong. With any change in the nature of the stimulus, however, the reflex recovers to full strength.

Covert Orienting

It has been assumed by most researchers that the *overt orienting* response to sudden changes in the environment is usually accompanied by another, unseen orienting response, the fixing of attention on the event or object that elicited the reflex, selecting that event from among the others simultaneously present for focused processing, which we call **covert orienting.** It is nearly always assumed that the combination of overt orienting and covert orienting to an event will result in enhanced perception of that event, including faster identification and awareness of its significance. Although this hidden orienting of attention usually occurs in association with an overt orienting response, whether reflexive or voluntary, several researchers have pointed out that it is possible to covertly attend to an event or stimulus without making any overt sign that we are doing so. For example, Helmholtz (1909/1962) observed that he could direct his visual attention without the necessity of an eye movement or change in accommodation or convergence. Thus, we can consider covert attention orienting separately from overt orienting behaviors, although the two are surely closely related.

A common example of covert orienting is when we become aware of a familiar voice and the conversation it is having somewhere else at a party even while we look at and nod to the person in front of us every once in a while. Most modern research on attention takes for granted that overt orienting is not necessary for paying attention. Typically, in attentional experiments, eye/head/body movements are strictly controlled, or they are made irrelevant by using headphones or such short stimulus presentations that there is no time to shift the eyes to fixate the stimulus. Such controlled presentations allow researchers to separate the effects of overt orienting from covert shifts of attention. Thus, in the following discussion we will use the words *covert orienting* to refer only to situations in which attention is focused on a particular object or event, but an overt orienting response is absent.

There are many ways your attention can be drawn to objects or events in the environment. A dramatic example capitalizes on the fact that visual stimuli seem to be more capable of drawing our attention to particular locations in space than do auditory stimuli. This is the phenomenon ventriloquists depend on, called **visual capture**, in which a sound is mislocated at its apparent visual source. This drawing of attention to the apparent visual source of a sound can actually enhance the processing of speech sounds in the presence of other distracting speech sounds (Driver, 1996). Demonstration Box 15-1 allows you to experience visual capture for yourself.

An important demonstration of how attention can be captured by a visual event was made by Yantis and Jonides (1984; Jonides & Yantis, 1988). They showed that under some conditions the abrupt appearance of a stimulus in the visual field captures visual attention and facilitates responding to that stimulus. In their experiment they asked observers to say whether a particular target

---

DEMONSTRATION BOX 15-1
Visual Capture

Visual capture is a phenomenon in which attention is caught by a visual stimulus in a way that results in an illusion of auditory localization. Whenever you are listening to a sound, such as a voice talking, there is a tendency to try to identify visual events, or objects, that could be causing the sound. When the ventriloquist's dummy is moving its mouth and limbs and the ventriloquist is talking without moving *his* mouth, then your visual attention is "captured" by the dummy's movements, and you *hear* the ventriloquist's voice coming from its mouth, even though it is really the ventriloquist speaking.

You can demonstrate this effect for yourself by obtaining two television sets (or going to a store that sells them and asking to use two of theirs for a "scientific demonstration"). Place them side by side, about 500 cm apart, and tune both sets to the same newscast, talk show, or other show in which the sound is highly corre-lated with the picture. (You could also use a radio and a television set, tuning in to a simulcast show such as some concerts.) Now turn off the sound on one of the sets and turn off the picture on the other. Move back a short distance and look at a place between the two sets while paying attention to the picture-displaying set. The sound seems to come from that set, even though its sound is turned off. It actually doesn't matter where you look; the sound will seem to come from the set with the picture. You could also try moving the sets apart to see how powerful the phenomenon is. You will be surprised at how far apart these sets can be before the actual sound source dominates. By the way, this also explains why when you are watching a film the sound seems to come from the actors' mouths, even though the speakers may be located at the side of the film screen, or even in the back of the room.

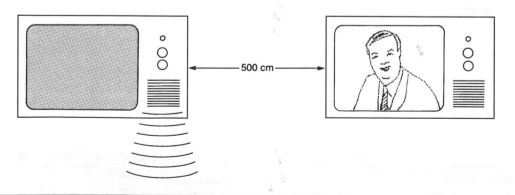

← 500 cm →

letter was present or not in a field of other distracting letters. On a typical trial, one letter appeared abruptly in the visual field while three others appeared gradually by the fading of selected lines in figures that had been displayed previously, as shown in Figure 15-2. Sometimes the target letter was the abruptly appearing letter; sometimes it was one of the gradually appearing letters. When the target appeared abruptly, observers detected it significantly more quickly than when it faded on. It seems that attention was drawn first to the abruptly appearing letter, and if it was the target, a positive response could immediately be made. If the abrupt-onset letter wasn't the target, then attention had to be directed toward the other letters before a response could be made, slowing the response.

Other studies have confirmed the ability of an abrupt-onset stimulus to attract attention (e.g., Müller & Findlay, 1988). They found that when such a stimulus preceded the occurrence of a target by about 100 ms the target information was processed optimally. It seems that attention is automatically attracted to the spatial location of the abrupt-onset stimulus within about 100 ms of its appearance, without the need to voluntarily orient (Jonides, 1981; Müller & Humphreys, 1991). It is not inevitable that attention is pulled toward such abrupt stimuli, however, because you can keep attention from being captured by voluntarily focusing your attention elsewhere (Yantis & Jonides, 1990). Moreover, if the observer's task does not require attending to abrupt-onset stimuli, for example, if the target is defined by a color difference, then abrupt-onset stimuli also may not capture attention, whereas color-difference stimuli will (Folk, Remington, & Johnston, 1992; Folk, Remington, & Wright, 1994; but see Theeuwes, 1994).

In Yantis and Jonides's experiments and in most others, the abrupt-onset stimuli are also new perceptual objects in the visual field. Is attention drawn to any abrupt luminance change in the visual field, or is it drawn only to those that represent new perceptual objects? Actually, attention seems to be tuned to notice the appearance of objects because it is drawn to the abrupt appearance of a new perceptual object even if its appearance is not accompanied by a luminance change—conversely, a salient luminance change that is not associated with the appearance of a new object does not capture attention (Yantis & Hillstrom, 1994). If attention is captured, it is possible to ask whether it is now oriented to the object itself or just toward the location of the object (see Duncan, 1984). Many studies have shown attention is associated with perceptual objects regardless of their location (or even if they move to new locations); however, some resources may also be allocated

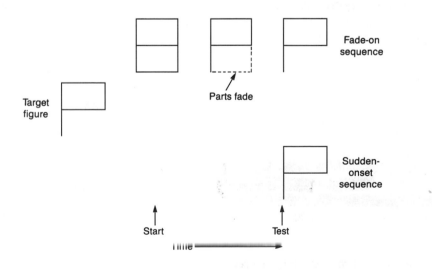

FIGURE 15-2 The upper sequence shows a gradual-onset stimulus, whereas the lower sequence shows a sudden-onset stimulus in the Yantis and Jonides (1984) study. Sudden-onset stimuli were more easily detected.

toward processing spatial location. Thus, attention is drawn both to a new perceptual object and to its location, and which dominates at any one moment depends on the perceptual task (see Egeth & Yantis, 1997, for a review).

Attention capture also happens in hearing. For example, in the early experiments on divided attention, subjects were given a different message in each of their two ears by means of headphones. They were asked to pay attention to and repeat the message they were hearing in one ear (shadowing) while another message was delivered to the other ear. When an abrupt or distinctive sound or an unexpected change, such as a switch from a male to a female voice, occurred in the unshadowed ear, subjects tended to "stumble" or lose the continuity of their shadowing (see, e.g., Kahneman, 1973). Apparently, their attention was drawn to the unshadowed message, causing them to fail to hear what they were supposed to be attending to and thus to interrupt the smooth flow of their shadowing. More recent experiments have confirmed the ability of an abrupt-onset sound to trigger involuntary orienting of auditory attention, both to the frequency of the abrupt-onset sound (Scharf, 1989; Schlauch & Hafter, 1991; Ward, 1997) and to its location (McDonald & Ward, 1998; Mondor & Zatorre, 1995; Spence & Driver, 1994; Ward, 1994). Moreover, as in visual orienting, whether an abrupt-onset sound orients attention to its location depends on the task. If the task is spatial, then attention is oriented to the location of abrupt-onset sounds, whereas if it is nonspatial, for example, a frequency discrimination task, then attention is not oriented to the location of previously occurring abrupt-onset sounds (McDonald & Ward, 1998).

In the situations discussed earlier, attention was drawn to some conspicuous stimulus somewhere in the visual or auditory field. In many modern studies of orienting, a special abrupt-onset stimulus, which we will call a **direct cue**, is presented in advance of a target to be responded to for just this purpose. Responses to targets that appear near the cued location are facilitated, relative to those to targets that appear elsewhere, for about 100–200 ms after cue onset if the cue doesn't predict the target's location and for up to 1 second if it does (see Wright & Ward, 1998, for a review). Orienting, filtering, and searching all depend on

the presence of one or more direct cues toward which attention is either automatically drawn (orienting) or voluntarily directed (filtering or searching). When we receive information in advance about where or when something is likely to happen (we call this a **symbolic cue**), attentional phenomena appear to be somewhat different. This suggests that our expectations interact with how we direct our attention, a matter discussed later under *preparing*.

The Attentional Gaze

A useful way of conceptualizing some of the findings in covert visual orienting and visual searching is a metaphor that we will call the **attentional gaze.** Other terms have been suggested for this concept (e.g., a *zoom lens* by Eriksen & Hoffman, 1972; Eriksen & Murphy, 1987 and Eriksen & St. James, 1986; a *spotlight* by Hernandez-Peon, 1964; and Treisman, 1982; the *mind's eye* by Jonides, 1980), but attentional gaze is the most general. In this metaphor, we imagine that your attention can "gaze" about, independently of where your eyes are looking. In the case of orienting, attention can be drawn to a direct cue anywhere in the visual field where there is adequate acuity and sensitivity to register it, either by an abrupt onset, as earlier, or by other conspicuous differences in movement, shape, or color (Egeth & Yantis, 1997; Joseph & Optican, 1996; Julesz, 1981; Nakayama & Silverman, 1986; Treisman, 1982).

Covert shifts in the attentional gaze seem to behave in a way similar to physical movements of the eye, in that attention seems to jump from Point A to Point B like a saccade, although it seems to take no longer to move a large distance than a small one (Tsal, 1983; see Wright & Ward, 1998, for a review). Another similarity between the attentional gaze and physical eye movements is that attention usually cannot be drawn to more than one location in the visual field at any instant in time (Eriksen & Yeh, 1985; Müller & Humphreys, 1991; van der Heijden, Wolters, Groep, & Hagenaar, 1987; Yantis & Jonides, 1984). Auditory attention also acts as if it has a direction of gaze. It can be drawn to particular spatial locations in a way similar to that of visual attention (McDonald & Ward, 1998; Mondor & Zatorre, 1995; Spence & Driver, 1994; Ward, 1994).

The fact that the attentional gaze can be shifted without accompanying eye (or head) movements raises the question of how these two systems are coordinated. Under normal circumstances a direct cue will attract both a shift in attentional gaze and an eye movement to the location of the stimulus. However, as you may have noted in listening to a boring conversation, an eye movement to a location of greater interest can be suppressed voluntarily (Klein, 1980; Posner, 1980), although it is rare for attention not to be attracted by a conspicuous event, at least momentarily. Experimental studies of the attentional gaze show that it can shift much faster than the eye—it reaches a stimulus location before the eye does and seems to help to guide the eye to the proper location (Fischer & Breitmeyer, 1987; Henderson & Pollatsek, 1989; Posner, 1988; Remington, 1980). These experiments suggest that the attentional gaze and the gaze of the eye are related, much like the gaze of the eye and movement of the hand are related in the everyday act of reaching. Under normal circumstances the eye will first move to the object of interest and then help guide the hand to the correct location. However, an eye movement can occur without a hand movement necessarily following, and hand movements can be made even with one's eyes closed.

Three aspects of the attentional gaze are important in the processing of sensory information. At any one moment attention may be described as having a *locus,* an *extent,* and a *detail set.* As noted earlier, the attentional gaze shifts around much as your eyes move to take in visual information. After attention is located at a particular place, or **locus,** in the visual field, processing of stimuli occurring at or near that locus is improved. It is improved more if the locus is near the fovea than if it is in the more peripheral regions of the retina (Shulman, Sheehy, & Wilson, 1986). The **extent** of the area over which attention is spread can be controlled by making the direct cue larger or smaller (LaBerge & Brown, 1989; Podgorny & Shepard, 1983). The greater the extent over which attention is spread, the lesser the processing efficiency. Processing also becomes less efficient for stimuli that are farther away from the center of the attended region (Eriksen & St. James, 1986).

Finally, there is some evidence that the attentional gaze is set or calibrated for a particular level of detail at any one time. In the visual modality, for example, this **detail set** tends to direct the focus of attention to elements of a particular relative size. Several studies have shown that observers can focus selectively on either the more global (relatively larger) aspects or the more local (relatively smaller) aspects in a visual form. Thus, if we have a large figure made up of smaller distinct components (such as the large letter made up of smaller letters that we saw in Figure 10-25), attention can be set for either the large figure or its smaller elements. When attention is set for one level of detail, processing of features at the other level is poorer (Hoffman, 1980; Kinchla, Solis-Macias, & Hoffman, 1983; L. M. Ward, 1985). This effect may be mediated by separate brain mechanisms that are invoked for the different levels of detail (Lamb & Yund, 1996; Robertson, Lamb, & Knight, 1988). Experiments in which observers searched for global or local forms of varying structures indicate that the global-level processing mechanism may be an attention-demanding grouping operation (Enns & Kingstone, 1995). An example of the effects of detail set is given in Demonstration Box 15-2.

The Neurophysiology of Orienting

Over the past 20 years researchers studying the physiology of the brain have begun to examine some of the neural mechanisms of orienting. Several areas of the monkey brain contain single nerve cells that fire more vigorously (firing *enhancement*) when the monkey is attending to target stimuli in their receptive fields than they do when the same target is not attended to (Mountcastle, Motter, Steinmetz, & Sestokas, 1987; Wurtz, Goldberg, & Robinson, 1980). (Recall from Chapter 3 that the *receptive field* of a particular cell is that region of the visual field in which a stimulus can produce a response from that cell.) The relevant cortical areas involved in orienting attention can be seen in Figure 15-3A. Deeper in the brain, the thalamus and the **superior colliculi** are involved in orienting attention. The superior colliculi are the upper pair of hill-like bumps on the top of the brain stem, and they can be seen in Figure 15-3B, which is a view of a brain that has been split down the middle to show the deeper structures. The superficial

---

DEMONSTRATION BOX 15-2
Level of Detail and Attention

How many times in your life have you looked at a penny? Probably thousands of times. Take a piece of paper and, from memory, draw both sides of a penny. There is no need to be artistic; just try to represent all the figures, words, numbers, and dates on a penny, each in its proper place. Next, compare your drawings to an actual penny. It is likely that you will find at least one error, and probably several, in the material you include and your placement of it. The reason for this is that it is possible to recognize a penny based on a fairly global set of characteristics, namely its size, shape, and color. So your *detail set* when attending to pennies has probably seldom been small enough to pick out the local characteristics, regardless of the thousands of times you have looked at one.

---

layers of the superior colliculi contain many cells that fire when a stimulus appears at a specific location in the visual field. These cells fire even more vigorously (enhancement) when the monkey makes an overt eye movement toward the stimulus at that location (Wurtz, Goldberg, & Robinson, 1980). These cells are not simply recording or initiating eye movements, however, because they do not respond at all when eye movements are made in complete darkness. Rather, they show enhanced firing only for eye movements accompanied by a shift in attention toward a visual target, with the increased firing rate of the cells beginning 50 ms after the target is flashed onto the screen, while the eye movement that follows might actually begin 200 ms later.

To differentiate overt from covert orienting, we can use an experimental situation like the one shown in Figure 15-4. This involves a screen on which a visual stimulus can be projected and a lever that a monkey can press or release to indicate that it has seen a particular stimulus. In Figure 15-4A the monkey is looking at a point in the center of the screen and neither overtly nor covertly orienting to the target. In Figure 15-4B the monkey has shifted its eyes to the stimulus, demonstrating overt orienting. In Figure 15-4C the monkey has responded to the stimulus with a lever press, indicating covert orienting, but has not moved its eyes, so there is no overt orienting. Recordings from the superior colliculi while monkeys performed the tasks in Figures 15-4B and 15-4C indicate that firing enhancement occurred only for the overt orienting displayed in Figure 15-4B and not for the covert orienting displayed in Figure 15-4C.

A similar experiment was done in which a direct cue was presented before the target appeared—no eye movement was made as in Figure 15-4C, and a recording was made of a superior colliculus superficial-layer cell's response to the target in its receptive field (Robinson & Kertzman, 1995). In this experiment, manual responding by the monkey was faster when the target appeared close to the cued location than when it appeared far away (such as in the opposite hemifield), regardless of whether the cue was in the target cell's receptive field or not. However, the response of the cell to the target was affected only if the cue previously appeared in the target cell's receptive field. These and other results indicate that the role of some superior colliculus cells might be to act as triggers for shifts of attention, which then may be followed with overt orienting via eye movements directed at the abrupt-onset stimuli (LaBerge, 1995; Robinson & Kertzman, 1995).

The **posterior parietal lobe,** a part of the cortex that lies toward the back of the brain and above the occipital lobes, has also been implicated in attention orienting. The response of cells in this area are enhanced both when a monkey makes an eye movement toward a target and when the monkey keeps its eyes fixed but responds to the target stimulus with a button press, as in Figure 15-4C (Mountcastle et al., 1987; Wurtz et al., 1980). Posterior parietal lobe cells have also been studied in a cue-target paradigm in the absence of eye movements, as discussed for the superior colliculus earlier (Robinson, Bowman, & Kertzman, 1995;

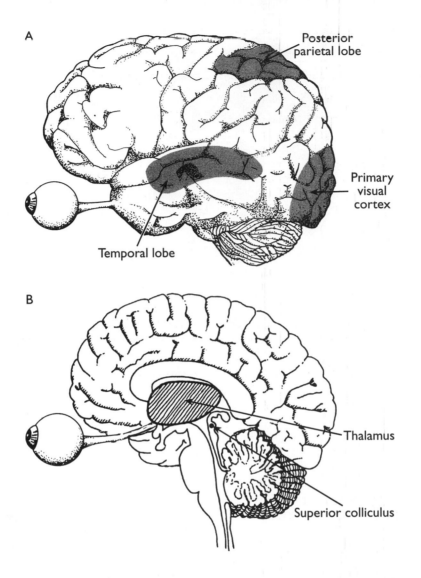

FIGURE 15-3 Areas of the brain involved in attention to visual stimuli. (A) The *posterior parietal lobe* (covert orienting and filtering) and the *temporal lobe* (site of enhanced activity for attended representations) are located on the cortical surface. (B) The *superior colliculus* (overt eye movements and covert orienting) and the *thalamus* (filtering) are located in the brain stem and midbrain, respectively, and are seen here in a sagittal section (slice vertically through the middle of the brain).

Steinmetz, Connor, Constantinidis, & McLaughlin, 1994). Again, manual responding was faster when a target appeared near a cued location. However, in this case, firing of cells was always affected when a target followed a cue in roughly the same location even if the cue was not in the cell's receptive field. These results suggest that the parietal lobe is an important brain area for directing the covert attentional gaze, although it is also involved in overt orienting. Because each hemisphere of the brain receives direct inputs from only one side of the visual field, this may explain why damage to the posterior parietal lobe can result in *hemifield neglect*, which is the inability to pay attention to and to notice stimuli from one half of the visual field (De Renzi, 1982; Posner, Inhoff, Friedrich, &

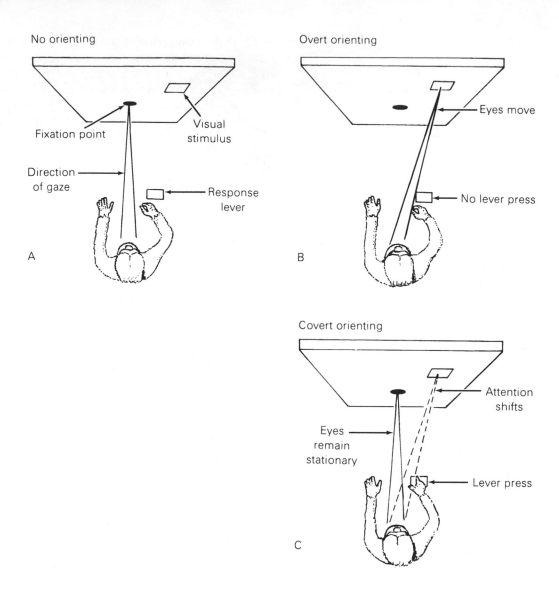

FIGURE 15-4   Conditions used to test for various attention functions in the brains of monkeys. (A) No eye movement or response (no orienting). (B) Eye movement only (overt orienting). (C) Lever press with no eye movement (covert orienting).

Cohen, 1987—see also Chapter 18). It also can explain why covert visual orienting in the cue-target paradigm is disrupted by lesions of the parietal lobe caused by strokes (Posner, Walker, Friedrich, & Rafal, 1984). Evidence from people with such lesions indicates that the two hemispheres may operate differently in covert orienting, with the left

posterior parietal cortex relatively more specialized for shifting attention between objects, in particular for disengaging attention from attended objects in order to shift to a new object (Egly, Driver, & Rafal, 1994). Injuries to either the left or right parietal cortex impair the ability to shift attention away from a currently attended location.

FILTERING

Having oriented, either covertly or overtly, to an environmental event, we may continue to attend to (look at, listen to) that event to the exclusion of other events. When we do this we are **filtering** out all information except that from the spatial location or perceptual object we are attending to, a single information channel. How well can we do this? What affects how efficiently we can select one information source and filter out others? What happens to the information to which we don't attend? Everyday experience suggests that things we attend to seem sharp and clear and are easy to recall, whereas unattended stimuli are less distinct and more difficult to remember. Careful experimental research confirms these informal impressions.

The Cocktail Party Phenomenon

A noisy party is a good example of a situation that requires attentional filtering. Imagine a typical party where there are loud music and many conversations going on simultaneously, including one in which you are involved. You hear a significant or familiar voice, and you covertly orient toward a conversation off to one side, even while you occasionally nod and say "uh-huh" in response to the person standing in front of you, who thinks you are paying attention to him. Suddenly you are startled to see the person with whom you had been "talking" give a sniff and walk away rapidly, obviously angry at you. You are puzzled because you can't remember a thing that person has said in the last 5 minutes. However, you remember perfectly what your former sweetheart said in the other conversation to which you *were* listening covertly. Apparently you very effectively filtered out everything else, including whatever it was that you nodded at that caused your conversational partner to walk away.

Colin Cherry (1953), in a classic article, investigated some of the problems exemplified in the behavior we just described. He introduced the experimental technique called **shadowing** in order to control how his observers oriented their auditory attention. In this technique, an observer is presented with two messages through two different information channels. For example, the two channels

could be the two ears (one message to each ear, a technique called **dichotic listening**), or one message could be presented visually and the other auditorially, or the two messages could be presented at different locations in space. The observer must repeat aloud (that is, follow along with, or "shadow") one of the messages as it is presented. In **phrase shadowing** the observer is allowed to lag slightly behind the message and to repeat entire phrases at once, whereas in **phonemic shadowing** the observer is required to repeat each syllable as it is presented. Cherry demonstrated that observers could orient to one message and filter out the other.

The difficulty of shadowing depends on the nature of the message: Shadowing prose, such as a selection from a story, is relatively easy; shadowing random lists of words is more difficult; and shadowing nonsense syllables (e.g., *orp, vak, bij*) is the most difficult of all. Clearly, meaning and grammatical structure help us to attend to one message and filter out others. Shadowing is also easier if the messages come from two different places in space, are different in pitch (e.g., one male voice and one female voice), or are presented at different speeds. For an example of how this works, try Demonstration Box 15-3.

What happens to inputs we don't attend to, which, we suggested earlier, are "filtered out"? Cherry (1953) found that listeners could remember very little of the rejected message in the shadowing task. Moray (1959) found that in difficult shadowing tasks, even though they knew that they would later be asked about it, listeners were unable to remember words that had been repeatedly presented in the unshadowed message. Did the listeners simply not hear the unshadowed message, or did the shadowed message somehow interfere with their memory of the unshadowed message? Both Cherry and Moray had waited for some time after the shadowing task was completed to ask about the unshadowed message. Perhaps the unshadowed message was heard, maybe the words were actually recognized, but they were forgotten quickly because they weren't entered into a long-lasting memory. Perhaps we must pay attention to an input in order to remember it for longer than a few seconds. This idea was tested by interrupting listeners' shadowing to ask them to report what had just been presented to the unshadowed ear

DEMONSTRATION BOX 15-3
Selective Attention and the Precedence Effect

You may remember our discussion of the precedence effect from Chapter 7, where we listed some variables that affect our ability to localize the position of sound sources in space. When sounds are emitted in enclosed spaces, they tend to cause echoes as they bounce from walls, ceilings, and floors. However, we can still make a correct localization of the sound source because the sound emanating directly from this source will reach our ears before its echoes. The auditory system is sensitive to these time differences and can use this information in the localization of sound-producing sources. The direction of the sound emanating directly from the sound source takes precedence over other sounds in localization, hence the name *precedence effect*.

The precedence effect can also be helpful in selective attention, when we are attempting to process one of many simultaneously occurring stimulus events. A good example of this is found in cocktail party situations, where you may try to follow one of many competing conversations. This aspect of selective attention is helped by the spatial and temporal separations of the auditory inputs. You can demonstrate this for yourself with the aid of two friends (preferably of the same sex) and a doorway. First have your friends stand as shown in Figure A, while each reads passages from a book or newspaper simultaneously. Notice that even with your eyes closed you can easily separate and locate the two messages. Now stand out of the direct line of sight (and sound) of each friend, as shown in Figure B. In this situation the messages must travel indirectly out through the open door. This means that they will tend to reach you at the same time and come from

the same direction. Now, again with your eyes closed, notice how difficult it is to locate the voices and to separate their messages.

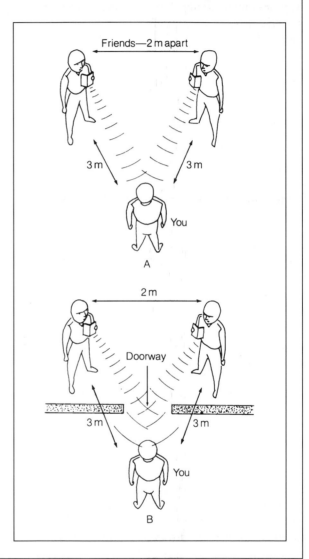

(Glucksberg & Cowen, 1970; Norman, 1969). When this happens, listeners can usually recall the last five to seven words, numbers, or whatever units are being shadowed.

More recent tests that have added a method to detect shifts to the unshadowed ear have found that people could remember material from the unshadowed channel only if they had shifted attention to that channel during the presentation of that material (Wood & Cowan, 1995a). Even a powerful stimulus such as their own name in the unshadowed ear was detected by only about 34% of listeners (Wood & Cowan, 1995b). The only people who recalled hearing their own name made attentional shifts to the unshadowed channel immediately after their name occurred, and in addition they recalled an average of two words following the occurrence of their name. It seems that material in the unshadowed ear is available for processing, and attention, for a short while after it occurs, but unless it is attended to it is not entered into a long-lasting memory.

The Video Overlap Phenomenon

An analog of the auditory shadowing task described earlier has been used to study visual filtering (Neisser & Becklin, 1975). Overlapping video programs, one of a hand game and the other of a ball game, were presented to observers. In the hand game, the players tried to slap each other's hands, and observers who "shadowed" this game had to report each attacking stroke (but not feints). In the ball game, players threw a basketball to one another while moving around irregularly. Observers who shadowed the ball game had to report each throw of the ball from one player to another (but not fakes and dribbles). "Odd" events were also sometimes inserted in the programs (for example, the hand game players shook hands, and then resumed play, or the ball game players threw the ball out of the picture, played with an imaginary ball for a few seconds, and then resumed playing with the real ball). Figure 15-5 shows examples of single frames from each game and the two frames superimposed.

The results of this study were remarkably similar to those from auditory shadowing experiments. Observers could easily follow the events in one program presented alone, as would be expected. They also had little difficulty following the events of one program when the other one was superimposed on it, although they did make a few more errors in this condition. Moreover, the odd events in the shadowed programs were almost always noticed, whereas the odd events in the unshadowed programs were almost never noticed. For example, only 1 of 24 subjects noticed the handshake in the hand game while shadowing the ball game; no subjects noticed the ball disappear in the ball game while they were watching the hand game. The

reports that did occur were vague and uncertain and usually not correct. When asked, a few subjects felt that there might be something unusual about the unshadowed program, but they didn't know what it was. Most subjects noticed nothing unusual at all. This indicates that, like auditory filtering, visual filtering allows little of the filtered-out information to make a lasting impression, a result that has been verified in many different situations (e.g., Rock & Guttman, 1981). You can experience a similar type of visual shadowing, and its effect on memory for the unshadowed message, by trying Demonstration Box 15-4. It is also possible to re-create Neisser and Becklin's display and to try their task by feeding the outputs of two video players through a cable splitter (reversed) into a single TV set cable input. You will have the most success with this latter approach if you use two prerecorded video programs that are set in stable scenes with very different content, for example, a basketball game and a hockey game. Don't forget to turn off the sound!

The Neurophysiology of Filtering

Where in the brain might filtering of this sort occur? We have described how the *superior colliculus* and the *posterior parietal lobe* of the brain are involved in shifting our attention to various locations or objects in the visual field. However, filtering involves more than simply attending to one object or location and ignoring others. We can choose to attend to one of several stimuli that appear in the same general location. We can also choose to focus on the color rather than the shape of an object or on its texture rather than on its size. One important brain area in which the behavior of single cells is affected by attention is the **temporal lobe** of the cortex (Desimone & Ungerleider, 1989; Moran & Desimone, 1985; Spitzer, Desimone, & Moran, 1988). The temporal lobe is pointed out in Figure 15-3A. You may recall from Chapter 3 that the temporal lobe seems to be specialized to answer the question "What is it?"—that is, to identify objects. To study how attention affects the activity of neurons in this area, researchers trained monkeys to attend to one of two stimuli. For example, a monkey might be rewarded with food for pressing a button every time a red

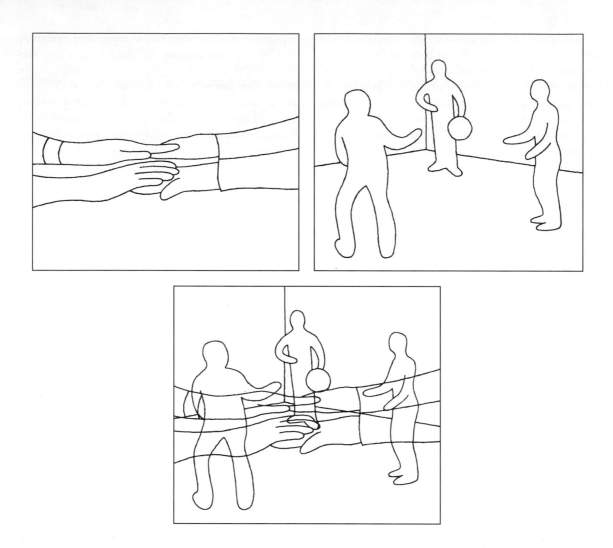

FIGURE 15-5   Outline tracings of isolated frames from the video overlap experiment. (A) Hand game only. (B) Ball game only. (C) Hand game and ball game superimposed (from Neisser & Becklin, 1975).

rectangle appeared on the screen. This was called the "attended" stimulus. Responses to other stimuli, such as a green rectangle, were not rewarded, and soon the monkey learned to ignore them. They were called the "unattended" stimuli. The researchers then recorded from a single cell in the temporal lobe that responded best to one of the stimuli, for example, a cell that normally responded to a red rectangle shown anywhere in its fairly large receptive field. If the monkey was paying attention to the red rectangle, the cell responded vigorously. Moreover, the cell seemed to become less sensitive to other stimuli simultaneously present in its receptive field, as if the receptive field had shrunk to fit the boundaries of the attended stimulus. When the red rectangle was present but was not being attended to, because it was no longer being reinforced, the cell's rate of firing was dramatically lower. Somehow attention had relatively enhanced the response of the temporal lobe neuron to the red rectangle.

This enhancement may be accomplished in part by the activity of the **thalamus,** in particular the pulvinar nucleus, the largest nucleus in the thalamus

---

DEMONSTRATION BOX 15-4
Visual Shadowing and Memory

In the accompanying passage, the relevant message is shaded, and the irrelevant message is printed in the normal fashion. You arc to read the shaded passage aloud as rapidly as possible, ignoring the irrelevant (unshaded) message. Now without cheating and looking back, write down all the words you remember from the irrelevant message. Go back and read the shaded passage again, but this time stop after each line to write down the words you recall from the irrelevant message (without looking back at it). You should find that the list of remembered words is longer when your reading is interrupted and you are not asked to recall all the

irrelevant message at once (from Lindsay & Norman, 1977).

In performing an experiment like this one by man attention car it house is boy critically hat important shoe that candy the old material horse that tree is pen being phone read cow by book the hot subject tape for pin the stand relevant view task sky be read cohesive man and car grammatically house complete boy but hat without shoe either candy being horse so tree easy pen that phone fully cow attention book is hot not tape required pin in stand order view to sky read red it not /too//difficult/

(LaBerge, 1995). Figure 15-3B shows the general location of the thalamus, which lies in the midbrain, underneath the cortex. The anatomy of several thalamic nuclei is ideally suited for involvement in attentional modulation of responses in sensory and motor areas (Guillery, Feig, & Lozsádi, 1998; LaBerge, 1995). These nuclei both send projections to and receive them from many cortical areas, including the temporal cortex, the posterior parietal cortex, and the prefrontal cortex (where voluntary actions are believed to originate). Several studies have indicated that the pulvinar nucleus in particular shows elevated activity when attention must be used to filter out distracting stimuli. For example, LaBerge and Buchsbaum (1990) and Liotta, Fox, and LaBerge (1994) monitored the activity of the pulvinar nucleus of human subjects by PET while the subjects performed either a task that required filtering as well as covert orienting (pressing a button when an *O* appeared at the center of the letter group to the left of the fixation dot in Figure 15-6A) or a task that required only covert orienting (pressing a button whenever an *O* appeared to the right of the fixation dot in Figure 15-6B). The activity of the pulvinar nucleus was significantly   elevated   when the task required filtering compared to when it did not. Similarly, another PET study found

that the thalamus was active when a person was required to respond to only a particular attribute of a visual object, for instance, its color or size, and to ignore other attributes (Corbetta, Miezin, Dobmeyer, Shulman, & Petersen, 1991). LaBerge (1995) has argued that this and other evidence imply that the pulvinar nucleus of the thalamus assists in attentional filtering (when instructed to do so by other parts of the brain) by selectively enhancing activity in sensory cortical areas such as the temporal lobe.

Divided Attention

An important question relevant to perception is whether it is possible to pay attention to more than one source of information at the same time and, if so, whether performance suffers compared to when only one channel is attended. In the visual filtering experiment (the hand game and the ball game) discussed earlier, observers were also asked to try to *divide* their attention and to shadow both programs simultaneously. That is, they had to report both attacks in the hand game and throws in the ball game. When they tried to do this, performance deteriorated dramatically. Observers missed many more events and typically said the task was

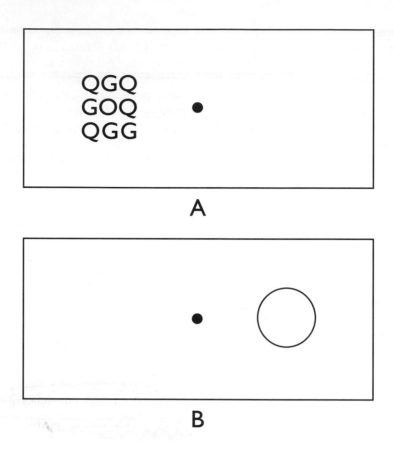

FIGURE 15-6 Stimuli used to ascertain which areas of the brain are involved in filtering. (A) Attending to the center *O*, and filtering out the other letters, causes much activity in the pulvinar nucleus of the thalamus. (B) Because attending to the large *O* does not involve filtering, activity in the thalamus is much lower than for the stimulus in *A*.

"demanding" or even "impossible" (Neisser & Becklin, 1975). Moreover, presenting the two programs to different eyes **(dichoptic presentation)** made the divided attention task no easier. Thus, dividing visual attention between two (or more) sources is very difficult; usually we can look at only one thing at a time. This effect is most dramatic when the competing channels are spatially separated. Under some conditions, attention can be paid to two aspects of a single object at once without depressing performance, whereas when the two aspects characterize two objects separated in space, performance is worse when attention must be divided between them (Bonnel & Prinzmetal, 1998).

Dividing attention between two auditory information channels is similarly difficult. Of course, it is impossible to verbally shadow two messages at once because we cannot say two things at once. However, people have been asked to listen to messages (in this case, word lists) in both ears and later to distinguish words they had heard from distracters (Levy, 1971, cited in Kahneman, 1973). Recognition performance was far poorer when people were trying to pay attention to both ears than when listening to only one ear and filtering out the other. You may have had similar experiences at a party when trying to listen to two interesting conversations at once. It is possible to switch back and forth between them, but if they are at all demanding, a great deal of the information of each one will be lost.

Divided attention is easier if the information channels are in different modalities, such as vision and audition, although performance still suffers in comparison to attention focused on only one channel, whenever the dual task is at all difficult, such as identifying words, lights, or sounds (Bonnel & Hafter, 1998; Treisman & Davies, 1972). Usually, the only time when there is no decline in performance under divided attention is when the task is very easy, such as responding to a simple signal as soon as it occurs in either of two modalities (Bonnel & Hafter, 1998; Miller, 1982). However, in the vast majority of cases, divided-attention performance is considerably worse than focused-attention performance.

Finally, it is worth mentioning that dividing attention between two demanding tasks does become easier with extensive practice. We all have experienced doing two, or more, things at once, such as driving a car and carrying on a conversation, or reading a book, chewing on a sandwich, and scratching our head. A skilled typist can type at a high rate and shadow a message at the same time with almost no loss of efficiency at either task (Shaffer, 1975). Extensive practice in typing has made that skill "automatic" for the typist. **Automatic processing** requires less attention than does **controlled processing,** allowing more attention to be allocated to the less-automatic skill (shadowing, in this case). We discuss *automaticity* more fully in the next section.

SEARCHING

Imagine you are waiting in an airport for a loved one to arrive home from a trip abroad. The plane arrives, and a flood of people surges through the arrival door. Your eyes flick back and forth across the confusion, searching for that beloved face. You don't bother looking at the people's clothes because you know she is wearing a new outfit, and you don't know what it looks like. You are looking for the peculiar combination of longish coal-black hair, large nose, and wide-set eyes that you remember so well. Someone near you suddenly shouts to a large man in a bright orange suit, who waves in reply. The shouter confides to you that she has an easy time finding her husband at the airport because he always wears that silly suit and "sticks out like a sore thumb." We have been describing a typical circumstance where we know

what we are looking (or listening) for and must search a field of "distracters" to find it. This task is one of the most popular for studying attention, partly because it is easy to implement in the laboratory and partly because it has important implications for everyday life.

Eye Movements and Visual Searching

It is much easier to study "looking for" than "listening for" because there is an obvious external indicator of visual searching—overt eye movements. Our eyes are constantly exploring the visual field with high-speed ballistic movements called **saccades.** Demonstration Box 15-5 will show you an easy way to observe saccades in someone who is reading.

The path taken by our eyes as they move (or, more correctly, jerk—*saccader* is French for "to jerk") over the visual field is determined by our intentions, by our previous experience, and by the way the eye movement system works. We will consider each of these influences in turn.

Meaning and expectation help to direct where we look in a visual scene (Antes & Penland, 1981; Findlay, 1981; Stark & Ellis, 1981). For example, Yarbus (1967) recorded eye movement patterns while observers looked at pictures with different intentions in mind. Figure 15-7 shows the eye movement patterns observers made for a typical picture (A) when asked to estimate either the ages of the individuals in the picture (B) or their wealth (C). Clearly, people looked at different places in order to find information relevant to the different questions.

People rapidly learn to inspect spatial locations in a systematic order to detect targets that may be present. Although this is a fairly efficient process for adults, it does not appear to be fully developed until children are about 6 or 7 years of age (e.g., Cohen, 1981; Green, Hammond, & Supramaniam, 1983) and unfortunately becomes more difficult again for the elderly (Rabbitt, 1984). People also use their knowledge of the world to guide visual inspection. If a scene has been jumbled by randomly interchanging different areas, as has been done in Figure 15-8 (p. 454), people have a harder time locating a target object, such as a store sign (Biederman, Glass, & Stacey, 1973). We also

---

DEMONSTRATION BOX 15-5
Saccadic Eye Movements

For this demonstration you will need a volunteer to help you. The materials you will need are a stiff piece of paper with a small hole punched in it and a piece of reading material for your partner. Sit facing your partner at a distance of 2 ft to 3 ft. Ask your partner to read the passage silently and to move his or her eyes as smoothly as possible. While your partner is reading, look at one of the eyes through the peephole in the stiff piece of paper. Adjust the viewing distance so that only your partner's eye is in view. You should now be able to see each small jerking movement (saccade) as the eye moves across the page. Note that you can identify the end of a line in the passage by the long saccade that is made every so often. You may also be able to tell when your partner goes back to reread some words that were not understood on the first scan.

---

look at unusual objects in a visual scene longer when we find them (A. Friedman, 1979; Antes & Penland, 1981; Friedman & Liebelt, 1981). Perhaps because of this, unexpected objects tend to be remembered and recognized more easily, and exchanges of one unusual object for another (a cow for a car in a living room) are noticed far more often than are exchanges of one usual object for another (a chair for a table in a living room; A. Friedman, 1979). Unfortunately, all of this efficient inspecting doesn't mean that we see everything in a scene. It seems that we must pay attention to a particular part of a natural scene in order to notice changes occurring in that part even if they are quite obvious. Rensink, O'Regan, and Clark (1997) have shown that if pictures are briefly flashed on and off, major changes in subsequent views might be missed, such as an engine that appears and disappears on a jumbo jet's wing or the repeated substitution of one person for another, unless that area of the visual field is being searched or attended to.

There is also evidence of an important process that could contribute to the constant search for novelty in our looking patterns. This process has been called inhibition of return because it refers to a conjectured decreased likelihood that people will move their eyes and their attentional gaze back to a location they have recently looked at (Maylor & Hockey, 1985; Posner & Cohen, 1984). Inhibition of return has been studied in several different experimental paradigms. In one of them, subjects are asked repeatedly to detect visual targets. Some targets occur in locations previously occupied by targets presented earlier,

whereas others occur in previously empty locations. Even after relatively long intervals between targets, from about ½ second to 2 seconds, responses to targets appearing where targets had appeared earlier are slower than to targets appearing in new locations (Maylor & Hockey, 1985). Responding to objects that have moved location is also slowed when a target appears in the new location (Tipper, Driver, & Weaver, 1991) or in the old location (Tipper, Weaver, Jerreat, & Burak, 1994). Inhibition of return has been observed even in infants as young as 6 months of age (Rothbart, Posner, & Boylan, 1990).

The study of inhibition of return is very active, and several proposals as to the mechanisms that cause it are currently being investigated. It has been proposed that this behavior arises from a bias against returning attention to a previously attended site or object because the information has already been extracted from it (Posner & Cohen, 1984; Pratt, Kingstone, & Kehoe, 1997; Tipper et al., 1994), arises from a sensory refractoriness at the previously stimulated site (Abrams & Dobkin, 1994; Posner & Cohen, 1984; Wright & Richard, 1998), or arises from various motor inhibitions, including those involved in suppressing an eye movement or other motor response relative to the site of an abrupt-onset stimulus (Abrams & Dobkin, 1994; Posner, Rafal, Choate, & Vaughan, 1985; Tassinari & Berlucchi, 1995). Inhibition of return has also been found in the auditory modality (McDonald & Ward, 1998; Mondor, Breau, & Milliken, 1998; Spence & Driver, 1998; Tassinari & Berlucchi, 1995; Ward, 1994) and across modalities

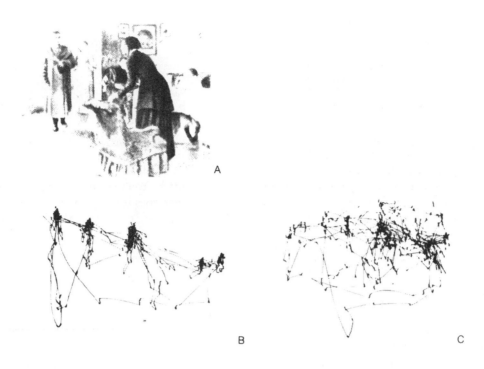

FIGURE 15-7 Eye-movement patterns made when viewing the picture (A) varied depending on whether the viewer was asked the ages of the individuals in the picture (Scan Pattern B) or their wealth (Scan Pattern C). (From Yarbus, 1967. Copyright Plenum Publishing Company. Reprinted by permission.)

(Spence & Driver, 1998), suggesting that whatever the mechanism, it is quite general. So far none of this evidence has been sufficient to rule out any of the aforementioned mechanisms. It is possible that inhibition of return arises from several mechanisms that often operate together to influence how we obtain information from the sensory world.

Feature Versus Conjunction Searching

A common laboratory task used to study visual search involves asking an observer to scan a collection of letters (or other forms) in order to find a specified target letter (or form). In one early study (Neisser, 1967), observers searched for particular targets in a list of letters arranged in 50 six-letter lines. With practice they came to perform a top-to-bottom search at great speed (as fast as 60 letters/second). Several factors, however, affected their search speed. For instance, when the target was an angular letter *(W, Z, X)* and the other

letters (distracters) were roundish *(O, Q, C)*, observers searched much more quickly than when the target was more similar to the distracters (e.g., *G*). When a search target differs from all distracters by possessing a feature they don't have (e.g., an angled line), the search is called a **feature search.** When the only way to detect the target is to detect a conjunction (or particular combination) of features (such as the particular angles and their orientations that distinguish between a *W* and an *M*), it is called a **conjunction search.** In general, feature searches are much easier than conjunction searches. Neisser's subjects typically reported that when they were searching the list, particularly when the target was very different from the distracters, the nontarget letters were just a blur, and the subjects did not "see" individual letters. In fact, the target often just "popped out" of the array. This is a characteristic phenomenon of feature search.

Neisser (1967) argued that there is a "preattentive" level of processing that segregates a visual

FIGURE 15-8   It is easier to find a target object in a coherent, natural scene (above) than in the same scene randomly jumbled (opposite page; from Biederman et al., 1973).

scene into figure and ground, a distinction we discussed in Chapter 10. When there are clear feature differences between the target and the distracting items, the target becomes readily visible because the distracters are lumped together as ground, and the target stands out as a figure by the action of this preattentive process alone. The notion is that similar elements are grouped together automatically, and the ones that don't fit seem to leap into consciousness. This isn't possible when the target and background items closely resemble each other (Duncan & Humphreys, 1989). Here, closer attention and scrutiny are needed to detect specific elements (e.g., Julesz, 1980).

The differences between feature and conjunction searching have been extensively explored (e.g., Pashler, 1987; Treisman, 1982, 1986a; Wolfe, Franzel, & Cave, 1989). The really striking result is that when feature search is possible, the number of distracting items doesn't seem to affect searching speed. The target simply pops out of the display,

and the search is said to be accomplished in **parallel** (meaning that all of the items are effectively processed at the same time). However, when conjunction search is required, the number of distracters does affect search speed. This can be seen clearly in some prototypical data illustrated in Figure 15-9. In a conjunction search we seem to be comparing each of the distracters, one at a time, with the image of the target and responding only when they match. Such an orderly and sequential set of comparisons is often referred to as a **serial search**.

To explain this kind of data, Treisman offered a *feature integration theory* (see Chapter 10). It suggests that each feature of a stimulus (such as color, size, or shape) is registered separately. When an object must be identified from a combination of features, a correct analysis can be achieved only if attention is focused on one location at a time. Recalling our discussion of the attentional gaze, we might say that features occurring in a single

FIGURE 15-8   (cont.)

attentional "glance" are combined to form an object. This process of combination and comparison takes time and effort. If attention is diverted or overloaded or if presentation is brief, errors in localization of features may occur (Prinzmetal, Henderson, & Ivry, 1995), and we may attribute the wrong features to a particular item and either miss the target or select a wrong target (Prinzmetal, 1981; Prinzmetal, Presti, & Posner, 1986; Treisman & Schmidt, 1982). Demonstration

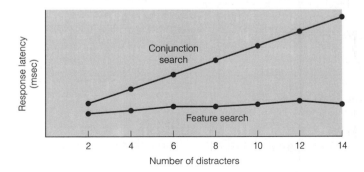

FIGURE 15-9   The relation between response latency to report the presence of a target and the number of distracting items that must be checked. The function is almost flat for feature search and much steeper for conjunction search (based on Treisman, 1982).

DEMONSTRATION BOX 15-6
Feature and Conjunction Search

In each of these arrays of visual forms there are targets to find. The target is a white *O*. Scan each array quickly, only once, and write down how many targets you see. Notice in each array how difficult or easy it is to find the targets. Do this before reading further.

Now you can know that Arrays A and B required a feature search (in *A* the feature was brightness; in *B* it was shape), whereas Array C required a conjunction search (for both brightness and shape). There were three targets in each array. Dud you get them all? Most people find the conjunction search to be the most difficult of these tasks, and if they are apt to miss any targets it will be in Array C.

A
```
O N O O N N O N O N O N N O O N
O O N N O N N O N O N N O O
N O O N O N N O N  O  N O O
N O N O N N  O  O N O O N N O
```

B
```
N  N  O  N  N  N  N  N  N  N  N  N
N  N  N  N  N  N  N  N  N  N  N  N
N  N  N  N  N  N  N  N  N  O  N  N
N  N  N  N  N  N  N  N  N  N  N  N
```

C
```
N  N  O  N  N  O  O  N  O  O  O  N
N  N  O  O  N  N  O  N  N  N  O
N  O  N  N  O  O  N  N  N  O  O
O  O  N  N  O  N  O  O  N  O  N
```

Box 15-6 gives you an opportunity to try feature and conjunction searches for yourself. Sometimes conjunctions of simple features also result in a very rapid search—even in "popout." Several examples of such displays are shown in Figure 15-10. Demonstrations such as these have been used to argue that the elementary features of forms with respect to attention are not *situation properties* but, rather, *object properties* (Enns & Rensink, 1990, 1991; Ramachandran, 1988). We saw in Chapter 11 that situation properties are the relatively variable features of a picture, such as the shapes and colors that change with viewpoint and lighting. In contrast, object properties, such as the relative orientation of an object and surface curvature, tend to remain constant over changes in the observer's viewpoint and scene lighting.

Feature integration theory asserts that attention must be moved sequentially from place to place in a conjunction search but that this is not necessary in a feature search, where the relevant feature pops out from the display. However, there is evidence that in some circumstances attention is used serially even in easy feature searches and that it tends to be allocated to features of the target in conjunction searches (Kim & Cave, 1995). Thus, the same mechanisms may underlie feature search and conjunction search. Moreover, it has also been argued that if the experimental data are carefully scrutinized, the differences described earlier between feature search and conjunction search are more apparent than real (Wolfe, 1998).

Automatic Versus Controlled Searching

Practice and the adopting of helpful strategies can improve search performance. For example, a conjunction search may be treated as two simple feature searches under some circumstances (Egeth, Virzi, & Garbart, 1984; Kaptein, Theeuwes, & van der Heijden, 1995; Wolfe, Cave, & Franzel, 1989). This has been called **guided search.** It means that in Demonstration Box 15-6 you might be able to look only at the white letters in Array C, ignoring the black letters, while searching for the white *O*. By treating the white objects as figures and the black objects as ground, you can rule out a large number of distracters on the basis of a simple feature difference from the target preattentively, leaving you with only a second simple feature search to complete. Guided search is apparently mediated by the left hemisphere of the brain, similar to language and other high-level cognitive processes (Kingstone, Enns, Mangun, & Gazzaniga, 1995).

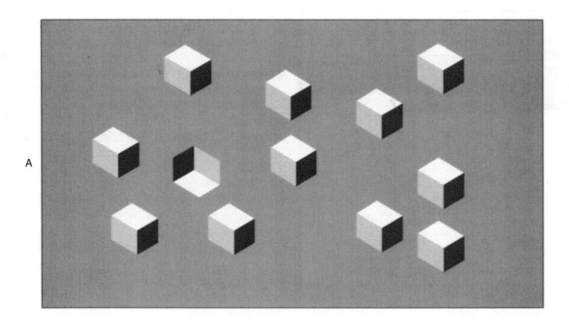

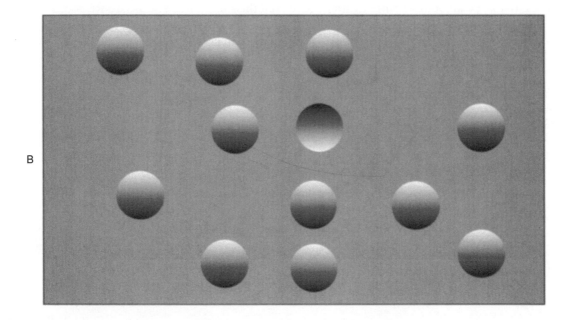

FIGURE 15-10 Examples of conjunctions of simple features that pop out in a visual search. In (A) each item consists of shapes defined by three diamonds—only the spatial relations of the diamonds distinguish the target item from the distracting items (based on Enns & Rensink, 1990). In (B) each item consists of a shaded circle—only the direction of the shading distinguishes the target item from the distracting items (based on Ramachandran, 1988).

Another strategy that sometimes speeds search is to group items together into smaller sets of stimuli. If stimulus sets are small enough (say, two to eight items), attention operates as if all items are checked at the same time **(parallel search)**, rather than sequentially as in serial search. Using such a grouping strategy, a person can search the smaller arrays in parallel for both features and conjunctions (Pashler, 1987).

When observers have been able to practice for a very long time on a task that always demands the same response under the same conditions, the nature of the search process seems to change—search time gradually becomes independent of the number of distracters present. In a typical study of this kind, some observers searched for a fixed set of targets (say, the letters *H, S,* and *T*) among a fixed set of distracters (say, the digits 1 to 9). At first, the more distracters in the display, the longer it took to find the target. However, after 14 days of practice (over 4,000 searches) on the same task, the number of distracters in the display ceased to matter. It took the same amount of time to find the target regardless of the number of distracters (Schneider & Shiffrin, 1977; Shiffrin & Schneider, 1977). Figure 15-11 shows this result graphically. It seems that before much practice the search is typical of conjunction searches and is serial in nature (this is often called *controlled processing*). After a lot of practice in a consistent environment the search is said to be **automatic,** rather like a simple feature search. A similar result has been obtained for an auditory detection task (Poltrock, Lansman, & Hunt, 1982), which indicates that automatic and controlled processing are not limited to vision, but occur in other modalities as well.

The shift from controlled to automatic processing that occurs with practice is accompanied by several other changes (Schneider, Dumais, & Shiffrin, 1984). On the negative side, for example, it becomes more difficult to prevent responding to targets for which search has become automatic, even if we wish to ignore them. We also don't remember as well the things found and responded to under automatic control. On the positive side, however, it is possible to do other tasks at the same time as engaging in an automatic search, and the added tasks won't interfere with the search. Actually, many lapses of attention in everyday life can be traced to such seemingly automatic processes and their inevitable effects (see Reason, 1984). You can experience for yourself the powerfully automatic nature of reading words, and how this can interfere with other tasks, by trying the demonstration of the **Stroop effect** in Demonstration Box 15-7.

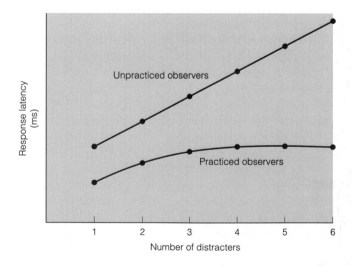

FIGURE 15-11   The relation between response latency to report the presence of a target and the number of distracters to be checked. This function is steeper for unpracticed than for practiced observers (based on Glass & Holyoak, 1986).

DEMONSTRATION BOX 15-7
The Stroop Effect

The *Stroop effect* is an interesting example of how well-learned material can interfere with our ability to attend to the demands of a task. In 1935 Stroop found that observers had difficulty screening out meaningful information even when it was irrelevant to the task. He devised three situations. In the first he recorded how long it took individuals to read a list of color names, such as *red* and *green*, printed in black ink. He then took an equal number of color patches and recorded how long it took observers to name each one of the series. Then he took a color name and printed it in a color of ink that did not coincide with the linguistic information (for example, the word *blue* printed in red ink). When he had observers name the ink color in this last series, he found that they often erroneously read the printed color name rather than the ink color name; therefore, it took them much longer to read through this last series.

The Stroop effect demonstrates that meaningful linguistic information is difficult to ignore, and the automatic expectations that have come to be associated with the presence of words often take over, resulting in difficulties in focusing attention.

Color Plate 8 is an example of the Stroop Color Word Test, so you can try this for yourself. Have a friend time you either with the second hand of a watch or with a stopwatch as you read each group. Start timing with the command "Go" and read across the lines in exactly the same fashion for each group. When the last response is made in each group, stop timing and note your response time. You should find that reading the color names will take the least amount of time, whereas naming the colors of the ink when the printed word names a different color will take you the most time. Naming the color patches will fall in between these two.

Is it possible that when a process is truly automatic it requires no attentional resources at all? A "yes" answer to this question is given by a clear but rather extreme position called **strong automaticity** (Schneider et al., 1984). However, several results are incompatible with this position. For example, reading in the Stroop effect demonstrated in Demonstration Box 15-7 is supposed to be automatic. However, the Stroop effect is much weaker when the colored ink and the incompatible color name are spatially separated than when they occur in the same place (Kahneman & Treisman, 1984). Strong automaticity would require that as long as the word could be read automatically it wouldn't matter where it was; yet it seems that it is possible to filter out the incompatible color word if it isn't part of the same perceptual object. This and other similar results favor a weaker notion of automatic processing (Cooke, Breen, & Schvaneveldt, 1987; Fisher, Duffy, Young, & Pollatsek, 1988; Hoffman, Nelson, & Houck, 1983).

A somewhat different approach to explaining the effect of practice on search speed emphasizes the acquisition of knowledge (Logan, 1988) or the development of **skill** in accomplishing various perceptual tasks (Neisser, 1976). Here the suggestion is that the effects of practice do not simply involve a switch from controlled to automatic processing but, rather, that a different *strategy* is being used to accomplish the same task (Cheng, 1985). A nonperceptual example would be adding a group of identical numbers, such as $2 + 2 + 2 + 2 + 2$. This could be accomplished by adding each of the numbers to a running sum, by learning the multiplication rule and calculating 5×2, or by simply committing to memory the answer to the question, "What is 5 times 2?" In this view, extensive practice allows a new strategy to be learned or new knowledge to be used, rather than causing a transition from controlled to automatic processing.

Vigilance and Arousal

Sometimes we are asked to search for targets that appear very rarely. Therefore, we must sustain a high level of readiness (see the next section on *preparation*) for an indefinite, sometimes long, period of time. Some examples include a radar technician who is watching for the signal of a particular type of aircraft that flies by only occasionally or a quality control inspector on an assembly line where damaged or substandard items seldom appear. In these cases the observer is said to be performing a **vigilance** task. Research into vigilance began after it was noticed that radar operators during World War II tended to become fatigued after a time on duty, resulting in a decrease in their ability to detect enemy planes. After the war, experiments began to explore how attention sustains itself, particularly in boring search tasks with infrequent target stimuli.

The original experiments on vigilance required observers to watch a display similar to a clock face around which a clock hand moved in steps. They had to press a key each time the hand took a double step. After only ½ hr of watching, observers began to report fewer and fewer double steps, missing almost 25% of them (Mackworth, 1948). Physical fatigue didn't seem to be a reasonable explanation of the drop in performance because the workload was very light. Perhaps the visual system itself was becoming less sensitive, or perhaps the observer was just as sensitive to the double steps but simply failed to respond on some occasions.

The scene was set for the application of signal detection theory (see Chapter 2). If the visual system was becoming less sensitive, it would be reflected in a decrease in d', the measure of the observer's sensitivity. If there was some change in the observer's motivation to report the double step, it would be reflected in a change in β, the observer's criterion that indicates response bias. Signal detection theory analysis showed that sensitivity, or d', did not change over time, but β did in this experiment. The longer they had to maintain vigilance, the less "willing" observers became to report that the rare event they searched for had actually occurred (Broadbent & Gregory, 1963, 1965). More recent research has indicated that extensive training can decrease or eliminate such vigilance decrements (Fisk & Schneider, 1981; Parasuraman, 1984). Apparently, setting the criterion for responding in such tasks is a function of alertness, or the way available attention is allocated to the task at hand (Parasuraman, 1984).

Does sensitivity ever change in a vigilance task? Yes, it does, and usually for the worse. A meta-analysis of many studies of the sensitivity decrement indicated that four major factors affect the size of the decrement (see Howe, Warm, & Dember, 1995). When the task is a *sensory* discrimination, as in detecting the presence of a particular visual stimulus, and individual stimuli are presented *successively*, the decrement increases dramatically with the number of events per unit of time that must be monitored *(event rate)*. However, if sensory stimuli are presented simultaneously for discrimination, as in saying which of two lines is longer, sensitivity actually increases as event rate increases. On the other hand, for cognitive discrimination tasks, as in classifying a letter, the trends are exactly the opposite: a modest increase in sensitivity with event rate for successive tasks and a dramatic decrease for simultaneous tasks. Moreover, for simultaneous presentation, the decrement is much larger for sensory tasks than for cognitive tasks, except at high event rates, whereas for successive presentation, the decrement is greater for cognitive tasks, again except for high event rates, where they are similar. Finally, the vigilance decrement also depends on overall sensitivity, with greater declines for tasks that have high initial sensitivity.

A major part of maintaining attention seems to be a certain degree of physiological arousal. We adopt certain body positions, tense specific muscle groups, and have the feeling of "concentrating" whenever we are vigilant. Apparently most of us already believe that if we are highly aroused physiologically, we will be better able to sustain attention because we often attempt to raise our arousal level in vigilance situations with stimulants such as the caffeine in coffee. In order to understand how arousal affects vigilance, it is important to know how arousal affects performance in general.

The relation between arousal and performance is perhaps most elegantly expressed in the well-known **Yerkes-Dodson Law** (Yerkes & Dodson, 1908). Figure 15-12 shows this relation graphically. Contrary to the belief expressed earlier, performance doesn't always get better the more highly aroused we are. In fact, overall performance of any task peaks at an intermediate level of arousal. This intermediate level is lower for difficult tasks than for easy tasks, suggesting that very difficult tasks are best performed under low levels of arousal (Easterbrook, 1959; Hockey, 1970).

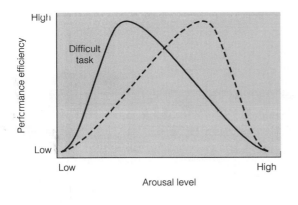

FIGURE 15-12 Yerkes-Dodson Law. Performance is best at intermediate levels of arousal, and performance peaks at lower levels of arousal for difficult tasks than for easy tasks.

The level of arousal also influences the way in which attention is allocated. This has been studied by artificially inducing arousal through the administration of mild electrical shocks to the subject's fingers (Johnson & Shapiro, 1989; Shapiro & Johnson, 1987) or by playing anxiety-inducing music (Shapiro & Lim, 1989). Subjects who were moderately aroused in this way were more likely to detect brief tones than they were to detect brief flashes of light, even though these signals were equally detectable when the subjects were not aroused (Shapiro & Egerman, 1984). Moderately aroused subjects were also more likely to detect brief visual flashes in the visual periphery than in the center of the visual field (Johnson & Shapiro, 1989; Shapiro & Lim, 1989). These findings suggest that arousal associated with negative outcomes assists our "early warning" mechanisms. When confronted with danger, humans are probably better off to be more vigilant to sounds than to sights (alerting them to dangers they cannot see) and to visual events in the periphery rather than those at fixation (alerting them to new dangers entering the visual field). Some recent work using brain imaging techniques has begun to uncover the complex relationship among arousal, attention, and vigilance. In one experiment, increasing reaction time to auditory targets over the vigilance period was associated with decreasing activity in the left medial thalamus, an area thought to mediate attentional preparation to respond (LaBerge, 1995; Paus et al., 1997).

PREPARING

Knowing exactly when or where an important signal will occur is often difficult. For this reason we have orienting mechanisms that draw our attention to conspicuous stimuli. We also have search strategies that allow us to investigate likely locations where important stimuli might be. However, sometimes our past experience predicts where or when an important event will happen, or we get an advance cue (called a **symbolic cue**) about where or when the event will happen. The information creates in us an *expectancy* about the event, and we may *prepare* for its occurrence by aligning attention with the location and time of the expected event (see LaBerge, 1995, for a discussion of expecting and preparing). For example, imagine you are back in the airport, this time trying to monitor two doors at once through only one of which your beloved will arrive. Suddenly the loudspeaker announces that most of the passengers disembarking from that flight will arrive through Gate 21 (the left one of the two doors). Although you know that still doesn't *guarantee* it will be *the* door, you find yourself more often shifting your attention to the left door. You are actively **preparing** for something to happen there by changing your attentional state.

Costs and Benefits of Symbolic Cues

A clear demonstration of the effects of symbolic cues on performance resulted from an experiment conducted by Posner (1980). He asked observers to press a key when they detected a flash of light either to the right or to the left of a fixation point. On half of the trials (the *neutral* trials), the observers fixated a plus sign in the middle of the visual field, and the flash occurred randomly on one side or the other. On the other half of the trials, observers received in advance of the flash a symbolic cue: an arrow pointing either right or left and located where the plus was located on the neutral trials. These were the *cued* trials. On 80% of the cued trials the flash occurred on the side to which the arrow pointed (*valid-cue* trials), and on the other 20% it occurred on the opposite side (*invalid-cue* trials). The observers were not allowed to move their eyes away from either the plus or the arrow; they could only orient their attention. Figure 15-13A shows a summary of these conditions.

Figure 15-13B shows the results of Posner's experiment. The average reaction time on neutral trials, about 245 ms, is a baseline that indicates what performance level we would expect without any location-specific attentional preparation stimulated by the symbolic cue. From Figure 15-13B you can see that it took about 30 ms less than that baseline to respond to the flash on the valid-cue trials (the **benefit** of a valid symbolic cue), but it

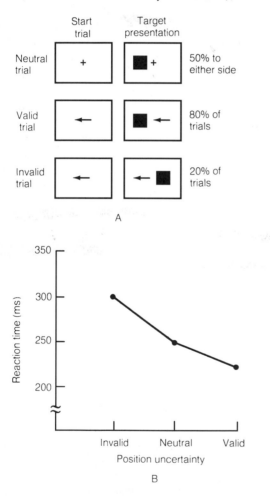

A

B

took over 50 ms more than the baseline to respond to the flash on invalid-cue trials (the **cost** of an invalid symbolic cue). The costs and benefits of symbolic cues have been interpreted by Posner (1980), and others, as indicating that an informative symbolic cue can stimulate the covert orienting of attention in preparation for an event, even in the absence of a stimulus at that location in the visual field on which to focus the attentional gaze.

The effects of preparing for an event by orienting attention directed by symbolic cues depend on a number of factors. A somewhat different experimental situation involves a visual field that contains several small empty boxes to which attention can be covertly oriented in response to a symbolic cue. Under these conditions it has been found that the maximum costs and benefits of symbolic cues do not occur immediately but, rather, take at least 300 ms to 500 ms after the appearance of the cue to produce their full effect (Shepard & Muller, 1989). Thus, preparatory attentional alignments in response to a symbolic cue take much longer than does covert orienting in response to an abruptly appearing direct cue, which occurs in about 100 ms. Part of this extra time must be the time necessary to decode the meaning of the symbolic cue and to initiate the indicated covert shift of attention voluntarily. The voluntary nature of such attention shifts is supported by the fact that symbolic cues can be ignored easily, especially if the subject discovers that, in a particular situation, the available symbolic cues are often wrong (Jonides, 1981). The slower, voluntary alignment of attention in response to a symbolic cue is not automatic. Orienting of attention in response to a symbolic cue can be interrupted by the occurrence of another, attention-grabbing, stimulus (Muller & Rabbitt, 1989), although highly informative symbolic cues can direct attention to a location where it can be sustained even in the face of the occurrence of abrupt-onset stimuli at other locations (Yantis & Jonides, 1990). The costs and benefits associated with symbolic cues affect a broad range of tasks, including detection, identification, and discrimination (Downing, 1988).

Our ability to prepare for expected events is not limited to visual cues and events. Auditory events (such as the howling of the wolves in the introduction) can be expected and prepared for as well. For instance, imagine you are expecting your mother

FIGURE 15-13 (A) Stimulus presentations used to study the effects of preparation on detection. (B) Results of reaction-time study of preparation showing the costs (invalid-cue reaction time minus neutral-cue reaction time) and benefits (neutral-cue reaction time minus valid-cue reaction time) of advance knowledge of stimulus location (based on Posner, 1980).

to come home any minute now. You are expecting to hear her cheery "Hello" in her usual rather high-pitched voice. At this moment your father shouts to you to come help him in the basement. You don't hear him calling, and a minute later he storms into the room, demanding to know why you weren't responding to him. You explain that you were listening for your mother's high-pitched voice and simply didn't hear his much lower pitched voice all the way from the basement. (If he doesn't believe you, you can always show him this discussion.) There is lots of evidence that detection of sounds is more difficult when they are of uncertain frequency; that is, there is a cost of not attending to the appropriate frequency region (e.g., Scharf, Quigley, Aoki, Peachy, & Reeves, 1987; Swets, 1963). However, if observers are told which frequency to listen for by a nonauditory symbolic cue, their detection of the sound (Hafter & Schlauch, 1991) and discrimination of its intensity (Ward & Mori, 1996) are improved. Thus, preparation can help us to "tune in" or "tune out" an auditory stimulus by allowing us to select a frequency region to which to orient our attention.

The Neurophysiology of Preparing

In addition to the effects that attentional preparation has on behavior, such as allowing us to respond more rapidly to stimuli for which we are prepared, researchers have found preparation to be reflected in patterns of brain activity. One way to examine brain activity is through the measurement of **event-related potentials** (Mangun & Hillyard, 1990), a technique that allows the researcher to measure tiny changes in the brain's electrical activity by recording from the scalp of the subject (see the Appendix). As shown in Figure 15-14A, recording electrodes are attached to various locations on the surface of the head with a small amount of paste. Recording is synchronized to start with the stimulus event, and many trials are averaged to produce an indication of the time course of the brain activity (as in Figure 15-14B). Monitoring the size of the voltage changes at the various electrode placements also determines the precise location of maximum activity. In Figure 15-14C the darkest areas indicate the strongest responses. There is an intriguing finding from

measurements of event-related potentials related to preparation: When an observer sees a target at an expected location, some components of the

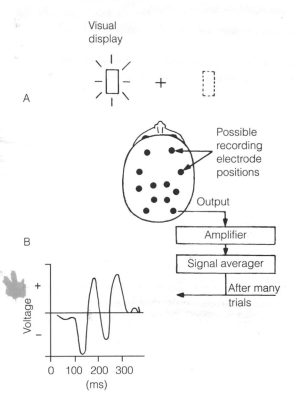

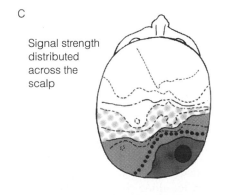

FIGURE 15-14 Event-related potentials measured from the scalp of a human subject. (A) A display is viewed while electrical responses from scalp electrodes are recorded. (B) Averages over many trials show the time course of the electrical responses. (C) A comparison of responses from several locations shows the location of the most vigorous brain responses (dark areas).

event-related brain potential are larger than when the same target falls on the same retinal location but is unexpected (Hillyard & Kutas, 1983; Van Voorhis & Hillyard, 1977). The differences in brain response associated with preparation are largest in the posterior parietal region of the brain.

Another technique that is sensitive to brain activity that accompanies changes in attention is **positron-emission tomography,** or PET (Posner & Petersen, 1990—see the Appendix). This method involves injecting a weakly radioactive dye into the bloodstream. Areas of the brain with active blood flow tend to collect more of the dye. The results can be imaged on a color computer screen, with the brain regions of high blood flow coded in a distinctive color, such as red. By comparing the "hot spots" associated with different tasks the subject is performing, researchers are able to locate the brain regions most active in a given task (Petersen, Fox, Posner, Mintun, & Raichle, 1988). As with event-related potentials, PET studies associate enhanced activity in the posterior parietal cortex with the perception of visual stimuli in expected locations (Posner & Petersen, 1990).

THEORIES OF ATTENTION

Ever since the first studies of attention, investigators have attempted to construct a coherent theoretical account of the major phenomena. As you have seen in this chapter, however, the concept of attention can mean many different things, and it has been studied in many different ways. Therefore, the goal of a coherent and widely accepted theory is still out of reach. At present there are several approaches to understanding attention. We will try to give you the flavor of a few of them here, but you must remember that no one of these approaches is adequate to explain all of the data described earlier, let alone the vast array of other data we do not have space to describe.

All theories of attention attempt to explain its filtering aspect. Probably the oldest surviving theoretical approach is the group of **structural theories.** As pointed out by Kahneman and Treisman (1984), the studies of stimulus filtering that were popular in the 1950s and 1960s seemed to imply that perceptual attention is *structurally* limited.

The notion was that there is a bottleneck or a filter somewhere in the information-processing system beyond which only one, or at most a few, stimulus input can pass at one time. The first studies suggested that this bottleneck occurs very early in the perceptual process, just after registration by the sensory system and before the meaning of an input can be determined (Broadbent, 1958). This **early selection** model is depicted schematically in Figure 15-15. Imagine that you are trying to listen to only one person in a room full of talking people. According to an early selection model, you would isolate that person's voice by means of the physical characteristics (such as frequency, intensity, and location) that distinguish it from the others, rather than by means of what the various speakers are saying. Although the physical qualities are registered for all of the voices, only the words associated with the particular physical characteristics admitted by this early filter (such as *low* frequency, *very* intense, and from over there) are processed for content and understanding.

Early selection models have difficulty with evidence that at least some analysis is done on information coming through unattended perceptual channels. This processing may affect our responses even if we are unaware of it (Cheeseman & Merikle, 1985; Holender, 1986; Marcel, 1983). A striking example is when someone, in a conversation that you are not paying direct attention to, mentions your name. In this instance you sometimes immediately become aware of that fact and may even switch your attention to that conversation (see our earlier discussion of filtering and Wood & Cowan, 1995b). This kind of evidence led to a set of structural theories that emphasized **late selection.** They hypothesized that *all* information entering sensory systems gets some preliminary analysis. The bottleneck is then believed to occur at a stage of more or less conscious processing, when material is being entered into a longer lasting memory (e.g., Deutsch & Deutsch, 1963; Norman, 1968). A schematic representation of this kind of model is shown in Figure 15-15. The debate between early and late selection still rages and has spilled over onto other approaches as well (Pashler, 1984, 1996).

A second general approach to attention has grown mostly from studies of search and preparation (Kahneman & Treisman, 1984), especially

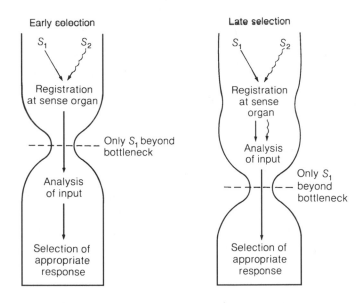

Early selection

S_1 S_2

Registration
at sense organ

Only S_1 beyond
bottleneck

Analysis
of input

Selection of
appropriate
response

Late selection

S_1 S_2

Registration
at sense
organ

Analysis
of input

Only S_1
beyond
bottleneck

Selection of
appropriate
response

FIGURE 15-15   Bottleneck models of attention (stimuli are indicated by S_1 *and* S_2). Early selection models locate the bottleneck (the structural limitation on information processing) just after registration of the stimulus, whereas late selection models locate it after some amount of analysis.

studies involving comparisons of focused and divided attention. The general finding that dividing attention between two tasks or searching for more than one target usually is more difficult than focusing on one task or target has led to the notion that there are **attentional resources** that can be "used up" by a task. If there is more demand than there are resources available, then performance suffers. The first theories of a limited attention capacity viewed attention as a single "pool" of capacity (e.g., Kahneman, 1973). A representation of such a model is shown in Figure 15-16. All of the available capacity is used for one task in Figure 15-16A, whereas in Figure 15-16B, involving divided attention, the capacity must be shared, leaving less processing resources for each task. This would predict that both of the processing tasks in a divided attention condition would be accomplished less efficiently because fewer resources are available to each.

Recently the attentional resource models have been revised. There have been some demonstrations of near-perfect division of attention, for instance, when sight-reading music and shadowing at the same time. This has led some theorists to suggest that there may be multiple resources, as

shown in Figure 15-16C (Navon & Gopher, 1979; Wickens, 1984). Some of these resources are probably specific to a particular sensory modality, whereas others may be attributable to an "executive" that monitors inputs from the various modalities and controls access to response selection. Whether attention to one task interferes with attention to another would then depend on the characteristics of the tasks and the processing required. For example, monitoring and analyzing two prose passages read into the two ears probably require that the same set of resources and analyzers be utilized for each of the two tasks. This is like the situation of Figure 15-16B; hence these two tasks would interfere with each other. In contrast, drawing a picture or doodling while monitoring someone speaking probably involves different types of mental capacity, and one task will not compete with the other for mental resources (more like the situation in Figure 15-16C). Recent research suggests that the bottleneck model and the capacity model can be combined, and it may make sense to think of selectivity and capacity limitations at both early and late processing stages (Dark, Johnston, Myles-Worsley, & Farah, 1985).

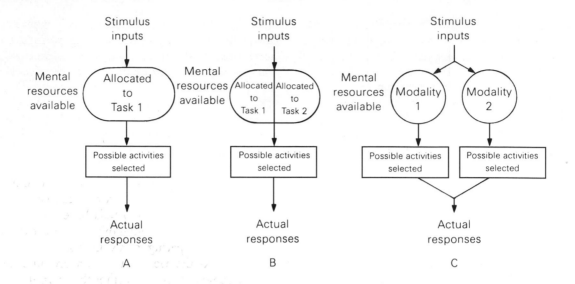

FIGURE 15-16 Attentional resource models. Parts A and B show a single resource model with either one (A) or two (B) tasks to accomplish simultaneously. In C separate resources are available for different sensory modalities or task types.

In addition to the models we have discussed, several newer types of attention theories have been proposed. These theories are based either on our growing knowledge of the neurophysiological underpinnings of attention and action (e.g., LaBerge, 1995) or on a more abstract, often mathematical or computational, conceptualization of attention (e.g., Logan, 1996; Weichselgartner & Sperling, 1996). None of these theories has yet gained universal acceptance, but the rapid pace of attention research—and the novel approaches being proposed—promises that our understanding of this elusive yet ubiquitous phenomenon will continue to advance in the new millennium.

CHAPTER SUMMARY

There are four major aspects of attention: **orienting, filtering, searching,** and **preparing.** In its simplest form, **orienting** refers to directing a sensory organ toward a source of stimulation. For example, the **orienting reflex** causes a person to move his or her eyes in the direction of a stimulus that suddenly appears. This is *overt orienting* as opposed to **covert orienting,** which involves directing attention to a stimulus. **Visual capture**

demonstrates that visual stimuli are more powerful at attracting and maintaining attention than are auditory stimuli. *Attentional capture* can also occur when a salient auditory cue pulls attention away from another auditory channel, as in a **dichotic listening** study, where an individual is **shadowing** (repeating the message) of the input in the attended ear but is pulled to the unattended ear's message by some powerful stimulus. Although the **attentional gaze** seems to be most focused on the object or meaningful properties of the stimulus, it is also tuned to a specific **locus** (region of space), **extent** (size of the area over which attention is spread), and **detail set** (whether larger global aspects or smaller local aspects are being processed). The **superior colliculi** and the **posterior parietal lobe** of the cortex seem to play major roles in the orienting of attention.

Filtering involves focusing attention on a specific set of stimuli and screening all others out of consciousness, as in the *cocktail party phenomenon* where it is possible to attend to the conversation of one person and to ignore all of the other noise and conversation. Dichotic listening studies have demonstrated that physical stimulus quality differences, such as location of the stimulus or differences in speakers' voice frequencies and identity, can make auditory filtering of particular information channels easier. The *video overlap phenomenon* demonstrates filtering in vision. Studies show that information in the unattended channels (those that are filtered out) is lost to the observer, although some low-level processing of the unattended-to information may still occur. Attempting not to filter, as in studies that have looked at **divided attention** where two channels of information must be simultaneously processed, is very difficult, and information processing is difficult, inefficient, and not very good. Filtering seems to involve enhancement of processing in the **temporal lobe** of the cortex, with the assistance of the *pulvinar nucleus* of the **thalamus.**

Searching involves seeking information from the sensory field, as when the eyes move over a scene to find something. Searching is strongly influenced by expectations and practice (e.g., children are less efficient at it), and unexpected items will elicit more attention. **Inhibition of return** refers to the fact that after an area is searched, the likelihood that the eyes and the attentional gaze will be directed to that location again is greatly reduced for a period of time—as if we are actively searching for novelty. **Feature searches** involving search for a target with one specific stimulus difference are easier and faster than **conjunction searches,** where several different features are involved. Feature searches often involve **parallel** processing, meaning that all of the items are effectively processed at the same time, and the number of distracters doesn't make much difference. Conjunction searches often involve serial processing, meaning that each item is sequentially scanned for the features, and the **serial search** takes longer if the number of distracters is greater. *Feature integration theory* suggests that each aspect of a target is registered in parallel but that objects composed of a conjunction of features must be processed separately and serially. **Guided searches** involve the conscious use of search strategies, and with much practice with particular stimuli the consciously guided and serial **controlled processing** gives way to *automaticity.* When conjunction searches become **automatic** they act as if parallel processing is being used, and little or no conscious attentional resources are needed. The **Stroop effect** is an example in which automatic processing can lead to difficulty in processing information. A special form of search involves **vigilance** tasks, where attention must be sustained over long periods and target events are infrequent. Under these conditions predictable decreases in search efficiency occur over each session. Vigilance performance will also interact with the observer's arousal level.

Preparing in attention often involves a **symbolic cue,** which allows the observer to begin orienting more quickly toward the expected stimulus. Although this produces processing **benefits** when the cue is valid, there may be **costs** in slowed processing time or lost information if the cue is invalid. **Event-related potentials** have shown that the posterior parietal region of the cortex reacts as a function of preparing for a stimulus.

Structural theories of attention presume that there is some bottleneck or filter that permits only attended-to stimuli to pass. **Early selection** theories say that this occurs at the sensory levels of processing before any meaning has been extracted, whereas **late selection** theories say that filtering occurs after some preliminary information processing has occurred. **Attentional resource** theories suggest that capacity to process information is limited, with large resources allotted to attended channels and information lost because resource capacity is not large enough for some tasks.

KEY TERMS

orienting	filtering
filtering	shadowing
information channels	dichotic listening
searching	phrase shadowing
preparing	phonemic shadowing
focused attention	temporal lobe
divided attention	thalamus
orienting response	dichoptic presentation
orienting reflex	automatic processing
covert orienting	controlled processing
visual capture	saccades
shadowing	inhibition of return
direct cue	feature search
symbolic cue	conjunction search
attentional gaze	parallel
locus	serial search
extent	guided search
detail set	parallel search
superior colliculi	controlled processing
posterior parietal lobe	automatic

Stroop effect

strong automaticity

skill

vigilance

Yerkes-Dodson Law

symbolic cue

preparing

benefit

cost

event-related potentials

positron-emission
 tomography (PET)

structural theories

early selection

late selection

attentional resources

Development

CHAPTER 16

The camp counselor turned to the newest arrival and asked, "And how old are you, son?"

"Well," said the boy, "it all depends. According to my latest set of anatomical tests I'm 7. According to my physical dexterity test I'm 10. I've got a mental age of 11, a moral age of 9, and a social age of 10. If you are referring to my chronological age, though, that's 8, but nobody pays any attention to that these days."

Although you might not relish the thought of spending a summer with this child, his comments point out that there are significant changes in many of our physical and psychological characteristics as we age. Each of these changes has its own time course. Some changes represent physiological transformations occurring as the body matures (such as a person's anatomical age). Others represent patterns of behavior that are learned as the individual grows older (such as social or moral age). Still others may represent a combination of both learning and maturation (such as mental age). Although no one refers to a perceptual age, changes in perceptual characteristics also occur as an individual develops and matures. These changes are usually improvements producing perceptual experiences that more accurately represent the physical environment. However, there are also some perceptual capacities that deteriorate with age.

In considering how an individual's perceptual functioning changes, we can adopt two different

469

perspectives. The first is long term, viewing people over their entire life span. This is the **life span developmental approach,** which assumes that knowledge of a person's chronological age will allow us to predict many aspects of perceptual behavior. The other approach is short term, viewing the changes that occur in perceptual responses as a result of a circumscribed set of experiences. This is the **perceptual learning approach.** It is based on the presumption that our interactions with the world can shape our percepts. These two approaches are not mutually exclusive; understanding the nature of perception often requires us to use both. Common to both approaches is the conclusion that, despite the fact that you may not be aware of it, your perceptual behavior is continually changing. Your experience of the world differs from that of individuals who are 10 years older or 10 years younger than you. Because the developmental and perceptual learning approaches use different techniques and often address somewhat different theoretical issues, we deal with these areas in separate chapters. Here we will begin with the developmental approach and then proceed to the effects of learning and experience in Chapter 17.

DEVELOPMENT OF THE NERVOUS SYSTEM

The Visual System

Before speaking about how perception changes as we develop and age, we must know something about the physiology of our sensory systems. What is our sensory apparatus capable of at birth, and how do these capacities change with age? Let us begin by looking at the infant's visual system.

In comparison to the rest of the body, the size of the eye changes very little after birth. The body may increase in volume about twentyfold, but the eye increases in volume merely twofold, as a consequence of the length from the cornea to the retina growing from about 16 mm to about 24 mm (Hickey & Peduzzi, 1987). The infant's retina contains rods and cones, as does the adult's. Electrical measures indicate that these receptors are functioning from birth, although the responses may not yet exactly match those of older children or adults (Aantaa, 1970; Maurer, 1975). Anatomically,

however, the retina is still quite immature at birth (Banks & Salapatek, 1983; Johnson, 1990). For instance, the region of the central fovea is not well defined in a 1-week-old infant—the cones in this region are stubby in appearance and much more sparsely packed than they will be eventually (Abramov, Gordon, Hendrickson, Hainline, Dobson, & La Bossiere, 1982).

Visual functioning of the retinal receptors is somewhat more developed at birth in the periphery of the eye than it is in the central region (Banks & Salapatek, 1983). By 11 to 12 months, however, the receptors in all regions of the retina have an adult-like function (Russoff, 1979). The optic nerve fibers that carry information from the retina to the brain become myelinated quite rapidly during the first 4 months of life, reaching adult levels by about 2 years of age (see the Appendix for a discussion of myelinization).

Our knowledge of the status of the visual pathways in newborns and infants comes mostly from animal studies, with the cat providing most of the data. If we measure the physiological functions of the various sites in the visual pathways of the cat at the time when the animal first opens its eyes, we get results like those in Table 16-1 (see Hickey & Peduzzi, 1987; Imbert, 1985; Norton, 1981a). The table shows that a number of adult-like and immature response patterns coexist in the newborn cat. Thus, in the retinal ganglion cell, we find the expected center-surround arrangement of excitatory and inhibitory responses. However, the receptive fields differ in size from those of the adult, and there is a general sluggishness in the response (e.g., Russoff & Dubin, 1977).

In Chapter 3 we discussed two different visual pathways, one originating from the small ganglion cells in the retina, called the *parvocellular* pathway, and one originating from the larger ganglion cells, called the *magnocellular* pathway. These pathways appear to process different types of information in parallel, with the parvocellular pathway associated principally with color and detailed form vision and the magnocellular pathway specialized for movement and depth perception. These two systems are also characterized by response pattern differences—parvo cells give a sustained response, magno cells a transient response. In the cat and monkey, however, at the retinal level, these two response types are not well defined at birth

Table 16-1   The Functional Condition of Various Sites in the Visual Pathways of the Newborn Cat

ADULT-LIKE RESPONSES	IMMATURE RESPONSES
Retinal Ganglion Cells	
Center-surround organization of receptive fields Adult percentage of on/off center	Low activity level Overly large receptive fields Slow responses to light and weak inhibition Parvo vs. magno responses not clear
Lateral Geniculate Nucleus	
Normal visual-field mapping Binocular separation of inputs	Low activity and silent areas Large receptive field diameter Slow, sluggish, fatigable responses
Superior Colliculus	
Normal visual-field mapping Center-surround receptive fields Adult percentage of on/off center	Slow, sluggish, fatigable responses Large receptive fields No movement direction sensitivity
Striate Cortex	
Normal visual-field mapping Adult separation of responses by eye of input	Sluggish, fatigable responses Many silent cells Fewer or absent orientation and direction-selective cells with broader tuning No binocular disparity cells

(Hamasaki & Sutija, 1979; Mooney, Dubin, & Russoff, 1979; Shiller, 1986).

Farther up in the visual pathways, at the lateral geniculate nucleus, we do find the adult division of two magnocellular layers and four parvocellular layers in the neonate. Here we also can observe the separation of the inputs from the two eyes into clearly defined layers that are interleaved. However, many of the cells in the geniculate don't seem to respond to any sort of visual input, and the responses that can be measured are often slow and easily fatigued (Daniels, Pettigrew, & Norman, 1978). The parvo cells in the lateral geniculate reach their adult size first, by about 12 months of age, whereas the magno cells are much slower, reaching full size only by 2 years of age (Hickey, 1977). A similar pattern emerges for the superior colliculus, with the general organization of cell layers and the center-surround organization of receptive fields resembling those of an adult by 3–6 months. However, at birth the receptive field size of these cells is much larger than that of adults,

and the responses are relatively slow, weak, and not very sensitive to direction (Norton, 1981a).

Finally, at the level of the primary visual cortex (V1), we find that the inputs from the two eyes separate into the expected columnar arrangement discussed in Chapter 3 and that directional and orientation-sensitive cells (both simple and complex) are present. In infant monkeys, single cell recordings show that some cells are orientation selective (Weisel & Hubel, 1974), although they are fewer in number, and their responses are slow and easily fatigued (Imbert, 1985). In human newborns, when behavioral measures are used, orientation-selective responses have not been observed until 5 to 6 months of age (Braddick, Wattam-Bell, & Atkinson, 1986). In addition, binocular-disparity-sensitive cells seem to be almost absent until several weeks of age in both monkeys and humans (Braddick, Atkinson, Julesz, Kropfl, Bodis-Wollner, & Raab, 1980; Held, 1985). Overall, many of the characteristics of the adult system seem to be present in the newborn visual system, but the full adult pattern of response clearly is not present (Banks & Salapatek, 1983). Of course, many of these statements are species specific, and humans appear to develop somewhat more slowly than do cats and monkeys. Thus, whereas those animals show separation of the two eyes into separate ocular dominance columns from birth, humans may take 4 to 6 months to develop similar complex neural structures (Hickey & Peduzzi, 1987).

It should be clear from this discussion that many components of the visual system mature at different rates. The parvocellular pathway to the cortex matures in some respects more quickly than the magnocellular pathway (Maurer & Lewis, 1979). The cells associated with the more peripheral retina (for both parvocellular and magnocellular pathways) mature more quickly than cells related to central vision. Within the primary visual cortex, the layers of cortex that receive inputs directly from the eye reach their mature size and complete the myelinization process before the layers that receive or send information to other brain centers (Rabinowicz, 1979). Also, even when neonatal cells are relatively mature in appearance, their responses are slower and less vigorous than those of the adult. Taken together, these observations suggest that the quality of information reaching the highest visual centers of the newborn's brain may be relatively poor and that different perceptual functions will emerge at different times during development.

Patterns of Brain Change in Development

Contrary to what you might be tempted to think at first, brain development does not primarily involve an increase in the number of neurons, nor does it involve even a systematic increase in the number of connections between neurons. In fact, the absolute number of cortical neurons for a well-defined brain region such as the primary visual cortex (Area V1) stays remarkably constant from gestational age 28 weeks (typical birth is at 40 weeks) to age 70 years in humans (Huttenlocher, 1990). This is quite different from some other animals, where cell death seems to play a more important role in brain development. For example, mice lose up to 30% of their cortical

neurons during development (Heumann & Leuba, 1983), and the monkey visual cortex loses 15% of its total cell population between birth and adulthood (O'Kusky & Colonnier, 1982).

One of the most important aspects of brain development in humans appears to be closely tied to the loss of connections between the various cortical neurons. This is referred to as **neuronal pruning** by some researchers because under the microscope the connections look like "branches" from the axon of one neuron making contact with the dendritic "branches" of another neuron. Reducing the number of these branches can then be viewed as pruning of the neuronal tree. Figure 16-1 shows how the total number of synaptic connections in the visual cortex changes quite remarkably with age. The number of connections increases rapidly until about 8 months of age, after which it begins to decrease, declining to almost one half the maximum level between the ages of 8 months and 10 years. There is another smaller, but significant, decline in the number of connections in old age.

What is the possible importance of the inverted U-shaped trend in the number of connections that neurons are making with one another over development? One very promising theory is that the decline in the number of connections reflects the development of specialized pathways of information flow and specialized regions of cortex devoted to particular functions (Johnson & Vecera, 1996). This theory proposes that in the young infant, different attributes of a visual stimulus, and even information from different sensory modalities, may be processed in a relatively diffuse and undifferentiated way. The emergence of specialized systems in development, through the loss of specific neuronal connections, results in information that is combined in early infancy being increasingly segregated or partitioned into relatively isolated modules as the child matures.

This theory makes some interesting predictions that are interesting because they contrast with the general trend that perceptual functions tend to improve with development. For example, consider the development of the ocular dominance columns in Area V1 of the visual cortex. We saw in the preceding section that in humans these may take between 4 and 6 months to develop into their adult-like forms (Held, 1985; Hickey & Peduzzi, 1987).

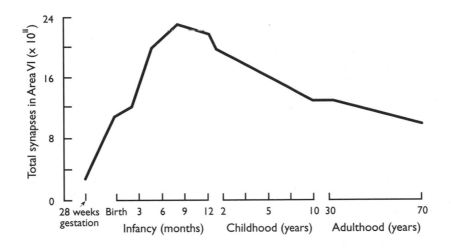

FIGURE 16-1   The estimated total number of synaptic connections in human brain Area V1 as a function of age. Drawn based on Huttenlocher (1990, p. 519).

This implies that before the columns have become segregated, both eyes project to the same cells in the visual cortex. This leads to the interesting prediction that a young infant should have an integrated neural representation of some stimulus inputs that would not be possible for older infants. Support for this prediction was found in one experiment in which infants were shown vertical stripes in one eye and horizontal stripes in the other eye (Held, 1993). Infants under 4 months of age behaved in the same way as when they were shown a gridlike pattern in only one eye (the composite of the two striped patterns). Infants older than 4 months behaved toward the composite pattern as though it were a new stimulus.

Another example of greater perceptual integration in young infants than in older infants can be seen in experiments on cross-modal communication. In some studies (e.g., Melzoff & Borton, 1979; Streri, 1987) infants were familiarized with an object either visually (by letting the infants view a picture) or tactilely (by placing it in the hand or the mouth of the infants). The exploratory behavior of an infant (either visual or tactile) was then examined when the infant was presented with the same shape in either the same or the opposite modality. Infants as young as 1 and 2 months of age showed transfer across modality in their exploratory behavior, whereas 5-month-old infants did not.

A second very important aspect of brain development in humans is the myelinization of neurons. Myelin is the fatty tissue that surrounds many neuronal axons; its presence speeds the transmission of neural information (see the Appendix). A very natural place to begin looking for links between developmental change in behavior and the brain is in the relative rates at which various brain regions become fully myelinated. Neuroanatomical studies indicate that myelinization is complete in early infancy for the brain stem and midbrain, is completed in young childhood for the primary cortical areas and parietal lobes, and is completed only in the early teen years for regions of the frontal cortex (Lecours, 1975; Yakolev & Lecours, 1967).

PERCEPTION IN INFANTS

Research Challenges in Testing Infants

The perceptions of newborn infants (neonates) are difficult to assess. In the first few months of life, infants spend much of their time sleeping, and they do not respond to instructions or answer our questions in any direct fashion. They also produce only a limited range of observable behaviors. These challenges require experimenters to be quite creative in devising techniques to measure the perceptual abilities of the very young. Furthermore, the use of these different techniques sometimes results in findings that do not agree with one another (Teghtsoonian, 1987; Trehub & Schneider, 1987).

To resolve these inconsistencies, researchers are sometimes forced to use animal subjects rather than humans, especially if direct physiological measures of functioning are desired. But, this can create its own problems, because those aspects of such measures that are species specific are often unknown. An alternative approach, which is rapidly increasing in popularity, is the use of brain-imaging techniques such as event-related potentials, positron-emission tomography, and functional magnetic imaging (see Chapter 15). These techniques can be used to acquire pictures of infant brain activity that can be correlated with visual or auditory stimuli. Thus, we are able to determine whether the infant brain "sees" a stimulus pattern even though the infant cannot indicate this to us using any observable behavior.

For example, we can determine how well the visual cortex of the infant is functioning by measuring event-related potentials in response to visual stimulation. The recordings are made by pasting electrodes (generally flat pieces of silver) to the scalp and connecting them to very sensitive amplifiers (see the Appendix). Plotting the output of these amplifiers over time reveals small changes in the electrical activity of the brain in response to stimulation. When the stimuli are visual, these recordings are called **visually evoked potentials** (abbreviated **VEP**). Some characteristics of the VEP signal are reliably related to visual detection and pattern identification (Cannon, 1983).

Almost all newborn infants (and even most premature infants) show some VEP, although it differs somewhat from the adult response in its pattern, size, and speed (Atkinson, 1984; Ellingson, 1968; Umezaki & Morrell, 1970). For instance, VEPs from subcortical regions of the brain are always present at birth, but only some of the VEPs from cortical regions can be seen (Vaughan & Kurtzberg, 1989). Over a period of about 3 to 6 months, the infant's electrical responses to visual stimuli come to look more and more like those of adults (Banks & Salapatek, 1983; Braddick, Wattam-Bell, & Atkinson, 1986; Harter & Suitt, 1970). It is generally agreed that during the first year of life

the visual system matures rapidly and that, although it shows many adult capabilities by the end of the second year (Ellingson, Lathrop, Nelson, & Donahy, 1972; Movshon & Van Sluyters, 1981), some brain centers continue to develop until the child is 10–12 years of age or older (Huttenlocher, DeCourten, Garey, & Van der Loos, 1982; Imbert, 1985).

Methods of testing infants' visual capacities that rely on observable behaviors by the infants must be very carefully devised because we can't use verbal instructions or obtain verbal responses from them. The researcher's only recourse is to use existing behaviors, which, for perceptual research, usually involve some form of a reflex such as overt orienting. The orienting reflex involves eye movements, head turns, and visual following behavior in response to a stimulus that appears suddenly or is moving. The eliciting stimulus may be auditory, visual, or even tactile (Banks & Dannemiller, 1987).

Given the limited response repertoire available to a young infant, we can appreciate the methodological breakthrough made by Fantz (1961). His procedure, called **preferential looking,** involves first placing a young infant in a special chamber (either on its back or in an infant chair). Visual stimuli are then placed on the walls or the roof of the chamber. There is a tiny hole through which the experimenter can watch the infant looking at the stimuli. An apparatus similar to Fantz's is shown in Figure 16-2. When the infant views one of a pair of stimulus patterns placed in the chamber, the experimenter determines which one is being looked at by simply noting the side to which the eyes turn. A timer is used to record how long the infant views each of the two stimuli. If the infant looks at one target longer than the other, this is taken as indicating a preference for that target. The simple existence of a preference for a pattern implies that the infant can discriminate between the patterns. Unfortunately, this simple result does not tell us *why* the infant preferred to look at one stimulus rather than the other, nor can we be sure that the absence of a viewing preference means that the infant cannot discriminate between the two stimuli.

There have been many elaborations of this technique, such as the one by Teller (1981) called the **forced-choice preferential looking** technique. Her procedure allows the study of stimulus

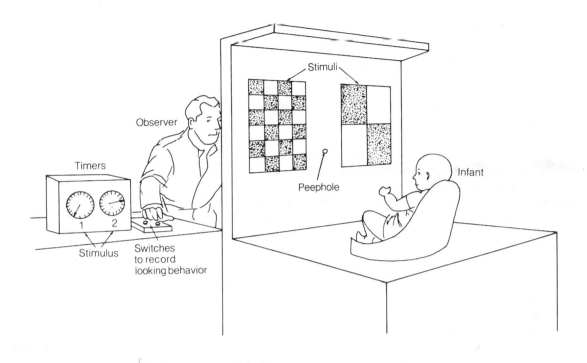

FIGURE 16-2   An apparatus for monitoring how long infants view particular stimuli.

detection as well as discrimination between stimuli. Here, the infant is presented with only a single stimulus while its response is monitored by a hidden observer or TV camera. If, on the basis of the infant's head and eye movements alone, an observer can reliably determine whether the test target was presented to the left or to the right side of the screen, it is presumed that the information concerning the position of the target has been transmitted from the screen, through the infant's visual system and behavior, to the observer. At the minimum, this suggests that the infant can see the stimulus.

A further variation of this technique allows researchers to determine whether an infant can notice any difference between stimuli. Again, only one stimulus is presented, and the viewing behavior is monitored. At first the infant will spend a good deal of time looking at the stimulus, but as time passes it will begin to look at it less and less. Researchers often informally say that the infant is becoming "bored" with the stimulus. The technical name for this process is **habituation.** If a different stimulus is now presented, the baby will again look. This renewed interest in the stimulus

suggests that the infant has recognized that something has changed and that the present stimulus is different from the former one (e.g., Kellman & Spelke, 1983; McCall, 1979). The technical name for the renewed interest in the stimulus is **dishabituation.** It is used by researchers as a measure that the infant has discriminated the current stimulus from the previous stimulus to which the infant had inhabituated.

Eye Movements and Visual Attention

In Chapter 9 we saw that certain aspects of spatial vision, such as the binocular perception of depth or distance, are not present at birth but, rather, develop as the infant grows (e.g., Held, 1985; Yonas & Granrud, 1985a). The perception of direction, however, is much better at birth. Newborn infants can move their eyes so as to bring visual targets onto or close to their foveas. Thus, if we present a young infant (about 2 weeks of age) with a target that suddenly appears 20° from the fovea, it will slowly turn its eyes toward that target (Aslin, 1987; Harris & MacFarlane, 1974).

Furthermore, 3-month-old infants seem to be able to identify targets in the periphery of their visual field well enough to guide their eyes to selected or preferred stimuli (Maurer & Lewis, 1991).

Although infants will look at a target that suddenly appears or moves, infants' eye movements are not exactly like those of adults. Each of the two main types of voluntary eye movements takes some time to develop fully. The first type is **saccadic eye movements,** which are fast, ballistic movements from one target to another that occur when you direct your attention toward a target. In adults, a saccade will start the eye moving toward a target some distance from the current fixation point within 200 ms to 250 ms. The actual time taken by the movement itself can be as short as 4 ms to 10 ms (e.g., Komoda, Festinger, Phillips, Duckman, & Young, 1973; Kowler & Martin, 1980; Rayner, 1978). Saccades are also accurate in positioning the eye so that the new target is centered on the fovea. A typical long saccade would bring the eye to within 5% to 10% of the desired position. A representative adult eye movement to a target 30° from the current fixation point is shown

in Figure 16-3. Infants are much slower to begin the saccade and tend to make a series of small saccades, often not reaching the target for well over a second, as shown in Figure 16-3 (Aslin, 1987; Regal, Ashmead, & Salapatek, 1983). However, even the immature saccadic eye movements of infants can reveal something of their perceptual capacities. For example, expectation (see Chapter 15) can be studied in infants by showing them a light that either consistently alternates between two locations (so that its "next" location can be anticipated) or appears randomly at various locations. Newborn infants' eye movements are similar in both conditions, indicating that they probably are not able to anticipate where the light will be next even when it alternates consistently. However, by 3 to 4 months of age infants move their eyes toward the "next" location when the light alternates consistently, indicating that they are expecting it to appear there (Haith, Hazan, & Goodman, 1988).

The other type of eye movement is **smooth pursuit eye movements.** Here the eyes track a steadily moving object, such as a ball flying through the air or a person swinging on a swing, with a

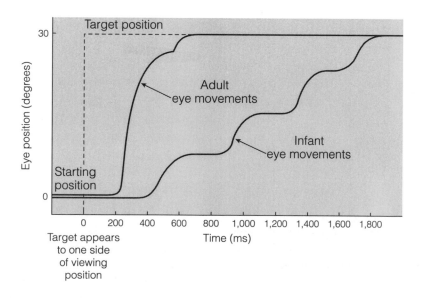

FIGURE 16-3 A typical adult eye movement to a target appearing 30 deg to one side of fixation will involve a single, fast, large saccade and a small corrective flick, whereas an infant will have a longer delay before moving, and the movement will involve a series of shorter saccades.

uniform and even motion. Smooth pursuit eye movements do not appear in newborns—instead they use short, jumpy saccadic eye movements to track even smoothly moving objects. Thus, rather than keep pace with the moving target, an infant grabs a glimpse of it, waits until it drifts from view, and then attempts to look at it again. As with saccades, newborns are unable to anticipate the path of an object that moves smoothly back and forth. Instead they seem always to be "catching up" with small stepwise movements that are the same size regardless of the speed of the object. This pattern does not simply reflect an immature motor system because infants can be shown to make much larger saccades under other circumstances (Aslin, 1981a). The adult pattern of smooth anticipatory movements begins to emerge at 8 to 10 weeks of age.

The fact that infants move their eyes in response to moving or suddenly appearing stimuli can be used to measure other capacities in the newborn. For instance, if we show an adult observer a continuously moving pattern (such as a screen full of stripes all moving in one direction) we get a characteristic eye-movement pattern. The eye will smoothly track in the direction of the movement for a distance and then flick back in the opposite direction. After this return movement the observer's eyes fixate another stripe and follow it, and this process repeats itself while the observer views the array. This repetitive eye movement sequence in the presence of a moving pattern is called optokinetic nystagmus. A similar (but not as smooth) pattern of eye movements is found in infants younger than 5 days (Kremenitzer, Vaughan, Kurtzberg, & Dowling, 1979). In fact, its appearance is so reliable that the absence of optokinetic nystagmus is used as an indication that there may be neurological problems (Brazelton, Scholl, & Robey, 1966). This eye-movement pattern seems to be automatic or reflexive in nature, rather than voluntary, and is probably controlled by the *tectopulvinar system* we described in Chapter 3 (Atkinson & Braddick, 1981; Hoffmann, 1979). If an infant cannot see a pattern of moving stripes (because they are not large enough or lack sufficient contrast), optokinetic nystagmus will be absent. This technique has been used to study brightness discrimination, visual acuity, and motion perception in infants (Banks & Salapatek, 1983).

Although newborns will move their eyes to suddenly appearing stimuli, they show a much more consistent response to stimuli in the temporal visual field (the peripheral portion of the visual field out toward the temples of the head) than to those in the nasal visual field (the central portion of the visual field, which could be conceived as being pointed to by the nose; Johnson, 1990; Lewis, Maurer, & Milewski, 1979). By 2 months of age, this asymmetry has diminished greatly, although it can still be observed to some extent in adults (Posner, 1980). An interesting finding is that eye movements toward stimuli in the temporal visual field can be elicited by the superior colliculus, a part of the tectopulvinar system, without any contribution from the visual cortex. However, movements toward the nasal field require activation of the visual cortex in addition to the superior colliculus (Johnson, 1990). This suggests that the movement asymmetry found in infants arises from an immaturity in the control over eye movements exerted by the visual cortex (Maurer & Lewis, 1991).

The eye movements of young infants are also easily disrupted by the appearance of more than one stimulus in the visual field. "Competing" stimuli increase the time required to complete an eye movement and decrease the accuracy with which a saccade will cause a target to be fixated (Atkinson, Hood, Braddick, & Wattam-Bell, 1988). One very vivid demonstration of competition between brain regions in the infant occurs when an initial flashing light at the center of gaze is accompanied some time later by a light flashing in the visual periphery (Hood & Atkinson, 1993). The infant at first orients to the central flashing light. When the peripheral light begins to flash, the infant's head is drawn in the direction of the peripheral light, but the eyes appear to remain fixated on the central flashing light. A reasonable explanation of this behavior is that some reflexive neural mechanism is guiding the head to orient to the new light in the periphery, while another mechanism has "locked" the eye movement system onto the central light. This conflict is much less evident in 6- to 7-month-old infants than in 2- to 3-month-old infants, suggesting that these reflexes are gradually coming under the control of central, cortical mechanisms (Atkinson, Hood, Wattam-Bell, & Braddick, 1992; Johnson, 1995).

Another phenomenon of visual competition occurs when infants are faced with the choice between looking again at a previously fixated stimulus and at a new one. Infants up to 3 months of age tend to look again at the original stimulus, whereas 6- to 7-month-olds will choose to fixate the new stimulus instead (Hood, 1993; Hood & Atkinson, 1991; Johnson & Tucker, 1996; Rothbart, Posner, & Boylan, 1990). This is similar to the *inhibition of return* phenomenon seen in adults (see Chapter 15) in that it biases the older infant observer to take in new information. This bias toward the examination of objects in novel locations assists the infant in a full exploration of its visual world.

Visual Acuity

The visual acuity of infants is rather poor, especially in the periphery of the nasal visual field of each eye (Courage & Adams, 1996). This fact has been established in several ways. For instance, the optokinetic response that we described earlier can be used to test the visual acuity of infants. This is done by finding the narrowest width of stripes that will still produce the tracking response. Other ways, such as preferential looking procedures, can be used to measure infant visual acuity. Although the level of acuity found for infants varies with the technique (Teller & Movshon, 1986) and with the specific acuity stimulus used (Shimojo & Held, 1987), there is a general agreement that visual acuity is around

20/800 (6/240 in metric units) at birth. This is less acuity than is needed to see the single big *E* on a standard Snellen acuity chart (which is a Snellen acuity of 20/200).

Newborns also act as if they have limited ability to change focus through lens accommodation. They act as if their lenses are fixed in focus to see something about 20 cm away (White, 1971). This is about the distance of the mother's face for a nursing infant. However, the poor acuity and accommodative ability of the infant do not last for long. There is a rapid increase in visual acuity during the first 3 months of age (e.g., Courage & Adams, 1990, 1996), and, as shown in Figure 16-4, the young child's acuity increases steadily with age (see Gwiazda & Bauer, 1989). Some tests show, however, that the improvement continues for quite a while, and the child may not finally reach average adult levels until more than 7 years of age (Scharre, Cotter, Block, & Kelly, 1990). If you have access to a young infant, you can see the effect of this limited accommodation by trying Demonstration Box 16-1.

Brightness and Color

Several techniques have been used to assess the basic sensitivity of infants to brightness and color. One-month-old infants are about ⅙₀ as sensitive to light

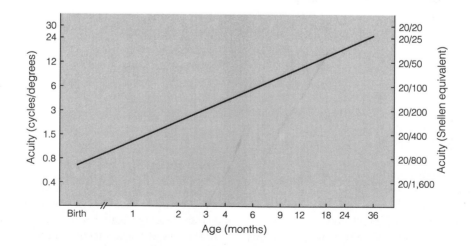

FIGURE 16-4   Steady improvement in visual acuity from birth to 3 years of age.

DEMONSTRATION BOX 16-1
Infant Accommodation

To demonstrate that an infant's accommodation is limited to close objects, you will, of course, need an infant, preferably 2 months of age or younger. If you can find one, catch its attention and then slowly move a pencil from side to side near the infant's face. Use a distance of about 20 cm, or around 8 in. Watch the child's head and eyes and notice that the infant will track, or at least try to track, the pencil. Now repeat this, but vary the distance to 1 m or 2 m away from the child. At this distance you should have exceeded the ability of the infant to accommodate, and you should notice that little, if any, tracking occurs.

---

as are adults, whereas 3-month-old infants are $\frac{1}{10}$ as sensitive to light both under dark-adapted (scotopic) and light-adapted (photopic) conditions (Peeples & Teller, 1978; Powers, Schneck, & Teller, 1981). However, despite these differences infants are still very sensitive to light. For example, in Chapter 4 we found that an adult can detect as few as 6 quanta of light hitting anywhere in a patch of 1,300 rod receptors. In comparison, a 3-month-old infant would need to receive about 60 quanta of light over the same region, and a 1-month-old infant would need about 300 quanta of light (Teller & Bornstein, 1987). Although that is substantially greater than that required by adults, it is still a very small amount of light.

Several studies show that despite differences in absolute sensitivity, the relative sensitivity of infants and adults to different wavelengths of light is about the same. Both are most sensitive to middle wavelengths and exhibit a gradual decrease in sensitivity to longer and shorter wavelengths (Dobson, 1976; Moskowitz-Cook, 1979; Werner, 1979). This does not mean, however, that infants have color vision equivalent to that of adults. In general, young infants do show some ability to discriminate between colors (Bornstein, 1985; Werner & Wooten, 1979). Infants have good color discrimination between the long and middle wavelengths of light (red and green), and, at least for large stimuli, this may be present as early as the first week of life (Adams, 1989, 1995). However, for the 1-month-old infant the short-wavelength (blue) discriminating mechanism seems to still be immature (Adams, 1995; Teller & Bornstein, 1987). Most 1-month-old infants have poor discrimination among the various short-wavelength stimuli. In fact, their discrimination appears much like that of tritanopic color-blind individuals (see Chapter 5). By the age of 2 months, however, most infants can make such short-wavelength discriminations (Adams & Courage, 1994; Varner, Cook, Schneck, McDonald, & Teller, 1985).

Pattern Discrimination

The preferential looking technique has been used extensively to explore pattern perception in infants. Using this technique it has been shown that even premature infants, born 1 to 2 months prior to a full-term gestation, often preferentially look at patterned stimuli rather than plain ones of equal average brightness and also sometimes discriminate between different patterns (Fantz & Miranda, 1977). This means that the optical and neural bases of pattern vision do not abruptly become functional at the end of the full term of pregnancy, which is the age at which infants ordinarily can first be observed. Rather, these mechanisms have already matured to a reasonable degree of function prior to the normal birth time.

Preferential looking studies have also shown that young infants can discriminate among a variety of different types of patterns. For instance, in one experiment newborn infants were shown pairs of targets. These infants showed a clear preference for viewing patterns of stripes over a simple square and also preferred patterns with high contrast between the figures and the background. They showed a preference for larger patterns, indicating that they can discriminate size, and also preferred patterns containing many rather than

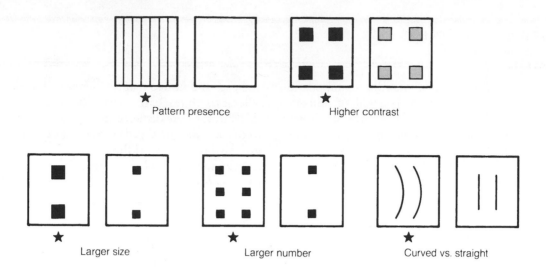

FIGURE 16-5 Patterns most looked at by newborns are indicated with a star for each pair of stimuli (based on Fantz & Yeh, 1979).

few elements. In addition, they showed some ability to discriminate certain aspects defining contours, such as curvature, by preferring curved to straight-line elements. Figure 16-5 shows some representative forms. In the figure, the star indicates those most preferred by newborns for each pair (Fantz & Yeh, 1979).

Generally, infants prefer moderately complex stimuli over those that are very simple or very complex, although preferences do change with age (Karmel & Maisel, 1975). Young infants prefer simple patterns with highly contrasting elements, whereas 5-month-olds can make more subtle distinctions in contrast and configuration (Fantz & Yeh, 1979). Banks and Salapatek (1983) suggested that pattern perception in infants reflects the developing ability to discriminate various spatial frequencies (see Chapter 4).

Preferences in viewing also show that some high-level aspects of pattern perception are possible for the young infant. Infants can discriminate the orientation of patterns within the first few weeks (Maurer & Martello, 1980) and perhaps even on the first day of life (Kessen, Salapatek, & Haith, 1972). Furthermore, they seem to be aware of certain forms of symmetry or its absence (Bornstein, 1981). Although infants respond to both the size and position of stimuli, at age 4 months they are relatively insensitive to changes in the configuration of the stimuli (Humphrey, Humphrey, Muir, & Dodwell, 1986). Furthermore, 3- to 4-month-old infants seem to pay attention to specific features (such as whether the dots making up a pattern are square rather than round) instead of to the global configuration (such as the pattern the dots make). By 6 or 7 months they are responding to these global aspects of the pattern as well (Dineen & Meyer, 1980). Figure 16-6 summarizes the sensitivity of the 4-month-old infant to various aspects of visual patterns. It shows a pattern to which the infant is habituated and then some test patterns. The patterns with a plus sign exemplify changes that the infant would be expected to notice; the pattern with a minus sign exemplifies a change that the infant would not notice (Dodwell, Humphrey, & Muir, 1987).

Object Perception

Certain meaningful patterns receive special attention, even from neonates. A number of researchers have studied the response of infants to targets that resemble the human face (Johnson, Dziurawiec,

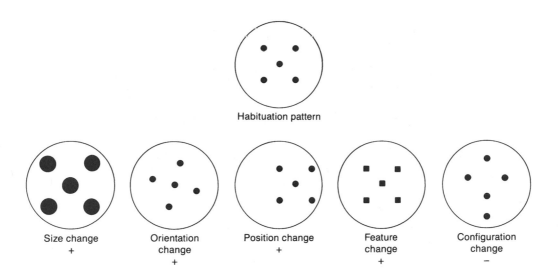

FIGURE 16-6   When 4-month-old infants habituate to the top pattern, they act as if they recognize changes in the pattern indicated by a plus (+) sign but do not recognize the change indicated by the minus (-) sign.

Ellis, & Morton, 1991; Nelson & Ludemann, 1989). One common procedure is to use some targets that are only head shaped, others containing only some facial features (such as a hairline or eyes), some containing scrambled facial features, and others that actually look like faces. Samples of such stimuli are shown in Figure 16-7. In general, it is found that by 2 months of age infants prefer to look at stimuli that contain facial features arranged in the normal configuration rather than scrambled, whereas children younger than 1 month of age do not make this discrimination (Carey, 1981; Haaf, 1977; Mauer & Barrera, 1981). Between 1

month and 4 months of age infants begin to take note of certain features in the facelike stimulus. By about 10 or 12 weeks of age, infants notice and recognize changes in hairline and eyes, although changes in mouth and nose configurations go unnoticed (Caron, Caron, Caldwell, & Weiss, 1973). However, the configurational and specific features picked up by infants only 1 month of age do seem to be sufficient to permit the infants to discriminate their own mother's face from that of a stranger (Maurer & Salapatek, 1976), which suggests that young infants can discriminate among certain classes of fairly complex patterns.

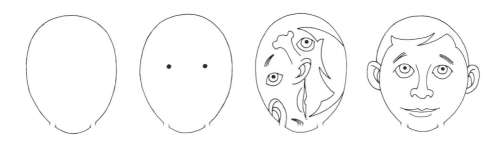

FIGURE 16-7   Schematic and scrambled facelike stimuli.

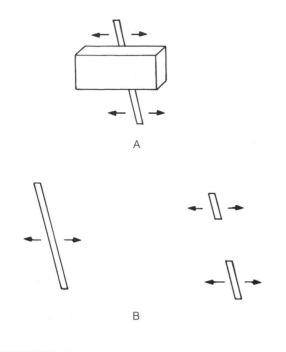

FIGURE 16-8 Stimuli to test whether objects are perceptually completed when they are partially obscured by other objects: (A) the original habituation stimulus; (B) two possible test stimuli (based on Kellman & Spelke, 1983).

One group of researchers looked at the ability of infants to integrate fragments of an object that are physically separated from each other in the visual image, as, for instance, when a nearer object blocks part of a farther object from view. In one study 4-month-olds were repeatedly shown a rod that moved back and forth but was partially occluded by a brick that lay in front of it. After the infants had habituated to this display, they were shown either a connected rod moving back and forth or two short rods that moved back and forth in synchrony. These displays are shown in Figure 16-8. The infants now looked longer at the broken-rod display, indicating that they perceived this display as different from the occluded-rod display (Kellman & Spelke, 1983). This suggests that the infants were perceptually completing the object when it was partially occluded from sight. This result has been shown under a number of conditions (Kellman & Short, 1987; Kellman, Spelke, & Short, 1986) and apparently also includes correction of certain shape

distortions that occur when a moving object passes behind a nearer object (Craton & Yonas, 1990).

Figure 16-9 summarizes how the child's visual competence develops over the first few months of life.

Infant Hearing

The ears of infants are functional at birth, but the auditory cortex is still rather immature and continues to develop over the first year (Kuhl, 1987). Several studies have suggested that infants less than 6 months of age have higher absolute thresholds than adults have (Berg & Smith, 1983; Trehub, Schneider, & Endman, 1980). An interesting feature of these data is that the differences are most noticeable in the frequency range below 10,000 Hz. The ability of adults to detect tones in this range is nearly twice as good as that of infants (Olsho, 1984). At the higher frequencies, however, infants show more adult-like sensitivity (Kuhl, 1987).

Newborns are able to indicate their ability to localize the direction of a sound source by turning either their head or eyes toward the sound (Butterworth, 1981; Muir & Field, 1979). Long stimulus durations and frequent stimulus repetitions increase the likelihood of a head turn in the direction of the sound (Clarkson, Swain, Clifton, & Cohen, 1991). Wertheimer (1961) probably tested the youngest child for this ability. A mere 3 min after birth, with the infant lying on her back, a loud click was sounded next to her right ear or left ear. Two observers noted whether the eyes moved to the infant's right or to her left or not at all. On 18 out of the 22 occasions when the infant's eyes moved, they moved in the direction of the click. When the experiment was completed the infant was still only 10 min old. Hence these data allow us to conclude that some directional aspects of auditory stimuli are accurately processed and may influence behavior from birth.

Recall from Chapter 7 that there are several binaural cues that help to indicate the direction of a sound relative to the listener. The two most important of these are the time differences between the arrival of low-frequency sounds to the two ears (earlier to the closer ear) and the intensity differences between the two ears caused by the lack of bending of higher frequencies of sound around the head (more intense to the closer ear—see Green,

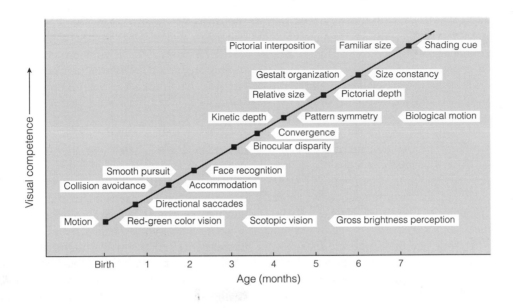

FIGURE 16-9 Various visual abilities, and sensitivity to various environmental or stimulus dimensions, appear at different ages.

1976; Moore, 1977). Which of these cues is most effective for the infant? By directly controlling both the time differences between the ears and intensity of sound reaching the two ears, Clifton, Morrongiello, and Dowd (1984) demonstrated that newborn infants, and those up to about 9 weeks of age, respond to intensity differences between the two ears by turning in the direction of the sound. At these young ages, the more complex time discrimination cue is not adequate to induce the infant to turn its head in the appropriate direction. However, by age 5 months both cues are effective and cause the infant to look in the direction of the sound source (Muir, Clifton, & Clarkson, 1989). If you have access to an infant, Demon-

stration Box 16-2 will show you how to demonstrate auditory localization.

One of the more interesting biases that newborns exhibit is a preference to orient their head and eyes toward the location of a relatively high-pitched speaking voice. This bias seems to coincide very conveniently with the tendency on the part of adults to speak in high-pitched and exaggerated voices to young infants. This kind of baby talk was once called *motherese* but is now referred to as **infant directed talk** because it can be heard when men, women, and even young children speak to infants (Werker & McLeod, 1989). Infants of 4–6 months respond to such talk by increasing their amount of smiling and vocalization (Fernald,

---

DEMONSTRATION BOX 16-2
Auditory Localization in Infants

If you have access to an infant, auditory localization is easily demonstrated. Simply look squarely at the child and then make a sharp sound near one ear. Good sound sources are a rattle, a snap of the fingers, or a toy "clicker." Watch the infant's head and eyes. You should see the eyes flick in the direction of the sound, or you may see the head turn in the direction of the stimulus.

1985; Trehub & Trainor, 1990; Wolff, 1987) and by engaging in a "conversational" exchange of vowel-like sounds (a sort of cooing) with the talker (Bloom, 1990).

There is now also growing evidence that infants perceptually group sounds in systematic ways, similar to the ways in which they (and adults) perceptually group visual patterns (Trehub & Trainor, 1990). In one study infants of 6 to 9 months of age listened to sequences of tones separated by equal time intervals, in which the first three tones were the same high frequency and the last three tones were the same low frequency (Thorpe & Trehub, 1989). Such sequences can be represented graphically as *HHHLLL* where *H* is the high tone and *L* the low. Following habituation to this tone sequence, the infants listened to a modified tone sequence. In one such sequence there was a longer silent interval—indicated by an apostrophe (')—at the boundary between the two frequencies (*HHH'LLL*), which is the place where adults will tend to perceptually separate the series into two groups, and hence the silent pause seems "natural" in that position. This is the auditory equivalent of grouping based on the Gestalt Law of Similarity, which we discussed in Chapter 10. Alternatively, the silent interval could be placed in another place (e.g., *HHHL'LL*). This is an unexpected place for the silent pause, and it seems a bit strange perceptually, causing adults to pay a bit more attention to this stimulus sequence. In this study, infants also directed more attention to this sequence. This shows that the infants had also grouped the tones in the original sequence on the basis of their frequency similarity, much the way that adults do; hence the novel grouping was more surprising to them. Other studies have shown that this kind of auditory grouping, or perceptual organization of sounds on the basis of their temporal

and frequency relationships, also occurs for infants' perceptions of classical music and lullabies (Juszcyk & Krumhansl, 1993; Krumhansl & Juszcyk, 1990; Trehub & Unyk, 1994) and their perceptions of infant directed talk (Kemler-Nelson, Hirsh-Pasek, Jusczyk, & Wright-Cassidy, 1989).

Touch, Pain, Taste, and Smell

Touch sensitivity and heat sensitivity appear to be among the first sensory modalities to emerge during the course of fetal development (Hall & Oppenheim, 1987). This can be demonstrated through the reflexes of the infant, which show the ability to feel and to localize touch stimuli immediately after birth. For instance, there is the rooting response, in which an infant will reflexively turn its head in the direction of a touch to the cheek. This response helps the infant to locate its mother's breast for nursing. Demonstration Box 16-3 shows you how to elicit this directional response.

There has been a widespread belief among many clinicians and other investigators that because the cortex is not fully developed in the neonate, infants do not experience pain as severely as do adults, nor is its impact believed to persist as long (e.g., Eland & Anderson, 1977). This has led to the practice of giving little treatment for pain to infants, even during or after major medical procedures and operations (see Liebeskind & Melzack, 1987; Owens, 1984). However, recent evidence (Craig & Hadjistavropoulos, 1994; Grunau & Craig, 1987; Hadjistavropoulos & Craig, 1994) suggests that this belief is wrong. Infants appear to be just as susceptible to the perception of pain as adults are and express it in similar ways in their facial muscle patterns.

DEMONSTRATION BOX 16-3
The Rooting Response

The easiest method to show tactile sensitivity and localization in infants is to elicit the reflex called the *rooting response*. To see how early this response exists, a very young baby of less than 2 months of age should be used (although the response can be elicited in older infants). To demonstrate tactile localization ability, you should stroke the infant's cheek lightly with your finger. If you stroke the right cheek, the infant should turn to the right. If you stroke the left cheek, the infant should turn to the left.

Taste receptors start to form early in fetal life and are apparent as early as 13 weeks after conception (Bradley & Stern, 1967). In general, then, neonates appear to be as well equipped with taste receptors as are adults. However, they respond to the taste primaries differently (Crook, 1987). Using sucking responses as an indicator, Lipsett (1977) found a preference for sweet stimuli in newborns. Even small differences in the concentration of sweetness produce differences in neonatal reactions. However, infants less than about 4 months of age seem to be insensitive to the taste of salt (Beauchamp & Cowart, 1985). And only strong concentrations of sour and bitter stimuli elicit facial expressions of disgust in young infants (Ganchrow, Steiner, & Daher, 1983).

Much work on infant olfactory ability has involved presenting newborns with cotton swabs saturated with various smell stimuli. A swab is placed under a newborn's nose, and responses such as heart rate, respiration, and general bodily activity are monitored using a polygraph (Engen, Lipsett, & Kaye, 1963). These studies have shown that infants can detect a number of strong odorants, such as anise oil, asafoetida (rotten smell), alcohol, and vinegar. Moreover, even newborn infants turn away from noxious odors and toward pleasant ones (Rieser, Yonas, & Wikner, 1976). This turning response has been used to show that infants respond to odorants of human body origin. Infants less than 2 weeks old will orient toward an object carrying their mother's scent, such as a breast pad (Cernoch & Porter, 1985; Russell, 1976). There is even the suggestion that, in contrast to some of the limitations on infant sensory capacities, children actually may be more responsive than adults to human body odors (Filsinger & Fabes, 1985).

PERCEPTUAL CHANGE THROUGH CHILDHOOD

Throughout childhood there is a general improvement in perceptual discrimination, identification, and information processing. Many of these improvements occur fairly rapidly within the first year or two of life, whereas others continue over much longer time spans. The most dramatic improvements seem to occur at around the age of 2–3 months (Atkinson & Braddick, 1981; Maurer & Lewis, 1979), when there is a sudden improvement in the infant's visual abilities. Acuity increases markedly (Braddick & Atkinson, 1979; Courage & Adams, 1990), tracking behavior becomes more adult-like (Atkinson, 1979), the ability to recognize individual elements surrounded by an enclosing contour appears (Milewski, 1976), and infants begin to show more adult-like eye-movement patterns when viewing figures (Hainline, 1978). By 3 to 4 months of age stereoscopic depth perception appears (Shea, Fox, Aslin, & Dumais, 1980), and this ability continues to improve over the first 2 years (Fox, Aslin, Shea, & Dumais, 1980; Held, 1985). Although the most rapid period of improvement in the ability to discriminate depth based on binocular disparity seems to have been completed by about 30 months of age (Ciner, Schanel-Klitsch, & Scheiman, 1991), binocular depth perception seems to improve throughout childhood and into early adolescence (Romano, Romano, & Puklin, 1975).

Other basic visual processes also seem to develop rapidly over the first 2 years. Thus, visual acuity, which is originally quite poor, improves steadily into early childhood (Gwiazda, Brill, Mohindra, & Held, 1980), and early astigmatic problems (lens flattening), which lower visual resolution in infants, also disappear (Atkinson, Braddick, & French, 1979; Ingram & Barr, 1979). By 5 years of age children seem to have fully developed scotopic and photopic visual systems, which show adaptation effects and sensitivities equivalent to those of adults.

A similar pattern is found for the other senses. Consider hearing as an example. Infants begin with a substantial low-frequency hearing deficit and a lesser high-frequency deficit. Over the first 2 years hearing improves quickly, especially for the low frequencies, and the improvement then continues more gradually until about 10 years of age (Kuhl, 1987; Trehub et al., 1980; Yoneshige & Elliott, 1981).

Eye Movements and Attention

In addition to changes in basic sensory processes, there appear to be changes in the patterns of attention and information encoding, which appear as developmental changes in perception. Theorists such as Hochberg (1981, 1982) have suggested that the way information is integrated over time changes as the child develops. The notion of **integration** involves the child's constructing mental models (like pictures or images), called **schemata**, to help make sense of the perceptual information available in a given situation. In addition, integration involves the child's selecting new information from the perceptual array through the process of **encoding**. After it is encoded, information has been modified into a form suitable for remembering. In this form it can be compared to other new information as well as to information from the existing schemata. Simply put, this means that attention and memory are playing a major role in the perceptual process.

As we learned in Chapter 15, one of the ways by which we can observe the pattern of overt attention is by monitoring eye movements. Developmental theorists, such as Piaget (1969), have argued that patterns of eye movements provide some clues as to which stimuli are being selected and compared by individuals of different ages. For instance, we know that adults display a strong tendency to look at forms that are informative, unusual, or of particular functional value (Antes, 1974; Friedman & Liebelt, 1981; Loftus & Mackworth, 1978). Thus, by monitoring eye-movement patterns in children, we can observe the **search** component of visual attention. Information about search should be helpful in determining how children are viewing, and hence constructing, their visual world.

We have already seen that infants from birth to 2 months of age do make a variety of eye movements (such as fixating stationary stimuli, tracking moving stimuli, or moving their eyes toward stimuli in the periphery of the visual field), although not as precisely as adults do. More important, they often do not move their eyes to the most informative parts of the stimulus (at least by adult standards) but, rather, seem to view only limited parts of the stimulus, usually around a border or corner (Day, 1975; Mackworth & Bruner, 1970). For instance, when there is a distinct contour within the visual field of an infant, its eye is drawn toward it. Infants of around 1 month of age tend to direct their eyes toward one distinctive feature of a visual stimulus, such as the corner of a triangle (Bronson, 1990; Haith, Bergman, & Moore, 1977). Their eyes seem to be "captured" by the feature because

they dwell on it for prolonged periods (Salapatek & Kessen, 1973). Because the gaze of a 1-month-old infant is caught by the first contour encountered, most of the viewing time is spent focused on the external contours of a form. If the stimulus has internal features, they are ignored or missed. This changes by the age of 2 months. Now the infant scans the contours a little more, and shorter periods are spent on each feature (Banks & Salapatek, 1983; Hainline, 1978; Salapatek, 1975). In addition, the 2-month-old dwells almost exclusively on the internal features of the stimulus, seemingly ignoring the overall pattern. These differences are shown in Figure 16-10. If the stimulus is unstable, however (such as when it is flickering), the eye movements seem to revert back to patterns typical of younger ages (Bronson, 1990).

The eye-movement patterns of 3- and 4-year-olds are similar to those of 2-month-olds. Children

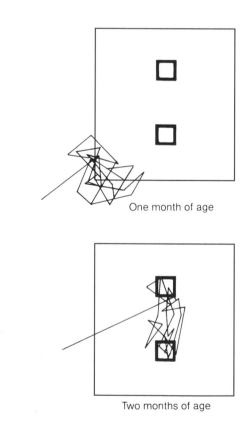

One month of age

Two months of age

FIGURE 16-10 Eye movements typical of 1- and 2-month-old infants.

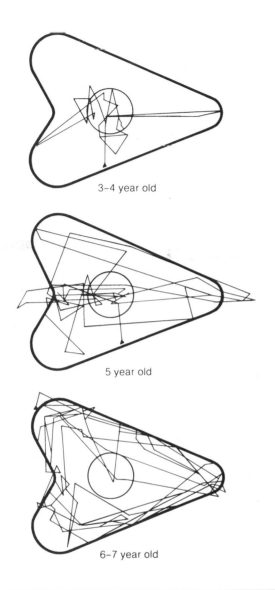

3–4 year old

5 year old

6–7 year old

FIGURE 16-11 Changes in eye movements from ages 3 to 7. (From Zaporozhets, 1965. Copyright The Society for Research in Child Development, Inc.)

of this age spend most of their time dwelling on the internal details of a figure, with only an occasional eye movement beyond the contour boundary. The 4- or 5-year-old child begins to make eye-movement excursions toward the surrounding contour. At 6 and 7 years of age, there is a systematic scan of the outer portions of the stimulus with occasional eye movements into the interior. This development is shown in Figure 16-11 (Zaporozhets, 1965).

Eye-movement patterns have important consequences for certain perceptual discrimination tasks. Vurpillot (1968) monitored the eye movements of children between the ages of 2 and 9 years. They were presented with pictures of houses with different kinds of windows and were asked to indicate whether or not the houses appeared to be the same, a task that required systematic comparison of the windows. She found that the youngest children did not conduct a systematic search. Rather, they often continued searching through the houses even after looking at two windows that were quite different. This lack of systematic viewing was accompanied by a low degree of accuracy in the discrimination judgments of the younger children. Older children, with more regular and systematic viewing patterns, were much more accurate. Similarly, Cohen (1981) found in a figure matching task that 5- and 8-year-old children take longer to decide where to move their eyes than adults do in the same task. In addition, they make more eye movements and are less likely than adults are to look directly at the matching target in their first eye movements. It is likely that these differences reflect differences in strategies of attention and information pickup, rather than differences in visual capacity because eye movements seem to be strongly affected by task demands, meaning, context, and expectations (Antes & Penland, 1981; Findlay, 1981; Stark & Ellis, 1981).

Such differences in observing strategy may explain why as a child becomes older there is a gradual change in the way it comes to view patterns and the elements that make them up (Elkind, 1978). For instance, consider Figure 16-12. It consists of several objects (fruits and vegetables) that are organized into a larger figure (a bird). Children 4 and 5 years old report seeing only the parts ("carrots and a pear and an orange"). By the age of 7, children report seeing both the parts and the global organization ("fruits and carrots and a bird"). By 8 or 9 years of age, most children show awareness of the relation between the parts and the global organization ("a bird made of fruits and vegetables").

Orienting and Filtering

Attention involves more than simply searching for targets and scanning the environment with eye

FIGURE 16-12 A vegetable-fruit-bird figure used to measure part-versus-whole perception in children.

movements. Several of these other aspects have also been shown to change systematically with age (Enns, 1990a; Enns & Cameron, 1987). For instance, the aspect we called covert orienting in Chapter 15 (a shift in attention without accompanying physical movement of the eye) shows changes with age for both *direct* and *information* cues. It is possible to measure covert orienting in response to a stimulus that suddenly appears in the visual periphery in children as young as 3 and 4 years of age (Enns, 1990a). However, when this ability has been studied systematically in 6- to 7-year-olds, it is still apparent that these children do not shift their visual attention as efficiently as adults do (Akhtar & Enns, 1989; Brodeur & Enns, 1997; Enns & Brodeur, 1989). Even larger developmental differences can be seen when attention must be reoriented voluntarily by a child in response to an information cue. Children as old as 11 years of age require more time than adults do to shift their attention between information from two visual locations (Pearson & Lane, 1991b) or to shift between their information pickup between the two ears (Pearson & Lane, 1991a).

Selective attention also involves the component we called filtering in Chapter 15. This refers to the ability to ignore irrelevant stimuli in the environment while more task-relevant stimuli are being processed. A number of studies have shown that children are more easily distracted by irrelevant stimuli (e.g., Day & Stone, 1980). Thus, in a card-sorting task where information from the patterns on each card is used to determine which pile it will be placed in, both children and adults show poorer performance if there are irrelevant as well as relevant features present in the patterns on the cards; however, children show a much greater reduction in efficiency than adults do (Well, Lorch, & Anderson, 1980).

There is an interesting set of phenomena that may show age changes in stimulus filtering more graphically. These are responses to visual-geometric illusions, which are simple line drawings in which the actual size, shape, or direction of some elements differs from the perceived size, shape, or direction (see Coren & Girgus, 1978). We have already encountered some of these illusions in Chapters 1 and 14; two of them are shown in Figure 16-13. Figure 16-13A shows the **Mueller-Lyer illusion,** in which the line marked *x* appears to be longer than the line marked *y*. Figure 16-13B shows the **Ponzo illusion,** in which the line marked *w* appears to be longer than the line marked *z*. This is the case in spite of the fact that *x* and *y* are physically equal in length, and *w* and *z* are also physically equal to each other.

One explanation for certain visual-geometric illusions is that the lines that induce the illusion become confused with the test lines, thus causing the distortion (Coren & Girgus, 1978). For instance, in the Mueller-Lyer illusion (Figure 16-13A), the upper figure *is* longer if you measure from wing tip to wing tip. Thus, confusing the wings with the horizontal line might add to the distortion. This explanation is supported by the fact that focusing attention on the lines, and ignoring the wings, reduces the strength of the illusion (Coren & Girgus, 1972b), whereas directing attention to certain parts of a figure can produce illusions (Coren & Porac, 1983a). If we accept this explanation and if children are poorer at filtering out extraneous stimuli, then we should expect that children will show stronger visual illusions than will adults. In general, we do find that visual illusions are stronger for children and decrease with age, suggesting that children are less able to ignore the inducing lines when making their judgments (Coren & Girgus, 1978; Enns & Girgus, 1985; Pick & Pick, 1970). In one study,

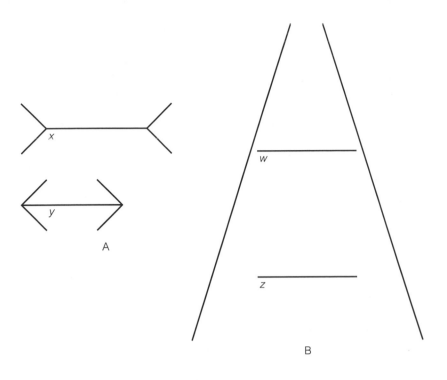

FIGURE 16-13   Two illusions that show age-related differences in their perception: (A) the Mueller-Lyer; (B) the Ponzo.

illusion magnitude was found to decrease until about the age of 25 years, after which it didn't change further (Porac & Coren, 1981).

Encoding and Memory

Another factor that can affect perceptual development is the change in encoding ability. For a child to integrate and compare stimuli, he or she must first have the ability to register the information obtained in a glance, as well as the ability to remember information from other glances and the schemata associated with a particular class of stimuli. Thus, it is not surprising that a number of studies have shown that the ability to discriminate between visual patterns improves with age (e.g., Cratty, 1979).

Studies that have directly compared the ability of children to encode versus to remember visual stimuli indicate that the largest developmental changes lie in the memory component. For in-stance, when children are presented with a brief (100 ms) visual display of eight items arranged in an imaginary circle, they can report the identity of the items with adult-like accuracy under some conditions (Morrison, Holmes, & Haith, 1974; Sheingold, 1973). Specifically, this is possible when a stimulus marker, indicating the item to be reported, appears within 50–200 ms of the onset of the display. When the delay between the display and the marker is longer than 200 ms, the children's accuracy is worse than adults'. This suggests that children are different from adults mainly in the memory processes associated with object identification, not in the initial stimulus encoding processes. Other studies have come to this same conclusion by varying the spatial and temporal distance between pieces of information that must be integrated before a response can be made (Enns & Girgus, 1986; Enns & King, 1990) and by varying the degree of symmetry in patterns that must be encoded only versus those that must be both encoded and remembered (Enns, 1987).

An interesting example of how pattern discrimination improves with age can be seen in the recognition of human faces. The impressive achievements we noted earlier for 5- to 7-month-old infants in discriminating face from nonface stimuli should not be interpreted to mean that these infants have full adult abilities in this area. The development of the ability to recognize faces continues for many years (Carey, 1981; Flin, 1980). For example, a dramatic increase in the ability of children to recognize unfamiliar faces occurs between the ages of 6 and 10 years. Under conditions where a 6-year-old will recognize about 60% of the faces previously shown her, a 10-year-old will recognize nearly all of them (95%). Furthermore, improvement in ability can be observed even through adolescence to the age of 16 (Carey, Diamond, & Woods, 1980).

There is one form of pattern discrimination error that seems to be characteristic of young children. This involves mirror reversals. Children confuse lateral mirror-image pairs (such as *p* and *q* or *b* and *d*) more frequently than up-down mirror-image pairs (such as *p* and *b* or *q* and *d*; Springer & Deutsch, 1985). These confusions are quite common in young children (around 3–4 years old) and gradually decrease until about the age of 10 or 11 (Gaddes, 1985; Serpell, 1971). Some of the improvement seems to be associated with educational processes because between the ages of 5½ and 6½ there is a sudden increase in the ability to make these discriminations. It is likely that the improvement is caused by the formal instruction in reading and writing that usually begins at about that age. With appropriate training, kindergarten-aged children can learn the lateral discrimination quite well, although it still seems to be more difficult than the up-down discrimination (Clark & Whitehurst, 1974).

When a child continues to have difficulties with left-right confusions, he can experience problems with reading. The specific term used for such reading disability (when it is not associated with other disturbances, such as mental retardation, sensory impairment, or emotional problems) is **dyslexia**. Estimates of the incidence of dyslexia vary widely, but it seems that the problem affects no less than 2% of all children in Western countries, with the incidence perhaps being as high as 10% (Bannatyne, 1971; Gaddes, 1985; Spreen,

1976). This problem seems to have a perceptual rather than an intellectual basis. A dyslexic individual may be highly talented in many other respects. There are many case histories of exceptional people who have been dyslexic, among them the inventor Thomas A. Edison, the surgeon Harvey Gushing, the sculptor Auguste Rodin, President Woodrow Wilson, and the author Hans Christian Andersen. One characteristic of all children who have been diagnosed as dyslexic is that they show confusions between the left-right mirror images of targets, although they have no problem with up-down mirror images (Gaddes, 1985; Newland, 1972; Sidman & Kirk, 1974).

Children's inability to discriminate letter reversals suggests that they are relatively insensitive to the orientation of a stimulus. There is an interesting phenomenon associated with this issue. Consider a stimulus, such as a human face, that has a familiar orientation. When a face is inverted it seems to lose much of its facelike quality, and even very familiar individuals are difficult to recognize when their photographs are turned upside down (Rock, 1973). Thus, it is not surprising to find that adult observers, who have had thousands of exposures to upright faces, show greater accuracy in identifying faces when the faces are upright than when they are inverted (Yin, 1970). However, the ability of 6-year-olds to identify faces is about the same regardless of whether the faces are presented in a normal or in an inverted position. By the age of 10 years, children's ability to identify faces is disrupted when the faces are inverted (Carey & Diamond, 1977; Carey, Diamond, & Woods, 1980). It seems that adults' sensitivity to orientation differences makes it more difficult for them to identify inverted familiar faces than for 6-year-olds tested on the same task. You can explore the adult sensitivity to orientation yourself by trying Demonstration Box 16-4.

The Other Senses

As for visual abilities of children, care must be taken in studying the other senses to separate developmental changes in the early perceptual registration process from changes in the conceptual processes that are important in perception. One study of odor perception examined both odor sensitivity and odor identification in children 8 to 14

DEMONSTRATION BOX 16-4
Orientation and Stimulus Recognition

Adults are more rigid in their reliance on normal orientations than are children. Look at the two figures here, and you will probably find them quite difficult to identify, but if you invert the page you will see them suddenly become identifiable. This effect is especially striking for faces and for handwritten script.

A   B

---

years of age (Cain & Stevens, 1995). Although children and young adults were equally able to discriminate various odors, the children performed poorly in being able to name the odors. This was true even though naming the same objects on the basis of visual cues was equally accurate at all ages. It therefore appears that the learning of associations between odors and specific objects is the aspect of odor perception that is slow to develop in childhood. An interesting aside is that adults are quite accurate in identifying the degree of pleasantness versus unpleasantness in odors simply by viewing videotapes of the faces of children who have been exposed to the odors (Soussignan & Schall, 1996).

PERCEPTUAL CHANGE IN ADULTS

Perceptual and sensory functions continue to change throughout the life span, although the rate of change is usually slower during adulthood than during infancy and childhood. Also, the earlier changes are toward increased efficiency in perceptual processing, whereas the later changes, beginning around age 40, are toward decreased functioning, as sensory receptors age and neural efficiency drops (Corso, 1981; Werner, Peterzell, & Scheetz, 1990).

Visual Function and Aging

We have all seen individuals who, on reaching their mid- to late 40s, suddenly begin to wear reading glasses or bifocals in order to see the details of objects within arm's reach. This reduction in the accommodative range of the eye is called **presbyopia** and was discussed in Chapter 3. However, there are a number of other, less obvious, changes that occur in aging individuals that reduce their visual sensitivity. For instance, the aged eye generally has a smaller pupil size; hence less light enters the eye (Corso, 1981; Weale, 1982). The optics of the eye also become less efficient with

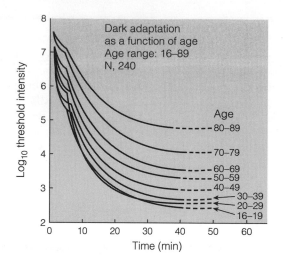

FIGURE 16-14 Age changes in dark adaptation (from McFarland et al., 1960).

increasing age because the crystalline lens continues to become yellower and darker (Coren, 1987; Coren & Girgus, 1972a), and the cornea yellows somewhat (Lerman, 1984). Of course, we would expect a decrease in sensitivity because of the resulting decrease in the amount of light reaching the retina. Between 20 and 70 years of age, we find a consistent increase in threshold sensitivities for the detection of spots of light (Fozard, Wolf, Bell, McFarland, & Podolsky, 1977). This is particularly evident in dark adaptation. Although the time to reach minimum threshold remains the same, the maximum sensitivity eventually achieved decreases with age. This is shown in Figure 16-14 (McFarland, Domey, Warren, & Ward, 1960).

Many studies have shown that visual acuity decreases with age; at age 40 nearly 94% of individuals have 20/20 visual acuity or better, whereas by age 80 only 6% have this level of acuity (Richards, 1977; Weale, 1986; Woo & Bader, 1978). The relationship between age and visual acuity can be seen in Figure 16-15.

The pattern of the acuity loss with age is quite interesting. Elder observers are still able to resolve visual details; however, the light level necessary for them to do so is greatly increased. In terms of our discussion in Chapter 4, we would say that the contrast threshold is higher for the elder observers (Crassini, Brown, & Bowman, 1988; Leibowitz,

Post, & Ginsburg, 1980). Furthermore, it appears that the neural system that processes depth and movement information (remember the *magnocellular* pathway discussed in Chapter 3) shows the greatest loss of sensitivity (Sekuler & Hutman, 1980). These findings suggest that in tasks such as night driving—where good acuity and responses to relatively fast moving stimuli are required, yet illumination conditions are low—elder individuals might be quite inefficient and may even be at risk.

Some deterioration of vision in the elderly may be due to a progressive decrease in the number of functioning rods and cones in the retina (Werner et al., 1990). For example, loss of cones sensitive to short-wavelength light may account for the gradual deterioration in color vision with age (Knoblauch et al., 1987). Sensitivity to the shorter wavelengths of light (those that appear bluish) continually diminishes from early childhood until death (Bornstein, 1977; Lakowski, 1962).

How do healthy elder adults perform on the standard tests used to assess aspects of attention? On tests of covert orienting, filtering, and rapid enumeration, they often perform in a very similar way to college-age adults (D'Aloisio & Klein, 1990; Nissen & Corkin, 1985; Plude & Hoyer, 1986; Trick, Enns, & Brodeur, 1996). Like the children we discussed earlier, they tend to diverge from the performance of college-age adults on orienting tasks that involve informational cues. As long as the situation involves automatic, involuntary shifts, such as when a target suddenly appears in the visual field, attention shifts are quite efficient (Madden, 1986). However, if the cue is informational only, thus requiring a voluntary effort to reorient attention, it appears that shifts in visual orientation can be quite slow for elderly adults (Hartley, Keiley, & Slabach, 1990; Madden, 1983; Nissen & Corkin, 1985). On tests of visual filtering, elderly observers also perform similarly to college-age observers (D'Aloisio & Klein, 1990), as long as there is no uncertainty about where the to-be-identified target will appear (Plude & Hoyer, 1986) and stimuli are not presented too far into the visual periphery (Ceralla, 1985). Under these more taxing conditions performance drops in the elderly.

The attentional aspect in which elder adults do show a consistent and substantial performance difference from younger adults is that of visual search (D'Aloisio & Klein, 1990; Plude, 1990; Rabbitt,

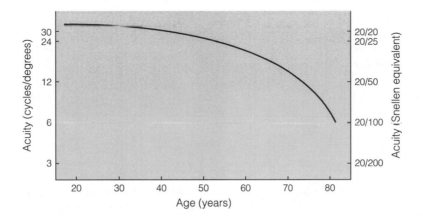

FIGURE 16-15   Age-related decrease in visual acuity.

1965). We discussed several examples of such tasks in Chapter 15, all of which involve scanning for the presence of a particular target stimulus. One possible explanation for this result is that the visual field of elder observers might be smaller because of loss of acuity in the periphery of the retina, where there are fewer receptors. Although this is certainly true at the farthest edges of the visual field, within approximately 70° on either side of the center of gaze peripheral the acuity variation with age is not as pronounced (Burg, 1968; Scialfa, 1990). Because all visual search tasks involve displays that fall well within this range, the loss in peripheral acuity would not seem to be the major cause of the poorer performance. An additional fact—which seems to argue against the decreased search efficiency arising from contracting of the visual field due to acuity losses in the periphery with age—is the finding that elder subjects do not appear to have any difficulty identifying or counting isolated stimuli in the peripheral visual field (Ceralla, 1985; Sekuler & Ball, 1986; Trick, Enns, & Brodeur, 1996).

Another possible explanation for poorer search performance with age is that elder observers are slower in moving their eyes across the various items in the display. However, this possibility can be eliminated when one considers that the difference in search speeds between elder and younger adults remains even after eye movements are not a factor, such as in briefly flashed stimulus presentations (D'Aloisio & Klein, 1990).

In order to distinguish these attentional aging effects from the receptor-related and muscular effects we have already discussed, some researchers refer to the useful field of view (or simply **UFOV**) in their descriptions of aging (Ball, Roenker, & Bruni, 1990; Sanders, 1970). The UFOV is defined simply as the area of the visual field that is functional for an observer at a given time and for a given task. Thus, for the tasks involving the detection of bright light flashes and the identification of briefly presented targets, we can say that the UFOV does not differ a great deal between younger and elder adults. In contrast, for the task of finding a specific target amidst many distracters, the UFOV is much smaller for older observers. It is of interest, then, that studies looking for relations between traffic accident records and the UFOV indicate that there is no relation between the two when the UFOV is measured with tasks involving simple detection and identification (Allen, 1970; Shinar, 1977). However, there is a significant relation between the number of traffic accidents that people have and the size of their UFOV when it is measured in a situation where they must identify targets in the presence of visual distracters (Avolio, Kroeck, & Panek, 1986).

Age Effects on the Other Senses

Hearing ability declines with age. Generally speaking, hearing impairments begin to appear during middle age and occur with increasing frequency after age 60. About 15% of all people over 65 could be classified as hearing impaired, and as many as 75% of all 70-year-olds have some hearing problems (Schaie & Geiwitz, 1982). The loss of hearing ability is much more marked for high-frequency stimuli (Corso, 1981). As can be seen from Figure 16-16, at age 70 there is still very little decrease in threshold sensitivity for a 1,000-Hz tone, but for an 8,000-Hz tone there is a reduction in threshold sensitivity of nearly 50 dB. The most handicapping aspect of hearing loss in the elderly is the inability to recognize speech, and the amount of loss of speech recognition can be directly predicted from the losses in pure tone hearing sensitivity (e.g., Coren & Hakstian, 1994). In terms of overall hearing ability, a loss of sensitivity of 25 dB represents a *slight hearing handicap*. This will produce a small but measurable effect on behavior, particularly with faint speech. At 55 dB of hearing loss, we have *marked hearing handicap*, where the individual has difficulty understanding loud speech. This level corresponds to a 45% hearing loss for speech range sounds.

It is possible to estimate a person's hearing sensitivity without using any audiometric equipment. This is done by simply asking people about their everyday experiences with sounds in the world. Because we normally use both ears, and our ability to hear a sound will depend on the ear with the better sensitivity, such an estimate will really be of our "better ear" sensitivity. Coren and Hakstian (1992) developed such a hearing screening inventory that correlates 0.81 with laboratory measures of pure tone hearing thresholds in the better ear. You can test yourself with it, using Demonstration Box 16-5. Using yourself, some friends, and some older family members such as your parents or grandparents, you can easily observe the age-related deterioration in hearing (and also get a good idea of your own hearing sensitivity at the moment).

Absolute sensitivity in other modalities also decreases with advancing age. For example, detection thresholds for vibrating stimuli applied to the hand increase quite steadily with age, indicating a reduced touch sensitivity (Gesheider & Bolanowski, 1994; Thornbury & Mistretta, 1981). This reduction becomes even greater after 65 years of age and seems to be substantially greater in the signals carried by the Pacinian corpuscles than in the NP I or NP II fibers (see Chapter 8 on touch). Further, although elder observers show lower sensitivity to touch, the decrease in their sensitivity to pain is not as great (Harkins & Chapman, 1977).

Some of the most noticeable changes with age occur in the realms of taste and smell. Odor sensitivity is greatly diminished, although the reduction is not uniform across all stimuli or individuals (Cain & Stevens, 1989). For instance, elderly subjects seem best able to discriminate among fruity odors, as compared to other classes of scents (Schiffman

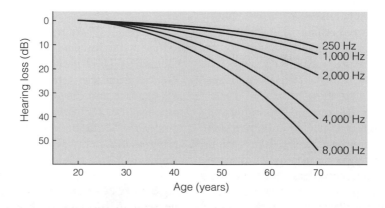

FIGURE 16-16   The age-related decrease in auditory sensitivity is particularly noticeable for the high frequencies.

DEMONSTRATION BOX 16-5
Hearing Screening Inventory

It is easy to get an estimate of your own better ear hearing sensitivity using this test, which is called the *Hearing Screening Inventory* (Coren & Hakstian, 1992). The inventory deals with a number of common situations. For the first eight items, you should select the response that best describes you and your behaviors from among these response alternatives: Never (or almost never), Seldom, Occasionally, Frequently, Always (or almost always). Simply circle the letter that corresponds to the first letter of your choice. (If you normally use a hearing aid, answer as if you were not wearing it.)

1. Are you ever bothered by feelings that your hearing is poor?   N S O F A
2. Is your reading or studying easily interrupted by noises in nearby rooms?   N S O F A
3. Can you hear the telephone ring when you are in the same room in which it is located?   N S O F A
4. Can you hear the telephone ring when you are in the room next door?   N S O F A
5. Do you find it difficult to make out the words in recordings of popular songs?   N S O F A
6. When several people are talking in a room, do you have difficulty hearing an individual conversation?   N S O F A
7. Can you hear the water boiling in a pot when you are in the kitchen?   N S O F A
8. Can you follow the conversation when you are at a large dinner table?   N S O F A

For the remaining four items answer using these response alternatives: Good, Average, Slightly below average, Poor, or Very poor. Again, simply circle the letter that corresponds to the first letter of your choice.

9. Overall I would judge my hearing in my *right* ear to be   G A S P V
10. Overall I would judge my hearing in my *left* ear to be   G A S P V
11. Overall I would judge my ability to make out speech or conversations to be   G A S P V
12. Overall I would judge my ability to judge the location of things by the sound they are making alone to be   G A S P V

Scoring instructions:

Items 1, 5, and 6 are scored 1 for "Never," 2 for "Seldom," 3 for "Occasionally," 4 for "Frequently," and 5 for "Always." Items 2, 3, 4, 7, and 8 are reverse scored, with 1 for "Always" up to 5 for "Never." For Items 9 through 12, scoring goes from 1 for "Good" to 5 for "Very poor." Your hearing sensitivity score is simply the sum of the 12 responses.

The higher the score, the poorer the hearing is in the better ear. A score of 27 or higher indicates a slight hearing handicap with 25 dB or more of hearing loss. A score of 37 or higher indicates a marked hearing handicap with a loss of 55 dB or more in the better ear. Now that you have your own scores, and maybe those of a couple of friends, give this test to some older relatives or acquaintances. In general, the older the individual, the higher the score that you will get, with some of the older individuals perhaps showing even marked hearing loss with scores of 37 or more.

& Pasternak, 1979). However, they adapt more quickly than younger adults to a particular odor and, once adapted, require considerably more time to return to their original level of sensitivity (Stevens, Cain, & Oatley, 1989; Stevens, Cain, Shiet, & Oatley, 1989). Odor memory also shows large age differences in adulthood. In one study many of the younger adults tested were able to recognize odors they had smelled one week earlier, whereas many of the elder adults failed to recognize such odors only several minutes after the initial exposure (Stevens, Cain, & Demarque, 1990).

A diminished sensitivity to some tastes can also be seen in the elderly. For instance, thresholds for the taste primaries of both salt and sugar rise measurably, although not dramatically, with age

Table 16-2 The Percentage of 20-Year-Olds Versus the Percentage of Elderly Individuals (Mean Age of 73 Years) Correctly Identifying Some Common Foods in Pureed Form (Based on Schiffman, 1977)

FOOD	20-YEAR-OLDS	ELDERLY
Apple	81	55
Lemon	52	24
Strawberry	78	33
Broccoli	30	0
Carrot	63	7
Corn	67	38
Beef	41	28
Coffee	89	70
Sugar	63	57

(Grzegorczyk, Jones, & Mistretta, 1979; Moore, Nielson, & Mistretta, 1982). Recovery from adaptation to these tastes is also slowed (Stevens & Wellen, 1989). This diminished sensitivity to odor and taste in the elderly can reduce their ability to identify foods, especially when blended or pureed so that they are not identifiable by sight or texture in the mouth (Cain, Reid, & Stevens, 1990; Schiffman, 1977; Stevens, Cain, Demarque, & Ruthruff, 1991). This has the potential of putting the elderly at risk for ingesting dangerous substances and overlooking important ingredients in their diet. Just how large a deficit is experienced by the elderly can be seen by comparing the performance of a group of 20-year-olds at identifying foods by taste and smell alone with a group of adults whose average age is 73 years. As can be seen in Table 16-2, in most instances the younger individuals do twice as well as the elderly, although on some common items, such as coffee, performance is about the same for both age groups.

Global Changes in Perceptual Performance

At least three types of change seem to affect all of the sensory modalities. The most important of these is a general slowing of neural responses, accompanied by an increasing persistence of the stimulus (actually slower recovery or clearing time) in the neural representation (Salthouse, 1985, 1996a, b). This means that elder individuals have more trouble with briefly presented stimuli (Hoyer & Plude, 1980), show slower reaction times to stimulus onsets (Stern, Oster, & Newport, 1980), have more difficulty identifying stimuli arriving in a rapid sequence (Birren, Woods, & Williams, 1980), and retrieve information more slowly from memory (Salthouse & Kail, 1983). This slowing of processing in the elderly individual becomes most apparent when the perceptual tasks are complex (Cerella, Poon, & Williams, 1980; Cunningham, 1980).

A second general change that accompanies aging involves control over the information that enters and is sustained in short-term or working memory (Hasher & Zacks, 1988). Because many theorists see working memory as being the mechanism for consciousness, having a reduced ability to guide and control these contents can have serious effects on perception. One of the more noticeable effects of aging on everyday behavior is a reduced ability to prevent nonrelevant material from being processed (Hasher & Quig, 1997). For instance, elderly people are more likely to engage in sudden switches in conversation (Gold, Andres, Arbuckle, & Schwartzman, 1988), they momentarily activate a broader range of ideas in processing a sentence (Hamm & Hasher, 1992; Stolzfus, 1992), and the activation of an idea often persists much longer for them than for younger adults after the idea has served its purpose (Hamm & Hasher, 1992; Hartman & Hasher, 1991). In tasks involving visual perception, this failure to control the contents of working memory reveals itself as a failure to suppress or ignore distracter items that are irrelevant to the task (Carlson & Hasher, 1995; Connelly & Hasher, 1993; Hasher & Quig, 1997).

A third general change that accompanies aging involves the distribution of attention to perceptual tasks (Botwinick, 1984). Much of this can be traced to the idea that a fixed amount of attentional resources can be divided among various tasks (see Chapter 15 and Kahneman, 1973). Elder individuals seem to have more difficulty dividing their attention between various stimuli or input channels (Craik & Simon, 1980). In addition, they seem to have more difficulty filtering or extracting relevant from irrelevant targets in search or recognition tasks (Rabbitt, 1977; Wright & Elias, 1979). The more similar the irrelevant stimuli are to the target stimuli, the greater the difficulty all observers have in detecting targets in a search task. However, elderly observers have their performance disrupted at levels of difficulty that do not seem to affect younger observers (Farkas & Hoyer, 1980).

CHAPTER SUMMARY

The **life span developmental approach,** which assumes knowledge of a person's chronological age will allow us to predict many aspects of perceptual behavior, and the **perceptual learning approach,** which assumes interactions with the world can shape a person's percepts, both have tried to explain perceptual development. Physiologically, the sensory systems of newborns contain both adultlike and immature response patterns because different components mature at different rates. Following an initial rapid growth of interconnections between neurons in sensory processing regions of the brain, **neuronal pruning** occurs. Many interconnections are then lost as cells are tuned for specific specialized information-processing tasks.

Measuring the perceptual abilities of infants is often difficult. **Visually evoked potentials** have been used to show rapid maturing of regions of the visual areas of the brain during the first year. **Preferential looking, forced-choice preferential looking,** and **habituation** techniques have been used to assess pattern perception in infants. **Saccadic eye movements** in infants are imprecise and slow, and looking at a distant target may require several short movements before it is reached. These movements are most consistent to objects in the **temporal visual field** and are often disrupted when there is "competition" due to more than one salient target in the field. **Smooth pursuit eye movements** do not even appear until 8 to 10 weeks of age. After they are present **optokinetic nystagmus** can be used to measure visual acuity and brightness perception. Visual acuity in infants is quite poor (20/800), and the accommodation of the lens is fixed at a distance of about 20 cm. Acuity steadily improves over the first 7 years of life. Light sensitivity of adults is 50 times better than that of 1-month-old children. Although infants have color vision, their ability to see short wavelengths of light is poor. Infants can discriminate size, location, and even symmetry from patterns. By age 2 months they can recognize human facelike stimuli. Most visual abilities show a marked improvement after 2 to 3 months.

The auditory thresholds of infants are much higher than those of adults. Infants can localize sounds from birth; however, young infants use only the intensity difference cue, not time differences, to do this. Infants also use **auditory grouping** to organize streams of sounds, much as adults do. Touch localization is present from birth, as demonstrated by the **rooting response.** Taste receptors are fully functional in infants, and they show a strong preference for sweet tastes. Infants may have an acute sense of smell, and infants less than 2 weeks of age will turn toward objects carrying their mother's scent.

Through childhood infants use **integration** processes to construct **schemata,** which will help in **encoding** perceptual information. Young infants' eye movements are captured by the first contour they encounter; from 2 months to about 4 years, children will dwell on internal details in the pattern, and systematic scanning of contours may not appear until 6 to 7 years of age. Visual searching and viewing strategies also change throughout childhood, moving from concentration on component elements to more global perception. **Covert orienting** of attention appears between 3 to 4 years of age. Children are not good at **filtering** out irrelevant stimuli, which may account for their strong susceptibility to **visual-geometric illusions** such as the **Ponzo illusion** and the **Mueller-Lyer illusion.** Children also have difficulty encoding perceptual information, which can cause mirror image confusions (e.g., *b* versus *d*); if the difficulty persists it can lead to reading difficulties such as **dyslexia.**

As part of the aging process adults begin to show sensory losses. Visual acuity decreases such that only 6% of the population has 20/20 vision at age 80. With a loss in near accommodative ability of the lens, older people develop **presbyopia.** Threshold sensitivities for light and movement increase, and color discrimination (especially for the short wavelengths) diminishes. Visual search becomes much less efficient, possibly because the **useful field of view (UFOV)** of elder individuals is much smaller when there are distracting stimuli present. Hearing sensitivity decreases, especially for the higher frequencies. Touch sensitivity, but not pain sensitivity, diminishes. The largest losses seem to be for taste and smell, particularly in the ability to recognize flavors and odors. There are three global effects of aging on perception: (1) Perceptual responses slow, and sometimes there is prolonged persistence of sensation; (2) perceptual processes that are guided by short-term working memory become less efficient; (3) it becomes more difficult to divide attention between various stimuli or input channels.

KEY TERMS

life span developmental
  approach
perceptual learning
  approach
neuronal pruning
visually evoked potentials
  (VEP)
preferential looking
forced-choice
  preferential looking
habituation
dishabituation
saccadic eye movements
smooth pursuit eye
  movements
optokinetic nystagmus
temporal visual field
nasal visual field

infant directed talk
auditory grouping
rooting response
integration
schemata
encoding
search
covert orienting
filtering
visual-geometric illusions
Mueller-Lyer illusion
Ponzo illusion
encoding
dyslexia
presbyopia
useful field of view
  (UFOV)

Learning and Experience

CHAPTER 17

An article in the *New York Times* spoke of a tea expert who was called in to determine the components of a blend of tea that an American company was about to market. A small cup of it was poured for him. He sniffed it gently, sipped a bit, swished it around in his mouth a little, and then looked up.

"I detect," he said crisply, "a rather good Assam, a run-of-the-mill Darjeeling, a mediocre Ceylon, and, of course, the tea bag" (Root, 1974).

Although we might be amazed at performances such as these, or similar ones of expert wine tasters, we must realize that this degree of perceptual discrimination has come about through years of training and experience. Such experts do not have some incredible native sensitivity and especially low thresholds for tastes and odors (e.g., Bende & Nordin, 1997). In other words, such experts have simply *learned* to taste, smell, and identify these flavors.

In some of the previous chapters we have mentioned some ways in which our history, experience, knowledge, and hypotheses affect our perception. Most people are willing to admit that some aspects of perception may be susceptible to the influences of experience, but they are often unaware of the magnitude of these influences. In fact, our past can influence even whether we perceive anything at all in certain circumstances. For example, suppose we briefly flash a visual stimulus (such as a word) in front of you. If we have chosen the duration and intensity of the stimulus carefully, you may be unaware of any aspect of the stimulus. If we flash the same stimulus again, we would expect that, again, you would see nothing. However, with repeated presentations something about its appearance will begin to change. Soon you will be able to make out fragments of this stimulus, and after a while these fragments will become more complex. Eventually the entire stimulus pattern will be identified on every trial (i.e., you can read the word), even though the luminance and exposure durations are the same as for the very first trials when you saw and identified nothing (Haber & Hershenson, 1965; Uhlarik & Johnson, 1978)! Your prior experience with this stimulus has changed your perceptual abilities in some manner, and now you can see what was formerly invisible. In other words, during the course of this experiment you have learned to see this pattern.

EXPERIENCE AND DEVELOPMENT

As an organism develops, its nervous system matures, and over the years many changes in physiology and perceptual ability also come about simply due to physiological maturation. Of course, as the months and years roll by, the organism is also accumulating new experiences with the environment and is encountering many chances to learn new perceptual coordinations. It is important for us to understand how the natural course of development interacts with an individual's life history to shape that individual's perception of the world.

Experience can affect the development of the individual's perceptual processes in several ways. We have outlined these in Figure 17-1 (see Aslin, 1985; Gottlieb, 1981).

The strongest form of interaction between experience and development is **induction.** Here, the presence of some sort of relevant experience actually determines both the presence and final level of the ability (Figure 17-1A). The weakest form of interaction effect we will call **maturation.** This actually represents no interaction at all, and the ability might be expected to develop regardless of the individual's experience or lack of it (Figure 17-1B). Another possible interaction is **enhancement.** Here the final level of an ability, which is already

present or developing, is improved because of experiential factors (Figure 17-1C). **Facilitation** increases the rate at which an ability develops, but not its final level, providing earlier acquisition of the skill but not greater proficiency (Figure 17-1D). Finally, **maintenance** serves to stabilize, or to keep, an ability that is already present (Figure 17-1E). Of course, different mechanisms might be expected to produce each of these patterns of interaction between development and experience.

Restricted and Selective Rearing

The most direct method for assessing the relationship between development and experience is to deprive the observer of the opportunity to use a particular sensory modality from the moment of birth. After the observer has fully matured, we test the perceptual capacities in the deprived modality. If they have developed poorly, we would have demonstrated the need for experience in the development of normal functions. This technique is called **restricted rearing.** (We previously encountered this technique in Chapter 10 when we discussed the development of depth perception.) A somewhat more elegant technique involves deliberately altering the pattern of experience that the developing organism is exposed to from birth. For example, an animal may be exposed to only diffuse light, vertical stripes, the color red, and so forth. Such a technique should selectively bias, rather than eliminate, certain perceptual abilities if experience plays a role in their development. This technique is known as **selective rearing.**

Neurophysiological Effects

Research indicates that experience may play a role in the development of sensory physiological structures themselves. For instance, as discussed in Chapter 16, the visual pathways and visual cortex of the newborn differ from those of the adult; there are fewer responsive cells, and these show lesser degrees of directional and orientational sensitivity, as you will see later (cf. Hickey & Peduzzi, 1987; Norton, 1981a). Visual experience, in addition to the growth and maturation of the nervous system, seems to be necessary for the development

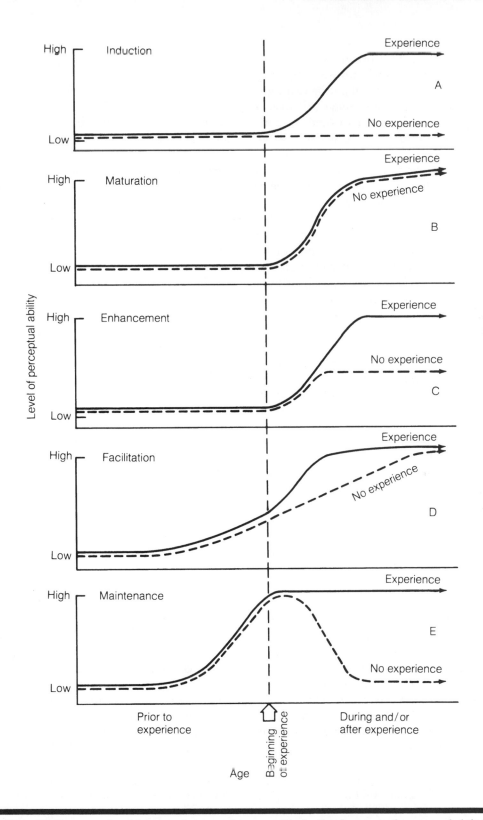

FIGURE 17-1   Various ways in which experience can interact with the development of perceptual abilities.

of normal visual functioning. This has been demonstrated through restricted-rearing studies.

Let us consider what happens if we completely deprive an animal of any visual input by rearing it in the dark from birth. This animal will have a visual cortex that shows reduced overall responsiveness to visual stimuli when tested using the electrode implantation techniques discussed in Chapter 3. Furthermore, those cells that are found to be responsive will not show the usual degree of orientation and movement selectivity (Blakemore, 1978; Leventhal & Hirsch, 1980), contrast sensitivity will be reduced (Gary-Bobo, Przybyslawski, & Saillour, 1995), and the usual separation of responses according to eye of input will not be as clear (Swindale, 1988). Overall, the visual cortex of such animals appears to be very immature because of the absence of the usual history of visual experience (Fagiolini, Pizzorusso, Berardi, Domenici, & Maffei, 1994).

Such neurophysiological disruption caused by the absence of visual experience can be found all along the visual pathways. Some effects are seen in the processing done by the retina, but they also appear in other places such as the superior colliculus, the lateral geniculate nucleus, and the visual cortex (Binns & Salt, 1997; Movshon & Van Sluyters, 1981). Different aspects of the visual pathways seem to be more or less susceptible to such damage. Thus, we find that parvo ganglion cells are relatively unaffected by dark rearing, whereas magno ganglion cells are readily lost if no visual experience is available (Hoffman & Sherman, 1975; Rothblat & Schwartz, 1978). Dark rearing can affect senses other than vision. For instance, in some animals, such as the guinea pig, restricting visual stimulation can also delay or disrupt development of the normal *auditory* maps in the brain, suggesting that the coordination of visual and auditory sensations requires simultaneous experiences (Withington, Binns, Ingham, & Thornton, 1994). In general, the effects of restricted rearing are not irreversible. There is evidence that even animals that have been raised for a year following birth in total darkness show some recovery after several months of exposure to illuminated surroundings, although recovery is never complete (Cynader, Berman, & Hein, 1976).

Much more subtle neurophysiological changes come about through selective-rearing practices.

For instance, in Chapter 3 we stated that cells in the visual cortex tend to show ocular dominance. This means that although most cells in the cortex can be activated by stimulation of either eye, they tend to respond more vigorously to one eye than to the other. The fact that most cells respond somewhat to each eye's input probably has to do with the depth cue of binocular disparity (see Chapter 10). Suppose that we rear an animal from birth so that it views the world through only one eye. Later we test separately the ability of the two eyes to produce a response in the visual cortex. We would probably find that the majority of the cells are activated by the experienced eye, and often less than 10% of the cells can be driven by the deprived eye (LeVay, Wiesel, & Hubel, 1980).

The degree of disruption of normal functioning seems to depend on when the period of deprivation begins. If the animal is deprived of binocular viewing during the period of 3 weeks to 3 months after birth, large disruptions of the normal pattern of binocular response occur. However, if the monocular viewing period is instituted after 3 months of age, even for periods of up to a year, virtually no effect is found (Cynader, Timney, & Mitchell, 1980; Held, 1985). This means that there is a particular time period during which the visual experience is most required and most effective. Such an interval is called a **critical period,** and it characterizes many aspects of the interaction between experience and development (Mitchell, 1981). Critical periods may correspond to periods of maximal growth and development in the nervous system (Aslin, 1985; Hickey, 1977). Any disruption of normal visual experience during the critical period, even for periods as short as 3 days, produces measurable changes in the responses of cells in the visual system (Freeman, Mallach, & Hartley, 1981).

Perhaps the most subtle form of selective visual rearing involves limiting an animal to a world containing contours oriented in only one direction. Thus, an animal might be exposed to only vertically oriented lines from birth. This is accomplished by either affixing to the animal goggles that contain only lines of one orientation or by giving the animal experience for a few hours each day in an apparatus similar to that shown in Figure 17-2. This is simply a large cylinder containing nothing but vertical stripes and a clear plastic floor

FIGURE 17-2 An apparatus for selectively rearing a kitten so that its only visual experience will be with vertical lines.

on which the animal stands. Notice that the animal is wearing a special collar that prevents it from seeing its own limbs.

What happens in the nervous system after exposure to this kind of selective rearing and stimulation might be called *environmental surgery*. Such surgery drastically alters the response characteristics of neurons in the visual cortex. Normally, when we insert an electrode into the visual cortex in order to map receptive fields, we find large numbers of cells that respond most strongly to lines in a particular orientation, as we saw in Chapter 3, and the particular preferred orientations are rather evenly distributed. The left side of Figure 17-3 depicts this distribution as a set of lines each of which represents a neuron responding best to that orientation. However, recording from an animal that has never seen horizontal stripes produces quite a different result. In this animal, virtually no cells are responsive to horizontally oriented lines, resulting in a distribution of preferred stimulus orientations much like that shown on the right in Figure 17-3 (Hirsch & Spinelli, 1970; Movshon & Van Sluyters, 1981). It is as if the absence of horizontally oriented stimuli in the environment has served as a (figurative) scalpel that has systematically cut

off any response to stimuli other than the vertical stripes to which the animal was exposed. Again, there is a critical period between 3 weeks and 3 months, during which this sort of selective stimulation seems to be most effective (Mitchell, 1981; Rothblat & Schwartz, 1978). The effect of selective experience is not confined to vision. For example, the tonotopic organization (different neurons respond best to different sound frequencies) of the primary auditory cortex is altered by experience with particular sound frequencies, with more cortical neurons more sharply tuned to the particular frequencies that have been frequently experienced during some form of training (Recanzone, Schreiner, & Merzenich, 1993).

Blake (1981) has summarized the evidence from such selective-rearing studies, saying, "In effect, the neurophysiologists have compiled a set of recipes for creating animals with specific kinds of neural deficits at sites along the visual pathways" (p. 97). The ingredients that go into these recipes are particular experiences, or the lack of certain normal experiences, with visual stimuli.

Perceptual Effects

How do all of these unusual environmental experiences affect what the organism perceives? There is a slight divergence between the physiological and the behavioral data when we answer this question. Consider a kitten reared in total darkness until the

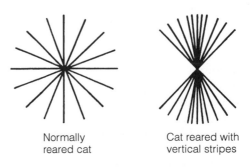

Normally reared cat   Cat reared with vertical stripes

FIGURE 17-3 Distribution of the preferred orientation of cortical receptive fields in a normally reared cat versus that in a cat reared with selective exposure to vertical lines. Each line indicates the preferred orientation of one cell.

age of 6 months. When we remove this kitten from darkness, it at first appears to be completely blind; however, within about 48 hr of exposure to illuminated surroundings the kitten begins to show some visual responsiveness. Various forms of sensory motor coordination begin to appear in a piecemeal fashion, and after a 6-week period of normal experience a great deal of recovery has occurred. Direct measures of visual acuity show a gradual improvement. If the animal had been dark reared for only about 4 months, the acuity gradually would return to that of a normally reared cat; however, visual acuity never reaches normal levels for animals that have been dark reared for longer periods (Timney, Mitchell, & Griffin, 1978). Although many of the physiological changes appear to be permanent, there seems to be enough plasticity in the animal to allow for considerable behavioral recovery of function after the initial period of deprivation. Still, there will be measurable deficits in many visual tasks, including obstacle avoidance, tracking, jumping under visual guidance, and eye blinks to oncoming objects, even after 2 years of normal experience (Rothblat & Schwartz, 1978). Dark-reared animals also seem less responsive to visual information and use it less efficiently in other tasks, such as maze or spatial learning (Tees & Buhrmann, 1990; Tees & Symons, 1987).

Because selective rearing is a more subtle procedure than restricted rearing, it should not be surprising to find that its behavioral effects are often somewhat indirect and elusive. For instance, the most dramatic behavioral effect of rearing animals with one eye occluded is a reduction in the visual acuity of the deprived eye (Mitchell, 1981). However, there are a number of interesting visual field effects as well. **Visual field** refers to the region of the outside world to which an eye will respond, measured in degrees around the head. For instance, Figure 17-4 shows the visual fields for the right and left eyes of a cat. There is a rather large region of overlap between the two eyes in the frontal part of the field. This is the region of binocular vision, where either or both eyes of the cat should be able to see an object. Generally, if an interesting stimulus appears in the visual field of a cat, it will immediately turn its eyes and head toward it, displaying an orienting response (see

Chapter 15). We can use this response to measure the effectiveness of stimuli in the visual field of the cat, and if we cover one eye at a time, we can measure each visual field separately.

Let us first consider an animal that has been completely dark reared. This animal shows a severe loss of response in the region of binocular overlap. Each eye seems to respond only to objects on its side of the head, as shown in the middle view of Figure 17-4. An animal reared with one eye occluded also does not show a binocularly responsive region of the visual field. The eye that had normal visual experience shows a normal visual field, overlapping well to the opposite side. However, the eye that did not receive visual experience acts as if it responds only to targets that are far to the side of the head and excludes all of the visual field that the normal eye covers, as shown in the bottom view of Figure 17-4 (Sherman, 1973). A similar effect has been reported in humans. A young man was born with a cataract that prevented any patterned vision in his left eye; thus his visual experience was similar to the monocularly reared animals we have been discussing. When this cataract was removed at age 19, the normal eye had its usual visual field size, but the patient simply could not detect any stimuli in a large portion of the region where the two eyes' views overlapped (the binocular region) with the deprived (cataract) eye. Although there was some recovery over the next 10 months, the visual field of the deprived eye never became as large as that of the normal eye (Moran & Gordon, 1982). There is some recent suggestion that depriving one eye of visual input may also reduce the visual field of the undeprived eye (Maire-Lepoivre & Przybyslawski, 1988).

The other form of selective rearing, where an animal is reared under conditions of exposure to horizontal or vertical stripes alone, also produces a behavioral deficit in addition to the change in the distribution of cells in the cortex with a specific set of preferred orientations. Here the results are not as dramatic as one might expect. Animals that have been reared only with vertical stripes are not blind to horizontal stripes; rather, they have measurably lower visual acuity for stripes in an orientation never seen during their rearing (Blasdel, Mitchell, Muir, & Pettigrew, 1977; Hirsch, 1972).

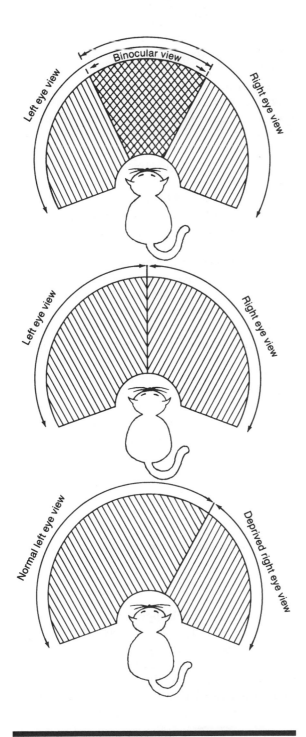

FIGURE 17-4   Regions of the visual field in which a cat will respond to visual stimuli presented to the right or left eye are altered by depriving one or both eyes of visual experience from birth (based on Sherman, 1973).

Human Studies

Restricted-rearing studies cannot be conducted with human observers because of the possibility of producing long-lasting perceptual deficits. However, some clinical conditions reproduce the circumstances needed to study the effects of experience on perception. Perhaps the best examples come from Senden (1960), who collected case reports of individuals who had suffered from lifelong blindness due to the presence of cataracts; these individuals later had vision restored through a surgical procedure. After the removal of the cataracts, these adults were unable to identify familiar objects by sight, although they were capable of identifying them if they were allowed to touch the objects. When asked to discriminate between a square and a triangle, they had to seek out and count the corners of the figure before the forms could be distinguished from each other.

These newly sighted observers seemed able to detect the presence or absence of an object in the visual field, but this seemed to be the extent of their abilities. For example, one patient was shown a watch and was asked whether it was round or square. When he seemed unable to answer, he was asked whether or not he knew the shape of a square or a circle. He was able to position his hands to form both a square and a circular shape, but he could not visually identify the shape of the watch. When the watch was placed in his hands, he immediately recognized it as being round. It appears that his sense of touch, although not more sensitive than that of a sighted person, had come through long experience to be a more reliable source of information about the world than was his untrained sense of vision (see Warren, 1984).

There is an interesting naturally occurring analogy to selective rearing of the type used with cats in which they see only contours in a single orientation. This analogy arises from a common visual problem known as **astigmatism.** Astigmatism usually occurs if the cornea of the eye is not perfectly spherical, perhaps being flatter in some places and more curved in others. This deviation from perfect sphericity brings contours of some orientations into sharper focus than those of other orientations. Thus, with a vertical astigmatism, horizontal lines will be clear, and vertical lines will be blurry, and so forth. The fact that this condition can mimic selective-rearing effects was shown by Freeman and Pettigrew (1973), who reared cats wearing cylindrical lenses that artificially created an astigmatism. They were able to show that such selective rearing can also alter the distribution of preferred orientations of visual cortical neurons, causing a reduction of the number of cells preferring the blurred orientation. Severe astigmatism at an early age in humans results in a permanent loss of visual acuity in the direction of the astigmatism. This is an acuity loss due to neural changes because it remains even after correcting for any optical errors and is probably the result of selective restriction of exposure to contours in the astigmatic direction (Mitchell, 1980).

A variation of this same selective-rearing effect is caused by living in an urbanized environment. The nature of our carpentered cities means that we have frequent exposure to vertical lines (defining walls, corners, furniture legs, etc.) and to horizontal lines (defining floors, ceilings, table edges, etc.). Proportionally, we have much less exposure to oblique lines. Therefore, as inhabitants of such a selectively stimulating environment, we might be expected to show reduced acuity for diagonal lines relative to horizontal and vertical lines. In fact, the human visual system is *anisotropic*, meaning that it often reacts differently to stimuli depending on their orientation. In general, the normal visual

system shows a slight, but well-defined, preference for horizontal or vertical stimuli over diagonal stimuli (Jenkins, 1985; Vogels & Orban, 1986). This is demonstrated in a number of acuity-related tasks, where resolution acuity and vernier acuity are poorer for stimuli oriented diagonally (Bowker & Mandler, 1981; Saarinen, & Levi, 1995), and has been shown even for moving stimuli (Coletta & Segu, 1993). This phenomenon is known as the **oblique effect** and can easily be demonstrated using Demonstration Box 17-1.

Some investigators feel that at least part of the oblique effect arises from genetic factors (Leehey, Moskowitz-Cook, Brill, & Held, 1975; Timney & Muir, 1976). There is, however, some interesting support for selective environmental effects. This came about from comparison of acuity for different line orientations between students from Queens University in Kingston, Ontario, and a group of Cree Indians from James Bay, Quebec (Annis & Frost 1973). The students had all grown up in typical North American buildings. The Cree Indians, however, were among the last to be raised in traditional housing consisting of a cook tent (or *meech-wop*) in summer and a winter lodge (or *matoocan*) during the rest of the year. Both the insides and outsides of these structures consist of a rich array of contours, with no obvious preponderance of verticals and horizontals. In addition, the natural environment of the Cree shows no excesses of

---

DEMONSTRATION BOX 17-1
The Oblique Effect

To demonstrate that visual acuity is better for horizontal or vertical stimuli than for obliquely oriented stimuli, prop this book up on a table so you can see the three stimulus patterns. Now slowly walk backward from the book until you can no longer resolve clearly the oblique lines in the center circle. It will appear uniform gray at this point, as your resolution acuity fails. Notice, however, that at this distance you still can see that the left circle contains vertical lines and the right contains horizontal lines, thus indicating your greater visual acuity for these orientations.

verticals and horizontals, in contrast to the urbanized environment of the students. In line with the selective exposure hypothesis, the students showed the expected reduction in acuity for obliquely oriented contours, whereas the Cree, without this selective exposure, did not. In the laboratory a learning factor has been shown for the oblique effect. With prolonged training (15 to 20 days), practice can improve ability to see obliquely oriented stimuli (Schoups, Vogels, & Orban, 1995).

Although we have emphasized the visual modality in our discussions thus far, it is important to recognize that selective rearing and restricted rearing in other senses also have measurable effects in humans and animals. In hearing, for example, it has been found that individuals who are deaf in one ear, or who are congenitally deaf, tend to have brain organizations different from those of normal-hearing subjects (Neville, 1985; Neville, Schmidt, & Kutas, 1983). In such individuals parts of the brain normally reserved for auditory processing appear to be available for visual functions.

SENSORY-MOTOR LEARNING

One variable that seems to be essential for the development of normal visual functioning involves not only the eyes but also the entire body. It seems that normal perceptual development depends on active bodily movement under visual guidance. Holst and Mittelstaedt (1950) offered a distinction between stimulation that acts on a passive observer, which they called **exafference,** and stimulation that changes as a result of an individual's own movements, called **reafference.**

Reafference was shown to be necessary for the development of accurate visually guided spatial behavior in a classic series of experiments by Richard Held and Alan Hein. In one study they reared kittens in the dark until they were 8–12 weeks of age (Held & Hein, 1963). From that age on, the kittens received 3 hr of patterned visual exposure in a "carousel" apparatus, shown in Figure 17-5. As you can see from the figure, one of the animals is active and can walk around freely. The other animal is passive and is carried around in a gondola that moves in exactly the same direction and at exactly the same speed as the movements of the active animal. Thus, the moving animal experiences

changing visual stimuli as a result of its own movements (reafference), whereas the passive animal experiences the same stimulation as exafference.

Both animals in each pair were later tested on a series of behaviors involving depth perception. These included dodging or blinking when presented with a rapidly approaching object and avoiding the deep side of the visual cliff (see Chapter 10). They were also tested for the visual placing response, a paw extension (as if to avoid collision) when the animals were moved quickly toward a surface. In all three measures, the active animals performed like normal kittens, and the passive animals showed little evidence of depth perception. It is interesting to note that if one eye receives active exposure and the other does not, only the actively exposed eye shows normal depth perception (Hein, Held, & Gower, 1970), indicating that the effects of experience are quite specific.

How much of the development of our visually guided behavior requires practice and exposure? Consider the simple tasks of reaching out and picking up an object with one hand. These involve not only the accurate assessment of the distance and the size of the object but also the ability to guide your limb on the basis of the perceptual information. Held and Hein (1967) reared kittens in the dark until they were 4 weeks old. After this period, they were allowed 6 hr of free movement each day in a lighted and patterned environment. However, during the time when the kittens received their exposure to patterned stimuli, they wore lightweight opaque collars that prevented them from seeing their bodies or paws while they moved about (see Figure 17-6). The remainder of the time, the kittens were placed in a dark room. After 12 days of such exposure, these animals showed normal depth perception, but their ability to accurately place their paws by visually directing them toward targets was quite poor. Nonetheless, after 18 hr of free movement in a lighted environment, with their paws visible, all directional confusions seemed to have disappeared. Similar effects were found in monkeys (Held & Bauer, 1967).

There are suggestions that human infants need experience to develop normal reaching behaviors. After the first month of life infants spend many hours watching their hands. Their reaching is quite inaccurate at first but improves steadily. Active practice seems to speed up this process. If

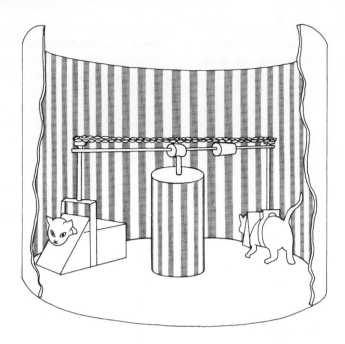

FIGURE 17-5 Kitten carousel for active or passive exposure to visual stimulation. (From R. Held & A. Hein, 1963, *Journal of Comparative and Physiological Psychology, 56.* Copyright 1963 by the American Psychological Association. Reprinted by permission.)

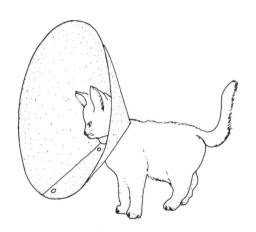

FIGURE 17-6 Kitten in a collar that prevents view of paws. (From A. Hein & R. Held, 1967, *Science, 158,* 390–392. Copyright 1967 by the American Association for the Advancement of Science.)

conditions are arranged so that there are many objects to reach for and to play with, infants develop accurate reaching behavior several weeks earlier than do children who have not received this type of enriched experience. This suggests that in humans, experience with the sight of actively moving parts of the body is also necessary for the successful development of visually guided behavior (Hein, 1980).

PERCEPTUAL REARRANGEMENT

In 1896 George Stratton reasoned that if some aspects of the perception of space and direction are learned, then it ought to be possible to learn a new set of spatial percepts. To test this, Stratton used a technique that altered spatial relations in the visual world (Stratton, 1897a, b). His technique involved wearing a set of goggles that optically rotated the field of view by 180° so that everything appeared to be upside down. Such a technique is called optical **rearrangement** (Welch, 1978).

In some prototypical experiments, Kohler (1962, 1964) elaborated on this procedure. Kohler's observers often wore optically distorting devices for several weeks. Observers reported that at first the world seemed very unstable, the visual field appearing to swing as the head was turned. During this stage of the experiments observers often had difficulty walking and needed help to perform very simple tasks. However, after about 3 days one observer was able to ride a bicycle, and after only a few weeks he was able to ski. The observers reported that they sporadically experienced the world as being upright. If they observed common events that have definite directional components, such as smoke rising from a cigarette or water pouring from a pitcher, they reported that the world appeared to be upright. This suggests that their ability to adapt to the optically rearranged visual input was facilitated by the notion of gravitational direction along with interaction with familiar events and objects. Kohler suggested that a real perceptual change had taken place because when the inverting lenses were removed, observers

experienced a sense of discomfort. The world suddenly appeared to be inverted again, and they had difficulty moving about. However, the readaptation to the normal upright world was accomplished within a period of about 1 hr. Demonstration Box 17-2 shows how you can experience this inverted visual stimulation.

Most rearrangement studies involve a less dramatic change of optical input. A common technique is to use a wedge prism, which is a wedge-shaped piece of glass that bends, or refracts, light. The locations of objects viewed through the prism seem to be shifted in the direction of the apex (the pointed end of the wedge). If an observer viewed the world through goggles containing such prisms and reached for an object, she would find herself missing it. After only a few minutes of practice, however, the observer's reaching would become quite accurate. We would say that she has adapted to the prismatic distortion; in other words, she has compensated for the optical distortion. If the observer is consciously correcting for the distortion (e.g., saying to herself, "I must reach 10° to the

---

DEMONSTRATION BOX 17-2
Optical Inversion

You can experience some of the effects associated with inverted optical stimulation by holding a mirror as shown in the accompanying figure. Walk around and view the world by looking up at the mirror. Notice that the world seems inverted, and also notice how the world swings as you turn. Now pour some water from a glass. Does the water pour up or down? Are you sure?

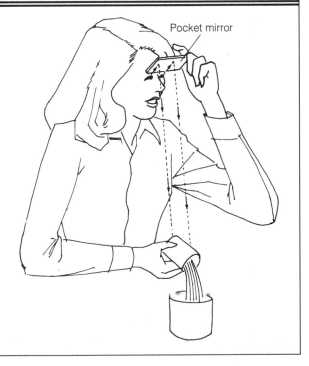

Pocket mirror

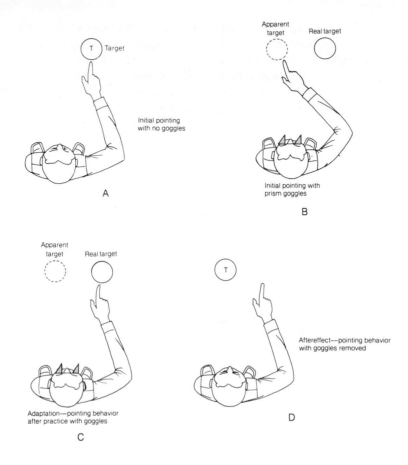

FIGURE 17-7 Prism adaptation and aftereffect.

right of where the object appears"), when the goggles were removed she would, of course, know that the distortion is no longer present. Being rational, she should then drop this conscious correction and reach for seen stimuli with her usual accuracy. However, suppose that some perceptual change has occurred. In this case we would expect that when the distorting prism is removed, the visual world would appear to be shifted several degrees to one side. When reaching for an object the observer should err in the direction opposite to that of the initial distortion. This is what actually does occur. These errors are called **aftereffects.** The occurrence of aftereffects in prism adaptation is evidence that some perceptual rearrangement has occurred (Harris, 1980). This process is outlined in Figure 17-7.

A number of investigators have attempted to specify what conditions are necessary for adaptation to rearranged stimulation. Held and Hein (1958) have argued that adaptation depends on active movements, as does the development of visually guided behavior discussed earlier. They tested this notion by having an observer view his hand through a prism under one of three conditions. The first was a no-movement condition, in which the observer viewed only his stationary hand. The second was a passive-movement condition, in which the observer's arm was swung back and forth by the experimenter. The third was an active-movement condition, in which the observer saw his hand through the prism while he actively moved it from side to side. There was considerable adaptation to the distortion produced by the prism under the active-movement condition, whereas in the other conditions there was not. These results have been verified several times (Pick & Hay, 1965).

Another series of experiments used conditions similar to the kitten carousel discussed earlier. Observers wearing displacing prism goggles either walked around for about 1 hr (active exposure) or were wheeled around in a wheelchair over the same path for about 1 hr (passive exposure). They were then measured to see if any perceptual change had taken place. Adaptation to the prismatic distortion occurred in the active-exposure condition but not in the passive-exposure condition (Held & Bossom, 1961; Mikaelian & Held, 1964).

One important aspect of active movement under optically distorted conditions seems to be that it provides observers with some sort of error feedback, which informs them of the direction and the extent of the distortion. This information provides a basis for learning a new correlation between the incoming stimuli and the conscious percept. The more information we give observers about the nature of their errors, the greater is the adaptation to the distortion (Coren, 1966; Welch, 1969, 1971). The timing and amount of information from feedback are important factors in adaptation (Redding & Wallace, 1990). For instance, not being able to see the starting position of your hand before you begin to point to the target can slow the rate of adaptation (Redding & Wallace, 1997). Simply delaying, by a mere 50 ms, individuals' ability to see how accurate their hand movements are can also slow the rate of adaptation by a marked amount (Kitazawa & Kohno, 1995).

Some investigators suggest that error information in the absence of active movement is sufficient to produce prism adaptation. Howard, Craske, and Templeton (1965) had two groups of observers watch a rotating rod through an optical system that displaced it to one side. For members of one group the rod appeared to be displaced to the side, and they merely watched it rotate. For members of the other group the rod appeared displaced to the same degree; however, as the rod swung about it brushed each observer across the lips, indicating that it was directly in front of the observer rather than off to the side as it appeared. Although both groups were passive, members of the group receiving the information that their percept was erroneous (being touched by a stimulus that looked like it would pass them by) showed perceptual adaptation, whereas members of the other group did not. Another study involved a more subtle manipulation. O'Leary and McMahon (1991) used cylindrical lenses that made stimuli appear too wide or too tall. When observers viewed photographs of faces distorted in this way, even though no active movement was engaged in, they still showed some adaptation to the distortion. When they viewed line drawings of simple figures (e.g., circles or squares), no adaptation occurred. Presumably, their familiarity with the normal dimensions of faces provided the cue that there was a distortion present and triggered the perceptual recalibration. Thus, information indicating how our percepts are in error may be sufficient to produce adaptation (Howard, Anstis, & Lucia, 1974).

What actually changes during the adaptation process? This issue is still being debated. Some researchers believe that adaptation simply alters the felt position of various parts of the body (Harris, 1980). This belief is based on the observation that after prism adaptation, when observers are asked to point to a straight-ahead position (by feel alone), they tend to point off to the side. This indicates some proprioceptive or "felt" component in the aftereffect (Harris, 1980). Other data indicate that this may be only part of the process (Mikaelian, 1974; Redding & Wallace, 1976). For example, animals can still adapt to the visual displacement when the nerves that provide information about the position of the arm are severed (Taub & Berman, 1968). The consensus is that a change is taking place in both proprioceptive and visual perception, which is the result of recalibration of the higher brain centers used to interpret perceptual input (Howard, 1982; Welch, 1978). Some direct evidence for this perceptual recalibration comes from an interesting experiment by Foley (1974). She placed wedge prisms in front of the eyes of observers so that the direction of displacement was different for each eye. Either one eye saw an upward displacement and the other a downward displacement, or one eye saw a displacement to the right and the other to the left. After several hours of exposure the two eyes were tested separately. The results indicated that each eye had adapted to its own particular distortion. This implies a perceptual recalibration. It seems likely that adaptation to optically rearranged stimuli involves a form of perceptual learning that alters the appearance of visual space, which, like many other forms of learning, is sensitive to what the observer is paying attention to (Redding, Clark, & Wallace, 1985). However, whether learning to deal with rearranged spatial stimuli involves the same mechanisms that may have gone into the original development of our perception of space is not clear.

Illusion Decrement

There is another form of perceptual learning that is similar to rearrangement in that it involves learning to compensate for a perceptual error. It differs from the situations we have been discussing in that the error is not optical in nature, and the observer usually is not conscious either of the erroneous perception or of any perceptual change. The situation involves visual-geometric illusions, which are simple line drawings that evoke percepts differing in size or shape from those expected on the basis of physical measurements of the stimuli. We have encountered several of these already, in Chapters 1, 11, 14, and 16, including the Mueller-Lyer illusion (Figure 17-8), in which the horizontal line with the outward-turned wings appears longer than the line with the inward-turned wings, despite the fact that the lines are physically equal in length. Suppose we present the Mueller-Lyer figure to an observer and measure her susceptibility to the line-length distortion. Next we instruct her to begin moving her eyes across the figure, scanning from one end of the horizontal line to the other on both portions of the figure. We ask her to be as accurate as possible with her eye movements. At 1-min intervals we stop the scanning process and take measurements of illusion magnitude until a total of 5 min of viewing time has elapsed. This simple process of inspection leads to a 40% reduction in the original illusion magnitude (Coren & Porac, 1984). This decrease, known as **illusion decrement,** has been demonstrated many times and for many different types of illusions, not just the Mueller-Lyer illusion (e.g., Beckett, 1989; Glaser & Slotnick, 1995; Porac & Coren, 1985; Predebon, 1990).

What is happening in this situation? Some researchers have suggested that continuously inspecting the illusion figure fatigues or adapts some

of the neural units that register or distort the pattern, and this is what accounts for a weakening of the illusion (Long, 1988; Porac, 1989). Although this may contribute to the process, it can't be a full explanation because inspection of fields of lines that have been designed to fatigue the same neural units does not result in a reduction of the illusion when the figure is viewed afterward (Coren, Girgus, & Schiano, 1986; Schiano & Jordan, 1990). If neural fatigue is not the answer, then it seems likely that we are looking at a form of perceptual learning (Coren & Girgus, 1978; Long, 1988).

Perceptual learning requires some information processing that will later affect how a stimulus is perceived. In this situation observers must somehow learn that there is an illusion present so that they can begin to correct their perception and eliminate the illusory distortion. Observers get this information not via rulers or measuring tapes but, rather, via information from their eye movements (see Coren, 1986). If we measure the actual pattern of eye movements an observer makes over an illusion figure, we find that the eyes are directed to move as if the distorted percept were actually correct. In other words, if the eyes were resting on the end of the line in the perceptually elongated portion of the Mueller-Lyer figure (Figure 17-8A), an attempt to look at the far end of the line would produce an eye movement that is too long. This eye-movement error is in agreement with the percept, which tends to overestimate the length of the line. A corrective adjustment in the eye movement must be made if the fovea is to come to rest on the exact end of the line. The opposite happens for the underestimated portion of the Mueller-Lyer figure (Figure 17-8B). Here the eye movements are too short (again in agreement with the perceptual underestimation of the line length), and a corrective adjustment must be made. The eye-movement patterns over the two portions of the figure are shown in Figure 17-8C.

In Chapters 15 and 16 we saw instances where patterns of eye movements could be used to tell us something about the information-processing abilities of an observer. The same reasoning can be applied to the study of eye-movement patterns across illusion configurations. As the observer views the illusory array, eye movements and eye-movement errors provide information about the existence (as well as the direction and the strength) of the

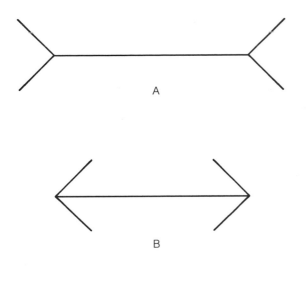

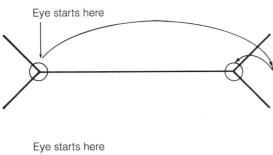

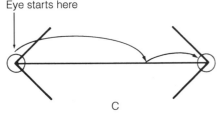

FIGURE 17-8 The overestimated (A) and underestimated (B) portions of the Mueller-Lyer illusion and (C) typical eye movements obtained when viewing them.

illusory distortion. This error information can be used by the observer to correct the percept. This point of view is supported by the fact that an illusion decrement does not occur unless the observer is allowed to scan the figure (Coren, Girgus, & Schiano, 1986; Coren & Hoenig, 1972; Festinger, White, & Allyn, 1968).

The phenomenon of illusion decrement implies that perceptual learning is taking place (Brosvic, Walker, Perry, Degnan, & Dihoff, 1997). The information obtained from the eye movements is being used to reduce a perceptual error, and the direction of this change (from greater to lesser illusion susceptibility) mimics that associated with perceptual rearrangement studies (see also Brosvic & Farrelly, 1993). The most interesting aspect of this form of perceptual adjustment, however, is the fact that nothing about it appears to be available to consciousness. Unless provided with a ruler or a direct explanation, the observer does not consciously know that the perception is in error, nor does she know that illusory error has been reduced as a result of her active interactions with the illusion figure! The percept simply becomes more accurate with no change in the observer's own awareness.

CONTEXT AND MEANING

Basically, all percepts are ambiguous. Consider a target that casts a square image on the retinal surface. The object the image represents could actually be one of an infinite number of different shapes at any distance or inclination relative to the observer, as is shown in Figure 17-9. Because any retinal image can be caused by a variety of different physical targets in the world, it is surprising that our normal perceptual experiences are generally so unambiguous. What we perceive seems to be the result of a decision-making process in which we deduce, on the basis of all available information, what the stimulus object is. This **transactional viewpoint** maintains that any current perceptual experience consists of a complex evaluation of the significance of stimuli reaching our receptors. Through our life experience we learn that certain objects or conditions have a high probability of being related to each other. On this basis we derive our "best bet" as to what we are viewing. In a sense, the world we are experiencing is more the *result* of perceptual processing than the *cause* of the perception (Coren, 1984; Ittelson, 1962). The transactional viewpoint implies that if our expectations change or our analysis of the situation changes, then our perceptual experience will also change (Ames, 1951; Brunswick, 1955). A simple example of the effect of context and expectations can be seen in Demonstration Box 17-3.

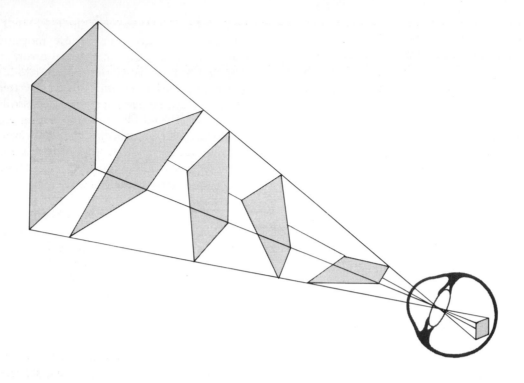

FIGURE 17-9 Many different objects at different distances and slants, all of which cast the same square retinal image (from Coren & Girgus, 1978).

Most of our percepts are constructed from incomplete stimuli. Look at Figure 17-10A. It is clear that this represents a dog, yet it should also be clear that there is no dog present. The figure is completely constructed in the mind's eye of the observer. The elephant in Figure 17-10B will probably be somewhat more difficult to identify. The less familiar the object, the more difficult is the identification. Furthermore, you must begin with the initial hypothesis that there is some object there in the first place; otherwise you may never see any pattern at all (Reynolds, 1985). However, after you have seen (or "constructed") the figure, the meaningful organization will be apparent immediately when you look at it again. Our ability to perceive these stimuli as objects depends on our prior experience. This was shown by Steinfield (1967), who found that when observers were told a story about an ocean cruise, they identified Figure 17-10C as a steamship in less than 5 seconds. Observers who were told an irrelevant story took six times longer to identify the figure.

In Chapter 14 we talked about the difference between stimuli that are *registered* and those that are *apprehended* (see also Coren, 1989). Apprehended stimuli are present in our conscious experience, whereas registered stimuli may be strong enough only to trigger some form of perceptual processing, without actually being strong enough to make us consciously aware of their presence. This means that some of the experiences that affect perception may take place without any conscious awareness. For instance, earlier in the chapter we spoke of an experiment in which researchers presented a word for so brief a time that it could not be identified. They found that if the word was presented several times, even though the length of time of each presentation was not increased, the word was eventually identified (Haber & Hershenson, 1965; Uhlarik & Johnson, 1978). If an observer could not identify the word on the first presentation, why should an observer be able to identify it after repeated exposures? It may be that very fast presentations of stimuli do

DEMONSTRATION BOX 17-3
A Context Effect on Perception

Read the accompanying handwritten message. You probably read it as "My phone number is area code 604, 876-1569. Please call!" If you did, you were being affected by several contextual influences on perception. Go back to the message and look carefully at the script. You will see that the two pairs of characters you read as the word *is* and the number 15 are identical. In addition, the *h* in the word *phone* and the *b* in the word *number* are identical, as are the *d* in the word *code* and the *l* in the word *please*. You saw each letter or number within a context when you first read the message, and this context determined how you interpreted the script character.

My phone number 15 area code 604, 876-1569. Please call!

not give the brain sufficient time to do the necessary computations required for recognition while still allowing some low-level processing of the stimulus (Cheesman & Merikle, 1986; Dodwell, 1971). The partially processed stimulus is held in memory, and as the information extraction continues, hypotheses are formed and checked until the stimulus appears to make sense. At this point, the conscious identification response may take place (Doherty & Keeley, 1972). Even when the stimulus is still not fully identified, sufficient information may be present to "prime" (make easier) the recognition of other stimuli that are related to it or fall in the same general class, because relevant perceptual hypotheses are now already activated and set up a context for new incoming stimuli (Bernstein, Bissonnette, Vyas, & Barclay, 1989; Dark, 1988).

A   B   C

FIGURE 17-10   Some degraded stimuli that may be seen as objects (based on Street, 1931).

The same perceptual hypotheses, allowing us to eventually formulate a percept from minimal or degraded input, can also modify our perception so that it no longer accurately represents the stimulus. For example, Ross and Schilder (1934) presented observers with a series of briefly flashed line drawings. Some of the drawings were incomplete or distorted, such as three-armed people and faces with a mouth missing. A look at some of the observers' comments is informative. When presented with the side view of a dog with the left hind leg missing, an observer reported: "It's a dog, a wolf, two ears stand upright, a round mouth, a long tail." The experimenter then instructed the observer: "Look at his legs." Observer: "He has five toes on each leg." Experimenter: "Look at the hind legs." Observer: "I saw two; the tail goes up."

Despite continued pressure from the experimenter, the observer continued to correct the percept, filling in the missing leg on the hypothesis that dogs have four legs.

These researchers also used a drawing of a woman's head facing forward. She had two large eyes as well as a large third eye on her forehead. One observer described the drawing as "a woman with long hair, black, two eyes, one nose, one mouth, two ears." The stimulus was presented again briefly, and the observer was asked if the forehead was in order, to which he replied, "Yes." After several other stimuli were presented again, the observer now reported: "The same woman I saw before. She is funny—big eyes, a big nose, and a big mouth." Experimenter: "Look at the forehead." Observer: "She has a small curl in the middle."

Even with more brief presentations, this observer still insisted that all that appeared on the forehead was a curl of hair. Third eyes do not occur normally, so we apparently correct our percept on the basis of our expectations—we see extra hair, not extra eyes. You may see how our expectations alter our perceptions in Demonstration Box 17-4.

It is interesting to note that even the perceptual comparisons that lead to various illusions and systematic distortions require a consideration of the context and meaning of the stimuli. Consider the familiar Ebbinghaus illusion that is shown in Figure 17-11A. In this illusion the central circle surrounded by large circles is seen as smaller than the circle surrounded by small circles even though both are the same size. This same illusion occurs if we use meaningful objects rather than circles, as in Figure 17-11B, where the dog surrounded by large dogs appears to be smaller than the dog surrounded by small dogs. It is important to note, however, that the conceptual nature or identity of the objects surrounding the test stimuli is important in determining the strength of this illusion. Coren and Enns (1993) showed that the illusion was strongest when the objects surrounding the test figures were absolutely identical to test objects, as in *B*. If the objects were drawn from the same class of stimuli as the test object (such as dogs) but were visually dissimilar (as in *C*, which shows only the large surround half of the illusion), the size of the distortion was reduced. It was reduced further if the surrounding figures were drawn from a near, but dissimilar, conceptual class (e.g., four-footed animals such as horses, as in *D*). The illusion virtually disappeared when surrounding objects were drawn from a distant and irrelevant class of items, such as shoes (as in *E*). Thus, it becomes clear that we first classify and identify items that form the context for the stimuli that we

---

DEMONSTRATION BOX 17-4
An Expectancy Effect on Perception

Turn to Color Plate 9 and *quickly* count the number of aces of spades you see. Then return to this demonstration box. Although you probably saw only two aces of spades, three are actually there. One of the aces of spades is printed in red ink, rather than black. The red spade is also upside down. Because you "expect" spades to be black, your identification process for incongruent or unexpected stimuli is impaired.

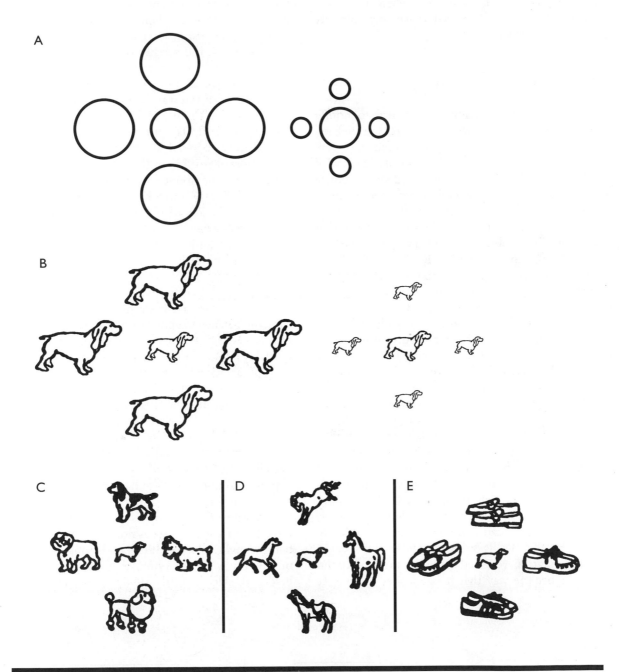

FIGURE 17-11   (A) The Ebbinghaus illusion, where the central item surrounded by large inducers is seen as smaller than that surrounded by small inducers, also occurs in meaningful objects (B). The strength of the illusion diminishes as we go from illusion variants with test and surrounding stimuli drawn from the same class but not identical in form (C), a conceptually near class of stimuli (D), or obviously different classes of objects (E; after Coren & Enns, 1993).

are looking at. Our final conscious perception of the stimulus (whether correct or distorted) will be strongly affected by our experience with such classes of stimuli and the way in which we identify and categorize them.

Eyewitness Testimony

Language and expectation can also serve to modify our reports of what we have seen. Carmichael, Hogan, and Walter (1932) presented observers with simple line drawings and associated each with a label. Observers were then asked to reproduce these drawings. In general, their reproductions were biased in the direction of the verbal label. When presented with Figure 17-12A and told that it was a broom, observers tended to reproduce patterns similar to Figure 17-12B. When told that it was a rifle, observers tended to reproduce patterns similar to Figure 17-12C. In this experiment the reproductions occurred only a few moments after the stimulus was taken away. Such distortions in our recollections of what we have seen may have important consequences for many behaviors. Our memory of scientific data presented in a graph or our ability to reproduce contours drawn on a map may be distorted by the context provided from someone's verbal description of it (Tversky & Schiano, 1989). It also may explain why eyewitness reports of events that occurred during a crime tend to be remarkably unreliable, even when obtained immediately after the event. Observers have a tendency to include details that they could not have seen. Such details are often provided on the basis of an observer's expectations or biases (Cutler & Penrod, 1995; Wells & Loftus, 1984).

Information received after a stimulus is seen can distort the way that it is encoded (Loftus & Donders, 1989; Zaragoza & Lane, 1994). In one often-cited experiment Loftus (1974) showed observers a brief videotape of an automobile accident and then asked them some questions about what they had just observed. For one group of observers one of the questions was, "How fast was the white sports car going while traveling along the country road?" For the other group the question was, "How fast was the white sports car going when it passed the barn while traveling along the country road?" In fact, there was no barn present. Yet when questioned about the incident a week later, more than 17% of the group exposed to the false suggestion about a barn answered the question "Did you see a barn?" by saying "Yes," as opposed to only 3% of the group that did not get such a suggestion.

There are limitations to how much perception (or a remembered perception) can be affected by later inputs (see McCloskey & Egeth, 1983; Zaragoza & McCloskey, 1989). For instance, some data suggest that when we have clearly perceived something, the perceptual memory resists any later change. It seems that the suggestions from later (possibly false) context provided after the actual perceptual event act only to fill in gaps in the perception (Ross, Read, & Toglia, 1994; Yuille, 1984). This is much like the observer's expectation that dogs have four legs, which caused the missing leg to be added perceptually in the experiment discussed earlier. This can lead to some problems, especially with eyewitness identifications made by children. Children seem to have the same accuracy as adults in identifying a person whom they saw before when that person is present in a lineup. However, if the lineup does not contain the person being sought, children are much more likely to misidentify a person whom they have never seen before (Dekle & Beal, 1996; Gross, & Hayne,

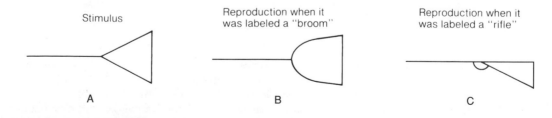

FIGURE 17-12   The effects of labels on later perceptual recall.

1996). This may well be due to the expectation that the guilty party must be present, which then provides pressure for an erroneous identification.

One of the most fascinating aspects of eyewitness identifications is that our feeling of certainty (namely, how certain we are that our identification is correct) is not a reasonable predictor of how accurate our description of what we saw actually is (Juslin & Olsson, 1996). Even though in trials juries tend to be swayed toward believing individuals who are very certain that they saw something and toward disbelieving individuals who are uncertain, both are equally likely to be correct or incorrect in their recollections. To a limited extent, structuring the questioning to fit the actual sequence of events may help to prevent some eyewitness errors, perhaps by restoring the original context that was present during the actual viewing of the event (Geiselman, Fisher, MacKinnon, & Holland, 1986; Morris & Morris, 1985).

ENVIRONMENTAL AND LIFE HISTORY DIFFERENCES

We have seen what effect the availability, or non-availability, of particular environmental stimuli can have on the development of sensory systems and hence on the observer's later perceptual abilities. There also are aspects of our environment and culture that may teach us different perceptual strategies and may alter the internal set of expectations and analyses that we bring to each new perceptual situation. Thus, if we live in the desert or on the pampas or the plains, we are exposed to broad vistas of open space that are never experienced by a forest dweller. If we live in a technologically advanced country, we are exposed to sets of visual stimuli (such as photographs and television) that are usually not available to someone dwelling in the African bush or the Australian outback. Such differences, especially when experienced over an entire lifetime, may have dramatic consequences for perceptual processes.

Picture Perception

In our civilized, urbanized, and media-intensive culture, we are inundated with images—not just the images of our immediate environment, but also images representing environments or objects that are not present. Some of these latter images are in the form of patterns of color or black and white shown on televisions and in cinemas. There are also photographs in magazines and newspapers, where we might "see" a baby elephant peaceably grazing a few feet in front of its gigantic mother, all in a 5-cm-square smudge of black ink on a perfectly flat surface. If you have some artistic talent, you may be able to represent such a scene with a few strokes of a pen on a sheet of paper and thus be able to let your friends "see for themselves" what you have seen. This seems like a perfectly natural fact of life.

Pictures, of the sort that we encounter daily, are often viewed as simply "windows" through which we see other worlds (Haber, 1980). Certainly these images must follow all of the same optical laws as the real world. Certainly every observer must follow these laws to interpret such stimuli in the same way that we do. Unfortunately, neither statement is completely "certain." Pictures do contain much information that mimics the optical patterns encountered in natural viewing (Gibson, 1979; Sedgwick, 1980), but there are many discrepancies between the pictured image and the real image. For instance, the actual sizes of the images are usually too large or too small, which in turn ruins the geometrical correspondence between the image and the actual scene (Lumsden, 1980). Furthermore, even if we could make the geometry of perspective perfect, it would be correct only for one viewing angle, and viewing any pictured image from a vantage point other than the viewpoint adopted by the camera or artist who produced the picture ought to lead to distorted percepts (Kennedy & Ostry, 1976). However, such distortions do not appear (Rosinski & Farber, 1980). We could enlarge this list of discrepancies between the real scene and a picture of it. For instance, the picture is flat, whereas the real world is three-dimensional; the picture is interpreted correctly even if its colors are all wrong, or even if there are no colors at all; and so forth. Such considerations have led some theorists to conclude that pictures may be statements in a sort of visual language that are created and interpreted according to the agreed-on set of conventions in any given culture. Thus, they are not simply representations of reality at all (Gombrich,

1972; Goodman, 1968). At the very least, they must be interpreted as hypotheses shared among individuals growing up with a common heritage (Gregory, 1971). By either of these two theories, however, the perception of pictures must be learned in some manner.

Before we investigate whether we must learn to interpret pictures, it is important for us to specify that we are really talking about two separate skills. The first is the ability to identify objects depicted in a picture, and the second is the ability to interpret the three-dimensional arrangement implied in the flat image.

Hochberg and Brooks (1962) conducted a heroic experiment, using one of their children as the subject. The child was reared to the age of 19 months carefully shielded from any sort of pictorial representation. This meant that the television was never used in the child's presence, nor were there magazines or picture books. Even the labels on cans and boxes of food were removed or covered. When the child was tested after this restricted rearing, he had no difficulty identifying pictures of common items. This implies that we need not learn to interpret patterns or drawings as representations of real-world objects.

The unlearned nature of picture identification seems to be supported by the fact that color photos are interpreted readily when shown to individuals who have lived in cultures where they have never experienced pictures (Hagen & Jones, 1978). However, when black-and-white photos or drawings are used, individuals reared in isolated cultures sometimes have difficulties that are strange to those who have been reared with the continuous company of graphic images. Deregowski (1980) collected a number of such reports, including one from a Scottish missionary working in Malawi (a country in southwestern Africa between northern Rhodesia and Mozambique) nearly 75 years ago:

> Take a picture in black and white, and the natives cannot see it. You may tell the natives: "This is a picture of an ox and a dog"; and the people will look at it and look at you, and that look says that they consider you a liar. Perhaps you say again, "Yes, this is a picture of an ox and a dog. Look at the horn of the ox, and there is his tail!" And the boy will say, "Oh, yes and there is the dog's nose and eyes and ears!" Then the old people will look again and clap their hands and say, "Oh yes, it is a dog."

Clearly, such a report indicates that the individuals involved did not respond to the photo with the immediate spontaneous object identification characteristic of our viewing of pictures. Still, when the individuals had their attention directed to the relevant aspects of the pattern, they did have an "Aha!" experience, indicating that the ability to identify the pattern was there, although they lacked training to direct their attention appropriately.

Although there may be a general ability to identify objects depicted in pictures, interpreting the implied spatial relationships seems to be more subject to cultural and educational influences. Identifying depth in a flat image requires a certain amount of selection among the perceptual cues available. For instance, a picture might include such cues for depth as *linear perspective, interposition,* and *texture gradients,* among others mentioned in Chapter 10. However, there are also cues indicating that the picture is flat; there is no *binocular disparity* between items in the picture, and all of the elements in the picture require the same degree of *accommodation* and *convergence* (see Chapter 10). Thus, to see a drawing or a photograph as representing an arrangement of objects in three dimensions, rather than as a flat surface with different shadings of dark and light, you must attend to some depth cues and ignore others (Pick, 1987). An observer's particular perceptual strategy may depend on her life history and the relative frequency with which certain cues are encountered in the immediate environment.

Hudson (1960, 1962) attempted to separate cultural factors associated with the use of pictorial depth information. His technique consisted of using a series of pictures that depicted certain combinations of pictorial depth cues. Figure 17-13 shows one picture similar to those used by Hudson; as you can see, it depicts a hunting scene containing two pictorial depth cues. The first is **interposition,** in which objects close to the observer block the view of portions of more distant objects. Because the hunter and the antelope are covering portions of the rocks, they appear to be closer to the observer than are the rocks.

The second pictorial depth cue contained in this picture is **familiar size.** We know the relative sizes of familiar objects; therefore, if an object is depicted as relatively small or large, we will judge its distance from us in a way consistent with our

FIGURE 17-13   A figure used to test ability to respond to pictorial depth cues (based on Hudson, 1962).

expectations based on its known size. For example, an elephant is a very large animal. However, in Figure 17-13 the elephant is one of the smallest items in the picture. If we are responding to the cue of familiar size, we would tend to see the elephant as being the most distant object in this hunting scene. When something as large as an elephant casts a smaller image than an antelope, the elephant must be farther away because we know it is physically larger than the antelope.

Hudson used these stimuli because they are uniquely constructed to allow for both **two-dimensional** (no use of pictorial depth) and **three-dimensional** (full use of pictorial depth) types of responses. Suppose we asked an observer to describe what she saw in this picture. First we would expect her to identify correctly all of the component objects in the picture. However, suppose we also asked her to describe the actions taking place. A correct three-dimensional response would indicate that the hunter is attempting to spear the antelope (which is, of course, nearer to him than is the elephant if pictorial depth is perceived). A two-dimensional response would state that the hunter is attempting to spear the elephant, which is actually physically closer to the tip of the spear in the picture. Such a response would indicate that the observer had not responded to either the interposition cue or the familiar-size cue, both of which place the elephant at a greater distance from the hunter than is the antelope.

Stimuli similar to these have been used in a number of studies conducted throughout Africa to test observers from a number of tribal and linguistic groups (Deregowski, 1980). The results indicate that compared to Western observers the African observers have difficulty seeing pictorial depth in these pictures, a fact that has been verified using other types of pictures (Jahoda & McGurk, 1974). Presumably this is because African observers have been relatively isolated from the sort of formal exposure and training with drawings that Western-style education and exposure to the mass media provide. The ability to perceive three-dimensionality in pictures seems to be improved if more depth cues are added (Hagen & Jones, 1978; Killbride & Leibowitz, 1975) or if formal education, involving the use of picture books, drawings, and so forth, has been experienced (Killbride & Robbins, 1968; Leibowitz & Pick, 1972; Pick, 1987). You can explore your own tendencies to use certain depth cues but not others by trying Demonstration Box 17-5.

Culturally determined conventions associated with the interpretation of pictures can be shown best in situations where the flat, stationary picture is supposed to depict not only three-dimensionality but also motion. For instance, Figure 17-14 depicts a scene in which there are three different forms of motion. From left to right, we see a speeding car, a boy rapidly whipping his head around, and a dog wagging its tail. Of course, there is no actual motion, yet we "read" such

---

DEMONSTRATION BOX 17-5
Cross-Cultural Differences in Perception

The figure accompanying this box is sometimes called the "devil's tuning fork." Look at the figure for about 30 seconds or so; then close the book and try to draw it from memory. Return to this box when you have done this.

Most of you probably found this task to be quite difficult. The source of your difficulty comes from the fact that your cultural experience with graphic representations has caused you to interpret this two-dimensional stimulus as a three-dimensional object. Unfortunately, such an interpretation leads to problems because the depth cues implied in this figure are ambiguous. It is interesting to note that Africans who have not received formal education have no difficulty reproducing the figure. Because they do not interpret the figure as three-dimensional, they merely see a pattern of flat lines, which is easy to reproduce.

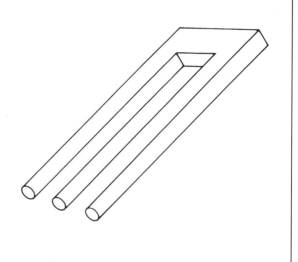

---

motion into the pictures. Within Western cultures, such interpretation of motion in pictorial arrays may appear as early as 4 years of age (Friedman & Stevenson, 1975). Non-Western cultures without pictorial experience, however, virtually never "see" movement in such representations. The likelihood that movement will be seen in such representations increases with education, urbanization, and exposure to pictorial materials (Duncan, Gourlay, & Hudson, 1973; Friedman & Stevenson, 1980).

An interesting feature of picture perception is that after we have learned to "see" pictures, we actually end up seeing more than was physically present. First, remember that any picture is just a small sample of information that would be present if we were actually looking at the actual scene in the real world. When we look at a photograph and are later asked to recall or to draw what we saw, we tend to remember seeing information that was not really in the picture but was likely to have existed just outside the camera's field of view. This tendency is called **boundary extension** (Intraub & Berkowits, 1996; Intraub & Gottesman, 1996). This is another example of the fact that our current perceptual experience consists of the "best bet" as to what was actually out there. Through

FIGURE 17-14 Scenes conventionally recognized as depicting motion by Western observers but not necessarily by non-Western observers.

our life experience we have learned that certain objects or aspects of view have a high probability of being related to each other, and so, even if they are not physically present, they are simply added to the conscious percept to make the scene "look right."

Illusion and Constancy

Certain facets of the environment make us more or less responsive to certain patterns of depth cues appearing in pictures. For instance, the **carpentered world hypothesis** begins with the observation that in the urbanized Western world, rooms and buildings are usually rectangular, many objects in the environment have right-angled corners, city streets have straight sides, and so forth. Surrounded by such an environment, we may learn to depend more heavily on depth cues based on linear perspective than would people who live in less "carpentered" and more rural environments (Coren & Girgus, 1978; Gregory, 1966; Segall, Campbell, & Herskovits, 1966). For example, rural, isolated Zulus have been described as surrounded by a circular culture. They live in round huts with round doors. They do not plow their land in straight furrows but instead tend to use curved furrows. Individuals living in such a world would not be expected to rely on linear perspective as heavily as do those of us living in a more linear environment.

In a classic study Segall, Campbell, and Herskovits (1966) compared the responsiveness of individuals in carpentered versus noncarpentered environments to certain types of depth cues. However, instead of using pictures like those that Hudson used, as stimulus materials they chose a more subtle class of patterns, namely the visual-geometric illusions. Some of these configurations have already been discussed in Chapter 11, where we pointed out how susceptibility to size distortions in some figures, such as the Mueller-Lyer illusion, may be dependent on a three-dimensional interpretation of the pattern (to refresh your memory refer back to Figure 11-0). As we discussed then, the apparently longer portion of the Mueller-Lyer figure may be interpreted as a corner of a room receding in depth because the wings of the illusion act as linear perspective cues. The inappropriate application

of size constancy based on this interpretation of the wings of the figure as perspective cues results in our overestimation of the size of this segment of the figure relative to the segment with the inward-turned wings. Because pictorial depth information is thought to play a role in the formation of these illusory percepts, these types of configurations are well suited to an exploration of the carpentered world hypothesis.

Segall and colleagues (1966) gathered data from throughout Africa and also from several groups of people living in Evanston, Illinois. Although there are variations within the noncarpentered samples, the average Mueller-Lyer illusion was greater for the more urban groups. Similar results have been reported for other perspective-related illusions (Coren & Girgus, 1978; Deregowski, 1980; Killbride & Leibowitz, 1975).

Although the observed differences in illusion susceptibility for different cultural groups may be partially caused by factors other than experience with a carpentered world (Berry, 1971; Coren & Porac, 1978; Pollack & Silvar, 1967), there is ample evidence that the absence of experience with certain types of depth cues impairs certain other perceptual functions (such as size constancy) that are dependent on depth perception. One of the most striking examples of this was provided by the anthropologist Turnbull (1961). He observed the behavior of the Bambuti Pygmies, who live in the Ituri forest in the Congo. Because they live in the dense rain forest, their vision is generally limited to short distances, with vistas that extend for, at most, only 30 m. Therefore, their life history seems to lack the visual experience needed to learn to use the depth cues responsible for the maintenance of size constancy at greater viewing distances. Turnbull noted one instance when he had taken his Bambuti guide, Kenge, out of the forest for the first time in his life. They were crossing a broad plain and happened to spot a herd of buffalo:

> . . . Kenge looked over the plains and down to where a herd of about a hundred buffalo was grazing some miles away. He asked me what kind of insects they were, and I told him they were buffalo, twice as big as the forest buffalo known to him. He laughed loudly and told me not to tell such stupid stories. . . . We got into the car and drove down to where the animals were grazing. He watched them getting larger and larger, and though he was as courageous

as any Pygmy, he moved over and sat close to me and muttered that it was witchcraft. . . . Finally, when he realized that they were real buffalo he was no longer afraid, but what puzzled him still was why they had been so small, and whether they really had been small and suddenly grown larger, or whether it had been some kind of trickery. (From C. Turnbull, *American Journal of Psychology*, 74. Copyright 1961 The University of Illinois Press.)

Turnbull's description of Kenge's perceptual impressions suggests that our experience with particular stimuli prevalent in our immediate environment can result in differences in how we perceive new stimuli and new situations. It seems that we learn to utilize stimulus information that we encounter frequently, but we fail to learn to utilize stimulus information that is rare. This holds for the auditory as well as the visual environment.

Speech

The most dominant feature in our auditory environment is the constant flow of language sounds that surrounds us. As discussed in Chapter 12, each language uses a small set of word-differentiating *phonemes*, which are the functionally characteristic sounds of that language. Because different languages use different subsets and combinations of these phonemes, experiments on people reared in different linguistic settings offer a unique opportunity to observe the effects of specific kinds of experience on perception (see Kuhl, 1987). Because some sounds may be treated as distinctively different in some languages and not in others—for instance, the sounds "r" as in *rope* and "l" as in *lope* are different phonemes in English, but not in Japanese—we would expect a bias in the auditory experience of individuals brought up surrounded by one or the other of these two languages. Numerous studies have shown that adults who have grown up with exposure to only one language often have difficulty discriminating certain linguistic contrasts characteristic of other languages (Strange & Jenkins, 1978; Werker & Tees, 1984). This type of difficulty may persist even if the adults have learned the other language and appear to be fluent in it. For example, Goto (1971) recorded pairs of words that contrasted the "r" and "l" sounds (such as *lead* versus *read* or *play* versus *pray*). Several

native Japanese speakers, who were bilingual in Japanese and English, could produce these sounds so that native English-speaking listeners could differentiate them without error. However, this seems to be a learned ability to *produce* rather than to perceive the phonemic difference because, when asked to listen to recordings of pairs of words that contrasted these phonemes, the native Japanese speakers could not perceive the difference, even when listening to their own speech productions!

The mechanism responsible for our ability to discriminate some speech sounds but not others is still somewhat mysterious. Surprisingly, infants seem to be born with the ability to discriminate certain sound pairs not used in their native tongue, and they appear to lose this ability as adults (Trehub, 1976; Werker & Tees, 1984). A striking example was provided by Werker, Gilbert, Humphrey, and Tees (1981), who presented English-speaking and Hindi-speaking adults with pairs of sounds that are different phonemes in Hindi but not in English. As we might expect, the adult Hindi speakers could make the discrimination, but the adult English speakers could not. The interesting result, however, is that 6-month-old infants from English-speaking homes could make the discrimination. It seems that at some time during the first year of exposure to the language, infants begin to respond selectively to certain aspects in their linguistic environment and to lose selectively their ability to respond to phonemic distinctions not used in their native language (Werker & Tees, 1984).

This is not to say that one cannot learn to make certain phonemic distinctions. Evidence suggests that learning through exposure and experience plays a role in the ability to discriminate between various linguistic sounds, and some linguistic discriminations seem to be learned during the childhood years (Eilers, Wilson, & Moore, 1979). However, this appears to be limited to certain dimensions of the sounds. Tees and Werker (1984) showed that short-term intensive training improved the ability of native English speakers to make certain nonnative (Hindi) speech discriminations, although after 5 years of language study the ability to make these discriminations was already apparent. An interesting additional finding pertained to individuals who spent their early years in a setting where Hindi was spoken (perhaps by a live-in relative). Even though these individuals had never studied the language and as adults were unable to speak, understand, or write more than a few words of Hindi, it was found that they could make the phonemic discriminations that nonnative Hindi speakers found impossible. Thus, their early experience seems to have "tuned" their speech-sound decoding capacity for certain phonemes even though they were not actually speaking the language.

In terms of our earlier discussion about the relationship between experience and development, these results suggest that different aspects of the perception of speechlike sounds follow different courses. Whereas some auditory discriminations are facilitated through contact with particular sounds in the linguistic environment, others are lost through their absence or rarity, thus showing that experience is necessary for their maintenance (cf. Walley, Pisoni, & Aslin, 1981). Overall, this confirms that much of what we perceive and many of the perceptual distinctions we make are strongly influenced by the culture and environment in which we were reared.

Effects of Occupation

Even within a given culture there is selective exposure to different sets of environmental stimuli. You are exposed to your occupational setting for about one half of your adult working life, and specific sets of occupational experiences can affect your perceptual abilities both at the physiological and at higher cognitive levels. One aspect of an occupation that may have physiological effects on a sensory system is the magnitude of sound, light, or chemical stimulation to which you are exposed.

Consider, for example, the amount of auditory input that bombards you in your occupational setting. Some work environments are relatively quiet (such as offices and small stores); others are associated with continuous high-intensity noise (e.g., factories, mills, or rock music bands). Figure 17-15 illustrates the effects of noise on hearing for different occupations. The horizontal axis represents the frequencies at which hearing was tested in a sample of male office, farm, and factory workers. The 0 dB point on the vertical axis represents the average minimum threshold for an auditory experience. The three curves on the graph plot the

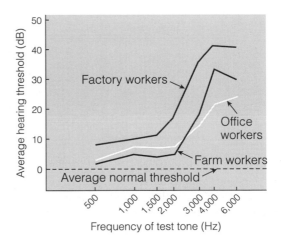

FIGURE 17-15 The effect of occupation on hearing (based on Glorig, Wheeler, Quigle, Grings, & Summerfield, 1970).

average threshold sound intensity at each of the frequencies used in the test. As you can see, the group of factory workers has a lowered sensitivity (higher average thresholds). Fortunately, many factory workers have begun to wear earphones while working; these help protect them from the destructive effects of continual noise exposure.

According to Kryter (1985), factory workers are not the only group who should be concerned about exposure to very loud sounds. For instance, soldiers exposed to the sound of gunfire and airline pilots exposed to engine noises have been shown to have hearing loss. The loss tends to be greatest in the high-frequency ranges and seems to increase in severity as the length of the exposure increases. Thus, airline pilots who had from 1,000 hr to 2,000 hr of flying time on the noisy planes of the 1960s had an average auditory threshold of approximately 0 dB at a sound frequency of 4,000 Hz, whereas more experienced pilots, with 10,000 hr to 16,000 hr of flying time, had an average auditory threshold of 10 dB at that sound frequency.

Rice, Ayley, Bartlett, Bedford, Gregory, and Hallum (1968) showed that performers of rock music may also suffer hearing losses. In Figure 17-16 average auditory thresholds are again plotted for various test frequencies. The lowest curve represents the thresholds of the control group of nonperformers. Notice that relative to nonperformers

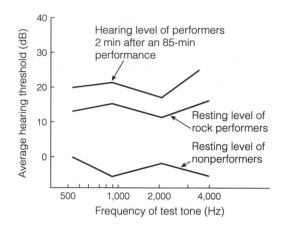

FIGURE 17-16 A comparison of the hearing of rock performers to that of nonperformers (based on Rice et al., 1968).

of the same age, the rock performers have elevated auditory thresholds (lower sensitivity). At 4,000 Hz there is approximately 20 dB difference between the thresholds of the performers and the controls. To give you a reference point, a 20-dB difference would be roughly equivalent to being able to hear a normal conversational tone as opposed to a shout. Figure 17-16 also shows the immediate effects of prolonged exposure to very loud sounds. The top curve on this graph plots the measured thresholds immediately after 85 min of exposure to very loud music; as you can see, the threshold at 4,000 Hz has risen to 25 dB.

In a similar vein, there are occupations that expose the eyes to high-intensity lights (such as welding arcs and furnace blazes). In the same manner that exposure to prolonged high-intensity sound can permanently impair hearing, exposure to prolonged high-intensity light can permanently impair vision (Noell, 1980).

Perhaps the most interesting occupational effect on vision pertains to **myopia** (nearsightedness). Physiologically this is a condition where the length of the eye is somewhat too great, and the parallel rays of light from distant objects come to a focus well in front of the retina, thus resulting in poor distance acuity. Myopia is actually the most prevalent visual disorder in the world, affecting over 2 billion individuals. Over the past 40 years a

number of studies have established that one of the major causes of myopia has to do with a life history of exposure to "near work," which would include reading and other activities restricted to close distances (see Birnbaum, 1981; Grosvenor & Flom, 1991; Lundervold, Lewin, & Irvin, 1987). It is believed that trying hard to see leads to overaccommodation of the crystalline lens and some increased internal pressure in the eye. Over a long period of time this may actually lengthen the eye and lead to myopia (Freidman, 1981). It has been demonstrated that after only a short span of near work (such as 3 hr of editing text on a visual display terminal), a person may become temporarily myopic (Jaschinski-Kruza, 1984). It is also possible to induce myopia in animals by using certain environmental and visual exposure conditions (e.g., Sivak, Barrie, Callender, Doughty, Seltner, & West, 1990). In monkeys this has been done by rearing them under conditions where for extended periods the maximum visual distance that they could see was around 50 cm (20 in.; e.g., Young, 1981).

The most common way to correct for myopia is, of course, to prescribe eyeglasses. In fact, with the high prevalence of myopia, we are very used to seeing people with glasses. It is so common that we seldom think about glasses, which must have been the case with the artist C. Schoneus, who depicted the circumcision of Jesus, shown here as Figure 17-17. Notice that the rabbi performing the operation is using *pince-nez* or "nose clip" eyeglasses that permit the use of both hands, even those these were not to be invented for another 1,500 years!

Glasses, however, are not the only solution to myopia that has been suggested. One attempted remedy is based on the assumption that if myopia comes about through a particular pattern of eye use, then it should be possible to develop a set of exercises that might reverse the process that is causing nearsightedness. Vision training to correct myopia has been discussed and debated extensively ever since 1920, when William Bates wrote his controversial book titled *Better Eyesight Without Glasses*. He and his successors emphasized certain eye exercises and discouraged the use of corrective spectacles. Since that time a number of different training techniques have been developed. Some use recognition training, some use focus exercises to accommodate to more distant targets, and some have used even biofeedback techniques, where

FIGURE 17-17   Part of an engraving by C. Schoneus, depicting the circumcision of Jesus by a rabbi wearing glasses, despite the fact that these were invented 1,500 years *after* Jesus' birth.

complex oculometers monitor the individual's state of lens accommodation (Freidman, 1981; Kaplan, 1995; Roscoe & Couchman, 1987; Woo & Wilson, 1990).

How well does vision training work for myopia or any other form of visual difficulty? There have been some reports of success, with at least some individuals showing measurable improvement in their ability to recognize familiar targets and letters (e.g., Lundervold, Lewin, & Irvin, 1987). Unfortunately, this success seems to be due to attentional changes, which allow individuals to recognize blurred stimuli better, rather than to any actual improvement in the refractive state of the eye (Goodson & Rahe, 1981). The most recent studies have shown that the vision training does not really change visual acuity at all (e.g., Long, 1994). It certainly does not allow individuals better distance vision in situations where the targets have few recognition clues when they are blurred or are much different from the ones that the individuals trained with (e.g., Koslowe, Spierer, Rosner, & Belkin, 1991; Woo & Wilson, 1990). A series of studies by Fahle and associates (e.g., Fahle, 1997; Fahle, Edelman, & Poggio, 1995; Herzog & Fahle, 1997) makes it clear why this is the case. Using tasks involving vernier acuity (see Chapter 4) they found that there was rapid improvement in acuity with practice, especially with appropriate feedback about errors. Unfortunately, the learning was quite specific for the stimuli used. If a stimulus is rotated, say, from horizontal to vertical, if the pattern is altered in any visible way, or even if it is moved to a different location on the retina, then all of the training effects seem to be lost. This lack of transfer from one set of learned discriminations to a new one is not unique to vision but also occurs in touch and other modalities (e.g., Sathian & Zangaladze, 1997). Thus, although an individual's viewing practices and near work habits are capable of causing myopia, simple training and exercise procedures do not seem to be able to reverse the condition after it has developed.

Perceptual Set

Experiences we have in an occupational or other setting may bias our perception and interpretation of various stimuli. This seems to be because specific past experiences produce a sensitization or predisposition to "see" a situation in a certain way, especially when several alternative perceptual experiences are

possible (as when the stimulus is ambiguous or degraded because of poor viewing conditions). Technically, this is known as a **perceptual set,** and it refers specifically to the expectancies or predispositions an observer brings to the perceptual situation (Coren, 1984). In many respects, set can be thought of as another example of selective attention (as we discussed in Chapter 15), in which the observer is set to process some but not all incoming information or to organize it in a specific manner. To get a better feeling for how set operates, you might try Demonstration Box 17-6.

As an example, let us consider police as observers and eyewitnesses because this is an occupation in which observation is important. Some findings suggest that perceptual set may influence the observations of police in certain situations. In one study, police officers and civilians were shown films of a street scene over a period of several hours. Their task was to categorize the people who appeared as wanted (photos on display below the screen) or unwanted and to categorize the actions they engaged in as normal exchanges of goods or as thefts. The police tended to report more alleged thefts than did the nonpolice, although there was no significant difference between the police and civilians in their actual detection of people and actions that were to be categorized (Clifford & Bull, 1978).

A more subtle demonstration of this effect of set was provided by Toch and Schulte (1961), who studied perception of violence and crime in ambiguous visual scenes. They simultaneously presented different pictures to each eye in a stereoscope (see Chapter 10). One eye was shown a

---

DEMONSTRATION BOX 17-6
Perceptual Set

Something of the flavor of perceptual set can be experienced by simply reading the set of words below out loud:
MACBETH MACARTHUR
MACWILLIAMS MACNAMARA
MACDILLON MACDONALD
MACMASTER MACDOWELL
MACHINES MACKENZIE

Now look back at the next-to-the-last word. Did you pronounce it as if it were organized as the name *Mac Hines*, or did you pronounce it as if it were organized as the more familiar and natural form that makes the common word *machines*? If you pronounced it as the name, organizing the prefix *Mac* into a separate unit, you were demonstrating the effects of perceptual set.

FIGURE 17-18 A stereogram used to test for occupational influences on the perception of violence (from H. H. Toch & R. Schulte, 1961, *British Journal of Psychology, 52*, 389–393).

violent scene and the other a nonviolent scene, as in the pair of stimuli in Figure 17-18. If these two views are seen simultaneously by the two eyes, perceptual confusion should result. Observers tend to resolve this ambiguous situation in favor of one scene or the other; that scene then dominates the percept. Toch and Schulte were interested in exploring the notion that police students would be predisposed to interpret this particular ambiguous situation in terms of the violent as opposed to the nonviolent scene. They compared the performance of advanced police administration students with two control groups: beginning police students and university students. In general, they found that the advanced police students interpreted the stereograms as depicting violence approximately twice as many times as did the other two groups. Thus, their data provide some evidence that certain occupations, especially those requiring intensive training, may set an individual to interpret ambiguous stimulation in a particular way.

We are not singling out the police for scrutiny. Perceptual set associated with occupational training, experience, and education can affect all groups of individuals. An example of how our educational background can bias our perception can be seen by looking at Figure 17-19A. Most Western observers will see a complex pattern of black shapes, which, by some stretching of the imagination, might appear to cohere into some sort of a boot. Conversely, Figure 17-19B is quite different. Here the white spaces clearly shape the word *FLY*, whereas the black spaces serve as the background. Our familiarity with the English language helps to focus our attention on this region of the figure, and we

supply the missing contours, subjectively, to complete the percept (see Chapter 11). Actually, if you were an educated native Chinese, you might be more captured by Figure 17-19A because it outlines in the white spaces between the black shapes the calligraphic character for the Chinese word *FLY*, and Figure 17-19B might appear to be merely five meaningless black shapes (see Coren, Porac, & Theodor, 1987).

Another interesting example of perceptual set based on language (here written language) has been provided by Diener (1990). Look at the two words printed in Figure 17-20. Pay particular attention to the letter *P* in both. In the one on the left the letter *P* appears to be a lowercase letter,

A

B

FIGURE 17-19 Although *A* may appear to be a relatively random collection of black shapes, perhaps depicting some sort of boot, it is actually similar to *B* in that it contains the word *FLY* depicted in the white areas, but in *A* the word is in Chinese calligraphy.

apt APt

FIGURE 17-20   The letter *P* in the word on the right appears to be in uppercase and also appears to be larger than the letter on the left. The two letters, however, are physically identical (based on Diener, 1990).

and on the right it appears to be a capital letter. Now look at the size of both of these letters. Notice that the capital *P* appears to be physically larger than its lowercase counterpart. Actually both are the same size. Your set and expectations based on your knowledge that capital letters are usually larger than lowercase letters have distorted your perception in this case.

Although we have singled out vision for most of our discussion, it is important to note that set effects can be found in all aspects of perception. For example, consider the case of the apparent intensity of an odor. It has been shown that a strawberry odor smells more intense when the solution in which it is presented is colored red than when it is colorless (Zellner & Kautz, 1990). It is as if the brain were saying "Strawberries are red, so something that is red must have more strawberry quality than something that is colorless." A similar effect occurred when attempts were made to market clear, colorless cola drinks. The product failed because many people complained that these drinks had "washed out" or "weak" flavors. This is because we are set to see our carbonated cola drinks as brown. In summary, then, much of what you perceive is determined by what your experience, culture, and education have set you to perceive.

CHAPTER SUMMARY

Many of the developmental changes in perception reflect the effects of experience rather than **maturation. Induction** is the process whereby experience triggers development of a perceptual capacity; in **enhancement** experience improves it; with **facilitation** experience speeds its appearance; whereas **maintenance** preserves a perceptual ability already acquired. Both **restricted rearing** and

selective rearing have been used to study the effect of experience on perception. Animals without adequate stimulation show neurophysiological deficits, reduced numbers of sensory neurons, and fewer interconnections. There are often **critical periods** during which stimulation is needed. Restricting sensory experience before or after the critical period produces few effects. In selective rearing the sensory inputs are biased and limited. Thus, it is possible to reduce the number of neurons tuned to a particular line orientation by restricting experience with those stimuli. The behavioral effects of such sensory restrictions are often subtle, and recovery is often possible when normal conditions are restored. People born with cataracts or **astigmatism** often experience the same kind of effects as produced by restricted and selective rearing conditions. The **oblique effect,** a phenomenon where the acuity for diagonally oriented stimuli is poorer than for horizontally or vertically oriented stimuli, may be a selective-rearing effect in urban humans who are most commonly exposed to contours oriented horizontally or vertically.

In terms of sensory-motor learning, feedback coordinating external stimulation with our own voluntary movements **(reafference)** seems to be more effective than feedback from passively induced or presented stimuli **(exafference)** in developing accurate spatial perception. **Rearrangement** studies involving distorting lenses and prisms have shown that with active movements and/or error feedback, we quickly show *adaptation* to the distortion. When the optical distortion is removed we then show **aftereffects** in the opposite direction, confirming that the change was perceptual. Such perceptual adaptation to visual rearrangement may involve several types of change. For instance, in addition to visual changes there may be changes in proprioception and eye position as well as other effects. Another form of perceptual learning involves **illusion decrement,** where the strength of a visual-geometric illusion diminishes with active scanning, which produces information feedback about the nature of the distortion.

Context is important in determining what we perceive because according to the **transactional viewpoint** our phenomenal perception of a situation is simply our "best bet" as to what is out there in the world. Through experience and learning we develop hypotheses that can improve or bias and distort our conscious perception in ambiguous stimulus situations. The conceptual classification or meaning of stimuli can affect our perception. For example, stimuli from the same conceptual class are more likely to interact to cause illusions than are stimuli from different classes. Language can sometimes set a context for perception. Labeling a stimulus can bias our perception of that stimulus toward attributes implied by the label. In the case of eyewitness testimony, even the pattern of questioning after the event can bias our recollection of what we actually saw or heard earlier.

Some common percepts require considerable learning and practice, such as the perception of depth and size constancy in a two-dimensional picture. The perception of motion in a flat, stationary picture also seems to require the kind of practice provided in literate cultures. If we have adequate experience with pictorial material, it is possible for us to see even more of the world than is actually presented in the picture, as shown in the case of **boundary extension.** In some schematic patterns that tend to cause visual illusions, the process involved is constancy scaling based on treatment of the pattern as if it were an attempt to represent three-dimensional space. The **carpentered world hypothesis** states that individuals living in urban environments characterized by straight lines and angles will tend to depend more on depth cues based on linear perspective than would people living in more primitive rural environments; hence they will be more susceptible to illusions that have implicit perspective cues that will trigger constancy scaling in them. Even in real-world situations experience may be required to evoke normal constancy corrections.

Probably the most frequently recognized situation where experience plays a role in our perception involves speech. Early experience with the phonemes in a language seems to be needed to maintain our ability to make those phonemic distinctions. Adults who have not had those early experiences simply cannot perceive differences, such as the difference between the "r" in *rice* and the "l" in *lice*, which is not heard by adult Japanese speakers.

Our occupations also alter our perceptual experiences. Noise in the workplace can have cumulative and permanent effects on an individual's hearing sensitivity. In vision, **myopia** can result from prolonged viewing of near objects. Vision training exercises are a deliberate attempt to use learning procedures to improve vision. Although such exercises can improve visual acuity for certain tasks, such as vernier acuity, the training effects are quite specific to the stimuli practiced on and do not transfer well to new situations or even to modifications of the training stimulus.

Perceptual set refers to the expectancies or predispositions that an observer brings to a perceptual situation. Our expectations that particular events will occur make it more likely that we will perceive such events if they do appear or interpret ambiguous stimuli as instances that fit our expectations. Thus, a clear cola drink tastes weaker and more "washed out," even though the ingredients are the same as those of a brown cola (except for food coloring), because we are set to believe that something clear colored is mostly water without any added flavors.

KEY TERMS

induction
maturation
enhancement
facilitation
maintenance
restricted rearing
selective rearing
critical period
visual field
astigmatism
oblique effect
exafference
reafference

rearrangement
aftereffects
illusion decrement
transactional viewpoint
interposition
familiar size
two-dimensional
three-dimensional
boundary extension
carpentered world
  hypothesis
myopia
perceptual set

Individual Differences

CHAPTER 18

How often have you heard people arguing over whether a color is green or blue, whether the room is too hot or too cold, or whether the coffee is too weak or too strong? Such arguments may represent real differences in the perceptions of the individuals involved. Remember that perception is not simply a process by which the qualities of the world get transferred from "out there" to "in here." Rather, your final conscious experience of a stimulus involves many levels of processing. Not only must the peripheral sensory receptors be stimulated, but also stimuli must be interpreted and encoded. As one ancient philosopher said, "The eyes are blind; only the mind sees." If this premise is true, it is quite probable that individuals can differ in the way that they perceive their worlds, because it is certainly true that no two minds seem to work in exactly the same way.

Many factors can cause individuals to have different perceptions even when encountering identical stimuli. For instance, consider Figure 18-1, which shows a common visual distortion called the **Poggendorff illusion.** For most people it appears that if the line marked *A* were extended, it would pass below the line marked *B* by several millimeters. Actually *A* and *B* are directly in line with each other. The magnitude of this illusion differs among individuals depending on their age, their education, whether they are male or female, and even how well they do on spatial skills tests, such as those that form

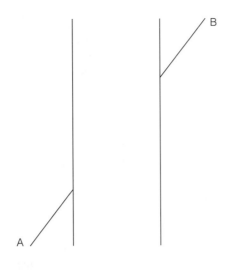

FIGURE 18-1 The Poggendorff illusion, in which Line A appears as if it would pass below Line B if extended, even though the two lines are exactly aligned.

part of many intelligence scales (Coren & Girgus, 1978; Coren & Porac, 1987; Girgus & Coren, 1987). Some of these factors are probably not surprising to you, because we have already discussed how age and past experience can affect perception (in Chapters 16 and 17). However, there are many other variables that operate to make each person's perceptual experiences somewhat unique. These variables include physiological factors, such as changes in the sensory receptors themselves or in the neural apparatus that decodes the sensory information. There is also a contribution from an individual's cognitive, or perceptual, style, which is actually a reflection of personality differences and different approaches to gathering information from the environment. Even an individual's gender seems to cause differences in the way sensory information is processed. All of these factors lead to individual differences in perception. One of the most interesting aspects of perception is the consideration of why the world you perceive may not necessarily be the same as the world perceived by others.

PHYSIOLOGICAL DIFFERENCES

Each of us can be seen as a complex physiological machine, and we certainly have seen how factors that alter the structure and function of our sensory apparatus will alter what we perceive. For example, nonfunctional retinal cones will cause color vision deficits. Calcium deposits on the bones of one's inner ear will lessen the intensity of sounds from the environment while making one's own voice seem very loud. In addition to such very specific factors, there are some physiological factors that affect the body generally and also alter perception as a side effect.

The Effects of Drugs

Many drugs can cause marked changes in sensory capacities. For instance, cigarette smokers are continually ingesting several active chemicals. The most important of these is the poison nicotine; next in importance is the gas carbon monoxide. Because these chemicals enter the body predominantly via the mouth, it is not surprising that the major sensory effects of smoking tobacco are on the sense of taste. Absolute taste thresholds are higher for smokers than for nonsmokers, with smokers being especially insensitive to bitter tastes such as quinine (Kaplan & Glanville, 1964; Sinnot & Rauth, 1937). However, you may be surprised to find that smoking also affects vision. Most of these effects are probably due to the inhalation of carbon monoxide, a substance that has been shown to produce alterations in performance on some visual tasks, particularly those involving sustaining visual attention (Gliner, Horvath, & Mihevic, 1983) or smoothly tracking targets with the eyes (Sibony, Evinger, & Manning, 1987). In addition, habitual smokers tend to have somewhat poorer contrast sensitivity (Fine & Kobrick, 1987) and reduced ability to make light-intensity discriminations, especially under scotopic illumination conditions (Rhee, Kim, & Kim, 1965). This latter fact might explain why smokers tend to have more nighttime driving accidents than nonsmokers. There is also evidence that ingestion of nicotine slows the rate of recovery from certain visual aftereffects (such as the afterimages associated with viewing bright targets or the fatigue effects of prolonged staring at certain types of patterns, as we discussed in Chapters 4 and 5). It has been hypothesized that nicotine slows recovery from aftereffects because it affects the balance of neural excitation and inhibition within the visual system (Amure, 1978).

One general theme that characterizes the data describing the effects of drugs on perception is that drugs that depress neural activity—such as sedatives, barbiturates, tranquilizers, or alcohol—also decrease sensory acuity. For example, Hellekant (1965) measured the effect of alcohol on taste sensitivity by recording directly from the chorda tympani nerve of a cat. This nerve conveys taste information from most of the tongue. Alcohol reduced responsiveness to sweet (sucrose), acid (acetic acid), salt (sodium chloride), and bitter (quinine) stimuli. The strongest reduction of taste response was for the bitter stimuli. Alcohol also may affect other sensory systems, and recent studies suggest that these effects may be cumulative. One study tested the auditory system and found that chronic alcoholics show delays in the neural response to auditory signals when compared to nonalcoholics (Begleiter, Porjesz, & Chou, 1981) and slower recognition responses to auditory signals (Gustafson, 1986). Studies of the effect of alcohol on visual abilities have produced similar findings. Research with chronic alcoholics has found differences in color vision, indicating that alcoholic observers have a higher incidence of color vision deficiencies than nonalcoholic observers (Granger & Ikeda, 1976; Reynolds, 1979).

One does not have to be an alcoholic or a habitual drinker to show the effects of alcohol on visual perception. In some studies of nonalcoholic observers, there are indications that high doses of alcohol decrease an individual's ability to follow a moving target with the eyes (Flom, Brown, Adams, & Jones, 1976; Levy, Lipton, & Holtzman, 1981) and also decrease the ability of the eye to accommodate or change the focus of the lens (Miller, Pigion, & Martin, 1985). Even a small amount of alcohol can decrease an observer's ability to detect the onset of movement in a visual stimulus (Bates, 1989; MacArthur & Sekuler, 1982). The Hollywood film stereotype of the intoxicated person with double vision has some basis in fact. Both fusion and stereoscopic depth perception deteriorate in proportion with a direct relationship to blood alcohol level (Miller, 1991; Wang & Taylor-Nicholson, 1992).

Alcohol also affects some more complex perceptual processes, such as size constancy (Farrimond, 1990). The breakdown of size constancy with alcohol is particularly dangerous for drivers. If,

under the influence of alcohol, individuals do not apply the size constancy scaling mechanism as usual, problems can arise because perceived size and distance interact, as we saw in Chapter 13. After ingesting enough alcohol, a driver perceives objects such as pedestrians or other vehicles as being smaller and more distant than when they are perceived under conditions when the driver is completely sober. This means that the intoxicated driver is less likely to think that it is necessary to apply the brakes or to slow down to avoid collisions even when such actions are called for.

The overall sensitivity of the visual and auditory systems is also affected by many depressant drugs. A popular technique for measuring visual responsiveness is the **critical flicker fusion frequency** task (usually abbreviated **CFF**). This task requires an observer to view a flickering light. As the flicker rate is increased the observer will eventually no longer see the successive on-and-off cycles but, rather, will see them fused into a steady, continuous light. The flicker speed that results in the perceptual shift from an apparently flickering to an apparently steady light is the CFF. The more sensitive the eye is to changes in illumination level, the faster the rate that the light must be cycled on and off to cause the perception of flicker to disappear. A similar task used in hearing is called the **auditory flutter fusion (AFF)** task. In measuring the AFF, a tone, rather than a light, is switched on and off repeatedly. The AFF is the rate that the tone must be cycled on and off for the listener to hear it as a continuous sound. Depressant drugs, such as alcohol and tranquilizers, tend to lower both the CFF and the AFF, thus indicating that the visual and auditory systems are acting sluggishly and with less sensitivity under the influence of such drugs (Besser, 1966; Holland, 1960). It is interesting to note that fasting, which also increases fatigue and makes individuals sluggish, also tends to lower the CFF (Ali & Amir, 1989).

Drugs that increase the arousal level of the observer, such as stimulants like caffeine or amphetamines (and even some of the B vitamins), may sometimes improve the sensitivity of the observer. For instance, the high-level stimulant cocaine may enhance recognition performance (Higgens & Bickel, 1990), whereas caffeine speeds and improves the localization of visual targets (Lorist & Snel, 1997). However, the effects of stimulants do

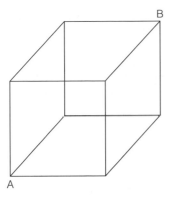

FIGURE 18-2 The Necker Cube, in which the face with Corner A sometimes appears nearer than the face with Corner B and sometimes reverses so that the face with Corner B appears nearer.

not seem to be as widespread or as reproducible as those obtained with depressant drugs. We do find that amphetamines and caffeine seem to increase the responsiveness of the visual and auditory systems and even the olfactory system (Turner, 1968). There are hints that some aspects of the superior perceptual performance with stimulants may be due to improved attention rather than to changes in threshold level (Fagen & Swift, 1988; Swift & Tiplady, 1988).

Another technique used to monitor drug effects involves reversible figures, such as the one shown in Figure 18-2. When you look steadily at this figure (which is called the **Necker Cube**), you will notice that it seems to reverse its apparent orientation from time to time. Sometimes the face with

the corner labeled *A* appears closer than the face with the corner labeled *B*, and at other times *B* seems closer. Most people have a fairly constant rate of reversal for this figure. Many factors can affect the reversal rate, such as the way you attend to it (Reisberg & O'Shaughnessy, 1984; Wallace & Priebe, 1985). Depressive drugs, such as some tranquilizers, will tend to slow the reversal rate (Phillipson & Harris, 1984). Demonstration Box 18-1 provides a procedure for testing the effects of a stimulant on this phenomenon.

The hallucinogenic and psychoactive drugs—including LSD, mescaline, psilocybin, and marijuana—are often reported to have profound perceptual effects. For instance, Aldous Huxley (1963) described his visual experiences after taking mescaline, saying: "First and most important is the experience of light . . . All colors are intensified to a pitch far beyond anything seen in the normal state, and at the same time the mind's capacity for recognizing fine distinctions of tone and hue is notably heightened." Unfortunately, although some aspects of the subjective experience seem to be heightened, actual measurements do not always show increased sensory sensitivity. Generally speaking, most tasks involving time discrimination and time estimation deteriorate under the influence of LSD (Frederick, Gillam, Lensing, & Paule, 1997). LSD, mescaline, and psilocybin all reduce the accuracy of color discriminations (Hartman & Hollister, 1963), reduce visual sensitivity in a threshold task (Carlson, 1958), blur vision (Hoffer & Osmond, 1967), and slow dark adaptation (Ostfeld, 1961). Even if individuals begin to abstain from LSD use, these negative visual effects may persist for periods of 2 years

---

DEMONSTRATION BOX 18-1
The Effects of Stimulants on Figure Reversals

For this demonstration you will need a friend and a watch. Have your friend monitor you while you look at Figure 18-2 for 1 min. Call out each time the figure reverses its orientation and have your friend keep count. Next, drink a cup of coffee. Don't use decaffeinated coffee because we want you to receive a dose of caffeine. Because caffeine is a stimulant, it should in-

crease your visual responsiveness (as well as keep you awake for the rest of the chapter). The effects take about 15 min to appear; after this interval, repeat the viewing process. Look at Figure 18-2 again for 1 min while your friend records the number of reversals. You should find that the stimulant has increased the number of perceptual shifts that you experience.

or more (Abraham & Wolf, 1988). Susceptibility to at least one visual-geometric illusion, the Mueller-Lyer, increases under the influence of LSD (Edwards & Cohen, 1961). However, LSD does seem to improve auditory acuity and seems to enhance the CFF (Hoffer & Osmond, 1967; Williams, 1979).

Similarly, when observers are asked to describe their experiences after smoking moderate doses of marijuana (cannabis), they often report improved visual clarity and acuity. Unfortunately, the experimental results indicate that, as with LSD, the actual perceptual effects involve losses in sensitivity (in some respects very similar to those of alcohol). For instance, in a vigilance task where observers were asked to fixate a target and report stimuli appearing in the periphery of vision, those who had smoked marijuana produced fewer accurate reports (Moskowitz, Sharma, & McGlothlin, 1972). Such an effect could be due to a narrowing of attention induced by the drug, which also could interfere with the perceptual motor skills needed when driving a car or flying a plane (Murray, 1986). Intake of marijuana has also been shown to increase the interstimulus interval at which visual masking occurs (visual masking is discussed in Chapter 11), suggesting that it acts like a sedative and decreases the speed of visual information processing (Braff, Silverton, Saccuzzo, & Janowsky, 1981). As with alcohol, prolonged use of marijuana seems to have a cumulative effect. This shows up as slower reaction times in perceptual-motor tasks (Varma & Malhotra, 1988). There is also evidence that color discrimination, particularly for short wavelengths (blues), is much poorer in habitual marijuana users (Adams, Brown, Haegerstrom-Portnoy, & Flom, 1976).

Some more complex sensory effects have been reported after the smoking of marijuana. Some observers experience changes in depth perception and distortions in the perception of size (Tart, 1971). In addition, there is a report that the autokinetic effect, which is the illusory movement of a stationary light viewed in total darkness (illustrated in Demonstration Box 14-7), may become exaggerated. This last observation has led one group of experimenters to caution against night driving while under the influence of marijuana (Sharma & Moskowitz, 1972). Yet marijuana, even at relatively high intake levels, does not seem to impair eye-movement facility, because neither saccadic eye movements nor the ability to pursue a moving visual stimulus with the eyes is affected by its ingestion (Flom, Brown, Adams, & Jones, 1976).

Although contact with hallucinogenic drugs involves a departure from everyday behavior for most people, many of the stimulants (such as caffeine) and depressants (such as tobacco and alcohol) that alter perception are used commonly. Everyday drugs, including antihistamines and aspirin, can cause the perceptual responses of individuals to differ. For instance, *aspirin* may cause dimness of vision or ringing in the ears (Allen, 1985; Goodman & Gilman, 1965). The auditory effects of aspirin can reduce threshold sensitivity (Bennett & Morgan, 1978) and even interfere with speech perception (Young & Wilson, 1982). Another common drug, the antiseasickness compound *scopolamine*, can cause blurred vision and alter the ability of the lens of the eye to accommodate to near targets (Parrott, 1988). Thus, an individual who has just had a cup of coffee or a martini, or who has tried to alleviate a headache or nausea, may differ from other individuals in perceptual responses because of the actions of the ingested drugs.

The Effects of Physical Pathology

Many pathological conditions affect perception. The most obvious of these are maladies that directly damage a particular receptor organ. Glaucoma, which causes a pressure increase inside the eye, can produce blindness if left untreated, and otosclerosis, which causes the bones of the middle ear to become immobile, will impair hearing. There are, however, some pathological conditions that cause disturbances in very special and complex aspects of perception, rather than simply causing a loss of sensitivity to a given stimulus dimension. These can affect such complex functions as the ability to identify objects or to place them in space, and they also may affect the ability to distribute attention. In general, such a problem is called an **agnosia,** from the Greek *a* meaning "not" and *gnosis* meaning "intuitive knowledge." People suffering from agnosias seem to perceive but are not capable of understanding the information presented to them. Such effects are often caused by severe toxic conditions, such as carbon monoxide poisoning (e.g., Patla & Goodale, 1996), as well as by diseases or injuries that damage or reduce the functioning in some parts of the brain, such as Alzheimer's disease (e.g., Kramer & Duffy, 1996) or strokes (Ramachandran, Altschuler, & Hillyer, 1997).

Freud (1953) noticed a form of perceptual disturbance that he called **visual object agnosia.** Some of his patients were unable to identify familiar objects, although there seemed to be no psychopathological disturbance or readily detectable elementary damage to the visual apparatus. Later, Luria (1973) suggested that agnosias might arise from lesions in the secondary visual areas of the cortex. These lesions do not cause blindness, nor do they seem to diminish visual acuity. Rather, they make it difficult for a person to combine parts of an object so as to identify it. Some of these effects might be quite subtle, such as not being able to see both aspects of a reversible figure, such as Figure 10-10 (p. 297) (Ricci & Blundo, 1990). Other errors are more dramatic. For instance, Luria (1973) gave a patient a line drawing of a pair of eyeglasses. The patient examined the drawing carefully in a manner indicating that he was confused and did not know exactly what it represented. He then started to guess. "There is a circle . . . and another circle . . . a cross bar . . . why, it must be a bicycle?"

Such a patient also has problems in separating the parts of the figure from the overall context. Thus, if the patient is shown a drawing of a clock, such as the one in Figure 18-3A, he can usually identify it correctly. However, if the clock is simply crossed out with a few lines, as in Figure 18-3B, the patient can no longer identify what the drawing represents. Such a patient may identify a telephone, with a dial, as a clock or perceive a sofa, upholstered in brown fabric, as a trunk. Such difficulties seem to be even more pronounced when the stimuli are presented for less than 500 ms. Some agnosic patients can recognize objects if they are presented in familiar orientations, but not if they are presented from an unusual angle (e.g., Turnbull, & McCarthy, 1996). The reverse of this occurs in some patients who can recognize the shape or form of an object—for instance, they can tell a + from an *O*—but they can't recognize its orientation. Thus, they can't discriminate between 6 and 9 (Turnbull, Beschin, & Della Sala, 1997). The fact that shape coding and orientation coding are quite different has also been demonstrated by creating agnosic monkeys of different types. Monkeys with lesions in the parietal cortex act like patients who can recognize shape but not orientation, whereas monkeys with lesions in the inferior temporal cortex cannot discriminate between different shapes but still can discriminate between shapes that differ only in orientation (Walsh, & Butler, 1996).

What sort of underlying mechanisms are involved in these perceptual disturbances? As long ago as 1909 the Hungarian neurologist Balint made some observations that suggest a problem with visual attention. Thus, researchers find that such patients have a definite decrease in attention

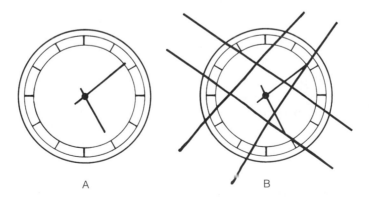

A   B

FIGURE 18-3   (A) A figure identified as a clock. (B) A figure no longer identifiable to a visual agnosic.

FIGURE 18-4   A test figure for simultagnosia.

those in Figure 18-4, she might report a single object, for example, the hammer, and deny that she can see any of the others (Williams, 1970). If such individuals are asked to copy a simple drawing, such as the one shown as the specimen in Figure 18-5, they depict only its individual parts. Essentially, they give a visual list of most of the details. Despite the fact that their ability to localize objects in space is still functional, they seem unable to meld the parts into an integrated and unified figure (Goodale & Milner, 1991). Visual object agnosia and simultagnosia are often found in the same patients and are sometimes grouped together under the label *visual integrative agnosia* (e.g., Grailet & Seron, 1990). A drawing typical of such a patient is shown as the copy in Figure 18-5.

Evidence from several physiological experiments implies that this defect is caused by disturbances in the temporal and sometimes the upper occipital regions of the cortex. It also seems to be specific to the way in which attention is distributed to the visual targets (Butters, Barton, & Brody, 1970; Gerbrandt, Spinelli, & Pribram, 1970). Luria (1973) claimed that injections of caffeine (to stimulate the appropriate region of the cortex) can reduce some of the symptoms, thus allowing the patient to be able to attend to two or three objects in the visual field simultaneously. Unfortunately, this improvement lasts only as long as the drug is active.

span, being able to see only one object at a time, regardless of its size (e.g., Rizzo & Robin, 1990). For instance, such patients could not place a dot in the center of a circle because this would require paying attention to both the circle and the dot simultaneously. This type of patient is said to be suffering from **simultagnosia.** Thus, if a patient were shown a series of overlapping objects, such as

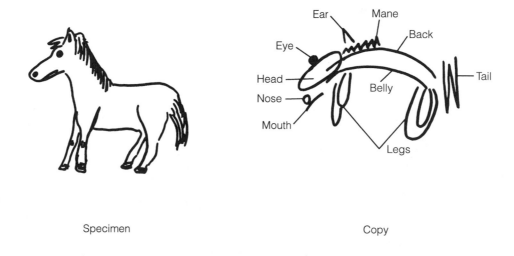

Specimen   Copy

FIGURE 18-5   A target figure to be copied and a reproduction typical of a person suffering from visual integrative agnosia.

Recently, patients have shown some improvement when given attentional training involving learning to look for certain cues and to organize the visual pattern (Perez, Tunkel, Lachmann, & Nagler, 1997).

Some of the agnosia effects are quite general in scope and may involve more than one sensory modality. Patients with diseases of the parietal lobe of the brain may show a **spatial agnosia.** They have difficulty negotiating their way through the world. They make wrong turns even in familiar surroundings, do not easily recognize landmarks, and can become lost in their own homes. This problem does not appear to be caused by a defect in a single sensory modality. These patients seem to be just as impaired when using their tactile or kinesthetic senses as when using their visual sense (Heaton, 1968; Weinstein, Cole, Mitchell, & Lyerly, 1964). Such patients often also show a tendency to ignore one side in space and are said to be suffering from **visual hemineglect,** where the term *hemi* refers to "half" (see Chamorro & Sacco, 1990; Ladavas & Petronio, 1990). For example, if asked to draw symmetrical objects, they will usually produce some sort of distortion on one side. Thus, an individual with left-sided spatial agnosia would reproduce the copy shown in Figure 18-6. Although hemineglect has always been considered to be an esoteric and rare problem, recent evidence suggests that this is not so. In the Copenhagen Stroke Study, Pedersen, Jorgensen, Nakayama, Raaschou, and Olsen (1997) examined 602 consecutive stroke patients and found that 23% of them showed at least some symptoms of hemineglect.

Whereas some of these perceptual effects are quite general, others are quite specific. For instance, there is a rare disorder called **prosopagnosia.** In this type of agnosia the patient has difficulty perceiving and identifying human faces (Damasio & Tranel, 1990; Levine & Calvanio, 1989). In extreme cases the patient may not identify even his or her own face in a mirror. Prosopagnosia is of interest because the human face is a very important stimulus. Our mother's face was probably one of the first visual forms to which we attended as an infant. When children draw, the face is usually the first part of the body to be depicted. So we find that face perception is one of the aspects of form perception that is lost only in cases of serious brain injury, usually involving the right hemisphere of the brain, and particularly the right temporal lobe (Wacholtz, 1996). The loss of face recognition is often quite specific to the identity of the face, leaving the ability to recognize the emotional expressions, gender, or age unaffected (Damasio & Tranel, 1990). Unfortunately, because the problem of facial recognition is perceptual in nature, training and practice at identifying faces seem to produce no improvement in prosopagnosic patients (Hadyn & Young, 1988; Polster, & Rapcsak, (1996).

A related disorder is called **autotopagnosia,** which is the distorted perception of body image

Specimen   Copy

FIGURE 18-6   A target figure to be copied and a reproduction typical of a person with hemineglect.

Table 18-1   **Some of the More Common Forms of Agnosia That Manifest Themselves as Complex Perceptual Deficits**

TYPE OF AGNOSIA	SENSORY MODALITY	PERCEPTUAL DEFICIT
Object agnosia	Visual	Inability to name, recognize, or use objects
Simultagnosia	Visual	Inability to attend to more than one visual object at a time
Integrative agnosia	Visual	Inability to combine parts of an object into a whole (often symptoms of both object agnosia and simultagnosia are combined with this)
Color agnosia	Visual	Inability to associate colors with objects
Drawing agnosia	Visual	Inability to recognize drawn stimuli
Spatial agnosia	Visual	Deficits in stereoscopic vision and ability to relate objects in space
Prosopagnosia	Visual	Inability to recognize faces
Hemineglect	Visual	Apparent deficit in processing stimuli on one side
Sensory amusia	Auditory	Inability to recognize melodies, often accompanied by inability to reproduce rhythm or tempo
Sound agnosia	Auditory	Inability to identify the meaning of nonverbal sounds (i.e., bells, dog bark)
Phonagnosia	Auditory	Inability to recognize familiar voices
Sensory aphasia	Auditory	Inability to comprehend speech, although verbal (Wernicke's aphasia) production is unimpaired (as opposed to motor or Broca's aphasia, which affects production but not comprehension)
Astereagnosia	Somatosensory	Inability to recognize objects by touch
Autotopagnosia	Somatosensory	Inability to name or localize body parts
Asomatagnosia	Somatosensory	Inability to recognize bodily states

and body parts (see Semenza, 1988). For example, one patient, when asked to point to her ear, looked around for it and replied that she must have lost it. Finger agnosias and finger-naming difficulties are the most widely known forms of specific autotopagnosias, and these are thought to be associated with lesions in the left parietal portion of the brain (Pirozzolo, 1978).

Although we have concentrated on the visual sense in this discussion, similar difficulties are found in speech and sound perception. These are usually grouped under the overall heading of **aphasia** (from *a* meaning "not" and *phasis* meaning "utterance"). Aphasia sufferers have an inability to name common objects and often fail to recall the

meanings of words designating common objects (Berndt & Mitchum, 1997). In addition, there are many varieties of specific *auditory agnosias*, resulting from damage to the auditory pathways. For instance, there are some that lead to the selective loss of the perception of words (e.g., Buchtel & Stewart, 1989), sometimes called *pure word deafness*. Loss of the perception of nonlinguistic sounds is called *sound agnosia*, whereas deficient perception of music is called *sensory amusia* (Pirozzolo, 1978), and loss of the ability to recognize familiar voices is called *phonagnosia* (Van Lancker & Kreiman, 1989). There is now evidence that the same kind of head injuries that cause these various forms of agnosia can also reduce our ability to recognize smells (Doty et al., 1997), although there is as yet not even an agreed-on label for an olfactory agnosia. It should be clear, however, that there are many different forms of agnosia, or high-level perceptual disruptions, and a sample of these is listed in Table 18-1.

Most agnosias seem to have been caused by physiological damage, usually of the high brain centers involved in the interpretation of stimuli. Thus, when we find agnosias, we tend often to find damage at particular brain sites. However, these are usually not the primary areas of the cortex for that particular sensory modality. Visual agnosias often are associated with damage to the more forward portions of the occipital cortex, generally Areas 18 and 19, which are the secondary visual areas, and to the temporal lobes, which are tertiary visual processing areas and seem to be associated with complex visual analysis, as we saw in Chapter 3. Similarly for the other sensory modalities, the various forms of agnosia are associated with secondary and tertiary areas of the cortex, rather than with the primary receiving areas. A map of areas often found to be damaged when an individual demonstrates various agnosias is shown as Figure 18-7.

Specifiable physiological differences are not the only source of individual differences in perception, however. In the next sections, we will consider factors affecting perception that may or may not have a physiological basis or that may be the result of a combination of physiological and experiential processes. Unlike drugs and specific sensory damage, the causes of gender and personality differences in perception are harder to specify, although both kinds of differences appear to exist.

SEX DIFFERENCES

The sex of an individual (whether a person is male or female) may partially determine what is perceived in any given stimulus situation. An individual's sex, of course, carries with it many physiological implications. One of the most important of these is the chemical differences between the bodies of men and women due to the presence of specific male or female hormones. Hormones are carried in the blood, which infuses and supplies all of our sensory receptors, and are found in many parts of the brain. Thus, it would not be surprising to find that men and women might differ in certain sensory and perceptual capacities.

Examples of sex differences in perception are found in both taste and olfaction (Velle, 1987). For instance, women, on average, have more acute senses of smell than do men (Money, 1965), and this difference holds over the entire life span (Doty, Shaman, & Applebaum, 1984). This difference seems to be directly attributable to hormonal influences because the acuity of a female's sense of smell varies over the course of the menstrual cycle, reaching its peak at midcycle when estrogen (one of the major female hormones) levels are at their highest (Mair, Bouffard, Engen, & Morton, 1978;

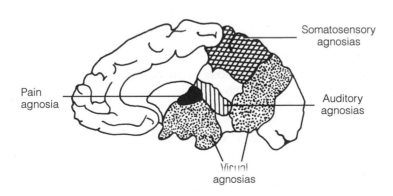

FIGURE 18-7   Damage to particular portions of the brain is often associated with the indicated agnosias.

Parlee, 1983). Women whose ovaries are less active than normal have decreased smell sensitivity, but this can be remedied by the administration of estrogen. Conversely, doses of androgen (such as the male hormone testosterone) make the sense of smell less sensitive (Schneider, Costiloe, Howard, & Wolf, 1958). Additionally, although men and women seem to remember visual and acoustic stimuli equally well, women seem to have a better memory for odors (Klutky, 1990).

There are also sex-related differences in taste. Women tend to have greater taste sensitivity, and the difference between men and women increases with age (Weiffenbach, Baum, & Burghauser, 1982). A more subtle difference between the sexes involves taste preference rather than taste sensitivity; females prefer the sweet taste more than males do, and this preference varies with the menstrual cycle (Aaron, 1975). This is true for rats as well as humans. When the ovaries of female rats are removed, their preference for the sweet taste diminishes; therapeutic doses of estrogen restore the preference (Zucker, Wade, & Ziegler, 1972). This may also help us to understand why women using contraceptive pills (which contain estrogen) often complain that they have a tendency to overeat sweets and, as a consequence, gain weight.

Male-female differences in sensory sensitivity are found in other modalities as well (McGuinness, 1976a; Velle, 1987). For example, women usually show greater touch sensitivity than do men (Ippolitov, 1973; Weinstein & Sersen, 1961). They also show superior hearing sensitivity, especially at high frequencies and in older people (Corso, 1959; McGuinness, 1972; Royster, Royster, & Thomas, 1980). Women generally are more sensitive than men to pain produced by electric shock, and women's pain thresholds also seem to vary over the menstrual cycle (Goolkasian, 1980; Tedford, Warren, & Flynn, 1977). These differences are not due simply to some "macho" denial of pain sensations on the part of the males because subtle autonomic measures of pain responses that are not under voluntary control, such as the change in the diameter of the pupil of the eye, show less male sensitivity to painful stimulation (Ellermeier & Westphal, 1995).

Sex differences in vision seem to be more complex. Males generally appear to have much better visual acuity under photopic conditions (Burg,

1966; Seymoure & Juraska, 1997), whereas females have lower absolute thresholds under scotopic conditions (McGuinness & Lewis, 1976). This difference seems to be present from childhood (see Brabyn & McGuinness, 1979). Additionally, men seem to have faster reaction times to visual stimuli over all ages tested (Bleecker & Bolla-Wilson, 1987). As with taste and smell, there is also some evidence that the visual abilities vary due to hormonal factors. Evidence supporting this comes from the fact that the visual acuity of women varies with their menstrual cycle (Parlee, 1983; Scher, Pionk, & Purcell, 1981), being poorest just prior to and during menstruation. The hormone progesterone (another predominantely female hormone) is often prescribed for women who suffer from severe anxiety or depression during menstruation. Progesterone relieves these symptoms and also restores visual acuity to its normal level in most patients (Dalton, 1964). When visual sensitivity is measured at different spatial frequencies (Chapter 4), females have lower contrast thresholds in the low spatial frequency ranges, and males have lower contrast thresholds for the high spatial frequency ranges (Brabyn & McGuinness, 1979). Also, there is some suggestion that females dark adapt more rapidly than males do (McGuinness, 1976b).

Men and women also differ in their perception of time and motion. Men tend to be more accurate than women in their discrimination of time durations (Rammsayer & Lustnauer, 1989). An interesting study by Schiff & Oldak (1990) combined time and motion estimates. Observers looked at a film of an oncoming vehicle. The view of the scene was then interrupted, and the observers had to estimate how long it would take from the moment when the view of the car was lost until the moment when the car would reach (or collide) with them. All observers tended to underestimate the time needed for collision. For the women, however, the underestimates of the time before collision were some 10% to 20% shorter than those for the men. This suggests that, compared to men, women judge the motion as faster and/or tend to underestimate the distance more relative to men. It may also provide a perceptual explanation for why many women complain that men are "more risk-taking" drivers, and seem to "cut things too close" or do not apply the brake soon enough in many traffic situations. This belief could come about simply because women judge the time to collision to be much shorter than men do rather than because of any social or personality differences as a function of sex.

Visual-Spatial Abilities

An interesting and complex sex difference concerns visual-spatial abilities. These are tasks that involve nonverbal cognitive manipulations of objects and may include the ability to visualize how objects will appear when they are rotated, to detect the orientations of and relationships between different stimuli, and to correctly perceive complex visual patterns (McGee, 1979). Such tasks seem to produce consistent sex differences favoring males (Halpern, 1986). One of these tasks involves **disembedding,** or the ability to disentangle a target object from a surrounding, and often confusing, context. For example, in Figure 18-8A you see a figure marked *Target* that is hidden, or embedded, in the more complex figure beside it. The observer's task is to find the

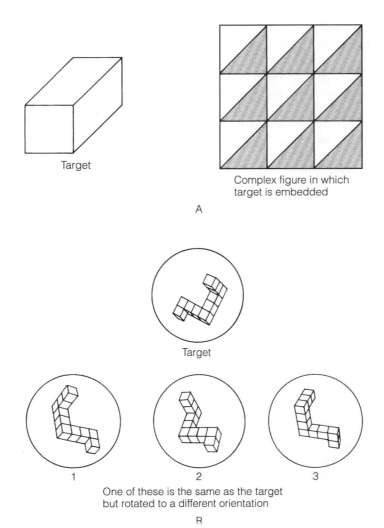

Target

Complex figure in which target is embedded

A

Target

1 2 3

One of these is the same as the target but rotated to a different orientation

B

FIGURE 18-8 (A) An embedded figures test in which the target is found in the more complex array. (B) A mental rotation test in which the target is found as one of the three test figures, but in a different orientation.

simple shape as quickly as possible. Such tasks are usually called the **embedded figures test** or the **hidden figures test.** A different spatial task involves the ability to recognize targets when they have been rotated. An example of this **mental rotation task** is shown in Figure 18-8B. The observer has to recognize the shape marked *Target* from among the three figures next to it. It is often difficult to recognize which shape is exactly the same as the target because the correct shape has been rotated into a different spatial orientation.

Both disembedding tasks and mental rotation tasks produce performance differences that favor males (Halpern, 1992; Wilson et al., 1975), and the differences hold up whether we are dealing with simple or complex patterns (Bryden & George, 1990). Sometimes the size of the performance difference is quite large, amounting to 16% or more, depending on the tests involved (Collins & Kimura, 1997; Sanders, Soares, & D'Aquila, 1982) and has remained unchanged over the years (Masters & Sanders, 1993). Males either are more accurate in their responses or show greater speed when completing such tasks (Blough & Slavin, 1987; Harris, 1981; Lohman, 1986). The male advantage in a task like mental rotation seems to be established by about 10 years of age (Johnson & Meade, 1987). In addition, McGlone (1981) has shown that females approach these tasks differently than males do. Females appear to make more rotational hand movements while completing cognitive rotations; in other words, they more frequently need concrete aids or verbal strategies to successfully complete the task (Clarkson-Smith & Halpern, 1983). Demonstration Box 18-2 provides an opportunity for you to test this sex-related difference in spatial ability for yourself.

Physiological Factors Disembedding a figure, or recognizing it when it has been rotated in space, is a complex task that would seem to involve many learned skills and would seem to be affected by a familiarity with such things as maps and blueprints, which might involve the use of similar skills. So it is somewhat surprising to find that evidence suggests that some of the same physiological factors distinguishing males from females might be partially responsible for their differences on these tasks. Dawson (1967) used a series of these tests on a number of West African males who suffered from a disease that results in estrogen levels higher than those usually found in males. When tested on a series of spatial tasks, these males showed reduced spatial ability relative to a sample of nonaffected males. Similar effects were found in certain South American tribes where the males habitually chew the leaves of the coca shrub, thus releasing cocaine, which when ingested decreases the secretion of the male hormone testosterone. Such males tend to show typical signs of feminization (including enlarged breasts, widened hips, softened skin texture, etc.) and also show reduced spatial abilities, similar to those of females. Male hormones influence these spatial abilities in the opposite way. Thus, males who produce little, or are insensitive to, androgen (e.g., testosterone) also show reduced spatial abilities, whereas females with high androgen (e.g., androstenedione) levels show greater spatial abilities (Hier & Crowley, 1982; Masica, Money, Ehrhardt, & Lewis, 1969; Peterson, 1976). Hormonal effects in these complex spatial abilities have also been implicated by the finding that the spatial abilities of pregnant women (who have higher than usual levels of estrogen) decrease relative to those of women who are not pregnant (Woodfield, 1984).

There are other factors consistent with physiological determination of spatial ability. For instance, the rate at which individuals mature seems to predict spatial performance. In this case, "mature" means to show their secondary sexual characteristics. Typically, late-maturing individuals are better on such spatial tasks than are early-maturing individuals (Gilger & Ho, 1989; Petersen & Crockett, 1985; Waber, 1976, 1977). This is consistent with the usually observed sex differences because males tend to mature later than females.

Psychosocial Factors We have been dealing with some of the physiological variables that seem to produce different patterns of perceptual abilities in males and females. Of course, many factors relating to experience, life history, and cultural influence also affect perceptual behaviors. This is because many aspects of perception are subject to learning influences, as we discussed in Chapter 17. Research has shown that even at an early age males and females may differ in the types of tasks and activities they prefer,

DEMONSTRATION BOX 18-2
Gender Differences in Mental Rotation

For this demonstration, you will need a stopwatch or a wristwatch that allows you to read seconds (either with a sweep hand or digitally). You will also need a couple of male and female friends. Test them one at a time. First show them what is meant by a mental rotation task by using Figure 18-8B. If they have difficulty, point out that only Stimulus 3 can be rotated to be identical to the target, whereas the other two are differently shaped figures. Next, tell your observers that they will see another target figure and a set of 12 test figures. Five of the test figures are identical in shape to the target figures, and your observers' task is to pick out those five as quickly as possible. Start your watch, show them the figure, and time how long it takes for them to find the five correct ones. If they get any wrong, tell them, but keep the time going until all five are found. The correct answers are on the bottom of page 550.

You should notice that, on average, females will take longer at this task than males. Another interesting observation should be that females are more likely to perceive the task as being difficult, as indicated by comments such as "I can never do this sort of thing" or "I'm terrible at this," and so forth.

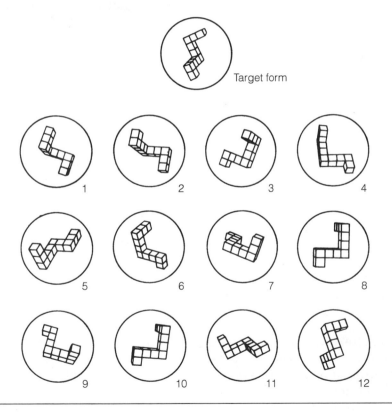

Target form

and also in the tools, implements, or utensils they use in their everyday activities (see Harris, 1981). These factors can also influence some aspects of perception. Demonstration Box 18-3 provides an object-identification task that occa-

sionally produces different responses from males and females. The task shows differences that are most likely to have an experiential basis rather than the kind of physiological basis we have discussed earlier.

DEMONSTRATION BOX 18-3
Sex Differences and Object Identification

Look at the three accompanying figures and decide what each looks like. Do this before reading any further.

Responses to patterns similar to these show differences depending on the sex of the observer. Most males view the top figure as a brush or a centipede, whereas females tend to view it as a comb or teeth. Most men view the middle figure as a target, whereas women tend to view it as a dinner plate (but both respond equally with "ring" and "tire"). Most men see the bottom figure as a head, whereas women tend to view it as a cup.

Perhaps the strongest data in favor of psychosocial factors contributing to sex differences in spatial skills come from studies in which specific training was given to boys and girls using toys and games that have a spatial component and that are typically preferred by boys (such as blocks, Tinker Toys, or paper cut into geometric shapes). Individuals who received such training tended to do better on spatial skills tests, such as the embedded figures task, suggesting that there is a learned component for spatial ability (Smith, Frazier, Ward, & Webb, 1983; Sprafkin, Serbin, Denier, & Conner, 1983). However, improvement does not occur with training for all of the spatial skills that usually show sex differences (Thomas, Jamison, & Hammel, 1973).

It seems likely that differences in spatial skills are due to the interaction between biological and psychosocial factors (Gilger & Ho, 1989; Halpern, 1986). Such interactions may explain why identification behavior differs for individuals who are more strongly sex typed, that is, who identify themselves as being "a typical male or female," versus those who are "androgynous," showing a mixture of typical male and female behaviors (Bem, 1981). Such interactions may also help to explain why male homosexuals resemble heterosexual females more than they resemble heterosexual males in terms of their performance on spatial tasks (Sanders & Ross-Field, 1986).

PERSONALITY AND COGNITIVE STYLE DIFFERENCES

There are myriad nonperceptual ways in which individuals differ from one another. Some individuals are outgoing and sociable; others are withdrawn and prefer to be alone. Some are careful and methodical in everything; others are haphazard and unsystematic. The total of all these behavior traits composes the individual's personality. People with different personalities tend to behave differently in many social situations and tend to respond differently to information of various sorts. Do they also perceive the world differently?

There have been many attempts to link individual differences in personality to individual differences in perception. Often the perceptual responses themselves are used to classify individuals as belonging to one personality type or another. There is a lot of evidence that individuals differ in their ability to disembed figures from one another in tasks such as the one we discussed earlier and illustrated in Figure 18-8A (e.g., T. B. Ward, 1985). Some investigators have suggested that these tasks not only separate individuals according to their spatial abilities but also separate individuals according to underlying personality type. Observers who have difficulty with these tasks are called **field dependent**. They have been classified by personality tests as being socially dependent, eager to make a good impression, conforming, and sensitive to their social surroundings (Konstadt & Forman, 1965; Linton & Graham, 1959; Ruble & Nakamura, 1972). Individuals who have little difficulty with such perceptual disembedding tasks are called **field independent**. They have been classified by the same tests as being self-reliant, inner directed, and individualistic (Alexander & Gudeman, 1965; Crutchfield, Woodworth, & Albrecht, 1958; Klein, 1970). Witkin has been one of the major proponents of this approach. He and his associates look on both the personality and perceptual effects as examples of an individual's **cognitive style** (Witkin & Berry, 1975). They maintain that perceptual, cognitive, personality, and social interactions all are affected by the same set of processes that determine how a person approaches the world. In effect, cognitive style is part of what we call in everyday language "lifestyle," affecting not only our habitual interpersonal and task-oriented behaviors but also the way we process information and, in effect, the way we perceive the world. Thus, by measuring how you normally respond in complex perceptual situations, we can predict to some extent how you will approach many nonperceptual aspects of your life.

Some investigators use perception as the starting point and move from there into predictions about personality; others have attempted to go in the opposite direction, predicting individual differences in perception from prior considerations of personality theory. Characteristic of this approach is the work of Eysenck (1967). He divided individuals into two groups on the basis of certain theoretical and physiological considerations. We can describe the first group as outgoing and sociable (**extrovert**), whereas the second group is more withdrawn and self-contained (**introvert**). Eysenck found that he could classify individuals along this dimension on the basis of a simple questionnaire, and he speculated on some physiological differences that might account for the differences in personality traits. He suggested that extroverts have a neural system that is slower to respond and is more weakly aroused by stimuli than that of introverts. In addition, extroverts generate neural inhibition more quickly. If this physiological speculation is correct, then introverts should be more perceptually sensitive than extroverts. Several studies have investigated the effect of introversion-extroversion on perception. Introverts do seem to have more sensitive perceptual systems as predicted by the theory. They show lower average thresholds for vision (Siddle, Morrish, White, & Mangen, 1969), hearing (Stelmack & Campbell, 1974), touch (Coles, Gale, & Kline, 1971), and pain (Halsam, 1967). In addition, introverts are better at tasks requiring sustained attention or vigilance (Harkins & Green, 1975).

When we study the effects of personality factors on perception, it is important to be sure that we are measuring perceptual sensitivity rather than simply detecting differences in how observers respond. It could be the case that introverts simply say, "Yes, I detected the stimulus" more often than extroverts. Signal detection theory (discussed in Chapter 2) allows us to separate these possibilities. When Stelmack and Campbell (1974) analyzed their data from this viewpoint, they found that introverts have more sensitive hearing than extroverts, even though extroverts are more biased toward saying yes.

Another way to ascertain sensitivity independent of the observer's response bias is to use direct physiological measurements. One technique is called **evoked response** recording. An electrode is placed on an observer's head over the region of the cortex receiving the primary sensory information for the sense modality being tested. Another electrode, elsewhere on the body, serves as a reference electrode. Any changes in the electrical activity of this brain region can be picked up by sensitive recording devices, and such activity presumably means that the sensory information has, at least, been registered in the brain. In this way, Stelmack, Achorn, and Michaud (1977) demonstrated that introverts seem to have greater auditory sensitivity than extroverts. Unfortunately, not all researchers have been able to verify these findings (Campbell, Baribeau-Braun, & Braun, 1981). This may mean that nonsensory factors, such as motivation or distribution of attention, or even the sort of cognitive style that we discussed earlier, rather than direct neurological differences, account for the differences between introverts and extroverts on sensory tasks.

It is surprising nonetheless that the answers to a few questions about how a person interacts with other individuals can be used to predict how one person's perceptual responses may differ from those of another. Demonstration Box 18-4 allows you to estimate your own degree of introversion and extroversion and to test a typical perceptual preference for yourself.

Because personality factors that differ among people in the general population are related to differences in processing of sensory information, it is not surprising that dramatic perceptual effects are associated with certain severe personality disorders. The perceptual responses that differentiate schizophrenic from nonschizophrenic observers is one area that has received a large amount of research attention. **Schizophrenia** (from the Greek for "split mind") is the most frequent diagnosis of a severe or psychotic personality disorder. It is usually characterized by a withdrawal (or "splitting off") from the environment, reduced levels of emotional response, a reduction in abstract thinking, and a general diminishing of daily activity. In other words, schizophrenia is a disorder that affects all aspects of the sufferer's social and cognitive life. Studies of the perceptual responses of schizophrenics have shown that they differ from control groups in their performance on time estimation (Wahl & Sieg, 1980), attentional tasks (Cegalis, & Deptula, 1981), and even on the perception of visual aftereffects (Tress & Kugler, 1979). Several studies have shown also that schizophrenics display eye-movement patterns that differ from those of control groups: They perform poorly when they are asked to track a moving target with their eyes (Levin, Lipton, & Holzman, 1981; Rea & Sweeney, 1989). Because poor eye-tracking behavior is also found in the close relatives of schizophrenics (who

---

DEMONSTRATION BOX 18-4
Introversion-Extroversion and Taste Perception

It is easy to determine your own standing on introversion versus extroversion by answering the following questions with a "Yes" or a "No."

Do you often wish for more excitement in life?
Do you often say things without stopping to think?
Do you like going out a lot?
Do you often think of you as being lively?
Do you like interacting with people?

If you answered all the questions "Yes," you are rather extroverted; if you answered them all "No," you are rather introverted.

Have some friends or relatives answer these questions, but add one additional item to the list:
Do you like spicy foods?

What answer do you expect extroverts versus introverts to give? What *sensory data* would lead you to expect that answer?

are not affected with the disorder), it has been suggested that eye-movement behavior may be a genetic marker for the disorder (Iacono, Peloquin, Lumry, Valentine, & Tuason, 1982). Other psychological disorders show different patterns of perceptual involvement. For example, patients suffering from depression may show increased sensitivity to light (Seggie & Canny, 1989).

Some investigators feel that these perceptual problems may be part of the cause of some personality disorders. For example, when infants with difficult temperaments were examined, well over half of them showed perceptual disturbances. These disturbances included poorly coordinated eye movements, excessive touch sensitivity, vestibular problems, and difficulty coordinating vision with touch (DeGangi & Greenspan, 1988). Similarly, 62% of schizophrenics report various visual distortions (including distortions in sensory processes as basic as brightness contrast), whereas 44% report various distortions in their auditory processing (Phillipson & Harris, 1985). The close association between perceptual difficulties and personality problems is intriguing. It has led to the speculation that alterations in sensory abilities, especially those that occur during the early phases of an individual's development, may play a key role in the later development of personality problems and even in the development of certain forms of psychopathology.

Overall, who you are, the kind of person you are, and the life history that you have had all affect what you perceive in any stimulus situation. Because you differ along many dimensions from those around you, your perception of the world has a unique flavor. What you perceive in any situation is not necessarily the same as what is perceived by the person next to you.

CHAPTER SUMMARY

Individual differences in age, sex, physiological status, and even personality and cognitive styles can alter perception. Various common chemicals and drugs can also have effects. Thus, smokers have higher taste and smell thresholds and may suffer from a variety of visual problems. Alcohol consumption also affects taste and smell, as well as slowing auditory recognition, impeding binocular fusion, reducing motion perception, and even affecting size constancy. Most depressant drugs slow perceptual processes, which is easily measured as a lowered **critical flicker fusion frequency (CFF)** or **auditory flutter fusion (AFF)** and reduced reversals on the **Necker Cube.** Common stimulants often lower detection thresholds and increase figure reversal rates. Hallucinogenic and psychoactive drugs tend to impair many perceptual processes and to reduce the efficiency of information processing. Some, such as marijuana, will have cumulative effects—such as damage to color vision, particularly in the blue range.

Physical damage to the brain can cause **agnosias,** where the individual seems to have unimpaired basic sensory functions but can't process sensory information correctly. These agnosias take many forms, such as **visual object agnosia,** where there is an inability to recognize familiar objects; **simultagnosia,** where an individual cannot attend to or process more than one stimulus at a time; **visual hemineglect,** in which one side of all objects in the visual field is not processed; **prosopagnosia,** in which an individual cannot identify human faces; **autotopagnosia,** which is the distorted perception of body image and body parts; and many others.

A person's sex is an important individual difference variable in perception. Generally speaking, women have more acute taste and olfactory capacities, and these may vary with the menstrual cycle or with the concentration of female hormones. Women also have lower pain thresholds and greater sensitivity to higher sound frequencies. Men have better photopic visual acuity, whereas women have better scotopic sensitivity. Again, hormonal factors are implicated. Men have more accurate time duration discrimination and are better at interpreting information from moving visual stimuli. Men also are better at complex spatial skills as measured by visual **disembedding** tasks and **mental rotation tasks.** As for other aspects of perception, hormonal factors seem to play a role; however, psychosocial factors and cultural influences may also explain some portion of the observed sex differences.

Certain personality dimensions also cause individual differences in perception. **Field dependent** individuals are more likely to have difficulty separating conflicting information streams and ignoring irrelevant stimuli than are **field independent** individuals. These two groups of individuals also show personality and **cognitive style** differences. **Introverted** individuals seem to have lower sensory thresholds for many sensory modalities than do **extroverted** individuals. Some severe personality disorders, such as **schizophrenia,** are also accompanied by perceptual problems, such as poorly coordinated eye movements, excessive touch sensitivity, vestibular problems, and difficulty coordinating vision with touch. In fact, the eye-movement problems are so common that it has been suggested that these may be a marker for physiologically based personality disorders.

KEY TERMS

Poggendorff illusion
critical flicker fusion
  frequency (CFF)
auditory flutter fusion
  (AFF)
Necker Cube
agnosia
visual object agnosia
simultagnosia
spatial agnosia
visual hemineglect
prosopagnosia
autotopagnosia

aphasia
disembedding
embedded figures test
hidden figures test
mental rotation task
field dependent
field independent
cognitive style
extrovert
introvert
evoked response
schizophrenia

Answers to Deomonstration Box 18-2: 3, 6, 7, 9, 11

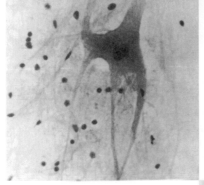

Primer of Neuro-physiology

APPENDIX

There are several places in this book where our discussions assume that you know some neurophysiology, specifically some of the terminology used for parts of the nervous system, how a neuron functions, and how we investigate neural activity in sensory systems. This appendix provides you with that information in a condensed form. More details are available from most basic texts in biopsychology (e.g., Carlson, 1998; Kalat, 1998; Pinel, 1990).

NEURONS AND THE NERVOUS SYSTEM

The human nervous system contains about 100 billion neurons. Figure A-1 shows some aspects of several types of neurons. A **sensory neuron** conducts information from sensory receptors (either part of the neuron itself or a separate cell) toward the brain; an **interneuron** conducts information between other neurons; and a **motor neuron** conducts nerve impulses outward to the muscles. Each of these neurons is a separate cell, generally composed of three distinct parts: a **cell body,** an **axon,** and **dendrites.** The cell body contains the nucleus (which contains the genetic material) and many different molecules that govern the functioning of the neuron. The dendrites are branching structures that receive information from incoming nerve

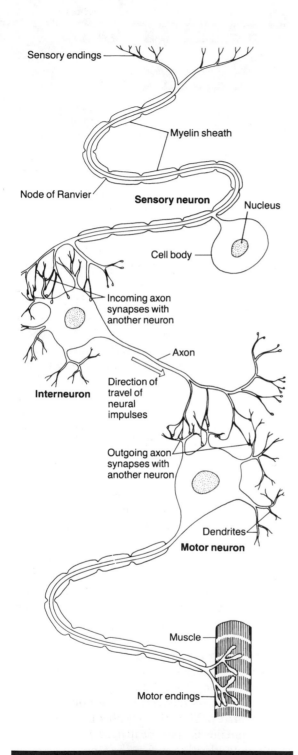

Sensory endings

Myelin sheath

Node of Ranvier

Sensory neuron

Nucleus

Cell body

Incoming axon synapses with another neuron

Axon

Interneuron

Direction of travel of neural impulses

Outgoing axon synapses with another neuron

Dendrites

Motor neuron

Muscle

Motor endings

FIGURE A-1 Neurons of various types and their important parts and connections with each other.

fibers from many other neurons. The axons are usually long fibers that conduct nerve impulses toward the many other neurons (or muscle fibers) with which each neuron connects. Axons typically terminate near dendrites of other neurons. Many, but not all, neurons have axons that are covered by protective and nutritive cells called **glial cells.** Some glial cells (including a variety called **Schwann cells**) form the myelin sheath around the axon, which, as you will see later, helps to increase the speed at which electrical changes travel. The myelin sheath is interrupted about every millimeter by **nodes of Ranvier,** which are the gaps between successive glial cells. Most sensory and motor nerves have a myelin sheath.

When many axons gather together into a pathway to carry information from one part of the body to another, that pathway is called a **nerve.** Sensory information usually is carried by nerves to the **central nervous system (CNS),** which consists of the brain and the spinal cord. In the central nervous system, a pathway is no longer called a nerve but, rather, a **tract,** although the terms *fasciculus* and *peduncle* are sometimes used for certain pathways. A bundle of nerve fibers ascending the spinal cord is quite often referred to as a **lemniscus.** In addition to pathways in the central nervous system, which appear as *white matter* because the myelin sheath is white, there are distinct regions containing cell bodies of many neurons grouped together that appear as *gray matter.* Distinct islands of gray matter are referred to as **nuclei.** Much of the sensory information processing and complex channeling of information takes place in nuclei of the brain and spinal cord.

THE NATURE OF NEURAL ACTIVITY

Information is passed along neurons, and from one neuron to another, by electrochemical changes in the neuron. When unstimulated, the inside of a neuron is electrically negative with respect to the outside, with a **resting potential** of about -70 millivolts (mV), mostly because of the presence of large negatively charged proteins inside the cell. In addition, millions of *ions* (atoms that have gained or lost an electron and hence are electrically charged) occur inside and outside the neuron. The most important ions for neural action are sodium (Na⁺), potassium (K⁺), and chloride (Cl⁻). These ions are not distributed equally on both sides of the cell membrane (the cell's outer covering made of fat and protein molecules). The negative chloride ion is many times more common outside. The positive sodium ion is more common outside and the positive potassium ion more common inside, mainly because of the **sodium-potassium pump,** a biochemical process that ejects three sodium ions for every two potassium ions it allows in. The resting state of the neuron represents a dynamic chemical equilibrium resulting from the flow of these and other ions across the membrane.

When a neuron is stimulated, either by a physical stimulus or another neuron, the difference in electrical potential across the cell membrane either becomes less negative by moving toward 0 mV **(depolarization)** or more negative **(hyperpolarization)**. This happens because the stimulation causes changes in the permeability of the cell membrane to various ions. For example, when sodium is blocked from its usual flow across the membrane into the cell, the negative charge inside the cell increases (hyperpolarization). Conversely, if sodium ions are allowed to flow more rapidly into the cell, the charge becomes less negative (depolarization).

There are several ways by which such stimulation occurs. Different sensory cells use different methods to transduce or change the received environmental stimulation into a depolarization or a hyperpolarization. We discuss some of these methods in the chapters devoted to particular sensory systems because they are rather specialized. For neurons stimulated by other neurons, however, the changes in permeability are fairly standard. They are caused by release of a **transmitter substance** across the **synapse,** which is a small gap separating two cells. Figure A-2 shows the most important parts of a synaptic connection. The transmitter substance is stored in the **synaptic vesicle** located in the **synaptic knob** near the **presynaptic membrane** and is released across the **synaptic cleft** in amounts determined by the amount of electrical activity in the neuron. Another positive ion, calcium (Ca²⁺), that is present outside the cell begins the process of transmitter substance release when it enters through tiny channels opened by an electrical change in the cell membrane. Although

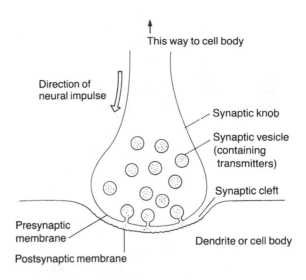

FIGURE A-2   A typical synapse. Transmitter substances are stored in the synaptic vesicles and released across the synaptic cleft.

there are many types of neurotransmitters, and some are selectively located and may be used to define particular neural circuits or systems in the central nervous system, at the functional level they can be grouped into two types. **Excitatory transmitters** depolarize the **postsynaptic membrane,** making it more likely that the adjacent neural cell will generate a neural impulse, whereas **inhibitory transmitters** hyperpolarize the postsynaptic membrane, making it less likely that a neural impulse will be generated by the receiving cell. Transmitter substances are active for only a short time after release and are either quickly neutralized by enzymes that are always present in the synaptic cleft or are collected back into the emitting neuron. Typically, a given neuron will itself possess only one type of neurotransmitter in its vesicles, although it may receive inputs from neurons that emit either type.

Usually, the stronger the excitatory stimulus to a neuron is, the greater the change in electrical potential that results. Such changes are called **graded potentials.** The neural responses in several sensory systems, such as parts of the retina that respond first (including rods, cones, and bipolar and horizontal cells), involve only a continuous graded change in electrical potential. For more central sensory neurons (such as retinal amacrine and ganglion cells) and for virtually all nonsensory neurons, the graded response is not the only response to stimulation. If a depolarization reaches a critical level, a more dramatic and rapid change in the electrical state of the neuron follows. It is referred to as the **action potential** or **spike potential.** In the action potential, the initial small depolarization is suddenly followed by a much larger and more rapid depolarization as sodium ions flow into the axon through tiny channels. This rapid depolarization occurs within about 1 ms and is quickly reversed and followed by a period of hyperpolarization as the sodium channels are closed and potassium ions flow out through other tiny channels. After this sudden swing in electrical charge, the potential returns to the resting level of −70 mV. During the time of hyperpolarization following a spike, there is a **refractory period,** during which the neuron is much more difficult to excite.

These changes in electrical potentials in the neuron can be recorded by various devices, and one such recording is shown in Figure A-3. Increased stimulation does not change the degree of depolarization in the spike potential but, rather, increases the number of such neural spike potentials that are produced by the neuron in any unit of time. This is often called the *firing rate* of the neuron. You might imagine that each neural response is a bark from a dog, and the excitement of the dog is measured by the speed at which it is barking. Thus, the frequency of responses shows the level of stimulation. Because of the refractory period, the maximum rate at which spikes can occur is less than 1,000 per second. Most of the information carried to the central nervous system is in the form of a series of spike potentials.

The spike potential moves as a wave of sudden depolarization along the axon of the neuron until it stimulates the release of transmitter substance where the neuron makes synapses with the dendrites or cell bodies of other neurons. The wave of depolarization moves more quickly along thick axons than along thin ones, with a maximum speed of about 35 m/s in squid "giant" axons, which are about 500 micrometers in diameter. However, even the thickest axons in humans and other animals require help in getting conduction speeds up to levels where they are useful for quick sensing and muscular action. This help is provided by the myelin sheath worn by many axons (see Figure A-1). In myelinated axons, spikes travel from one node of Ranvier to the next at the speed of electrical conduction, which is about 300 million m/s. However, the spike occurs anew by the usual ion-exchange process at each node of Ranvier. The slower ion-exchange process of conduction through the nodes of Ranvier limits the speed with which spike potentials can travel down a myelinated axon to a rate far less than that of electricity in a wire. However, speeds may still reach 120 m/s in myelinated axons only 20 micrometers in diameter.

TECHNIQUES TO MEASURE NEURAL FUNCTION

Investigation of the brain and neural function has tended to be at two levels. At the micro level, individual neurons have been isolated in known sensory pathways or processing centers. At the macro level, the function of neural systems or larger brain regions is studied. Each of these requires its own technology and study methods.

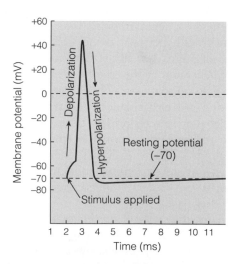

FIGURE A-3 Voltage changes over time that describe a typical spike or action potential.

Individual Neural Response Techniques

Neural responses, mainly in the form of spikes, are measured using microelectrodes. These consist of tiny glass tubes (the tip might be .01 mm in size or smaller) filled with salt water. The electrode is inserted into the cell body or the axon, and the potential difference between the test electrode and a comparison or reference electrode located outside the cell is amplified and then recorded by a computer, which converts the continuous voltages to digital numbers and stores them many times per second. The continuous changes in electrical activity can also be displayed visually on an **oscilloscope,** which is a sensitive voltmeter that displays voltage changes over time by tracing them out on a screen. Oscilloscope recordings of typical spike responses are shown in Figure A-4, which shows two neurons responding at different rates.

The use of microelectrode techniques to record the activity of single neurons has produced some of the most exciting data in the field of sensory physiology. Generally, the procedure involves the application of a muscle relaxant combined with local anesthetics to eliminate the discomfort from the restraining device used to hold an animal, in accordance with strict ethical guidelines. A **stereotaxic instrument** is used to allow the researcher to accurately place electrodes in the brain. Figure A-5 shows a cat with its head in a stereotaxic instrument. Note that the cat is viewing a screen on which visual stimuli may be presented. The electrode is attached through a set of amplifiers to the computer, the oscilloscope, and also often to a speaker. The loudspeaker transforms the amplified neural response into a series of pops or clicks, each click caused by a single neural spike potential. Researchers can then listen to the neural response, keeping their eyes free to attend to other matters. An increase in the rate of clicking means an increase in the frequency of cell firing, and a decrease means a decrease. An increase in firing rate when a stimulus is applied means that the neuron is being excited by the stimulus or whatever other neurons it is connected to that are responding to the stimulus. A decrease in the firing rate indicates that the stimulus or other neurons are inhibiting the neuron from which the recordings are being made. Typically, the records of neural activity along with the conditions under which they occurred are analyzed by the computer for patterns that indicate their functional significance.

Measurement of Brain Function

The earliest attempts to study the function of large areas of the nervous system involved **lesions** (places where neural tissue is destroyed) or

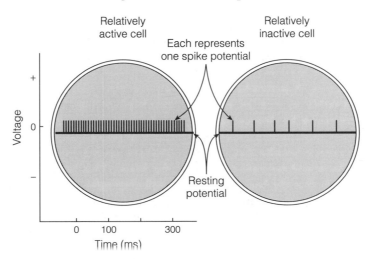

FIGURE A-4   Oscilloscope records of spikes generated by two neurons penetrated by recording microelectrodes.

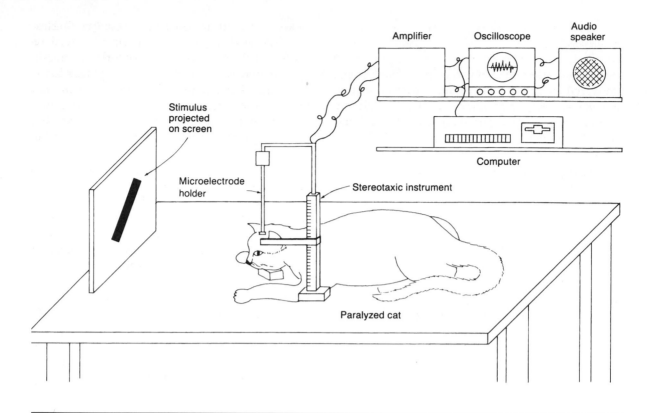

FIGURE A-5 Setup to record neural activity from the visual cortex of the cat.

ablations (places where part of the brain is removed). By observing the relation between where a lesion or ablation was made and which functions were affected, much information was gained about sensory processing. Unfortunately, the results of lesion or ablation experiments are often difficult to interpret because the loss of function may be due to many factors. A somewhat crude example is that it is possible to stop an animal from further visual processing by destroying the centers in the brain stem that control breathing because an animal that cannot breathe dies, and a dead animal can't see. We would *not* want to conclude from this lesion study that the brain stem is directly involved in processing visual stimuli!

Electrical recordings have also been used to study the function of brain regions by attaching electrodes to the scalp. This produces the familiar **electroencephalogram** or **EEG,** which measures the average activity of thousands of cells in a particular region. Locating a number of electrodes over various regions of the skull allows precise pinpointing of the areas of the brain that are most active (e.g., John, Prichep, Fridman, & Easton, 1988). Localized EEGs measured in response to brief sensory stimuli, which are called *event related potentials* or *ERP*s, are now routinely used in studies of vision, audition, and speech perception and are the main tool of a new field called "cognitive psychophysiology." Recent variations of electrical recording involve the measurement of magnetic fields produced as a side effect of the electrical changes caused by neural activity in regions of the brain. This technique is called **magnetoencephalography** or **MEG,** and it allows more precise localization of regions of neural activity and also allows researchers to isolate the areas that respond most quickly, those that respond slightly later, and so forth. In this way researchers can trace the entire chain of sensory processing in the brain (see Hari, 1994; Salmelin, Hari, Lounasmaa, & Sams, 1994).

Other techniques for measuring the dynamic functioning of the brain take advantage of normal metabolic functioning. One of the most exciting is **positron-emission tomography** or **PET** scans. Most typically it involves the injection of a radioactive form of glucose (2-deoxyglucose or 2-DG), which is the major fuel for brain activity, although other radioactively tagged chemicals can be used. This substance is picked up by the active energy-consuming brain areas that are seeking fuel to sustain their continued activity. However, the 2-DG is difficult to metabolize and accumulates in the active neurons. Thus, if the person were viewing a picture, we would expect more 2-DG in the visually active areas. The radioactive glucose in the brain regions is detectable by sensitive recorders that detect the gamma ray bursts that result as positrons (subatomic particles) emitted by the decay of the radioactive 2-DG collide with normal matter and mutually annihilate. Maps of the active regions of the brain can then be made (e.g., Fox, Mintun, Reiman, & Raichle, 1988). Two such maps (one for visual and another for auditory activities) are shown in Color Plate 10. PET scans can give a spatial resolution of a few millimeters and can pick up responses with a resolution of about 1 to 2 seconds.

Two other techniques for measuring brain activity also depend on metabolic changes (Andreasen, 1988). Specifically, they rely on the fact that there is increased blood flow to active brain areas. Because this change in blood flow occurs fairly quickly, it can allow the measurement of rapid changes in the pattern of brain activity. The original method for monitoring these activity changes is called the **regional cerebral blood flow** method or **rCBF.** The technique involves injecting into a person a relatively inert, radioactively tagged substance that goes where the blood goes without being absorbed. One of the side effects of neural activity is to briefly dilate the small blood vessels nearby (Iadecola, 1993). Detectors placed around the head can then determine the blood flow by detecting the radioactive emissions, hence indicating the most active regions in the brain (Berman, Zec, & Weinberger, 1986).

The second technique for determining function based on blood flow is **magnetic resonance imaging** or **MRI,** which also goes under the name

nuclear magnetic resonance or **NMR.** This technique does not involve any added radioactive substances. Rather, it depends on the fact that the ordinarily randomly oriented axes of rotation of atoms, such as the hydrogen bound in water and blood, can be aligned by an outside magnetic field and then made to spin like tiny gyroscopes by a radio-frequency electromagnetic field. When the radio-frequency field is turned off, the hydrogen atoms release electromagnetic energy as their spinning slows. The released energy can be measured and from it can be deduced the concentration of hydrogen atoms in the region being monitored. This can give precise pictures of brain structures with no need to expose individuals to radioactive substances. Recently MRI has been modified to provide information about localized brain activity. This modified form is called **functional magnetic resonance imaging** or **fMRI** (Cohen, Noll, & Schneider, 1993). This procedure takes advantage of the fact that the blood protein *hemoglobin*, which normally binds with oxygen, will show a slight change in its paramagnetic properties when it releases the oxygen. Because blood flow and oxygen use by neurons increase when neural activity increases, this can pinpoint the most active regions of neural activity during a sensory, perceptual, or cognitive task (e.g., Belliveau et al., 1991; Moonen, van Zijl, Frank, Le Bihan, & Becker, 1990). This technique has a spatial resolution of 1 mm or 2 mm and a temporal resolution of less than 1 second; hence it promises to give us a better idea of the regions of the brain involved in information processing and the sequence of events that occurs in those regions.

These new techniques are beginning to expand our knowledge of how the brain processes sensory information. Although researchers are just beginning to tap the potential of these techniques, we have already learned enough that we can begin to form "maps" of how the brain goes about interpreting and responding to sensory inputs (e.g., Posner & Raichle, 1994). The really exciting aspect of these techniques is that they allow us to comfortably test human beings, who are conscious and responding to the stimuli in the world around them, without any surgical interventions or pain.

KEY TERMS

sensory neuron
interneuron
motor neuron
cell body
axon
dendrites
glial cells
Schwann cells
nodes of Ranvier
nerve
central nervous system
  (CNS)
tract
lemniscus
nuclei
resting potential
sodium-potassium pump
depolarization
hyperpolarization
transmitter substance
synapse
synaptic vesicle
synaptic knob
presynaptic membrane
synaptic cleft
excitatory transmitters

postsynaptic membrane
inhibitory transmitters
graded potentials
action potential
spike potential
refractory period
oscilloscope
stereotaxic instrument
lesions
ablations
electroencephalogram
  (EEG)
magnetoencephalog-
  raphy (MEG)
positron-emission
  tomography (PET)
regional cerebral blood
  flow (rCBF)
magnetic resonance
  imaging (MRI)
nuclear magnetic
  resonance (NMR)
functional magnetic
  resonance imaging
  (fMRI)

Glossary

All items that appear in boldface in the text and in the list of key terms at the end of each chapter are listed in this glossary. The definitions are specific to this book.

Ablation Surgical removal of neural tissue.

Absolute Distance The distance of an object from the observer.

Absolute Threshold The minimal amount of energy required to detect a stimulus; defined as the 50th percentile of a psychometric function from a method of constant stimuli experiment.

Acceleration Change in rate of motion.

Accommodation The change in focus of the lens of the eye. This may serve as a depth cue.

Acoustic-Phonetic Invariance The idea that there must be some fixed set of acoustic features associated with each phoneme.

Across-Fiber Pattern A pattern of neural activity in which various neural units have different stimulus-specific response rates.

Action Potential The large depolarization of a neuron, 1 ms in duration, that occurs when a graded depolarization exceeds a certain threshold.

Active Process A process by which energy is added to the traveling wave on the basilar membrane just before it peaks, possibly by means of outer hair cell motions.

Active Processing Models of speech perception that incorporate the effects of expectations, context, memory, and attention. Processing may vary depending on previous computations.

Adaptation A reversible change in sensitivity as a result of prolonged or ongoing stimulation.

Adaptation Level A subjective reference point against which stimuli are both quantitatively and qualitatively assessed.

Adaptive Testing A method for measuring threshold in which the sequence of stimuli presented to an observer is adapted to the observer's responses to previous stimuli.

Additive Color Mixing Color mixing resulting from the addition of light of one wavelength to light of another, for example, projection of a blue light on top of a red light on a screen to produce magenta.

Aerial Perspective A distance cue in which objects appear hazy, less distinct, and bluer the farther away they are because of the interaction of light with dust and moisture particles in the air.

Afference Copy Information about eye movement arising from the muscles actually effecting an eye movement.

Affordances A set of actions that a specific object or environmental situation *affords* or makes available to the perceiver.

Aftereffects Errors in hand-eye coordination that follow adaptation to wedge-prism distortion.

Afterimage A visual sensation that appears after an intense or prolonged exposure to a visual stimulus.

Agnosia A pathological condition in which an individual can no longer attach meaning to a sensory impression.

Aguesia Relative insensitivity to a taste.

Amacrine Cells Large, laterally interconnecting neurons found in the retina near the ganglion cell layer.

Anomalous Trichromatism A defect in color vision in which color matches made by an individual are systematically different from normal, although the three primary color systems are still functioning.

Anosmia Relative insensitivity to an odor.

Anterior-Insular Cortex Cortical center for taste information.

APB A neurotransmitter that, when applied to the retina, causes all the on-center ganglion cells to become unresponsive to light but leaves the off-center cells intact.

Aperture Problem The inherent motion ambiguity associated with the output of a single Reichardt detector.

Aphasia A disorder characterized by difficulties involving speech and sound perception.

Apparent Motion Perceived movement of spatially separated static stimuli flashed successively at appropriate interstimulus intervals.

Aqueous Humour The fluid occupying the small chamber between the cornea and the lens of the eye.

Articulators Parts of the vocal tract that are used to produce speech, such as teeth, tongue, lips, and palates.

Astigmatism A selective visual bias caused by physical distortion of the cornea.

Attached Shadow A shading pattern on an object that is determined by the shape of the object itself. For example, a ball that is illuminated from above will appear to be lighter on top and darker on the bottom.

Attentional Gaze A metaphor for how attention is drawn to or directed to stimuli in the visual field.

Attentional Resources The capacity for processing stimulus inputs. These can be "used up" by a task, resulting in poorer performance in divided-attention situations.

Aubert-Fleischl Effect A moving target being tracked with the eyes seems to move more slowly than when a stationary background behind the moving target is fixated.

Auditory Adaptation Transient reduction in auditory sensitivity arising from prior or concurrent exposure to sound stimuli.

Auditory Continuity Illusion The perception that a steady tone can be heard despite being briefly interrupted by a burst of noise.

Auditory Fatigue Prolonged reduction in auditory sensitivity following exposure to very high-level sounds.

Auditory Flutter Fusion (AFF) The rate of interruption of a continuous tone at which an observer first hears the tone as continuous.

Auditory Grouping The perceptual organization of sound on the basis of temporal and frequency relationships.

Auditory Scene The array of sounds produced by the events in our environment; these sounds are mixed when they arrive at the ear.

Auditory Scene Analysis The process of building separate mental representations of sound-producing events in the auditory scene based on the mixture of sound received from those events.

Auditory Stream A perception of a group of sounds as belonging together or coming from a single source.

Autokinetic Effect The illusion of movement of a stationary point of light viewed in an otherwise totally dark field.

Automatic Processing A type of information processing characterized by parallel, capacity-free, and involuntary comparison of stimulus items with target representations.

Autotopagnosia The distorted perception of body image and body parts.

Axon The long, slender part of a neuron that conducts membrane potential changes away from the cell body and makes synapses with other neurons or their dendrites or with muscle fibers.

Azimuth The direction of a sound source indicated as degrees right or left around a horizontal circle, with 0° straight ahead of and 180° directly behind an observer.

Back Projections Signals coming to a particular region of the brain from another region that is further along the visual stream. These signals may provide feedback based on previous information that has already been processed by the brain.

Background Stimuli Adaptation-level theory term for stimuli that form a context for a focal stimulus but are not judged by an observer.

Backward Masking When the second of the two stimuli presented in succession impairs perception of the first.

Bandwidth The range of frequencies (frequency *band*) making up a complex sound.

Bar A stripe in an image with sharp changes in light intensity.

Basilar Membrane The membrane within the cochlea on which the organ of Corti lies.

Beats Fluctuations in loudness of a complex sound caused by interactions of the simple sound waves composing it.

Bel The basic unit used to measure the relative intensity of a sound wave.

Benefit When a valid symbolic cue results in improved performance relative to neutral-cued performance.

Benham's Top A black-and-white pattern that when rotated produces subjective colors.

Beta In signal detection theory, the criterion for sensation level that separates a "yes" response from a "no" response.

Bezold-Brucke Effect The shift in the apparent hue of a color as the intensity is changed.

Binaural Sound presentation to both ears simultaneously.

Binocular Pertaining to two eyes.

Binocular Disparity The difference in the monocular views of the two eyes.

Biological Clock A physiological mechanism that underlies our experience of time.

Biological Motion The movement patterns of the skeletal structure of a human engaged in activities such as walking or running.

Biological Reductionism The theoretical premise that each sensory experience is associated with particular physiological events.

Bipolar Cells Neural cells in the retina between the photoreceptor and ganglion cells.

Bit The amount of information in a stimulus; measured by the logarithm to the base 2 of the number of stimulus alternatives.

Blind Spot Region of the retina through which the optic nerve passes and therefore an area without photoreceptors. This region shows no response to light.

Blobs Regions of cells in Layers 2 and 3 of Area V1 that become dark in response to chemical staining. These cells receive signals from both the parvo cells and the magno cells of Layer 4C and are sensitive to color and to contrast.

Bloch's Law $T \times I = C$ is the relationship between intensity (I) and time (T) in determining the critical amount of light (C) needed in a brief flash to reach the threshold of visibility.

Bodycentric Direction with the midline of the body used as a reference point.

Bony Labyrinth The structure inside the head that contains the cochlea and the vestibular organs. It is made of very hard bone.

Boundary Extension The tendency to remember seeing information that was not really in a photograph but was likely to have existed just outside the camera's field of view.

Brightness The phenomenal impression of the intensity of a light stimulus.

Brightness Assimilation The reverse of brightness contrast. Here, added light elements lighten the percept of a stimulus, and added dark elements darken it.

Bril A unit for measuring the apparent brightness of stimuli.

Buildup Cells Cells in the intermediate layers of the superior colliculus that are active prior to an eye movement.

Bunsen-Roscoe Law The physical law defining the photochemical reaction of any light-sensitive substance as a function of the intensity and duration of light exposure.

Burst Cells Cells in the upper layers of the superior colliculus that are briefly active during an eye movement.

Calcarine Fissure A major convolution of the cortical surface, running horizontally, separating the representation of the upper and lower visual fields.

Carpentered World Hypothesis States that individuals living in urban environments characterized by straight lines and angles will tend to depend more on depth cues based on linear perspective than would individuals living in more primitive rural environments characterized by curved lines.

Cast Shadow A shading pattern that is produced when one object falls between the light source and another object or surface. For example, a ball that lies between the light and a surface will cast an elliptical shadow on the surface.

Catch Trials Trials where no stimulus is presented. Used in threshold measuring experiments.

Categorical Perception When an entire speech feature continuum, such as voice onset time, gives rise to only a few, usually two, distinct percepts, rather than a gradual change in perception of the continuum.

Cell Body The part of a neuron that contains the nucleus.

Central Masking Masking resulting from presentation of target sound and masking sound to different ears.

Central Nervous System (CNS) The brain and spinal cord.

Cerebral Achromatopsia Color blindness that occurs as the result of cortical damage.

Cerebral Akinetopsia Motion blindness that occurs as the result of cortical damage.

Change Monitoring The theory that the tick rate of the cognitive clock reflects the number of events, or changes, that occur in an interval.

Channel Capacity The limit to the number of bits of information an observer can transmit on a single stimulus dimension.

Chlorolabe Green-sensitive cone pigment.

Choice Reaction Time Reaction time to make different responses to different stimuli.

Chopper Neurons Cochlear nucleus neurons that, in response to presentation of a pure tone, give repeated bursts of firing followed by short pauses, with the vigor of successive bursts decreasing.

Chord Simultaneous presentation of three or more musical tones.

Chroma A "circular" dimension of musical pitch that connects similar notes of different octaves.

Chromatic Adaptation A weakened response to a color stimulus due to previous exposure to other chromatic stimuli.

CIE The Commission Internationale de l'Eclairage; an international organization responsible for light measurement.

CIE Chromaticity Space *See* CIE Color Space.

CIE Color Space A standard system used to describe colors based on the mixture of three primary wavelengths.

Circadian Rhythm A rhythmic biological cycle occurring over an approximately 24-hr period.

CNS *See* Central Nervous System.

Coarticulation In normal speech, movements of our articulators producing sounds relevant to three phones simultaneously (the end of one, the middle of another, and the beginning of a third).

Cochlea A snail-shaped part of the labyrinth of the ear that contains the auditory receptors.

Cochlear Duct One of the three canals in the cochlea; also called the *scala media*.

Cochlear Implant A device implanted in the cochlea that electrically stimulates the auditory nerve similarly to the way it is stimulated by hair cell activity.

Cochlear Nucleus A structure in the lower back part of the brain that receives input from the auditory nerve.

Cognition The process of knowing, incorporating both perception and learning.

Cognitive Clock A cognitive mechanism that determines our experience of time.

Cognitive Style The overall personality and perceptual predispositions that are characteristics of a particular individual.

Cohort Theory A model of word identification in which early passive stages of analysis extract the first phoneme(s) of words, activating a cohort of words in memory with the same beginning; other acoustic or phonetic information and higher level expectations then eliminate all the candidates except one, which is identified.

Color Atlas A book in which each page represents a horizontal or a vertical slice through the color space.

Color Blindness A condition in which individuals lack the ability to make discriminations on the basis of wavelength of light.

Color Circle *See* Color Wheel.

Color Solid *See* Color Spindle.

Color Spindle A three-dimensional model in which the relationship between hue, brightness, and saturation is depicted.

Color Wheel A circular scheme in which colors are separated according to hue, with complementary colors placed directly across from each other.

Common Fate A Gestalt law of perceptual organization that states that portions of an image that move together tend to be seen as belonging to the same object or surface.

Comparison Stimuli A graded set of stimuli differing along a specific dimension that are to be judged relative to a standard stimulus.

Complementary Colors Colors whose mixture produces an achromatic gray or white.

Complex Cells Cells in the visual cortex that respond to features such as line orientation and direction of movement.

Computational Approach *See* Computational Theories.

Computational Theories Theories involving the presumption that certain perceived qualities must be computed from stimulus information and that these computations can be precisely described mathematically.

Conceptually Driven Processing Perceptual information processing that is guided by conceptual processes, such as memories and expectations concerning the nature of the incoming stimulation.

Cones Short, thick, tapering cells in the photoreceptive layer of the retina, used in bright-light and color vision.

Confusion Matrix Matrix or table in which the entries are the number of occasions on which a given response was made to a given stimulus in an absolute identification experiment.

Conjunction Search A type of search for a target defined by a conjunction, or particular combination, of features, each of which is also possessed by some distracters.

Consonance The quality of two tones blending or "going together."

Consonant A basic speech sound produced by closing the vocal tract.

Constrained Scaling A scaling procedure in which observers learn a standard scale for a set of reference stimuli and then judge other psychological magnitudes on the same scale.

Constructive Theories Theories maintaining that perception may involve the integration of several sources of information and may be affected by cognitive factors and experience.

Contour In vision, any place in the perceived visual field where the light intensity seems to change abruptly. In music, the general "shape" of a musical sequence of sounds defined by the rises and drop in frequency of the notes.

Contrast Matching A psychophysical procedure in which observers are asked to match two targets (often sine wave gratings) by adjusting the intensities of the light and the dark regions until the two patterns are apparently equal in brightness.

Contrast Ratio A physical measure of the difference between the light and dark regions in an image that is unaffected by overall changes in illumination. One common form of the ratio is: $(L_{max} - L_{min}) / (L_{max} + L_{min})$, where L_{max} refers to the maximum luminance, and L_{min} refers to the minimum luminance in the image.

Controlled Processing A type of information processing characterized by a serial, capacity-limited, voluntary comparison of stimulus items with target representations.

Convergence The inward rotation of both eyes toward the nose as a fixated object becomes closer.

Cooperative Algorithm A method for solving the correspondence problem, based on the idea that disparity detectors tuned to the same disparity will cooperatively excite one another, whereas those with different disparities will inhibit one another.

Cornea The transparent, domelike part of the eye formed by the bulged sclera.

Correct Negative A signal detection theory term for a signal absent trial on which the observer's response is "no."

Correspondence Problem The task of identifying the elements in one eye that correspond to the same elements in the other eye, when each eye is given a slightly different view of the world.

Corresponding Retinal Points Areas in the two retinas that share a common visual direction when the two monocular inputs are processed in the brain.

Cortical Blindness A loss of vision due to damage to the visual cortex.

Cortical Magnification Factor The inverse relationship between distances from the center of gaze and cortical tissue devoted to processing stimuli appearing at those distances.

Cost When an invalid symbolic cue results in poorer performance relative to neutral-cued performance.

Covert Orienting Part of selective attention that involves shifting attention from one source of information to another, without any accompanying movements of the eyes, ears, or head.

Criterion In signal detection theory, a sensation level that differentiates "yes" from "no" responses. (*See* Beta.)

Critical Band A band of sound frequencies within which sounds of different frequencies interact, either by summating when all are beneath absolute threshold or by masking each other's individual detectability when all are above threshold.

Critical Flicker Fusion Frequency (CFF) The minimum rate at which a light must be flickered on and off to be perceived as continuous.

Critical Period An interval during which sensory experience is essential if perceptual development is to proceed normally.

Cross-Adaptation A phenomenon in which exposure to one tastant (or odorant) affects the absolute threshold or sensation intensity of other tastants (or odorants).

Crossed Disparity A cue for relative distance, where, when there are double images, the unfused image in the right eye appears on the left and that in the left eye on the right.

Crossed Olivocochlear Bundle Bundle of efferent nerve fibers extending from cells in the superior olive to the outer hair cells in the contralateral cochlea.

Cross-Modality Matching A scaling procedure in which the observer adjusts the intensity of a stimulus until it appears to be as intense as another stimulus from a different sensory continuum.

Crowding A reduction in visual acuity that occurs when nontarget shapes are placed in close proximity to the target shape.

Cues Features of visual stimuli that prompt the perception of depth or distance.

Cyanolabe Blue-sensitive cone pigment.

Cycle In sound, the completion of a full sequence of air rarefaction and compression.

Cycles Per Second The unit used to measure frequency of sound waves, usually referred to as *Hertz* (Hz).

Cyclopean Eye An imaginary point midway between the eyes thought to be used as a reference point for the straight-ahead direction.

d′ In signal detection theory, the distance between the means of the signal absent and the signal present distributions; a measure of sensory sensitivity.

Dark Adaptation The increase in visual sensitivity after a change from a higher to a lower level of illumination.

Data-Driven Processing Perceptual information processing that responds directly to properties of the incoming stimuli according to fixed procedures and without influence from memories, expectations, or the like.

Day Blindness Visual difficulty under bright-light conditions, caused by the absence or nonfunctioning of cones.

Decibel (dB) The logarithmic unit used to measure sound amplitude; ¹⁄₁₀ of a Bel. Zero dB is average absolute threshold.

Dendrites The branching parts of a neuron that make synapses with other neurons and serve as receivers of excitatory or inhibitory neural stimulation.

Density The quality of compactness or hardness of a sound.

Depolarization A change from the resting level of −70 mV toward 0 mV of electrical potential across the cell membrane of a neuron.

Dermis The inner layer of skin, containing most of the nerve endings.

Detail Set The level of detail—for example, the relative size of elements—for which the attentional gaze is set.

Detection A psychophysical problem involving being aware that a stimulus is present.

Deuteranomaly A condition in which an individual's color matches require more green than those of a color-normal individual.

Deuteranopia A form of color blindness associated with the confusion of reds and greens due to insensitivity in the green system.

Dichoptic Masking A method for studying visual masking, in which the target is presented to one eye and the mask to the other.

Dichotic Listening A technique in which two different messages are simultaneously played through earphones, with a different message to each ear.

Dichromats Individuals whose color vision is defective, allowing all hues to be matched with two rather than three primaries.

Difference of Gaussian Filter A mathematical description of a spatial filter based on the difference between two bell-shaped curves of different widths. Performs the function of a center-surround ganglion cell. Also called a DOG filter.

Difference Threshold The minimum amount of stimulus change needed for two stimuli to be perceived as different; defined as the interval of uncertainty divided by 2 in a method of constant stimuli experiment.

Diplopia Double vision.

Direct Cue A conspicuous stimulus somewhere in the visual or auditory field toward which attention is drawn or directed.

Direct Perception The theoretical position that all of the information needed for the final conscious percept is in the stimulus array and requires no computations or inferences to extract the meaning.

Direct Scaling A procedure in which individuals are asked to assess directly the intensity of a sensation.

Direction Constancy The stability of an object's perceived direction despite changes in eye position.

Directional Acuity *See* Vernier Acuity.

Discrimination A psychophysical problem involving noticing a difference between stimuli.

Disembedding The ability to disentangle a target object from a surrounding, and often confusing, context.

Dishabituation The process by which an observer shows renewed interest in a stimulus.

Dissonance The quality of two sounds being discordant or "clashing."

Divergence The outward rotation of both eyes away from the nose as a fixated object becomes more distant.

Divided Attention Attention directed toward more than one source of stimulus information or more than one perceptual task.

DOG Filter *See* Difference of Gaussian Filter.

Dol Scale A scale of pain intensity based on the discriminability of painful stimuli.

Dolorimeter A device that delivers precise quantities of radiant heat; used to measure pain thresholds.

Dominant Wavelength The wavelength of a monochromatic stimulus that best approximates the hue of a color mixture.

Dorsal Cochlear Nucleus The back half of the nucleus in the lower back part of the brain where the auditory nerve fibers end.

Dorsal Column One of the two major nerve pathways in the spinal cord; it receives input mostly from A β fibers and carries mostly touch information.

Double Pain The phenomenon of two distinct peaks of pain, differing in quality and separated in time, from a single pain stimulus.

Duplex Perception Perception of both speech and nonspeech sounds simultaneously from a single auditory stimulus.

Duplex Retina Theory The concept of two separate visual systems, rod-dependent for dim-light vision, and cone-dependent for bright-light vision.

Dynamic Range For a particular frequency, the difference between the absolute threshold and the pain threshold, measured in decibels.

Dyschromatopsias Acquired color vision losses.

Dyslexia A form of impaired reading ability characterized by confusion of letters that are left-right mirror images.

Eardrum The membrane at end of the auditory canal that vibrates in resonance with incoming sound waves.

Early Selection Attentional selection occurs immediately following sensory registration, before the meaning of an input can be determined.

Echolocation System System used by some animals, such as bats and whales, to locate objects by analyzing self-emitted sound waves reflected from them.

Eeg *See* Electroencephalography.

Efference Copy Information about eye movement arising from the commands issued to the ocular musculature to rotate the eye.

Efferent Fibers Neural fibers that carry outgoing commands from the brain to muscles or other action systems.

Egocenter The position in the head that serves as the reference point for the determination of head-centered straight ahead.

Egocentric Localization The awareness of where our bodies are positioned relative to other objects in the external environment.

Electroencephalography (EEG) Recordings of the activity of brain neurons by measuring electrical potentials between electrodes affixed to the scalp and reference electrodes on the body.

Embedded Figures Test A task used to determine spatial abilities, in which a subject is asked to find a simple shape hidden in a more complex figure.

Emergent Feature A feature that characterizes a particular configuration of parts and is at least as perceptually salient as any of the parts.

Emmetropic Referring to an eye with normal accommodative ability.

Encoding Entering the perceptual information in a glance into some form of memory storage to allow identification and comparison with other stimuli.

Endogenous Opiates Analgesia-inducing opiates produced naturally in the brain and other areas of the body.

Endorphins One of the major groups of endogenous opiates.

Enhancement An improvement in the final level of an existing ability caused by a relevant experience.

Enkephalins One of the major groups of endogenous opiates.

Entrainment The process by which the biological clock is synchronized to physical time cycles.

Epidermis The outer layer of skin.

Equal Loudness Contour A curve describing the sound pressure levels at which tones of different frequencies appear to be equally loud.

Equal Pitch Contour A curve describing the frequencies at which tones of varying sound pressure levels appear to have the same pitch.

Equal Temperament Scale A version of the musical scale where each octave is divided into 12 equal parts, called *semitones*, each of which is further divided into 100 *cents*.

Erythrolabe Red-sensitive cone pigment.

Eustachian Tube A channel from the back of the throat to the middle ear; when we swallow it opens and allows the air pressure in the middle ear to equalize with the outside.

Event A perceptual unit consisting of a set of relations among objects and actions.

Event Processing *See* Change Monitoring.

Event-Related Potentials Specific patterns of the EEG evoked by sensory events, such as lights or sounds.

Evoked Response Overall electrical response of the brain to presentation of a stimulus.

Exafference Stimulus input that acts on a passive observer.

Excitatory Transmitter A substance released across a synapse that causes the postsynaptic membrane to depolarize.

Extent The area of the visual or auditory field over which the attentional gaze is spread.

External Auditory Meatus The canal conducting sound waves to the eardrum; also called the *ear canal*.

Extrastriate Cortex Regions of the occipital lobe beyond Area V1 that contain visual maps.

Extrinsic Contour A contour in the retinal image that occurs simply as a consequence of one object occluding another.

Extrovert An outgoing and sociable person.

Eye Dominance Refers to the fact that most cortical receptive cells can be driven better by one eye than by the other.

Eye-Head System A movement-perception system that monitors and differentiates eye- or head-generated from object-generated movement of the visual image on the retina.

Facilitation An increase in the rate at which an ability develops, but not in its final level.

False Alarm A signal detection theory term for a signal absent trial to which the observer's response is "yes."

Familiar Size A cue to depth based on the known or remembered size of objects.

Feature Attributes of a shape that distinguish it from other shapes.

Feature Integration Theory A theory of how features are integrated to form perceptual objects; it assumes that features are extracted in parallel and automatically but that attention must be paid to a particular spatial locus in order for perceptual objects to be formed from the features.

Feature Search A type of search for a target when the target differs from all distracters by possessing a feature they don't have.

Fechner's Law The logarithmic relation, proposed by Fechner, between the intensity of sensation and the intensity of physical stimulus, $S = (1/k) \log_e (I/I_0)$.

Field Dependent Descriptive of individuals exhibiting some difficulty with embedded-figures tasks.

Field Independent Descriptive of individuals exhibiting little difficulty with embedded-figures tasks.

Figure Integrated visual experience that "stands out" in the center of attention.

Filled Duration Illusion An interval filled with stimulus events is perceived as being longer than an identical interval without stimulus events.

Filtering Part of selective attention that involves screening out irrelevant stimuli while attending to relevant stimuli.

Fixation Cells Cells in the upper layers of the superior colliculus that are active when a visual target is fixated by the eyes.

Flanker Effects *See* Simultaneous Masking.

Flow The perception of time passing.

fMRI *See* Functional Magnetic Resonance Imaging.

Focal Attention Active attention focused on a particular spatial location.

Focal Stimuli Adaptation level theory term for stimuli at the center of an observer's attention, usually those being judged.

Focus of Expansion A point in space around which all other stimuli seem to expand as we move forward toward it.

Focused Attention Attention directed toward only a single source of stimulus information or a single perceptual task.

Forced Choice A paradigm in which several observation intervals are presented to an observer who must make a choice as to which interval contained the stimulus with a specified property (for example, the more intense stimulus).

Forced-Choice Preferential Looking An experimental method in which observers watch infants and attempt to determine, solely on the basis of their orienting responses, on which side of the visual field a stimulus was presented.

Formant Band of especially intense frequency components of a speech signal, seen as dark smudges on a spectrogram.

Formant Transitions Changes in formants over relatively short intervals of time (less than 100 ms) that are related to consonant sounds.

Forward Masking When a masking stimulus impairs the perception of a target presented later in time. *See* **Masking.**

Fourier Components Simple sine waves that add together to form a complex waveform.

Fourier's Theorem States that any periodic wave can be mathematically analyzed into a series of simple sine or cosine waves.

Fovea Centralis A small depression in the retina that contains mostly cones and where acuity is best.

Frame Duration The duration of each stimulus presentation in an apparent motion display.

Free Nerve Endings Noncorpuscular, branching nerve endings in skin, joints, and so on, that may be receptors for pain and temperature.

Frequency The number of cycles a sound wave completes in 1 second.

Frequency Principle Asserts that sound frequency is encoded by the overall frequency of firing in the auditory nerve.

Frequency Sweep Detector A auditory cortical neuron that responds only to sounds that change frequency in a specific direction and range.

Functional Magnetic Resonance Imaging (fMRI) A modified form of magnetic resonance imaging that allows mapping of brain function by recording the change in the paramagnetic properties of hemoglobin when it gives up its oxygen during neural activity. *See also* Magnetic Resonance Imaging.

Fundamental The lowest-frequency, and usually highest-level, sine wave component in a complex sound; greatest common denominator of the *harmonics*.

Fusion The process by which disparate views are synthesized into one percept.

Gabor Filter A mathematical description of a spatial filter based on multiplying a bell-shaped curve with a sine wave. Performs the function of an oriented simple cortical cell.

Ganglion Cells Third layer of the retina through which neural signals travel, after the photoreceptor and bipolar cells.

Ganzfeld A visual field that contains no abrupt luminance changes and thus no visible contours.

Gate-Control Theory A conceptual model of pain based on the interaction of slow, high-threshold nerve fibers and fast, low-threshold nerve fibers via the substantia gelatinosa (the "pain gate").

Geniculostriate System The primary visual pathway passing through the lateral geniculate nucleus to the striate cortex.

Geon One of the primitive components from which perceptual objects are constructed in identification-by-components theory.

Gestalt A concept and school of psychology emphasizing the notion of meaningful and coherent form, or "whole."

Glabrous Skin A type of skin that has no hairs (e.g., on lips); it is highly sensitive to stimulation.

Glial Cells Cells that protect and feed neurons; some types form the myelin sheath as well.

Global The overall arrangement of parts of a figure, as opposed to the local details.

Global Precedence The hypothesis that the processing of the more global aspects of a visual form is faster than processing of the more local aspects.

Global Stereopsis Stereopsis that is not dependent on local contour elements (e.g., as in random-dot stereograms).

Graded Potential A change in electrical potential across the cell membrane of a neuron that varies in magnitude with the intensity of the stimulation.

Grating Acuity *See* Resolution Acuity.

Ground The background against which figures appear.

Guided Search A strategy for increasing the speed of conjunction search. Some of the display items are rejected first by looking only at those with one of the target features, requiring only a second simple feature search to find the target.

Habituation The process by which an observer ceases to respond, or reduces the magnitude of a response, to a repeated or continuously exposed stimulus.

Hair Bundle A graded set of hairs protruding from a hair cell in the cochlea and tending to move, or bend, as a unit.

Hairy Skin Covering of the human body from which numerous hairs protrude; it is both a protective and stimulus-sensitive covering. *See* Glabrous Skin.

Haptic Perception Experience of the world based on a combination of cutaneous and kinesthetic sensations.

Harmonics Sine wave components at frequencies that are whole-number multiples of the fundamental frequency in complex sounds.

Headcentric Direction judged using the midline of the head as a reference point.

Head-Related Transfer Function (HRTF) A mathematical description of the effect on each frequency of sound from each location of the pinnae, head, neck, shoulders, and other body parts near the ears; used to create virtual auditory space for sound presented through headphones.

Height The "vertical" dimension of pitch in musical scales.

Height in the (Picture) Plane A cue for distance referring to where an object is relative to the horizon.

Helicotrema An opening, between the vestibular and tympanic canals, at the apex of the cochlea.

Hemianopia Complete loss of vision on one side of the field of view because of damage to the visual cortex on the opposite side of the brain.

Hemifield One half of the visual field, usually relative to a vertical division through the fovea.

Hertz (Hz) The unit (cycles per second) used to measure frequency of sound waves.

Hick's Law A law stating that choice reaction time is a linear function of the amount of information in the stimuli to be differentiated.

Hidden Figures Test *See* Embedded Figures Test.

Hierarchical Clustering A psychological scaling procedure that represents the relations among stimuli as "leaves" on a "tree."

Hit A signal detection theory term for a signal present trial on which the response is "yes."

Homophenes Different words that are produced by almost identical patterns of lip movements, such as *married* and *buried*.

Homophones Words that are pronounced similarly, but spelled differently, such as *brake* and *break*.

Horizontal Cells Retinal cells with short dendrites and a long axonal process that extends horizontally.

Horopter An imaginary plane in external space used to describe the region of fused images.

Hue The term denoting the psychological dimension most clearly corresponding to wavelength of light and most often termed *color* in common language.

Hughes's Law Describes temporal summation in detection of sounds, in which energy level (E) and duration (D) of a threshold sound trade off according to the equation $T = E \times D$, where T is a constant threshold energy level.

Hyperacuity Resolution of details that are smaller than the diameter of one retinal receptor; usually, any acuity less than 10 seconds of visual angle.

Hypercolumn A small piece of visual cortex, sensitive to input from both eyes and to a full range of orientational specificity.

Hypercomplex Cells Cortical cells that respond to complex stimulus features regardless of where they occur in the receptive field.

Hypermetropia Farsightedness.

Hyperpolarization An increase in the negative electrical potential across the cell membrane.

Identification A psychophysical task involving naming a stimulus.

Illuminance The amount of light falling on a surface.

Illusion Decrement The decrease in the strength of a visual illusion with prolonged viewing.

Illusions Distortions or incongruities between percept and reality.

Illusory Contours *See* Subjective Contours.

Image-Retina System A movement-perception system that detects movement within the retinal image.

Incus One of the three middle-ear bones involved in sound conduction to the cochlea. Also known as the *anvil*.

Indirect Scaling Any method, often based on discrimination ability, by which sensation intensity is measured indirectly.

Induced Motion An illusion of movement of a stationary object created by movement of the background or surround context.

Induction A process in development whereby experience determines the presence and final level of an ability.

Infant Directed Talk The tendency on the part of adults to speak in a high-pitched and exaggerated voice to infants.

Inferior Colliculi Auditory processing centers in the midbrain that are the termini for cells of the superior olives.

Inferotemporal Cortex A cortical region located in the temporal lobes of the brain that may be associated with recognition abilities and, pathologically, with visual agnosia.

Inflow Theory The suggestion that motion is detected via feedback information from the six extraocular muscles controlling eye movement.

Information Channel A separable source of stimulus information, such as each of the two ears or a particular spatial location in the visual field.

Information Processing The process by which stimuli are registered in the receptors, identified, and stored in memory.

Information Theory A quantitative system for measuring the difficulty of an identification task in terms of the logarithm to the base 2 of the number of stimulus alternatives that must be distinguished.

Information Transmission The degree to which the output of an information channel (for example, an observer in an identification experiment) reflects the information input to it.

Informational Masking Simultaneous masking of a pure tone by a complex sound made up of several frequencies that vary randomly from trial to trial. *See* Masking.

Inhibition of Return The tendency to react more slowly to a second stimulus that occurs where a recently processed location or object has been; possibly allows attention to be directed preferentially to locations of novel or yet-unprocessed objects.

Inhibitory Transmitter A substance released across a synapse that causes the postsynaptic membrane to hyperpolarize.

Inner Ear The part of the ear containing the cochlea.

Inner Hair Cells Cells found on the inner side of the tunnel of Corti.

Integration The process by which an observer builds an internal model of perceptual objects based on incoming stimulation and knowledge from previous perceptions.

Intelligent Perception The theoretical presumption that cognitive processes and experience can affect perception.

Interblob Regions See Interblobs.

Interblobs Regions between the blobs of Layers 2 and 3 in Area V1. These cells receive signals from the parvo cells of Layer 4C and are sensitive to the orientation of a visual edge, but not to the color of the edge.

Interneuron A neuron that conducts information from one neuron to another.

Interposition The depth cue based on the blocking of an object or part of an object from view by another closer object.

Interstimulus Interval The time span between the end of one stimulus presentation and beginning of the next.

Interval of Uncertainty In a discrimination experiment, the difference between the stimulus intensity judged greater than the standard 25% of the time and that judged greater 75% of the time.

Interval Scale A scale in which differences between adjacent values are meaningful, but in which no absolute zero point exists.

Intrinsic Contour A contour in the retinal image that is part of the true shape of an object.

Introvert A withdrawn and self-contained person.

Invariants Aspects of the stimulus situation that are always present in the stimulus and are good predictors of object properties such as size, shape, or distance.

Iodopsin The cone pigment present in some birds.

Iris The opaque, colored membrane controlling the amount of light entering the eye by changing the size of the pupil.

Isoluminant Stimuli These stimuli contain lines or forms of equal brightness and are distinguished from their backgrounds on the basis of color only.

J-Shaped Masking As the interval between a target and a backward mask is increased, target visibility first decreases before it begins to increase at longer intervals.

Just Noticeable Difference (*jnd*) The subjective experience of the difference threshold; the sensation difference between two stimuli separated by one difference threshold.

Kinesthesis Sensations of force, weight, and limb position and movement.

Kinetic Depth Effect The perception of the three-dimensional shape of an object based on cues generated by the object's motion.

Labeled-Line Theory A theory of taste in which each taste fiber encodes the intensity of a single basic taste quality.

Labyrinth A structure of fluid-filled canals and chambers in the head that contains organs of hearing and the vestibular senses.

LAFS Acronym for Klatt's (1980) theory of word recognition: stands for *lexical access from spectra*.

Late Selection All information entering a sensory system gets preliminary analysis, and attentional selection occurs at the stage where material is entered into longer lasting memory.

Lateral Geniculate Nucleus The first major relay center in the geniculostriate system for optic nerve fibers leaving the retina. It is in the thalamus in primates.

Lateral Inhibition The process of adjacent sensory units inhibiting one another.

Lateral Olfactory Tract The main route, composed of axons, from the olfactory bulb to the smell cortex.

Lateral Posterior Nuclei A visual center in the thalamus, part of the tectopulvinar system.

Law of Closure The Gestalt law stating that contours that form a closed region tend to be attracted to each other and form a figure.

Law of Good Continuation The Gestalt law stating that figural elements that form smooth curves tend to be grouped together.

Law of Pragnanz The Gestalt law stating that the psychological organization of the percept will always be as "good" as prevailing conditions allow.

Law of Proximity The Gestalt law stating that elements close to one another tend to be grouped together.

Law of Similarity The Gestalt law stating that the more similar figural elements are, the more likely they are to be grouped together.

Lemniscus A bundle of neural fibers ascending the spinal cord.

Lens A transparent body in the eye. It can change shape, thus altering the focus of the retinal image.

Lesion The destruction or functional disruption of neural pathways or nuclei.

Levels-of-Processing Analysis Analysis of the contribution of each stage of processing to the final percept, beginning with the receptor and continuing through cognitive mechanisms.

Life Span Developmental Approach An approach to perception that presumes that chronological age is the best predictor of perceptual ability.

Light Adaptation The decrease in visual sensitivity after a change from a lower to a higher level of illumination.

Light Source The direction and intensity of the one or more light sources in the visual environment. This property, together with the reflectance, surface orientations, and viewing position of the observer, completely determines the retinal image.

Lightness The phenomenal impression of the "grayness" of a surface. This judgment is related to the percentage of light that is reflected from a surface.

Limbic System A part of the brain, old in an evolutionary sense, involved in emotion and memory.

Linear Perspective The apparent convergence of physically parallel lines as they recede into the distance.

Linearity The idea that for each phoneme in an utterance there must correspond a segment of the physical speech signal.

Local The detailed aspects of a figure as opposed to the global aspects.

Lock-And-Key Theory A theory of smell mechanism in which variously shaped molecules fit into holes in the walls of olfactory receptor cells like a key into a lock, causing an electrochemical change that in turn causes an action potential in the axon.

Locus A particular spatial location to which the attentional gaze has been drawn or directed.

Long-Range Motion Apparent motion seen in displays where successive frames are separated by more than 100 ms in time and the spatial displacement of corresponding elements is more than 15 min of visual angle.

Loudness The psychological attribute of sound most closely associated with the sound pressure level.

Lumen The unit of radiance equal to the light emanating from a standard candle, which is slightly more than .001 watt at a wavelength of 555 nm.

Luminance The amount of light reflected from a surface.

Luminosity Curve A plot of the relative brightness of different wavelengths.

Mach Bands The perception of dark and light lines at regions near abrupt changes in an intensity gradient.

Macula The receptor organ of the utricle and saccule. It is responsive to linear acceleration.

Macula Lutea A yellow-pigmented area centered over the fovea.

Magnetic Resonance Imaging (MRI) Mapping brain activity by measuring blood flow and volume by monitoring changes in a magnetic field that occur after hydrogen atoms in the brain are exposed to a strong radio frequency signal.

Magnetoencephalography (MEG) Mapping of brain activity from changes in the brain's magnetic field caused by the electrical activity of neurons.

Magnitude Estimation A psychophysical scaling procedure requiring the observer to assign numbers to stimuli on the basis of the intensity of the sensations they arouse.

Magno Cells Large, fast conducting visual cells that are important for motion perception.

Magnocellular Channel Refers to the information carried from the large cell layers of the lateral geniculate, which is mostly concerned with brightness, motion, form, and depth.

Maintenance Preservation of a developed ability by relevant experience.

Malleus The inner ear bone that is attached to the eardrum; also called the *hammer*.

Masker A sound that, when presented, makes perception of another sound more difficult.

Masking When a usually audible sound can no longer be heard because of the presentation of another sound close to it in time and frequency composition.

Maturation Development of an ability independent of experience.

McGurk Effect The perception of an "intermediate" phoneme when auditory and visual speech cues conflict.

Medial Geniculate The brain structure that receives inputs from the inferior colliculus and sends axons to the auditory cortex.

Medial Lemniscus A part of the spinal cord composed of fibers that conduct sensory information to the thalamus.

MEG *See* Magnetoencephalography.

Mel A scale used to measure apparent pitch; the unit of that scale—a 1,000-Hz tone at 40 dB—has a pitch of 1,000 mels.

Mental Rotation Task A task in which observers are asked to recognize a visual target in different spatial orientations (rotations).

Metameric Colors Colors that appear to be the same but are composed of different wavelengths.

Metathetic Continuum A stimulus continuum for which quantitative stimulus differences give rise to qualitative sensation differences, such as wavelength of light and hue.

Method of Constant Stimuli A method for determining thresholds in which each of a number of stimuli above and below the proposed threshold is presented and judged repeatedly.

Method of Limits A method for determining thresholds in which stimulus intensity is systematically increased or decreased until a change in response occurs.

Microsaccades Small, involuntary eye movements that keep our eyes shivering in their sockets.

Microspectrophotometer A device for measuring the amount and wavelengths of light emanating from microscopic target areas.

Middle Ear The part of the ear consisting of the ossicles (malleus, incus, and stapes) that transmit the eardrum vibrations to the inner ear.

Minimum Audible Angle The smallest amount of difference in location of a sound source that can be detected.

Minimum Audible Field The absolute threshold for a sound stimulus presented and measured in a free field.

Minimum Audible Pressure The absolute threshold for a sound stimulus presented through earphones and measured at the eardrum.

Miss A signal detection theory term for a signal present trial on which the observer's response is "no."

Missing Fundamental When a complex sound has a fundamental frequency that is not actually present in the sound.

Model-Based Theory of object identification in which the image of a real object is compared with the image of a model object.

Molar Concentration A measure of the amount of a tastant present; 1 *mole* equals the molecular weight of a substance in grams added to enough water to make 1 L of solution.

Monaural Sound presentation to one ear.

Monochromatic Stimuli Stimuli that contain only one wavelength of light.

Monochromats Individuals who see color as simply gradations of intensity, due to the absence of any functioning cones.

Monocular Cues Depth cues requiring only one eye to be used.

Monoptic Masking A method for studying visual masking, in which the target and mask are presented to only one eye.

Motion Aftereffect An illusion of movement that occurs in the direction opposite to a moving stimulus that an observer has viewed for an extended time.

Motion Coherence The spatiotemporal correlation between randomly located dots in successive frames of a random-dot kinematogram.

Motion Correspondence Problem This refers to the fact that in apparent motion the visual system must first identify which elements shown at Time 1 correspond to which elements shown in a different position at Time 2, in order to determine the path of the apparent motion.

Motion Parallax The apparent relative motion of objects in the visual field as the observer moves his head or body.

Motion Smear The trail of visible persistence left by an object in motion.

Motor Neuron A neuron that conducts activity from the central nervous system outward toward the muscles.

MRI *See* Magnetic Resonance Imaging.

Mueller-Lyer Illusion An illusion of size in which the apparent length of a line is affected by the direction of its contextual wings.

Multidimensional Scaling A psychological scaling procedure in which the perceived similarities between stimuli are represented as physical distances in a spatial map.

Musical Interval The perception of the separation in musical pitch between two musical sounds.

Myelin Sheath A covering of glial cells on the axons of neurons that allows an increase in the speed of transmission of neural activity.

Myopia Nearsightedness resulting in poor acuity for distant targets.

Nanometer (NM) A billionth of a meter (a millionth of a millimeter).

Nasal Visual Field The half of the visual field of each eye that lies toward the nose.

Near Point Distance The nearest point to which an object may be brought to an eye and still remain in focus on the retina.

Necker Cube The drawing in Figure 18-2 in which the three-dimensional interpretation alternates between two equally compelling possibilities.

Negative Time Error In discrimination experiments, when the point of subjective equality is less than the value of the standard stimulus.

Neospinothalamic Pathway A part of the spinal cord, which is a recent evolutionary development, that conducts information (representing sharp, pricking pain, temperature, and rudimentary touch) from the skin, muscles, and joints to the brain.

Nerve A bundle of axons that carries information from one part of the body to another.

Neural Adaptation Progressive decrease in the firing rate of a neuron in response to a stimulus as time since stimulus onset increases.

Neural Filter Cells in the brain that are able to perform a crude Fourier analysis of the visual image by behaving like feature detectors for particular spatial frequencies.

Neural Satiation A process in which specific groups of neurons fatigue in response to optimal and continuous stimulation. The presumed cause of selective adaptation.

Neuronal Pruning A reduction in the number of connections between neurons that occurs with development and aging.

Night Blindness The inability to see under low-light (twilight) conditions, caused by an absence of functioning rods.

NMR *See* Magnetic Resonance Imaging.

Nodes Of Ranvier Interruptions in the myelin sheath (about every millimeter) that increase the speed of neural spike transmission.

Nominal Scale A scale in which scale values can be used only as names of objects or events, thus reflecting only identity.

Now The interval of time that we interpret as "the present."

Nuclear Magnetic Resonance (NMR) *See* Magnetic Resonance Imaging.

Nuclei Groups of cell bodies of neurons found in the spinal cord and brain.

Nystagmus A reflexive, jerky eye movement caused by stimulation of the vestibular organs (cristas) in the semicircular canals.

Object-Relative Change The movement of objects in relation to one another.

Object-Relative Localizations The estimation of the relative positions of objects (other than the observer) within the environment.

Oblique Effect The phenomenon whereby acuity for diagonally oriented stimuli is poorer than for horizontally or vertically oriented stimuli.

Occipital Lobe The rear portion of the cortex, which serves as the primary visual processing center.

Occipital Pole The extreme rear point of the occipital lobe, where central vision is represented in Area V1.

Occlusion See Interposition.

Off Response A neural response commencing with the termination of a stimulus.

Offset Neurons Cochlear nucleus neurons that reduce their firing rate below background at the onset of a tone and then give a burst of firing at the tone's termination.

Ohm's Acoustical Law The principle that the auditory system separates complex sounds into simple (Fourier) components.

Olfactory Binding Protein (OBP) A type of protein molecule found in the watery mucus covering the olfactory epithelium; it may transport hydrophobic odorant molecules to and from olfactory receptor molecules.

Olfactory Bulb A complex brain nucleus where the axons of primary olfactory neurons terminate; sends axons to various brain centers, including the olfactory cortex and limbic system.

Olfactory Cilia Hairlike projections extending from the knoblike end of the olfactory rod, protruding through the surface of the olfactory epithelium.

Olfactory Epithelium The small area in the upper nasal passages containing primary olfactory neurons that respond to smell stimuli.

Olfactory Nerve The bundle of axons of primary olfactory neurons that passes through the top of the nasal cavity and terminates in the olfactory bulb.

Olfactory Rod A long extension from smell receptor cells toward the surface of the olfactory epithelium.

On-Off Response A burst of neural responses given both at the onset and at the termination of a stimulus.

On Response A neural response commencing with the onset of a stimulus.

Onset Neurons Cochlear nucleus neurons that fire immediately and exclusively after the onset of a tone.

Opponent Process Neural process that signals the presence of one color by increasing its activity and of an opposing color by decreasing its activity.

Opsin Protein part of the rhodopsin pigment.

Optacon A system, similar to the vision substitution system, that converts printed letters into vibration patterns on the fingertip.

Optic Axis Imaginary line from the center of the pupil to the fovea, used as a reference point for distances across the eye.

Optic Chiasm The point at which the two optic nerves meet and the nasal fibers cross to the contralateral side.

Optic Disk The region of the retina where the optic nerve leaves the eye. *See* Blind Spot.

Optic Nerve The collection of axons from retinal ganglion cells as they exit the eye.

Optic Radiations The large fans of neural fibers spreading out from the lateral geniculate nucleus to the occipital cortex.

Optic Tract The path of the optic nerve after it is past the optic chiasm.

Optokinetic Nystagmus An eye-movement sequence in which smooth-tracking eye movements alternate with saccades in the opposite direction in the presence of a moving pattern.

Ordinal Scale A scale involving the ranking of items on the basis of more or less of some quantity.

Organ Of Corti The part of the cochlear duct that transduces mechanical sound wave energy into electrochemical energy interpretable by the nervous system.

Orientation Specificity A property whereby cortical cells respond selectively to visually presented lines or edges of a particular orientation.

Orienting When attention is drawn toward a sudden change in the environment. Often accompanied by an orienting reflex.

Orienting Reflex A constellation of responses to a novel or dramatic stimulus, including the orienting response and various physiological changes such as pupil dilation and heart rate decrease.

Orienting Response When an observer turns toward and orients sensory receptors toward a novel or dramatic stimulus.

Oscilloscope A sensitive voltmeter that displays voltage changes over time as a tracing on a screen.

Otoacoustic Emissions Emissions of sound by the ear, either spontaneously or in response to stimulation.

Out of Phase When the peaks and valleys of sound waves do not coincide over time.

Outcome Matrix In signal detection theory, a matrix containing the proportions of trials on which the four possible outcomes occurred.

Outer Ear The pinna, the auditory canal, and the eardrum.

Outer Hair Cells Cells found on the outer side of the tunnel of Corti.

Outflow Theory The suggestion that brain commands initiating eye movements enable the eye-head movement system to differentiate object-generated from observer-generated movement of the retinal image.

Oval Window A membrane in the cochlea that receives sound vibrations from the stapes.

Pacemaker The mechanism that sets the speed of the biological clock.

Pacinian Corpuscle A corpuscular nerve ending found in skin and joints, sensitive to mechanical deformation.

Paleospinothalamic Pathway A part of the spinal cord, evolutionarily older, that conducts information (representing dull, burning pain, temperature, and rudimentary touch) from the skin, muscles, and joints to the brain.

Pandemonium A computer model of pattern identification based on a series of successive stages of feature analysis and recombination.

Panum's Area The region around the horopter where all images in space are fused.

Papillae Small bumps on the tongue in which taste buds are located.

Parallel Search A pattern of visual search in which all the items in a searched array can be compared to a target representation at the same time.

Parietal Cortex The upper central region of the brain housing the somatosensory cortex.

Parietal Lobe A portion of the cortex above the occipital lobe and one of the tertiary visual centers involved in the processing of information about object location.

Parvo Cells Small, slow conducting ganglion cells that are important for detailed pattern and color vision.

Parvocellular Channel Refers to the information carried to the cortex from the small cell layers of the lateral geniculate. When sent to the blobs in primary visual cortex (V1), this is mostly color information.

Passive Processing A model of speech perception based on detecting features in the speech signal but with no higher-level interactions.

Pauser Neurons Cochlear nucleus neurons, similar to onset neurons, that exhibit an initial response to a tone, followed by a pause, and then a weaker, sustained response until the tone stops.

Payoff Matrix In signal detection theory, a matrix depicting the set of rewards and penalties given an observer based on performance.

Perceived Duration The length of time a sound appears to last.

Perceived Location Where in space a sound seems to come from.

Perception The conscious experience of objects and object relationships.

Perceptual Learning Approach An approach to perception that maintains that the primary determinant of our perceptual abilities is our previous experience with certain environmental stimuli.

Perceptual Moment The hypothetical basic psychological unit of time, about 100 ms.

Perceptual Object The perceptual experience of a part of the retinal image forming a whole entity, an "object," that usually corresponds to a real-world object.

Perceptual Set The expectancies or predispositions that an observer brings to a perceptual situation.

Pet See Positron Emission Tomography.

Phase Angle The particular point in the compression-rarefaction cycle of a sound wave at one instant of time; 0° to 360° for one cycle of a sine wave.

Phase Difference The difference in the phase of a sound wave between the two ears caused by the different distances the sound wave has to travel to reach each ear; cue to localization of lower-frequency sounds.

Phase Locking The tendency of individual neurons to fire at fixed points in the cycle of a sound wave.

Pheromones Chemicals secreted by animals that transmit information to other animals, usually of the same species.

Phonagnosia Inability to recognize familiar voices.

Phone The basic sound unit used by linguists to describe speech.

Phoneme A phone used in a language to distinguish one word from another.

Phonemic Boundary The point on a speech feature continuum where the perception of the phoneme changes from one category to another, for example, 35 ms for voice onset time (VOT), with "ba" heard for VOTs less than 35 ms and "pa" heard for VOTs greater than that.

Phonemic Restoration Effect When a listener hearing a spoken sentence fills in a missing phoneme based on the context.

Phonemic Shadowing When a listener must repeat each syllable of a shadowed message as it occurs.

Photometry The measurement of light.

Photon The minimum unit of light energy.

Photopic A term for high light (daylight) conditions and vision under these light levels.

Photopsin The protein segment of the photochemical in cones.

Photoreceptors Photo-sensitive cells in the retina (rods and cones).

Phrase Shadowing When a listener is allowed to lag somewhat behind a shadowed message and repeat entire phrases at once.

Physiological Cues *See* Structural Cues.

Pictorial Depth Cues Cues for distance that can be found in photographs and pictures.

Pigment Epithelium The light-absorbing dark layer backing the retina in diurnal animals.

Pinna The fleshy, visible part of the outer ear.

Piper's Law The tradeoff relationship between area and intensity in the detection of stimuli between 10′ and 24° of visual angle in size; $\sqrt{A} \times I = C$.

Pitch The psychological attribute of sound most closely associated with sound frequency; described by the words *high* or *low*.

Pixel A picture element in a television or computer screen. Each screen consists of many rows and columns of pixels.

Place Principle Asserts that sound frequency is encoded by what *place* on the basilar membrane vibrates most to each frequency.

Poggendorff Illusion An illusion of direction that shows both age and sex differences.

Point of Subjective Equality The comparison stimulus intensity that appears most like the standard in a discrimination experiment.

Ponzo Illusion An illusion of size in which the length of a line is perceptually affected by its place in the context of surrounding converging lines.

Position Constancy Stable perceived position of objects despite body, eye, or head movements.

Positron Emission Tomography (PET) Mapping of brain activity by detecting the metabolic uptake of a radioactively tagged form of glucose molecule.

Posterior Parietal Lobe Area of cortex toward the back of the brain and above the occipital lobes, involved in the orienting of attention, both when attention is drawn to an abrupt-onset stimulus and when attention is voluntarily directed toward a location in preparation for an event there.

Postsynaptic Membrane The cell membrane of a neuron that is *receiving* transmitter substance across a synapse.

Potentiation A case of cross-adaptation in which exposure to one taste stimulus lowers the threshold to another taste stimulus.

Power Law The statement that the magnitude of sensation varies as the intensity of the physical stimulus raised to some power. Also known as Stevens's Law, $S = aI^m$.

Precedence Effect The first of a group of sounds (for example, a sound and its echoes) to arrive at the ear is the major determinant of where in space the sound source is perceived to be.

Preferential Looking A behavioral measure of infant discrimination in which target fixation time is assumed to be positively related to stimulus preference.

Preparing When an observer is in possession of advance information about where or when a stimulus event will happen and aligns attention with that place or time.

Presbyopia Farsightedness found in older individuals.

Pressure Amplitude A measure of the degree of compression or rarefaction at the peaks or valleys of a sound wave.

Presynaptic Membrane The cell membrane of a neuron that is *sending* transmitter substance across a synapse.

Primaries Three monochromatic light sources that when combined in appropriate amounts can match any other hue.

Primary Auditory Projection Area The area of the temporal cortex that receives most of the fibers from the medial geniculate; also known as *A1*.

Primary Olfactory Neurons The receptive cells of the olfactory system, containing olfactory rods and cilia, on the latter of which are located the receptor molecules.

Primary Visual Cortex Primary area of visual function in the occipital lobe. Also known as *Area V1* and *striate cortex*.

Primary-Like Neurons Cochlear nucleus neurons that give an initial burst of firing in response to a tone and then continue to fire at a lower level until the tone stops.

Primers Pheromones that trigger glandular and other physiological responses.

Probability Distribution A graphic representation of the likelihood that a given event will occur.

Processing Effort Model A theory that time is measured internally by the amount of cognitive work or processing that an individual does during an interval.

Profile Analysis Detection of a level increment ("bump") or other difference between complex sounds that differ in their profiles (amplitudes at the various frequencies making them up).

Prosopagnosia A perceptual disorder in which an individual cannot identify human faces.

Protanopia A form of color blindness resulting in the confusion of reds and greens due to insensitivity in the red system.

Prothetic Continuum A stimulus continuum for which quantitative differences in stimulus intensity give rise to quantitative differences in sensation intensity, such as sound intensity and loudness.

Protoanomaly A condition in which an individual's color matches require more green than those of a color-normal individual.

Psychic Blindness The condition in which animals are able to locate objects yet are unable to identify them.

Psychometric Function The relation between the proportion of responses of a particular type (for example, "heavier") and the intensity of the stimulus.

PTC Phenylthiocarbamide, a substance that shows large variations in absolute threshold across different individuals; some people are "taste-blind" to it.

Pulvinar Nucleus A visual center in the thalamus.

Pupil The opening in the iris of the eye through which light enters.

Purity A spectrally pure stimulus is composed of only one wavelength. The more wavelengths, the less pure.

Purkinje Shift The change in the apparent brightness of different wavelengths as one goes from a light- to a dark-adapted state.

Quadrantanopia A blind spot that covers a quarter of the field of view.

Radiance The amount of energy emitted by a light source.

Random-Dot Kinematogram (RDK) An apparent motion display consisting of randomly located dots.

Ratio Scale A measurement scale in which the rank order, spacing, and ratios of the numbers assigned to events have meaning; it also has an absolute zero point.

rCBF. *See* Regional Cerebral Blood Flow.

Reaction Time The interval between the onset of a stimulus and the beginning of an overt response.

Reafference Stimulus input that results from an observer's own movements.

Real Movement Physical movement of a stimulus.

Rearrangement An experimental technique that alters spatial relations in the visual world.

Receptive Field For any particular cells, the region of the visual field in which a stimulus can produce a response.

Recognition The experience of perceiving something as previously known.

Recognition Acuity A type of visual acuity commonly measured by means of letter recognition and scaled relative to a norm of recognition at 6 m distance from the observer (6/6).

Red-Green-Blue (or simply **RGB**) **Space** A three-dimensional model of color used in television and computer screens in which the relationship between three primary colors—red, green, and blue—is depicted.

Reduction Conditions An experimental procedure in which an attempt is made to eliminate or reduce most depth cues.

Reflectance Light-reflecting property of the surfaces in the visual environment. This property, together with the light source, surface orientations, and viewing position of the observer, completely determines the retinal image. *Also*, the proportion of incident light that a surface reflects.

Reflecting Tapetum The shiny surface backing the retina in some nocturnal animals.

Reflex Pursuit Movements Smooth eye movements, under vestibular control, that are made to keep the image of a target on the fovea despite head movements.

Refractive Error Light-bending or focusing error.

Refractory Period A period of time shortly after a spike during which it is difficult to stimulate the neuron sufficiently to produce another spike.

Regional Cerebral Blood Flow (rCBF) Mapping of brain activity by monitoring blood flow with a relatively inert but radioactively tagged material dissolved in the blood.

Reichardt Detector A neural arrangement for the detection of motion in an image.

Reissner's Membrane One of two membranes making up the cochlear duct.

Relative Brightness A depth cue in which the brighter of two otherwise identical objects will be seen as closer.

Relative Distance Distance of one object relative to another.

Relative Phase The difference between the phase angles of two waves expressed in degrees (0 to 360).

Releasers Pheromones that trigger specific behavioral responses.

Relevant Features Attributes such as color, size, and texture that differentiate one shape from another.

Residual Stimuli In adaptation level theory, stimuli that are no longer present but affect the current adaptation level.

Resolution Acuity The observer's ability to detect a gap between two lines, or the orientation of a grid of lines.

Resting Potential The usual electrical potential difference across the cell wall of a neuron, typically with the inside about −70 mV with respect to the outside.

Restricted Environmental Stimulation Technique A procedure in which a subject remains in a dark, sound-deadened room for specified intervals of time.

Restricted Rearing An experimental technique in which an animal is reared without exposure to a particular class of sensory inputs.

Retina The rear portion of the eye containing photoreceptors and several types of sensory neurons.

Retinal Part of the rhodopsin pigment, similar to vitamin A.

Retinal Illuminance The amount of light reaching the retina.

Retinal Image The two-dimensional distribution of light of various intensities and wavelengths on the retina.

Retinal Image Size A potential depth cue based on the size of the image on the retina.

Reverberation Sound Sound that reaches the ears after having bounced off some surface; proportion of reverberation sound is a cue to the distance of a sound source.

Rhodopsin The photopigment found in rods.

Rhythm The perceived organization in time of a sequence of sounds.

Ricco's Law The tradeoff relationship between area and intensity in the detection of stimuli smaller than 10′ of visual angle in size: $A \times I = C$.

Rods Long, thin, cylindrical photoreceptors in the retina, used in low-light vision.

Rooting Response An infant reflex consisting of head turning in the direction of a touch to the face.

Round Window The membrane at the base of the cochlea facing the middle ear.

S Potentials Graded electrical retinal-cell responses that vary in direction and strength depending on the wavelength of the stimulus.

Saccades *See* Saccadic Eye Movements.

Saccadic Eye Movements Fast, ballistic eye movements used to explore the visual field and to place the images of objects on the fovea.

Saturated The state in which a neuron cannot fire any faster, even if stimulus intensity is increased.

Saturation The psychological attribute of a color associated with "how much" of a hue is present.

Scale A rule by which numbers are assigned to objects or events.

Scaling A psychophysical problem involving the measurement of sensation magnitude.

Schemata Internal models or hypotheses about the external world that organize perceptual information.

Schizophrenia A psychotic disorder characterized by withdrawal from the environment, reduced levels of emotional response, a reduction in abstract thinking, and a general diminishing of daily activity.

Schwann Cells One type of glial cells forming the myelin sheath around axons.

Sclera Strong, elastic outer covering, seen as the "white" of the eye.

Scotoma A localized blind spot caused by damage to the visual cortex.

Scotopic A term for low-light (night) visibility conditions and vision under these light levels.

Scotopsin The protein portion of rhodopsin—a type of opsin.

Search The process of scanning a scene or a display for a particular target stimulus.

Selective Adaptation A psychophysical technique in which motion-specific cells in the visual system are fatigued, causing reduced sensitivity to other visual stimuli moving in the same direction and at the same speed as the previously exposed adapting pattern. *See also* Neural Satiation.

Selective Rearing An experimental technique in which an animal is reared under conditions that bias the stimulus input it receives toward a particular class of stimuli (e.g., it sees only vertical stripes).

Self-Adaptation A phenomenon in which exposure to a tastant (or odorant) raises the absolute threshold or decreases the sensory intensity of the same tastant (or odorant).

Self-Motion The perception that the body is moving through space.

Semicircular Canals Vestibular organs contained in the bony labyrinth, next to the cochlea of the ear.

Sensation Simple conscious experience associated with a stimulus.

Sensitive Period An age range during which the development of a perceptual ability may be strongly influenced by the presence or absence of relevant stimulation or experience.

Sensory Convergence The notion that several different sensory inputs, from different modalities and sources, combine to form an apparently simple perceptual experience.

Sensory Neuron A neuron that carries information from a sensory receptor toward the brain or spinal cord.

Sequential Integration Integration of a group of sounds into a single auditory stream by virtue of their temporal proximity.

Serial Search A pattern of visual search in which items in an array are compared one at a time with a target representation.

Set *See* Perceptual Set.

Shadowing When listeners are asked to repeat the verbal input they are receiving, usually in a particular ear; used to study filtering and divided attention.

Shape A region of the retinal image surrounded by contours.

Short-Range Motion Apparent motion seen in displays where successive frames are separated by less than 100 ms in time and the spatial displacement of corresponding elements is less than 15 min of visual angle.

SI System The System International d'Unites; a uniform system of measurement.

Sighting-Dominant Eye The eye whose use is preferred in monocular tasks such as looking through a telescope.

Signal Detection Theory A mathematical, theoretical system that formally deals with both decisional and sensory components in detection and discrimination tasks.

Similarity Matrix A matrix whose entries are the perceived similarities between pairs of stimuli; *see* Multidimensional Scaling.

Simple Cell A cortical cell that responds to lines or edges of a particular orientation and location.

Simple Reaction Time Reaction time for detecting the onset of a stimulus.

Simultagnosia An attentional disorder in which an individual cannot pay attention to more than one stimulus at a time.

Simultaneous Brightness Contrast A target area of a given luminance appears brighter when surrounded by a darker background than when surrounded by a lighter background.

Simultaneous Color Contrast A process in which inhibitory interactions between adjacent color systems cause hue shifts.

Simultaneous Integration Integration of a group of sounds into a single auditory stream by virtue of the similarity of their frequency spectra.

Simultaneous Masking A reduction in target detectability that occurs when nontarget stimuli are presented at the same time.

Sine-Wave Grating A pattern of light intensity that varies from light to dark following sinusoidal gradations.

Skill An approach to attention that emphasizes learning how to process stimuli optimally, rather than shifting between modes of processing, as an explanation for good divided-attention performance.

Smooth Pursuit Eye Movement The continuous eye movement involved in following a smoothly and steadily moving object.

Sodium-Potassium Pump A mechanism that ejects three sodium ions from inside the neuron for every two potassium ions it lets in, thus helping to maintain the −70 mV resting potential.

Solitary Tract Region of the brain stem that receives information from cranial nerves about taste.

Somatosensory Cortex The part of the cerebral cortex, located in the parietal lobe, that receives input from the thalamus and other brain regions representing touch, temperature, pain, and kinesthesis.

Sone A scale for the loudness of a sound; the unit of that scale—a 1,000-Hz, 40-dB tone—has a loudness of 1 sone.

Sound Level Difference A difference in sound pressure level at the two ears caused by the presence of a sound shadow; cue to localization of higher-frequency sounds.

Sound Pressure Level (SPL) The amount by which the pressure amplitude of a sound wave differs from atmospheric pressure, measured in decibels.

Sound Shadow An area in which only sounds diffracted by the edge of the head are received by the ear, resulting in lower intensity, especially for sounds of higher frequencies.

Spatial Agnosia A perceptual disorder in which individuals cannot accurately localize objects or themselves.

Spatial Modulation Transfer Function A graphical description of the way in which an optical system's ability to resolve spatial modulations (intensity changes across space) varies with spatial frequency.

Spatial Summation A facilitation in contour detection that occurs when a second subthreshold contour is placed in near proximity to the target contour.

Spectral Colors Pure monochromatic stimuli, such as those in a prismatic spectrum.

Speech Spectrogram A representation of the speech signal in terms of the frequencies and amplitudes of its sine wave components as these change over time.

Spike Potential *See* Action Potential.

Spinothalamic Pathway A slow pathway of short fibers in the spinal cord that conducts information (representing pain, temperature, and rudimentary touch) to the brain from the skin, muscles, tendons, and organs.

Spiral Ganglion The cells whose axons form the auditory nerve.

Square-Wave Grating Sharply alternating light and dark stripes.

Stabilized Retinal Image A technique for making the retinal image stay in one place in spite of where or how the eye moves.

Staircase Method A method for measuring absolute thresholds in which the experimenter alters the direction of changes in stimulus intensity each time the observer's response changes.

Standard A stimulus against which the comparison stimuli are judged in a discrimination experiment.

Standard Units Internationally agreed-on measures of photic energy.

Stapes The bone in the chain of middle ear ossicles that makes contact with the oval window; also called the *stirrup*.

Statocysts In primitive invertebrates, motion-sensitive cavities lined with hair cells.

Statolith A tiny stonelike body resting on the hairs of statocysts and causing them to bend in response to the motion or change of position of an animal.

Stereomotion A dynamic cue to depth based on the relative rates of motion in the two eyes.

Stereopsis The ability to see depth based solely on the disparity of the two retinal images.

Stereoscope An optical instrument enabling two different images to stimulate the two eyes simultaneously to produce an effect of depth.

Stereotaxic Instrument A device that allows accurate placement of electrodes in the brains of experimental animals.

Stevens's Law *See* Power Law.

Stimulus Onset Asynchrony (SOA) The elapsed time between the onset of one frame and the onset of the next frame in an apparent motion display.

Storage Size Model A model that contends that time is measured internally by the number of items processed and stored in memory during an interval.

Streaming Perspective The optical flow of stimuli as we move through space, centered around the direction of movement.

Striate Cortex Area 17 in the occipital lobe. Also known as *V1* and *primary visual cortex*.

Stroop Effect The difficulty of observers to eliminate meaningful but conflicting information from a task even when that information is irrelevant to the task.

Structural Cues Depth and distance cues arising from adjustments of the eye(s) in interaction with the visual stimulus.

Structural Theories Theories of attention that emphasize a structural limitation on the ability to attend to multiple perceptual inputs.

Structure From Motion The perception of a three-dimensional surface or shape that is given only by the pattern of relative motion in an image.

Subjective Colors Colors that are consciously experienced but not associated with any wavelength change in the physical stimulus.

Subjective Contours Contours that are consciously experienced but not associated with physical stimulus change.

Subject-Relative Change The movement of objects relative to the body.

Substantia Gelatinosa The part of the spinal cord implicated in pain transmission through the gate-control theory.

Subtractive Color Mixture A color mixture resulting from the subtraction or absorption of light of various wavelengths, for example, the mixture of yellow and blue pigments to produce green.

Successive Brightness Contrast Brightness perception that is influenced by events occurring immediately prior to the test stimulus. It is the temporal analog of simultaneous brightness contrast.

Superior Colliculi The upper pair of hill-like bumps on the top of the brain stem. These are involved in the overt and possibly covert orienting of attention.

Superior Olives The brain termini for axons from the ventral cochlear nuclei.

Superior Temporal Cortex An area of the temporal lobe whose cells show a high degree of response specificity to visual stimuli.

Suppression of Motion Smear The decrease in motion smear that occurs when a moving object follows a predictable trajectory.

Suprachiasmatic Nucleus (SCN) A center in the hypothalamus that is believed to be responsible for circadian rhythms.

Surface Deletion and **Surface Accretion** An emergent property signaling relative depth between two objects. Portions of a more distant object's surface will be deleted (disappear) and then be accreted (reappear) as the nearer object moves past the more distant one.

Surface Orientation The orientation of the light-reflecting surfaces in the visual environment. This property, together with the light source, reflectance, and viewing position of the observer, completely determines the retinal image.

Symbolic Cue Advance information about where or when a stimulus event will happen.

Synapse The place where two neurons almost touch each other.

Synaptic Cleft The gap between two neurons at a synapse, into which neural transmitters are released.

Synaptic Knob Swelling at the ends of an axon. It contains the synaptic vesicles.

Synaptic Vesicles Small reservoirs in the synaptic knobs that contain neural transmitters.

Tadoma A method of assistance to speech perception in which the "listener" places her hand on the face and neck of the speaker and deduces what is said from the haptically perceived actions of the articulators.

Target The sound to be detected in a masking situation.

Taste Buds The group of cells in which the major receptors for taste are located, on the tongue and parts of the mouth.

Taste Pore An opening in the surface of the tongue leading to the taste cells extending from the taste bud.

Tectopulvinar System A secondary pathway to the visual cortex that includes nuclei in the brain stem and thalamus.

Tectorial Membrane Within the cochlear duct, the membrane, extending from Reissner's membrane, in which hairs of the outer hair cells are embedded.

Tectum A primitive visual center in the brain stem.

Tempo The perceived speed with which the sequence of sounds is proceeding.

Temporal Integration A unified percept obtained from separate flashes of light, resulting when the flashes are presented within 100 ms of each other and there is no overlap in the spatial patterns.

Temporal Lobe Area of the cortex toward the bottom of the brain and in front of the occipital lobes, involved in the analysis of shape and form. Neurons in this area are sensitive to the intentions of the subject to filter out unwanted stimuli.

Temporal Processing Model The theory that your experience of the passage of time depends on the amount of attention that you direct toward monitoring time.

Temporal Summation The auditory system adds the sound energy received over about 200 ms for near-threshold stimuli, giving rise to the relationship $T = E \times D$. See Hughes's Law.

Temporal Visual Field The half of the visual field of each eye that lies toward the temple.

Textons Elongated blobs of a particular color, length, width, or orientation, line ends, or line crossings; differences between regions of the visual array in the textons they contain define textural contours.

Textural Contour A contour created by a boundary between two areas differing in visual texture.

Texture Gradient Distance cue based on variations in surface texture as a function of distance from the observer.

Texture Segregation A perceptual task in which subjects must find an "odd" region of form elements amongst a larger region of "background" form elements.

Thalamus Area of the midbrain through which sensory pathways pass on the way to the cortex. It serves as a major "switching center" for sensory information, and several nuclei, particularly the pulvinar, are implicated in attentional filtering.

Three-Dimensional Possessing pictorial depth.

Threshold Response Curve A graph of neural absolute threshold as a function of sound frequency.

Timbre A psychological attribute of sound associated with its harmonic structure.

Time Difference The difference between the time taken by a sound wave to travel to the two ears when starting from an azimuth other than 0° or 180°; a cue to the direction of a low-frequency sound source.

Tip Link A thin filament, possibly made of actin, that connects the tips of shorter hairs to the sides of neighboring longer hairs of hair cells; probably involved in transduction of sound.

Tonotopic Characteristic of the place of response to a sound depending on the frequency of the sound.

Topographic Map An area of the brain in which points in visual space are represented in the neural tissue in a spatially related manner.

Trace McClelland and Elman's (1986) theory of word identification.

Tract The most common name for a nerve in the central nervous system.

Transactional View Point Maintains that any perceptual experience consists of a complex evaluation of the significance of available stimuli based on expectations and experience.

Transmission (T) Cells In the gate-control theory of pain, these transmit pain impulses to the brain.

Transmitter Substance Chemicals released into the synaptic cleft that polarize or hyperpolarize the post-synaptic membrane.

Trichromatic Theory The theory that color vision is based on three primary responses.

Tristimulus Values The combination of the stimulus hue and brightness used in the CIE color system for determining any color stimulus.

Tritanopia The color defect in which yellows and blues are confused due to reduced blue sensitivity.

Tuned Neuron A neuron that responds optimally to tones of a particular frequency.

Tuning Curve A graph showing the rate of firing of an auditory neuron for different tone frequencies; it usually has a single peak.

Tunnel of Corti A structure in the cochlea.

Two-Dimensional Lacking pictorial depth.

Two-Point Threshold The minimum distance necessary between two pointed touch stimuli (such as two toothpicks) so that they will be felt as two distinct sensations.

Two-Tone Suppression Inhibition of neural response to a tone at the characteristic frequency of the neuron that occurs when a second tone of a different frequency is presented; suppression occurs during and briefly after the presentation of the second tone.

Tympanic Canal One of three canals running through the cochlea.

Tympanum *See* Eardrum.

Type 1 Fibers Fibers extending from the spiral ganglion to the inner hair cells.

Type 2 Fibers Fibers extending from the spiral ganglion to the outer hair cells.

UFOV *See* Useful Field of View.

Uncrossed Disparity A cue for relative distance in which, when there are double images, the unfused image in the right eye appears on the right and that in the left eye on the left.

Unilateral Neglect A form of spatial agnosia in which only one side of all objects and of the visual field is not processed.

Useful Field of View (UFOV) The area of the visual field that is functional for an observer performing a given task. In general, the more difficult a task, the smaller the useful field of view.

Utricle A vestibular organ contained in the bony labyrinth.

V1 The first region of the occipital lobe to receive visual input in the geniculostriate pathway. Also known as the *primary visual cortex* and *striate cortex*.

V2, V3, V4, V5 Visual areas within the occipital lobe that receive their inputs from Area V1. Also known as *prestriate* and *extrastriate visual cortex*.

Vanishing Point In linear perspective a point on the horizon at which converging parallel lines seem to meet.

Vection An illusion of induced motion, in which you experience your body moving through space or tilting because of changes in the optical flow.

Ventral Cochlear Nucleus The front half of the nucleus in the lower back part of the brain where the auditory nerve fibers end.

VEP *See* Visually Evoked Potential.

Vergence Movements Movements of the eyes in which the two eyes move together but in opposite directions, either converging or diverging.

Vernier Acuity The measure of an individual's ability to distinguish a broken line from an unbroken line.

Vestibular Canal One of three canals running through the cochlea.

Vestibular Nuclei In the brain stem, way stations along the route of nerve fibers from the crista and macula to the cerebellum and cortex.

Vestibular System The system that monitors the body's movement and orientation in space. Its receptors are located in the bony labyrinth.

Viewing Position The position of the viewer with respect to the objects in the visual environment. This property, together with the light source(s), reflectances, and surface orientations in the visual environment, completely determines the retinal image.

Vigilance Maintaining overt attention to a perceptual task, often with infrequent stimulus events, for prolonged time periods.

Visible Persistence The experience of seeing a light persist after photons have stopped hitting the retina.

Vision Substitution System An instrument that converts a visual pattern from a television camera into a pattern of vibrating points on the skin of the back; used for the visually impaired.

Visual Acuity The ability of the eye to resolve details.

Visual Agnosia Syndrome in which all parts of a visual field are seen, but the objects seen are without meaning.

Visual Angle A measure of the size of the retinal image.

Visual Capture When sound seems to be originating from a spatial location where appropriate visual movement is occurring, as in ventriloquism.

Visual Cliff A table with shallow and deep sides overlaid by a sheet of glass; used for measuring depth perception in young animals.

Visual Context Visual stimuli that surround or accompany other stimuli.

Visual Field All the parts of the environment that are sending light to the eyes at any moment.

Visual-Geometric Illusions Simple line drawings in which the actual physical characteristics of certain elements differ from the perceived characteristics of those elements.

Visual Integrative Agnosia Inability to integrate parts of a figure into a whole (usually combines symptoms of visual object agnosia and simultagnosia).

Visual Masking The reduced visibility of a stimulus presented in close temporal and spatial proximity to a second stimulus.

Visual Object Agnosia An inability to recognize familiar objects in the absence of psychopathological or organic damage to the visual apparatus.

Visual Search A perceptual task in which the subject looks for the presence of a "target" item amidst a number of other "distracter" items.

Visual Texture Aggregates of many small elements in the retinal image that do not differ in average brightness or color from one another.

Visually Evoked Potential (VEP) The change in the electrical activity of the brain produced in response to a visual stimulus.

Vitreous Humour The jelly-like substance filling the large chamber of the eye.

Voice Onset Time The latency in producing a vowel sound following a stop-consonant sound.

Volley Principle The theory that neurons fire in groups, one group of neurons firing while another group "recharges."

Volume The psychological quality of sound associated with the degree to which a sound fills space and seems large or small.

Voluntary Pursuit Movements The eye movements by which you voluntarily track a moving target.

Vomeronasal Organ A special set of reptilian and mammalian odor receptors that detects very heavy molecules, usually pheromones and sometimes dissolved in fluid.

Vowel A basic speech sound produced by opening the vocal tract and vibrating the vocal cords.

Waterfall Illusion Staring at a waterfall and then shifting your gaze to the bank beside the waterfall can produce the vivid impression that the bank is moving in a direction opposite to the waterfall.

Wave The pattern of air molecule motion that characterizes sound.

Wavelength The distance from one peak to the next of a sound wave.

Weber Fraction The proportion by which the standard stimulus must be increased in order to detect change, $k = \Delta I / I$.

Weber's Law The statement that the size of the difference threshold increases linearly with the size of the standard, $\Delta I = KI$.

Westheimer Function The ability to detect a small spot of light first declines and then improves as the diameter of a background disk is increased. This psychophysical procedure demonstrates the operation of center-surround ganglion cells.

Yerkes-Dodson Law The principle that arousal and performance are related, with the best performance occurring for a medium amount of arousal.

Zeitgeber The stimulus used to calibrate, or entrain, the biological clock.

References

Aantaa, E. (1970). Light-induced and spontaneous variations in the amplitude of the electro-oculogram. *Acta Otolaryngologica, Supplementum, 267.*

Aaron, M. (1975). Effect of the menstrual cycle on subjective ratings of sweetness. *Perceptual and Motor Skills, 40,* 974.

Abbs, J. H., & Sussman, H. M. (1971). Neurophysiological feature detectors and speech perception: Discussion of theoretical implications. *Journal of Speech and Hearing Research, 14,* 23–36.

Abraham, H. D., & Wolf, E. (1988). Visual function in past users of LSD: Psychophysical findings. *Journal of Abnormal Psychology, 97,* 443–447.

Abramov, I., Gordon, J., Henderson, A., Hainline, L., Dobson, V., & La Brossiere, E. (1982). The retina of the newborn human infant. *Science, 217,* 265–267.

Abrams, R. A., & Dobkin, R. S. (1994). Inhibition of return: Effects of attentional cueing on eye movement latencies. *Journal of Experimental Psychology: Human Perception and Performance, 20,* 467–477.

Adam, N., Rosner, B. S., Hosick, E. C., & Clark, D. L. (1971). Effect of anesthetic drugs on time production and alpha rhythm. *Perception & Psychophysics, 10,* 133–136.

Adams, A. S., Brown, B., Haegerstrom-Portnoy, G., & Flom, M. C. (1976). Evidence for acute effect of alcohol and marijuana on color discrimination. *Perception & Psychophysics, 20,* 119–124.

Adams, C. L., & Molfese, D. L. (1987). Electrophysiological correlates of categorical speech perception for voicing contrasts in dogs. *Developmental Neuropsychology, 3,* 175–189.

Adams, J. (1989). Newborns' discrimination among mid- and long-wavelength stimuli. *Journal of Experimental Child Psychology, 47,* 130–141.

Adams, R. D. (1977). Intervening stimulus effects on category judgments of duration. *Perception & Psychophysics, 21,* 527–534.

Adams, R. J. (1995). Further exploration of human neonatal chromatic achromatic discrimination. *Journal of Experimental Child Psychology, 60,* 344–360.

Adams, R. J., & Courage, M. L. (1994). Systematic measurement of human neonatal color vision. *Vision Research, 34,* 1691–1701.

Adelson, E. H., & Movshon, J. A. (1982). Phenomenal coherence of moving visual patterns. *Nature, 300,* 523–525.

Agostini, T., & Proffitt, D. R. (1993). Perceptual organization evokes simultaneous lightness contrast. *Perception, 22,* 263–272.

Aitkin, L., & Martin, R. (1990). Neurons in the inferior colliculus of cats sensitive to sound-source elevation. *Hearing Research, 50,* 97–106.

Akhtar, N., & Enns, J. T. (1989). Relations between covert orienting and filtering in the development of visual attention. *Journal of Experimental Child Psychology, 48,* 315–334.

Akil, H., & Watson S. J. (1980). The role of endogenous opiates in pain control. In H. W. Kosterlitz & L. Y. Terenius (Eds.), *Pain and society* (pp. 201–222). Weinheim: Verlag Chemie Gmblt.

Aks, D. J., & Enns, J. T. (1996). Visual search for size is influenced by a background texture gradient. *Journal of Experimental Psychology: Human Perception and Performance, 22,* 1467–1481.

Alexander, J. B., & Gudeman, H. E. (1965). Personal and interpersonal measures of field dependence. *Perceptual and Motor Skills, 20,* 70–86.

Alexander, K. R., & Shansky, M. S. (1976). Influence of hue, value, and chroma on the perceived heaviness of colours. *Perception & Psychophysics, 19,* 72–74.

Algom, D., Ben-Aharon, B., & Cohen-Raz, L. (1989). Dichotic, diotic, and monaural summation of loudness: A comprehensive analysis of composition and psychophysical functions. *Perception & Psychophysics, 46,* 567–578.

Algom, D., & Lubel, S. (1994). Psychophysics in the field: Perception and memory for labor pain. *Perception & Psychophysics, 55,* 133–141.

Algom, D., & Marks, L. E. (1990). Range and regression, loudness scales, and loudness processing: Toward a context-bound psychophysics. *Journal of Experimental Psychology: Human Perception and Performance, 16,* 706–727.

Algom, D., Raphaeli, N., & Cohen-Raz, L. (1986). Integration of noxious stimulation across separate somatosensory communications systems: A functional theory of pain. *Journal of Experimental Psychology: Human Perception and Performance, 12,* 92–102.

Algom, D., Rubin, A., & Cohen-Raz, L. (1989). Binaural and temporal integration of the loudness of tones and noises. *Perception & Psychophysics, 46,* 155–166.

Alho, K., Teraniemi, M., Huotilainen, M., Lavikainen, J., Tiitinen, H., Ilmoniemi, R. J., Knuutila, J., & Näätänen, R. (1996). Processing of complex sounds in the human auditory cortex as revealed by magnetic brain responses. *Psychophysiology, 33,* 369–375.

Ali, M. R., & Amir, T. (1989). Effects of fasting on visual flicker fusion. *Perceptual and Motor Skills, 69,* 627–631.

Allan, L. G., & Siegel, S. (1986). McCollough effects as conditioned responses: Reply to Skowbo. *Psychological Bulletin, 100,* 388–393.

Allen, J. R. (1985). Salicylate-induced musical perceptions. *New England Journal of Medicine, 313,* 642–643.

Allen, M. (1970). *Vision and highway safety.* Radnor, PA: Chilton Books.

Allison, A. C. (1953). The structure of the olfactory bulb and its relation to the olfactory pathways in the rabbit and the rat. *Journal of Comparative Neurology, 98,* 309–348.

Allman, J., Miezin, F., & McGuinness, E. (1985). Direction- and velocity-specific responses from beyond the classical receptive field in the middle temporal visual area (MT). *Perception, 14,* 105–126.

Alpern, M. (1979). Lack of uniformity in color matching. *Journal of Physiology, 288,* 85–105.

Ames, A. Jr. (1951). Visual perception and the rotating trapezoid window. *Psychological Monographs, 65* (14, Whole No. 324).

Ames, A. Jr. (1955). *The nature of our perception, apprehensions and behavior.* Princeton, NJ: Princeton University Press.

Amoore, J. E. (1969). A plan to identify most of the primary odors. In C. Pfaffman (Ed.), *Olfaction and taste III* (pp. 158–171). New York: Rockefeller University Press.

Amoore, J. E. (1970). *Molecular basis of odor.* Springfield, IL: Thomas.

Amoore, J. E. (1975). Four primary odor modalities of man: Experimental evidence and possible significance. In D. A. Denton & J. P. Coghlan (Eds.), *Olfaction and taste V* (pp. 283–289). New York: Academic Press.

Amoore, J. E., Pelosi, P., & Forrester, L. J. (1977). Specific anosmias to 5a-androst-16en-3one and w-penta-decalone: The urinous and musky odors. *Chemical Senses and Flavor, 5,* 401–425.

Amure, B. O. (1978). Nicotine and decay of the McCollough effect. *Vision Research, 18,* 1449–1451.

Andersen, G. J. (1986). Perception of self-motion: Psychophysical and computational approaches. *Psychological Bulletin, 99,* 52–65.

Andersen, G. J., & Braunstein, M. L. (1985). Induced self-motion in central vision. *Journal of Experimental Psychology: Human Perception and Performance, 11,* 122–132.

Anderson, N. H. (1975). On the role of context effects in psychophysical judgment. *Psychological Review, 82,* 462–482.

Anderson, N. H. (1992). Integration psychophysics and cognition. In D. Algom (Ed.), *Psychophysical approaches to cognition* (pp. 13–113). New York: North Holland.

Anderson, N. S., & Fitts, P. M. (1958). Amount of information gained during brief exposures of numerals and colors. *Journal of Experimental Psychology, 56,* 362–369.

Andreasen, N. C. (1988). Brain imaging: Applications in psychiatry. *Science, 239,* 1381–1388.

Andrews, B. W., & Pollen, D. A. (1979). Relationship between spatial frequency selectivity and receptive field profile of simple cells. *Journal of Physiology, 287,* 163–176.

Annis, R. C., & Frost, B. (1973). Human visual ecology and orientation anisotropies in acuity. *Science, 182,* 729–731.

Anstis, S. M. (1975). What does visual perception tell us about visual coding? In M. S. Gazzaniga & C. Blakemore (Eds.), *Handbook of psychobiology* (pp. 267–234). New York: Academic Press.

Anstis, S. M. (1978). Apparent movement. In R. Held, H. W. Leibowitz, & H. L. Teuber (Eds.), *Handbook of sensory physiology* (pp. 655–673). New York: Springer-Verlag.

Anstis, S. M., & Mather, G. (1985). Effects of luminance and contrast on direction of ambiguous motion. *Perception, 14,* 167–179.

Anstis, S. M., Rogers, B., & Henry, J. (1978). Interactions between simultaneous contrast and colored afterimages. *Vision Research, 18,* 899–911.

Antes, J. R., & Penland, J. (1981). Picture context effects on eye movement patterns. In D. Fisher, R. Monty, & J. Senders (Eds.), *Eye movements: Cognition and visual perception* (pp. 157–170). New Jersey: Erlbaum.

Antes, J. R. (1974). The time course of picture viewing. *Journal of Experimental Psychology, 103,* 62–70.

Arend, L. E. (1993). Mesopic lightness, brightness and brightness contrast. *Perception & Psychophysics, 54,* 469–476.

Arend, L. E., & Goldstein, R. (1987). Lightness models, gradient illusions, and curl. *Perception & Psychophysics, 42,* 65–80.

Arend, L. E., & Spehar, B. (1993a). Lightness, brightness and brightness contrast: 1. Illuminance variation. *Perception & Psychophysics, 54,* 446–456.

Arend, L. E., & Spehar, B. (1993b). Lightness, brightness and brightness contrast: 2. Reflectance variation. *Perception & Psychophysics, 54,* 457–468.

Arlin, M. (1986). The effects of quantity, complexity, and attentional demand on children's time perception. *Perception & Psychophysics, 40,* 177–182.

Arterberry, M., & Yonas, A. (1989). Self-produced locomotion and the development of responsiveness to linear perspective and texture gradients. *Developmental Psychology, 25,* 976–982.

Arvidson, K., & Friberg, U. (1980). Human taste response and taste bud number in fungiform papillae. *Science, 209,* 807–808.

Asano, F., Suzuki, Y., & Sone, T. (1990). Role of spectral cues in median plane localization. *Journal of the Acoustical Society of America, 88,* 159–168.

Aschoff, J. (1979). Circadian rhythms: General features and endocrinological aspects. In D. T. Krieger (Ed.), *Endocrine rhythms* (pp. 1–61). New York: Raven Press.

Aschoff, J. (1981). *Handbook of behavioral neurobiology: Vol. 4.* New York: Plenum Press.

Aschoff, J. (1984). Circadian timing. *Annals of the New York Academy of Sciences, 423,* 442–468.

Ashby, F. G., & Perrin, N. A. (1988). Toward a unified theory of similarity and recognition. *Psychological Review, 95,* 124–150.

Ashmead, D. H., Davis, D. L., & Northington, A. (1995). Contributions of listeners' approaching motion to auditory distance perception. *Journal of Experimental Psychology: Human Perception and Performance, 21,* 239–256.

Ashmead, D. H., LeRoy, D., & Odom, R. D. (1990). Perception of the relative distances of nearby sound sources. *Perception & Psychophysics, 47,* 326–331.

Aslin, R. N. (1981a). Development of smooth pursuit in human infants. In D. Fisher, R. Monty, & J. Senders (Eds.), *Eye movements: Cognition and visual perception* (pp. 31–52). Hillsdale, NJ: Erlbaum.

Aslin, R. N. (1981b). Experiential influences and sensitive periods in perceptual development: A unified model. In R. N. Aslin, J. R. Alberts, & M. R. Peterson (Eds.), *Development of perception* (pp. 45–93). New York: Academic Press.

Aslin, R. N. (1985). Effects of experience on sensory and perceptual development: Implications for infant cognition. In J. Mehler & R. Fox (Eds.), *Neonate cognition: Beyond the blooming buzzing confusion* (pp. 157–184). Hillsdale, NJ: Erlbaum.

Aslin, R. N. (1987). Motor aspects of visual development in infancy. In P. Salapatek & L. Cohen (Eds.), *Handbook of infant perception: Vol. 1. From sensation to perception* (pp. 43–113). Orlando: Academic Press.

Aslin, R. N., & Dumais, S. (1980). Binocular vision in infants: A review and a theoretical framework. In H. Reese & L. Lipsett (Eds.), *Advances in child development and behavior: Vol. 15* (pp. 54–95). New York: Academic Press.

Aslin, R. N., & Smith, L. B. (1988). Perceptual development. *Annual Review of Psychology, 39,* 435–473.

ASVA 97. (1997). *Proceedings of the International Symposium on Simulation, Visualization and Auralization for Acoustic Research and Education.* Tokyo: Acoustical Society of Japan.

Atkinson, J. (1979). Development of optokinetic nystagmus in the human infant and monkey infant: An analogue to development in kittens. In R. D. Freeman (Ed.), *Developmental neurobiology of vision* (pp. 277–288). New York: Plenum Press.

Atkinson, J. (1984). Human visual development over the first six months of life: A review and a hypothesis. *Human Neurobiology, 3,* 61–74.

Atkinson, J., & Braddick, O. (1981). Acuity, contrast, sensitivity, and accommodation in infancy. In R. Aslin, J. Alberts, & M. Petersen (Eds.), *Development of perception: Psychobiological perspectives: Vol. 2. The visual system* (pp. 243–278). New York: Academic Press.

Atkinson, J., Braddick, O., & French, J. (1979). Contrast sensitivity of the human neonate measured by the visual evoked potential. *Investigative Ophthalmology and Visual Sciences, 18,* 210–213.

Atkinson, J., Hood, B., Braddick, O. J., & Wattam-Bell, J. (1988). Infants' control of fixation shifts with single and competing targets: Mechanisms for shifting attention. *Perception, 17,* 367–368.

Atkinson, J., Hood, B., Wattam-Bell, J., & Braddick, O. (1992). Changes in infants' ability to switch visual attention in the first three months of life. *Perception, 21,* 643–653.

Attneave, F. (1954). Some informational aspects of visual perception. *Psychological Review, 61,* 183–193.

Attneave, F. (1955). Symmetry, information and memory for patterns. *American Journal of Psychology, 68,* 209–222.

Aubert, H. (1886). Die Bewegungsempfindung. *Archiv fuer die Gesamte Physiologie des Menschen and der Tiere, 39,* 347–370.

Augenstine, L. G. (1962). A model of how humans process information. *Biometrics, 18,* 420–421.

Avant, L. L. (1965). Vision in the Ganzfeld. *Psychological Bulletin, 64,* 246–258.

Avant, L. L., & Lyman, P. J. (1975). Stimulus familiarity modifies perceived duration in prerecognition visual processing. *Journal of Experimental Psychology: Human Perception and Performance, 1,* 205–213.

Avant, L. L., Lyman, P. J., & Antes, J. R. (1975). Effects of stimulus familiarity upon judged visual duration. *Perception & Psychophysics, 17,* 253–262.

Avolio, B., Kroeck, K., & Panek, P. (1986). Individual differences in information processing ability as a predictor of motor vehicle accidents. *Human Factors, 27,* 577–588.

Bachman, T., & Allik, J. (1976). Integration and interruption in the masking of form by form. *Perception, 5,* 79–97.

Baddeley, A. D. (1966). Time estimation at reduced body temperature. *American Journal of Psychology, 79,* 475–479.

Bailey, P. J., & Herrmann, P. (1993). A reexamination of duplex perception evoked by intensity differences. *Perception & Psychophysics, 54,* 20–32.

Baird, J. C. (1975). Psychophysical study of numbers: IV. Generalized preferred state theory. *Psychological Research, 38,* 175–187.

Baird, J. C., Green, D. M., & Luce, R. D. (1980). Variability and sequential effect in cross modality matching of area and loudness. *Journal of Experimental Psychology: Human Perception and Psychophysics, 6,* 277–289.

Baird, J. C., & Noma, E. (1978). *Fundamentals of scaling and psychophysics.* New York: Wiley.

Bakalyar, H. A., & Reed, R. R. (1990). Identification of specialized adenylyl cyclase that may mediate odorant detection. *Science, 250,* 1403–1406.

Baker, C. L., & Braddick, O. J. (1985). Temporal properties of the short-range process in apparent motion. *Perception, 14,* 181–192.

Balint, R. (1909). Seelenlahmung des "Schauens," optische Ataxie, raumliche Storung der Aufmerksamkeit. *Monatsschr. Psychiatr. Neurol., 25,* 51–81.

Ball, K. K., Roenker, D. L., & Bruni, J. R. (1990). Developmental changes in attention and visual search throughout adulthood. In J. T. Enns (Ed.), *The development of attention: Research and theory* (pp. 489–508). Amsterdam: Elsevier.

Ball, W., & Vurpillot, E. (1976). La perception du mouvement en profondur chez le nourrisson. *L'Annee Psychologique, 67,* 393–400.

Ballard, D. H., Hinton, G. E., & Sejnowski, T. J. (1983). Parallel visual computation. *Nature, 306,* 21–26.

Ballas, J. A. (1993). Common factors in the identification of an assortment of brief everyday sounds. *Journal of Experimental Psychology: Human Perception and Performance, 19,* 250–267.

Balogh, R. D., & Porter, R. H. (1986). Olfactory preferences resulting from mere exposure in human neonates. *Infant Behavior and Development, 9,* 395–401.

Baltes, P. B., & Lindenberger, U. (1997). Emergence of a powerful connection between sensory and cognitive functions across the adult life span: A new window to the study of cognitive aging? *Psychology and Aging, 12,* 12–21.

Banks, M. S., & Dannemiller, J. L. (1987). Infant visual psychophysics. In P. Salapatek & L. Cohen (Eds.), *Handbook of infant perception: Vol. 1. From sensation to perception* (pp. 115–184). Orlando: Academic Press.

Banks, M. S., & Ehrlich, S. M. (1996). Estimating heading during real and simulated eye movements. *Vision Research, 36,* 431–443.

Banks, M. S., & Salapatek, P. (1983). Infant visual perception. In M. M. Haith & J. J. Campos (Eds.), *Handbook of child psychology* (pp. 435–571). New York: Wiley.

Bannatyne, A. (1971). *Language, reading and learning disabilities.* Springfield, IL: Thomas.

Barac-Cikoja, D., & Turvey, M. T. (1993). Haptically perceiving size at a distance. *Journal of Experimental Psychology: General, 122,* 331–346.

Barac-Cikoja, D., & Turvey, M. T. (1995). Does perceived size depend on perceived distance? An argument from extended haptic perception. *Perception & Psychophysics, 57,* 216–224.

Barbeito, R. (1981). Sighting dominance: An explanation based on the processing of visual direction in tests of sighting dominance. *Vision Research, 21,* 855–860.

Barclay, C. D., Cutting, J. E., & Kozlowski, L. T. (1978). Temporal and spatial factors in gait perception that influence gender recognition. *Perception & Psychophysics, 23,* 145–152.

Barlow, H. B. (1985). The role of single neurons in the psychology of perception. *Quarterly Journal of Experimental Psychology, 37A,* 121–145.

Barlow, H. B., Hill, R. M., & Levick, R. E. (1964). Retinal ganglion cells responding selectively to direction and speed of image motion in the retina. *Journal of Physiology, 173,* 377–407.

Barsz, K. (1991). Auditory pattern perception: The effect of tone location on the discrimination of tonal sequences. *Perception & Psychophysics, 50,* 290–296.

Bartleson, C. J. (1960). Memory colors of familiar objects. *Journal of the Optical Society of America, 50,* 73–77.

Bartoshuk, L. M. (1974). Taste illusions: Some demonstrations. *Annals of the New York Academy of Sciences, 237,* 279–285.

Bartoshuk, L. M (1978). Gustatory system. In R. B. Masterton (Ed.), *Handbook of behavioral neurobiology: Vol. I. Sensory integration* (pp. 503–567). New York: Plenum Press.

Bartoshuk, L. M. (1988). Clinical psychophysics of taste. *Gerodontics, 4,* 249–255.

Bartoshuk, L. M. (1990). Distinctions between taste and smell relevant to the role of experience. In E. Capaldi & T. L. Powley (Eds.), *Taste, experience, and feeding* (pp. 62–72). Washington, DC: American Psychological Association.

Bartoshuk, L. M. (1993). Genetic and pathological taste variation: What can we learn from animal models and human disease? In D. Chadwick, J. Marsh, & J. Goode (Eds.), *The molecular basis of smell and taste transduction* (pp. 251–267). New York: Wiley.

Bartoshuk, L. M., & Beauchamp, G. K. (1994). Chemical senses. *Annual Review of Psychology, 45,* 419–449.

Bartoshuk, L. M., Rifkin, B., Marks, L. E., & Hooper, J. E. (1988). Bitterness of KCl and benzoate: Related to genetic status for sensitivity to PTC/PROP. *Chemical Senses, 13,* 517–528.

Bashford, J. A., & Warren, R. M. (1987). Multiple phonemic restorations follow the rules for auditory induction. *Perception & Psychophysics, 42,* 114–121.

Bashford, J. A., Warren, R. M., & Brown, C. A. (1996). Use of speech-modulated noise adds strong "bottom-up" cues for phonemic restoration. *Perception & Psychophysics, 58,* 342–350.

Bates, M. E. (1989). The effect of repeated occasions of alcohol intoxication on two processes involved in the visual discrimination of movement. *Journal of Studies on Alcohol, 50,* 143–154.

Batteau, D. W. (1967). The role of the pinna in human localization. *Proceedings of the Royal Society of London, Series B, 168,* 158–180.

Beal, A. L. (1985). The skill of recognizing musical structures. *Memory and Cognition, 13,* 405–412.

Beauchamp, G. K., & Cowart, B. J. (1985). Congenital and experiential factors in the development of human flavor preferences. *Appetite, 6,* 357–372.

Beck, J. (1965). Apparent spatial position and the perception of lightness. *Journal of Experimental Psychology, 69,* 170–179.

Beck, J. (1966). Effects of orientation and of shape similarity on perceptual grouping. *Perception & Psychophysics, 1,* 300–302.

Beck, J. (1982). Textural segmentation. In J. Beck (Ed.), *Organization and representation in perception* (pp. 285–317). Hillsdale, NJ: Erlbaum.

Beck, J., & Rosenfeld, A. (1989). Line segregation. *Spatial Vision, 4,* 75–101.

Beck, J., & Schwartz, T. (1979). Vernier acuity with dot test objects. *Vision Research, 19,* 313–319.

Beck, J., Sutter, A., & Ivry, R. (1987). Spatial frequency channels and perceptual grouping in texture perception. *Computer Vision, Graphics, and Image Processing, 37,* 299–325.

Beck, N. C., & Siegel, L. J. (1980). Preparation for childbirth and contemporary research on pain, anxiety, and stress reduction: A review and critique. *Psychosomatic Medicine, 42,* 429–447.

Beckett, P. A. (1989). Illusion decrement and transfer of illusion decrement in real- and subjective-contour Poggendorff figures. *Perception & Psychophysics, 45,* 550–556.

Begleiter, H., Porjesz, B., & Chou, C. L. (1981). Auditory brain-stem potentials in chronic alcoholics. *Science, 211,* 1064–1066.

Beidler, L. M., & Smallman, R. L. (1965). Renewal of cells within taste buds. *Journal of Cell Biology, 27,* 263–272.

Bekesy, G. von. (1947). A new audiometer. *Acta oto-laryngologica, 35,* 411–422.

Bekesy, G. von. (1959). Synchronism of neural discharges and their demultiplication in pitch perception on the skin and in learning. *Journal of the Acoustical Society of America, 31,* 338–349.

Bekesy, G. von. (1960). *Experiments in hearing.* New York: McGraw-Hill.

Bekesy, G. von. (1967). *Sensory inhibition.* Princeton, NJ: Princeton University Press.

Belliveau, J. W., Kennedy, D. N., McKinstry, R. C., Buchbinder, R. R., Weisskopff, R. M., Cohen, M. S., Vevea, J. M., Brady, T. J., & Rosen, B. R. (1991). Functional mapping of the human visual cortex by magnetic resonance imaging. *Science, 254,* 716–719.

Bem, S. L. (1981). Gender schema theory: A cognitive account of sex typing. *Psychological Review, 88,* 354–364.

Bende, M., & Nordin, S. (1997). Perceptual learning in olfaction: Professional wine tasters versus controls. *Physiology & Behavior, 62,* 1065–1070.

Benedetti, F. (1985). Processing of tactile spatial information with crossed fingers. *Journal of Experimental Psychology: Human Perception and Performance, 11,* 517–525.

Bennett, T. L., & Morgan, R. J. (1978). Temporary threshold shifts in auditory sensitivity produced by the combined effects of noise and sodium salicylate. *Bulletin of the Psychonomic Society, 12,* 95–98.

Bentham, J. van (1985). Semantics of time. In J. A. Michon & J. L. Jackson (Eds.), *Time, mind and behavior* (pp. 266–278). Berlin: Springer-Verlag.

Bentin, S., & Mann, V. A. (1990). Masking and stimulus intensity effects on duplex perception: A confirmation of the dissociation between speech and nonspeech modes. *Journal of the Acoustical Society of America, 88,* 64–74.

Berbaum, K., Bever, T., & Chung, C. S. (1983). Light source position in the perception of object shape. *Perception, 12,* 411–416.

Berbaum, K., Bever, T., & Chung, C. S. (1984). Extending the perception of shape from known to unknown shading. *Perception, 13,* 479–488.

Berbaum, K., & Lenel, J. C. (1983). Objects in the path of apparent motion. *American Journal of Psychology, 96,* 491–501.

Berbaum K., Tharp, D., & Mroczek, K. (1983). Depth perception of surfaces in pictures: Looking for conventions of depiction in Pandora's box. *Perception, 12,* 5–20.

Berg, B. G., & Green, D. M. (1990). Spectral weights in profile listening. *Journal of the Acoustical Society of America, 88,* 758–766.

Berg, K. M., & Smith, M. C. (1983). Behavioral thresholds for tones during infancy. *Journal of Experimental Child Psychology, 35,* 409–425.

Bergeijk, W. A. van. (1967). The evolution of vertebrate hearing. In W. D. Neff (Ed.), *Contributions to sensory physiology:*

Vol. 2 (pp. 1–49). New York: Academic Press.

Berger, G. O. (1896). Uber den Einfluss der Reizstarke auf die Dauer einfacher psychischer Vorgange mit besonderer Rucksicht auf Lichtreize. *Philosophische Studien (Wundt), 3,* 38–93.

Berglund, B., Hogman, L., & Johansson, I. (1988). Reliability of odor measurements near threshold. *Reports from the Department of Psychology.* Stockholm: The University of Stockholm.

Berglund, M. B. (1991). Quality assurance in environmental psychophysics. In S. J. Bolanowski & G. A. Gescheider (Eds.), *Ratio scaling of psychological magnitude* (pp. 140–162). Hillsdale, NJ: Erlbaum.

Berkley, M. A. (1982). Neural substrates of the visual perception of movement. In A. H. Wertheim, W. A. Wagenaar, & H. W. Leibowitz (Eds.), *Tutorials on motion perception* (pp. 201–229). New York: Plenum Press.

Berlin, B., & Kay, P. (1969). *Basic color terms.* Berkeley: University of California Press.

Berman, E. R. (1991). *Biochemistry of the eye.* New York: Plenum Press.

Berman, K. F., Zec, R. F., & Weinberger, D. R. (1986). Physiologic dysfunction of dorsolateral prefrontal cortex in schizophrenia: II. Role of neuroleptic treatment, attention and mental effort. *Archives of General Psychiatry, 43,* 126–135.

Berndt, R. S., & Mitchum, C. C. (1997). Lexical-semantic organization: Evidence from aphasia. *Clinical Neuroscience, 4,* 57–63.

Bernstein, I. H., Bissonnette, V., Vyas, A., & Barclay, P. (1989). Semantic priming: Subliminal perception or context. *Perception & Psychophysics, 45,* 153–161.

Bernstein, L. R., & Green, D. M. (1987). Detection of simple and complex changes of spectral shape. *Journal of the Acoustical Society of America, 82,* 1587–1592.

Berry, J. W. (1971). Mueller-Lyer susceptibility: Culture, ecology, race? *International Journal of Psychology, 7,* 193–196.

Besser, G. (1966). Centrally acting drugs and auditory flutter. In A. Herxheimer (Ed.), *Proceedings of the Symposium on Drugs and Sensory Functions* (pp. 199–200). London: SS Churchill, Ltd.

Besson, M., & Faita, F. (1995). An event-related potential (ERP) study of musical expectancy: Comparison of musicians with nonmusicians. *Journal of Experimental Psychology: Human Perception and Performance, 21,* 1278–1296.

Best, C. T. (1992). The emergence of language-specific phonemic influences in infant speech perception. In J. Goodman & H. C. Nusbaum (Eds.), *Speech perception and word recognition.* Cambridge, MA: MIT Press.

Betke, K. (1991). New hearing threshold measurements for pure tones under free-field listening conditions. *Journal of the Acoustical Society of America, 89,* 2400–2403.

Bharucha, J. J. (1996). Melodic anchoring. *Music Perception, 13,* 383–400.

Bhatia, B. (1975). Minimum separable as function of speed of a moving object. *Vision Research, 15,* 23–33.

Biederman, I. (1987). Recognition-by-components: A theory of human image understanding. *Psychological Review, 94,* 115–147.

Biederman, I., Glass, A. L., & Stacey, E. W. Jr. (1973). Searching for objects in real-world scenes. *Journal of Experimental Psychology, 97,* 22–27.

Bigand, E. (1997). Perceiving musical stability: The effect of tonal structure, rhythm, and musical expertise. *Journal of Experimental Psychology: Human Perception and Performance, 23,* 808–822.

Bigand, E., Parncutt, R., & Lerdahl, F. (1996). Perception of musical tension in short chord sequences: The influence of harmonic function, sensory dissonance, horizontal motion, and musical training. *Perception & Psychophysics, 58,* 125–141.

Billings, B. L., & Stokinger, T. E. (1977). Investigation of several aspects of low-frequency (200 Hz) central masking. *Journal of the Acoustical Society of America, 61,* 1260–1263.

Binder, J. R., Frost, J. A., Hammeke, T. A., Cox, R. W., Rao, S. M., & Prieto, T. (1996). Human brain language areas identified by functional magnetic resonance imaging. *The Journal of Neuroscience, 17,* 353–362.

Binder, J. R., Rao, S. M., Hammeke, T. A., Yetkin, F. Z., Jesmanowicz, A., Bandettini, P. A., Wong, E. C., Estkowski, L. D., Goldstein, M. D., Haughton, V. M., & Hyde, J. S. (1994). Functional magnetic resonance imaging of human auditory cortex. *Annals of Neurology, 35,* 662–672.

Binns, K. E., & Salt, T. E. (1997). Post eye-opening maturation of visual receptive field diameters in the superior colliculus of normal- and dark-reared rats. *Brain Research: Developmental Brain Research, 99,* 263–266.

Birch, E. E., Shimojo, S., & Held, R. (1985). Preferential-looking assessment of fusion and stereopsis in infants aged 1–6 months. *Investigative Ophthalmology and Visual Science, 26,* 366–370.

Birnbaum, M. H. (1981). Clinical management of myopia. *American Journal of Optometry and Physiological Optics, 58,* 554–559.

Birren, J. E., Woods, A., & Williams, M. (1980). Behavioral slowing with age: Causes, organization, and consequences. In L. Poon (Ed.), *Aging in the 1980s* (pp. 293–308). Washington, DC: American Psychological Association.

Birren, J. E., Casperson, R. C., & Botwinick, J. (1950). Age changes in pupil size. *Journal of Gerontology, 5,* 267–271.

Bishop, P .O. (1981). Binocular vision. In R. A. Moses (Ed.), *Adler's physiology of the eye: Clinical applications* (7th ed.) (pp. 575–649). St. Louis, MO: Mosby.

Bishop, P. O. (1984). Processing of visual information within the retinostriate system. In I. Darian-Smith (Ed.), *Handbook of physiology: Section I. The nervous system. Volume III: Sensory processes* (pp. 340–424). Bethesda, MD: American Physiological Society.

Bishop, P. O., & Pettigrew, J. D. (1986). Neural mechanisms of binocular vision. *Vision Research, 26,* 1587–1600.

Blake, R. (1981). Strategies for assessing visual deficits in animals with selective neural deficits. In R. N. Aslin, J. R. Alberts, & M. R. Petersen (Eds.), *Development of perception: Vol. 2. The visual system* (pp. 95–110). New York: Academic Press.

Blakemore, C. (1978). Maturation and modification in the developing visual system. In R. Held, M. W. Leibowitz, & H. L. Teuber (Eds.), *Handbook of sensory physiology: Vol. VIII. Perception* (pp. 377–436). New York: Springer-Verlag.

Blakemore, C., & Nachmias, J. (1971). Orientation specificity on two visual aftereffects. *Journal of Physiology, 171,* 286–288.

Blakeslee, A. F., & Salmon, T. H. (1935). Genetics of sensory thresholds: Individual taste reactions for different substances. *Proceedings of the National Academy of Sciences of the U.S.A., 21,* 84–90.

Blamey, P. J., Dowell R. C., Brown, A. M., Clark, G. M., & Seligman, P. M. (1987). Vowel and consonant recognition of cochlear implant patients using formant–estimating speech processors. *Journal of the Acoustical Society of America, 82,* 48–57.

Blasdel, G. G., Mitchell, D. E., Muir, D. W., & Pettigrew, J. D. (1977). A combined physiological and behavioral study of the effect of early visual experience with contours of a single orientation. *Journal of Physiology, 265,* 615–636.

Blazynski, C., & Ostroy, S. E. (1981). Dual pathways in the photolysis of rhodopsin: Studies using a direct chemical method. *Vision Research, 21,* 833–841.

Bleeker, M. L., & Bolla-Wilson, K. (1987). Simple visual reaction time: Sex and age differences. *Developmental Neuropsychology, 3,* 165–172.

Bliss, J. C., Katcher, M. H., Rogers, C. H., & Shepard, R. P. (1970). Optical-to-tactile image conversion for the blind. *IEEE Transactions on Man–Machine Systems, 11,* 58–65.

Block, R. A. (1974). Memory and the experience of duration in retrospect. *Memory and Cognition, 2,* 153–160.

Block, R. A. (1978). Remembered duration: Effects of event and sequence complexity. *Memory and Cognition, 6,* 320–326.

Block, R. A., George, E. J., & Reed, M. A. (1980). A watched pot sometimes boils: A study of duration experience. *Acta Psychologica, 46,* 81–94.

Bloom, K. (1990). Selectivity and early infant vocalization. In J. T. Enns (Ed.), *The development of attention: Research and theory* (pp. 121–136). Amsterdam: Elsevier.

Blough, P. M., & Slavin, K. (1987). Reaction time assessments of gender differences in visual-spatial performance. *Perception & Psychophysics, 41,* 276–281.

Boer, K., & Keuss, P. (1982). Global precedence as a post-perceptual effect: An analysis of speed accuracy trade off functions. *Perception & Psychophysics, 31,* 358–366.

Bolanowski, S. J. Jr., Gescheider, G. A., Verrillo, R. T., & Checkosky, C. M. (1988). Four channels mediate the mechanical aspects of touch. *Journal of the Acoustical Society of America, 84,* 1680–1694.

Bolton, T. L. (1894). Rhythm. *American Journal of Psychology, 6,* 145–238.

Bonnel, A.-M., & Hafter, E. R. (1998). Divided attention between simultaneous auditory and visual signals. *Perception & Psychophysics, 60,* 179–190.

Bonnel, A.-M., & Prinzmetal, W. (1998). Dividing attention between the color and the shape of objects. *Perception & Psychophysics, 60,* 113–124.

Bonnet, C. (1984). Discrimination of velocities and mechanisms of motion perception. *Perception, 13,* 275–282.

Borg, G., Diamant, H., Oakley, B., Strom, L., & Zotterman, Y. (1967). A comparative study of neural and psychophysical responses to gustatory stimuli. In T. Hayashi (Ed.), *Olfaction and taste II* (pp. 253–264). Oxford: Pergamon Press.

Borg, G. A. V. (1982). Psychophysical bases of perceived exertion. *Medicine and Science in Sports and Exercise, 14,* 377–381.

Bornstein, M. H. (1973). Color vision and color naming: A psychophysiological hypothesis of cultural difference. *Psychological Bulletin, 80*, 257–285.

Bornstein, M. H. (1975). The influence of visual perception on culture. *American Anthropologist, 77*, 774–798.

Bornstein, M. H. (1977). Developmental pseudocyanapsia: Ontogenetic change in human color vision. *American Journal of Optometry and Physiological Optics, 54*, 464–469.

Bornstein, M. H. (1981). Two kinds of perceptual organization near the beginning of life. In W. Collins (Ed.), *Aspects of the development of competence* (pp. 39–91). Hillsdale, NJ: Erlbaum.

Bornstein, M. H. (1985). Infant into adult: Unity to diversity in the development of visual categorization. In J. Mehler & R. Fox (Eds.), *Neonate cognition: Beyond the blooming buzzing confusion* (pp. 115–138). Hillsdale, NJ: Erlbaum.

Bornstein, M. H., Kessen, W., & Weiskopf, S. (1976). Color vision and hue categorization in young human infants. *Journal of Experimental Psychology: Human Perception and Performance, 2*, 115–129.

Bornstein, M. H., & Monroe, M. D. (1978). Color-naming evidence for tritan vision in the fovea. *American Journal of Optometry and Physiological Optics, 55*, 627–630.

Botstein, D. (1986). The molecular biology of color vision. *Science, 232*, 142–143.

Botte, M. C., Baruch, C., & Scharf, B. (1986). Loudness reduction and adaptation induced by a contralateral tone. *Journal of the Acoustical Society of America, 80*, 73–81.

Botte, M. C., & Mönikheim, S. (1994). New data on the short-term effects of tone exposure. *Journal of the Acoustical Society of America, 95*, 2596–2605.

Botte, M. C., Canévet, G., & Scharf, B. (1982). Loudness adaptation induced by an intermittent tone. *Journal of the Acoustical Society of America, 72*, 727–739.

Botwinick, J. (1984). *Aging and behavior: A comprehensive integration of research findings* (3rd ed.). New York: Springer.

Bouma, H. (1970). Interaction effects in parafoveal letter recognition. *Nature, 226*, 177–178.

Bowen, R. W. (1981). Latencies for chromatic and achromatic visual mechanisms. *Vision Research, 2*, 1457–1466.

Bowker, D. O., & Mandler, M. B. (1981). Apparent contrast of suprathreshold gratings varies with stimulus orientation. *Perception & Psychophysics, 29*, 585–588.

Bowmaker, J. K., & Dartnall, H. J. A. (1980). Visual pigments of rods and cones in a human retina. *Journal of Physiology, 298*, 501–511.

Boycott, B. B., & Waessle, H. (1974). The morphological types of ganglion cells of the domestic cat's retina. *Journal of Physiology, 240*, 397–419.

Boynton, R. M. (1971). Color vision. In J. W. King & L. A. Riggs (Eds.), *Woodworth and Schlossberg's experimental psychology* (3rd ed.; pp. 315–368). New York: Holt, Rinehart and Winston.

Boynton, R. M. (1979). *Human color vision*. New York: Holt, Rinehart and Winston.

Boynton, R. M. (1988). Color vision. *Annual Review of Psychology, 39*, 69–100.

Boynton, R. M., & Gordon, J. (1965). Bezold-Brucke hue shift measured by color-naming technique. *Journal of the Optical Society of America, 55*, 78–86.

Brabyn, L. B., & McGuinness, D. (1979). Gender differences in response to spatial frequency and stimulus orientation. *Perception & Psychophysics, 26*, 319–324.

Braddick, O. (1974). A short-range process in apparent motion. *Vision Research, 14*, 519–527.

Braddick, O. J. (1980). Low-level and high-level processes in apparent motion. *Philosophical Transactions of the Royal Society of London, Series B, 290*, 137–151.

Braddick, O. J., & Atkinson, J. (1979). Accommodation and acuity in the human infant. In R. D. Freeman (Ed.), *Developmental neurobiology of vision* (pp. 289–300). New York: Plenum Press.

Braddick, O. J., Atkinson, J., Julesz, B., Kropfl, W., Bodis–Wollner, I., & Raab, E. (1980). Cortical binocularity in infants. *Nature, 288*, 363–385.

Braddick, O. J., Wattam-Bell, J., & Atkinson, J. (1986). Orientation-specific cortical responses develop in early infancy. *Nature, 320*, 617–619.

Bradley, A., & Skottun B. C. (1987). Effects of contrast and spatial frequency on vernier acuity. *Vision Research, 27*, 1817–1824.

Bradley, R. M., & Stern I. B. (1967). The development of the human taste bud during the foetal period. *Journal of Anatomy, 101*, 743–752.

Braff, D. L., Silverton, L., Saccuzzo, D. P., & Janowsky, D. S. (1981). Impaired speed of visual information processing in marihuana intoxication. *American Journal of Psychiatry, 138*(5), 613–617.

Braida, L. D., & Durlach, N. D. (1988). Peripheral and central factors in intensity perception. In G. M. Edelman, W. E. Gall, & M. W. Cowan (Eds.), *Auditory function: Neurobiological bases of hearing* (pp. 559–583). New York: Wiley.

Brainard, D. H., Wandell, B. A., & Chichilnisky, E. (1993). Color constancy: From physics to appearance. *Current Directions in Psychological Science, 2*, 365–370.

Braine L. G., Plastow, E., & Greene, S. I. (1987). Judgments of shape orientation: A matter of contrasts. *Perception & Psychophysics, 41*, 335–344.

Brass, D., & Kemp, D. T. (1993). Suppression of stimulus frequency otoacoustic emissions. *Journal of the Acoustical Society of America, 93*, 920–939.

Braun, C. M., & Daigneault, S. (1989). Color discrimination testing reveals early printshop solvent neurotoxicity better than a neuropsychological test battery. *Archives of Clinical Neuropsychology*, 4–13.

Braunstein, M. L., & Liter, J. C. (1993). Recovering three-dimensional shape from perspective translations and orthographic rotations. *Journal of Experimental Psychology: Human Perception and Performance, 19*, 598–614.

Brazelton, T., Scholl, M., & Robey, J. (1966). Visual responses in the newborn. *Pediatrics, 37*, 284–290.

Bregman, A. S. (1978). Auditory streaming: Competition among alternative organizations. *Perception & Psychophysics, 23*, 391–398.

Bregman, A. S. (1981). Asking the "What for?" question in auditory perception. In M. Kubovy & J. R. Pometrantz (Eds.), *Perceptual organization* (pp. 99–118). Hillsdale, NJ: Erlbaum.

Bregman, A. S. (1990). *Auditory scene analysis*. Cambridge, MA: Bradford/MIT Press.

Breitmeyer, B. G. (1984). *Visual masking: An integrative approach*. New York: Oxford University Press.

Breitmeyer, B. G. (1989). A visually based deficit in specific reading disability. *Irish Journal of Psychology, 10*, 534–541.

Brennan, P., Kaba, H., & Keverne, E. B. (1990). Olfactory recognition: A simple memory system. *Science, 250*, 1223–1226.

Brenowitz, E. A. (1991). Altered perceptions of species-specific song by female birds after lesions of a forebrain nucleus. *Science, 251*, 303–305.

Breslin, P. A. S., Beauchamp, G. K., & Pugh, A. N. Jr. (1996). Monogeusia for fructose, glucose, sucrose and maltose. *Perception & Psychophysics, 58*, 327–341.

Bridgeman, B., Cragiano, J. A. (1989). Effect of context and efference copy on visual straight ahead. *Vision Research, 29*, 1729–1736.

Bridges, C. D. B. (1986). Biochemistry of vision—A perspective. *Vision Research, 26*, 1317–1337.

Brillat-Savarin, J. A. (1971). *The physiology of taste: Or meditations on transcendental gastronomy.* (M. K. F. Fisher, Trans.). New York: Knopf. (Original work published 1825)

Broadbent, D. (1958). *Perception and communication.* Oxford: Pergamon.

Broadbent, D. E., & Gregory, M. (1963). Vigilance considered as a statistical decision. *British Journal of Psychology, 54,* 309–323.

Broadbent, D. E., & Gregory, M. (1965). Effects of noise and of signal rate upon vigilance analyzed by means of decision theory. *Human Factors, 7,* 155–162.

Brodeur, D. A., & Enns, J. T. (1997). Lifespan differences in covert visual orienting. *Canadian Journal of Experimental Psychology, 51,* 20–35.

Brodmann, K. (1914). Physiologie des gehirng. In F. Krause (Ed.), *Allsemaie chirurgie der gehirnkankheiten.* Stuttgart: F. Enke.

Bronkhorst, A. W., Bosman, A. J., & Smoorenburg, G. F. (1993). A model for context effects in speech recognition. *Journal of the Acoustical Society of America, 93,* 499–509.

Bronkhurst, A. W. (1995). Localization of real and virtual sound sources. *Journal of the Acoustical Society of America, 98,* 2542–2553.

Bronson, G. W. (1990). Changes in infants' scanning across the 2- to 14-week age period. *Journal of Experimental Child Psychology, 49,* 101–125.

Brooks, P. L., & Frost, B. J. (1983). Evaluation of a tactile vocoder for word recognition. *Journal of the Acoustical Society of America, 74,* 34–39.

Brooks, R. A. (1981). Symbolic reasoning among 3-D models and 2-D images. *Artificial Intelligence, 17,* 205–244.

Brosvic, G. M., & Farrelly, M. (1993). Nonequivalent roles for motor and visual feedback in the Mueller Lyer and horizontal-vertical illusions. *Bulletin of the Psychonomic Society, 31,* 42–44.

Brosvic, G. M., Walker, M. A., Perry, N., Degnan, S., & Dihoff, R E. (1997). Illusion decrement as a function of duration of inspection and figure type. *Perceptual & Motor Skills, 84,* 779–783.

Brou, P., Sciancia, T. R., Linden, L., & Lettvin, J. Y. (1986). The colors of things. *Scientific American, 255*(3), 84–91.

Brown, A. C., Beeler, W. J., Kloka, A. C., & Fields, R. W. (1985). Spatial summation of pre-pain and pain in human teeth. *Pain, 21,* 1–16.

Brown, B. (1972). Resolution thresholds for moving targets at the fovea and in the peripheral retina. *Vision Research, 12,* 293–304.

Brown, E. L., & Deffenbacher, K. (1979). *Perception and the senses.* New York: Oxford University Press.

Brown, J. M., & Koch, C. J. (1991). *Influences of closure and occlusion on the perception of fragmented pictures.* Paper presented at ARVO, Sarasota, FL.

Brown, J. W. (1990). Psychology of time awareness. *Brain and Cognition, 14,* 144–164.

Brown, L. G. (1996). Additional rules for the transformed up-down method in psychophysics. *Perception & Psychophysics, 58,* 959–962.

Brown, P. E. (1972). Use of acupuncture in major surgery. *Lancet, 1,* 1328–1330.

Brown, P. K., & Wald, G. (1964). Visual pigments in single rods and cones of the human retina. *Science, 144,* 45–52.

Brown, R. E., & MacDonald, D. W. (Eds.). (1985a). *Social odours in mammals: Vol. 1.* Oxford: Clarendon Press.

Brown, R. E., & MacDonald D. W. (Eds.). (1985b). *Social odours in mammals: Vol. 2.* Oxford: Clarendon Press.

Brown, S. W. (1985). Time perception and attention: The effects of prospective versus retrospective paradigms and task demands on perceived duration. *Perception & Psychophysics, 38,* 115–124.

Brown, T. S. (1975). General biology of sensory systems. In B. Scharf (Ed.), *Experimental sensory psychology* (pp. 69–111). Glenview, IL: Scott-Foresman.

Brown, W. (1910). The judgment of difference. *University of California, Berkeley, Publications in Psychology, 1,* 1–71.

Brownell, W. E., Bader, C. R., Bertrand, D., & de Ribaupierre, Y. (1985). Evoked mechanical responses of isolated cochlear outer hair cells. *Science, 227,* 194–196.

Bruce, C., Desimone, R., & Gross, C. G. (1981). Visual properties of neurons in a polysensory area in superior temporal sulcus of the macaque. *Journal of Neurophysiology, 46,* 369–384.

Bruce, V., & Green, P. (1985). *Visual perception physiology, psychology and ecology.* Hillsdale, NJ: Erlbaum.

Bruner, J. S., Postman, L., & Rodrigues, J. (1951). Expectations and the perception of color. *American Journal of Psychology, 64,* 216–227.

Bruno, N., Bernardis, P., & Schirillo, J. (1997). Lightness, equivalent backgrounds, and anchoring. *Perception & Psychophysics, 59,* 643–654.

Bruno, N., & Bertamini, M. (1997). Amodal completion of partly occluded surfaces: Is there a mosaic stage? *Journal of Experimental Psychology: Human Perception and Performance, 23,* 1412–1426.

Bruno, N., & Cutting, J. E. (1988). Minimodularity and the perception of layout. *Journal of Experimental Psychology: General, 117,* 161–170.

Brunswick, E. (1955). Representative design and probabilistic theory in a functional psychology. *Psychological Review, 62,* 193–217.

Brussell, E. M., & Festinger, L. (1973). The Gelb effect: Brightness contrast plus attention. *American Journal of Psychology, 86,* 225–235.

Bryden, M. P., & George, J. (1990). Sex differences and the role of figural complexity in determining the rate of mental rotation. *Perceptual and Motor Skills, 70,* 467–477.

Buchtel, H. A., & Stewart, J. D. (1989). Auditory agnosia: Apperceptive or associative disorder? *Brain and Language, 37,* 12–25.

Bujas, Z., Szabo, S., Ajdukovic, D., & Mayer, D. (1989). Individual gustatory reaction times to various groups of chemicals that provoke basic taste qualities. *Perception & Psychophysics, 45,* 385–390.

Bujas, Z., Szabo, S., Ajdukovic, D., & Mayer, D. (1991). Time course of recovery from gustatory adaptation to NaCl. *Perception & Psychophysics, 49,* 517–521.

Bundesen, C., Larsen, A., & Farrell, J. E. (1983). Visual apparent movement: Transformations of size and orientation. *Perception, 12,* 549–568.

Burg, A. (1966). Visual acuity as measured by dynamic and static tests: A comparative evaluation. *Journal of Applied Psychology, 50,* 460–466.

Burg, A. (1968). Lateral visual field as related to age and sex. *Journal of Applied Psychology, 52,* 10–15.

Burns, E. M. (1981). Circularity in relative pitch judgments for inharmonic complex tones: The Shepard demonstration revisited, again. *Perception & Psychophysics, 30,* 467–472.

Burr, D. C., Ross, J., & Morrone, M. C. (1986). Smooth and sampled motion. *Vision Research, 26,* 643–652.

Burt, P., & Julesz, B. (1980). A disparity gradient limit for binocular fusion. *Science, 208,* 615–617.

Burt, P., & Sperling, G. (1981). Time, distance and feature trade-offs in visual apparent motion. *Psychological Review, 88,* 137–151.

Burton, G., Turvey, M. T., & Solomon, H. Y. (1990). Can shape be perceived by dynamic touch? *Perception & Psychophysics, 48,* 477–487.

Burton, G. J., Nagshineh, S., & Ruddock, K. H. (1977). Processing by the human visual system of the light and dark contrast components of the retinal image. *Biological Cybernetics, 27,* 189–197.

Burton, H., & Sinclair, R. (1996). Somatosensory cortex and tactile perceptions. In L. Kruger (Ed.), *Pain and touch* (pp. 105–177). San Diego: Academic Press.

Busby, P. A., Tong, Y. C., & Clark, G. M. (1993). Electrode position, repetition rate, and speech perception by early- and late-deafened cochlear implant patients. *Journal of the Acoustical Society of America, 93,* 1058–1067.

Bushnell, M. C., & Duncan, G. H. (1989). Sensory and affective aspects of pain perception: Is medial thalamus restricted to emotional issues? *Experimental Brain Research, 78,* 415–418.

Butler, D. L., & Kring, A. M. (1987). Integration of features in depictions as a function of size. *Perception & Psychophysics, 41,* 159–164.

Butler, R. A. (1987). An analysis of the monaural displacement of sound in space. *Perception & Psychophysics, 41,* 1–7.

Butler, R. A., & Humanski, R. A. (1992). Localization of sound in the vertical plane with and without high-frequency spectral cues. *Perception & Psychophysics, 51,* 182–186.

Butler, R. A., Levy, E. T., & Neff, W. D. (1980). Apparent distance of sounds recorded in echoic and anechoic chambers. *Journal of Experimental Psychology: Human Perception and Physiology, 6,* 745–750.

Butters, N., Barton, M., & Brody, B. A. (1970). Right parietal lobe and cross-model associations. *Cortex, 6,* 19–46.

Butterworth, G. (1981). The origins of auditory-visual perception and visual proprioception in human development. In R. D. Walk & H. L. Pick Jr. (Eds.), *Intersensory perception and sensory integration* (pp. 37–70). New York: Plenum Press.

Buus, S. (1985). Release from masking caused by envelope fluctuations. *Journal of the Acoustical Society of America, 78,* 1958–1965.

Cacace, A. T., & Margolis, R. H. (1985). On the loudness of complex stimuli and its relationship to cochlear excitation. *Journal of the Acoustical Society of America, 78,* 1568–1573.

Caelli, T. (1982). On discriminating visual textures and images. *Perception & Psychophysics, 31,* 149–159.

Caelli, T. (1984). On the specification of coding principles for visual image processing. In P. C. Dodwell & T. Caelli (Eds.), *Figural synthesis* (pp. 153–184). Hillsdale, NJ: Erlbaum.

Caelli, T. (1988). An adaptive computational model for texture segregation.

IEEE transactions on systems, man, and cybernetics, 18, 9–17.

Cahoon, D., & Edmonds, E. M. (1980). The watched pot still won't boil: Expectancy as a variable in estimating the passage of time. *Bulletin of the Psychonomic Society, 16,* 115–116.

Cain, D. P., & Bindra, D. (1972). Response of amygdala single units to odors in the rat. *Experimental Neurology, 35,* 98–110.

Cain, W. S. (1969). Odor intensity: Differences in the exponent of the psychophysical function. *Perception & Psychophysics, 6,* 349–354.

Cain, W. S. (1977). Differential sensitivity for smell: "Noise" at the nose. *Science, 195,* 796–798.

Cain, W. S. (1979). To know with the nose: Keys to odor identification. *Science, 203,* 467–470.

Cain, W. S., & Engen, T. (1969). Olfactory adaptation and the scaling of odor intensity. In C. Pfaffman (Ed.), *Olfaction and taste III* (pp. 127–141). New York: Rockefeller University Press.

Cain, W. S., & Johnson, F. Jr. (1978). Lability of odor pleasantness: Influence of mere exposure. *Perception, 7,* 459–465.

Cain, W. S., Reid, F., & Stevens, J. C. (1990). Missing ingredients: Aging and the discrimination of flavor. *Journal of Nutrition for the Elderly, 9,* 3–15.

Cain, W. S., & Stevens, J. C. (1989). Uniformity of olfactory loss in aging. *Annals of the New York Academy of Sciences, 561,* 29–38.

Cain, W. S., & Stevens, J. C. (1995). Lifespan development of odor identification, learning, and olfactory sensitivity. *Perception, 24,* 1457–1472.

Cajal, S. R. (1893). La retine des vertebres. *Cellule, 9,* 17–257.

Calis, G., & Leeuwenberg, E. (1981). Grounding the figure. *Journal of Experimental Psychology: Human Perception and Performance, 7,* 1386–1397.

Callaghan, T. C. (1989). Interference and dominance in texture segregation: Hue, geometric form, and line orientation. *Perception & Psychophysics, 46,* 299–311.

Callaghan, T. C., Lasaga, M. L., & Garner, W. R. (1986). Visual texture segregation based on orientation and hue. *Perception & Psychophysics, 39,* 32–38.

Calvert, G. A., Bullmore, E. T., Brammer, M. J., Campbell, R., Williams, S. C. R., McGuire, P. K., Woodruff, P. W. R., Iverson, S. D., & David, A. S. (1997). Activation of auditory cortex during silent lipreading. *Science, 276,* 593–596.

Campbell, F. W., & Maffei, L. (1981). The influence of spatial frequency and

contrast on the perception of moving patterns. *Vision Research, 21,* 713–721.

Campbell, F. W., & Robson, J. G. (1968). Application of Fourier analysis to the visibility of gratings. *Journal of Physiology, 197,* 551–566.

Campbell, K. B., Baribeau-Braun, J., & Braun, C. (1981). Neuroanatomical and physiological foundations of extraversion. *Psychophysiology, 18,* 263–267.

Canévet, G., Hellman, R., & Scharf, B. (1986). Group estimation of loudness in sound fields. *Acustica, 60,* 277–282.

Cannon, M. W. Jr. (1983). Contrast sensitivity: Psychophysical and evoked potential methods compared. *Vision Research, 23,* 87–95.

Cansino, S., Williamson, S. J., & Karron, D. (1994). Tonotopic organization of human auditory association cortex. *Brain Research, 663,* 38–50.

Capaldi, E., & Powley, T. L. (Eds.). (1990). *Taste, experience, and feeding.* Washington, DC: American Psychological Association.

Carey, S. (1981). The development of face perception. In G. Davies, H. Ellis, & J. Shepherd (Eds.), *Perceiving and remembering faces* (pp. 9–38). London: Academic Press.

Carey, S., & Diamond, R. (1977). From piecemeal to configurational representation of faces. *Science, 195,* 312–314.

Carey, S., Diamond, R., & Woods, B. (1980). The development of face recognition: A maturational component. *Developmental Psychology, 16,* 257–269.

Carlson, C. R. (1983). A simple model for vernier acuity. *Investigations in Ophthalmology and Visual Science, 24* (Suppl. 276).

Carlson, M. C., & Hasher, L. (1995). Aging, distraction, and the benefits of predictable location. *Psychology & Aging, 10,* 427–436.

Carlson, V. R. (1958). Effect of lysergic acid diethylamide (LSD-25) on the absolute visual threshold. *Journal of Comparative and Physiological Psychology, 51,* 528–531.

Carlson, V. R. (1977). Instructions and perceptual constancy judgments. In W. Epstein (Ed.), *Stability and constancy in visual perception: Mechanisms and processes* (pp. 217–254). New York: Wiley.

Carlyon, R. P. (1988). The development and decline of forward masking. *Hearing Research, 65,* 80.

Carmichael, L., Hogan, H. P., & Walter, A. A. (1932). An experimental study of the effect of language on the reproduction of visually perceived forms. *Journal of Experimental Psychology, 15,* 73–86.

Caron, A., Caron, R., Caldwell, R., & Weiss, S. (1973). Infant perception of the structural properties of the face. *Developmental Psychology, 9,* 385–399.

Carpenter, D. L., & Dugan, M. P. (1983). Motion parallax information for direction of rotation in depth: Order and direction components. *Perception, 12,* 559–569.

Carroll, J. D., & Chang, J. J. (1970). Analysis of individual differences in multidimensional scaling via an N-way generalization of Ekhart-Young decomposition. *Psychometrika, 48,* 157–169.

Casey, K. L. (1978). Neural mechanisms of pain. In E. C. Carterette & M. P. Friedman (Eds.), *Handbook of perception: Vol. VIB. Feeling and hurting* (pp. 183–230). New York: Academic Press.

Casey, K. L., & Morrow, T. J. (1983). Ventral posterior thalamic neurons differentially responsive to noxious stimulation of the awake monkey. *Science, 221,* 675–677.

Cassone, V. M. (1990). Effects of melatonin on vertebrate circadian systems. *Trends in Neurosciences, 13,* 457–464.

Cataliotti, J., & Gilchrist, A. (1995). Local and global processes in surface lightness perception. *Perception & Psychophysics, 57,* 125–135.

Cattell, J. M. (1886). The influence of the intensity of the stimulus on the length of the reaction time. *Brain, 9,* 512–514.

Cavanagh, P. (1984). Image transforms in the visual system. In P. C. Dodwell & T. Caelli (Eds.), *Figural synthesis* (pp. 185–218). Hillsdale, NJ: Erlbaum.

Cavanagh, P. (1988). Pathways in early vision. In Z. Pylyshyn (Ed.), *Computational processes in human vision* (pp. 239–261). Norwood, NJ: Ablex.

Cavanagh, P., & Leclerc, Y. G. (1989). Shape from shadows. *Journal of Experimental Psychology: Human Perception and Performance, 15,* 3–27.

Cavanagh, P., & Mather, G. (1989). Motion: The long and short of it. *Spatial Vision, 4,* 103–129.

Cavanagh, P., Tyler, C. W., & Favreau, O. E. (1984). Perceived velocity of moving chromatic gratings. *Journal of the Optical Society of America A, 1,* 893–899.

Cegalis, J. A., & Deptula, D. (1981). Attention in schizophrenia: Signal detection in the visual periphery. *Journal of Nervous and Mental Health Diseases, 169,* 751–760.

Ceralla, J. (1985). Age-related decline in extra–foveal letter perception. *Journal of Gerontology, 40,* 727–736.

Cerella, J., Poon, L., & Williams, D. (1980). Age and the complexity hypothesis. In L. Poon (Ed.), *Aging in the 1980s* (pp. 332–345). Washington, DC: American Psychological Association.

Cernoch, J. M., & Porter, R. H. (1985). Recognition of maternal axillary odors by infants. *Child Development, 56,* 1593–1598.

Chamorro, A., & Sacco, R. L. (1990). Visual hemineglect and hemihallucinations in a patient with subcortical infarction. *Neurology, 40,* 1463–1464.

Chapman, C. R. (1978). The hurtful world: Pathological pain and its control. In E. C. Carterette & M. P. Friedman (Eds.), *Handbook of perception: Vol. VIB. Feeling and hurting* (pp. 264–301). New York: Academic Press.

Cheeseman, J., & Merikle, P. M. (1984). Priming with and without awareness. *Perception & Psychophysics, 36,* 387–395.

Cheeseman, J., & Merikle, P. M. (1985). Word recognition and consciousness. *Reading Research: Advances in Theory and Practice, 5,* 311–352.

Cheeseman, J., & Merikle, P. M. (1986). Distinguishing conscious from unconscious perceptual processes. *Canadian Journal of Psychology, 40,* 343–367.

Cheng, P. W. (1985). Restructuring versus automaticity: Alternative accounts of skill acquisition. *Psychological Review, 92,* 414–423.

Cheng, T. O. (1973). Acupuncture anesthesia. *Science, 179,* 521.

Cherry, E. C. (1953). Some experiments on the recognition of speech, with one and with two ears. *Journal of the Acoustical Society of America, 25,* 975–979.

Cheour-Luhtanen, M., Alho, K., Saino, K., Rinne, T., Reinikainen, K, Pohjavouri, M., Renlund, M., Aaltonen, O., Eerola, O., & Näätänen, R. (1996). The ontogenetically earliest discriminative response of the human brain. *Psychophysiology, 33,* 478–481.

Chevrier, J., & Delorme, A. (1983). Depth perception in Pandora's box and size illusion: Evolution with age. *Perception, 12,* 177–185.

Chocolle, R. (1940). Variations des temps de réaction auditifs en fonction de l'intensité à diverses frequences. *Année Psychologique, 41,* 65–124.

Chocolle, R. (1962). Les effets des interactions interaurales dans l'audition. *Journale de psychologie, 3,* 255–282.

Cholewiak, R. W., & Collins, A. A. (1997). Individual differences in the vibrotactile perception of a "simple" pattern set. *Perception & Psychophysics, 59,* 850–866.

Cholewiak, R. W., & Craig, J. C. (1984). Vibrotactile pattern recognition and discrimination at several body sites. *Perception & Psychophysics, 35,* 503–514.

Chomsky, N., & Miller, G. A. (1963). Introduction to the formal analysis of natural languages. In R. D. Luce, R. Bush, & E. Galanter (Eds.), *Handbook of mathematical psychology: Vol. 2* (pp. 269–231). New York: Wiley.

Choudhurt, B. P., & Crossey, A. D. (1981). Slow-movement sensitivity in the human field of vision. *Physiology and Behavior, 26,* 125–128.

Cicerone, C. M., & Nerger, J. L. (1989). The density of cones in the fovea centralis of the human dichromat. *Vision Research, 29,* 1587–1595.

Ciner, E. B., Schanel-Klitsch, E., & Scheiman, M. (1991). Stereoacuity development in young children. *Optometry & Vision Science, 68,* 533–536.

Clark, H. H., & Clark, E. V. (1977). *Psychology and language: An introduction to psycholinguistics.* New York: Harcourt.

Clark, J. C., & Whitehurst, G. S. (1974). Asymmetrical stimulus control and the mirror-image problem. *Journal of Experimental Child Psychology, 17,* 147–166.

Clark, W. C., & Yang, J. C. (1974). Acupunctural analgesia? Evaluation by signal detection theory. *Science, 184,* 1096–1098.

Clarkson, M. G., Swain, I. U., Clifton, R. K., & Cohen, K. (1991). Newborns' head orientation toward trains of brief sounds. *Journal of the Acoustical Society of America, 89,* 2411–2420.

Clarkson-Smith, L., & Halpern, D. F. (1983). Can age-related deficits in spatial memory be attenuated through the use of verbal coding? *Experimental Aging Research, 9,* 179–184.

Clifford, B. R., & Bull, R. (1978). *The psychology of person identification.* London: Routledge & Kegan Paul.

Clifton, R. K., Freyman, R. L., Litovsky, R. Y., & McCall, D. (1994). Listeners' expectations about echoes can raise or lower echo threshold. *Journal of the Acoustical Society of America, 95,* 1525–1533.

Clifton, R. K., Morrongiello, B. A., & Dowd, J. M. (1984). A developmental look at an auditory illusion: The precedence effect. *Developmental Biology, 17,* 519–536.

Coffield, K. E., & Buckalew, L. W. (1988). A study of color preferences for drugs and implications for compliance and drug-taking. *Journal of Alcohol and Drug Education, 34,* 28–36.

Cogan, R., & Spinnato, J. A. (1986). Pain and discomfort thresholds in late pregnancy. *Pain, 27,* 63–68.

Coghill, R. C., Talbot, J. D., Evans, A. C., Meyer, E., Gjedde, A., Bushnell, M. C., & Duncan, G. H. (1994). Distributed processing of pain and vibration by the human brain. *Journal of Neuroscience, 14,* 4095–4108.

Cohen, J. D., Noll, D. C., & Schneider, W. (1993). Functional magnetic resonance imaging: Overview and methods for psychological research. *Behavior Research Methods, Instruments & Computers, 25,* 101–113.

Cohen, K. (1981). The development of strategies of visual search. In D. Fisher, R. Monty, & J. Senders (Eds.), *Eye movements: Cognition and visual perception.* Hillsdale, NJ: Erlbaum.

Cohen, W. (1958). Color-perception in the chromatic Ganzfeld. *American Journal of Psychology, 71,* 390–394.

Cole, R. A., Rudnicky, A. I., Zue, V. W., & Reddy, D. R. (1980). Speech as patterns on paper. In R. A. Cole (Ed.), *Perception and production of fluent speech* (pp. 3–50). Hillsdale, NJ: Erlbaum.

Coles, M. G., Gale, A., & Kline, P. (1971). Personality and habituation of the orienting reaction: Tonic and response measures of electrodermal activity. *Psychophysiology, 8,* 54–63.

Coletta, N. J., & Segu, P. (1993). An oblique effect in parafoveal motion perception. *Vision Research, 33,* 2747–2756.

Collings, V. B. (1974). Human taste response as a function of locus of stimulation on the tongue and soft palate. *Perception & Psychophysics, 16,* 169–174.

Collins, A. A., & Cholewiak, R. W. (1994). The shape of the vibrotactile loudness function: The effect of stimulus repetition and skin-contactor coupling. *Perception & Psychophysics, 55,* 465–472.

Collins, D. W., & Kimura, D. (1997). A large sex difference on a two-dimensional mental rotation task. *Behavioral Neuroscience, 111,* 845–849.

Collins, S. C. (1985). Duplex perception with musical stimuli: A further investigation. *Perception & Psychophysics, 38,* 172–177.

Comfort, A. (1971). Likelihood of human pheromones. *Nature, 230,* 432–433.

Condon, W. S., & Sander, L. W. (1974). Neonate movement is synchronized with adult speech: Interactional participation and language acquisition. *Science, 183,* 99–101.

Connelly, S. L., & Hasher, L. (1993). Aging and the inhibition of spatial location. *Journal of Experimental Psychology: Human Perception and Performance, 19,* 1238–1250.

Cooke, N. M., Breen, T. J., & Schvaneveldt, R. W. (1987). Is consistent mapping necessary for high-speed search? *Journal of Experimental Psychology: Learning, Memory, and Cognition, 13,* 223–229.

Cooper, B. Y., Vierck, C. J. Jr., & Yeomans, D. C. (1986). Selective reduction of second pain sensations by systemic morphine in humans. *Pain, 24,* 93–116.

Corbetta, M., Miezin, F. M., Dobmeyer, S., Shulman, G. L., & Petersen, S. E. (1991). Selective and divided attention during visual discrimination of shape, color, and speed: Functional anatomy by positron emission tomography. *Journal of Neuroscience, 11,* 2383–2402.

Coren, S. (1966). Adaptation to prismatic displacement as a function of the amount of available information. *Psychonomic Science, 4,* 407–408.

Coren, S. (1969). Brightness contrast as a function of figure-ground relations. *Journal of Experimental Psychology, 80,* 517–524.

Coren, S. (1972). Subjective contours and apparent depth. *Psychological Review, 79,* 359–367.

Coren, S. (1984). Set. In R. J. Corsini (Ed.), *The encyclopedia of psychology: Vol. 3* (pp. 296–298). New York: Wiley.

Coren, S. (1986). An efferent component in the visual perception of direction and extent. *Psychological Review, 93,* 391–410.

Coren, S. (1987). In vivo measures of the density of human lens pigmentation: A rapid and simple psychophysical procedure. *Acta Ophthalmologica, 65,* 575–578.

Coren, S. (1989). The many moon illusions: An integration through analysis. In M. Hershenson (Ed.), *The moon illusion* (pp. 351–370). Hillsdale, NJ: Erlbaum.

Coren, S. (1990). Perceptual constancies. In M. W. Eysenck (Ed.), *The Blackwell dictionary of cognitive psychology* (pp. 255–257). Oxford: Basil Blackwell.

Coren, S. (1991). Retinal mechanisms in the perception of subjective contours: The contribution of lateral inhibition. *Perception, 20,* 181–191.

Coren, S. (1992). Psychophysical scaling: Context & illusion. *Behavioral and Brain Sciences, 15,* 563–564.

Coren, S. (1992). The moon illusion: A different view through the legs. *Perceptual and Motor Skills, 75,* 827–831.

Coren, S. (1993). *The left-hander syndrome: The causes and consequences of left-handedness* (pp. i–x, 1–317). New York: Vintage Books.

Coren, S. (1994). Constraints on context effects in perception: Evidence from visual illusions. In L. M. Ward (Ed.), *Fechner Day 94. Proceedings of the International Society for Psychophysics* (pp. 54–61). Vancouver, Canada: The International Society of Psychophysics.

Coren, S. (1997). *Sleep thieves.* New York: Free Press.

Coren, S., & Aks, D. J. (1990). Moon illusion in pictures: A multimechanism approach. *Journal of Experimental*

Psychology: Human Perception and Performance, 16, 365–380.

Coren, S., Bradley, D. R., Hoenig, P., & Girgus, J. S. (1975). The effect of smooth tracking and saccadic eye movements on the perception of SIE: The shrinking circle illusion. *Vision Research, 15,* 49–55.

Coren, S., & Enns, J. T. (1993). Size contrast as a function of conceptual similarity between test and inducers. *Perception & Psychophysics, 54,* 579–588.

Coren, S., & Girgus, J. S. (1972a). Density of human lens pigmentation: In vivo measures over an extended age range. *Vision Research, 12,* 343–346.

Coren, S., & Girgus J. S. (1972b). Differentiation and decrement in the Mueller-Lyer illusion. *Perception & Psychophysics, 12,* 466–470.

Coren, S., & Girgus, J. S. (1977). Illusions and constancies. In W. Epstein (Ed.), *Stability and constancy in visual perception: Mechanisms and processes* (pp. 255–284). New York: Wiley.

Coren, S., & Girgus, J. S. (1978). *Seeing is deceiving: The psychology of visual illusions.* Hillsdale, NJ: Erlbaum.

Coren, S., & Girgus, J. S. (1980). Principles of perceptual organization and spatial distortion: The Gestalt illusions. *Journal of Experimental Psychology: Human Perception and Performance, 6,* 404–412.

Coren, S., Girgus, J. S., & Schiano, D. (1986). Is adaptation of orientation-specific cortical cells a possible explanation of illusion decrement? *Bulletin of the Psychonomic Society, 24,* 207–210.

Coren, S., & Hakstian, A. R. (1987). Visual screening without the use of technical equipment: Preliminary development of a behaviorally validated questionnaire. *Applied Optics, 26,* 1468–1472.

Coren, S., & Hakstian, A. R. (1988). Color vision screening without the use of technical equipment: Scale development and cross-validation. *Perception & Psychophysics, 43,* 115–120.

Coren, S., & Hakstian, A. R. (1989). A behaviorally validated self-report inventory of the measurement of visual acuity. *International Journal of Epidemiology, 18,* 451–456.

Coren, S., & Hakstian, A. R. (1992). The development and cross-validation of a self-report inventory to assess pure tone threshold hearing sensitivity. *Journal of Speech and Hearing Research, 35,* 921–928.

Coren, S., & Hakstian, A. R. (1994). Predicting speech recognition thresholds from pure tone hearing thresholds. *Perceptual and Motor Skills, 79,* 1003–1008.

Coren, S., & Hakstian, A. R. (1995). Testing color discrimination without the use of special stimuli or technical equipment. *Perceptual and Motor Skills, 81*, 931–938.

Coren, S., & Hakstian, A. R. (1996). Screening for stereopsis without the use of technical equipment: Scale development and cross-validation. *International Journal of Epidemiology, 25*, 146–152.

Coren, S., & Harland, R. E. (1994). Subjective contours and visual-geometric illusions: Do they share common mechanisms? *Italian Journal of Psychology [Giornale Italiano di Psicologia], 20*, 709–730.

Coren, S., & Hoenig, P. (1972). Eye movements and decrement in the Oppel-Kundt illusion. *Perception & Psychophysics, 12*, 224–225.

Coren, S., & Keith, B. (1970). Bezold-Brucke effect: Pigment or neural locus? *Journal of the Optical Society of America, 60*, 559–562.

Coren, S., & Komoda, M. K. (1973). Apparent lightness as a function of perceived direction of incident illumination. *American Journal of Psychology, 86*, 345–349.

Coren, S., & Porac, C. (1978). Iris pigmentation and visual-geometric illusions. *Perception, 7*, 473–478.

Coren, S., & Porac, C. (1983a). The creation and reversal of the Mueller-Lyer illusion through attentional manipulation. *Perception, 12*, 49–54.

Coren, S., & Porac, C. (1983b). Subjective contours and apparent depth: A direct test. *Perception & Psychophysics, 33*, 197–200.

Coren, S., & Porac, C. (1984). Structural and cognitive components in the Mueller-Lyer illusion assessed via cyclopean presentation. *Perception & Psychophysics, 35*, 313–318.

Coren, S., & Porac, C. (1987). Individual differences in visual-geometric illusions: Predictions from measures of spatial cognitive abilities. *Perception & Psychophysics, 41*, 211–219.

Coren, S., Porac, C., Aks, D. J., & Morikawa, K. (1988). A method to assess the relative contribution of lateral inhibition to the magnitude of visual-geometric illusions. *Perception & Psychophysics, 43*, 551–558.

Coren, S., Porac C., & Duncan, P. (1981). Lateral preference in pre-school children and young adults. *Child Development, 52*, 443–450.

Coren, S., Porac, C., & Theodor, L. H. (1987). Set and subjective contour. In S. Petry & G. E. Meyer (Eds.), *The perception of illusory contours* (pp. 237–245). New York: Springer-Verlag.

Coren, S., Whitehead, L. A., Baca, M. J., & Patten, R. (1995). Navigational range lights: The effect of stimulus configuration on alignment accuracy. *Ergonomics, 38*, 1360–1367.

Cormack, R. H. (1984). Stereoscopic depth perception at far viewing distances. *Perception & Psychophysics, 35*, 423–428.

Cornsweet, T. N. (1956). Determination of the stimuli for involuntary drifts and saccadic eye movements. *Journal of the Optical Society of America, 46*, 987–993.

Cornsweet, T. N. (1962). The staircase-method in psychophysics. *American Journal of Psychology, 75*, 485–491.

Cornsweet, T. N. (1970). *Visual perception.* New York: Academic Press.

Cornsweet, T. N. (1985). Prentice Award Lecture: A simple retinal mechanism that has complex and profound effects on perception. *American Journal of Optometry and Physiological Optics, 62*, 427–438.

Correia, M. J., & Guedry, F. E. (1978). The vestibular system: Basic biophysical and physiological mechanisms. In R. B. Masterton (Ed.), *Handbook of sensory neurobiology: Vol. I. Sensory integration.* New York: Plenum Press.

Corso, J. F. (1959). Age and sex differences in thresholds. *Journal of the Acoustical Society of America, 31*, 498–509.

Corso, J. F. (1981). *Aging sensory systems and perception.* New York: Praeger.

Costanzo, R. M., & Graziadei, P. P. C. (1987). Development and plasticity of the olfactory system. In T. E. Finger & W. L. Silver (Eds.), *Neurobiology of taste and smell* (pp. 233–250). New York: Wiley.

Courage, M. L., & Adams, J. (1990). The early development of visual acuity in the binocular and monocular peripheral fields. *Infant Behavioral Development, 13*, 123–128.

Courage, M. L., & Adams, R. J. (1996). Infant peripheral vision: The development of monocular visual acuity in the first 3 months of postnatal life. *Vision Research, 36*, 1207–1215.

Cowan, R. S. C., Alcantara, J. I., Blamey, P. J., & Clark, G. M. (1988). Preliminary evaluation of a multichannel electrotactile speech processor. *Journal of the Acoustical Society of America, 83*, 2328–2338.

Cowey, A. (1981). Why are there so many visual areas? In F. O. Schmitt, F. G. Worden, G. Adelman, & S. G. Dennis (Eds.), *The organization of the cerebral cortex.* (pp. 395–413). Cambridge, MA: MIT Press.

Cowley, J. J., & Broolsbank, B. W. L. (1991). Human exposure to putative pheromones and changes in aspects of social behavior. *Journal of Steroid Biochemistry and Molecular Biology, 39*, 647–659.

Cowley, J. J., Johnson, A. L., & Brooksbank, B. W. L. (1977). The effect of two odorous compounds on performance in an assessment-of-people test. *Psychoneuroendocrinology, 2*, 159–172.

Craig, J. C. (1978). Vibrotactile pattern recognition and masking. In G. Gordon (Ed.), *Active touch: The mechanism of recognition of objects by manipulation* (pp. 229–242). Oxford: Pergamon Press.

Craig, J. C. (1981). Tactile letter recognition: Pattern duration and modes of pattern generation. *Perception & Psychophysics, 30*, 540–546.

Craig, J. C. (1983a). The role of onset in the perception of sequentially presented vibrotactile patterns. *Perception & Psychophysics, 34*, 421–432.

Craig, J. C. (1983b). Some factors affecting tactile pattern recognition. *International Journal of Neuroscience, 19*, 47–58.

Craig, J. C. (1989). Interference in localizing tactile stimuli. *Perception & Psychophysics, 45*, 343–355.

Craig, J. C. (1995). Vibrotactile masking: The role of response competition. *Perception & Psychophysics, 57*, 1190–1200.

Craig, J. C., & Evans, P. M. (1987). Vibrotactile masking and the persistence of tactual features. *Perception & Psychophysics, 42*, 309–317.

Craig, K. D. (1978). Social modeling influences on pain. In R. A. Sternbach (Ed.), *The psychology of pain.* New York: Raven Press.

Craig, K. D., Best, H., & Ward, L. M. (1975). Social modelling influences on psychophysical judgments of electrical stimulation. *Journal of Abnormal Psychology, 84*, 366–373.

Craig, K. D., & Coren, S. (1975). Signal detection analysis of social modelling influences on pain expressions. *Journal of Psychosomatic Research, 19*, 105–112.

Craig, K. D., & Hadjistavropoulos, H. D. (1994). A comparison of two measures of facial activity during pain in the newborn child. *Journal of Pediatric Psychology, 19*, 305–318.

Craig K. D., & Prkachin, K. M. (1978). Social modeling influences on sensory decision theory and psychophysiological indexes of pain. *Journal of Personality and Social Psychology, 36*, 805–815.

Craik, F., & Simon, E. (1980). The roles of attention and depth of processing in understanding age differences in memory. In L. Poon, J. Fozard, L. Cermak, & L. Thompson (Eds.), *New directions in memory and aging: Proceedings of the George A. Talland*

Memorial Conference (pp. 95–112). Hillsdale, NJ: Erlbaum.

Crassini, B., Brown, B., & Bowman, K. (1988). Age-related changes in contrast sensitivity in central and peripheral retina. *Perception, 17,* 315–332.

Craton, L. G., & Yonas, A. (1990). The role of motion in infants' perception of occlusion. In J. T. Enns (Ed.), *The development of attention: Research and theory* (pp. 21–46). Amsterdam: Elsevier.

Cratty, B. (1979). *Perceptual and motor development in infants and children.* New Jersey: Prentice-Hall.

Crick, F. (1994). *The astonishing hypothesis.* New York: Simon & Schuster.

Crook, C. (1987). Taste and olfaction. In P. Salapatek & L. Cohen (Eds.), *Handbook of infant perception: Vol. 2. From perception to cognition* (pp. 237–264). Orlando: Academic Press.

Crossman, E. R. F. W. (1953). Entropy and choice time: The effect of frequency unbalance on choice response. *Quarterly Journal of Experimental Psychology, 5,* 41–51.

Crutchfield, R. S., Woodworth, D. G., & Albrecht, R. E. (1958). *Perceptual performance and the effective person.* (WADC-TN-58-60). Lackland Air Force Base, TX: Wright Air Development Center. (NTIS No. AD-151-039).

Cuddy, L. L., Cohen, A. J., & Mewhort, D. J. K. (1981). Perception of structure in short melodic sequences. *Journal of Experimental Psychology: Human Perception and Performance, 7,* 869–883.

Cunningham, W. (1980). Speed, age and qualitative differences in cognitive functioning. In L. Poon (Ed.), *Aging in the 1980s* (pp. 327–331). Washington, DC: American Psychological Association.

Curcio, C. A., Sloan, K. R., Packer, O., Hendrickson, A. E., & Kalina, R. E. (1987). Distribution of cones in human and monkey retina: Individual variability and radial asymmetry. *Science, 236,* 579–582.

Cutler, B. L., & Penrod, S. D. (1995). *Mistaken identification: The eyewitness, psychology and the law.* New York: University of Cambridge Press.

Cutler, W. B., Preti, G., Krieger, A., Huggins, G. R., Garcia, C. R., & Lawley, H. J. (1986). Human axillary secretions influence women's menstrual cycles: The role of donor extract from men. *Hormones and Behavior, 20,* 463–473.

Cutting, J. E. (1976). Auditory and linguistic processes in speech perception: Inferences from six fusions in dichotic listening. *Psychological Review, 83,* 114–140.

Cutting, J. E. (1978). Generation of synthetic male and female walkers through manipulation of a biomechanical invariant. *Perception, 7,* 393–405.

Cutting, J. E. (1986). *Perception with an eye for motion.* Cambridge, MA: MIT Press.

Cutting, J. E. (1987). Perception and information. *Annual Review of Psychology, 38,* 61–90.

Cutting, J. E., & Kozlowski, L. T. (1977). Recognizing friends by their walk: Gait perception without familiarity cues. *Bulletin of the Psychonomic Society, 9,* 353–356.

Cutting, J. E., Proffitt, D. R. (1981). Gait perception as an example of how we may perceive events. In R. Walk & H. L. Pick Jr. (Eds.), *Intersensory perception and sensory integration* (pp. 249–273). New York: Plenum Press.

Cutting, J. E., Proffitt, D. R., & Kozlowski, L. T. (1978). A biomechanical invariant for gait perception. *Journal of Experimental Psychology: Human Perception and Performance, 4,* 357–372.

Cutting, J. E., & Vishton, P. M. (1997). Heading and path information from retinal flow in naturalistic environments. *Perception & Psychophysics, 59,* 426–441.

Cynader, M., Berman, N., & Hein, A. (1976). Recovery of function in cat visual cortex following prolonged deprivation. *Experimental Brain Research, 25,* 139–156.

Cynader, M., & Regan, D. (1978). Neurons in cat parastriate cortex sensitive to the direction of motion in three-dimensional space. *Journal of Physiology, 274,* 549–569.

Cynader, M., Timney, B. N., & Mitchell, D. E. (1980). Period of susceptibility of kitten visual cortex to the effects of monocular deprivation extends beyond 6 months of age. *Brain Research, 191,* 545–550.

Daan, S., Beersma, D. G. M., & Borbely, A. A. (1984). Timing of human sleep: Recovery process gated by a circadian pacemaker. *American Journal of Physiology, 246,* 161–178.

Dacey, D. M. (1988). Dopamine-accumulating retinal neurons revealed by in vitro fluorescence display a unique morphology. *Science, 240,* 1196–1198.

Dai, H., & Green, D. M. (1993). Discrimination of spectral shape as a function of stimulus duration. *Journal of the Acoustical Society of America, 93,* 957–965.

Dai, H., Versfeld, N. J., & Green, D. M. (1996). The optimum decision rules in the same-different paradigm. *Perception & Psychophysics, 58,* 1–9.

Dallenbach, K. M. (1939). Pain: History and present status. *American Journal of Psychology, 52,* 331–347.

D'Aloisio, A., & Klein, R. M. (1990). Aging and the deployment of attention. In J. T. Enns (Ed.), *The development of attention: Research and theory* (pp. 447–466). Amsterdam: Elsevier.

Dallos, P. (1978). Biophysics of the cochlea. In E. C. Friedman & M. P. Carterette (Eds.), *Handbook of perception: Vol. IV. Hearing* (pp. 125 162). New York: Academic Press.

Dallos, P., Santos-Sacchi, J., & Flock, A. (1982). Intracellular recordings from cochlear outer hair cells. *Science, 18,* 582–584.

Dalton, K. (1964). *The premenstrual syndrome.* Springfield, IL: Thomas.

Dalziel, C. C., & Egan, D. J. (1982). Crystalline lens thickness changes as observed by pachometry. *American Journal of Optometry and Physiological Optics, 59,* 442–447.

Damasio, A. R. (1994). *Descartes' error.* New York: Putnam.

Damasio, A. R., & Tranel, D. (1990). Face agnosia and the neural substrates of memory. *Annual Review of Neuroscience, 13,* 89–109.

Daniels, J. D., Pettigrew, J. D., & Norman, J. L. (1978). Development of single-neuron responses in kittens' lateral geniculate nucleus. *Journal of Neurophysiology, 41,* 1373–1393.

Dannemiller, J. L. (1989). Computational approaches to color constancy: Adaptive and ontogenetic considerations. *Psychological Review, 96,* 225–266.

Dannemiller, J. L., & Freedland, R. L. (1991). Detection of relative motion by human infants. *Developmental Psychology, 27,* 67–78.

Darian-Smith, I., Sugitani, M., Heywood, J., Karita, K., & Goodwin, A. (1982). Touching textured surfaces: Cells in somatosensory cortex respond both to finger movement and to surface features. *Science, 218,* 906–909.

Dark, V., Johnston, W., Myles-Worsley, M., & Farah, M. (1985). Levels of selection and capacity limits. *Journal of Experimental Psychology: General, 114,* 472–497.

Dark, V. J. (1988). Semantic priming, prime reportability, and retroactive priming are interdependent. *Memory and Cognition, 16,* 299–308.

Dartnall, H. M. A. (1957). *The visual pigments.* London: Methuen.

Daugman, J. G. (1980). Two-dimensional spectral analysis of cortical receptive field profiles. *Vision Research, 20,* 847–856.

Davidoff, J. B. (1975). *Differences in visual perception: The individual eye.* New York: Academic Press.

Dawkins, R. (1996). *Climbing Mount Improbable.* New York: Random House.

Dawson, J. L. (1967). Cultural and physiological influences upon spatial processes in West Africa: I. *International Journal of Psychology, 2,* 115–128.

Dawson, M. R. W. (1991). The how and why of what went where in apparent motion: Modelling solutions to the motion correspondence problem. *Psychological Review, 98,* 569–603.

Dawson, M. R. W., & Di Lollo, V. (1990). Effects of adapting luminance and stimulus contrast on the temporal and spatial limits of short-range motion. *Vision Research, 30,* 415–429.

Dawson, M. R. W., & Pylyshyn, Z. W. (1988). Natural constraints on apparent motion. In Z. W. Pylyshyn (Ed.), *Computational processes in human vision* (pp. 99–120). Norwood, NJ: Ablex.

Day, M. C. (1975). Developmental trends in visual scanning. In H. W. Reese (Ed.), *Advances in child development and behavior: Vol. 10* (pp. 154–193). New York: Academic Press.

Day, M. C., & Stone, C. A. (1980). Children's use of perceptual set. *Journal of Experimental Child Psychology, 29,* 428–445.

Day, R. H. (1990). The Bourdon illusion in haptic space. *Perception & Psychophysics, 47,* 400–404.

Day, R. H., Stuart G. W., & Dickinson, R. G. (1980). Size constancy does not fail below half a degree. *Perception & Psychophysics, 28,* 263–265.

Day, R. H., & Webster, W. R. (1989). Negative afterimages and the McCollough effect. *Perception & Psychophysics, 46,* 419–424.

Day, R. S. (1968). *Fusion in dichotic listening.* Unpublished doctoral dissertation, Stanford University, Stanford, CA.

Day, R. S. (1970). Temporal order judgments in speech: Are individuals language-bound or stimulus-bound? *Haskins Laboratories Status Report* (SR-21/22), 71–87.

DeGangi, G. A., & Greenspan, S. I. (1988). The development of sensory functions in infants. *Physical & Occupational Therapy in Pediatrics, 8,* 21–33.

Dekle, D. J., & Beal, C. R. (1996). Children as witnesses: A comparison of lineup versus showup identification methods. *Applied Cognitive Psychology, 10,* 1–12.

Delgutte, B. (1990). Physiological mechanisms of psychophysical masking: Observations from auditory-nerve fibers. *Journal of the Acoustical Society of America, 87,* 791–809.

Deliege, I., & Melen, M. (1996). Musical schemata in real-time listening to a piece of music. *Music Perception, 14,* 117–160.

Delk, J. L., & Fillenbaum, S. (1965). Differences in perceived color as a function of characteristic color. *American Journal of Psychology, 78,* 290–293.

Delorne, A., & Martin, C. (1986). Roles of retinal periphery and depth periphery in linear vection and visual control of standing in humans. *Canadian Journal of Psychology, 40,* 176–187.

Dennet, D. C. (1991). *Consciousness explained.* New York: Little, Brown.

De Monasterio, F. M. (1978). Center and surround mechanisms of opponent-color X and Y ganglion cells of retina of macaques. *Journal of Neurophysiology, 41,* 1418–1434.

Deregowski, J. (1980). *Illusions, patterns and pictures: A cross-cultural perspective.* London: Academic Press.

De Renzi, D. E. (1982). *Disorders of space exploration and cognition.* New York: Wiley.

Derrington, A. M., & Fuchs, A. F. (1981). The development of spatial-frequency selectivity in kitten striate cortex. *Journal of Physiology, 316,* 1–10.

Desimone, R., Albright, T. D., Gross, C. G., & Bruce, C. (1980). Responses of inferior temporal neurons to complex visual stimuli. *Society of Neurosciences. Abstracts, 6,* 581.

Desimone, R., & Gross, C. G. (1979). Visual areas in the temporal cortex of the macaque. *Brain Research, 178,* 363–380.

Desimone, R., Schein, S. J., Moran, J., & Ungerleider, L. G. (1985). Contour, color and shape analysis beyond the striate cortex. *Vision Research, 25,* 441–452.

Desimone, R., & Ungerleider, L. G. (1989). Neural mechanisms of visual processing in monkeys. In I. Boller & J. Grafman (Eds.), *Handbook of neuropsychology: Vol. 2* (pp. 267–299). Amsterdam: Elsevier.

Desjardins, R. N., Rogers, J., & Werker, J. F. (1997). An exploration of why preschoolers perform differently than do adults in audiovisual speech perception tasks. *Journal of Experimental Child Psychology, 66,* 85–110.

Deutsch, D. (1975). Two channel listening to musical scales. *Journal of the Acoustical Society of America, 57,* 1156–1160.

Deutsch, D. (1978). The psychology of music. In E. C. Carterette & M. P. Friedman (Eds.), *Handbook of perception: Vol. X. Perceptual ecology* (pp. 191–224). New York: Academic Press.

Deutsch, D. (Ed.). (1982). *The psychology of music.* New York: Academic Press.

Deutsch, D. (1986). A musical paradox. *Music Perception, 3,* 275–280.

Deutsch, D. (1987). The tritone paradox: Effects of spectral variables. *Perception & Psychophysics, 41,* 563–575.

Deutsch, D. (1995). *Musical illusions and paradoxes.* La Jolla, CA: Philomel Records, Inc.

Deutsch, D., & Feroe, J. (1981). The internal representation of pitch sequences in tonal music. *Psychological Review, 88,* 503–522.

Deutsch, D., & Kuyper, W. L. (1987). The tritone paradox: Its presence and form of distribution in a general population. *Music Perception, 5,* 79–92.

Deutsch, J. A., & Deutsch, D. (1963). Attention: Some theoretical considerations. *Psychological Review, 70,* 80–90.

DeValois, K. K. (1977). Independence of black and white: Phase specific adaptation. *Vision Research, 17,* 209–215.

DeValois, R. L., Albrecht D. G., & Thorell, L. G. (1982). Spatial frequency selectivity of cells in the macaque visual cortex. *Vision Research, 22,* 545–559.

DeValois, R.L., & DeValois, K. K. (1975). Neural coding of color. In E. C. Carterette & M. P. Friedman (Eds.), *Handbook of perception: Vol. V. Seeing* (pp. 117–168). New York: Academic Press.

DeValois, R. L., & DeValois, K. K. (1980). Spatial vision. *Annual Review of Psychology, 31,* 309–341.

DeValois, R. L., & DeValois, K. K. (1987). *Spatial vision.* New York: Oxford University Press.

DeValois, R. L., & DeValois, K. K. (1991). Vernier acuity with stationary moving Gabors. *Vision Research, 31,* 1619–1626.

DeValois, R. L., Yund, E. W., & Hepler, N. (1982). The orientation and direction selectivity of cells in macaque visual cortex. *Vision Research, 22,* 531–544.

De Vries, H., & Stuiver, M. (1961). The absolute sensitivity of the human sense of smell. In W. A. Rosenblith (Ed.), *Communication processes* (pp. 159–167). New York: Wiley.

De Vries, J. V. (1968). *Perspective.* New York: Dover. (Original work published 1604)

DeWitt, L. A., & Samuel, A. G. (1990). The role of knowledge-based expectations in music perception: Evidence from musical restoration. *Journal of Memory & Language, 26,* 36–56.

DeYoe, E. A., & van Essen, D. C. (1988). Concurrent processing streams in monkey visual cortex. *Trends in Neuroscience, 11,* 219–226.

Diamant, H., Funakoshi, M., Strom, L., & Zotterman, Y. (1963). Electrophysiological studies on human taste nerves. In Y. Zotterman (Ed.), *Olfaction and taste* (pp. 191–203). Oxford: Pergamon Press.

Diamant, H., & Zotterman, Y. (1969). A comparative study on the neural and psychophysical response to taste stimuli. In C. Pfaffman (Ed.), *Olfaction and taste III* (pp. 428–435). New York: Rockefeller University Press.

DiCarlo, L. T., & Cross, D. V. (1990). Sequential effects in magnitude scaling: Models and theory. *Journal of Experimental Psychology: General, 119,* 375–396.

Dichgans, J., & Brandt, T. (1978). Visual-vestibular interaction: Effects on self-motion perception and postural control. In R. Held, H. W. Leibowitz, & H. L. Teuber (Eds.), *Handbook of sensory physiology: Vol. 7. Perception* (pp. 755–804). New York: Springer-Verlag.

Dickhaus, H., Pauser, G., & Zimmerman, M. (1985). Tonic descending inhibition affects intensity coding of nociceptive responses of spinal dorsal horn neurones in the cat. *Pain, 23,* 145–158.

Dichl, R. L. (1981). Feature detectors for speech: A critical reappraisal. *Psychological Bulletin, 89,* 1–18.

Diener, D. (1990). The P&P illusion. *Perception & Psychophysics, 47,* 65–67.

Di Lollo, V. (1980). Temporal integration in visual memory. *Journal of Experimental Psychology: General, 109,* 75–97.

Di Lollo, V. (1984). On the relationship between stimulus intensity and duration of visible persistence. *Journal of Experimental Psychology: Human Perception & Performance, 10,* 144–151.

Di Lollo, V., & Bischof, W. F. (1995). Inverse-intensity effect in duration of visible persistence. *Psychological Bulletin, 118,* 223–237.

Dineen, I. T., & Meyer, W. J. (1980). Developmental changes in visual orienting behavior to featural versus structural information in the human infant. *Developmental Psychology, 13,* 123–130.

Ditchburn, R. W. (1973). *Eye movements and perception.* Oxford: Clarendon Press.

DiZio, P. A., & Lackner, J. R. (1986). Perceived orientation, motion, and configuration of the body during viewing of an off-vertical rotating surface. *Perception & Psychophysics, 39,* 39–46.

Dobson, V. (1976). Spectral sensitivity of the 2-month-old infant as measured by the visual evoked cortical potential. *Vision Research, 16,* 367–374.

Dobson, V., & Teller, D. Y. (1978). Visual acuity in human infants: A review and comparison of behavioral and electrophysiological studies. *Vision Research, 18,* 1169–1103.

Dodwell, P. C. (1971). On perceptual clarity. *Psychological Review, 78,* 275–279.

Dodwell, P. C., & Humphrey, G. K. (1990). A functional theory of the McCollough effect. *Psychological Review, 97,* 78–89.

Dodwell, P. C., Humphrey, G. K., & Muir, D. W. (1987). Shape and pattern perception. In P. Salapatek & L. Cohen (Eds.), *Handbook of infant perception: Vol. 2. From perception to cognition* (pp. 1–80). Orlando: Academic Press.

Doetsch, G. S., Ganchrow, J. J., Nelson, L. M., & Erickson, R. P. (1969). Information processing in the taste system of the rat. In C. Pfaffman (Ed.), *Olfaction and taste III* (pp. 492–511). New York: Rockefeller University Press.

Doherty, M. E., & Keeley, S. M. (1972). On the identification of repeatedly presented visual stimuli. *Psychological Bulletin, 78,* 142–154.

Donaldson, I. M. L., & Long, A. C. (1980). Interactions between extraocular proprioceptive and visual signals in the superior colliculus of the cat. *Journal of Physiology, 298,* 85–110.

Donchin, E. (1981). Surprise! . . . Surprise? *Psychophysiology, 18,* 493–513.

Doner, J., Lappin, J. S., & Perfetto, G. (1984). Detection of three-dimensional structure in moving optical patterns. *Journal of Experimental Psychology: Human Perception and Performance, 10,* 1–11.

Dooley, G. J., & Moore, B. C. J. (1988). Detection of linear frequency glides as a function of frequency and duration. *Journal of the Acoustical Society of America, 84,* 2045–2057.

Dorr, S., & Neumeyer, C. (1996). The goldfish—A colour-constant animal. *Perception, 25,* 243–250.

Doty, R. L. (1985). The primates: III. Humans. In R. E. Brown & D. W. MacDonald (Eds.), *Social odours in mammals: Vol. 2* (pp. 804–832). Oxford: Clarendon Press.

Doty, R. L., Applebaum, S., Zusho, H., & Settle, R. G. (1985). Sex differences in odor identification ability: A cross-cultural analysis. *Neuropsychologia, 23,* 667–672.

Doty, R. L., Green, P. A., Ram, C., & Yankell, S. L. (1982). Communication of gender from human breath odors: Relationship to perceived intensity and pleasantness. *Hormones and Behavior, 16,* 13–22.

Doty, R. L., Shaman, P., & Applebaum, S. L. (1984). Smell identification ability: Changes with age. *Science, 226,* 1441–1443.

Doty, R. L., Yousem, D. M., Pham, L. T., Kreshak, A. A., Geckle, R., & Lee, W. W. (1997). Olfactory dysfunction in patients with head trauma. *Archives of Neurology, 54,* 1131–1140.

Dowling, W. J., & Carterette, E. C. (Eds.). (1987). The understanding of melody and rhythm [Special issue]. *Perception & Psychophysics, 41,* 482–656.

Dowling, W. J., & Harwood, D. L. (1986). *Music cognition.* Orlando: Academic Press.

Dowling, W. J., Kwak, S., & Andrews, M. W. (1995). The time course of recognition of novel melodies. *Perception & Psychophysics, 57,* 134–139.

Downing, C. J. (1988). Expectancy and visual-spatial attention: Effects on perceptual quality. *Journal of Experimental Psychology: Human Perception and Performance, 14,* 188–202.

Driver, J. (1996). Enhancement of selective listening by illusory mislocation of speech sounds due to lip-reading. *Nature, 381,* 66–68.

Driver, J., & McLeod, P. (1992). Reversing visual search asymmetries with conjunctions of movement and orientation. *Journal of Experimental Psychology: Human Perception and Performance, 18,* 22–33.

Droscher, V. B. (1971). *The magic of the senses: New discoveries in animal perception.* New York: Harper.

Drum, B. (1980). Relation of brightness to threshold for light-adapted and dark-adapted rods and cones: Effects of retinal eccentricity and target size. *Perception, 9,* 633–650.

Drum, B. (1981). Brightness interactions between rods and cones. *Perception & Psychophysics, 29,* 505–510.

Duncan, H. F., Gourlay, N., & Hudson, W. (1973). *A study of pictorial perception among the Bantu and white primary school children in South Africa.* Johannesburg: Witwatersrand University Press.

Duncan, J. (1984). Selective attention and the organization of visual information. *Journal of Experimental Psychology: General, 113,* 501–517.

Duncan, J., & Humphreys, G. W. (1989). Visual search and stimulus similarity. *Psychological Review, 96,* 433–458.

Duncker, K. (1929). Uber induzierte Bewegung (ein Beitrag zur Theorie optisch warigenommener Bewegung). *Psychologische Forschung, 2,* 180–259.

Durlach, N. I., Delhorne, L. A., Wong, A., Ko, W. Y., Rabinowitz, W. M., & Hollerbach, J. (1989). Manual discrimination and identification of length by the finger-span method. *Perception & Psychophysics, 46,* 29–38.

Easterbrook, J. A. (1959). The effect of emotion on cue utilization and the organization of behavior. *Psychological Review, 66,* 183–201.

Easton, R. D., & Basala, M. (1982). Perceptual dominance during lipreading. *Perception & Psychophysics, 32,* 562–570.

Edwards, A., & Cohen, S. (1961). Visual illusions, tactile sensibility and reaction time under LSD-25. *Psychopharmacologia, 2,* 297–303.

Efron, R. (1967). The duration of the present. *Annals of the New York Academy of Sciences, 138,* 713–729.

Efron, R. (1973). Conservation of temporal information by perceptual systems. *Perception & Psychophysics, 14,* 518–530.

Egan, J. P. (1975). *Signal detection theory and ROC-analysis.* New York: Academic Press.

Egeth, H. E., Virzi, R. A., & Garbart, H. (1984). Searching for conjunctively defined targets. *Journal of Experimental Psychology: Human Perception and Performance, 10,* 32–39.

Egeth, H. E., & Yantis, S. (1997). Visual attention: Control, representation, and time course. *Annual Review of Psychology, 48,* 269–297.

Eggermont, J. J. (1995). Representation of a voice onset time continuum in primary auditory cortex of the cat. *Journal of the Acoustical Society of America, 98,* 911–920.

Egly, R., Driver, J., & Rafal, R. D. (1994). Shifting visual attention between objects and locations: Evidence from normal and parietal lesion subjects. *Journal of Experimental Psychology: General, 123,* 161–177.

Eichengreen, J. M., Coren, S., & Nachmias, J. (1966). Visual-cliff preference by infant rats: Effects of rearing and test conditions. *Science, 151,* 830–831.

Eijkman, E. G. J., Jongsma, H. J., & Vincent, J. (1981). Two dimensional filtering, oriented line detectors and figural aspects as determinants of visual illusions. *Perception & Psychophysics, 29,* 352–358.

Eilers, R., Wilson, W., & Moore, T. (1979). Speech perception in the language innocent and the language wise: A study in the perception of voice onset time. *Journal of Child Language, 6,* 1–18.

Eimas, P. D., & Corbit, J. D. (1973). Selective adaptation of linguistic feature detectors. *Cognitive Psychology, 4,* 99–109.

Eimas, P. D., & Miller, J. D. (1980). Contextual effects in infant speech perception. *Science, 209,* 1140–1141.

Eimas, P. D., Siqueland, E. R., Jusczyk, P., & Vigorito, J. (1971). Speech perception in infants. *Science, 171,* 303–306.

Einstein, A., & Besso, M. (1972). *Correspondance 1903–1955.* Paris: Hermann.

Ekman, G. (1954). Dimensions of color vision. *Journal of Psychology, 38,* 467–474.

Eland, J. M., & Anderson, J. E. (1977). The experience of pain in children. In A. Jacox (Ed.), *Pain: A sourcebook for nurses and other professionals.* Boston: Little, Brown.

Elder, J., & Zucker, S. (1993). The effect of contour closure on the rapid discrimination of two-dimensional shapes. *Vision Research, 33,* 981–991.

Elder, J., & Zucker, S. (1994). A measure of closure. *Vision Research, 34,* 3361–3369.

Elkind, D. (1978). *The child's reality: Three developmental themes.* Hillsdale, NJ: Erlbaum.

Ellermeier, W., & Westphal, W. (1995). Gender differences in pain ratings and pupil reactions to painful pressure stimuli. *Pain, 61,* 435–439.

Ellingson, R. (1968). Clinical applications of evoked potential techniques in infants and children. *Electroencephalography and Clinical Neurophysiology, 24,* 293.

Ellingson, R., Lathrop, G., Nelson, G., & Donahy, T. (1972). Visual evoked potentials of infants. *Revue d'Electroencéphalographie et de Neurophysiologie Clinique, 2,* 395–400.

Ellis, H. (1905). *Sexual selection in man.* New York: Davis.

Ellis, H. D., & Young, A. W. (1988). Training in face-processing skills for a child with acquired prosopagnosia. *Developmental Neuropsychology, 4,* 283–294.

Emmerson, P. G., & Ross, H. E. (1986). The effect of brightness on colour recognition under water. *Ergonomics, 29,* 1647–1658.

Emmerton, J. (1983). Pattern discrimination in the near-ultraviolet by pigeons. *Perception & Psychophysics, 34,* 555–559.

Engel, A. K., Konig, P., Kreiter, A. K., & Singer, W. (1991). Interhemispheric synchronization of oscillatory neural responses in cat visual cortex. *Science, 252,* 1177–1179.

Engen, T. (1982). *Perception of odors.* New York: Academic Press.

Engen, T. (1987). Remembering odors and their names. *American Scientist, 75,* 497–503.

Engen, T., Lipsett, L. P., & Kaye, H. (1963). Olfactory responses and adaptation in the human neonate. *Journal of Comparative and Physiological Psychology, 56,* 73–77.

Enns, J. T. (1986). Seeing textons in context. *Perception & Psychophysics, 39,* 143–147.

Enns, J. T. (1987). A developmental look at pattern symmetry in perception and memory. *Developmental Psychology, 23,* 839–850.

Enns, J. T. (1990a). Relations between components of visual attention. In J. T. Enns (Ed.), *The development of attention: Research and theory* (pp. 447–466). Amsterdam: Elsevier.

Enns, J. T. (1990b). Three dimensional features that pop out in visual search. In D. Brogan (Ed.), *Visual search* (pp. 37–45). London: Taylor & Francis.

Enns, J. T. (1992). Sensitivity of early human vision to 3-D orientation in line-drawings. *Canadian Journal of Psychology, 46,* 143–169.

Enns, J. T., & Brodeur, D. A. (1989). A developmental study of covert orienting to peripheral visual cues. *Journal of Experimental Child Psychology, 48,* 171–189.

Enns, J. T., & Cameron, S. (1987). Selective attention in young children: The relations between visual search, filtering and priming. *Journal of Experimental Child Psychology, 44,* 38–63.

Enns, J. T., & Coren, S. (1995). The Box Alignment Illusion: An orientation illusion induced by pictorial depth. *Perception & Psychophysics, 57,* 1163–1174.

Enns, J. T., & Di Lollo, V. (1997). Object substitution: A new form of visual masking in unattended visual locations. *Psychological Science, 8,* 135–139.

Enns, J. T., & Girgus, J. S. (1985). Perceptual grouping and spatial distortion: A developmental study. *Developmental Psychology, 21,* 241–246.

Enns, J. T., & Girgus, J. S. (1986). A developmental study of shape integration over space and time. *Developmental Psychology, 22,* 491–499.

Enns, J. T., & King, K. A. (1990). Components of line-drawing interpretation: A developmental study. *Developmental Psychology, 26,* 469–479.

Enns, J. T., & Kingstone, A. (1995). Access to global and local properties in visual search for compound stimuli. *Psychological Science, 5,* 283–291.

Enns, J. T., & Prinzmetal, W. (1984). The role of redundancy in the object-line effect. *Perception & Psychophysics, 35,* 22–32.

Enns, J. T., & Rensink, R. A. (1990). Influence of scene-based properties on visual search. *Science, 247,* 721–723.

Enns, J. T., & Rensink, R. A. (1991). Preattentive recovery of three-dimensional orientation from line drawings. *Psychological Review, 98,* 335–351.

Enright, J. T. (1987a). Art and the oculomotor system: Perspective illustrations evoke vergence changes. *Perception, 16,* 731–746.

Enright, J. T. (1987b). Perspective vergence: Oculomotor responses to line drawings. *Vision Research, 27,* 1513–1526.

Epstein, W. (1973). The process of taking into account in visual perception. *Perception, 2,* 267–285.

Epstein, W., & Baratz, S. S. (1964). Relative size in isolation as a stimulus for relative perceived distance. *Journal of Experimental Psychology, 67,* 507–513.

Epstein, W., & Broota, K. D. (1986). Automatic and attentional components in perception of size-at-a-distance. *Perception & Psychophysics, 40,* 256–262.

Epstein, W., & Hanson, S. (1977). Discrimination of unique motion-path length. *Perception & Psychophysics, 22,* 152–158.

Epstein, W., Hatfield, G., & Muise, G. (1977). Perceived shape at a slant as a function of processing time and processing load. *Journal of Experimental Psychology: Human Perception and Performance, 3,* 473–483.

Epstein, W., & Lovitts, B. E. (1985). Automatic and attentional components in perception of shape-at-a-slant. *Journal of Experimental Psychology: Human Perception and Performance, 11,* 355–366.

Epstein, W., & Park, J. N. (1964). Shape constancy: Functional relationships and theoretical formulations. *Psychological Bulletin, 62,* 180–196.

Erickson, R. P. (1963). Sensory neural patterns and gustation. In Y. Zotterman (Ed.), *Olfaction and taste* (pp. 205–213). Oxford: Pergamon Press.

Eriksen, C. W., & Collins, J. F. (1968). Sensory traces versus the psychological movement in the temporal organization of form. *Journal of Experimental Psychology, 77,* 376–382.

Eriksen, C. W., & Hake, H. W. (1955). Absolute judgments as a function of stimulus range and number of stimulus and response categories. *Journal of Experimental Psychology, 49,* 323–332.

Eriksen, C. W., & Hoffman, J. E. (1972). Some characteristics of selective attention in visual perception determined by vocal reaction time. *Perception & Psychophysics, 11,* 169–171.

Eriksen, C. W., & Murphy, T. D. (1987). Movement of attentional focus across the visual field: A critical look at the evidence. *Perception & Psychophysics, 42,* 299–305.

Eriksen, C. W., & St. James, J. D. (1986). Visual attention within and around the field of focal attention: A zoom lens model. *Perception & Psychophysics, 40,* 225–240.

Eriksen, C. W., & Yeh, Y. (1985). Allocation of attention in the visual field. *Journal of Experimental Psychology: Human Perception and Performance, 11,* 583–597.

Ernst, M., Lee, M. H. M., Dworkin, B., & Zaretsky, H. H. (1986). Pain perception decrement produced through repeated stimulation. *Pain, 26,* 221–231.

Erulkar, S. C. (1972). Comparative aspects of spatial localization of sound. *Physiological Review, 52,* 237–360.

Evans, E. F. (1975). Cochlear nerve and cochlear nucleus. In W. D. Keidel & W. D. Neff (Eds.), *Handbook of sensory physiology: Vol. V/2. Auditory system: Physiology (CNS). Behavioral studies. Psychoacoustics* (pp. 1–108). New York: Springer-Verlag.

Evans, P. M. (1987). Vibrotactile masking: Temporal integration, persistence, and strengths of representation. *Perception & Psychophysics, 42,* 515–525.

Evans, P. M., & Craig, J. C. (1986). Temporal integration and vibrotactile backward masking. *Journal of Experimental Psychology: Human Perception and Performance, 12,* 160–168.

Eysenck, H. J. (1967). *The biological basis of personality.* Springfield, IL: Thomas.

Fagen, D., & Swift, C. G. (1988). Effects of caffeine on vigilance and other performance tests in normal subjects. *Journal of Psychopharmacology, 2,* 19–25.

Fagiolini, M., Pizzorusso, T., Berardi, N., Domenici, L., & Maffei, L. (1994). Functional postnatal development of the rat primary visual cortex and the role of visual experience: Dark rearing and monocular deprivation. *Vision Research, 34,* 709–720.

Fahle, M. (1997). Specificity of learning curvature, orientation, and vernier discriminations. *Vision Research, 37,* 1885–1895.

Fahle, M., Edelman, S., & Poggio, T. (1995). Fast perceptual learning in hyperacuity. *Vision Research, 35,* 3003–3013.

Falmagne, J. C. (1985). *Elements of psychophysical theory.* New York: Oxford University Press.

Fant, G. (1967). Auditory patterns of speech. In W. Wathen-Dunn (Ed.), *Models for the perception of speech and visual form* (pp. 111–125). Cambridge, MA: MIT Press.

Fantz, R. L. (1961). The origin of form perception. *Scientific American, 204,* 66–72.

Fantz, R. L. (1965). Ontogeny of perception. In A. M. Schrier, H. F. Harlow, & F. Stollnitz (Eds.), *Behavior of nonhuman primates* (Vol. 2, pp. 365–403). New York: Academic Press.

Fantz, R. L., & Miranda, S. B. (1977). Visual processing in the newborn preterm, and mentally high-risk infant. In L. Gluck (Ed.), *Intrauterine asphyxia and the developing fetal brain* (pp. 453–471). Chicago: Year Book Medical Publishers.

Fantz, R. L., & Yeh, J. (1979). Configurational selectives: Critical for development of visual perception and

attention. *Canadian Journal of Psychology, 33,* 277–287.

Farbman, A. I. (1992). *Cell biology of olfaction.* New York: Cambridge University Press.

Farkas, M., & Hoyer, W. (1980). Processing consequences of perceptual grouping in selective attention. *Journal of Gerontology, 35,* 27–216.

Farrell, J. E. (1983). Visual transformations underlying apparent movement. *Perception & Psychophysics, 33,* 85–92.

Farrimond, T. (1990). Effect of alcohol on visual constancy values and possible relation to driving performance. *Perceptual and Motor Skills, 70,* 291–295.

Favreau, O. E., & Cavanagh, P. (1981). Color and luminance: Independent frequency shifts. *Science, 212,* 831–832.

Fechner, G. T. (1966). *Elements of psychophysics.* (H. E. Alder, Trans.). New York: Holt, Rinehart and Winston. (Original work published 1860)

Fender, D. H. (1971). Time delays in the human eye-tracking system. In P. Bach-y-Rita, C. C. Collins, & J. E. Hyde (Eds.), *The control of eye movements* (pp. 539–543). New York: Academic Press.

Fernald, A. (1985). Four-month-old infants prefer to listen to motherese. *Infant Behavior and Development, 8,* 181–195.

Festinger, L., Allyn, M. R., & White, C. W. (1971). The perception of color with achromatic stimulation. *Vision Research, 11,* 591–612.

Festinger, L., Coren, S., & Rivers, G. (1970). The effect of attention on brightness contrast and assimilation. *American Journal of Psychology, 83,* 189–207.

Festinger, L., & Easton, M. (1974). Inference about the efferent system based on a perceptual illusion produced by eye movements. *Psychological Review, 81,* 44–58.

Festinger, L., White, C. W., & Allyn, M. R. (1968). Eye movements and decrement in the Mueller-Lyer illusion. *Perception & Psychophysics, 3,* 376–382.

Field, D. J., & Hayes, A. (1993). Contour integration by the human visual system: Evidence for a local "association field." *Vision Research, 33,* 173–193.

Fiez, J. A., & Raichle, M. E. (1995). PET studies of auditory and phonological processing: Effects of stimulus characteristics and task demands. *Journal of Cognitive Neuroscience, 7,* 357–375.

Filsinger, E. E., & Fabes, R. A. (1985). Odor communication, pheromones, and human families. *Journal of Marriage and the Family, 47,* 349–360.

Findlay, J. (1981). Local and global influences on saccadic eye movements. In

D. Fisher, R. Monty, & J. Senders (Eds.), *Eye movements: Cognition and visual perception* (pp. 171–179). Hillsdale, NJ: Erlbaum.

Fine, B. J., & Kobrick, J. L. (1987). Cigarette smoking, field-dependence and contrast sensitivity. *Aviation, Space and Environmental Medicine, 58,* 777–782.

Fiorentini, A., Baumgartner, G., Magnussen, S., Shiller, P. H., & Thomas, J. P. (1990). The perception of brightness and darkness. In L. Spillman & J. S. Werner (Eds.), *Visual perception: The neurophysiological foundations* (pp. 129–161). New York: Academic Press.

Firestein, S., & Werblin, F. (1989). Odor-induced membrane currents in vertebrate-olfactory receptor neurons. *Science, 244,* 79–82.

Fisher, D. L., Duffy, S. A., Young, C., & Pollatsek, A. (1988). Understanding the central processing limit in consistent-mapping visual search tasks. *Journal of Experimental Psychology: Human Perception and Performance, 14,* 253–266.

Fisher, R. (1967). The biological fabric of time. In *Interdisciplinary perspectives of time, Annals of the New York Academy of Sciences, 138,* 451–465.

Fisk, A. D., & Schneider, W. (1981). Control and automatic processing during tasks requiring sustained attention: A new approach to vigilance. *Human Factors, 23,* 737–750.

Fitzpatrick, V., Pasnak, R., & Tyer, Z. E. (1982). The effect of familiar size at familiar distances. *Perception, 11,* 85–91.

Flandrin, J. M., & Jeannerod, M. (1981). Effects of unilateral superior colliculus ablation on oculomotor and vistibulo-ocular responses in the cat. *Experimental Brain Research, 42,* 73–80.

Flannery, R., & Butler, R. A. (1981). Spectral cues provided in the pinna for monaural localization in the horizontal plane. *Perception & Psychophysics, 29,* 438–444.

Flin, R. H. (1980). Age effects in children's memory for unfamiliar faces. *Developmental Psychology, 16,* 373–374.

Flock, H. R., & Freedberg, E. (1970). Perceived angle of incidence and achromatic surface color. *Perception & Psychophysics, 8,* 251–256.

Flock, H. R., & Nusinowitz, S. (1984). Visual structures for achromatic color perceptions. *Perception & Psychophysics, 36,* 111–130.

Flom, M. C., Brown, B., Adams, A. J., & Jones, R. T. (1976). Alcohol and marihuana effects on ocular tracking. *American Journal of Optometry and Physiological Optics, 53,* 764–773.

Florentine, M. (1986). Level discrimination of tones as a function of duration. *Journal of the Acoustical Society of America, 79,* 792–798.

Florentine, M., Buus, S., & Mason, C. R. (1987). Level discrimination as a function of level for tones from 0.25 to 16 kHz. *Journal of the Acoustical Society of America, 81,* 1528–1541.

Fogel, I., & Sagi, D. (1989). Gabor filters as texture discriminator. *Biological Cybernetics, 61,* 103–113.

Foley, J. E. (1974). Factors governing interocular transfer of prism adaptation. *Psychological Review, 81,* 183–186.

Folk, C. L., Remington, R. W., & Johnston, J. C. (1992). Involuntary covert orienting is contingent on attentional control settings. *Journal of Experimental Psychology: Human Perception and Performance, 18,* 1030–1044.

Folk, C. L., Remington, R. W., & Wright, J. H. (1994). The structure of attentional control: Contingent attentional capture by apparent motion, abrupt onset, and color. *Journal of Experimental Psychology: Human Perception and Performance, 20,* 317–329.

Forge, A., Li, L., Corwin, J. T., & Nevill, G. (1993). Ultrastructural evidence for hair cell regeneration in the mammalian inner ear. *Science, 259,* 1616–1619.

Foulke, E., & Sticht, T. (1969). Review of research on the intelligibility and comprehension of accelerated speech. *Psychological Bulletin, 72,* 50–62.

Fowler, C. A. (1996). Listeners do hear sounds, not tongues. *Journal of the Acoustical Society of America, 99,* 1730–1741.

Fowler, C. A., & Rosenblum, L. D. (1990). Duplex perception: A comparison of monosyllables and slamming doors. *Journal of Experimental Psychology: Human Perception and Performance, 16,* 742–754.

Fox, P. T., Mintun, M. A., Reiman, E. M., & Raichle, M. E. (1988). Enhanced detection of focal brain responses using intersubject averaging and change-distribution analysis of subtracted PET images. *Journal of Cerebral Blood Flow and Metabolism, 8,* 642–653.

Fox, R., Aslin, R. N., Shea, S. L., & Dumais, S. T. (1980). Stereopsis in infants. *Science, 207,* 323–324.

Fox, R., & McDaniel, C. (1982). The perception of biological motion by human infants. *Science,* 486–487.

Fozard, J., Wolf, E., Bell, B., McFarland, R., & Podolsky, S. (1977). Visual perception and communication. In J. Birren & K. Schaie (Eds.), *Handbook of the psychology of aging* (pp. 497–534). New York: Van Nostrand Reinhold.

Fraisse, P. (1963). *The psychology of time.* New York: Harper & Row.

Frankenhauser, M. (1959). *The estimation of time.* Stockholm: Almqvist & Wiksell.

Fraser, J. (1908). A new illusion of direction. *British Journal of Psychology, 8,* 49–54.

Frederick, D. L., Gillam, M. P., Lensing, S., & Paule, M. G. (1997). Acute effects of LSD on rhesus monkey operant test battery performance. *Pharmacology, Biochemistry & Behavior, 57,* 633–641.

Freeman, D. M., & Weiss, T. F. (1990). Hydrodynamic analysis of a two-dimensional model for micromechanical resonance of free-standing hair bundles. *Hearing Research, 48,* 37–68.

Freeman, R., Mallach, R., & Hartley, S. (1981). Responsivity of normal kitten striate cortex deteriorates after brief binocular deprivation. *Journal of Neurophysiology, 45,* 1074–1084.

Freeman, R., & Pettigrew, J. (1973). Alteration of visual cortex from environmental asymmetries. *Nature, 246,* 359–360.

Freidman, E. (1981). Vision training program for myopia management. *American Journal of Optometry and Physiological Optics, 58,* 546–553.

Freud, S. (1953). *An aphasia.* London: Imago.

Frey, M. von, & Kiesow, F. (1899). Uber die Function der Tastkorperchen. *Zeitschrift feur Psychologie, 20,* 126–163.

Frey, M. von, & Goldman, A. (1915). Der zeitliche Verlauf det Einstellung bei den Druckempfindungen. *Zeitschrift feur Biologie, 65,* 183–202.

Freyd, J., & Tversky, B. (1984). Force of symmetry in form perception. *American Journal of Psychology, 97,* 109–126.

Friedman, A. (1979). Framing pictures: The role of knowledge in automatized encoding and memory for gist. *Journal of Experimental Psychology: General, 108,* 316–355.

Friedman, A., & Liebelt, L. (1981). On the time course of viewing pictures with a view towards remembering. In D. Fisher, R. Monty, & J. Senders (Eds.), *Eye movements: Cognition and visual perception* (pp. 137–155). Hillsdale, NJ: Erlbaum.

Friedman, R. B. (1980). Identity without form: Abstract representations of letters. *Perception & Psychophysics, 28,* 53–60.

Friedman, S. L., & Stevenson, M. (1975). Developmental changes in the understanding of implied motion in two-dimensional pictures. *Child Development, 46,* 773–778.

Friedman, S. L., & Stevenson, M. (1980). Perception of movements in pictures. In M. Hagen (Ed.), *Perception of pictures;*

Vol. I. Alberti's window: The projective model of pictural information (pp. 225–255). New York: Academic Press.

Frisby, J. P. (1980). *Seeing: Illusion, brain and mind*. Oxford: Oxford University Press.

Fuld, K., Wooten, B. R., & Whalen, J. J. (1981). The elemental hues of shortwave and extraspectral lights. *Perception & Psychophysics, 29*, 317–322.

Fuller, C. A., Lydic, R., Sulzman, F. M., Albers, H. E., Tepper, B., & Moore-Ede, M. C. (1981). Circadian rhythm of body temperature persists after suprachiamatic lesions in the squirrel monkey. *American Journal of Physiology, 241*, R385–R391.

Fulton, J. F., & Bailey, P. (1929). Tumors in the region of the third ventricle: Their diagnosis and relation to pathological sleep. *Journal of Nervous and Mental Disorders, 69*, 1–25,145–164, 261–277.

Funakoshi, M., Kasahara, Y., Yamamoto, T., & Kawamura, Y. (1972). Taste coding and central perception. In D. Schneider (Ed.), *Olfaction and taste IV* (pp. 336–342). Stuttgart: Wissenshaftliche Verlagsgesellschaft MBH.

Funkenstein, H. H., Nelson, P. G., Winter, P. L., Wolberg, Z., & Newman, J. D. (1971). Unit responses in auditory cortex of awake squirrel monkeys to vocal stimulation. In M. B. Saschs (Ed.), *Physiology of the auditory system* (pp. 307–326). Baltimore: National Educational Consultants, Inc.

Gaddes, W. H. (1985). *Learning disabilities and brain function: A neuropsychological approach* (2nd ed.). New York: Springer-Verlag.

Gagne, J. P. (1988). Excess masking among listeners with a sensorineural hearing loss. *Journal of the Acoustical Society of America, 83*, 2311–2321.

Gaik, W. (1993). Combined evaluation of interaural time and intensity differences: Psychoacoustic results and computer modelling. *Journal of the Acoustical Society of America, 94*, 98–110.

Galanter, E. (1962). Contemporary psychophysics. In R. Brown, E. Galanter, E. Hess, & G. Mandler (Eds.), *New directions in psychology* (pp. 87–157). New York: Holt, Rinehart and Winston.

Ganchrow, J. R., Steiner, J. E., & Daher, M. (1983). Neonatal facial expressions in response to different qualities and intensities of gustatory stimuli. *Infant Behavior and Development, 6, 189–200.*

Garbin, C. P. (1988). Visual-haptic perceptual nonequivalence for shape information and its impact upon cross-modal performance. *Journal of Experimental Psychology: Human Perception and Performance, 14*, 547–553.

Gardner, E. P. (1983). Cortical neuronal mechanisms underlying the perception of motion across the skin. In C. von Euler, O. Franzen, U. Lindblom, & D. Ottoson (Eds.), *Somatosensory mechanisms* (pp. 93–112). New York: Plenum Press.

Garner, W. R. (1953). An informational analysis of absolute judgments of loudness. *Journal of Experimental Psychology, 46*, 373–380.

Garner, W. R. (1962). *Uncertainty and structure as psychological concepts*. New York: Wiley.

Garner, W. R. (1974). *The processing of information and structure*. Potomac, MD: Erlbaum.

Garner, W. R. (1978). Aspects of a stimulus: Features, dimensions and configurations. In E. H. Rosch & B. B. Lloyd (Eds.), *Cognition and categorization* (pp. 99–139). Hillsdale, NJ: Erlbaum.

Garner, W. R., & Clement, D. E. (1963). Goodness of pattern and pattern uncertainty. *Journal of Verbal Learning and Verbal Behavior, 2*, 446–452.

Garner, W. R., & Hake, H. W. (1951). The amount of information in absolute judgments. *Psychological Review, 58*, 446–459.

Gary-Bobo, E., Przybyslawski, J., & Saillour, P. (1995). Experience-dependent maturation of the spatial and temporal characteristics of the cell receptive fields in the kitten visual cortex. *Neuroscience Letters, 189*, 147–150.

Geiselman, R. E., Fisher, R. P., MacKinnon, D. P., & Holland, H. L. (1986). Enhancement of eyewitness memory with the cognitive interview. *American Journal of Psychology, 99*, 385–401.

Geisler, C. D. (1991). A cochlear model using feedback from motile outer hair cells. *Hearing Research, 54*, 105–117.

Geisler, C. D., Yates, G. K., Patuzzi, R. B., & Johnstone, B. M. (1990). Saturation of outer hair cell receptor currents causes two-tone suppression. *Hearing Research, 44*, 241–256.

Gelb, A. (1929). Die "Farbenkonstanz" der Sehdinge. *Handbuch der normalen und pathologische physiologie, 12*, 549–678.

Geldard, F. A. (1972). *The human senses* (2nd ed.). New York: Wiley.

Gent, J. F. (1979). An exponential model for adaptation in taste. *Sensory Processes, 3*, 303–316.

Gerbino, W., & Salmaso, D. (1987). The effect of amodal completion on visual matching. *Acta Psychologica, 65*, 25–46.

Gerbrandt, L. K., Spinelli, D. N., & Pribram, K. H. (1970). Interaction of visual attention and temporal cortex stimulation on electrical activity evoked in striate cortex. *Electroen-*

cephalography and Clinical Neurology, 29, 146.

Gerkema, M. P., & Groos, G. A. (1990). Differential elimination of circadian and ultradian rhythmicity by hypothalamic lesions in the common vole, *Microtus arvalis. Journal of Biological Rhythms, 5*, 81–95.

Gescheider, G. A. (1988). Psychophysical scaling. *Annual Review of Psychology, 39*, 169–200.

Gescheider, G. A. (1997). *Psychophysics, the fundamentals*. Mahwah, NJ: Lawrence Erlbaum Associates.

Gescheider, G. A., & Bolanowski, S. J. (1991). Final comments on ratio scaling of psychological magnitudes. In S. J. Bolanowski & G. A. Gescheider (Eds.), *Ratio scaling of psychological magnitude* (pp. 295–311). Hillsdale, NJ: Erlbaum.

Gescheider, G. A., & Bolanowski, S. J. (1994). The effects of aging on information-processing channels in the sense of touch: I. Absolute sensitivity. *Somatosensory and Motor Research, 11*, 345–357.

Gescheider, G. A., Bolanowski, S. J. Jr., & Verrillo, R. T. (1989). Vibrotactile masking: Effects of stimulus onset asynchrony and stimulus frequency. *Journal of the Acoustical Society of America, 85*, 2059–2064.

Gescheider, G. A., Bolanowski, S. J., Verrillo, R. T., Arpajian, D. J., & Ryan, T. F. (1990). Vibrotadile intensity discrimination measured by three methods. *Journal of the Acoustical Society of America, 87*, 330–338.

Gescheider, G. A., & Verrillo, R. T. (1982). Contralateral enhancement and suppression of vibrotactile sensation. *Perception & Psychophysics, 32*, 69–74.

Gesteland, R. C. (1986). Speculations on receptor cells as analyzers and filters. *Experientia, 42*, 287–291.

Gesteland, R. C., Lettvin, J. Y., Pitts, W. H., & Rojas, A. (1963). Odor specificities of the frog's olfactory receptors. In Y. Zotterman (Ed.), *Olfaction and taste* (pp. 19–34). Oxford: Pergamon Press.

Getchell, T. V., & Getchell, M. L. (1987). Peripheral mechanisms of olfaction: Biochemistry and neurophysiology. In T. E. Finger & W. L. Silver (Eds.), *Neurobiology of taste and smell* (pp. 91–124). New York: Wiley.

Giachetti, I., & MacLeod, P. (1975). Cortical neuron responses to odours in the rat. In D. A. Denton & J. P. Coghlan (Eds.), *Olfaction and taste V* (pp. 303–307). New York: Academic Press.

Gibson, J. J. (1966). *The senses considered as perceptual systems*. Boston: Houghton Mifflin.

Gibson, J. J. (1979). *The ecological approach to visual perception*. Boston: Houghton Mifflin.

Gibson, R. H., & Tomko, D. L. (1972). The relation between category and magnitude estimates of tactile intensity. *Perception & Psychophysics, 12,* 135–138.

Gilbert, A. N., & Martin, R. (1996). Cross-modal correspondence between vision and olfaction: The color of smells. *American Journal of Psychology, 109,* 335–351.

Gilchrist, A. L. (1980). When does perceived lightness depend on perceived spatial arrangement? *Perception & Psychophysics, 28,* 527–538.

Gilchrist, A. L. (1988). Lightness contrast and failures of constancy: A common explanation. *Perception & Psychophysics, 43,* 415–424.

Gilchrist, A. L., & Bonato, F. (1995). Anchoring of lightness values in center-surround displays. *Journal of Experimental Psychology: Human Perception & Performance, 21,* 1427–1440.

Gilchrist, A. L., Delman, S., & Jacobsen, A. (1983). The classification and integration of edges as critical to the perception of reflectance and illumination. *Perception & Psychophysics, 33,* 425–436.

Gilchrist, A. L., & Jacobsen, A. (1984). Perception of lightness and illumination in a world of one reflectance. *Perception, 13,* 5–19.

Gilger, J. W., & Ho, H. (1989). Gender differences in adult spatial information processing: Their relationship to pubertal timing, adolescent activities and sex-typing of personality. *Cognitive Development, 4,* 197–214.

Gilinsky, A. S. (1989). The moon illusion in a unified theory of visual space. In M. Hershenson (Ed.), *The moon illusion* (pp. 167–192). Hillsdale, NJ: Erlbaum.

Gillam, B. (1980). Geometrical illusions. *Scientific American, 242,* 102–111.

Gilmore, M. M., & Murphy, C. (1989). Aging is associated with increased Weber ratios for caffeine, but not for sucrose. *Perception & Psychophysics, 46,* 555–559.

Gintzler, A. R. (1980). Endorphin-mediated increases in pain threshold during pregnancy. *Science, 210,* 193–195.

Girgus, J. S., & Coren, S. (1987). The interaction between stimulus variations and age trends in the Poggendorff illusion. *Perception & Psychophysics, 41,* 60–66.

Glaser, A. L., & Slotnick, B. M. (1995). Visual inspection alone produces a decrement in the horizontal vertical illusion. *Perceptual & Motor Skills, 81,* 323–330.

Glass, A. L., & Holyoak, K. J. (1986). *Cognition.* New York: Random House.

Gliner, J. A., Horvath, S. M., & Mihevic, P. M. (1983). Carbon monoxide and human performance in a single and dual task methodology. *Aviation, Space and Environmental Medicine, 54,* 714–717.

Glorig, A., Wheeler, D., Quigle, R., Grings, W., & Summerfield, A. (1970). 1954 Wisconsin State Fair hearing survey: Statistical treatment of clinical and audiometric data. Cited in D. D. Kryter, *The effects of noise on man* (p. 116). New York: Academic Press.

Glucksberg, S., & Cowen, G. N. Jr. (1970). Memory for nonattended auditory material. *Cognitive Psychology, 1,* 149–156.

Gogel, W. C., & DaSilva, J. A. (1987a). A two-process theory of the response to size and distance. *Perception & Psychophysics, 41,* 220–238.

Gogel, W. C., & DaSilva, J. A. (1987b). Familiar size and the theory of off-sized perceptions. *Perception & Psychophysics, 41,* 318–328.

Gogel, W. C., Gregg, J. M., & Wainwright, A. (1961). *Convergence as a cue to absolute distance.* (Report No. 467, pp. 1–16). Fort Knox, KY: U.S. Army Medical Research Laboratory.

Gogel, W. C., & Koslow, M. (1972). The adjacency principle and induced movement. *Perception & Psychophysics, 11,* 309–324.

Gold, D., Andres, D., Arbuckle, T., & Schwartzman, A. (1988). Measurement and correlates of verbosity in elderly people. *Journal of Gerontology: Psychological Sciences, 43,* P27-P33.

Goldfoot, D. A. (1981). Olfaction, sexual behavior and the pheromone hypothesis in the rhesus monkey: A critique. *American Zoologist, 21,* 153–164.

Goldfoot, D. A., Essock-Vitale, S. M., Asa, C. S., Thornton, J. E., & Leshner, A. I. (1978). Anosmia in male rhesus monkeys does not alter copulatory activity with cycling females. *Science, 199,* 1095–1096.

Goldstein, E. B. (1980). *Sensation and perception.* Belmont, CA: Wadsworth.

Goldstein, J. L. (1973). An optimum processor theory for the central formation of the pitch of complex tones. *Journal of the Acoustical Society of America, 54,* 1496–1516.

Goldstone, S., Boardman, W. K., & Lhamon, W. T. (1958). Effect of quinal barbitone dextro-amphetamine, and placebo on apparent time. *British Journal of Psychology, 49,* 324–328.

Gombrich, E. H. (1972). The mask and the face: The perception of physiognomic likeness in life and in art. In E. H. Gombrich, J. Hochberg, & M. Black (Eds.), *Art, perception and reality* (pp. 1–46). Baltimore: Johns Hopkins Press.

Goodale, M. A., & Milner, A. D. (1991). A neurological dissociation between perceiving objects and grasping them. *Nature, 349,* 154–156.

Goodman, L., & Gilman, A. (Eds.). (1965). *The pharmacological basis of therapeutics.* New York: Macmillan.

Goodman, N. (1968). *Languages of art.* New York: Bobbs-Merrill.

Goodson, R., & Rahe, A. (1981). Visual training effects on normal vision. *American Journal of Optometry and Physiological Optics, 58,* 787–791.

Goodwin, M., Gooding, K. M., & Regnier, F. (1979). Sex pheromone in the dog. *Science, 203,* 559–561.

Goolkasian, P. (1980). Cyclic changes in pain perception: A ROC analysis. *Perception & Psychophysics, 27,* 499–504.

Goto, H. (1971). Auditory perception by normal Japanese adults of the sounds "L" or "R." *Neuropsychologia, 9,* 317–323.

Gottlieb, M. D., Kietzman, M. I., & Bernhaus, I. J. (1985). Two-pulse measures of temporal integration in the fovea and peripheral retina. *Perception & Psychophysics, 37,* 135–138.

Gottlieb, G. (1981). Roles of early experience in species-specific perceptual development. In R. Aslin, J. Alberts, & M. Petersen (Eds.), *Development of perception: Psychobiological perspectives, Vol. 1. Audition, somatic perception and the chemical senses* (pp. 5–44). New York: Academic Press.

Gouras, P., & Zrenner, E. (1981). Color coding in primate retina. *Vision Research, 21,* 1591–1598.

Gracely, R. H., & Naliboff, B. D. (1996). Measurement of pain sensation. In L. Kruger (Ed.), *Pain and touch* (pp. 243–313). San Diego: Academic Press.

Graham, C. H. (1965). Visual space perception. In C. H. Graham (Ed.), *Vision and visual perception* (pp. 504–547). New York: Wiley.

Graham, C. H., & Hisa, Y. (1958). Color defect and color theory. *Science, 127,* 657–682.

Graham, N. (1980). Spatial-frequency channels in human vision: Detecting edges without edge detectors. In C. S. Harris (Ed.), *Visual coding and adaptability* (pp. 215–262). New York: Erlbaum.

Graham, N. (1981). Psychophysics of spatial-frequency channels. In M. Kubovy & J. Pomerantz (Eds.), *Perceptual organization* (pp. 1–26). Hillsdale, NJ: Erlbaum.

Graham, N. V. S. (1989). *Vision pattern analyzers*. New York: Oxford University Press.

Grailet, J. M., & Seron, X. (1990). Case report of a visual integrative agnosia. *Cognitive Neuropsychology, 7*, 275–309.

Granger, G. W., & Ikeda, H. (1976). Drugs and visual thresholds. In A. Herxheimer (Ed.), *Drugs and sensory functions* (pp. 299–344). London: Churchill.

Granrud, C. E. (1986). Binocular vision and spatial perception in 4- and 5-month-old infants. *Journal of Experimental Psychology: Human Perception and Performance, 12*, 36–49.

Granrud, C. E., Haake, R. J., & Yonas, A. (1985). Infants' sensitivity to familiar size: The effect of memory on spatial perception. *Perception & Psychophysics, 37*, 459–466.

Granrud, C. E., & Yonas, A. (1985). Infants' sensitivity to the depth cue of shading. *Perception & Psychophysics, 37*, 415–419.

Granrud, C. E., Yonas, A., & Pettersen, L. (1984). A comparison of monocular and binocular depth perception in 5- and 7-month-old infants. *Journal of Experimental Child Psychology, 38*, 19–32.

Grau, J. W., & Nelson, D. G. K. (1988). The distinction between integral and separable dimensions: Evidence for the integrality of pitch and loudness. *Journal of Experimental Psychology: General, 117*, 347–370.

Gravetter, F., & Lockhead, G. R. (1973). Criterial range as a frame of reference for stimulus judgment. *Psychological Review, 80*, 203–216.

Gray, C. M., Konig, P., Engel, A. K., & Singer, W. (1989). Oscillatory responses in cat visual cortex exhibit intercolumnar synchronization which reflects global stimulus properties. *Nature, 338*, 334–337.

Green, B. G. (1985). Heat pain thresholds in the oral-facial region. *Perception & Psychophysics, 38*, 110–114.

Green, B. G. (1987). The effect of cooling on the vibrotactile sensitivity of the tongue. *Perception & Psychophysics, 42*, 423–430.

Green, D. G., & Powers, M. K. (1982). Mechanisms of light adaptation in rat retina. *Vision Research, 22*, 209–216.

Green, D. M. (1976). *An introduction to hearing*. New York: Academic Press.

Green, D. M. (1987). *Profile analysis: Auditory intensity discrimination*. New York: Oxford University Press.

Green, D. M., Nachmias, J., Kearny, J. K., & Jeffress, L. A. (1979). Intensity discrimination with gated and continuous sinusoids. *Journal of the Acoustical Society of America, 66*, 1051–1056.

Green, D. M., & Swets, J. A. (1974). *Signal detection theory and psychophysics* (reprint). New York: Krieger. (Original work published 1966)

Green, D. W., Hammond, E. J., & Supramaniam, S. (1983). Letters and shapes: Developmental changes in search strategies. *British Journal of Psychology, 74*, 11–16.

Green, K. P., Tomiak, G. R., & Kuhl, P. K. (1997). The encoding of rate and talker information during phonetic perception. *Perception & Psychophysics, 59*, 675–692.

Green, P. R., & Davies, I. B. (1993). Interaction of visual and tactile information in the control of chicks' locomotion in the visual cliff. *Perception, 22*, 1319–1331.

Greene, H. A., & Madden, D. J. (1987). Adult age differences in visual acuity, stereopsis, and contrast sensitivity. *American Journal of Optometry and Physiological Optics, 64*, 749–753.

Greenberg, M. J. (1981). The dependence of odor intensity on the hydrophobic properties of molecules. In H. R. Moskowitz & C. B. Warren (Eds.), *Odor quality and chemical structure* (pp. 177–194). Washington, DC: American Chemical Society.

Greenspan, J. D., & Bolanowski, S. J. (1996). The psychophysics of tactile perception and its physiological basis. In L. Kruger (Ed.), *Pain and touch* (pp. 25–103). San Diego: Academic Press.

Greenwood, D. D. (1990). A cochlear frequency-position function for several species—29 years later. *Journal of the Acoustical Society of America, 87*, 2592–2605.

Gregory, R. L. (1966). *Eye and brain*. New York: World University Library.

Gregory, R. L. (1971). *Concepts and mechanisms of perception*. London: Duckworth.

Gregory, R. L. (1978). *Eye and brain* (3rd ed.). New York: McGraw-Hill.

Grice, G. R., Nullmeyer, R., & Schnizlein, J. M. (1979). Variable criterion analysis of brightness effects in simple reaction time. *Journal of Experimental Psychology: Human Performance and Perception, 5*, 303–314.

Groos, G., & Daan, S. (1985). The use of the biological clocks in time perception. In J. A. Michon & J. L. Jackson (Eds.), *Time, mind and behavior* (pp. 65–74). Berlin: Springer-Verlag.

Groos, G., & Meijer, J. H. (1985). The effects of illumination on suprachiasmatic nucleus electrical discharge. *Annals of the New York Academy of Sciences, 453*, 134–146.

Gross, C. G., Rocha-Miranda, E. C., & Bender, D. B. (1972). Visual properties of neurons in inferotemporal cortex of the macaque. *Journal of Neurophysiology, 35*, 96–111.

Gross, J., & Hayne, H. (1996). Eyewitness identification by 5- to 6-year-old children. *Law & Human Behavior, 20*, 359–373.

Grossberg, J. M., & Grant, B. F. (1978). Clinical psychophysics. *Psychological Bulletin, 85*, 1154–1176.

Grossberg, S. (1983). The quantized geometry of visual space: The coherent computation of depth, form, and lightness. *Behavioral and Brain Sciences, 6*, 625–692.

Grossberg, S. (1987). Cortical dynamics of three-dimensional form, color, and brightness perception: I. Monocular theory. *Perception & Psychophysics, 41*, 87–116.

Grossberg, S. (1995). The attentive brain. *American Scientist, 83*, 438–449.

Grosvenor, T., & Flom, M. C. (Eds.). (1991). *Refractive anomalies: Research and clinical applications*. Boston: Butterworth-Heineman.

Grunau, R. V. E., & Craig, K. D. (1987). Pain expression in neonates: Facial action and cry. *Pain, 28*, 395–410.

Grzegorczyk, P. B., Jones, S. W., & Mistretta, C. M. (1979). Age-related differences in salt taste acuity. *Journal of Gerontology, 34*, 834–940.

Guenther, F. H., & Gjaja, M. N. (1996). The perceptual magnet effect as an emergent property of neural map formation. *Journal of the Acoustical Society of America, 100*, 1111–1121.

Guillery, R. W., Feig, S. L., & Lozsádi, D. A. (1998). Paying attention to the thalamic reticular nucleus. *Trends in Neuroscience, 21*, 28–32.

Guirao, M. (1991). A single scale based on ratio and partition estimates. In S. J. Bolanowski & G. A. Gescheider (Eds.), *Ratio scaling of psychological magnitude* (pp. 59–78). Hillsdale, NJ: Erlbaum.

Guitton, D., Crommelink, M., & Roucoux, A. (1980). Stimulation of the superior colliculus in the alert cat: Eye movement and neck EMG activity evoked when the head is restrained. *Experimental Brain Research, 39*, 63–74.

Gulick, W. L. (1971). *Hearing: Physiology and psychophysics*. London and New York: Oxford University Press.

Gurnsey, R., & Browse, R. A. (1987). Micropattern properties and presentation conditions influencing visual texture discrimination. *Perception & Psychophysics, 41*, 239–252.

Gurnsey, R., & Browse, R. A. (1989). Asymmetries in visual texture discrimination. *Spatial Vision, 4*, 31–44.

Gustafson, R. (1986). Effect of moderate doses of alcohol on simple auditory reaction time in a vigilance setting. *Perceptual and Motor Skills, 62,* 683–690.

Guzman, A. (1971). Analysis of curved line drawings using context and global information. *Machine Intelligence, 6,* 325–375. Edinburgh: Edinburgh University Press.

Gwiazda, J., & Bauer, J. (1989). From visual acuity to hyperacuity: A 10-year update. *Canadian Journal of Psychology, 43,* 109–120.

Gwiazda, J., Brill, S., Mohindra, I., & Held, R. (1980). Preferential looking acuity in infants from 2 to 58 weeks of age. *American Journal of Optometry and Physiological Optics, 57,* 428–432.

Haaf, R. (1977). Visual responses to complex facelike patterns by 15 and 20 week old infants. *Developmental Psychology, 38,* 893–899.

Haber, R. N. (1980). Perceiving space from pictures: A theoretical analysis. In M. Hagen (Ed.), *Perception of pictures. Vol. 1. Alberti's window: The projective model of pictorial information* (pp. 3–31). New York: Academic Press.

Haber, R. N., & Hershenson, M. (1965). The effects of repeated brief exposures on the growth of a percept. *Journal of Experimental Psychology, 69,* 40–46.

Hadjistavropoulos, H. D., & Craig, K. D. (1994). Judging pain in newborns: Facial and cry determinants. *Journal of Pediatric Psychology, 19,* 485–491.

Hafter, E. R., & Buell, T. (1990). Restarting the adapted binaural system. *Journal of the Acoustical Society of America, 88,* 806–812.

Hafter, E. R., & Schlauch, R. S. (1991). Cognitive factors and selection of auditory listening bands. In A. L. Dancer, D. Henderson, R. J. Salvi, & R. P. Hammernik (Eds.), *Noise induced hearing loss* (pp. 303–310). Philadelphia: B. C. Decker.

Hagen, M., & Jones, R. (1978). Cultural effects on pictorial perception: How many words is one picture really worth? In R. Walk & H. Pick (Eds.), *Perception and experience* (pp. 171–212). New York: Plenum Press.

Hahn, H. (1934). Die Adaptation des Geschmackssinnes. *Zeitschrift fuer Sinnesphysiologie, 65,* 105–145.

Hainline, L. (1978). Developmental changes in the scanning of face and nonface patterns by infants. *Journal of Experimental Child Psychology, 25,* 90–115.

Haith, M. M., Bergman, T., & Moore, M. J. (1977). Eye contact and face scanning in early infancy. *Science, 198,* 853–855.

Haith, M. M., Hazan, C., & Goodman, G. S. (1988). Expectation and anticipation of dynamic visual events by 3.5-month-old babies. *Child Development, 59,* 467–479.

Hall, J. W., & Grose, J. H. (1995). Amplitude discrimination in masking release paradigms. *Journal of the Acoustical Society of America, 98,* 847–852.

Hall, J. W., Haggard, M. P., & Fernandes, M. A. (1984). Detection in noise by spectro-temporal pattern analysis. *Journal of the Acoustical Society of America, 76,* 50–56.

Hall, J. W. III, & Peters, R. W. (1982). Change in the pitch of a complex tone following its association with a second complex tone. *Journal of the Acoustical Society of America, 71,* 142–146.

Hall, M. D., & Pastore, R. E. (1992). Musical duplex perception: Perception of figurally good chords with subliminal distinguishing tones. *Journal of Experimental Psychology: Human Perception and Performance, 18,* 752–762.

Hall, M. J., Bartoshuk, L. M., Cain, W. S., & Stevens, J. C. (1975). PTC taste blindness and the taste of caffeine. *Nature (London), 253,* 442–443.

Hall, W. G., & Oppenheim, R. W. (1987). Developmental psychobiology: Prenatal, perinatal and early postnatal aspects of behavioral development. *Annual Review of Psychology, 38,* 91–128.

Halpern, B. P., & Meiselman, H. L. (1980). Taste psychophysics based on a simulation of human drinking. *Chemical Senses, 5,* 279–294.

Halpern, D. F. (1986). *Sex differences in cognitive abilities.* Hillsdale, NJ: Erlbaum.

Halpern, D. F. (1992). *Sex differences in cognitive ability.* Hillsdale, NJ: Erlbaum.

Halpern, D. L., Blake, R., & Hillenbrand, J. (1986). Psychoacoustics of a chilling sound. *Perception & Psychophysics, 39,* 77–80.

Halsam, D. (1967). Individual differences in pain threshold and level of arousal. *British Journal of Psychology, 58,* 139–142.

Hamalainen, H., & Jarvilehto, T. (1981). Peripheral neural basis of tactile sensations in man: I. Effect of frequency and probe area on sensations elicited by single mechanical pulses on hairy and glabrous skin of the hand. *Brain Research, 219,* 1–12.

Hamasaki, D. J., & Sutija, V. G. (1979). Development of X- and Y-cells in kittens. *Experimental Brain Research, 35,* 9–23.

Hamid, P N., & Newport, A. G. (1989). Effect of colour on physical strength and mood in children. *Perceptual and Motor Skills, 69,* 179–185.

Hamm, V.P., & Hasher, L. (1992). Age and the availablity of inferences. *Psychology & Aging, 7,* 56-64.

Handel, S., & Garner, W. R. (1965). The structure of visual pattern associates and pattern goodness. *Perception & Psychophysics, 1,* 33–38.

Handel, S., & Oshinsky, J. S. (1981). The meter of syncopated auditory polyrhythms. *Perception & Psychophysics, 30,* 1–9.

Hanna, T. E., von Gierke, S. M., & Green, D. M. (1986). Detection and intensity discrimination of a sinusoid. *Journal of the Acoustical Society of America, 80,* 1335–1340.

Hantz, E. C., & Kreilick, K. G. (1995). Effects of musical training and absolute pitch on a pitch memory task: An event-related potential study. *Psychomusicology, 14,* 53–76.

Hardie, R. C., & Kirschfeld, K. (1983). Ultraviolet sensitivity of fly photoreceptors R7 and R8: Evidence for a sensitizing function. *Biophysics of Structure and Mechanism, 9,* 171–180.

Hardy, J. D., Stolwijk, J. A. J., & Hoffman, D. (1968). Pain following step increase in skin temperature. In D. R. Kenshalo (Ed.), *The skin senses* (pp. 444–457). Springfield, IL: Thomas.

Hardy, J. D., Wolff, H. G., & Goodell, B. S. (1943). The pain threshold in man. *Research Publications Association for Research in Nervous and Mental Disease, 23,* 1–15.

Hardy, J. D., Wolff, H. G., & Goodell, H. (1947). Studies on pain: Discrimination of differences in intensity of a pain stimulus as a basis of a scale of pain intensity. *Journal of Clinical Investigation, 26,* 1152–1158.

Hari, R. (1994). Human cortical functions revealed by magnetoencephalography. *Progress in Brain Research, 100,* 163–168.

Harkins, S., & Green, R. G. (1975). Discriminability and criterion differences between extraverts and introverts during vigilance. *Journal of Research in Personality, 9,* 335–340.

Harkins, S. W., & Chapman, C. R. (1977). The perception of induced dental pain in young and elderly women. *Journal of Gerontology, 32,* 428–435.

Harmon, L. D. (1973). The recognition of faces. *Scientific American, 229,* 70–82.

Harmon, L. D., & Julesz, B. (1973). Masking in visual recognition: Effects of two dimensional filtered noise. *Science, 180,* 1194–1197.

Harper, R. S. (1953). The perceptual modification of coloured figures. *American Journal of Psychology, 66,* 86–89.

Harris, C. S. (1980). Insight or out of sight?: Two examples of perceptual plasticity in the human adult. In C. S. Harris (Ed.), *Visual coding and adaptability* (pp. 95–149). Hillsdale, NJ: Erlbaum.

Harris, L. J. (1981). Sex related variations in spatial skill. In L. S. Liben, A. H. Patterson, & N. Newcombe (Eds.), *Spatial representation and behavior across the lifespan: Theory and application* (pp. 83–128). New York: Academic Press.

Harris, P., & MacFarlane, A. (1974). The growth of the effective visual field from birth to seven weeks. *Journal of Experimental Child Psychology, 18*, 340–348.

Harrison, R. V., Nagasawa, A., Smith, D. W., Stanton, S., & Mount, R. J. (1991). Reorganization of auditory cortex after neonatal high frequency cochlear hearing loss. *Hearing Research, 54*, 11–19.

Harrison, W. A., & Burns, E. M. (1993). Effects of contralateral acoustic stimulation on spontaneous otoacoustic emissions. *Journal of the Acoustical Society of America, 94*, 2649–2658.

Harter, M., & Suitt, C. (1970). Visually-evoked cortical responses and pattern vision in the infant: A longitudinal study. *Psychonomic Science, 18*, 235–237.

Hartley, A. A., Keiley, J. M., & Slabach, E. H. (1990). Age differences and similarities in the effects of cues and prompts. *Journal of Experimental Psychology: Human Perception and Performance, 16*, 523–537.

Hartline, H. K. (1940). The receptive fields of optic nerve fibers. *American Journal of Physiology, 130*, 690–699.

Hartline, H. K., & Ratliff, F. (1957). Inhibitory interaction of receptor units in the eye of Limulus. *Journal of General Physiology, 40*, 357–376.

Hartman, A., & Hollister, L. (1963). Effect of mescaline, lysergic acid diethylamide and psilocybin on color perception. *Psychopharmacologia, 4*, 441–451.

Hartman, M., and Hasher, L. (1991). Aging and suppression: Memory for previously relevant information. *Psychology & Aging, 6*, 587-594.

Hartmann, W. M., & Rakerd, B. (1993). Auditory spectral discrimination and the localization of clicks in the sagittal plane. *Journal of the Acoustical Society of America, 94*, 2083–2092.

Hartmann, W. M., & Rakerd, B. (1989). On the minimum audible angle—a decision theory approach. *Journal of the Acoustical Society of America, 85*, 2031–2141.

Harvey, L. O. Jr., & Leibowitz, H. (1967). Effects of exposure duration, cue reduction, and temporary monocularity on size matching at short distances.

Journal of the Optical Society of America, 57, 249–253.

Hasher, L., & Quig, M. B. (1997). Inhibitory control over no longer relevant information: Adult age differences. *Memory and Cognition, 25*, 286–295.

Hasher, L., & Zacks, R. T. (1988). Working memory, comprehension, and aging: A review and a new view. In G. H. Bower (Ed.), *The psychology of learning and motivation: Advances in research and theory, Vol. 22* (pp. 193–225). New York: Academic Press.

Hatfield, G., & Epstein, W. (1985). The status of the minimum principle in the theoretical analysis of visual perception. *Psychological Bulletin, 97*, 155–186.

Haug, B. A., & Kolle, R. U. (1995). Predominant affection of the blue cone pathway in Parkinson's disease. *Brain, 118*, 771–778.

Hausen, K. (1982). Movement sensitive interneurons in the optomotor system of the fly. II. The horizontal cells: Receptive field organization and response characteristics. *Biological Cybernetics, 46*, 67–79.

He, J., Hashikawa, T., Ojima, H., & Kinouchi, Y. (1997). Temporal integration and duration tuning in the dorsal zone of cat auditory cortex. *The Journal of Neuroscience, 17*, 2615–2625.

He, L. (1987). Involvement of endogenous opioid peptides in acupuncture analgesia. *Pain, 31*, 99–122.

He, L., Lu, R., Zhuang, S., Zhang, X., & Pan, X. (1985). Possible involvement of opioid peptides of caudate nucleus in acupuncture analgesia. *Pain, 23*, 83–93.

He, S., Cavanagh, P., & Intriligator, J. (1996). Attentional resolution and the locus of visual awareness. *Nature, 383*, 334–337.

He, Z. J., & Nakayama, K. (1992). Surfaces versus features in visual search. *Nature, 359*, 231–233.

Head, H. (1920). *Studies in neurology*. London & New York: Oxford University Press.

Heaton, J. M. (1968). *The eye: Phenomenology and psychology of function and disorder*. London: Tavistock.

Hecht, H., & Proffitt, D. (1991). Apparent extended body motions in depth. *Journal of Experimental Psychology: Human Perception and Performance, 17*, 1090–1103.

Hecht, S., & Mandelbaum, M. (1938). Rod-cone dark adaptation and vitamin A. *Science, 88*, 219–221.

Hecht, S., Shlaer, S., & Pirenne, M. H. (1942). Energy quanta and vision. *Journal of General Physiology, 25*, 819–840.

Heckmann, T., Post, R. B., & Deering, L. (1991). Induced motion of a fixated target: Influence of voluntary eye deviation. *Perception & Psychophysics, 50*, 230–236.

Heffner, H. E., & Heffner, R. S. (1984). Temporal lobe lesions and perception of species-specific vocalizations by macaques. *Science, 226*, 75 76.

Heggelund, P. (1981a). Receptive field organization of simple cells in cat striate cortex. *Experimental Brain Research, 42*, 89–98.

Heggelund, P. (1981b). Receptive field organization of complex cells in cat striate cortex. *Experimental Brain Research, 42*, 99–107.

Hein, A., & Held, R. (1967). Dissociation of the visual placing response into elicited and guided components. *Science, 158*, 390–392.

Hein, A., Held, R., & Gower, E. C. (1970). Development and segmentation of visually controlled movement by selective exposure during rearing. *Journal of Comparative and Physiological Psychology, 73*, 181–187.

Hein, A., & Diamond, R. M. (1971). Contrasting development of visually triggered and guided movements in kittens with respect to interocular and interline equivalence. *Journal of Comparative and Physiological Psychology, 76*, 219–224.

Heinemann, E. G., & Chase, S. (1995). A quantitative model for simultaneous brightness induction. *Vision Research, 35*, 2007–2020.

Held, R. (1985). Binocular vision—behavioral and neuronal development. In J. Mehler & R. Fox (Eds.), *Neonate cognition: Beyond the blooming buzzing confusion* (pp. 37–44). Hillsdale, NJ: Erlbaum.

Held, R. (1993). Binocular vision—Behavioral and neuronal development. In M. H. Johnson (Ed.), *Brain development and cognition: A reader* (pp. 152–166). Oxford, UK: Blackwell.

Held, R., & Bauer, J. A. (1967). Visually guided reaching in infant monkeys after restricted rearing. *Science, 155*, 718–720.

Held, R., & Bossom, J. (1961). Neonatal deprivation and adult rearrangement: Complementary techniques for analyzing plastic sensory-motor coordinations. *Journal of Comparative and Physiological Psychology, 54*, 33–37.

Held, R., Dichgans, J., & Bauer, J. (1975). Characteristics of moving visual scenes influencing spatial orientation. *Vision Research, 15*, 357–365.

Held, R., & Hein, A. (1958). Adaptation of disarranged hand-eye coordination contingent upon reafferent stimulation. *Perceptual and Motor Skills, 8*, 87–90.

Held, R., & Hein, A. (1963). Movement-produced stimulation in the development of visually guided behavior. *Journal of Comparative and Physiological Psychology, 56*, 872–876.

Held, R., & Hein, A. (1967). On the modifiability of form perception. In W. Wathen-Dunn (Ed.), *Models for the perception of speech and visual form* (pp. 296–304). Cambridge, MA: MIT Press.

Hellekant, G. (1965). Electrophysiological investigation of the gustatory effect of ethyl alcohol: The summated response of the chorda tympani in the cat, dog and rat. *Acta Physiologica Scandinavica, 64*, 392–397.

Heller, M. A. (1989). Texture perception in sighted and blind observers. *Perception & Psychophysics, 45*, 49–54.

Heller, M. A., Calcaterra, J. A., Burson, L. L., & Green, S. L. (1997). The tactual-horizontal-vertical illusion depends on radial motion of the entire arm. *Perception & Psychophysics, 59*, 1297–1311.

Hellman, R. P., & Zwislocki, J. J. (1968). Loudness determination at low sound frequencies. *Journal of the Acoustical Society of America, 43*, 60–64.

Hellstrom, A. (1979). Time errors and differential sensation weighting. *Journal of Experimental Psychology: Human Perception and Performance, 5*, 460–477.

Hellstrom, A. (1985). The time-order error and its relatives: Mirrors of cognitive processes in comparing. *Psychological Bulletin, 97*, 35–61.

Helmholtz, H. E. F. von (1930). *The sensations of tone* (A. J. Ellis, Trans.). New York: Longmans, Green. (Original work published 1863)

Helmholtz, H. E. F. von (1962). *Treatise on physiological optics* (J. P. C. Southall, Ed. and Trans.). New York: Dover. (Original work published 1909)

Helson, H. (1964). *Adaptation level theory: An experimental and systematic approach to behavior.* New York: Harper.

Henderson, J. M., & Pollatsek, A. (1989). Covert visual attention and extrafoveal information use during object identification. *Perception & Psychophysics, 45*, 196–208.

Henmon, V. A. C. (1906). The time of perception as a measure of differences in sensations. *Archives of Philosophy, Psychology and Scientific Methods*, No. 8.

Henn, V., Cohen, B., & Young, L. (1980). Visual-vestibular interaction in motion perception and the generation of nystagmus. *Neurosciences Research Program Bulletin, 18*, 459–651.

Henn, V., Young, L. R., & Finley, C. (1974). Vestibular nucleus units in alert monkeys are also influenced by moving visual field. *Brain Research, 71*, 144–149.

Henning, H. (1916). Die Qualitatenreihe des Geschmaks. *Zeitschrift fuer Psychologie, 74*, 203–219.

Hensel, H. (1981). *Thermoreception and temperature regulation.* New York: Academic Press.

Hermes, D. J. (1990). Vowel-onset detection. *Journal of the Acoustical Society of America, 87*, 866–873.

Hernandez-Peon, R. (1964). Psychiatric implications of neurophysiological research. *Bulletin of the Meninger Clinic, 28*, 165–185.

Hershberger, W. (1987). Saccadic eye movements and the perception of visual direction. *Perception & Psychophysics, 41*, 35–44.

Hershberger, W. A., & Misceo, G. F. (1996). Touch dominates haptic estimates of discordant visual-haptic size. *Perception & Psychophysics, 58*, 1124–1132.

Hershenson, M. (1989). *The moon illusion.* Hillsdale, NJ: Erlbaum.

Hershenson, M., & Bader, P. (1990). Development of the spiral aftereffect. *Bulletin of the Psychonomic Society, 28*, 300–301.

Herz, R. S., & Engen, T. (1996). Odor memory: Review and analysis. *Psychonomic Bulletin & Review, 3*, 300–313.

Herzog, M. H., & Fahle M. (1997). The role of feedback in learning a vernier discrimination task. *Vision Research, 37*, 2133–2141.

Hess, E. H. (1950). Development of the chick's response to light and shade cues of depth. *Journal of Comparative and Physiological Psychology, 43*, 112–122.

Hess, R. H., Baker, C. L., & Zihl, J. (1989). The "motion-blind" patient: Low-level spatial and temporal filters. *Journal of Neuroscience, 9*, 1628–1640.

Heumann, D., & Leuba, G. (1983). Neuronal death in the development and aging of the cerebral cortex of the mouse. *Neuropathology and Applied Neurobiology, 9*, 297–311.

Heywood, C. A., & Cowey, A. (1987). On the role of cortical area V4 in the discrimination of hue and pattern in macaque monkeys. *Journal of Neuroscience, 7*, 2601–2617.

Heywood, C. A., Wilson, B., & Cowey, A. (1987). A case study of cortical colour "blindness" with relatively intact achromatic discrimination. *Journal of Neurology, Neurosurgery, and Psychiatry, 50*, 22–29.

Hick, W. E. (1952). On the rate of gain of information. *Quarterly Journal of Experimental Psychology, 4*, 11–26.

Hickey, T. L. (1977). Postnatal development of the human lateral geniculate nucleus: Relationship to a critical period for the visual system. *Science, 198*, 836–838.

Hickey, T. L., & Peduzzi, J. D. (1987). Structure and development of the visual system. In P. Salapatek & L. Cohen (Eds.), *Handbook of infant perception: Vol. 1. From sensation to perception* (pp. 1–43). Orlando: Academic Press.

Hicks, R. E., Miller, G. W., Gaes, G., & Bierman, K. (1977). Concurrent processing demands and the experience of time in passing. *American Journal of Psychology, 90*, 431–446.

Hicks, R. E., Miller, G. W., & Kinsbourne, M. (1976). Prospective and retrospective judgments of time as a function of amount of information processed. *American Journal of Psychology, 89*, 719–730.

Hier, D. B., & Crowley, W. F. Jr. (1982). Spatial ability in androgen-deficient men. *New England Journal of Medicine, 306*, 1202–1205.

Higashiyama, A. (1985). The effects of familiar size on judgments of size and distance: An interaction of viewing attitude with spatial cues. *Perception & Psychophysics, 35*, 305–312.

Higgins, S. T., & Bickel, W. K. (1990). Effects of intranasal cocaine on human learning, performance and physiology. *Psychopharmacology, 102*, 451–458.

Hillyard, S. A., & Kutas, M. (1983). Electrophysiology of cognitive processing. *Annual Review of Psychology, 34*, 33–61.

Hirsch, H. V. (1972). Visual perception in cats after environmental surgery. *Experimental Brain Research, 15*, 409–423.

Hirsch, H. V., & Spinelli, D. N. (1970). Visual experience modifies distribution of horizontally and vertically oriented receptive fields in cats. *Science, 168*, 869–871.

Hirsh, I. J., & Watson, C. S. (1996). Auditory psychophysics and perception. *Annual Review of Psychology, 47*, 461–484.

Hoagland, H. (1933). The physiological control of judgment of duration: Evidence for a chemical clock. *Journal of General Psychology, 9*, 267–287.

Hochberg, J. (1971). Perception: II. Space and movement. In J. W. Kling & L. A. Riggs (Eds.), *Woodworth and Schlossberg's experimental psychology* (3rd ed., pp. 475–550). New York: Holt, Rinehart and Winston.

Hochberg, J. (1974). Higher-order stimuli and interresponse coupling in the perception of the visual world. In R. B. Macleod & H. L. Pick (Eds.), *Perception: Essays in honor of James J. Gibson* (pp. 17–39). Ithaca: Cornell University Press.

Hochberg, J. (1981). On cognition in perception: Perceptual coupling and unconscious inference. *Cognition, 10,* 127–134.

Hochberg, J. (1982). How big is a stimulus? In J. Beck (Ed.), *Organization and representation in perception* (pp. 191–218). Hillsdale, NJ: Erlbaum.

Hochberg, J., & Beck, J. (1954). Apparent spatial arrangement and perceived brightness. *Journal of Experimental Psychology, 47,* 263–266.

Hochberg, J., & Brooks, V. (1960). The psychophysics of form: Reversible-perspective drawings of spatial objects. *American Journal of Psychology, 73,* 337–354.

Hochberg, J., & Brooks, V. (1962). Pictorial recognition as an unlearned ability: A study of one child's performance. *American Journal of Psychology, 75,* 624–628.

Hockey, G. R. (1970). Effect of loud noise on attentional selectivity. *Quarterly Journal of Experimental Psychology, 22,* 28–36.

Hoffer, A., & Osmond, H. (1967). *The hallucinogens.* New York: Academic Press.

Hoffman, J. E. (1980). Interaction between global and local levels of form. *Journal of Experimental Psychology: Human Perception and Performance, 6,* 222–234.

Hoffman, J. E., Nelson, B., & Houck, M. R. (1983). The role of attentional resources in automatic detection. *Cognitive Psychology, 51,* 379–410.

Hoffman, K. P. (1979). Optokinetic nystagmus and single cell responses in the nucleus tractus opticus after early monocular deprivation in the cat. In R. D. Freeman (Ed.), *Developmental neurobiology of vision* (pp. 63–72). New York: Plenum Press.

Hoffmann, K. P., & Sherman, S. (1975). Effects of early binocular deprivation on visual input to cat superior colliculus. *Journal of Neurophysiology, 38,* 1049–1059.

Hogben, J. H., & Di Lollo, V. (1985). Suppression of visible persistence in apparent motion. *Perception & Psychophysics, 38,* 450–460.

Holender, D. (1986). Semantic activation without conscious identification in dichotic listening, parafoveal vision, and visual masking: A survey and appraisal. *The Behavioral and Brain Sciences, 9,* 1–23.

Holland, H. (1960). Drugs and personality: XII. A comparison of several drugs by the flicker-fusion method. *Journal of Mental Science, 106,* 858–861.

Holst, E. von, & Mittelstaedt, H. (1950). Das Reafferenzprincip (wechselwirkungen zeischen zentral Nervensystem und Periphere). *Naturwissenschaften, 37,* 464–476.

Holway, A. F., & Boring, E. G. (1941). Determinants of apparent visual size with distance variant. *American Journal of Psychology, 54,* 21–37.

Honda, H. (1984). Functional between-hand differences and outflow eye position information. *Quarterly Journal of Experimental Psychology, 36A,* 75–88.

Hood, B. M. (1993). Inhibition of return produced by covert shifts of visual attention in 6-month-old infants. *Infant Behavior and Development, 16,* 245-254.

Hood, B. M., & Atkinson, J. (1991). Sensory visual loss and cognitive deficits in the selective attentional system of normal infants and neurologically impaired children. *Developmental Medicine and Child Neurology, 32,* 1067–1077.

Hood, B. M., & Atkinson, J. (1993). Disengaging visual attention in the infant and adult. *Infant Behavior & Development, 16,* 405–422.

Horn, B. K. P. (1977). Understanding image intensities. *Artificial Intelligence, 8,* 201–231.

Horn, B. K. P. (1986). *Robot vision.* Cambridge, MA: MIT Press.

Horner, D. T. (1991). The effects of complexity on the perception of vibrotactile patterns. *Perception & Psychophysics, 49,* 551– 562.

Horner, D. T. (1997). The effect of shape and location on temporal masking of spatial vibrotactile patterns. *Perception & Psychophysics, 59,* 1255–1265.

Horton, J. C., & Sherk, H. (1984). Receptive field properties in the cat's lateral geniculate nucleus in the absence of on-center retinal input. *Journal of Neuroscience, 4,* 374–380.

Houck, M. R., & Hoffman, J. E. (1986). Conjunction of color and form with-out attention: Evidence from an orientation-contingent color aftereffect. *Journal of Experimental Psychology: Human Perception and Performance, 12,* 186–199.

Houtsma, A. J. M., & Goldstein, J. L. (1972). The central origin of the pitch of complex tones: Evidence from musical interval recognition. *Journal of the Acoustical Society of America, 51,* 520–529.

Howard, I. P. (1982). *Human visual orientation.* Chichester: Wiley.

Howard, I. P., Anstis, T., & Lucia, H. C. (1974). The relative lability of mobile and stationary components in a visual-motor adaptation task. *Quarterly Journal of Experimental Psychology, 26,* 293–300.

Howard, I. P., Craske, B., & Templeton, W. B. (1965). Visuomotor adaptation to discordant exafferent stimulation. *Journal of Experimental Psychology, 70,* 189–191.

Hoyer, W., & Plude, D. (1980). Attentional and perceptual processes in the study of cognitive aging. In L. Poon (Ed.), *Aging in the 1980s* (pp. 227–238). Washington, DC: American Psychological Association.

Hu, S., Grant, W. F., Stern, R. M., & Koch, K. (1991). Motion sickness severity and physiological correlates during repeated exposures to a rotating optokinetic drum. *Aviation, Space and Environmental Medicine, 62,* 308–314.

Hubbell, W. L., & Bownds, M. D. (1979). Visual transduction in vertebrate photoreceptors. *Annual Review of Neurosciences, 2,* 17–34.

Hubel, D. H., & Wiesel, T. N. (1962). Receptive fields, binocular interaction and functional architecture in the cat's visual cortex. *Journal of Physiology (London), 160,* 106–154.

Hubel, D. H., & Wiesel, T. N. (1968). Receptive fields and functional architecture of monkey striate cortex. *Journal of Physiology (London), 195,* 215–243.

Hubel, D. H., & Wiesel, T. N. (1979). Brain mechanisms of vision. *Scientific American, 82,* 84–97.

Hudson, W. (1960). Pictorial depth perception in subcultural groups in Africa. *Journal of Social Psychology, 52,* 183–208.

Hudson, W. (1962). Pictorial perception and educational adaptation in Africa. *Psychologia, Africana, 9,* 226–239.

Hudspeth, A. J. (1985). The cellular basis of hearing: The biophysics of hair cells. *Science, 230,* 745–752.

Hughes, H. C. (1986). Asymmetric interference between components of suprathreshold compound gratings. *Perception & Psychophysics, 40,* 241–250.

Hughes, H. C., Layton, W. M., Baird, J. C., & Lester, L. S. (1984). Global precedence in visual pattern recognition. *Perception & Psychophysics, 35,* 361–371.

Hughes, J. W. (1946). The threshold of audition for short periods of stimulation. *Proceedings of the Royal Society of London, Series B, 133,* 486–490.

Hukin, R. W., & Darwin, C. J. (1995). Comparison of the effect of onset asynchrony on auditory grouping in pitch matching and vowel identification. *Perception & Psychophysics, 57,* 191–196.

Hulse, S. H., & Page, S. C. (1988). Toward a comparative psychology of music perception. *Music Perception, 5,* 427–452.

Humphrey, G. K., Humphrey, D. E., Muir, D. W., & Dodwell, P. C. (1986). Pattern perception in infants: Effects of structure and transformation. *Journal of Experimental Child Psychology, 41,* 128–148.

Humphreys, G. W (1984). Shape constancy: The effects of changing shape orientation and the effects of changing the position of focal features. *Perception & Psychophysics, 36,* 50–64.

Humphries, S. A., Johnson, M. H., & Long, N. R. (1996). An investigation of the gate control theory of pain using the experimental pain stimulus of potassium iontophoresis. *Perception & Psychophysics, 58,* 693–703.

Hung, P., & Berns, R. S. (1995). Determination of constant hue loci for a CRT gamut and their predictions using color appearance spaces. *Color Research & Application, 20,* 285–295.

Hunzelmann, N., & Spillman, L. (1984). Movement adaptation in the peripheral retina. *Vision Research, 24,* 1765–1769.

Hurlbert, A. C., & Poggio, T. A. (1988). Synthesizing a color algorithm from examples. *Science, 239,* 482–485.

Hurvich, L. M. (1981). *Color vision.* Sunderland, MA: Sinauer Associates.

Hurvich, L. M., & Jameson, D. (1974). Opponent processes as a model of neural organization. *American Psychologist, 29,* 88–102.

Huttenlocher, P. R. (1990). Morphometric study of human cerebral cortex development. *Neuropsychologia, 28,* 517–527.

Huttenlocher, P. R., DeCourten, C., Garey, L. J., & Van der Loos, H. (1982). Synaptic development in human cerebral cortex. *International Journal of Neurology, 16,* 144–154.

Hutz, C. S., & Bechtoldt, H. P. (1980). The development of binocular discrimination in infants. *Bulletin of the Psychonomic Society, 16,* 83–86.

Huxley, A. (1963). *The doors of perception and heaven and hell.* New York: Harper.

Hyman, A., Mentyer, T., & Calderone, L. (1979). The contribution of olfaction to taste discrimination. *Bulletin of the Psychonomic Society, 13,* 359–362.

Iacono, W. G., Pelouqin, L. J., Lumry, A. E., Valentine, R.H., & Tuason, V. B. (1982). Eye tracking in patients with unipolar and bipolar affective disorders in remission. *Journal of Abnormal Psychology, 91,* 35–44.

Iadecola, C. (1993). Regulation of cerebral microcirculation during neural activity: Is nitric oxide the missing link? *Trends in Neurosciences, 16,* 206–214.

Iida, T. (1983). Accommodative response under reduced visual conditions. *Japanese Psychological Research, 25,* 222–227.

Imbert, M. (1985). Physiological underpinnings of perceptual development. In J. Mehler & R. Fox (Eds.), *Neonate cognition: Beyond the blooming buzzing confusion* (pp. 69–88). Hillsdale, NJ: Erlbaum.

Ingram, R. M., & Barr, A. (1979). Changes in refraction between the ages of 1 and 3 1/2 years. *British Journal of Ophthalmology, 63,* 39–342.

Intraub, H. (1985). Visual dissociation: An illusory conjunction of pictures and forms. *Journal of Experimental Psychology: Human Perception and Performance, 11,* 431–442.

Intraub, H., & Berkowits, D. (1996). Beyond the edges of a picture. *American Journal of Psychology, 109,* 581–598.

Intraub, H., & Gottesman, C. V. (1996). Boundary extension for briefly glimpsed photographs: Do common perceptual processes result in unexpected memory distortions? *Journal of Memory & Language, 35,* 118–134.

Ippolitov, F. W. (1973). Interanalyzer differences in the sensitivity-strength parameter for vision, hearing and cutaneous modalities. In V. D. Nebylitsyn & J. A. Gray (Eds.), *Biological bases of individual behavior* (pp. 43–61). New York: Academic Press.

Irwin, R. J., & Hautus, M. J. (1997). Likelihood-ratio decision strategy for independent observations in the same-different task: An approximation to the detection-theoretic model. *Perception & Psychophysics, 59,* 313–316.

Irwin, R. J., Hautus, M. J., Dawson, N. J., Welch, D., & Bayly, M. F. (1994). Discriminability of electrocutaneous stimuli after topical anesthesia: Detection-theory measurement of sensitivity to painful stimuli. *Perception & Psychophysics, 55,* 125–132.

Irwin, R. J., & Whitehead, P. R. (1991). Towards an objective psychophysics of pain. *Psychological Science, 2,* 230–235.

Ittelson, W. H. (1951). Size as a cue to distance: Static localization. *American Journal of Psychology, 64,* 54–67.

Ittelson, W. H. (1960). *Visual space perception.* Berlin and New York: Springer-Verlag.

Ittelson, W. H. (1962). Perception and transactional psychology. In S. Koch (Ed.), *Psychology: A study of a science: Vol. 4* (pp. 660–704). New York: McGraw-Hill.

Iverson, P. (1995). Auditory stream segregation by musical timbre: Effects of static and dynamic acoustic attributes. *Journal of Experimental Psychology: Human Perception and Performance, 21,* 751–763.

Jacobs, G. H. (1976). Color vision. *Annual Review of Psychology, 27,* 63–89.

Jacobs, G. H. (1986). Cones and opponency. *Vision Research, 26,* 1533–1541.

Jacobsen, A., & Gilchrist, A. (1988). The ratio principle holds over a million-to-one range of illumination. *Perception & Psychophysics, 43,* 1–6.

Jahoda, G., & McGurk, H. (1974). Pictorial depth perception: A developmental study. *British Journal of Psychology, 65,* 141–149.

James, W. (1890). *The principles of psychology.* New York: Holt, Rinehart and Winston.

Jameson, D., & Hurvich, L. M. (1959). Note on factors influencing the relation between stereoscopic acuity and observation distance. *Journal of the Optical Society of America, 49,* 639.

Jameson, D., & Hurvich, L. M. (1964). Theory of brightness and color contrast in human vision. *Vision Research, 4,* 135–154.

Jameson, D., & Hurvich, L. M. (1989). Essay concerning color constancy. *Annual Review of Psychology, 40,* 1–22.

Janal, M. N., Clark, W. C., & Carroll, J. D. (1991). Multidimensional scaling of painful and innocuous electrocutaneous stimuli: Reliability and individual differences. *Perception & Psychophysics, 50,* 108–116.

Jarvis, J. R. (1977). On Fechner-Benham subjective colour. *Vision Research, 17,* 445–451.

Jaschinski-Kruza, W. (1984). Transient myopia after visual work. *Ergonomics, 27,* 1181–1189.

Javel, E. (1981). Suppression of auditory nerve responses I: Temporal analysis, intensity effects and suppression contours. *Journal of the Acoustical Society of America, 69,* 1735–1745.

Javel, E. (1996). Long-term adaptation in cat auditory nerve fiber responses. *Journal of the Acoustical Society of America, 99,* 1040–1052.

Jeka, J. J., Easton, R. D., Bentzen, B. L., & Lackner, J. R. (1996). Haptic cues for orientation and postural control in sighted and blind individuals. *Perception & Psychophysics, 58,* 409–423.

Jenkins, B. (1985). Orientational anisotropy in the human visual system. *Perception & Psychophysics, 37,* 125–134.

Jenness, J. W., & Shevell, S. K. (1995). Color appearance with sparse chromatic context. *Vision Research, 35,* 797–805.

Jennings, J. A. M., & Charman, W. N. (1981). Off-axis image quality in the human eye. *Vision Research, 21,* 445–455.

Jesteadt, W., Bacon, S. P., & Lehman, J. R. (1982). Forward masking as a function of frequency, masker level, and signal delay. *Journal of the Acoustical Society of America, 71,* 950–962.

Jesteadt, W., & Wier, C. C. (1977). Comparison of monaural and binaural discrimination of intensity and frequency. *Journal of the Acoustical Society of America, 61,* 1599–1603.

Jesteadt, W., Wier, C. C., & Green, D. M. (1977). Intensity discrimination as a function of frequency and sensation level. *Journal of the Acoustical Society of America, 61,* 169–177.

Jin, E. W., & Shevell, S. K. (1996). Color memory and color constancy. *Journal of the Optical Society of America A-Optics & Image Science, 13,* 1981–1991.

Johansson, G. (1976a). Visual motion perception. In R. Held & W. Richards (Eds.), *Recent progress in perception: Readings from Scientific American* (pp. 67–75). San Francisco: Freeman.

Johansson, G. (1976b). Spatio-temporal differentiation and integration in visual motion perception. *Psychological Research, 38,* 379–393.

Johansson, G., von Hofsten, C., & Jansson, G. (1980). Event perception. *Annual Review of Psychology, 31,* 27–63.

John, E. R., Prichep, L. S., Fridman, J., & Easton, P. (1988). Neurometrics: Computer-assisted differential diagnosis of brain dysfunctions. *Science, 239,* 162–169.

Johnson, C. H., & Hastings, J. W. (1986). The elusive mechanism of the circadian clock. *American Scientist, 74*(1), 29–36.

Johnson, D. H. (1980). The relationship between spike rate and synchrony in responses of auditory-nerve fibers to single tones. *Journal of the Acoustical Society of America, 68,* 1115–1122.

Johnson, E. S., & Meade, A. C. (1987). Developmental patterns of spatial ability: An early sex difference. *Child Development, 58,* 725–740.

Johnson, M. A. (1986). Color vision in the peripheral retina. *American Journal of Optometry and Physiological Optics, 63,* 97–103.

Johnson, M. H. (1990). Cortical maturation and the development of visual attention in early infancy. *Journal of Cognitive Neuroscience, 2,* 81–95.

Johnson, M. H. (1995). The inhibition of automatic saccades in early infancy. *Developmental Psychobiology, 28,* 281-291.

Johnson, M. H., Dziurawiec, S., Ellis, H., & Morton, J. (1991). Newborns' preferential tracking of facelike stimuli and its subsequent decline. *Cognition, 40,* 1–19.

Johnson, M. H., & Tucker, L. A. (1996). The development and temporal dynamics of spatial orienting in infants. *Journal of Experimental Child Psychology, 63,* 171–188.

Johnson, M. H., & Vecera, S. P. (1996). Cortical differentiation and neurocognitive development: The parcellation conjecture. *Behavioural Processes, 36,* 195–212.

Johnson, S. C. (1967). Hierarchical clustering schemes. *Psychometrika, 32,* 241–254.

Johnson, T. L., & Shapiro, K. L. (1989). Attention to auditory and peripheral visual stimuli: Effects of arousal and predictability. *Acta Psychologica, 72,* 233–245.

Jones, D. T., & Reed, R. R. (1989). Golf: An olfactory neuron specific-G protein involved in odorant signal transduction. *Science, 244,* 790–795.

Jonides, J. (1980). Towards a model of the mind's eye's movements. *Canadian Journal of Psychology, 34,* 103–112.

Jonides, J. (1981). Voluntary versus automatic control over the mind's eye's movement. In J. B. Long & A. D. Baddely (Eds.), *Attention & performance: Vol. 9* (pp. 187–203). Hillsdale, NJ: Erlbaum.

Jonides, J., & Yantis, S. (1988). Uniqueness of abrupt visual onset in capturing attention. *Perception & Psychophysics, 43,* 346–355.

Joseph, J. S., & Optican, L. M. (1996). Involuntary attentional shifts due to orientation differences. *Perception & Psychophysics, 58,* 651–665.

Joubert, C. E. (1983). Subjective acceleration of time: Death anxiety and sex differences. *Perceptual and Motor Skills, 57,* 49–50.

Joubert, C. E. (1990). Subjective expectations of the acceleration of time with aging. *Perceptual and Motor Skills, 70,* 334.

Julesz, B. (1964). Binocular depth perception without familiarity cues. *Science, 145,* 356–362.

Julesz, B. (1971). *Foundations of cyclopean perception.* Chicago: University of Chicago Press.

Julesz, B. (1978). Perceptual limits of texture discrimination and their implications to figure-ground separation. In E. Leeuwenberg & H. Buffart (Eds.), *Formal theories of perception* (pp. 205–216). New York: Wiley.

Julesz, B. (1980). Spatial nonlinearities in the instantaneous perception of textures with identical power spectra. In C. Longuet-Higgins & N. S. Sutherland (Eds.), *The psychology of vision. Philosophical transactions of the Royal Society, London, 290,* 83–94.

Julesz, B. (1981). Textons, the elements of texture perception and their interactions. *Nature, 290,* 91–97.

Julesz, B. (1984). A brief outline of the texton theory of human vision. *Trends in Neuroscience, 7,* 41–45.

Julesz, B. (1986). Stereoscopic vision. *Vision Research, 26,* 1601–1612.

Julesz, B., & Bergen, J. R. (1983). Textons, the fundamental elements in preattentive vision and perception of textures. *The Bell System Technical Journal, 62,* 1619–1645.

Julesz, B., & Payne, R. A. (1968). Differences between monocular and binocular stroboscopic movement perception. *Vision Research, 8,* 433–444.

Julesz, B., & Schumer, R. A. (1981). Early visual perception. *Annual Review of Psychology, 32,* 575–627.

Jung, R. (1961). Korrelationen von Neuronentaetigkeit und Sehen. In R. Jung & H. H. Kornhuber (Eds.), *Neurophysiologie und Psychophysik des visuellen Systems* (pp. 410–435). New York: Springer-Verlag.

Jusczyk, P. W. (1986). Toward a model of the development of speech perception. In J. S. Perkell & D. H. Klatt (Eds.), *Invariance and variability in speech processes* (pp. 1–19). Hillsdale, NJ: Erlbaum.

Jusczyk, P. W., & Krumhansl, C. L. (1993). Pitch and rhythmic patterns affecting infants' sensitivity to musical phrase structure. *Journal of Experimental Psychology: Human Perception and Performance, 19,* 627–640.

Juslin, P., & Olsson, N. (1996). Calibration and diagnosticity of confidence in eyewitness identification: Comments on what can be inferred from the low confidence-accuracy correlation. *Journal of Experimental Psychology: Learning, Memory, and Cognition, 22,* 1304–1316.

Kaas, J. H. (1983). The organization of somatosensory cortex in primates and other mammals. In C. von Euler, O. Franzen, U. Lindblom, & D. Ottoson (Eds.), *Somatosensory mechanisms* (pp. 51–60). New York: Plenum Press.

Kaernbach, C. (1990). A single-interval adjustment-matrix (SIAM) procedure for unbiased adaptive testing. *Journal of the Acoustical Society of America, 88,* 2645–2655.

Kaernbach, C. (1991). Simple adaptive testing with the weighted up-down method. *Perception & Psychophysics, 49,* 227–229.

Kaess, D. W. (1980). Instructions and decision times of size-constancy responses. *Perception & Psychophysics, 27,* 477–482.

Kahneman, D. (1966). Time-intensity reciprocity in acuity as a function of luminance and figure-ground contrast. *Vision Research, 6,* 207–215.

Kahneman, D. (1967). An onset-onset law for one case of apparent motion and metacontrast. *Perception & Psychophysics, 2,* 577–584.

Kahneman, D. (1968). Method, findings, and theory in studies of visual masking. *Psychological Bulletin, 70*, 404–425.

Kahneman, D. (1973). *Attention and effort.* Englewood Cliffs, NJ: Prentice-Hall.

Kahneman, D., Norman, J., & Kubovy, M. (1967). Critical duration for the resolution of form: Centrally or peripherally determined? *Journal of Experimental Psychology, 73*, 323–327.

Kahneman, D., & Treisman, A. (1984). Changing views of attention and automaticity. In R. Parasuraman & D. R. Davies (Eds.), *Varieties of attention.* (pp. 29–61). Orlando: Academic Press.

Kaiser, M., & Calderone, J. B. (1991). Factors influencing perceived angular velocity. *Perception & Psychophysics, 50*, 428–434.

Kaiser, P. K., & Boynton, R. M. (1985). Role of the blue mechanism in wavelength discrimination. *Vision Research, 25*, 523–529.

Kalat, J. W. (1998). *Biological psychology, 6th ed.* Belmont, CA: Wadsworth.

Kaneko, A., Nishimura, Y., Tachibana, M., Tauchi, M., & Shimai, K. (1981). Physiological and morphological studies of signal pathways in the carp retina. *Vision Research, 21*, 1519–1526.

Kanisza, G. (1979). *Organization in vision: Essays on Gestalt perception.* New York: Praeger.

Kanizsa, G., Renzi, P., Conte, S., Compostela, C., & Guerani, L. (1993). Amodal completion in mouse vision. *Perception, 22*, 713–721.

Kaplan, A., & Glanville, E. (1964). Taste thresholds for bitterness and cigarette smoking. *Nature (London), 202*, 1366.

Kaplan, G. (1969). Kinetic disruption of optical texture: The perception of depth at an edge. *Perception & Psychophysics, 6*, 193–198.

Kaplan, R-M. (1995). *The power behind your eyes: Improving your eye sight with integrated vision therapy.* Rochester, VT: Healing Arts Press.

Kaptein, N. A., Theeuwes, J., & van der Heijden, A. H. C. (1995). Search for a conjunctively defined target can be selectively limited to a color-defined subset of elements. *Journal of Experimental Psychology: Human Perception and Performance, 21*, 1053–1069.

Karmel, B. Z., & Maisel, E. B. (1975). A neuronal activity model for infant visual attention. In L. B. Cohen & P. Salapatek (Eds.), *Infant perception: From sensation to cognition: Vol. 1. Basic visual processes* (pp. 78–133). New York: Academic Press.

Kasamatsu, T. (1976). Visual cortical neurons influenced by the oculomotor input: Characterization of their receptive field properties. *Brain Research, 113*, 271–292.

Kauer, J. S. (1980). Some spatial characteristics of central information processing in the vertebrate olfactory pathway. In H. van der Starre (Ed.), *Olfaction and taste VII* (pp. 227–236). London: IRL Press.

Kauer, J. S. (1987). Coding in the olfactory system. In T. E. Finger & W. L. Silver (Eds.), *Neurobiology of taste and smell* (pp. 205–232). New York: Wiley.

Kaufman, L. (1974). *Sight and mind: An introduction to visual perception.* London and New York: Oxford University Press.

Kaufman, L., & Rock, I. (1989). The moon illusion thirty years later. In M. Hershenson (Ed.), *The moon illusion* (pp. 193–234). Hillsdale, NJ: Erlbaum.

Kaufmann, R., Maland, J., & Yonas, A. (1981). Sensitivity of 5- and 7-month-old infants to pictorial depth information. *Journal of Experimental Child Psychology, 32*, 162–168.

Kaye, M., Mitchell, D. E., & Cynader, M. (1982). Depth perception, eye dominance and cortical binocularity of dark-reared cats. *Developmental Brain Research, 2*, 37–53.

Kellman, P. J. (1984). Perception of three-dimensional form by human infants. *Perception & Psychophysics, 36*, 353–358.

Kellman, P. J., & Shipley, T. F. (1990). A theory of visual interpolation in object perception. *Cognition, 23*, 141–221.

Kellman, P. J., & Short, K. R. (1987). Development of three-dimensional form perception. *Journal of Experimental Psychology: Human Perception and Performance, 13*, 545–557.

Kellman, P. J., & Spelke, E. S. (1983). Perception of partly occluded objects in infancy. *Cognitive Psychology, 15*, 483–524.

Kellman, P. J., Spelke, E. S., & Short, K. R. (1986). Infant perception of object unity from translatory motion in depth and vertical translation. *Child Development, 57*, 72–86.

Kemler-Nelson, D. G., Hirsh-Pasek, K., Jusczyk, P. W., & Wright-Cassidy, K. (1989). How the prosodic cues in motherese might assist language learning. *Journal of Child Language, 16*, 66–68.

Kemp, D. T. (1978). Stimulated acoustic emissions from within the human auditory system. *Journal of the Acoustical Society of America, 64*, 1386–1391.

Kendrick, K. M., & Baldwin, B. A. (1987). Cells in the temporal cortex of conscious sheep can respond preferentially to the sight of faces. *Science, 236*, 448–450.

Kennedy, J. M., & Domander, R. (1985). Shape and contour: The points of maximum change least useful for recognition. *Perception, 14*, 367–370.

Kennedy, J. M., & Ostry, D. (1976). Approaches to picture perception: Perceptual experience and ecological optics. *Canadian Journal of Psychology, 30*, 90–98.

Kenshalo, D. R., & Isensee, O. (1983). Responses of primate SI cortical neurons to noxious stimuli. *Journal of Neurophysiology, 50*, 1479–1496.

Keren, G., & Baggen, S. (1981). Recognition models of alphanumeric characters. *Perception & Psychophysics, 29*, 234–245.

Kersten, D., & Knill, D. C. (1996). Illusory motion from shadows. *Nature, 379*, 31.

Kessen, W., Salapatek, P., & Haith, M. M. (1972). The visual response of the human newborn to linear contour. *Journal of Experimental Child Psychology, 13*, 9–20.

Khanna, S. M., & Leonard, D. G. B. (1982). Basilar membrane tuning in the cat cochlea. *Science, 215*, 305–306.

Kiang, K. Y. S., Rho, J. M., Northrop, C. C., Liberman, M. C., & Ryugo, D. K. (1982). Hair-cell innervation by spiral ganglion cells in adult cats. *Science, 217*, 175–177.

Kidd, G. Jr., Mason, C. R., Deliwala, P. S., Woods, W. S., & Colburn, H. S. (1994). Reducing informational masking by sound segregation. *Journal of the Acoustical Society of America, 95*, 3475–3480.

Kidd, G. Jr., Mason, C. R., Uchanski, R. M., Brantley, M. A., & Shah, P. (1991). Evaluation of simple models of auditory profile analysis using random reference spectra. *Journal of the Acoustical Society of America, 90*, 1340–1354.

Kilbride, P. E., Hutman, L. P., Fishman, M., & Read, J. S. (1986). Foveal cone pigment density difference in the aging human eye. *Vision Research, 26*, 321–325.

Killbride, P. L., & Leibowitz, H. W. (1975). Factors affecting the magnitude of the Ponzo illusion among the Baganda. *Perception & Psychophysics, 17*, 543–548.

Killbride, P. L., & Robbins, M. (1968). Linear perspective pictorial depth perception and education among the Baganda. *Perception and Motor Skills, 27*, 601–602.

Kim, D. O. (1985). Functional roles of the inner- and outer-hair-cell subsystems in the cochlea and brainstem. In C. J. Berlin (Ed.), *Hearing science: Recent advances* (pp. 241–262). San Diego: College Hill.

Kim, M-S., & Cave, K. R. (1995). Spatial attention in visual search for features and feature conjunctions. *Psychological Science, 6,* 376–380.

Kimchi, R. (1992). Primacy of wholistic processing and global/local paradigm: A critical review. *Psychological Bulletin, 112,* 24–38.

Kimura, K., & Beidler, L. M. (1961). Microelectrode study of taste receptors of rat and hamster. *Journal of Cellular and Comparative Physiology, 58,* 131–140.

Kinchla, R. A., Solis-Macias, V., & Hoffman, J. E. (1983). Attending to different levels of structure in a visual image. *Perception & Psychophysics, 33,* 1–10.

Kinchla, R. A., & Wolfe, J. (1979). The order of visual processing: "Top-down," "bottom-up," or "middle-out." *Perception & Psychophysics, 25,* 225–231.

King, M. C., & Lockhead, G. R. (1981). Response scales and sequential effects in judgment. *Perception & Psychophysics, 30,* 599–603.

Kingstone, A., Enns, J. T., Mangun, G. R., & Gazzaniga, M. S. (1995). Guided visual search is a left-hemisphere process in split-brain patients. *Psychological Science, 6,* 118–121.

Kirk-Smith, M. D., & Booth, D. A. (1980). Effects of androstenone on choice of location in other's presence. In H. van der Starre (Ed.), *Olfaction and taste VII* (pp. 397–400). London: IRL Press.

Kirk-Smith, M. D., Booth, D. A., Caroll, D., & Davies, P. (1978). Human social attitudes affected by androstenol. *Research Communications in Psychology, Psychiatry and Behavior, 3,* 379–384.

Kitazawa, S., & Kohno, T. (1995). Effects of delayed visual information on the rate and amount of prism adaptation in the human. *Journal of Neuroscience, 15,* 7644–7652.

Kitzes, L. M., Gibson, M. M., Rose, J. E., & Hind, J. E. (1978). Initial discharge latency and threshold considerations for some neurons in cochlear nucleus complex of the cat. *Journal of Neurophysiology, 41,* 1165–1182.

Klatt, D. H. (1980). Speech perception: A model of acoustic-phonetic analysis and lexical access. In R. Cole (Ed.), *Perception and production of fluent speech* (pp. 243–288). Hillsdale, NJ: Erlbaum.

Klatzky, R. L., Lederman, S. J., & Reed, C. (1987). There's more to touch than meets the eye: The salience of object attributes for haptics with and without vision. *Journal of Experimental Psychology: General, 116,* 356–369.

Klatzky, R. L., Lederman, S. J., & Reed, C. (1989). Haptic integration of object properties: Texture, hardness and planar contour. *Journal of Experimental Psychology: Human Perception and Performance, 15,* 45–57.

Klatzky, R. L., Lederman S. J., & Metzger, V. A. (1985). Identifying objects by touch: An "expert system." *Perception & Psychophysics, 37,* 299–302.

Klatzky, R. L., & Lederman, S. J. (1995). Identifying objects from a haptic glance. *Perception & Psychophysics, 57,* 1111–1123.

Klatzky, R. L., Lederman, S. J., & Matula, D. E. (1993). Haptic exploration in the presence of vision. *Journal of Experimental Psychology: Human Perception & Performance, 19,* 726–743.

Klein, G. S. (1970). *Perception, motives and personality.* New York: Knopf.

Klein, R. (1980). Does oculomotor readiness mediate cognitive control of visual attention? In R. S. Nickerson (Ed.), *Attention and performance VIII* (pp. 259–276). Hillsdale, NJ: Lawrence Erlbaum.

Klein, R. (1988). Inhibitory tagging system facilitates visual search. *Nature, 334,* 430–431.

Klein, S. A., & Levi, D. M. (1985). Hyperacuity threshold of 1.0 second: Theoretical predictions and empirical validation. *Journal of the Optical Society of America A2,* 1170–1190.

Kluender, K. R., Diehl, R. L., & Killeen, P. R. (1987). Japanese quail can learn phonetic categories. *Science, 237,* 1195–1197.

Kluender, K. R., & Jenison, R. L. (1992). Effects of glide slope, noise intensity, and noise duration on the extrapolation of FM glides through noise. *Perception & Psychophysics, 51,* 231–238.

Kluender, K. R., & Lotto, A. J. (1994). Effects of first formant onset frequency on [-voice] judgments results from auditory processes not specific to humans. *Journal of the Acoustical Society of America, 95,* 1044–1052.

Klutky, N. (1990). Geschlechtsunterschiede in der Gedachtnisleistung für Geruche, Tonfolgen und Farben. *Zeitschrift für Experimentelle und Angewandte Psychologie, 37,* 437–446.

Kluver, H., & Bucy, P. C. (1937). "Psychic blindness" and other symptoms following bilateral temporal lobectomy in rhesus monkeys. *American Journal of Physiology, 119,* 352–353.

Klymenko, V., & Weisstein, N. (1986). Spatial frequency differences can determine figure–ground organization. *Journal of Experimental Psychology: Human Perception and Performance, 12,* 324–330.

Knoblauch, K., Saunders, F., Kusuda, M., Hynes, R., Podgor, M., Higgins, K. E., & deMonasteriod, F. M. (1987). Age and illuminance effects in the Farnsworth-Munsell 100-hue test. *Applied Optics, 26,* 1441–1448.

Knudsen, E. I., & Brainard, M. S. (1991). Visual instruction of the neural map of auditory space in the developing optic tectum. *Science, 253,* 85–87.

Knudsen, E. I., & Knudsen, P. F. (1989). Vision calibrates sound localization in developing barn owls. *The Journal of Neuroscience, 9,* 3306–3313.

Knudsen, E. I., & Konishi, M. (1978a). A neural map of auditory space in the owl. *Science, 200,* 795–797.

Knudsen, E. I., & Konishi, M. (1978b). Center-surround organization of auditory receptive fields in the owl. *Science, 202,* 778–780.

Kobler, J. B., Isbey, S. F., & Casseday, J. H. (1987). Auditory pathways to the frontal cortex of the mustache bat, Pteronotus parnelli. *Science, 236,* 824–826.

Koffka, K. (1935). *Principles of Gestalt psychology.* New York: Harcourt, Brace & World.

Kohl, J. V., & Francoeur, R. T. (1995). *The scent of eros.* New York: Continuum.

Kohler, I. (1962). Experiments with goggles. *Scientific American, 206,* 62–86.

Kohler, I. (1964). The formation and transformation of the perceptual world. *Psychological Issues, 3* (Whole No. 4).

Kohler, W. (1923). Zur Theories des Sukzessivvergleichs und der Zeitfehler. *Psychologische Forschung, 4,* 115–175.

Kohlston, P. J. (1988). Sharp mechanical tuning in a cochlear model without negative damping. *Journal of the Acoustical Society of America, 83,* 1481–1487.

Kolb, B., & Whishaw, I. O. (1985). *Fundamentals of human neuropsychology* (2nd ed.). New York: Freeman.

Kolb, H., Nelson, R., & Mariani, A. (1981). Amacrine cells, bipolar cells and ganglion cells of the cat retina: A Golgi study. *Vision Research, 21,* 1081–1114.

Kolers, P. A., & Brewster, J. M. (1985). Rhythms and responses. *Journal of Experimental Psychology: Human Perception and Performance, 11,* 150–167.

Kolers, P. A., & Green, M. (1984). Color logic of apparent motion. *Perception, 13,* 249–254.

Kolers, P. A., & von Grunau, M. (1976). Shape and color in apparent motion. *Vision Research, 16,* 329–335.

Komoda, M. K., Festinger, L., Phillips, L. J., Duckman, R. H., & Young, R. A. (1973). Some observations concerning saccadic eye movement. *Vision Research, 13,* 1009–1020.

Konstadt, N., & Forman, E. (1965). Field dependence and external directedness. *Journal of Personality and Social Psychology, 1,* 490–493.

Koslowe, K. C., Spierer, A., Rosner, M., & Belkin, M. (1991). Evaluation of accommotrac biofeedback training for myopia control. *Optometry and Vision Science, 68,* 338–343.

Kosterlitz, H. W., & McKnight, A. T. (1981). Opioid peptides and sensory function. In D. Ottoson (Ed.), *Progress in sensory physiology: Vol. 1* (pp. 31–95). Heidelberg: Springer-Verlag.

Kowler, E., & Martin, A. J. (1980). Eye movements in preschool children. *Science, 215,* 997–999.

Kozlowski, L. T., & Cutting, J. E. (1977). Recognizing the sex of a walker from a dynamic point-light display. *Perception & Psychophysics, 21,* 575–580.

Kramer, J. H., & Duffy, J. M. (1996). Aphasia, apraxia, and agnosia in the diagnosis of dementia. *Dementia, 7,* 23–26.

Krauskopf, J., & Reeves, A. (1980). Measurement of the effect of photon noise on detection. *Vision Research, 20,* 193–196.

Kremenitzer, J. P., Vaughan, H. G., Kurtzberg, D., & Dowling, K. (1979). Smooth-pursuit eye movements in the newborn infant. *Child Development, 50,* 442–448.

Kries, J. von. (1895). Uber die Natur gewisser mit den spychischen Vorgangen verknupfter Ghirnzustande. *Zeitschrift fur Psychologie, 8,* 1–33.

Krueger, L. E. (1982). A word superiority effect with print and Braille characters. *Perception & Psychophysics, 31,* 345–352.

Krueger, L. E. (1991). Toward a unified psychophysical law and beyond. In S. J. Bolanowski Jr. & G. A. Gescheider (Eds.), *Ratio scaling of psychological magnitude* (pp. 101–114). Hillsdale, NJ: Lawrence Erlbaum.

Kruger, J. (1981). The difference between x- and y-type responses in ganglion cells of the cat's retina. *Vision Research, 21,* 1685–1687.

Krumhansl, C. L. (1985). Perceiving tonal structure in music. *American Scientist, 73,* 371–378.

Krumhansl, C. L. (1990). *Cognitive foundations of musical pitch.* Oxford: Oxford University Press.

Krumhansl, C. L., Bharucha, J. J., & Kessler, E. J. (1982). Perceived harmonic structure of chords in three related musical keys. *Journal of Experimental Psychology: Human Perception and Performance, 8,* 24–36.

Krumhansl, C. L., & Iverson, P. (1992). Perceptual interactions between musical pitch and timbre. *Journal of Experimental Psychology: Human Perception and Performance, 18,* 739–751.

Krumhansl, C. L., & Jusczyk, P. W. (1990). Infants' perception of phrase structure in music. *Psychological Science, 1,* 70–73.

Krumhansl, C. L., & Kessler, E. J. (1982). Tracing the dynamic changes in perceived tonal organization in a spatial representation of musical keys. *Psychological Review, 89,* 334–368.

Krumhansl, C. L., & Shepard, R. N. (1979). Quantification of the hierarchy of tonal functions within a diatonic context. *Journal of Experimental Psychology: Human Perception and Performance, 5,* 579–594.

Kruskal, J. B. (1964). Multidimensional scaling by optimizing goodness of fit to a nonmetric hypothesis. *Psychometrika, 29,* 1–27.

Kryter, K. D. (1985). *The effects of noise on man* (2nd ed.). Orlando: Academic Press.

Kubovy, M., & Wagemans, J. (1995). Grouping by proximity and multistability in dot lattices: A quantitative Gestalt theory. *Psychological Science, 6,* 225–234.

Kuffler, S. W. (1953). Discharge patterns and functional organization of mammalian retina. *Journal of Neurophysiology, 16,* 37–68.

Kuhl, P. K. (1987). Perception of speech and sound in early infancy. In P. Salapatek & L. Cohen (Eds.), *Handbook of infant perception: Vol. 2: From perception to cognition* (pp. 275–382). Orlando: Academic Press.

Kuhl, P. K. (1991). Human adults and human infants show a "perceptual magnet effect" for prototypes of speech categories, monkeys do not. *Perception & Psychophysics, 50,* 93–107.

Kuhl, P. K., & Meltzoff, A. N. (1982). The bimodal perception of speech in infancy. *Science, 218,* 1138–1141.

Kuhl, P. K., & Padden, D. M. (1983). Enhanced discriminability at the phonetic boundaries for the place feature in macaques. *Journal of the Acoustical Society of America, 73,* 1003–1010.

Kuhl, P. K., Williams, K. A., Lacerda, F., Stevens, K. N., & Lindbloom, B. (1992). Linguistic experience alters phonetic perception in infants by 6 months of age. *Science, 255,* 606–608.

Kulikowski, J. J., Walsh, V., McKeefry, D., Butler, S. R., & Carden, D. (1994). The electrophysiological basis of colour processing in macaques with V4 lesions. *Behavioural Brain Research, 60,* 73–78.

Kupchella, C. (1976). *Sights and sounds.* Indianapolis: Bobbs-Merrill.

Kuriki, I., & Uchikawa, K. (1996). Limitations of surface-color and apparent-color constancy. *Journal of the Optical Society of America A-Optics & Image Science, 13,* 1622–1636.

Kurtz, D., & Butter, C. M. (1980). Impairments in visual discrimination performance and gaze shifts in monkeys with superior colliculus lesions. *Brain Research, 196,* 109–124.

Kuyk, T., Veres, J. G. III, Lahey, M. A., & Clark, D. J. (1986). The ability of protan color defectives to perform color-dependent air traffic control tasks. *American Journal of Optometry and Physiological Optics, 63,* 582–586.

LaBerge, D. (1995). *Attentional processing: The brain's art of mindfulness.* Cambridge, MA: Harvard University Press.

LaBerge, D., & Brown, V. (1989). Theory of attentional operations in shape identification. *Psychological Review, 96,* 101–124.

LaBerge, D., & Buchsbaum, M. S. (1990). Positron emission tomographic measurements of pulvinar activity during an attention task. *Journal of Neuroscience, 10,* 613–619.

Ladavas, E., & Petronio, A. (1990). The deployment of visual attention in the intact field of hemineglect patients. *Cortex, 26,* 307–317.

Ladefoged, P. (1975). *A course in phonetics.* New York: Harcourt Brace Jovanovich.

Lakotos, S., McAdams, S., & Caussé, R. (1997). The representation of auditory source characteristics: Simple geometric form. *Perception & Psychophysics, 59,* 1180–1190.

Lakowski, R. (1962). Is the deterioration of colour discrimination with age due to lens or retinal changes? *Farbe, 11,* 69–86.

Lakowski, R., Aspinall, P. A., & Kinnear, P. R. (1972). Association between colour vision losses and diabetes mellitus. *Ophthalmic Research, 4,* 145–159.

Lakowski, R., & Drance, S. M. (1979). Acquired dyschromatopsias: The earliest functional losses in glaucoma. *Documenta Ophthalmologica,* Proceedings Series 19, 159–165.

Lakowski, R., & Morton, B. A. (1977). The effect of oral contraceptives on colour vision in diabetic women. *Canadian Journal of Ophthalmology, 12,* 89–97.

Lamb, M. R., & Yund, E. W. (1996). Spatial frequency and attention: Effects of level-, target-, and location-repetition on the processing of global and local forms. *Perception & Psychophysics, 58,* 363–373.

Lamour, Y., Willer, J. C., & Guilbaud, G. (1983). Rat somatosensory (SmI) cortex: I. Characteristics of neuronal responses to noxious stimulation and comparison with responses to nonnoxious stimulation. *Experimental Brain Research, 49,* 35–45.

Land, E. H. (1986). Recent advances in retinex theory. *Vision Research, 26,* 7–21.

Land, E. H., & McCann, J. J. (1971). Lightness and retinex theory. *Journal of the Optical Society of America, 61,* 1–11.

Landolt, E. (1889). Tableau d'optotypes pour la determination de l'acuité visuelle. *Societé Francais d'Ophthalmologie, 1,* 385ff.

Lappin, J. S., & Preble, L. D. (1975). A demonstration of shape constancy. *Perception & Psychophysics, 17,* 439–444.

Larish, J. F., & Flach, J. M. (1990). Sources of optical information useful for the perception of speed of rectilinear self–motion. *Journal of Experimental Psychology: Human Perception and Performance, 16,* 295–302.

Lauter, J. L., Herscovitch, P., Formby, C., & Raichle, M. E. (1985). Tonotopic organization in human auditory cortex revealed by positron emission tomography. *Hearing Research, 20,* 199–205.

Lawless, H. T., & Stevens, D. A. (1988). Responses by humans to oral chemical irritants as a function of locus of stimulation. *Perception & Psychophysics, 43,* 72–78.

Lea, S. E. G. (1984). *Instinct, environment, and behaviour.* London: Methuen.

Lecours, A. R. (1975). Myelogenetic correlates of development of speech and language. In E. H. Lemlich, R. N. (1975). Subjective acceleration of time with aging. *Perceptual and Motor Skills, 41,* 235–205.

Lenneberg & E. Lenneberg (Eds.). *Foundations of language and development: A multidisciplinary approach* (pp. 121–135). New York: Academic Press.

Lederman, S. J., Browse, R. A., & Klatzky, R. L. (1988). Haptic processing of spatially distributed information. *Perception & Psychophysics, 44,* 222–232.

Leehey, S. C., Moskowitz-Cook, A., Brill, S., & Held, R. (1975). Orientational anisotropy in infant vision. *Science, 190,* 900–902.

Leek, M. R., Brown, M. E., & Dorman, M. F. (1991). Informational masking and auditory attention. *Perception & Psychophysics, 50,* 205–214.

Leek, M. R., Hanna, T. E., & Marshall, L. (1992). Estimation of psychometric functions from adaptive tracking procedures. *Perception & Psychophysics, 51,* 247–256.

Leeuwenberg, E. L. J. (1971). A perceptual coding language for visual and auditory patterns. *American Journal of Psychology, 84,* 307–346.

Leeuwenberg, E. L. J. (1988). *On geon and global precedence in form perception.* Paper presented at the meetings of the Psychonomic Society, Chicago.

Lefebvre, P. P., Malgrange, B., Staecker, H., Moonen, G., & Van de Water, T. R. (1993). Retinoic acid stimulates regeneration of mammalian auditory hair cells. *Science, 260,* 692–695.

Lefton, L. A. (1973). Metacontrast: A review. *Perception & Psychophysics, 13,* 161–171.

Lehmkuhle, S., & Fox, R. (1980). Effect of depth separation of metacontrast masking. *Journal of Experimental Psychology: Human Perception and Performance, 6,* 605–621.

Lehmkuhle, S., Kratz, K. E., Mangel, S. C., & Sherman, S. M. (1980). Spatial and temporal sensitivity of x- and y-cells in dorsal lateral geniculate nucleus of the cat. *Journal of Neurophysiology, 43,* 520–541.

Lehmkuhle, S., Kratz, K. E., & Sherman, S. M. (1982). Spatial and temporal sensitivity of normal and amblyopic cats. *Journal of Neurophysiology, 48,* 372–387.

Leibowitz, H. W., & Moore, D. (1966). Role of changes in accommodations and convergence in the perception of size. *Journal of the Optical Society of America, 56,* 1120–1123.

Leibowitz, H. W., & Owens, D. A. (1977). Nighttime accidents and selective visual degradation. *Science, 197,* 422–423.

Leibowitz, H. W., & Pick, H. (1972). Cross-cultural and educational aspects of the Ponzo perspective illusion. *Perception & Psychophysics, 12,* 430–432.

Leibowitz, H. W., Post, R. B., Brandt, T., & Dichgans, J. (1982). Implications of recent developments in dynamic spatial orientation and visual resolution for vehicle guidance. In A. H. Wertheim, W. A. Wagenaar, & H. W. Leibowitz (Eds.), *Tutorials on motion perception* (pp. 231–260). New York: Plenum Press.

Leibowitz, H. W., Post, R. B., & Ginsburg, A. (1980). The role of fine detail in visually controlled behavior. *Investigative Ophthalmology and Visual Science, 19,* 846–848.

Leibowitz, H. W., Shupert, C. L., Post, R. B., & Dichgans, J. (1983). Autokinetic drifts and gaze deviation. *Perception & Psychophysics, 33,* 455–459.

Leibowitz, H. W., Wilcox, S. B., & Post, R. B. (1978). The effect of refractive error on size constancy and shape constancy. *Perception, 7,* 557–562.

Leinonen, L. (1983). Integration of somatosensory events in the posterior parietal cortex of the monkey. In C. von Euler, O. Franzen, U. Lindblom, & D. Ottoson (Eds.), *Somatosensory mechanisms* (pp. 113–124). New York: Plenum Press.

Lemlich, R. N. (1975). Subjective acceleration of time with aging. *Perceptual and Motor Skills, 41,* 235–238.

Lenneberg, E. H. (1967). *Biological foundations of language.* New York: Wiley.

Lennie, P., Trevarthen, C., Van Essen, D., & Waessle, H. (1990). Parallel processing of visual information. In L. Spillman & J. S. Werner (Eds.), *Visual perception: The neurophysiological foundations* (pp. 103–128). Orlando: Academic Press.

Leonards, U., & Singer, W. (1997). Selective temporal interactions between processing streams with differential sensitivity for colour and luminance contrast. *Vision Research, 37,* 1129–1140.

LePage, E. L. (1987). A spatial template for the shape of tuning curves in the mammalian cochlea. *Journal of the Acoustical Society of America, 82,* 155–164.

LePage, E. L. (1989). Functional role of the olivo-cochlear bundle: A motor unit control system in the mammalian cochlea. *Hearing Research, 38,* 177–198.

Lerdahl, F., & Jackendoff, R. (1983). *A generative theory of tonal music.* Cambridge, MA: MIT Press.

Lerman, S. (1984). Biophysical aspects of corneal and lenticular transparency. *Current Eye Research, 3,* 3–14.

LeVay, S., Wiesel, T. N., & Hubel, D. H. (1980). The development of ocular dominance columns in normal and visually deprived monkeys. *Journal of Comparative Neurology, 191,* 1–51.

Levelt, W. J. M., Riemersma, J. B., & Bunt, A. A. (1972). Binaural additivity of loudness. *British Journal of Mathematical and Statistical Psychology, 25,* 51–68.

Leventhal, A., & Hirsch, H. (1980). Receptive-field properties of different classes of neurons in visual cortex of normal and dark-reared cats. *Journal of Neurophysiology, 43,* 1111–1132.

Levin, A., Lipton, R. B., & Holzman, P. S. (1981). Pursuit eye movements in psychopathology: Effects of target characteristics. *Biological Psychiatry, 16,* 255–267.

Levine, D. N., & Calvanio, R. (1989). Prosopagnosia: A defect in visual configural processing. *Brain and Cognition, 10,* 149–170.

Levine, M. W., & Shefner, J. M. (1981). *Fundamentals of sensation and perception.* Reading, MA: Addison-Wesley.

Levitin, D. J., & Cook, P. R. (1996). Memory for musical tempo: Additional evidence that auditory memory is absolute. *Perception & Psychophysics, 58,* 927–935.

Levitt, H. (1971). Transformed up-down methods in psychoacoustics. *Journal of the Acoustical Society of America, 49,* 467–477.

Levy, D. L., Lipton, R. B., & Holzman, P. S. (1981). Smooth pursuit eye movements: Effects of alcohol and chloral hydrate. *Journal of Psychiatric Research, 16,* 1–11.

Lewis, J. W., Terman, G. W., Shavit, Y., Nelson, L. R., & Liebeskind, J. C. (1984). Neural, neurochemical, and hormonal bases of stress-induced analgesia. In L. Kruger & J. C. Liebeskind (Eds.), *Neural mechanisms of pain* (pp. 277–288). New York: Raven Press.

Lewis, T. L., Maurer, D., & Milewski, A. (1979). The development of nasal detection in young infants. *Investigating Ophthalmology and Visual Science Supplement,* 271.

Liberman, A. M. (1982). On finding that speech is special. *American Psychologist, 37,* 148–167.

Liberman, A. M., Cooper, F. S., Shankweiler, D. P., & Studdert-Kennedy, M. (1967). Perception of the speech code. *Psychological Review, 74,* 431–461.

Liberman, A. M., Harris, K. S., Hoffman, H. A., & Griffith, B. C. (1957). The discrimination of sounds within and across phoneme boundaries. *Journal of Experimental Psychology, 54,* 358–368.

Liberman, A. M., & Mattingly, I. G. (1985). The motor theory of speech perception revised. *Cognition, 21,* 1–36.

Liberman, A. M., & Mattingly, I. G. (1989). A specialization for speech perception. *Science, 243,* 489–494.

Liberman, M. C. (1982). Single-neuron labeling in the cat auditory nerve. *Science, 216,* 1239–1241.

Lichte, W. H., & Borresen, C. R. (1967). Influence of instructions on degree of shape constancy. *Journal of Experimental Psychology, 74,* 538–542.

Lichtenstein, M. (1963). Spatio-temporal factors in cessation of smooth apparent motion. *Journal of the Optical Society of America, 53,* 302–306.

Lie, I. (1980). Visual detection and resolution as a function of retinal locus. *Vision Research, 20,* 967–974.

Liebeskind, J. C., & Melzack, R. (1987). The International Pain Foundation: Meeting a need for education in pain management. *Pain, 30,* 1.

Light, A. R. (1992). *The initial processing of pain and its descending control: Spinal and trigeminal systems.* Basel: Karger.

Lim, D. J. (1980). Cochlear anatomy related to cochlear micromechanics: A review. *Journal of the Acoustical Society of America, 67,* 1686–1695.

Lindblom, B. (1996). Role of articulation in speech perception: Clues from pro-

duction. *Journal of the Acoustical Society of America, 99,* 1683–1692.

Lindsay, P. H., & Norman, D. A. (1977). *Human information processing* (2nd ed.). New York: Academic Press.

Lindsey, D. T., & Teller, D. Y. (1990). Motion at isoluminance: Discrimination detection ratios for moving isoluminant gratings. *Vision Research, 30,* 1751–1761.

Link, S. (1993). *The wave theory of similarity and difference.* Mahwah, NJ: Lawrence Erlbaum Associates.

Linton, H., & Graham, E. (1959). Personality correlates of persuasibility. In I. Janis (Ed.), *Personality and persuasibility.* New Haven, CT: Yale University Press.

Liotti, M., Fox, P. T., & LaBerge, D. (1994). PET measurements of attention to closely spaced visual shapes. *Society for Neurosciences Abstracts, 20,* 354.

Lipsett, L. P. (1977). Taste in human neonates: Its effect on sucking and heart rate. In J. M. Weiffenbach (Ed.), *Taste and development: The ontogeny of sweet preference* (pp. 125–140). Washington, DC: U.S. Government Printing Office.

Lisker, L., & Abramson, A. (1970). The voicing dimension: Some experiments in comparative phonetics. *Proceedings of the 6th International Congress of Phonetic Sciences* (pp. 563–567).

Livingstone, M. S., & Hubel, D. H. (1988). Segregation of form, color, movement and depth: Anatomy, physiology, and perception. *Science, 240,* 740–749.

Locke, J. L. (1983). *Phonological acquisition and change.* New York: Academic Press.

Lockhead, G. R. (1966). Effects of dimensional redundancy on visual discrimination. *Journal of Experimental Psychology, 72,* 95–104.

Lockhead, G. R. (1970). Identification and the form of multidimensional discrimination space. *Journal of Experimental Psychology, 85,* 1–10.

Lockhead, G. R., & Byrd, R. (1981). Practically perfect pitch. *Journal of the Acoustical Society of America, 70,* 387–389.

Loewenstein, W. R. (1960). Biological transducers. *Scientific American, 203,* 98–108.

Loftus, E. (1974). Reconstructing memory: The incredible eye witness. *Psychology Today, 8,* 116–119.

Loftus, E. F., & Donders, K. (1989). Creating new memories that are quickly accessed and confidently held. *Memory and Cognition, 17,* 607–616.

Loftus, G., & Mackworth, N. (1978). Cognitive determinants of fixation location during picture viewing. *Journal of Experimental Psychology: Human Perception and Performance, 4,* 565–572.

Logan, G. D. (1988). Toward an instance theory of automatization. *Psychological Review, 95,* 492–527.

Logan, G. D. (1996). The CODE theory of visual attention: An integration of space-based and object-based attention. *Psychological Review, 103,* 603–649.

Lohman, D. F. (1986). The effect of speed–accuracy tradeoff on sex differences in mental rotation. *Perception & Psychophysics, 39,* 427–436.

Long, G. M. (1988). Selective adaptation vs. transfer of decrement: The conjoint effects of neural fatigue and perceptual learning. *Perception & Psychophysics, 43,* 207–209.

Long, G. M. (1994). Exercises for training vision and dynamic visual acuity among college students. *Perceptual & Motor Skills, 78,* 1049–1050.

Long, G. R., & Cullen, J. K. Jr. (1985). Intensity difference limens at high frequencies. *Journal of the Acoustical Society of America, 78,* 507–513.

Longstreth, L. E. (1987). Hick's law: Its limit is 3 bits. *Bulletin of the Psychonomic Society, 26,* 8–10.

Lonsbury-Martin, B. L., Harris, F. P., Stagner, B. B., Hawkins, M. D., & Martin, G. K. (1990). Distortion product emissions in humans: I. Basic properties in normally hearing subjects. *Annals of Otology, Rhinology and Laryngology, 99,* 3–14.

Loomis, J. M. (1978). Lateral masking in foveal and eccentric vision. *Vision Research, 18,* 335–338.

Loomis, J. M. (1981). Tactile pattern perception. *Perception, 10,* 5–27.

Loop, M. S. (1984). Effect of duration on detection by the chromatic and achromatic systems. *Perception & Psychophysics, 36,* 65–67.

Loosen, F. (1994). Tuning of diatonic scales by violinists, pianists and nonmusicians. *Perception & Psychophysics, 56,* 221–226.

Loosen, F. (1995). The effect of musical experience on the conception of accurate tuning. *Music Perception, 12,* 291–306.

Lord, T., & Kasprzak, M. (1989). Identification of self through olfaction. *Perceptual and Motor Skills, 69,* 219–224.

Lorist, M. M., & Snel, J. (1997). Caffeine effects on perceptual and motor processes. *Electroencephalography & Clinical Neurophysiology, 102,* 401–413.

Lovegrove, W. J., & Over, R. (1973). Color selectivity in orientation masking and aftereffect. *Vision Research, 13,* 895–902.

Lowe, D. (1987). Three-dimensional object recognition from single two-dimensional images. *Artificial Intelligence, 31,* 355–395.

Lowenstein, O., & Sand, A. (1940). The mechanism of the semicircular canal: A study of the responses of single-fibre preparations to angular accelerations and to rotation at constant speed. *Proceedings of the Royal Society of London, Series B, 129*, 256–275.

Luce, R. D. (1990). "On the possible psychophysical laws" revisited: Remarks on cross-modality matching. *Psychological Review, 97*, 66–77.

Luce, R. D., & Mo, S. S. (1965). Magnitude estimation of heaviness and loudness by individual observers: A test of a probabilistic response theory. *The British Journal of Mathematical and Statistical Psychology, 18*, 159–174.

Luce, R. D., & Narens, L. (1987). Measurement scales on the continuum. *Science, 236*, 1527–1532.

Lueck, C. J., Zeki, S., Friston, K. J., Deiber, M. P., Cope, P., Cunningham, V. J., Lammertsma, A. A., Kennard, C., & Frackowiak, R. S. J. (1989). The colour centre in the cerebral cortex of man. *Nature, 340*, 386–389.

Lufti, R. A. (1990). How much masking is informational masking? *Journal of the Acoustical Society of America, 88*, 2607–2610.

Lufti, R. A. (1993). A model of auditory pattern analysis based on component-relative-entropy. *Journal of the Acoustical Society of America, 94*, 748–758.

Lumsden, E. (1980). Problems of magnification and minification: An explanation of the distortions of distance, slant, shape, and velocity. In M. Hagen (Ed.), *Perception of pictures: Vol. I, Alberti's window: The projective model of pictorial information* (pp. 91–135). New York: Academic Press.

Lunch, E. D., Lee, M. K., Morrow, J. E., Welsch, P. L., León, P. E., & King, M-C. (1997). Nonsyndromic deafness DFNA1 associated with mutation of a human homolog of the *Drosophila* gene *diaphanous*. *Science, 278*, 1315–1318.

Lundervold, D., Lewin, L. M., & Irvin, L. K. (1987). Rehabilitation of visual impairments: A critical review. *Clinical Psychology Review, 7*, 169–185.

Luria, A. R. (1973). *The working brain.* London: Penguin.

Lynch, M. P., & Eilers, R. E. (1990). Innateness, experience, and music perception. *Psychological Science, 1*, 272–276.

Lynn, P. A., & Sayers, B. M. A. (1970). Cochlear innervation, signal processing, and their relation to auditory time–intensity effects. *Journal of the Acoustical Society of America, 47*, 523–533.

MacArthur, R. O., & Sekuler, R. (1982). Alcohol and motion perception. *Perception & Psychophysics, 31*, 502–505.

MacDonald, D. W., & Brown, R. E. (1985). Introduction: The pheromone concept in mammalian chemical communication. In R. E. Brown & D. W. MacDonald (Eds.), *Social odours in mammals: Vol. 1* (pp. 1–18). Oxford: Clarendon Press.

MacFarlane, A. (1975). Olfaction in the development of social preferences in the human neonate. In *Ciba Foundation Symposium 33: The human neonate in parent–infant interaction* (pp. 103–177). Amsterdam: Elsevier.

Mach, E. (1959). *The analysis of sensations and the relation of the physical to the psychical.* New York: Dover. (Originally published 1886)

Mack, A., & Herman, E. (1972). A new illusion: The underestimation of a distance during pursuit eye movements. *Perception & Psychophysics, 12*, 471–473.

Mack, A., Heuer, F., Fendrich, R., Vilardi, K., & Chambers, D. (1985). Induced motion and oculomotor capture. *Journal of Experimental Psychology: Human Perception and Performance, 11*, 329–345.

Mack, A., Tang, B., Tuma, R., Kahn, S., & Rock, I. (1992). Perceptual organization and attention. *Cognitive Psychology, 24*, 475–501.

MacKain, K., Studdert-Kennedy, M., Spieker, S., & Stern, D. (1983). Infant intermodal speech perception is a left hemisphere function. *Science, 219*, 1347–1349.

Mackworth, N. H. (1948). The breakdown of vigilance during prolonged visual search. *Quarterly Journal of Experimental Psychology, 1*, 6–21.

Mackworth, N. H., & Bruner, J. S. (1970). How adults and children search and recognize pictures. *Human Development, 13*, 149–177.

MacLeod, D. I. (1978). Visual sensitivity. *Annual Review of Psychology, 29*, 613–645.

MacLeod, P. (1971). An experimental approach to the peripheral mechanisms of olfactory discrimination. In G. Ohloff & A. F. Thomas (Eds.), *Gustation and olfaction* (pp. 28–44). New York: Academic Press.

MacLeod, R. (1947). The effects of "artificial penumbra" on the brightness of included areas. In A. Michotte (Ed.), *Miscellanea psychologica* (pp. 1–22). Paris: Librairie Philosophique.

Macmillan, N. A., & Creelman, C. D. (1991). *Detection theory: A user's guide.* Cambridge: Cambridge University Press.

MacNichol, E. F. Jr. (1986). A unifying presentation of photopigment spectra. *Vision Research, 29*, 543–546.

Madden, D. J. (1983). Aging and distraction by highly familiar stimuli during visual search. *Developmental Psychology, 19*, 499–507.

Madden, D. J. (1986). Adult age differences in the attentional capacity demands of visual search. *Cognitive Development, 2*, 100–107.

Madden, T. M., & Burt, G. S. (1981). Inappropriate constancy scaling theory and the Mueller-Lyer illusion. *Perceptual and Motor Skills, 52*, 211–218.

Mair, R. G., Bouffard, J. A., Engen, T., & Morton, T. (1978). Olfactory sensitivity during the menstrual cycle. *Sensory Process, 2*, 90–98.

Maire-Lepoivre, E., & Przybyslawski, J. (1988). Visual field in dark-reared cats after an extended period of recovery. *Behavioural Brain Research, 28*, 245–251.

Makous, J. C., & Middlebrooks, J. C. (1990). Two-dimensional sound localization by human listeners. *Journal of the Acoustical Society of America, 87*, 2188–2200.

Mandler, G. (1980). Recognizing: The judgment of previous occurrence. *Psychological Review, 87*, 252–271.

Mangun, G. R., & Hillyard, S. A. (1990). Electrophysiological studies of visual selective attention in humans. In A. B. Scheibel & A. F. Wechsler (Eds.), *Neurobiology of higher cognitive function* (pp. 271–295). New York: Guildford Press.

Marcel, A. J. (1983). Conscious and unconscious perception: Experiments on visual masking and word recognition. *Cognitive Psychology, 15*, 197–237.

Marks, L. E. (1968). Stimulus range, number of categories, and form of the category scale. *American Journal of Psychology, 81*, 467–479.

Marks, L. E. (1974). On scales of sensation: Prolegomena to any future psychophysics that will be able to come forth as science. *Perception & Psychophysics, 16*, 358–376.

Marks, L. E. (1979a). Summation of vibrotactile intensity: An analogy to auditory critical bands? *Sensory Processes, 3*, 188–203.

Marks, L. E. (1979b). A theory of loudness and loudness judgments. *Psychological Review, 86*, 256–285.

Marks, L. E. (1988). Magnitude estimation and sensory matching. *Perception & Psychophysics, 43*, 511–525.

Marks, L. E. (1993). Contextual processing of multidimensional and unidimensional auditory stimuli. *Journal of Experimental Psychology: Human Perception and Performance, 19*, 227–249.

Marks, L. E. (1994). "Recalibrating" the auditory system: The perception of loudness. *Journal of Experimental Psychology: Human Perception and Performance, 20*, 382–396.

Marks, L. E., Galanter, E., & Baird, J. C. (1995). Binaural summation after learning psychophysical functions for loudness. *Perception & Psychophysics, 57,* 1209–1216.

Marks, L. E., Szczesiul, R., & Ohlott, P. (1986). On the cross-modal perception of intensity. *Journal of Experimental Psychology: Human Perception and Performance, 12,* 517–534.

Marks, W. B., Dobelle, W. H., & Mac-Nichol, E. F. (1964). Visual pigments of single primate cones. *Science, 143,* 1181–1183.

Marr, D. (1982). *Vision.* San Francisco: W. H. Freeman.

Marr, D., & Poggio, T. (1979). A computational theory of human stereo vision. *Proceedings of the Royal Society (London), Series B, 204,* 301–328.

Marr, D., & Ullman, S. (1981). Directional selectivity and its use in early visual processing. *Proceedings of the Royal Society of London, Series B, 211,* 151–180.

Marshall, D. A., & Moulton, D. G. (1981). Olfactory sensitivity to a-ionine in humans and dogs. *Chemical Senses, 6,* 53–61.

Marslen-Wilson, W. D. (1980). Speech understanding as a psychological process. In J. C. Simon (Ed.), *Spoken language generation and understanding* (pp. 39–67). Dordrecht, Netherlands: Reidel.

Marslen-Wilson, W. (1989). Access and integration: Projecting sound onto meaning. In W. Marslen-Wilson (Ed.), *Lexical representation and process* (pp. 3–24). Cambridge, MA: MIT Press.

Martin, D. K., & Holden, B. A. (1982). A new method for measuring the diameter of the in vivo human cornea. *American Journal of Optometry and Physiological Optics, 59,* 436–441.

Martin, G. K., Lonsbury-Martin, B. L., Probst, R., & Coats, A. C. (1988). Spontaneous otoacoustic emissions in a nonhuman primate: I. Basic features and relations to other emissions. *Hearing Research, 33,* 49–68.

Martin, M. (1979). Local and global processing: The role of sparsity. *Memory and Cognition, 7,* 476–484.

Martin, R. L., Webster, W. R., & Service, J. (1988). The frequency organization of the inferior colliculus of the guinea pig: A [14C]-2-deoxyglucose study. *Hearing Research, 33,* 245–256.

Masica, D. N., Money, J., Ehrhardt, A. A., & Lewis, V. G. (1969). IQ, fetal sex hormones and cognitive patterns studies in testicular feminizing syndrome of androgen insensitivity. *Johns Hopkins Medical Journal, 124,* 34.

Masland, R. H. (1986). The functional architecture of the retina. *Scientific American, 255,* 102–111.

Massaro, D. (1988). Ambiguity in perception and experimentation. *Journal of Experimental Psychology: General, 117,* 417–421.

Massaro, D. W. (1987). *Speech perception by ear and eye: A paradigm for psychological inquiry.* Hillsdale, NJ: Erlbaum.

Masters, M. S., & Sanders, B. (1993). Is the gender difference in mental rotation disappearing? *Behavior Genetics, 23,* 337–341.

Mather, J. A., & Fisk, J. D. (1985). Orienting to targets by looking and pointing: Parallels and interactions in ocular and manual performance. *Quarterly Journal of Experimental Psychology, 37A,* 315–338.

Matin, L. (1982). Visual localization and eye movements. In A. H. Wertheim, W. A. Wagenaar, & H. W. Leibowitz (Eds.), *Tutorials on motion perception* (pp. 101–156). New York: Plenum Press.

Matin, L., & MacKinnon, G. E. (1964). Autokinetic movement: Selective manipulation of directional components by image stabilization. *Science, 143,* 147–148.

Maturana, H. R., & Frenk, S. (1963). Directional movement and horizontal edge detectors in the pigeon retina. *Science, 142,* 977–979.

Maturana, H. R., Lettvin, J. Y., McCulloch, W. S., & Pitts, W. H. (1960). Anatomy and physiology of vision in the frog (Rana pipins). *Journal of General Physiology, 43*(Suppl. 2), 129–171.

Maunsell, J. H. R., & Newsome, W. T. (1987). Visual processing in monkey extrastriate cortex. *Annual Review of Neuroscience, 10,* 363–401.

Maunsell, J. H. R., & Van Essen, D. C. (1983). Functional properties of neurons in middle temporal visual area of the macaque monkey: I. Selectivity for stimulus direction, speed, and orientation. *Journal of Neurophysiology, 49,* 1127–1147.

Maurer, D. (1975). Infant visual perception: Methods of study. In L. B. Cohen & P. Salapatek (Eds.), *Infant perception: From sensation to cognition, basic visual processes: Vol. 1* (pp. 1–77). New York: Academic Press.

Maurer, D., & Barrera, M. (1981). Infant's perception of natural and distorted arrangements of a schematic face. *Child Development, 52,* 196–202.

Maurer, D., & Lewis, T. L. (1979). A physiological explanation of infants' early visual development. *Canadian Journal of Psychology, 33,* 232–251.

Maurer, D., & Lewis, T. L. (1991). The development of peripheral vision and its physiological underpinnings. In M. J. Weiss & P. R. Zelazo (Eds.), *Newborn attention* (pp. 218–255). Norwood, NJ: Ablex.

Maurer, D., & Martello, M. (1980). The discrimination of orientation by young infants. *Vision Research, 20,* 201–204.

Maurer, D., & Salapatek, P. (1976). Development changes in the scanning of faces by young infants. *Child Development, 47,* 523–527.

Maxwell, J. C. (1873). *Treatise on electricity and magnetism.* Oxford: Clarendon Press.

May, B., & Moody, D. B. (1989). Categorical perception of conspecific communication sounds by Japanese macaques, *Macaca fuscata. Journal of the Acoustical Society of America, 85,* 837–847.

Mayer, D. J., & Watkins, L. R. (1984). Multiple endogenous opiate and nonopiate analgesia systems. In L. Kruger & J. C. Liebeskind (Eds.), *Neural mechanisms of pain* (pp. 253–276). New York: Raven Press.

Mayhew, J. E. W., & Frisby, J. P. (1979). Convergent disparity discriminations in narrow-band-filtered random-dot stereograms. *Vision Research, 19,* 63–71.

Mayhew, J. E. W., & Frisby, J. P. (1980). The computation of binocular edges. *Perception, 9,* 69–86.

Maylor, E. A., & Hockey, R. (1985). Inhibitory component of externally controlled covert orienting in visual space. *Journal of Experimental Psychology: Human Perception and Performance, 11,* 777–787.

McAdams, S., Winsberg, S., Donnadieu, S., De Soete, G., & Krimphoff, J. (1995). Perceptual scaling of synthesized musical timbres: Common dimensions, specificities, and latent subject classes. *Psychological Research, 58,* 177–192.

McAnally, K. I., & Calford, M. B. (1990). A psychophysical study of spectral hyperacuity. *Hearing Research, 44,* 93–96.

McBride, R. L. (1987). Taste psychophysics and the Beidler equation. *Chemical Senses, 12,* 323–332.

McBride, R. L. (1993). Three models for taste mixtures. In D. G. Laing, W. S. Cain, R. L. McBride, & B. W. Ache (Eds.), *Perception of complex smells and tastes* (pp. 265–282). New York: Academic Press.

McBurney, D. H. (1969). Effects of adaptation on human taste function. In C. Pfaffman (Ed.), *Olfaction and taste III* (pp. 407–419). New York: Rockefeller University Press.

McBurney, D. H., Levine, J. M., & Cavanaugh, P. H. (1977). Psychophysical and social ratings of human body odor. *Personality and Social Psychology Bulletin, 3*, 135–138.

McCall, R. B. (1979). Individual differences in the pattern of habituation at five and 10 months of age. *Developmental Psychology, 15*, 559–569.

McClain, L. (1983). Interval estimation: Effect of processing demands on prospective and retrospective reports. *Perception & Psychophysics, 34*, 185–189.

McClellan, P. G., & Bernstein, I. H. (1984). What makes the Mueller a liar: A multiple-cue approach. *Perception & Psychophysics, 36*, 234–244.

McClelland, J. L., & Elman, J. L. (1986). The TRACE model of speech perception. *Cognitive Psychology, 18*, 1–86.

McClintock, M. K. (1971). Menstrual synchrony and suppression. *Nature (London), 229*, 244–245.

McCloskey, M., & Egeth, H. E. (1983). Eyewitness identification: What can a psychologist tell a jury? *American Psychologist, 38*, 550–553.

McColgin, F. H. (1960). Movement threshold in peripheral vision. *Journal of the Optical Society of America, 50*, 774–779.

McCready, D. (1986). Moon illusions redescribed. *Perception & Psychophysics, 39*, 64–72.

McDonald, J. J., & Ward, L. M. (1999). Spatial relevance determines facilitatory and inhibitory effects of auditory covert spatial orienting. *Journal of Experimental Psychology: Human Perception and Performance.*

McFadden, D., & Pasanen, E. G. (1994). Otoacoustic emissions and quinine sulfate. *Journal of the Acoustical Society of America, 95*, 3460–3474.

McFarland, R. A., Domey, R. G., Warren, A. B., & Ward, D. C. (1960). Dark-adaptation as a function of age: I. A statistical analysis. *Journal of Gerontology, 15*, 149–154.

McGee, M. G. (1979). Human spatial abilities: Psychometric studies and environmental, genetic, hormonal, and neurological influences. *Psychological Bulletin, 86*, 889–918.

McGlone, J. (1981). Sexual variations in behavior during spatial and verbal tasks. *Canadian Journal of Psychology, 35*, 277–282.

McGuinness, D. (1972). Hearing: Individual differences in perceiving. *Perception, 1*, 465–473.

McGuinness, D. (1976a). Away from a unisex psychology: Individual differences in visual sensory and perceptual processes. *Perception, 5*, 279–294.

McGuinness, D. (1976b). Sex differences in the organization of perception and cognition. In B. Lloyd & U. Archer (Eds.), *Exploring sex differences* (pp. 123–156). New York: Academic Press.

McGuinness, D., & Lewis, I. (1976). Sex differences in visual persistence: Experiments on the Ganzfeld and the after image. *Perception, 5*, 295–301.

McGurk, H., & MacDonald, J. (1976). Hearing lips and seeing voices. *Nature, 264*, 746–748.

McLaughlin, S. K., McKinnon, P. J., Robichon, A., Spickofsky, N., & Margolskee, R. F. (1993). Gustducin and transducin: A tale of two G proteins. In D. Chadwick, J. Marsh, & J. Goode (Eds.), *The molecular basis of smell and taste transduction* (pp. 186–196). New York: Wiley.

McManus, I. C. (1997). Note: Half-a-million basic colour words: Berlin and Kay and the usage of colour words in literature and science. *Perception, 26*, 367–370.

Meddis, R. (1988). Simulation of auditory-neural transduction: Further studies. *Journal of the Acoustical Society of America, 83*, 1056–1063.

Meehan, J. W. (1993). Apparent minification in an imaging display under reduced viewing conditions. *Perception, 22*, 1075–1084.

Meese, T. S. (1995). Using the standard staircase to measure the point of subjective equality: A guide based on computer simulations. *Perception & Psychophysics, 57*, 267–281.

Meiselman, H. L., Bose, H. E., & Nykvist, W. F. (1972). Magnitude production and magnitude estimation of taste intensity. *Perception & Psychophysics, 12*, 249–252.

Melara, R. D., & Marks, L. E. (1990). Interaction among auditory dimensions: Timbre, pitch, and loudness. *Perception & Psychophysics, 48*, 169–178.

Meltzoff, A. N., & Borton, R. W. (1979). Intermodal matching by human neonates. *Nature, 282*, 403–404.

Melzack, R., & Casey, K. L. (1968). Sensory, motivational, and central control determinants of pain. In D. R. Kenshalo (Ed.), *The skin senses* (pp. 423–443). Springfield, IL: Thomas.

Melzack, R., & Wall, P. D. (1965). Pain mechanisms: A new theory. *Science, 150*, 971–979.

Melzack, R., & Wall, P. D. (1988). *The challenge of pain* (2nd ed.). London: Penguin.

Melzack, R., Wall, P. D., & Ty, T. C. (1982). Acute pain in an emergency clinic: Latency of onset and descriptor patterns related to different injuries. *Pain, 14*, 33–43.

Mercer, M. E., Courage, M. L., & Adams, R. J. (1991). Contrast/color card procedure: A new test of young infants' color vision. *Optometry and Vision Science, 68*, 522–532.

Mergler, D., Bowler, R., & Cone, J. (1990). Colour vision loss among disabled workers with neuropsychological impairment. *Neurotoxicology and Teratology, 12*, 669–672.

Mergner, T., Anastasopoulos, D., Becker, W., & Deecke, L. (1981). Discrimination between trunk and head rotation: A study comparing neuronal data from the cat with human psychophysics. *Acta Psychologica, 48*, 291–302.

Merkel, J. (1885). Die zeitlichen Verhaltnisse der Willensthatigkeit. *Philosophische Studien (Wundt), 2*, 73–127.

Mershon, D. H., Ballenger, W. L., Little, A. D., McMurtry, P. L., & Buchanan, J. L. (1989). Effects of room reflectance and background noise on perceived auditory distance. *Perception, 18*, 403–416.

Mershon, D. H., & Bowers, J. N. (1979). Absolute and relative cues for the auditory perception of egocentric distance. *Perception, 8*, 311–322.

Mershon, D. H., Desaulniers, D. H., & Amerson, T. L. Jr. (1980). Visual capture in auditory distance perception: Proximity image effect reconsidered. *Journal of Auditory Research, 20*, 129–136.

Mershon, D. H., Desaulniers, D. H., Kiefer, S. A., & Amerson, T. L. Jr. (1981). Perceived loudness and visually determined auditory distance. *Perception, 10*, 531–543.

Mershon, D. H., & Gogel, W. C. (1970). Effect of stereoscopic cues on perceived whiteness. *American Journal of Psychology, 83*, 55–67.

Mershon, D. H., & King, L. E. (1975). Intensity and reverberation as factors in the auditory perception of egocentric distance. *Perception & Psychophysics, 18*, 409–415.

Merzenich, M. M., Knight, P. L., & Roth, G. L. (1975). Representation of cochlea within primary auditory cortex in the cat. *Journal of Neurophysiology, 38*, 231–249.

Messerli, P., Pegna, A., & Sordet, N. (1995). Hemispheric dominance for melody recognition in musicians and non-musicians. *Neuropsychologia, 33*, 395–405.

Metzler, D. E., & Harris, C. M. (1978). Shapes of spectral bands of visual pigments. *Vision Research, 18*, 1417–1420.

Michael, C. R. (1966). Receptive fields of directionally selective units in the optic nerve of the ground squirrel. *Science, 152*, 1092–1095.

Michael, C. R. (1985). Laminar segregation of color cells in the monkey's striate cortex. *Vision Research, 25,* 415–423.

Michael, R. P., Keverne, E. B., & Bonsall, R. W. (1971). Pheromones: Isolation of male sex attractants from a female primate. *Science, 172,* 964–966.

Michael, S., & Sherrick, M. F. (1986). Perception of induced visual motion: Effects of relative position, shape and size of the surround. *Canadian Journal of Psychology, 40,* 122–125.

Michaels, C. F., & Carello, C. (1981). *Direct perception.* Englewood Cliffs, NJ: Prentice-Hall.

Michaels, C. F., & Turvey, M. T. (1979). Central sources of masking: Indexing structures supporting seeing at a single, brief glance. *Psychological Research, 41,* 1–61.

Michell, J. (1986). Measurement scales and statistics: A clash of paradigms. *Psychological Bulletin, 100,* 398–407.

Michon, J. (1985). The compleat time experiencer. In J. A. Michon & J. L. Jackson (Eds.), *Time, mind and behavior* (pp. 20–52). Berlin: Springer-Verlag.

Middlebrooks, J. C., Clock, A. C., Xu, L., & Green, D. M. (1994). A panoramic code for sound location by cortical neurons. *Science, 264,* 842–844.

Middlebrooks, J. C., Makous, J. C., & Green, D. M. (1989). Directional sensitivity of sound-pressure levels in the human ear canal. *Journal of the Acoustical Society of America, 86,* 89–108.

Mikaelian, H. (1974). Adaptation to displaced hearing: A nonproprioceptive change. *Journal of Experimental Psychology, 103,* 326–330.

Mikaelian, H., & Held, R. (1964). Two types of adaptation to an optically-rotated visual field. *American Journal of Psychology, 77,* 257–263.

Miles, F. A., & Fuller, J. E. (1975). Visual tracking and the primate flocculus. *Science, 189,* 1000–1002.

Milewski, A. E. (1976). Infant's discrimination of internal and external pattern elements. *Journal of Experimental Child Psychology, 22,* 229–246.

Mill, J. (1829). *Analysis of the phenomena of the human mind.* London.

Millan, M. J. (1986). Multiple opioid systems and pain. *Pain, 27,* 303–347.

Miller, D. L., Moore, R. K., & Wooten, B. R. (1984). When push comes to pull: Impressions of visual direction. *Perception & Psychophysics, 36,* 396–397.

Miller, G. A. (1956). The magical number seven, plus or minus two: Some limits on our capacity for processing information. *Psychological Review, 63,* 81–97.

Miller, G. W., Hicks, R. E., & Willette, M. (1978). Effects of concurrent verbal rehearsal and temporal set upon judgments of temporal duration. *Acta Psychologica, 42,* 173–179.

Miller, J. (1982). Divided attention: Evidence for coactivation with redundant signals. *Cognitive Psychology, 14,* 247–279.

Miller, J. (1996). The sampling distribution of d'. *Perception & Psychophysics, 58,* 65–72.

Miller, J. L., & Eimas, P. D. (1995). Speech perception: From signal to word. *Annual Review of Psychology, 46,* 467–492.

Miller, J. L., & Liberman, A. M. (1979). Some effects of later-occurring information on the perception of stop consonants and semivowel. *Perception & Psychophysics, 25,* 457–465.

Miller, J. M., & Spelman, F. A. (1990). *Cochlear implants: Models of the electrically stimulated ear.* New York: Springer-Verlag.

Miller, N. D. (1965). Visual recovery from brief exposures to high luminance. *Journal of the Optical Society of America, 55,* 1661–1669.

Miller, R. J. (1991). The effect of ingested alcohol on fusion latency at various viewing distances. *Perception & Psychophysics, 50,* 575–583.

Miller, R. J., Pigion, R. G., & Martin, K. D. (1985). The effects of ingested alcohol on accommodation. *Perception & Psychophysics, 37,* 407–414.

Mills, A. W. (1958). On the minimum audible angle. *Journal of the Acoustical Society of America, 30,* 127–246.

Mills, A. W. (1960). Lateralization of high-frequency tones. *Journal of the Acoustical Society of America, 32,* 132–134.

Milne, J., & Milne, M. (1967). *The senses of animals and men.* New York: Atheneum.

Miron, D., Duncan, G. H., & Bushnell, M. C. (1989). Effects of attention on the intensity and unpleasantness of thermal pain. *Pain, 39,* 345–352.

Mishkin, M., & Lewis, M. E. (1982). Equivalence of parieto-preoccipital subareas for visuospatial ability in monkeys. *Journal of Brain and Behavioral Sciences, 6,* 41–55.

Mishkin, M., & Ungerleider, L. G. (1982). Contribution of striate inputs to the visuospatial functions of parieto-preoccipital cortex in monkeys. *Journal of Brain and Behavioral Sciences, 6,* 57–77.

Mishkin, M., Ungerleider, L. G., & Macko, K. A. (1983). Object vision and spatial vision: Two cortical pathways. *Trends in Neuroscience, 6,* 414–417.

Mitchell, D. (1978). Effect of early visual experience on the development of certain perceptual abilities in animals and man. In R. Walk & H. Pick (Eds.), *Perception and experience.* New York: Plenum Press.

Mitchell, D. (1980). The influence of early visual experience on visual perception. In C. Harris (Ed.), *Visual coding and adaptability* (pp. 1–50). Hillsdale, NJ: Erlbaum.

Mitchell, D. (1981). Sensitive periods in visual development. In R. Aslin, J. Alberts, & M. Petersen (Eds.), *Development of perception* (pp. 1–43). New York: Academic Press.

Miyazaki, K. (1995). Perception of relative pitch with different references: Some absolute-pitch listeners cannot tell musical interval names. *Perception & Psychophysics, 57,* 962–970.

Mollon, J. (1995). Seeing colour. In T. Lamb & J. Bourriau (Eds.), *Colour: Art & science* (pp. 127–150). Cambridge, England: Cambridge University Press.

Moncrieff, R. W. (1956). Olfactory adaptation and colour likeness. *Journal of Physiology (London), 133,* 301–316.

Mondor, T. A., Breau, L. M., & Milliken, B. (1998). Inhibitory processes in auditory selective attention: Evidence of location-based and frequency-based inhibition of return. *Perception & Psychophysics, 60,* 296–302.

Mondor, T. A., & Zatorre, R. J. (1995). Shifting and focusing auditory spatial attention. *Journal of Experimental Psychology: Human Perception and Performance, 21,* 387–409.

Money, J. (1965). Psychosexual differentiation. In J. Money (Ed.), *Sex research: New developments* (pp. 3–23). New York: Holt.

Montellese, S., Sharpe, L. T., & Brown, J. L. (1979). Changes in critical duration during dark-adaptation. *Vision Research, 19,* 1147–1153.

Montgomery, J. C., & MacDonald, J. A. (1987). Sensory tuning of lateral line receptors in Antarctic fish to the movements of planktonic prey. *Science, 235,* 195–196.

Moonen, C. T. W., van Zijl, P. C. M., Frank, J. A., Le Bihan, D., & Becker, E. D. (1990). Functional magnetic resonance imaging in medicine and physiology. *Science, 250,* 53–61.

Mooney, R. D., Dubin, M. W., & Rusoff, A. C. (1979). Interneuron circuits in the lateral geniculate nucleus of monocularly deprived cats. *Journal of Comparative Neurology, 187*(3), 533–544.

Moore, B. (1977). *Introduction to the psychology of hearing.* Baltimore: University Park Press.

Moore, L. M., Nielson, C. R., & Mistretta, C. M. (1982). Sucrose taste thresholds: Age-related differences. *Journal of Gerontology, 37,* 64–69.

Moran, J., & Desimone, R. (1985). Selective attention gates visual processing in the extrastriate cortex. *Science, 229,* 782–784.

Moran, J., & Gordon, B. (1982). Long term visual deprivation in a human. *Vision Research, 22,* 27–36.

Moray, N. (1959). Attention in dichotic listening: Affective cues and the influence of instructions. *Quarterly Journal of Experimental Psychology, 11,* 56–60.

Moray, N. (1969). *Attention: Selective processes in vision and hearing.* London: Hutchinson Educational.

Mori, S., & Ward, L. M. (1991). Listening versus hearing: Attentional effects on intensity discrimination. *Technical Report on Hearing: The Acoustical Society of Japan,* No. H-91-36.

Mori, S., & Ward, L. M. (1992). Listening versus hearing II: Attentional effects on intensity discrimination by musicians. *Technical Report on Hearing: The Acoustical Society of Japan,* No. H-92-48.

Morris, V., & Morris, P. E. (1985). The influence of question order on eyewitness accuracy. *British Journal of Psychology, 76,* 365–371.

Morrison, F. J., Holmes, D. L., & Haith, M. M. (1974). A developmental study of the effect of familiarity on short-term visual memory. *Journal of Experimental Child Psychology, 18,* 412–425.

Morrison, J. D., & Whiteside, T. C. D. (1984). Binocular cues in the perception of distance of a point source of light. *Perception, 13,* 555–566.

Morse, P. A., & Molfese, D. L. (1987). Categorical perception for voicing contrasts in normal and lead-treated rhesus monkeys: Electrophysiological indices. *Brain and Language, 30,* 63–80.

Moskowitz, H., Sharma, S., & McGlothlin, W. (1972). Effect of marijuana upon peripheral vision as a function of the information processing demands in central vision. *Perceptual and Motor Skills, 35,* 875.

Moskowitz-Cook, A. (1979). The development of photopic spectral sensitivity in human infants. *Vision Research, 9,* 113–1142.

Mountain, D. C., & Hubbard, A. E. (1994). A piezoelectric model of outer hair cell function. *Journal of the Acoustical Society of America, 95,* 350–354.

Mountcastle, V. B., Motter, B. C., Steinmetz, M. A., & Sestokas, A. K. (1987). Common and differential effects of attentive fixation on the excitability of parietal and prestriate (V4) cortical visual neurons in the macaque monkey. *Journal of Neuroscience, 7,* 2239–2255.

Movshon, J. A., Adelson, E. H., Gizzi, M. S., & Newsome, W. T. (1985). The analysis of moving visual patterns. In C. Chagas, R. Gattass, & C. Gross (Eds.), *Pattern recognition mechanisms* (pp. 117–151). Rome: Vatican Press.

Movshon, J. A., & Newsome, W. T. (1992). Neural foundations of visual motion perception. *Current Directions in Psychological Science, 1,* 35–39.

Movshon, J. A., & Van Sluyters, R. C. (1981). Visual neural development. *Annual Review of Psychology, 32,* 477–522.

Mozel, M. M., Smith, B., Smith, P., Sullivan, R., & Swender, P. (1969). Nasal chemoreception in flavor identification. *Archives of Otolaryngology, 90,* 367–373.

Muir, D., & Field, J. (1979). Newborn infants orient to sounds. *Child Development, 50,* 431–436.

Muir, D. W., Clifton, R. K., & Clarkson, M. G. (1989). The development of a human auditory localization response: A U-shaped function. *Canadian Journal of Psychology, 43,* 199–216.

Mullen, K. T. (1990). The chromatic coding of space. In C. Blakemore (Ed.), *Vision: Coding and efficiency* (pp. 150–158). New York: Cambridge University Press.

Muller, H. J., & Findlay, J. M. (1988). The effect of visual attention on peripheral discrimination thresholds in single and multiple element displays. *Acta Psychologica, 69,* 129–155.

Muller, H. J., & Humphreys, G. W. (1991). Luminance-increment detection: Capacity-limited or not? *Journal of Experimental Psychology: Human Perception and Performance, 17,* 107–124.

Muller, H. J., & Rabbitt, P. M. A. (1989). Reflexive and voluntary orienting of visual attention: Time course of activation and resistance to interruption. *Journal of Experimental Psychology: Human Perception and Performance, 15,* 315–330.

Mulligan, R. M., & Schiffman, H. R. (1979). Temporal experience as a function of organization in memory. *Bulletin of the Psychonomic Society, 14,* 417–420.

Munoz, D. P., & Wurtz, R. H. (1993). Fixation cells in monkey superior colliculus: I: Characteristics of cell discharge. *Journal of Neurophysiology, 70,* 559–575.

Munoz, D. P., & Wurtz, R. H. (1995). Saccade-related activity in monkey superior colliculus: I: Characteristics of burst and buildup neurons. *Journal of Neurophysiology, 73,* 2313–2333.

Munsell, A. H. (1915). *Atlas of the Munsell color system.* Maldin, MA: Wadsworth, Howland.

Murphy, C., & Cain, W. S. (1980). Taste and olfaction: Independence vs. interaction. *Physiology and Behavior, 24,* 601–605.

Murray, J. B. (1986). Marijuana's effects on human cognitive functions, psychomotor functions, and personality. *Journal of General Psychology, 113,* 23–55.

Mustillo, P. (1985). Binocular mechanisms mediating crossed and uncrossed stereopsis. *Psychological Bulletin, 97,* 187–201.

Myers, A. K. (1982). Psychophysical scaling and scales of physical stimulus measurement. *Psychological Bulletin, 92,* 203–214.

Näätänen, R., Lehtokoski, A., Lennes, M., Cheour, M., Houtilainen, M., Ilvonen, A., Vainlo, M., Alkus, P., Ilmoniemi, Luuk, A., Allik, J., Sinkonen, J., & Alho, K. (1997). Language-specific phoneme representations revealed by electric and magnetic brain responses, *Nature, 385,* 432–434.

Nagy, A. L. (1980). Short-flash Bezold-Brucke hue shifts. *Vision Research, 20,* 361–368.

Naka, Ken-Ichi. (1982). The cells horizontal cells talk to. *Vision Research, 22,* 653–660.

Nakayama, K. (1985). Biological image motion processing: A review. *Vision Research, 25,* 625–660.

Nakayama, K., Shimojo, S., & Silverman, G. H. (1989). Stereoscopic depth: Its relation to image segmentation, grouping, and the recognition of occluded objects. *Perception, 18,* 55–68.

Nakayama, K., & Silverman, G. H. (1986). Serial and parallel processing of visual feature conjunctions. *Nature, 320,* 264–265.

Narens, L., & Luce, R. D. (1986). Measurement: The theory of numerical assignments. *Psychological Bulletin, 99,* 166–180.

Narens, L., & Mausfeld, R. (1992). On the relationship of the psychological and the physical in psychophysics. *Psychological Review, 99,* 467–479.

Nathans, J. (1987). Molecular biology of visual pigments. *Annual Review of Neuroscience, 10,* 163–164.

Nathans, J., Plantanida, T. P., Eddy, R. L., Shows, T. B., & Hogness, D. S. (1986). Molecular genetics of inherited variation in human color vision. *Science, 232,* 203–210.

Navon, D. (1977). Forest before trees: The precedence of global features in visual perception. *Cognitive Psychology, 9*, 353–383.

Navon, D., & Gopher, D. (1979). On the economy of the human-processing system. *Psychological Review, 86*, 214–255.

Navon, D., & Norman, J. (1983). Does global precedence really depend on visual angle? *Journal of Experimental Psychology: Human Perception and Performance, 9*, 955–965.

Neely, S. T. (1993). A model of cochlear mechanics with outer hair cell motility. *Journal of the Acoustical Society of America, 94*, 137–146.

Neff, D. L. (1991). Forward masking by maskers of uncertain frequency content. *Journal of the Acoustical Society of America, 89*, 1314–1323.

Neff, D. L., & Green, D. M. (1987). Masking produced by spectral uncertainty with multicomponent maskers. *Perception & Psychophysics, 41*, 409–415.

Neisser, U. (1967). *Cognitive psychology.* New York: Appleton.

Neisser, U. (1976). *Cognition and reality: Principles and implications of cognitive psychology.* San Francisco: Freeman.

Neisser, U., & Becklin, R. (1975). Selective looking: Attending to visually specified events. *Cognitive Psychology, 7*, 480–494.

Neitz, J., & Jacobs, G. H. (1986). Polymorphism of the long-wavelength cone in normal human colour vision. *Nature, 323*, 623–625.

Nelson, C. A., & Ludemann, P. M. (1989). Past, current, and future trends in infant face perception research. *Canadian Journal of Psychology, 43*, 183–198.

Nelson, R., Kolb, H., Robinson, M. M., & Mariani, A. P. (1981). Neural circuitry of the cat retina: Cone pathways to ganglion cells. *Vision Research, 21*, 1527–1537.

Neuhoff, J. G., & McBeath, M. K. (1996). The Doppler illusion: The influence of dynamic intensity change on perceived pitch. *Journal of Experimental Psychology: Human Perception and Performance, 22*, 970–985.

Nevatia, R. (1982). *Machine perception.* Englewood Cliffs, NJ: Prentice-Hall.

Neville, H. J. (1985). Effects of early sensory and language experience on the development of the human brain. In J. Mehler & R. Fox (Eds.), *Neonate cognition: Beyond the bloom buzzing confusion* (pp. 349–364). Hillsdale, NJ: Erlbaum.

Neville, H. J., Schmidt, A., & Kutas, M. (1983). Altered visual evoked potentials in congenitally deaf adults. *Brain Research, 266*, 127–132.

Newhall, S. M., Burnham, R. W., & Clark, J. R. (1957). Comparison of successive with simultaneous color matching. *Journal of the Optical Society of America, 47*, 43–56.

Newhall, S. M., Nickerson, D., & Judd, D. B. (1943). Final report of the O.S.A. subcommittee on spacing of the Munsell colors. *Journal of the Optical Society of America, 33*, 385–418.

Newland, J. (1972). *Children's knowledge of left and right.* Unpublished master's thesis, University of Auckland. Cited in M. C. Corballis & J. L. Beale (1976), *The psychology of left and right* (p. 167). Hillsdale, NJ: Erlbaum.

Newsome, W. T., Britten, K. H., & Movshon, J. A. (1989). Neuronal correlates of a perceptual decision. *Nature, 341*, 52–54.

Newsome, W. T., & Pare, E. B. (1988). A selective impairment of motion processing following lesions of the middle temporal visual area (MT). *Journal of Neuroscience, 8*, 2201–2211.

Niall, K. K. (1990). Projective invariance and picture perception. *Perception, 19*, 637–660.

Nickell, W. T. (1997). Basic anatomy and physiology of olfaction. In A. M. Seiden (Ed.), *Taste and smell disorders* (pp. 20–37). New York: Thieme.

Nihjawan, R. (1994). Motion extrapolation in catching. *Nature, 370*, 256–257.

Nijhawan, R. (1991). Three-dimensional Mueller-Lyer illusion. *Perception & Psychophysics, 49*, 333–341.

Nissen, M. J., & Corkin, S. (1985). Effectiveness of attentional cueing in older and younger adults. *Journal of Gerontology, 40*, 185–191.

Noda, H., Freeman, R. B., & Creutzfeldt, O. D. (1972). Neuronal correlates of eye movements in the cat visual cortex. *Science, 175*, 661–664.

Noell, W. (1980). Possible mechanisms of photoreceptor damage by light in mammalian eyes. *Vision Research, 20*, 1163–1172.

Nordin, S. (1994). Context effects, reliability, and internal consistency of intermodal joint scaling. *Perception & Psychophysics, 55*, 180–189.

Norman, D. A. (1968). Toward a theory of memory and attention. *Psychological Review, 75*, 522–536.

Norman, D. A. (1969). Memory while shadowing. *Quarterly Journal of Experimental Psychology, 21*, 85–93.

Norman, D. A., Rumelhart, D. E., and the LNR Research Group. (1975). *Explorations in cognition.* San Francisco: Freeman.

Norman, J. F., Todd, J. T., Perotti, V. J., & Tittle, J. S. (1996). The visual perception of three-dimensional length. *Journal of Experimental Psychology: Human Perception & Performance, 22*, 173–186.

Norton, S. J., Schultz, M. C., Reed, C. M., Braida, L. D., Durlach, N. I., Rabinowitz, W. M., & Chomsky, C. (1977). Analytic study of the Tadoma method: Background and preliminary results. *Journal of Speech and Hearing Research, 20*, 574–595.

Norton, T. T. (1981a). Development of the visual system and visually guided behavior. In R. Aslin, J. Alberts, & M. Petersen (Eds.), *Development of perception: Psychobiological perspectives: Vol. 2. The visual system* (pp. 113–156). New York: Academic Press.

Norton, T. T. (1981b). Geniculate and extrageniculate visual systems in the tree shrew. In A. R. Morrison and P. L. Strick (Eds.), *Changing concepts of the nervous system* (pp. 377–410). New York: Academic Press.

Norwich, K. H. (1983). To perceive is to doubt: The relativity of perception. *Journal of Theoretical Biology, 102*, 175–190.

Norwich, K. H. (1984). The psychophysics of taste from the entropy of the stimulus. *Perception & Psychophysics, 35*, 269–278.

Norwich, K. N. (1993). *Information, sensation and perception.* Orlando: Academic Press.

Nusbaum, H. C., & Schwab, E. C. (1986). The role of attention and active processing in speech perception. In E. C. Schwab & H. C. Nusbaum (Eds.), *Pattern recognition by humans and machines: Vol. 1. Speech perception* (pp. 113–157). Orlando: Academic Press.

Nygaard, L. C. (1993). Phonetic coherence in duplex perception: Effects of acoustic differences and lexical status. *Journal of Experimental Psychology: Human Perception and Performance, 19*, 268–286.

O'Connell, R. J., & Mozell, M. M. (1969). Quantitative stimulation of frog olfactory receptors. *Journal of Neurophysiology, 32*, 51–63.

Ogasawara, K., McHaftie, J. G., & Stein, B. E. (1984). Two visual corticotectal systems in the cat. *Journal of Neurophysiology, 52*, 1226–1245.

Ohala, J. J. (1986). Phonological evidence for top-down processing in speech perception. In J. S. Perkell and D. H. Klatt (Eds.), *Invariance and variability in speech processes* (pp. 386–397). Hillsdale, NJ: Erlbaum.

Ohala, J. J. (1996). Speech perception is hearing sounds, not tongues. *Journal of the Acoustical Society of America, 99*, 1718–1725.

O'Kusky, J., & Colonnier, M. (1982). Postnatal changes in the number of neurons and synapses in the visual cortex (A17) of the macaque monkey.

Journal of Comparative Neurology, 210, 291–296.

Oldfield, S. R., & Parker, S. P. A. (1984). Acuity of sound localization: A topography of auditory space: II. Pinna cues absent. *Perception, 13,* 601–617.

Oldfield, S. R., & Parker, S. P. A. (1986). Acuity of sound localization: A topography of auditory space: III. Monaural hearing conditions. *Perception, 15,* 67–81.

O'Leary, A., & McMahon, M. (1991). Adaptation to form distortion of a familiar shape. *Perception & Psychophysics, 49,* 328–332.

Olsho, L. W. (1984). Infant frequency discrimination. *Infant Behavior and Development, 7,* 27–35.

Olson, R., & Attneave, F. (1970). What variables produce similarity grouping? *American Journal of Psychology, 83,* 1–21.

Olzak, L. (1986). Widely separated spatial frequencies: Mechanism interactions. *Vision Research, 26,* 1143–1154.

O'Mahony, M., & Heintz, C. (1981). Direct magnitude estimation of salt taste intensity with continuous correction for salivary adaptation. *Chemical Senses, 6,* 101–112.

Ono, H. (1969). Apparent distance as a function of familiar size. *Journal of Experimental Psychology, 79,* 109–115.

Ono, H., & Rogers, B. J. (1988). Dynamic occlusion and motion parallax in depth perception. *Perception, 17,* 255–256.

Ono, H., & Weber, E. U. (1981). Nonveridical visual direction produced by monocular viewing. *Journal of Experimental Psychology: Human Perception and Performance, 7,* 937–947.

Ono, M. E., Rivest, J., & Ono, H. (1986). Depth perception as a function of motion parallax and absolute-distance information. *Journal of Experimental Psychology: Human Perception and Performance, 12,* 331–337.

Orban, G. A. (1984). *Neuronal operations in the visual cortex.* Berlin: Springer-Verlag.

Orban, G. A., Kennedy, H., & Maes, H. (1981a). Response to movement of neurons in areas 17 and 18 of the cat: Velocity sensitivity. *Journal of Neurophysiology, 45,* 1043–1058.

Orban, G. A., Kennedy, H., & Maes, H. (1981b). Response to movement of neurons in areas 17 and 18 of the cat: Direction sensitivity. *Journal of Neurophysiology, 45,* 1059–1073.

Ornstein, R. E. (1969). *On the experience of time.* London: Penguin.

Osaka, N. (1981). Brightness exponent as a function of flash duration and retinal eccentricity. *Perception & Psychophysics, 30,* 144–148.

Osborne, M. P., Comis, S. D., & Pickles, J. O. (1988). Further observations on the fine structure of tip links between stereocilia of the guinea pig cochlea. *Hearing Research, 35,* 99–108.

O'Shaughnessy, D. (1996). Critique: Speech perception: Acoustic or articulatory? *Journal of the Acoustical Society of America, 99,* 1726–1729.

Osterberg, G. (1935). Topography of the layer of rods and cones in the human retina. *Acta Ophthalmologica* (Suppl. 6).

Ostfeld, A. (1961). Effects of LSD-25 and JB318 on tests of visual and perceptual functions in man. *Federation Proceedings, Federation of American Societies for Experimental Biology, 20,* 876–883.

Ottoson, D. (1956). Analysis of the electrical activity of the olfactory epithelium. *Acta Physiologica Scandinavica, 35*(Suppl. 122), 1–83.

Owens, M. E. (1984). Pain in infancy: Conceptual and methodological issues. *Pain, 20,* 213–220.

Owsley, C. (1983). The role of motion in infants' perception of solid shape. *Perception, 12,* 707–717.

Owsley, C. J., Sekuler, R., & Siemensen, D. (1983). Contrast sensitivity throughout adulthood. *Vision Research, 23,* 689–699.

Oyama, T. (1968). A behavioristic analysis of Stevens's magnitude estimation method. *Perception & Psychophysics, 317–320.*

Oyama, T. (1986). The effect of stimulus organization on numerosity discrimination. *Japanese Psychological Research, 28,* 77–86.

Pagano, C. C., Kinsella-Shaw, J. M., Cassidy, P. E., & Turvey, M. T. (1994). Role of the inertia tensor in haptically perceiving where an object is grasped. *Journal of Experimental Psychology: Human Perception & Performance, 20,* 276–285.

Palmer, A. R., Winter, I. M., & Darwin, C. J. (1986). The representation of steady-state vowel sounds in the temporal discharge pattern of the guinea pig cochlear nerve and primarylike cochlear nucleus neurons. *Journal of the Acoustical Society of America, 79,* 100–113.

Palmer, C., & Krumhansl, C. L. (1987). Independent temporal and pitch structures in determination of musical phrases. *Journal of Experimental Psychology: Human Perception and Performance, 13,* 116–126.

Palmer, C., & Krumhansl, C. L. (1990). Mental representations for musical meter. *Journal of Experimental Psychology: Human Perception and Performance, 16,* 728–741.

Palmer, J. (1986). Mechanisms of displacement discrimination with and without perceived movement. *Journal of Experimental Psychology: Human Perception and Performance, 12,* 411–421.

Palmer, S. E. (1975a). The effects of contextual scenes on the identification of objects. *Memory and Cognition, 3,* 519–526.

Palmer, S. E. (1975b). Visual perception and world knowledge: Notes on a model of sensory-cognitive interaction. In D. A. Norman & D. E. Rumelhart (Eds.), *Explorations in cognition* (pp. 297–307). San Francisco: Freeman.

Palmer, S. E., Neff, J., & Beck, D. (1996). Late influences on perceptual grouping: Amodal completion. *Psychonomic Bulletin & Review, 3,* 75–80.

Palmer, S. E., & Rock, I. (1994). Rethinking perceptual organization: The role of uniform connectedness. *Psychonomic Bulletin & Review, 1,* 29–55.

Pantev, C., Hoke, M., Lutkenhoner, B., & Lehnertz, K. (1989). Tonotopic organization of the auditory cortex: Pitch versus frequency representation. *Science, 246,* 486–488.

Papert, S. (1961). Centrally produced geometric illusions. *Nature, 191,* 733.

Paquet, L., & Merikle, P. M. (1984). Global precedence: The effect of exposure duration. *Canadian Journal of Psychology, 38,* 45–53.

Paramei, G. V. (1996). Color space of normally sighted and color deficient observers reconstructed from color naming. *Psychological Science, 7,* 311–317.

Parasuraman, R. (1984). Sustained attention in detection and discrimination. In R. Parasuraman & D. R. Davies (Eds.), *Varieties of attention* (pp. 243–271). Orlando: Academic Press.

Parducci, A. (1965). Category judgment: A range-frequency model. *Psychological Review, 72,* 407–418.

Parker, D. E. (1980). The vestibular apparatus. *Scientific American, 243,* 118–135.

Parks, T. E. (1965). Post-retinal visual storage. *American Journal of Psychology, 78,* 145–147.

Parlee, M. B. (1983). Menstrual rhythms in sensory processes: A review of fluctuations in vision, olfaction, audition, taste and touch. *Psychological Bulletin, 93,* 539–548.

Parrott, A. C. (1988). Transdermal scopolamine: Effects upon psychological performance and visual functioning at sea. *Human Psychopharmacology Clinical & Experimental, 3,* 119–125.

Pashler, H. (1984). Evidence against late selection: Stimulus quality effects in previewed displays. *Journal of Experimental Psychology: Human Perception and Performance, 10,* 429–448.

Pashler, H. (1987). Detecting conjunctions of color and form: Reassessing the serial search hypothesis. *Perception & Psychophysics, 41,* 191–201.

Pashler, H. (1996). *The psychology of attention.* Cambridge, MA: MIT Press.

Pasnak, R., Tyer, Z. A., & Allen, J. A. (1985). Effect of distance instructions on size judgements. *American Journal of Psychology, 98,* 297–304.

Pastore, R. E., & Li, X. F. (1990). Categorical perception of nonspeech chirps and bleats. *Perception & Psychophysics, 48,* 151–156.

Pastore, R. E., Schmeckler, M. A., Rosenblum, L., & Szczesiul, R. (1983). Duplex perception with musical stimuli. *Perception & Psychophysics, 33,* 469–474.

Patla, A. E., & Goodale, M. A. (1996). Obstacle avoidance during locomotion is unaffected in a patient with visual form agnosia. *Neuroreport, 8,* 165–168.

Patterson, R. D. (1969). Noise masking of a change in residue pitch. *Journal of the Acoustical Society of America, 45,* 1520–1524.

Paulus, K., & Haas, E. M. (1980). The influence of solvent viscosity on the threshold values of primary tastes. *Chemical Senses, 5,* 23–32.

Paulus, K., & Reisch, A. M. (1980). The influence of temperature on the threshold values of primary tastes. *Chemical Senses, 5,* 11–21.

Paus, T., Zatorre, R. J., Hofle, N., Caramanos, Z., Gotman, J., Petrides, M., & Evans, A. C. (1997). Time-related changes in neural systems underlying attention and arousal during the performance of an auditory vigilance task. *Journal of Cognitive Neuroscience, 9,* 392–408.

Pearson, D. A., & Lane, D. M. (1991a). Auditory attention switching: A developmental study. *Journal of Experimental Child Psychology, 51,* 320–334.

Pearson, D. A., & Lane, D. M. (1991b). Visual attention movements: A developmental study. *Child Development, 61,* 1779–1795.

Pedersen, P. M., Jorgensen, H. S., Nakayama, H., Raaschou, H. O., & Olsen, T. S. (1997). Hemineglect in acute stroke—incidence and prognostic implications. The Copenhagen Stroke Study. *American Journal of Physical Medicine & Rehabilitation, 76,* 122–127.

Peeples, D. R., & Teller, D. Y. (1978). White-adapted photopic spectral sensitivity in human infants. *Vision Research, 18,* 39–53.

Peichl, L., & Wassle, H. (1979). Size, scatter and coverage of ganglion-cell receptive-field centers in the cat retina. *Journal of Physiology (London), 291,* 117.

Pelosi, P., & Pisanelli, A. M. (1981). Specific anosmia to 1,8-cineole: The camphor primary odor. *Chemical Senses, 6,* 87–93.

Pelosi, P., & Tirindelli, R. (1989). Structure/activity studies and characterization of an odorant-binding protein. In J. G. Brand, J. H. Teeter, R. H. Cagan, & M. R. Kare (Eds.), *Chemical senses. Vol. 1: Receptor events and transduction in taste and olfaction* (pp. 207–226). New York: Marcel Dekker, Inc.

Penfield, W., & Rasmussen, T. (1950). *The cerebral cortex of man.* New York: Macmillan.

Pentland, A. P. (1986). Perceptual organization and the representation of natural form. *Artificial Intelligence, 28,* 293–331.

Perez, F. M., Tunkel, R. S., Lachmann, E. A., & Nagler, W. (1997). Balint's syndrome arising from bilateral posterior cortical atrophy or infarction: Rehabilitation strategies and their limitation. *Disability & Rehabilitation, 18,* 300–304.

Perkell, J. S., & Klatt, D. H. (Eds.). (1986). *Invariance and variability in speech processes.* Hillsdale, NJ: Erlbaum.

Perl, E. R. (1984). Characterization of nociceptors and their activation of neurons in the superficial dorsal horn: First steps for the sensation of pain. In L. Kruger & J. C. Liebeskind (Eds.), *Neural mechanisms of pain* (pp. 23–52). New York: Raven Press.

Perlman, M., & Krumhansl, C. L. (1996). An experimental study of interval standards in Javanese and Western musicians. *Music Perception, 14,* 95–116.

Perrett, D. I., & Mistlin, A. M. (1987). Visual neurones responsive to faces. *Trends in Neuroscience, 10,* 358–364.

Perrett, S., & Noble, W. (1995). Available response choices affect localization of sound. *Perception & Psychophysics, 57,* 150–158.

Perrott, D. R., & Saberi, K. (1990). Minimum audible angle thresholds for sources varying in both elevation and azimuth. *Journal of the Acoustical Society of America, 87,* 1728–1731.

Perrott, D. R., Constantino, B., & Bell, J. (1993). Discrimination of moving events which accelerate or decelerate over the listening interval. *Journal of the Acoustical Society of America, 93,* 1053–1057.

Perrott, D. R., & Tucker, J. (1988). Minimum audible movement angle as a function of signal frequency and the velocity of the source. *Journal of the Acoustical Society of America, 83,* 1522–1527.

Perry, V. H., & Silveira, L. C. (1988). Functional lamination in the ganglion cell layer of the macaque's retina. *Neuroscience, 12,* 1101–1123.

Pessoa, L., Mingolla, E., & Arend, L. E. (1996). The perception of lightness in 3-D curved objects. *Perception & Psychophysics, 58,* 1293–1305.

Petersen, A. C., & Crockett, L. (1985, August). Factors influencing sex differences in spatial ability during adolescence. In S. L. Willis (Chair), *Sex Differences in Spatial Ability Across the Lifespan.* Symposium conducted at the Ninety-Third Annual Convention of the American Psychological Association, Los Angeles, CA.

Petersik, J. T. (1989). The two-process distinction in apparent motion. *Psychological Bulletin, 106,* 107–127.

Peterson, A. C. (1976). Physical androgyny and cognitive functioning in adolescence. *Developmental Psychology, 12,* 524–533.

Petitto, L. A., & Marentette, P. F. (1991). Babbling in the manual mode: Evidence for the ontogeny of language. *Science, 251,* 1493–1496.

Petrig, B., Julesz, B., Kropfl, W., Baumgartner, G., & Anliker, M. (1981). Development of stereopsis and cortical binocularity in human infants: Electrophysiological evidence. *Science, 213,* 1402–2405.

Petry, S., & Meyer, G. E. (1987). *The perception of illusory contours.* New York: Springer-Verlag.

Pevsner, J., Sklar, P. B., Hwang, P. M., & Snyder, S. H. (1989). Odorant binding protein: Sequence analysis and localization suggest an odorant transport function. In J. G. Brand, J. H. Teeter, R. H. Cagan, & M. R. Kare (Eds.), *Chemical senses. Vol. 1: Receptor events and transduction in taste and olfaction* (pp. 227–242). New York: Marcel Dekker, Inc.

Pfaff, D. (1968). Effects of temperature and time of day on judgment. *Journal of Experimental Psychology, 76,* 419–422.

Pfaffman, C. (1955). Gustatory nerve impulses in rat, cat, and rabbit. *Journal of Neurophysiology, 18,* 429–440.

Pfaffman, C. (1974). Specificity of the sweet receptors of the squirrel monkey. *Chemical Senses and Flavor, 1,* 61–67.

Pfaffman, C., Bartoshuk, L., & McBurney, D. H. (1971). Taste psychophysics. *Handbook of Sensory Physiology, 1,* 75–101.

Pfeiffer, R. R. (1966). Classification of response patterns of spike discharges for units in the cochlear nucleus: Toneburst stimulation. *Experimental Brain Research, 1,* 220–235.

Phillips, C. G., Zeki, S., & Barlow, H. B. (1984). Localization of function in the cerebral cortex. *Brain, 107,* 328–360.

Phillips, D. F. (1993). Representation of acoustic events in the primary auditory cortex. *Journal of Experimental Psychology: Human Perception and Performance,* *19,* 203–216.

Phillips, D. P., & Brugge, J. F. (1985). Progress in neurophysiology of sound localization. *Annual Review of Psychology, 36,* 245–274.

Phillipson, O. T., & Harris, J. P. (1984). Effects of chlorpromazine and promazine on the perception of some multi-stable visual figures. *Quarterly Journal of Experimental Psychology, 36A,* 291–308.

Phillipson, O. T., & Harris, J. P. (1985). Perceptual changes in schizophrenia: A questionnaire survey. *Psychological Medicine, 15,* 859–866.

Piaget, J. (1969). *The mechanisms of perception.* (G. N. Seagrine, Trans.). New York: Oxford University Press.

Pick, H. L. Jr. (1987). Information and the effects of early perceptual experience. In N. Eisenberg (Ed.), *Contemporary topics in developmental psychology* (pp. 59–76). New York: Wiley.

Pick, H. L. Jr. (1992). Eleanor J. Gibson: Learning to perceive and perceiving to learn. *Developmental Psychology, 28,* 787–794.

Pick, H. L. Jr., & Hay, J. C. (1965). A passive test of the Held reafference hypothesis. *Perceptual and Motor Skills, 20,* 1070–1072.

Pick, H. L. Jr., & Pick, A. D. (1970). Sensory and perceptual development. In P. H. Mussen (Ed.), *Carmichael's manual of child development* (pp. 773–848). New York: Wiley.

Pickles, J. O. (1988). *An introduction to the physiology of hearing* (2nd ed.). San Diego: Academic Press.

Pickles, J. O., Comis, S. D., & Osborne, M. P. (1984). Cross-links between stereocilia in the guinea pig organ of Corti, and their possible relation to sensory transduction. *Hearing Research, 15,* 103–112.

Pickles, J. O., Osborne, M. P., Comis, S. D., Köppl, C., Gleich, O., Brix, J., & Manley, G. A. (1989). Tip-link organization in relation to the structure and orientation of stereovillar bundles. In J. P. Wilson & D. T. Kemp (Eds.), *Cochlear mechanisms: Structure, function and models.* New York: Plenum Press.

Pierce, J. D. Jr., & Wysocki, C. J. (1996). The role of perceptual and structural similarity in cross adaptation. *Chemical Senses, 21,* 223–237.

Piggins, D. J., Kingham, J. R., & Holmes, S. M. (1972). Colour, colour saturation and pattern induced by intermittent illumination: An initial study. *British Journal of Physiological Optics, 27,* 120–125.

Pind, J. (1995). Speaking rate, voice-onset time, and quantity: The search for higher-order invariants for two Ice-
landic speech cues. *Perception & Psychophysics, 57,* 291–304.

Pinel, J. P. J. (1990). *Biopsychology.* Boston: Allyn & Bacon.

Pinker, S. (1997). *How the mind works.* New York: W. W. Norton.

Pinkers, A., & Marre, M. (1983). Basic phenomena in acquired colour vision deficiency. *Documenta Ophthalmologica, 55,* 251–271.

Pirozzolo, F. J. (1978). *The neuropsychology of developmental reading disorders.* New York: Praeger.

Pisoni, D. B. (1973). Auditory and phonetic codes in the discrimination of consonants and vowels. *Perception & Psychophysics, 13,* 253–260.

Pisoni, D. B., & Luce, P. A. (1986). Speech perception: Research, theory, and the principal issues. In E. C. Schwab & H. C. Nusbaum (Eds.), *Pattern recognition by humans and machines: Vol. 1. Speech perception* (pp. 1–50). Orlando: Academic Press.

Pitt, M. A. (1994). Perception of pitch and timbre by musically trained and untrained listeners. *Journal of Experimental Psychology: Human Perception and Performance, 20,* 976–986.

Plateau, M. H. (1872). Sur la mesure des sensations physiques, et sur la loi qui lie l'intensité de la cause excitante. *Bulletin de l'Academie Royale de Belgique, 33,* 376–388.

Plude, D. J. (1990). Aging, feature integration, and visual attention. In J. T. Enns (Ed.), *The development of attention: Research and theory* (pp. 467–487). Amsterdam: Elsevier.

Plude, D. J., & Hoyer, W. J. (1986). Age and the selectivity of visual information processing. *Psychology and Aging, 1,* 4–10.

Plug, C., & Ross, H. E. (1994). The natural moon illusion: A multifactor angular account. *Perception, 23,* 321–333.

Podgorny, P., & Shepard, R. N. (1983). Distribution of visual attention over space. *Journal of Experimental Psychology: Human Perception and Performance, 9,* 380–393.

Poggio, G. F., & Fischer, B. (1977). Binocular interaction and depth sensitivity in striate cortical neurons of behaving rhesus monkeys. *Journal of Neurophysiology, 40,* 1392–1405.

Poggio, G. F., & Mountcastle, V. B. (1960). A study of the functional contributions of the lemniscal and spinothalamic systems to somatic sensibility: Central nervous mechanisms in pain. *Bulletin of the Johns Hopkins Hospital, 106,* 266–316.

Poggio, G. F., & Poggio, T. (1984). The analysis of stereopsis. *Annual Review of Neuroscience, 7,* 379–412.

Poggio, G. F., & Talbot, W. H. (1981). Mechanisms of static and dynamic stereopsis in foveal cortex of rhesus monkey. *Journal of Physiology, 315,* 469–492.

Pohl, W. (1973). Dissociation of spatial discrimination deficits following frontal and parietal lesions in monkeys. *Journal of Comparative Physiology and Psychology, 82,* 227–239.

Pokorny, J., & Smith, V. C. (1986). Eye disease and color defects. *Vision Research, 26,* 1573–1584.

Pola, J., & Wyatt, H. J. (1989). The perception of target motion during smooth pursuit eye movements in the open-loop condition: Characteristics of retinal and extraretinal signals. *Vision Research, 29,* 471–483.

Polka, L., & Werker, J. F. (1994). Developmental changes in perception of nonnative vowel contrasts. *Journal of Experimental Psychology: Human Perception and Performance, 20,* 421–435.

Pollack, I. (1952). The information of elementary auditory displays. *Journal of the Acoustical Society of America, 24,* 745–749.

Pollack, I. (1953). The information of elementary auditory displays: II. *Journal of the Acoustical Society of America, 25,* 765–769.

Pollack, I. (1975). Auditory informational masking. *Journal of the Acoustical Society of America, 57,* S5.

Pollack, I. (1978). Decoupling of auditory pitch and stimulus frequency: The Shepard demonstration revisited. *Journal of the Acoustical Society of America, 63,* 202–206.

Pollack, I., & Pickett, J. M. (1964). Intelligibility of excerpts from fluent speech: Auditory vs. structural context. *Journal of Verbal Learning and Verbal Behavior, 3,* 79–84.

Pollack, R. H., & Silvar, S. D. (1967). Magnitude of the Mueller-Lyer illusion in children as a function of pigmentation of fundus oculi. *Psychonomic Science, 8,* 83–84.

Pollen, D. A., Lee, J. R., & Taylor, J. H. (1971). How does the visual cortex begin the reconstruction of the visual world? *Science, 173,* 74–77.

Polster, M. R., & Rapcsak, S. Z. (1996). Representations in learning new faces: Evidence from prosopagnosia. *Journal of the International Neuropsychological Society, 2,* 240–248.

Poltrock, S. E., Lansman, M., & Hunt, E. (1982). Automatic and controlled attention processes in auditory target detection. *Journal of Experimental Psychology: Human Perception and Performance, 8,* 37–45.

Pomerantz, J. R. (1983). Global and local precedence: Selective attention in form and motion perception. *Journal of Experimental Psychology: General, 112,* 511–535.

Pomerantz, J. R. (1986). Visual form perception: An overview. In E. C. Schwab & H. C. Nusbaum (Eds.), *Pattern recognition by humans and machines: Vol. 2. Visual perception* (pp. 1–30). Orlando: Academic Press.

Pomerantz, J. R., Goldberg, D., Golder, P., & Tetewsky, S. (1981). Subjective contours can facilitate performance in a reaction-time task. *Perception & Psychophysics, 29,* 605–611.

Pomerantz, J. R., Sager, L. C., & Stoever, R. J. (1977). Perception of wholes and of their component parts: Some configural superiority effects. *Journal of Experimental Psychology: Human Perception and Performance, 1,* 422–435.

Pons, T. P., Garraghty, P. E., Friedman, D. P., & Mishkin, M. (1987). Physiological evidence for serial processing in somatosensory cortex. *Science, 237,* 417–420.

Pons, T. P., Garraghty, P. E., Ommaya, A. K., Kaas, J. H., Taub, E., & Mishkin, M. (1991). Massive cortical reorganization after sensory deafferentation in adult macaques. *Science, 252,* 1857–1860.

Pont, S. C., Kappers, A. M. L., & Koenderink, J. J. (1997). Haptic curvature discrimination at several regions of the hand. *Perception & Psychophysics, 59,* 1225–1240.

Poppel, E. (1978). Time perception. In R. Held, H. W. Leibowitz, & H. L. Teuber (Eds.), *Handbook of sensory physiology: Vol. VIII. Perception* (pp. 713–729). New York: Springer-Verlag.

Popper, R., Parker, S., & Galanter, E. (1986). Dual loudness scales in individual subjects. *Journal of Experimental Psychology: Human Perception and Performance, 12,* 61–69.

Porac, C. (1989). Is visual illusion decrement based on selective adaptation? *Perception & Psychophysics, 46,* 279–283.

Porac, C., & Coren, S. (1976). The dominant eye. *Psychological Bulletin, 83,* 880–897.

Porac, C., & Coren, S. (1981). Life-span age trends in the perception of the Mueller-Lyer: An additional evidence for the existence of two illusions. *Canadian Journal of Psychology, 35,* 58–62.

Porac, C., & Coren, S. (1985). Transfer of illusion decrement: The effects of global versus local figural variations. *Perception & Psychophysics, 37,* 515–522.

Porac, C., & Coren, S. (1986). Sighting dominance and egocentric localization. *Vision Research, 26,* 1709–1713.

Porter, R. H., Balogh, R. D., Cernoch, J. M., & Franchi, C. (1986). Recognition of kin through characteristic body odors. *Chemical Senses, 11,* 389–395.

Porter, R. H., & Moore, J. D. (1981). Human kin recognition by olfactory cues. *Physiology & Behavior, 27,* 493–495.

Posner, M. I. (1978). *Chronometric exploration of mind.* Hillsdale, NJ: Erlbaum.

Posner, M. I. (1980). Orienting of attention. *Quarterly Journal of Experimental Psychology, 32,* 3–25.

Posner, M. I. (1988). Structures and functions of selective attention. In T. Boll & B. Bryant (Eds.), *Master lectures in clinical neuropsychology* (pp. 173–202). Washington, DC: American Psychological Association.

Posner, M. I., & Cohen, Y. (1984). Components of visual attention. In H. Bouma & D. G. Bouhuis (Eds.), *Attention and performance X.* Hillsdale, NJ: Erlbaum.

Posner, M. I., Inhoff, A., Friedrich, F. J., & Cohen, A. (1987). Isolating attentional systems: A cognitive–anatomical analysis. *Psychobiology, 15,* 107–121.

Posner, M. I., & Petersen, S. E. (1990). The attention system of the human brain. *Annual Review of Neuroscience, 13,* 25–42.

Posner, M. I., Rafal, R. D., Choate, L. S., & Vaughan, J. (1985). Inhibition of return: Neural basis and function. *Cognitive Neuropsychology, 2,* 211–228.

Posner, M. I., & Raichle, M. E. (1994). *Images of the mind.* New York: Scientific American Library.

Posner, M. I., Walker, J. A., Friedrich, F. J., & Rafal, R. D. (1984). Effects of parietal injury on covert orienting of attention. *Journal of Neuroscience, 4,* 1863–1874.

Post, B., & Leibowitz, H. W. (1985). A revised analysis of the role of efference in motion perception. *Perception, 14,* 631–643.

Postman, L., & Egan, J. P. (1949). *Experimental psychology.* New York: Harper.

Poulton, E. C. (1989). *Bias in quantifying judgments.* Hillsdale, NJ: Erlbaum.

Powers, M. K., Schneck, M., & Teller, D. Y. (1981). Spectral sensitivity of human infants at absolute visual threshold. *Vision Research, 21,* 1005–1016.

Poynter, W. D., & Holma, D. (1985). Duration judgment and the experience of change. *Perception & Psychophysics, 33,* 548–560.

Pratt, J., Kingstone, A., & Kehoe, W. (1997). Inhibition of return in location- and identity-based choice decision tasks. *Perception & Psychophysics, 59,* 964–971.

Predebon, J. (1990). Illusion decrement and transfer of illusion decrement in

obtuse- and acute-angle variants of the Poggendorff illusion. *Perception & Psychophysics, 48,* 467–476.

Predebon, J. (1993). The familiar-size cue to distance and stereoscopic depth perception. *Perception, 22,* 985–995.

Preti, G., Cutler, W. B., Garcia, C. R., Huggins, G. R., & Lawley, H. J. (1986). Human axillary secretions influence women's menstrual cycles: The role of donor extract of females. *Hormones and Behavior, 20,* 474–482.

Previc, F. H. (1994). The relationship between eye dominance and head tilt in humans. *Neuropsychologia, 32,* 1297–1303.

Price, J. L. (1987). The central and accessory olfactory systems. In T. E. Finger & W. L. Silver (Eds.), *Neurobiology of taste and smell* (pp. 179–204). New York: Wiley.

Prinzmetal, W. (1981). Principles of feature integration in visual perception. *Perception & Psychophysics, 30,* 330–340.

Prinzmetal, W., Henderson, D., & Ivry, R. (1995). Loosening the constraints on illusory conjunctions: Assessing the roles of exposure duration and attention. *Journal of Experimental Psychology: Human Perception and Performance, 21,* 1362–1375.

Prinzmetal, W., & Millis-Wright, M. (1984). Cognitive and linguistic factors affect visual feature integration. *Cognitive Psychology, 16,* 305–340.

Prinzmetal, W., Presti, D. E., & Posner, M. I. (1986). Does attention affect visual feature integration? *Journal of Experimental Psychology: Human Perception and Performance, 12,* 361–369.

Pritchard, R. M., Heron, W., & Hebb, D. O. (1960). Visual perception approached by the method of stabilized images. *Canadian Journal of Psychology, 14,* 67–77.

Puckett, J. de W., & Steinman, R. M. (1969). Tracking eye movements with and without saccadic correction. *Vision Research, 9,* 295–303.

Puel, J. L., Bobbin, R. P., & Fallon, M. (1988). An ipsilateral cochlear efferent loop protects the cochlea during intense sound exposure. *Hearing Research, 37,* 65–70.

Purghé, F., & Coren, S. (1992). Subjective contours 1900–1990: Research trends and bibliography. *Perception & Psychophysics, 51,* 291–304.

Quinn, P. C., Wooten, B. R., & Ludman, E. J. (1985). Achromatic color categories. *Perception & Psychophysics, 37,* 198–204.

Rabbitt, P. M. A. (1965). An age decrement in the ability to ignore irrelevant information. *Journal of Gerontology, 20,* 233–238.

Rabbitt, P. M. A. (1977). Changes in problem solving ability in old age. In J. Birren & K. Schaie (Eds.), *Handbook of the psychology of aging*. New York: Van Nostrand Reinhold.

Rabbitt, P. M. A. (1984). The control of attention in visual search. In R. Parasuraman & D. R. Davies (Eds.), *Varieties of attention* (pp. 273–291). Orlando: Academic Press.

Rabbitt, R. D. (1990). A hierarchy of examples illustrating the acoustic coupling of the eardrum. *Journal of the Acoustical Society of America, 87,* 2566–2582.

Rabin, M. D. (1988). Experience facilitates olfactory quality discrimination. *Perception & Psychophysics, 44,* 532–540.

Rabin, M. D., & Cain, W. S. (1984). Odor recognition: Familiarity, identifiability, and encoding consistency. *Journal of Experimental Psychology: Learning, Memory, and Cognition, 10,* 316–325.

Rabinowicz, T. (1979). The differential maturation of the human visual cortex. In F. Faulkner & J. M. Tanner (Eds.), *Human growth: Vol. 3. Neurobiology and nutrition* (pp. 97–123). New York: Plenum Press.

Rabinowitz, W. M., Houtsma, A. J. M., Durlach, N. I., & Delhorne, L. A. (1987). Multidimensional tactile displays: Identification of vibratory intensity, frequency, and contactor area. *Journal of the Acoustical Society of America, 82,* 1243–1252.

Radvansky, G. A., Hartmann, W. M., & Rakerd, B. (1992). Structural alterations of an ambiguous musical figure: The scale illusion revisited. *Perception & Psychophysics, 52,* 256–262.

Raftenberg, M. N. (1990). Flow of endolymph in the inner spiral sulcus and the subtectorial space. *Journal of the Acoustical Society of America, 87,* 2606–2620.

Rakerd, B., & Hartmann, W. M. (1985). Localization of sound in rooms: II. The effects of a single reflecting surface. *Journal of the Acoustical Society of America, 78,* 524–533.

Ramachandran, V. S. (1986). Capture of stereopsis and apparent motion by illusory contours. *Perception & Psychophysics, 39,* 361–373.

Ramachandran, V. S. (1988). Perceiving shape from shading. *Scientific American, 259,* 76–83.

Ramachandran, V. S., & Anstis, S. M. (1986). The perception of apparent motion. *Scientific American, 254,* 80–87.

Ramachandran, V. S., Altschuler, E. L., & Hillyer, S. (1997). Mirror agnosia. *Proceedings of the Royal Society of London—Series B: Biological Sciences, 264,* 645–647.

Ramachandran, V. S., & Gregory, R. L. (1978). Does colour provide an input to human motion perception? *Nature, 275,* 55–56.

Rammsayer, T., & Lustnauer, S. (1989). Sex differences in time perception. *Perceptual and Motor Skills, 68,* 195–198.

Rand, T. C. (1974). Dichotic release from masking for speech. *Journal of the Acoustical Society of America, 55,* 678–680.

Randsom-Hogg, A., & Spillman, L. (1980). Perceptive field size in fovea of the light and dark adapted. *Vision Research, 20,* 221–228.

Ratliff, F. (1965). *Mach bands: Quantitative studies on neural networks in the retina*. San Francisco: Holden-Day.

Rayleigh, Lord. (1907). On our perception of sound direction. *Philosophical Magazine, 13*(6), 214–232.

Raymond, J. E., Shapiro, K. L., & Rose, D. J. (1984). Optokinetic backgrounds affect perceived velocity during ocular tracking. *Perception & Psychophysics, 36,* 221–224.

Rayner, K. (1978). Eye movements in reading and information processing. *Psychological Bulletin, 85,* 618–660.

Rea, M. M., & Sweeney, J. A. (1989). Changes in eye tracking during clinical stabilization in schizophrenia. *Psychiatry Research, 28,* 31–39.

Reason, J. (1984). Lapses of attention in everyday life. In R. Parasuraman & D. R. Davies (Eds.), *Varieties of attention* (pp. 515–549). Orlando: Academic Press.

Reason, J., & Brand, J. (1975). *Motion sickness*. London: Academic Press.

Redding, G. M., Clark, S. E., & Wallace, B. (1985). Attention and prism adaptation. *Cognitive Psychology, 17,* 1–25.

Redding, G. M., & Wallace, B. (1976). Components of displacement adaptation in acquisition and decay as a function of hard and hall exposure. *Perception & Psychophysics, 20,* 453–459.

Redding, G. M., & Wallace, B. (1990). Effects on prism adaptation of duration and timing of visual feedback during pointing. *Journal of Motor Behavior, 22,* 209–224.

Redding, G. M., & Wallace, B. (1997). Prism adaptation during target pointing from visible and nonvisible starting locations. *Journal of Motor Behavior, 29,* 119–130.

Reddy, D. R. (1976). Speech recognition by machine: A review. *Proceedings of the IEEE, 64,* 501–531.

Reed, C. F. (1989). Terrestrial and celestial passage. In M. Hershenson (Ed.), *The moon illusion* (pp. 267–280). Hillsdale, NJ: Erlbaum.

Regal, D. M., Ashmead, D. H., & Salapatek, P. (1983). The coordination of eye and head movements during early infancy: A selective review. *Behavioral and Brain Research, 10,* 125–132.

Regan, D. M., & Beverley, K. (1973). Disparity detectors in human depth perception: Evidence for directional selectivity. *Science, 181,* 877–879.

Regan, D. M., & Beverley, K. (1979). The visual perception of motion in depth. *Scientific American, 241,* 136–151.

Regan, D. M., & Beverly, K. (1982). How do we avoid confounding the direction we are looking and the direction we are moving? *Science, 215,* 194–196.

Regan, D. M., Frisby, J. P., Poggio, G. F., Schor, C. M., & Tyler, C. W. (1990). The perception of stereodepth and stereomotion: Cortical mechanisms. In L. Spillman & J. S. Werner (Eds.), *Visual perception* (pp. 317–347). New York: Academic Press.

Regolin, L., & Vallortigara, G. (1995). Perception of partly occluded objects by young chicks. *Perception & Psychophysics, 57,* 971–976.

Rehn, T. (1978). Perceived odor intensity as a function of airflow through the nose. *Sensory Processes, 2,* 198–205.

Reichardt, W. (1961). Autocorrelation: A principle for the evaluation of sensory information by the central nervous system. In W. A. Rosenblith (Ed.), *Principles of sensory communication*. New York: Wiley.

Reichardt, W., & Poggio, T. (1979). Figure-ground discrimination by relative movement in the visual system of the fly. *Biological Cybernetics, 35,* 81–100.

Reisberg, D., & O'Shaughnessy, M. (1984). Diverting subjects' concentration slows figural reversals. *Perception, 13,* 461–468.

Remez, R. E. (1996). Critique: Auditory form and gestural topology in the perception of speech. *Journal of the Acoustical Society of America, 99,* 1695–1698.

Remez, R. E., Rubin, P. E., Pisoni, D. B., & Carrell, T. D. (1981). Speech perception without traditional speech cues. *Science, 212,* 947–950.

Remington, R. (1980). Attention and saccadic eye movements. *Journal of Experimental Psychology: Human Perception and Performance, 6,* 726–744.

Rencanzone, G. H., Schreiner, C. E., & Merzenich, M. M. (1993). Plasticity in the frequency representation of primary auditory cortex following discrimination training in adult owl monkeys. *The Journal of Neuroscience, 13,* 87–103.

Rensink, R. A., O'Regan, K., & Clark, J. J. (1997). To see or not to see: The need for attention to perceive changes in scenes. *Psychological Science, 8,* 368–373.

Repp, B. H. (1987). The sound of two hands clapping: An exploratory study. *Journal of the Acoustical Society of America, 81,* 1100–1109.

Reuter, G., & Zenner, H. P. (1990). Active radial and transverse motile responses of outer hair cells in the organ of Corti. *Hearing Research, 43,* 219–230.

Reynolds, D. C. (1979). A visual profile of the alcoholic driver. *American Journal of Optometry and Physiological Optics, 56,* 241–251.

Reynolds, R. I. (1985). The role of object-hypotheses in the organization of fragmented figures. *Perception, 14,* 49–52.

Rhee, K., Kim, D., & Kim, Y. (1965). The effects of smoking on night vision. *14th Pacific Medical Conference (Professional Papers).*

Rhode, W. S., & Greenberg, S. (1994). Encoding of amplitude modulation in the cochlear nucleus of the cat. *Journal of Neurophysiology, 71,* 1797–1825.

Rhodes, G. (1987). Auditory attention and the representation of spatial information. *Perception & Psychophysics, 42,* 1–14.

Ricci, C., & Blundo, C. (1990). Perception of ambiguous figures after focal brain lesions. *Neuropsychologia, 28,* 1163–1173.

Rice, C. G., Ayley, J. B., Bartlett, B., Bedford, W., Gregory, W., & Hallum, G. (1968). A pilot study on the effects of pop group music on hearing. Cited in K. D. Kryter (1970). *The effects of noise on man* (p. 203). New York: Academic Press.

Richards, W. (1977). Lessons in constancy from neurophysiology. In W. W. Epstein (Ed.), *Stability and constancy in visual perception: Mechanisms and processes* (pp. 421–436). New York: Wiley.

Rieser, J., Yonas, A., & Wikner, K. (1976). Radial localization of odors by human newborns. *Child Development, 47,* 856–859.

Riesz, R. R. (1928). Differential intensity sensitivity of the ear for pure tones. *Physical Review, 31,* 867–875.

Riggs, L. A., Ratliff, F., Cornsweet, J. C., & Cornsweet, T. N. (1953). The disappearance of steadily fixated visual test objects. *Journal of the Optical Society of America, 43,* 495–501.

Rijnsdorp, A., Daan, S., & Dijkstra, C. (1981). Hunting in the kestrel (Falco tinnunculus) and the adaptive significance of daily habits. *Oecologia, 50,* 391–406.

Rivest, J., & Ono, H. (1989). The roles of convergence and apparent distance in depth constancy with motion parallax. *Perception & Psychophysics, 46,* 401–408.

Rizzo, M., & Robin, D. (1990). Simultagnosia: A defect of sustained attention yields insights on visual information processing. *Neurology, 40,* 447–455.

Roberts, M., & Summerfield, A. Q. (1981). Audio-visual adaptation in speech perception. *Perception & Psychophysics, 30,* 309–314.

Robertson, L. C., Lamb, M. R., & Knight, R. T. (1988). Effects of lesions of temporal-parietal junction on perceptual and attentional processing in humans. *Journal of Neuroscience, 8,* 3757–3769.

Robertson, P. W. (1967). Color words and colour vision. *Biology and Human Affairs, 33,* 28–33.

Robinson, D. L., Bowman, E. M., & Kertzman, C. (1995). Covert orienting of attention in macaques. II. Contributions of parietal cortex. *Journal of Neurophysiology, 74,* 698–712.

Robinson, D. L., & Kertzman, C. (1995). Covert orienting of attention in macaques. III. Contributions of the superior colliculus. *Journal of Neurophysiology, 74,* 713–721.

Robinson, D. W., & Dadson, R. S. (1956). A redetermination of the equal-loudness relations for pure tones. *British Journal of Applied Physics, 7,* 166–181.

Robinson, K., & Patterson, R. D. (1996). The stimulus duration required to identify vowels, their octave, and their pitch chroma. *Journal of the Acoustical Society of America, 98,* 1858–1865.

Robinson, L. R., & Green, D. M. (1988). Detection of changes in spectral shape: Uniform vs. non-uniform background spectra. *Hearing Research, 32,* 157–166.

Robson, J. G. (1980). Neural images: The physiological basis of spatial vision. In C. S. Harris (Ed.), *Visual coding and adaptability* (pp. 177–214). Hillsdale, NJ: Erlbaum.

Rock, I. (1973). *Orientation and form.* New York: Academic Press.

Rock, I. (1975). *An introduction to perception.* New York: Macmillan.

Rock, I. (1983). *The logic of perception.* Cambridge, MA: MIT Press.

Rock, I. (1997). *Indirect perception.* Cambridge, MA: MIT Press.

Rock, I., & Brosgole, L. (1964). Grouping based on phenomenal proximity. *Journal of Experimental Psychology, 67,* 531–538.

Rock, I., & Guttman, D. (1981). The effect of inattention on form perception. *Journal of Experimental Psychology: Human Perception and Performance, 7,* 275–285.

Rock, I., & Halper, F. (1969). Form perception without a retinal image. *American Journal of Psychology, 82,* 425–440.

Rock, I., & Linnett, C. M. (1993). Is a perceived shape based on its retinal image? *Perception, 22,* 61–76.

Rock, I., Nijhawan, R., Palmer, S. E., & Tudor, L. (1992). Grouping based on phenomenal similarity of achromatic color. *Perception, 21,* 779–789.

Rockland, K. S., & Pandya, P. N. (1981). Cortical connections of the occipital lobe in the rhesus monkey: Interconnections between areas 17, 18, 19 and the superior temporal sulcus. *Brain Research, 212,* 249–270.

Rodieck, R. W. (1965). Quantitative analysis of the cat retinal ganglion cell response to visual stimuli. *Vision Research, 5,* 583–601.

Rodieck, R. W. (1973). *The vertebrate retina: Principles of structure and function.* San Francisco: Freeman.

Rodieck, R. W. (1979). Visual pathways. *Annual Review of Neuroscience, 2,* 193–226.

Roelofs, C. O. (1935). Optische Lokalisation, *Archiv fuer Augenheilkunde, 109,* 395–415.

Rogel, M. J. (1978). A critical evaluation of the possibility of higher primate reproductive and sexual pheromones. *Psychological Bulletin, 85,* 810–830.

Rogers, B. J., & Collett, T. S. (1989). The appearance of surfaces specified by motion parallax and binocular disparity. *Quarterly Journal of Experimental Psychology: Human Experimental Psychology, 41,* 697–717.

Rogers, B. J., & Graham, M. (1979). Motion parallax as an independent cue for depth perception. *Perception, 8,* 125–134.

Rohrbaugh, J. W. (1984). The orienting reflex: Performance and central nervous system manifestations. In R. Parasuraman & D. R. Davies (Eds.), *Varieties of attention.* (pp. 323–373). Orlando: Academic Press.

Rollman, G. B., & Harris, G. (1987). The detectability, discriminability, and perceived magnitude of painful electric shock. *Perception & Psychophysics, 42,* 257–268.

Romani, G. L., Williamson, S. J., & Kaufman, L. (1982). Tonotopic organization of the human auditory cortex. *Science, 216,* 1339–1340.

Romano, P. E., Romano, J. A., & Puklin, J. E. (1975). Stereoactivity development in children with normal single vision. *American Journal of Ophthalmology, 79,* 966–971.

Root, W. (1974, December 22). Of wine and noses. *New York Times Magazine,* pp. 14 et seq.

Roscoe, S. N. (1989). The zoom-lens hypothesis. In M. Hershenson (Ed.), *The moon illusion* (pp. 31–58). Hillsdale, NJ: Erlbaum.

Roscoe, S. N., & Couchman, D. H. (1987). Improving visual performance through volitional focus control. *Human Factors, 29,* 311–325.

Rose, J. E., Brugge, J. F., Anderson, D. J., & Hind, J. E. (1967). Phase-locked response to low frequency tones in single auditory nerve fibers of the squirrel monkey. *Journal of Neurophysiology, 30,* 769–793.

Rose, J. E., Galambos, R., & Hughes, J. (1959). Microelectrode studies of the cochlear nuclei of the cat. *Johns Hopkins Hospital Bulletin, 14,* 211–251.

Rose, J. E., Galambos, R., & Hughes, J. (1960). Organization of frequency sensitive neurons in the cochlear nuclear complex of the cat. In G. L. Rasmussen & W. F. Windle (Eds.), *Neural mechanisms of the auditory and vestibular systems* (pp. 116–136). Springfield, IL: Thomas.

Rosinski, R., & Farber, J. (1980). Compensation for viewing point in the perception of pictured space. In M. Hagen (Ed.), *Perception of pictures: Vol. 1. Albert's window: The projective model of pictorial information.* New York: Academic Press.

Ross, D. F., Read, J. D., & Toglia, M. P. (1994). *Adult eyewitness testimony: Current trends and developments.* New York: University of Cambridge Press.

Ross, H. (1975, June 19). Mist, murk and visual perception. *New Scientist,* pp. 658–660.

Ross, N., & Schilder, P. (1934). Tachistoscopic experiments on the perception of the human figure. *Journal of General Psychology, 10,* 152–172.

Rossi, A. F., Rittenhouse, C. D., & Paradiso, M. A. (1996). The representation of brightness in primary visual cortex. *Science, 273,* 1104–1107.

Rothbart, M. K., Posner, M. I., & Boylan, A. (1990). Regulatory mechanisms in infant development. In J. T. Enns (Ed.), *The development of attention: Research and theory* (pp. 47–66). Amsterdam: Elsevier.

Rothblat, L., & Schwartz, M. (1978). Altered early environment: Effects on the brain and visual behavior. In R. Walk & H. Pick (Eds.), *Perception and experience* (pp. 7–36). New York: Plenum Press.

Rouiller, E. M., Rodrigues-Dagaeff, C., Simm, G., De Ribaupierre, Y., Villa, A., & De Ribaupierre, F. (1989). Functional organization of the medial division of the medial geniculate body of the cat: Tonotopic organization, spatial distribution of response properties and cortical connections. *Hearing Research, 39,* 127–142.

Royden, C. S., & Hildreth, E. C. (1996). Human heading judgments in the presence of moving objects. *Perception & Psychophysics, 58,* 836–856.

Royster, L. H., Royster, J. D., & Thomas, W. G. (1980). Representative hearing levels by race and sex in North Carolina industry. *Journal of the Acoustical Society of America, 68,* 551–566.

Rozin, P. (1978). The use of characteristic flavorings in human culinary practice. In C. M. Apt (Ed.), *Flavor: Its chemical, behavioral, and commercial aspects* (pp. 101–127). Boulder, CO: Westview Press.

Rozin, P. (1982). "Taste-smell confusions" and the duality of the olfactory sense. *Perception & Psychophysics, 31,* 397–401.

Rubin, E. (1915). *Synoplevede figuren.* Copenhagen: Gyldendalske.

Rubin, E. (1921). *Visuell wahrgenommene figuren.* Copenhagen: Gyldendalske.

Ruble, D. N., & Nakamura, C. Y. (1972). Task orientation versus social orientation in young children and their attention to relevant social cues. *Child Development, 43,* 471–480.

Ruggieri, V., Cei, A., Ceridono, D., & Bergerone, C. (1980). Dimensional approach to the study of sighting dominance. *Perceptual and Motor Skills, 51,* 247–251.

Runeson, S., & Frykholm, G. (1983). Kinematic specifications of dynamics as an informational basis for person-and-action perception: Expectation, gender recognition, and deceptive intention. *Journal of Experimental Psychology: General, 112,* 585–615.

Rusak, B., & Groos, G. (1982). Suprachiasmatic stimulation phase shifts rodent circadian rhythms. *Science, 215,* 1407–1409.

Rusak, B., & Zucker, I. (1979). Neural regulation of circadian rhythms. *Physiological Review, 59,* 449–526.

Rushton, W. A. H. (1962). Visual pigments in man. *Scientific American, 205,* 120–132.

Rushton, W. A. H. (1965). Cone pigment dynamics in the deuteranope. *Journal of Physiology (London), 176,* 38–45.

Russell, M. J. (1976). Human olfactory communication. *Nature (London), 260,* 520–522.

Russoff, A. C. (1979). Development of ganglion cells in the retina of the cat. In R. D. Freeman (Ed.), *Developmental neurobiology of vision* (pp. 19–30). New York: Plenum Press.

Russoff, A. C., & Dubin, M. W. (1977). Development of receptive-field properties of retinal ganglion cells in kittens. *Journal of Neurophysiology, 40,* 1188–1198.

Saarinen, J., & Levi, D. M. (1995). Orientation anisotropy in vernier acuity. *Vision Research, 35,* 1449–1461

Saberi, K., & Perrott, D. R. (1990). Minimum audible movement angles as a function of sound source trajectory. *Journal of the Acoustical Society of America, 88,* 2639–2644.

Sachs, M. B., & Kiang, N. Y. S. (1968). Two-tone inhibition in auditory nerve fibers. *Journal of the Acoustical Society of America, 43,* 1120–1128.

Sacks, O. (1987). *The man who mistook his wife for a hat.* New York: Summit.

Sahley, T. L., Nodar, R. H., & Musiek, F. E. (1997). *Efferent auditory system: Structure and function.* San Diego: Singular Publishing Group.

Salapatek, P. (1975). Pattern perception in early infancy. In L. B. Cohen & P. Salapatek (Eds.), *Infant perception: From sensation to cognition: Vol. 1* (pp. 133–248). New York: Academic Press.

Salapatek, P., & Kessen, W. (1973). Prolonged investigation of a plane geometric triangle by the human newborn. *Journal of Experimental Child Psychology, 15,* 22–29.

Salmelin, R., Hari, R., Lounasmaa, O. V., & Sams, M. (1994). Dynamics of brain activation during picture naming. *Nature, 368,* 463–465.

Salthouse, T. A. (1985). *A theory of cognitive aging.* Amsterdam: North-Holland.

Salthouse, T. A. (1996a). The processing-speed theory of adult age differences in cognition. *Psychological Review, 103,* 403–428.

Salthouse, T. A. (1996b). Constraints on theories of cognitive aging. *Psychonomic Bulletin & Review, 3,* 287–299.

Salthouse, T. A., & Kail, R. (1983). Memory development throughout the life span: The role of processing rate. In P. B. Baltes & O. G. Brim (Eds.), *Life-span development and behavior: Vol. 5* (pp. 90–116). New York: Academic Press.

Samuel, A. G. (1981). Phonemic restoration: Insights from a new methodology. *Journal of Experimental Psychology: General, 110,* 474–494.

Samuel, A. G. (1987). Lexical uniqueness effects on phonemic restoration. *Journal of Experimental Psychology: General, 110,* 132–144.

Samuel, A. G. (1996). Phoneme restoration. *Language and Cognitive Processes, 11,* 647–653.

Samuel, A. G. (1997). Lexical activation produces potent phonemic percepts. *Cognitive Psychology, 32,* 97–127.

Samuel, A. G., & Kat, D. (1996). Early levels of analysis of speech. *Journal of Experimental Psychology: Human Perception and Performance, 22,* 676–694.

Sanders, A. (1970). Some aspects of the selective process in the functional field of view. *Ergonomics, 13,* 101–107.

Sanders, B., Soares, M. P., & D'Aquila, J. M. (1982). Sex difference on one test of spatial visualization: A nontrivial difference. *Child Development, 53,* 1106–1110.

Sanders, G., & Ross-Field, L. (1986). Sexual orientation and visuospatial ability. *Brain and Cognition, 5,* 280–290.

Sanford, E. C. (1898). *A course in experimental psychology: Part I, sensation and perception.* Boston: Heath.

Sanocki, T. (1987). Visual knowledge underlying letter perception: Font-specific, schematic tuning. *Journal of Experimental Psychology: Human Perception and Performance, 13,* 267–278.

Sathian K., & Zangaladze A. (1997). Tactile learning is task specific but transfers between fingers. *Perception & Psychophysics, 59,* 119–128.

Sawusch, J. R. (1986). Auditory and phonetic coding of speech. In E. C. Schwab & H. C. Nusbaum (Eds.), *Pattern recognition by humans and machines: Vol. 1. Speech perception* (pp. 51–88). Orlando: Academic Press.

Sawusch, J. R., & Gagnon, D. A. (1995). Auditory coding, cues, and coherence in phonetic perception. *Journal of Experimental Psychology: Human Perception and Performance, 21,* 635–652.

Schab, F. R. (1991). Odor memory: Taking stock. *Psychological Bulletin, 109,* 242–251.

Schab, F. R., & Crowder, R. G. (Eds.). (1995). *Memory for odors.* Mahwah, NJ: Lawrence Erlbaum Associates.

Schaie, K. W., & Geiwitz, J. (1982). *Adult development and aging.* Boston: Little, Brown.

Scharf, B. (1964). Partial masking. *Acustica, 14,* 16–23.

Scharf, B. (1975). Audition. In B. Scharf (Ed.), *Experimental sensory psychology* (pp. 112–149). Glenview, IL: Scott, Foresman.

Scharf, B. (1978). Loudness. In E. C. Carterette & M. P. Friedman (Eds.), *Handbook of perception: Vol. IV. Hearing.* New York: Academic Press.

Scharf, B. (1989). Spectral specificity in auditory detection: The effect of listening on hearing. *Journal of the Acoustical Society of Japan, 10,* 309–317.

Scharf, B., Quigley, S., Aoki, C., Peachey, N., & Reeves, A. (1987). Focused auditory attention and frequency selectivity. *Perception & Psychophysics, 42,* 215–223.

Scharre, J. E., Cotter, S. A., Block, S. S., & Kelly, S. A. (1990). Normative contrast sensitivity data for young children. *Optometry and Vision Science, 67,* 826–832.

Schefrin, B. E., & Werner, J. S. (1990). Loci of spectral unique hues throughout the life span. *Journal of the Optical Society of America A, 7,* 305–311.

Schenkel, K. D. (1967). Die beidohrigen Mithorschoellen von Impulsen. *Acustica, 18,* 38–46.

Scher, D., Pionk, M., & Purcell, D. G. (1981). Visual sensitivity fluctuations during the menstrual cycle under dark and light adaptation. *Bulletin of the Psychonomic Society, 18,* 159–160.

Schiano, D. J., & Jordan, K. (1990). Mueller-Lyer decrement: Practice or prolonged inspection? *Perception, 19,* 307–316.

Schiff, W., & Oldak, R. (1990). Accuracy of judging time to arrival: Effects of modality, trajectory, and gender. *Journal of Experimental Psychology: Human Perception and Performance, 16,* 303–316.

Schifferstein, H. N. J., & Frijters, J. E. R. (1993). Perceptual integration in heterogeneous taste percepts. *Journal of Experimental Psychology: Human Perception & Performance, 19,* 661–675.

Schiffman, S. S. (1974). Physiochemical correlates of olfactory quality. *Science, 185,* 112–117.

Schiffman, S. S. (1977). Food recognition by the elderly. *Journal of Gerontology, 32,* 586–592.

Schiffman, S. S., & Erikson, R. P. (1971). A theoretical review: A psychophysical model for gustatory quality. *Physiology and Behavior, 1,* 617–633.

Schiffman, S. S., & Pasternak, M. (1979). Decreased discrimination of food odors in the elderly. *Journal of Gerontology, 84,* 73–79.

Schiller, P. H. (1986). The central visual system. *Vision Research, 26,* 1351–1386.

Schiller, P. H., & Logothetis, N. K. (1990). The color-opponent and broad-band channels of the primate visual system. *Trends in Neurosciences, 13,* 392–398.

Schindler, R. A., & Merzenich, M. M. (Eds.). (1985). *Cochlear implants.* New York: Raven Press.

Schirillo, J. A., & Arend, L. E. (1995). Illumination change at a depth edge can reduce lightness constancy. *Perception & Psychophysics, 57,* 225–230.

Schlauch, R. S., & Hafter, E. R. (1991). Listening bandwidths and frequency uncertainty in pure-tone signal detection. *Journal of the Acoustical Society of America, 90,* 1332–1339.

Schlaug, G., & Jäncke, L. (1995). In vivo evidence of structural brain asymmetry in musicians. *Science, 267,* 699–701.

Schlaug, G., Jäncke, L., Huang, Y., Staiger, J. F., & Steinmetz, H. (1995). Increased corpus callosum size in musicians. *Neuropsychologia, 33,* 1047–1055.

Schleidt, M., Hold, B., & Attili, G. (1981). A cross-cultural study on the attitude towards personal odors. *Journal of Chemical Ecology, 7,* 19–31.

Schmiedt, R. A., Zwislocki, J. J., & Hamernik, R. P. (1980). Effects of hair cell lesions on responses of cochlear nerve fibers: I. Lesions, tuning curves, two-tone inhibition, and responses to trapezoidal-wave patterns. *Journal of Neurophysiology, 43,* 1367–1389.

Schnapf, J. L., & Baylor, D. A. (1987). How photoreceptor cells respond to light. *Scientific American, 256,* 40–47.

Schneider, B., & Parker, S. (1990). Does stimulus context affect loudness or only loudness judgments? *Perception & Psychophysics, 48,* 409–418.

Schneider, B. A., & Bissett, R. J. (1981). The dimensions of tonal experience: A nonmetric scaling approach. *Perception & Psychophysics, 30,* 39–48.

Schneider, B. A., & Cohen, A. J. (1997). Binaural additivity of loudness in children and adults. *Perception & Psychophysics, 59,* 655–664.

Schneider, D. (1969). Insect olfaction: Deciphering system for chemical messages. *Science, 163,* 1031–1037.

Schneider, G. E. (1969). Two visual systems. *Science, 163,* 895–902.

Schneider, R., Costiloe, J., Howard, R., & Wolf, S. (1958). Olfactory perception thresholds in hypogonadal women: Changes accompanying administration of androgen and estrogen. *Journal of Clinical Endocrinology, 18,* 379–390.

Schneider, S. L., Hughes, B., Epstein, W., & Bach-y-Rita, P. (1986). The detection of length and orientation changes in dynamic vibrotactile patterns. *Perception & Psychophysics, 40,* 290–300.

Schneider, W., Dumais, S. T., & Shiffrin, R. M. (1984). Automatic and control processing and attention. In R. Parasuraman & D. R. Davies (Eds.), *Varieties of attention* (pp. 1–27). Orlando: Academic Press.

Schneider, W., & Schiffrin, R. M. (1977). Controlled and automatic human information processing: I. Detection, search and attention. *Psychological Review, 84,* 1–66.

Schoenlein, R. W., Peteanu, L. A., Mathies, R. A., & Shank, C. V. (1991). The first step in vision: Femtosecond isomerization of rhodopsin. *Science, 254,* 412–415.

Schoups, A. A., Vogels, R., & Orban, G. A. (1995). Human perceptual learning in identifying the oblique orientation: Retinotopy, orientation specificity and monocularity. *Journal of Physiology*, *483*, 797–810.

Schouten, M. E. H. (1980). The case against a speech mode of perception. *Acta Psychologica, 44*, 71–98.

Schubert, E. D. (1978). History of research on hearing. In E. C. Carterette & M. P. Friedman (Eds.), *Handbook of perception: Vol. IV. Hearing* (pp. 41–80). New York: Academic Press.

Schull, J., Kaplan, H., & O'Brien, C. P. (1981). Naloxone can alter experimental pain and mood in humans. *Physiological Psychology, 9*, 245–250.

Schulman, P. H. (1979). Eye movements do not cause induced motion. *Perception & Psychophysics, 26*, 381–383.

Schulze, H. H. (1989). Categorical perception of rhythmic patterns. *Psychological Research, 51*, 10–15.

Schwartz, S. H., & Loop, M. S. (1984). Effect of duration on detection by the chromatic and achromatic systems. *Perception & Psychophysics, 36*, 65–67.

Scialfa, C. T. (1990). Adult age differences in visual search: The role of non-attentional processes. In J. T. Enns (Ed.), *The development of attention: Research and theory* (pp. 509–526). Amsterdam: Elsevier.

Scott, T. R. (1987). Coding in the gustatory system. In T. E. Finger & W. L. Silver (Eds.), *Neurobiology of taste and smell* (pp. 355–378). New York: Wiley.

Scott, T. R. (1990). The effect of physiological need on taste. In E. Capaldi & L. T. Powley (Eds.), *Taste, experience, and feeding* (pp. 45–61). Washington, DC: American Psychological Association.

Scott, T. R., & Erickson, R. P. (1971). Synaptic processing of taste-quality information in the thalamus of the rat. *Journal of Neurophysiology, 34*, 868–884.

Scott, T. R., & Giza, B. K. (1990). Coding channels in the taste system of the rat. *Science, 249*, 1585–1587.

Sedgwick, H. (1980). The geometry of spatial layout in pictorial representation. In M. Hagen (Ed.), *Perception of pictures: Vol. I. Alberti's window: The projective model of pictorial information* (pp. 33–90). New York: Academic Press.

See, J. E., Howe, S. R., Warm, J. S., & Dember, W. N. (1995). Meta-analysis of the sensitivity decrement in vigilance. *Psychological Bulletin, 117*, 230–249.

Segall, M. H., Campbell, D. T., & Herskovits, M. J. (1966). *The influence of culture on visual perception.* Indianapolis: Bobbs-Merrill.

Seggie, J., & Canny, C. (1989). Antidepressant medication reverses increased sensitivity to light in depression: Preliminary report. *Progress in Neuro-*

Psychopharmacology and Biological Psychiatry, 13, 537–541.

Sekuler, A. B. (1996). Axis of elongation can determine reference frames for object perception. *Canadian Journal of Experimental Psychology, 50*, 270–279.

Sekuler, A. B., & Lee, J. A. J. (1996). Pigeons do not complete partly occluded figures. *Perception, 25*, 1109–1120.

Sekuler, A. B., & Palmer, S. E. (1992). Perception of partly occluded objects: A microgenetic analysis. *Journal of Experimental Psychology: General, 121*, 95–111.

Sekuler, R. (1975). Visual motion perception. In E. C. Carterette & M. P. Friedman (Eds.), *Handbook of perception: Vol. 5* (pp. 387–433). New York: Academic Press.

Sekuler, R., & Ball, K. (1986). Visual localization: Age and practice. *Journal of the Optical Society of America A, 3*, 864–867.

Sekuler, R., Ball, K., Tynan, P., & Machmer, J. (1982). Psychophysics of motion perception. In A. H. Wertheim, W. A. Wagenaar, & H. W. Leibowitz (Eds.), *Tutorials on motion perception* (pp. 81–100). New York: Plenum Press.

Sekuler, R., & Ganz, L. (1963). A new aftereffect of seen movement with a stabilized retinal image. *Science, 139*, 419–420.

Sekuler, R., & Hutman, L. P. (1980). Spatial vision and aging: I. Contrast sensitivity. *Journal of Gerontology, 35*, 692–699.

Selfridge, O. G. (1959). Pandemonium: A paradigm for learning. In D. V. Blake & A. M. Uttley (Eds.), *Proceedings of the Symposium on the Mechanisation of Thought Processes* (pp. 511–529). London: HM Stationery Office.

Sellick, P. M., Patuzzi, R., & Johnstone, B. M. (1982). Measurement of basilar membrane motion in the guinea pig using the Mössbauer technique. *Journal of the Acoustical Society of America, 72*, 131–141.

Semenza, C. (1988). Impairment in localization of body parts. *Cortex, 24*, 443–449.

Semple, M. N., & Kitzes, L. M. (1987). Binaural processing of sound pressure level in the inferior colliculus. *Journal of Neurophysiology, 57*, 1130–1147.

Senden, M. von. (1960). *Space and sight: The perception of space and shape in congenitally blind patients before and after operation.* London: Methuen.

Serafine, M. L., & Glassman, N. (1989). The cognitive reality of hierarchic structure in music. *Music Perception, 6*, 397–430.

Serafini, S. (1995). Timbre judgments of Javanese gamelan instruments by

trained and untrained adults. *Psychomusicology, 14*, 137–153.

Serpell, R. (1971). Discrimination of orientation by Zambian children. *Journal of Comparative Physiology, 75*, 312.

Seymoure, P., & Juraska, J. M. (1997). Vernier and grating acuity in adult hooded rats: The influence of sex. *Behavioral Neuroscience, 111*, 792–800.

Shaffer, H. L. (1975). Multiple attention in continuous verbal tasks. In P. M. A. Rabbitt & S. Dornic (Eds.), *Attention and performance V.* London: Academic Press.

Shaffer, L. H. (1985). Timing in action. In J. A. Michon & J. L. Jackson (Eds.), *Time, mind and behavior* (pp. 226–242). Berlin: Springer-Verlag.

Shallice, T., & Vickers, D. (1964). Theories and experiments on discrimination times. *Ergonomics, 7*, 37–49.

Shannon, C. E., & Weaver, W. (1949). *The mathematical theory of communication.* Urbana: University of Illinois Press.

Shannon, R. V., & Otto, S. R. (1990). Psychophysical measures from electrical stimulation of the human cochlear nucleus. *Hearing Research, 47*, 159–168.

Shapiro, K. L., & Egerman, B. (1984). Effects of arousal on human visual dominance. *Perception & Psychophysics, 35*, 547–552.

Shapiro, K. L., & Johnson, T. L. (1987). Effects of arousal on attention to central and peripheral visual stimuli. *Acta Psychologica, 66*, 157–172.

Shapiro, K. L., & Lim, A. (1989). The impact of anxiety on visual attention to central and peripheral events. *Behaviour Research & Therapy, 27*, 345–351.

Shapley, R. (1986). The importance of contrast for the activity of single neurons, the VEP and perception. *Vision Research, 26*, 45–61.

Shapley, R. (1990). Visual sensitivity and parallel retino-cortical channels. *Annual Review of Psychology, 41*, 635–658.

Shapley, R., & Enroth-Cugell, C. (1984). Visual adaptation and retinal gain controls. *Progress in Retinal Research, 3*, 263–346.

Shapley, R., & Kaplan, E. (1989). Responses of magnocellular LGN neurons and M retinal ganglion cells to drifting heterochromatic gratings. *Investigative Ophthalmology and Visual Science, 30* (Suppl.), 323.

Shapley, R., & Reid, R. C. (1985). Contrast and assimilation in the perception of brightness. *Proceedings of the National Academy of Science, USA, 82*, 5983–5986.

Sharma, S., & Moskowitz, H. (1972). Effect of marijuana on the visual autokinetic phenomenon. *Perceptual and Motor Skills, 35*, 891.

Sharpe, L. T., & Nordby, K. (1989). Total color-blindness: An introduction. In R. F. Hess, L. T. Sharpe, & K. Nordby (Eds.), *Night vision: Basic, clinical and applied aspects*. Cambridge: Cambridge University Press.

Shea, S. L., Fox, R., Aslin, R. N., & Dumais, S. T. (1980). Assessment of stereopsis in human infants. *Investigative Ophthalmology, 19*, 1400–1404.

Shebilske, W. L. (1976). Extraretinal information in corrective saccades and inflow vs. outflow theories of visual direction constancy. *Vision Research, 16*, 621–628.

Shebilske, W. L. (1977). Visuomotor coordination in visual direction and position constancies. In W. Epstein (Ed.), *Stability and constancy in visual perception: Mechanisms and processes* (pp. 23–70). New York: Wiley.

Sheedy, J. E., Bailey, I. L., Buri, M., & Bass, E. (1986). Binocular vs. monocular task performance. *American Journal of Optometry and Physiological Optics, 63*, 839–846.

Sheingold, K. (1973). Developmental differences in the uptake and storage of visual information. *Journal of Experimental Child Psychology, 16*, 1–11.

Shepard, M., & Muller, H. J. (1989). Movement versus focusing of attention. *Perception & Psychophysics, 46*, 146–154.

Shepard, R. N. (1962). The analysis of proximities: Multidimensional scaling with an unknown distance function: I & II. *Psychometrika, 27*, 125–246.

Shepard, R. N. (1964). Circularity in judgments of relative pitch. *Journal of the Acoustical Society of America, 36*, 2346–2353.

Shepard, R. N. (1974). Representation of structure in similarity data: Problems and prospects. *Psychometrika, 39*, 373–421.

Shepard, R. N. (1980). Multi-dimensional data, tree-fitting, and clustering. *Science, 210*, 290–298.

Shepard, R. N. (1982). Geometrical approximations to the structure of musical pitch. *Psychological Review, 89*, 305–333.

Shepard, R. N., & Zare, S. L. (1983). Path-guided apparent motion. *Science, 220*, 632–634.

Shera, C. A., & Zweig, G. (1991). Asymmetry suppresses the cochlear catastrophe. *Journal of the Acoustical Society of America, 89*, 1276–1289.

Sherk, H., & Horton, J. C. (1984). Receptive field properties in the cat's area 17 in the absence of on-center geniculate input. *Journal of Neuroscience, 4*, 381–393.

Sherman, S. M. (1973). Visual field defects in monocularly and binocularly deprived cats. *Brain Research, 49*, 25–45.

Sherman, S. M. (1985). Parallel W-, X- and Y-cell pathways in the cat: A model for visual function. In D. Rose & V. G. Dobson (Eds.), *Models of the visual cortex* (pp. 71–84). Chichester: Wiley.

Sherrington, C. S. (1906). *Integrative action of the nervous system*. New Haven, CT: Yale University Press.

Shiffman, S. S., Reynolds, M. L., & Young, F. W. (1981). *Introduction to multidimensional scaling*. New York: Academic Press.

Shiffrin, R. M., & Schneider, W. (1977). Controlled and automatic human information processing: II. Perceptual learning, automatic attending and a general theory. *Psychological Review, 84*, 127–190.

Shiller, P. H. (1984). Central connections on the retinal on- and off-pathways. *Nature, 297*, 580–583.

Shiller, P. H., Sandell, J. H., & Maunsell, J. H. R. (1986). Functions of the on and off channels of the visual system. *Nature, 322*, 824–825.

Shimojo, S., & Held, R. (1987). Vernier acuity is less than grating acuity in 2- and 3-month olds. *Vision Research, 27*, 77–86.

Shimojo, S., & Richards, W. (1986). "Seeing" shapes that are almost totally occluded: A new look at Park's camel. *Perception & Psychophysics, 39*, 418–426.

Shinar, D. (1977). *Driver visual limitations: Diagnosis and treatment*. Institute for Research in Public Safety, DOT-HS-5-1275, Indiana University.

Shinn-Cunningham, B. G., Zurek, P. M., Durlach, N. I., & Clifton, R. K. (1995). Cross-frequency interactions in the precedence effect. *Journal of the Acoustical Society of America, 98*, 164–171.

Shipley, T. F., & Kellman, P. J. (1994). Spatiotemporal boundary formation: Boundary, form, and motion perception from transformations of surface elements. *Journal of Experimental Psychology: General, 123*, 3–20.

Shockey, L., & Reddy, R. (1974, August). *Quantitative analysis of speech perception: Results from transcription of connected speech from unfamiliar languages*. Paper presented at the Speech Communications Seminar, Stockholm.

Shore, D. I., & Enns, J. T. (1997). Shape completion time depends on the size of the occluded region. *Journal of Experimental Psychology: Human Perception & Performance, 23*, 980–998.

Shower, E. G., & Biddulph, R. (1931). Differential pitch sensitivity of the ear. *Journal of Acoustical Society of America, 3*, 275–287.

Shulman, G. L., Sheehy, J. B., & Wilson, J. (1986). Gradients of spatial attention. *Acta Psychologica, 61*, 167–181.

Shulman, G. L., Wilson, J., & Sheehy, J. B. (1985). Spatial determinants of the distribution of attention. *Perception & Psychophysics, 37*, 59–65.

Shurtleff, D., Raslear, T. G., & Simmons, L. (1990). Circadian variations in time perception in rats. *Physiology and Behavior, 47*, 931–939.

Sibony, P. A., Evinger, C., & Manning, K. A. (1987). Effects of tobacco on pursuit eye movements and blinks. *Investigative Ophthalmology and Visual Science, 28*, 316.

Siddle, D. A., Morish, R. B., White, K. D., & Mangen, G. L. (1969). Relation of visual sensitivity to extraversion. *Journal of Experimental Research in Personality, 3*, 264–267.

Sidman, M., & Kirk, B. (1974). Letter reversals in naming, writing, and matching to sample. *Child Development, 45*, 616–625.

Sillito, A. M., Jones, H. E., Gerstein, G. L., & West, D. C. (1994). Feature-linked synchronization of thalamic relay cell firing induced by feedback from the visual cortex. *Nature, 369*, 479–482.

Silver, W. L. (1987). The common chemical sense. In T. E. Finger & W. L. Silver (Eds.), *Neurobiology of taste and smell* (pp. 65–87). New York: Wiley.

Simmons, F. B., Epley, J. M., Lummis, R. C., Guttman, N., Frishkopf, L. S., Harmon, L. D., & Zwicker, E. (1965). Auditory nerve: Electrical stimulation in man. *Science, 148*, 104–106.

Simmons, J. A. (1989). A view of the world through the bat's ear: The formation of acoustic images in echolocation. *Cognition, 33*, 155–199.

Simpson, W. A. (1988). The method of constant stimuli is efficient. *Perception & Psychophysics, 44*, 433–436.

Sinclair, D. C., & Stokes, B. A. R. (1964). The production and characteristics of "second pain." *Brain, 87*, 609–618.

Sinnot, J., & Rauth, J. (1937). Effect of smoking on taste thresholds. *Journal of General Psychology, 17*, 155–162.

Sinnott, J. M., Brown, C. H., Malik, W. T., & Kressley, R. A. (1997). A multidimensional analysis of vowel discrimination in humans and monkeys. *Perception & Psychophysics, 59*, 1214–1224.

Sivak, J. G., Barrie, D. L., Callender, M. G., Doughty, M. J., Seltner, R. L., & West, J. A. (1990). Optical causes of experimental myopia. In *Myopia and the control of eye growth. Ciba Foundation Symposium 155* (pp. 160–177). Chichester: Wiley.

Sivian, L. S., & White, S. D. (1933). On minimum audible sound fields. *Journal of the Acoustical Society of America, 4*, 288–321.

Skarda, C. A., & Freeman, W. J. (1987). How brains make chaos in order to make sense of the world. *Behavioral and Brain Sciences, 10,* 161–195.

Skowbo, D. (1984). Are McCollough effects conditioned responses? *Psychological Bulletin, 96,* 215–226.

Slaughter, M. M., & Miller, R. F. (1981). 2-Amino-4-phosphonobutyric acid: A new pharmacological tool for retina research. *Science, 211,* 182–184.

Sloane, M. E., Ost, J. W., Etheredge, D. B., & Henderlite, S. E. (1989). Overprediction and blocking in the McCollough effect. *Perception & Psychophysics, 45,* 110–120.

Sloane, S. A., Shea, S. L., Proctor, M. M., & Dewsbury, D. A. (1978). Visual cliff performance in 10 species of muroid rodents. *Animal Learning and Behavior, 6,* 244–248.

Sloboda, J. A. (1985). *The musical mind: The cognitive psychology of music.* Oxford: Oxford University Press.

Small, L. H., & Bond, Z. S. (1986). Distortions and deletions: Word-initial consonant specificity in fluent speech. *Perception & Psychophysics, 40,* 20–26.

Smith, A., & Over, R. (1979). Motor aftereffect with subjective contours. *Perception & Psychophysics, 25,* 95–98.

Smith, D. V. (1985). Brainstem processing of gustatory information. In D. W. Pfaff (Ed.), *Taste, olfaction, and the central nervous system.* (pp. 151–177). New York: Rockefeller University Press.

Smith, D. V. (1997). Basic anatomy and physiology of taste. In A. M. Seiden (Ed.), *Taste and smell disorders* (pp. 128–145). New York: Thieme.

Smith, J., Hausfeld, S., Power, R. P., & Gorta, A. (1982). Ambiguous musical figures and auditory streaming. *Perception & Psychophysics, 32,* 454–464.

Smith, W. S., Frazier, N. I., Ward, S., & Webb, F. (1983). Early adolescent girls' and boys' learning of spatial visualization skill-replications. *Journal of Education, 67,* 239–243.

Snellen, H. (1862). *Probebuchstaben zur Bestimmung der Sehscharfe.* Utrecht: Weijer.

Snodgrass, J. G., & Corwin, J. (1988). Pragmatics of measuring recognition memory: Applications to dementia and amnesia. *Journal of Experimental Psychology: Human Perception and Performance, 117,* 34–50.

Snyder, S. H. (1977). Opiate receptors and internal opiates. *Scientific American, 236, 44–56.*

Söderfeldt, B., Ingvar, M., Rönnberg, J., Eriksson, L., Serrander, M., & Stone-Elander, S. (1997). Signed and spoken language perception studied by positron emission tomography. *Neurology, 49,* 82–87.

Sokolov, E. N. (1975). The neuronal mechanisms of the orienting reflex. In E. N. Sokolov & O. S. Vinogradova (Eds.), *Neuronal mechanisms of the orienting reflex* (pp. 217–238). New York: Wiley.

Soussignan, R., & Schall, B. (1996). Children's facial responsiveness to odors: Influences of hedonic valence of odor, gender, age, and social presence. *Developmental Psychology, 32,* 367–379.

Sparks, D. L. (1978). Functional properties of neurons in the monkey superior colliculus: Coupling of neuronal activity and saccade onset. *Brain Research, 113,* 21–34.

Spence, C. J., & Driver, J. (1994). Covert spatial orienting in audition: Exogenous and endogenous mechanisms facilitate sound localization. *Journal of Experimental Psychology: Human Perception and Performance, 20,* 555–574.

Spence, C. J., & Driver, J. (1997). Audiovisual links in exogenous covert spatial orienting. *Perception & Psychophysics, 59,* 1–22.

Spence, C. J., & Driver, J. (1998). Auditory and audiovisual inhibition of return. *Perception & Psychophysics, 60,* 125–139.

Sperling, H. G. (1986). Spectral sensitivity, intense spectral light studies and the color receptor mosaic of primates. *Vision Research, 26,* 1557–1571.

Sperling, G., & Weichselgartner, E. (1995). Episodic theory of the dynamics of spatial attention. *Psychological Review, 102,* 503–532.

Sperry, R. W. (1943). Effect of 180 degree rotation of the retinal field on visuomotor coordination. *Journal of Experimental Zoology, 92,* 263–277.

Spillman, L., Randsom-Hogg, A., & Oehler, R. (1987). A comparison of perceptive and receptive fields in man and monkey. *Human Neurobiology, 6,* 51–62.

Spitzer, H., Desimone, R., & Moran, J. (1988). Increased attention enhances both behavioral and neuronal performance. *Science, 240,* 338–340.

Spitzer, M. W., & Semple, M. N. (1991). Interaural phase coding in auditory midbrain: Influence of dynamic stimulus features. *Science, 254,* 721–724.

Spoendlin, H. H. (1978). The afferent innervation of the cochlea. In R. F. Naunton & C. Fernandey (Eds.), *Evoked electrical activity in the auditory nervous system* (pp. 21–42). New York: Academic Press.

Spoendlin, H. H., & Schrott, A. (1989). Analysis of the human auditory nerve. *Hearing Research, 43,* 25–38.

Sprafkin, C., Serbin, L. A., Denier, C., & Conner, J. M. (1983). Sex-differentiated play: Cognitive consequences and early

interventions. In M. B. Liss (Ed.), *Social and cognitive skills* (pp. 167–192). New York: Academic Press.

Spreen, O. (1976). Neuropsychology of learning disorders: Post conference review. In R. M. Knights & D. J. Bakker (Eds.), *The neuropsychology of learning disorders* (pp. 445–467). Baltimore: University Park Press.

Srulovicz, P., & Goldstein, J. L. (1983). A central spectrum model: A synthesis of auditory-nerve timing and place cues in monaural communication of frequency spectrum. *Journal of the Acoustical Society of America, 73,* 1266–1276.

Stark, L., & Bridgeman, B. (1983). Role of corollary discharge in space constancy. *Perception & Psychophysics, 34,* 371–380.

Stark, L., & Ellis, S. (1981). Scanpaths revisited: Cognitive models direct active looking. In D. Fisher, R. Monty, & I. Senders (Eds.), *Eye movements: Cognition and visual perception* (pp. 193–226). Hillsdale, NJ: Erlbaum.

Stebbins, W. C. (1980). The evolution of hearing in the mammals. In A. N. Popper & R. R. Fay (Eds.), *Comparative studies of hearing in vertebrates* (pp. 421–436). New York: Springer-Verlag.

Stein, B. E., & Meredith, M. A. (1993). *The merging of the senses.* Cambridge, MA: MIT Press.

Steinberg, A. (1955). Changes in time perception induced by an anaesthetic drug. *British Journal of Psychology, 46,* 273–279.

Steinfield, G. J. (1967). Concepts of set and availability and their relation to the reorganization of ambiguous pictorial stimuli. *Psychological Review, 74,* 505–525.

Steinmetz, M. A., Connor, C. E., Constantinidis, C., & McLaughlin, J. R. (1994). Covert attention suppresses neuronal responses in Area 7a of the posterior parietal cortex. *Journal of Neurophysiology, 72,* 1020–1023.

Steinschneider, M., Schroeder, C. E., Arezzo, J. C., & Vaughan, H. G. Jr. (1995). Physiologic correlates of the voice onset time boundary in primary auditory cortex (A1) of the awake monkey: Temporal response patterns. *Brain and Language, 48,* 326–340.

Stelmach, L. B., & Herdman, C. M. (1991). Directed attention and perception of temporal order. *Journal of Experimental Psychology: Human Perception & Performance, 17,* 539–550.

Stelmack, R. M., Achorn, E., & Michaud, A. (1977). Extravision and individual differences in auditory evoked response. *Psychophysiology, 14,* 368–374.

Stelmack, R. M., & Campbell, K. B. (1974). Extraversion and auditory sensitivity to high and low frequency. *Perceptual and Motor Skills, 38*, 875–879.

Stephan, F. K., & Nunez, A. A. (1977). Elimination of circadian rhythms in drinking activity, sleep, and temperature by isolation of suprachiasmatic nuclei. *Behavioral Biology, 20*, 1–16.

Stephens, P. R., & Young, J. Z. (1982). The stacocyst of the squid Loligo. *Journal of Zoology, London, 197*, 241–266.

Stern, J. A., Oster, P. J., & Newport, K. (1980). Reaction time measures, hemispheric specialization, and age. In L. Poon (Ed.), *Aging in the 1980s* (pp. 309–326). Washington, DC: American Psychological Association.

Stern, R. M., Koch, K. L., Leibowitz, H. W., Lindblad, I. M., Shupert, C. L., & Stewart, W. R. (1985). Tachygastria and motion sickness. *Aviation, Space and Environmental Medicine, 56*, 1074–1077.

Sternbach, R. A. (1963). Congenital insensitivity to pain: A review. *Psychological Bulletin, 60*, 252–264.

Sternbach, R. A., & Tursky, B. (1964). On the psychophysical power function in electric shock. *Psychonomic Science, 1*, 247–248.

Sternberg, S. (1975). Memory scanning: New findings and current controversies. *Quarterly Journal of Experimental Psychology, 27*, 1–32.

Stevens, D. A., & Lawless, H. T. (1986). Putting out the fire: Effects of tastants on oral chemical irritation. *Perception & Psychophysics, 39*, 346–350.

Stevens, J. C. (1990). Perceived roughness as a function of body locus. *Perception & Psychophysics, 47*, 298–304.

Stevens, J. C. (1995). Detection of heteroquality taste mixtures. *Perception & Psychophysics, 57*, 18–26.

Stevens, J. C., & Cain, W. S. (1986). Smelling via the mouth: Effects of aging. *Perception & Psychophysics, 40*, 142–146.

Stevens, J. C., Cain, W. S., & Burke, R. J. (1988). Variability of olfactory thresholds. *Chemical Senses, 13*, 643–653.

Stevens, J. C., Cain, W. S., & Demarque, A. (1990). Memory and identification of simulated odors in elderly and young persons. *Bulletin of the Psychonomic Society, 28*, 293–296.

Stevens, J. C., Cain, W. S., Demarque, A., & Ruthruff, A. M. (1991). On the discrimination of missing ingredients: Aging and salt flavor. *Appetite, 16*, 129–140.

Stevens, J. C., Cain, W. S., & Oatley, M. W. (1989). Aging speeds olfactory adaptation and slows recovery. *Annals of the New York Academy of Sciences, 562*, 323–325.

Stevens, J. C., Cain, W. S., Shiet, F. T., & Oatley, M. W. (1989). Olfactory adaptation and recovery in old age. *Perception, 18*, 265–276.

Stevens, J. C., & Marks, L. E. (1980). Cross-modality matching functions generated by magnitude estimation. *Perception & Psychophysics, 27*, 379–389.

Stevens, J. C., & Wellen, D. G. (1989). Recovery from adaptation to NaCl in young and elderly. *Chemical Senses, 14*, 633–635.

Stevens, K. N. (1996). Critique: Articulatory-acoustic relations and their role in speech perception. *Journal of the Acoustical Society of America, 99*, 1693–1694.

Stevens, K. N., & House, A. S. (1972). Speech perception. In J. V. Tobias (Ed.), *Foundations of modern auditory theory: Vol. 2* (pp. 3–62). New York: Academic Press.

Stevens, S. S. (1935). The relation of pitch to intensity. *Journal of the Acoustical Society of America, 6*, 150–154.

Stevens, S. S. (1946). On the theory of scales of measurement. *Science, 103*, 677–680.

Stevens, S. S. (1956). The direct estimation of sensory magnitudes—loudness. *American Journal of Psychology, 69*, 1–25.

Stevens, S. S. (1959). Tactile vibration: Dynamics of sensory intensity. *Journal of Experimental Psychology, 57*, 210–218.

Stevens, S. S. (1961). The psychophysics of sensory function. In W. A. Rosenblith (Ed.), *Sensory communication* (pp. 1–33). Cambridge, MA: MIT Press.

Stevens, S. S. (1975). *Psychophysics: Introduction to its perceptual, neural, and social prospects.* New York: Wiley.

Stevens, S. S., & Galanter, E. (1957). Ratio scales and category scales for a dozen perceptual continua. *Journal of Experimental Psychology, 54*, 377–411.

Stevens, S. S., & Newman, E. B. (1934). The localization of pure tones. *Proceedings of the National Academy of Sciences of the USA, 20*, 593–596.

Stevens, S. S., Volkman, J., & Newman, E. B. (1937). A scale for the measurement of the psychological magnitude of pitch. *Journal of the Acoustical Society of America, 8*, 185–190.

Stevens, S. S., & Warshovsky, F. (1965). *Sound and hearing.* New York: Time-Life Books.

Stinson, M. R., & Khanna, S. M. (1989). Sound propagation in the ear canal and coupling to the eardrum, with measurements on model systems. *Journal of the Acoustical Society of America, 85*, 2481–2491.

Stoffregen, T. A. (1985). Flow structure versus retinal location in the optical control of stance. *Journal of Experimental Psychology: Human Perception and Performance, 11*, 554–565.

Stolzfus, E. R. (1992). Aging and breadth of availability during language processing. Unpublished doctoral dissertation, Duke University.

Stone, J., & Fabian, M. (1966). Specialized receptive fields of the cat's retina. *Science, 152*, 1277–1279.

Stone, L. S. (1960). Polarization of the retina and development of vision. *Journal of Experimental Zoology, 145*, 85–93.

Strange, W., & Jenkins, J. (1978). Role of linguistic experience in the perception of speech. In R. Walk & H. Pick (Eds.), *Perception and experience* (pp. 125–169). New York: Plenum Press.

Stratton, G. M. (1896). Some preliminary experiments on vision without inversion of the retinal image. *Psychological Review, 3*, 611–617.

Stratton, G. M. (1897a). Upright vision and the retinal image. *Psychological Review, 4*, 182–187.

Stratton, G. M. (1897b). Vision without inversion of the retinal image. *Psychological Review, 4*, 341–360.

Street, R. F. (1931). *A Gestalt completion test: A study of a cross section of intellect.* New York: Bureau of Publication, Columbia University.

Streitfeld, B., & Wilson, M. (1986). The ABCs of categorical perception. *Cognitive Psychology, 18*, 432–451.

Streri, A. (1987). Tactile discrimination of shape and intermodal transfer in 2- to 3-month-old infants. *British Journal of Developmental Psychology, 5*, 213–220.

Stromeyer, C. F., III. (1978). Form-color aftereffects in human vision. In R. Held, H. Leibowitz, & H. L. Teuber (Eds.), *Handbook of sensory physiology: Vol. 8* (pp. 97–142). New York: Springer-Verlag.

Stroop, J. (1935). Studies of interference in serial verbal reactions. *Journal of Experimental Psychology, 18*, 624–643.

Stroud, J. M. (1955). The fine structure of psychological time. In H. Quastler (Ed.), *Information theory in psychology: Problems and methods* (pp. 174–207). Glencoe, IL: Free Press.

Stryer, L. (1987). The molecules of visual excitation. *Scientific American, 257*, 42–50.

Stuart, G. W., & Day, R. H. (1988). The Fraser illusion: Simple figures. *Perception & Psychophysics, 44*, 409–420.

Suedfeld, P. (1980). *Restricted environmental stimulation: Research and clinical applications.* New York: Wiley.

Supra, M., Cotzin, M. E., & Dallenbach, K. M. (1944). "Facial vision": The perception of obstacles by the blind. *American Journal of Psychology, 57*, 133–183.

Sussman, H. M. (1991a). The representation of stop consonants in three-dimensional acoustic space. *Phonetica, 48*, 18–31.

Sussman, H. M. (1991b). An investigation of locus equations as a source of relational invariance for stop place categorization. *Journal of the Acoustical Society of America, 90*, 1309–1325.

Sutter, A., Beck, J., & Graham, N. (1989). Contrast and spatial variables in texture segregation: Testing a simple spatial-frequency channels model. *Perception & Psychophysics, 46*, 312–332.

Svaetichin, G. (1956). Spectral response curves of single cones. *Acta Physiologica Scandinavica, 1*, 93–101.

Svaetichin, G., & MacNichol, E. F. Jr. (1958). Retinal mechanisms for achromatic vision. *Annals of the New York Academy of Sciences, 74*, 385–404.

Swarbrick, L., & Whitfield, I. C. (1972). Auditory cortical units selectively responsive to stimulus "shape." *Journal of Physiology (London), 224*, 68–69.

Swensson, R. G. (1980). A two-stage detection model applied to skilled visual search by radiologists. *Perception & Psychophysics, 27*, 11–16.

Swets, J. A. (1963). Central factors in auditory frequency selectivity. *Psychological Bulletin, 60*, 429–441.

Swift, C. G., & Tiplady, B. (1988). The effects of age on the response to caffeine. *Psychopharmacology, 94*, 29–31.

Swindale, N. V. (1988). Role of visual experience in promoting segregation of eye dominance patches in the visual cortex of the cat. *Journal of Comparative Neurology, 267*, 472–488.

Swindale, N. V., & Cynader, M. S. (1986). Vernier acuity of neurones in cat visual cortex. *Nature, 319*, 591–593.

Szabo, S., Bujas, Z., Ajdukovic, D., Mayer, D., & Vodanovic, M. (1997). Influence of the intensity of NaCl solutions on adaptation degree and recovery time course. *Perception & Psychophysics, 59*, 180–186.

Szentagothai, J. (1950). The elementary vestibulo-ocular reflex arc. *Journal of Neurophysiology, 13*, 395–407.

Takami, S., Getchell, M. L., Chen, Y, Monti-Bloch, L., Berliner, D. L., Stensaas, L. J., & Getchell, T. V. (1993). Vomeronasal epithelial cells of the adult human express neuron-specific molecules. *Neuroreport, 4*, 375–378.

Talbot, J. D., Marrett, S., Evans, A. C., Meyer, E., Bushnell, M. C., & Duncan, G. H. (1991). Multiple representations of pain in human cerebral cortex. *Science, 251*, 1355–1358.

Tan, H. Z., Rabinowitz, W. M., & Durlach, N. I. (1989). Analysis of a synthetic Tadoma system as a multidimensional tactile display. *Journal of the Acoustical Society of America, 86*, 981–988.

Tart, C. (1971). *On being stoned.* Palo Alto: Science and Behavior Books.

Tassinari, G., & Berlucci, G. (1995). Covert orienting to non-informative cues: Reaction time studies. *Behavioral Brain Research, 71*, 101–112.

Tassinari, Campara, Laercia, Chilosi, Martignoni, & Marzi (1994), *Neuroreport, 5*, 1425–1428.

Taub, E., & Berman, A. J. (1968). Movement and learning in the absence of sensory feedback. In S. J. Freedman (Ed.), *The neuropsychology of spatially oriented behavior* (pp. 173–192). Homewood, IL: Dorsey.

Taylor, S. P., & Woodhouse, J. M. (1980). A new illusion and possible links with the Munsterberg and Fraser illions of direction. *Perception & Psychophysics, 9*, 479–481.

Tedford, W. H., Warren, D. E., & Flynn, W. E. (1977). Alternation of shock aversion thresholds during menstrual cycle. *Perception & Psychophysics, 21*, 193–196.

Tees, R. C. (1974). Effect of visual deprivation on development of depth perception in the rat. *Journal of Comparative and Physiological Psychology, 86*, 300–308.

Tees, R. C., & Buhrmann, K. (1990). The effect of early experience on water maze spatial learning and memory in rats. *Developmental Psychobiology, 23*, 427–439.

Tees, R. C., & Midgley, G. (1978). Extent of recovery of function after early sensory deprivation in the rat. *Journal of Comparative and Physiological Psychology, 92*, 768–777.

Tees, R. C., & Symons, L. A. (1987). Intersensory coordination and the effects of early sensory deprivation. *Developmental Psychobiology, 20*, 497–507.

Tees, R. C., & Werker, J. F. (1984). Perceptual flexibility: Maintenance or recovery of the ability to discriminate non-native speech sounds. *Canadian Journal of Psychology, 38*, 579–590.

Teghtsoonian, M. (1987). The structure of an experiment. In M. Teghtsoonian & R. Teghtsoonian (Eds.), *Fechner Day '87* (pp. 49–52). Northampton, MA: International Society for Psychophysics.

Teghtsoonian, M., & Teghtsoonian, R. (1983). Consistency of individual exponents in cross-modality matching. *Perception & Psychophysics, 33*, 203–214.

Teghtsoonian, R. (1971). On the exponents in Stevens' law and the constant in Ekman's law. *Psychological Review, 78*, 71–80.

Teghtsoonian, R. (1975). Review of Psychophysics by S. S. Stevens. *American Journal of Psychology, 88*, 677–684.

Teghtsoonian, R., Teghtsoonian, M., Bergulund, B., & Berglund, U. (1978). Invariance of odor strength with sniff vigor: An olfactory analogue to size constancy. *Journal of Experimental Psychology: Human Perception and Performance, 4*, 144–152.

Telford, L., & Howard, I. P. (1996). Role of optical flow field asymmetry in the perception of heading during linear motion. *Perception & Psychophysics, 58*, 283–288.

Teller, D. Y. (1980). Locus questions in visual science. In C. S. Harris (Ed.), *Visual coding and adaptability* (pp. 151–176). Hillsdale, NJ: Erlbaum.

Teller, D. Y. (1981). Color vision in infants. In R. Aslin, J. Alberts, & M. Petersen (Eds.), *Development of perception, physiological perspectives: Vol. 2* (pp. 298–312). New York: Academic Press.

Teller, D. Y., & Bornstein, M. H. (1987). Infant color vision and color perception. In P. Salapatek & L. Cohen (Eds.), *Handbook of infant perception: Vol. 1. From sensation to perception* (pp. 185–237). Orlando: Academic Press.

Teller, D. Y., & Movshon, J. A. (1986). Visual development. *Vision Research, 26*, 1483–1506.

Terheardt, E. (1974). Pitch, consonance and harmony. *Journal of the Acoustical Society of America, 55*, 1061–1069.

Theeuwes, J. (1994). Stimulus-driven capture and attentional set: Selective search for color and visual abrupt onsets. *Journal of Experimental Psychology: Human Perception and Performance, 20*, 799–806.

Thomas, E. A. C., & Weaver, W. B. (1975). Cognitive processing and time perception. *Perception & Psychophysics, 17*, 363–367.

Thomas, H. (1983). Parameter estimation in simple psychophysical models. *Psychological Bulletin, 93*, 396–403.

Thomas, H., Jamison, W., & Hammel, D. D. (1973). Observation is insufficient for discovering that the surface of still water is invariantly horizontal. *Science, 181*, 173–174.

Thornbury, J. M., & Mistretta, C. M. (1981). Tactile sensitivity as a function of age. *Journal of Gerontology, 36*, 34–39.

Thorpe, L. A., & Trehub, S. E. (1989). Duration illusion and auditory grouping in infancy. *Developmental Psychology, 24*, 484–491.

Timney, B. (1985). Visual experience and the development of depth perception. In D. J. Ingle, M. Jeannerod, & D. N. Lee (Eds.), *Brain mechanisms and spatial vision* (pp. 147–174). Dordrecht: Martinus Nijhoff.

Timney, B., Mitchel, D. E., & Griffin, F. (1978). The development of vision in cats after extended periods of dark rearing. *Experimental Brain Research, 31*, 547–560.

Timney, B., & Muir, D. W. (1976). Orientation anisotropy: Incidence and magnitude in Caucasian & Chinese subjects. *Science, 193*, 699–700.

Tipper, S. P., Driver, J., & Weaver, B. (1991). Object-centered inhibition of return of visual attention. *Quarterly Journal of Experimental Psychology, 43A*, 289–298.

Tipper, S. P., Weaver, B., Jerreat, L. M., & Burak, A. L. (1994). Object-based and environment-based inhibition of return of visual attention. *Journal of Experimental Psychology: Human Perception and Performance, 20*, 478–499.

Toch, H. H., & Schulte, R. (1961). Readiness to perceive violence as a result of police training. *British Journal of Psychology, 52*, 389–393.

Todd, J. T. (1983). Perception of gait. *Journal of Experimental Psychology: Human Perception and Performance, 9*, 31–42.

Todd, J. T., & Akerstrom, R. A. (1987). Perception of three-dimensional form from patterns of optical texture. *Journal of Experimental Psychology: Human Perception and Performance, 13*, 242–255.

Toet, A., & Levi, D. M. (1992). The two-dimensional shape of spatial interaction zones in the parafovea. *Vision Research, 32*, 1349–1357.

Tomlinson, R. W. W., & Schwarz, D. W. F. (1988). Perception of the missing fundamental in nonhuman primates. *Journal of the Acoustical Society of America, 84*, 560–565.

Tootell, R. B. H., Silverman, M. S., Hamilton, S. L., DeValois, R. L., & Switkes, E. (1988). Functional anatomy of the macaque striate cortex: III. Color. *Journal of Neuroscience, 8*, 1569–1593.

Torebjork, H. E., & Hallin, R. G. (1973). Perceptual changes accompanying controlled, preferential blocking of A and C fibre responses in intact human skin nerves. *Experimental Brain Research, 16*, 321–332.

Torgerson, W. S. (1958). *Theory and methods of scaling.* New York: Wiley.

Torgerson, W. S. (1961). Distances and ratios in psychophysical scaling. *Acta Psychologica, 19*, 201–205.

Tougas, Y., & Bregman, A. S. (1990). Auditory streaming and the continuity illusion. *Perception & Psychophysics, 47*, 121–126.

Townshend, B., Cotter, N., Van Compernolle, D., & White, R. L. (1987). Pitch perception by cochlear implant subjects. *Journal of the Acoustical Society of America, 82*, 106–115.

Townsend, J., & Ashby, F. G. (1982). Experimental test of contemporary mathematical models of visual letter recognition. *Journal of Experimental Psychology: Human Perception and Performance, 8*, 834–864.

Trainor, L. J., & Trehub, S. E. (1992). A comparison of infants' and adults' sensitivity to Western musical structure. *Journal of Experimental Psychology: Human Perception and Performance, 18*, 394–402.

Trainor, L. J., & Trehub, S. E. (1994). Key membership and implied harmony in Western tonal music: Developmental perspectives. *Perception & Psychophysics, 56*, 125–132.

Trehub, S. (1976). The discrimination of foreign speech contrasts by infants and adults. *Child Development, 47*, 466–472.

Trehub, S. E., & Schneider, B. A. (1987). Problems and promises of developmental psychophysics: Throw out the bath water but keep the baby. In M. Teghtsoonian & R. Teghtsoonian (Eds.), *Fechner Day '87* (pp. 43–47). Northampton, MA: International Society for Psychophysics.

Trehub, S. E., Schneider, B. A., & Endman, M. (1980). Developmental changes in infants sensitivity to octave-band noises. *Journal of Experimental Child Psychology, 29*, 282–293.

Trehub, S. E., & Trainor, L. J. (1990). Rules for listening in infancy. In J. T. Enns (Ed.), *The development of attention: Research and theory* (pp. 87–119). Amsterdam: Elsevier.

Trehub, S. E., & Unyk, A. M. (1994). Children's songs to infant siblings: Parallels with speech. *Journal of Child Language, 21*, 735–744.

Treisman, A. M. (1982). Perceptual groupings and attention in visual search for features and for objects. *Journal of Experimental Psychology: Human Perception and Performance, 8*, 194–214.

Treisman, A. M. (1986a). Features and objects in visual processing. *Scientific American, 255*, 114B–125.

Treisman, A. M. (1986b). Properties, parts, and objects. In K. R. Boff, L. Kaufman, & J. P. Thomas (Eds.), *Handbook of perception and human performance* (pp. 35-1– 35-70). New York: Wiley.

Treisman, A. M., Cavanagh, P., Fischer, B., Ramachandran, V. S., & von der Heydt, R. (1990). Form perception and attention: Striate cortex and beyond. In L. Spillman & J. S. Werner (Eds.), *Visual perception* (pp. 273–316). New York: Academic Press.

Treisman, A. M., & Davies, A. (1972). Divided attention to ear and eye. In S. Kornblum (Ed.), *Attention and performance IV* (pp. 101–118). New York: Academic Press.

Treisman, A. M., & Gelade, G. (1980). A feature-integration theory of attention. *Cognitive Psychology, 12*, 97–136.

Treisman, A. M., & Gormican, S. (1988). Feature analysis in early vision: Evidence from search asymmetries. *Psychological Review, 95*, 15–48.

Treisman, A. M., & Schmidt, H. (1982). Illusory conjunctions in the perception of objects. *Cognitive Psychology, 14*, 107–141.

Treisman, A. M., & Souther, J. (1985). Search asymmetry: A diagnostic for preattentive processing of separable features. *Journal of Experimental Psychology: General, 114*, 285–310.

Treisman, M. (1963). Temporal discrimination and the indifference interval: Implications for the model of an internal clock. *Psychological Monographs, 77* (1–31, Whole No. 576).

Treisman, M. (1976). On the use and misuse of psychophysical terms. *Psychological Review, 83*, 246–256.

Tress, K. H., & Kugler, B. T. (1979). Interocular transfer of movement aftereffects in schizophrenia. *British Journal of Psychology, 70*, 389–392.

Trick, L., Enns, J. T., & Brodeur, D. A. (1996). Lifespan changes in visual enumeration: The number discrimination task. *Developmental Psychology, 32*, 925–932.

Tronick, E. (1972). Stimulus control and the growth of the infant's effective visual field. *Perception & Psychophysics, 11*, 373–376.

Troscianko, T., & Fahle, M. (1988). Why do isoluminant stimuli appear slower? *Journal of the Optical Society of America A, 5*, 871–880.

Trout, J. D., & Poser, W. J. (1990). Auditory and phonemic influences on phonemic restoration. *Language & Speech, 33*, 121–135.

Tsal, Y. (1983). Movements of attention across the visual field. *Journal of Experimental Psychology: Human Perception and Performance, 9*, 523–530.

Tsotsos, J. K. (1988). A "complexity level" analysis of immediate vision. *International Journal of Computer Vision, 1*, 303–320.

Tuck, J. P., & Long, G. M. (1990). The role of small-field tritanopia in two measures of color vision. *Ophthalmic and Physiological Optics, 10,* 195–199.

Turnbull, C. (1961). Some observations regarding the experiences and behavior of the Bambuti Turnbull, O. H., Beschin, N., & Della Sala, S. (1997). Agnosia for object orientation: Implications for theories of object recognition. *Neuropsychologia, 35,* 153–163.

Turnbull, O. H., & McCarthy, R. A. (1996). When is a view unusual? A single case study of orientation-dependent visual agnosia. *Brain Research Bulletin, 40,* 497–502. Pygmies. *American Journal of Psychology, 74,* 304–308.

Turner, P. (1968). Amphetamines and smell threshold in man. In A. Herxheimer (Ed.), *Drugs and sensory functions* (pp. 91–100). Boston: Little, Brown.

Turvey, M. T., Burton, G., Pagano, C. C., Solomon, H. Y., & Runeson, S. (1992). Role of the inertia tensor in perceiving object orientation by dynamic touch. *Journal of Experimental Psychology: Human Perception & Performance, 18,* 714–727.

Tversky, A. (1977). Features of similarity. *Psychological Review, 84,* 327–352.

Tversky, B., & Schiano, D. J. (1989). Perceptual and conceptual factors in distortions in memory for graphs and maps. *Journal of Experimental Psychology: General, 118,* 387–398.

Tyler, C. W. (1975). Stereoscopic tilt and size aftereffects. *Perception, 4,* 187–192.

Uchikawa, K., Uchicawa, H., & Boynton, R. M. (1989). Partial color constancy of isolated surface colors examined by a color-naming method. *Perception, 18,* 83–91.

Uhlarik, J., & Johnson, R. (1978). Development of form perception in repeated brief exposures to visual stimuli. In R. Walk & L. Pick Jr. (Eds.), *Perception and experience.* New York: Plenum.

Ullman, S. (1979). The interpretation of structure from motion. *Proceedings of the Royal Society of London, Series B, 203,* 405–426.

Ulrich, R. (1987). Threshold models of temporal-order judgments evaluated by a ternary response task. *Perception & Psychophysics, 42,* 224–239.

Umezaki, H., & Morrell, F. (1970). Developmental study of photic evoked responses in premature infants. *Electroencephalography and Clinical Neurophysiology, 28,* 55–63.

Ungerleider, L. G., Mishkin, M. (1982). Two cortical visual systems. In D. J. Ingle, M. A. Goodale, & R. J. W. Mansfield (Eds.), *Analysis of visual behavior* (pp. 549–586). Cambridge, MA: MIT Press.

Uttal, W. (1981). *A taxonomy of visual processes.* Hillsdale, NJ: Erlbaum.

Vallbo, A. B. (1981). Sensations evoked from the glabrous skin of the human hand by electrical stimulation of unitary mechano-sensitive afferents. *British Research, 215,* 359–363.

Vallbo, A. B. (1983). Tactile sensation related to activity in primary afferents with special reference to detection problems. In C. von Euler, O. Franzen, U. Lindblom, & D. Ottoson (Eds.), *Somatosensory mechanisms* (pp. 163–172). New York, Plenum Press.

Van Doren, C. L. (1989). A model of spatiotemporal sensitivity linking psychophysics to tissue mechanics. *Journal of the Acoustical Society of America, 85,* 2065–2080.

van der Heijden, A. H. C., Wolters, G., Groep, J. C., & Hagenaar, R. (1987). Single-letter recognition accuracy benefits from advance cuing of location. *Perception & Psychophysics, 42,* 503–509.

van der Meer, H. C. (1979). Interrelation of the effects of binocular disparity and perspective cues on judgments of depth and height. *Perception & Psychophysics, 26,* 481–488.

Van Essen, D. C. (1979). Visual areas of the mammalian cerebral cortex. *Annual Review of Neurosciences, 2,* 227–263.

Van Essen, D. C. (1984). Functional organization of primate visual cortex. In A. Peters & E. G. Jones (Eds.), *Cerebral cortex: Vol. 3* (pp. 259–329). New York: Plenum Press.

Van Essen, D. C., Anderson, C. H., & Felleman, D. J. (1992). Information processing in the primate visual system: An integrated systems perspective. *Science, 255,* 419–423.

Van Lancker, D. R., & Kreiman, J. (1989). Voice perception deficits: Neuroanatomical correlates of phonagnosia. *Journal of Clinical and Experimental Neuropsychology, 11,* 665–674.

van Santen, J. P. H., & Sperling, G. (1985). Elaborated Reichardt detectors. *Journal of the Optical Society of America A, 2,* 300–321.

Van Voorhis, S., & Hillyard, S. A. (1977). Visual evoked potentials and selective attention to points in space. *Perception & Psychophysics, 22,* 54–62.

Varma, V. K., & Malhotra, A. K. (1988). Cannabis and cognitive functions: A prospective study. *Drug & Alcohol Dependence, 21,* 147–152.

Varner, D., Cook, J. E., Schneck, M. E., McDonald, M., & Teller, D. (1985). Tritan discriminations by 1- and 2-month-old human infants. *Vision Research, 6,* 821–831.

Vaughan, H. G., & Kurtzberg, D. (1989). Electrophysiologic indices of normal and aberrant cortical maturation. In P. Kelaway & J. Noebels (Eds.), *Problems and concepts of developmental neurophysiology* (pp. 263–287). Baltimore: Johns Hopkins University Press.

Vautin, R. G., & Berkley, M. A. (1977). Responses of single cells in cat visual cortex to stimulus movement: Neural correlates of visual after-effects. *Journal of Neurophysiology, 40,* 1051–1065.

Velle, W. (1987). Sex differences in sensory functions. *Perspectives in Biology and Medicine, 30,* 490–522.

Verrey, L. (1888). Hemiachromatopsie droite absolue. *Archives of Ophthalmology* (Paris), *8,* 289–301.

Verriest, G. (1974). Recent advances in the study of the acquired deficiencies of color vision. *Fondazione "Gorgio Ranchi," 24,* 1–80.

Verrillo, R. T. (1968). A duplex mechanism of mechanoreception. In D. R. Kenshalo (Ed.), *The skin senses* (pp. 139–159). Springfield, IL: Thomas.

Verrillo, R. T., & Bolanowski, S. J. Jr. (1986). The effects of skin temperature on the psychophysical responses to vibration on glabrous and hairy skin. *Journal of the Acoustical Society of America, 80,* 528–532.

Verrillo, R. T., Fraioli, A. J., & Smith, R. L. (1969). Sensation magnitude of vibrotactile stimuli. *Perception & Psychophysics, 6,* 366–372.

Viemeister, N. F. (1988). Intensity coding and the dynamic range problem. *Hearing Research, 34,* 267–274.

Vierck, C. (1978). Somatosensory system. In R. B. Masterston (Ed.), *Handbook of sensory neurobiology: Vol. I. Sensory integration* (pp. 249–310). New York: Plenum Press.

Vimal, R. L. P., Pokorny, J., & Smith, V. C. (1987). Appearance of steadily viewed lights. *Vision Research, 27,* 1309–1318.

Vogels, R., & Orban, G. A. (1986). Decision factors affecting line orientation judgments in the method of single stimuli. *Perception & Psychophysics, 40,* 74–84.

Vurpillot, E. (1968). The development of scanning strategies and their relation to visual differentiation. *Journal of Experimental Child Psychology, 6,* 632–650.

Waber, D. P. (1976). Sex differences in cognition. A function of maturation rate? *Science, 192,* 572–574.

Waber, D. P. (1977). Sex differences in mental abilities, hemispheric lateralization and rate of physical growth at adolescence. *Developmental Psychology, 13,* 29–38.

Wacholtz, E. (1996). Can we learn from the clinically significant face processing deficits, prosopagnosia and Capgras delusion? *Neuropsychology Review, 6,* 203–257.

Wade, N. J. (1984). *Brewster & Wheatstone on vision.* New York: Academic Press.

Waespe, W., & Henn, V. (1977). Neuronal activity in the vestibular nuclei of the alert monkey during vestibular and optokinetic stimulation. *Experimental Brain Research, 27,* 523–538.

Wahl, O. F., & Sieg, D. (1980). Time estimation among schizophrenics. *Perceptual and Motor Skills, 50,* 535–541.

Wald, G. (1968). The molecular basis of visual excitation. *Nature (London), 219,* 800–807.

Walk, R. D., & Gibson, E. J. (1961). A comparative and analytic study of visual depth perception. *Psychological Monographs, 75,* 1–44.

Walker, J. L. (1977). Time estimation and total subjective time. *Perceptual and Motor Skills, 44,* 527–532.

Walker, J. T. (1975). Visual texture as a factor in the apparent velocity of objective motion and motion aftereffects. *Perception & Psychophysics, 18,* 175–180.

Walker, J. T., & Shank, M. D. (1988). Real and subjective lines and edges in the Bourdon illusion. *Perception & Psychophysics, 43,* 475–484.

Wall, P. D. (1979). On the relation of injury to pain. *Pain, 6,* 253–264.

Wallace, B., & Priebe, F. A. (1985). Hypnotic susceptibility, interference and alternation frequency to the Necker cube illusion. *Journal of General Psychology, 112,* 271–277.

Wallace, P. (1977). Individual discrimination of humans by odor. *Physiology and Behavior, 19,* 577–579.

Wallach, H. (1972). The perception of neutral colors. In R. Held & W. Richards (Eds.), *Perception: Mechanisms and models: Readings from Scientific American* (pp. 278–285). San Francisco: Freeman. (Originally published in *Scientific American,* 1963)

Wallach, H. (1987). Perceiving a stable environment when one moves. *Annual Review of Psychology, 38,* 1–27.

Wallach, H., & Becklen, R. (1983). An effect of speed on induced motion. *Perception & Psychophysics, 34,* 237–242.

Wallach, H., Becklen, R., & Nitzberg, D. (1985). Vector analysis and process combination in motion perception. *Journal of Experimental Psychology: Human Perception and Performance, 11,* 93–102.

Wallach, H., Newman, E. B., & Rosenzweig, M. R. (1949). The precedence effect in sound localization. *American Journal of Psychology, 62,* 315–336.

Walley, A., Pisoni, D., & Aslin, R. (1981). The role of early experience in the development of speech perception. In R. Aslin, J. Alberts, & M. Petersen (Eds.), *Development of perception: Psychobiological perspectives: Vol. 1. Audition, somatic perceptions, and the chemical senses* (pp. 219–256). New York: Academic Press.

Walls, G. L. (1951). A theory of ocular dominance. *AMA Archives of Ophthalmology, 45,* 387–412.

Walraven, J., Enroth-Cugell, C., Hood, D. C., McLeod, D. I., & Schnapf, J. L. (1990). The control of visual sensitivity: Receptoral and postreceptoral processes. In L. Spillman & J. S. Werner (Eds.), *Visual perception: The neurophysiological foundations* (pp. 53–101). New York: Academic Press.

Walsh, V., & Butler, S. R. (1996). The effects of visual cortex lesions on the perception of rotated shapes. *Behavioural Brain Research, 76,* 127–142.

Wang, M. Q., & Taylor-Nicholson, M. E. (1992) Psychomotor and visual performance under the time-course effect of alcohol. *Perceptual and Motor Skills, 75,* 1095–1106.

Warchol, M. E., Lambert, P. R., Goldstein, B. J., Forge, A., & Corwin, J. T. (1993). Regenerative proliferation in inner ear sensory epithelia from adult guinea pigs and humans. *Science, 259,* 1619–1622.

Ward, L. M. (1971). *Some psychophysical properties of category judgments and magnitude estimations.* Unpublished doctoral dissertation, Duke University, Durham, NC.

Ward, L. M. (1972). Category judgments of loudness in the absence of an experimenter-induced identification function: Sequential effects and power function fit. *Journal of Experimental Psychology, 94,* 179–184.

Ward, L. M. (1973). Repeated magnitude estimations with a variable standard: Sequential effects and other properties. *Perception & Psychophysics, 13,* 193–200.

Ward, L. M. (1974). Power functions for category judgments of duration and line length. *Perceptual and Motor Skills, 38,* 1182.

Ward, L. M. (1975). Sequential dependencies and response range in cross-modality matches of duration to loudness. *Perception & Psychophysics, 18,* 217–223.

Ward, L. M. (1982a). Mixed-modality psychophysical scaling: Sequential dependencies and other properties. *Perception & Psychophysics, 31,* 53–62.

Ward, L. M. (1982b). Determinants of attention to local and global features of visual forms. *Journal of Experimental Psychology: Human Perception and Performance, 8,* 562–581.

Ward, L. M. (1983). On processing dominance: Comment on Pomerantz. *Journal of Experimental Psychology: General, 112,* 541–546.

Ward, L. M. (1985). Covert focussing of the attentional gaze. *Canadian Journal of Psychology, 39,* 546–563.

Ward, L. M. (1986). Mixed-modality psychophysical scaling: Double cross-modality matching for "difficult" continua. *Perception & Psychophysics, 39,* 407–417.

Ward, L. M. (1987). Remembrance of sounds past: Memory and psychophysical scaling. *Journal of Experimental Psychology: Human Perception and Performance, 13,* 216–227.

Ward, L. M. (1990). Critical bands and mixed-frequency scaling: Sequential dependencies, equal-loudness contours, and power function exponents. *Perception & Psychophysics, 47,* 551–562.

Ward, L. M. (1991). Associative measurement of psychological magnitude. In S. J. Bolanowski & G. A. Gescheider (Eds.), *Ratio scaling of psychological magnitude* (pp. 79–100). Hillsdale, NJ: Erlbaum.

Ward, L. M. (1992). Mind in psychophysics. In D. Algom (Ed.), *Psychophysical approaches to cognition.* (pp. 187–249). Amsterdam: North-Holland (Elsevier).

Ward, L. M. (1994). Supramodal and modality-specific mechanisms for stimulus-driven shifts of auditory and visual attention. *Canadian Journal of Experimental Psychology, 48,* 242–259.

Ward, L. M. (1997). Involuntary listening aids hearing. *Psychological Science, 8,* 112–118.

Ward, L. M., Armstrong, J., & Golestani, N. (1996). Intensity resolution and subjective magnitude in psychophysical scaling. *Perception & Psychophysics, 58,* 793–801.

Ward, L. M., & Davidson, K. P. (1993). Where the action is: Weber fractions as a function of sound pressure at low frequencies. *Journal of the Acoustical Society of America, 94,* 2587–2594.

Ward, L. M., & Lockhead, G. R. (1970). Sequential effects and memory in category judgments. *Journal of Experimental Psychology, 854,* 27–34.

Ward, L. M., McDonald, J. J., & Golestani, N. (1998). Cross-modal control of attention shifts. In R. D. Wright (Ed.), *Visual attention* (pp. 232–268). New York: Oxford University Press.

Ward, L. M., & Mori, S. (1996). Attention cueing aids auditory intensity resolution. *Journal of the Acoustical Society of America, 100,* 1722–1727.

Ward, L. M., Porac, P., Coren, S., & Girgus, J. S. (1977). The case for misapplied constancy scaling: Depth associations elicited by illusion configurations. *American Journal of Psychology, 90,* 609–620.

Ward, T. B. (1985). Individual differences in processing stimulus dimensions: Relation to selective processing ability. *Perception & Psychophysics, 37,* 471–482.

Ward, W. D. (1970). Musical perception. In J. V. Tobias (Ed.), *Foundations of modern auditory theory. Vol. 1* (pp. 407–47). New York: Academic Press.

Ware, C. (1981). Subjective contours independent of subjective brighteners. *Perception & Psychophysics, 29,* 500–504.

Ware, C., & Cowan, W. B. (1987). Chromatic Mach bands: Behavioral evidence for lateral inhibition in human color vision. *Perception & Psychophysics, 41,* 173–178.

Warm, J. S., & McCray, R. E. (1969). Influence of word frequency and length on the apparent duration of tachistoscopic presentations. *Journal of Experimental Psychology, 79,* 56–58.

Warren, D. H. (1984). *Blindness and early childhood development.* New York: American Foundation for the Blind.

Warren, R. M. (1970). Perceptual restoration of missing speech sounds. *Science, 167,* 392–393.

Warren, R. M. (1984). Perceptual restoration of obliterated sounds. *Psychological Bulletin, 96,* 371–383.

Warren, R. M., Obusek, C. J., Farmer, R. M., & Warren, R. P. (1969). Auditory sequence: Confusion of patterns other than speech or music. *Science, 164,* 586–587.

Warren, R. M., Reiner, K. R., Bashford, J. A. Jr., & Brubaker, B. S. (1995). Spectral redundancy: Intelligibility of sentences heard through narrow spectral slits. *Perception & Psychophysics, 57,* 175–182.

Warren, W. H., & Hannon, D. J. (1988). Direction of self-motion is perceived from optical flow. *Nature, 336,* 162–163.

Wassle, H., Peichl, L., & Boycott, B. B. (1983). A spatial analysis of on- and off-ganglion cells in the cat retina. *Vision Research, 23,* 1151–1160.

Watanabe, T., & Katsuki, Y. (1974). Response patterns of single auditory neurons of the cat to species-specific vocalization. *Japanese Journal of Physiology, 24,* 135–155.

Watkins, L. R., & Mayer, D. J. (1982). Organization of endogenous opiate and nonopiate pain control systems. *Science, 216,* 1185–1192.

Watson, A. B. (1983). Detection and recognition of simple spatial forms. In O. J. Braddick & A. C. Sleigh (Eds.), *Physical and biological processing of images* (pp. 100–114). New York: Springer-Verlag.

Watson, A. B., & Fitzhugh, A. (1990). The method of constant stimuli is inefficient. *Perception & Psychophysics, 47,* 87–91.

Watson, C. S., Kelly, W. J., & Wroten, H. W. (1976). Factors in the discrimination of tonal patterns: II. Selective attention and learning under various levels of stimulus uncertainty. *Journal of the Acoustical Society of America, 60,* 1176–1185.

Weale, R. A. (1979). Discoverers of Mach-bands. *Investigative Ophthalmology and Visual Sciences, 18,* 652–654.

Weale, R. A. (1982). *Focus on vision.* Cambridge, MA: Harvard University Press.

Weale, R. A. (1986). Aging and vision. *Vision Research, 26,* 1507–1512.

Weber, E. H. (1834). *De pulen, resorptione, auditu et tactu: Annotationes anatomicae et physiologicae.* Leipzig: Koehler.

Webster, M., & DeValois, R. (1985). Relationship between spatial frequency and orientation tuning of striate cortex cells. *Journal of the Optical Society of America A, 2,* 1124–1132.

Webster, M. A., & Mollon, J. D. (1995). Colour constancy influenced by contrast adaptation. *Nature, 373,* 694–698.

Webster, W. R., & Atkin, L. M. (1975). Central auditory processing. In M. S. Gazzaniga & C. Blakemore (Eds.), *Handbook of sensory psychobiology* (pp. 325–364). New York: Academic Press.

Weiffenbach, J. M., Baum, B. J., & Burghauser, B. (1982). Taste thresholds: Quality specific variation with human aging. *Journal of Gerontology, 37,* 372–377.

Weil, A. T., Zinberg, E., & Nelson, J. N. (1968). Clinical and psychological effects of marijuana in man. *Science, 162,* 1234–1242.

Weinstein, E. A., Cole, M., Mitchell, M. S., & Lyerly, O. G. (1964). Anosagnosia and aphasia. *Archives of Neurology, 10,* 376–386.

Weinstein, S. (1968). Intensive and extensive aspects of tactile sensitivity as a function of body part, sex, and laterality. In D. R. Kenshalo (Ed.), *The skin senses* (pp. 195–218). Springfield, IL: Thomas.

Weinstein, S., & Sersen, E. A. (1961). Tactual sensitivity as a function of handedness and laterality. *Journal of Comparative and Physiological Psychology, 54,* 665–669.

Weisel, T. N., & Hubel, D. H. (1974). Ordered arrangement of orientation columns in monkeys lacking visual experience. *Journal of Comparative Neurology, 158,* 307–318.

Weisenberg, M. (1984). Cognitive aspects of pain. In P. D. Wall & R. Melzack (Eds.), *Textbook of pain* (pp. 162–172). Edinburgh: Churchill Livingstone.

Weisenberger, J. M., Broadstone, S. M., & Saunders, F. A. (1989). Evaluation of two multichannel tactile aids for the hearing impaired. *Journal of the Acoustical Society of America, 86,* 1764–1775.

Weisstein, N. A. (1968). Rashevsky-Landahl neural net: Simulation of metacontrast. *Psychological Review, 75,* 494–521.

Weisstein, N. A. (1980). Tutorial: The joy of Fourier analysis. In C. S. Harris (Ed.), *Visual coding and adaptability* (pp. 365–380). Hillsdale, NJ: Erlbaum.

Weisstein, N. A., Harris, C., Berbaum, K., Tangney, J., & Williams, A. (1977). Contrast reduction by small localized stimuli: Extensive spatial spread of above-threshold orientation-selective masking. *Vision Research, 17,* 341–350.

Weisstein, N. A., Mantalvo, F. S., & Ozog, G. (1972). Differential adaptation to gratings blocked by cubes and gratings blocked by hexagons: A test of the neural symbolic activity hypothesis. *Psychonomic Science, 27,* 89–91.

Weisstein, N. A., Matthews, M., & Berbaum, K. (1974, November). *Illusory contours can mask real contours.* Paper presented at the meeting of the Psychonomic Society, Boston.

Weisstein, N. A., Ozog, G., & Szoc, R. (1975). A comparison and elaboration of two models of metacontrast. *Psychological Review, 82,* 325–343.

Weisstein, N. A., & Wong, E. (1986). Figure-ground organization and the spatial and temporal responses of the visual system. In E. C. Schwab & H. C. Nusbaum (Eds.), *Pattern recognition by humans and machines: Vol. 2. Visual perception* (pp. 31–64). Orlando: Academic Press.

Welch, R. B. (1969). Adaptation to prism-displaced vision: The importance of target pointing. *Perception & Psychophysics, 5,* 305–309.

Welch, R. B. (1971). Prism adaptation: The "target pointing effect" as a function of exposure trials. *Perception & Psychophysics, 5,* 102–104.

Welch, R. B. (1978). *Perceptual modification, adapting to altered sensory environments.* New York: Academic Press.

Welford, A. T. (1980). *Reaction times.* London: Academic Press.

Well, A. D., Lorch, E. P., & Anderson, D. R. (1980). Developmental trends in distractability: Is absolute or proportional decrement the appropriate measure of interference? *Journal of Experimental Child Psychology, 30,* 109–124.

Wells, G. L., & Loftus, E. (1984). *Eyewitness testimony: Psychological perspectives*. Cambridge: Cambridge University Press.

Wenderoth, P., Criss, G., & van der Zwan, R. (1990). Determinants of subjective contour: Bourdon illusions and "unbending" effects. *Perception & Psychophysics, 48,* 497–508.

Wenzel, E. M., Arruda, M., Kistler, D. J., & Wightman, F. L. (1993). Localization using nonindividualized head-related transfer functions. *Journal of the Acoustical Society of America, 94,* 111–123.

Werker, J. F. (1989). Becoming a native listener. *American Scientist, 77,* 54–59.

Werker, J. F. (1992). Cross–language speech perception: Developmental change does not involve loss. In J. Goodman & H. C. Nusbaum (Eds.), *Speech perception and word recognition.* Cambridge, MA: MIT Press.

Werker, J. F., Gilbert, J., Humphrey, K., & Tees, R. (1981). Developmental aspects of cross-language speech perception. *Child Development, 52,* 349–355.

Werker, J. F., & Logan, J. S. (1985), Cross-language evidence for three factors in speech perception. *Perception & Psychophysics, 37,* 35–44.

Werker, J. F., & McLeod, P. J. (1989). Infant preference for both male and female infant directed talk: A development of attention and affective responsiveness. *Canadian Journal of Psychology, 43,* 230–246.

Werker, J. F., & Tees, R. C. (1984). Cross-language speech perception: Evidence for perceptual reorganization during the first year of life. *Infant Behavior and Development, 7,* 49–63.

Werner, H. (1935). Studies on contour. *American Journal of Psychology, 47,* 40–64.

Werner, J. S. (1979). *Developmental change in scotopic sensitivity and the absorption spectrum of the human ocular media.* Unpublished doctoral dissertation, Brown University, Providence, RI.

Werner, J. S., Peterzell, D. H., & Sheetz, A. J. (1990). Light, vision and aging. *Optometry and Vision Science, 67,* 214–229.

Werner, J. S., & Walraven, J. (1982). Effect of chromatic adaptation on the achromatic locus: The role of contrast, luminance and background color. *Vision Research, 22,* 929–943.

Werner, J. S., & Wooten, B. R. (1979). Human infant color vision and color perception. *Infant Behavior and Development, 2,* 241–274.

Wertheimer, M. (1912). Experimentelle Studien uber das Sehen von Bewegung. *Zeitschrift fur Psychologie, 61,* 161–265.

Wertheimer, M. (1923). Principles of perceptual organization (Abridged trans. by M. Wertheimer). In D. S. Beardslee & M. Wertheimer (Eds.), *Readings in perception* (pp. 115–137). Princeton, NJ: Van Nostrand-Reinhold. (Original work published 1923, *Psychologishe Forschung, 41,* 301–350)

Wertheimer, M. (1961). Psychomotor coordination of auditory and visual space at birth. *Science, 134,* 1692.

West, R. L. (1996). Constrained scaling: Calibrating individual subjects in magnitude estimation. Doctoral Dissertation, University of British Columbia (Dissertation Abstracts International-B, 58/01, p. 438, July 1997 ATT NNI 4853).

West, R. L., & Ward, L. M. (1994). Constrained scaling. In L. M. Ward (Ed.), *Fechner Day 94* (pp. 225–230). Vancouver, Canada: International Society for Psychophysics.

Westerman, L. A., & Smith, R. L. (1988). A diffusion model of the transient response of the cochlear inner hair cell synapse. *Journal of the Acoustical Society of America, 83,* 2266–2276.

Westheimer, G. (1965). Spatial interaction in the human retina during scotopic vision. *Journal of Physiology, 181,* 812–894.

Westheimer, G. (1967). Spatial interaction in human cone vision. *Journal of Physiology, 190,* 139–154.

Westheimer, G. (1979). Spatial sense of the eye. *Investigative Ophthalmology and Visual Science, 18,* 893–912.

Wever, E. G. (1970). *Theory of hearing.* New York: Wiley.

Wever, R. A. (1979). *The circadian system of man.* New York: Springer-Verlag.

Wever, R. A. (1989). Light effects on human circadian rhythms: A review of recent Andechs experiments. *Journal of Biological Rhythms, 4,* 161–185.

Whalen, D. H., & Liberman, A. M. (1987). Speech perception takes precedence over nonspeech perception. *Science, 237,* 169–171.

Whalen, D. H., & Liberman, A. M. (1996). Limits on phonetic integration in duplex perception. *Perception & Psychophysics, 58,* 857–870.

White, B. W., Saunders, F. A., Scadden, L., Bach-y-Rita, P., & Collins, C. C. (1970). Seeing with the skin. *Perception & Psychophysics, 7,* 23–27.

White, C. (1963). Temporal numerosity and the psychological unit of duration. *Psychological Monographs, 77* (1–37, Whole No. 575).

White, C. W., Lockhead, G. R., & Evans, N. J. (1977). Multidimensional scaling of subjective color-blind observers. *Perception & Psychophysics, 21,* 522–526.

White, C. W., & Montgomery, D. A. (1976). Memory colours in after-images: A bicentennial demonstration. *Perception & Psychophysics, 19,* 371–374.

Whitfield, I. C. (1967). *The auditory pathway.* London: Arnold.

Whitfield, I. C. (1968). The organization of the auditory pathways. *Journal of Sound and Vibration Research, 8,* 108–117.

Whitfield, I. C. (1978). The neural code. In E. C. Carterette & M. P. Friedman (Eds.), *Handbook of perception: Vol. IV. Hearing* (pp. 163–183). New York: Academic Press.

Whitfield, I. C. (1980). Auditory cortex and the pitch of complex tones. *Journal of the Acoustical Society of America, 67,* 644–647.

Whitfield, I. C., & Evans, E. F. (1965). Responses of auditory cortical neurons to stimuli of changing frequency. *Journal of Neurophysiology, 28,* 655–672.

Whitsel, B. L., Dreyer, D. A., Hollins, M., & Young, M. G. (1979). The coding of direction of tactile stimulus movement: Correlative psychophysical and electrophysiological data. In D. R. Kenshalo (Ed.), *Sensory functions of the skin of humans* (pp. 79–108). New York: Plenum Press.

Whytt, R. (1751). *An essay on the vital and other involuntary motions of animals.* Edinburgh: Balfour & Neill.

Wickens, C. D. (1984). Processing resources in attention. In R. Parasuraman & D. R. Davies (Eds.), *Varieties of attention* (pp. 63–101). Orlando: Academic Press.

Wiener, N. (1961). *Cybernetics* (2nd ed.). Cambridge, MA: MIT Press.

Wier, C. C., Jesteadt, W., & Green, D. M. (1977). Frequency discrimination as a function of frequency and sensation level. *Journal of the Acoustical Society of America, 61,* 178–184.

Wier, C. C., Pasanen, E. G., & McFadden, D. (1988). Partial dissociation of spontaneous otoacoustic emissions and distortion products during aspirin use. *Journal of the Acoustical Society of America, 84,* 230–237.

Wightman, F. L., & Kistler, D. J. (1989). Headphone simulation of free-field listening II: Psychophysical validation. *Journal of the Acoustical Society of America, 85,* 868–878.

Wild, H. M., Butler, D., Carden, D., & Kulikowski, J. J. (1985). Primate cortical area V4 important for colour constancy but not wavelength discrimination. *Nature, 313,* 133–135.

Wilkinson, F., Wilson, H., R., & Ellemberg, D. (1997). Lateral interactions in peripherally viewed texture arrays.

Journal of the Optical Society of America, *14,* 2057–2068.

Willer, J. C., Dehen, H., & Cambier, J. (1981). Stress-induced analgesia in humans: Endogenous opioids and naloxone-reversible depression of pain reflexes. *Science, 212,* 689–690.

Williams, D. R., MacLeod, D. I. A., Hayhoe, M. M. (1981). Foveal tritanopia. *Vision Research, 21,* 1341–1356.

Williams, J. M. (1979). Distortions of vision and pain: Two functional facets of D-lysergic diethylamide. *Perceptual and Motor Skills, 49,* 499–528.

Williams, M. (1970). *Brain damage and the mind.* London: Penguin.

Willis, W. D. (1983). Descending control of nociceptive transmission by primate spinothalamic neurons. In C. von Euler, O. Franzen, U. Lindblom, & D. Ottoson (Eds.), *Somatosensory mechanisms* (pp. 296–308). New York: Plenum Press.

Willis, W. D. (1985). *The pain system: The neural basis of nociceptive transmission in the mammalian nervous system.* Basel: Karger.

Wilson, E. O. (1971). *The insect societies.* Cambridge, MA: Harvard University Press.

Wilson, H. C. (1987). Female axillary secretions influence women's menstrual cycles: A critique. *Hormones and Behavior, 21,* 536–546.

Wilson, H. C. (1988). Male axillary secretions influence women's menstrual cycles: A critique. *Hormones and Behavior, 22,* 266–271.

Wilson, H. R. (1986). Responses of spatial mechanisms can explain hyperacuity. *Vision Research, 26,* 453–469.

Wilson, H. R., & Bergen, J. R. (1979). A four mechanism model for threshold spatial vision. *Vision Research, 19,* 19–32.

Wilson, H. R., & Gelb, D. J. (1984). Modified line element theory for spatial frequency and width discrimination. *Journal of the Optical Society of America A, 1,* 124–131.

Wilson, H. R., Levi, D., Maffei, L., Rovamo, J., DeValois, R. (1990). The perception of form: Retina to striate cortex. In L. Spillman & J. S. Werner (Eds.), *Visual perception: The neurophysiological foundations* (pp. 231–272). New York: Academic Press.

Wilson, J. R., DeFries, J. C., McClearn, G. C., Vandenberg, S. G., Johnson, R. C. & Rashad, M. N. (1975). Cognitive abilities: Use of family data as a control to assess sex and age differences in two ethnic groups. *International Journal of Aging and Human Development, 6,* 261–275.

Wilson, M. (1957). Effects of circumscribed cortical lesions upon somesthetic and visual discrimination in the monkey. *Journal of Comparative and Physiological Psychology, 50,* 630–635.

Withington, D. J., Binns, K. E., Ingham, N. J., & Thornton, S. K. (1994). Plasticity in the superior collicular auditory space map of adult guinea-pigs. *Experimental Physiology, 79,* 319–325.

Witkin, H. A., & Berry, J. W. (1975). Psychological differentiation in cross-cultural perspective. *Journal of Cross-Cultural Psychology, 6,* 4–87.

Wolfe, J. M. (1998). What can 1 million trials tell us about visual search? *Psychological Science, 9,* 33–39.

Wolfe, J. M., Cave, K. R., & Franzel, S. L. (1989). Guided search: An alternative to the feature integration model for visual search. *Journal of Experimental Psychology: Human Perception and Performance, 15,* 419–433.

Wolfe, J. M., & O'Connell, K. M. (1986). Fatigue and structural change: Two consequences of visual pattern adaptation. *Investigative Ophthalmology and Visual Science, 28,* 173–212.

Wolff, H. G., & Goodell, B. S. (1943). The relation of attitude and suggestion to the perception of and reaction to pain. *Research Publications, Association for Research in Nervous and Mental Disease, 23,* 434–448.

Wolff, P. H. (1987). *The development of behavioral states and the expression of emotions in early infancy.* Chicago: University of Chicago Press.

Wong, C., & Weisstein, N. (1982). A new perceptual context-superiority effect: Line segments are more visible against a figure than against a ground. *Science, 218,* 587–589.

Wong, E., & Weisstein, N. (1987). The effects of flicker on the perception of figure and ground. *Perception & Psychophysics, 41,* 440–448.

Wong-Riley, M. T. T. (1979). Changes in the visual system of monocularly sutured or enucleated cats demonstrable with cytochrome oxidase histochemistry. *Brain Research, 171,* 11–28.

Woo, G., & Bader, D. (1978). Age and its effect on vision. *Canadian Journal of Optometry, 40,* 29–34.

Woo, G. C., & Wilson, M. A. (1990). Current methods of treating and preventing myopia. *Optometry and Vision Science, 67,* 719–727.

Wood, N. L., & Cowan, N. (1995a). The cocktail party phenomenon revisited: Attention and memory in the classic selective listening procedure of Cherry (1953). *Journal of Experimental Psychology: General, 124,* 243–262.

Wood, N. L., & Cowan, N. (1995b). The cocktail party phenomenon revisited: How frequent are attention shifts to one's name in an irrelevant auditory channel? *Journal of Experimental Psychology: Learning, Memory, and Cognition, 21,* 255–260.

Wood, R. W. (1985). The "haunted swing" illusion. *Psychological Review, 2,* 277–278.

Woodfield, R. L. (1984). Embedded figures test performance before and after childbirth. *British Journal of Psychology, 75,* 81–88.

Woodrow, H. (1951). Time perception. In S. S. Stevens (Ed.), *Handbook of experimental psychology* (pp. 1224–1236). New York: Wiley.

Woodworth, R. S. (1938). *Experimental psychology.* New York: Holt, Rinehart and Winston.

Woolard, H. H., Weddell, G., & Harpman, J. A. (1940). Observations of the neuro-historical basis of cutaneous pain. *Journal of Anatomy, 74,* 413–440.

Worchel, P., & Dallenbach, K. M. (1947). "Facial vision": Perception of obstacles by the deaf-blind. *American Journal of Psychology, 60,* 502–553.

Worthey, J. A., & Brill, M. H. (1986). Heuristic analysis of von Kries color constancy. *Journal of the Optical Society of America A, 3,* 1708–1712.

Wright, L. L., Elias, J. W. (1979). Age differences in the effects of perceptual noise. *Journal of Gerontology, 34,* 704–708.

Wright, M. J., & Johnston, A. (1985). Invariant tuning of motion aftereffect. *Vision Research, 25,* 1947–1955.

Wright, N. H. (1964). Temporal summation and backward masking. *Journal of the Acoustical Society of America, 36,* 927–932.

Wright, R. D., & Richard, C. M. (1998). Inhibition-of-return is not reflexive. In R. D. Wright (Ed.), *Visual attention* (pp. 330–347). New York: Oxford University Press.

Wright, R. D., & Ward, L. M. (1998). Control of visual attention. In R. D. Wright (Ed.), *Visual attention* (pp. 132–186). New York: Oxford University Press.

Wright, R. H. (1982). *The sense of smell.* Boca Raton, FL: CRC Press.

Wright, W. D. (1929). A re-determination of the trichromatic mixture data. *Medical Research Council (Great Britain), Special Report Series, SRS–139,* 1–38.

Wright, W. D. (1952). The characteristics of tritanopia. *Journal of the Optical Society of America, 42,* 509–521.

Wurtz, R. H. (1996). Vision for the control of movement. *Investigative Ophthalmology & Visual Science, 37,* 2131–2145.

Wurtz, R. H., & Goldberg, M. E. (1971). Superior colliculus cell responses related to eye movements in awake monkeys. *Science, 171,* 82–84.

Wurtz, R. H., Goldberg, M. E., & Robinson, D. L. (1980). Behavioral modulation of visual responses in monkeys. *Progress in Psychobiology and Physiological Psychology, 9,* 42–83.

Wyburn, G. M., Pickford, R. W., & Hurst, R. J. (1964). *Human senses and perception.* Toronto: University of Toronto Press.

Wysocki, C. J., & Meredith, M. (1987). *The vomeronasal system.* New York: Wiley.

Wyszecki, G., & Stiles, W. S. (1967). *Color science: Concepts and methods, quantitative data and formulas.* New York: Wiley.

Wyttenbach, R. A., & Hoy, R. R. (1993). Demonstration of the precedence effect in an insect. *Journal of the Acoustical Society of America, 94,* 777–784.

Wyttenbach, R. A., May, M. L., & Hoy, R. R. (1996). Categorical perception of sound frequency by crickets. *Science, 273,* 1542–1544.

Xu, Y., Liberman, A. M., & Whalen, D. H. (1997). On the immediacy of phonetic perception. *Psychological Science, 8,* 358–362.

Yakolev, P. I., & Lecours, A-R. (1967). The myelogenetic cycles of regional maturation of the brain. In A. Minkowsky (Ed.), *Regional development of the brain in early life* (pp. 3–70). Oxford, UK: Blackwell.

Yaksh, T. L. (1984). Multiple spinal opiate receptor systems in analgesia. In L. Kruger & J. C. Liebeskind (Eds.), *Neural mechanisms of pain* (pp. 197–216). New York: Raven Press.

Yamamoto, T., Yayama, N., & Kawamura, Y. (1981). Central processing of taste perception. In Y. Katsuki, R. Norgren, & M. Sato (Eds.), *Brain mechanisms of sensation* (pp. 197–208). New York: Wiley.

Yantis, S. (1992). Multielement visual tracking: Attention and perceptual organization. *Cognitive Psychology, 24,* 295–340.

Yantis, S., & Hillstrom, A. P. (1994). Stimulus-driven attentional capture: Evidence from equiluminant visual objects. *Journal of Experimental Psychology: Human Perception and Performance, 20,* 95–107.

Yantis, S., & Jonides, J. (1984). Abrupt onsets and selective attention: Evidence from visual search. *Journal of Experimental Psychology: Human Perception and Performance, 10,* 601–621.

Yantis, S., & Jonides, J. (1990). Abrupt visual onsets and selective attention: Voluntary versus automatic allocation. *Journal of Experimental Psychology: Human Perception and Performance, 16,* 121–134.

Yarbus, A. L. (1967). *Eye movements and vision.* New York: Plenum Press.

Yates, G., Robertson, D., & Johnstone, B. M. (1985). Very rapid adaptation in the guinea pig auditory nerve. *Hearing Research, 17,* 1–12.

Yen, W. (1975). Sex-linked major gene influence on selected types of spatial performance. *Behavior Genetics, 5,* 281–298.

Yerkes, R. M., & Dodson, J. D. (1908). The relation of strength of stimulus to rapidity of habit formation. *Journal of Comparative Neurology and Psychology, 18,* 459–482.

Yin, R. K. (1970). Face recognition by brain injured patients — a dissociable ability. *Neuropsychologia, 8,* 395.

Yodogawa, E. (1982). Symmetropy, an entropy-like measure of visual symmetry. *Perception & Psychophysics, 32,* 230–240.

Yonas, A. (1981). Infants' response to optical information for collision. In R. N. Aslin, J. R. Alberts, & M. R. Petersen (Eds.), *Development of perception* (pp. 313–334). New York: Academic Press.

Yonas, A., Cleaves, W., & Pettersen, L. (1978). Development of sensitivity to pictorial depth. *Science, 200,* 77–79.

Yonas, A., & Craton, L. G. (1987). Relative motion: Kinetic information for the order of depth at an edge. *Perception & Psychophysics, 41,* 53–59.

Yonas, A., & Craton, L. G. (1990). Kinetic occlusion: Further studies of the boundary-flow cue. *Perception & Psychophysics, 47,* 169–179.

Yonas, A., Goldsmith, L. T., & Hallstrom, J. (1978). Development of sensitivity to information provided by cast shadows in pictures. *Perception, 7,* 333–341.

Yonas, A., & Granrud, C. E. (1985a). Development of visual space perception in young infants. In J. Mehler & R. Fox (Eds.), *Neonate cognition: Beyond the blooming buzzing confusion* (pp. 45–68). Hillsdale, NJ: Erlbaum.

Yonas, A., & Granrud, C. E. (1985b). The development of sensitivity to kinetic, binocular and pictorial depth information in human infants. In D. Ingle, D. Lee, & M. Jeannerod (Eds.), *Brain mechanisms and spatial vision* (pp. 113–145). Dordrecht, Netherlands: Nijoff.

Yonas, A., & Granrud, C. E. (1986). Infants' distance perception from linear perspective and texture gradients. *Infant Behavior and Development, 9,* 247–256.

Yoneshige, Y., & Elliott, L. L. (1981). Pure-tone sensitivity and ear canal pressure at threshold in children and adults. *Journal of the Acoustical Society of America, 70,* 1272–1276.

Young, F. A. (1981). Primate myopia. *American Journal of Optometry and Physiological Optics, 58,* 560–566.

Young, L. L., & Wilson, K. A. (1982). Effects of acetylsalicylic acid on speech discrimination. *Audiology, 21,* 342–349.

Young, L. R. (1971). Pursuit eye tracking movements. In P. Bach-y-Rita, C. C. Collins, & J. E. Hyde (Eds.), *The control of eye movements* (pp. 429–443). New York: Academic Press.

Young, R. A. (1977). Some observations on temporal coding of color vision: Psychophysical results. *Vision Research, 17,* 957–965.

Yuille, J. (1984). Research and teaching with police: A Canadian example. *International Review of Applied Psychology, 33,* 5–23.

Yund, E. W., Morgan, H., & Efron, R. (1983). The micropattern effect and visible persistence. *Perception & Psychophysics, 34,* 209–213.

Zakay, D., Nitzan, D., & Glicksohn, J. (1983). The influence of task difficulty and external tempo on subjective time estimation. *Perception & Psychophysics, 34,* 451–456.

Zaporozhets, A. V. (1965). The development of perception in the pre-school child. *Monographs of the Society for Research in Child Development, 30,* 82–101.

Zaragoza, M. S., & Lane, S. M. (1994). Source misattributions and the suggestibility of eyewitness memory. *Journal of Experimental Psychology: Learning, Memory, and Cognition, 20,* 934–945.

Zaragoza, M. S., & McCloskey, M. (1989). Misleading postevent information and the memory impairment hypothesis: Comment on Belli and reply to Tversky and Tuchin. *Journal of Experimental Psychology: General, 118,* 92–99.

Zatorre, R. J. (1985). Discrimination and recognition of tonal melodies after unilateral cerebral excisions. *Neuropsychologia, 23,* 31–41.

Zatorre, R. J. (1988). Pitch perception of complex tones and human temporal-lobe function. *Journal of the Acoustical Society of America, 84,* 566–572.

Zatorre, R. J., Evans, A. C., Meyer, E., & Gjedde, A. (1992). Lateralization of phonetic and pitch discrimination in speech processing. *Science, 256,* 846–849.

Zatorre, R. J., & Jones-Gotman, M. (1990). Right-nostril advantage for discrimination of odors. *Perception & Psychophysics, 47,* 526–531.

Zatorre, R. J., Meyer, E., Gjede, A., & Evans, A. C. (1996). PET studies of phonetic processing of speech: Review, replication and reanalysis. *Cerebral Cortex, 6,* 21–30.

Zeigler, H. P., & Leibowitz, H. (1957). Apparent visual size as a function of distance for children and adults. *American Journal of Psychology, 70,* 106–109.

Zeki, S. (1973). Colour coding in rhesus monkey prestriate cortex. *Brain Research, 53,* 422–427.

Zeki, S. (1977). Colour coding in the superior temporal sulcus of rhesus monkey cortex. *Proceedings of the Royal Society of London, B 197,* 195–223.

Zeki, S. (1990). A century of cerebral achromatopsia. *Brain, 113,* 1721–1777.

Zeki, S. (1991). Cerebral akinetopsia (cerebral visual motion blindness). *Brain, 114,* 811–824.

Zeki, S. (1993). *A vision of the brain.* Cambridge, MA: Blackwell Scientific Publications.

Zeki, S. (1993). *A vision of the brain.* Oxford: Blackwell.

Zeki, S., & Shipp, S. (1988). The functional logic of cortical connections. *Nature, 335,* 311–317.

Zellner, D. (1991). How foods get to be liked: Some general mechanisms and some special cases. In R. C. Boles (Ed.), *The hedonics of taste* (pp. 199–217).

Hillsdale, NJ. Lawrence Erlbaum Associates.

Zellner, D. A., & Kautz, M. A. (1990). Color affects perceived odor intensity. *Journal of Experimental Psychology: Human Perception and Performance, 16,* 391–397.

Zigler, M. J. (1932). Pressure adaptation time: A function of intensity and extensity. *American Journal of Psychology, 44,* 709–720.

Zihl, J., von Cramon, D., & Mai, N. (1983). Selective disturbance of movement vision after bilateral brain damage. *Brain, 106,* 313–340.

Zrenner, E., Abramov, I., Akita, M., Cowey, A., Livingstone, M., & Valberg, A. (1990). Color perception: Retina to cortex. In L. Spillman & J. Werner (Eds.), *Visual perception: The neurophysiological foundations.* New York: Academic Press.

Zucker, I., Wade, G., & Ziegler, R. (1972). Sexual and hormonal influences on eating, taste preferences, and body weight of hamsters. *Physiology and Behavior, 8,* 101–111.

Zucker, S. (1987). Early vision. In S. C. Shapiro (Ed.), *The encyclopedia of artificial intelligence* (pp. 1131–1152). New York: Wiley.

Zuidema, P., Gresnight, A. M., Bouman, M. A., & Koenderink, J. J. (1978). A quanta coincidence model for absolute threshold vision incorporating deviations from Ricco's law. *Vision Research, 18,* 1685–1689.

Zurek, P. M. (1980). The precedence effect and its possible role in the avoidance of interaural ambiguities. *Journal of the Acoustical Society of America, 67,* 952–964.

Zwicker, E. (1958). Uber psychologische und methodosche Grundlagen der Lautheit. *Acustica, 8,* 237–258.

Zwicker, E. (1986). A hardware cochlear nonlinear preprocessing model with active feedback. *Journal of the Acoustical Society of America, 80,* 146–153.

Zwislocki, J. J. (1978). Masking: Experimental and theoretical aspects of simultaneous, forward, backward, and central masking. In E. C. Carterette & M. P. Friedman (Eds.), *Handbook of perception: Vol. IV. Hearing* (pp. 283–336). New York: Academic Press.

Zwislocki, J. J., Damianopoulos, E. N., Buining, E., & Glantz, J. (1967). Central masking: Some steady-state and transient effects. *Perception & Psychophysics, 2,* 59–64.

Author Index

Subject Index

Literary Permissions

Page 44
Figure 2-17
From S. S. Stevens, in W. A. Rosenbluth (Ed.), *Sensory Communication*. New York: Wiley, 1961. Copyright © 1961 by the MIT Press.

Page 135
The Color Vision Screening Inventory is copyrighted by SC Psychological Enterprises, Ltd., and is reprinted here with permission.

Page 191
Figure 7-9
Copyright © 1971 by Oxford University Press, Inc. Reprinted by permission.

Page 198
Figure 7-13
Copyright © 1971 by Oxford University Press, Inc. Reprinted by permission.

Page 231
Figure 8-12
From *The Cerebral Cortex of Man* by W. Penfield and T. Rasmussen. Copyright © 1950 by Macmillan Publishing Co., Inc., renewed 1978 by Theodore Rasmussen.

Page 272
From *Foundations of Cyclopean Perception* by B. Juless, copyright © 1971 by the University of Chicago Press.

Page 299
Figure 10-12
Copyright © 1972 by the American Psychological Assocation. Reprinted by permission.

Page 315
Figure 10-28
Copyright © 1975 by W.H. Freeman & Co. Used by permission.

Page 386
Figure 13-4
Belvedere by M. C. Escher. Copyright © 1998 Cordon Art-Baarn, Holland. All rights reserved.

Page 453
Figure 15-7
From Yarbus, *Eye Movements in Vision*. Copyright © 1967 by Plenum Publishing Company. Reprinted by permission.

Page 487
Figure 16-11
Copyright © 1965 by The Society for Research in Child Development, Inc.

Page 508
Figure 17-5
Copyright © 1963 by the American Psychological Association. Reprinted by permission.

Page 508
Figure 17-6
From "Dissociation of the Visual Placing Response into Elicited and Guided Components," by A. Hein & R. Held, 1967, *Science*, *158*, pp. 390–392. Copyright © 1967 by the American Association for the Advancement of Science.

Page 523
From "Some Observations Regarding the Experience and Behavior of the Bambuti Pygmies" by C. Turnbull, 1961, *American Journal of Psychology*, *74*. Copyright © 1961 by the University of Illinois Press.

Page 529
Figure 17-18
From "Readiness to Perceive Violence as a Result of Police Training," by H. H. Toch and R. Schutle, 1961, *British Journal of Psychology*, *52*, 389–393.

Photo Permissions

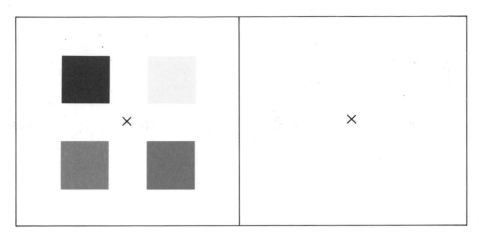

Color Plate 7

A   Read through this list of color names as quickly as possible.
    Read from right to left across each line.

RED	**YELLOW**	**BLUE**	**GREEN**
RED	**GREEN**	**YELLOW**	**BLUE**
YELLOW	**GREEN**	**BLUE**	**RED**
BLUE	**RED**	**GREEN**	**YELLOW**
RED	**GREEN**	**BLUE**	**YELLOW**

B   Name each of these color patches as quickly as possible.
    Name from left to right across each line.

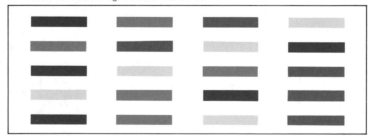

C   Name the color of ink in which each word is printed as quickly as possible.
    Name from left to right across each line.

RED	**BLUE**	**GREEN**	**YELLOW**
YELLOW	**BLUE**	**RED**	**GREEN**
BLUE	**YELLOW**	**GREEN**	**RED**
GREEN	**BLUE**	**YELLOW**	**RED**
BLUE	**YELLOW**	**RED**	**GREEN**

Color Plate 8